Handbook of
Racial & Ethnic Minority Psychology

Racial and Ethnic Minority Psychology Series

Series Editor: Frederick T. L. Leong, *The Ohio State University*

This series of scholarly books is designed to advance theories, research, and practice in racial and ethnic minority psychology. The volumes published in this new series focus on the major racial and ethnic minority groups in the United States, including African Americans, Hispanic Americans, Asian Americans, and Native American Indians. The series features original materials that address the full spectrum of methodological, substantive, and theoretical areas related to racial and ethnic minority psychology and that are scholarly and grounded in solid research. It comprises volumes on cognitive, developmental, industrial/organizational, health psychology, personality, and social psychology. While the series does not include books covering the treatment and prevention of mental health problems, it does publish volumes devoted to stress, psychological adjustment, and psychopathology among racial and ethnic minority groups. The state-of-the-art volumes in the series will be of interest to both professionals and researchers in psychology. Depending on their specific focus, the books may be of greater interest to either academics or practitioners.

Editorial Board

Please address all correspondence to the Series Editor:

Frederick T. L. Leong
The Ohio State University
Department of Psychology
142 Townshend Hall
1885 Neil Avenue
Columbus, Ohio 43210-1222
Phone: (614) 292-8219
Fax: (614) 292-4537
E-mail: leong.10@osu.edu

Books in This Series:

Assessing Intelligence: Applying a Bio-Cultural Model
by Eleanor Armour-Thomas and Sharon-Ann Gopaul-McNicol

Chinese America: Mental Health & Quality of Life in the Inner City
by Chalsa M. Loo

Intelligence Testing and Minority Students: Foundations, Performance Factors, & Assessment Issues
by Richard R. Valencia & Lisa A. Suzuki

Handbook of Racial and Ethnic Minority Psychology
by Guillermo Bernal, Joseph E. Trimble, A. Kathleen Burlew, & Frederick T. L. Leong

Handbook of
Racial & Ethnic Minority Psychology

Editors

Guillermo Bernal
University of Puerto Rico

Joseph E. Trimble
Western Washington University

A. Kathleen Burlew
University of Cincinnati

Frederick T. L. Leong
The Ohio State University

SAGE Publications
International Educational and Professional Publisher
Thousand Oaks ■ London ■ New Delhi

For information:

 Sage Publications, Inc.
2455 Teller Road
Thousand Oaks, California 91320
E-mail: order@sagepub.com

Sage Publications Ltd.
6 Bonhill Street
London EC2A 4PU
United Kingdom

Sage Publications India Pvt. Ltd.
B-42, Panchsheel Enclave
Post Box 4109
New Delhi 110 017 India

Printed in the United States of America

Library of Congress Cataloging-in-Publication Data

Handbook of racial and ethnic minority psychology / edited by Guillermo
Bernal . . . [et al.].
    p. cm. — (Racial & ethnic minority psychology series)
Includes bibliographical references and index.
  ISBN 0-7619-1965-1 (c)
  1. Ethnopsychology. 2. Minorities—United States—Psychology.
I. Bernal, Guillermo. II. Racial and ethnic minority psychology series.
  GN502 .H3635 2003
  155.8′2—dc21

                  2002006456

This book is printed on acid-free paper.

02 03 04 05 10 9 8 7 6 5 4 3 2 1

Acquisitions Editor:	Jim Brace-Thompson
Editorial Assistant:	Karen Ehrmann
Production Editor:	Olivia Weber
Typesetter:	C&M Digitals (P) Ltd
Cover Designer:	Ravi Balasuriya

Contents

PART II. ETHNIC MINORITY RESEARCH AND METHODS 177

PART III. SOCIAL AND DEVELOPMENTAL PROCESS 237

PART IV. STRESS AND ADJUSTMENT   375

PART V. CLINICAL INTERVENTIONS   485

PART VI. APPLIED AND PREVENTIVE PSYCHOLOGY   571

Series Editor's Introduction

As I have indicated in previous Introductions to volumes in the Racial & Ethnic Minority Psychology Series (REMP), a brief review of studies published on racial and ethnic differences in journals cataloged by PsychInfo provides a clear indication of the increasing importance of the subfield of racial and ethnic minority psychology. Between 1970 and 1990 (21 years), PsychInfo cataloged 6,109 articles related to racial and ethnic differences. Between 1991 and 2001 (11 years), the number of such articles was 7,892. As a convenient means of representing the increase in attention paid to racial and ethnic minority issues in psychology, one can easily divide the number of articles published during the time period by the number of years. Such a computation reveals that between 1970 and 1990, an average of 290 articles were published each year on racial and ethnic differences. For the period from 1990 to 2001, that number had jumped to an annual average of 717, or an increase of nearly 150%. All indications are that this pattern of growth will continue.

There is also other converging evidence that racial and ethnic minority psychology is becoming an important and central theme in psychology in the United States. Within the American Psychological Association (APA), the Society for the Psychological Study of Racial and Ethnic Minority Issues was formed as Division 45. The division has now acquired its own journal devoted to ethnic minority issues in psychology—namely, *Cultural Diversity and Ethnic Minority Psychology*. Also, we have seen the publication of five APA bibliographies devoted to racial and ethnic minority groups. The first was focused on Black males (Evans & Whitfield, 1988), and a companion volume focused on Black females (Hall, Evans, & Selice, 1989). In 1990, APA published a bibliography on Hispanics in the United States (Olmedo & Walker, 1990) followed by one on Asians in the United States (Leong & Whitfield, 1992). The fifth bibliography focused on American Indians (Trimble & Bagwell, 1995). In recognition of these developments, the REMP book series was launched at Sage Publications in 1995.

The REMP series is designed to advance our theories, research, and practice related to racial and ethnic minority psychology. It focuses on, but is not limited to, the major racial and ethnic minority groups in the United States (i.e., African Americans, Hispanic Americans, Asian Americans, and American Indians). For example, books concerning Asians and Asian Americans are also considered, as are books on racial and ethnic minorities in other countries. The books in the series contain original materials that address the full spectrum of methodological, substantive, and theoretical areas related to racial and ethnic minority psychology. With the exception of counseling and psychotherapeutic interventions, all aspects of psychology as it relates to racial and ethnic minority groups in the United States are covered by the series. This includes topics in cognitive, developmental, industrial/organizational, personality, abnormal, and social psychology. The series includes books that examine a single racial or ethnic group (e.g., *Chinese America: Mental Health & Quality of Life in the Inner City*) as well as books that undertake a comparative approach (e.g., *Intelligence Testing & Minority Students*). As a series devoted to racial and ethnic minority groups in the United States and other countries, this series will not cover the usual cross-cultural issues and topics such as those covered by the Sage Series on Cross-Cultural Research and Methodology.

As editor of the REMP series, it gives me great pleasure to introduce the fourth volume: the *Handbook of Racial and Ethnic Minority Psychology*. Its publication serves not only as the "anchor" volume for the series but also as another indicator of the increasing importance and impact of the subfield on mainstream psychology. The breadth of the *Handbook* speaks to the richness of the work being done in the subfield. With 32 chapters covering the whole range of topics represented in psychology, the *Handbook* has been divided into six parts: (a) conceptual, professional, and training issues; (b) ethnic minority research and methods; (c) social and developmental process; (d) stress and adjustment; (e) clinical interventions; and (f) applied and preventive psychology. I am confident that this volume will serve as a standard reference and eventually become "a classic" within the field. As the most comprehensive state-of-the-art review for racial and ethnic minority psychology, it is a most welcomed addition to the series and, it is hoped, will stimulate further interest and expansion of the subfield of racial and ethnic minority psychology.

— Frederick T. L. Leong
Series Editor

REFERENCES

Evans, B. J., & Whitfield, J. R. (1988). *Black males in the United States: Abstracts of the psychological and behavioral literature, 1967-1987* (Bibliographies in Psychology, No. 1). Washington, DC: American Psychological Association.

Hall, C. C. I., Evans, B. J., & Selice, S. (1989). *Black females in the United States: Abstracts of the psychological and behavioral literature, 1967-1987* (Bibliographies in Psychology, No. 3). Washington, DC: American Psychological Association.

Leong, F. T. L., & Whitfield, J. R. (1992). *Asians in the United States: Abstracts of the psychological and behavioral literature, 1967-1991* (Bibliographies in Psychology, No. 11). Washington, DC: American Psychological Association.

Olmedo, E. L., & Walker, V. R. (1990). *Hispanics in the United States: Abstracts of the psychological and behavioral literature, 1980-1989* (Bibliographies in Psychology, No. 8). Washington, DC: American Psychological Association.

Trimble, J. E., & Bagwell, W. M. (1995). *North American Indians and Alaskan Natives: Abstracts of the psychological and behavioral literature, 1967-1994* (Bibliographies in Psychology, No. 15). Washington, DC: American Psychological Association.

Foreword

S uch dynamic changes are occurring within the U.S. population that diversity in ethnic/cultural backgrounds will soon be the norm, with some states already fast reaching such changes. By the year 2030, 14.4% of the population are expected to be African American, 18.9% Hispanic, 7.0% Asian/Pacific Islander, and 1.0% Native American. By the year 2050, the number of ethnic minorities is expected to be 50% of the U.S. population (U.S. Bureau of the Census, 1996). Moreover, 75% of those entering the workforce is anticipated to be ethnic minorities and women, and 45% of students in public schools would be from culturally diverse backgrounds (Sue, Parham, & Bonilla-Santiago, 1998). During the 1990s, the Asian American population itself grew by 45%, thus becoming the fastest-growing American ethnic population in the United States, and the expectation is that this group will triple within the next 50 years. There are more than 34 million African American persons and more than 29 million Hispanic persons currently living in the United States (U.S. Bureau of the Census, 2000). Thus, the various minority populations that have been a small segment of the population are quickly becoming a larger majority requiring equal attention, appreciation, and representation in educational, research, political, and human services environments. In fact, the term *ethnic minority group* is already being replaced by the newer term *people of color*.

Psychology has often been defined as the discipline and profession that involves the systematic study of human behavior. However, the history of American psychology demonstrates that for about a century, the study of human behavior really meant the study of the behavior of White persons. Early psychological data relied on Euro-American samples and did not consider ethnic minority populations as normative. Guthrie (1976) called attention to this attitude in the title of his incisive book *Even the Rat Was White*. Furthermore, research on ethnic minority issues was initially devalued in academic circles as not meeting psychological standards for "good research," and hence such research studies were often not counted in considerations for the promotion of faculty doing such research.

In addition, minority scholars often experienced rejection of their submitted manuscripts on minority samples, based on the criticism that a

White sample had not been included, and hence valid conclusions could not be drawn. Indeed, American psychology was a psychology of the majority population and nonrepresentative of the ethnic minority populations. There was no ethnic minority psychology.

The current volume therefore represents a significant statement about the current status of ethnic psychology in several ways. The volume's very title, *Handbook,* demonstrates that ethnic psychology has developed to the extent that a substantive knowledge base is available. The part and chapter headings display a full range of relevant topics, including theoretical models, research methodologies, professional practice, and applied psychology issues. It is noteworthy that ideas and directions unique to ethnic populations have already reached the level of development as to truly reflect an ethnic minority psychology. Among these are descriptions and discussion of multiculturalism and ethnic and racial identity development, as well as specific attention to topics involving developmental, educational, social, clinical, counseling, and community psychology. No longer is it sufficient to assume that data on the majority culture are adequate for understanding ethnic populations. Instead, the *Handbook* aims at providing the needed conceptual and theoretical foundations, normative data, research findings, and pragmatic strategies distinctive to work with persons of color.

Not to be overlooked is the historical background that is the baseline against which to evaluate the current achievements within ethnic psychology.

This background is comprehensively covered in the *Handbook* regarding the general sociopolitical environment in the United States as well as the history of the ethnic psychology movement. Of added relevance in this volume is the extensive discussion of the many implicit meanings underlying the terms *ethnic, racial,* or *cultural psychology,* meanings that are a foundation of ethnic minority psychology. Also to be found in the chapters are discussions of racism and discrimination, which might be interpreted as more political than psychological; however, prejudice and social injustices are in fact variables relevant to ethnic minority experiences and therefore to ethnic minority psychological studies.

Further evidence of the status of ethnic psychology is the authors' ability to document their information by citing relevant published research.

The presence of such publications confirms that such research has now achieved respectability among journal editors and publishers of scholarly materials. Furthermore, articles have been published not only in ethnically oriented journals but also in other mainstream periodicals previously focused on data based only on the majority population.

Hence, the *Handbook of Racial and Ethnic Psychology* represents the enormous progress of ethnic psychology as a major field within American psychology. The American Psychological Association's Society for the Psychological Study of Ethnic Minority Issues (Division 45) has achieved a major contribution by pulling together the many voices to speak to this topic. The authors of the chapters are leading scholars and elders who approach their topics sometimes with words of passion, always with the underlying respect and caring the authors have for those populations being studied.

The topics are diverse enough to be valuable for informing the new researcher or practitioner or educator. The writings are also relevant for the student seeking to gain an overview of existing knowledge or to identify what challenges exist. And for all ethnic minority psychologists, the writings are an anchoring source of identity and pride.

I believe this volume provides an outstanding resource that will aid current and future researchers, educators, and professionals to acquire new and fuller understanding of this important American population—persons of color.

— Richard Suinn
1999 APA President
Emeritus Professor
Colorado State University

REFERENCES

Guthrie, R. (1976). *Even the rat was White.* New York: Harper & Row.

Sue, D., Parham, T., & Santiago, G. (1998). The changing face of work in the United States: Implications for individual, institutional, and societal survival. *Cultural Diversity & Ethnic Minority Psychology, 4,* 153-164.

U.S. Bureau of the Census. (1996). *Statistical abstracts of the U.S.* Washington, DC: Government Printing Office.

U.S. Bureau of the Census. (2000). *Statistical abstracts of the U.S.* Washington, DC: Government Printing Office.

Acknowledgments

In the late 19th century, Lone Man (isna la-wica), a Teton Lakota (Sioux), allegedly stated that "I have seen that in any great undertaking it is not enough for a man to depend simply upon himself." The preparation of this volume of original articles depended on the hard work and dedication of a vast number of friends and colleagues. We want to take this occasion to acknowledge their assistance and contributions because, as Lone Man so aptly pointed out, we could not have produced this volume simply by one solitary man or woman.

The idea for the *Handbook* occurred around 1995 in an airport lounge in Washington, D.C. At the time, Amado Padilla and Joseph Trimble were returning home after spending 3 days at a meeting on ethnic minority issues and topics sponsored by the American Psychological Association. Although weary from the 3-day marathon of talks, arguments, presentations, and intense deliberations, their attention was still keenly focused on the future of the presence of ethnic minorities in psychology. Although the memory of the conversation has been cluttered by the passage of time, Joseph suggested to Amado that they should compile a series of linked articles focusing on the myriad of psychological topics in the emerging field of ethnic minority psychology and publish it as a handbook. Months later, Amado flew to Bellingham, Washington, from his home at Stanford University and met with Joseph to lay out a list of prospected chapters, potential authors, and a publication schedule.

By that time, Sage Publications through Jim Nageotte already had expressed a strong interest in the concept and was willing to consider it for publication. Progress on the *Handbook* languished, and eventually Amado indicated that he no longer had the time to work on it. Another year went by. All the while, Jim Nageotte kept pressing, still keen on publishing the *Handbook*. Fred Leong, who had initiated his book series on *Racial and Ethnic Minority Psychology* with Sage, then approached Guillermo Bernal to take the lead on this project. Guillermo consulted with Joseph, who was presiding over Division 45. On the basis of these discussions, Guillermo graciously agreed to take over Amado's role as the first editor. The editorial team (Guillermo, Joseph, and Fred) was then able to persuade Kathy Burlew to join the venture and see it to its closure. We are grateful for Amado Padilla's initial commitment and efforts and also for Jim Nageotte's support for the project before he moved on to Guilford Press.

This volume could not have been produced without the thoughtful contributions of some 80 authors and coauthors. Thank you all for your persistence, your wisdom, and your well-written chapters. Most of all, thank you for putting up with our constant badgering through e-mail messages and telephone calls.

We are deeply indebted to the skillful assistance, patience, perseverance, and guidance provided us by our editors James Brace Thompson and Karen Ehrmann at Sage Publications. Their enthusiastic support, unending professionalism, and extraordinary patience were most helpful especially during times when the compilation of the chapters was experiencing untoward difficulty.

Numerous colleagues, students, and staff too numerous to mention by name at the following institutions provided us with support, resources, encouragement, and advice. We wish to extend our warm appreciation and deep gratitude to them: the University Center for Psychological Services and Research (CUSEP) at the University of Puerto Rico, Río Piedras; the Radcliffe Institute for Advanced Study at Harvard University; the University of Cincinnati, Department of Psychology; The Ohio State University, Department of Psychology; and Western Washington University, Department of Psychology.

We wish to acknowledge the support of our ancestors whose careful nurturance and wisdom came alive for us through their stories, folktales, legends, and gentle guidance through many of the best of our times and the turbulent and often trying times. It is our hope that our experiences and accomplishments will live on through our children and families. It is to them that we truly wish to dedicate our accomplishment: Ana Isabel Alvarez; Jennifer Susan Trimble (Genevieve Sage), Lee Erin Trimble, and Casey Ann Trimble; Robin and Randi Burlew; and Sandy, Kate, and Sarah Leong. Finally, we want to acknowledge the support we received from the Society for the Psychological Study of Ethnic Minority Issues, Division 45 of the American Psychological Association. We are dedicating all of the royalties to the Society to assist it in its mission and the support of students. To all of you in the Society and for your support, we say, *muchas gracias, lela pilamayaye, medawase,* and *dao xie.*

— Guillermo Bernal
San Juan, Puerto Rico

— Joseph E. Trimble
Bellingham, WA

— A. Kathleen Burlew
Cincinnati, OH

— Frederick T. L. Leong
Columbus, OH

Introduction

The Psychological Study of Racial and Ethnic Minority Psychology

GUILLERMO BERNAL
University of Puerto Rico

JOSEPH E. TRIMBLE
Western Washington University

A. KATHLEEN BURLEW
University of Cincinnati

FREDERICK T. L. LEONG
The Ohio State University

Never look for a psychological explanation unless every effort to find a cultural one has been exhausted.

—Margaret Mead (1959, p. 16), quoting William Fielding Ogburn,
one of her mentors at Columbia University

In her quote, the esteemed anthropologist Margaret Mead referred to the "psychological" as innate, generic characteristics of the mind, whereas the "cultural" referred to the behavior that one learned in her or his culture. The quote was in reference to cultural anthropologist William Fielding Ogburn's approach to the study of humankind that,

AUTHORS' NOTE: Work on this chapter was supported in part by a grant from the National Institute of Mental Health (G. Bernal), R24-MH49368 and the Latino Research Program Project (M. Alegría), No. P01-MH59876. Guillermo Bernal is grateful to the administrative and secretarial staff at the University Center for Psychological Studies and Research at the University of Puerto Rico, and in particular to Carmen Reyes, who assisted him in the preparation and organization of the *Handbook*. In addition, he is appreciative of Betzaida Castro's help in conducting searches of the PsycINFO database. Joseph E. Trimble extends his deepest gratitude to the administration and research staff at the Radcliffe Institute for Advanced Study at Harvard University for providing him with the time, resources, and support to conduct research for this chapter. In addition, he wishes to extend his appreciation to his Radcliffe Research Partners—Harvard College seniors Peggy Ting Kim and Maiga Miranda—who assisted him with his research and writing.

in the 1920s, was lacking any formative psychological theory that could explain humankind in a holistic manner; psychoanalysis was an exception as it was taking firm hold in Europe and North America, but Ogburn was reluctant to use it. At the time, psychologists were not at all interested in cultural explanations or explorations of human affect, behavior, and cognition. In fact, most psychologists then firmly believed that "all humans were alike"; hence, the need to identify and study cultural correlates exceeded what was sufficient to understand the sum total of the conscious and unconscious events that make up an individual's life. Indeed, and in word, psychologists ignored the robustness and salience of culture and ethnicity for 80 years of its legitimate existence; some continue to hold firmly to this belief today, arguing in the main that the study of culture belongs with anthropology (see Chapter 1 by Holliday, this volume, for more details).

With all due respect to the original intent of Margaret Mead's (1959) quotation, we would like to offer our interpretation. In a word, and from our perspective, Ogburn was correct. Before anyone can begin to apply conventional psychological principles and theories to an ethnic or cultural group, they must understand their unique lifeways and thoughtways. Unfortunately, most psychologists do not subscribe to this principle, often arguing that it takes too much time to completely familiarize oneself with an ethnic group. Others argue that they are merely interested in testing hypotheses "so that the universal validity of psychological theories can be effectively examined" (Dawson, 1971, p. 291). They often add that deep cultural influences are not likely to influence outcomes. Such attitudes and beliefs are mind-numbing, incredulous, and ethnocentric. Even a cursive review of the scientific literature in cultural, cross-cultural, and ethnic minority psychology indicates that culture and ethnic lifeways and thoughtways contribute immensely to the social and psychological character of humans.

In the face of overwhelming cultural evidence, long-standing academic and scientific psychological traditions are too entrenched to accommodate the evidence. For example, American social psychology is a cultural contradiction. The field's theories and findings are typically riddled with cultural biases and ethnocentric perspectives while claiming that the findings have universal applicability. There is mounting evidence, though, that the universality claims may be unfounded. Amir and Sharon (1987) provided compelling evidence that certain social psychological studies conducted in the United States cannot be fully replicated in Israel, suggesting that findings in American social psychology may be culturally distinct and ethnocentric. Jahoda (1979) agreed with this point and added, "It is by no means self-evident that a concept embodied in a theory that has its origins within a particular culture can necessarily be operationalized into a conceptual equivalent in a different culture" (p. 143). On the absence of cultural explanations in social psychology, Jahoda (1988) accused "mainstream social psychology of being guilty of *suggestio falsi* (as the fields) textbooks and articles commonly imply universality without seeking to provide any grounds for their implicit claims" (p. 93).

Culture matters, but it did not seem to matter enough in the history of the development of psychology. Culture matters so pervasively in the enculturation process that it begs for attention and recognition. It is this very attention that the field of racial and ethnic minority is giving to the cultural construct. Culture matters so much that it behooves the investigator to spend considerable time with the ethnic or cultural group of interest to learn about the deep cultural elements of one's lifeways and thoughtways and how they contribute to social and psychological character. Once that is understood, then the investigator may be in a position to explore and apply conventional and traditional psychological principles to understanding. We say "may" because the collection of the information will undoubtedly influence the nature of the research and data collection procedures and measures; that introduces a whole new set of methodological considerations.

The long absence of culture in the web of psychological inquiry did not go unnoticed. In 1968, the Association of Black Psychologists was organized out of a concern that ethnic and minority considerations were not adequately addressed within the American Psychological Association (APA). In 1972, a group of psychologists from different countries convened in Hong Kong to critically examine and discuss culture's influence on the human experience. The meeting led to the founding of the International Association for Cross-Cultural Psychology (IACCP). Two years earlier, the well-established and distinguished *Journal of Cross-Cultural Psychology* was launched under the editorship of Walter Lonner at Western Washington University. There are several definitions of this field, but most agree that the field is "the study of similarities and differences in individual psychological functioning in various cultural and ethnic groups; of the relationships between psychological variables and sociocultural, ecological, and biological variables; and of current changes in these variables" (Berry, Poortinga, Segall, & Dasen, 1992, p. 2). It is interesting to point out that in 1973, there were 1,125 cross-cultural psychologists representing numerous countries listed in an IACCP-sponsored directory.

The attention given to culture by the international psychologists in the early 1970s was a reflection of the growing concerns already present among ethnic minority psychologists and students in the United States. Organizations representing ethnic minority psychologists had already begun to raise serious and daunting questions about the meaning of psychology as it then existed for them. IACCP became another voice echoing concerns about the absence of culture and ethnicity in psychology. The student who is reading this should be mindful that the field of cultural and ethnic

psychology is not that old and to not take it for granted that all psychologists embrace culture and ethnic research and inquiry in psychology. There is still a long way to go.

During the past 30 years, the study of racial and ethnic minority issues in psychology has evolved into what can now be considered a significant and rapidly growing field or subfield of study. Based on this observation and the mounting accumulation of research findings, the foundation for the publication of the *Handbook of Racial and Ethnic Minority Psychology* was set. This *Handbook* is unique, as no other volume or compendium of original papers addresses the breadth of issues on racial and ethnic minority psychology presented in these pages. However, we acknowledge the edited book by Organista, Chun, and Marin (1998), titled *Readings in Ethnic Psychology*, which predates the *Handbook* by 4 years. The book is a collection of republished journal articles and chapters depicting many areas of ethnic psychology. This *Handbook,* however, is a response to the pressing and growing need for a comprehensive resource for students, investigators, and practitioners to critically evaluate the debates, concepts, issues, and approaches to the psychological study of race and ethnicity. The *Handbook* examines an evolving area of psychology in terms of conceptual, professional, and training issues; offers reviews of current research and methodological tools; and examines the role of race and ethnicity in social and developmental processes, as well as in stress and development, clinical interventions, and applied and preventive approaches. As a new area of psychology emerges, focusing on the social construction of racial and ethnic minority considerations in psychology, this *Handbook* serves as a comprehensive resource.

For the past 6 years, the *Handbook* has been a project sponsored by the Society for the Psychological Study of Ethnic and Minority Issues, Division 45 of the American Psychological Association. This society, also known as Division 45, is an association of psychologists who carry out research on ethnic, racial, and minority issues and who apply psychological knowledge and practices to minority policy issues. This *Handbook* is a result of putting into action the goals of the division—namely, to "advance psychology as a science and to promote public welfare through research." All of the chapters address racial and ethnic minority concerns and apply research findings to these concerns, another purpose of Division 45. As such, the *Handbook* stands as an exemplary volume on the research, teaching, and practices of a cadre of professionals engaged in the psychological study of racial and ethnic minority issues.

Diversity and ethnic minority considerations in psychology have not been well represented in traditional publication venues. A few authors have documented the lack of attention to issues of diversity in mainstream journals and other publications (Graham, 1992). Others have questioned the relevance and applicability of a body of psychological knowledge that has unknown external validity to ethnic and racial groups (Bernal & Scharrón del Río, 2001; Sue, 1999; Washington & McLoyd, 1982). Clearly, there are major disparities between the psychological knowledge base on Latinos and their numbers in contemporary society. The same holds true for other ethnic minority groups (Bernal, 1994). With the changing demographic profile of contemporary society, it is essential that the construction of psychology be based on the widest possible representation, which includes, at least, the major ethnic minority and racial groups that make up contemporary North American society. This *Handbook* is a step in the direction of a psychology that embraces racial and ethnic minority concerns within a society that is rapidly growing in its ethnic and cultural diversity.

CHANGING DEMOGRAPHICS

The U.S. Bureau of the Census predicts that by 2050, the U.S. population will reach more than 400 million, about 47% larger than in the year 2000 (U.S. Bureau of the Census, 2001b, 2001d). The primary ethnic minority groups—namely, Latinos and Latinas, African Americans, Asian Americans, and American Indians, Alaska Natives, and Pacific Islanders—will constitute almost 50% of the population. About 57% of the population younger than age 18 and 34% older than age 65 will be ethnic minorities (U.S. Bureau of the Census, 2001d).

The demographic profile based on the 2000 census indicates that during the past decade (1990s), the growth rate of Latinos was eight times faster than that of Whites. Asian Americans and Pacific Islanders also had a rapid growth rate in part due to immigration from Southeast Asia. For Latinos, increased immigration and high birth rates explain the population increase. Projections for the year 2010 suggest that Latinos will be the largest ethnic group, second only to White Americans, and followed by African Americans.

Currently, Latinos and Latinas number 35.3 million persons, about 12.5% of the U.S. population (U.S. Bureau of the Census, 2001c), and comprise a diversity of races and countries of origin. The largest groups of Latinos and Latinas are Mexican Americans (62.6%); next are Puerto Ricans (11.1%), followed by Cubans (4.9%) and Central and South Americans (13.8%), with another 7.6% from Spain and others who do not identify their country of origin. These estimates, however, do not include the 3.8 million U.S. citizens who live on the island of Puerto Rico.

The census estimates that African Americans number about 35 million people (U.S. Bureau of the Census, 2000). Among them are notable group differences in terms of socioeconomic levels, urban or rural areas, and within-group cultural variation. Much of the psychological treatment of African Americans has focused on the relation of social conditions, such as poverty and unemployment, to adverse health and mental health outcomes (Rodríguez, Allen, Frongillo, & Chandra, 1999). However, a growing number of African

American scholars have demonstrated the need for more examination of how cultural strengths such as communalism (Mattis et al., 2000), spirituality, and an interpersonal orientation (emphasis on group over individual) (Randolph & Banks, 1993). The chapters in this *Handbook* reflect a deliberate goal of providing a more balanced presentation about the psychology of various ethnic groups than the deficit model so evident in U.S. psychology. The rate of unemployment for African Americans is more than double that of the White population and has been associated with poor health and higher rates of depression (Rodríguez et al., 1999). Racism, prejudice, and discrimination have been documented as significant sources of stress for African Americans (Clark, Anderson, Clark, & Williams, 1999).

Asian Americans and Pacific Islanders number 10.6 million in the United States (U.S. Bureau of the Census, 2001b). There are 32 different cultural groups with distinct ethnic or national identities and different religions, histories, languages, and traditions that are included within the category of Asian American and Pacific Islander. The most numerous Asian groups in the United States are Filipinos, Chinese, Koreans, Japanese, Vietnamese, and Asian Indians. As with other immigrants, Asian immigrants have migrated to the United States for political and economic reasons and face the stresses of acculturation, racism, and language barriers.

On the basis of the 2000 census, the U.S. Bureau of the Census (2001a) declared that 2,475,956 citizens are American Indians and Alaska Natives—a 26.4% difference from the 1990 census, when the figure was 1,959,234. The 2000 count represents less than one tenth of 1% of the total U.S. population of 281 million. On the basis of the 1960 census, the Census Bureau reported that 552,000 residents of the United States were American Indians (in 1960, the Census Bureau did not include an Alaska Native category, so this figure may be an undercount). Thus, between 1960 and 2000, the American Indian population apparently grew by 349%. This rapid population increase is staggering and strains credulity, as such rates of increase are almost unheard of in the field of demography. One explanation for the increase may be that many more individuals chose to identify with their American Indian heritage in 2000 than did so in 1960 (U.S. Bureau of the Census, 2001b).

In the 2000 census, individuals had the option of marking more than one "race" category and so were able to declare identification with more than one group. Whereas less than 3% of the total U.S. population chose to do so, more than 4,119,000 individuals who chose to mark multiple categories marked "American Indian and Alaska Native" along with one or more others. The "race alone or in combination" count is much higher than the "race alone" count of 2,475,956 (U.S. Bureau of the Census, 2001a). The discrepancy raises the question about which count is more accurate or representative of the "true" Indian population, 2,475,956 or 4,119,000.

American Indians and Alaska Natives are considered to have the poorest health status and the lowest life expectancy of any ethnic group in the United States (U.S. Congress, 1986). They have poor indicators in social, health, and mental health areas (Renfrey, 1998). The poor physical and mental health status of American Indians and Alaska Natives is associated with poverty and substance use. Historical and current racism and discrimination have been described as sources of stress that help explain the health disparities in American Indians and Alaska Natives (Belcourt-Dittloff & Stewart, 2000).

The changing demographic context calls into question the relevance of a psychology that historically has not been inclusive of ethnic and racial groups and that fostered a research agenda that is ethnocentric and bound by time and place. How well prepared will practitioners be in the delivery of quality mental health services to ethnic and language minorities? How will psychology programs handle the teaching of an increasingly diverse student population? How will the science of psychology build a knowledge base that can be generalized to the population as a whole? New priorities for research, teaching, and practice must be developed so that the body of knowledge within psychology holds greater relevance and applicability. The changing demographics will inevitably move the field toward the full consideration of diversity in ways that are inclusive and truly reflect diversity of our changing demographic context. The question is how soon and with what tools? This *Handbook* provides a valuable compendium of resources for teaching, research, and action.

DIVERSITY AND MULTICULTURALISM AS AN EMERGING AREA

An emerging area of study is often defined by a community of scholars and professionals that begins to establish societies and proceeds to publish their work through a variety of venues. For this reason, we take special note of the formation of associations, the publication of key volumes, and the development of journals as indicators of a growing scholarly community concerned with the study of race and ethnic minority issues, diversity, and multiculturalism in psychology.

In part because of the problems with publishing manuscripts on ethnic minority issues in mainstream periodicals, a number of ethnicity-specific publications were established in the 1970s. For example, in 1974, the first issue of the *Journal of Black Psychology* appeared. In 1978, the *White Cloud Journal of American Indian/ Alaska Native Mental Health* was founded; in June 1987, the journal was renamed *American Indian and Alaska Native Mental Health Research, the Journal of the National Center*. In 1979, the *Hispanic Journal of Behavioral Sciences* and the *Journal of Asian American Psychological Association* were published. In 1980, the National Hispanic Psychological

Association was established. However, it was not until 1999 that a journal completely focused on diversity and ethnic minority psychology came to light, when the APA's Division 45 published its journal *Cultural Diversity and Ethnic Minority Psychology*, with Lillian Comas-Diaz as its first editor.

There are rich stories behind all of these publications, and there is an evolving context that dates back in decades. In the first chapter of this *Handbook*, Bertha Holliday offers a unique view of the history of ethnic minorities in psychology. For our purpose, it is important to consider that by the late 1960s and early 1970s, a number of psychological associations were established, such as the Association of Black Psychologists, the Network of Indian Psychologists (now the Society of Indian Psychologists of the Americas), and later the Asian American Psychological Association, which gave way to important publications in psychology. Within the APA, a number of important developments set the stage for what later influenced the field and its capacity to publish. For example, the Minority Fellowship Program was established under the direction of Dalmas Taylor in 1974. Later, in 1979, the Office of Ethnic Minority Affairs was formed, and by 1984, the Board of Ethnic Minority Affairs was established. By 1986, the Society for the Psychological Study of Ethnic Minority Issues (Division 45) and the Society for the Clinical Psychology of Ethnic Minorities (Section VI, within Division 12) were founded. These organizations provided the human and physical infrastructure to pursue publication projects.

The organization of psychological societies, special interest groups within organizations such as the APA, and the publication of journals are signs of a maturing field of study. Another sign of the emerging field of diversity and multiculturalism is the increased number of publications and citations on ethnic minorities. An analysis of the past 40 years of citations cataloged in PsycINFO shows a remarkable increase in the number of citations that reference ethnic minorities.[1]

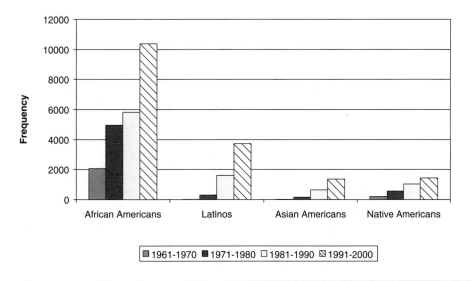

Figure I.1   Citations of Ethnic Minorities by Decade

Figure I.1 shows the frequency of citations for each ethnic minority group during the past four decades. We do not mean to suggest that a citation alone is evidence that all these works focus on an ethnic minority. Nevertheless, a notable increase for citations on all ethnic minority groups is evident over time. Citations making references to African Americans increased from less than 2,063 in the 1960s to 10,382 in the 1990s. Latinos also showed a remarkable increase, from only 22 references in the 1960s to 3,720 in the 1990s. References on Asian Americans increased from 17 citations in the 1960s to 1,360 in the 1990s, and for American Indians and Alaska Natives, they increased from 203 to 1,434 during the same period. As can be appreciated, the increase in citations is indeed remarkable and provides further evidence of an emerging field of study within psychology. Given the increase in the number of articles that reference race and ethnic minorities in psychology, the *Handbook* is, perhaps, a reflection of a maturing of this subfield.

Since 1988, the APA has been publishing a series of annotated bibliographies focusing on the gradual accumulation of ethnic literature citations. The series' topics include African Americans (Keita & Petersen, 1996),

African American males (Evans & Whitfield, 1988), Hispanics (Olmedo & Walker, 1990), Asians (Leong & Whitfield, 1992), and North American Indians (Trimble & Bagwell, 1995). APA also sponsors edited books dealing with ethnic and cultural topics in fields such as feminist theory (Landrine, 1995) and testing Hispanics (Geisinger, 1992). As racial and ethnic minority citations increase in the literature, we are hopeful that the APA will continue the publication series.

Despite these notable increases in the citation of racial and ethnic minorities in the psychological literature, the overall production of knowledge is still limited. When the relationship of ethnic minority citations to the overall number of citations is examined (even after eliminating from the search infrahuman research), the overall production of psychological knowledge for ethnic minorities is quite limited. In the 1960s, the percentage of ethnic minority references to the total number of references was .0026%. In the 1970s, this percentage increased to .0053%. In the 1980s, the percentage remained essentially the same, at .0057%. In the 1990s, the percentage increased to .0079%. The overall percentage of ethnic minority citations to the total during the past 40 years, again after eliminating infrahuman research, is .022%. Thus, more than 99% of the psychological literature during the past 40 years does not make reference to ethnicity, race, or diversity. In other words, less than 1% of this body of knowledge makes reference to racial and ethnic minority considerations.

In a similar analysis on the diversity of the psychological literature, Martha Bernal (1994) questioned whether clinical psychologists were prepared to provide services and conduct research with ethnic minorities. She noted that the fundamental knowledge base required for both understanding and serving the needs of racial and ethnic minorities was "limited and narrow and in need of vigorous expansion" (p. 797). As we have shown here, the gap between the available knowledge base and the current demographic profile of the minority populations is enormous. The percentage of citations on racial and ethnic minorities to their current population estimates is far from equal. The result is a body of knowledge with unknown validity and dubious relevance to an increasingly diverse population. The *Handbook* aims to bridge this disturbing gap in the disparity of our knowledge base.

THE CHALLENGE OF UNDERSTANDING AND DEFINING ETHNICITY: SHARED LEGACIES

Understanding the meaning of race, ethnicity, and the minority experience is a challenge that requires conceptual and methodological tools. Despite the findings of the Human Genome Project that race does not appear to have a biological basis, race and ethnicity are constructs or categories that continue to be an integral aspect of our social fabric. Racial and ethnic categories are used to establish political and social structures, and these categories in turn are the result of social, historical, and political processes that continue to influence and define the experience of ethnic minorities,

as well as that of nonethnic minorities. It is often difficult to separate ethnicity and race from socioeconomic status, the experience of migration, acculturation, and discrimination. At times, the issue of race and ethnicity may serve as a proxy for other variables (e.g., socioeconomic status [SES], ethnic identity, acculturation, acculturative stress, racism, discrimination, etc.). The challenge ahead is to move away from simplistic categories of race and ethnicity and toward the development of constructs that reflect the true complexity of culture and ethnicity and its relationship to psychological phenomena. Another challenge rests on focusing efforts in the study of prevention and remediation to the consequences of racism, oppression, and discrimination. This *Handbook* offers both conceptual and methodological tools that move the field closer to the consideration of more complex and ecologically valid constructs that underlie notions of race and ethnicity.

Despite a growing and compelling body of work that argues against a universal approach to the study of human behavior, too many graduate programs, scholars, and researchers carry out their affairs as though a universal approach was appropriate. Perhaps one reason for this pattern is the absence of a comprehensive resource on some of the critical issues that need to be considered in understanding and studying the psychology of ethnic minorities. This *Handbook* addresses that shortage by providing a comprehensive body of work as a resource for professionals seeking to incorporate diversity into their training or work. The myth of ethnic minority uniformity is nearly dead, although researchers continue to use an "ethnic gloss" when describing ethnic minority groups (Trimble, 1991, 1995). This *Handbook* challenges the false notion that minorities are alike and highlights differences within racial and ethnic minority groups such as African Americans, Latinos, Asian Americans, and American Indians and Alaska Natives. A number of chapters in this volume address the rich mosaic of diversity and heterogeneity within ethnic minorities (see Chapter 12 by Trimble, Helms, and Root, this volume). There are, however, important similarities for certain ethnic minority groups that share a legacy of oppression, genocide, slavery, colonization, and/or conquest. The counterpart of these legacies, such as resistance, survival, and resiliency in the face of overwhelming odds, merits serious study as these processes can point the way to preventive and remediational strategies.

If we are to understand how racism and discrimination affect the physical and mental health of the African American community, it is essential that we first understand the legacy of Black slavery in U.S. history. American Indians and Alaska Natives share a legacy of conquest, defeat, and genocide. The population of American Indians and Alaska Natives in the 18th century actually decreased from its original population to 10% (Sue & Sue, 1990). Chinese Americans share a legacy of discrimination during the 19th century as nearly enslaved workers in the U.S. railroads.

Some Latinos and Latinas in the United States share a history of conquest and colonization (Bernal & Enchautegui, 1994; also see Chapter 19 by Sáez-Santiago and Bernal, this volume). For example, Puerto Ricans and Mexican Americans share in a legacy of subordination and defeat. With the doctrine of "Manifest Destiny" in 1845, the United States expanded its territory and occupied Mexican lands. The Mexican-American War resulted in Mexico giving up 45% of its territory (today the states of Texas, New Mexico, Arizona, and California). Puerto Rico has a similar history of conquest and resistance when the United States invaded it in 1898. To date, Puerto Rico remains a colony of the United States.

A consideration of these legacies of genocide, slavery, conquest, and discrimination is basic to understanding the social and psychological processes linked to stress, health, and behavior. Conceptual models of human behavior need to incorporate the legacies of oppression, discrimination, and the strength inherent in resistance, resilience, and survival to fully appreciate the unique experiences specific to ethnic minorities. This *Handbook* examines common historical experiences, as well as differences among ethnic minorities, and explores ways in which such experiences are critical to the teaching, research, and practice of racial and ethnic minority psychology.

AIMS AND ORGANIZATION OF THE VOLUME

The *Handbook* was written with several audiences in mind: educators, students, researchers, and other professionals interested in the psychological study of racial and ethnic minority issues. One of the objectives of this volume is to address race, culture, and ethnicity across the broad spectrum of psychological knowledge. Authors with expertise in their respective areas of research, training, or practice were invited to submit chapters. Initially, the authors were asked to address each of the four major ethnic minority groups with the objective of presenting reviews of the psychological knowledge for each minority group in specific areas of psychology. It soon became evident, however, that this approach would result in repetitive information. In addition, some authors were unwilling to write or review the literature for ethnic groups about which they were unfamiliar. Thus, we settled on chapters that offer both depth and breadth on the current knowledge base, accepting a number of chapters that focused on a particular ethnicity because of the new insights or the novel approach such chapters offered. The *Handbook* is composed of 32 chapters, with 61 contributors.

The *Handbook* is organized into six parts. The seven chapters that comprise Part I explore conceptual, professional, practice, and training issues. This part begins with a chapter on the history of ethnic minority psychology and another on conceptualizations and models. The remaining chapters focus on professional issues, teaching racial identity development, teaching multiculturalism, and ethics. Part II is about ethnic minority research and methods. This part opens with a conceptual and methodological review of ethnic minority research. Subsequently, specific issues are addressed in three other chapters: ethnic research as good science, acculturation research, and instrument development. Part III explores social and development processes. It begins with a chapter on psychological perspectives on ethnic and racial psychology, followed by another piece on constructing race and deconstructing racism. Five other chapters address different aspects of current social and developmental processes. Part IV focuses on stress and adjustment. A chapter on stress, coping, and minority health introduces the section. Separate chapters on depression, anxiety, drug abuse, and violence offer reviews of the literature as it relates to ethnic minorities. Part V is on clinical interventions. The five chapters in this part address cutting-edge issues in counseling and clinical interventions, ranging from developing culture-centered interventions to cognitive-behavioral therapy to drug abuse treatment and mental health issues. Part VI is on applied and preventive psychology. It opens with a chapter on the legacy of community psychology in ethnic minority populations. Subsequent chapters address the issues in creating culturally valid interventions, HIV prevention, strategies for reducing prejudice and racism, and the prevention of drug abuse among ethnic minorities.

In closing, this volume seeks to disseminate key professional writings and research advances in an emerging area of psychology, namely, the study of racial and ethnic minority psychology. The *Handbook* is oriented toward students, academics, practitioners, and other professionals working in the field, in the hope that collaborative links can be established and a new generation of researchers will venture into this promising and rapidly growing area of scholarship and research.

NOTE

1. Field-restricted searches were made in the PsycINFO online database. The frequency of articles for each ethnic group was obtained by writing two or three possible words or phrases that described the minority group, separated by an OR (e.g., African American OR Black OR Negro). The "OR" was used so that the articles found had any of the words/phrases used and not necessarily all of them. For each search, both the "all fields" and "keywords" alternatives were selected. The "all fields" selection was supposed to provide us with the number of articles that mentioned any of the words/phrases used in the search, even if the article did not involve a study with the particular population searched. The "keywords" selection, on the other hand, provided only the articles that focused their research on the minority groups on which the search was made. These searches were made by decade, starting with 1961-1970 and ending with 1991-2000. Separate searches were done for the following groups of words/phrases: (a) African American, Black, Negro; (b) Asian American, Pacific Islander; (c) Native American, American Indian; (d) Latino, Hispanic, Spanish-speaking; and (e) Ethnic Minority, Cultural Minority, Minority Group. The first four searches were used to construct graphs of each minority group by decade. These were then added to build a graph that summed up all the articles referencing ethnic groups, by decade. For this same purpose, a fifth search was performed. Subsequently, a search was performed by decade, with no words or phrases written in the search blanks, to identify the total number of articles published in each time frame

(decade). Finally, a last search was made with the phrases "Animal Research" OR "Animal Psychology," so that the number of articles based on infrahuman research could be estimated. The number of references on infrahuman and neuroscience research was then subtracted from the total to estimate the total number of articles referencing human psychology. These two last searches permitted the corresponding estimates to determine the percentage of PsycINFO articles on human psychology (by decade) that referenced ethnic minorities.

REFERENCES

Amir, Y., & Sharon, I. (1987). Are social psychological laws cross-culturally valid? *Journal of Cross-Cultural Psychology, 18,* 383-470.

Belcourt-Dittloff, A., & Stewart, J. (2000). Historical racism: Implications for Native Americans. *American Psychologist, 55*(10), 1166-1167.

Bernal, G., & Enchautegui, N. (1994). Latinos and Latinas in community psychology: A review of the literature. *American Journal of Community Psychology, 22,* 531-555.

Bernal, G., & Scharrón del Río, M. R. (2001). Are empirically supported treatments valid for ethnic minorities? Toward an alternative approach for treatment research. *Journal of Cultural Diversity and Ethnic Minority Psychology, 7,* 328-342.

Bernal, M. E. (1994). Are clinical psychologists prepared for service and research with ethnic minorities? A report of a decade of progress. *American Psychologist, 49*(9), 797-805.

Berry, J., Poortinga, Y., Segall, M., & Dasen, P. (1992). *Cross-cultural psychology: Research and applications.* New York: Cambridge University Press.

Clark, R., Anderson, N. B., Clark, V., & Williams, D. R. (1999). Racism as a stressor for African Americans: A biopsychosocial model. *American Psychologist, 54,* 805-816.

Dawson, J. (1971). Theory and research in cross-cultural psychology. *Bulletin of the British Psychological Society, 24,* 291-306.

Evans, B., & Whitfield, J. (Eds.). (1988). *Black males in the United States: An annotated bibliography from 1967-1987* (Bibliographies in Psychology No. 1). Washington, DC: American Psychological Association.

Geisinger, K. (Ed.). (1992). *Psychological testing of Hispanics.* Washington, DC: American Psychological Association.

Graham, S. (1992). Most of the subjects were White and middle class: Trends in published research on African Americans in selected APA journals, 1970-1989. *American Psychologist, 47,* 629-639.

Jahoda, G. (1979). A cross-cultural perspective on experimental social psychology. *Personality and Social Psychology Bulletin, 5,* 142-148.

Jahoda, G. (1988). J'Accuse. In M. Bond (Ed.), *The cross-cultural challenge to social psychology* (pp. 86-95). Newbury Park, CA: Sage.

Keita, G., & Petersen, A. (Eds.). (1996). *Blacks in the United States: Abstracts of the psychological and behavioral literature, 1987-1995* (Bibliographies in Psychology No. 16). Washington, DC: American Psychological Association.

Landrine, H. (Ed.). (1995). *Bringing cultural diversity to feminist psychology: Theory, research, and practice.* Washington, DC: American Psychological Association.

Leong, F., & Whitfield, J. R. (Eds.). (1992). *Asians in the United States: Abstracts of the psychological and behavioral literature, 1967-1991* (Bibliographies in Psychology No. 11). Washington, DC: American Psychological Association.

Mattis, J. S., Jagers, R. J., Hatcher, C. A., Lawhon, G. D., Murphy, E. J., & Murray, Y. F. (2000). Religiosity, volunteerism, and community involvement among African American men: An exploratory analysis. *Journal of Community Psychology, 28,* 391-406.

Mead, M. (1959). *An anthropologist at work: Writings of Ruth Benedict.* Boston: Houghton Mifflin.

Olmedo, E., & Walker, V. (Eds.). (1990). *Hispanics in the United States: Abstracts of the psychological and behavioral literature, 1980-1989* (Bibliographies in Psychology No. 8). Washington, DC: American Psychological Association.

Organista, P. B., Chun, K., & Marin, G. (Eds.). (1998). *Readings in ethnic psychology.* Florence, KY: Taylor & Francis/Routledge.

Randolph, S., & Banks, H. D. (1993). Making a way out of no way: The promise of Africentric approaches to HIV prevention. *Journal of Black Psychology, 19,* 204-214.

Renfrey, G. (1998). Cognitive-behavior therapy and the Native American client. In P. Balls Organista & G. Marín (Eds.), *Readings in ethnic psychology* (pp. 335-352). New York: Routledge.

Rodríguez, E., Allen, J. A., Frongillo, E. A., & Chandra, P. (1999). Unemployment, depression, health: A look at the African-American community. *Journal of Epidemiology Community Health, 53*(6), 335-342.

Sue, S. (1999). Science, ethnicity, and bias: Where have we gone wrong? *American Psychologist, 54,* 1070-1077.

Sue, S., & Sue, D. (1990). *Counseling the culturally different.* New York: John Wiley.

Trimble, J. (1991). Ethnic specification, validation prospects and future of drug abuse research. *International Journal of the Addictions, 25,* 149-169.

Trimble, J. (1995). Ethnic minorities. In R. Coombs & D. Ziedonis (Eds.), *Handbook on drug abuse prevention: A comprehensive strategy to prevent the abuse of alcohol and other drugs* (pp. 379-410). Needham Heights, MA: Allyn & Bacon.

Trimble, J., & Bagwell, W. (Eds.). (1995). *North American Indians and Alaska Natives: Abstracts of psychological and behavioral literature, 1967-1995.* Washington, DC: American Psychological Association.

U.S. Bureau of the Census. (2000). *Overview of race and Hispanic origin* (C2KBR/01-1). Washington, DC: U.S. Department of Commerce, Economics and Statistical Administration.

U.S. Bureau of the Census. (2001a). *Census of the population: General population characteristics, American Indians and Alaska Natives areas, 2000.* Washington, DC: Government Printing Office.

U.S. Bureau of the Census. (2001b). *Overview of race and Hispanic origin.* Washington, DC: U.S. Department of Commerce, Economics and Statistical Administration.

U.S. Bureau of the Census. (2001c, January 13). *Projections of the total resident population by 5-year age groups, race, and Hispanic origin with special age categories: Middle series, 2050 to 2070.* Retrieved January 29, 2001, from the World Wide Web: www.census.gov/population/projections/nation/summary/np-t4-g.txt

U.S. Bureau of the Census. (2001d, January 2). *Resident population estimates of the United States by sex, race, and Hispanic origin: April 1, 1990 to November 1, 1999, with short-term projection to November 1, 2000.* Retrieved January 29, 2001, from the World Wide Web: www.census.gov/population/estimates/nation/intfile3-1.txt

U.S. Congress. (1986). *Indian health care.* Springfield, VA: National Technical Information Service.

Washington, E. D., & McLoyd, V. (1982). The external validity of research involving American minorities. *Human Development, 25,* 324-339.

Part I

CONCEPTUAL, PROFESSIONAL, AND TRAINING ISSUES

CHAPTER 1

A Tale of Challenge and Change
A History and Chronology of Ethnic Minorities in Psychology in the United States

BERTHA GARRETT HOLLIDAY
American Psychological Association

ANGELA L. HOLMES
University of the District of Columbia

The history of ethnic minority psychology in the United States is characterized by four major themes:

1. the promulgation of theories and data that were used by psychologists and others to support notions of scientific racism—especially as these relate to the legitimacy of White advantage/superiority and the inferiority, exploitation, discrimination, and dispossession of U.S. peoples of color;

2. the critique and challenge of psychological theories and interventions that support stereotypic notions of the negative and deficit individual psychological characteristics and behaviors of ethnic minority peoples, as well as nonprogressive social policy in ethnic minority communities;

3. the pursuit of ethnic minority inclusion and participation in psychology's scientific and professional associations and literature; and

4. the development and promulgation of theories and interventions derived from the cultures, traditional values and worldviews, and historical experiences of ethnic minority peoples.

BACKGROUND AND OVERVIEW

The content, timing, and significance of many events in the history of ethnic minority

AUTHORS' NOTE: An earlier version of this chapter's "Timeline of Challenge and Change" was prepared by the first author for the final report of the American Psychological Association's Commission on Ethnic Minority Recruitment, Retention, and Training in Psychology (Holliday et al., 1997).

psychology are in response to a major nemesis: psychology's involvement in scientific racism and resulting implications for the development of ethnic minority communities and peoples. Scientific racism is derived from 19th-century theories of evolution, genetics, and heredity. These theories support the cardinal assumption that differences among the world's peoples reflect differences in evolutionary development and that these differences can be viewed hierarchically and valued differentially. The scientific underpinnings of this assumption were hallmarked by the 1859 publication of Charles Darwin's *The Origins of the Species by Means of Natural Selection.*

In addition, during the 19th century, the pervasiveness of the domination, colonization, and enslavement of non-European peoples by Europeans served to create a distinctive racial spin to this assumption. Indeed, by the beginning of the 20th century, scientific racism was cloaked in White racism and White superiority. White Europeans dominated the world. And the justification for this domination was often found in the numerous scientific studies documenting the differences in the cultures, values, social behaviors, and physiology of non-Europeans, which were judged as inferior to those of White Europeans, who were viewed as the inevitable standard for comparison.

The discipline of psychology, which came into existence during the latter half of the 19th century, contributed to the support of scientific racism. Examples of such contributions are evident in the works of Francis Galton and G. Stanley Hall—both of whom were founders of psychology in the United States. Francis Galton, who developed psychometrics and parametric statistical techniques and conducted the first experimental studies of psychological process, devised a 15-point scale of "grades of [psychological] ability." According to Galton, on this scale, the Negro race was, on average, two grades below the Anglo-Saxon,

and the "Australian type" was a further grade lower (Galton, 1869/1962, as cited by Richards, 1997, p. 18). Galton, a cousin of Darwin, also championed eugenics.

G. Stanley Hall, the holder of the first Ph.D. granted in the United States (Harvard University, 1878) and a founder of the American Psychological Association (Street, 1994, chap. 1), advocated a more humane form of scientific racism. Hall argued that compared to White Europeans, "lower races" were at a different, more adolescent stage of their life cycle. To address this situation, Hall supported the development of "civilizing programs" tailored to specific needs of a given group (Hall, 1904, as cited in Richards, 1997, pp. 22-24). Thus, Hall accepted racial hierarchies but rejected the permanence both of the hierarchical rankings and their assumption of White superiority and dominance.

Thus, by the beginning of the 20th century, the major components were in place for the scientific background of the stage on which the history of ethnic minority psychology would be played. These major components related to the scientific racism perspective. And the relationship of the emerging discipline of psychology to that perspective would serve to dictate several conditions of the forthcoming drama, including the following:

1. Due to assumptions of innate inferiority and associated conditions of social dominance and restricted opportunities, ethnic minorities or persons of color would not be involved in establishing the new discipline of psychology, defining its major issues of concerns and procedures, or establishing its major organizational structures and professional standards of conduct, academic departments, and scholarly journals.

2. Psychological theories, perspectives, and extant knowledge emanating from non-European peoples and their communities would not be valued by or readily incorporated into the new discipline.

3. In the main, assumptions and derivatives of scientific racism would be integral to the sustenance and legitimization of the emerging discipline of psychology; in turn, the theories and procedures of that discipline would be used to support the assumptions of scientific racism and its derivatives.

4. As symbolized by the differences in the perspectives of Galton and Hall, from its inception, psychology in the United States would be characterized by its simultaneous tendencies to serve as tools for both oppression and development of the nation's communities of color.

It was the existence of this latter possibility that has attracted and continues to attract persons of color to the discipline, despite its historical embeddedness in scientific racism.

But the stage for the history of people of color in psychology involved far more than scientific factors; it also involved social contextual factors grounded in indigenous and traditional customs, values, and beliefs; historical experience; and political-economic realities. Descriptions of such factors are incorporated into the following history of ethnic minority psychology in the United States.

NARRATIVE ON THE HISTORY OF ETHNIC MINORITIES IN U.S. PSYCHOLOGY

The Mid-19th Century

During the last half of the 19th century, and consistent with the imperialistic adventures of major European nations, the United States engaged in a multifaceted program of colonialism and national expansion that was marked not only by vast land acquisitions but also by the conquest, oppression, and exploitation of peoples of color. The scope and intensity of such activity are readily apparent when one considers that at the beginning of the 19th century, more than 80% of what are now the contiguous

48 states was Indian land (Nies, 1996, chap. 7). But that quickly changed.

The Louisiana Purchase of 1803 extended the boundaries of the United States from the Mississippi River to the Rocky Mountains and sparked public policies of removal of American Indians from their lands. Florida (i.e., what is now Florida, Alabama, and parts of Georgia) was purchased from Spain in 1819. In 1844, U.S. claims to the Oregon Territory were recognized by Britain. In 1845, the Republic of Texas was admitted to the United States, and in 1848, Mexico ceded to the United States the southwestern and western lands that later became the territories of New Mexico, Arizona, California, and part of the state of Texas. Remaining Mexican land in these territories was sold to the United States in 1853, thus completing acquisition of the continental portion of the United States.

The land acquisitions of the mid-19th century also were associated with both the racial/ethnic diversification of the U.S. population and the emergence and institutionalization of strategies for the management of indigenous, enslaved, and immigrant populations (cf. Gonzalez, 2000, chap. 5; Nies, 1996, chap. 7; Sanchez, 1966). For example, in 1823, the Office of Indian Affairs was established within the U.S. War Department. In the 1830s, the forcible removal of the Five Civilized Tribes (i.e., the Chickasaw, the Cherokee, the Creek, the Choctaw, and the Seminole) from southern states to Oklahoma marked the beginning of the Indian reservation system and ensured the continuation and expansion of the Southern plantation economy, which was grounded on the labor of enslaved Africans (Nies, 1996, chap. 7). Furthermore, the acquisition of southwestern and western lands included more than 100,000 persons of Spanish and/or Mexican descent who became the object of land theft, violence, and disenfranchisement (Gonzalez, 2000, chap. 5; Samura, 1996; Sanchez, 1966).

Timeline of Challenge and Change: The Inclusion of People of Color
in Psychology in the United States

1869	Major General Canby, military commander of Union forces occupying Virginia, authorizes the establishment of the first U.S. institution for the exclusive care of African American mental patients. Howard's Grove Asylum, later named Central State Hospital, was opened in April 1885 near Petersburg (Street, 1994, p. 42).
1892	The American Psychological Association is founded by 26 [White] men (Street, 1994).
1899	Howard University offers its first psychology course, "Psychology: The Brief Course" (Hopkins, Ross, & Hicks, 1994).
1917	U.S. War Department adopts the Army Alpha and Army Beta Tests developed by psychologist Robert Yerkes (Street, 1994).
1920	Francis C. Sumner is the first African American awarded the Ph.D. in psychology from a U.S. institution (Clark University); dissertation title: "Psychoanalysis of Freud and Adler" (Guthrie, 1994; Street, 1994). J. Henry Alston is first African American to publish a research article (titled "Psychophysics of the Spatial Condition of the Fusion of Warmth and Cold in Heat") in an exclusively psychological journal, the *American Journal of Psychology* (T. C. Cadwallader, as cited by Benimoff, 1995).

Immediately after the United States acquired California lands, the Gold Rush of the 1850s sparked not only an onslaught of speculators but also the start of Asian immigration to the United States, which intensified during the building of the Pacific Railroad in the 1860s (Daniels & Kitano, 1970, chap. 3; Gossett, 1963/1965, chap. 12). Furthermore, economic factors—related to the use of enslaved Africans and the South's plantation economy, northern industrialization, and federal policies affecting the nation's western expansion—were at the root of the nation's Civil War of 1861-1865. After the Civil War, the employment of former soldiers in the army of the West ensured that the Indian wars took on the characteristics of major military campaigns (Nies, 1996, chap. 7). And then, after the Civil War, there was also the cost of Reconstruction.[1]

During this era, psychology as a scientific discipline had not as yet emerged in the United States.

The Last Quarter of the 19th Century

This era began in the midst of a national economic depression, which shifted national concern from issues such as the rebuilding of the South (i.e., Reconstruction) to national economic policy. Imperialistic ambitions continued as reflected in the Paris Treaty of 1898, which signaled the end of the Spanish-American war and ceded Puerto Rico, Cuba, Guam, and the Philippines to the United States.[2]

As previously noted, psychology as a discipline began to emerge during this era. In 1878, G. Stanley Hall was awarded the first Ph.D. in psychology granted by a U.S. institution (Harvard University). Later, Hall established the first U.S. psychology research laboratory in 1883 at Johns Hopkins University; in 1887, he edited and published the first issue of the *American Journal of Psychology* (Street, 1994, pp. 49, 56, 64). The first meeting of the International

Congress of Psychology was conducted in 1889. And in 1892, the American Psychological Association was founded by 26 White men of European descent (Street, 1994, pp. 67, 77). Much of the psychological research of the times focused on studies of basic psychological/sensory processes.

During this era, the history of people of color in psychology was limited to their occasional mention as subjects of various speculative theories, and descriptive and experimental studies often focused on physiological or sensory racial differences (cf. Gossett, 1963/1965, pp. 364-365; Guthrie, 1976; Richards, 1997, chaps. 2, 4). However, in general, these studies were fundamentally of academic and scientific interest, with relatively few social policy implications.[3] Racism was just beginning to place its indelible stamp on psychology.

The First Quarter of the 20th Century

This was an era of new beginnings punctuated by massive movements of people both to and within the United States. In the midst of these massive movements of human populations, World War I occurred. The war served to somewhat mute the social dislocation, economic competition, and political discomfort occasioned by the "newcomer" immigrants and migrants. But after the war, social and political debate increasingly focused on means for understanding and controlling the impact of the "newcomers."

The largest voluntary immigration of Europeans to the United States occurred during the decade of 1900-1910. This immigration continued until the outbreak of World War I, which diverted the use of transatlantic ships (the primary means of immigrant transcontinental transport) to war purposes.

In addition, the Southwest's Mexican American population radically increased by more than 1 million persons as a result of displacement resulting from the Mexican Revolution (1910-1920) and the massive recruitment of Mexican labor as agricultural, mining, railroad, and industrial workers (Gonzalez, 2000, chap. 3). Japanese immigration also began to boom during the early part of the 20th century. In 1900, there were only 10,000 Japanese among California's population of nearly 1.5 million; by 1920, California's Japanese population had increased to 72,000 (Daniels & Kitano, 1970, chap. 3; Gossett, 1963/1965, chap. 12).[4] Filipino immigration also became prominent between 1920 and 1930, during which that group's U.S. population increased from 5,000 to 45,000 (Daniels & Kitano, 1970, p. 66; Okamura & Agbayani, 1991).

Prior to the U.S. entry into World War I in 1917, the Great Migration began of an estimated 500,000 to 1 million African Americans from southern rural areas to northern urban areas and, to a much lesser extent, to the West (Great Migration, 1999, pp. 869-872). In contrast, American Indians were distinguished by the absence of their involvement in any "new beginnings" during the early 20th century. Federal policies of isolation, exploitation, and assimilation continued to ensure that Indians were outside the mainstream of historical and social developments. Indeed, for Indians, the early years of the 20th century were marked by continued disruption of culture, loss and theft of natural resources (especially oil and water), and social neglect as a result of the enactment of more allotment laws (which broke up traditional systems of collective land tenure of reservation lands, fostered the destruction of tribal leadership, and defined *Indian* based on the race-based notion of "blood quantum") and other governmental actions (cf. Nies, 1996, chap. 8).[5]

After World War I, in the nation's communities of color—especially in the South—the continuing entrenchment of oppression and discrimination and the increased incidence of racial intimidation and terrorism (as epitomized by the resurgence of lynching and the Ku Klux Klan[6]) served to institutionalize the color coding of the nation's social relations and political-economic activities.

In contrast, most European American communities prospered after World War I. Nevertheless, new European immigrants and migrants continued to be a source of discomfort for the nation. Consequently, immigration policy became a topic of public debate (cf. Gossett, 1963/1965, chaps. 12-15). So, in 1924, a more stringent Immigration Act was enacted that limited the number of immigrants to 2% of immigrants from a given country living in the United States as of 1890 and extended the ban against Asian immigration. This served to favor the older immigrant groups from northern and western Europe over the newer immigrant groups from southern and eastern Europe (Daniels & Kitano, 1970, pp. 54-56; Gossett, 1963/1965, pp. 405-406).

For the discipline of psychology, the first quarter of the 20th century was a period of consolidation and entrenchment. It also was an era when psychology actively championed tenets of scientific racism. All of these developments were, to a large extent, spurred by refinements in psychometric and experimental techniques and the applications of these techniques to problems of national concern.

For example, Binet and Simon introduced intelligence testing in 1905. In 1916, U.S. psychologist Lewis Terman and his associates published the Stanford-Binet Test—a revision of the Binet-Simon Test. This event, coupled with Binet's death, served to shift the center of IQ testing from France to the United States.

Later, the American Psychological Association (APA), under the leadership of Robert M. Yerkes, spearheaded psychologists' involvement in World War I, which resulted in the creation of Army Alpha and Army Beta Tests of mental and performance abilities. These tests, which were the first intelligence tests developed for large-group administration, were adopted by the army in 1917 and administered to more than 1.7 million men, primarily for the purpose of identifying those who might be suitable for officer training (Gossett, 1963/1965, pp. 365-367; Richards, 1997, chap. 4; Street, 1994, pp. 74, 138). The Psychological Corporation, a major publisher of assessment instruments, was founded in 1921 (Street, 1994, p. 75). Psychologists also contributed to the medical treatment and rehabilitation of soldiers (Street, 1994, p. 74).

As a result of such activities, psychology was enabled to represent itself as an empirically based science whose findings were not biased by value-laden theoretical assumptions but rather were the results of unbiased empirical techniques. Social and scientific entrenchment and legitimacy of the new discipline were ensured when it was demonstrated that these techniques could be used in service of national goals and to address perceived "threats" to national interests, including those occasioned by the era's European immigration and increased racial competition.

In the case of immigration, and to a large degree, as a result of the massive administration of the Army Alpha and Beta Tests, psychological studies of intelligence and other psychological characteristics were explicitly used in the service of the eugenics aspects of scientific racism.[7] Thus, intelligence and other psychological tests were used to identify "less desirable" immigrant groups, and psychologists used such findings to justify immigration restrictions and associated differential immigration preference for persons based on their nation of origin.[8]

Although data from the Army Alpha Test indicated that racial differences in mental test scores varied across geographical areas—thus suggesting significant environmental influences on intellectual functioning—the assumed innateness of intelligence was the more dominant and prevailing idea of the day.

Consequently, the army tests spawned a large number of studies on racial differences in psychological (both intellectual and personality) characteristics. The stated implications of these studies most often focused on issues related to the management, socialization, and education of the nation's people of color.[9] Indeed, the bulk of this era's psychological research on persons of color was used to justify racially differential treatment—especially in educational opportunity for children of color, which emerged as an issue of public debate during Reconstruction. Thus, psychologists used their psychometric and empirical techniques to justify both different and separate education for children of color.

Richards (1997) has characterized the body of psychological studies addressing both immigrant and racial intellectual and learning attributes that emerged during this era as "race psychology" (cf. Klineberg, 1945). In general, race psychology sought to refine and document scientific racism assumptions—especially those related to the innate, biologically based, inheritable aspects of race differences and related eugenetic concerns, as well as its "mulatto hypothesis," whereby biracial individuals are viewed as having psychological attributes that are intermediate to those of their parents' racial group (Richards, 1997, chap. 4).

It was also during this era that ethnic minorities first began participating in the discipline of psychology as scholars. In 1920, African American Francis C. Sumner became the first person of color awarded a Ph.D. in psychology from a U.S. institution (Guthrie, 1998; Street, 1994). In the same year, J. Henry Alston, an African American, became the first person of color to publish a research article in an exclusively psychological journal (T. C. Cadwalleder, as cited by Benimoff, 1995).

Thus, the first quarter of the 20th century is notable in the history of ethnic minority psychology as the era when tenets of scientific racism were incorporated into mainstream psychology and when ethnic minorities first lay claim to inclusion and participation in the young discipline of psychology. Both developments, to a great extent, were centered on (differing) concerns about the capabilities and education of children of color, and both occurred against a common historical background marked by economic progress, war, increased racial competition, and increased concern among European Americans about control of both ethnic minority and newly arrived immigrant populations. Thus, one can presume there was a tension—a divergence of interests—between the first psychologists of color and their White fellow psychologists.

The Second Quarter of the 20th Century

This was an era of high drama involving worldwide economic depression and world war. During this era, the world heaved and began reorganizing itself politically, economically, and socially.

The Great Depression and the New Deal

The stock market crashed in 1929, and during the next 10 years, the United States and Europe experienced a severe economic depression. In the United States, no attempt was made to stimulate the economy until Franklin D. Roosevelt (FDR) and his "New Dealers" were swept into the presidency in 1932. The devastation of the Great Depression forced the U.S. citizenry to rethink major assumptions of U.S. American society—including those undergirding scientific racism. Political, economic, and social class analyses became far more salient. And increasingly, citizens looked to the federal government to actively provide for their well-being. In response to the economic situation and changing ideologies and expectations, the FDR administration developed the "New Deal"—a domestic reform program, including

Timeline of Challenge and Change: The Inclusion of People of Color
in Psychology in the United States

1928	Psychology department is established at Howard University, chaired by Francis C. Sumner (Hopkins et al., 1994).
1930s	Four historically Black colleges and universities (HBCUs) offer psychology as an undergraduate major (Evans, 1999a, 1999b, Guthrie, 1998).
1933	Inez B. Prosser is first African American woman awarded a doctorate (Ed.D.) in psychology from a U.S. institution (University of Cincinnati); dissertation title: "Non-Academic Development of Negro Children in Mixed and Segregated schools" (Guthrie, 1976; Task Force, 1995).
1937	Alberta Banner Turner is first African American woman awarded a Ph.D. in psychology from a U.S. institution (Ohio State University) (Guthrie, 1976; T. C. Cadwallader, as cited by Benimoff, 1995).
1938	The first ethnic minority psychological association is established as Division 6, the Department of Psychology, at the meeting of the all-Black American Teachers Association (ATA) for ATA members interested in "the teaching and application of the science of psychology and related fields, particularly in Negro institutions," with Herman Canady, psychologist at West Virginia State College elected as its chairman (Guthrie, 1998).
1943	Robert Chin is first Chinese American awarded a Ph.D. in psychology from a U.S. institution (Columbia University) (S. Sue, 1994).
1949	The National Institute of Mental Health (NIMH) is established (Street, 1994).

both temporary initiatives and permanent reforms.[10] The related effects on both psychology and communities of color were unprecedented (cf. Sellman, 1999a).

Indeed, the dramatic changes occasioned by the Great Depression and the New Deal brought to head a schism, or internal contradiction, within psychology that continues to affect the discipline to this day. Psychology up until the Great Depression had taken great pains to position itself as a(n) (experimental) scientific discipline of a traditional positivist character. In other words, psychology, intellectually and publicly, claimed to be rooted in that type of objectivity wherein fact was not influenced by value. However, the realities of the Great Depression—the sheer scope of its human misery, the vast political will and social and economic interventions that would be required to respond affirmatively to its reality, and its negative impact

on the careers and livelihood of psychologists—challenged positivist assumptions. Psychologists increasingly were confronted with the realities of the need for not only a scientific methodology but also a value or ideological framework that enabled an understanding of the effects of social-economic factors on behavior (cf. Harris, 1986).

Consequently, before and during the Great Depression, on one hand, psychology continued in a very steadfast, almost blinders-on manner to institutionalize the accouterments of an established scientific discipline, despite the fact that about 40% of APA members were unemployed (Miller, 1986, p. 127). Thus, APA purchased and began publishing five psychological journals in 1925; launched a journal of abstracts, *Psychological Abstracts,* in 1927; and issued its first publication manual (i.e., instructions to authors of psychological manuscripts) in

1928. Psi Chi, the national honor society in psychology, was established in 1929, and the first of a series of thirty 15-minute weekly radio lectures titled "Psychology Today" was broadcast over 50 NBC-affiliated stations in 1931. During this era, behaviorism began to flower, and testing and psychometrics continued to flourish as suggested by the premier administrations of the College Entrance Examination Board's Scholastic Aptitude Test (SAT) in 1926 and the Iowa Tests of Basic Skills standardized achievement tests in 1935, the conduct of the first Educational Testing Service Invitation Conference in 1936, and the publication of David Weschler's *The Measurement of Adult Intelligence* in 1939 (Street, 1994, chap. 3).

In addition, clinical psychology began its professionalization through the 1935 publication of the "Report of the Clinical Section of the APA," which defined clinical psychology, described standards for training, and provided a guide to all of the psychological clinics in the United States (Street, 1994, chap. 3).

The race psychologists continued their studies. But increasingly, their findings tended to disconfirm major tenets of scientific racism. In attempting to demonstrate the innateness of racial differences, these researchers increasingly sought to control the effects of a variety of nongenetic factors and met with highly mixed success. Furthermore, such attempts often resulted in highlighting the potential effects that environmental variables could in fact have on human behavior in general and on the observed racial differences in particular.[11] Also, the biological integrity of racial categories (not to mention that of the "mulatto") was increasingly challenged by a variety of interests, including other scientific disciplines (cf. Guthrie, 1998, p. 30; Richards, 1997, chaps. 4, 5).

On the other hand, during this same era, there emerged a distinct clamor within psychology for recognition that social issues and social problems are not separate from science but instead should be a subject of psychological theory and methodology. Paradoxically, in consideration of psychologists' active involvement in the immigration policies some 10 years earlier, this call for psychology's involvement in social issues was (and continues to be) viewed as a stance advocated by the more "radical" (and "softer") element of psychologists.

During the Depression era, attempts to engage psychology in social issues were best represented by the establishment of the Psychologists League (PL) in 1934 in New York City and the Society for the Psychological Study of Social Issues (SPSSI—Division 9 of the APA) in 1936. The founding of both of these organizations was stimulated by the socialist, Marxist, Marxist-Leninist, and social democrat interests of most of their founding members. The Psychologists League was an activist organization committed both to ideological critique of issues pertinent to psychological theory and to direct political action. More specifically, PL consistently published articles in its journal that subjected psychological theory to sociopolitical critique, conducted forums on social psychological topics such as racial differences and issues of war and peace, and continuously and directly advocated for the expansion of the roles of psychologists and the employment of psychologists in New Deal programs. Most PL members were clinicians, and many were master's-level psychologists (Finison, 1986; Miller, 1986).

In contrast, SPSSI, whose early members were mostly academic, nonclinical, Ph.D.-level psychologists, was primarily concerned with the application of psychological theory and methods to the scholarly study of such social issues as war, industrial conflict, and racial prejudice and the testing of hypotheses regarding social change (Finison, 1986; Morawski, 1986).

Both PL and SPSSI actively critiqued intelligence testing and many of its scientific racism assumptions. PL held forums and published articles critiquing such testing, and SPSSI issued public statements in 1939 on the misuse and misinterpretations of these tests (Finison, 1986; Morawski, 1986). SPSSI, in conjunction with the Yale Institute of Human Relations (which was established in 1929), also initiated what would be landmark investigations into the roots and nature of prejudice (Sitkoff, 1978, pp. 194-201; Street, 1994, p. 175). As a result of such efforts, there emerged within psychology a distinct sector that sought to apply psychology to social problems. Indeed, the study of social attitudes became a major defining topic of the then emerging field of experimental social psychology.

Richards (1997) argued that those efforts of the new applied psychologists that focused on the problems of the nation's communities of color, along with the newer findings of the race psychologists, served to promote an anti-racist perspective that successfully challenged most of the traditional assumptions of scientific racism related to the innate sources of racial differences as well as the claim these assumptions had on mainstream scientific theory.

Major tenets of this anti-racism perspective were as follows: (a) Racial/ethnic differences in psychological characteristics can be attributed to environmental differences; (b) racial comparison studies are methodologically insufficient and flawed, as extant methodology has not and cannot identify and control presumed innate ethnic/racial differences; and (c) race is a category that cannot be justified scientifically, and therefore race should best be construed as either a myth or social construction that is used to justify domination, oppression, and injustice (Richards, 1997, chap. 4).

Consequently, during this era, scholarly and social opinion began shifting to a type of revisionist scientific racism wherein racial minorities were assumed to be "disadvantaged" and "damaged" relative to European Whites as a result of differences in social culture situation and experience rather than by reason of genetic endowment.[12]

For scholars of color in psychology, the Depression was of great significance. This in part was due to the New Deal's provision of new opportunities for people of color to be involved in federal policymaking.[13] In addition, private foundations (e.g., the Rosenwald Fund, the General Education Board) along with various New Deal programs provided both higher educational opportunities and jobs for a small but growing number of social scientists of color, including psychologists (cf. Holliday, 1989, 1999). This served to help strengthen an emerging institutional base for African Americans in psychology.[14]

Indeed, at the 1938 meeting of the all-Black American Teachers Association (ATA), a division was organized for ATA members interested in "the teaching and application of the science of psychology and related fields, particularly in Negro institutions." Herman Canady, psychologist at West Virginia State College, was elected president. However, the impending war blunted the future of this first organized group of ethnic minority psychologists (Guthrie, 1998, pp. 142-145).

Likewise, the active participation of then psychology graduate student/young professional Kenneth B. Clark, an African American, in SPSSI marked the beginning of meaningful minority participation in the national psychological associations (Finison, 1986, pp. 31-32). Clark would later become president of the American Psychological Association.

In conclusion, the Great Depression era in the history of ethnic minority psychology is marked by a significant change in psychology's ideology, including a modification of its positivist perspective to include the legitimacy of the confluence of science and social ideology and the explicit recognition that psychological science can be used in the solution of social problems. This ideological shift was accompanied by the advent of experimental social psychology, the expansion of applied psychology, and the demise of assumptions of the innateness of racial differences in mainstream psychology. This is not to say that such assumptions disappeared from psychology. It is to say that from the Great Depression era to the present, assumptions of such innate racial differences (especially in intelligence) have been continuously challenged by various sectors of psychology and have progressively assumed a fringe position relative to mainstream theory and assumptions in psychology.

Ethnic minority psychologists—especially African Americans—witnessed some minor expansion in their numbers and a significant expansion in their roles and stature as a result of the political liberalization of psychology and the opportunities of the New Deal. For the first time, ethnic minority psychologists were visible in intellectual and policy debates related to the study of racial differences and social and educational problems in minority communities.[15] Their involvement in such issues would prove to be a harbinger of future activities. In addition, African American psychologists organized the first ethnic minority psychological association and also began to participate in the major U.S. psychological associations.

All of this occurred against a background of the economic crisis and large-scale human misery that occasioned political radicalization, including increasing public expectations of a greater role of federal government in regulation and support of the nation's social and economic activities, as well as growing political turmoil abroad that would soon erupt into a world war.

World War II and Its Aftermath

New Deal programs served to blunt the misery of the Great Depression. But it took a world war to restore the nation to economic prosperity. For communities of color, prosperity often came with a high price.

War broke out in Europe in September 1939 when Britain and the allied powers declared war on Germany after it invaded Poland. The United States immediately began mobilizing for war but did not officially enter the war until the Japanese bombed the U.S. military at Pearl Harbor in December 1941. The war ended in 1945.

Two months after the bombing, Executive Order 9066 required the forced relocation of all persons of Japanese ancestry (both citizens and aliens who numbered more than 110,000) living in the western halves of the states of California, Oregon, and Washington and the southern half of Arizona to 10 internment or concentration camps (with barrack-type accommodations, barbed wire, and armed guards) located in inaccessible, barren areas in the Southern and Southwestern United States and administered by the War Relocation Authority (WRA) (cf. O'Brien & Fugita, 1991, chaps. 3, 4).[16]

The war did not stop Indians' continuing loss of land. For example, an estimated 900,000 acres of Indian lands in Alaska and 16 Indian reservations in the West were taken by the U.S. government to use as air bases, gunnery ranges, nuclear test sites, training installations, or internment camps (Nies, 1996, pp. 343-344). Discrimination also continued for African Americans, which resulted in a great deal of discontent and civil rights activism. For example, during the summer of 1943, there were 250 racial conflicts in 47 cities; the National Association for the Advancement of Colored People (NAACP) and the Black press launched a "Double V" campaign for victory over fascism abroad and racism at home; and between 1940 and 1946, the NAACP membership grew from 50,000 to 450,000 (Sellman, 1999c). In the case of Hispanics, although the Great Depression occasioned a federal program of deportation by the trainloads, war occasioned the opposite. For example, the Bracero Agreement of 1942 allowed the temporary immigration of up to 100,000 contracted laborers per year from Mexico, who were to be paid prevailing wages (Gonzalez, 2000, chap. 5; Scholes, 1966). All of the major U.S. populations of color participated in the military in World War II—albeit usually in segregated units.[17] Many of these men of color became politically radicalized upon returning after the war to discrimination, racial segregation, and restricted opportunities.

For psychology, the prosperity of the war years served to take the edge off of its new-found social activism. Instead, as was the case in World War I, psychology took advantage of wartime needs to expand its spheres of influence and expertise and to further entrench itself into the institutional and cultural fabric of U.S. society. But this time, the vehicle to such ends primarily involved the contributions of clinical psychology, as well as the alignment of scientific psychological research with compelling national interests.

Cognizant of its success in World War I, U.S. psychology formally mobilized for ensuring its active involvement in World War II.[18] As part of the mobilization, the American Psychological Association was reorganized in 1944 to include its present divisional and Council of Representatives structures and initiated use of a professional staff (Street, 1994, chap. 4.)

The significant role of clinical psychology to U.S. war efforts was heralded by the 1940 release of the U.S. Selective Service System's Medical Circular #1, which provided guidance for conducting minimal mental and personality inspection of draftees (Street, 1994, p. 205). In 1944, 244 enlisted persons (including 5 women and 1 African American) were appointed officers in the army and given short, intensive courses in clinical psychology. In addition, the 1944 GI Bill of Rights authorized the Veterans Administration (VA) to provide mental health assistance to veterans. In 1946, the Veterans Administration adopted the doctoral degree and internship as the minimum qualification for clinical psychologists and initiated a field training program in clinical psychology for doctoral psychology students having both academic and clinical training (i.e., a forerunner of psychology's scientist-practitioner model of clinical training). At the same time, the VA appointed its first chief clinical psychologist for the VA Central Office, who in turn appointed psychology chiefs at the 13 VA branch offices (Baker, 1992; Guthrie, 1998, p. 141).

In response to the VA's need to identify psychology programs that provided both academic and clinical training, the APA established standards for training clinical psychologists and prepared its first list of APA-evaluated graduate clinical psychology programs in 1947, thus initiating the accreditation process of professional psychology programs. The first state licensing law regulating professional psychology was enacted by Connecticut in 1945, and the American Board of Professional Psychology was established in 1946 (Street, 1994, pp. 212-219).

The modern fate of scientific psychology was shaped by the 1941 establishment of a federal Office of Scientific Research and Development (OSRD) for the purpose of entering into contracts for basic and applied research related to national defense, as well as medical research pertinent to military concerns (National Academy of Sciences, 1964, pp. 22-23). As a result, the military-industrial complex was born, and the funding of research became a proper concern of federal government.

Near the end of the war, an OSRD committee issued a report on the federal role in postwar scientific research. As a result of the report's recommendations, a number of federal research funding agencies were established, including the National Institutes of Health in 1944, the National Institute of Mental Health in 1949, and the National Science Foundation in 1950 (National Academy of Sciences, 1964, pp. 22-49; Street, 1994, pp. 210, 215, 222). These developments served to enormously strengthen the research missions and institutional budgets of U.S. universities, including those of departments of psychology, and, in so doing, ensured the viability of scientific psychology (cf. Holliday, 1999).

During and after World War II, persons of color continued to slowly increase their participation in psychology. In 1943, Robert Chin became the first Chinese American to be awarded a Ph.D. in psychology in the United States (S. Sue, 1994). Guthrie (1998, chap. 7) reported that by 1950, 32 African Americans had received a Ph.D. or Ed.D. in psychology or educational psychology. Psychology also continued to flourish in the nation's Black colleges and universities—especially after World War II, when these institutions were strengthened due to the influx of former Black soldiers using their GI education benefits. Psychologists of color also began gaining access to clinical psychology jobs in the Veterans Administration system (Evans, 1999a, 1999b; Guthrie, 1998, chap. 6).[19]

In addition, the scholarly attacks against the assumptions of scientific racism continued, aided by the increasing stature of research guided by theories and methods related to social attitudes, culture and personality, and social learning. For example, psychologist John Dollard (1937) made use of these new paradigms in his study of racial prejudice in *Caste and Class in a Southern Town*. In 1944, Swedish social economist Gunnar Myrdal published his classical work on U.S. racism, *An American Dilemma*, which sought to debunk lingering assumptions of scientific racism and turned the discussion of racism on its head by declaring that the Negro problem was fundamentally "a White man's problem," requiring developmental intervention targeted on those social and institutional practices that White men had created (Myrdal, 1944). This study, which involved collaboration with several Black social scientists, served to provide scientific legitimacy and scholarly stature to the efforts of researchers of color.

Additional challenges to scientific racism emerged in response to the anti-Semitism of the Nazis and the resulting Jewish Holocaust. In 1944, the American Jewish Committee authorized a series of studies on prejudice, several of which were conducted by psychologists. Examples of these studies are Adorno, Frenkel-Brunswik, Levinson, and Sanford's (1950) *The Authoritarian Personality* and Bettelheim and Janowitz's (1950) *Dynamics of Prejudice*.

The use of IQ tests as measures of innate intelligence also continued to be challenged. One of the most notable such projects, which defined the parameters of culturally biased and culturally fair tests, was chaired by African American social anthropologist Allison Davis of the University of Chicago (Eells, Davis, Havinghurst, Herrick, & Tyler, 1951; cf. Guthrie, 1998, p. 78), who in 1941 was also the first African American awarded a full-time faculty appointment at a predominantly White U.S. university.[20]

In general, during the second quarter of the 20th century, the professional status of psychology in ethnic minority communities in many ways mirrored that of mainstream U.S. psychology some 50 to 75 years earlier. That is, ethnic minority psychologists, who at that time were mostly African Americans, were involved in establishing departments of psychology in historically Black colleges and identifying other limited professional opportunities—primarily in education and government sectors.

This first small cadre of psychologists of color confronted a racially segregated social order and highly restricted professional opportunities. Furthermore, psychology's affiliation with scientific racism also presented ideological barriers. Consequently, these African American psychologists had few opportunities to model their careers after those of their European American psychology colleagues (who had initially modeled themselves after German psychologists).

Instead, these early psychologists of color tended to model their behavior and values after those of other African American scholars and intellectuals while drawing their ambitions and intellectual affinities from those of their communities. As a result, this first major cadre of psychologists of color tended to adopt a scholar-activist role (cf. Holliday, 1999) and gravitated to psychological issues with practical applications—especially related to education (Guthrie, 1998, p. 123). Their research typically was tools for community development and advocacy. And their legacy continues to mark the efforts of contemporary psychologists of color.

The second quarter of the 20th century also was an era when the scholarly framework for critique of the assumptions and tenets of scientific racism and related nonprogressive social policy was cogently formulated and formally articulated.

The Third Quarter of the 20th Century

The end of the world war and the dawn of the 1950s spawned self-examination and challenge. Oppressed and colonized people throughout the world initiated liberation and decolonization efforts—especially among people and nations of color. In the world's western and northern nations, industrialization resulted in a tremendous increase in capital and wealth. Thus, this era involved the creation of new situations and new identities: It was an era of reinvention.

In the United States, the postwar years were characterized by economic growth, an increased emphasis on consumerism, and associated rising expectations. These were bolstered by generous veterans benefits that enabled millions of U.S. citizens to obtain a college education and become homeowners. These programs, along with those of the New Deal, served to reaffirm the U.S. ethos of upward social mobility.

In the nation's growing communities of color, returning soldiers made active use of veterans benefits, thus laying the groundwork for both an entrenched ethnic minority middle class and what would decades later emerge as the first massive intergenerational transfer of wealth in communities of color. Nevertheless, returning soldiers of color evidenced dissatisfaction and unrest on returning to segregated communities after risking life and limb on battlefields in defense of democracy.

Consequently, it was almost inevitable (although rarely predicted by psychologists or others) that this unrest and dissatisfaction would become manifest in organized social agitation and protest. The agitation and protests of communities of color were punctuated and informed by other events, including urban civil uprisings of the 1960s, the domestic social-political dynamics of the Vietnam War, and federal programs of the 1960s and 1970s (e.g., the U.S. Office of Economic Opportunity—i.e., the Johnson administration's "War Against Poverty" and the Model Cities program), which emphasized the development of grassroots leadership and decision making.

In addition, the Immigration Act of 1965 turned the U.S. pattern of immigration upside down by eliminating immigration quotas based on national origins with favor given to European nationals (Min, 1995, p. 11). These were replaced by three criteria related to (a) occupational skills needed in the U.S. labor market, (b) relationships with persons residing in the United States (family unification), and (c) vulnerability to political and religious persecution. Provision also was made for admission under certain circumstances of "special immigrants" (Min, 1995, p. 11). This policy change would result in catapulting both the growth and diversity of U.S. communities of color.

In regard to unrest and protest, 1954 became a watershed year when the U.S. Supreme Court ruled in favor of the plaintiff in *Brown v. Topeka Board of Education*.

Timeline of Challenge and Change: The Inclusion of People of Color
in Psychology in the United States

1950   The National Science Foundation is established (Street, 1994).

1951   Efraín Sanchez-Hidalgo is the first Puerto Rican awarded a Ph.D. in psychology
        (Columbia University); dissertation title: "A Study of Symbiotic Relationships Between
        Friends" (Roca de Torres, 1994b).

1953   The first InterAmerican Congress of Psychology is convened in the Dominican Republic,
        with Andres Aviles (of that country) elected as president (Street, 1994).

1954   The Puerto Rican Psychological Association is established with Efraín Sanchez-Hidalgo,
        Ph.D., as its first president (Padilla, 1980a, 1980b; Roca de Torres, 1994b).

        U.S. Supreme Court rules on *Brown v. Topeka Board of Education* and requires the
        dismantling of racially segregated systems of education "with all deliberate speed."
        Decision in part relied on psychological and social science data on the effects of segregation
        that were prepared by a committee of the Society for the Psychological Study of Social
        Issues (SPSSI—APA Division 9) that included Kenneth B. Clark, Ph.D., Isidor Chein, Ph.D.,
        and Stuart Cook, Ph.D. (Benjamin & Crouse, 2002).

1955   APA Council of Representatives approves its first model legislation for state licensure of
        professional psychologists (Street, 1994).

1955   Publication of *Prejudice and Your* Child by African American psychologist
        Kenneth B. Clark.

1958   Publication of Audrey Shuey's *The Testing of Negro Intelligence,* which argues the
        existence of native [innate] racial IQ differences of 13 to 15 points (Richards, 1997).

1962   Martha Bernal is first Mexican American woman awarded the Ph.D. in psychology
        (Indiana University) (Bernal, 1994; Street, 1994).

1963   The APA Ad Hoc Committee on Equality of Opportunity in Psychology (CEOP) is
        established by the APA Board of Directors in response to a proposal from Division 9
        (SPSSI) relative to the training and employment of Negroes. The committee is charged "to
        explore the possible problems encountered in training and employment in psychology as a
        consequence of race" (APA, 1963; Comas-Diaz, 1990; Wispe et al., 1969).

        The Community Mental Health Center Act, which provided funding for construction and
        operation of community facilities, is signed into law (Street, 1994).

1965   A graduate program in psychology is established at the University of Puerto Rico,
        Rio Piedras campus (Guillermo Bernal, personal communication, July 24, 1996).

1967   Martin Luther King, Jr., at the Invitation of SPSSI (APA Division 9) delivers a distinguished
        address at the APA convention on the topic of "The Role of the Behavioral Scientist in the
        Civil Rights Movement."

1968   The Association of Black Psychologists (ABPsi) is established at the APA Convention in
        San Francisco, with Charles L. Thomas, Ph.D., and Robert L. Green, Ph.D., elected as
        co-chairs (Street, 1994; Williams, 1974).

        ABPsi Co-Chair Charles L. Thomas presents a *Petition of Concerns* to the APA Council of
        Representatives that addresses three major issues: (a) the extremely limited number of
        Black psychologists and Black graduate and undergraduate students in psychology, (b) the
        APA's failure to address social problems such as poverty and racism, and (c) the inadequate
        representation of Blacks in the APA governance structure (Guzman, Schiavo, & Puente,
        1992; Williams, 1974).

(continued)

Timeline of Challenge and Change *(Continued)*

Howard University, an HBCU, establishes a Ph.D. program in psychology (Hopkins et al., 1994).

1969   The Black Students Psychological Association (BSPA) is established at the Western Psychological Association meeting in Vancouver, British Columbia (Williams, 1974).

BSPA President Gary Simpkins presents demands to the APA related to the recruitment, retention, and training of Black students and faculty (Figueroa-Garcia, 1994; Guzman et al., 1992; Street, 1994; Williams, 1974).

Publication of Arthur Jensen's *Harvard Educational Review* monograph, "How Much Can We Boost IQ and Scholastic Achievement?" which argues that race IQ differences reflect innate differences assuming hereditability of IQ (Richards, 1997, chap. 9).

1970   The Association of Psychologists Por La Raza (APLR) is founded at the APA convention in Miami (Bernal, 1994).

The APA establishes the Commission for Accelerating Black Participation in Psychology (CABPP), composed of representatives of BSPA, ABPsi, and APA, and charges CABPP to address BSPA's concerns (Blau, 1970; Williams, 1974).

ABPsi provides all graduate departments of psychology its "Ten-Point Program" for increasing the representation of Blacks in psychology; 35 departments agree to immediately implement the entire program (Williams, 1974).

ABPsi and APA develop a 3-year Black Visiting Scientist program to historically Black colleges and universities (Williams, 1974).

BSPA opens offices in the APA building in Washington, D.C., with APA providing 3 years of funding; Ernestine Thomas is the office's director and BSPA national coordinator (Figueroa-Garcia, 1994; Williams, 1974).

First issue of *Network of Indian Psychologists* is published by Carolyn Attneave, Ph.D. (LaFromboise & Fleming, 1990).

Patrick Okura, M.A., a Japanese American psychologist, becomes the executive assistant to the NIMH director and the first ethnic minority psychologist to assume an administrative position at the NIMH.

Kenneth B. Clark, Ph.D., an African American, becomes the first person of color to become the APA president (Pickren & Tomes, 2002; Street, 1994).

1971   In response to demands of the Black Psychiatrists of America, the NIMH Center for Minority Group Mental Health Programs is established with a focus on (a) funding investigator-initiated studies on the mental health concerns of ethnic minorities; (b) establishing and administering six research and development centers, each of which focus on mental health needs of a particular racial/cultural group; and (c) initiating the Minority Fellowship Program, which provides funding to five professional associations to administer minority fellowships for research and clinical training in psychiatry, psychology, psychiatric nursing, psychiatric social work, and sociology (Guzman et al., 1992; Parron, 1990).

An early form of the System of Multicultural Pluralistic Assessment (SOMPA) is published by Jane Mercer and June Lewis (Street, 1994).

(continued)

Timeline of Challenge and Change *(Continued)*

1972   The Asian American Psychological Association (AAPA) is founded with seed monies provided by APA Division 9 (SPSSI); Derald W. Sue, Ph.D., is elected as president (Leong, 1995; S. Sue, 1994).

The First National Conference on Asian American Mental Health is convened in San Francisco with funding provided by NIMH's Center for Minority Mental Health Programs (Leong, 1995).

Publication of the first edition of *Black Psychology*, edited by Reginald L. Jones, Ph.D., which heralds a proactive perspective of the psychology of African Americans.

Psychologist Leon Kamin challenges the authenticity of Sir Cyril Burt's twin study data, which were frequently cited as proof of the hereditability of IQ.

The Bay Area Chapter of the Association of Black Psychologists issues a "Position Statement on Use of IQ and Ability Test," which demands that the California State Department of Education declare a moratorium on these tests' use in assessing Black children (Richards, 1997).

1973   As a result of a vote of the APA membership, the APA Board for Social and Ethical Responsibility for Psychology is established with a mandate that includes issues related to minority participation in psychology (Pickren & Tomes, 2002).

Participants at the Vail Conference on "Levels and Patterns of Professional Training" form a Task Group on Professional Training and Minority Groups and recommend that the APA create an office and board on ethnic minority affairs (Bernal, 1994; Comas-Diaz, 1990).

Publication of the first edition of *Asian Americans: Psychological Perspectives,* edited by Stanley Sue, Ph.D., and Nathaniel Wagner, Ph.D.

A national conference on Chicano psychology is convened at the University of California at Riverside by Manuel Ramirez III and Alfred Casteñeda with funding provided by NIMH (Bernal, 1994; Padilla & Lindhom, 1980).

Jack Sawyer and David J. Senn publish the landmark *Journal of Social Issues* article, "Institutional Racism and the American Psychological Association," which describes how the APA, through an absence of concern about the employment practices of its printers and other suppliers, engaged in institutional racism (Holliday, 1992).

Freda Cheung, Ph.D., is appointed special assistant to the director of NIMH's Minority Programs and thus becomes the first doctoral-level ethnic minority psychologist hired at NIMH (K. P. Okura, personal communication to A. Homes, July, 2001).

1974   The APA Minority Fellowship Program is established with funding provided by NIMH and Dalmas Taylor, Ph.D., as director (Comas-Diaz, 1990; Guzman et al., 1992).

The Association of Black Psychologists publishes the first issue of the *Journal of Black Psychology,* edited by William David Smith, Ph.D. (Street, 1994).

This decision resulted in dismantling the nation's legally sanctioned segregated public education systems with "all deliberate speed." This decision also was notable for two other reasons: (a) It was the first Supreme Court decision to involve the citation of psychological data, and (b) the primary architect in the compilation and use of those data was an African American psychologist—Kenneth B. Clark, Ph.D. (Benjamin & Crouse, 2002).

The *Brown* decision can be viewed as the beginning of the civil rights era, which lasted for nearly a quarter of a century and primarily involved various social-legal tactics and challenges as instruments both for securing protections guaranteed by the Reconstruction era's 14th and 15th Amendments to the U.S.

Constitution and for eliminating racially differential, legally sanctioned practices that existed throughout U.S. society (cf. Sullivan, 1999). The success of these efforts served to increase the movement's self-consciousness and concern with group solidarity and self-reliance. It also sparked a revolution in electoral politics in many communities of color.

However, among the nation's ethnic minority communities, differences in responses to and participation in the civil rights era were grounded in differences among these communities in the types, functions, and maturity of their indigenous organizations and institutions, as well as differences in their contemporary public policy challenges and historical relationships to White America.[21]

Street (1994, chap. 5) has characterized the third quarter of the 20th century as a period when U.S. psychology "comes of age." Indeed, during this era, psychology did not change as much as it broadened and deepened its areas of interest and public influence. During this quarter century, the number of APA divisions nearly doubled in number, increasing from 19 to 36; the first version of the APA's *Ethical Standards of Psychologists* was published in 1953, and the American Psychological Foundation was established in that same year; APA built a new headquarters building (1200 17th St., NW, in Washington, D.C.), which it occupied in 1964; and the Archives of the History of American Psychology was established at the University of Akron in 1965 (Street, 1994, chap. 5).

Professional psychology expanded tremendously, with nearly every state enacting a law for the licensing of psychologists during this era. The APA approved its first standards for predoctoral internships in clinical psychology in 1950, standards for counseling psychology programs were approved in 1951, the organizing meeting of the American Association of State Psychology Boards (now the Association of State and Provincial Psychology Boards) was held in 1960, and the first independent self-standing graduate professional school of psychology was established in 1968 (i.e., the California School of Professional Psychology, now the Alliant International University) (Street, 1994, chap. 5).

Professional psychology also was influenced profoundly by two other developments. Psychotherapeutic drugs were introduced in the 1950s, which radically changed the manner in which mentally ill and emotionally distressed persons were treated and managed. And in 1963, Congress enacted the Community Mental Health Centers Act, which provided an alternative to inpatient care, facilitated deinstitutionalization of the nation's mental hospitals, and resulted in the establishment of nearly 300 centers within 4 years (Street, 1994, chap. 5).

Testing continued to expand as an industry, and the APA continued to actively support this expansion. In 1950, the APA created a Committee on Test Standards, and the first Graduate Record Examination (GRE) was published; the Wechsler Adult Intelligence Scale (WAIS) was published in 1955; the first administration of the American College Test (ACT) occurred in 1959; and the APA published its first *Standards for Educational and Psychological Testing* in 1966 (Street, 1994, chap. 5).

But as testing continued to expand its spheres of use and influence, it also increasingly confronted legal challenges. Often, these challenges involved racial discrimination issues. In 1971, the Supreme Court ruled in *Griggs v. Duke Power Co.* that the irrelevant use of intelligence tests as employment screening instruments constituted racial discrimination. In 1975, a similar Supreme Court ruling was made regarding "inappropriate psychological testing" in *Albermarle Paper Company v. Moody*. In the early 1970s, California courts ruled in the cases *Larry P. v. Riles* and *Diana v. State Board of Education* that, respectively for Black and

Hispanic students, racial bias resulted when intelligence tests were used as the basis for placement in special education (Street, 1994, chap. 6). African American psychologist Asa G. Hilliard III, Ph.D., was the principal architect and lead expert witness of the *Larry P.* challenge.[22]

Psychologists continued to conduct research on social attitudes, social learning, and culture and personality that challenged scientific racism's assumptions of innate racial differences (e.g., Clark, 1955, 1965; Pettigrew, 1964). But this research, which most frequently involved racial comparative research paradigms that subtly promoted assumptions of White superiority, resulted in alternative explanations of the behavior of peoples of color that were equally troubling (cf. Katz, 1969; Pearl, 1970; Rainwater, 1970; Valentine, 1971). For example, Kardiner and Ovesey's (1951/1962) study of Black personality, *The Mark of Oppression,* suggested that Blacks' adaptive response to racism involved the development of pathological personality characteristics, matriarchal families, and emasculated Black males.

Debate related to the appropriate type of education for Black children continued and was expanded to include Hispanic/Latino and other children of color. Educational and developmental researchers such as Riessman (1962) promoted the notion that children of color demonstrated poor educational achievement because they were "culturally deprived." Cognitive psychology researchers ascribed the poor educational achievement of children of color to their "cognitive style differences" (e.g., Hess, 1970; Hess & Shipman, 1965). Psycholinguistics researchers argued about racial/ethnic differences in the surface and deep structures of language, the effects of linguistic structures and bilingualism on cognitive abilities, and whether "Black English" had characteristics of a dialect or a separate language (e.g., Baratz, 1973; Peal & Lambert, 1962). And, of course, issues

related to racial/ethnic differences in IQ scores continued (e.g., Deutsch & Brown, 1964; Dreger, 1973; Lesser, Fifer, & Clark, 1965; Stodolsky & Lesser, 1967). The findings of such research and debates served to influence the design of federally funded programs such as Head Start, various Title I curricular programs for educationally disadvantaged children, and educational television programming, including *Sesame Street* (Laosa, 1984; Washington, 1988).

Nevertheless, the scientific racists, then as now, continued to exhibit remarkable resilience in the face of increasing countervailing evidence. For example, Audrey Shuey's (1958) *The Testing of Negro Intelligence* presented 240 studies that collectively indicated a racial IQ difference of 13 to 15 points (Richards, 1997, pp. 245-246). Arthur Jensen's (1969) *Harvard Educational Review* monograph also argued that race differences reflect innate differences indicative of the heritability of IQ (Richards, 1997, chap. 9).

During the latter part of this era, the APA increasingly became involved in advocacy related to both professional issues and social concerns. In 1957, the APA convention was moved from Miami Beach to New York City due to the former's racial discrimination in public accommodations. In 1962, the APA filed its first amicus curiae brief in *Jenkins v. U.S.,* which challenged the competence of psychologists to testify regarding determinations of sanity. In 1967, SPSSI (Division 9) asked Martin Luther King, Jr. to speak at the APA convention. In 1969, in protest to the brutality inflicted on Vietnam War protesters in Chicago the previous year, the APA convention was moved from Chicago to Washington, D.C. (Pickren & Tomes, 2002; Street, 1994). However, generally in regard to civil rights issues in communities of color, Richards (1997) has argued that the APA was "politically paralyzed by the sheer breadth of its members' interests and political attitudes. Any general statement about

U.S. Psychology and the Civil Rights movement is thus impossible" (p. 238).[23] It was in fact the growing cadre of psychologists of color and their allies that began unparalyzing the APA and its membership.

For psychologists of color, the third quarter of the 20th century was marked by increased diversification and organization. For example, Hispanics/Latinos started gaining a presence in psychology. In 1951, a Puerto Rican (Efrain Sanchez-Hidalgo) was awarded a Ph.D. for the first time. The Puerto Rican Psychological Association was established in 1954, and a graduate program in psychology was established at the University of Puerto Rico, Rio Piedras campus, in 1965. In 1962, Martha Bernal became the first Mexican American woman awarded a Ph.D. in psychology.

In 1963, at the urging of the SPSSI (APA Division 9), the APA established the Ad Hoc Committee on Equality of Opportunity in Psychology (CEOP) as an initial effort to "explore the possible problems encountered in training and employment in psychology as a consequence of race"(APA, 1963, p. 769). The committee's final report (Wispe et al., 1969) documented the underrepresentation of Black psychologists and their alienation from mainstream U.S. psychology.

And then there was the drama of the wake-up call that instigated the APA's de-paralysis. The call was delivered at the 1968 APA convention in San Francisco, when the Association of Black Psychologists (ABPsi) was established and its representatives walked in on the meeting of the APA Board of Directors and presented the ABPsi's "Petition of Concern." This petition addressed the three major issues that would serve as organizing principles for future activities of persons of color in organized psychology. These issues were (a) the low numbers of Black psychologists and Black graduate students in psychology, (b) the APA's failure to address social problems of concern to communities of color (e.g., IQ testing), and (c) the

inadequate representation of Blacks in the APA governance structure (Pickren & Tomes, 2002; Williams, 1974).

The ABPsi example resonated with other psychologists of color. In 1969, a newly established independent Black Students Psychological Association (BSPA) took control of the APA convention podium and demanded that the APA take action to increase ethnic minority recruitment and retention. In response, the APA later provided 3 years of funding for a BSPA office in the APA building. This marked the first time the APA had embraced any organized group of psychology graduate students (Figueroa-Garcia, 1994; Guzman, Schiavo, & Puente, 1992; Pickren & Tomes, 2002; Street, 1994).

By 1975, independent psychological associations had been formed by the other three major racial/ethnic minority groups. These associations, in turn, established newsletters and journals. Once organized, these associations not only strategically challenged the APA and pressed for greater inclusion of people of color but also promoted issues of special concern to their communities. Of even greater significance, the ethnic minority psychological associations became catalysts for the development and promotion of distinctly ethnic-centric psychological theories and practices.

Other developments during this era that supported and further legitimized the concerns of psychologists of color included the following. In 1970, the APA established a Commission for Accelerating Black Participation in Psychology (CABPP). In that same year, African American psychologist Kenneth B. Clark, in his role as APA president, urged the APA Board of Directors to place high priority on issues of social responsibility. Consequently, in 1971, the APA established a Department of Social and Ethical Responsibility and an ad hoc Committee on Social and Ethical Responsibility for Psychology (CSERP). By vote of the APA membership, the ad hoc committee became a standing board (BSERP) in 1973 with responsibility for aspects of psychology involving solutions to problems of social justice—including issues related to minority participation in psychology (Pickren & Tomes, 2002). Also in 1971, the National Institute of Mental Health (NIMH) established its Center for Minority Group Mental Health Programs, which sought to develop a major focus on minority mental health issues and increase the number of ethnic minorities mental health researchers and providers by funding a Minority Fellowship Program. In 1974, the APA established its Minority Fellowship Program with funding provided by NIMH.[24]

In summary, the third quarter of the 20th century was an era when psychologists of color began to come into their own—comprising sufficient numbers to have a sense of cohort; articulating distinct identities and destinies relative to their communities and the discipline of psychology; assuming leadership roles in organized psychology for the first time; and developing ethnocentric professional networks and organizations where their contributions were wanted and valued, where they could be affirmed as scholars, professionals, and community leaders, and where they could devise strategies for promoting group interests. Consequently, psychologists of color increasingly assumed postures of challenge, protest, and change. Such "coming into their own" was a well-earned prize of the civil rights era.[25]

The Fourth Quarter of the 20th Century

The first three quarters of the 20th century were marked by the breaking down or "modernization" of old social and political boundaries, categories, hierarchies, and systems of privileges and obligations. But in the last quarter of the 20th century, increased efforts were devoted to fashioning new, more global relationships and rules for political, economic, and human interactions that would be compatible with emerging and increasingly "unbounded" social realities marked by increased worldwide demand for limited natural resources, global communication and markets, and a plethora of emerging technologies. Such efforts, though often chaotic and wrenching, were integral to the movement toward a postmodern world.

Walls between the Western and Eastern worlds continued to fall either as a result of intrusion or decay. For example, Islam and Muslim discontent began to enter into the contemporary American imagination when Iranian Muslim militants seized 52 hostages at the U.S. embassy in Tehran in 1979, who were not released until more than a year later. The breadth and depth of this discontent were further reinforced by the 1990-1991 Gulf War and the assassination of Egypt's premier Anwar Sadat in 1991. Communist regimes fell throughout Eastern Europe, culminating in the collapse of the U.S.S.R. (Soviet Union) in 1991. Apartheid in South Africa came under international attack when economic sanctions were imposed in 1986. As a result of these and other events, political conceptualizations of the world began shifting from West-East (democratic-nondemocratic governments) to North-South (Western/European–non-European peoples/cultures; consumers of natural resources–holders of natural resources; former colonialists–former colonized; rich-poor).

In the United States, the pull of immigration policies that were revamped in the mid-1960s and a fairly continually growing U.S. economy, coupled with the push of political and ecological turmoil throughout the world, caused the U.S. population to become increasingly diverse and colored. For example, among Latinos, in the 1970s, political turmoil sparked a significant immigration of Colombians, which was subsequently followed by waves of immigration from Central America (e.g., Salvadorans, Guatemalans, and Nicaraguans) (Gonzalez, 2000, pp. 77, 78). Similarly, the U.S. evacuation of Saigon in 1975 marked the beginning

(text continued on p. 41)

Timeline of Challenge and Change: The Inclusion of People of Color
in Psychology in the United States

1975   As a result of the California Supreme Court's decision in *Larry P. v. Riles* that use of
        intelligence tests results in racial bias in the placement of students into programs for the
        educable mentally retarded, the California Board of Education declares a moratorium on
        the uses of such tests for such purposes. African American psychologist Asa G. Hilliard III
        served as principal architect and lead expert witness of this challenge of the use of IQ tests
        (Bowser, 1996; Street, 1994)

        The Society of Indian Psychologists (SIP) is established (LaFromboise, 1994).

1976   The National Asian American Psychology Training Conference is convened at California
        State University at Long Beach with a focus on "Models of Psychology for Asian
        Americans" and "Training Psychologists for Asian Americans" (Leong, 1995; Street,
        1994; S. Sue, 1994).

1977   Publication of the first edition of *Chicano Psychology,* edited by Joe Martinez, Ph.D.
        (Bernal, 1994).

1978   With the leadership of Dalmas Taylor, Ph.D., the Dulles Conference is convened by the
        APA Board of Directors, the APA Board of Social and Ethical Responsibility, and NIMH
        on the topic of "Expanding the Roles of Culturally Diverse Peoples in the Profession of
        Psychology" and recommends the establishment of an APA office and board on ethnic
        minority affairs (Comas-Diaz, 1990; Guzman et al., 1992; Street, 1994; S. Sue, 1994).

        Kenneth B. Clark, Ph.D., receives the first APA Award for Distinguished Contributions to
        Psychology in the Public Interest (Street, 1994).

        John Garcia, Ph.D., is first Mexican American/Latino elected to the Society of Experimental
        Psychologists (Padilla, 1980a, 1980b).

        The APA Ad Hoc Committee on Minority Affairs is established and later notes that major
        areas of ethnic minority concern include (a) psychological and educational testing,
        (b) APA accreditation criteria and procedures, (c) ethnic minority curriculum issues,
        (d) licensure/certification issues, (e) publication/editorial activities, (f) underrepresentation
        of ethnic minorities in APA's governance structure, and (g) APA's involvement in court and
        legislative advocacy (Comas-Diaz, 1990; Holliday, Figueroa-Garcia, & Perry, 1994).

1979   The APA Office of Ethnic Minority Affairs is established, with Estaban Olmedo, Ph.D.,
        as its director (Comas-Diaz, 1990).

        The National Hispanic Psychological Association (NHPA) is established with Carlos
        Albizu-Miranda elected as president (Bernal, 1994; Padilla & Lindhom, 1980).

        The first issue of the *Hispanic Journal of Behavioral Science* is published with Amado
        Padilla, Ph.D., as editor (Bernal, 1994; Jones & Campagna, 1995; Street, 1994).

        The first issue of the *Journal of Asian American Psychological Association* is published
        with Roger Lum, Ph.D., as editor (Leong, 1995; Street, 1994).

        U.S. District Court rules that in regards to *Larry P. v. Riles,* California's use of
        standardized intelligence testing in schools for purposes of placing children in special
        education was discriminatory and therefore illegal (Guthrie, 1998; Hilliard, 1983;
        Street, 1994).

(continued)

Timeline of Challenge and Change *(Continued)*

APA approves revised Criteria for Accreditation of Doctoral Training Programs and Internships in Professional Psychology, one of which (Criterion II) relates to cultural and individual diversity (e.g., "Social and personal diversity of faculty and student is an essential goal if the trainees are to function optimally within our pluralistic society. Programs must develop knowledge and skills in their students relevant to human diversity.") (Guzman et al., 1992, pp. 202-203).

John Garcia, Ph.D., is the first Mexican American/Latino selected for receipt of a major APA award—the APA Distinguished Scientific Contribution Award (Bernal, 1994; Padilla, 1980a; Street, 1994).

Logan Wright, Ph.D., is the first person of American Indian heritage elected to the APA Board of Directors.

1980   By vote of the APA membership, the APA Board of Ethnic Minority Affairs (BEMA) is established; Henry Tomes, Ph.D., is elected as chair.

1981   BEMA establishes the Task Force on Minority Education and Training.

1984   BEMA establishes the Task Force on Communication With Minority Constituents, which is charged to (a) identify and increase ethnic minority membership in divisions and state associations, (b) help divisions and state associations establish ethnic minority-oriented committees, and (c) increase ethnic minority participation in APA governance (Comas-Diaz, 1990).

The APA Publication and Communication (P&C) Board establishes the Ad Hoc Committee on Increasing the Representation of Underrepresented Groups in the Publication Process (Comas-Diaz, 1990).

First issue of the *Puerto Rican Journal of Psychology* is published by the Puerto Rican Association of Psychologists (Roca de Torres, 1994a).

1985   BEMA, with the approval of the APA Council of Representatives, establishes the BEMA Committee on Ethnic Minority Human Resources Development (CEMHRD) to address ethnic minority student and faculty recruitment and retention, as well as development of ethnic minority education and training resources, and appoints Martha Bernal, Ph.D., as CEMHRD's chair.

The first national convention of the Asian American Psychological Association is held in Los Angeles (Leong, 1995; Street, 1994).

NIMH is reorganized; ethnic minority research is "mainstreamed"—all of NIMH's three research divisions assume responsibility for funding ethnic minority-focused research and ethnic minority investigators (Parron, 1990).

1986   The Society for the Psychological Study of Ethnic Minority Issues (APA's Division 45) is established (Comas-Diaz, 1990; Street, 1994).

The Society for the Clinical Psychology of Ethnic Minorities is established as Section VI of APA's Division 12 (Clinical Psychology) (M. Jenkins, 1994).

Logan Wright is the first person of American Indian heritage to be elected president of the APA (Street, 1994).

(continued)

Timeline of Challenge and Change *(Continued)*

1987	The APA Central Office is restructured into three directorates (Science, Practice, and Public Interest); James M. Jones, Ph.D., an African American, serves as interim director of the Public Interest directorate (Street, 1994).
	The BEMA/BSERP Task Force on the Status of Black Men and Its Impact on Families and Communities is established (Comas-Diaz, 1990).
	The BEMA Task Force on the Delivery of Services to Ethnic Minority Populations is established and later issues APA council-approved *Guidelines for Providers of Psychological Services to Ethnic, Linguistic and Culturally Diverse Populations,* under the chairship of Joseph Pine, Ph.D. (Comas-Diaz, 1990).
	As an outcome of the Publication and Communications Board's Ad Hoc Committee on Increasing the Representation of Underrepresented Groups in the Publication Process, the *Journal of Educational Psychology* establishes the Underrepresented Groups Project (UGP), whose major activities include creating a position of associate editor for a person of color who, with the assistance of an ethnic minority advisory group, assumes responsibility for both encouraging the publication of research on educational psychology issues of concern to ethnic minorities and developing a mentoring process for ethnic minority scholars (Comas-Diaz, 1990).
	APA sponsors the Utah National Conference on Graduate Education in Psychology, which incorporates a focus on "Cultural Diversity: How Do We Enhance Graduate Education in a Multicultural World?"—including issues related to curricula and increased participation of people of color as students and teachers (Comas-Diaz, 1990).
1988	Publication of the first edition of the *Directory of Ethnic Minority Professionals in Psychology,* edited by Christine Iijima Hall, Ph.D. (Figueroa-Garcia, 1994).
1990	APA governance structure is reorganized; the Board of Ethnic Minority Affairs (BEMA) and the Board for Social and Ethical Responsibility (BSERP) are sunset, and in their stead the Board for the Advancement of Psychology in the Public Interest (BAPPI) is established with Melba J. Vazquez, Ph.D., as its elected chair; the APA Committee on Ethnic Minority Affairs (CEMA) is established with Bertha G. Holliday, Ph.D., as its elected chair (Holliday, 1992; Street, 1994).
	Richard Suinn, Ph.D., is the first Asian American to serve on the APA Board of Directors.
	The Ethnic Minority Caucus of the APA Council of Representatives is established with Lillian Comas-Diaz, Ph.D., elected as its chair, and Alice F. Chang, Ph.D., elected as its secretary/treasurer.
1991	The National Conference on Enhancing the Quality of Undergraduate Education in Psychology is convened at St. Mary's College of Maryland with ethnic minority student issues as one of its seven topics of focus, including discussions on such issues as (a) broadening the curriculum to include more ethnic minority issues and researchers, (b) creating a sense of community and managing classes with diverse students, and (c) ethnic minority recruitment strategies (Guzman et al., 1992; Street, 1994).
1992	APA's Public Interest Directorate sponsors the first APA mini-convention (at the Washington, D.C., APA Centennial Convention) focused on ethnic minorities: "Ethnic Minorities: Issues and Concerns for Psychology, Now and in the Future." The mini-convention was organized by OEMA Director L. Philip Guzman, Ph.D. (Holliday, 1992).

Timeline of Challenge and Change *(Continued)*

At the Centennial APA Convention in Washington, D.C., the Council of National Psychological Associations for the Advancement of Ethnic Minority Interests is established on adoption of the CNPAAEMI Governing Rules. CNPAAEMI is composed of the presidents of the nation's ethnic minority psychological associations and the APA (Council of National Psychological Associations, 1992).

Joseph Horvat, Ph.D., an American Indian of the Seneca-Coyuga tribe, is the first ethnic minority person elected president of the Rocky Mountain Psychological Association.

Gail E. Wyatt, Ph.D., an African American, is the first person of color to receive a NIMH Research Scientist Career Award (Street, 1994).

Joseph Horvat, Ph.D., an American Indian of the Seneca-Coyuga tribe, is the first ethnic minority elected as president of the Psi Chi National Honor Society.

1993   With the leadership of Jessica Henderson Daniel, Ph.D., and chair of the Massachusetts Board of Registration of Psychologists, Massachusetts becomes the first state to require program and experience related to racial/ethnic basis of behavior for licensure (Daniel, 1994).

APA Council of Representatives passes a resolution declaring ethnic minority recruitment and retention as a high priority.

1994   Alice Chang, Ph.D., is the first ethnic minority female to serve on the APA Board of Directors.

The APA Commission on Ethnic Minority Recruitment, Retention, and Training in Psychology is established by the APA Board of Directors with Richard M. Suinn, Ph.D., appointed as chair by APA President Ronald Fox, Ph.D.

Publication of Murray and Herrnstein's *The Bell Curve,* which argues the existence of innate racial IQ differences and sets forth associated public policy recommendations.

Publication of J. P. Rushton's *Race, Evolution and Behavior,* which promotes a sociobiological evolutionary approach to racial IQ differences.

African American psychologist Brian Smedley, Ph.D., becomes the first ethnic minority to direct the APA's Public Interest Public Policy Office. During his tenure, ethnic minority issues are formally placed on the APA's legislative advocacy agenda for the first time.

1995   Volume 1 of the *AAPA Monograph Series* is issued with Nolan Zane, Ph.D., and Yoshito Kawahara, Ph.D., as coeditors.

Jennifer Friday, Ph.D., is the first African American to be elected president of the Southeast Psychological Association (SEPA).

APA Council of Representatives approves revised "guidelines and principles for accreditation of programs in professional psychology," including "Domain D: Cultural and individual differences and diversity," which calls for programs to make "systematic, coherent and long-term efforts to attract and retain students and faculty [or interns and staff]" from diverse backgrounds; "ensure a supportive and encouraging learning environment appropriate for the training of diverse individuals"; and provide a "coherent plan to provide students [or interns] with relevant knowledge and experience about the role of cultural and individual diversity in psychological phenomena and professional practice" (APA, Office of Program Consultation and Accreditation, 1996).

The XXV Interamerican Congress is held in San Juan, Puerto, with Irma Serrano-Garcia as Congress president.

(continued)

Timeline of Challenge and Change *(Continued)*

1996   With funding provided by the Office of Special Populations of the Center for Mental Health Services, APA initiates "HBCU Training Capacity Grant" program through which small grants are competitively awarded to psychology departments at historically Black colleges and universities for activities that will strengthen a department's capacity to effectively recruit, retain, and train students of color for careers in psychology (APA, Office of Ethnic Minority Affairs, 1996).

Publication of *Handbook of Tests and Measurements for Black Populations* (2 volumes), edited by Reginald L. Jones, Ph.D.

APA's Office of Ethnic Minority Affairs is awarded a $750,000 grant from the National Institute of General Medical Sciences (NIGMS) for the purpose of demonstrating the effectiveness of a "systemic approach" for increasing the number of persons of color in the educational pipeline for biomedical research careers in psychology. Later, in the year 2000, the grant is renewed for $1.43 million.

1997   APA's Office of Ethnic Minority Affairs organizes within the annual APA convention a mini-convention on "Psychology and Racism," focusing on the three themes of (a) the psychology of racism, (b) racism in psychology, and (c) the psychology of anti-racism and involving 121 events and 449 speakers (APA, 1997).

1998   Japanese American psychologist Patrick Okura and his wife, Lily, establish the Okura Mental Health Leadership Foundation through use of their 1988 federal reparations payments of $20,000 to each Japanese American interned in camps during World War II. The foundation seeks to assist and develop emerging Asian American leaders in human services fields to become national leaders (Chamberlain, 1998; Okura Mental Health Leadership Foundation, 1998; Yoshioka, 2001).

1999   APA's Division 45 (Society for the Psychological Study of Ethnic Minority Issues), in collaboration with Divisions 17 (Counseling) and 35 (Psychology of Women), organize the first National Multicultural Conference and Summit in Newport Beach, California, chaired by Derald W. Sue, Ph.D.

APA's Division 45 initiates publication of its journal *Cultural Diversity and Ethnic Minority Psychology* with Lillian Comas-Diaz, Ph.D., as its first editor.

The APA Council of Representatives passes a resolution on affirmative action and equal opportunity that encourages "psychological and public policy research that would illuminate sources of bias in institutional policies and practices."

2000   The APA Council of Representatives authorizes funding for a CEMRRAT Textbook Initiatives Work Group that is charged to develop guidelines on the inclusion of information and research on diverse populations for publishers and authors of introductory psychology textbooks (APA, 2001).

The APA's Office of Ethnic Minority Affairs establishes its Psychology in Ethnic Minority Services Institutions (PEMSI) initiative, aimed at strengthening relationships between the APA and these institutions and promoting increased psychological education, training and research at these institutions (APA, Office of Ethnic Minority Affairs, 2000).

2001   The APA Council of Representatives passes a resolution on "Racial/Ethnic Profiling and Other Racial/Ethnic Disparities in Law and Security Enforcement Activities" (APA, Office of Ethnic Minority Affairs, 2001).

The APA Council of Representatives passes a resolution on "Racism and Racial Discrimination: A Policy Statement in Support of the Goals of the 2001 World Conference Against Racism, Racial Discrimination, Xenophobia, and Related Intolerance" (APA, Office of Ethnic Minority Affairs, 2001a).

(continued)

Timeline of Challenge and Change *(Continued)*

The APA's Office of International Affairs and Office of Ethnic Minority Affairs provide financial support for an APA six-member delegation to the United Nations (UN) World Conference Against Racism, Racial Discrimination, Xenophobia, and Related Intolerance in Durban, South Africa. Delegates are Corann Okorodudu, Ed.D. (delegation chair and the APA main representative to the UN); Thema Bryant, Ph.D. (an APA representative to the UN); A. J. Franklin, Ph.D. (president, Division 45); Bertha G. Holliday, Ph.D. (director, OEMA); James Jackson, Ph.D. (member of APA's Committee on International Relations in Psychology); and William Parham, Ph.D. (member of APA's Committee on Ethnic Minority Affairs APA, Office of Ethnic Minority Affairs, 2001b; APA, 2002).

Congress authorizes a major center and initiative at the National Institutes of Health on minority health and health disparities. The APA successfully advocated for the participation of psychologists in this initiative.

2002   APA's Council of Representatives unanimously confirms African American psychologist Norman B. Anderson, Ph.D., as the APA Chief Executive Officer, effective January 1, 2003.

---

of significant immigration of Southeast Asians, including persons from Vietnam, Cambodia, and Laos. Between 1975 and 1985, more than 700,000 Southeast Asian refugees settled in the United States (Nishio & Bilmes, 1987/1998). Immigration from East Asia (e.g., Pakistan, India), Africa, and the Caribbean also increased dramatically during this era. Documented and undocumented immigration from Mexico also continued and increased. Demographers began projecting that by the year 2050, the majority of the nation's population would be of non-European descent. And the nation's political culture became increasingly conservative.

During the last quarter of the 20th century, U.S. psychology increased its organization and established more state psychological associations and APA divisions. Despite the financial mishap involving the 1983 purchase and later 1988 sale of the magazine *Psychology Today,* the APA prospered financially as a result of its continuously growing membership, its expanded publication and research literature abstracting activities, and its real estate development successes. The visibility of ethnic minorities, women, and lesbian, gay, and bisexual persons significantly increased within the discipline and the association. This was accompanied by demands that attention also be paid to those persons at the intersections of such special interest and identity groups.

In addition, the influence of professional psychology (i.e., clinical and counseling psychologists) continued to grow. When a 1987-1988 proposal to enhance the power of academic and scientist interests through reorganization of the APA's governance structure into two to five autonomous/semi-autonomous assemblies or societies was not approved by the APA Council of Representatives and membership, many academics left the APA and formed a second national psychological association, the American Psychological Society.

Nevertheless, the APA continued its growth and development. For example, in 1987, the APA's Central Office was reorganized into a directorate structure (Practice, Science, Public Interest, and Education). With an eye toward its future growth, in 1988, the APA approved the establishment of the American Psychological Association of Graduate Students (APAGS). In 1991, the APA's governance structure was modified to align it with the reorganized staff structure. Boards of Education, Professional, and

Scientific Affairs were maintained. A Board for the Advancement of Psychology in the Public Interest was created, and the Boards for Ethnic Minority Affairs (BEMA) and Social and Ethical Responsibility (BSERP) were sunset. In 1991, the APA Public Policy Office was established to engage in federal legislative advocacy on behalf of APA's Science, Education, and Public Interest directorates. And in 1992, the APA occupied its newly built headquarters building (750 First St., NE, in Washington, D.C.).

Despite the loss of some important and well-earned gains,[26] the community of psychologists of color significantly strengthened during this era—in terms of not only number but also increased diversity and greater influence within organized psychology and the general society. This strengthening enabled these psychologists to mount comprehensive programs of research and action that focused primarily on crystallizing two of the major themes of ethnic minority psychology: the pursuit of ethnic minority inclusion and participation in psychology, as well as the development and promulgation of theories and interventions derived from the cultures, traditional values and worldviews, and historical experiences of ethnic minority peoples. Examples of such efforts are provided below.

The Pursuit of Ethnic Minority Inclusion and Participation

One of the major strategies for ethnic minority inclusion and participation focused on ethnic minority leadership development and opportunities. A major catalyst for this strategy was the set of recommendations resulting from the 1978 Dulles Conference on "Expanding the Roles of Culturally Diverse Peoples in the Profession of Psychology," which was sponsored by the APA Board of Directors, the APA Board of Social and Ethical Responsibility (which tended to be dominated by SPSSI members), and the NIMH. Major conference recommendations related to the need for an institutionalized ethnic minority presence in the governance and organizational structures of organized psychology. As a result, the APA Office of Ethnic Minority Affairs was established in 1979, the APA Board of Ethnic Minority Affairs (BEMA) was established in 1980 after a successful related bylaws vote by the APA membership, and the Society for the Psychological Study of Ethnic Minority Issues (APA Division 45) was established in 1986 (Comas-Diaz, 1990; Guzman et al., 1992; Street, 1994; S. Sue, 1994).

Over time, each of these entities assumed a role that was distinct but mutually supportive. For example, Division 45, as a "speciality area" group, focused its efforts on promoting the stature and visibility of scientific and practice issues of concern to ethnic minority psychologists and communities, primarily through establishment of its journal and the biennial National Multicultural Conference and Summit.

BEMA (and its successor—the APA Committee on Ethnic Minority Affairs [CEMA]), in its role as an APA governance group, not only monitored and contributed to greater equity and less racial/ethnic bias in APA policymaking but also identified and legitimized major issues and initiatives needed to increase the participation and stature of ethnic minorities in psychology.

In turn, many of these initiatives were actually carried out by staff of the Office of Ethnic Minority Affairs. Examples of such initiatives during this era include encouraging the development of division and state psychological association Committees on Ethnic Minority Affairs as a strategy for increasing minority membership and participation, publishing a directory of minority psychologists, advocating accreditation criteria that specifically address diversity and multicultural training issues, identifying multicultural experts who could serve as members of accreditation site visit teams, and developing formats for communicating with ethnic minority psychologists (Comas-Diaz, 1990; Figueroa-Garcia, 1994; Holliday, 1992; Street, 1994).

Ethnic minority recruitment, retention, and training were a second major strategy for increasing minority inclusion and participation in psychology. Such efforts were guided by a series of surveys and studies that documented the underrepresentation of ethnic minorities in psychology as both students and faculty (e.g., Kennedy & Wagner, 1979; Padilla, Boxley, & Wagner, 1973; Ponterotto et al., 1995; Suinn & Witt, 1982; Wyche & Graves, 1992). In 1981, the APA reported the results of its first comprehensive study of ethnic minorities in psychology (Russo, Olmedo, Strapp, & Fulcher, 1981). A follow-up to this study was released in 1990 (Kohout & Pion, 1990). Other studies sought to document strategies for eliminating such underrepresentation and improving training on minority-related issues (e.g., Bernal & Padilla, 1982; Fisher & Stricker, 1979; Hammond & Yung, 1993; Korchin, 1980; Quintana & Bernal, 1995; Rogers, Ponterotto, Conoley, & Wiese, 1992; Thomason, 1999). In 1988, an edited book, *Is Psychology for Them? A Guide to Undergraduate Advising,* included chapters that focused on minority recruitment and retention issues (Woods, 1988). In response to the minimal numbers of American Indians in psychology, in 1993, the first federally funded Indians into Psychology Doctoral Education (InPsyDE) was established in the clinical psychology training program at the University North Dakota (McDonald, 1994).

Coupled with these scholarly works and efforts, during the 7-year period from 1985 to 1992, no less than 14 federal and professional association task forces, committees, and conferences focused their efforts on ethnic minority recruitment, retention, and training issues in psychology (Holliday, Figueroa-Garcia, & Perry, 1994; Holliday et al., 1997).

The sheer volume and unyielding persistence related to the need for increased numbers of ethnic minorities in psychology of the various ethnic minority constituencies and their supporters were bound to move even a prone-to-paralysis APA. The breakthrough came in 1994, when the APA Council of Representatives, at the urging of the APA Education Directorate, passed a resolution declaring that "APA places a high priority on issues related to the education of ethnic minorities" (APA Council of Representatives, 1994). This was a green light for action.

Shortly thereafter, APA President Ronald E. Fox, Ph.D., authorized the establishment of a 15-member Commission on Ethnic Minority Recruitment, Retention, and Training in Psychology (CEMRRAT) to assess the status of and barriers to the participation of persons of color in American psychology and to develop a 5-year plan to guide the association's efforts in this area. The commission also engaged in a major education and information effort involving the development of various pamphlets, Web documents, and association newsletter articles that were widely distributed to all of the nation's departments of psychology (Holliday et al., 1997, pp. 33-35).

The commission's final report (Holliday et al., 1997) included six major recommendations as well as a 5-year Plan for Transformation.[27] In 1996, consistent with those plan proposals related to increasing ethnic minority student recruitment, retention, and training, the APA's Office of Ethnic Minority Affairs (OEMA) applied for and was awarded a $750,000 grant from the National Institute for General Medical Sciences to demonstrate a "systemic" approach for recruiting, retaining, and training ethnic minority students interested in the biomedical areas of psychology at 14 major research and predominantly minority institutions. In the year 2000, the grant was renewed for $1.43 million.

Furthermore, in 1999, at the urging of the APA Council of Representatives, the APA chief executive officer authorized the allocation of $100,000 per year for at least 5 years for implementing the CEMRRAT 5-Year Plan. The bulk of these funds has been used for a CEMRRAT Implementation Grant Program that provides modest support for various innovative efforts of psychology departments, state psychological associations, and other organized entities of psychology, APA offices, and individual psychologists that are consistent with the plan's strategies.

As a result of these and other efforts within the APA and other psychological associations and societies, ethnic minority participation in organized psychology increased significantly during this quarter century—although minorities continue to be significantly underrepresented in psychology. For example, in 1978, the APA had an estimated 1,384 ethnic minority members; by 1999, that number had increased nearly fourfold to 5,297 or 6.1% of all APA associates, members, and fellows (APA, Research Office, 2001; Russo et al., 1981). Even more encouraging are data indicating that in 1999-2000, 17.9% of all full-time first-year students in doctoral-level departments of psychology were ethnic minorities (APA, Research Office, 2001).

Development of Ethnocentric Theories and Interventions

In response to the prevailing deficit orientation of the era's psychological research on ethnic minorities, psychologists of color increasingly assumed postures of challenge by focusing on the strengths, positive adaptations, and resilience of children and families and persons of color. In doing so, these psychologists and their allies adopted explicitly nonnormative perspectives that did not require presumptions of universal normative standards. Consequently, psychologists of color increasingly embraced cultural-specific and ethnocentric values, beliefs, and

perspectives as tools for both guiding their research and practice and understanding the behaviors of persons of color. This served to not only mute some of the more controversial conclusions of the deficit orientation; it also served to affect paradigmatic shifts away from universal theories and normative assumptions toward more population- and cultural-specific approaches to psychological knowledge, research, training, and practice. What follows is a brief overview of the focus of this increasing body of culture-specific and ethnocentric efforts of psychologists of color.

In general, in articulating ethnocentric psychological theories and perspectives, psychologists of color have either revived such theories from those existing in the cultural group or constructed such theories in response to unique characteristics and experiences of the ethnic/racial group. For example, Ramirez (1998) has constructed a bicultural theory of Mestizo psychology in response to what he views as "a new race and new culture" resulting from the European colonization of the indigenous peoples of the Americas and the Caribbean, the importation of enslaved Africans into those areas, and the associated intermarriage among these groups.

Similar psychological theories reflecting a bicultural perspective have been developed to explain the psychological experiences and triumphs of African Americans. Examples include A. Jenkins's (1982) humanistic theory and Franklin's (1998) theory of invisibility. Other more African-centered theories have been constructed in response both to the need to explain the African American experience and to the assumptions that enslavement resulted in African Americans having no cultural referent other than that of the United States (i.e., European). These theories draw heavily on a wide-ranging array of African philosophical, spiritual, and cultural concepts. Examples include Nobles's (1972) theory, which builds on the African notion of the importance of the group to the individual's sense of identity; Akbar's (1977) theory, which highlights the African cultural emphasis on affective orientation, including caring, empathy, and cooperative efforts as significant sources of behavioral motivation; Baldwin's (1981) theory, in which cultural traits of African people are viewed as at least partially biogenetic in origin, and maladjustment is viewed as the result of cognitive misorientation associated with loss of contact with one's cultural roots; and L. J. Myers's (1988) optimal psychology theory, which emphasizes the oneness of all, the individual's embeddedness in a larger spiritual force, and the individual's construction of reality.

Recently articulated ethnocentric psychological theories also emphasize the critical role of ethnic/racial identity development. These theories, which often take the form of dynamic stage models, typically attempt to describe how people seek to develop a positive sense of self in the context of minority and nondominant group status. Examples include Cross's (1971, 1991) model of Negro-to-Black conversion; Parham's (1989) African-centered theory of cycles of Nigrescence, which postulates identity development processes throughout the life cycle; Helms's (1990) Black and White racial identity theory; and Ramirez's (1998) model of stages and patterns of bicultural identity development.

Other psychologists of color have noted the pivotal role of acculturation in ethnic minority identity and behavior (e.g., Amaro, Russo, & Pares-Avila, 1987; Padilla, 1980b; Rogler, Cortes, & Malgady, 1991; Tomine, 1991) and argue that acculturation need not result in assimilation (i.e., a loss of connection to one's culture of origin) but also may result in biculturalism (LaFromboise, Trimble, & Mohatt, 1998; Szapocznik, Kurtines, & Fernandez, 1980).

It should be noted that many concepts of the various constructed ethnocentric theories are mirrored in American Indian psychological perspectives, which are embedded in extant traditional Indian core values and beliefs that emphasize the life force and interconnectedness of all things and the associated need for harmony, balance, and cooperation. Wellness reflects balance and integration in one's life, harmony with the universe, and respectful coexistence (cf. Duran & Duran, 1995; Garrett, 1999; Garrett & Garrett, 1994). Also, traditional Native Hawaiian psychological perspectives reflect similar core values and beliefs (Ito, 1987; Marsella, Oliveira, Plummer, & Crabbe, 1998).

Traditional Chinese psychological perspectives emphasize interconnectiveness, maintenance of harmonious interpersonal relations and avoidance of confrontation, subordination of the individual to the group, and social control through shame and loss of face (Huang, 1991). Similar perspectives have been documented for other Asian groups such as the Japanese (Fugita, Ito, Abe, & Takeuchi, 1991) and Koreans (Lee & Cynn, 1991), although significant differences exist among such Asian groups related to a great extent on the religious or spiritual orientation of a given culture (Chung & Okazaki, 1991; D. Sue, 1998).

Psychologists of color also have participated in the development of a research literature on cultural-specific conceptions of mental illness. For example, Stanley Sue (1976) has documented the differences in the conceptions of European American and Asian American students, whereas T'ien (1985) has documented the traditional beliefs of Chinese about mental illness. Nishio and Bilmes (1987/1998) have described the somatization of mental illness among Southeast Asian refugees. Others have described American Indian concepts of mental health and illness (e.g., Garrett, 1999; Trimble, 1981; Trimble, Manson, Dinges, & Medicine, 1984).

Often, such conceptions are linked with unique patterns of symptomatology. For example, Mezzich, Ruiz, and Munoz (1999) noted that ethnic/racial-specific symptomatology is of three types: (a) group-based manifestations of standard diagnostic categories, (b) culture-bound syndromes (i.e., folk illness categories), and (c) cultural idioms of distress. Examples of the former have been noted for depression (Marsella, Kinzie, & Gordon, 1973; Mezzich & Raab, 1980), whereas the last category is exemplified by *Ataque de nervios* (Guarnaccia, De La Cancela, & Carrilo, 1989). In addition, Duran and Duran (1995) have elaborated the unique intergenerational posttraumatic stress syndrome resulting from the colonization and forced acculturation of American Indians. Unique forms of posttraumatic stress also have been noted among Southeast Asian immigrants and refugees (Chung & Okazaki, 1991; Kinzie et al., 1990; Mollica, Wyshak, & Lavelle, 1987). Rezentes (1996) has described two cultural-specific syndromes rooted in the historical experiences of Native Hawaiians. One is a type of depression—*kaumaha syndrome*—that is rooted in collective sadness and moral outrage of the colonial experience, as well as a pattern of spiritually empty selfish behavior termed the *ha'ole syndrome.*

Such ethnic/racial-specific symptomatologies often are associated with various indigenous interventions or treatments, which have been described by psychologists of color. Such treatments traditionally are provided by varying types of traditional healers who engage in such curative activities as confession, atonement, and absolution; restoration of balance, harmony, and wholeness; involvement of the family and community in treatment (reinforcement of community values); and communication with the supernatural or ancient world (cf. Garrett, Garrett, & Brotherton, 2001; Grills & Rowe, 1998; LaFromboise, 1998; Ramirez, 1998).

Examples of traditional treatments that have been incorporated into contemporary psychological practice include *Ho'oponopono*—a traditional Native Hawaiian practice used for conflict resolution and group and family therapy (Ito, 1985; Marsella et al., 1998; Mokuau, 1990); the Morita and Naikan therapies, which are rooted in Buddhism (Fugita et al., 1991); acupuncture; various American Indian practices, including dream and vision therapies, the medicine wheel, and healing circles (Duran & Duran, 1995; Garrett & Garrett, 1994; Garrett et al., 2001); and African-inspired rites of passage.

It also should be noted that in addition to the clinical and counseling areas, psychologists of color have made and are making equally significant contributions to scientific areas of psychology. Psychologists of color have engaged in innovative research aimed at rehabilitating the reputations of children of color and their families, as well as documenting and enhancing their academic achievement, resilience, and cognitive, behavioral, and psychological strengths (e.g., Harrison, Serafica, & McAdoo, 1984; Jones, 1999; McAdoo & McAdoo, 1985; McLoyd & Steinberg, 1998; Spencer, Brookins, & Allen, 1985). Psychologists of color also have addressed issues related to research methods and procedures in communities of color (e.g., Caldwell, Jackson, Tucker, & Bowman, 1999; Council of National Psychological Associations, 2000; Jones, 1996). Currently, psychologists of color are conducting some of the most significant seminal research in such areas as racial/ethnic psychopharmacology (e.g., Lawson, 1998; Strickland, Lawson, & Lin, 1993) and mental health disparities (e.g., Carpenter, 2002; Haynes & Smedley, 1999; Myers, Anderson, & Strickland, 1998; Smedley, Stith, & Nelson, 2002).

This very brief and selective overview of research during the last quarter of the 20th century is indicative of the exceptional giftedness and productivity associated with both the maturation of the first major cohort of U.S. psychologists of color and their nurturance and mentorship of a younger second cohort, who will help define U.S. psychology in the 21st century.

LOOKING BACKWARDS TOWARD THE FUTURE

The tale of challenge and change of ethnic minorities in U.S. psychology is remarkable in its uniqueness. For it is the tale of people who endured enslavement, colonization, internment, and other forms of blatant oppression and exclusion. It is the tale of people who were objects of a concept and ideology—scientific racism—that was integral to the justification of their oppression and exclusion. It is the tale of a scientific discipline that embraced that concept, contributed to its legitimacy, and simultaneously struggled against it. It is the tale of people who, not withstanding all of this, had faith that the discipline of psychology could somehow make an important difference in communities of color. It is the tale of people who, less than a lifetime ago, were being documented by that discipline as innately inferior human beings and who are now that discipline's major transformational force for a psychological science, practice, and ideology appropriate for the multicultural and global realities of the 21st century. It is quite simply a tale of wonder.

This tale also is a primer for the value and significance of diversity. In contrast to popular conceptions, diversity is not simply a matter of appropriate representational numbers of persons of color in the service of a colorblind society. Diversity is a transformational and revitalization change strategy that recognizes the unique benefits to all of multicultural/multiracial experiences and perspectives. In psychology, that change is resulting in a substantive broadening of knowledge and skills that is serving to significantly expand the range of psychological practice and research.

Nevertheless, important barriers continue to exist to the full participation of persons of color in psychology. These include continuing racial/ethnic inequities in student and faculty recruitment, retention, training, and curricular representation. Much more substantial barriers and ethnic/racial underrepresentation exist in the discipline's two major knowledge "gatekeeper" functions: (a) editors of scientific and professional journals in psychology and (b) federal and foundation grant administrators of psychological research. These gatekeeper functions undoubtedly will be the next target of the focused and coordinated action that consistently has been demonstrated by psychologists of color and their allies. For access to these functions is essential for a transformed U.S. psychology.

Indeed, U.S. psychology is undergoing a paradigm shift. Ramirez's (1998) perspective suggests that this shift from a Eurocentric psychology toward a multicultural/multiracial psychology is characterized by (a) recognition of the unity of spirit, mind, body, and behavior; (b) development of new terminology, concepts, and methods that are more appropriate for and respectful of communities of color and diverse populations; (c) increased use of multidisciplinary knowledge and methods; (d) research questions and professional practices that recognize the individual's embeddedness in a variety of cultural/ historical and social/ecological systems; and (e) increased emphasis on psychologists' social responsibility, including the need to incorporate advocacy and service into research, educator, and practitioner roles.

This is the future of ethnic minority psychology—as well as the future of U.S. psychology.

NOTES

1.   Immediately after the Civil War, southern states began enacting Black Codes, which were laws that severely limited the rights of newly freed African American slaves, including the right to vote. As a result, the U.S. Congress passed the Reconstruction Act of 1867, which divided the South into five military districts and required southern states to ratify the 14th Amendment (which forbids abridgement of citizen rights without due process and guaranteed equal protection under the law) prior to their readmission to the Union (Fay, 1999, pp. 1595-1599).

2.   Prior to the signing of the Paris Treaty, the U.S. Congress passed the Teller Amendment, which blocked future U.S. claims on Cuban sovereignty. However, in 1900, Congress passed the Foraker Act, which declared Puerto Rico a U.S. territory, authorized the president to appoint its governor and top administrators, and replaced the peso with the U.S. dollar as that island's official currency. In 1917, U.S. citizenship was imposed upon the Puerto Rican people despite the unanimous objection of their House of Delegates (Gonzalez, 2000, chap. 3). Similarly, after the signing of the Paris Treaty, the United States sent troops to the Philippines and battled those who sought an independent Philippines. The war began in 1899 and ended in 1902, with the Philippines remaining a U.S. colony. It has been estimated that between 200,000 to 1 million Filipinos lost their lives during this conflict (Agbayani-Siewart & Revilla, 1995).

3.   Early examples of psychological assessment of racial differences included a 1895 *Psychological Review* article by R. M. Bache that reported that on a test of quickness of sensory perception, American Indians had the quickest reactions, Negro subjects were second, followed by Whites. These findings were interpreted as indicating that Whites belonged to a more deliberate and reflective race than did the members of the other two groups. Similarly, in 1897, B. R. Stetson compared 500 White children with 500 Black children on a test of memory on which the Black children scored slightly higher. Stetson attributed this finding to the Black children's higher average chronological age (as cited in Gossett, 1963/1965, p. 364). Thus, consistent with the tenets of scientific racism, during the late 19th century, even when African Americans or American Indians scored higher than European Americans on such psychological experiments and tests, these results were often interpreted as indicators of Black and Indian inferiority relative to Whites.

4.   In 1917, all Asians except Japanese persons were barred from immigrating to the United States. But in 1922, in *Ozawa v. U.S.*, the U.S. Supreme Court ruled that naturalization statutes that limited citizen applications to "free white persons" and "persons of African descent" served to exclude Japanese from becoming naturalized citizens (Daniels & Kitano, 1970, chap. 3).

5.   Federal policies of allotment were initiated by the General Allotment Act of 1887 (or the Dawes Act). This act authorized the division of Indian reservation lands into 160-acre parcels to individual families listed on government-administered tribal rolls (by virtue of being documentably of 50% or more Indian blood), with "surplus" lands put up for sale to White settlers or development companies. Proceeds from land sales were to be held in trust by the federal government "for the benefit of the tribe." During the 40-year allotment period, more than 60% of affected land (86-96 million acres) passed into non-Indian hands (Churchill & Morris, 1992, p. 14; Jaimes, 1992, pp. 126-128; Nies, 1996, chaps. 7, 8).

6.   The Ku Klux Klan was reborn in 1905 and developed chapters in both the North and South. It has been reported that between 1914 and 1920, a total of 382 African Americans were lynched (Sellman, 1999c, p. 2028).

7. See Guthrie (1998, pp. 93-101) for an excellent discussion of the role of psychology in the eugenics movement and its relationship to scientific racism.

8. Psychologist and eugenicist H. H. Goddard tested immigrants at Ellis Island as early as 1913 and concluded that 40% of immigrants were "feeble-minded" (Richards, 1997, pp. 68, 83). In 1921, R. M. Yerkes stated in the official report on "Psychological Examining in the United States Army" that the army tests "measure native intellectual ability. They are to some extent influenced by educational acquirement, but in the main, the soldier's inborn intelligence and the accidents of environment determine his mental rating or grade in the Army" (p. 794; also cited in Gossett, 1963/1965, p. 368). Later, in a foreword to psychologist Carl C. Brigham's (1923) book *A Study of American Intelligence,* Yerkes observed that "no one of us as a citizen can afford to ignore the menace of race deterioration or the evident relations of immigration to national progress and welfare" (p. viii; also cited in Richards, 1997, p. 88). In this book, Brigham reported large differences in mean scores between most northern European groups and those of the Irish and southern and eastern Europeans, concluding, "The intellectual superiority of our Nordic group over the Alpine, Mediterranean and Negro groups has been demonstrated" (p. 192; also cited in Richards, 1997, p. 89; cf. Gossett, 1963/1965, pp. 374-376). According to Richards (1997), "Yerkes urged Brigham's publisher to bring the book out in time for the immigration-restriction hearings and generally lobbied the chairmen of relevant Congressional committees regarding the importance of the Army Alpha findings" (p. 90).

9. Examples of such studies include the following: In 1913, Marion J. Mayo published a monograph on *The Mental Capacity of the American Negro,* which reports findings on students in integrated New York schools and concludes that the scholastic efficiency of Black children is 76% that of Whites. Alice Strong (1913) conducted a study of the intelligence of 350 South Carolina Black and White children ages 6 to 12 years using the Simon-Binet scale. She concluded that the Black children were mentally younger than White children of the same age. George O. Ferguson Jr. (1916/1970) compared 486 White and 421 Black fifth-, sixth- and seventh-grade students living in Virginia on five performance tests of cognitive abilities. In general, Black children performed less well than did White children. Ferguson concluded that Black subjects with the greater amount of White blood (as visually assessed) performed superior to those of pure Negro blood, and these two groups were differentiated by native ability and not as a result of acquired capacity (p. 111). Ferguson further argued that Blacks should be provided segregated education with differing curricula emphases than that of White schools because "no expenditure of time or money is likely to raise Negro scholastic attainment to that of the whites" (p. 125). S. D. Porteus (1924) studied intelligence differences among Hawaiian groups of students, including Whites, using the Stanford-Binet and various maze tests. On the Stanford-Binet, he found that the Whites rank first, the Chinese second, the Japanese third, and the Portuguese last. But on the maze tests, the ethnic minority children often had the superior scores. Thomas Garth (1925) assessed the intelligence of 1,050 Indian children (Pueblo, Navajo, and Apache tribes) who were in the fourth through eighth grades at a U.S. Indian school, using the National Intelligence Test. Garth concluded that the IQ of these full-blood Indians was 69, thus indicating that Whites on average had a mental age 14% higher. Paschal and Sullivan (1925) conducted an extensive psychological and anthropological investigation of Mexican children who were 9 and 12 years of age and attending Tuscon public schools. A variety of cognitive and IQ tests were administered, and the children were examined and measured for the physiological and racial

characteristics. Based on these assessments, Paschal concluded that, on average, Tuscon Mexicans who are partially of Indian origin, when compared to those of wholly White origin, have lower mental scores, lower social or economic status, and lower school standings in grades. Also see Richards (1997, chap. 4) and Gossett (1963/1965, chap. 15).

10.   New Deal temporary initiatives included work projects programs for the unemployed of the Works Progress Administration (WPA) and the Public Works Administration (PWA), as well as the federal program of assistance to individuals of the Federal Emergency Relief Administration (FERA). Permanent reforms included the guaranty of bank deposits through the Federal Deposit Insurance Corporation (FDIC), regulation of the stock market through the Securities Exchange Commission (SEC), regional development projects of the Tennessee Valley Authority (TVA) and the Rural Electrification Authority (REA), and the universal pension system of the Social Security Administration (SSA) (Sellman, 1999b, pp. 1417-1418).

11.   The following are some examples of the "newer" race psychology research conducted during the second quarter of the 20th century: In 1926, Wang tested the verbal intelligence of Chinese, Russian, African, and American college students and observed that conclusions concerning the relative intelligence of such groups could not be drawn unless there is some control of the language factor (Wang, 1926, as reported in Richards, 1997, chap. 4). Sandiford and Kerr (1926) reached a similar conclusion in their study comparing the intelligence of foreign-born Chinese and Japanese children with that of Chinese and Japanese children of foreign-born parents. Klineberg (1928) reported that when various performance tests were administered to American Indian and White children, the White children exhibited greater speed but made more errors, whereas Indian children were slower and made fewer errors. These findings were at variance with most prior IQ studies of Indians, which had emphasized verbal abilities and educational tasks. Similarly, Garth, Smith, and Abell (1928) conducted several studies of Indian intelligence that challenged assumptions of the innateness of intelligence and instead suggested the influence of educational achievement on IQ scores.

12.   Critical landmark research related to the effect of social-cultural experience on intelligence is the 1932 *Journal of Applied Psychology* article authored by Mexican American George I. Sanchez, Ed.D., which challenged the biased research literature on intelligence testing in Chicano children that failed to take into account these children's "dual language handicap" (Guthrie, 1976; Padilla, 1980a; Street, 1994).

13.   Examples of the involvement of peoples of color in federal policymaking during the New Deal era include the following: Based on the recommendation of a coalition of philanthropic foundations, the FDR administration created a position for a Special Advisor Concerned With the Economic Status of the Negro as a means for advocating the participation of Blacks in all of the administration's social reforms. This position served as a springboard for inclusion of Blacks in major positions within the Roosevelt administration (Kirby, 1980, pp. 13-21). Likewise, for the first time, Indians were appointed to policy positions within the Bureau of Indian Affairs (Nies, 1996, p. 345).

14.   A few examples of the strengthened emerging institutional base for African American psychologists during the second quarter of the 20th century include the following: In 1928, a psychology department was established at Howard University (one of the nation's largest historically Black universities) under the chairmanship of Francis C. Sumner, Ph.D. (Hopkins, Ross, & Hicks,

1994). In 1934, the *Journal of Negro Education* (published by Howard University) issued a historic issue of 14 papers (many authored by African American education and social science scholars) that examined and challenged race differences research (Richards, 1997, chaps. 4, 5). Results of a 1936 survey of Black colleges also indicated that 28% of responding schools had a department of psychology, and 8% awarded a B.A. or B.S. in psychology. Indeed, Black colleges had a total of 88 psychology faculty in 1936 (Canady, 1939, as reported by Guthrie, 1998, pp. 126-129).

15.   Examples of research and public policy studies focusing on educational and psychological issues by early African American psychologists include the following: A. S. Beckham (1933) explored the effects of differing social economic statuses on the intelligence of Black adolescents, H. G. Canady (1936, 1943) examined the effect of rapport on IQ and issues involved in equating the environment of Negro-White groups for intelligence testing in racial comparative studies, and H. H. Long (1935) explored psychological hazards of segregation on Black youth.

16.   Although relocation of Japanese Americans was deemed a "military necessity," it is generally acknowledged that its major impetus resulted from anti-Japanese hysteria, racism, and scapegoating of Japanese citizens in the United States and Hawaii by the press, as well as military leaders who asserted themselves in the face of an absence of political leadership (Commission on Wartime Relocation and Internment of Civilians, 1982; Daniels & Kitano, 1970, chap. 3; O'Brien & Fugita, 1991, chaps. 2, 3).

17.   Some illustrative data on the participation of ethnic minorities in World War II include the following: More than 24,500 American Indian men served in the armed services—including 400 Navajo who served in special code units (the Navajo codetalkers) as radio operators for units in the Pacific Islands (Nies, 1996, pp. 341-343). More than 10,000 men volunteered for the two all-Japanese combat units, but most were from Hawaii, where Japanese were not interned. Less than 1,200 of these volunteers came from the internment camps (O'Brien & Fugita, 1991, p. 75). More than 375,000 Mexican Americans saw active duty with the U.S. armed forces (Gonzalez, 2000, chap. 5). African Americans accounted for more than 8% of army personnel and 5% of navy personnel during the war (Sellman, 1999c).

18.   Examples of psychology's World War II mobilization efforts included the 1940 establishment of the Conference on Morale, which consisted of representatives from several psychological associations and societies; the 1940 appointment of the National Research Council's Emergency Committee in Psychology; the 1941 founding of the National Council of Women Psychologists; and the 1943 formation of the Intersociety Constitutional Convention. All of these groups sought to promote the use of psychology as part of the war effort (Finison, 1986; Street, 1994, pp. 204-209).

19.   An example of an early ethnic minority psychologist in the Veterans Administration system is African American psychologist C. Kermit Phelps, Ph.D., who began a clinical psychology internship at the Topeka, Kansas, VA hospital in 1949. He joined the staff of the Kansas City, Missouri, VA hospital in 1952 and became a staff psychologist in 1953. In 1957, Phelps became the chief of that hospital's Psychological Services, and in 1975 he became its associate chief of staff for education. During the early 1950s, he served as president of the then fledgling Missouri Psychological Association. Phelps reports that his greatest difficulty with the VA system was in gaining promotions through the GS federal grades (C. K. Phelps, personal communication to A. Holmes, July 2001).

20.   Allison Davis became the first African American academic to be appointed to a major White university on a full-time basis, when the Rosenwald

Foundation in 1941 agreed to pay his salary if the University of Chicago would appoint him to its faculty (Guthrie, 1998, p. 139).

21. Some of the differences in responses to the civil rights era of various ethnic minority groups are noted below. In African American communities, the civil rights struggle drew heavily on and in turn further strengthened those indigenous community organizations and institutions that had been created and nurtured in response and adaptation to the experiences of enslavement, reconstruction, Black Codes, Jim Crowism, and segregation. Because of the existence of these local community organizations and institutions, many of which were linked by national structures and networks, the civil rights movement was enabled to spawn thousands of independent community-based protests and challenges. The ability of African American communities to readily act autonomously and independently was critical to the success of the civil rights era, given the structure of law in the United States and the relationships and boundaries of local, state, and federal legal jurisdiction.

In American Indian country, U.S. industrialists continued to gain control of mineral resources on Indian land by promoting public policies for dismantling the reservation system, increasing Indian assimilation, terminating federal relationships with tribes, and encouraging relocation of Indians to urban areas. This sparked a new type of Indian political involvement and consciousness and increased multitribal cooperation and action involving both legal strategies and direct action. The former most frequently involved land claims, state voting rights, and water rights. The latter (e.g., sit-ins, takeovers) most frequently involved fishing rights, treaty rights, bureaucratic abuses, and Indian rights in general. Thus, in American Indian communities, the civil rights era involved activism related to civil rights guaranteed by the U.S. Constitution but, even more so, to issues of tribal rights derived from indigenous tradition, treaty, and federal law (Nies, 1996, pp. 306, 355, 361-370; Robbins, 1996, pp. 98-107).

In Mexican American or Chicano communities, the beginning of a new militancy was symbolized by a 1954 Supreme Court decision on *Hernandez v. Texas* (which was announced 2 weeks before the *Brown v. Topeka Board of Education* decision), when the Court ruled that based on their history of disenfranchisement in Texas where none of the 6,000 jurors called during a 25-year period in Jackson County had been Chicano, Mexican Americans were "a distinct class" who could claim protection from discrimination (Gonzalez, 2000, p. 173). This enabled Mexican Americans to file civil rights suits similar to those filed on behalf of African Americans. For example, in 1957, a federal district court outlawed segregated schools for Chicanos, and in 1966, a federal judge declared the Texas poll tax as illegal (Gonzalez, 2000, pp. 170-173). Mexican American or Chicano communities also established newer, more radical organizations during the civil rights era (Gonzalez, 2000, pp. 170-176). Chicanos also were successful in gaining increased voice through electoral politics. Thus, based on a history of disenfranchisement, segregation, and discrimination that somewhat paralleled that of African Americans, the Chicano response to the civil rights era in many respects mirrored that of African Americans.

Puerto Rican communities, which often served as "buffers" and "linchpins" between African American and White ethnic communities (especially in New York City), mirrored much of the militancy and activism of African American communities during the civil rights era. However, Puerto Rican activism also was informed by both their experiences of colonialism in Puerto Rico and their continuing familial and cultural linkages to that island (Gonzalez, 2000).

In contrast, the relatively new (and more affluent) Cuban American communities generally did not participate in the activism of the civil rights era. Instead, these communities tended to be more politically conservative and focused on their possible return to Cuba by maintaining support for U.S. anti-Castro sentiments and efforts. This support also served to advantage and empower this new immigrant group during the anticommunist cold war politics of this historical era. Significant interest in local politics did not occur until 1973, when two Cubans were elected to local political offices in Miami. Later that year, county legislation declared Dade County as officially bilingual. During the 1970s, riots in Miami's Black community underscored the lack of alliance between Miami's African American and Cuban American communities (Gonzalez, 2000, pp. 180-182).

Due to changes in immigration (which for decades had included exclusionary policies for Asians), Asian American communities grew rapidly during this era. But the response of these communities to the civil rights era was quite mixed. Although many (especially among Japanese Americans, who were the former objects of a targeted federal policy of dispersion and assimilation as a requirement for resettlement from internment camps) actively sought to "blend" into America's social fabric, others saw parallels in their own experiences and those of the increasingly vocal and visible African American community. For example, Japanese American psychologist Patrick Okura, M.A., has observed that in 1963, during his tenure as national president of the Japanese Americans Citizens League (JACL), the organization's members strongly opposed public support of Martin Luther King Jr. Despite this, Okura marched with King: "I felt that since we were placed in internment camps, we should take a firm stand as well" (Chamberlain, 1998, p. 34). Nevertheless, the civil rights era's emphasis on self-determination and reparations for past wrongs was not lost on the JACL: In 1970, the JACL passed a resolution calling for reparations for interned Japanese (O'Brien & Fugita, 1991, p. 79).

22. The *Larry P. v. Riles* case was a class action suit supported by the National Association for the Advancement of Colored People in which the placement of five African American children into classes for the mentally retarded was challenged. Psychologists from the Bay Area Association of Black Psychologists retested children on the same IQ test that had been used in determining their need for placement in classes for the educable mentally retarded but varied procedures to enable the establishment of rapport with the children. None of the children were found to be retarded on the retest. A detailed analysis of the case is provided by Hilliard (1983).

23. A most glaring example of the paralysis of the APA on civil rights issues was the failure of APA to salute or acknowledge, in any formal manner, the contributions of psychological research and psychologists to the 1954 *Brown v. Topeka Board of Education* Supreme Court school desegregation decision (Benjamin & Crouse, 2002).

24. The APA Minority Fellowship Program (MFP), which was initially directed by Dalmas Taylor, Ph.D., and is currently directed by James Jones, Ph.D., has expanded since its initiation. Nearly 1,000 persons have received financial support from the MFP for doctoral study and research in psychology and neuroscience.

25. Examples of ways in which the civil rights era served to dramatically increase the number of psychologists of color include the following: During the civil rights era, educational opportunities for persons of color expanded exponentially. Educational systems, including state postsecondary systems, were desegregated, thus greatly expanding education access for ethnic minorities. Affirmative action requirements (i.e., legally mandated strategies for inclusion of persons who are representative of those who were systematically discriminated against and/or excluded in the past by an

institution or company) spurred even the most elite higher educational institutions to actively seek more diverse faculties and student bodies. Changes in federal financial aid (e.g., the establishment of the National Defense Student Loan Program, the Pell Grant, various state and federally insured student loan programs, etc.) also served to promote greater diversity in postsecondary education. Open enrollment policies and federal support for the establishment and strengthening of community colleges and minority-serving postsecondary institutions were other major strategies for providing universal access to post-secondary education during this era. In addition, voting rights laws coupled with increased group identity and solidarity resulted in a tremendous increase in the number of elected public officials of color, who provided hard-core political and legislative leadership support for educational and employment access legislation. Furthermore, community mental health centers, the flood of Vietnam veterans into both colleges and the VA hospital system, the various War Against Poverty programs, and the clamor of empowered communities of color all served to greatly expand job opportunities for psychologists of color. This convergence, during a single historical era, of such employment opportunities with other types of opportunities associated with the civil rights era resulted in a sudden and significant increase in the numbers of psychologists of color.

26.   Two examples of loss of gains for ethnic minority psychologists include the elimination of NIMH's Office of Minority Mental Health Research as a result of a 1985 NIMH reorganization that included "mainstreaming" minority research activities throughout NIMH's three research divisions and sunsetting the APA's Board of Ethnic Minority Affairs in 1990 (Holliday, 1992; Parron, 1990; Street, 1994).

27.   The CEMRRAT 5-Year Plan for Transformation identified strategies related to the following five major objectives: (a) promote and improve multicultural education and training in psychology; (b) increase ethnic minority faculty recruitment and retention in psychology; (c) increase ethnic minority student recruitment, retention, and graduation in psychology; (d) provide national leadership for diversity and multiculturalism in education, science, and human services; and (e) promote data collection, research, and evaluation on ethnic minority recruitment, retention and graduation, and education and training (Holliday et al., 1997).

REFERENCES

Adorno, T. W., Frenkel-Brunswik, E., Levinson, D. J., & Sanford, R. N. (1950). *The Authoritarian personality*. New York: Harpers.

Agbayani-Siewart, P., & Revilla, L. (1995). In P. G. Min (Ed.), *Asian Americans: Contemporary trends and issues* (pp. 134-168). Thousand Oaks, CA: Sage.

Akbar, N. (1977). *Natural psychology and human transformation*. Chicago: Nation of Islam Office of Human Development.

Albermarle Paper Co. v. Moody, 422 U.S. 405 (1975).

Amaro, H., Russo, N. F., & Pares-Avila, J. A. (1987). Contemporary research on Hispanic women: A selected bibliography. *Women Quarterly, 11*, 523-532.

American Psychological Association (APA). (1963). Proceedings of the APA. *American Psychologist, 18*(12), 769.

American Psychological Association (APA). (1997). Psychology and racism. *Monitor, 28*(10), 38-46.

American Psychological Association (APA). (2001). A primer of diversity. *Monitor, 32*(10), 76-77.

American Psychological Association (APA). (2002). Psychology bolsters the world's fight against racism. *Monitor, 33*(1), 52-53.

American Psychological Association (APA) Council of Representatives. (1994). *February 1994 minutes of the APA Council of Representatives: APA resolution, ethnic minority recruitment and retention.* Washington, DC: Author.

American Psychological Association (APA), Office of Ethnic Minority Affairs. (1996, February). APA launches training capacity grants for the recruitment, retention, and training of psychologists of color in historically Black colleges and universities. *Communique*, pp. 13-14.

American Psychological Association (APA), Office of Ethnic Minority Affairs. (2000, May). Psychology and ethnic minority serving institutions. *Communique*, pp. 43-53.

American Psychological Association (APA), Office of Ethnic Minority Affairs. (2001, February). Taking a position on racial profiling and other related racial/ethnic disparities in law and security enforcement. *Communique*, pp. 38-50.

American Psychological Association (APA), Office of Ethnic Minority Affairs. (2001a, July). APA Board approves resolution on racism. *Communique*, pp. 32-48.

American Psychological Association (APA), Office of Ethnic Minority Affairs. (2001b, July). APA to participate in the World Conference Against Racism, Racial Discrimination, Xenophobia, and Related Intolerance. *Communique*, pp. 3-5.

American Psychological Association (APA), Office of Program Consultation and Accreditation. (1996). *Book 1: Guidelines and principles for accreditation of programs in professional psychology.* Washington, DC: Author.

American Psychological Association (APA), Research Office. (2001). *Graduate study in psychology 2000.* Washington, DC: Author.

Baker, R. R. (1992). *VA psychology: 1946-1992.* Oklahoma City, OK: Association of VA Chief Psychologists.

Baldwin, J. A. (1981). Notes on an Africentric theory of Black personality. *The Western Journal of Black Psychology, 5*(3), 172-179.

Baratz, J. C. (1973). Language abilities of Black Americans. In K. Miller & R. Dreger (Eds.), *Comparative studies of Blacks and Whites in the United States* (pp. 127-177). New York: Seminar.

Beckham, A. S. (1933). A study of intelligence of colored adolescents of differing social-economic status in typical metropolitan areas. *Journal of Social Psychology, 4,* 70-91.

Benimoff, M. (1995). Eastern Psychological Association: Report of the sixty-sixth annual meeting. *American Psychologist, 50*(12), 1086-1088.

Benjamin, L. T., Jr., & Crouse, E. M. (2002). The American Psychological Association's response to *Brown v. Board of Education:* The case of Kenneth B. Clark. *American Psychologist, 57*(1), 38-50.

Bernal, M. (1994). Hispanics in psychology. *Focus* (APA Division 45 Newsletter), *8*(2), 9-10.

Bernal, M. E., & Padilla, A. (1982). Status of minority curricula and training in clinical psychology. *American Psychologist, 37,* 780-787.

Bettelheim, B., & Janowitz, M. (1950). *Dynamics of prejudice: A psychological and sociological study of veterans.* New York: Harper & Brothers.

Blau, T. H. (1970). APA Commission on Accelerating Black Participation in Psychology. *American Psychologist, 25*(2), 1103-1104.

Bowser, B. (1996). Towards a liberated education: Asa G. Hilliard, III. *Sage Race Relations Abstracts, 21*(1), 6-24.

Brigham, C. C. (1923). *A study of American intelligence.* Princeton, NJ: Princeton University Press.

Brown v. Topeka Board of Education, 347 U.S. 483 (1954).

Caldwell, C. H., Jackson, J. S., Tucker, M. B., & Bowman, P. J. (1999). Culturally-competent research methods. In R. L. Jones (Ed.), *Advances in African American psychology* (pp. 101-127). Hampton, VA: Cobb & Henry.

Canady, H. G. (1936). The effect of rapport on the "IQ." *Journal of Negro Education, 5,* 209-219.

Canady, H. G. (1939, June). Psychology in Negro institutions. *West Virginia State Bulletin, 26*(3), 24.

Canady, H. G. (1943). The problem of equating the environment of Negro-White groups for intelligence testing in comparative studies. *Journal of Social Psychology, 17,* 3-15.

Carpenter, S. (2002). What can resolve the paradox of mental health disparities? *Monitor on Psychology, 33*(4), 46.

Chamberlain, J. (1998). A lifetime of leadership aids Asian professionals [Electronic version]. *APA Monitor, 29*(8), 34. Retrieved from www.apa.org/monitor/aug98/asia.html

Chung, R. C., & Okazaki, S. (1991). Counseling Americans of Southeast Asia descent: The impact of the refugee experience. In C. C. Lee & B. L. Richardson (Eds.), *Multicultural issues in counseling: New approaches to diversity* (pp. 107-126). Alexandria, VA: American Association for Counseling and Development.

Churchill, W., & Morris, G. T. (1992). Table: Key Indian laws and cases. In M. A. Jaimes (Ed.), *The state of Native America* (pp. 13-22). Boston: South End.

Clark, K. B. (1955). *Prejudice and your child*. Middletown, CT: Wesleyan University Press.

Clark, K. B. (1965). *Dark ghetto: Dilemmas of social* power. New York: Harper & Row.

Comas-Diaz, L. (1990). Ethnic minority mental health: Contributions and future directions of the American Psychological Association. In F. C. Serafica, A. E. Schwebel, R. K. Russell, P. D. Isaac, & L. B. Myers (Eds.), *Mental health of ethnic minorities* (pp. 275-301). New York: Praeger.

Commission on Wartime Relocation and Internment of Civilians. (1982). *Personal justice denied*. Washington, DC: Government Printing Office.

Council of National Psychological Associations for the Advancement of Ethnic Minority Interests. (1992). *Governing rules*. Washington, DC: American Psychological Association, Office of Ethnic Minority Affairs.

Council of National Psychological Associations for the Advancement of Ethnic Minority Interests. (2000, January). *Guidelines for research in ethnic minority communities*. Washington, DC: American Psychological Association.

Cross, W. E., Jr. (1971). The Negro to Black conversion experience: Towards a psychology of Black liberation. *Black World, 20*(9), 13-27.

Cross, W. E., Jr. (1991). *Shades of Black: Diversity in African American identity*. Philadelphia: Temple University Press.

Daniel, J. H. (1994). Leadership and legacy in psychology. *Focus* (Division 45 Newsletter), *8*(2), 14-15.

Daniels, R., & Kitano, H. H. L. (1970). *American racism: Exploration of the nature of prejudice*. Englewood Cliffs, NJ: Prentice Hall.

Darwin, C. (1859). *The origin of species by means of natural selection*. London: John Murray.

Deutsch, M., & Brown, B. (1964). Social influences in Negro-White intelligence differences. *Journal of Social Issues, 20,* 24-35.

Diana v. State Board of Education. (1970). No. C-70 37 RFP (District Court of California).

Dollard, J. (1937). *Caste and class in a southern town*. New York: Doubleday Anchor.

Dreger, R. M. (1973). Intellectual functioning. In K. Miller & R. Dreger (Eds.), *Comparative studies of Blacks and Whites in the United States* (pp. 185-230). New York: Seminar.

Duran, E., & Duran, B. (1995). *Native American postcolonial psychology.* Albany: State University of New York Press.

Eells, K., Davis, A., Havinghurst, R. J., Herrick, V. E., & Tyler, R. (1951). *Intelligence and cultural difference.* Chicago: University of Chicago Press.

Evans, R. B. (1999a, December). The long road to diversity. *The APA Monitor,* p. 24.

Evans, R. B. (1999b, December). A once fledgling field comes of age. *The APA Monitor,* p. 14.

Fay, R. (1999). Reconstruction. In K. A. Appiah & H. L. Gates (Eds.), *Africana: The encyclopedia of the African and African American experience* (pp. 1595-1599). New York: Basic Books.

Ferguson, G. O., Jr. (1970). The psychology of the Negro: An experimental study. In R. S. Woodsworth (Series Ed.), *Archives of Psychology,* No. 36, 1-136. Westport, CT: Negro Universities Press. (Original work published 1916, New York: The Science Press).

Figueroa-Garcia, A. (1994, August). *The making of an ethnic minority psychologist.* Paper presented at the annual convention of the APA, Los Angeles.

Finison, L. J. (1986). The psychological insurgency: 1936-1945. *Journal of Social Issues, 42*(1), 21-33.

Fisher, M., & Stricker, G. (1979). Minority candidacy in professional psychology. *Professional Psychology, 10*(5), 740-743.

Franklin, A. J. (1998). The invisibility syndrome in psychotherapy with African American males. In R. L. Jones (Ed.), *African American mental health: Theory, research and intervention* (pp. 395-411). Hampton, VA: Cobb & Henry.

Fugita, S., Ito, K. L., Abe, J., & Takeuchi, D. T. (1991). Japanese Americans. In N. Mokuaua (Ed.), *Handbook of social services for Asian and Pacific Islanders* (pp. 61-77). New York: Greenwood.

Galton, F. (1962). *Hereditary genius: An inquiry into its laws and consequences.* London: Fontana. (Original work published 1869)

Garrett, J. T., & Garrett, M. W. (1994). The path of good medicine: Understanding and counseling Native American Indians. *Journal of Multicultural Counseling and Development, 22,* 134-144.

Garrett, M. T. (1999). Understanding the "medicine" of Native American traditional values: An integrative review. *Counseling and Values, 43,* 84-98.

Garrett, M. T., Garrett, J. T., & Brotherton, D. (2001). Inner circle/outer circle: A group technique based on Native American healing circles. *Journal for Specialists in Group Work, 26*(1), 17-30.

Garth, T. R. (1925). The intelligence of full-blood Indians. *Journal of Applied Psychology, 9,* 382-389.

Garth, T. R., Smith, H. W., & Abell, W. (1928). A study of the intelligence and achievement of full-blood Indians. *Journal of Applied Psychology, 12,* 511-516.

Gonzalez, J. (2000). *Harvest of empire: A history of Latinos in America.* New York: Penguin.

Gossett, T. F. (1965). *Race: The history of an idea in America.* New York: Schocken. (Original work published 1963)

Great Migration. (1999). In K. A. Appiah & H. L. Gates (Eds.), *Africana: The encyclopedia of the African and African American experience* (pp. 869-872). New York: Basic Books.

Griggs v. Duke Power Co., 401 U.S. 424 (1971).

Grills, C., & Rowe, D. (1998). African traditional medicine: Implications for African-centered approaches to healing. In R. L. Jones (Ed.), *African American mental health: Theory, research and intervention* (pp. 71-100). Hampton, VA: Cobb & Henry.

Guarnaccia, P. J., De La Cancela, V., & Carrilo, E. (1989). The multiple meanings of "ataques de nervios" in the Latino community. *Medical Anthropology, 11*(1), 47-62.

Guthrie, R. (1976). *Even the rat was white: A historical view of psychology.* Boston: Allyn & Bacon.

Guthrie, R. (1994, November). African Americans in psychology. *Focus* (APA Division 45 Newsletter), *8*(2), 4-6.

Guthrie, R. V. (1998). *Even the rat was white: A historical view of psychology* (2nd ed.). Boston: Allyn & Bacon.

Guzman, L. P., Schiavo, S., & Puente, A. E. (1992). Ethnic minorities in the teaching of psychology. In A. E. Puente, J. R. Matthews, & C. L. Brewer (Eds.), *Teaching psychology in America: A history* (pp. 182-213). Washington, DC: American Psychological Association.

Hall, G. S. (1904). *Adolescence: Its psychology and its relation to physiology, anthropology, sociology, sex, crime, religion and education* (Vols. 1-2). New York: Appleton.

Hammond, W. R., & Yung, B. (1993). Minority student recruitment and retention practices among schools of professional psychology: A national survey and analysis. *Professional Psychology: Research and Practice, 24*(1), 3-12.

Harris, B. (1986). Reviewing 50 years of the psychology of social issues. *Journal of Social Issues, 42*(1), 1-20.

Harrison, A., Serafica, F., & McAdoo, H. (1984). Ethnic families of color. In R. Parke (Ed.), *Review of child development research* (pp. 329-371). Chicago: University of Chicago Press.

Haynes, M. A., & Smedley, B. D. (Eds.). (1999). *The unequal burden of cancer: An assessment of NIH research and programs for ethnic minorities and the medically underserved.* Washington, DC: National Academy Press.

Helms, J. (1990). *Blacks and White racial identity: Theory, research and practice.* Westford, CT: Greenwood.

Hernandez v. Texas, 347 U.S. 475 (1954).

Hess, R. D. (1970). The transmission of cognitive strategies in poor families: The socialization of apathy and underachievement. In V. Allen (Ed.), *Psychological factors in poverty* (pp. 73-92). Chicago: Markham.

Hess, R. D., & Shipman, V. (1965). Early experience and socialization of cognitive modes in children. *Child Development, 36*(4), 869-886.

Hilliard, A. G. (1983). IQ and the courts' *Larry P. vs. Wilson Riles* and *PASE vs. Hannon. Journal of Black Psychology, 10*(1), 1-18.

Holliday, B. G. (1989). Trailblazers in Black adolescent research. In R. L. Jones (Ed.), *Black adolescents* (pp. 39-54). Berkeley, CA: Cobb & Henry.

Holliday, B. G. (1992, August). *Roots of the mini-convention on ethnic minorities at the Centennial Convention of the American Psychological Association.* Paper presented at the annual APA convention, Washington, DC.

Holliday, B. G. (1999). The American Council on Education's studies on Negro youth development: An historical note with lessons on research, context, and social policy. In R. L. Jones (Ed.), *African American children, youth and parenting* (pp. 3-30). Hampton, VA: Cobb & Henry.

Holliday, B. G., Figueroa-Garcia, A., & Perry, D. (Eds.). (1994). *APA Commission on ethnic minority recruitment, retention and training: Resource book.* Washington, DC: American Psychological Association, Office of Ethnic Minority Affairs.

Holliday, B. G., Suinn, R. M., Bernal, M. E., Myers, H. F., Vazquez-Nuttal, E., Adams, D., et al. (1997). *Visions and transformations: The final report of the*

Commission on Ethnic Minority Recruitment, Retention and Training in Psychology. Washington, DC: American Psychological Association.

Hopkins, R., Ross, S., & Hicks, L. H. (1994). A history of the Department of Psychology at Howard University. *Journal of the Washington Academy of Sciences, 82*(2), 161-167.

Huang, K. (1991). Chinese American. In N. Mokuau (Ed.), *Handbook of social services for Asian and Pacific Islanders* (pp. 79-96). New York: Greenwood.

Immigration Act of 1924, Pub. L. No. 68-139, ch. 190, 43 Stat. 153.

Immigration Act of 1965, Pub. L. No. 89-236, 79 Stat. 911.

Ito, K. (1985). Affective bonds: Hawaiian interrelationships of self. In G. M. White & J. Kirkpatrick (Eds.), *Person, self, and experience: Exploring Pacific ethnopsychologies* (pp. 301-327). Berkeley: University of California Press.

Ito, K. (1987). Emotions, proper behavior (Hana Pono) and Hawaiian concepts of self, person, and individual. In A. B. Robillard & A. J. Marsella (Eds.), *Contemporary issues in mental health research in the Pacific Islands* (pp. 45-71). Honolulu: University of Hawaii Press.

Jaimes, M. A. (1992). Federal Indian identification policy: A usurpation of indigenous sovereignty in North America. In M. A. Jaimes (Ed.), *The state of Native America: Genocide, colonization and resistance* (pp. 123-138). Boston: South End.

Jenkins, A. (1982). *The psychology of the Afro-American.* New York: Pergamon.

Jenkins, M. (1994). Section VI, Clinical psychology of ethnic minorities. *The Clinical Psychologist, 47*(1), 16.

Jenkins v. United States, 307 F.2d 637 (1962).

Jensen, A. R. (1969). How much can we boost IQ and educational achievement? *Harvard Educational Review, 39,* 1-123.

Jones, R. L. (Ed.). (1996). *Handbook of tests and measurements for Black populations* (2 vols.). Hampton, VA: Cobb & Henry.

Jones, R. L. (Ed.). (1999). *African American children, youth and parenting.* Hampton, VA: Cobb & Henry.

Jones, S. L., & Campagna, R. V. (1995). Contributions of Hispanics to psychology. *History of Psychology Newsletter* (APA Division 26), *27*(22), 19-23.

Kardiner, A., & Ovesey, L. (1962). *The mark of oppression: Explorations in the personality of the American Negro.* Chicago and New York: Meridian Books, World Publishing Company. (Original work published 1951)

Katz, I. (1969). A critique of personality approaches to Negro performance, with research suggestions. *Journal of Social Issues, 25*(3), 13-27.

Kennedy, C. D., & Wagner, N. N. (1979). Psychology and affirmative action: 1977. *Professional Psychology, 10*(2), 234-243.

Kinzie, J., Boehnlein, J. K., Leung, P. K. Moore, L. J., Riley, C., & Smith, D. (1990). The prevalence of post-traumatic stress disorder and its clinical significance among Southeast Asian refugees. *American Journal of Psychiatry, 147,* 913-917.

Kirby, J. H. (1980). *Black Americans in the Roosevelt era: Liberalism and race.* Knoxville: University of Tennessee Press.

Klineberg, O. (1928). An experimental study of speed and other factors in "racial" differences. *Archives of Psychology, 93,* 111.

Klineberg, O. (1945). Racial psychology. In R. Linton (Ed.), *The science of man in the world crisis* (pp. 63-77). New York: Columbia University Press.

Kohout, J., & Pion, G. (1990). Participation of ethnic minorities in psychology: Where do we stand today? In G. Strickler, E. Davis-Russell, E. Bourg, E. Duran, W. R. Hammond, J. McHolland, K. Polite, & B. E. Vaughn (Eds.), *Toward ethnic diversification in psychology education and training* (pp. 153-160). Washington, DC: American Psychological Association.

Korchin, S. J. (1980). Clinical psychology and minority problems. *American Psychologists, 35,* 262-269.

LaFromboise, T. (1994). American Indians in psychology: A journey through the life of Carolyn Atteneave. *Focus* (APA Division 45 Newsletter), *8*(2), 11-13.

LaFromboise, T. (1998). American Indian mental health policy. In D. R. Atkinson, G. Morten, & D. W. Sue (Eds.), *Counseling American minorities* (pp. 137-158). Boston: McGraw-Hill.

LaFromboise, T., & Fleming, C. (1990, May/June). Keeper of the fire: A profile of Carolyn Atteneave. *Journal of Counseling and Development, 68,* 537-547.

LaFromboise, T., Trimble, J. E., & Mohatt, G. V. (1998). Counseling intervention and American Indian tradition: An integrative approach. In D. R. Atkinson, G. Morten, & D. W. Sue (Eds.), *Counseling American minorities* (5th ed., pp. 159-182). Boston: McGraw-Hill.

Laosa, L. M. (1984). Social policies toward children of diverse ethnic, racial, and language groups in the United States. In H. W. Stevenson & A. E. Siegel (Eds.), *Child development research and social policy* (pp. 1-109). Chicago: University of Chicago Press.

Larry P. v. Riles, 793 F.2d 969 (9th Cir. 1984).

Lawson, W. B. (1998). Psychopharmacology and African American mental health. In R. L. Jones (Ed.), *African American mental health: Theory, research and intervention* (pp. 303-314). Hampton, VA: Cobb & Henry.

Lee, J. C., & Cynn, V. E. H. (1991). Issues in counseling 1.5 generation Korean Americans. In C. C. Lee & B. L. Richardson (Eds.), *Multicultural issues in counseling: New approaches to diversity* (pp. 127-140). Alexandria, VA: American Association for Counseling and Development.

Leong, F. (1995). *History of Asian American psychology* (Asian American Psychological Association Monograph Series No. 1). Phoenix, AZ: Asian American Psychological Association.

Lesser, G., Fifer, G., & Clark, D. (1965). Mental abilities of children from different social-class and cultural groups. *Monographs of the Society for Research in Child Development, 30*(4, Serial No. 102).

Long, H. H. (1935). Some psychogenic hazards of segregated education of the Negro. *Journal of Negro Education, 4,* 336-350.

Marsella, A. J., Kinzie, D., & Gordon, P. (1973). Ethnic variations in expression of depression. *Journal of Cross-Cultural Psychology, 4,* 435-458.

Marsella, A. J., Oliveira, J. M., Plummer, C. M., & Crabbe, K. M. (1998). Native Hawaiian (Kanaka Maoli) culture, mind, and well-being. In H. J. McCubbin, A. E. Thompson, A. I. Thompson, & J. E. Fromer (Eds.), *Resiliency in Native American and immigrant families* (pp. 93-113). London: Sage.

Mayo, M. J. (1913). The mental capacity of the American Negro. *Archives of Psychology, 28.*

McAdoo, H. P., & McAdoo, J. L. (Eds.). (1985). *Black children: Social, educational and parental environments.* Beverly Hills, CA: Sage.

McDonald, D. (1994). New frontiers in clinical training: The UND Indians into Psychology Doctoral Education (InPsyDE). *American Indian and Alaska Native Mental Health Research, 5*(3), 52-56.

McLoyd, V. C., & Steinberg, L. (Eds.). (1998). *Studying minority adolescents: Conceptual, methodological and theoretical issues.* Mahwah, NJ: Lawrence Erlbaum.

Mezzich, J. E., & Raab, E. S. (1980). Depressive symptomatology across the Americas. *Archives of General Psychiatry, 37,* 818-823.

Mezzich, J. E., Ruiz, P., & Munoz, R. A. (1999). Mental health care for Hispanic Americans: A current perspective. *Cultural Diversity and Ethnic Minority Psychology, 5*(2), 91-102.

Miller, D. K. (1986). Screening people in, not out: Comment on Morawski. *Journal of Social Issues, 42*(1), 127-131.

Min, P. G. (1995). An overview of Asian Americans. In P. G. Min (Ed.), *Asian Americas: Contemporary trends and issues* (pp. 10-37). Thousand Oaks, CA: Sage.

Mokuau, N. (1990). A family-centered approach in Hawaiian culture. *Families in Society: Journal of Contemporary Social Services, 71*(10), 607-613.

Mollica, R. F., Wyshak, G., & Lavelle, J. (1987). The psychological impact of war trauma and torture on Southeast Asian refugees. *American Journal of Psychiatry, 144*(12), 1567-1572.

Morawski, J. G. (1986). Psychologist for society and societies for psychologists: SPSSI's place among professional organizations. *Journal of Social Issues, 42*(1), 111-126.

Myers, H. F., Anderson, N. B., & Strickland, T. L. (1998). Biobehavioral perspective for research on stress and hypertension in African American adults: Theoretical and empirical issues. In R. L. Jones (Ed.), *African American mental health: Theory, research and intervention* (pp. 209-245). Hampton, VA: Cobb & Henry.

Myers, L. J. (1988). *Understanding an Afrocentric world view: Introduction to an optimal psychology.* Dubuque, IA: Kendall/Hunt.

Myrdal, G. (1944). *An American dilemma: The Negro problem and modern democracy.* New York: Harper & Row.

National Academy of Sciences, Committee on Science and Public Policy. (1964). *Federal support of behavior research in institutions of higher learning.* Washington, DC: Author.

Nies, J. (1996). *Native American history: A chronology of the vast achievements of a culture and their links to world events.* New York: Ballantine.

Nishio, K., & Bilmes, M. (1987). Psychotherapy with Southeast Asian American clients. *Professional Psychology: Research and Practice, 18,* 342-364. (Also reprinted in *Counseling American minorities,* pp. 235-243, by D. R. Atkinson, G. Morten, & D. W. Sue, Eds., 1998, Boston: McGraw-Hill)

Nobles, W. W. (1972). African philosophy: Foundations for Black psychology. In R. L. Jones (Ed.), *Black psychology* (pp. 99-105). New York: Harper & Row.

O'Brien, D. J., & Fugita, S. S. (1991). *The Japanese American experience.* Bloomington: Indiana University Press.

Okamura, J. Y., & Agbayani, A. (1991). Filipino Americans. In N. Mokuau (Ed.), *Handbook of social services for Asian and Pacific Islanders* (pp. 97-115). New York: Greenwood.

Okura Mental Health Leadership Foundation. (1998). *Ten-year activities report: 1988-1998.* Bethesda, MD: Author.

Ozawa v. United States, 260 U.S. 178 (1922).

Padilla, A. M. (1980a). Notes on the history of Hispanic psychology. *Hispanic Behavioral Science, 6,* 13-32.

Padilla, A. M. (1980b). The role of cultural awareness and ethnic loyalty in acculturation. In A. Padilla (Ed.), *Acculturation: Theory, models, and some new findings* (pp. 47-84). Boulder, CO: Westview.

Padilla, A. M., & Lindhom, K. J. (1980). Notes on the history of Hispanic psychology. *Hispanic Behavioral Science, 6,* 13-32.

Padilla, E. R., Boxley, R., & Wagner, N. N. (1973). The desegregation of clinical psychology training. *Professional Psychology, 4,* 259-264.

Parham, T. A. (1989). Cycles of psychological Nigrescence. *The Counseling Psychologist, 17,* 187-226.

Parron, D. L. (1990). Federal initiatives in support of mental health research on ethnic minorities. In F. C. Serafica, A. E. Schwebel, R. K. Russell, P. D. Isaac, & L. B. Myers (Eds.), *Mental health of ethnic minorities* (pp. 302-309). New York: Praeger.

Paschal, F. C., & Sullivan, L. R. (1925). Racial influences in the mental and physical development of Mexican children. *Comparative Monographs, 3*, 1-76.

Peal, E., & Lambert, W. E. (1962). The relation of bilingualism to intelligence. *Psychological Monographs, 76* (Whole No. 546), 1-23.

Pearl, A. (1970). The poverty of psychology—an indictment. In V. Allen (Ed.), *Psychological factors in poverty* (pp. 348-364). Chicago: Markham.

Pettigrew, T. F. (1964). *A profile of the Negro American.* New York: Van Nostrand.

Pickren, W. E., & Tomes, H. (2002). The legacy of Kenneth B. Clark to the APA: The Board of Social and Ethical Responsibility for Psychology. *American Psychologist, 57*(1), 51-59.

Ponterotto, J. G., Burkhard, A., Yoshida, R. K., Cancelli, A. A., Giovanni, M., Wasilewski, L., et al. (1995). Prospective minority students' perceptions of application packets for professional psychology programs: A qualitative study. *Professional Psychology: Research and Practice, 26*(2), 196-204.

Porteus, S. D. (1924). Temperament and mentality in maturity, sex and race. *Journal of Applied Psychology, 8*, 57-74.

Quintana, S. M., & Bernal, M. E. (1995). Ethnic minority training in counseling psychology: Comparisons with clinical psychology and proposed standards. *The Counseling Psychologist, 23*(1), 102-121.

Rainwater, L. (1970). Neutralizing the disinherited: Some psychological aspects of understanding the poor. In V. Allen (Ed.), *Psychological factors in poverty* (pp. 9-28). Chicago: Markham.

Ramirez, M. (1998). *Multicultural/multiracial psychology: Mestizo perspectives in personality and mental health.* Northvale, NJ: Jason Aronson

Rezentes, W. C., III. (1996). *Ka lama kuki—Hawaiian psychology: An introduction.* Honolulu, HI: 'A'ali'i Books.

Richards, G. (1997). *"Race," racism and psychology: Towards a reflexive history.* New York: Routledge Kegan Paul.

Riessman, F. (1962). *The culturally deprived child.* New York: Harper & Row.

Robbins, R. L. (1996). Self-determination and subordination: The past, present and future of American Indian governance. In M. A. Jaimes (Ed.), *The state of Native America: Genocide colonization and resistance* (pp. 87-122). Boston: South End.

Roca de Torres, I. (1994a). La APPR: Una perspective historica [The APPR: A historical perspective]. *Revista Puertorriqueña de Psicologia, 9,* 109-128.

Roca de Torres, I. (1994b). Reseñas biograficas de algunos precursores de la psicologia en Puerto Rico [Biographical sketches of some psychology pioneers in Puerto Rico]. *Revista Puertorriqueña de Psicologia, 9,* 31-60.

Rogers, M., Ponterotto, K., Conoley, J., & Wiese, M. (1992). Multicultural training in school psychology: A national survey. *School Psychology Review, 21,* 603-616.

Rogler, L. H., Cortes, D. E., & Malgady, R. G. (1991). Acculturation and mental health status among Hispanics: Convergence and new directions for research. *American Psychologist, 46*(6), 585-597.

Russo, N. F., Olmedo, E. L., Strapp, J., & Fulcher, R. (1981). Women and minorities in psychology. *American Psychologist, 36*(11), 1315-1363.

Samura, J. (1966). Introduction. In J. Samura (Ed.), *La Raza: Forgotten Americans* (pp. 1-26). Notre Dame, IN: University of Notre Dame Press.

Sanchez, G. I. (1932). Group differences and Spanish-speaking children: A critical review. *Journal of Applied Psychology, 16,* 549-558.

Sanchez, G. I. (1966). History, culture and education. In J. Samura (Ed.), *La Raza: Forgotten Americans* (pp. 1-26). Notre Dame, IN: University of Notre Dame Press.

Sandiford, P., & Kerr, R. (1926). Intelligence of Chinese and Japanese children. *Journal of Educational Psychology, 17*(6), 361-367.

Scholes, W. E. (1966). The migrant worker. In J. Samura (Ed.), *La Raza: Forgotten Americans* (pp. 63-94). Notre Dame, IN: University of Notre Dame Press.

Sellman, J. C. (1999a). Great Depression. In K. A. Appiah & H. L. Gates (Eds.), *Africana: The encyclopedia of the African and African American experience* (pp. 867-869). New York: Basic Books.

Sellman, J. C. (1999b). New Deal. In K. A. Appiah & H. L. Gates (Eds.), *Africana: The encyclopedia of the African and African American experience* (pp. 1417-1418). New York: Basic Books.

Sellman, J. C. (1999c). World War II and African Americans. In K. A. Appiah & H. L. Gates (Eds.), *Africana: The encyclopedia of the African and African American experience* (pp. 2028-2030). New York: Basic Books.

Shuey, A. (1958). *The testing of Negro intelligence.* New York: Social Science Press.

Sitkoff, H. (1978). *A new deal for Blacks: The emergence of civil rights as a national issue: Vol. 1. The Depression decade.* New York: Oxford University Press.

Smedley, B. D., Stith, A. Y., & Nelson, A. R. (Eds.). (2002). *Unequal treatment: Confronting racial and ethnic disparities in health care.* Washington, DC: National Academy Press.

Spencer, M. B., Brookins, G. K., & Allen, W. R. (Eds.). (1985). *Beginnings: The social and affective development of Black children.* Hillsdale, NJ: Lawrence Erlbaum.

Stodolsky, S. S., & Lesser, G. (1967). Learning patterns in the disadvantaged. *Harvard Educational Review, 37,* 546-593.

Street, W. R. (1994). *A chronology of noteworthy events in American psychology.* Washington, DC: American Psychological Association.

Strickland, T. L., Lawson, W. B., & Lin, K. M. (1993). Interethnic variation in response to lithium therapy among African American and Asian American populations. In K. M. Lin, R. E. Poland, & G. Nakasaki (Eds.), *Psychopharmacology and psychobiology of ethnicity* (pp. 107-123). Washington, DC: American Psychiatric Association.

Strong, A. (1913). Three hundred fifty White and colored children measured by the Binet-Simon measuring scale of intelligence: A comparative study. *Pedagogical Seminary, 20,* 485-512.

Sue, D. (1998). The interplay of sociocultural factors on the psychological development of Asians in America. In D. R. Atkinson, G. Morten, & D. W. Sue (Eds.), *Counseling American minorities* (5th ed., pp. 205-213). Boston: McGraw-Hill.

Sue, S. (1976). Conceptions of mental illness among Asian and Caucasian American students. *Psychological Report, 38,* 703-708.

Sue, S. (1994). Asian Americans in psychology. *Focus* (APA Division 45 Newsletter), *8*(2), 6-8.

Suinn, R. M., & Witt, J. C. (1982). Survey on ethnic minority faculty recruitment and retention. *American Psychologist, 37*(11), 1239-1244.

Sullivan, P. (1999). Civil rights movement. In K. A. Appiah & H. L. Gates (Eds.), *Africana: The encyclopedia of the African and African American experience* (pp. 441-455). New York: Basic Books.

Szapocznik, J., Kurtines, W., & Fernandez, T. (1980). Bicultural involvement and adjustment in Hispanic-American youths. *International Journal of Intercultural Relations, 4,* 353-365.

Task Force on Representation in the Curriculum of the Division of Psychology of Women of the American Psychological Association. (1995). *Including diverse women in the undergraduate curriculum: Reasons and resources.* Washington, DC: Author.

Thomason, T. C. (1999). Improving the recruitment and retention of Native American students in psychology. *Cultural Diversity and Ethnic Minority Psychology, 5*(4), 308-316.

T'ien, J. K. (1985). Traditional Chinese beliefs and attitudes toward mental illness. In W. S. Tseng & D. Y. Wu (Eds.), *Chinese culture and mental health* (pp. 67-79). San Diego: Academic Press.

Tomine, S. I. (1991). Counseling Japanese Americans: From internment to reparation. In C. C. Lee & B. L. Richardson (Eds.), *Multicultural issues in counseling: New approaches to diversity* (pp. 91-105). Alexandria, VA: American Association for Counseling and Development.

Trimble, J. E. (1981). Value differentials and their importance in counseling American Indians. In P. Pederson, J. Dragnus, W. Lonner, & J. Trimble (Eds.), *Counseling across cultures* (pp. 203-226). Honolulu: University of Hawaii Press.

Trimble, J. E., Manson, S. M., Dinges, N. G., & Medicine, B. (1984). American Indian concepts of mental health: Reflections and directions. In P. Pedersen, N. Satorius, & A. Marsella (Eds.), *Mental health services: The cross-cultural context* (pp. 199-220). Beverly Hills, CA: Sage.

Valentine, C. (1971). Deficit, difference and bicultural models of Afro-American behavior. *Harvard Educational Review, 41*, 137-157.

Wang, S. L. (1926). A demonstration of the language involved in comparing racial groups by means of verbal intelligence tests. *Journal of Applied Psychology, 10*, 102-106.

Washington, V. (1988). Historical and contemporary linkages between Black child development and social policy. In D. T. Slaughter (Ed.), *New directions for child development: No. 24. Black children and poverty: A developmental perspective* (pp. 93-105). San Francisco: Jossey-Bass.

Williams, R. (1974). A history of the Association of Black Psychologists: Early formation and development. *Journal of Black Psychology, 1*(91), 9-24.

Wispe, L., Awkard, J., Hoffman, M., Ash, P., Hicks, L. H., & Porter, J. (1969). The Negro psychologist in America. *American Psychologist, 24*(2), 142-150.

Woods, P. J. (Ed.). (1988). *Is psychology for them? A guide to undergraduate advising.* Washington, DC: American Psychological Association.

Wyche, K. F., & Graves, S. B. (1992). Minority women in academia: Access and barriers to professional participation. *Psychology of Women Quarterly, 16*(4), 429-437.

Yerkes, R. M. (1921). Psychological examining in the United States Army. *Memoirs of the National Academy of Science, 15*, 1-890.

Yoshioka, M. (2001). *Okura Mental Health Leadership Foundation.* Retrieved from www.columbia.edu/cu/ssw/projects/pmap/okura.htm

CHAPTER 2

Conceptualization and Models

The Meaning(s) of Difference
in Racial and Ethnic Minority Psychology

RANDOLPH G. POTTS
Holy Cross College

RODERICK J. WATTS
Georgia State University

Psychology has historically provided a variety of labels and taxonomies of individual and group differences. In this discourse on difference, however, the language of psychology is not just descriptive, and it is certainly not value neutral. Several general models have been used in conceptualizing differences in racial and ethnic minority psychology. One model is "universalism" (Bourne, 1991), in which work in the field is put forth explicitly or implicitly as equally applicable to all populations, when in fact it is undergirded by a particular cultural worldview. Historically, European American psychology has favored this "main effects" view, seeing all human behavior and experience as generalizable. For example, in Erikson's (1968) influential theory of human development, Black racial identity is treated as a special case of

identity and relegated to a separate section at the end of the book. Tacit in this and similar theories that have come to dominate U.S. psychology is that culture-related values, such as individualism, are cultural universals. In the universal model, cultural variations are marginalized to maintain the facade of a "univocal science" (Gergen, Gulerce, Lock, & Misra, 1996). Within this model of difference, European American psychological concepts and methods are held as "universals," whereas indigenous conceptualizations of the self and ways of knowing are regarded as "particulars." This denial of racial and ethnic differences in psychology has been referred to as a *"beta bias"* (Hare-Mustin & Marecek, 1988), whereas the pervasive tendency to formulate theories and applications of psychology based mainly on studies of European

Americans has been called *"cultural malpractice"* (Iijima Hall, 1997).

Another model of difference acknowledges cultural differences but ranks them hierarchically. In a hierarchical or evolutionary model, difference from the European American middle-class cultural standard is interpreted as incipient and less adequately developed (Bourne, 1991). A third model sees differences in the psychology of people defined as "racial and ethnic minorities" as a consequence of racism and social oppression. This model is valuable in that it acknowledges the effects of inequities and injustices associated with racism but risks basing our understanding of people mainly on their trauma rather than their cultural heritage. What constitutes a "racial and ethnic minority" depends on historical and social location. "Minority" status is just one feature of a group's cultural and psychological experience.

Finally, there is a model of difference that views differences in cultural systems as equivalent and complementary. Within this model are population-specific psychologies, multicultural psychology, cultural psychology, and what has been called "cultural relativist" approaches to psychology. Population-specific psychologies focus on understanding a particular population (e.g., a specific Latino population, a specific Asian or Asian American population, etc.) on its own terms rather than in comparative terms (as is the case with cross-cultural psychology). Cultural psychology is the study of how cultural traditions, practices, and systems of meaning contribute to culturally specific constructions of mind, self, and emotion (Shweder, 1991). The value of cultural relativism, according to Wagner (quoted in Stein, 1986, p. 169), is that it "poses a constant question, keeps a persistent radical doubt. . . . [It serves] . . . as a critique of ethnocentrism and scientific imperialism" (quoted in Stein, 1986, p. 169). We would argue that one-standard, context-independent judgments of fitness and goodness are culture bound.

This way of understanding distinctiveness sets the stage for hegemony and population-based notions of superiority and supremacy. If it is to remedy the shortcomings of many existing ideas in psychology, racial and ethnic minority psychology (REMP) should take a very different approach. It must fully incorporate cultural distinctiveness in an affirmative way while seeking to eradicate the threats to well-being and justice posed by racism and oppression.

At its best, there will be no tendency in REMP to understand differences as inferior or superior based on a single standard of goodness and without regard to the social and ecological context of population differences. However, REMP is a young field, and it has some distance to go before resolving the many challenges associated with these goals. In this chapter, we will raise some questions and highlight what may be weaknesses of REMP as it currently exists, as well as critique anti-diversity perspectives in the field. We will also take note of its strengths—its affirmation of pluralism and the variety of culturally distinctive ways of knowing and providing relief from human suffering. In this chapter, we will continue the discussion on ideas of difference in racial and ethnic minority psychology and how these have influenced research and practice. We will focus our discussion on (a) difference as antagonism, (b) difference as complementary relationship, and (c) shared and distinctive themes in racial and ethnic minority psychology.

Difference as Antagonism

One of the first challenges in any paradigm of diversity is overcoming a long history of antagonistic attitudes toward difference in U.S. psychology. Psychological testing has been one of the more potent means of operationalizing human differences in a way that privileges certain cultural notions of competence at the expense of others. For example, "high-stakes testing" (National Research Council,

1999) can be misused in a way that rationalizes and sustains educational and social inequity. Test constructors in psychology could profit from what the National Research Council (1999) stated on this topic: "Fairness, like validity cannot be addressed as an afterthought. . . . It must be confronted through the interconnected phases of the testing process, from test design and development to administration, scoring, interpretation, and use" (pp. 4, 7). Psychology has also done its part to frame notions in a way that implies the superiority of certain traits, regardless of context. Terms such as *impulsive* versus *thoughtful* and *submissive* versus *assertive* are part of standard psychology vocabulary and examples of this tendency. Prejudicial word choices encourage implicit if not explicit value judgments, and often the word choices reflect some underlying cultural value such as rationality (vs. intuition), autonomy (vs. interdependence), or the like. This whole approach serves to perpetuate an antagonistic, hierarchically ordered approach to understanding differences. As Ani (1994) argued in her critique of certain European cultural imperatives, "Once the 'person' was artificially split into conflicting faculties or tendencies it made sense to think in terms of one faculty 'winning' or controlling the other(s)" (p. 33). In addition to these problems with the construction of differences, there is the notion of individual differences itself. A focus on traits and other differences at the individual level risks reducing problems that are associated with groups and social systems to dysfunctions within the individual.

Overcoming antagonistic, hierarchically ordered conceptualizations of difference is a formidable task, given the wide dissemination of psychological literature promoting these conceptualizations (e.g., Herrnstein & Murray, 1994; Rushton, 1999).[1] Making this task even more daunting, two of the most prolific and strident theorists on hierarchical models of racial difference—Arthur Jensen and J. Philippe Rushton—have been recognized in the newspaper of the American Psychological Association as "frontier scientists" producing some of the best psychological research.

Difference as Complementary Relationship

Some cultural traditions offer alternatives to framing differences as antagonistic opposites. T'Shaka (1995) described ancient Kemetic (Egyptian) cosmological principles that have led to African principles of "twinness" as a means of understanding complementarity. In the case of life and death, the story of Re illustrates the twinness principle:

> Re symbolizes the birth and rise of the sun; during the evening the sun Re enters the world of Osiris, the "realm of death." . . . The main theme of the Litany of Re is the meeting of opposites, Re and Osiris, who become united and form an entity. (Piankoff, 1964, quoted in T'Shaka, 1995, p. 110)

The Asian notion of yin and yang is similar to twinness. More than 2,000 years ago, Chinese cosmology gave birth to what would become the Tao Te Ching. The Tao provides a poetic vision of complementarity and how unity gives rise to diversity:

> The Tao is the One,
> From the One come yin and yang;
> From these two, creative energy;
> From energy, ten thousand things;
> The forms of all creation.
> All life embodies the yin
> And embraces yang,
> Through their union
> Achieving harmony.

> Dreher (1990, p. 102)

The point of bringing forth these philosophical ideas is to encourage emerging theories of racial and ethnic psychology to recognize complementarity at the foundation of racial and ethnic minority psychology—for instance, viewing spirituality as a parallel and contrasting rather than as an antagonistic counterpart to science, as well as viewing diversity as differing but compatible expressions of wholeness ("the One"). A useful intellectual exercise for us is to constantly strive to reframe hierarchically ordered notions of difference in our personal and professional lives. Another is to resist quick judgments of goodness and instead focus on the interdependence of ideas.

SHARED AND DISTINCTIVE THEMES IN RACIAL AND ETHNIC MINORITY PSYCHOLOGY

Within racial and ethnic minority psychology, there is the creative tension between shared and distinctive concepts in the field. According to Watts (1994), some of these shared concepts are cultural identity, oppression and culture, and the salience of the context. In this chapter, we add to these recognition of population-specific psychologies and the quest for liberation.

Cultural Identity

Even at this early point in the development of racial and ethnic minority psychology, virtually all populations have worked to identify the meaning of culture for their group and the degree of psychological kinship felt by members. Culture, acculturation, (cross) cultural psychology, racial socialization, racial centrality, and ethnic and racial identity are all part of this domain. Several chapters in this *Handbook* describe the current research on ethnic identity (Chapter 11), acculturation (Chapter 9), and biculturalism (Chapter 12).

One question for racial and ethnic minority psychology is the place of European Americans. In locations beyond the United States, they may be similar to other racial or ethnic minorities, but within the United States, they are participants in the hegemonic culture as well. And although European Americans as a group are racial and ethnic minorities on the world stage, they benefit from White supremacy and its global reach. Just as "minority" status does not fully explicate the cultural and psychological experience of people of African origin in the United States, "hegemonic" status does not fully reveal the cultural realities of European Americans. At this historical and social juncture, do they constitute a cultural or ethnic group? Or is "being White" mainly a social construction designed to grant privilege to those having certain physical characteristics? To what extent must we investigate and understand the psychology of Whites to understand the development and functioning of populations of color? We suggest that acculturation in the United States cannot be understood without a study of the hegemonic culture and the processes through which hegemony is reproduced. Similarly, our understanding of the experience of oppression is enhanced through investigating the experience of privilege. Just as the dominant theories of psychology with their origins in Western culture have failed the field by their distortions and omissions with respect to people of color, a racial and ethnic minority psychology that lacks a critical, historical understanding of the thought and behavior of Whites will fall short of being a psychology that can reshape society. Some progressive Whites are taking steps toward meeting this challenge by creating the field loosely defined as "White studies" (e.g., Frankenberg, 1997).

Oppression and Culture

The notions of *minority* and *people of color* are collective terms that combine a wide range of populations that are culturally distinct. If these populations do not share a common culture, what do they share? An obvious common feature is the experience of oppression and the cultural transformation in response to it. Given the experiences of conquest by indigenous peoples of the Americas, slavery by people of African descent, the generations of discrimination and worse by Asian immigrants, and the contemporary racism experienced by all, oppression and the struggle for liberation are salient features of our psychologies. Concepts such as discrimination, marginalization, alienation, segregation, hegemony, and internalized racism (constructing one's identity vis-à-vis the hegemonic culture of the socially oppressive other) are among the concepts of interest in this domain. Racial and ethnic minority psychology must come to grips with the construct of oppression and, even more important, the construct and practice of liberation.

Elsewhere, Watts and his colleagues (Watts, Griffith, & Abdul-Adil, 1999) defined oppression as the unjust use of power by one socially salient group over another in a way that creates and sustains inequity in the distribution of coveted resources. Particularly influential in the theory is recent work by Serrano-García and Lopez-Sanchez (1992). Serrano-García (1994) described this as an "asymmetry" maintained through a power relationship between oppressors and the oppressed. Typically, the rationale for maintaining this inequity is an ideology of group superiority (e.g., racism, sexism, heterosexism). The use of power to create and sustain inequity suggests that oppression is a process, whereas the circumstance or state that results from this use of power is an outcome. For sociopolitical development to proceed, a person becomes increasingly aware of group-based power relationships and is able to distinguish both the processes (e.g., policies and practices) and the outcomes (e.g., subjugation, trauma, and social and personal dysfunction) that result from long-term oppression. Based on work by Gramsci, Hopper (1999) provided a helpful definition of the reflective aspect of sociopolitical development in his discussion of "the importance of symbolic forays against cultural 'hegemony' to the larger struggle": It is

> learning to think critically about accepted ways of thinking and feeling, discerning the hidden interests in underlying assumptions and framing notions (whether these be class-, gender-, race/ethnicity- or sect-based). It means learning to see, in the mundane particulars of ordinary lives, how history works, how received ways of thinking and feeling serve to perpetuate existing structures of inequality. (p. 13)

Another task of racial and ethnic minority psychology is to clarify how cultures meet the challenges of oppression. In meeting these challenges, ideas and survival strategies that undermine the integrity and authenticity of the culture may be incorporated. On the other hand, authentic cultural practices and strategies may be accessed that support resistance to oppression, survival, and well-being. (The latter will be discussed more in the next section on population-specific psychologies.) But can a clear line be drawn between practices that are strategies for resisting oppression and those that reflect "deeper" cultural continuities? For example, some theorists have interpreted elements of machismo in Latin American cultures as a stereotypic, hypermasculine response to the experience of conquest and subjugation by Spanish invaders (Zinn, 1992). From this perspective, the emphasis on strength, honor, and respect in machismo behavior and attitudes can be seen as a compensation for the emasculating effects of oppression. How much is this the case, and how much is it an extension of preexisting cultural factors or just another myth that paints people of color in an unfavorable way?

As the example above suggests, responses to "cultural trauma" and the incorporation of alien ideas may introduce self-destructive tendencies and contradictions into a culture. Because culture is dynamic, changing constantly to meet environmental challenges of all kinds, those that occur due to oppression may be incorporated into culture as well. To better understand such cultural changes, a critical, historically conscious cultural analysis would be a valuable element in racial and ethnic minority psychology. We must gain a clear understanding of cultural change processes under conditions of oppression. It is important to note that oppression can give rise to creativity as well as misery. Some African American music traditions arose from the unceasing drudgery of work (and the need for secret communication) in the fields. Similarly, work by Sue and Okazaki (1990) suggests that the outstanding academic performance of Asian Americans, stronger than that found in many of their home countries, can be understood in part as a response to the experience of oppression in the United States.

A critical, cultural analysis in racial and ethnic minority psychology would more closely investigate contemporary cultural strategies for responding to oppression vis-à-vis what may be the more enduring, authentic essence of a culture, the *asili* (Ani, 1994). The optimal approach to such a cultural analysis may vary across populations, just as cultural traditions, histories, and experiences of oppression may differ substantially. One population-specific example of a process of cultural analysis is provided by Banks (1982, cited in Akbar, 1998), who identified three critical methods in the development of Black psychology. These three methods are defined as deconstruction, reconstruction, and construction. Murrell (1997) contended that before "digging again" the wells of traditional cultural resources, an essential first step is deconstructing or countering misrepresentations by the hegemonic culture. Using a slightly different emphasis, Freire (1998) described this first step as a process of "denunciation."

Reconstruction, the second method in a critical, cultural analysis, attempts to develop a racial and ethnic minority psychology that honors and incorporates specific cultural resources or *asili*. According to Martín-Baró (1994), this recovery of "historical memory" is an essential component of a liberatory psychology. In recent years, a few researchers have also turned their attention to the *process* of recovery, believing that "indigenous methodologies" are needed for the optimal reconstruction of the story of a people. As a member of the indigenous Maori people of New Zealand, Smith (1999), drawing on ideas from Egan (1987), argued that the Western scientific method is not a culture-free lingua franca for systematic inquiry:

> Rationality in the Western tradition enabled knowledge to be produced and articulated in a scientific and "superior" way . . . notions of rationality and conceptualizations of knowledge became the "convenient" tool for dismissing from serious comparison with Western forms of thought those forms of "primitive" thought which were being encountered. (p. 170)

Recovering historical memory is not just a cognitive or intellectual process but a healing and spiritual process. Consequently, it does not just involve academic technologies but spiritual technologies. In African philosophy, it is believed that historical memory may be best accessed through ritual (Somé, 1998). "Ritual provides not only healing but the recovery of memory and the reaffirmation of each individual's life purpose" (Somé, 1998, p. 32). Within the sacred space of ritual, consciousness can be moved through time from the present to the ancestral past—from the *Sasa* to the *Zamani* (Mbiti, 1970).

The third method, construction, is a particularly creative process. It simultaneously involves action to enhance the social well-being of the group and advance the growth of critical knowledge in psychology (Nobles, 1986, cited in Akbar, 1998). The constructionist method synthesizes the body of population-specific knowledge gained through reconstructionist methods into the multivocal forms of dialogue called for by Gergen et al.

(1996) in proposing a multicultural psychology. In using this knowledge for social justice and well-being, construction is similar to *annunciation*, the affirmative process that complements Freire's (1998) "denunciation." The finished product is a psychology of a population that is built from the ground up, based on the distinctive cultural patterns of the group of interest. Through the process of deconstruction and reconstruction, the maladaptive and self-depreciative elements are removed, and elements based on preoppression heritage are restored. In reality, all three phases just described are part of an ongoing process of "becoming" that never reaches a perfect, final destination. Instead, it responds to contemporary demands and evolving insights constantly over time.

The Salience of the Context

A third shared theme in racial and ethnic minority psychology is the significance of the context—the setting and circumstances that surround, influence, respond to, and interact with human behavior. For example, the dynamics of cultural identity in the first shared theme, or oppression in the second, are influenced by environmental and social contexts, as noted in Lewin's (1936) famous equation: Behavior is a function of the person and the environment—$B:f$ (P, E). Elements of each theme respond to and influence their context. Ecological models have also been applied to human behavior in an effort to better understand the interaction. However, unlike creatures of the forest, the ability humans have to consciously and planfully shape their environment is not limited to instinct. Another way of understanding context that takes human cognition into account is intergroup theory. Racial and ethnic populations respond to both within- and between-group relations, and thus the process and structure of intergroup contact constitute a context. Intergroup theory helps us understand how group definition and boundaries, social identity theory, intergroup prejudice, ethnocentrism, and similar intergroup dynamics operate in and respond to various circumstances.

Population-Specific Psychologies

The shared or crosscutting themes in racial and ethnic minority psychology described above exist in creative tension with population-specific psychologies (Watts, 1994). Although a variety of populations have experienced oppression, in the United States, mainly people of African descent have experienced the legacy of chattel slavery, and only the Japanese have experienced "internment." Similarly, only the indigenous people of the Americas have experienced conquest and subjugation by European invaders on their own soil followed by either immigration or "reservation" experiences in the United States. These unique histories, in combination with the varying cultural origins of the affected populations, produce a distinctive collective experience that cannot be captured fully by general constructs such as oppression.

One of the clear advantages of population-specific psychologies is the focus on understanding a single population and building theories and interventions from its unique heritage and cultural imperatives. Again, we must emphasize that there is more to a population than its experience of oppression, and population-specific psychologies ought to reflect that in theory, research, and practice. Population-specific psychologies can illuminate aspects of cultural experience that exist not because of social oppression but, rather, survived in spite of it. A population-specific psychology is a culture-conscious alternative to the frequent arguably hegemonic practice of developing an intervention with one population and then adapting it for use with a culturally different population in a different ecological setting. The typical example is developing an interpersonal problem-solving program with

European American children in a suburban setting and then adapting it for use with low-income urban, immigrant Latin American children. A universalist scientific worldview assumes that potent main effects are universal in their benefits and that only superficial changes (such as the race or language of the children in the instructional video) are needed to achieve external validity. But what of the underlying worldview and cultural ethos of the original intervention? It may persist and be in conflict with the culture of other recipients of the intervention. A population-specific approach starts with identifying and understanding a culture's underlying values and worldview, and from that unique foundation, an intervention approach is developed.

Certain preferences, conceptualizations of the person, ways of relating to ancestors, ways of relating to nature, styles of speaking, linguistic items, notions of time, ways of worshipping God, attitudes, and so on, are retentions of traditional culture (Jones, 1991; Nobles, 1991). Central in many indigenous cultural systems are distinctive traditions for healing, promoting resilience, and restoring harmony. Rediscovering cultural resources for healing has stimulated several therapeutic practices in population-specific psychologies based on traditional wisdom teachings such as NTU therapy (Foster, Phillips, Belgrave, Randolph, & Braithwaite, 1993), *cuento* therapy (Costantino, Malgady, & Rogler, 1986), Morita therapy (Morita, Kondo, & LeVine, 1998), rites of passage programs (Warfield-Coppock, 1992), sacred Inipi or sweat lodges (Lame Deer & Sarkis, 1993), and Oshodi empty pot ceremonies. Beyond healing at the level of the person and family, methods for restoring harmony and resisting social oppression may have become imbedded in the cultural heritage of ethnic minorities in the United States.

A number of theorists have argued that there is indeed conflict between different cultural worldviews—including conflicting systems of beliefs, values, and conceptions of "self"—and they argue that we ignore this conflict at our peril. For example, Ramirez (1998) and Kambon (1996) argued that there are irreconcilable differences between cultural worldviews. Citing several other psychologists and scholars, Kambon contended, "It has also been convincingly argued by African social scientists that not only are the African and European worldviews distinct in nature, but they are oppositional as well" (p. 8). It follows by his and similar arguments that maintaining the integrity of a cultural system in the face of conquest, denigration, and domination is essential to the health of a culture and its people. Native American postcolonial psychology and Smith's (1999) work on "decolonizing methodologies" are similar examples of how new psychologies are developing out of catastrophic experiences. An intellectually honest psychology must recognize population-specific paradigms and their perspectives on theory and research.

It is tempting to view the population-specific psychologies as intrinsically anti-hegemonic and thus not requiring an incisive critique from within. But these psychologies are dynamic and tend to have their own internal tensions and contradictions. The glorification of one's own culture without critical reflection can lead to the denigration of others. Another challenge, which may be encountered in the "reconstruction" method noted earlier, is determining more clearly when "traditional cultures" exist or existed. What is traditional Mexican culture? Is it that of the Aztecs prior to invasion by the Spaniards, or is it the resulting Mestizo amalgam that Ramirez (1998) argued is itself a culture—a fusion of indigenous and European worldviews? Should all cultural amalgams involving oppression or other external incursions be excluded from consideration as "traditional culture"? It is hoped that the continuing work in population-specific psychologies will bring greater clarity to these and other important questions.

Another challenge for REMP more generally is for researchers to remain appreciative of differences in theoretical paradigms. As captured in the model proposed by Banks (1982, cited in Akbar, 1998) earlier, a constructionist method integrates shared constructs and serves to remind us of our common humanity, whereas reconstructionist methods and population-specific perspectives affirm our diversity.

The Quest for Liberation

A major question still to be answered is how racial and ethnic minority psychology can play a greater role in countering the structural asymmetries of oppression. Expanding psychosocial inquiry to include actions beneficial to oppressed groups and society as a whole is the focus in constructionist and annunciation approaches discussed earlier. But how can racial and ethnic minority psychology participate more fully in creating a just, equitable, and culturally pluralistic society? Some answers to this question may be found in this *Handbook* in chapters that discuss community psychology (Chapter 28), community interventions (Chapter 29), reducing racism (Chapter 31), and community-based prevention (Chapters 29 and 32).

Martín-Baró (1994) suggested several elements of a psychology in service of liberation that include a preferential option for the poor, a new epistemology, and a new praxis. According to Martín-Baró, in reflecting on conceptualizations and models of racial and ethnic minority psychology, we must ask ourselves how these formulations will have an impact on the urgent issues and harsh circumstances facing people of color. He cautioned against "scientist mimicry"—prioritizing our own recognition and status as individuals (or as an American Psychological Association Division) within mainstream U.S. psychology over aligning ourselves with and representing the voices of the oppressed in our scholarly work. Within a new and ultimately liberating praxis in racial and ethnic minority psychology, we may begin to discover creative ways of integrating indigenous ways of seeking knowledge (Smith, 1999) with critically revitalized versions of Western scientific methods in the service of social justice.

> It is not easy to figure out how to place ourselves within the process alongside the dominated rather than alongside the dominator. It is not even easy to leave our role of technocratic or professional superiority and to work hand in hand with community groups. But if we do not embark upon this new type of praxis that transforms ourselves as well as transforming reality, it will be hard indeed to develop a Latin American psychology that will contribute to the liberation of our peoples. (Martín-Baró, 1994, p. 29)

NOTE

1. A large number of American Psychological Association members, especially from Divisions 6, 7, 8, 9, 14, and 15, recently received by mail a version of *Race, Evolution and Behavior* by J. Philippe Rushton (1999). Herrnstein and Murray's (1994) *The Bell Curve* and Rushton's (1999) *Race, Evolution and Behavior* are recent examples of research on human differences that purport to demonstrate how group differences are indicative of inferiority on the part of African Americans, in particular. These are not the best examples, however, because many dispute the methodology that produced the differences these authors attempt to explain. Nonetheless, they are contemporary examples of a tradition in psychology that uses the gloss of the

scientific method to affirm oppressive social policies, much as the now-discredited pseudo-science of eugenics and, more recently, the use of testing and psychology aimed at showing the inferiority of certain Europeans seeking immigration to the United States (see Albee, 1988).

REFERENCES

Akbar, N. (1998). *Know thy self*. Tallahassee, FL: Mind Productions.

Albee, G. (1988). The politics of nature and nurture. *American Journal of Community Psychology, 10*, 4-28.

Ani, M. (1994). *Yurugu: An African-centered critique of European cultural thought and behavior*. Trenton, NJ: Africa World Press.

Bourne, E. J. (1991). Does the concept of the person vary cross-culturally? In R. A. Shweder (Ed.), *Thinking through cultures: Expeditions in cultural psychology* (pp. 113-155). Cambridge, MA: Harvard University Press.

Costantino, G., Malgady, R. G., & Rogler, L. H. (1986). Cuento therapy: A culturally sensitive modality for Puerto Rican children. *Journal of Consulting and Clinical Psychology, 54*(5), 639-645.

Dreher, D. (1990). *The Tao of inner peace*. New York: Harper Perennial.

Egan, K. (1987). Literacy and the oral foundations of education. *Harvard Educational Review, 57*(4), 446.

Erikson, E. (1968). *Identity: Youth and crisis*. New York: Norton.

Foster, P. M., Phillips, F., Belgrave, F. Z., Randolph, S. M., & Braithwaite, N. (1993). An Africentric model for AIDS education, prevention, and psychological services within the African American community. *Journal of Black Psychology, 19*(2), 123-141.

Frankenberg, R. (1997). Local whiteness, localizing whiteness. In R. Frankenberg (Ed.), *Displacing Whiteness: Essays in social and cultural criticism*. Durham, NC: Duke University Press.

Freire, P. (1998). *Education for critical consciousness*. New York: Continuum.

Gergen, K. J., Gulerce, A., Lock, A., & Misra, G. (1996). Psychological science in cultural context. *American Psychologist, 51*(5), 496-503.

Hare-Mustin, R. T., & Marecek, J. (1988). The meaning of difference: Gender theory, postmodernism, and psychology. *American Psychologist, 43*(6), 455-464.

Herrnstein, R. J., & Murray, C. (1994). *The bell curve: Intelligence and class structure in American life*. New York: Free Press.

Hopper, K. (1999). John Berger and Erick Holtsman. *Social Policy 30*(2), 13-21.

Iijima Hall, C. (1997). Cultural malpractice: The growing obsolescence of psychology with the changing US population. *American Psychologist, 52*(6), 642-651.

Jones, J. M. (1991). Racism: A cultural analysis of the problem. In R. L. Jones (Ed.), *Black psychology* (3rd ed., pp. 609-635). Berkeley, CA: Cobb & Henry.

Kambon, M. (1996). Afrikan (Black) psychologists answer the healing drum. In E. Addae (Ed.) *To heal a people: Afrikan scholars defining a new reality* (pp. 163-176). Columbia, MD: Kujichaguilia.

Lame Deer, A. F., & Sarkis, H. (1993). *The Lakota sweat lodge cards: Spiritual teachings of the Sioux*. Rochester, VT: Inner Traditions International.

Lewin, K. (1936). *Principles of topological psychology*. New York: McGraw-Hill.

Martín-Baró, I. (1994). *Writings for a liberation psychology* (A. Aron & S. Corne, Eds.). Cambridge, MA: Harvard University Press.

Mbiti, J. S. (1970). *African religions and philosophies*. Garden City, NY: Anchor.

Morita, S., Kondo, A., & LeVine, P. (1998). *Morita therapy and the true nature of anxiety-based disorders*. Albany: State University of New York Press.

Murrell, P. C. (1997). Digging again the family wells: A Freirian literacy framework as emancipatory pedagogy for African-American children. In P. Freire (Ed.), *Mentoring the mentor: A critical dialogue with Paulo Freire* (pp. 19-55). New York: Peter Lang.

National Research Council. (1999). *High stakes: Testing for tracking, promotion and graduation.* Washington, DC: Author.

Nobles, W. W. (1991). African philosophy: Foundations for Black psychology. In R. L. Jones (Ed.), *Black psychology* (3rd ed., pp. 47-63). Berkeley, CA: Cobb & Henry.

Ramirez, M. (1998). *Multicultural/multiracial psychology: Mestizo perspectives in personality and mental health.* Northvale, NJ: Jason Aronson.

Rushton, J. P. (1999). *Race, evolution and behavior.* London, Ontario: Charles Darwin Research Institute.

Serrano-García, I. (1994). The ethics of the powerful and the power of ethics. *American Journal of Community Psychology, 22,* 1-20.

Serrano-García, I., & Lopez-Sanchez, G. (1992, August). *Asymmetry and oppression: Pre-requisites of power relationships.* Paper presented at the annual convention of the American Psychological Association, Washington, DC.

Shweder, R. A. (1991). Cultural psychology: What is it? In R. A. Shweder (Ed.), *Thinking through cultures: Expeditions in cultural psychology* (pp. 73-110). Cambridge, MA: Harvard University Press.

Smith, L. T. (1999). *Decolonizing methodologies: Research and indigenous peoples.* New York: Zed Books.

Somé, M. P. (1998). *The healing wisdom of Africa.* New York: Plenum.

Stein, H. (1986). Cultural relativism as the central organizing resistance in cultural anthropolgy. *Journal of Psychoanalytic Anthropology, 9,* 157-175.

Sue, S., & Okazaki, S. (1990). Asian-American educational achievements: A phenomenon in search of an explanation. *American Psychologist, 45,* 913-920.

T'Shaka, O. (1995). *Return to the Afrikan mother principle of male and female equality* (Volume 1). Oakland, CA: Pan Afrikan.

Warfield-Coppock, N. (1992). The rites of passage movement: A resurgence of African-centered practices for socializing African American youth. *Journal of Negro Education, 61,* 471-482.

Watts, R. (1995). Paradigms of diversity. In E. Trickett, R. Watts, & D. Birman (Eds.) *Human diversity: Perspectives on people in context.* San Francisco: Jossey-Bass.

Watts, R. J., Griffith, D. M., & Abdul-Adil, J. (1999). Sociopolitical development as an antidote for oppression: Theory and action. *American Journal of Community Psychology, 27*(2), 225-240.

Zinn, M. (1992). Chicano men and masculinity. In S. Kimmel & M. Messner (Eds.), *Men's lives* (2nd ed.). New York: Macmillan.

CHAPTER 3

A Profile of Ethnic Minority Psychology

A Pipeline Perspective

FREDERICK T. L. LEONG
The Ohio State University

JESSICA KOHOUT
American Psychological Association

JAMIE SMITH
The Ohio State University

MARLENE WICHERSKI
American Psychological Association

INTRODUCTION AND ORGANIZATION

Tracking demographics among scientists and engineers has a relatively recent history. It was only in the mid-1970s that organizations, researchers, and policymakers began paying close attention to the gender and racial/ethnic composition of their workforces, among the first demographics to be tracked (census excluded). Since that time, however, measuring diversity has become an accepted part of research and policy. Gender and race/ethnicity data are collected by the American Psychological Association (APA) and other associations and agencies in membership surveys, employment and salary surveys, surveys of departments, as well as in surveys of APA governance. Diversity is important because it tells us how representative psychology is of the larger population and, by implication, how relevant it may be deemed to be by consumers, students, employers, and policymakers. Diversity itself has broadened in definition over the years and now includes gender, race/ethnicity, sexual orientation, and physical and mental challenges, among other characteristics.

This chapter focuses on only one of these components of diversity, race/ethnicity. As the population of the United States diversifies and the world becomes one global community, the goal of increasing the participation of racial/ethnic minorities in psychology has been of great concern to the field. On our way to this goal, it is useful to periodically assess where we stand with respect to the representation of various racial and ethnic groups within psychology. It is also useful to gauge the representation and experiences of minorities in the various stages of the educational pipeline.

For these reasons, the organization of this chapter follows closely one written about 10 years ago by Kohout and Pion (1990), who addressed the participation of ethnic minorities in psychology by looking back at psychology's success in attracting minorities to the field. They stressed that it is important to look at all stages of the formal educational pipeline, not just at the graduate level, for every stage provides a potential point for intervention. As Kohout and Pion reported, although psychology had seen success in attracting ethnic minorities, the percentages of non-White doctoral psychologists remained relatively small.

EARLIER STUDIES

Before discussing the current situation with respect to the educational pipeline, new doctorates, and employed psychologists, it is worthwhile to consider several earlier studies that took a similar broad look at ethnic minority representation in psychology. Using data from the 1978 APA Human Resources Survey (Gottfredson & Dyer, 1978), the APA Survey of Graduate Departments of Psychology, and the National Research Council, Russo, Olmedo, Stapp, and Fulcher (1981) documented the underrepresentation of women and minorities in the APA, in the doctoral population, and among new doctorates in an article for a special issue of *American Psychologist*. Because the focus of this chapter is on the representation of minorities in psychology, we will be focusing on these data rather than on the gender data. First, with respect to the APA membership, Russo et al. found that just over 3% of APA members were members of a minority group and 29% were women, supporting the notion that women and minorities were underrepresented in the APA. Blacks were most numerous at 1.2%, followed by Asians at 1%, Hispanics at .7%, and American Indians at .2%. They revealed that gender distribution varied by race/ethnicity, with Blacks having the highest proportion of women at around 40%, whereas all other groups had proportions between 20% and 26%. The authors uncovered variations by subfield but cautioned that detailed comparisons were difficult given the small numbers. Russo et al. also relied on data from the 1980-1981 Survey of Graduate Departments of Psychology (American Psychological Association, 2001b). Approximately 5% of graduate faculty were minorities. Minority representation varied by subfield, and the distribution of women varied by minority group.

Finally, trends for minority doctorate recipients and current students were discussed using data from the National Research Council (Syverson, 1981) and the Survey of Graduate Departments of Psychology (American Psychological Association, 2001b). Data on new Ph.D.s revealed that minorities comprised 8% of the new doctorates in 1980 (Syverson, 1981), and material from the 1980-1981 APA Survey of Graduate Departments of Psychology indicated that just under 11% of full-time doctoral students were members of a minority group. The pipeline data appeared to indicate that increases in the representation of minorities could be expected. Nonetheless, Russo et al. (1981) pointed out that factors such as budget cuts in federal support for psychology training could reverse the trends, and they called for a renewed commitment to the goal of increasing the representation and status for minorities in the field of psychology.

In "The Changing Face of American Psychology," Howard et al. (1986) showed that psychology had made progress in attracting minorities to psychology over the past decade, particularly in reference to other science and engineering fields. The authors did state that minority groups remained underrepresented when compared to numbers in the general population. They reported that members of minority groups made up 8.6% of new Ph.D.s in 1984. In 1983, Blacks and Hispanics represented only 2% and 1.4%, respectively, of all doctoral-level psychological personnel in the United States, whereas nationally, they comprised 11.7% and 6.4% of the U.S. population in 1984 (Coyle & Syverson, 1986).

Howard et al. (1986) presented data that indicated that the degree of underrepresentation among new Ph.D.s varied by ethnic group. Psychology was doing as well as other science and engineering fields with respect to attracting new Black and Hispanic Ph.Ds., but it was not doing as well in attracting Asians, and Native Americans remained grossly underrepresented in most major fields. Howard et al. also noted variation in minority participation by subfield. Blacks had been moving into the health services subfields, such as clinical, and away from the traditional research/academic subfields. Hispanics had moved strongly into all subfields. However, enrollment data from 1984-1985 revealed that both Black and Hispanic students were more likely to be enrolled in the health service provider subfields, leading to the conclusion that the numbers of Blacks and Hispanics in health service provision would only increase.

New doctorates of Asian heritage were somewhat more apt to graduate with a doctorate in a traditional research/academic subfield rather than in a health service provider subfield.

Howard et al. (1986) concluded by urging organized psychology to focus on all levels of the educational pipeline—elementary/secondary, baccalaureate, and graduate. They reminded policymakers that because minority representation was better at the undergraduate level than at the graduate level and that more than half of the psychology doctorates took a baccalaureate in psychology, the pool exists from which to recruit. In 1998, almost 59% of new psychology Ph.D.s did have a baccalaureate in psychology (National Science Foundation, 2001a, 2001b). The authors went on to recommend steps to improve minority representation.

DEMOGRAPHIC PROFILE

National Counts

Before moving to a discussion of the educational pipeline and psychology and the current situation with regard to the distribution and representation of racial and ethnic minority psychologists and psychologists-in-training, it is useful to present a brief overview of the national demographic profile that forms the background for the current chapter.

In 1980, Blacks comprised 11.6% of the U.S. population; Hispanics were at 6.4%, Asians made up 1.6%, and American Indians were at 0.6% (U.S. Census of Population, 1983). Minorities comprised 19.6% of the U.S. population. By 2000, Blacks had inched up to 12.9%; Hispanics and Asians were at 11.4% and 4.1%, respectively; and American Indians rose slightly to 0.9%—minorities represented 29% of the U.S. population. The numbers for all groups have grown, but some have grown more than others, yielding the proportionate shifts. Whites only increased in number approximately 16% between 1980 and 2000. Asians increased more than 200%, whereas Hispanics went up 115%. Blacks and American Indians showed more modest gains of 33% and 69%, respectively. The census counts clearly reveal a nation that has become far more diverse in the past two decades. This diversity largely has occurred not as a result of growth or increases in the Black and American Indian populations but as a consequence of growth, via migration and births, among Asians and Hispanics.

Looking back 15 years at the doctoral scientists and engineers in the United States in 1985, we can see that 88.7% were White, 1.4% were Black, 1.5% were Hispanic, and 8.6% and 0.1% were Asians and Native Americans, respectively. Those numbers today are Whites at 81%, Blacks at 2.3%, Hispanics at 2.4%, Asians at 13.9%, and American Indians at 0.3%. All minority groups have made gains, but, most especially, Asians have moved into science and engineering fields at the doctoral level.

PIPELINE

As mentioned, this chapter will follow a pipeline perspective that involves examining data regarding the representation and distribution of racial and ethnic minority psychologists and those in training in a chronological fashion. Beginning with the situation in the high schools and colleges, we then move on to graduate studies. This is followed by an analysis of recent graduates and, last, the doctoral population.

High School

The educational pipeline that culminates in a career in psychology can begin with high school, as students begin to consider possible career paths and interests. Although data are sparse on the rate at which students enroll in high school psychology courses, there is

information on the race ethnicity of high school students, as well as information on the plans of high school seniors following graduation. Unpublished analyses from the College Board databases indicate that about one fourth of college-bound seniors (high school graduates from 2001) took psychology while in high school. It is not unreasonable to infer that nationally, 25% of college-bound students have had some psychology while in high school (Camara, personal communication, January 29, 2002).

Census data from 1998 indicate that 93.6% of White 25- to 29-year-olds had completed high school, as had 88.2% of Black 25- to 29-year-olds and 62.8% of Hispanic 25- to 29-year-olds. In addition, U.S. Census and Labor Department data from 1999 show that there were 2,287,000 White high school graduates, 453,000 Black high school graduates, and 329,000 Hispanic graduates from high school in 1998.

According to data from the U.S. Department of Education, National Center for Education Statistics, in 1992, 91.4% of all graduating seniors planned to go to college at some point after high school. Breaking this down into more specific plans, 76.6% planned to go immediately, 10.7% after 1 year, and 4.1% after more than 1 year. Table 3.1 shows that this pattern differed little among White, Black, and Hispanic students. The patterns for Asian and American Indian students, however, did differ. Asian seniors, at 83.4%, were more apt to plan to go to college immediately than were all the other racial ethnic groups. American Indian seniors were less likely to plan to go to college immediately, with only 65.7% planning on doing so. However, 15.5% planned to go after 1 year and 5.3% after more than a year. Overall, more than 85% of all minority students planned on attending college at some point following graduation and, therefore, had the possibility of entering the field of psychology (computed from Table 3.1). Census data for

Table 3.1   Percentage of High School Seniors Who Plan to Go to College After Graduation, by Race/Ethnicity: 1992

	No College	Right After High School	After 1 Year	After More Than a Year	Don't Know
All seniors	4.0	76.6	10.7	4.1	4.6
White	3.9	76.6	10.6	4.4	4.5
Black	5.4	75.2	11.2	3.2	5.2
Hispanic	3.5	75.4	11.6	3.6	5.9
Asian	2.6	83.4	8.6	2.4	3.1
American Indian	5.8	65.7	15.5	5.3	7.7

SOURCE: U.S. Department of Education (n.d.-a, n.d.-c).

1999 indicated that 68.2% of White high school graduates, 59.2% of Black graduates, and 42.2% of Hispanic graduates went on to college in the year following graduation from high school.

Undergraduate Training in Psychology

Having entered college, the undergraduate has a myriad of majors from which to choose. Frequently, the choices made may change throughout the course of the undergraduate career, and often the degree earned is in a field that was not the original major. This section examines the enrollment patterns by race/ethnicity in psychology as well as the baccalaureates awarded in psychology to undergraduates. The data came from both the National Science Foundation and the American Psychological Association.

Enrollments. At least 79,045 undergraduates were enrolled as psychology majors in the United States and Canada in 1998-1999 (Kyle & Williams, 2000) (see Table 3.2). This included enrollment in both 4-year and 2-year institutions, as well as other institutions such as satellite campuses, comprehensive colleges, and technical schools. It is important to note that these numbers are based on departments choosing to respond to the survey and are therefore a partial count of the population.

The survey was mailed to 2,724 departments across the United States, with just over 29%, or 795, responding with useable data. Thus, the actual count of undergraduate majors could be much higher. Overall, White undergraduates made up the greatest percentage of psychology majors at just under 75%. This was followed by African Americans (10%), Hispanics (7%), Asian/Pacific Islander students (4%), and American Indian/Alaskan Native undergraduates at just under 1%. The remaining undergraduate psychology majors identified themselves as "other" (just under 3%). The vast majority of the students in all the racial/ethnic groups were located in 4-year institutions, including both those institutions with and without graduate programs. This pattern may be skewed somewhat by the dearth of responses from the 2-year institutions. Although the largest single proportion in each racial/ethnic group was most apt to be enrolled in a 4-year institution, the American Indian/Alaskan Natives were also found in greater concentration in 2-year institutions. Specifically, White students were most often enrolled in 4-year institutions (97%), followed by African American/Black students and "other" students (96% each), Asian/Pacific Islander students (95%), Hispanic students (92%), and American Indian/Alaskan Native students (70%). Thirty percent of all American Indian/Alaskan Native psychology majors were enrolled in 2-year settings,

Table 3.2   Enrollment of Undergraduate Psychology Majors in Departments of Psychology, by Race/Ethnicity and Institution Type: 1998-1999

	4-Year Institution w/ Grad Program		*4-Year Institution w/o Grad Program*		*Institution Type* *2-Year Institution*		*Other*[a]		*Total*	
	(n = 395)	*%*	*(n = 302)*	*%*	*(n = 186)*	*%*	*(n = 11)*	*%*	*(n = 795)*	*%*
Total	64,448	100	11,450	100	2,848	100	299	100	79,045	100
White	47,882	74.3	9,379	81.9	1,854	65.1	108	36.1	59,223	74.9
African American/Black	6,429	10.0	1,260	11.0	294	10.3	6	2.0	7,989	10.1
Hispanic	4,572	7.1	367	3.2	238	8.4	182	60.9	5,359	6.8
Asian/Pacific Islander	2,947	4.6	314	2.7	161	5.7	2	0.7	3,424	4.3
American Indian/ Alaskan Native	410	0.6	92	0.8	217	7.6	0	0.0	719	0.9
Other	2,208	3.4	38	0.3	84	2.9	1	0.3	2,331	2.9

SOURCE: American Psychological Association (2000).

a. "Other" includes satellite campuses for 4-year institutions, comprehensive colleges, and combination 2-year, 4-year, and technical schools.

Table 3.3 Baccalaureate Recipients From Undergraduate Departments of Psychology, by Gender and Race/Ethnicity: 1998

	White/Non-Hispanic		Black/Non-Hispanic		Hispanic		Asian		Native American/Alaskan Native		Total	
	n	%	n	%	n	%	n	%	n	%	n	%
All recipients	54,304	75.9	6,910	9.7	5,510	7.7	4,267	6.0	517	0.7	71,508	100
Male recipients	13,927	73.0	1,553	8.1	1,382	7.3	1,223	6.4	149	0.8	18,234	100
Female recipients	30,377	72.8	5,357	9.6	4,128	7.5	3,044	5.5	368	0.7	43,274	100

SOURCE: U.S. Department of Education (n.d.-b).

compared with no more than 5% of any one of the other racial/ethnic groups.

In summary, psychology majors were mostly White, followed by African American/Black, Hispanic, Asian/Pacific Islander, "other," and, making up the smallest percentage, American Indian/Alaskan Native. All psychology majors were most likely to be enrolled in 4-year institutions, regardless of their race/ethnicity. All racial/ethnic minorities displayed the same pattern with respect to type of institution in which they were enrolled, with the exception of American Indian/Alaskan Native students, who were less likely than other racial/ethnic minorities to be enrolled in a 4-year institution and more likely to be enrolled in a 2-year institution. In addition, Hispanic students were more likely to be enrolled in "other" institutions.

Degrees. According to data from the Department of Education, in 1998, 74,640 students received a baccalaureate in psychology. Of these students, 71,508 were U.S. citizens and had provided a racial/ethnic designation. The majority of the recipients were White/non-Hispanic (75.9%), followed by Black/non-Hispanic (9.7%), Hispanic (7.7%), Asian (6.0%), and Native American/Alaskan Native (0.7%). Overall, female recipients outnumbered male recipients at a consistent rate, regardless of race/ethnicity. The gender distribution was similar across all students, regardless of race/ethnicity, with approximately 25% of the degrees going to men and 75% to women (Table 3.3). Although it may be tempting to make comparisons between the two preceding data sets to determine the graduation rate compared to the enrollment rate, this is not possible because they are from different samples.

Graduate Training in Psychology

Given the nature of the field, it is difficult to forge a career in psychology without earning a graduate degree. It is not enough that students interested in psychology receive a baccalaureate in psychology or some other field; they must continue along the educational pipeline to graduate school in psychology. This section examines the enrollment and graduation patterns of racial/ethnic minorities at the graduate level in psychology. The data are drawn from the most recent reports from the American Psychological Association's Research Office and from analyses of data from the 2002 Graduate Study in Psychology. Other good sources of data are those that can be found at www.nsf.gov/sbe/srs/nsf01324/start.htm. An important caveat about the Research Office data is that they reflect responses from only part of the population of graduate departments and thus underrepresent the actual number of psychology graduate students in the pipeline. For example, in 1999, the National Science Foundation (NSF) counted 49,634 full- and part-time graduate students in psychology (Burrelli, 2001). This is far greater than the 4,845 reported by graduate departments to the APA. However, the APA numbers do appear to yield results similar to those found by NSF. Essentially, just over three fourths of the graduate students in psychology were White in 1999, whereas just over one fifth were members of a minority group. APA data do appear to underrepresent the Asian/Pacific Islander and Hispanic students slightly.

Master's Students. In 1998-1999, the majority of master's students attended school full-time. Roughly 87% of these full-time students identified themselves as White. White students were also the majority among the part-time students, at 78%. Racial/ethnic minority students did not display this pattern of lower part-time enrollment, with all except Asian/Pacific Islander students comprising a greater percentage of the part-time students than the full-time students.

Table 3.4   Enrollment in Graduate Departments of Psychology, by Enrollment Status, Degree Sought, and Race/Ethnicity: 1998-1999

	White/Non-Hispanic		Black/Non-Hispanic		Hispanic		Asian/Pacific Islander		Native American/ Alaskan Native		Total	
	n	*%*	*n*	*%*	*n*	*%*	*n*	*%*	*n*	*%*	*n*	*%*
Ph.D.												
Full-time	2,103	78.7	187	7.0	135	5.1	217	8.1	30	1.1	2,672	100
Part-time	57	72.2	19	24.1	1	1.3	1	1.3	1	1.3	79	100
M.A.												
Full-time	1,505	86.7	91	5.2	55	3.2	76	4.4	8	0.5	1,735	100
Part-time	280	78.0	47	13.1	17	4.7	13	3.6	2	0.6	359	100

SOURCE: American Psychological Association (2000).
NOTE: *n* = 345 graduate departments in psychology in the United States and Canada.

Doctoral Students. A similar pattern is found when looking at enrollment in doctoral programs. Few programs provided data on part-time enrollments. Consequently, little can be said about the part-time students using the APA data. White/non-Hispanic students made up the majority, at just under 79% of the full-time students and 72% of part-time students. Students who were members of a racial/ethnic minority were better represented among the full-time students seeking a doctorate than they were among those seeking a master's degree. Black, non-Hispanic students were 7% of full-time doctoral students; Hispanic students were at 5%; Asian/Pacific Islander enrollees were 8%; and Native American/Alaskan Natives were just over 1%. The numbers of part-time doctoral students reported by the graduate programs were so small as to make comparisons across racial ethnic groups very shaky. We can say that just under three fourths of the part-time doctoral students were White, which means that about 28% of the part-time doctoral students were members of a minority group. Data from the Graduate Study in Psychology (American Psychological Association, 2002) showed that minorities represented 26% of full-time first-year graduate students and 21% of part-time first-year graduate students in Psy.D. programs in the fall of 2000-2001. For Ph.D. programs, the percentage of minorities among full-time first-year students was 19%, and for part-time first-year students, it was 21%.

Subfield. If we look at the data to see what proportion of each of the racial/ethnic categories has chosen one of the subfield clusters, certain patterns emerge. At the doctoral level, almost two thirds of Black and Hispanic students were in the health service provider subfields compared to 56% of White students, 54% of Asian students, and 46% of Native American doctoral students. Conversely, 43% of Native American and 34% of Asian doctoral students were enrolled in a research subfield compared to 32% of White students, 37% of Hispanic enrollees, and 23% of Black students. This leaves 12% or less of the doctoral students in each of the categories in the "other" category (e.g., special education, marriage and family, counseling).

At the master's level, we see similar patterns for representation in the health service provider subfields, with 56% of Black and Hispanic students in this cluster, compared to 52% of White students, 42% of Asian students, and 37% of Native American master's students. On the other hand, 21% of White students, 22% of Black students, and 18% of Hispanic students chose a research subfield. We found that 33% of Asian master's students and 25% of Native American master's students did likewise. The master's students, unlike the doctoral students, were much more likely to choose an "other" psychology subfield. In fact, with the exception of Native American students at 37%, approximately one fourth of each racial/ethnic group of master's students chose "other."

In summary, the data indicate that full-time enrollment was more frequent than part-time enrollment; indeed, the NSF data support this. The NSF (Burrelli, 2001) found that part-time enrollments were about half the size of full-time graduate enrollments in psychology. Whites remained the majority through sheer numbers, but minority students represented a solid fifth of graduate enrollees in 1999. Doctoral students were much less likely to choose the "other" subfields than were master's students, primarily because these "other" subfields are predominantly aimed at the master's-level student (e.g., counseling, marriage and family).

The Minority Fellowship Program at the American Psychological Association

The Minority Fellowship Program (MFP) at the American Psychological Association has

Table 3.5 Enrollment in Graduate Departments of Psychology, by Degree Sought, Subfield, and Race/Ethnicity: 1998-1999

	White/Non-Hispanic		Black/Non-Hispanic		Hispanic		Asian/Pacific Islander		Native American/Alaskan Native		Total	
	n	%	n	%	n	%	n	%	n	%	n	%
Ph.D.												
Health service provider subfields	1,170	77.4	123	8.1	87	5.8	117	7.7	14	0.9	1,511	100
Research subfields	687	80.5	43	5.0	36	4.2	74	8.7	13	1.5	853	100
Other psychology-related subfields	246	79.9	21	6.8	12	3.9	26	8.4	3	1.0	308	100
M.A.												
Health service provider subfields	779	86.9	51	5.7	31	3.5	32	3.6	3	0.3	896	100
Research subfields	314	84.6	20	5.4	10	2.7	25	6.7	2	0.5	371	100
Other psychology-related subfields	412	88.0	20	4.3	14	3.0	19	4.1	3	0.6	486	100

SOURCE: American Psychological Association (2000).
NOTE: n = 345 graduate departments in psychology in the United States and Canada.

played a significant role in the training of racial and ethnic minority psychologists over the past three decades. An analysis of the graduate training of ethnic minority psychologists would not be complete without an overview of the MFP and its achievements. At the APA, the MFP was begun under the directorship of Dalmas A. Taylor, Ph.D., as a federally funded program to support doctoral training in psychology. In 1977, James M. Jones, Ph.D., became the second director of the MFP.

Since 1979, 249 trainees have received support from the MFP at the American Psychological Association, and more than 80% of those who entered the program prior to 1990 have received their doctorates (Jones & Nickerson, 2001). During the past 5 years (1996-2000), the racial/ethnic distribution of the applicant pool was as follows: Asian Americans, 15.4%; American Indians, 3.3%; African Americans, 51.1%; Hispanics, 24.7%; and other, 4.0%. Whereas the applicant base continues to be dominated by African Americans, the selection process considers each ethnic group and makes sure there is reasonable representation in the final group. So, the distribution of selected fellows in the past 5 years is as follows: Asian Americans, 23.2%; American Indians, 20.9%; African Americans, 27.9%; and Hispanics, 18.6%. It is important to note that this distribution is close to *parity* across the groups, even though Blacks are almost 50% of the applicant pool, and Hispanics are nearly 30% (Jones & Nickerson, 2001).

In terms of geographical distribution, fellows in the program have come from 36 states in the United States, including Puerto Rico. The largest group of fellows has come from the following states: California (39), New York (26), Michigan (24), Massachusetts (15), Washington, D.C. (11), and Pennsylvania (10) (National Institute of Mental Health, n.d.). The fellows have received their training at some of the top universities in the country, with large numbers of trainees attending the University of Michigan (20), Howard University (13), City University of New York (10), UC–Berkeley (9), UCLA (7), and University of Pittsburgh (7).

Graduate Degree Recipients

Getting into a graduate program is only half the battle, as students must actually complete their degrees before moving out into the field. This is the final stage in the pipeline and, for many, the most difficult to complete. This section examines the master's and doctoral degrees awarded to racial/ethnic minority graduate students. This section uses data from the National Science Foundation/Division of Science Resources Studies and the U.S. Department of Education, National Center for Education Statistics.

In 1998, 14,449 graduate students were the recipients of a master's degree in psychology (U.S. Department of Education, 2001). This total excludes 539 non-U.S. students and 708 unknown students. Minorities comprised 18.7% of the graduates (those with U.S. citizenship or those who had permanent visas). Of the graduates, 27% were men and 73% were women. African Americans earned 8.3% of the master's degrees, Asian graduates earned 3%, and Hispanic graduates accounted for 6.5%. Native American students earned just less than 1% of the master's degrees granted, and White graduates accounted for 81.3%.

The pattern of master's degree by subfield was as expected, with the top five subfields being counseling psychology, general psychology, educational psychology, clinical psychology, and "other" psychology, in descending order (U.S. Department of Education, 2001).

In 2000, a total of 3,623 graduate students received their Ph.D.s (Hoffer et al., 2001). Of these new Ph.D.s, 3,221 provided a racial/ethnic category and were U.S. citizens or on permanent visas and are included in the following analyses. The U.S.

Table 3.6 Master's Degree Recipients From Graduate Departments of Psychology, by Gender and Race/Ethnicity: 1997-1998

	White/Non-Hispanic		Black/Non-Hispanic		Hispanic		Asian		Native American/Alaskan Native		Total	
	n	%	*n*	%	*n*	%	*n*	%	*n*	%	*n*	%
All recipients	11,744	81.3	1,203	8.3	937	6.5	440	3.0	125	0.9	14,449	100
Male recipients	3,136	61.3	906	17.7	700	13.7	335	6.5	39	0.8	5,116	100
Female recipients	8,608	92.2	297	3.2	237	2.5	105	1.1	86	0.9	9,333	100

SOURCE: U.S. Department of Education (n.d.-b).

NOTE: A total of 1,956 bachelor's, 708 master's, and 226 doctorate degrees were awarded to individuals for whom no race/ethnicity data are available. These individuals are excluded from this table.

Department of Education (DOE) counted some 4,735 new doctorates in 1997-1998; 454 of these were non-U.S. citizens on temporary visas or were students for whom we had no race/ethnicity, and they have been excluded (U.S. Department of Education, 2001). This leaves 4,281 new doctorates who were U.S. citizens or on a permanent visa and for whom we had a racial/ethnic category. Besides the fact that they are from different years, the two data sources are collected differently, which may help to explain some of the great difference. The data on new Ph.D.s are gathered directly from the graduating students. The DOE data on new doctorates are reported by the institutions. The number of new Ph.D.s in psychology has been fairly steady for a number of years, so the large difference between the two sources is surprising. However, it appears that DOE data include counts of Psy.D. degrees (doctors of psychology), whereas the NSF data do not (Ph.D.s only). It will be useful to look at the degree of convergence between the two data sets with respect to minority representation.

The 2000 NSF data (Hoffer et al., 2001) indicated that 82% of new Ph.D.s were earned by Whites; American Indians earned just under 1%, Asians earned 5%, and Black and Hispanics graduates earned 6% each. The DOE data on new doctorates in 1997-1998 showed that 85% were White, just under 6% were Hispanic, just over 5% were African American, just over 1% were American Indian, and almost 3% were Asian. Interestingly, 1997-1998 data from the NSF on new Ph.D.s (the corollary to the 1997-1998 DOE data) continued to reflect a slightly more diverse population of new graduates than that reported by the DOE in 1997-1998. The minority representation in the 1997-1998 NSF data was just over 16%. The differences are small, and it is important to remember that the numbers of minorities on which the percentages are based are also small and that slight increases or decreases in

numbers can have a large effect on the resulting percentage. The representation of women among new Ph.D.s was 67% in 2000 (Hoffer et al., 2001). The percentage of women appeared to be somewhat higher among Asian, African American, and Native American doctorates than was the case for Hispanic and White doctorates, but again, changes in small numbers can have major effects on the percentages that are found.

Although psychology graduates earned degrees across all the various subfields, comparisons are useful. With the exception of American Indian Ph.D.s, the highest percentage of new Ph.D.s in each racial/ethnic group received a Ph.D. in clinical psychology. Overall, clinical psychology represented 39% of the Ph.D.s granted in psychology in 2000. The second most "popular" field was counseling psychology. Social psychology was a third choice for White and Black graduates, whereas Asian graduates chose comparative psychology and Hispanic graduates earned degrees in general psychology.

In summary, just under 19% of the master's degree recipients in psychology in 1998 and 18% of the doctorate recipients in 2000 were members of a minority group. Around 73% of master's degree recipients and 67% of the Ph.D. recipients were women. The graduates earned degrees across the range of subfields open to psychology students. However, counseling psychology was paramount among master's graduates, and clinical psychology was dominant at the doctoral level.

Comparison of Psychology and Other Science Fields

It is helpful to look at how psychology compares to similar fields when attempting to gauge how well psychology as a field and discipline has done in recruiting and retaining racial/ethnic minority students. This section will focus on comparing psychology with the biological sciences, social sciences, and

Table 3.7 Doctorate Recipients From Graduate Departments of Psychology, by Race/Ethnicity: 2000

	White/Non-Hispanic		Black/Non-Hispanic		Hispanic		Asian		Native American/ Alaskan Native		Total	
	n	%	*n*	%	*n*	%	*n*	%	*n*	%	*n*	%
All recipients	2,601	80.8	193	6.0	194	6.0	149	4.6	22	0.7	3,221	100

SOURCE: National Science Foundation (2001a, 2001b).
NOTE: Percentages are row percentages and may not add up to 100% due to the exclusion of unknown ethnicity.

engineering in the awarding of baccalaureate, master's, and doctorate degrees to minorities in 1998. Information was taken from the U.S. Department of Education (2001) (see Table 3.8). These percentages do not include non-U.S. citizens, those on temporary visas, or those whose race/ethnicity was unknown. These groups do not comprise a significant portion of students in psychology as they do with other fields, such as engineering and biology. For this reason, it is important to exclude them when talking about the representation of minorities across fields because these groups tend to artificially inflate the minority representation found in other fields.

White graduates earned the majority of baccalaureates for all fields. Social sciences was at the top of the list, with just over 76% of the bachelor's degrees going to Whites. They were followed by psychology at just under 76%, engineering at a little over 72%, and biological sciences at almost 72%. These percentages are not very different. The notable differences across the fields are revealed when minority representation is considered in each field. Blacks represented almost 10% of the degrees in psychology, 9% of the degrees in the social sciences, 6.6% in engineering, and 7% in the biological sciences. Hispanics earned almost 8% of the baccalaureates in psychology compared to nearly 7% in engineering and the biological sciences and a little over 7% in the social sciences. American Indians represented between six and seven tenths of the baccalaureates granted across the different subfields. It is among the percentage of Asians that larger differences were observed across the fields. In engineering and biology, Asians represented 13.5% and 13.9%, respectively, of the baccalaureates granted. Asians earned about 6% each of the bachelor's degrees granted in 1997-1998 in psychology and the social sciences.

A similar pattern was found for master's degree recipients in these fields. Whites comprised the majority of all degrees awarded for all fields, and again, the social sciences had the highest percentage at 81.5%, psychology was at 81.3%, the biological sciences were at 81%, and engineering granted 77% of its master's degrees to Whites. Blacks earned around 8% of the master's degrees in psychology and the social sciences and about 4% in the biological sciences and engineering. Hispanics earned about 4.5% of the master's degrees in engineering, 3.7% in the biological sciences, and 5% and 6.5%, respectively, in the social sciences and psychology. American Indians took .4% of the master's degrees in engineering and the biological sciences, each in 1997-1998. Psychology and the social sciences granted .9% and .7%, respectively, of their master's degrees to American Indian students. Continuing the pattern noted for baccalaureate degrees, Asians were better represented among the graduates in engineering and biological sciences (13.7% and 11.2%, respectively) than among the social sciences (5%) and psychology (3%).

Doctoral degrees followed suit. White students comprised the majority of all degrees awarded for all fields, with psychology at the top of the list with 85% of the doctorate recipients in psychology identifying themselves as White. Psychology was followed by the social sciences at just over 84%, the biological sciences at 82%, and engineering at 81%. Blacks were granted 6% of the doctorates in social sciences, 5% of the doctorates in psychology, and just under 3% each of the degrees granted in engineering and the biological sciences. Hispanics comprised fewer than 6% of the doctorates in psychology, about 3.4% of those in the social sciences, 3.7% of those in the biological sciences, and 3.6% of those in engineering. American Indians earned .3% of the doctorates in the biological sciences and engineering, .7% of the doctorates in the social sciences, and 1.1% of the doctorates granted in psychology. Asians earned a little over 12% of the doctorates in engineering, slightly more than 11% of those granted in the

Table 3.8. Comparison of Psychology and Other Sciences on B.A., M.A., and Ph.D. Degrees, by Race/Ethnicity: 1998

	White/Non-Hispanic		Black/Non-Hispanic		Hispanic		Asian/Pacific Islander		Native American/Alaskan Native		Total	
	n	%	n	%	n	%	n	%	n	%	n	%
B.A.												
Social science	90,023	76.3	11,106	9.4	8,499	7.2	7,572	6.4	857	0.7	118,057	100
Biological science	45,862	71.7	4,553	7.1	4,283	6.7	8,867	13.9	399	0.6	63,964	100
Engineering	132,272	72.3	12,126	6.6	12,692	6.9	24,741	13.5	1,051	0.6	182,882	100
Psychology	54,304	75.9	6,910	9.7	5,510	7.7	4,267	6.0	517	0.7	71,508	100
M.A.												
Social science	9,404	81.5	906	7.9	577	5.0	572	5.0	75	0.7	11,534	100
Biological science	4,161	81.0	190	3.7	188	3.7	576	11.2	21	0.4	5,136	100
Engineering	20,527	77.3	1,097	4.1	1,186	4.5	3,628	13.7	100	0.4	26,538	100
Psychology	11,744	81.3	1,203	8.3	937	6.5	440	3.0	125	0.9	14,449	100
Ph.D.												
Social science	2,537	84.3	188	6.2	101	3.4	162	5.4	21	0.7	3,009	100
Biological science	2,844	82.1	92	2.7	127	3.7	394	11.4	9	0.3	3,466	100
Engineering	8,021	81.1	266	2.7	358	3.6	1,215	12.3	28	0.3	9,888	100
Psychology	3,649	85.2	220	5.1	242	5.7	123	2.9	47	1.1	4,281	100

SOURCE: U.S. Department of Education (n.d.-b).
NOTE: Individuals for whom no race/ethnicity data are available are excluded from this table.

biological sciences, 5.4% of the doctorates in the social sciences, and less than 3% of those granted in psychology (2.9%).

Overall, psychology has done well with regard to the percentage of its minority graduates at the baccalaureate, master's, and doctoral levels compared to the social sciences, the biological sciences, and engineering. The notable exception is Asian/Pacific Islander graduates, who make up the smallest percentage of racial/ethnic minorities across all degrees in psychology. Furthermore, although psychology is doing well overall, it should be noted that the pipeline constricts for minorities as one progresses from the baccalaureate to the doctoral level. This suggests that in addition to targeting efforts to increase the numbers of all racial/ethnic minorities who are recruited into the field, especially Asian/Pacific Islanders, strategies for retaining students in the pipeline must be devised.

NEW DOCTORATES

This section relies on data on new Ph.D.s drawn from the NSF as well as data gathered by the APA on new doctorates. Data from the NSF indicate that minorities comprised almost 18% of the new Ph.D.s in psychology in 2000 (Hoffer et al., 2001). APA's biennial Doctorate Employment Survey shows a 17% minority representation among 1999 doctorates in psychology (Kohout & Wicherski, in press). The Doctorate Employment Survey is sent to all new doctorates in psychology in the spring following their graduation and asks for demographic, educational, and employment data from the new doctorates.

Demographics

The representation of women was highest among Blacks in comparison with the other racial/ethnic groups (88%) and lowest among American Indians (56%) (Kohout & Wicherski, in press). For the most part, the new doctorates were in their mid-30s. With the exception of Hispanic graduates, 75% or more of all new doctorates earned a Ph.D. degree, with 81% of Asians doing so. Psy.D.s were claimed by between 20% and 24% of each of the racial ethnic groups, except for Hispanics, of whom 32% earned a Psy.D. As a group, just over two thirds of all new doctorates earned their degree in a health service provider subfield (mostly in clinical, counseling, or school, in that order). However, Hispanics were most apt to have earned a doctorate in a health service provider subfield (83%), whereas Asians were least apt to have done so (56%). Seventy-one percent of African Americans, 69% of Whites, and 78% of American Indians earned a degree in a health service provider subfield. Almost 42% of Asian doctorates had earned their degrees in a research subfield, compared to 30% of Whites, 28% of Blacks, 15% of Hispanics, and 22% of American Indians. Although there were differences in representation within specific subfields across the different ethnic groups, members of minority groups earned 17% of the doctorates granted in the health service provider subfields and 15% of the doctorates granted in the research subfields in 1999 (Kohout & Wicherski, in press). NSF data on new Ph.D.s in 2000 (Hoffer et al., 2001) reported that 18% of the Ph.D.s in health service provider subfields had been awarded to a member of a minority group, whereas minority group members earned 17% of the Ph.D.s granted in the research subfields. Small Ns made more detailed comparisons difficult in these data as well as in NSF data on the Ph.D. population. The NSF data indicated that minorities ranged from a low of just less than 6% in experimental psychology to a high of almost 13% in educational psychology in the psychology Ph.D. workforce in 1999. The average across all subfields was 9% (National Science Foundation, 2001a, 2001b).

Employment Setting and Activity

Minority doctorates were somewhat more apt to be employed full-time than were Whites (74% vs. 66%), were less likely to be working part-time, and were found about as often in postdoctoral positions. There is some variation across the minority groups: 81% of Blacks were employed full-time compared with 58% of Hispanic doctorates. Blacks were less apt to be in postdoctorates than were Hispanics, Asians, or Whites (13% vs. 18%, 15%, 18%, respectively). The number of American Indians among new doctorates was so small as to render these comparisons trivial; however, 22% were in postdoctorates. Members of the various racial/ethnic groups were found across the spectrum of employment settings. Universities and 4-year colleges claimed 27% of Blacks, almost 15% of Hispanics, just less than 27% of Asians, and 14% of American Indians. Medical schools claimed 8% of new Black doctorates and 5% of Asian doctorates. Other academic settings, including professional schools, accounted for less than 5% in each of the minority groups, whereas schools (primary and secondary) were listed as a primary employment setting by 8% of Hispanics, almost 3% of Asians, and 22% of Blacks. Just over one fifth of Blacks, almost a third of Hispanics, almost one fourth of Asians, and more than one fourth of American Indians were located in organized health care settings. Independent practice is not a frequent employment option among new doctorates because of the supervised hours that are needed to sit for licensure. Finally, business and government settings (e.g., business and industry, criminal justice system) claimed 11% of Hispanics, 13% of Asians, and almost 5% of Blacks. In summary, patterns of employment setting appear to be pretty much as expected. Most new doctorates, regardless of race/ethnicity, were employed in universities, 4-year colleges, and organized health care settings. Interestingly,

schools and other educational settings were a large draw for new Black doctorates.

The largest single proportion of each of the racial/ethnic groups chose human services as a primary activity (43% of Blacks, 60% of Hispanics, 44% of Asians, 57% of American Indians, and 50% of Whites.) These percentages are not surprising in that the majority of new doctorates were earned in a health service provider subfield. Education, teaching, and research also were listed frequently as primary activities. One fifth or more of Blacks, Asians, and American Indians gave research as a primary activity, as did just over one tenth of Whites and just less than one tenth of Hispanics. One fifth of Blacks and just over one tenth each of Hispanics and Asians listed education and teaching. Just over 13% of Whites and 12% of Hispanics chose education/teaching as a primary activity. These patterns follow the top employment setting choices of higher education and organized health care. When asked about their involvement in all work activities rather than just a primary activity, the percentages claiming research, education, and health service provision climbed. In addition, sizable proportions of the new doctorates identified management and administrative duties. This was the case across all racial/ethnic groups.

Salaries, Education-Related Debt, and Sources of Support for Training

With a few exceptions, salaries for new doctorates appear to be equitable. Minorities reported a median salary of $47,333 in 2000 compared to $47,000 reported by White doctorates. The salaries reported by African American and Hispanic doctorates were a little higher than the overall median reported by minorities, whereas those reported by Asian and American Indian doctorates were slightly lower. The exceptions included independent practice settings, hospital settings, and school settings (Kohout & Wicherski, in press).

Almost 68% of Whites reported some education-related debt upon graduation compared to 83% of Black graduates, 81% of Hispanic graduates, 57% of Asian doctorates, and 78% of American Indian graduates. The actual level of debt varied by racial/ethnic group such that only 5% of Whites, 11% of Blacks, 5% of Hispanics, 11% of Asians, and no American Indians reported debt levels of $5,000 or less. Debt levels of $6,000 to $10,000 were reported by between 7% and 10% of the graduates. Fifteen percent of Whites, 15% of Blacks, 14% of Hispanics, and 31% of Asian graduates reported $11,000 to $20,000 in debt. Between $21,000 and $40,000 of debt were claimed by 25% of Whites, 31% of Blacks, 19% of Hispanics, and 18% of Asians. Between $40,000 and $75,000 in debt were reported by 25% of White graduates, 13% of Black graduates, 30% of Hispanic graduates, and 13% of Asian graduates. Finally, 21% of White doctorates said they owed more than $75,000, as did 21% of Black doctorates, 24% of Hispanic doctorates, and 20% of Asian graduates. The number of American Indian graduates was so low as to render these detailed breakouts meaningless; however, only 1 of 7 American Indian doctorates on whom we have data reported a debt level of $10,000 or less.

The tendency of psychology graduates to rely on loans as a primary source of support is one reason that the debt levels are so high (Kohout & Wicherski, in press). With two exceptions, the largest single proportion in each racial/ethnic group claimed loans as the primary source of support. The two exceptions were Asian and Black graduates. In the case of the Asian graduates, we found a heavy reliance on university support, which, of course, does not have to be paid back (41%), and on their own earnings or family support (26%). Among Black graduates, the tendency was to rely on university assistance (31%) but also on loans (29%) and grants (19%). Whites primarily used loans (32%), as well as assistantships

(31%) and their own earnings (26%). Hispanic doctorates relied on loans (39%), university assistance (21%), and their own earnings (16%). American Indian graduates used loans (33%) as well but also relied on grants and assistantships (56%). When we look at sources of support used by graduates during their graduate careers, we see that at least two thirds of White graduates used a loan sometime during their graduate career, as did at least three fourths each of Black, Hispanic, and American Indian graduates. However, only half of Asian doctorates used a loan as a means of support while in graduate school.

WORKFORCE DATA

Although this next section will focus primarily on the doctoral-level workforce in psychology, because the data are more current and more complete at this level, we will briefly present some data on the master's-level personnel in psychology. We do not use the term *master's-level psychologist* because the term *psychologist* has been reserved for those with a doctoral degree. The only exception to this is among school psychologists, many of whom are practicing psychologists with master's degrees.

Master's-Level Personnel in Psychology. In 1997, there were 328,800 individuals with a master's degree in psychology in the United States. Almost two thirds of the master's-level personnel were women, and 12% were members of a minority group—7% were Black, almost 3% were Hispanic, and just under 2% were Asian. Of the master's-level personnel, 83% were employed. About one fourth was employed in psychology, and just under 7% were employed in some other science and engineering field. Thirty-eight percent were employed in a closely related occupation but not in science or engineering, 18% were in a somewhat related occupation, and 12% were working in a completely unrelated field (NSF, http://srsstats.sbe.nsf.gov/performatted.tables/ 1997/dst1997.htm). In 1999, the NSF counted 28,800 White, Black, and Hispanic graduates with a master's degree in psychology from 1997 or 1998 (National Science Foundation, 2001a, 2001b). They did not disclose the numbers of Asian or American Indian graduates because the numbers were too small. The data indicate that a sizable proportion of each of the three groups for whom there were data was working in another occupation (Whites, 43%; Blacks, 65%; Hispanics, 42%).

Doctoral-Level Psychologists. Data on the doctoral-level workforce were drawn from the National Science Foundation's Survey of Earned Doctorates (National Science Foundation, 2001a, 2001b). In 1999, there were at least 93,540 doctoral-level psychologists in the United States. Just under 91% of the doctoral psychologists in the United States were White, 3.2% were Black, 3.0% were Hispanic, 2.3% were Asian, and .5% were American Indian. Ethnic minorities as a whole remain underrepresented among doctoral psychologists in relation to their representation in the U.S. population.

If we consider degree subfields, we will see that the highest number of ethnic minorities was to be found in clinical psychology. Fully 39% of the minorities in the doctoral workforce were located in clinical psychology; 11% were in counseling psychology and 9% were in general psychology. In comparison, 37% of Whites in the doctoral workforce were located in clinical psychology, 11% in counseling psychology, and 9% in experimental psychology. Proportionally speaking, minorities had a stronger representation in educational, industrial/organizational, general, and social psychology. They had a low representation in experimental psychology, making up just under 6% of the psychologists in that field.

Psychologists were employed across a range of settings. In general, just over a third were employed in educational settings in 1999, just under 10% were in government settings, and 45% were employed in business and industry (almost 50% were self-employed). Salaries appear to have improved for all racial/ethnic groups, but without specific comparisons and controls for such variables as years of experience, measures of productivity, and rank, it would be difficult to draw any conclusions. It does appear to be the case that faculty salaries for racial/ethnic minorities in the doctoral workforce lag behind those paid to White faculty, but this may be true only for those who have more experience. Younger and newer faculties are being paid salaries that appear to be more equitable.

Faculty in Psychology

Since 1981-1982, faculties in U.S. graduate departments of psychology have slowly become more diverse, from a 5% minority representation to 10% by 2001 (American Psychological Association, 2001b). In 2000-2001, Blacks comprised 4% of graduate faculty, up from 3% twenty years ago. Hispanics were at 3% of graduate faculty in 2001, up from 1% over the past 20 years. Asian graduate faculty were also at 3%, up from 1% in 1981-1982, and Native American faculty remained at under 1%. There was some variation by subfield in minority representation among graduate faculty. The three fields with the highest proportion of minorities were also the fields that were small in number—psycholinguistics, community, and psychopharmacology. However, counseling psychology, one of the larger subfields, reports 18% minority faculty and is better diversified. Obviously, given the overall percentage reported above, it is the case that the graduate faculty in most fields is no more than 10% minority.

Diversity in the APA Membership

Racial/ethnic minorities represented a little over 9% of the APA membership among those members who provided a racial/ethnic identity in 1999 (American Psychological Association, 2001a). Women were more strongly represented among Blacks and Hispanics than among the other racial/ethnic groups. Of the various racial/ethnic groups, 78% or more had a Ph.D., whereas between 4% and 7% had a Psy.D. Asians were most apt to have earned a Ph.D. (84%), and Hispanics were most likely of all the groups to have earned a Psy.D.

CONCLUSION
AND RECOMMENDATIONS

Given the current updated profile, it appears that Kohout and Pion's (1990) observation that a great deal more needs to be done for psychology to successfully attract and retain talented ethnic minorities is still valid today. The field of psychology must "enhance the attractiveness of psychology as a profession and as a scientific endeavor" (Kohout & Pion, 1990). Furthermore, examination of current trends and the different levels of representation throughout the educational pipeline showed that psychology has had more success recruiting and retaining certain ethnic groups (e.g., Blacks and Hispanics) than others (Asians and Native Americans). It is important for programs to increase outreach efforts, improve availability of financial support, provide culturally diverse environments, and continue to assess and meet the needs of ethnic minority groups.

There are large gaps in our knowledge of the exposure to psychology that students are receiving in high school. More data are needed, not just on the number of psychology courses taken and who is taking them but also on the quality of the courses. Low-quality classes may discourage students from considering the field of psychology as an area of study or may present the field so narrowly that students do not realize the breadth of the field.

Ensuring that psychology is accurately portrayed as a legitimate field of study will help to increase enrollment rates of racial/ethnic minority students in undergraduate programs in psychology. Overall, enrollment in and graduation from these programs need to be increased, particularly for Native American/Alaskan Native and Asian/Pacific Islander students. Males of all racial/ethnic minorities should also be targeted. In addition, differences in undergraduate graduation rates and subsequent entry into graduate school based on type of undergraduate institution (4-year, 2-year, etc.) should be examined. American Indian/Alaskan Native students in particular are more likely to attend 2-year institutions and may be at risk for lower graduation rates and, consequently, may be less likely to pursue an advanced degree.

At the graduate level, psychology is doing well compared to other fields with regard to racial/ethnic minority student enrollment and graduation, lagging behind others only in attracting Asian/Pacific Islander students. Specific measures should be taken to entice this population into considering psychology as a viable career option. Despite psychology's standing in relation to other fields, there is still much to do. Enrollment should be targeted at doctoral programs, with strong efforts to improve retention, particularly for African American and Hispanic students.

Differences in graduation rates from graduate programs based on enrollment status, either full-time or part-time, need to be explored. Minority students, particularly Black/non-Hispanic students, are more likely to be enrolled part-time. Part-time enrollment increases the amount of time until degree completion and may increase the odds that part-time students do not graduate, contributing to retention problems. Finally, effort should be spent in distributing enrollment across the breadth of psychology. African American and Hispanic students, especially, are heavily represented in service provider areas but lacking in other areas. Asian students, on the other hand, are more heavily concentrated in the research subfields. As the population of the United States continues to diversify, so too should psychology. Psychology's relevance to future generations hinges on its success in presenting a face that is reflective of the larger world and a body of knowledge that is informed by a diversity of perspectives.

REFERENCES

American Psychological Association. (2000). *1998-99 APA survey of undergraduate departments of psychology.* Washington, DC: Author.

American Psychological Association. (2001a). *2000 membership profile* (Internal report from the APA Research Office). Washington, DC: Author.

American Psychological Association. (2001b). *Surveys of graduate departments of psychology: 1981-82 through 2000-2001* (Internal report from the APA Research Office). Washington, DC: Author.

American Psychological Association. (2002). *Graduate study in psychology.* Washington, DC: Author.

Burrelli, J. (2001). *Graduate students in science and engineering, fall 1999* (NSF 01-315). Arlington, VA: National Science Foundation, Division of Science Resource Studies.

Coyle, S., & Syverson, P. (1986). *Doctorate recipients from United States universities: Summary report 1984.* Washington, DC: National Academy Press.

Gottfredson, G., & Dyer, S. (1978). Health service providers in psychology. *American Psychologist, 33,* 314-338.

Hoffer, T., Dugoni, B., Sanderson, A., Sederstrom, S., Shadialy, R., & Roeque, P. (2001). *Doctorate recipients from United States universities: Summary report 2000.* Chicago: National Opinion Research Center.

Howard, A., Pion, G., Gottfredson, G., Ebert-Flattau, P., Bray, D., Oskamp, S., Burstein, A., & Pfafflin, S. (1986). The changing face of American psychology: A report from the Committee of Employment and Human Resources. *American Psychologist, 41,* 763-779.

Jones, J. M., & Nickerson, K. J. (2001). *Annual progress report: Minority Fellowship Program.* Washington, DC: American Psychological Association.

Kohout, J., & Pion, G. (1990). Participation of ethnic minorities in psychology: Where do we stand today? In G. Stricker, E. Davis-Russell, E. Bourg, E. Duran, W. R. Hammond, J. McHolland, K. Polite, & B. E. Vaughn (Eds.), *Towards ethnic diversification in psychology education and training* (pp. 153-165). New York: National Council of Schools of Professional Psychology.

Kohout, J., & Wicherski, M. (in press). *1999 doctorate employment survey.* Washington, DC: American Psychological Association.

Kyle, T., & Williams, S. (2000, April). *1998-1999 APA survey of undergraduate departments of psychology.* Washington, DC: American Psychological Association.

National Institute of Mental Health. (n.d.). *NIMH training programs for underrepresented racial/ethnic minorities NIMH interim staff report.* Retrieved from www.nimh. nih.gov/council/minority.pdf

National Science Foundation, Division of Science Resources Studies. (2001a). *Characteristics of recent science and engineering graduates: 1999* (Early release tables). Arlington, VA: Author.

National Science Foundation, Division of Science Resources Studies. (2001b). *Characteristics of doctoral scientists and engineers in United States: 1999.* Arlington, VA: Author.

Russo, N. F., Olmedo, E. L., Stapp, J., & Fulcher, R. (1981). Women and minorities in psychology. *American Psychologist, 36,* 1315-1363.

Syverson, P. (1981). *Doctorate recipients from United States universities: Summary report 1980.* Washington, DC: National Academy Press.

U.S. Census of Population. (1983). *General social and economic characteristics 1980.* Washington, DC: Government Printing Office.

U.S. Department of Education, National Center for Education Statistics. (2001). [From the Integrated Postsecondary Education Data System Completions surveys]. Analyses by the American Psychological Association Research Office.

U.S. Department of Education, National Center for Education Statistics. (n.d.-a). *High school and beyond: First followup survey.* Retrieved December 2001 from http://nces.ed.gov/

U.S. Department of Education, National Center for Education Statistics. (n.d.-b). *Integrated Postsecondary Education Data System Completions Survey.* Retrieved December 2001 from http://nces.ed.gov/

U.S. Department of Education, National Center for Education Statistics. (n.d.-c). *National Education Longitudinal Study of 1988: Second followup student survey.* Retrieved December 2001 from http://nces.ed.gov/

CHAPTER 4

The Psychology of Tokenism
Psychosocial Realities of Faculty of Color

YOLANDA FLORES NIEMANN
Washington State University

People's stereotypical image of university professors is one of White males who wear eyeglasses, whose work is considered important and valuable by the university and the community of scholars, and who are accorded high status and respect by their students and colleagues. Professors are generally considered to have a very good quality of life. Indeed, a job as a tenure-stream faculty member in a research institution, a position that is expected to lead to job security, is considered one of high status and prestige and is coveted by many Ph.D. graduates (Menges, 1999). However, the reality of faculty of color is very likely quite different from the rosy picture of the stereotypical White professor. Most faculty of color find themselves working in situations where they are numerical minorities in their universities and departments and, sometimes, in their communities outside the university. Some of these faculty members are not only numerical minorities but are also the only people of color in their departments, and they are among a relative few in their universities. As a result, the majority of ethnic/racial minority faculty members work in institutions where they may be subject to the psychological effects of tokenism (Kanter, 1977; Niemann, 1999; Niemann & Dovidio, 1998a, 1998b; Olmedo, 1990; Pollak & Niemann, 1998).

What Is Tokenism? Tokenism is a situation that handicaps members of racial/ethnic minority groups who find themselves working alone or nearly alone among members of another social category (Kanter, 1977; Mullen, 1991; Niemann, 1999; Niemann & Dovidio, 1998a; Pollak & Niemann, 1998; Taylor, Fiske, Etcoff, & Ruderman, 1978). Tokens report feeling three overarching perceptual phenomena. The first of these is visibility; tokens become more visible than they are in more ethnically balanced groups (Kanter, 1977; Niemann & Dovidio, 1998a). The second is contrast; differences between Whites and ethnic/racial minorities are exaggerated (Fiske & Taylor, 1991). The third is assimilation; perceptions of tokens are distorted to conform to preexisting stereotypes and generalizations about members of their group (Crosby & Clayton, 1990; Kanter, 1977).

The Role of Numbers in Tokenism. Tokenism occurs when those in the numerical minority account for 15% or less of the total workforce in a given context. As the following numbers indicate, the paucity of minorities in academia makes it likely that members of minority groups will be in token positions. As of 1995, Whites, African Americans, Latinas/Latinos, Asian Americans, and Native Americans made up 90%, 2.5%, 1.7%, 5%, and .3% of full professors, respectively; 88%, 5%, 1.9%, 4.8%, and .4% of associate professors; and 84%, 10.8%, 3.2%, 7.1%, and .4% of assistant professors (Rai & Critzer, 2000). In addition, most university administrators and students are also White. It is rarity and scarcity, rather than being an ethnic/racial minority, that shapes the environment and sets the stage for tokenism of minorities. The negative experiences of the token are exacerbated for those minorities who are also in solo status. *Solo status* refers to a situation in which these faculty members are the only ethnic/racial minority in their department or unit (Dovidio, Gaertner, Niemann, & Snider, 2001; Niemann & Dovidio, 1998a, 1998b).

THE PSYCHOLOGICAL EFFECTS OF TOKENISM

Distinctiveness

Novelty within groups attracts disproportional attention (Taylor & Fiske, 1978). Due to their low numbers in academia, minority faculty members work in situations that make them particularly distinctive and visible (Kanter, 1977; Niemann, 1999; Niemann & Dovidio, 1998a, 1998b; Pollak & Niemann, 1998; Taylor et al., 1978). Minority faculty members often feel as if they are in a glass house (Kanter, 1977; Niemann & Dovidio, 1998a, 1998b). Majority White group members have better recollection of their words and behaviors (Taylor & Fiske, 1978), whether they are positive or negative. Tokens are assigned disproportionate causality (Fiske & Taylor, 1991; Kanter, 1977; Kunda, 2000). When things go well, they receive some credit; however, when outcomes are not good, they receive much of the blame. The distinctiveness of tokens also results in exaggeration of differences between tokens and nontokens.

The effects of distinctiveness on tokens may depend on the extent to which their social group is a culturally stigmatized group in a given context (Crocker & Quinn, 2000; Frable, 1993; Frable, Blackstone, & Scherbaum, 1990; McGuire, McGuire, Child, & Fujioka, 1978). African Americans and Latinas/Latinos are the most negatively stereotyped and stigmatized groups within academic domains in the United States (Niemann, 2001), so members of those groups are likely to be most at risk for the negative feelings of distinctiveness.

The distinctiveness described by tokens is largely negative. It is not the type of distinctiveness felt by a Nobel Prize winner or high-ranking officer of the university. Tokens' salience creates psychological discomfort and places them on constant guard about the implications of their words, behaviors, and their very presence. This distinctiveness becomes uncomfortable to the extent that tokens report fearing visibility (Kanter, 1977).

Tokens as Symbols of Diversity

Tokens report feeling like they are in special mascot-like roles (Kanter, 1977). They are often deliberately thrust into the limelight as the university's representative when it is in the interest of the institution to demonstrate a belief in diversity (Kanter, 1977; Niemann, 1999). Ironically, officials who engage in using minorities as symbols of their nonracist, liberal values do not see the racism inherent in this behavior (Niemann, 1999). They seem to fail to understand that the reason they require the use of the same few minorities as their symbols is because of the paucity of minorities in their institutions. Tokens also report being listed as consultants on grants, projects, or committees to enhance the diversity component of these projects. Often, this use of the token happens without their consent or knowledge (Niemann, 2001).

These situations present a dilemma for tokens. If they speak up and "call" their colleagues and administrators on their display or listing of minorities as symbols, they stand to be seen as people who are not team players and who do engage in the cause of advancing the university. If they do not speak up, their own personal integrity is challenged. They also stand to be ridiculed and seen as traitors by other minorities in the institution who are less frequently placed in these symbolic roles (e.g., minority students). As is the case with the negative consequences of distinctiveness, when tokens are placed on display in the interest of the institution, the situation is not flattering. Indeed, it can lead to feelings of helplessness and a destruction of personal pride (Kanter, 1977; Niemann, 1999).

Tokens as Representative of Their Ethnic Group

Not only do token faculty experience treatment as the institution's symbols of diversity, but they are also perceived and treated as symbolic representatives of their ethnic/racial groups (Kanter, 1977; Niemann, 1999; Pollak & Niemann, 1998). Tokens are often asked to provide a point of view representing their ethnic/racial group. There is a general assumption that they know what "their" group wants or thinks. Tokens' individuality seems nonexistent.

Tokens are simultaneously representative and exceptions. They serve as symbols of their category, especially when they fumble, yet they are also seen as unusual examples of

their kinds, especially when they succeed (Kanter, 1977; Fiske & Taylor, 1991; Kunda, 2000). Tokens must be continually aware of putting their best foot forward so as to not negatively affect perceptions of other members of their demographic groups. They seem to be in a situation of constantly examining and second-guessing their behavior. This experience is related to the feeling of excessive distinctiveness. There is a sense of having no privacy or freedom to be themselves. These experiences are very stressful and exacerbate the stress and anxiety typical of all faculty, especially those who are untenured.

Stereotyping

The perception that tokens are representative of their group may be a function of ethnic/racial stereotyping. As the size of the minority group decreases relative to the majority, minorities become perceived as increasingly distinctive and homogeneous (Mullen, 1991), both of which fuel the stereotyping of tokens. Stereotypes are "pictures in our heads" (Lippmann, 1922). The pictures are structured sets of beliefs that contain perceivers' organized knowledge, beliefs, and expectancies about some human group (Fiske & Taylor, 1991; Hamilton & Trolier, 1986; Smith & Zarate, 1990; Zarate & Smith, 1990). Stereotypes serve both descriptive and prescriptive functions (Fiske & Taylor, 1991). Some stereotyping may be overt and intentional. However, White colleagues may unintentionally distort characteristics of tokens to fit preexisting, stereotypical assumptions about what tokens must be like (e.g., "You know those Latinos, they're really macho") (Niemann, 2001). This process happens because stereotypes involve the unintentional or spontaneous activation of a well-learned set of associations or responses. They do not require conscious effort and appear to be initiated by the mere presence of a member of a different ethnic group (Devine, 1989). Part of the insidious nature of stereotyping is that those who are engaging in it may not be aware of the inherent unfairness and, very likely, the inaccuracy of their perception. Tokens who believe that majority group members are evaluating them stereotypically usually cannot prove their belief to their own satisfaction or to that of others.

Because they are perceived to have veridical validity, stereotypes seem to reveal a "kernel of truth," or an accurate and seemingly objective reflection of these groups (Lee, Jussim, & McCauley, 1995; Niemann & Secord, 1995; Oakes, Haslam, & Turner, 1994). However, what is less readily apparent is that many of the behaviors and traits that become stereotypes and are seen as inherent to ethnic/racial minorities are actually a function of societal oppression and discrimination (Niemann, 2001; Niemann & Secord, 1995; Sue & Sue, 1999). That is, historical and current racism in the United States has deprived ethnic/racial minorities of the opportunities to pursue and achieve in higher education (Thomas & Neville, 1999). The pervasiveness of stereotypes is such that once these token faculty members are identified by race/ethnicity, the stereotypes of their category group follow them. Their presence in the academic context does not change the stereotypical perception (Niemann, Pollak, Rogers, & O'Connor, 1998).

One of the most damaging stereotypes about Latinas/Latinos, African Americans, and American Indians is that they are not competent in academic domains (Niemann, 2001). This stereotype is maintained, in part, by statistics reflecting the small numbers of these professors and students in universities. Although ethnic/racial minority faculty have clearly achieved academic qualifications for their positions, such as Ph.D.s, they are often stereotyped as not belonging in their positions and/or as simply unqualified and undeserving beneficiaries of affirmative action (Crosby & Clayton, 1990; McCombs, 1989). There is a widely held belief among Whites that minorities are less competent than White faculty and would not have been hired if it were not for affirmative action policy.

Ethnic/racial group stereotypes are among the most powerful forces that affect out-group perception, self-image, and personal identity (Jussim & Fleming, 1996; Kunda, 2000). Tokens seem to operate in a state of reflective expectancy, believing that others hold general stereotypical expectancies of them (Niemann & Dovidio, 1998a, 1998b; Pollak & Niemann, 1998; Steele, 1997). This awareness that others perceive them in a negative, stereotypical manner can have damaging consequences for tokens' interactions and relations with colleagues and other university personnel. This situation may hinder the formation of friendships that could alleviate feelings of isolation and loneliness, which will be discussed later in this chapter. It could also preclude formations of alliances and relations with potential mentors, which could have strong implications for the success of these ethnic/racial minority faculty members. Their awareness of their colleagues' stereotypic beliefs may also place tokens at risk for internalizing the stereotypes about their own groups.

Tokens and Stereotype Threat. Cooley (1902) referred to the looking-glass metaphor of the self, whereby we come to see ourselves in ways that we believe others see us. More recently, Steele (1997) has documented the insidious consequences of internalizing prevailing social attitudes, a situational phenomenon that he calls *stereotype threat.* Stereotype threat is

> the event of a negative stereotype about a group to which one belongs becoming self-relevant, usually as a plausible interpretation for something one is doing, for an experience one is having, or for a situation one is in, that has relevance to one's self-definition. It happens when one is in the field of the stereotype . . . such that one can be judged or treated in terms of a racial stereotype. (Steele, 1997, p. 616)

Steele (1997) stated that stereotype threat may be cued by the mere recognition that a negative group stereotype could apply to oneself in a given situation. Due to their distinctiveness and negative stereotypes about their groups, tokens are at particular risk for the effects of stereotype threat.

The effects of stereotype threat within the educational system extend to ethnic/racial minority university faculty (Garza, 1992; Niemann, 1999; Niemann & Dovidio, 1998a, 1998b). The self-perceptions of these faculty members may begin positively, with feelings of self-competence and self-efficacy. However, the undermining attitudes and behavior of fellow faculty members may change those self-perceptions to ones of incompetence and lack of confidence in their ability to succeed in their departments or even in any university (Niemann, 1999). These beliefs may then lead to self-undermining behavior, thereby sabotaging tokens' ability to succeed. In effect, stereotype threat may lower overall feelings of self-efficacy across various domains. They may also lead to increasing consciousness of their own stigmatization in the academy.

Stigma Consciousness of Tokens

Numerical minority status, the related distinctiveness, and negative stereotyping may arouse feelings of stigma consciousness among tokens. *Stigma consciousness* refers to the extent to which people expect to be stereotyped. People high in stigma consciousness are more likely to perceive discrimination directed toward their group and toward them personally, and they are also more likely to provide sound evidence for these perceptions (Pinel, 1999). High levels of group consciousness associated with tokenism often coincide with stigma consciousness. People high in stigma consciousness might be more likely to fight against discrimination than people low in stigma consciousness (Pinel, 1999). Therefore, tokens may not only be more consciously

aware of racism and its consequences, but they also may feel a moral obligation to fight racism. As these faculty members engage in a fight against racism in the university system and in the community at large, they consume energy and time that might be otherwise put to use toward their success in the university system. In addition, these fights frequently do not have intended results, which can lead to feelings of hopelessness. Pinel (1999) argued that tokens' concern about their stigmatized status consumes energy and can have the unintended effect of spoiling their opportunities to move beyond it.

Stigma consciousness may also be related to stereotypes that ethnic/racial minorities owe their faculty positions not to their competence and qualifications but to the dictates of affirmative action policy. That is, minorities are presumed to be in the university because of affirmative action and not because they are qualified (Crosby & Clayton, 1990; McCombs, 1989). Minority faculty carry a stigma of incompetence that accompanies the affirmative action label:

> In eyes of respondents, not only were the skills and talents of those individuals believed to be hired on an affirmative action basis considered irrelevant to the selection process, but these individuals also were considered to have been ill equipped for their jobs. (Heilman, Block, & Lucas, 1992, p. 543)

Affirmative action provides the truly prejudiced with an easy mark for their intolerance, thus increasing the stigmatization of minority faculty (Crosby & Clayton, 1990).

Tokens' awareness of Whites' beliefs that minorities have been hired only because of affirmative action policies may perpetuate disadvantage through a process of self-fulfilling negative prophecies (Crosby & Clayton, 1990). For instance, when people perceive that affirmative action is imposed on their departments, the policy has been negatively related to department climate and job satisfaction (Niemann & Dovidio, 1998a, 1998b). On the other hand, departmental support for affirmative action is negatively related to personal doubt and job satisfaction. Therefore, in departments with strong anti–affirmative action sentiments, which are usually related to the stigmatization of ethnic minority faculty, an insidious and potential fatal effect of the policy is the undermining of self-confidence and loss of self-esteem (Crosby & Clayton, 1990).

Tokens are not the only members of the university who may be aware of the stigmatization and stereotypes of ethnic/racial minorities. Many of their White colleagues are also acutely aware of the institutional stereotypes about minority faculty. Some of these White faculty make a conscious effort to avoid seeming racist by scrutinizing messages to and from stigmatized sources. The least prejudiced White faculty members are the most likely to engage in enhancing scrutiny of messages from stigmatized sources (Petty, Fleming, & White, 1999). However, this constant vigilance by Whites also consumes psychic energy, such that White colleagues may limit their interactions with faculty of color. This may account, in part, for evidence of limited relationships between faculty of color and White faculty. However, it is the token faculty member who is most likely to experience negative consequences of these limited relationships with the more numerous and, in most cases, more powerful White colleagues. One negative consequence may be Whites' benign neglect of ethnic/racial minorities (Hall, 1990).

In some cases, to avoid stigmatization, ethnic minority faculty who can "pass" as White (e.g., a Latina with an Anglicized last name) may conceal their ethnic/racial identity for the first few years in the department (Niemann, 2001). Unfortunately, these faculty members then live in fear of having their ethnicity "discovered" before they are ready. They also further isolate themselves from other minority faculty, who may be their main source of support in the university. This hidden ethnicity also fuels anxiety over identity issues.

Identity Issues

People's self-perception is predicated largely by distinctiveness in situations (Cota & Dion, 1986; McGuire et al., 1978). Due to their salience, tokens focus attention on themselves and become more concerned with discrepancies between members of their demographic group and others (Mullen, 1991). When people's social identity is activated, they perceive themselves more as interchangeable exemplars of their social category than as unique individuals (Mullen, 1991; Tajfel & Turner, 1986). Tokens may lose their individuality behind stereotyped roles and expectations and their public personae, which can distort their sense of self. As a result, the goals and values of the collective group take precedence over those of the individual (Crocker & Luhtanen, 1990).

Because of their visibility and stigmatization, tokens may engage in self-monitoring (Snyder, 1979) and defensive impression management strategies (Tedeschi & Norman, 1985). These strategies occur in situations in which people believe others may attribute negative qualities to them. The strategies are initiated by the actor to establish particular attributes in the eyes of others (Tedeschi & Norman, 1985). Even during times intended to be informal and relaxing, such as after-work drinks, celebratory dinners, or sports events, tokens are on guard (Kanter, 1977; Niemann, 2001). Tokens must often pretend that racial differences do not exist or have no implications (Niemann, 2001). Their White colleagues will often talk about being "color-blind." White colleagues do not typically understand that comments such as "I don't see you as a Chicana" are insulting by their very denial of tokens' identity and experiences in the institution. Tokens may don a "white mask" to fit in with White colleagues (Alexander-Snow &

Johnson, 1999). This constant self-monitoring and impression management may leave tokens little freedom to just be themselves.

Tokens may be in a constant quandary about which group they most identify with in different situations. The pressure that tokens feel to be like everybody else represents an intrapsychic conflict and a role conflict (Fine, 1992; Shaw, 1981; Winnikow, 1991). If tokens choose to align themselves with the majority, they may feel they are betraying members of their ethnic group. Other persons of color may accuse them of ingratiating behaviors or of being "white-washed," a euphemism meaning that one has completely assimilated into White culture. Impression management concerns, coupled with and related to identity issues, increase the energy it takes to socialize with other members of the university, so many tokens will simply choose to keep to themselves. As such, identity issues can underlie isolation and feelings of loneliness.

Isolation of Tokens

There is a positive relationship between the level of in-group identification and the level of intergroup differentiation (Tajfel & Turner, 1986). As tokens identify with their ethnic in-group, they psychologically distance themselves from the mainstream group they work with, resulting in increased isolation at the university. Tokens are subjected to informal isolation, often kept on the periphery of colleagues' interaction, but also still expected to demonstrate loyalty to peers in the dominant groups (Kanter, 1977; Niemann, 1999, 2001; Wolman & Frank, 1975).

Tokens suffer from their loneliness and marginalization (Johnsrud, 1993; Niemann, 2001). Symptoms of alienation of faculty include being emotionally, intellectually, and philosophically spent (burnout); being intensely cynical; seeing students as enemies; seeing life activities as valueless; feeling psychologically entrenched; feeling deep alienation; and pretending elitism (arrogance) (Machell, 1988-1989). The dynamics of interaction around them create pressure for them to seek advantage by dissociating themselves from others of their category and, hence, to remain alone. Gatherings with others of their group increase stereotyping and increase perception of their differences from majority department members. In addition, tokens do not want department members to feel threatened by their associations with other minorities, which sometimes adds to their decision to isolate themselves.

In addition, people tend to socialize with members of their own ethnic groups. Because there are few minorities in these communities, it is not unusual for tokens to rarely or never receive an invitation to socialize with those community members not affiliated with the university. Also, tokens may have the freedom and luxury to be themselves only in their homes. Therefore, although some colleagues may extend invitations after work hours, tokens often see these situations as further work situations and politely decline these. Tokens are not only isolated within their universities; those who work in predominantly White communities are also isolated after work. The loneliness and isolation of tokens seem to be especially pervasive in White universities and exacerbated in White communities (Niemann, 2001). In these White communities, tokens' awareness of racism and its possible consequences is also part of their psychosocial realities.

Tokenism and Racism

In addition to having the recognized difficulties of all untenured faculty, ethnic/racial minority faculty tokens encounter effects of overt hostility, unconscious racism, classism, elitism, and sexism (McKay, 1988, p. 47). In tokenized contexts, the burdens of institutional and individual racism weigh heavily.

The special problems that confront minority group faculty in mainstream White colleges and universities are rooted in the premises that informed Western culture's White, male-dominated, closed intellectual system for hundreds of years. This system originated in the self-serving dictates of race, class, and gender. (McKay, 1988, p. 48)

Tokens need to be aware that on a day-to-day basis, they are likely to encounter humiliating, difficult, and insulting behavior in a variety of ways, including overt hostility, subtle and less easily detected expressions of prejudices or biases, and unconscious racism, classism, and elitism (McKay, 1988).

These racist behaviors may be grounded in ambivalence on the part of the White majority. Ambivalence refers to feelings of aversions and hostility, on one hand, and sympathy and compassion, on the other. Ambivalence creates a tendency toward behavioral instability. Extreme reactions to minorities may be mediated by conflicted attitudes, yet these attitudes and feelings may be an important feature of attitudes toward the stigmatized (Katz, Wackenhut, & Glass, 1986). According to ambivalence-amplification theory, these behaviors toward minorities result because (a) feelings and beliefs about certain out-groups tend to be ambivalent rather than unambiguously hostile or friendly, (b) stimulus events that make salient an individual's ambivalence about a group create a threat to self-esteem, and (c) efforts at threat reduction may take the form of extreme behavior toward attitudinal object (Katz et al., 1986, p. 116). This theory is supported by research on aversive racism (Dovidio & Gaertner, 1996). Aversive racists outwardly proclaim egalitarian values but express racism in subtle, rationalizable ways such as believing that persons are in low-status positions because they have not worked hard (Dovidio & Gaertner, 1996). Aversive racists may engage in subtle, perhaps unconscious, behaviors that token faculty members recognize as racist. Although aversive racism

is largely unconsciousness, it affects how Whites interact with minorities.

Although overt hostility toward the minority faculty may be easier to detect and deal with, the subtler forms of racism cause greater frustration (McKay, 1988). The minority person is often unable to be absolutely sure that offense was intended (e.g., "I never think of you as a Black person"). Tokens must also deal with their White colleagues' attitudes about "color-blindness." At the same time, tokens often find themselves exposed to derogatory remarks about minority group students (McKay, 1988). "Minority group faculty often complain that they are the ones on whom the burdens of being tactful, of causing no offense, and of 'educating' (sensitizing) their mainstream colleagues fall" (McKay, 1988, p. 53; Persico, 1990).

Among the day-to-day effects of institutionalized racism for tokens are that they have few friends; the few faculty of color are spread out across campus, so these faculty have no way of getting to know other faculty of color; there are no built-in support mechanisms for these faculty; racial/cultural groups are not valued in some colleges; administrators do not support cultural/racial projects; there is little flexibility for teachers of color who spend lots of time mentoring; and research, service, and teaching are all evaluated from the perspective of the White majority (Garza, 1993).

Overcoming racism and insensitivity may be psychologically debilitating. As long as numbers remain low, disruptions of interaction around tokens (such as complaints about lack of focus on diversity) are seen by the organizations as a deflection from its central purposes, a drain of energy; yet disruptions are primarily a function of the numbers being low and could be remedied by proportional increases (Kanter, 1977).

Where there are a very small number of African-American or Hispanic faculty members in a given institution, the burdens of institutional and individual racism weigh heavily. The psychological safety associated with numbers is not available to persons who work in these isolated situations. (Washington & Harvey, 1989, p. 26)

Tokenism and Different Ethnic/Racial Groups

The psychological effects of tokenism may also depend on the extent to which the social group of the token is a culturally stigmatized group in a given context. The psychological effects of tokenism are thus likely to be most pronounced for Blacks and Latinas/Latinos, who are members of the most stigmatized groups in academic contexts and may represent a distinctive focus of prejudice among their White colleagues (Niemann & Dovidio, 1998a, 1998b). There may also be regional differences for the level of stigmatization for a given group. For instance, in South Dakota, where American Indians have been historically visible and oppressed but Latinas/Latinos have been less so, American Indians are likely at greater risk of negative effects of tokenism in the academy.

Tokenism and Interactions of Race/Ethnicity and Gender

For ethnic/racial minority women in token situations, the intersections of race/ethnicity and gender are particularly pronounced. Women of color are doubly disadvantaged in their efforts to advance (Fontaine & Greenlee, 1993). Women of color faculty report increased pressure to outperform others and outshine and outthink their colleagues, feelings of isolation, pressures to assimilate, lack of mentors, difficulty communicating with majority group members, gender discrimination, being left out of the "old boy" network, role complexity, and doubts from their majority group counterparts regarding their competency (Fontaine & Greenlee, 1993; McCombs, 1989).

Minority women, especially those in token situations, may be at particular risk for sexual harassment. These women tend to be exoticized in White environments. They may be stereotyped as easy or passive targets that want the attention of White men. Token women also experience sexism from men from their own ethnic/racial groups, especially those from especially patriarchal communities. These women fight both gender and race stereotypes and may be at particular risk for success in academia.

Third world women face unique difficulties in these institutions because of their race and gender. Their presence, as bearers of knowledge is in direct contradiction to Western concepts of accepted knowledge. Of all groups, as bona fide intellectuals, they are the furthest removed from society's expectations of their "place," the least expected to succeed on merit, and the most vulnerable to insult. (McKay, 1988, p. 58)

THE ROAD TO TENURE

The psychological effects of token status can affect every aspect of tokens' working life, including their survival within the academy, which usually means the attainment of tenure. Achievement of tenure is a primary goal for faculty members.

The conferral of tenure means that the institution, after utilizing a probationary period of as long as six years in which it has had ample opportunity to determine the professional competence and responsibility of its appointees, has rendered a favorable judgment establishing a rebuttable presumption of the individual's professional excellence. (Finkin, 1988, p. 92)

Tenured faculty members are typically ensured of a job for life within the tenure-granting institution. Exceptions are made almost exclusively for unethical behavior or misconduct within or affecting the institution. Being fired after having been granted tenure is a very rare occasion

(Finkin, 1988). The achievement of tenure means academic freedom, including freedom of speech, freedom in teaching, and freedom as a citizen. Finally, tenure means the end of the probationary period. A tenured faculty member is "welcomed to the ranks." To achieve tenure, however, tokens must overcome numerous obstacles.

Tokens and Cognitive Busyness

The pretenure time period is stressful. The tenure clock ticks increasingly loudly as that pretenure time period begins to run out. For faculty to be successful, they must produce a significant number and quality of publications, prepare for and teach new courses, advise students, and serve on institutional and department committees. This work requires their time, energy, and concentration. However, tokens have more memory and problem-solving deficits than do nontokens (Lord & Saenz, 1985; Saenz, 1994). These deficits are interpreted to be a function of minorities' cognitive busyness with their minority status, rather than with any inherent personal deficits (Lord & Saenz, 1985; Saenz & Lord, 1989). That is, tokens are preoccupied with issues pertaining to self-distinctiveness and self-presentation strategies. In addition, after experiencing instances of racism, tokens may spend time and cognitive energy ruminating about the experiences and their responses, or lack of responses, to the situation (Niemann, 1999).

Minorities often do not share a common culture or values with the majority. The unique perspective of these groups may lead to problems in communicating, which could affect achievement (Cantor, 1989; Fine, Johnson, & Ryan, 1990). Furthermore, racial heterogeneity tends to create interpersonal tension, which is reflected in the feelings and behaviors of group members; this tension may also affect tokens' performance (Shaw, 1981). In addition, minority group members are more competitive than majority counterparts in high-salience conditions (Espinoza & Garza, 1985), which can further increase cognitive busyness. Tokens may also deliberately not perform to the best of their ability for several reasons, including fear of seeming more competent than majority groups members, fear of retaliation out of jealousy and racism (belief that Whites are superior to minorities), and because it may add to distinctiveness (Kanter, 1977).

Self-protective attributions also add to a state of cognitive busyness (Crocker & Major, 1989). Tokens do not have the luxury of time to engage in cognitive busywork that will not lead to scholarly production. The experience begins a viscous circle. The more that tokens ruminate about experiences or events not directly related to their scholarly achievement, the more stressed they become, and the more they ruminate about how they are wasting time to do the work necessary to achieve tenure. The tenure process is one of solitude, as minority faculty members seem to be largely on their own in this endeavor (Ellsworth, 1993).

Attributional Ambiguity

A key component of success for faculty members is mentorship that sees them through the tenure process. This mentorship includes constructive, critically analytical feedback on their work. Because of their few numbers in academia, feedback to minorities is usually provided by out-group members. However, tokens live in a state of attributional ambiguity regarding causes of positive and negative feedback from White peers (Crocker, Voelkl, Testa, & Major, 1991). They do not know if the negative feedback is racist or if positive feedback is overly kind from aversive racists who do not have the confidence or courage to provide negative feedback to minorities. Tokens often do know who to trust or what feedback to trust (Niemann, 1999). To the extent that positive feedback is seen as due to group status, it may be discounted (Crocker & Major, 1989, p. 621).

For instance, attributional ambiguity may be grounded in self-protection strategies such as (a) attributing negative feedback to prejudice against their group, (b) selectively comparing their outcomes with those of members of their own groups, and (c) selectively devaluing those attributes on which their group typically fares poorly and valuing those on which their group excels (Crocker & Major, 1989). These strategies may help protect self-esteem, but they do little to help tokens understand what they need to do to improve the quality of their work. That understanding is critical for faculty to be successful. Furthermore, these strategies are not guaranteed to protect self-esteem. Indeed, people who attribute negative feedback to discrimination experience a drop in social self-esteem and lowered perception of control over their performance in subsequent tasks and social interactions (Pinel, 1999).

The attributional ambiguity in which the stigmatized exist may have other unanticipated negative consequences. Not knowing whether feedback from Whites is genuine or is related to prejudice makes it difficult for the stigmatized to predict their future outcomes, select tasks of appropriate difficulty, and accurately assess their own skills and abilities (Crocker & Major, 1989; Dovidio et al., 2001; Niemann, 1999; Niemann & Dovidio, 1998a, 1998b). In general, attributional ambiguity is difficult, results in isolation from collaborative research and intellectual and professional stimulation, and greatly increases the risks of not achieving tenure (Hall, 1990).

Evaluation of Research

Among the top-ranked reasons for nonachievement of tenure for ethnic/racial minorities are insufficient publications due to insufficient research activity, insufficient publications due to inexperience in writing research, and insufficient data-based publications (Suinn & Witt, 1982). Additionally, faculty members' work is evaluated by tenured members of the department and university, the majority of whom are White.

As such, White definitions of learning and scholarship prevail as research is evaluated. Achievement of tenure is difficult for ethnic/racial minorities because reviews are given by a closed "old boy" network, research pertaining to minorities is not seen as legitimate, and publishing in specialty journals is seen as less prestigious (Suinn & Witt, 1982). Minorities sometimes radically redefine issues, research paradigms, and approaches to teaching (Suinn & Witt, 1982). These different approaches are often perceived by senior academics as provocative and threatening to the status quo (Alexander-Snow & Johnson, 1999). Scholarly work that focuses on ethnic/racial minorities is devalued and seen as soft or illegitimate and not sufficient to survive scrutiny of tenure and promotion reviews (De la Luz Reyes & Halcon, 1991). Minorities' research is often not accepted for publication in mainstream journals, so the status of journals in which minority-oriented research usually appears also compounds problems of tenure (Suinn & Witt, 1982). Tokens are likely to be evaluated more extremely than their White counterparts (Linville & Jones, 1980). So if the token's portfolio is clearly excellent, evaluations are high; if his or her achievements are somewhat less than stellar or optimal, evaluations will be lower than they are for Whites with comparable achievements. In addition, lack of information about the research topic, the minority researcher, or performance tends to be filled in with stereotypes (Devine, 1989; Fiske & Taylor, 1991). Tenure portfolios may thus be interpreted in a stereotype-consistent manner that devalues and minimizes the tokens' research.

The overriding value in academia is merit, with the belief that meritocracies are predicated on clear standards. This belief ignores the subjective evaluation of every perceiver, who uses his or her own values in evaluating scholarly work. Differences on most job performance criteria increase when the number of minority members in the group being rated is relatively small (Mellor, 1996; Schmitt & Noe, 1986). Furthermore, race effects of variables for performance criteria decline as the percentage of minorities in the work group increases (Kraiger & Ford, 1985). Suinn and Witt (1982) suggested that more racism and discrimination are perpetrated under the cloak of maintaining high academic standards than under any guise in the academy.

Evaluation of Teaching

Token faculty not only have to prove the worth of their scholarship to their colleagues, but they must also work harder than their White counterparts to prove their competence in the classroom. Students also carry stereotypes about minority groups. Tokens may thus be seen as unintelligent. Token faculty experience more resistance in the classroom than do their White counterparts. This resistance is especially felt when these faculty incorporate issues relative to minorities into their lectures and coursework. Tokens who talk about racism and challenge students' naive and/or racist perceptions and ideas may receive lower teaching evaluations than do those faculty who do not discuss these issues in the classroom. Their White colleagues and chairs often do not take into consideration that these faculty members are dealing with issues that create tension in the classroom and are met with resistance. Lower teaching evaluations may provide the justification to give tokens poor annual reviews and/or to deny them tenure. The quality and choice of service are also evaluated for tenure purposes.

Tokens and Excessive Service

The number one barrier to retention and promotion for ethnic/racial minority faculty is engaging in too much minority-related service in addition to other duties expected of all faculty (Garza, 1993; Suinn & Witt, 1982). Ethnic/racial minority faculty members are assigned excess committee work because most committees want minority representation (Suinn & Witt, 1982). However, service with respect to the minority community is not valued as much as more academically oriented work in the direct service of the institution (e.g., curriculum committees). Tokens also engage in formal and informal student advising. As Suinn and Witt (1982) pointed out, minority students often automatically gravitate toward a minority group faculty member for informal advising and even for counseling on private matters. Minority students generally fail to understand that minority faculty must focus on research to survive the academy. White faculty often deny tokens' realities by telling them that all faculty have an equal workload (Alexander-Snow & Johnson, 1999).

Although minority faculty are quite aware that they should limit the amount of time they spend on minority-related service, most do not believe that they really have a choice in the matter. Because there are so few minorities in their institutions, these faculty members find it a matter of personal values and integrity to engage in this work (Schneider, 1997). However, service is typically not valued highly in the institution's criterion for the evaluation for tenure. Therefore, many minorities believe that the system sets them up for failure.

Role Encapsulation of Tokens

The excessive service conducted by ethnic/racial minority faculty is related to the perception of ethnic/ racial minorities as homogeneous. The perception of minority group homogeneity leads to stereotyping and encapsulation in roles. Tokens are often asked to play the role of a minority rather than that of an individual scholar. Because of mistaken, stereotypical attributions, tokens may be forced to play limited and caricatured roles (e.g., they are readily placed on "diversity" committees or committees where a "person of color voice" is seen as beneficial). Tokens are "typecast" as specialists in ethnic matters rather than being perceived as "qualified" in their particular disciplines (Kanter, 1977; Niemann, 1999; Spangler, Gordon, & Pipkin, 1978). It is a function of biased perceptions and institutionalized racism that White faculty and administrators assume that ethnic/racial minorities are specialists in minority-related issues. Even when their research and teaching are not at all related to minority issues, tokens are still placed on these committees and assigned to teach any "diversity"-related courses in the department. In more ethnically balanced groups, members have more freedom to assume nontraditional roles (Rozell & Vaught, 1988). These racist assumptions are understandably resented by many minority faculty members, especially as these assignments detract from their own scholarship related to achieving tenure. Role stress represented in role encapsulation has been linked to feelings of tension, decreased job satisfaction, and employee turnover (Niemann & Dovidio, 1998a).

Job Satisfaction of Tokens

Tokens' job satisfaction is related to their potential to achieve tenure. Ethnic/racial minority group members report less job satisfaction than their White counterparts (Niemann & Dovidio, 1998a, 1998b; Rozell & Vaught, 1988). Turnover is higher among minorities than Whites (Frierson, 1990). The extent to which ethnic/racial minority faculty members are satisfied may affect their motivation to do the work necessary for success and their ability to concentrate on their work.

SUGGESTIONS TO MINORITIES FOR AVOIDING EFFECTS OF TOKENISM

The effects of tokenism can affect ethnic/racial minorities' overall quality of life, mental and physical health, and potential for success (Niemann, 1999). However, minority faculty members are not without personal agency in preventing some of these negative effects for themselves. By being very aware of potential land mines, minorities can avoid some of them. This awareness must begin during the interview process.

Job Interviews. During job interviews, assess the institutional climate by asking the following key questions: How many minority faculty and students are there on campus? What percentage of minority faculty achieves tenure? What percentage of minority students graduates? What is the retention rate for minority faculty? What journals or other publication outlets are valued in the tenure evaluation? Are faculty protected from committee work in pretenure years? How is service evaluated? Is there consideration for the amount of service by reducing teaching load? Are department chairs motivated to nurture faculty and help them develop? Are administrators held accountable for the recruitment and retention of faculty of color? What roles do your colleagues envision faculty filling? Are travel funds available for faculty to travel to conferences during which they might make key networking and mentoring connections? What mentoring structures are available in the department and university? What services are available for minority students? Are students required to take diversity-related courses? Is the Confederate flag widely displayed? Are pictures of ethnic/racial minority persons visible? The answers to these questions determine a great deal about the institutional and department climate for ethnic/racial minorities.

Tokenized Situations. For faculty members who find themselves in tokenized situations, the following are some suggestions: Find mentors you trust; these persons can be contacts made at conferences. Do network at conferences; you need professional colleagues you trust. Ask these trusted mentors to critically evaluate your work. Trusted feedback is critical for stress reduction (Alexander-Snow & Johnson, 1999). Say no to committee work that is not meaningful to you or that involves a great deal of your time. Find others in the university who will provide caring guidance to minority students; you need to have other faculty (especially caring White faculty) to whom you can refer students who come to you. Remember that you are only one person; you can't do everything for everyone. Publish! When you receive rejections, follow reviewers' suggestions that do not compromise your intent and resubmit your manuscripts or artistic works. Manage your time; stay home 2 days a week to write. Hold those days sacred and don't schedule any meetings on those days. Find one or two people you can share your experiences with and who will validate your feelings so that you do not spend an excessive amount of time ruminating about racist or sexist experiences. Pick your battles; you cannot fight every racist statement and/or behavior on campus.

Do not volunteer to teach courses that are new to you; you need to spend the majority of your time on your scholarship. When possible, teach courses that will facilitate your scholarship. You must communicate with your students. Let them know you want to help them grow and learn. Conduct teaching evaluations at regular intervals during the term. Share the patterns of results with your students and let them know how you will respond to their concerns and requests. If students believe you care about them, their resistance to you and/or your message will decrease. They will also be likely to give you more positive teaching evaluations. When you do receive negative evaluations that are reflected in your annual reviews, respond to the review in writing and explain the circumstances of the class. Ask that your response be attached to the review.

Be aware of your feelings; validate yourself. Strive for a reduction of stress and a sense of control over your daily activities. Remember that excess stress is related to high blood pressure, heart disease, and other chronic health issues (Alexander-Snow & Johnson, 1999). Strive for well-being and a holistic sense of self. Maintain your identity and integrity. When all is said and done, success will feel empty if you feel you have compromised your values. It is therefore important to do work that is important to you; don't conduct research you do not value. Conducting work that is meaningful to you will also keep you motivated to continue your work. Remember that the best way to get out of a negative situation is by ensuring that you remain an attractive candidate on the job market.

SUGGESTIONS FOR INSTITUTIONAL CHANGE IN CLIMATE

Fewer than 10% of Ph.D.s are awarded to ethnic/racial minorities. Therefore, as these new graduates become faculty members, they will likely continue to be subjected to the psychological effects of tokenism felt by their forebears in the academy. Universities that recognize the effects of tokenism can do much to improve the quality of life for their minority faculty. First, it is critical for White faculty and administrators to understand why minority faculty are important to the university (Persico, 1990; see also Vaughn, 1990, for a detailed list of the importance of minority faculty). This top-down understanding will eventually affect university climate. Deans and chairs must be held accountable for the recruitment and retention of minority faculty. To be effective, this accountability must be tied to their unit funding. Academic institutions must design and implement review procedures that honor cultural diversity and respect cultural differences. Chairs must be trained to conduct constructive annual reviews and to provide clear expectations. It is not enough for White faculty and administrators to believe that tenure review procedures are fair to minorities; faculty of color must also believe that they are fair.

During new faculty orientations, provide opportunities for faculty to create networks with colleagues from various parts of the institution. In that way, when minorities cannot find support in their own units, they will turn to other faculty members. Provide a promotion and tenure handbook with advice from other faculty members, especially faculty of color. In the same way, mentors from within and outside of the faculty members' departments will be helpful. Focus on retention; most universities place their greatest efforts on recruitment of minority faculty, then lose them after a few years. Provide a structure through which minority faculty can come together, form networks, and receive support. Additionally, there must be bidirectionality in the faculty socialization processes. That is, acknowledge and respect that faculty and institutions will influence each other (Lenze, 1999).

Finally, university members must remember that tokenism and its consequences are a function of the numbers of ethnic/racial minorities and not inherent to minorities themselves. Reduce the proportional discrepancy between White and minority faculty and administrators, and tokenism and its devastating effects will be reduced.

> Change is tied inexorably to changes in institutional status quo. . . . Once the process of ethnic diversification was set in motion, it, itself, would initiate profound transformations within the institution. There is an essential relationship between institutional change and ethnic diversification. (McHolland, 1990, p. 37)

FUTURE DIRECTIONS FOR RESEARCH

Although empirical knowledge about the psychology of tokenism is fairly limited, basic social psychological knowledge on group dynamics, prejudice, and other areas is applicable to this experience. More direct research is needed to examine the mediating effects on token status of the following: department collegiality, the demographic makeup of the community outside the university, mentorship, salary, numbers of minority faculty in the department, numbers of minority student majors and in the university, faculty rank, number of cultural/ethnic events on campus, level of racial hostility on campus, the national political climate (e.g., Latinas/Latinos are subject to anti-immigration rhetoric), department chair's skills, and quality of annual evaluations. More information on the similarities of experiences between minority and White faculty is needed so that the differences specific to race may be teased out and examined. Much more information about the interactions of race, social class, and gender is also needed. Finally, not all faculty of color experience tokenism; future research can help us understand and predict which contexts facilitate these negative effects.

REFERENCES

Alexander-Snow, M., & Johnson, B. J. (1999). Perspectives from faculty of color. In R. J. Menges & Associates (Eds.), *Faculty in new jobs* (pp. 88-117). San Francisco: Jossey-Bass.

Cantor, B. (1989). Minority hiring shows problems in corporate America. *Communication World, 6*(8), 22-25.

Cooley, C. H. (1902). *Human nature and the social order.* New York: Scribner.

Cota, A. A., & Dion, K. L. (1986). Salience of gender and sex composition of ad hoc groups: An experimental test of distinctiveness theory. *Journal of Personality and Social Psychology, 50*(4), 770-776.

Crocker, J., & Luhtanen, R. (1990). Collective self esteem and ingroup bias. *Journal of Personality & Social Psychology, 58*(1), 60-67.

Crocker, J., & Major, B. (1989). Social stigma and self-esteem: The self-protective properties of stigma. *Psychological Review, 96,* 608-630.

Crocker, J., & Quinn, D. M. (2000). Social stigma and the self: Meanings, situations, and self-esteem. In T. F. Heatherton, R. E. Kleck, M. R. Hebl, & J. G. Hull (Eds.), *The social psychology of stigma* (pp. 153-183). New York: Guilford.

Crocker, J., Voelkl, K., Testa, M., & Major, B. (1991). Social stigma: The affective consequences of attributional ambiguity. *Journal of Personality and Social Psychology, 60,* 218-228.

Crosby, F., & Clayton, S. (1990). Affirmative action and the issue of expectancies. *Journal of Social Issues, 46*(2), 61-79.

De la Luz Reyes, M., & Halcon, J. (1991). Practices of the academy: Barriers to access for Chicano academics. In P. G. Altback & K. Lomotrey (Eds.), *The racial crisis in American higher education* (pp. 167-186). Albany: State University of New York Press.

Devine, P. G. (1989). Stereotypes and prejudice: Their automatic and controlled components. *Journal of Personality and Social Psychology, 56,* 5-18.

Dovidio, J. F., & Gaertner, S. L. (1996). Affirmative action, unintentional racial biases, and intergroup relations. *Journal of Social Issues, 52,* 51-76.

Dovidio, J. F., Gaertner, S. L., Niemann, Y. F., & Snider, K. (2001). Racial, ethnic, and cultural differences in responding to distinctiveness and discrimination on campus: Stigma and common group identity. *Journal of Social Issues, 57*(1), 167-188.

Ellsworth, E. (1993). Claiming the tenured body. In D. Wear (Ed.), *The center of the web* (pp. 63-74). New York: Statue University of New York Press.

Espinoza, J., & Garza, R. (1985). Social group salience and interethnic cooperation. *Journal of Experimental Social Psychology, 21*(4), 380-392.

Fine, M. G., Johnson, F. L., & Ryan, M. S. (1990). Cultural diversity in the workplace. *Public Personnel Management, 19*(3), 305-319.

Fine, T. S. (1992). The impact of issue framing on public opinion: Toward affirmative action programs. *The Social Science Journal, 29*(3), 323-334.

Finkin, M. W. (1988). The tenure system. In A. L. Deneef, C. D. Goodwin, & E. S. McCrate (Eds.), *The academic's handbook* (pp. 136-149). Durham, NC: Duke University Press.

Fiske, S. T., & Taylor, S. E. (1991). *Social cognition.* New York: McGraw-Hill.

Fontaine, D. C., & Greenlee, S. P. (1993). Black women: Double solos in the workplace. *The Western Journal of Black Studies, 17*(3), 121-125.

Frierson, H., Jr. (1990). The situation of Black educational researchers: Continuation of a crisis. *Educational Research, 19,* 12-17.

Frable, D. E. S. (1993). Dimensions of marginality: Distinctions among those who are different. *Personality and Social Psychology Bulletin, 19,* 370-380.

Frable, D. E. S., Blackstone, T., & Scherbaum, C. (1990). Marginal and mindful: Deviants in social interactions. *Journal of Personality and Social Psychology, 59,* 140-149.

Garza, H. (1992). Academic power, discourse, and legitimacy: Minority scholars in US universities. In M. Romero & C. Candelaria (Eds.), *Community empowerment and Chicano scholarship* (pp. 35-52). Los Angeles: National Association of Chicano Studies.

Garza, H. (1993). Second-class academics: Chicano/Latino faculty in U.S. universities. In J. Gainen & R. Boice (Eds.), *Building a diverse faculty* (New Directions for Teaching and Learning No. 53, pp. 33-42). San Francisco: Jossey-Bass.

Hall, C. C. I. (1990). Qualified minorities are encouraged to apply: The recruitment of ethnic minority and female psychologists. In G. Stricker, E. Davis-Russell, E. Bourg, E. Duran, W. R. Hammond, J. McHolland, K. Polite, & B. E. Vaughn (Eds.), *Toward ethnic diversification in psychology education and training* (pp. 105-112). Washington, DC: American Psychological Association.

Hamilton, D. L., & Trolier, T. K. (1986). Stereotypes and stereotyping: An overview of the cognitive approach. In J. F. Dovidio & S. L. Gaertner (Eds.), *Prejudice, discrimination and racism* (pp. 127-163). New York: Academic Press.

Heilman, M. E., Block, C. J., & Lucas, J. A. (1992). Presumed incompetent? Stigmatization and affirmative action efforts. *Journal of Applied Psychology, 77*(4), 536-544.

Johnsrud, L. K. (1993). Women and minority faculty experiences: Defining and responding to diverse realities. In J. Gainen & R. Boice (Eds.), *Building a diverse faculty* (New Directions for Teaching and Learning No. 53, pp. 3-16). San Francisco: Jossey-Bass.

Jussim, L., & Fleming, C. (1996). Self-fulfilling prophecies and the maintenance of social stereotypes: The role of dyadic interactions and social forces. In C. N. Macrae, C. Stangor, & M. Hewstone (Eds.), *Stereotypes and stereotyping* (pp. 161-191). New York: Guilford.

Kanter, R. M. (1977). *Men and women of the corporation.* New York: Basic Books.

Katz, I., Wackenhut, J., & Glass, D. C. (1986). An ambivalence-amplification theory of behavior toward the stigmatized. In S. Worchel & W. G. Austin (Eds.), *Psychology of intergroup relations* (pp. 103-117). Chicago: Nelson-Hall.

Kraiger, K., & Ford, J. K. (1985). A meta-analysis of ratee race effects in performance ratings. *Journal of Applied Psychology, 70,* 56-65.

Kunda, Z. (2000). *Social cognition: Making sense of people.* Cambridge: MIT Press.

Lee, Y. T., Jussim, L. J., & McCauley, C. R. (1995). *Stereotype accuracy: Toward appreciating group differences.* Washington, DC: American Psychological Association.

Lenze, L. F. (1999). Accountability for faculty welfare. In R. J. Menges & Associates (Eds.), *Faculty in new jobs* (pp. 310-327). San Francisco: Jossey-Bass.

Linville, P. W., & Jones, E. E. (1980). Polarized appraisals of outgroup members. *Journal of Personality and Social Psychology, 38,* 689-703.

Lippmann, W. (1922). *Public opinion.* New York: Harcourt, Brace.

Lord, C. G., & Saenz, D. S. (1985). Memory deficits and memory surfeits: Differential cognitive consequences of tokenism for tokens and observers. *Journal of Personality and Social Psychology, 49*(4), 918-926.

Machell, D. F. (1988-1989). A discourse on professorial melancholia. *Community Review, 9,* 41-50.

McCombs, H. G. (1989). The dynamics and impact of affirmative action processes on higher education, the curriculum, and Black women. *Sex Roles, 21*(1/2), 127-143.

McGuire, W. J., McGuire, C. V., Child, P., & Fujioka, T. (1978). Salience of ethnicity in the spontaneous self-concept as a function of one's ethnic distinctiveness in the social environment. *Journal of Personality and Social Psychology, 36*(5), 511-520.

McHolland, J. (1990). Addressing institutional change. In G. Stricker, E. Davis-Russell, E. Bourg, E. Duran, W. R. Hammond, J. McHolland, K. Polite, & B. E. Vaughn

(Eds.), *Toward ethnic diversification in psychology education and training* (pp. 37-42). Washington, DC: American Psychological Association.

McKay, N. Y. (1988). Minority faculty in [mainstream White] academia. In A. L. Deneef, C. D. Goodwin, & E. S. McCrate (Eds.), *The academic's handbook* (pp. 48-61). Durham, NC: Duke University Press.

Mellor, S. (1996). Gender composition and gender representation in local unions: Relationships between women's participation in local office and women's participation in local activities. *Journal of Applied Psychology, 80,* 706-720.

Menges, R. J. (1999). Dilemmas of newly hired faculty. In R. J. Menges & Associates (Eds.), *Faculty in new jobs* (pp. 19-38). San Francisco: Jossey-Bass.

Mullen, B. (1991). Group composition, salience, and cognitive representations: The phenomenology of being in a group. *Journal of Experimental Social Psychology, 27,* 297-323.

Niemann, Y. F. (1999). The making of a token: A case study of stereotype threat and racism in academe. *Frontiers: A Journal of Women Studies, 20*(1), 111-135.

Niemann, Y. F. (2001). Stereotypes about Chicanas and Chicanos: Implications for counseling. *The Counseling Psychologist, 29*(1), 55-90.

Niemann, Y. F., & Dovidio, J. (1998a). Relationship of solo status, academic rank, and perceived distinctiveness to job satisfaction of racial/ethnic minorities. *Journal of Applied Psychology, 83*(1), 55-71.

Niemann, Y. F., & Dovidio, J. (1998b). Tenure, race/ethnicity and attitudes toward affirmative action. *Sociological Perspectives, 41,* 783-796.

Niemann, Y. F., Pollak, K., Rogers, S., & O'Connor, E. (1998). The effects of physical context on stereotyping of Mexican American males. *Hispanic Journal of Behavioral Sciences, 20*(3), 349-362.

Niemann, Y. F., & Secord, P. (1995). The social ecology of stereotyping. *Journal for the Theory of Social Behavior, 25*(1), 1-14.

Oakes, P. J., Haslam, A., & Turner, J. C. (1994). *Stereotyping and social reality.* Oxford, UK: Blackwell.

Olmedo, E. L. (1990). Minority faculty development: Issues in retention and promotion. In G. Stricker, E. Davis-Russell, E. Bourg, E. Duran, W. R. Hammond, J. McHolland, K. Polite, & B. E. Vaughn (Eds.), *Toward ethnic diversification in psychology education and training* (pp. 99-104). Washington, DC: American Psychological Association.

Persico, C. F. (1990). Creating an institutional climate that honors diversity. In G. Stricker, E. Davis-Russell, E. Bourg, E. Duran, W. R. Hammond, J. McHolland, K. Polite, & B. E. Vaughn (Eds.), *Toward ethnic diversification in psychology education and training* (pp. 55-64). Washington, DC: American Psychological Association.

Petty, R. E., Fleming, M. A., & White, P. H. (1999). Stigmatized sources and persuasion: Prejudice as a determinant of argument scrutiny. *Journal of Personality and Social Psychology, 76*(1), 19-34.

Pinel, E. C. (1999). Sigma consciousness: The psychological legacy of social stereotypes. *Journal of Personality and Social Psychology, 76*(1), 114-128.

Pollak, K., & Niemann, Y. F. (1998). Black and White tokens in academia: A difference of chronic vs. acute distinctiveness. *Journal of Applied Social Psychology, 11,* 954-972.

Rai, K. B., & Critzer, J. W. (2000). *Affirmative action and the university: Race ethnicity, and gender in higher education employment.* Lincoln: University of Nebraska Press.

Rozell, E., & Vaught, B. C. (1988). The interaction effects of women in groups: A review of the interaction and implications. *Arkansas Business and Economic Review, 21*(3), 1-15.

Saenz, D. S. (1994). Token status and problem solving deficits: Detrimental effects of distinctiveness and performance monitoring. *Social Cognition, 12,* 61-74.

Saenz, D. S., & Lord, C. G. (1989). Reversing roles: A cognitive strategy for undoing memory deficits associated with token status. *Journal of Personality and Social Psychology, 56*(5), 698-708.

Schneider, A. (1997, June 20). Proportion of minority professor inches up to 10 percent. *Chronicle of Higher Education,* pp. A12-A14.

Shaw, M. (1981). *Group dynamics: The psychology of small group behavior.* New York: McGraw-Hill.

Schmitt, N., & Noe, R. A. (1986). Personnel selection and equal employment opportunity. In C. L. Cooper & I. T. Robertson (Eds.), *International review of industrial and organizational psychology* (pp. 71-116). New York: John Wiley.

Smith, E. R., & Zarate, M. A. (1990). Exemplar and prototype use in social categorization. *Social Cognition, 8,* 243-262.

Snyder, M. (1979). Self monitoring processes. *Advances in Experimental Social Psychology, 12,* 86-130.

Spangler, E., Gordon, M. A., & Pipkin, R. M. (1978). Token women: Am empirical test of Kanter's hypothesis. *American Journal of Sociology, 84,* 160-170.

Steele, C. M. (1997). A threat in the air: How stereotypes shape intellectual identity and performance. *American Psychologist, 52,* 613-629.

Sue, D. W., & Sue, D. (1999). *Counseling the culturally different* (3rd ed.). New York: John Wiley.

Suinn, R. M., & Witt, J. C. (1982). Survey on ethnic minority faculty recruitment and retention. *American Psychologist, 37,* 1239-1244.

Tajfel, H., & Turner, J. C. (1986). The social identity theory of intergroup behavior. In S. Worchel & W. G. Austin (Eds.), *Psychology of intergroup relations* (pp. 7-24). Chicago: Nelson-Hall.

Taylor, S. E., & Fiske, S. T. (1978). Salience, attention, and attribution: Top of the head phenomena. *Advances in Experimental and Social Psychology, 11,* 249-288.

Taylor, S. E., Fiske, S. T., Etcoff, N., & Ruderman, A. (1978). The categorical and contextual bases of person memory and stereotyping. *Journal of Personality and Social Psychology, 36,* 778-793.

Tedeschi, J. T., & Norman, N. (1985). Social power, self presentation, and the self. In B. R. Schlenker (Ed.), *The self and social life* (pp. 293-322). New York: McGraw-Hill.

Thomas, C. E., & Neville, H. A. (1999). Racism, mental health, and mental health practice. *The Counseling Psychologist, 27,* 155-223.

Vaughn, B. E. (1990). Recruitment and retention of ethnic minority faculty in professional schools of psychology. In G. Stricker, E. Davis-Russell, E. Bourg, E. Duran, W. R. Hammond, J. McHolland, K. Polite, & B. E. Vaughn (Eds.), *Toward ethnic diversification in psychology education and training* (pp. 91-98). Washington, DC: American Psychological Association.

Washington, V., & Harvey, W. (1989). *Affirmative rhetoric, negative action: African American and Hispanic faculty at predominantly White institutions* (Rep. No. 2). Washington, DC: George Washington University, School of Education and Human Development.

Winnikow, L. (1991). How women and minorities are reshaping corporate America. *Vital Speeches, 57*(8), 242-244.

Wolman, C., & Frank, H. (1975). The solo woman in professional peer group. *American Journal of Orthopsychiatry, 45,* 164-171.

Zarate, M. A., & Smith, E. R. (1990). Person categorization and stereotyping. *Social Cognition, 8,* 161-185.

CHAPTER 5

On Teaching Multiculturalism
History, Models, and Content

JEFFERY SCOTT MIO

California State Polytechnic University, Pomona

Why is it important to teach issues of multiculturalism to graduate students in the mental health field? Models of intervention were developed to be general models, so shouldn't these models apply to diverse populations a therapist will encounter? Isn't a good therapist simply a good therapist, and shouldn't this good therapist do well across diverse populations? If a therapist does not know how to treat those from diverse populations, why not just keep assigning that therapist diverse clients until that therapist gets it right?

For those of us who teach multicultural courses or present multicultural material at conferences, the above questions are familiar. They seem to reveal at least three stances of students or colleagues who express them. The first stance is a naive view of the world, one that has a "people are people" orientation. Individuals who hold this position are genuine in their beliefs but minimize the complexity of people and the importance of this complexity. The second stance is an intentionally or unintentionally racist stance. Individuals who hold

this position feel that general models of therapy (developed by White theorists) are superior and that the inclusion of issues of diversity is a nuisance factor that should be ignored. The third stance is an intellectually lazy stance. Individuals who hold this position may feel that there is an importance to issues of diversity, but they are too lazy to improve their skills, so they justify their stance by adopting a "people are people" orientation. All of these stances are forms of resistance to multiculturalism (Mio & Awakuni, 2000), and they represent real obstacles to overcome before issues of multiculturalism can be fully received.

History of Inclusion of a Multicultural Component to Graduate Training

As most people who are concerned about the inclusion of multiculturalism and other forms of diversity in graduate training know, the formal inclusion of such issues was mandated by the American Psychological Association (APA) in a famous conference, known as the 1973 Vail Conference (Bernal & Padilla, 1982; Korman, 1973). The Vail Conference asserted that the treatment of culturally diverse clients without knowledge about services relevant to such populations is considered unethical. Moreover, denial of such services simply because of a lack of expertise is equally unethical. Essentially, the Vail Conference stated that culturally competent therapists should be hired, and therapists should obtain training to become culturally competent themselves.

Although this mandate was disseminated in 1973 to all directors of clinical training, there were very few road maps to implement such a mandate. Although various articles and book chapters were published in the area of multiculturalism at that time, there were no textbooks or so-called "standard" articles that would constitute the core of a course dealing with multiculturalism. Thus, those who wanted to resist the mandate could do so by pointing out the dearth of material for a course of this sort.

Resistance to the inclusion of multicultural issues in graduate curricula was rendered moot with the publication of some landmark books in the late 1970s and early 1980s. These books include Pedersen, Lonner, and Draguns's (1976) Counseling Across Cultures; Atkinson, Morten, and Sue's (1979) Counseling American Minorities: A Cross-Cultural Perspective; Sue's (1991b) Counseling the Culturally Different: Theory and Practice; and an ambitious series of books called the Handbook of Cross-Cultural Psychology (Triandis & Berry, 1980; Triandis & Brislin, 1980; Triandis & Draguns, 1980; Triandis & Herron, 1981; Triandis & Lambert, 1980; Triandis & Lonner, 1980). The principal argument (resistance) against the inclusion of multicultural issues in graduate curricula having been addressed, such courses should have been flooding graduate programs across the country, right?

As has been documented elsewhere (Mio & Awakuni, 2000; Mio & Morris, 1990; Sue et al., 1998), programs across the country still resisted the inclusion of multicultural issues in graduate curricula. Sue et al. (1982) initially published a set of multicultural competencies that could be used to measure both how competent trainees were in the multicultural area and how successful programs were in training their students to be culturally competent. Although this article was one of the most cited in the literature (Ponterotto & Sabnani, 1989), support for the article was principally verbal and not behavioral (Sue et al., 1998). Those in power to change graduate curricula seemed not to be moved to change their curricula to seriously incorporate multicultural competencies.

Part of the resistance against the multicultural competency standards was that they were too vague, general, and/or abstract (Sue et al., 1998). Despite the fact that the Accreditation Handbook (American Psychological Association, 1986) states that competence in conducting therapy with diverse populations is a criterion for accreditation by the discipline (Criterion II in the Accreditation Handbook), many programs fail to meet these standards. Rickard and Clements (1993) suggested that many directors of clinical training genuinely wanted to comply with the standard, but they felt that the guidelines were unclear. Altmaier (1993) pointed out that Criterion II was no less unclear than other guidelines set forth by the Accreditation Handbook. Thus, suggestions that the multicultural guidelines were unclear were just another form of resistance to this standard. Payton (1993) stated that more clarity would not necessarily produce better therapists. Multicultural competency was aspirational, so one must strive to become more and more competent in this area and not think that reaching a certain plateau was sufficient.

In response to criticisms of needing more clarity, more specific criteria of multicultural competence were developed (Arredondo et al., 1996; D. W. Sue, 1991a, 1995; Sue, Arredondo, & McDavis, 1992). However, a new set of criticisms was then presented: These standards were too specific (Sue et al., 1998). Quite clearly, taken together, these two fundamentally opposing criticisms revealed what was underlying them: There was simply a resistance to incorporating these standards at all into graduate training, despite the fact that the lack of competence in multiculturalism is considered to be unethical as defined by our own profession.

Different Models of Multicultural Training

In a series of articles taking a retrospective perspective on the history of psychology's scientist-practitioner model of clinical psychology (Albee, 2000; Baker & Benjamin, 2000; Belar, 2000; Benjamin & Baker, 2000; Nathan, 2000; Peterson, 2000; Routh, 2000; Stricker, 2000), most congratulated our profession for taking such an empirically based approach to the understanding of psychological phenomena. However, Albee (2000) took exception to this stance. He criticized our profession for uncritically accepting the medical model of psychological disorders. This forever placed psychology under the control of medicine/psychiatry. Instead of the medical/organic/brain-defect model, Albee contended that psychology should have taken a social learning/stress-related model:

> The social model . . . seeks to end or to reduce poverty with all its associated stresses, as well as discrimination, exploitation, and prejudices as other major sources of stress leading to emotional problems. By aligning itself with the conservative view of causation, clinical psychology has joined the forces that perpetuate social injustice. (p. 248)

Had the profession of psychology adopted Albee's (2000) suggested model, perhaps we would not have experienced as much resistance as we historically have experienced in attempting to include issues of multiculturalism in clinical graduate curricula. However,

we did not adopt that model, and we are now encountering resistance to such inclusion.

For years, people had been fighting for the inclusion of just a single course that dealt with multicultural issues to help trainees understand that there were different perspectives to the traditional models of psychopathology, assessment, and treatment they were learning. However, as the profession evolved, and as more and more information about this area informed us of how we conceptualized the field of clinical psychology, the single-course model seemed inadequate. Thus, we have emerged from a single-course model to a cluster model to an integrative model (Barker-Hackett, 1999; D'Andrea & Daniels, 1991; Hills & Strozier, 1992; Peterson, Peterson, Abrams, & Stricker, 1997). The single-course model suggests that a single course on multicultural issues is sufficient enough to sensitize therapists in training to such issues. The cluster model suggests that because of the amount of information in the area of multiculturalism, such material can only be covered by multiple courses dealing with the topic. The integrative model is a fundamental shift in philosophy about multiculturalism. It suggests that multiculturalism is so important that it should be integrated throughout the curriculum in the graduate training program. This philosophical stance underlies Paul Pedersen's call for multiculturalism to be considered the "fourth force" in therapy (Essandoh, 1996; Pedersen, 1990, 1991, 1999).

In general, those who are exposed to more multicultural experience with respect to formal courses and practicum experiences are more culturally competent therapists than those not having as much experience in these areas (Holcomb-McCoy & Myers, 1999; Pope-Davis, Reynolds, Dings, & Ottavi, 1994; Rogers, Hoffman, & Wade, 1998; Rogers, Ponterotto, Conoley, & Wiese, 1992). This underscores the importance of such training; those who do not receive such training do their clients a disservice. Unfortunately, commitment to this area is uneven within our discipline. Counseling psychology programs seem to take multiculturalism much more seriously than clinical psychology programs (Pope-Davis, Reynolds, Dings, & Nielson, 1995; Quintana & Bernal, 1995). For example, Pope-Davis et al. (1995) found that "counseling psychology students complete an average of 1.6 multicultural counseling courses, and clinical psychology students complete an average of 0.9, a difference of nearly a standard deviation" (p. 325). Thus, the older, more established segment of our profession would appear to be more resistant to the inclusion of multicultural issues in its curricula.

As suggested by those who have taught multicultural courses at both the undergraduate and graduate levels, students enrolled in these courses experience uncomfortable or even resistant feelings (Gloria, Rieckmann, & Rush, 2000; Golding & Kraemer, 2000; Mio & Awakuni, 2000; Mio & Morris, 1990; Organista, Chun, & Marín, 2000; Ponterotto, 1988). Although there are many ways of addressing such feelings, one of the more popular models for helping individuals overcome their feelings of discomfort are activity-based interventions (Goldstein, 2000; Mio, 1989; Singelis, 1998). For example, Mio (1989) had students engaging in cross-cultural activities and writing about their experiences. These students were judged by independent raters as being more culturally sensitive than those who did not engage in such activities.

In one of the most comprehensive models of activity-based learning, Pedersen presented what he called the counselor–client–anti-counselor triad (Pedersen, 1977, 1988; Pedersen, Holwill, & Shapiro, 1978). In this exercise, students play roles of counselor, client, and anti-counselor. "Counselor" and "client" are self-explanatory. A student plays the role of a counselor, and another student plays the role of an ethnic minority client. The "anti-counselor" is a student who stands or sits to

the side of the counselor and reveals either underlying or racist/culturally insensitive interpretations of the counselor's interventions or the self-doubts that the counselor may hold. Pedersen et al. (1978) found that those who participated in the triad model were more empathic toward the simulated ethnic minority client after the training than before.

Ridley, Mendoza, and Kanitz (1994) proposed a multicultural training model they called the multicultural counseling training program development pyramid. This model contained five elements of training: training philosophy, learning objectives, instructional strategies, program designs, and evaluation. At the base of the pyramid, training philosophy provided the foundation. Here, it was proposed that the philosophy of the training program should hold multiculturalism at its core. Upon this foundation, learning objectives of multicultural training could be built. Then, instructional strategies for how to deliver multicultural training could be devised. Program designs that gave students multicultural experiences was next. Finally, such programs should have an evaluation component built in to demonstrate the effectiveness of the training program. Those who reviewed this model were in general agreement with the objectives that Ridley et al. were attempting to accomplish (Arredondo, 1994; Atkinson, 1994; Cheatham, 1994; Fukuyama, 1994).

One of the more enduring and powerful models of teaching cultural sensitivity is the racial/ethnic/minority identity model. This model was first formalized by William E. Cross (1971), who discussed the Negro-to-Black process of identity. This model formed the basis for many similar models (e.g., Atkinson et al., 1979; Parham, 1989). This model was presented primarily as a description of the processes through which "Negroes" moved through an acceptance of the White norms and preferences to an understanding of the importance of a Black identity. Atkinson et al. (1979) discussed how this process was true for all

Peoples of Color, and Parham (1989) discussed how one cycles through the stages of encountering bigotry or extremely positive affirmations of one's own ethnicity to withdrawal into one's own ethnic group to an emergence of valuing one's own ethnicity while appreciating ethnic differences of other groups. Cross's general model has been adapted for biracial identity (Poston, 1990) and gay and lesbian identity (Cass, 1979; Sophie, 1985).

Although the Cross model was extremely influential among ethnic minority communities, it was not until Janet Helms (Helms, 1984, 1986, 1990, 1995; Helms & Carter, 1991) adapted the Cross model to understand how White individuals went through similar stages that this model became a general training model for all individuals. Some reported on how this White racial identity was important in the understanding gained by their graduate students in training (Corvin & Wiggins, 1989; Ponterotto, 1988). This model not only helped individuals to understand the racial/ethnic barriers placed in front of People of Color, but it also gave these students experiential involvement in multicultural issues.

As stated before, one of the most consistent voices in trying to infuse multicultural training in graduate curricula has been Derald Wing Sue. Beginning from Sue et al. (1982), Sue attempted to establish multicultural competencies that would be adopted by all training programs. Sue et al. (1998) discussed three dimensions that are important in developing multicultural competence as a therapist: (a) awareness of one's attitudes and beliefs about issues of diversity, (b) knowledge about one's own worldview and the worldview of those from other perspectives, and (c) specific skills in working with those from differing groups. Within each of these three dimensions, Sue et al. (1998) also specified areas of awareness, knowledge, and skills. For example, within the first dimension of awareness, culturally skilled therapists need to be aware of how their own cultural background

may influence the process of therapy, be knowledgeable of communication style differences, and have the skills to seek out training in areas they have identified as being insufficient in their therapy repertoire. This competency-based model subsumed the identity development model, especially in the areas of awareness and knowledge. However, both models stand as different ways of getting students to become aware of the importance of the multicultural arena.

In one of the first articles published about teaching a multicultural course, McDavis and Parker (1977) discussed elements of the more formal awareness–knowledge–skills model proposed by Sue and his colleagues. They reported five basic goals of their course: (a) becoming aware of one's own and others' attitudes toward ethnic minorities, (b) learning skills to effectively treat ethnic minorities in group experiences, (c) learning about ethnic minority perceptions toward the counseling process, (d) learning skills for rapport building, and (e) learning skills to effectively treat ethnic minorities in one-to-one therapy situations. In addressing the knowledge area, the authors reported that students needed to write a term paper that contained resources in dealing with ethnic minority populations. Other articles discussed the structures of their courses as well (Mio & Morris, 1990; Parker, Moore, & Neimeyer, 1997). Parker et al. (1997), in particular, did a nice job of combining both the racial/ethnic identity model with the competency-based model.

General Issues to Cover in a Multicultural Curriculum

In this section, I will be covering all of the topic areas that should or could be covered in a graduate curriculum in multiculturalism. Although this list will not be comprehensive, it demonstrates the breadth of topics covered in courses, clusters of courses, or entire curricula on multiculturalism. Accompanying the topic areas will be some selected references that are relevant to the topic. Again, this will not be a comprehensive list but will be exemplary of articles in the area of discussion. For those interested in some relevant terms that multicultural researchers, theorists, and practitioners encounter, I refer you to a multicultural dictionary edited by myself and my colleagues (Mio, Trimble, Arredondo, Cheatham, & Sue, 1999).

What Do We Mean by "Culture"? One question with which I begin my courses on multiculturalism is on what is meant by *culture* (Mio & Awakuni, 2000; Mio & Morris, 1990). This typically stimulates a lively discussion by students as they grapple with this seemingly innocent question. Kluckhohn and Strodtbeck (1961) asked this question years ago and presented areas in which different cultures vary, such as if they were past, present, or future oriented or if they perceived the essence of being human to be good, evil, or a combination of the two. Vontress (1988) discussed how there was not a single culture but five cultures (universal, ecological, national, regional, and racioethnic), so a simplistic question of what culture is does not make sense.

Assimilation/Acculturation of Immigrants. Issues of assimilation/acculturation of immigrants need to be discussed. In her very influential books, McGoldrick and her colleagues (McGoldrick, Giordano, & Pearce, 1996; McGoldrick, Pearce, & Giordano, 1982) discussed important questions to keep in mind regarding ethnic minority clients. Such questions include what the immigrant history of clients or their families were, if they were living in ethnic enclaves or not, what type of religious or cultural practices they may observe, and if their families came with large groups of immigrants or if they came separately. All of these questions have implications for the degree to which they are or want to be absorbed into the larger community.

Mendoza (1989) presented an empirically validated scale to measure acculturation in Mexican American adolescents and adults. This scale measured five dimensions along which such individuals could vary in acculturation, thus making the concept of acculturation multidimensional as opposed to unidimensional. This scale measured areas such as language spoken, the ethnicity of friends and coworkers, and food preferences.

One important distinction a therapist must make is between an *immigrant* family versus a *refugee* family. Immigrants are those families who voluntarily came to the United States. They typically begin their acculturation process before they come to the United States by preparing for their voyage, reading about the culture to which they will be absorbed, and learning English. On the other hand, refugees are those families who are fleeing from political oppression and even the threat of death. These individuals sometimes only have days or even hours to decide to come to the United States. Thus, their acculturation process occurs almost entirely after they have arrived here, and there may still be a resistance to acculturate because of the hopes of returning to their homeland at some time in the future. Some researchers who have written about these issues are Baptiste (1993) and Gonsalves (1992).

Intelligence Testing. As Sue has repeatedly indicated (Sue, 1991a; Sue & Sue, 1990, 1999), intelligence testing has long been a political issue that often attempted to scientifically "prove" the inferiority of ethnic minorities to the White majority population. Sue and Sue (1999) wrote,

> For example, de Gobineau's (1915) *The Inequality of Human Races* and Darwin's (1859) *On the Origin of Species by Natural Selection* were used to support the genetic intellectual superiority of Whites and the genetic inferiority of the lower races. Galton (1869) wrote explicitly that African

"Negroes" were "half-witted men who made childish, stupid and simpleton-like mistakes," while Jews were inferior physically and mentally and only designed for a parasitical existence on other nations of people. In 1916 Terman, using the Binet scales in testing Black, Mexican American, and Spanish Indian families, concluded that they were *uneducable*. (p. 19)

Although other, more contemporary examples have challenged the intelligence of ethnic minority populations besides Darwin, Galton, and Terman, one of the most recent and celebrated assaults on the intelligence of ethnic minorities came in the 1994 publishing of Herrnstein and Murray's *The Bell Curve*. Others have refuted Herrnstein and Murray's claims (Gould, 1996; Ryan, 1995; Samuda, 1998; Suzuki, Meller, & Ponterotto, 1996; Willie, 1995), but such debates continue to raise the question of scientific evidence of racial superiority. Before the Herrnstein and Murray book came out, another important book by Paniagua (1994) dealt with intelligence testing and other forms of assessment of ethnic minorities.

White (Majority) Privilege. One of the more emotionally evocative topics covered in multicultural courses is the issue of White privilege. Of course, the individual most quoted in this area is Peggy McIntosh (McIntosh, 1988, 1995; McIntosh & Hu-Dehart, 1998). McIntosh's stance is that in the United States, Whites may not realize that they are privileged in this society and that many things that they accomplish or that affirm their positive images are due to this unearned privilege. This lack of awareness prevents them from fully understanding the pervasiveness of racism and how this racism prevents many individuals from succeeding—or even trying. For example, McIntosh (1995) suggested that one of her privileges as a White woman is, "I can turn on the television or open to the front page of the paper and see people of my race widely and positively represented" (p. 79). In my own

courses on multicultural issues, I discuss this privilege and challenge students to think of the last time they have seen *any* Asian male in a romantic situation. (Asian females are being portrayed more and more as objects of desire, but this is only for White males.) Asian males tend to either not be seen at all or are on martial arts–based programs and films. Pack-Brown (1999) underscored the importance in getting White therapists and counselors to understand their privileged status in their professional development.

Racism. One of the most important topics to cover in courses on multiculturalism is that of racism. Because this is such a well-known topic, I will not go into a long discussion here. However, as Jones (1997) and Ridley (1995) have pointed out, it is important for individuals to understand how some modern forms of racism are presented in a disguised form. As I have pointed out elsewhere (Mio & Awakuni, 2000), these more subtle forms of racism are ways of resisting the inclusion of multiculturalism into curricula. Some of the more cited references in racism are Dovidio and Gaertner (1986), Guthrie (1976, 1998), Jones (1972, 1997), Ridley (1995), and Tatum (1997). Related topics are stereotyping (Casas, Ponterotto, & Sweeney, 1987; McGoldrick & Rohrbaugh, 1997; Mok, 1998), prejudice (Ponterotto & Pedersen, 1993), and affirmative action (Pratkanis & Turner, 1994).

Attribution Theory. Attribution theory has long been influential in social psychology. At least dating back to Heider (1958), social psychologists have discussed how we attribute causes of behavior to internal (dispositional) or external (situational) variables. Others who have contributed to the early formulation of attribution theory are Jones and Davis (1965), Kelley (1967, 1972, 1973), and McArthur (1972). The reason why attribution theory is important to understand is because of two important offshoots of the theory. Jones and

Davis reported that there is a difference between attributions made by "actors" and "observers." *Actors* are those who engage in behaviors, whereas *observers* are those who observe the actors' behaviors. Actors tend to attribute behaviors to external or situational factors, whereas observers tend to attribute behaviors to internal or dispositional factors. For example, an actor who trips might attribute the trip to a crack in the sidewalk, whereas an observer may attribute the trip to the actor being clumsy. Lee Ross (1977) labeled the observer's tendency to overemphasize dispositional factors and underemphasize situational factors as "the fundamental attribution error." Ross believed this to be an error of attribution because of the lack of appreciation of environmental factors that may actually be the cause of the behavior. He believed this error to be common and pervasive. Thomas Pettigrew (1979) extended the fundamental attribution error to an attribution to an entire group. He labeled this "the ultimate attribution error." For example, if one were to observe an actor stealing a loaf of bread, the observer may attribute this theft to the actor being a bad person. If the actor also happens to be a member of an ethnic minority group, the observer may attribute the theft to ethnic minorities being bad. Pettigrew asserted that this perpetuates prejudice and racism because if the actor is a member of the White majority group, observers tend *not* to make this attribution to the White majority but only to the disposition of the actor.

According to Claude Steele (Steele & Aronson, 1995), the ultimate attribution error interacts with stereotypes to cause members of groups on the downside of power to perform worse on tasks, thus perpetuating the stereotypes. Steele termed this *stereotype threat*. Steele found that when highly intelligent African Americans were placed in an extremely intellectually challenging situation, they actually performed as well if not better than their White counterparts. However, if one were to make race salient by suggesting that the test would help determine if there is a difference between African Americans and Whites, these highly intelligent African Americans performed worse than their White counterparts. Steele replicated these findings with women highly accomplished in mathematics. When these women were taking an extremely challenging mathematics examination, they performed just as well as their male counterparts unless they were led to believe that the test would be diagnostic about gender differences in mathematical ability. Steele has suggested that when making the negative stereotypes salient, the stereotypes created an added pressure on the targets of the stereotypes, and the resultant anxiety fed on itself and distracted the targets from concentrating on the task at hand.

Worldviews. An important issue in multicultural courses is that of worldview. Students need to understand how their view of the world may differ from those of others. Some of these differences may be subtle, but some may be profound. Differing perspectives of the world have been discussed by Ho (1995), Kluckhohn and Strodtbeck (1961), Merchant and Dupuy (1996), Pedersen (1977, 1988, 1997, 1999), Pedersen et al. (1978), Robin and Spires (1983), Sue and Sue (1999), Tamura and Lau (1992), Ting-Toomey (1994), and Triandis (1995). For example, Sue and Sue discussed a model of worldview that Sue presented long ago (D. W. Sue, 1978) that crossed locus of control with locus of responsibility. This resulted in a 2×2 matrix with four worldviews: internal locus of control–internal locus of responsibility (IC–IR), external locus of control–internal locus of responsibility (EC–IR), external locus of control–external locus of responsibility (EC–ER), and internal locus of control–external locus of responsibility (IC–ER). The typical Western worldview is the IC–IR perspective, in which people feel that they hold both the control and responsibility for their position in life. This contrasts with those cultures that place more control of lives to fate (external locus of control). Issues such as individualism and collectivism (Triandis, 1995) also form the basis of differing worldviews.

Emic Versus Etic Distinction. One of the distinctions made by multicultural researchers is that of *emic,* or culture-specific, versus *etic,* or generalizable, phenomena. Among the most prominent researchers in this area is Harry Triandis and his colleagues (Triandis, 1989; Triandis et al., 1986; Triandis, Bontempo, Villareal, Asai, & Lucca, 1988; Triandis et al., 1993). Elsewhere, I (Mio & Awakuni, 2000) have summarized a particularly illustrative research finding by Triandis et al. (1988) on the emic versus etic distinction:

> For example, Triandis, Bontempo, Villareal, Asai, and Lucca (1988) discussed how the term "self-reliance" was interpreted differently in individualistic versus collectivistic societies. In individualistic societies, "self-reliance" meant the freedom to pursue one's own goals and to be in competition with others. In collectivistic societies, it meant not burdening the in-group, whereas competition was unrelated. Even the word "competition" had different connotations in these two societies. In individualistic societies, "competition" meant individuals would compete with one another, whereas in collectivistic societies, it meant that different in-groups would compete. (p. 12)

Other more recent researchers who discuss the importance of the emic–etic distinction are Fischer, Jome, and Atkinson (1998) and S. Sue (1999).

Individualism Versus Collectivism. Triandis and his colleagues have been one of the leading voices in examining the emic–etic distinction; they have also examined the individualism–collectivism distinction (Hui & Triandis, 1996; Triandis, 1989, 1995; Triandis et al., 1986; Triandis et al., 1988; Triandis

et al., 1993). Individualism tends to be a Western (i.e., North American, Western European, Australian, and New Zealand) perspective, in which individual rights, needs, and freedoms tend to be placed above the needs of the society when there is a conflict between these two needs. Collectivism is associated with most of the rest of the world, in which the individual subjugates his or her rights, needs, and freedoms in deference to societal needs. This dimension can be examined apart from the etic–emic distinction studied by Triandis and his colleagues (Dien, 1999; Hofstede, 1980, 1982, 1983; Hofstede & Bond, 1984; Tamura & Lau, 1992; Ting-Toomey, 1994). For example, one of the important additions to the individualism–collectivism literature was Hofstede's (1980) discussion of power distance in connection with the individualism–collectivism dimension. Triandis (1995) called this dimension a horizontal–vertical dimension. This resulted in a 2×2 matrix yielding four relevant quadrants: horizontal individualism, horizontal collectivism, vertical individualism, and vertical collectivism. The horizontal segment of the dimension suggests an equal status among society members, whereas the vertical segment suggests a hierarchical structure. For example, societies that emphasize horizontal individualism tend to value uniqueness among its citizens, whereas horizontal collectivistic societies value cooperativeness among its citizens. Societies that can be characterized by vertical individualism value achievement orientation, whereas vertical collectivistic societies value dutifulness.

Research/Methodological Issues. As discussed earlier, emic and etic distinctions are important research issues when investigating cultural differences. This topic is perhaps the most important one in the area of multiculturalism, for it not only relates to data collection within ethnic minority communities but also has implications for simple terms one uses in conducting therapy or even communicating with communities different from one's own. Other areas of research/methodological importance are the following: how to conduct culturally sensitive research (Council of National Psychological Associations for the Advancement of Ethnic Minority Interests, 2000; Merchant & Dupuy, 1996; S. Sue, 1999), therapist–client match (Atkinson, 1985; Atkinson & Schein, 1986), the measurement of multicultural competence (Coleman, 1996; Sodowsky, Taffe, Gutkin, & Wise, 1992), assessment of ethnic minority clients (Malgady, 1996; Paniagua, 1994), racial identity and the counseling process (Helms, 1990; Pope-Davis, Menefee, & Ottavi, 1993), and White researchers studying ethnic minority populations (Atkinson, 1993; Casas & San Miguel, 1993; Helms, 1993; Ivey, 1993; Mio & Iwamasa, 1993; Parham, 1993; Pedersen, 1993; Ponterotto, 1993; D. W. Sue, 1993).

Acculturative Stress and Psychopathology. Society can be the source of support or stress. To the extent that racism exists in society, society as a source of stress is a given. Some have found such a connection between acculturation into the broader society and stress, health risks, and psychopathology (Anderson, 1991; Clark, Anderson, Clark, & Williams, 1999; Smart & Smart, 1995). For example, in their review of the literature on racism and stress, Clark et al. (1999) concluded, "Despite the different sampling schemes and data quantification methodologies and the paucity of studies, the results of the research reviewed in this section were generally consistent. The perception of racism usually resulted in psychological and physiological stress responses" (p. 812). Such responses included "low birth weight and infant mortality . . . depression . . . the healing process . . . breast cancer survival . . . hearth disease . . . mean arterial blood pressure changes . . . and chronic obstructive pulmonary disease" (p. 812).

Racial Identity Development. One of the most vigorous areas of research has been in the area of racial identity development. As mentioned previously, the theory of racial identity has been so powerful that it represents one of the major theoretical models for teaching multicultural courses. As discussed earlier, Cross's (1971) Negro-to-Black model of identity development was one of the very first formal models published in this area. Helms's (1984) White racial identity model was the next major advancement in this area because it was one of the first models that applied ethnic minority identity development to White identity development. Throughout much of the history of models such as these, it was suggested that all individuals went through stages of awareness—the first stage involved complete unawareness of the racial oppression of the broader society; intervening stages included awareness, withdrawal, and activism; and finally, individuals developed a deep understanding of racial/ethnic differences and an integration of their identity with their own race/ethnicity and others' race/ethnicity. The concept of "stages" has been attacked, and more recently, Helms (1995) suggested that the term *statuses* should replace *stages*. Other resources on racial identity development issues are Burkard, Ponterotto, Reynolds, and Alfonso (1999); Corvin and Wiggins (1989); Cross (1995); Gushue (1993); Helms (1990); Neville et al. (1996); Pack-Brown (1999); Parham (1989); Parker et al. (1997); Ponterotto (1988); and Pope-Davis et al. (1993). Those studying biracial/multiracial identity development have been Kerwin and Ponterotto (1995), Poston (1990), Root (1992, 1996, 1998), and Stephan and Stephan (1989).

General Therapy Issues. As many have pointed out, multicultural issues in therapy are general therapy issues (Arredondo, 1998; Essandoh, 1996; Fischer et al., 1998;

Pedersen, 1999; Rooney, Flores, & Mercier, 1998; Sue et al., 1998). As Sue and Zane (1987) discussed, simple knowledge about a culture is a distal element to conducting therapy; what is most important (proximal) in the therapy situation is the credibility of the therapist. Cultural competence adds to the credibility of the therapist, and it is here that multicultural training adds to the therapeutic environment. Thus, knowledge about cultural issues needs to be integrated within one's presentation of self as a therapist so that the client can feel comfortable enough to allow therapy to proceed. As S. Sue (1977) long ago pointed out, ethnic minority clients tend to drop out of therapy after only one session at a much higher rate than their White majority counterparts. This dropout rate can at least in part be explained by the clients' perceived cultural insensitivity of the therapist.

In my estimation, one of the most important general issue articles on cultural transference and countertransference in multiculturalism was written by Comas-Diaz and Jacobsen (1991). This article discusses two types of therapeutic dyads: a White therapist with an ethnic minority client and an ethnic minority therapist with an ethnic minority client. The authors discuss the types of transference feelings that an ethnic minority client may have toward either a White therapist or an ethnic minority therapist. Such reactions may include having resentment, being overly cooperative, and feeling that the ethnic minority therapist is a "sell-out." The authors also discuss the types of countertransference feelings that a White or ethnic minority therapist may have toward an ethnic minority client. Such reactions may include being a cultural anthropologist (e.g., analyzing the client as an interesting "specimen" from a culture not yet encountered), feeling guilt, and discounting the importance of racial/ethnic issues.

Books designed for courses on multiculturalism should include general issues such as racism, worldviews, values, immigration, individualism–collectivism, and ethnic-specific chapters dealing with at least the following four racial/ethnic groups: African Americans/ Blacks, Hispanics/Latinos/Latinas, Native American Indians, and Asians. Such recent books that meet these criteria include *Using Race and Culture in Counseling and Psychotherapy: Theory and Process* (Helms & Cook, 1999), *Counseling and Psychotherapy: A Multicultural Perspective* (Ivey, Ivey, & Simek-Morgan, 1993), *Ethnicity & Family Therapy* (McGoldrick et al., 1996), *Counseling Across Cultures* (Pedersen, Draguns, Lonner, & Trimble, 1996), *Handbook of Multicultural Counseling* (Ponterotto, Casas, Suzuki, & Alexander, 1995), and *Counseling the Culturally Different: Theory and Practice* (Sue & Sue, 1999). Other supplementary books include *Resistance to Multiculturalism: Issues and Interventions* (Mio & Awakuni, 2000); *Multiculturalism as a Fourth Force* (Pedersen, 1999); *Multicultural Counseling Competencies: Assessment, Education and Training, and Supervision* (Pope-Davis & Coleman, 1997); and *Working With Culture: Psychotherapeutic Interventions With Ethnic Minority Children and Adolescents* (Vargas & Koss-Chioino, 1992).

Group-Specific Therapy Issues

Every course on multicultural/diversity issues deals with ethnic-specific groups. Groups almost always discussed are African Americans/Blacks, Hispanics/Latinos/Latinas, Native American Indians, and Asians. Some books discuss even more groups, including subdivisions within the four above categories, Middle Eastern cultures, Jewish cultures, European cultures, and Slavic cultures (McGoldrick et al., 1996). However, courses on multiculturalism/diversity are now beginning to include populations other than race/ ethnic-based ones, including issues dealing with gender, gay/lesbian/bisexual concerns, disabilities, and the elderly. Although other chapters in this volume will deal with all of these subpopulations, I will briefly mention the specific populations and resources that may be of interest to the reader.

African Americans/Blacks. Just as there was a movement in the late 1960s and early 1970s of moving from *Negro* to *Black,* so too was there a movement in the late 1980s and early 1990s of moving from *Blacks* to *African Americans.* However, the term *African American* leaves out those individuals in the United States who are actually from Africa, Jamaica, or Haiti, and other Blacks not born in America. All such individuals are targets of discrimination based on skin color; articles based on such forms of racism are relevant to all of these individuals, and such issues are brought into the therapy situation. Such resources dealing with racism include Anderson (1991), Clark et al. (1999), Harris (1995), and Pinderhughes (1982). Other resources having a broader scope include Greene (1996); Hines and Boyd-Franklin (1996); McNair (1992); Taylor, Chatters, Tucker, and Lewis (1990); Whaley (2000); White (1984); White and Parham (1990); and White, Parham, and Ajamu (1999).

Hispanics/Latinos/Latinas. One of the major issues when dealing with Hispanics/ Latinos/Latinas is the issue of immigration and acculturation status (Buriel, 1993; Smart & Smart, 1995). Other resources examining general issues when dealing with Hispanics/ Latinos/Latinas are Bernal and Enchautegui (1994), Bernal and Shapiro (1996), Falicov (1996), Garcia-Preto (1996), and Vega (1990). Such issues include the role of religion, language, machismo, and fatalism. Finally, a major issue with which Hispanics/Latinos/ Latinas must deal is the particular form of institutionalized racism related to the Immigration and Naturalization Service (INS)

(Falicov, 1996). As has been pointed out by many, how many of us carry around proof of our citizenship or permanent residence status? However, Hispanics/Latinos/Latinas are routinely stopped by the INS and asked to produce exactly such documentation.

Native American Indians. As Trimble, Fleming, Beauvais, and Jumper-Thurman (1996) have pointed out,

> Most scholars know the term *American Indian* is an imposed ethnic category with little relevant meaning. At best, it is a generalized gloss that was first foisted upon the Arawak, a now-extinct tribe once indigenous to islands off the southeastern coast of the United States, by a wayward Italian sailor who thought he had reached India. (pp. 178-179)

Thus, naming and self-identity are two of the major issues within Native American Indian populations. Other resources that deal with general issues involving Native American Indians are Attneave (1982); Choney, Berryhill-Paapke, and Robbins (1995); Garrett and Garrett (1994); Heinrich, Corbine, and Thomas (1990); McWhirter and Ryan (1991); and Tafoya and Del Vecchio (1996). I might add that when students first learn about the program of stealing Native American Indian children from their families and sending them to boarding schools, feelings of sadness, guilt, and anger are stirred.

Asians. Asians are an extremely diverse group of people, with each group having its own language. However, the issue of collectivism seems to cut across all Asian groups. Collectivism is evidenced in different ways across Asian communities, especially in the form of power distance, as discussed before (Dien, 1999; Hofstede, 1980). Issues such as duty, saving face, giving face, and cooperation are related to collectivism. Some of the resources that discuss Asian issues include Berg and Jaya (1993); Lee and Zane (1998);

Leong, Wagner, and Kim (1995); Leung and Boehnlein (1996); Mok (1998, 1999); Okazaki (1997); Shon and Ja (1982); Tamura and Lau (1992); and Ting-Toomey (1994).

Gender Issues. Despite the fact that women are in the numerical majority in this country, the major theories of intervention were developed from a male perspective. Issues of the patriarchal structure of society have been raised by feminist theorists, and such issues have resulted in treatments that have been unfair to women. Resources that discuss such issues include Brown (1994), Comas-Diaz and Greene (1994), Enns (1993), Hays (1996), Landrine (1995), and Worell and Johnson (1997).

Gay/Lesbian/Bisexual Issues. As stated earlier, issues of identity development have been applied to gay and lesbian identity (Cass, 1979; Sophie, 1985). Although issues of identity development may occur either within or without the context of therapy, a major issue that therapists in training need to confront is their own countertransference feelings about homosexuality (Gelso, Fassinger, Gomez, & Latts, 1995; Hayes & Erkis, 2000). Other resources that discuss more general issues include Greene (1997) and Pope (1994).

Individuals With Disabilities. Perhaps the major issue related to issues of individuals with disabilities is simply the awareness of nondisabled individuals that the issue of disability is an important issue of concern. Nondisabled individuals need to be aware of issues such as physical access to facilities, assumptions of impairment beyond the disability, and the disability not necessarily being the main issue for the need for services. Some helpful resources in this area include Asch and Russo (1985); Barnartt (1996); Esten and Willmott (1993); Henwood and Pope-Davis (1994); Kemp and Mallinckrodt (1996); Leigh, Corbett, Gutman, and Morere (1996); Mackelprang and Salsgiver (1999); Raifman

and Vernon (1996); Swain, Finkelstein, French, and Oliver (1993); and Yuker (1988).

Elderly Populations. A growing recognition is that America is getting older. Therapists need to know how to treat older adults (Abeles et al., 1998). Older adults have issues that are specific to them as opposed to a general model of treatment. Such issues include the wide gender disparity due to women living longer than men, generational or cohort differences, language differences among older immigrants, issues of mortality, and dementia. Some important resources in this area include Division 20 (1994); Duffy (1999); Gatz et al. (1998); Hartman-Stein (1998); Knight, Teri, Santos, and Wohlford (1995); Niederehe and Schneider (1998); Storandt and VandenBos (1994); and Zarit and Knight (1996).

ADDRESSING RESISTANCE TO MULTICULTURAL MATERIAL

As I have pointed out elsewhere (Mio & Awakuni, 2000), resistance to multiculturalism comes in many forms, both at the broader level and at the individual level. Those who have written about teaching multicultural courses (McDavis & Parker, 1977; Mio & Morris, 1990; Organista et al., 2000) have pointed out how emotionally evocative discussions of this topic are, which lead to resistance against the perceived source of such troubling thoughts. Such emotions need to be addressed. Because I have already pointed out the resistance of the broader profession, I will restrict my comments in this section to addressing resistance to two specific populations in training: White majority students and ethnic minority students.

Resistance Among White/Majority Individuals

As has been pointed out a while ago, resistance to White students' resistance to multicultural issues can be conceptualized within the context of White identity development models (Corvin & Wiggins, 1989; Helms, 1990; Ponterotto, 1988). Kiselica (1998) noted that this resistance is in part due to the difficult and painful nature of the journey from racism to multiculturalism:

> White racial identity growth also is painful because it is a provocative, personal voyage marked by the disturbing discovery that one is racist, a self-revelation that poses an intense and soul-searching conflict for the Anglo: Do I deny my racism, retreat from multicultural training, and avoid contact with the culturally different? Or do I confront this reprehensible facet of my identity, attempt to change it, and pursue multiculturalism? (p. 9)

To address these painful experiences, Kiselica (1998) suggested that the enriching aspects of this journey also be discussed:

> Although confronting ethnocentrism and racism is a critical component to multicultural training, an overemphasis of these tasks can obscure what may be the most enriching aspect of cross-cultural counseling and psychotherapy: experiencing the beauty of different cultures and sensing one's personal development toward a multicultural identity. The multicultural training literature has done little to adequately emphasize the potential for mental health professionals to discover these joys, which are inherent in multicultural counseling. Much more attention needs to be devoted in the multicultural literature and throughout the multicultural training process to this subject, for it can be a major motivator for professionals to pursue cross-cultural encounters. (p. 17)

Lark and Paul (1998), in responding to Kiselica's (1998) article, agreed with its conclusions. They also extended it to discuss the importance of their mentor, who was a White individual strongly supportive of multicultural issues. They identified with him, saw him as a possible future self, and appreciated his multicultural perspective. Tatum

(1997) would agree with this position. She discussed how White allies who come into her courses on multiculturalism to discuss their allied activities have a profound effect on White students. These students were burdened with the weight of racism and felt powerless by its enormity. However, when a White ally comes into her courses, these students suddenly see how their individual actions may make a difference, and they feel empowered by the experience.

Roades and Mio (2000) noted that although many discuss the importance of allies both in the multicultural literature and in workshops they have attended, little actual empirical evidence is collected on this important group of individuals. In their preliminary examination of their data, it appeared that allies seem to have a particularly strong sense of social justice. This not only motivated them into becoming allies, but it also helped to sustain their current efforts. Another important motivating force seems to be their connection with groups on the downside of power and their own victimization in some settings. For example, a White woman may advocate for ethnic minorities both due to her connection and friendship with ethnic minority individuals and also because of her own sense of victimization in a patriarchal society.

Still, despite efforts to make the journey of multiculturalism less painful for individuals, some White students and even professionals are resistant to this domain. Although students in training and professionals alike have criticized their graduate programs for the paucity of multicultural courses and training opportunities, there is evidence that many failed to take such courses when the opportunity presented itself (Mintz, Bartels, & Rideout, 1995), or they failed to take additional training in multiculturalism despite working with large populations of ethnic minority clients (Ramirez, Wassef, Paniagua, & Linskey, 1996). This resistance has found evidence in professional writings (Weinrach & Thomas,

1997), claiming that multicultural sensitivity amounts to little more than "political correctness" in our profession.

To address such resistance (at least in the classroom), I have advocated for a number of different techniques, exercises, and experiences (Mio, 1989; Mio & Awakuni, 2000; Mio & Morris, 1990). First, I have revealed my own resistance to multiculturalism, which was not overcome until well into my teaching years. In so doing, I hope to model for my students my vulnerability and invite them to do the same. I have also advocated for experiential involvement with ethnic minority communities as an adjunct to learning about such communities. I also use a number of videotaped television programs, educational materials, and commercially released films that deal with multicultural issues (to be discussed in the last section of this chapter). Moreover, I feel that it is important for instructors to allow for a confidential, safe environment for particularly resistant but shy students to be able to express their opinions. Therefore, I have used a "reaction paper" exercise, which requires students to turn in a weekly 1- to 2-page paper to react to any topic between papers, such as the readings, the course lectures, or the weekly news. I give every student feedback on their papers, responding to their particular concerns. Some may feel that students will still hold back from "politically incorrect" statements, but this is not the case. I have published such exchanges elsewhere (Mio & Awakuni, 2000).

Resistance Among Ethnic Minority Individuals

Although most efforts on resistance deal with the resistance to multiculturalism by White students, resistance among ethnic minorities is also an issue in multicultural courses. Such resistance is evidenced among ethnic minority students who are (a) still in denial of the importance of their ethnic minority status in this country (Atkinson et al., 1979; Cross, 1971, 1995; Parham, 1989), (b) simply tired of being the ethnic minority "educator" (Jackson, 1996; Mio & Awakuni, 2000), and (c) trying to get out of additional work (Mio & Awakuni, 2000).

The first form of ethnic minority resistance is an important one that cannot be ignored. Some ethnic minority students feel that they have never been the targets of racism, so racism must not exist. Others who have experienced racism and felt that they have overcome it have a sense that "if I overcame racism, then anyone can overcome racism." Still others may even feel that this is a White majority country, so ethnic minorities are not deserving of equal status. Many have felt that resistance from ethnic minority students is particularly difficult to address (personal communication from the Asian American Psychological Association listserv, 1998, 1999). If we were to consider this form of resistance to be an early stage or status in the ethnic minority identity development model, we can at least be mollified in the assumption that time will address this resistance. Even though this may not feel very good to us in the short run, it should theoretically turn out positively in the long run. As an illustration, I taught an undergraduate course in multiculturalism recently. There was one ethnic minority student who completely denied that racism existed in this country, and if it did, those who blamed a hindrance in their progress were "weak" and not deserving of anything better. Although other students in the class were visibly upset by this student, they were not able to break through his resistance. In his weekly reaction papers, he continued discounting the importance of racism. However, the next term, this student e-mailed me, apologizing for his behavior. He said that he had changed jobs, and he ran into racism that hindered his progress. He said that everything we had discussed in the class was true, and he was sorry that he had so vehemently denied the truths he now discovered.

The second form of resistance from ethnic minority students—that of being the class "educator"—is being voiced more and more. Often, students have felt that whenever issues of race/ethnicity were discussed in classes, other students would turn to them and ask them what their opinion was. The tenor of these discussions is, "What do people of your ethnicity think about this?" As McIntosh (1995) indicated, White individuals have the privilege of never being asked, "What do White people feel about this issue?" If one is White, one gets to express one's opinion as one's own, not as a representation of an entire people. Because ethnic minorities often feel that they are being asked to speak for their entire group, they sometimes shut down from this burden. Another reaction is anger that they have to educate otherwise bright individuals about issues of multiculturalism. They feel that they do not want to contribute to the intellectual laziness of their student colleagues because if they were truly interested in the answer to their questions, they would go out and research these answers on their own.

The third form of resistance from ethnic minority students—that of getting out of work—is disappointing for me to admit. However, the truth is that sometimes this happens. As discussed in the first section of this chapter, for years there was a fight for the inclusion of multicultural courses in graduate curricula. This fight was in part a response to some ethnic minority student complaints that courses in these curricula were not relevant to their existence or their communities. Now that multiculturalism is required in graduate training programs, some ethnic minority students feel that because of their personal experiences, they need not take such courses. As I stated elsewhere (Mio & Awakuni, 2000), I had a reputation of being a demanding instructor, and two ethnic minority students asked both the director of graduate training and me if they could be given credit for having fulfilled the multicultural requirement because they had a multicultural course at the undergraduate level from a well-respected leader in the field. Although we allowed them to receive such credit, two other ethnic minority students who had taken the same course also took my course, and they felt that they gained immeasurable knowledge from it.

In addressing these latter two forms of resistance, I would recommend that instructors particularly watch themselves when they call on ethnic minority students for their opinions. Questions should always be framed as "What do *you* feel?" as opposed to "What do *your people* feel?" Instructors should also be advocates for ethnic minority students when other students ask well-intentioned but naive questions that hint of the ethnic minority student speaking for everyone in their ethnic minority group. With respect to the resistance of trying to get out of work, I would suggest that instructors recognize that identity development is a process that takes time and maturity. Students who may have felt that they understood issues at the undergraduate level are much more mature at the graduate level, and another look at the same issues may be understood in a totally different light. Also, I know that for myself, I assign much more work at the graduate level, and I have much higher expectations for my graduate students than for my undergraduate students.

THE USE OF FILMS TO UNDERSCORE COURSE MATERIAL

As I have stated elsewhere (Mio & Awakuni, 2000; Mio & Morris, 1990), many videotapes are available to help supplement courses in multiculturalism. Others have advocated the use of videotapes as well (Pinterits & Atkinson, 1998; Williams, 1999). Some films I have found to be of particular value include *Eyes on the Prize* (Hampton, 1986), *The Color of Fear*

(Lee, 1994), *Black in White America* (Nunn, 1989), and *A Class Divided* (Peters, 1985). Other commercially released films that have also contributed to my students' understanding of multicultural issues include *Stand and Deliver, My Family/Mi Familia,* and *Who Killed Vincent Chin?* Finally, a series of videotapes by APA Division 45 and Microtraining Associates, Inc. (2000) has been developed to demonstrate culturally competent therapy. In this series of videotapes, ethnic minority therapists discuss theoretical issues involved in culturally competent therapy and act out therapy scenarios to demonstrate these issues.

The importance of these videotaped resources as an adjunct to multicultural courses is that they provide an emotionally evocative and dramatic component to these courses. Although the troubling experience of grappling with racism is also emotionally evocative, these videotaped resources present issues in a manner that is difficult to deny or resist. They pull for discussion as opposed to pushing for withdrawal. I have typically found vigorous discussion after showing these videotapes, and the reaction paper assignments I have students do on a weekly basis are generally in response to these videotapes and ensuing class discussions.

CONCLUSION

Teaching courses on multiculturalism presents challenges, difficulties, and opportunities. The profession of psychology itself has put up roadblocks along the way to the inclusion of multicultural issues throughout the years. However, even though many of these barriers have been removed, those who teach multicultural issues still encounter resistance to this material both from their colleagues and from students. These resistances are embedded within a cultural context of resistance to such issues. To the extent that these issues are addressed within the larger society, the teaching of multiculturalism will encounter less and less resistance.

This chapter was written with the assumption that many of those reading it may have never taught a course in multiculturalism before. Therefore, I have included models of teaching multiculturalism along with key issues covered in a course or curriculum in multiculturalism. Thus, I have tried to be as inclusive as possible in citing the relevant literature in the field. Such topics typically covered in courses on multiculturalism include assimilation/acculturation, intelligence testing, White privilege, racism, emic–etic distinctions, individualism–collectivism distinctions, research and methodological issues, racial identity, and norms, values, and other issues related to specific groups of diversity. These groups of diversity are broadening, including more than just ethnic minority populations, such as women, gays and lesbians, individuals with disabilities, and older adults. As the scope of diversity becomes larger and larger, one can truly see how this area is becoming a "fourth force" in psychology.

REFERENCES

Abeles, N., Cooley, S., Deitch, I. M., Harper, M. S., Hinrichsen, G., Lopez, M. A., & Molinari, V. A. (1998). What practitioners should know about working with older adults. *Professional Psychology: Research and Practice, 29,* 413-427.

Albee, G. W. (2000). The Boulder model's fatal flaw. *American Psychologist, 55,* 247-248.

Altmaier, E. M. (1993). Role of Criterion II in accreditation. *Professional Psychology: Research and Practice, 24,* 127-129.

American Psychological Association. (1986). *Accreditation handbook.* Washington, DC: Author.

Anderson, L. P. (1991). Acculturative stress: A theory of relevance to Black Americans. *Clinical Psychology Review, 11,* 685-702.

APA Division 45 & Microtraining Associates, Inc. (2000). *Culturally-competent counseling & therapy.* North Amherst, MA: Microtraining Associates, Inc.

Arredondo, P. (1994). Multicultural training: A response. *The Counseling Psychologist, 22,* 308-314.

Arredondo, P. (1998). Integrating multicultural counseling competencies and universal helping conditions in culture-specific contexts. *The Counseling Psychologist, 26,* 592-601.

Arredondo, P., Toporek, R., Brown, S. P., Jones, J., Locke, D. C., Sanchez, J., & Stadler, H. (1996). Operationalization of the multicultural counseling competencies. *Journal of Multicultural Counseling and Development, 24,* 24-78.

Asch, A., & Russo, H. (1985). Therapists with disabilities: Theoretical and clinical issues. *Psychiatry, 48,* 1-12.

Atkinson, D. R. (1985). A meta-review of research on cross-cultural counseling and therapy. *Journal of Multicultural Counseling and Development, 13,* 138-153.

Atkinson, D. R. (1993). Who speaks for cross-cultural counseling research? *The Counseling Psychologist, 21,* 213-217.

Atkinson, D. R. (1994). Multicultural training: A call for standards. *The Counseling Psychologist, 22,* 300-307.

Atkinson, D. R., Morten, G., & Sue, D. W. (1979). *Counseling American minorities: A cross-cultural perspective.* Dubuque, IA: W. C. Brown.

Atkinson, D. R., & Schein, S. (1986). Similarity in counseling. *The Counseling Psychologist, 14,* 319-354.

Attneave, C. (1982). American Indians and Alaska Native families: Emigrants in their own homeland. In M. McGoldrick, J. K. Pearce, & J. Giordano (Eds.), *Ethnicity & family therapy* (pp. 55-83). New York: Guilford.

Baker, D. B., & Benjamin, L. T. (2000). The affirmation of the scientist-practitioner: A look back at Boulder. *American Psychologist, 55,* 241-247.

Baptiste, D. A., Jr. (1993). Immigrant families, adolescents and acculturation: Insights for therapists. *Marriage & Family Review, 19,* 341-363.

Barker-Hackett, L. (1999). Cross-cultural training. In J. S. Mio, J. E. Trimble, P. Arredondo, H. E. Cheatham, & D. Sue (Eds.), *Key words in multicultural interventions: A dictionary* (pp. 57-58). Westport, CT: Greenwood.

Barnartt, S. (1996). Disability culture or disability consciousness. *Journal of Disability Policy Studies, 7,* 1-19.

Belar, C. D. (2000). Scientist-practitioner ≠ science + practice: Boulder is bolder. *American Psychologist, 55,* 249-250.

Benjamin, L. T., Jr., & Baker, D. B. (2000). Boulder at 50: Introduction to the section. *American Psychologist, 55,* 233-236.

Berg, I. K., & Jaya, A. (1993). Different and same: Family therapy with Asian-American families. *Journal of Marital and Family Therapy, 19,* 31-38.

Bernal, G., & Enchautegui, N. (1994). Latinos and Latinas in community psychology: A review of the literature. *American Journal of Community Psychology, 22,* 531-557.

Bernal, G., & Shapiro, E. (1996). Cuban families. In M. McGoldrick, J. Giordano, & J. K. Pearce (Eds.), *Ethnicity & family therapy* (2nd ed., pp. 155-168). New York: Guilford.

Bernal, M. E., & Padilla, A. M. (1982). Status of minority curricula and training in clinical psychology. *American Psychologist, 37,* 780-787.

Brown, L. S. (1994). *Subversive dialogues: Theory in feminist therapy.* New York: Basic Books.

Buriel, R. (1993). Childrearing orientations in Mexican American families: The influence of generation and sociocultural factors. *Journal of Cross-Cultural Psychology, 18*, 45-57.

Burkard, A. W., Ponterotto, J. G., Reynolds, A. L., & Alfonso, V. C. (1999). White counselor trainees' racial identity and working alliance perceptions. *Journal of Counseling and Development, 77*, 324-329.

Casas, J. M., Ponterotto, J. G., & Sweeney, M. (1987). Stereotyping the stereotyper: A Mexican American perspective. *Journal of Cross-Cultural Psychology, 18*, 45-57.

Casas, J. M., & San Miguel, S. (1993). Beyond questions and discussions, there is a need for action: A response to Mio and Iwamasa. *The Counseling Psychologist, 21*, 233-239.

Cass, V. C. (1979). Homosexual identity formation: A theoretical model. *Journal of Homosexuality, 4*, 219-235.

Cheatham, H. E. (1994). A response. *The Counseling Psychologist, 22*, 290-295.

Choney, S. K., Berryhill-Paapke, E., & Robbins, R. R. (1995). The acculturation of American Indians: Developing frameworks for research and practice. In J. G. Ponterotto, J. M. Casas, L. A. Suzuki, & C. M. Alexander (Eds.), *Handbook of multicultural counseling* (pp. 73-92). Thousand Oaks, CA: Sage.

Clark, R., Anderson, N. B., Clark, V. R., & Williams, D. R. (1999). Racism as a stressor for African Americans: A biopsychosocial model. *American Psychologist, 54*, 805-816.

Coleman, H. L. K. (1996). Portfolio assessment of multicultural counseling competency. *The Counseling Psychologist, 24*, 216-229.

Comas-Diaz, L., & Greene, B. (Eds.). (1994). *Women of color: Integrating ethnic and gender identities in psychotherapy.* New York: Guilford.

Comas-Diaz, L., & Jacobsen, F. M. (1991). Ethnocultural transference and counter-transference in the therapeutic dyad. *American Journal of Orthopsychiatry, 61*, 392-402.

Corvin, S., & Wiggins, F. (1989). An antiracism training model for White professionals. *Journal of Multicultural Counseling and Development, 17*, 105-114.

Council of National Psychological Associations for the Advancement of Ethnic Minority Interests. (2000). *Guidelines for research in ethnic minority communities.* Washington, DC: American Psychological Association.

Cross, W. E. (1971). The Negro-to-Black conversion experience: Toward a psychology of Black liberation. *Black World, 20*, 13-27.

Cross, W. E. (1995). The psychology of Nigrescence: Revising the Cross model. In J. G. Ponterotto, J. M. Casas, L. A. Suzuki, & C. M. Alexander (Eds.), *Handbook of multicultural counseling* (pp. 93-122). Thousand Oaks, CA: Sage.

D'Andrea, M., & Daniels, J. (1991). Exploring the different levels of multicultural counseling training in counselor education. *Journal of Counseling and Development, 70*, 78-85.

Dien, D. S.-F. (1999). Chinese authority-directed orientation and Japanese peer-group orientation: Questioning the notion of collectivism. *Review of General Psychology, 3*, 372-385.

Division 20. (1994). *Guide to doctoral study in the psychology of adult development and aging.* Washington, DC: Author.

Dovidio, J. F., & Gaertner, S. L. (Eds.). (1986). *Prejudice, discrimination and racism.* Orlando, FL: Academic Press.

Duffy, M. (Ed.). (1999). *Handbook of counseling and psychotherapy with older adults.* New York: John Wiley.

Enns, C. Z. (1993). Twenty years of feminist counseling and therapy: From naming biases to implementing multifaceted practice. *The Counseling Psychologist, 21,* 3-87.

Essandoh, P. K. (1996). Multicultural counseling as the "fourth force": A call to arms. *The Counseling Psychologist, 24,* 126-137.

Esten, G., & Willmott, L. (1993). Double bind messages: The effects of attitude towards disability on therapy. *Women & Therapy, 14,* 29-41.

Falicov, C. J. (1996). Mexican families. In M. McGoldrick, J. Giordano, & J. K. Pearce (Eds.), *Ethnicity & family therapy* (2nd ed., pp. 169-181). New York: Guilford.

Fischer, A. R., Jome, L. M., & Atkinson, D. R. (1998). Reconceptualizing multicultural counseling: Universal healing conditions in a culturally specific context. *The Counseling Psychologist, 26,* 525-588.

Fukuyama, M. A. (1994). Multicultural training: If not now, when? If not you, who? *The Counseling Psychologist, 22,* 296-299.

Garcia-Preto, N. (1996). Puerto Rican families. In M. McGoldrick, J. Giordano, & J. K. Pearce (Eds.), *Ethnicity & family therapy* (2nd ed., pp. 183-199). New York: Guilford.

Garrett, J. T., & Garrett, M. W. (1994). The path of good medicine: Understanding and counseling Native American Indians. *Journal of Multicultural Counseling and Development, 22,* 134-144.

Gatz, M., Fiske, A., Fox, L. S., Kaskie, B., Kasl-Godley, J. E., McCallum, T. J., & Wetherell, J. L. (1998). Empirically validated psychological treatments for older adults. *Journal of Mental Health and Aging, 4,* 9-46.

Gelso, C. J., Fassinger, R. E., Gomez, M. J., & Latts, M. G. (1995). Countertransference reactions to lesbian clients: The role of homophobia, counselor gender, and countertransference management. *Journal of Counseling Psychology, 42,* 356-364.

Gloria, A. M., Rieckmann, T. R., & Rush, J. D. (2000). Issues and recommendations for teaching an ethnic/culture-based course. *Teaching of Psychology, 27,* 102-107.

Golding, J. M., & Kraemer, P. J. (2000). Integrating psychology into a multidisciplinary-multicultural undergraduate program at a research I university. *Teaching of Psychology, 27,* 169-173.

Goldstein, S. (2000). *Cross-cultural explorations: Activities in culture and psychology.* Boston: Allyn & Bacon.

Gonsalves, C. J. (1992). Psychological stages of the refugee process: A model for therapeutic interventions. *Professional Psychology: Research and Practice, 23,* 382-389.

Gould, S. J. (1996). *The mismeasurement of man.* New York: Norton.

Greene, B. (1996). African American women. In L. Comas-Diaz & B. Greene (Eds.), *Women of color: Integrating ethnic and gender identities in psychotherapy* (pp. 10-29). New York: Guilford.

Greene, B. (Ed.). (1997). *Ethnic and cultural diversity among lesbians and gay men.* Thousand Oaks, CA: Sage.

Gushue, G. V. (1993). Cultural-identity development and family assessment: An interaction model. *The Counseling Psychologist, 21,* 487-513.

Guthrie, R. V. (1976). *Even the rat was White.* New York: Harper & Row.

Guthrie, R. V. (1998). *Even the rat was White* (2nd ed.). Boston: Allyn & Bacon.

Hampton, H. (Producer). (1986). *Eyes on the prize.* Boston: WGBH.

Harris, S. M. (1995). Psychosocial development and Black male masculinity: Implications for counseling economically disadvantaged African American male adolescents. *Journal of Counseling and Development, 73,* 279-287.

Hartman-Stein, P. E. (Ed.). (1998). *Innovative behavioral healthcare for older adults.* San Francisco: Jossey-Bass.

Hayes, J. A., & Erkis, A. J. (2000). Therapist homophobia, client sexual orientation, and source of client HIV infection as predictors of therapist reactions to clients with HIV. *Journal of Counseling Psychology, 47*, 71-78.

Hays, P. A. (1996). Addressing the complexities of culture and gender in counseling. *Journal of Counseling and Development, 74*, 332-338.

Heider, F. (1958). *The psychology of interpersonal relations.* New York: John Wiley.

Heinrich, R. K., Corbine, J. L., & Thomas, K. R. (1990). Counseling Native Americans. *Journal of Counseling and Development, 69*, 128-133.

Helms, J. E. (1984). Toward a theoretical explanation of the effects of race on counseling: Black/White interactional model. *The Counseling Psychologist, 12*, 153-165.

Helms, J. E. (1986). Expanding racial identity theory to cover counseling process. *Journal of Counseling Psychology, 33*, 62-64.

Helms, J. E. (1990). *Black and White racial identity: Theory, research and practice.* Westport, CT: Greenwood.

Helms, J. E. (1993). I also said, "White racial identity influences White researchers." *The Counseling Psychologist, 21*, 240-243.

Helms, J. E. (1995). An update of Helms's White and people of color racial identity models. In J. G. Ponterotto, J. M. Casas, L. A. Suzuki, & C. M. Alexander (Eds.), *Handbook of multicultural counseling* (pp. 181-191). Thousand Oaks, CA: Sage.

Helms, J. E., & Carter, R. T. (1991). Relationships of White and Black racial identity attitudes and demographic similarity to counselor preferences. *Journal of Counseling Psychology, 38*, 446-457.

Helms, J. E., & Cook, D. A. (1999). *Using race and culture in counseling and psychotherapy: Theory and process.* Boston: Allyn & Bacon.

Henwood, P. G., & Pope-Davis, D. B. (1994). Disability as cultural diversity. *The Counseling Psychologist, 22*, 489-503.

Herrnstein, R., & Murray, C. (1994). *The bell curve: Intelligence and class structure in American life.* New York: Free Press.

Hills, H. I., & Strozier, A. L. (1992). Multicultural training in APA-approved counseling psychology programs: A survey. *Professional Psychology: Research and Practice, 23*, 43-51.

Hines, P. M., & Boyd-Franklin, N. (1996). African American families. In M. McGoldrick, J. Giordano, & J. K. Pearce (Eds.), *Ethnicity & family therapy* (2nd ed., pp. 66-84). New York: Guilford.

Ho, D. Y. F. (1995). Internalized culture, culturocentrism, and transcendence. *The Counseling Psychologist, 23*, 4-24.

Hofstede, G. (1980). *Culture's consequences.* Beverly Hills, CA: Sage.

Hofstede, G. (1982). *Cultural pitfalls for Dutch expatriates in Indonesia.* Maastricht, the Netherlands: Institute for Research on Intercultural Cooperation.

Hofstede, G. (1983). Dimensions of national cultures in fifty countries and three regions. In J. Deregowski, S. Dzuirawiee, & R. Annis (Eds.), *Explications in cross-cultural psychology* (pp. 335-355). Lisse, the Netherlands: Swets and Zeitlinger.

Hofstede, G., & Bond, M. H. (1984). Hofstede's cultural dimensions: An independent validation using Rokeach's Value Survey. *Journal of Cross-Cultural Psychology, 15*, 417-433.

Holcomb-McCoy, C. C., & Myers, J. E. (1999). Multicultural competence and counselor training: A national survey. *Journal of Counseling and Development, 77*, 294-302.

Hui, C. H., & Triandis, H. C. (1996). Individualism-collectivism: A study of cross-cultural researchers. *Journal of Cross-Cultural Psychology, 17*, 225-248.

Ivey, A. E. (1993). On the need for reconstruction of our present practice of counseling and psychotherapy. *The Counseling Psychologist, 21*, 225-228.

Ivey, A. E., Ivey, M. B., & Simek-Morgan, L. (1993). *Counseling and psychotherapy: A multicultural perspective.* Boston: Allyn & Bacon.

Jackson, L. C. (1996, August). Teaching diversity in clinical programs: Resistance and students of color. In J. S. Mio (Chair), *Institutional and individual resistances to multicultural issues—Discussions and interventions.* Symposium presented at the 106th annual convention of the American Psychological Association, Toronto, Canada.

Jones, E. E., & Davis, K. E. (1965). From acts to dispositions: The attribution process in person perception. In L. Berkowitz (Ed.), *Advances in experimental social psychology* (Vol. 2, pp. 219-266). New York: Academic Press.

Jones, J. M. (1972). *Prejudice and racism.* Reading, MA: Addison-Wesley.

Jones, J. M. (1997). *Prejudice and racism* (2nd ed.). New York: McGraw-Hill.

Kelley, H. H. (1967). Attribution theory in social psychology. In D. Levine (Ed.), *Nebraska Symposium on Motivation* (Vol. 15, pp. 192-241). Lincoln: University of Nebraska Press.

Kelley, H. H. (1972). Attribution in social interaction. In E. E. Jones, D. E. Kanouse, H. H. Kelley, R. E. Nisbett, S. Valins, & B. Weiner (Eds.), *Attribution: Perceiving the causes of behavior* (pp. 1-26). Morristown, NJ: General Learning Press.

Kelley, H. H. (1973). The process of causal attribution. *American Psychologist, 28,* 107-128.

Kemp, N., & Mallinckrodt, B. (1996). Impact of professional training on case conceptualization of clients with a disability. *Professional Psychology: Research and Practice, 27,* 378-385.

Kerwin, C., & Ponterotto, J. G. (1995). Biracial identity development: Theory and research. In J. G. Ponterotto, J. M. Casas, L. A. Suzuki, & C. M. Alexander (Eds.), *Handbook of multicultural counseling* (pp. 199-215). Thousand Oaks, CA: Sage.

Kiselica, M. S. (1998). Preparing Anglos for the challenges and joys of multiculturalism. *The Counseling Psychologist, 26,* 5-21.

Kluckhohn, F. R., & Strodtbeck, F. L. (1961). *Variations in value orientations.* Evanston, IL: Row, Paytterson, & Co.

Knight, B. G., Teri, L., Santos, J., & Wohlford, P. (Eds.). (1995). *Mental health services for older adults: Implications for training and practice in geropsychology.* Washington, DC: American Psychological Association.

Korman, M. (1973). *Levels and patterns of professional training in psychology.* Washington, DC: American Psychological Association.

Landrine, H. (Ed.). (1995). *Bringing cultural diversity to feminist psychology: Theory, research, and practice.* Washington, DC: American Psychological Association.

Lark, J. S., & Paul, B. D. (1998). Beyond multicultural training: Mentoring stories from two White American doctoral students. *The Counseling Psychologist, 26,* 33-42.

Lee, L. C., & Zane, N. W. S. (Eds.). (1998). *Handbook of Asian American psychology.* Thousand Oaks, CA: Sage.

Lee, M. W. (Producer and Director). (1994). *The color of fear* [Film]. (Available from Stir-Fry Productions, 1222 Preservation Park Way, Oakland, CA 94612.)

Leigh, I. W., Corbett, C. A., Gutman, V., & Morere, D. A. (1996). Providing psychological services to Deaf individuals: A response to new perceptions of diversity. *Professional Psychology: Research and Practice, 27,* 364-371.

Leong, F. T. L., Wagner, N. S., & Kim, H. H. (1995). Group counseling expectations among Asian American students: The role of culture-specific factors. *Journal of Counseling Psychology, 42,* 217-222.

Leung, P. K., & Boehnlein, J. (1996). Vietnamese families. In M. McGoldrick, J. Giordano, & J. K. Pearce (Eds.), *Ethnicity & family therapy* (2nd ed., pp. 295-306). New York: Guilford.

Mackelprang, R., & Salsgiver, R. (1999). *Disability: A diversity model approach in human service practice.* Pacific Grove, CA: Brooks/Cole.

Malgady, R. G. (1996). The question of cultural bias in assessment and diagnosis of ethnic minority clients: Let's reject the null hypothesis. *Professional Psychology: Research and Practice, 27,* 73-77.

McArthur, L. A. (1972). The how and what of why: Some determinants and consequences of causal attribution. *Journal of Personality and Social Psychology, 22*, 171-193.

McDavis, R. J., & Parker, M. (1977). A course on counseling ethnic minorities: A model. *Counselor Education & Supervision, 17*, 146-149.

McGoldrick, M., Giordano, J., & Pearce, J. K. (Eds.). (1996). *Ethnicity & family therapy* (2nd ed.). New York: Guilford.

McGoldrick, M., Pearce, J. K., & Giordano, J. (Eds.). (1982). *Ethnicity & family therapy.* New York: Guilford.

McGoldrick, M., & Rohrbaugh, M. (1997). Researching ethnic family stereotypes. *Family Process, 26*, 89-99.

McIntosh, P. (1988). *White privilege and male privilege: A personal account of coming to see correspondences through work in women's studies* (Working Paper No. 189). Wellesley, MA: Wellesley College.

McIntosh, P. (1995). White privilege and male privilege: A personal account of coming to see correspondences through work in women's studies. In M. L. Andersen & P. H. Collins (Eds.), *Race, class, and gender: An anthology* (pp. 76-87). Belmont, CA: Wadsworth.

McIntosh, P., & Hu-Dehart, E. (1998, February). *White privilege: Unpacking the invisible knapsack and proposing to distribute the contents: From the perspective of a White woman and a woman of color.* Paper presented at the Interactive Conference for Exploring Issues Related to White Racial Identity in the United States, Riverside, CA.

McNair, L. D. (1992). African American women in therapy: An Afrocentric and feminist synthesis. *Women & Therapy, 12*, 5-17.

McWhirter, J. J., & Ryan, C. A. (1991). Counseling the Navajo: Cultural understanding. *Journal of Multicultural Counseling and Development, 19*, 74-82.

Mendoza, R. H. (1989). An empirical scale to measure type and degree of acculturation in Mexican-American adolescents and adults. *Journal of Cross-Cultural Psychology, 20*, 372-385.

Merchant, N., & Dupuy, P. (1996). Multicultural counseling and qualitative research: Shared worldview and skills. *Journal of Counseling and Development, 74*, 537-541.

Mintz, L. B., Bartels, K. M., & Rideout, C. A. (1995). Training in counseling ethnic minorities and race-based availability of graduate school resources. *Professional Psychology: Research and Practice, 26*, 316-321.

Mio, J. S. (1989). Experiential involvement as an adjunct to teaching cultural sensitivity. *Journal of Multicultural Counseling and Development, 19*, 38-46.

Mio, J. S., & Awakuni, G. I. (2000). *Resistance to multiculturalism: Issues and interventions.* Philadelphia: Brunner/Mazel.

Mio, J. S., & Iwamasa, G. (1993). To do, or not to do: That is the question for White cross-cultural researchers. *The Counseling Psychologist, 21*, 197-212.

Mio, J. S., & Morris, D. R. (1990). Cross-cultural issues in psychology training programs: An invitation for discussion. *Professional Psychology: Research and Practice, 21*, 434-441.

Mio, J. S., Trimble, J. E., Arredondo, P., Cheatham, H. E., & Sue, D. (Eds.). (1999). *Key words in multicultural interventions: A dictionary.* Westport, CT: Greenwood.

Mok, T. A. (1998). Getting the message: Media images and stereotypes and their effect on Asian Americans. *Cultural Diversity and Mental Health, 4*, 185-202.

Mok, T. A. (1999). Asian American dating: Important factors in partner choice. *Cultural Diversity and Ethnic Minority Psychology, 5*, 103-117.

Nathan, P. E. (2000). The Boulder model: A dream deferred—or lost? *American Psychologist, 55*, 250-252.

Neville, H. A., Heppner, M. J., Louie, C. E., Thompson, C. E., Brooks, L., & Baker, C. E. (1996). The impact of multicultural training on White racial identity attitudes and therapy competencies. *Professional Psychology: Research and Practice, 27,* 83-89.

Niederehe, G., & Schneider, L. S. (1998). Treatment of depression and anxiety in the aged. In P. E. Nathan & J. M. Gorman (Eds.), *A guide to treatments that work* (pp. 270-287). New York: Oxford University Press.

Nunn, R. (1989). *Black in White America.* New York: American Broadcasting Corporation.

Okazaki, S. (1997). Sources of ethnic differences between Asian American and White American college students on measures of depression and social anxiety. *Journal of Abnormal Psychology, 106,* 52-60.

Organista, P. B., Chun, K. M., & Marín, G. (2000). Teaching an undergraduate course on ethnic diversity. *Teaching of Psychology, 27,* 12-17.

Pack-Brown, S. P. (1999). Racism and White counselor training: Influence of White racial identity theory and research. *Journal of Counseling and Development, 77,* 87-92.

Paniagua, F. A. (1994). *Assessing and treating culturally diverse clients.* Thousand Oaks, CA: Sage.

Parham, T. A. (1989). Cycles of psychological Nigrescence. *The Counseling Psychologist, 17,* 187-226.

Parham, T. A. (1993). White researchers conducting multicultural counseling research: Can their efforts be "mo betta"? *The Counseling Psychologist, 21,* 250-256.

Parker, W. M., Moore, M. A., & Neimeyer, G. J. (1997). Altering White racial identity and interracial comfort through multicultural training. *Journal of Counseling and Development, 76,* 302-310.

Payton, C. R. (1993). Review of APA accreditation Criterion II. *Professional Psychology: Research and Practice, 24,* 130-132.

Pedersen, P. (1977). The triad model of cross-cultural counselor training. *Personnel and Guidance Journal, 56,* 94-100.

Pedersen, P. (1988). *A handbook for developing multicultural awareness.* Alexandria, VA: American Association for Counseling and Development.

Pedersen, P. (1990). The multicultural perspective as a fourth force in counseling. *Journal of Mental Health Counseling, 12,* 93-95.

Pedersen, P. (1991). Multiculturalism as a generic approach to counseling. *Journal of Counseling and Development, 70,* 6-12.

Pedersen, P. (1993). The multicultural dilemma of White cross-cultural researchers. *The Counseling Psychologist, 21,* 229-232.

Pedersen, P. (1997). The cultural context of the American Counseling Association code of ethics. *Journal of Counseling and Development, 76,* 23-28.

Pedersen, P. (Ed.). (1999). *Multiculturalism as a fourth force.* Philadelphia: Brunner/Mazel.

Pedersen, P., Draguns, J. D., Lonner, W. J., & Trimble, J. E. (Eds.). (1996). *Counseling across cultures* (4th ed.). Thousand Oaks, CA: Sage.

Pedersen, P., Holwill, C. F., & Shapiro, J. (1978). A cross-cultural training procedure for classes in counselor education. *Counselor Education and Supervision, 17,* 233-237.

Pedersen, P., Lonner, W. J., & Draguns, J. G. (Eds.). (1976). *Counseling across cultures.* Honolulu: University of Hawaii Press.

Peters, W. (1985). A class divided. In D. Fanning (Producer), *Frontline.* Boston: WGBH.

Peterson, D. R. (2000). Scientist-practitioner or scientific practitioner? *American Psychologist, 55,* 252-253.

Peterson, R. L., Peterson, D. R., Abrams, J. C., & Stricker, G. (1997). The National Council of Schools and Programs of Professional Psychology education model. *Professional Psychology: Research and Practice, 28,* 373-386.

Pettigrew, T. F. (1979). The ultimate attribution error: Extending Allport's cognitive analysis of prejudice. *Personality and Social Psychology Bulletin, 5,* 461-476.

Pinderhughes, E. (1982). Afro-American families and the victim system. In M. McGoldrick, J. K. Pearce, & J. Giordano (Eds.), *Ethnicity & family therapy* (pp. 108-122). New York: Guilford.

Pinterits, E. J., & Atkinson, D. R. (1998). The diversity video forum: An adjunct to diversity sensitivity training in the classroom. *Counselor Education and Supervision, 37,* 203-216.

Ponterotto, J. G. (1988). Racial consciousness development among White counselor trainees: A stage model. *Journal of Multicultural Counseling and Development, 16,* 146-156.

Ponterotto, J. G. (1993). White racial identity and the counseling professional. *The Counseling Psychologist, 21,* 213-217.

Ponterotto, J. G., Casas, J. M., Suzuki, L. A., & Alexander, C. M. (Eds.). (1995). *Handbook of multicultural counseling.* Thousand Oaks, CA: Sage.

Ponterotto, J. G., & Pedersen, P. B. (1993). *Preventing prejudice.* Newbury Park, CA: Sage.

Ponterotto, J. G., & Sabnani, H. B. (1989). "Classics" in multicultural counseling: A systematic 5-year content analysis. *Journal of Multicultural Counseling and Development, 17,* 23-37.

Pope, M. (1994). The "salad bowl" is big enough for us all: An argument for the inclusion of lesbians and gay men in any definition of multiculturalism. *Journal of Counseling and Development, 73,* 301-304.

Pope-Davis, D. B., & Coleman, H. L. K. (1997). *Multicultural counseling competencies: Assessment, education and training, and supervision.* Thousand Oaks, CA: Sage.

Pope-Davis, D. B., Menefee, L. A., & Ottavi, T. M. (1993). The comparison of White racial identity attitudes among faculty and students: Implications for professional psychologists. *Professional Psychology: Research and Practice, 24,* 443-449.

Pope-Davis, D. B., Reynolds, A. L., Dings, J. G., & Nielson, D. (1995). Examining multicultural counseling competencies of graduate students in psychology. *Professional Psychology: Research and Practice, 26,* 322-329.

Pope-Davis, D. B., Reynolds, A. L., Dings, J. G., & Ottavi, T. M. (1994). Multicultural competencies of doctoral interns at university counseling centers: An exploratory investigation. *Professional Psychology: Research and Practice, 25,* 466-470.

Poston, W. S. C. (1990). The biracial identity development model: A needed addition. *Journal of Counseling and Development, 69,* 152-155.

Pratkanis, A. R., & Turner, M. E. (1994). The year Cool Papa Bell lost the batting title: Mr. Branch Rickey and Mr. Jackie Robinson's plea for affirmative action. *NINE: A Journal of Baseball History and Social Policy Perspectives, 2,* 260-276.

Quintana, S. M., & Bernal, M. E. (1995). Ethnic minority training in counseling psychology: Comparisons with clinical psychology and proposed standards. *The Counseling Psychologist, 23,* 102-121.

Raifman, L., & Vernon, M. (1996). Important implications for psychologists of the Americans With Disabilities Act: Case in point, the patient who is deaf. *Professional Psychology: Research and Practice, 27,* 372-377.

Ramirez, S. M., Wassef, A., Paniagua, F. A., & Linskey, A. O. (1996). Mental health providers' perceptions of cultural variables in evaluating ethnically diverse clients. *Professional Psychology: Research and Practice, 27,* 284-288.

Rickard, H. C., & Clements, C. B. (1993). Critique of APA accreditation Criterion II: Cultural and individual differences. *Professional Psychology: Research and Practice, 24,* 123-126.

Ridley, C. R. (1995). *Overcoming unintentional racism in counseling and therapy: A practitioner's guide to intentional intervention.* Thousand Oaks, CA: Sage.

Ridley, C. R., Mendoza, D. W., & Kanitz, B. E. (1994). Multicultural training: Reexamination, operationalization, and integration. *The Counseling Psychologist, 22,* 227-289.

Roades, L. A., & Mio, J. S. (2000). Allies: How are they created and what are their experiences? In J. S. Mio & G. I. Awakuni (Eds.), *Resistance to multiculturalism: Issues and interventions* (pp. 63-82). Philadelphia: Brunner/Mazel.

Robin, M. W., & Spires, R. (1983). Drawing the line: Deviance in cross-cultural perspective. *International Journal of Group Tensions, 13,* 106-131.

Rogers, M. R., Hoffman, M. A., & Wade, J. (1998). Notable multicultural training in APA-approved counseling psychology and school psychology programs. *Cultural Diversity and Mental Health, 4,* 212-226.

Rogers, M. R., Ponterotto, J. G., Conoley, J. C., & Wiese, M. J. (1992). Multicultural training in school psychology: A national survey. *School Psychology Review, 21,* 603-616.

Rooney, S. C., Flores, L. Y., & Mercier, C. A. (1998). Making multicultural education effective for everyone. *The Counseling Psychologist, 26,* 22-32.

Root, M. P. P. (Ed.). (1992). *Racially mixed people in America.* Newbury Park, CA: Sage.

Root, M. P. P. (Ed.). (1996). *The multiracial experience.* Thousand Oaks, CA: Sage.

Root, M. P. P. (1998). Experiences and processes affecting racial identity development: Preliminary results from the biracial sibling project. *Cultural Diversity and Mental Health, 4,* 237-247.

Ross, L. D. (1977). The intuitive psychologist and his shortcomings: Distortions in the attribution process. In L. Berkowitz (Ed.), *Advances in experimental social psychology* (Vol. 10, pp. 174-221). New York: Academic Press.

Routh, D. K. (2000). Clinical psychology training: A history of ideas and practices prior to 1946. *American Psychologist, 55,* 236-241.

Ryan, A. (1995). Apocalypse now? In R. Jacoby & N. Glauberman (Eds.), *The bell curve debate* (pp. 14-29). New York: Times Books.

Samuda, R. J. (1998). *Psychological testing of American minorities.* Thousand Oaks, CA: Sage.

Shon, S. P., & Ja, D. Y. (1982). Asian families. In M. McGoldrick, J. K. Pearce, & J. Giordano (Eds.), *Ethnicity & family therapy* (pp. 208-228). New York: Guilford.

Singelis, T. M. (Ed.). (1998). *Teaching about culture, ethnicity, & diversity: Exercises and planned activities.* Thousand Oaks, CA: Sage.

Smart, J. F., & Smart, D. W. (1995). Acculturative stress: The experience of the Hispanic immigrant. *The Counseling Psychologist, 23,* 25-42.

Sodowsky, G. R., Taffe, R. C., Gutkin, T. B., & Wise, S. L. (1992). Development of the Multicultural Counseling Inventory: A self-report measure of multicultural competencies. *Journal of Counseling Psychology, 41,* 137-148.

Sophie, J. (1985). A critical examination of stage theories of lesbian identity development. *Journal of Homosexuality, 12,* 39-51.

Steele, C. M., & Aronson, J. (1995). Stereotype threat and the intellectual test performance of African Americans. *Journal of Personality and Social Psychology, 69,* 797–811.

Stephan, C. W., & Stephan, W. G. (1989). After intermarriage: Ethnic identity among mixed-heritage Japanese-Americans and Hispanics. *Journal of Marriage and the Family, 51,* 507-519.

Storandt, M., & VandenBos, G. R. (Eds.). (1994). *Neuropsychological assessment of dementia and depression in older adults: A clinician's guide.* Washington, DC: American Psychological Association.

Stricker, G. (2000). The scientist-practitioner model: Ghandi was right again. *American Psychologist, 55,* 253-254.

Sue, D. W. (1978). Eliminating cultural oppression in counseling: Toward a general theory. *Journal of Counseling Psychology, 25,* 419-428.

Sue, D. W. (1991a). A conceptual model for cultural diversity training. *Journal of Counseling and Development, 70,* 99-105.

Sue, D. W. (1991b). *Counseling the culturally different: Theory & practice.* New York: John Wiley.

Sue, D. W. (1993). Confronting ourselves: The White and racial/ethnic-minority researcher. *The Counseling Psychologist, 21,* 244-249.

Sue, D. W. (1995). Toward a theory of multicultural counseling and therapy. In J. A. Banks & C. A. M. Banks (Eds.), *Handbook of research on multicultural education* (pp. 647-659). New York: Macmillan.

Sue, D. W., Arredondo, P., & McDavis, R. J. (1992). Multicultural competencies/ standards: A pressing need. *Journal of Counseling and Development, 70,* 477-486.

Sue, D. W., Bernier, J. B., Durran, M., Feinberg, L., Pedersen, P., Smith, E., & Vazquez-Nuttal, E. (1982). Position paper: Cross-cultural counseling competencies. *The Counseling Psychologist, 10,* 45-52.

Sue, D. W., Carter, R. T., Casas, J. M., Fouad, N. A., Ivey, A. E., Jensen, M., LaFromboise, T., Manese, J. E., Ponterotto, J. G., & Vazquez-Nuttal, E. (1998). *Multicultural counseling competencies: Individual and organizational development.* Thousand Oaks, CA: Sage.

Sue, D. W., & Sue, D. (1990). *Counseling the culturally different: Theory and practice* (2nd ed.). New York: John Wiley.

Sue, D. W., & Sue, D. (1999). *Counseling the culturally different: Theory and practice* (3rd ed.). New York: John Wiley.

Sue, S. (1977). Community mental health services to minority groups: Some optimism, some pessimism. *American Psychologist, 32,* 616-624.

Sue, S. (1999). Science, ethnicity, and bias: Where have we gone wrong? *American Psychologist, 54,* 1070-1077.

Sue, S., & Zane, N. (1987). The role of culture and cultural techniques in psychotherapy: A critique and reformulation. *American Psychologist, 42,* 37-45.

Suzuki, L. A., Meller, P. J., & Ponterotto, J. G. (Eds.). (1996). *Handbook of multicultural assessment: Clinical, psychological, and educational applications.* San Francisco: Jossey-Bass.

Swain, J., Finkelstein, V., French, S., & Oliver, M. (Eds.). (1993). *Disabling barriers—Enabling environments.* Newbury Park, CA: Sage.

Tafoya, N., & Del Vecchio, A. (1996). Back to the future: An examination of the Native American holocaust experience. In M. McGoldrick, J. Giordano, & J. K. Pearce (Eds.), *Ethnicity & family therapy* (2nd ed., pp. 45-54). New York: Guilford.

Tamura, T., & Lau, A. (1992). Connectedness versus separateness: Applicability of family therapy to Japanese families. *Family Process, 31,* 319-340.

Tatum, B. D. (1997). *"Why are all the Black kids sitting together in the cafeteria?" and other conversations about race.* New York: Basic Books.

Taylor, R. J., Chatters, L. M., Tucker, M. B., & Lewis, E. (1990). Developments in research on Black families: A decade review. *Journal of Marriage and the Family, 52,* 993-1014.

Ting-Toomey, S. (Ed.). (1994). *The challenge of facework.* Albany: State University of New York Press.

Triandis, H. C. (1989). The self and social behavior in differing cultural contexts. *Psychological Review, 96,* 506-520.

Triandis, H. C. (1995). *Individualism & collectivism.* Boulder, CO: Westview.

Triandis, H. C., & Berry, J. W. (Eds.). (1980). *Handbook of cross-cultural psychology: 2. Methodology.* Boston: Allyn & Bacon.

Triandis, H. C., Bontempo, R., Betancourt, H., Bond, M., Leung, K., Brenes, A., Georgas, J., Hui, C. H., Marin, G., Setiadi, B., Sinha, J. B. P., Verma, J., Spangenberg, J., Touzard, H., & de Montmollin, G. (1986). The measurement of etic aspects of individualism and collectivism across cultures. *Australian Journal of Psychology, 38,* 257-267.

Triandis, H. C., Bontempo, R., Villareal, M. J., Asai, M., & Lucca, N. (1988). Individualism and collectivism: Cross-cultural perspectives on self-ingroup relationships. *Journal of Personality and Social Psychology, 54*, 323-338.

Triandis, H. C., & Brislin, R. W. (Eds.). (1980). *Handbook of cross-cultural psychology: 5. Social psychology*. Boston: Allyn & Bacon.

Triandis, H. C., & Draguns, J. G. (Eds.). (1980). *Handbook of cross-cultural psychology: 6. Psychopathology*. Boston: Allyn & Bacon.

Triandis, H. C., & Heron, A. (Eds.). (1981). *Handbook of cross-cultural psychology: 4. Developmental issues*. Boston: Allyn & Bacon.

Triandis, H. C., & Lambert, W. W. (Eds.). (1980). *Handbook of cross-cultural psychology: 1. Perspectives*. Boston: Allyn & Bacon.

Triandis, H. C., & Lonner, W. (Eds.). (1980). *Handbook of cross-cultural psychology: 3. Basic processes*. Boston: Allyn & Bacon.

Triandis, H. C., McCusker, C., Betancourt, H., Iwao, S., Leung, K., Salazar, J. M., Seiadi, B., Sinha, J. B. P., Touzard, H., & Zaleski, Z. (1993). An etic-emic analysis of individualism and collectivism. *Journal of Cross-Cultural Psychology, 24*, 366-383.

Trimble, J. E., Fleming, C. M., Beauvais, F., & Jumper-Thurman, P. (1996). Essential cultural and social strategies for counseling Native American Indians. In P. B. Pedersen, J. G. Draguns, W. J. Lonner, & J. E. Trimble (Eds.), *Counseling across cultures* (4th ed., pp. 177-209). Thousand Oaks, CA: Sage.

Vargas, L. A., & Koss-Chioino, J. D. (Eds.). (1992). *Working with culture: Psychotherapeutic interventions with ethnic minority children and adolescents*. San Francisco: Jossey-Bass.

Vega, W. A. (1990). Hispanic families in the 1980s: A decade of research. *Journal of Marriage and the Family, 52*, 1015-1024.

Vontress, C. E. (1988). An existential approach to cross-cultural counseling. *Journal of Multicultural Counseling and Development, 16*, 73-83.

Weinrach, S. G., & Thomas, K. R. (1997). Diversity-sensitive counseling today: A postmodern clash of values. *Journal of Counseling and Development, 76*, 115-122.

Whaley, A. L. (2000). Sociocultural differences in the developmental consequences of the use of physical discipline during childhood for African Americans. *Cultural Diversity and Ethnic Minority Psychology, 6*, 5-12.

White, J. L. (1984). *The psychology of Blacks: An Afro-American perspective*. Englewood Cliffs, NJ: Prentice Hall.

White, J. L., & Parham, T. A. (1990). *The psychology of Blacks: An African-American perspective* (2nd ed.). Upper Saddle River, NJ: Prentice Hall.

White, J. L., Parham, T. A., & Ajamu, A. (1999). *The psychology of Blacks: An Afrocentric perspective* (3rd ed.). Upper Saddle River, NJ: Prentice Hall.

Williams, C. B. (1999). *The Color of Fear* and *Blue-Eyed*: Tools for multicultural counselor training. *Counselor Education and Supervision, 39*, 76-79.

Willie, C. V. (1995). The relativity of genotypes and phenotypes. *Journal of Negro Education, 64*, 267–276.

Worell, J., & Johnson, N. G. (Eds.). (1997). *Shaping the future of feminist psychology: Education, research, and practice*. Washington, DC: American Psychological Association.

Yuker, H. (Ed.). (1988). *Attitudes towards persons with disabilities*. New York: Springer.

Zarit, S. H., & Knight, B. G. (Eds.). (1996). *A guide to psychotherapy and aging: Effective clinical interventions in a life-stage context*. Washington, DC: American Psychological Association.

CHAPTER 6

Teaching Racial Identity Development and Racism Awareness
Training in Professional Psychology Programs

SHAWN O. UTSEY
Howard University

CAROL A. GERNAT
Seton Hall University

MARK A. BOLDEN
Howard University and Seton Hall University

The increasing racial, ethnic, and cultural diversity of the consumers of psychological services has forced mental health practitioners to seek new, more culturally appropriate techniques and interventions. Consequently, the past 25 years have witnessed an explosion in the counseling and applied psychology literature with regard to cross-cultural (*cross-cultural* and *multicultural* are used interchangeably throughout this chapter) counseling and training. With increased attention directed toward preparing counseling and psychology trainees (henceforth referred to as *trainees*) for work with diverse client populations, a number of scholars have developed models for graduate-level cross-cultural training (e.g., Carter, 1995; Johnson, 1982; Pedersen, 1973). A review of the literature revealed that early approaches to multicultural training (MCT) focused on increasing trainees' sensitivity and awareness to issues affecting

AUTHORS' NOTE: We thank Rheeda L. Walker for her editorial assistance with this chapter.

individuals from various racial/ethnic groups. This approach later evolved into teaching culturally specific knowledge and skills related to working with various racial/ethnic groups (Holcomb-McCoy & Myers, 1999). More recently, however, there has been a shift toward fostering trainees' self-awareness with regard to racism and racial identity development (Brown, Parham, & Yonker, 1996; Pack-Brown, 1999; Parker, Moore, & Neimeyer, 1998).

Despite the recent emphasis on racial identity development and racism awareness training, few graduate programs have actually developed a course focusing specifically on the trainee's racial awareness training. With few exceptions, most graduate training programs in counseling and professional psychology continue to offer MCT models that focus on increasing knowledge, developing awareness, and encouraging sensitivity. The purpose of this chapter is to discuss the historical evolution of cross-cultural training in professional psychology; introduce issues and concepts related to race, racial identity, and racism awareness in training; and present a model for a graduate course in racial identity development and racism awareness training. The course presented in this chapter is intended for graduate-level (master's and doctoral) professional training programs in counseling and psychology.

We begin this chapter by delineating our political and conceptual opposition to multiculturalism. Next, we provide the reader with a presentation of the developmental history of MCT in counselor education and professional psychology programs. As part of this discussion, the current status of MCT, as well as new directions in the discipline's development, is examined. Next, we present our model for teaching racial identity development and racism awareness in counselor training programs. A case study of the racial identity development and racism awareness course is offered to illustrate the challenges of racism awareness and racial identity training. The chapter concludes with some thoughts about the importance of increasing counselor trainees' awareness regarding issues related to race, racism, and racial identity in the psychotherapy process.

POLITICAL AND CONCEPTUAL CONCERNS WITH MULTICULTURALISM

Prior to discussing the evolution of the multicultural movement in professional psychology and counselor training programs, it is appropriate to first voice our fundamental objection to multiculturalism per se. As will be discussed below, the cross-cultural movement in part developed out of the demands made by African Americans during the 1960s and 1970s for racial equality. It is our position that the multiculturalism movement thwarted the attempts of African Americans to dismantle institutional racism in the United States. Multiculturalism dilutes demands for racial equality by advancing an all-inclusive, pluralistic (or multicultural) perspective (Helms, 1994). For example, a premise of multicultural counseling is that all counseling is multicultural when *culture* is broadly defined to include race, nationality, ethnicity, social class, gender, sexual orientation, and disability (Das, 1995).

Multiculturalism maintains the status quo because it generally tends to ignore oppression, White privilege, and White racism. There is no attempt to deconstruct the White ethnocentric (supremacist) epistemological, ontological, and axiological framework that undergirds White psychology (Akintunde, 1999). An example of the White supremacist assumptions inherent in multicultural counseling and psychology, as highlighted by Akintunde (1999), are its goals of helping White trainees understand and respect the culture of "others." This "otherization" (Akintunde, 1999) reinforces for Whites the notion that they are at the center of the universe and everyone else is a nonentity—"other." Consequently, scholars, educators, and clinicians must look beneath the surface-level, "feel-good" cosmetics of multiculturalism and examine the social and political mechanisms that maintain the status quo. This challenge is particularly important given that the majority of clients for whom multicultural training is intended to benefit are members of oppressed racial/ethnic/social groups.

DEVELOPMENTAL HISTORY OF MULTICULTURAL TRAINING

Black Psychology: The Beginning

Although seldom acknowledged, it was the struggle of African Americans for civil and human rights during the 1960s and 1970s that spawned the cross-cultural movement in counseling and psychology (Das, 1995). For example, during the 1968 American Psychological Association (APA) convention in San Francisco, a small cadre of Black psychologists (among them were Robert L. Williams, Charles Thomas, Ernestine Thomas, and Joseph L. White) convened a meeting with the larger group (approximately 200) of Black psychologists who were in attendance (Guthrie, 1998). They met to discuss their concerns regarding (a) the lack of diversity reflected in the APA governing body and workforce, (b) the lack of Blacks in graduate psychology training programs, (c) publication of racist scholarship in APA journals, and (d) the lack of attention given to minority concerns by the APA. It was out of these efforts that the National (now International) Association of Black Psychologists (ABPsi) was founded. Since its inception, ABPsi's charge has been to advocate on the behalf of the mental health needs of African Americans, to eradicate and counter racist interpretations of African American behavior, and to develop

new, more culturally appropriate theoretical frameworks for understanding the behavior of African Americans (Williams, 1981).

The activities of ABPsi had a tremendous impact on the field of psychology, particularly with regard to the emergence of multicultural counseling and psychology. From the outset, members of ABPsi challenged popular notions of Black behavior that had been propagated by racist factions in the mainstream psychology community (Guthrie, 1998; Williams, 1981). Deficit models that had proliferated in the professional journals and psychology texts of the day were rejected. Moreover, the members of ABPsi called for the development of psychological theories that were culturally applicable to African Americans (Williams, 1981).

Another milestone in the development of contemporary cross-cultural psychology was the publication of a 1970 *Ebony* magazine article titled "Toward a Black Psychology." The author, Joseph White, argued that it was not possible to understand the behavior of African Americans using traditional psychological theories developed by White psychologists to explain the behavior of White people (Guthrie, 1998). White (1984) further advanced this new direction in the study of Black behavior in *The Psychology of Blacks: An African American Perspective,* where he explored Black family life, Black language patterns, and Black philosophical ideas that had previously been ignored by the White psychological establishment. White's work set the stage for a host of scholars to advance their own theories espousing a cross-cultural framework for understanding the behavior of racial/ethnic groups in the United States.

Clemmont Vontress is another pioneer in the cross-cultural counseling movement. His article, titled "Counseling Negro Adolescents" and published in the *School Counselor* (see Vontress, 1967), represents some of the earliest scholarship espousing a culturally congruent counseling approach for working with specific racial/ethnic populations. Vontress was among the first to discuss how race affects the transference-countertransference dynamics of the White counselor–Black client counseling dyad (Vontress, 1971). In this article, he concluded that racial differences between the therapist and client impede the process of establishing a therapeutic rapport. Vontress (1971) was also among the first to identify issues related to racial identity development for African Americans engaged in the counseling process. Specifically, he noted that self-labeling (i.e., Black, Negro, or colored) was a reflection of the client's level of racial consciousness and had implications for establishing rapport in the counseling relationship. The work of Clemmont Vontress has played a major role in shaping the contemporary direction of multicultural training.

PIONEERING MULTICULTURAL TRAINING MODELS

Paul Pedersen is credited with developing one of the earliest MCT models for counselors (McRae & Johnson, 1991). The triad training method involves a cross-cultural counseling role-play that is videotaped. This technique requires the participation of three individuals, each functioning in a different role. One individual plays the role of counselor and the other, client. The third participant has a particularly interesting role in the triad training method, serving as either a supportive, pro-counselor ally or an anti-counselor antagonist. The role of this individual is to emphasize the importance of cultural issues relevant to the counseling process (Pedersen, 1973). The ally/antagonist is required to be from the same cultural background as the client. Following the role-play, students review the videotape and discuss their experiences in the counseling session. The discussion centers on the counselor's awareness of, and sensitivity to, the client's cultural background. Research

conducted on the triad training method found the technique to be effective for increasing counselor trainees' sensitivity and awareness in cross-cultural counseling situations (Sue, 1979).

The Minnesota Multiethnic Counselor Education Curriculum (MMCEC), developed by Samuel Johnson (1982), is the forerunner to contemporary multicultural training models that emphasize developing knowledge, skills, and awareness as prerequisites to achieving competence in cross-cultural counseling. A core component of Johnson's training model was the experiential exercises that allowed counselor trainees to apply the knowledge and skills they had acquired through the program's teaching modules. The MMCEC provided the groundwork for a two-part graduate course that Johnson would later develop. Part one of this course was didactic and included theory and research on topics related to cross-cultural counseling. The second part of the course was an experiential laboratory that provided counselor trainees with opportunities to explore cultural group differences and to enhance their intercultural communications skills (McRae & Johnson, 1991).

A significant pedagogical advancement in MCT was the recognition that simply teaching trainees about cultural factors of clients from a particular ethnic/racial group had limited value (McRae & Johnson, 1991; Richardson & Molinaro, 1996). Educators had similar reservations regarding the focus on teaching specific counseling skills for working with clients from diverse cultural groups (Carter, 1995). Similarly, it was acknowledged that simply increasing a trainee's sensitivity to cultural factors in the counseling relationship was inadequate for developing multicultural competence (Holcomb-McCoy & Myers, 1999). Instead, educators determined that self-awareness was a precursor to cross-cultural competence. To become culturally competent, trainees must engage in a systematic process of cultural self-analysis with the aim of discovering how their beliefs, cultural values, and worldview have been shaped by their cultural/race group (Carter, 1995; Richardson & Molinaro, 1996).

CONTEMPORARY STATUS OF MULTICULTURAL TRAINING

Most doctoral programs in counseling psychology require at least one course in multicultural counseling (Das, 1995; Kiselica, 1998). However, many scholars consider these efforts alone to be inadequate in preparing trainees for working with diverse racial and ethnic groups. Some proponents of cross-cultural counseling have advocated that issues related to race, ethnicity, gender, class, and sexual orientation be infused into all aspects of the training curriculum for counselors and psychologists (Das, 1995; Holcomb-McCoy & Myers, 1999). In fact, the accrediting organizations for counselors (Council of Accreditation of Counseling and Related Educational Programs [CACREP]) and psychologists (APA) have incorporated cross-cultural issues into their standards for evaluating the accreditation worthiness of training programs (Holcomb-McCoy & Myers, 1999). Both CACREP and APA require graduate training programs to go beyond the "single-course" approach to cross-cultural training (CCT) and ensure adequate representation throughout the training curriculum (APA, 1993; CACREP, 1988). Despite these mandates, many counseling and psychology training programs have been slow in adhering to even the minimal standards set forth by their respective accrediting bodies.

With regard to pedagogy, most counseling and psychology training programs adhere to a *generic* framework that assumes the universal application of psychological theory to all human beings without regard to culture (Ridley, Mendoza, & Kanitz, 1994). Moreover, the generic or modernist approach operates from a Western, Eurocentric framework for assessing and treating human beings

from diverse backgrounds (Akintunde, 1999). Unquestioned by practitioners and trainees alike, the generic approach functions to maintain the status quo. An *etic* approach is similar to the generic approach, except that a deliberate effort is made to avoid cultural encapsulation and ethnocentrism. In contrast, *emic* approaches view training goals and outcome criteria as being grounded in the value system, behavioral patterns, and worldview of a given cultural group (Ridley et al., 1994).

A review of the multicultural counseling literature indicated that most contemporary training models focus on developing the knowledge, skills, and awareness of trainees. A more recent study conducted by Holcomb-McCoy and Myers (1999) found the knowledge/skills/awareness model to be inadequate in its ability to represent all the domains of cross-cultural competence. They recommended the inclusion of racial identity and definitions of important multicultural concepts as components contributing to multicultural competence in this area. Many scholars and educators consider racial identity development (i.e., achieving a nonracist White identity) as the most important contribution to CCT technology in the past decade (Helms, 1994; Holcomb-McCoy & Myers, 1999; Kiselica, 1998; Ponterotto, 1988; Richardson & Molinaro, 1996). Since 1990, several texts have been devoted entirely to the subject of race and racial identity in the psychotherapy process (see Carter, 1995; Helms, 1990; Helms & Cook, 1999). This trend provides a glimpse of what the future holds for CCT for counselors and psychologists.

NEW DIRECTIONS IN MULTICULTURAL COUNSELOR TRAINING

Racial Identity Development

Because the majority of cross-cultural counseling situations consist of the White therapist and the global majority person (misnamed "person of color" and "ethnic minority") dyad, the focus of this discussion will center on the inclusion of White racial identity models in the MCT curriculum. Janet Helms, considered by many to be the mother of White racial identity theory, developed one of the first conceptual frameworks for understanding the process by which Whites come to terms with their "White-ness" and work toward developing a nonracist identity (Helms, 1990). She postulated that because racism is embedded into the social and cultural milieu of the United States, the racial identity of Whites develops as a sense of superiority relative to other racial groups. Consequently, a goal of White racial identity development training is to assist Whites in developing a nonracist racial identity (Helms, 1990).

The White racial identity model posited by Helms (1990) initially consisted of a five-stage cognitive model describing the phases Whites experienced as they moved toward a nonracist identity. She later expanded her model to include six statuses (formerly stages) that delineate the abandonment of racism by Whites (Helms, 1995). The six statuses of White racial identity development are as follows: (a) Contact, (b) Disintegration, (c) Reintegration, (d) Pseudo-Independence, (e) Immersion-Emersion, and (f) Autonomy (see Helms, 1995, for a complete description of the six statuses). According to Helms (1990), the six statuses comprise the following two themes: (a) the abandonment of racism (Contact, Disintegration, and Reintegration) and (b) the development of a positive, nonracist White identity (Pseudo-Independence, Immersion-Emersion, and Autonomy). Research has consistently demonstrated that the racial identity of White trainees benefits (i.e., moves toward a nonracist identity) from MCT (Holcomb-McCoy & Myers, 1999; Parker et al., 1998).

Racism Awareness Training

Racism permeates the social and cultural fabric of the United States and is deeply embedded in the collective psyche of White America. All of society's social and cultural institutions abound with the mechanism of racism and oppression (Akintunde, 1999). Moreover, according to D'Andrea and Daniels (1991), all members of the dominant (White Anglo) culture have racist tendencies. Given these assertions, it follows that trainees are not immune to the omnipresence of racism and White supremacy. Therefore, MCT instructors are ethically bound to explore issues related to racism and White privilege as part of the MCT experience. To do so, however, requires that the instructors themselves be prepared to address their own racist attitudes and beliefs (Kiselica, 1998). Furthermore, it is essential that MCT instructors create a psychologically safe environment where trainees can confront their racism without the fear of being judged. Trainees who have had an opportunity to examine their tendencies to think, feel, and behave in racist ways will likely be more effective in working with racially and ethnically diverse client populations (Constantine, 1999).

Locke and Kiselica (1999) provided several strategies for teaching about racism in a cross-cultural counseling course. First, the instructor must be willing to relinquish power and move away from the comfort of traditional didactic teaching models. The trainees are encouraged to take responsibility for their own learning and must actively participate in classroom discussions. The course instructor must be supportive and should not hesitate to model what is expected behavior by sharing personal stories of how he or she has struggled and continues to struggle to confront his or her own racism. Course objectives should be clearly delineated and linked to measurable outcomes related to cross-racial counseling competence. Teaching strategies should be flexible and varied. The course instructor is responsible for keeping students focused on issues related to race and racism or related topics (e.g., White privilege). In our own racism and racial identity course (chronicled later in this chapter), we have noted the tendency by White trainees to prefer discussions of ethnicity, gender, social class, sexual orientation, and so on, over potentially charged discussions related to race and racism. Managing the anxiety and related feelings associated with such a highly volatile subject matter will be challenging, and the course instructor must be diligent in ensuring the psychological safety of the students and self. Furthermore, it would be wise for professors to secure the support and backing of one's program, department, and school before undertaking the risky but necessary business of confronting racism and White privilege.

Teachers College Training Model

Robert Carter has been teaching a course on racism and racial identity for the past 15 years at Columbia University's Teachers College. The course, initiated by Samuel Johnson, consists of a didactic component and an experiential lab. All doctoral and master's students are required to take the course sequence, and failure to obtain a passing grade results in having to repeat the course. The racism and racial identity course is intended to increase trainees' awareness of the role of racial and social factors in the psychotherapy relationship and process (Carter, 1995).

Conceptually, Carter's racism and racial identity course sequence (i.e., didactic lecture and experiential lab) is grounded in the *race-based approach* to the racially inclusive model of psychotherapy (Carter, 1995). The race-based approach asserts that sociopolitical history and intergroup power dynamics are central to understanding the culture and worldview of global majority peoples. Moreover, race-based theorists posit that variations in culture occur as a result of the sociopolitical racial categories assigned to

individuals who are phenotypically distinct from White Anglo-Americans. A core assumption of the race-based approach to CCT, though controversial, is that membership in a devalued racial group is the most defining experience for an individual living in the United States. It also assumes that White trainees are the beneficiaries of undeserved privileges associated with belonging to the dominant social and cultural group (Carter, 1995). Typically, White trainees functioning in the contact status of racial identity are oblivious to the privileges received because of their race-group membership (Helms, 1990). Therefore, it is incumbent on MCT instructors to employ race-based approaches to CCT in an effort to raise trainees' consciousness regarding racism and factors relating to racial identity development (Carter, 1995).

As previously mentioned, the Teachers College racism and racial identity course sequence is delivered in the form of a didactic course and experiential lab. The didactic course provides a theoretical foundation for understanding racism, racial identity, and related concepts (e.g., White privilege, oppression, "isms," etc.) in the psychotherapy process (Carter, 1995). The racial-cultural counseling lab, as it is referred to at Teachers College, consists of group discussions, lectures, and skill-building sessions. In the small-group experience, trainees are engaged in discussion (through the use of a structured interview protocol) regarding the salience of their group identities (e.g., race, ethnicity, sex, sexual orientation, etc.). Trainees are given feedback concerning their progress in developing racial-cultural competencies throughout the lab experience. The criterion for demonstrating racial-cultural counseling competence is the ability to integrate one's understanding of issues related to reference group factors into counseling interactions, skill sessions, and at a personal level (Carter, 1995).

A MODEL FOR TEACHING RACISM AWARENESS AND RACIAL IDENTITY

Overall Course Philosophy and Rationale

White power and privilege pervade the training atmosphere in a myriad of ways such that the trauma of racism and the eventual recovery process are avoided. For example, MCT is typically understood in a conventional context. That is, courses are often constructed and instructed according to a survey paradigm with emphasis on student presentation of a chosen culture. Diversity is often conceptualized by counting practicum clients who were of a different racial and ethnic heritage than the counselor's own. These perspectives discourage introspection, and students, in conjunction with their supervisors and faculty, do not look within to their own cognitive schema to be responsible for their racism and its transformation. It is infinitely easier to maintain this privileged stance than it is to confront one's own participation in institutionalized racism. It is also safer to consider the difficulties of European ethnic groups in their struggles to become assimilated—in essence, to have one's family pain validated. In so doing, the boundaries of White hegemony remain invincible because Whites do not move past internal defenses to the discovery that they may not be special, unique, entitled. The largely unquestioned "White privilege" underpinning to multicultural training is maintained when practitioners do not open to critical examination of their own racial identities.

For these reasons, a course was designed that represented a shift in consciousness in a department of professional psychology in a small, Catholic university in the Northeast, through which students would be introduced to race and racial identity in counseling. In contrast to being conducted in lab format, this course was delivered in didactic style, and a lab was considered as an additional component for future versions of the course. The readings were chosen to normalize anxiety given the unlikelihood that students had previously engaged in guided explorations of race and racial identity in a counseling context. This was an attempt to balance self-observation and inquiry with provocative subject material and class discussions. Although open to all graduate students in professional psychology, the course was required for first-year doctoral students in the Counseling Psychology Program. Moreover, given the racial composition of the student cohort, it was anticipated that the class would be primarily composed of White students. The sections that follow represent the general design of the course, including the opening, and brief overviews of the modules of (a) White privilege, (b) power, (c) history, (d) worldview conceptualizations, and (e) racial identity development theory. Finally, special considerations and implications for training are discussed with particular attention devoted to resistance.

The course was developed and run in fall 1998, and Locke and Kiselica (1999) touched on many of the same points in their article concerning teaching about racism in cross-cultural counseling courses. For example, racism was defined, and the chief responsibility for its transformation was located with Whites. Similarly, privilege was considered along with merit in both courses. We integrated the concepts of privilege and power to further understand the proliferation of institutional racism in addition to the affects of the power-privilege matrix on the counseling relationship. In contrast to Locke and Kiselica, the course we created did not use in-class exercises to more deeply probe beliefs in class; rather, guest speakers and structured class discussions were selected as first-line techniques to trigger initial self-observation. Moreover, given that the entire course was devoted to race and racial identity in counseling, modules highlighting historical foundations of race relations, worldview conceptualizations, and racial identity development were included to complete the course.

COURSE CONTENT AREAS

Opening of the Course

We begin this section in similar fashion to the approach taken in the opening class—by defining *racism*. At its core, racism is the abuse of power by a privileged group relative to arbitrarily assigned out-groups. In the United States, this distinction is based on skin color in conjunction with other physical characteristics socially constructed to define race, as noted by Helms (1995), whereby Whites enjoy privilege based on physical features as opposed to merit. Because Whites benefit from institutionalized racism, automatically and most often unconsciously, only Whites can be racist, as noted by the National Education Association (1973). Furthermore, we assumed that racism is a matter of degree, rejecting the notion that some Whites are somewhat racist some of the time. Rather, the question we posed to White counselors is, "How are you racist?" in contrast to, "Are you racist?" We constructed parameters as broad and inclusive as these so that White trainees could see their personal collusion in maintaining racism (i.e., White privilege).

This catalyst to self-examination is in marked contrast to definitions that distinguish between forms of racism such as *overt, covert, individual,* or *institutional.* In a training context, definitions of racism that locate responsibility for racism and its eradication on Whites are often experienced as attacking and traumatic, as evidenced by shouting, red faces, angry silence, and so on. These definitions directly challenge the privilege that Whites have enjoyed such that they have not had to confront, acknowledge, and work through the pain of racism and their responsibility for its maintenance. hooks (1992) illustrated this phenomenon in describing heated classroom debates during which Whites often react with disbelief, shock, and rage when Black students discuss representations of Whiteness in the Black perspective (e.g., terror, mystery). Often, rage erupts, according to hooks, because the White students believe that ways of examining difference threaten the liberal notion that we are all the same, and sameness equals Whiteness. This pluralistic fantasy, held in place by White privilege and power, is what Whites think will make racism disappear.

White Privilege and Power

The course continued with a discussion of White privilege and power, with a focus on the work of McIntosh (1989), who suggested that White privilege is an invisible package of unearned assets that Whites are carefully taught not to acknowledge. McIntosh also noted that this obliviousness is itself oppressive. In a training context, White privilege is exemplified in various ways, such as Whites speaking for themselves as individuals, not as representatives of the White race. In addition, White trainees are often not confronted by their White supervisors concerning their roles in the failures of cross-racial counseling relationships. Failures are most often attributed to the client's pathology. Moreover, if a White student complains about a Black professor, the White student can most often expect that the person hearing the complaint is White, and his or her success in the program will not be threatened by such action. This is not the case, however, for the Black professor, who would likely be censored in some way. Congruent with McIntosh's thoughts on White privilege and socialization, Dobbins and Skillings (2000) proposed that this position of privilege and dominance isolates Whites in such a way that a sense of entitlement and self-centeredness is activated. This then gives rise to an emerging compulsion to eliminate or explain away threats to an illusory sense of a morally superior order. Perhaps, then, these illusory constellations form the fuel for resistance commonly encountered in courses of this kind.

Pinderhughes (1989) offered a paradigm through which the complexities of power dynamics in the context of race and ethnicity may be explored. Most important, this work was chosen because it examines the relationship between power and anxiety, and consequently, students may be able to process thoughts and feelings that may arise in this regard without necessarily relying on automatic defensive reactions. Nevertheless, Pinderhughes's guide for understanding power, race, and ethnicity in clinical situations is practical and grounded in experience and thus lent itself to this course.

A number of clinician reactions to power and powerlessness may be observed whereby therapeutic effectiveness is hampered. Pinderhughes (1989) made the point that gratification derived from dominant, power-over positions is less easily acknowledged than is the pleasure experienced as the result of competence, and often, individuals in dominant power roles attempt to deny they have power. Thus, ambivalence concerning one's power can jeopardize clinical efficacy. Another troublesome reaction to power, as noted by Pinderhughes, is guilt, which in clinical work may motivate therapists to overcompensate, thus trapping the client into being less competent and autonomous. Also according to Pinderhughes, Whites, because they are in positions of power reinforced by systemic racism, learn and subsequently teach other Whites that they are entitled and superior. This position is illusory, so, by definition, Whites learn to distort reality. Paradoxically, in training situations, when required to confront their own racism, those in power are vulnerable to feelings of powerlessness. It is not uncommon that they project these feelings onto the instructor or onto

students, faculty, or global majority clients, thus managing their anxiety and maintaining a dominant stance. Pinderhughes posited that when one is accustomed to having power, any infringement of it is experienced as severe. Moreover, powerlessness, pain, and vulnerability may be denied. Clearly, then, a desirable objective of counselor training is the examination of the power-powerlessness matrix, taking racial identity into consideration.

History

Given the current state of race relations, a module concerning the racial history of the United States, in addition to an overview of the history of racism worldwide, was incorporated into the design of this course. Typically, Whites are undereducated and thus removed from the genocidal atrocities of American slavery and the institutionalization of racism. If we were to ask a group of Whites, even a group of White trainees, about the White history of the United States, the question would likely be met with shock and/or confusion. It may even be seen as reverse racism. On the other hand, Whites may understand the question as being related to the immigrant history of Europeans. That is, it would not be seen as racial history, or memory, but one of ethnicity—thus denying the role, at the collective level, that Whites have played in establishing and maintaining racism in this society. Furthermore, reactions to this question would be related to the notion that the unspoken counterpart to *White* is the word *supremacist*, or its synonyms. The brutal legacy of American racism is terrifying to consider, particularly for those Whites who construct defensive arrays to protect the "good self." This terror is then projected onto (or into) others, most notably Blacks. Similarly, hooks (1992) noted that Whiteness is represented in the Black imagination as terror. She suggested that the written histories of the past must be faced, given that the past has been reinvented to make the current illusion of racial harmony more plausible.

Worldview Conceptualizations

The work of Myers (Myers, 1988; Myers et al., 1991) was selected to continue to develop an understanding of the conceptual systems that form the foundations of worldview. Grounded in Afrocentric epistemology, the optimal conceptual system is a holistic paradigm in which connectedness transcends time, space, and external experience. Therefore, by definition, the optimal worldview is spiritual in nature. On the other hand, the suboptimal conceptual system is a fragmented worldview that is essentially externally focused and materialistic. Myers et al. (1991) emphasized that race does not determine one's underlying conceptual system; rather, it is the degree of adherence to a self-alienating framework that is the salient factor. This point in the course represented a conceptual shift to a more individual understanding of one's underlying schema and its connection to the wider social environment. The stage is now set to wrap up the course by focusing on the development of one's own racial identity.

Racial Identity Development

Racial identity development theory was integrated into the course to examine our evolution as racial beings. Although other models of Whiteness exist (e.g., Hardiman, 1982; Ponterotto, 1988), Helms's (1990, 1995) model was used particularly because racial identity development is understood as being a dynamic process in which Whites develop a sense of Whiteness in the context of "meaningful" interracial contact. There are two superstages—abandoning racism and developing a nonracist White identity, whereby automatic mechanisms for processing race-related stimuli are abandoned in favor of

more complex, flexible strategies. Similarly, Cross (1971) developed a model of Black racial identity in which the general developmental issue for Blacks is surmounting internalized racism in its various manifestations. To present a more complete picture of Africanity, we presented a module such that Black identity was not assumed to develop in relation to Whites. Rather, African self-consciousness and the African self-extension orientation (Kambon, 1992) were incorporated into the course design. This model highlights the spiritual-centered worldview that forms the foundation of the African personality, absent the influence of Whites.

SPECIAL CONSIDERATIONS AND IMPLICATIONS FOR TRAINING

Addressing the psychological configuration of anxiety, defense, guilt, and shame in a training context poses a number of significant challenges, particularly because Whites are also often in positions of power in professional psychology training programs. As Skillings and Dobbins (1991) noted, even in monoracial situations, feelings of shame and guilt that arise may be intense and difficult to work through. When global majority people are present, an array of reactions may arise. For example, some Whites may be completely unable to confront their racism, whereas others may seek absolution for past (or current) wrongs. In addition, global majority peoples in a mixed-race training context may be set up by the group to speak as authorities for their entire race. Therefore, it may be argued that course content is a secondary consideration to context in terms of departmental politics and support of the course (or lack thereof). In addition, history of MCT in the program, choice and qualifications of facilitators, supervision of the course if applicable, grades, course requirements, and the integration of global majority students and Whites should be well thought out in the design process.

Psychological Defense Mechanisms and Whiteness

Given the defensive posture many students assume in courses of this kind, the work of Thompson and Neville (1999), which outlined a number of ego defenses used by Whites to preserve racism, may be used to identify them in the training context. *Denial* and *selective attention* are believed to be the most pervasive and primitive ego defenses used by Whites to avoid the distress associated with race-related anxiety. Denial is characterized by attempts to suppress from one's consciousness the painful realities of racism. Selective attention, on the other hand, refers to the tendency of Whites to attend to certain realities of racism while ignoring the more harsh and painful truths about racism's insidiousness. *Rationalization* or *transference of blame* occurs when Whites present "reasonable" justifications for the racial inequalities that exist in society. This defensive style often includes placing blame for these inequalities on members of the oppressed groups themselves. The defensive style of *intellectualization* is characterized by an acknowledgment of racism's existence but without any affective connection to its deleterious effects on global majority people. *Identification* or *introjection* is reflected in the attempts by Whites to identify with or adopt various aspects of the behaviors, attitudes, and cultural practices of global majority people. Last, *projection* is the psychological process used by Whites to relocate undesirable and despised self-aspects or in-group characteristics onto global majority people. Constantine (1999) echoed these notions, suggesting that denial or minimization of the impact of racism may be used as defenses against both the reality of racism and the benefits derived from White privilege, particularly in earlier stages of racial self-awareness.

CASE STUDY

This section presents a case study of the racism and racial identity course referenced in the prior section. The course is analyzed through racial identity statuses (Helms, 1990, 1995) and uses journal notes from the African American male student in the course. The terms *African American, African Caribbean, Asian American, Iranian American,* and *European American* are used to respect the differences in ethnic realities of the individuals in the course. However, when race is salient, the terms *Black, White,* and *Asian* are used.

Background Information

Students

There were 10 students in the class, including 1 master's-level African American male; 1 post-master's-level African Caribbean female; 4 doctoral European American females, 3 of whom were in the Counseling Psychology Program (CP); 1 doctoral Asian American (CP) female; 1 doctoral Iranian American female (CP); and 2 doctoral European American males (CP).

Course

The course, which had been defunct for numerous years, was listed as "Cross-Cultural Psychology" but taught as "Race and Racial Identity." Attendance counted for full class participation credit. This requirement sought to lessen the potential discomfort by allowing silence as an outlet and appeared to make the classroom less competitive.

The Experience

Initial Dynamics

The first-year CP students comprised the core of the class, as did the theme of Whiteness among students and professor. Among the White students, a first-year cohort developed. The presence of a first-year cohort also created dynamics with other students due to the cohort and racial coalition salience. This was observable by the seating arrangements in which the three White females in the first year sat next to each other and on the same side with the White female in the clinical program and the Iranian female in the CP cohort. On the other side of the table were the two White males, the professor, the two Black students, and the Asian student.

First Class

The first task was to complete a racial identity scale. However, the professor neglected to have any of the Black Racial Identity Attitude Scales (BRIAS) available; hence, the Asian female and the Black male and female students had to wait while the White students completed the White Racial Identity Attitude Scales (WRIAS). This appeared to foreshadow the focus on attending to the issues that White students present in racial dynamics. Shortly after the White students began completing the WRIAS, the professor handed the BRIAS to the Asian American, African American, and African Caribbean students with an apology. In hindsight, the Asian female may have been offended by having to take a racial identity scale that did not measure Asian identity. However, the turn of events appeared to validate the African American and African Caribbean and Asian students in ways unbeknownst to anyone.

A climax came soon after scale completion. At this point, the professor defined racism and allowed dialogue to ensue. A few of the White students in the first-year cohort immediately became defensive toward the definition. Setting the semester tone, an atmosphere of anxiety led to various outward expressions of hostility, discomfort, and validation seeking from the majority of the White students. The Asian female, the African American male, and the Caribbean American female hesitated to speak while the class discussed racism. To the African American male, this appeared to be an issue for Whites to discuss because their defensiveness could result in backlash (Jackson, 1998) against him through racial/cultural transference.

The White students appeared to be in the Pseudo-Independence status as viewed by the rationalizations against a racist status, which failed to examine the possible veracity of an "all Whites are racist" premise, inherently suggesting that they could not be racist. The defensive posture was predictable due to the students' naïveté of racism as a function of White skin privilege and a matter of degree. Moreover, the professor's confrontational approach compounded the defensiveness and forced some White students to examine their Whiteness, consequently inducing a spontaneous Contact experience.

The term *racist* appeared to cause some students to fight for their self-esteem, which apparently could not coexist with being a racist. Thus, in losing the "good self" position, students sought self-validation through asserting the historical struggles of the respective ethnic groups. However, the denial of self as racist due to Whiteness was also an expression of the discomfort with self as a racial being and the loss of privilege. Conversely, this reaction may not be considered a Contact experience because there was an awareness of race as a construct, but only for "others," "non-Whites," or "people of color."

The idea that only "others" have a race is part and parcel of the universal racist assumption that "Whiteness is rightness," White is norm, or White is culture and other is multiculture. The historic stigmatization of race, compounded by the implications of being compartmentalized and thus limited by categorization—in essence, consumed—makes having a race a bad thing. There appears to be an unconscious understanding that when one becomes part of a group, or race in this case, one is implicitly responsible for the psychohistorical behavior of the group, or race, and the stereotypes that plague and emasculate people.

White students, in feeling that race is negative, tend to deny their race because of its association and potential for guilt. Some of the White students discussed the race of the Black students but dealt with it superficially and did not delve into the deep structure of race's cultural connection. Hence, the discussion of race became a discussion of color—the most obvious difference between Whites and "others." In fairness, however, this approach was taken by only a few of the White students. There may have been another reason for attempting to address the Asian and Black students in the class.

Using the case study, it becomes evident that White students in these courses use a myriad of defense mechanisms to protect their nonracist persona. For instance, one of the defense mechanisms asserts validation both aggressively, through the aforementioned defensiveness, and passively, by extending pseudo-power to African Americans via asking questions. However, what appears to be a genuine cross-racial/cultural experience can also be viewed as an exploration of "otherness."

The false exploration of race is an ostentatious cultural probing that seeks to minimize differences and accentuate similarities for the sake of maintaining the false perception of a nonracist facade. Moreover, the exploration of the Black students was an act of objectification and passive diversion of attention away from self into a dialogue in which White students may be seen as favorable because they can engage in intellectual discussions. Yet true dialogue, according to Freire (1993), can only occur between equals who share profound love, humility, and hope. Indeed, there was no reciprocity throughout the course because the students passively refused to answer any questions asked by the Black students. "I never thought about that" or "That's a good

question," they retorted in a politically correct, evasive fashion. In this context, there was no dialogue; there was only objectification for self-serving reasons.

The defense mechanisms typify resistance, which can occur through denying racism. Through "other" exploration, pseudo-validation, and de facto objectification of the Black students, there was an attempt to minimize the presence and power of the White professor, the definition of racism, and the confrontation with self as a racial being. Exemplary of this subtle, passive resistance is the statement "I have a Black friend, client, etc.," which is supposed to reflect diversity. For example, in a later class, one of the more defensive, outspoken White females argued her family's status as nonracist by noting that her father delivered Thanksgiving turkeys to a Black church.

The notions of charity and philanthropy have historically been used to assuage the White guilt of unintentional racists; "giving to minorities" allows one to reduce the guilt of historic racism. (Notice that the reduction was in guilt, not racism.) This process fulfills the Eurocentric style of helping in which symptoms are attended to as opposed to attention toward the causal relationships between oppressor and oppressed. Reduction in racism needs to occur at the systemic level because racism is a systemic phenomenon (Utsey, Bolden, & Brown, 2001). Throughout the class, the student was more willing to explore how she was not racist than to discuss how she was racist.

Another example of more aggressive objectification and "other" exploration in the class occurred when White students probed the African American for information from a Black perspective. Using the African American male student's journal notes, the incident occurred as follows:

> One student remarked that he "didn't mean to put me on the spot." Another male student affirmed, "Yeah. I figure it's just better if I hear it from the *horse's mouth*." I had to laugh at that. Laughter is an example of a

sophisticated defense mechanism that Cross (1991) suggests develops in the Internalization stage.

This passage lends itself to an analysis of the African and Asian students in the class.

The Semester

The global majority students appeared to be at different statuses throughout the duration of the semester. The African American male suggested through journal notes that he made a conscious effort to be at the Internalization status (for a review of Black racial identity development, see Cross, 1991; Helms, 1990). He affirmed this by noting that discussions of race often turn polemical, and in an academic setting, the notion of rationality often gives way to resistance through emotionally charged discussions that maintain racism:

> The Internalization stage would also allow me to use defense tactics that keep "the focus on racism as a form of human evil, rather than on the demonization of White people (Cross, 1991, p. 216)." ... Within the Internalization stage, I had the freedom to recycle the previous statuses dependent upon the stimuli (Cross, 1991).

The African Caribbean student appeared to be somewhat naive about racism's impact on Blacks. This may have been due to her African Caribbean status and lack of academic and personal exploration of race. The Asian female appeared to also be in the Preencounter status due to her ambiguity toward the topic of race (for a review of Black racial identity development, see Cross, 1991; Helms, 1990). However, it appeared that race was not a salient theme for her; cultural validation appeared to be more of a concern for her as the class progressed. Bonds based on experiential similarity relative to the course formed between the Asian and Black male and the two Black students.

During class discussions, it became evident that some of the students were not reading.

Students' comments and behavior reflected lower levels of racial development according to the readings. For instance, the discussions of power (Pinderhughes, 1989) turned into discussions about how the White students did not have power through the virtue of their ethnicity. Thus, there was a process of de-identifying with the self as a White racial being to preserve the nonracist identity in the ethnic being status. In addition, students did not appear to focus on the notion of privilege as discussed in McIntosh (1989). Some students were not processing what their "knapsack of privilege" contained. Subsequently, the levels of conversation fostered neither growth nor alliance with the White students; the conversations for the African, Asian, and Iranian students necessitated different issues.

Another climactic moment in class revealed yet another form of resistance—the "conspiracy of silence" or the "silent protest." One of the White males used aggressive defensiveness, which became offensive during a class discussion in which an African American professor presented African personality development (Kambon, 1992). Disinterested in the topic, some White students used silence as a form of protest. The ensuing silence was replete with composure and lack of eye contact, which could have been maintained for the duration of the class. However, the silence was broken when the African American professor spoke of a "vibe" existing in the class. In traditional T-Group form, he suggested that the students process their feelings. The professor noted that he was not interested in abusing power as a professor of their future courses. Finally, after the immediacy of processing, a group spokesperson emerged and broke the silence.

Using the power of cohort cohesion, one White male agreed that the professor could not abuse power. Following his statement, he discussed student power by noting how a student contingent redressing concerns with the dean and provost could be capable of causing trouble for the professor. The student detailed a potential plan and suggested that it would be easy to execute. No other student spoke in disagreement at that point, suggesting that (a) he was the identified spokesperson and (b) other students in the cohort were in support of his contention. Although speculative, the lack of objection suggests that the CP cohort dynamics were volatile enough to allow open hostility and threaten the professor's stability, possibly tenure. This is the "conspiracy of silence," in which unassuming racists support racism by not confronting racism. Confronting racism would lead to a loss of privilege for outspoken Whites.

In the following class, the peculiar responses to the professor's presence continued. During a review of the previous class, there were outward manifestations of resistance. In fact, the responses appeared to be of a psychosomatic nature. One of the more defensive White females began to gag and excused herself from the room during the peak of the discussion. One White male suddenly caught a back spasm and stood up to stretch. He informed the class of his back problems; however, it is the timing of the spasms that is relevant to this discussion. In fact, the two disturbances served as a precursor to a 10-minute class break. A third occurrence, for which no student was responsible, happened in a sort of metaphysical resistance—a shelved book fell. Indeed, the tension in the room was rank with resistance.

Conversely, the Asian student and the Black students identified with the professor. In fact, by this point in class, these students were more vocal in their disagreement and questioning of the status quo in the course and in psychology. Clearly, the Asian student felt validated, as evidenced by voicing her desire to finish her education in the United States and return to Asia to practice psychotherapy. The African Caribbean student voiced her concerns over the lack of culturally aware or sensitive therapy as seen in the students and in psychology in general. There was one brief end to the tension in the class near the end of the semester.

Final Class

A White professor prominent in the field of White racial identity guest lectured in the class. His approach gave focus to the career and professional benefits of diversity training. He spoke of how the White students could become more marketable with diversity training. In addition, he gave the White students a much-needed ego validation by asserting that all Whites were not racist, which he justified by saying that many Whites are able to purge themselves of racism. After that statement, there appeared to be a collective sense of ease among the oppositional White students. They were validated by a "giant" in the field, and thus the "traitor" White professor and the provocative, "agenda-wielding" African American professor were thereby invalidated in the eyes of the resistant White students.

This final sense of validation proved to be the most critical point in the class. The resistant White students were allowed to maintain their ego status and, unfortunately, their racism. The Asian student and two students of African descent appeared to be surprised that the resistant students would hold onto their racist conviction and defensive posture for the entire semester. There was no assessment of the guest lecturer's timing, but it was clear that the theme of White skin privilege remained through the professor's affirmations of the White students' attitudes.

The guest professor's approach appeared to undo the tension in the room and the potential gains made during the entire class with the resistant students, which reflects a recycled identity. A collective sigh of relief released the tension after the professor spoke. The silence that followed was a relatively healthy silence that begged for the end of the semester. The guest professor's approach caused the African American male to question his motivations. However, as Glausser (1999) noted, "It is a struggle to move beyond ethnocentric views, but it is also a challenge that provides an opportunity for growth. The rewards are an escape from cultural encapsulation and a bigger, better worldview" (p. 64).

CONCLUSION

In this chapter, we argued implicitly that multiculturalism has limited use as an approach to raising racial consciousness in White counseling and psychology trainees. Given the salience of race in this society, accentuating less relevant, though not irrelevant, demographic variables (e.g., gender, sexual orientation, socioeconomic status, etc.) in relation to the mental health functioning of oppressed groups, as multiculturalism does, maintains the status quo. We are advocating that counseling and psychology training programs develop a separate course that focuses on the dynamics of race in a race-conscious society, encourages White trainees to examine the meaning of their Whiteness in relation to the self (i.e., ego), and increases their awareness with regard to the insidious nature of White racism. Global majority trainees would benefit from a separate course geared toward exploring their own racial identity development and how it affects their work with

same- and different-race clients. More important, concepts of race, racial identity development, and racism awareness should be infused into the curriculum of training programs and not be isolated to one course, as has historically been the case with multicultural counseling.

Focusing on issues related to race, racial identity, and racism awareness is a relatively new endeavor in counseling and professional psychology training programs. Despite its relatively brief history, race, racial identity, and racism awareness training has received a great deal of attention in the counseling and psychology literature. A consensus among scholars conducting research in this area is that increased racial consciousness on the part of White trainees is a precursor to becoming cross-culturally competent (Brown et al., 1996; Carter, 1995; Pack-Brown, 1999; Parker et al., 1998; Richardson & Molinaro, 1996). Given the importance of race, racial identity, and racism awareness training in the repertoire of cross-counseling skills for trainees, it behooves training directors to develop courses (plural) that address these topics. We hope that this chapter will provide counselor educators and psychology training directors with the vision, rationale, and technology to develop courses that address racial factors in counseling and psychotherapy.

REFERENCES

Akintunde, O. (1999). White racism, White supremacy, White privilege, and the social construction of race: Moving from modernist to postmodernist multiculturalism. *Multicultural Education, 7,* 1-9.

American Psychological Association (APA). (1993). Guidelines for providers of psychological services to ethnic, linguistic, and culturally diverse populations. *American Psychologist, 48,* 45-48.

Brown, S. P., Parham, T. A., & Yonker, R. (1996). Influence of a cross-cultural training course on racial identity attitudes of White women and men: Preliminary perspectives. *Journal of Counseling and Development, 74,* 510-516.

Carter, R. T. (1995). *The influence of race and racial identity in psychotherapy: Toward a racially inclusive model.* New York: John Wiley.

Constantine, M. G. (1999). Racism's impact on counselors' professional and personal lives: A response to the personal narratives on racism. *Journal of Counseling and Development, 77,* 68-72.

Council for Accreditation of Counseling and Related Educational Programs (CACREP). (1988). *Accreditation procedures manual and application.* Alexandria, VA: Author.

Cross, W. E., Jr. (1971). The Negro-to-Black conversion experience. *Black World, 20,* 13-27.

Cross, W. E., Jr. (1991). *Shades of Black: Diversity in African-American identity.* Philadelphia: Temple University Press

D'Andrea, M., & Daniels, J. (1991). Exploring different levels of multicultural counseling training in counselor education. *Journal of Counseling and Development, 70,* 78-85.

Das, A. K. (1995). Rethinking multicultural counseling: Implications for counselor education. *Journal of Counseling and Development, 74,* 45-52.

Dobbins, J. E., & Skillings, J. H. (2000). Racism as a clinical syndrome. *American Journal of Orthopsychiatry, 78,* 14-27.

Freire, P. (1993). *Pedagogy of the oppressed* (New rev. 20th-anniversary ed.). New York: Continuum.

Glausser, A. S. (1999). Legacies of racism. *Journal of Counseling and Development, 77*(1), 62-67.

Guthrie, R. V. (1998). *Even the rat was White: A historical view of psychology* (2nd ed.). Boston: Allyn & Bacon.

Hardiman, R. (1982). *White racial identity development: A process oriented model for describing the racial consciousness of White Americans.* Unpublished doctoral dissertation, University of Massachusetts, Amherst.

Helms, J. E. (Ed.). (1990). *Black and White racial identity: Theory, research, and practice.* Westport, CT: Greenwood.

Helms, J. E. (1994). How multiculturalism obscures racial factors in the therapy process: Comment on Ridley et al. (1994), Sodowsky et al. (1994), Ottavi et al. (1994), and Thompson et al. (1994). *Journal of Counseling Psychology, 41,* 162-165.

Helms, J. E. (1995). An update on Helms' White and people of color racial identity models. In J. Ponterotto, J. M. Casas, L. A. Suzuki, & C. M. Alexander (Eds.), *Handbook of multicultural counseling* (pp. 181-198). Thousand Oaks, CA: Sage.

Helms, J. E., & Cook, D. A. (1999). *Using race and culture in counseling and psychotherapy: Theory and process.* Boston: Allyn & Bacon.

Holcomb-McCoy, C. C., & Myers, J. E. (1999). Multicultural competence and counselor training: A national survey. *Journal of Counseling and Development, 77,* 294-302.

hooks, b. (1992). *Black looks: Race and representation.* Boston: South End.

Jackson, G. G. (1998). The roots of the backlash theory in mental health. In G. Weaver (Ed.), *Culture, communication and conflict: Readings in intercultural relations* (pp. 322-340). Needham Heights, MA: Simon & Schuster.

Johnson, S. D. (1982). *The Minnesota multiethnic counselor education curriculum: The design and evaluation of an intervention for cross-cultural counselor education.* Unpublished doctoral dissertation, University of Minnesota, Minneapolis.

Kambon, K. K. (1992). *The African personality in America: An African-centered framework.* Tallahassee, FL: Nubian Nation Publications.

Kiselica, M. S. (1998). Preparing Anglos for the challenges and joys of multiculturalism. *The Counseling Psychologist, 26,* 5-21.

Locke, D. C., & Kiselica, M. S. (1999). Pedagogy of possibilities: Teaching about racism in multicultural counseling courses. *Journal of Counseling and Development, 77,* 80-86.

McIntosh, P. (1989, July/August). White privilege: Unpacking the invisible knapsack. *Peace and Freedom,* pp. 10-12.

McRae, M. B., & Johnson, S. D., Jr. (1991). Toward training for competence in multicultural counselor education. *Journal of Counseling and Development, 70,* 131-141.

Myers, L. J. (1988). *Understanding an Afrocentric world view: Introduction to an optimal psychology.* Dubuque, IA: Kendall Hunt.

Myers, L. J., Speight, S. L., Highlen, P. S., Cox, C. I., Reynolds, A. L., Adams, E. M., & Hanley, C. P. (1991). Identity development and worldview: Toward an optimal conceptualization. *Journal of Counseling and Development, 70,* 54-63.

National Education Association. (1973). *Education and racism: An action manual.* Washington, DC: Author.

Pack-Brown, S. P. (1999). Racism and White counselor training: Influence of White racial identity theory and research. *Journal of Counseling and Development, 77,* 87-92.

Parker, W. M., Moore, M. A., & Neimeyer, G. J. (1998). Altering White racial identity and interracial comfort through multicultural training. *Journal of Counseling and Development, 76,* 302-310.

Pedersen, P. B. (1973, September). *A cross-cultural coalition training model for educating mental health professionals to function in multi-cultural populations.* Paper presented at the Ninth International Congress of Ethnological and Anthropological Science, Chicago.

Pinderhughes, E. (1989). *Understanding race, ethnicity, and power: The key to efficacy in clinical practice.* New York: Free Press.

Ponterotto, J. G. (1988). Racial consciousness development among White counselor trainees: A stage model. *Journal of Multicultural Counseling and Development, 16,* 146-156.

Richardson, T. Q., & Molinaro, K. L. (1996). White counselor self-awareness: A prerequisite for developing multicultural competence. *Journal of Counseling and Development, 74,* 238-242.

Ridley, C. R., Mendoza, D. W., & Kanitz, B. E. (1994). Multicultural training: Reexamination, operationalization, and integration. *The Counseling Psychologist, 22,* 227-289.

Skillings, J. H., & Dobbins, J. E. (1991). Racism as a disease: Etiology and treatment implications. *Journal of Counseling and Development, 70,* 206-212.

Sue, D. W. (1979). *Preliminary data from the DISC evaluation report, No. 1.* Hayward: California State University.

Thompson, C. E., & Neville, H. A. (1999). Racism, mental health, and mental health practice. *The Counseling Psychologist, 27,* 155-223.

Utsey, S. O., Bolden, M. A., & Brown, A. L. (2001). Visions of revolution from the spirit of Franz Fanon: A psychology of liberation for counseling African Americans confronting societal racism and oppression. In J. G. Ponterotto, J. M. Casas, L. A. Suzuki, & C. M. Alexander (Eds.), *Handbook of multicultural counseling* (2nd ed., pp. 311-336). Thousand Oaks, CA: Sage.

Vontress, C. E. (1967). Counseling Negro adolescents. *The School Counselor, 15,* 86-91.

Vontress, C. E. (1971). Racial differences: Impediments to rapport. *Journal of Counseling Psychology, 18,* 7-13.

White, J. (1984). *The psychology of Blacks: An African American perspective.* Englewood Cliffs, NJ: Prentice Hall.

Williams, R. L. (1981). *The collective Black mind: An Afro-centric theory of Black personality.* St. Louis, MO: Williams & Associates.

CHAPTER 7

The Ethical Practice of Psychology
Ethnic, Racial and Cultural Issues

LEONARDO M. MARMOL
Seattle Pacific University

Concerns about the role of culture and ethnicity on the theory and practice of psychology have had a checkered history in American psychology. Some may say the same about psychology's concern about ethics in general. The American Psychological Association (APA) was founded in 1892 and incorporated legally in 1925. It functioned for 13 years without an Ethics Committee. This was established in 1938 but without written codes or guidelines to govern its activities.

But today we have come to the realization that ethnicity, race, and culture are ethical issues. The future of psychology as a force in human affairs may well hang on how it addresses the multicultural milieu of 21st-century America in a way that is relevant to all the people and not just a privileged few.

In 1947, Carl Rogers, as president of the APA, appointed a committee to define psychotherapy and suggested the idea of writing a code of ethics for the practice of psychotherapy. In 1948, a letter went out to 7,500 psychologists requesting reports of ethical dilemmas they had encountered in practice. One thousand reports came back.

The Boulder Conference of 1949, which promulgated the scientist-practitioner model for clinical psychology, actually left psychotherapy purposely vague and "undefined." The conference did not explicitly make any pronouncements about ethical practice. It was assumed that all practitioners would adhere to high standards. The impetus for writing a code was, however, strong, and such an effort continued.

Despite the opposition of such well-known psychologists as Calvin Hall, who in 1952 stated that an ethics code would "play into the hands of the crooked operator [who] reads the code to see how much he can get away with" (Hall, 1952), the first *Ethical Standards of Psychologists* was adopted in 1953 (APA,

AUTHOR'S NOTE: I acknowledge the contribution of my graduate assistant, Dean Coffey, M.A., in aiding in the research for this chapter.

1953). This is a national association of professionals that essentially practiced for 61 years without a written code of ethics.

This first code was revised in 1958, 1963, 1968, 1977, 1979, and 1981. The 1990 revision changed the name to *Ethical Principles of Psychologists* (APA, 1990). Finally, the current version of 1992 changed the title again to *Ethical Principles of Psychologists and Code of Conduct* (APA, 1992).

Historical Background

Perhaps the earliest call in the literature for attention to the role of race and ethnicity for psychotherapy was sounded by I. S. Lindsay (1947), writing in the *Journal of Social Casework*. In 1962, G. G. Wren, writing in the *Harvard Educational Review,* warned psychology of its cultural encapsulation (Wren, 1962) and again revisited the issue in 1985 in his chapter in Pedersen's edited volume, *Handbook of Cross-Cultural Counseling and Therapy*. The civil rights and feminist movements within the general society were beginning to sensitize many in psychology about the etic quality of most theories and practices of the profession, especially its assessment practices with its terrible history of racism and bias (e.g., Eysenck, 1971; Jensen, 1973; Putnam, 1961).

Etic and *emic* are concepts that have come into psychology from anthropology research. Etic refers to those theories, values, and practices that are considered to be not only universal but also normative for all people. Usually these came from the Eurocentric background of the researchers. Emic, on the other hand, refers to those values, mores, and practices that are specific to a given community, tribe, or nation. Traditionally, psychology has considered its theories to be etic—that is, universal—applicable to all people. The multicultural movement has tried to sensitize psychology to the validity of emic forms of practice. In fact, all psychology should be considered emic

because traditional psychology is always emic to White, Anglo-Saxon populations. It needs to be reinterpreted and retranslated for each and every racial, ethnic, and cultural group.

Not surprisingly, then, the Vail Conference of 1973 (reported by Korman, 1974) was permeated by a new awareness of the importance of incorporating emic concerns into the theory and practice of psychology, especially clinical and professional practices. For the first time in its history, "official" psychology promulgated as a principle that "counseling persons of culturally different backgrounds by persons not trained or competent to work with them should be regarded as unethical" (Pedersen & Marsella, 1982, p. 492).

To this day, this remains the strongest statement on the subject ever pronounced by an APA entity. The 1992 *Ethical Principles of Psychologists and Code of Conduct* refrains from such a strong position. Only Ethical Standards 1.08, 2.04, and 2.05 can obliquely be interpreted to address the issue.

After Vail, many things began to happen. In 1982, Division 17 (Counseling Psychology) adopted a position paper recommending that APA consider cross-cultural counseling competencies to become a criterion for the accreditation of training programs in counseling psychology (Ponterotto & Casas, 1991). APA also created committees and boards, such as the Committee for Equality of Opportunity in Psychology, the Board of Social and Ethical Responsibilities in Psychology, the Office of Minority Affairs, and the Board of Ethnic and Minority Affairs (BEMA).

In 1984, BEMA established a task force for "conversation" with minority constituents. Also, in 1986, Division 45, the Society for the Psychological Studies of Ethnic Minority Issues, was chartered. Eventually, 9 years later, the APA adopted the "Guidelines for Providers of Psychological Services to Ethnic, Linguistic, and Culturally Diverse Populations" (APA, 1993). It is interesting to note that the "Guidelines" were adopted 1 year after the 1992 code. Had this code addressed the issues adequately, the BEMA guidelines might not have been necessary.

In summary, we have 46 years from Lindsey, 31 years from Wren, and 20 years from Vail for the APA to officially go on record recognizing the importance of emic factors in counseling and psychotherapy. Psychology's concern for ethnic and cultural issues moved as slowly as its general concern for ethics as such.

Ethnicity as an Ethical Issue

Before moving on to the present, we need to raise some questions. Is a professional standard for ethical cross-cultural practice a feasibly attainable goal, given the diversity of the nation (and world) we practice in? Are there minimal competency standards for culturally sensitive therapy that can be compared to the minimal standards for licensure used by the state boards? Are there standards for excellence in the field comparable to American Board of Professional Psychology (ABPP) standards? In the field of medicine, there are "universal precautions" taken with every patient (gloves, masks, disposable sterile instruments). Can we develop "universal precautions" to guard against biases that might misconstrue diagnoses and interventions with culturally different clients?

Any attempt to answer those questions has to keep in mind the history of colonialism that lies behind all interactions between European White peoples and people of color in the rest of the world. The historical facts of how the great empires—be they British, German, Dutch, or Spanish—imposed their cultures on the weaker, less developed cultures of Africa and America permeate all interactions between these peoples to this day.

It must be acknowledged that the conquerors deceived themselves in thinking that their mission was to bring civilization and Christianity to the underdeveloped nations

(Venditti & Venditti, 1996). Nevertheless, the objective accounts of the conquest demonstrate that colonialism was nothing less than aggression and exploitation (Neil, 1964; Rivera Pagan, 1991).

In psychology, many have lamented the damage done on ethnic persons by the thoughtless application of White, Anglo-American values and behavioral expectations to persons of color. Some of these are documented in the articles in the volume edited by Janet Helms (1990), *Black and White Racial Identity: Theory, Research and Practice.* Perhaps the strongest indictment of this practice was voiced by T. Gordon (1973): "White psychology stands accused of unethical conduct in its relation with the black community. . . . Instead of service to black people, white psychology has been flagrantly self-serving and opportunistic" (p. 88).

The 1992 code tried very hard to steer away from a deontic approach of categorical imperatives toward a more utilitarian philosophy. There are only two categorical prohibitions in the entire code. One is about sexual relations with current patients, students, supervisees, and research subjects, and the other is against abandoning patients. Everything else is couched in what Bersoff (1999) has called "weasel words" (p. 112)—wording such as "whenever feasible," "as soon as possible," and so on. The legalistic protection of the psychologists seems to often overrule the optimal concern for the recipients of psychological services.

Others have related the issue to a philosophy of ethics embodied in the APA codes that is at odds with the basic values of minority communities. Underlying the 1992 (and all other versions) of the APA code is a ground floor of individually oriented values, such as autonomy, individualism, independence, and self-centeredness, that ignore values of community and interdependence important to other cultures (LaFromboise, Foster, & James, 1996).

There are more subtle implications in the code such as concepts of consumerism (e.g., more is better, strive for acceptance through success and competition). These differences in value orientation may lead psychologists to negatively evaluate those who are different from themselves, even stereotyping them as "inferior."

Some writers have even identified gender biases in the code by reflecting concepts of "rights" and "independence," which are judged to be "male," while ignoring concepts of caring and relationships that are judged to be "female," which are prevalent in cultures with a more altruistic outlook (Harding, 1987, cited by Ponterotto & Casas, 1991).

Despite other world cultures being more collectivistic, the APA code has had a strong influence on the ethics codes of many countries. The work of Triandis (1995) and others clearly establishes how it is that the ethnic cultures represented in the minority populations of the United States tend to be less individualistic than the dominant Anglo-American culture. Mark Leach and J. Judd Harbin (1997) surveyed and compared the APA code with those of psychological associations of 24 countries. They found the Canadian code to be most similar to the U.S. code and, not surprisingly, China's to be the most dissimilar. Most European and even several South American codes reflect major values of the U.S. code.

Training programs on cultural awareness and attitude change have proliferated since the 1980s, but how effective they are remains to be seen. A survey by Katz (1997) does not present a very optimistic picture of their effectiveness. Jane Guishard (1992) from the United Kingdom considers these as "seance-type group work . . . [which has] rightly received a cool response from a wide range of professionals" (p. 43). LaFromboise and her colleagues (1996) felt that most training models assume that increased knowledge translates into improved skills, so that after some modest training, European American counselors overestimate their multicultural skills.

Professional clinical psychology training programs are not much better. Most ethics classes in clinical programs boil down to rote learning of the APA code and are divorced from the practicum experiences. Abeles (1980) proposed teaching ethics through empirical analysis from clinical practice—that is, a grappling with ethical dilemmas that arise from the conflicts between the codes and the day-to-day struggles of clients. Confronting conflicting cultural values would enhance this process significantly. The courage to risk disagreeing with the codes from specific cultural and ethnic practices is lacking in the field. Casas, Ponterotto, and Gutierrez (1986) proposed a scathing indictment of the current training in both research and counseling from an ethical point of view.

LaFromboise et al. (1996) surveyed 10 popular casebooks used in ethics classes and found only 5 pages of cases related to ethnic minority issues. Even the most respected book, considered by many the classic "bible" in ethics—Koocher and Keith-Spiegel's (1998) *Ethics in Psychology,* now in its second edition—devotes only 2½ pages to the subheading "Ethics and Cultural Diversity," with only five cases cited. And only half a page is given to the heading "Subgroup Norming," without citing any cases.

The issue of assessment instruments with ethnic minority persons raises multiple ethical issues. The racism espoused by the works of Jensen (1969, 1973), Eysenck (1971), and Putnam (1961) is well known in the field—not to mention the recently published onerous volume, *The Bell Curve* (Herrnstein & Murray, 1994) (see Andrews & Nelkin's 1996 comments on *The Bell Curve* in *Science*). The cultural biases in test construction manifested in content, internal structure, and item selection are dealt with in more detail in the "Diagnoses and Assessment" section of this volume. The works of Richard Dana (1993, 1996) in this area are also well known in the field.

But the history of the misuse of assessment instruments with ethnic and minority populations goes back to early attempts to import the Binet test into America. Such a history, so expertly documented by Stephen Jay Gould (1981) in his seminal work, *The Mismeasure of Man,* is a shameful beginning for American psychology. The conclusions reached by such luminaries of psychology as H. H. Goddard, L. M. Terman, and R. M. Yeakes from their early use of intelligence tests are appalling. Statements to the effect that Negroes (as African Americans were called then), Mexicans, and American Indians as a group were "feeble-minded" due to their low scores on these tests give the modern reader conniptions. The offensive language was not spared for Caucasians of foreign birth. Tests performed at Ellis Island led Goddard to astounding results:

> 83 percent of the Jews, 80 percent of the Hungarians, 79 percent of the Italians, and 87 percent of the Russians were feeble-minded; that is below age 12 on the Binet scale. Goddard himself was flabbergasted: could anyone be made to believe that four-fifths of any nation were morons? (Gould, 1981, p. 166)

In the 1980s, the U.S. Employment Service (USES) tried to reduce the impact of standardized testing on ethnic minority groups by using within-group scoring, also known as *subgroup norming.* But the Civil Rights Act of 1991 banned its use in the name of avoiding reverse discrimination. Brown (1994) questioned this practice, considering it a case of reverse discrimination. But Gottfredson (1994) and Sackett and Wilk (1994) provided a more objective view of the practice of race or subgroup norming.

Ethics and Ethnicity in Multicultural Practice

On the question of whether the therapist and client should be racially or ethnically matched, the literature provides more heat than light. Gender and sexual orientation matching between therapist and client has also entered the discussion. A complete summary of the literature on these issues is beyond the scope of this chapter. Suffice it here to say that Sanchez and Atkinson (1983) investigated the subject among Mexican Americans; Atkinson, Furlung, and Poston (1986) among African Americans; and Atkinson, Maruyama, and Matsui (1978) among Asian Americans. Stanley Sue (1988) reviewed the research findings on ethnic matches in general and found no significant differences in therapeutic outcomes, provided the White therapists were culturally sensitive.

The question of whether multiple relationships that often happen in ethnic communities are considered unethical by APA codes is a more complicated subject. Ethical Standard 1.17 acknowledges that "in many communities and situations, it may not be feasible or reasonable for psychologists to avoid social or other nonprofessional contacts with persons such as patients, clients, students, supervisees, or research participants" (APA, 1992, p. 1601). Stockman (1990) illustrated this dilemma in rural communities.

In Hispanic communities, for example, a therapist who is well known in the community for his or her involvement in social groups, churches, political organizations, and so on, is a more respected and desirable person to be accepted as a therapist than someone from outside the community. Even someone who is an outright relative or the relative of a friend is preferable as a therapist. In Native American communities and especially in the reservations, all persons are considered part of the extended family. Tribal kinship "requires" familial designations. Anyone who is older than you should be addressed as "uncle" or "aunt" (LaFromboise et al., 1996). The culturally sensitive therapist must blend with the community values and, in a sense, ignore the codes.

The first of the four questions raised earlier as to whether a professional standard for ethical cross-cultural practice is an attainable goal can now be answered. The answer is in the affirmative if we agree to espouse two emphases.

The first is to acknowledge what Pedersen proposed in 1990 and later expanded on in the volume he edited in 1999, titled *Multiculturalism as a Fourth Force*. He suggested that multiculturalism has become a "fourth force" in psychology, with the other three being psychoanalysis, behaviorism, and humanism. Accepting multiculturalism on an equal standing with these other forces puts all research and developments in multiculturalism in the midst of "mainstream" psychology and not a "side issue" of interest only to a small cadre of devotees or rebels.

The work of Division 45 would no longer be that of consciousness raising for the profession but of promoting the newly acknowledged fourth force. It would include seeing that multiculturalism takes its rightful place in the pantheon of psychology, alongside the theories of psychoanalysis, behaviorism, and humanistic psychology. There should be at least two representatives of Division 45 on the APA's Committee on Accreditation to make sure that all training programs are teaching multiculturalism at the same level of importance and depth as they teach cognitive-behavioral, psychodynamic, and systemic psychotherapy. State licensing boards should be lobbied to begin requiring a minimum number of hours of supervised experience with ethnic and cultural clients for admission to licensure.

A further purpose for Division 45 would be to promote that "ethical relativism" is an appropriate and legitimate approach to practice. This concept, first proposed by Casas and Thompson (1991) and endorsed by LaFromboise et al. (1996), allows for an interpretation of the ethics codes of APA and others (e.g., American Association for Counseling and Development's 1988 *Ethical Standards*),

taking into account the value differences underlying the codes and how they are relevant to the lives of ethnic cultures and communities. This principle allows for the reinterpretation or "translation" of concepts of altruism, responsibility, justice, and caring (Casas & Thompson, 1991). Ethical relativism allows us to look at "ethnic life," avoiding the ethical lapse on the part of researchers whose fascination with pathology does not allow them to see the positive aspects of ethnic life.

Ethical relativism should not be confused with cultural relativity. Because we have come to accept that certain things that were thought to be absolute are actually relative to culture, and because mores are relative to culture and enforced by social pressure, some have argued that as long as a practice is acceptable in a subculture, it should be allowed by the larger U.S. society. An example of this problem is the old custom of polygamy among Mormon settlers of the territory of Utah, which had to be abolished so that Utah could be recognized as a state. Cultural practices that impinge on moral judgments have to live in harmony with the host cultures of which they are a part. So, then, moral judgments are only valid for the culture in which they arise. Wellman (1985) made the point that "generically similar acts may be right and good in one society and wrong or bad in another. Any comparison between the ethical views of the members of different societies can only be partial" (p. 45).

Recommendations for Training and Research

The second question we raised had to do with standards of minimal competency for a multiculturally sensitive practice. Teaching of ethics is required in all accredited programs, and classes in ethics are expected to show on the transcripts of applicants for licensure in most states. A separate class on multicultural issues in therapy is also expected by APA's accreditation standards.

But the two are kept distant and separate in most training programs. By separating ethical training from cultural sensitivity training, knowledge, and skills, clinical practitioners run the risk of perpetuating oppression and racism without being aware of doing it. As Lakin (1991) has pointed out,

> Some contemporary critics of the mental health establishment claim that the values represented in most psychotherapies in our society are in fact sexist and racist. They argue that much treatment is actually disguised social control and functions, perhaps inadvertently, to ensure a perpetuation of the traditional subordinacy of women by males and to justify the racist attitudes of the society. (p. 62)

Standard textbooks for the teaching of ethics in graduate clinical programs all contain chapters on individual differences, and many specifically address issues of culture and ethnicity (Bersoff, 1999; Bowie, 1985; Ibrahim & Arredondo, 1990; Koocher & Keith-Spiegel, 1998; Lakin, 1991; Pope & Vasquez, 1991). They all have illustrative case vignettes, but as we noted before, cases dealing specifically with the ethical implications of factors of ethnicity and culture are few in number. On the other side, texts used in multicultural classes tend to be heavy on techniques of how to address, diagnose, and treat in therapy persons of different ethnicities (Paniagua, 1994; Pedersen, 1985; Ponterotto, Casas, Suzuki, & Alexander, 1995; Sue & Sue, 1990; Vargas & Koss-Chioino, 1992). However, the ethical implications of misdiagnosis, mistreatment, lack of treatment, or outright malpractice perpetuated on ethnic minority persons due to lack of sensitivity and poor education of practitioners do not get addressed directly. Only by implication do these issues become ethical issues. That is why many commit what Iijima Hall (1997) calls "cultural malpractice." Gil and Bob (1999) made a similar point about research that is not culturally informed.

The third question we have raised regarding standards of excellence in the diagnosis and treatment of ethnic persons is still being debated. The ABPP has clear standards for diplomate status in clinical psychology and several other specialties. The ABPP should be encouraged to develop a diplomate in multiculturalism with clearly defined standards of excellence in the field. Some training programs have developed multicultural "tracks" or specialties. One example is the California School of Professional Psychology at its Alameda campus. But this is training for minimal competency, similar to the competency standards required for the independent practice of psychology by state boards. We need clear standards for excellence in the field.

The last question of "universal precautions," such as the ones in medicine that are used to operationalize the Hippocratic principle of *primo non nocere* (first do no harm), can be expressed as follows. The culturally competent and sensitive psychotherapist must be able to articulate certain knowledge, beliefs, attitudes, and skills:

- *Knowledge:* They understand the impact of racist concepts on psychological theory and on their own professional lives. They understand the role of oppression in the etiology of mental illness. They are aware of institutional barriers that prevent minorities from using mental health services. They acquire specific knowledge about the historical traditions and values of the group they are working with, as well as the history of oppression and colonization that group has suffered.
- *Beliefs and attitudes:* They are aware of their own values, attitudes, and biases and how these are likely to affect minority clients. They are able to monitor their own functioning and obtain consultation, supervision, and continuing education. They believe that it is possible to integrate different value systems in the interest of health and growth. They are willing to refer a client because of their own limitations.

- *Skills:* They are able to use styles and techniques that are congruent with the value system of their clients. They are not threatened by having to adapt conventional approaches to accommodate cultural differences. They are able to receive and send both verbal and nonverbal messages that are appropriate to the clients. They are willing to engage in institutional interventions on behalf of their clients, sometimes out of the office.

As cultural sensitivity becomes more and more an expected ethical "requirement" of all psychologists, the beliefs, attitudes, knowledge, and skills needed to become a culturally sensitive therapist will be required subjects in all clinical training programs. Accreditation standards will become more explicit in making sure that issues of race, ethnicity, and cultural diversity are in the forefront of psychological research and practice. As Sue and Sue (1990) have so cogently stated,

> Becoming culturally skilled is an active process, that is ongoing, and never reaches an end point. Implicit is recognition of the complexity and diversity of the client populations, and acknowledgement of our personal limitations and the need to always improve. (p. 146)

REFERENCES

Abeles, N. (1980). Teaching ethical principles by means of value confrontation. *Psychotherapy: Theory, Research, and Practice, 7,* 384-391.

American Association for Counseling and Development. (1988). *Ethical standards.* Alexandria, VA: Author.

American Psychological Association (APA). (1953). *Ethical standards of psychologists: A summary of ethical principles.* Washington, DC: Author.

American Psychological Association (APA). (1990). Ethical principles of psychologists (revised edition). *American Psychologist, 45,* 390-395.

American Psychological Association (APA). (1992). Ethical principles of psychologists and code of conduct. *American Psychologist, 47,* 1597-1611.

American Psychological Association (APA). (1993). Guidelines for providers of psychological services to ethnic, linguistic, and culturally diverse populations. *American Psychologist, 48,* 45-48.

Andrews, L. B., & Nelkin, D. (1996). The bell curve: A statement. *Science, 271,* 13-14.

Atkinson, D. R., Furlung, M. J., & Poston, W. C. (1986). Afro-American preferences for counselor characteristics. *Journal of Counseling Psychology, 33,* 326-330.

Atkinson, D. R., Maruyama, M., & Matsui, S. (1978). Effects of counselor race and counseling approach on Asian Americans' perception of counselor credibility and utility. *Journal of Counseling Psychology, 25,* 76-85.

Bersoff, D. N. (1999). *Ethical conflicts in psychology* (2nd ed.). Washington, DC: APA.

Bowie, N. E. (Ed.). (1985). *Making ethical decisions.* New York: McGraw-Hill.

Brown, D. C. (1994). Subgroup norming: Legitimate testing practice or reverse discrimination? *American Psychologist, 49,* 927-928.

Casas, J. M., Ponterotto, J. G., & Gutierrez, J. M. (1986). An ethical indictment of counseling research and training: The cross-cultural perspective. *Journal of Counseling and Development, 64,* 347-352.

Casas, J. M., & Thompson, C. E. (1991). Ethical principles and standards: A racial-ethnic minority research perspective. *Counseling and Values, 35*(3), 186-195.

Civil Rights Act of 1991, Pub. L. No. 102-166, § 106 (1991).

Dana, R. H. (1993). *Multicultural assessment perspectives for professional psychology.* Boston: Allyn & Bacon.

Dana, R. H. (1996). Culturally competent assessment practice in the United States. *Journal of Personality Assessment, 66*(3), 472-487.

Eysenck, H. (1971). *Race, intelligence and education.* London: Temple-Smith.

Gil, E. F., & Bob, S. (1999). Culturally competent research: An ethical perspective. *Clinical Psychology Review, 19*(1), 45-55.

Gordon, T. (1973). Notes on White and Black psychology. *Journal of Social Issues, 29*(1), 87-95.

Gottfredson, L. S. (1994). The science and politics of race-norming. *American Psychologist, 49,* 955-963.

Gould, S. J. (1981). *The mismeasure of man.* New York: Norton.

Guishard, J. (1992). People who live in posh houses shouldn't throw stones. *Educational and Child Psychology, 9*(3), 42-47.

Hall, C. S. (1952). Crooks, codes and cant. *American Psychologist, 7,* 430-431.

Helms, J. E. (Ed.). (1990). *Black and White racial identity: Theory, research and practice.* New York: Greenwood.

Herrnstein, R. J., & Murray, C. (1994). *The bell curve: The reshaping of American life by differences in intelligence.* New York: Free Press.

Ibrahim, F. A., & Arredondo, P. (1990). Ethical issues in multicultural counseling. In B. Herlihy & L. B. Golden (Eds.), *Ethical standards casebook* (pp. 137-145). Alexandria, VA: American Association for Counseling and Development.

Iijima Hall, C. C. (1997). Cultural malpractice: The growing obsolescence of psychology with the changing U. S. population. *American Psychologist, 52*(6), 642-651.

Jensen, A. R. (1969). How much can we boost I.Q. and scholastic achievement? *Harvard Educational Review, 39,* 1-123.

Jensen, A. R. (1973). *Educability and group differences.* London: Methuen.

Katz, J. H. (1997). The effects of a systematic training program on the attitudes and behavior of White people. *International Journal of Intercultural Relations, 1,* 77-89.

Koocher, G. P., & Keith-Spiegel, P. (1998). *Ethics in psychology: Professional standards and cases* (2nd ed.). New York: Oxford University Press.

Korman, M. (1974). National conference on levels and patterns of professional training in psychology. *American Psychologist, 29,* 441-449.

Kroeber, A., & Kluckholn, C. (1952). *Culture: A critical review of concepts and definitions.* Cambridge, MA: Peabody Museum.

LaFromboise, T. D., Foster, S., & James, A. (1996). Ethics in multicultural counseling. In P. B. Pedersen, J. G. Draguns, W. J. Lonner, & J. E. Trimble (Eds.), *Counseling across cultures* (pp. 47-72). Thousand Oaks, CA: Sage.

Lakin, M. (1991). *Coping with ethical dilemmas in psychotherapy.* New York: Pergamon.

Leach, M. N. M., & Harbin, J. J. (1997). Psychological ethics codes: A comparison of twenty-four countries. *International Journal of Psychology, 32*(3), 181-192.

Lindsay, I. S. (1947). Race as a factor in the caseworker's role. *Journal of Social Casework, 28,* 101-107.

Neil, S. (1964). *A history of Christian missions.* London: Penguin.

Paniagua, F. A. (1994). *Assessing and treating culturally diverse clients: A practical guide.* Thousand Oaks, CA: Sage.

Pedersen, P. (Ed.). (1985). *Handbook of cross-cultural counseling and therapy.* Westport, CT: Greenwood.

Pedersen, P. (1990). The multicultural perspective as a fourth force in counseling. *Journal of Mental Health Counseling, 12,* 93-95.

Pedersen, P. (Ed.). (1999). *Multiculturalism as a fourth force.* Philadelphia: Brunner/Mazel.

Pedersen, P. B., & Marsella, A. J. (1982). The ethical crisis for cross-cultural counseling and therapy. *Professional Psychology, 13*(4), 492-500.

Ponterotto, J. G., & Casas, J. M. (1991). *Handbook of racial/ethnic minority counseling research.* Springfield, IL: Charles C Thomas.

Ponterotto, J. G., Casas, J. M., Suzuki, L. A., & Alexander, C. M. (Eds.). (1995). *Handbook of multicultural counseling.* Thousand Oaks, CA: Sage.

Pope, K. S., & Vasquez, M. J. T. (1991). *Ethics in psychotherapy and counseling: A practical guide for psychologists.* San Francisco: Jossey-Bass.

Putnam, C. (1961). *Race and reason.* Washington, DC: Public Affairs Press.

Rivera Pagan, L. N. (1991). *Evangelizacion y violencia: La conquista de America* [Evangelism and violence: The conquest of America]. San Juan, Puerto Rico: Editorial CEMI.

Sackett, P. R., & Wilk, S. L. (1994). Within group norming and other forms of score adjustment in preemployment testing. *American Psychologist, 49,* 799-812.

Sanchez, A. R., & Atkinson, D. R. (1983). Mexican-American cultural commitment, preference of counselor ethnicity, and willingness to use counseling. *Journal of Counseling Psychology, 30,* 215-220.

Stockman, A. F. (1990). Dual relationships in rural mental health practice: An ethical dilemma. *Journal of Rural Community Psychology, 11*(2), 31-45.

Sue, D. W., & Sue, D. (1990). *Counseling the culturally different: Theory and practice.* New York: John Wiley.

Sue, S. (1988). Psychotherapeutic services for ethnic minorities: Two decades of research findings. *American Psychologist, 43*(4), 301-308.

Triandis, H. C. (1995). *Individualism and collectivism.* Boulder, CO: Westview.

Vargas, L. A., & Koss-Chioino, J. D. (Eds.). (1992). *Working with culture: Psychotherapeutic interventions with ethnic minority children and adolescents.* San Francisco: Jossey-Bass.

Venditti, N., & Venditti, L. (1996). *Historia de la iglesia 2: Renovacion en la edad moderna* [History of the church 2: Renewal in the modern age]. Des Moines, IA: Open Bible Standard Churches.

Wellman, C. (1985). The ethical implications of cultural relativity. In N. E. Bowie (Ed.), *Making ethical decisions* (pp. 41-46). New York: McGraw-Hill.

Wren, C. G. (1962). The culturally encapsulated counselor. *Harvard Educational Review, 32,* 444-449.

Wren, C. G. (1985). Afterward: The culturally encapsulated counselor revisited. In P. B. Pedersen (Ed.), *Handbook of cross-cultural counseling and therapy* (pp. 323-329). Westport, CT: Greenwood.

Part II

ETHNIC MINORITY RESEARCH AND METHODS

CHAPTER 8

Research With Ethnic Minorities
Conceptual, Methodological, and Analytical Issues

A. KATHLEEN BURLEW
University of Cincinnati

In 1990, the National Institutes of Health (NIH) and Alcohol, Drug Abuse, and Mental Health Administration (ADAMHA) enacted policies requiring the inclusion of women and minorities in study populations (NIH, 1990). These policies are consistent with findings on the underrepresentation of ethnic minorities that have been documented in published empirical studies elsewhere. For example, Graham (1992) conducted a study of the representation of African Americans in selected American Psychological Association (APA) journals. The findings revealed a consistent decline in the articles about African Americans in these journals between the early 1970s (1970-1974) and the late 1980s (1985-1989). Similarly, Hagen and Conley (1994) reported a disproportionately low number of empirical articles on either Latinos or Asian Americans.

In the NIH Revitalization Act of 1993 (*Federal Register*, 1994), the NIH reaffirmed its commitment to the fundamental principle of inclusion. Moreover, the policies were strengthened to ensure that analyses would be conducted in an appropriate manner and to prohibit the use of cost as an acceptable reason to exclude these groups. The intent of the legislation was to ensure that women and minorities would be included in all clinical research unless a clear and compelling justification existed to do otherwise. That mandate applies to all NIH-supported biomedical and behavioral research.

According to the 2000 census, Latinos, African Americans, American Indians and Alaska Natives, and Asian Americans (including Native Hawaiians and other Pacific Islanders) constitute 12.5%, 12.3%, .9%, and 3.7 %, respectively, of the population. Census projections predict that ethnic minorities will constitute about one third of the total population of the United States as soon as 2010 (U.S. Bureau of the Census, 1994) and almost half by the year 2050 (U.S. Bureau of the Census, 1994). As ethnic minorities grow in numbers in the United States, clearly it is important to the field of psychology and to the American society, in general, that adequate information is available on the psychological processes within various ethnic groups.

Despite the intent of the NIH regulations, inclusion alone does not guarantee that accurate information will be available on various ethnic minority groups. Instead, along with increasing the numbers of ethnic minority research participants, it is also important to conduct research on ethnic minorities in a manner that yields the most accurate information on these groups. Previous researchers have raised concerns regarding conceptual, methodological, and analytical issues that need to be addressed in studies that include ethnic minorities. The objective of this chapter is to summarize the issues in each of these areas.

Although the number of different ethnic minority groups in the United States is growing, most of the research on ethnic minority groups primarily focuses on the following four groups: American Indians and Alaska Natives, African Americans, Asian Americans, and Latinos. Accordingly, this chapter emphasizes the extant literature with these four groups. Nevertheless, many of the conclusions may apply to other ethnic minorities as well.

CONCEPTUAL ISSUES

The initial stage in the design of a research project is the development of a set of beliefs regarding the topic under investigation. This stage of the research is especially important because it shapes the type of questions examined, the variables included in the research, the research design, and, ultimately, how the results are interpreted.

The assumption of the universality of the American mainstream experience is a core issue at the conceptual level. This assumption is embedded (sometimes subtly) in much of the research that pertains to ethnic minorities. At best, this approach overlooks some

fundamental cultural differences that warrant further investigation. At worst, as Nobles (1995) stated, to the extent that psychology accepts the behaviors and mores of American mainstream as the standard by which all other groups are understood, the universality assumption, in effect, renders "European psychology as a powerful tool of oppression."

The assumption of universality has several specific implications for the conceptual phase of the research. First, the researcher is easily tempted to adopt the conceptual models and to accept prematurely research conclusions acquired from other groups. This approach ignores the obvious reality that the theoretical perspectives developed on one group may not necessarily fit the life experiences of another group. The research on locus of control is one example in which racial differences have been demonstrated. Specifically, research on locus of control among Whites has led to conclusions that an internal orientation is preferable because it is associated with positive outcomes such as persistence, performance, and participation in social activism (Rotter, 1990; Strickland, 1989). However, research on African Americans has revealed that an external orientation may reflect a realistic appraisal of the role of external factors such as discrimination and lack of economic support. Perhaps the most extreme example of the inadequacy of a universal approach is when theories previously tested on White college students are assumed to be automatically generalizable to ethnic group members with markedly different life experiences. Clearly, such an approach is inconsistent with literature, suggesting that cultural norms and belief systems of Asians (Kim, McLeod, & Shantzis, 1992), American Indians and Alaska Natives (Fleming, 1992), African Americans (Randolph & Banks, 1993), and Latinos (Casas, 1992) are unique.

A second implication of the assumption of universality is that it does not encourage researchers to develop alternative models and associated variables that may be more helpful for understanding the psychology of ethnic group members. Two examples illustrate this point. First, numerous studies have demonstrated the importance of acculturation (Casas, 1992) and racial identity, (Castro, Sharp, Barrington, & Walton, 1991; Gary & Berry, 1985; Goddard, 1993; Resnicow, Soler, Braithwaite, Ben Selassie, & Smith, 1999) in understanding the psychology of ethnic minority group members. However, because those variables are not particularly useful for understanding the psychology of Whites (Walsh, 2001), such variables are sometimes excluded in studies on ethnic minorities that are based on a White conceptual framework. The impact of language barriers on social arrangements (i.e., family life) is a second example of a phenomenon that may not be included in studies of the American culture but may be critical for understanding an ethnic minority group. Because it is not uncommon for some children in immigrant families to understand English better than the parent, the language barrier has sometimes created conditions in which the child actually has to negotiate for the family in the outside world because the child can speak English. This reality has led to role reversals in parent-child relationships among some Asian American children and their parents (Kim et al., 1992). However, this dynamic may be overlooked if a researcher is relying on a conceptual framework derived from studies on normative White families in which language barriers are not an issue.

Similarly, the assumption of universality overlooks the possibility of specific cultural strengths that may serve as protective factors for surviving the challenges of minority status. For example, spirituality has been identified as a strength of the African American culture (Boyd-Franklin, 1989; Goddard, 1993; Randolph & Banks, 1993). On the basis of that assumption, Oler (1995) found that the level of spirituality predicted intolerant drug attitudes among African American adolescents.

Even if other ethnic groups are just as spiritual, those groups may have other cultural strengths that buffer them from the potential consequences of negative risk factors. For instance, according to Triandis (1995), some Asian cultures are collectivistic in their orientation. That is, they favor cooperation and group harmony over purely personal goals. Theories derived on American samples are more likely to emphasize an individualistic orientation. Those researchers who frame questions on Asian Americans using the individualistic orientation of the American mainstream may not adequately address the potential protective role of the collectivistic orientation in facilitating a sense of belonging during immigration. Ignoring cultural strengths may be a particular problem in research designed to test the efficacy of a variety of interventions.

Finally, Jones (1993) reported a tendency for research on ethnic minority groups to focus on differences from the White culture. That approach (even if inadvertent) supports a viewpoint that mainstream behavior patterns are the standard and deviations from mainstream are problematic (Nobles, 1995). Such an approach may result in a focus on maladaptations, dysfunctions, and deficiencies when studying an ethnic group (Jones, 1993).

The assumption of universality may prevent researchers from uncovering some important information about the psychology of diverse groups. The point is that there is good reason to consider ethnicity at the conceptual stage. However, as the section on methodology will reveal, the assumption of universality is not just a conceptual issue. Rather, it is often embedded in methodology as well.

METHODOLOGICAL ISSUES

The methodology of a research project includes, among other issues, the selection of the sample, the selection of appropriate measurement tools, and the determination of the appropriate procedures for gathering information. These issues, along with recruitment and retention, are discussed in this section.

Sampling

Addressing the shortage of ethnic minorities in psychological research samples was the objective of the NIH Revitalization Act. This challenge was introduced earlier in the chapter. The adequacy of the sample is directly tied to the recruitment procedures. Moreover, in longitudinal studies or other situations in which more data collection is involved, an effective strategy for retention is essential. In addition, a representative sample should reflect the within-group diversity of the ethnic group. Each of these issues is discussed in this section.

Recruitment. Some groups may have a healthy skepticism about the value of research for their communities. Some of this skepticism may reflect a distrust of academic researchers and concerns regarding how the findings will be used (or misused) (Guerra & Jagers, 1998). Moreover, the difficulties may be even greater among illegal immigrant groups or others who may be understandably concerned that participation in a scientific project might uncover their identity. That healthy skepticism may mean that researchers have to take some extra steps to recruit a sample.

Other researchers have described the difficulties of recruiting African Americans (Ward, 1992) and other ethnic minority groups (Traugott, 1987). The NIH published its *Outreach Notebook for the NIH Guide on the Inclusion of Women and Minorities as Subjects in Clinical Research* in 1997. That document offers suggestions for recruiting and retaining these groups in research studies.

Despite the potential difficulties, some researchers have reported success in recruiting the overwhelming majority (85%-100%) of those approached (Capaldi & Patterson,

1987; Stouthamer-Loeber, van Kammen, & Loeber, 1992; Streissguth & Guinta, 1992). Cauce, Ryan, and Grove (1998) reported a number of recruitment strategies that work for ethnic minorities, including the following: (a) using monetary incentives, (b) securing endorsements from ethnic minority organizations or prominent community leaders, (c) building in personal contact, (d) collecting the information in the person's home or at a familiar site in the community, (e) avoiding study names that might stigmatize the participants (i.e., using a neutral name instead of the Family Drug Study), and (f) building persistence into the data collection process (i.e., numerous follow-up calls).

The advantages of including community leaders (or members) on the research team have been noted in previous research. For example, Beauvais and Trimble (1992) described the plight of a researcher who wished to collect data from the residents in a small Cree village in the Manitoba province of Canada. Instead of seeking the support of community leaders, the researcher entered the community uninvited despite tribal policies against such actions. Eventually, the researcher was asked to leave the reservation. Similarly, Casas (1992) argued that to obtain an adequate Latino sample, one might need to use strategies such as (a) soliciting the aid of community leaders in introducing the project to the targeted community, (b) obtaining signatures of respected community leaders to include on cover letters, and (c) (when appropriate) developing both English and Spanish versions of all materials. Others encourage those seeking to collect data from African American (Grace, 1992) and Asian American (Kim et al., 1992) groups also to develop community support before initiating the project.

In one of our prevention projects with high-risk youth in a small African American township, the principal investigator first met with the city council, city manager, and local leaders to see if they thought it was a good idea.

With their endorsement, she approached school officials and other leaders. Eventually, she set up an office in the community YWCA. Finally, she hired community residents on the project and established a community advisory board. By the time she approached individual families to participate, all these steps had been completed. For that reason, community response was much more favorable than if she had simply shown up on the scene indicating that she had government funds to work with the children in the community.

Beauvais and Trimble (1992) warned that the researcher should not expect community leaders simply to "rubber-stamp" the project. Rather, the researcher should be open to making changes based on the preferences and advice of the community representatives. The researcher should be prepared to make compromises with the community on issues related to both the objectives and the strategies.

Retention. In longitudinal studies and other studies that involve data collection in more than one administration, retention is a major concern. Some limited evidence suggests that it is more difficult to track ethnic minorities (Call, Otto, & Spenner, 1982). In a school-based study, for example, Seidman, Allen, Aber, Mitchell, and Feinman (1993) reported that the retention rates were highest for Whites, then Latinos, and lowest for African Americans.

This difference in retention may be due to factors associated with lower socioeconomic status (SES) such as lower home ownership rates, single parenthood, unstable employment patterns, and concentration in urban areas where contact with neighbors may be more limited. Nevertheless, numerous researchers have obtained respectable retention rates (Mason, Cauce, Gonzales, & Hiraga, 1996; Seidman et al., 1993; Stouthamer-Loeber et al., 1992) with ethnic minority samples. For example, Gregory, Lohr, and Gilchrist (1992) were able to retain 97% of their sample of low-SES,

pregnant adolescents in which data were collected five times over the course of a 5-year period. Cauce et al. (1998) suggested that the following retention strategies might reduce the attrition rate: (a) collecting accurate information such as the correct spelling of the name, birth date, place of employment, and driver's license number at the beginning along with information on significant others who may know how to reach the family if they move; (b) planning interim contacts with birthday cards, holiday greeting cards, newsletters, and so on, to learn early if a family has relocated; (c) designing incentive strategies that increase in amount from the beginning to the end of the study period; (d) adding staff to maintain regular contact; and (e) making the first experience especially pleasant so individuals will want to participate again.

Sehwan Kim and associates (1992) developed a list of strategies for the recruitment and retention of Asian American samples. These strategies include (a) collecting data in private settings; (b) providing refreshments at research activities; (c) using informal, personal approaches (i.e., telephone calls or personal visits) to recruit and retain research participants; (d) providing compensation for time given to evaluation tasks; and (e) providing logistical support such as transportation and child care.

Within-Group Diversity. The within-group diversity for the four ethnic minority groups considered in this chapter—Latinos, Asian/Pacific Islanders, American Indians and Alaska Natives, and African Americans—presents a formidable challenge for collecting a representative sample. Each of these four groups is quite diverse. The term *Hispanic* or *Latino* is the name for subgroups that vary by Latin American national origin, racial stock, and generational status in the United States (Casas, 1992). The subgroups include those whose cultural origins are in Mexico, Puerto Rico, Central America, Cuba, and other Latin

American countries (Padilla & Snyder, 1992). Similarly, Fleming (1992) reported 365 state-recognized American Indian and Alaska Native tribes, each with its own social, religious, economic, and legal-political norms. The term *Asian/Pacific Islander* includes more than 60 separate ethnic/racial groups or subgroups (Kim et al., 1992). These subgroups include unassimilated Asians living in separate enclaves such as various Chinatowns to third-generation Asians who might be quite integrated into the American culture. Moreover, people of African descent include individuals whose ancestors may have lived in one of the many countries of Africa, the West Indies, or one of the Americas. In addition to diversity in the region of the world from which their ancestors immigrated, important within-group differences in the social conditions and lifestyles should not be ignored in developing a sampling plan. Accordingly, those researchers who limit their study of any of these ethnic minority groups to a sample of college students run the risk of generating findings that may not be generalizable to other segments of these communities.

Within-Group Diversity in Survey Samples. Addressing the heterogeneity of the various ethnic groups is even more essential in survey research. A common practice in survey research is to increase the number of respondents recruited from a specific ethnic minority group by oversampling in pockets of the community that are densely populated with that particular ethnic group (i.e., inner-city neighborhoods). To the extent that this practice ignores the fact that members of that ethnic group reside in other settings, the practice violates a general tenet of probability sampling that every member has some chance of being selected.

The Institute of Social Research (ISR) at the University of Michigan has developed a strategy for generating a diverse sample of African Americans that may be applicable to other groups as well. If used appropriately, the design yields an equal probability, self-weighting sample of working household numbers. The sampling plan is an extension of a sampling plan developed by Waksberg (1978), commonly referred to as the random digit dialing (RDD) design.

The ISR plan is a modification of the Waksberg (1978) strategy for sampling the African American population (Inglis, Groves, & Heeringa, 1985). The plan takes advantage of two circumstances. First, telephone companies assign telephone prefixes geographically. For example, all the households with the same prefix are likely to be in close geographic proximity to each other. Second, racial segregation in housing increases the probability that households with the same prefix are likely to be of the same race.

The plan has two stages. In Stage 1, numbers are randomly selected from the pool of numbers in a specific locale. These numbers are considered the "primary numbers," and an attempt is made to reach each household. If the number belongs to an African American, it is considered an eligible cluster and retained. If not, it is eliminated.

For the purpose of this sampling strategy, telephone numbers with the same prefix can be grouped into 100 (or 200) member series. For example, the number 624-8890 belongs to the 100 series that ranges from 624-8800 to 624-8899. These are called clusters. Primary numbers that belong to African American households were retained in Stage 1 because they are assumed to belong to clusters where a larger proportion of the households within the cluster is African American as well. However, a small but disproportionate subset of the selected primary numbers should be randomly selected that belong to African Americans who live in mixed or predominately White communities. This latter group of clusters ensures within-group diversity because the African Americans contacted in those clusters live in mixed or predominately White neighborhoods.

The 100 telephone numbers in the eligible (or retained) clusters are then randomly ordered. The interviewer calls each number on the list and screens the household in that order to determine whether an African American individual or family lives in it. If so, an African American member of the household is invited to participate in the survey. These calls continue until a predetermined quota of African American households per cluster is enrolled.

The eventual sample is considered to be self-weighting because it automatically includes a proportionate number of African Americans in Stage 1 who live in other communities. If two thirds of African Americans in a given city live in African American communities and another third live either in mixed or predominately White communities, these two groups are expected to be represented proportionately in the sample of primary numbers. Blair and Czaja (1982) found that this two-stage process increased the number of hits (i.e., reaching an African American family) from 9% in Stage 1 to 25% in Stage 2. Moreover, they argued that it might be useful to enlarge the primary stage clusters to 200 or larger to increase the likelihood of obtaining the desired quota of African American households from each cluster.

Of course, one drawback of the strategy is the exclusion of the approximately 15% of the U.S. African American population without telephones. Members of that subgroup tend to be poorer and younger than those living in households with telephones (Thornberry & Massey, 1983).

Measurement

Adequate measurement is critical for meeting the challenge of the NIH Revitalization Act. Any biases inherent in the use of measurement detract from the goal of gathering accurate information on ethnic minorities. The assumption of the universality of the American mainstream can be evident in measurement as well.

When an investigator proposes to use a specific instrument for a specific ethnic group, it is becoming more common to ask whether that instrument has been used in the past with that ethnic group. However, clearly the fact that others have used the instrument with a specific group does not guarantee that the utility of that measure for that group has been sufficiently examined. In this section, we will discuss the issues that arise when using measurements that were standardized on predominately White samples.

To address those issues, let's consider an example of a race comparison study. Race comparison studies are studies in which ethnicity or race is the independent variable. Imagine a hypothetical clinical study in which a researcher is comparing the effect of divorce on the adjustment of Asian American and White males. A sample of adults from both groups is recruited to participate. For the purpose of this example, let's assume that the recruitment procedures are adequate. We decide that our operational definition of adjustment is the degree of anxiety or distress indicated on Scale 7 of the Minnesota Multiphasic Personality Inventory (MMPI-2). The MMPI-2 is administered to both groups, and the validity indicators indicate that the scores are appropriate. Elevated scores on the MMPI-2 suggest more problems. In our hypothetical study, the MMPI-2 scores of the Asian American sample are significantly higher than the MMPI-2 scores for the White sample. How do we interpret the findings?

The standardization sample of the MMPI-2 was carefully developed to reflect the composition of the U.S. population based on census data. Accordingly, Whites and Asian Americans constituted 83.7% and .5% of the sample, respectively, because these groups made up a similar proportion of the U.S. population at that time. Stated differently, there were 933 Whites and 6 Asian Americans in the MMPI restandardization male sample. (A small sample raises the issue

Table 8.1 Demonstration of the Assumption of Universality With Data From the MMPI-2

	Means Based on Actual Proportion of Caucasians and Asians in the Standardization Sample of the MMPI-2			Means if the Proportion of Caucasians and Asians in the Standardization Sample of the MMPI-2 Were Reversed		
	Overall Mean (n = 939)	Caucasian Mean (n = 933)	Asian Mean (n = 6)	Overall Mean (n = 939)	Caucasian Mean (n = 6)	Asian Mean (n = 933)
Pa	11.06	11.04	14.33	14.30	11.04	14.33
Sc	10.79	10.75	16.50	16.46	10.75	16.50

of representativeness, and that risk is, by definition, more of an issue for the smaller sample that is typically the ethnic sample. However, let's disregard that issue for the moment as well.) According to the *MMPI-2: Manual for Administration and Scoring* (Hathaway & McKinley, 1991), the means for the White and Asian American males in the standardization sample are fairly different on several scales, including Scale 7 (see Table 8.1). For simplicity's sake, let's imagine for a moment that the population only included Whites and Asian Americans. In that event, the overall mean would have been 11.06.[1] The means for the White and Asian American samples were 11.04 and 14.33, respectively. Obviously, the overall mean is much more similar to the mean of the larger than the smaller group.

Now imagine that we were norming the sample in a region that was largely Asian American to the point where it would be appropriate to have the reverse—6 Whites and 933 Asian Americans. Then, the corresponding overall mean would be 14.30—close to the mean for the Asian American sample. The main point here is that including a small, albeit proportionate, representation of an ethnic minority group in the standardization sample does little mathematically to change the mean from the mean for the majority group. Consequently, if the resulting scale mean is then used in the same manner for both groups, in effect, the mean for the majority group is being used to interpret the scores for the ethnic

minority group. Although this is a clinical issue, it is also clearly a research issue in studies that not only compare two or more ethnic groups but also use the universal mean or cutoff scores to evaluate findings of within-group designs of the ethnic minority group. For example, if scores above a uniform *T* score of 65 on the MMPI-2 are considered elevated, then the score of an ethnic minority, especially a score near the cutoff, could conceivably be defined as pathological even though the score may be fairly normative within one's own ethnic group. In essence, the assumption of universality is still in effect here even though the researcher has chosen a measure in which an ethnic group is included in proportion to its representation in the population.

One might argue that there are legitimate reasons why ethnic minorities may have higher scores on the attributes measured by the MMPI-2, so it is reasonable that higher scores be assigned to them. Those who accept that point of view might use this argument to justify evaluating the scores of ethnic minority groups against an overall group mean. However, that conclusion is unsatisfactory for several reasons. First, our hypothetical study, as it is designed, does not consider any preexisting ethnic differences. Hence, the researcher may be tempted to attribute the differences to divorce rather than to preexisting differences. Moreover, if we look at the female standardization sample, Asian American females (10.00) actually had lower scores than White females (12.27) on this same scale and six other clinical scales. However, the higher scores among the White females raise the mean. Hence, the higher scores of White females are not interpreted as elevated. The point is that the use of standardization samples that are predominantly drawn from one group essentially makes that group the standard and can lead to interpretations of the normative scores of the other groups as deviant. This is a particular problem when conducting race comparison research.

This issue is certainly not limited to the MMPI-2. Tanner-Halverson, Burden, and Sabers (1993) objected to the use of the Wechsler Intelligence Scale for Children–Third Edition (WISC-III) norms to interpret the responses of the Tohono O'odham children when that ethnic group only comprised 4% of the sample. Instead, Tanner et al. created local norms on the WISC-III for that group of children.

Clearly, this issue has the potential to be a concern in race comparison research. However, more generally, it is an issue whenever the scores of members of an ethnic group are being interpreted using scores derived from a standardization sample mainly composed of another group. Ironically, this issue should not just be viewed as a concern relevant to ethnic minority group members. Rather, if the predictions regarding the increases in the proportion of the U.S. population that are ethnic minority are realized, then Whites also could eventually find themselves in the unenviable position of being judged by norms developed in large part on other groups.

Equivalence. Equivalence is achieved when a measure assesses the same underlying concept in two separate groups. Berry (1980) and Brislin (1993) asserted that equivalence is a prerequisite condition for using an assessment tool developed in one culture but used in a different culture. The issue of equivalence is an especially important concern when trying to determine if group differences (or similarities) are indications of true differences (or similarities) in psychological processes or measurement issues (Knight & Hill, 1998). Test bias occurs when "an existing test does not measure the equivalent underlying psychological construct in a new group or culture as was measured within the original group in which it was standardized" (Allen & Walsh, 2000, p. 67). Cultural bias is a source of nonequivalence of measures that occurs when unintended systematic variance is present due to factors that vary across cultures or subcultures (Knight & Hill, 1998).

Brislin (1993) identified three types of equivalence, including translation, metric, and conceptual equivalence. Translation equivalence occurs when the scale is accurately translated to another language in a manner that promotes linguistic equivalence. Allowing members of groups in which English may be a second language to select the language for any paper-and-pencil instruments is the preferred strategy. However, it is important that the versions of the measure be identical. This usually requires a back-translation procedure in which the translation of an instrument into a new language is followed by a translation back into the original language by a different translator.

Okazaki and Sue (1995) noted that linguistic equivalence may even be an issue when an ethnic group speaks the dominant language. For example, many American Indians and Alaska Natives may only have exposure to reservation English (Allen, 1998). Similarly, Dunnigan, McNall, and Mortimer (1993) described a group of Laotian Hmong adolescents who spoke sufficient English to complete their academic requirements. Nevertheless, they interpreted the common meanings of words and metaphors so differently that it shaped their responses on psychological measures. Accordingly, the reliability and validity coefficients of instruments used to assess their mental health were poor.

Metric equivalence is generally assumed to be adequate when the reliability and validity of a measure are just as adequate in the new group as they were for the original group. However, Beauvais and Trimble (1992) suggested another indicator of metric equivalence—whether the factor structure of the measure is the same in the original and the new sample. Still another indicator of metric equivalence may be whether the response patterns for the two groups are equivalent. Bachman and O'Malley (1984a, 1984b) have demonstrated ethnic group differences in the predominant response patterns. For example, in a study of adolescents, African American youth were more likely than White youth to use the extreme response options. Moreover, some argue that the tendency to say yes or to indicate agreement within some Latino cultures is so prominent that a term exists for it—si-ismo. Clearly, cultural differences in response patterns may account for differences between ethnic groups in race comparison studies. Such differences might be a problem for establishing metric equivalence.

Conceptual equivalence is achieved if the underlying psychological construct is the same in the new group as it was in the original group. For example, a study by Milstein, Guarnaccia, and Midlarsky (1993) illustrates group differences in how Latinos, African Americans, and White caretakers conceptualize the mental illness of a family member. In that study, Latino caretakers described their family member's problem as emotional twice as often as the other two groups. However, both African American and White caretakers were more likely than Latino caretakers to interpret similar problems in a family member as "medical" in nature. Clearly, these differences raise the possibility of critical group differences in how other psychological concepts are understood. These differences may not be fully addressed in race comparison studies.

Allen and Walsh (2000) added a fourth type of equivalence known as functional equivalence. *Functional equivalence* refers to whether a specific behavior has the same meaning in the new group that it had in the group on which the measure was standardized. For example, Beauvais and Trimble (1992) described how excessive drinking in the presence of the family might be viewed as shameful among certain groups but an acceptable social behavior among certain American Indian and Alaska Native groups. They added that there may be instances when an underlying concept measured by one scale within one culture might best be measured by a different scale in a different culture.

Assessing the Appropriateness of Measures for Ethnic Populations. It is fairly common to consider the internal consistencies or any other form of reliability information available on a measure when it is to be used in a culture other than the one in which it was developed. However, internal consistency alone does not address the appropriateness of a measure. A number of other strategies are available for assessing validity.

Strategies developed by Campbell and Fiske (1959) for examining validity in general are useful for examining the validity of a measure in a new population. Generally, these strategies take advantage of the fact that variables do not occur in isolation from other variables but are related to each other. Accordingly, if variables have a conceptual relationship, then these relationships should be apparent empirically. For example, Knight, Tein, Shell, and Roosa (1992) used an r-to-Z transformation to examine whether the intercorrelations among a group of socialization and family interaction measures were the same for Latino and White samples. If the patterns of intercorrelations are similar across groups, then the measure may be equivalent across groups. However, differences in the pattern of intercorrelations raise the possibility of group differences in what the measure is tapping.

Allen and Walsh (2000) described three other promising strategies for screening measures for potential cross-cultural or multicultural adaptation. These are factor analysis, regression, and item response theory. In factor analysis, the researcher is examining whether the factor structure of a scale that was determined in a sample from another group applies to the new group to which the scale is to be applied. Allen and Walsh noted that findings from samples as small as 50 with loadings of .80 can be stable. Consequently, it is possible to examine similarities in the factor structure, even in small sample factor analyses. Differences in the factor analyses raise the possibility of cultural differences in what the measure is assessing. Manson (1994), for example, reported important ethnic group differences in the factor structure of the Center for Epidemiological Studies—Depression Scale (CES-D). This led Manson to conclude that the underlying concept of depression measured by the CES-D differed among Chinese American, Mexican American, and American Indian and Alaska Native groups.

A second strategy is the use of regression. This strategy is based on the Cleary (1968) rule, which states that

> a test developed for use in measurement of a construct is equivalent if it has the same regression equation with some external correlate of behavior in the new culture or ethnic group as with the group with which it was developed. (Allen & Walsh, 2000, p. 74)

Similarly, structural equation modeling (SEM) provides another method for examining the comparability of measures across groups. Again, the relationship of the measure to an external correlate is assessed. In SEM, the covariances (of the relationship of the measure to an external correlate) can be constrained to be equal in the groups (i.e., Whites and African Americans). If the constraint lowers the goodness-of-fit indices, then it is possible that the measure is not equivalent across groups.

The third strategy involves item response theory. It is possible to estimate the probability that an item will be endorsed based on item characteristics (or parameters) and available information regarding the actual presence of the trait. The probability of endorsing the item at any level of the trait is a function of item parameters and the extent to which the characteristic is actually present. This probability can be estimated. This information can be used to produce a line sometimes referred to as an item characteristic curve. Group differences in the item characteristic curve suggest that at any level of the trait, the two groups differ in their likelihood of endorsing the item. Hence, group differences in the item characteristic curve raise the possibility that the measure is not equivalent across groups.

Finally, one might examine whether race or ethnic group membership moderates the regression coefficient between two variables (including the variable being measured by the test measure). If group membership moderates the relationship between the two variables, then the measure may not be equivalent across groups.

If these various tests do not support the equivalence of a specific measure, then Allen and Walsh (2000) argued that the investigator can choose any of three potential options: (a) choose a different instrument, (b) develop a culture-specific instrument, or (c) investigate the item pool for items that display differential functioning across groups. The first and third strategies might be more feasible than the second for projects on limited budgets.

Of course, it is possible to gather some useful information regarding the equivalence of measures just by asking representatives of a group to critique the measure. Focus groups (Knight & Hill, 1998) and pilot studies (Beauvais & Trimble, 1992) are both useful for such purposes. Beauvais and Trimble (1992) described how an item as innocent as "Other boys like to play with me" had a double meaning among a specific group of young people.

The researchers only recognized this flaw when they received some unprintable responses! Focus groups may be particularly helpful for catching subtle differences in meaning earlier.

Use of Observations and Ratings to Measure Behavior. The difficulties associated with standardized paper-and-pencil instruments might persuade some researchers to use observations and ratings rather than paper-and-pencil instruments. However, clinical research has demonstrated that these types of measures also present challenges for the researcher. For example, a study by Loring and Powell (1988) presented the same case scenario to four different groups of psychiatrists. One group was told the patient was a White male. The others were told that the patient was a White female, African American female, or African American male. The psychiatrists were to use the information provided to render a diagnosis. The case was more likely to be diagnosed as paranoid schizophrenic when described as an African American male. Although this study illustrates an important clinical issue, it certainly suggests that researchers need to be aware of the potential for bias when subjective ratings are used to measure behavior.

Data Collection

The three common methods for collecting survey data are mail surveys, telephone surveys, and face-to-face or personal interviews. Survey researchers typically agree that response rates are lowest with mail surveys (average about 30%) and highest with personal interviews (70%-75%) (Cauce et al., 1998). This pattern may be especially important to consider when collecting data from ethnic minorities. Rogers (1976) asked Whites, African Americans, and Latinos how they preferred to be contacted for surveys. Both Latinos and African Americans preferred to be interviewed in person, whereas Whites preferred telephone contact. Similarly, Casas (1992) argued that either mail or telephone surveys may be a challenge for interviewing Latino samples. Rather, he argued that potential Latino respondents would cooperate more if they had a chance to meet and interact with the interviewer.

Previous research has demonstrated that participant responses may also vary depending on the ethnicity of the interviewer (Cauce et al., 1998). Matching the ethnicity of the interviewer and the participant may be especially important when asking about attitudes about another ethnic group or other sensitive information. However, Cauce et al. (1998) added that it may not be sufficient for the interviewer to be a member of the same ethnic group as the participant. Rather, it may also be important to select interviewers who were raised with sufficient contact with their own ethnic group and who are familiar with and comfortable interacting with members of their own ethnic group. For that reason, it may not always be appropriate to send those college students who were raised in a predominately White community to interview members of their own ethnic group if they are not accustomed to interacting with that subgroup. Instead, cultural sensitivity may be the key component.

ANALYTICAL ISSUES

Steinberg and Fletcher (1998) argued that despite increasing pressures by journals to disclose the ethnic composition of their samples, requiring that information alone does little to ensure the adequate analyses of samples that include ethnic minorities. Rather, even if the researcher addresses the concerns at the conceptual and methodological levels adequately, Steinberg and Fletcher pointed out that other concerns face the researcher once the data have been collected, coded, and prepared for data analyses. Conducting the appropriate analyses is particularly critical when a study includes two or more different ethnic groups (e.g., either Whites and an ethnic minority group or two or more ethnic minority groups). A number of the issues that face the researcher during the data analyses are discussed in this section.

Race-Comparison Research

The goal of such studies frequently is to determine group differences between ethnic groups on some dependent variable. Some shortcomings of race comparison studies—studies in which race or ethnicity is the independent variable—were discussed earlier in the section on measurement. However, the adequacy of race comparison research is an analytical issue as well. According to McLoyd (1998, p. 10), research on minority children traditionally has been dominated by studies that compare minority group children to White children. For example, McLoyd and Randolph (1985) reported that twice as many studies were published between 1936 and 1980 that compared African Americans to White children as studies that included only African American children. Moreover, Graham (1992) reported that 78% of the studies that appeared in *Developmental Psychology* and the *Journal of Educational Psychology* in 1989 were race comparative.

Our discussion in the chapter up to this point has raised a number of concerns about the potential pitfalls of race comparison studies. Some researchers argue that it is rarely appropriate to conduct this type of comparison research. Steinberg and Fletcher (1998) pointed out that ethnicity commonly covaries with other sociodemographic variables, and for that reason, it is difficult to determine whether racial differences are truly attributable to ethnicity or to group difference on other sociodemographic variables. Some

researchers address this issue by conducting preliminary analyses to determine if any group differences need to be controlled in the main analyses. However, Steinberg and Fletcher argued that it is not always possible to identify and include all the sociodemographic variables that may covary with ethnicity.

Azibo (1988) has identified several appropriate situations for conducting race comparison studies. According to Azibo, the appropriate basis for race comparison studies is the following: (a) to refute prevailing beliefs about African Americans (deconstructive compulsion), (b) to detect racial differences on social indices such as income or health status (research question compulsion), and (c) to compare groups on worldview (construct compulsion). However, he also argued that it is not proper to make race comparisons when the groups differ on any relevant variable.

Ethnicity as a Control Variable

Sometimes researchers add race or ethnicity as a control variable. When a variable is added as a control variable, the researcher is concerned that one's status on that control variable may be obscuring the relationship between the independent and the dependent variables. In that sense, Steinberg and Fletcher (1998) contended that control variables are treated as nuisance variables. Accordingly, the use of ethnicity as a control variable diminishes the importance of ethnicity in the research. Moreover, Steinberg and Fletcher cited the work of Applebaum and McCall (1983), who have demonstrated that such controls introduce a different set of confounds.

Alternatives to Comparative Studies

Heretofore, we have been discussing some controversial strategies for including ethnic group membership in research studies (i.e., race comparison studies). However, one should not conclude that it is inevitably unproductive to consider ethnic group membership in research. When the researcher decides that it is appropriate to compare ethnic groups, several questions other than mean differences may be more informative. These include research that examines group differences in variability and research that considers ethnic group membership in mediator and moderator studies.

Group Differences in Variability. Matsumoto (1994) argued that it may be just as interesting to compare the variances of the two groups as to compare the means. This information may be useful for identifying differences in the within-group heterogeneity of the two groups. Differences in variability are determined by examining the *F* ratio. This statistic is easily calculated by dividing the variance of one group by the variance of the other group. An *F* ratio larger than the critical value suggests that the response set for the two groups is different. If the *F* ratio is large enough to suggest group differences in variability, then Matsumoto suggested that the data be converted into standard scores within each culture, and then the standard scores can be used in subsequent analyses (except comparisons of the means of the various ethnic groups). Matsumoto pointed out that this strategy is only useful in a multifactor study.

Mediator Studies. A mediator is a third variable that serves as the vehicle through which one variable (the independent variable) influences a second variable (the dependent) variable. In this case, ethnicity may serve as the independent variable that ultimately influences the dependent variable indirectly by first influencing status on a third variable (the mediator), which subsequently influences status on the dependent variable. For example, ethnicity may influence access to medical care, and access ultimately influences one's

medical status. To test for a mediator, one must meet the following three conditions: (a) The independent variable (ethnicity) must have a relationship to the proposed mediator (access to medical care), (b) the proposed mediator (access) must have a relationship to the dependent variable (medical status), and (c) a preexisting relationship between the independent variable (ethnicity) and the dependent variable (medical status) is either eliminated or reduced substantially once the relationship between the mediator (access) and the dependent variable (medical status) is controlled (Baron & Keney, 1986).

Moderator Studies. Steinberg and Fletcher (1998) pointed out the value of examining group differences on patterns of relationships between variables. Such studies are sometimes referred to as moderator studies. A *moderator study* examines whether the relationship between two or more variables varies depending on one's status on the proposed moderator. A moderator variable study differs from the race comparison studies described earlier by examining group differences in the correlations between variables, whereas the other race comparison studies mentioned earlier examine whether group differences are present on the actual variables.

If ethnicity is proposed as a moderator, the question being addressed is whether the relationship between the other two variables is the same for various ethnic groups. The results of such an approach can reveal interesting group differences in the relationships between variables. For example, in a recent study of the relationship of discrepancies in SES to marital satisfaction, Enoch-Morris (2001) first conducted a preliminary examination to determine whether racial differences were present on any of her study variables. Although no racial differences were evident in these bivariate analyses, she still continued to examine the role of race. Her independent variable was

SES discrepancy (whether the spouses differed in SES). Couples were classified as being in marriages in which the husband had the higher SES according to the Hollingshead Four Factor Index of Social Economic Status (HH), the wife had the higher SES (WH), or the SES of the husband and wife were equal (SM). The dependent variable was the husband's marital satisfaction. Race was the proposed moderator. African Americans and Whites did not differ on either the SES discrepancy or the husband's marital satisfaction. However, the pattern of the relationship between SES discrepancy and marital satisfaction was different for African American and White males. Among White males, those in HH marriages reported more marital satisfaction than those in either WH or SM marriages. However, among African American males, those in WH reported the highest level of marital satisfaction. If that researcher had prematurely collapsed her sample after finding no mean differences between races on the individual variables, she would not have discovered this very interesting difference.

Steinberg and Fletcher (1998) warned that the test for a moderator effect (adding the product term to the regression equation) is a very conservative test and, consequently, may underestimate group differences in the relationship between two variables. Accordingly, they argued that it may sometimes be just as appropriate to examine the relationship between two variables separately in two different analyses—one for each ethnic group.

Addressing Within-Group Differences in the Analyses

When the study includes only one ethnic minority group, the researcher still needs to consider within-group heterogeneity. For example, it may be useful to report if a Latino sample is primarily Puerto Rican, so the reader will not assume that the results are automatically generalizable to other Latino groups. However, if the composition of the ethnic group is heterogeneous, then sufficient information should be collected on the ethnic background of the members of the sample. When the sample size is sufficient, then subanalyses can examine whether differences exist among the subgroups within a particular ethnic group. Even if those subanalyses are not feasible, at least the researcher can report the diversity within the subgroup when describing the sample.

CONCLUSIONS

In summary, the need for more psychological research on ethnic minorities is apparent. However, even though the inclusion of ethnic minorities in all kinds of research is necessary, inclusion alone is insufficient for ensuring the adequate treatment of ethnic minorities in future research. Instead, researchers face challenges at the conceptual, methodological, and analytical stages. At the conceptual stage, the assumption of the universality of the American mainstream experience sometimes leads to the blind adoption of theoretical approaches developed on other populations while failing to develop alternative models that consider the cultural strengths and other unique characteristics of a specific ethnic group. The methodological challenges include sampling, recruitment, retention, and measurement equivalence. At the analytical stage, the use of race comparison research is viewed as a flawed approach except in specific situations. Nevertheless, previous researchers have described other more effective strategies for considering race, such as the inclusion of race as an independent variable in mediator studies and the inclusion of race as a moderator variable.

NOTE

1. The actual mean for the male MMPI-2 is 11.24 on Scale 7. The difference is due to the inclusion of other ethnic groups in the standardization sample, not just Whites and Asian Americans. Nevertheless, the heavy influence of the White sample of 83.7% is still clearly evident in the overall mean.

REFERENCES

Allen, J. (1998). Personality Assessment with American Indians and Alaska Natives: Instrument considerations and service delivery style. *Journal of Personality Assessment, 70,* 17-42.

Allen, J., & Walsh, J. (2000). A construct-based approach to equivalence: Methodologies for cross-cultural/multicultural personality assessment research. In R. Dana (Ed.), *Handbook of cross-cultural and multicultural personality assessments* (pp. 63-85). Mahwah, NJ: Lawrence Erlbaum.

Applebaum, M., & McCall, R. (1983). Design and analysis in developmental psychology. In W. Kessen (Ed.), *History, theory, and methods.* In P. H. Mussen (Ed.), *Handbook of child psychology* (4th ed., Vol. 1, pp. 415-445). New York: John Wiley.

Azibo, D. (1988). Understanding the proper and improper usage of the comparative research framework. *Journal of Black Psychology, 15,* 81-91.

Bachman, J., & O'Malley, P. (1984a). Black-White differences in self esteem: Are they affected by response style? *American Journal of Sociology, 90*(3), 624-629.

Bachman, J., & O'Malley, P. (1984b). Yea-saying, nay-saying, and going to extremes: Black-White differences in response style. *Public Opinion Quarterly, 48*(2), 491-509.

Baron, R. M., & Keney, D. S. (1986). The moderator-mediator variable distinction in social psychological research: Conceptual, strategic, and statistical considerations. *Journal of Personality and Social Psychology, 51,* 1173-1182.

Beauvais, F., & Trimble, J. (1992). The role of the researcher in evaluating American Indian alcohol and other drug abuse treatment programs. In M. Orlandi (Ed.), *Cultural competence for evaluators: A guide for alcohol and other drug abuse prevention practitioners working with ethnic/racial communities* (pp. 173-201). Rockville, MD: OSAP.

Berry, J. W. (1980). Introduction to methodology. In H. C. Triandis & J. W. Berry (Eds.), *Handbook of cross-cultural psychology* (Vol. 2, pp. 1-28). Boston: Allyn & Bacon.

Blair, J., & Czaja, R. (1982). Locating a special population using random digit dialing. *Public Opinion Quarterly, 46,* 585-590.

Boyd-Franklin, N. (1989). *Black families in therapy: A multisystems approach.* New York: Guilford.

Brislin, R. W. (1993). *Understanding culture's influence on behavior.* New York: Harcourt Brace.

Call, V. R. A., Otto, L. B., & Spenner, K. I. (1982). *Tracking respondents: A multimethod approach.* Lexington, MA: Lexington Books.

Campbell, D. T., & Fiske, D. W. (1959). Convergent and discriminant validation by the multitrait-multimethod matrix. *Psychological Bulletin, 56,* 81-105.

Capaldi, D., & Patterson, G. R. (1987). An approach to the problem of recruitment and retention rates for longitudinal research. *Behavioral Assessment, 9,* 169-177.

Casas, J. M. (1992). A culturally sensitive model for evaluating alcohol and other drug abuse prevention programs: A Hispanic perspective. In M. Orlandi (Ed.), *Cultural competence for evaluators: A guide for alcohol and other drug abuse prevention practitioners working with ethnic/racial communities* (pp. 75-116). Rockville, MD: OSAP.

Castro, F., Sharp, E., Barrington, E. H., & Walton, M. (1991). Drug abuse and identity in Mexican Americans: Theoretical and empirical considerations. *Hispanic Journal of Behavioral Sciences, 13,* 209-225.

Cauce, A. M., Ryan, K., & Grove, K. (1998). Children and adolescents of color, where are you? Participation, selection, recruitment and retention in developmental research. In V. McLoyd & L. Steinberg (Eds.), *Studying minority adolescents* (pp. 147-166). Mahwah, NJ: Lawrence Erlbaum.

Cleary, T. (1968). Test bias: Prediction of grades of Negro and White students in integrated colleges. *Journal of Educational Measurement, 10,* 43-56.

Dunnigan, T., McNall, M., & Mortimer, J. T. (1993). The problem of metaphorical nonequivalence in cross-cultural survey research: Comparing the mental health statuses of Hmong refugee and general population adolescents. *Journal of Cross-Cultural Psychology, 24,* 344-365.

Enoch-Morris, A. (2001). *An examination of spousal values as a potential moderator of the association between discrepant socioeconomic status and marital satisfaction.* Unpublished doctoral dissertation, University of Cincinnati.

Federal Register. (1994, March 28). *59,* 14508-14513.

Fleming, C. (1992). American Indians and Alaska Natives: Changing societies past and present. In M. Orlandi (Ed.), *Cultural competence for evaluators: A guide for alcohol and other drug abuse prevention practitioners working with ethnic/racial communities* (pp. 147-171). Rockville, MD: OSAP.

Gary, L., & Berry, G. (1985). Predicting attitudes toward substance use in a Black community: Implication for prevention. *Community Mental Health Journal, 21,* 42-51.

Goddard, L. (1993). *An African centered model of prevention for African American youth at high risk.* Rockville, MD: OSAP.

Grace, C. (1992). Practical considerations for program professionals and evaluators working with African American communities. In M. Orlandi (Ed.), *Cultural competence for evaluators: A guide for alcohol and other drug abuse prevention practitioners working with ethnic/racial communities* (pp. 55-74). Rockville, MD: OSAP.

Graham, S. (1992). "Most of the subjects were White and middle class": Trends in published research on African Americans in selected APA journals 1970-1989. *American Psychologist, 47,* 629-639.

Gregory, M. M., Lohr, M. J., & Gilchrist, L. D. (1992). Methods for tracking pregnant and parenting adolescents. *Evaluation Review, 17,* 69-81.

Guerra, N., & Jagers, R. (1998). The importance of culture in the assessment of children and youth. In V. McLoyd & L. Steinberg (Eds.), *Studying minority adolescents* (pp. 167-181). Mahwah, NJ: Lawrence Erlbaum.

Hagen, J., & Conley, A. (1994, **MONTH**). Ethnicity and race of children studied in *Child Development,* 1980-1993. *Society for Research in Child Development Newsletter,* pp. 6-7.

Hathaway, S., & McKinley, J. (1991). *MMPI-2: Manual for administration and scoring.* Minneapolis: University of Minnesota Press.

Inglis, K., Groves, R., & Heeringa, S. (1985). *Telephone sample designs for the U.S. Black household population.* Unpublished manuscript.

Jones, J. (1993). The concept of race in social psychology. In L. Wheler & P. Shaver (Eds.), *Review of personality and social psychology* (Vol. 4, pp. 117-150). Newbury Park, CA: Sage.

Kim, S., McLeod, J., & Shantzis, C. (1992). Cultural competence for evaluators working with Asian-American communities: Some practical considerations. In M. Orlandi (Ed.), *Cultural competence for evaluators: A guide for alcohol and other drug abuse prevention practitioners working with ethnic/racial communities* (pp. 203-260). Rockville, MD: OSAP.

Knight, G., & Hill, N. (1998). Measurement equivalence in research involving minority adolescents. In V. McLoyd & L. Steinberg (Eds.), *Studying minority adolescents* (pp. 183-210). Mahwah, NJ: Lawrence Erlbaum.

Knight, G., Tein, J., Shell, T., & Roosa, M. (1992). The cross-ethnic equivalence of parenting and family interaction measures among Hispanic and Anglo American families. *Child Development, 63,* 1392-1403.

Loring, B., & Powell, B. (1988). Gender, race, and *DSM-II:* A study of the objectivity of psychiatric diagnostic behavior. *Journal of Health and Social Behavior, 29,* 1-22.

Manson, S. M. (1994). Culture and depression: Discovering variations in the experience of illness. In W. J. Lonner & R. S. Malpass (Eds.), *Psychology and culture* (pp. 285-290). Boston: Allyn & Bacon.

Mason, C., Cauce, A. M., Gonzales, N., & Hiraga, Y. (1996). Neither too sweet nor too sour: Problem peers, maternal control and problem behavior in African American adolescents. *Child Development, 67,* 2115-2130.

Matsumoto, D. (1994). *Cultural influences on research methods and statistics.* Pacific Grove, CA: Brooks/Cole.

McLoyd, V. C. (1998). Changing demographics in the American population: Implications for research on minority children and adolescents. In V. McLoyd & L. Steinberg (Eds.), *Studying minority adolescents* (pp. 3-28). Mahwah, NJ: Lawrence Erlbaum.

McLoyd, V. C., & Randolph, S. M. (1985). Secular trends in the study of Afro-American children: A review of *Child Development, 1936-1980. Monographs of the Society for Research in Child Development, 50,* 78-92.

Milstein, G., Guarnaccia, P., & Midlarsky, E. (1993, August). *Ethnic differences in the interpretation of mental dysfunction.* Paper presented at the 101st Annual Convention of the American Psychological Association.

National Institutes of Health (NIH). (1990). *NIH/ADAMHA policy concerning the inclusion of women in study populations.* Bethesda, MD: Author.

National Institutes of Health (NIH). (1997). *Outreach notebook for the NIH guide on inclusion of women and minorities as subjects in clinical research* (NIH Pub. No. 97-4160). Bethesda, MD: Author.

Nobles, W. (1995). Psychological research and the Black self-concept: A critical review. In N. Goldberger & J. Veroff (Eds.), *The culture and psychology reader* (pp. 164-183). New York: New York University Press.

Okazaki, S., & Sue, S. (1995). Methodological issues in assessment research with ethnic minorities. *Psychological Assessment, 7,* 367-375.

Oler, C. (1995). *Spirituality, racial identity, and intentions to use alcohol and other drugs among African American youth.* Unpublished doctoral dissertation, University of Cincinnati.

Padilla, A., & Snyder, V. (1992). Hispanics: What the culturally informed evaluator needs to know. In M. Orlandi (Ed.), *Cultural competence for evaluators: A guide for alcohol and other drug abuse prevention practitioners working with ethnic/racial communities* (pp. 117-146). Rockville, MD: OSAP.

Randolph, S. M., & Banks, H. D. (1993). Making a way out of no way: The promise of Afrocentric approaches to HIV prevention. *Journal of Black Psychology, 19*(2), 204-214.

Resnicow, K., Soler, R., Braithwaite, R., Ben Selassie, M., & Smith, M. (1999). Development of a racial and ethnic identity scale for African American adolescents: The survey of Black life. *Journal of Black Psychology, 25*(2), 171-188.

Rogers, T. (1976). Interviews by telephone and in person: Quality of response and field performance. *Public Opinion Quarterly, 40,* 51-65.

Rotter, J. B. (1990). Internal versus external control of reinforcement: A case history of a variable. *American Psychologist, 45,* 489-493.

Seidman, E., Allen, L., Aber, L., Mitchell, C., & Feinman, J. (1993, April). *The impact of school transitions in early adolescence on the self-system and social context of poor urban youth.* Paper presented at the meetings of the Society for Research on Child Development, New Orleans, LA.

Steinberg, L., & Fletcher, A. (1998). Data analytic strategies in research on ethnic minority youth. In V. McLoyd & L. Steinberg (Eds.), *Studying minority adolescents* (pp. 279-294). Mahwah, NJ: Lawrence Erlbaum.

Stouthamer-Loeber, M., van Kammen, W., & Loeber, R. (1992). The nuts and bolts of implementing large scale longitudinal studies. *Violence and Victims, 7,* 63-78.

Streissguth, A. P., & Guinta, C. T. (1992). Subject recruitment and retention for longitudinal research: Practical considerations for a nonintervention model. *NIDA Research Monographs, 117,* 137-154.

Strickland, B. R. (1989). Internal-external control expectancies: From contingency to creativity. *American Psychologist, 44,* 1-12.

Tanner-Halverson, P., Burden, T., & Sabers, D. (1993). WISC-III normative data for Tohono O'odham Native American children. *Journal of Psychoeducational Assessment: Monograph Series, Advances in Psychoeducational Assessment,* 125-133.

Thornberry, O., & Massey, J. (1983). *Coverage and response in random digit dialed national surveys.* Alexandria, VA: American Statistical Association.

Traugott, M. W. (1987). The importance of persistence in respondent selection for preelection surveys. *Public Opinion Quarterly, 51,* 48-57.

Triandis, H. C. (1995). *Individualism and collectivism.* Boulder, CO: Westview.

U.S. Bureau of the Census. (1994). *Statistical abstract of the United States: 1994.* Washington, DC: Government Printing Office.

Waksberg, J. (1978). Sampling methods for random digit dialing. *Journal of the American Statistical Association, 73,* 40-46.

Walsh, J. (2001). The Multidimensional Inventory of Black Identity: A validation study in a British sample. *Journal of Black Psychology, 27,* 172-189.

Ward, C. O. (1992). Cross-cultural methods for survey research in Black urban areas. *Journal of Black Psychology, 3,* 72-87.

CHAPTER 9

Ethnic Research Is Good Science

STANLEY SUE
University of California, Davis

LESLIE SUE
Butte-Glenn Community College, California

Over the years, a number of researchers and scholars have pointed to the paucity of social science research on ethnic minority populations and the lack of attention to cultural variables in the research. These are significant problems that face the social sciences. Without more research, we cannot be in a position to understand the status of these populations and their needs. On the other hand, the lack of ethnic research is instructive. It points to certain processes that plague our scientific practices. In this chapter, we assume that a consensus exists over the importance of accurately understanding the experiences of ethnic minority populations. Given this assumption, we argue that the quality and quantity of ethnic research are uneven and handicapped by the (a) difficulties in conducting such research and (b) current practices in scientific psychology. We conclude by suggesting the kinds of changes that are needed in scientific practices to increase the quality and quantity of ethnic research.

PROBLEMS IN CONDUCTING ETHNIC RESEARCH

The fact that research on ethnic minority populations is sparse has been well documented (Graham, 1992; Iwamasa & Smith, 1996; Padilla & Lindholm, 1995). Relatively few journal articles have been published that involved ethnic minority individuals. Although all researchers must grapple with theoretical and methodological issues in research, ethnic research requires additional considerations because theoretical models, assessment instruments, and methodologies have largely been developed on one population—namely, Americans in general and White Americans in particular. Psychology and the social sciences are well developed in the United States, and the subject of the research has been typically White Americans. Therefore, this means that investigators cannot simply assume that existing theories and assessment instruments have validity with ethnic minority populations, and they must expend some efforts in validating instruments or testing the applicability of existing theories before the examination of target research questions. They must take into account cultural considerations into every phase of research (Rogler, 1989). Sue, Kurasaki, and Srinivasan (1999) have outlined the difficulties in conducting ethnic research in critical research phases. They listed seven such phases: planning research, defining variables, selecting valid measures, sampling research participants, gaining cooperation from research participants, designing research, and interpreting findings. In all of these phases, special challenges and difficulties are posed for ethnic minority research, as shown in Table 9.1.

Planning for Research

In planning for research, the research questions must be addressed. The problem in this beginning stage is that there is often a smaller knowledge base on which to guide the research. For example, if a researcher is interested in the responsiveness of African American clients to culturally based psychotherapeutic interventions, the researcher is limited by the fact that there are very few rigorous empirical studies of the efficacy of therapy with African Americans, let alone culturally based therapies. A researcher often does not have the benefit of a direct body of knowledge on which to base the work. Furthermore, because theories and measures used in previous research are largely based on Anglo populations, it is unclear whether they are applicable to African Americans. Although theories and measures may have cross-cultural validity, one does not know

a priori. Most researchers use existing theories and measures with the assumption that they are applicable, try to validate them with the ethnic population, or modify measures and theories so that they are pertinent to the ethnic population. In any event, even in this beginning stage of research, complexities confront researchers.

Definition of Variables

Increasingly, social scientists are confronting the fact that certain concepts such as race have been inaccurately defined. Race has been used to refer to a subgroup of people who have certain genetically determined, physical characteristics that are more or less distinct from other subgroups (Jones, 1997). Yet as knowledge has accumulated over the human genome, it is clear that physical characteristics (hair, skin color, facial features, etc.) cannot be used to distinctly separate groups into races—that differences in physical characteristics are largely quantitative rather than qualitative in nature. In fact, race is more of a social, rather than biological, concept. Psychological scientists primarily use self-designation (one's self-reported race), not biological markers, to divide people. Similarly, ethnicity is also defined by self-report in most studies. Given self-definitions and reports, race and ethnicity are broad concepts that encompass a great deal of heterogeneity so that researchers may find it difficult to characterize members of a race or ethnicity (Trimble, 1988). Furthermore, race and ethnicity are often used as proxy variables that are mediated by, or correlated with, other variables (Walsh, Smith, Morales, & Sechrest, 2000). These other variables may be of greatest interest in explaining findings. For example, a researcher may find that Asian Americans tend to avoid the use of mental health services. Although this is an important finding, Asian Americans may be more susceptible to feelings of shame and stigma, which are the important

Table 9.1   Phases in Ethnic Minority Research

Planning for research
    Paucity of baseline research
    Unknown validity of theories based on other populations
    Unknown validity of assessment instruments
Definition of variables
    Operational definition of race and ethnicity
    Race or ethnicity as a distal variable
    Between- versus within-group emphasis
Selecting measures
Translation or language equivalence
Conceptual equivalence
Metric equivalence
Selection of subjects and sampling
    Sampling of small populations
    Representativeness of samples to the population
Gaining cooperation
    Problems in informed consent
Cultural differences in cooperativeness
Research designs and strategies
    Qualitative and quantitative designs
    Explanatory research
Interpretation of data
    Insider versus outsider perspectives
    Drawing inferences
    Generalizations

variables in explaining the avoidance of services. The definition of variables and identification of explanatory variables are important and often difficult tasks.

Selecting Measures and Establishing Cross-Cultural/Language Equivalency

When studying members of ethnic minority groups, some of whom may have limited English proficiency, what assessment instruments or measures should be used? Care must be taken to ensure that the instruments measure meaningful psychological concepts in a valid fashion. Brislin (1993) has noted that in studying ethnic minority populations with instruments primarily constructed for White or mainstream populations, establishing several types of equivalence is critical: (a) translation or language equivalence (when the descriptors and measures of psychological concepts can be translated well across languages), (b) conceptual equivalence (whether the construct being measured exists in the thinking of the target culture and is understood in the same way), and (c) metric equivalence (whether the scale of the measure can be directly compared for different cultural groups, e.g., whether an IQ score of 100 on an English intelligence scale may be truly equivalent to a score of 100 on the translated version of the same intelligence scale).

Thus, researchers interested in the study of ethnic minority populations cannot simply use existing psychological measures and tools without first considering the equivalence of the measures. Sometimes, in working with ethnic minority populations, innovative means must often be found to measure characteristics. For example, in the National Latino and Asian American Survey (NLAAS), a creative strategy was used to survey the mental health of Latinos and Asian Americans in the community. Because interviewers conducting household surveys might find respondents who speak a different language or dialect (e.g., a Chinese-speaking interviewer who encountered a Vietnamese-speaking respondent), NLAAS equipped interviewers with cell phones. If a respondent spoke a language different from that of the interviewer, the interviewer would then dial into a waiting group of interviewers who collectively could speak many different languages so that the respondent could be language-matched with an interviewer over the phone.

Selection and Sampling of the Population

Scientific research principles of selection and sampling of the population are no different for a cross-cultural or ethnic population as for research in the general population. However, complications exist because of the size of ethnic minority populations and possible differences in responding because of culture. Given the relatively small size of ethnic minority populations, it is often difficult to find representative samples and adequate sample sizes. Furthermore, some respondents, because of their cultural background, may find participation in research to be intrusive or taboo in nature, strange because of unfamiliarity with the research process, and anxiety provoking because of fears over how the collected information can be used. Refugees in particular may fear that their responses can somehow be used against them. Because of the problems in finding a representative sample of a relatively small minority group, ethnic minority research can be very costly and difficult to initiate. For example, in one study of Chinese Americans, the project cost $1.5 million to conduct a two-wave study (see Takeuchi et al., 1998). Nearly 20,000 households were approached to find 1,700 Chinese respondents.

The difficulties in finding adequate samples of certain ethnic minority populations have often led researchers to find convenience samples from quite different sources. For example, the samples may come from lists of ethnic organizations, names suggested by other respondents (the snowballing technique), and universities rather than communities at large. Another strategy is to combine groups so that an adequate sample size is reached. Instead of just studying Puerto Rican Americans, a researcher may broaden the base by including all Hispanics. Although these strategies can help to increase sample sizes, they obviously run the risk of subject self-selection, lack of representation of the population, and increased heterogeneity.

Gaining Cooperation From Research Participants

In conducting research requiring self-disclosure, ethnic minority respondents may be reticent in answering questions on their feelings or emotions, making the process of collecting data longer than anticipated. Respondents may be hesitant in discussing issues openly when they fear being overheard by other members of their family and community. Although respondents may be reluctant in participating in research, cultural variables may affect how cooperative respondents are.

The very act of obtaining consent to participate in the research may make prospective participants less likely to cooperate. For example, in the United States, respondents are asked to read a description of the research and then sign an informed consent statement. Although the procedure is common in the United States, respondents from other countries and cultures may be unfamiliar with the notion of informed consent. Respondents may be concerned over providing their signature or alarmed at the possible negative impact that the research may have, as stated in the description given to participants. Many may decline to participate.

Research Design and Strategies

The field of psychology is scientific as well as professional. It is perhaps accurate to characterize the scientific field as quantitative in nature. Knowledge is primarily acquired by the numerical analysis of observations or experiments. As mentioned earlier, mainstream diagnostic concepts, theoretical orientations, and treatment models are laden with values, beliefs, and attitudes, representative of the mainstream U.S. culture from which they were derived.

How, then, do we establish an understanding of relevant concepts and theoretical frameworks across diverse cultures, and how do we ensure that research findings are interpreted within the appropriate cultural context? A number of cultural investigators have emphasized qualitative methodologies that are more holistic in approach to understand the meanings, patterns, rules, and behaviors that exist in ethnic minority communities. Qualitative methodologies are often used when phenomena are difficult to quantify or measure using existing instruments. A number of qualitative strategies can be found, including ethnographic research (the study of the practices and beliefs of cultures and communities), case study, phenomenological research, participative inquiry, and focus groups (Mertens, 1998).

Most of the training in psychology is based on quantitative methodology. Although the learning of such methodology is necessary, training in qualitative approaches has typically been neglected. Thus, many investigators who want to study ethnicity find themselves ill trained.

Interpretation of Findings/Validity

Cultural issues also arise in the interpretation of research findings. For many years, African American researchers have objected to the pervasive view that African Americans are deficient—coming from broken families, low achieving, having poor verbal communication skills, and exhibiting self-hatred (Jones, 1997). Asian Americans have objected to interpretations of research findings on well-being that characterize them as being extraordinarily adjusted, well functioning, and educated compared to other Americans. When comparisons are made between various ethnic minority groups, differences between the groups cannot be assumed to reflect desirable or undesirable characteristics because the value assigned to the characteristics may be simply a reflection of one's own norms. This does not mean one should adopt absolute relativism, in which there are no standards that cross all groups. Rather, researchers must always consider whether their conclusions are biased in the direction of ethnic stereotypes and misunderstandings. They must also be sensitive to how characterizations are viewed by members of the ethnic group. The interpretation of findings should take into account the perspectives of insiders and outsiders to the ethnic group being investigated.

It should be noted that in the study of ethnicity and race, the research can be highly controversial. Genetic differences in physical features and in intellectual functioning, socioeconomic status, rates of crime, health and mental health disparities, personality characteristics, racism and discrimination, stereotyping, social relations, and hate crimes are issues that have been associated with race and ethnicity. These issues often raise strong emotions, feelings of discomfort, and political controversy. Ethnic researchers are sometimes subjected not only to professional scrutiny and standards of science but also to more personal criticisms about positions taken or conclusions drawn. Thus, researchers who wish to avoid controversy may be reluctant to study race and ethnicity. This is unfortunate because ethnic research is beneficial not only for ethnics but also for all Americans and for our science.

In conclusion, becoming involved in ethnic research has taught us that such research is very difficult to conduct, and many researchers have not been exposed or trained to deal with these difficulties. The unfortunate effect is that investigators, who find the research difficult or expensive to conduct, may prefer not to study ethnicity or prefer to treat ethnicity as a nuisance variable to be controlled. In either case, collection of data is jeopardized, and little knowledge on ethnic minority groups is gained. In each phase of research, efforts must be made to increase the meaningfulness and fidelity of the tasks.

SCIENTIFIC PRACTICE

In the previous section, we argued that conducting ethnic research requires cultural sensitivity and awareness in all phases of the research endeavor. Researchers may be reluctant to engage in ethnic research because of the difficulties. At a more fundamental level, the lack of more research on ethnic minority groups is attributable to the very practices used in psychological science. In particular, there is a selective enforcement of scientific principles (Sue, 1999). Table 9.2 outlines the arguments in selective enforcement. First, internal validity is emphasized over external validity in scientific practices. Second, because of the de-emphasis on external validity, there is little interest in testing the generalizability of findings, measurement instruments, or theories derived from one (usually the mainstream) population to another. Third, researchers interested in studying an ethnic minority group population must then either accept the generality of findings from the mainstream population (and run the risk of using findings that do not apply to the ethnic population) or reject the generality of findings (and then be forced to conduct baseline studies simply to establish a baseline of knowledge). Fourth, ethnic research has a difficult time being published because reviewers can question the validity of ethnic research because it may be based on findings that cannot be generalized or because a baseline level of knowledge has not been established.

The Selective Enforcement of Scientific Principles

In psychological science, the goal of research is to describe, understand, predict, and control phenomena. Underlying this goal is the need to determine cause-and-effect relationships. If, say, the etiology of schizophrenia is found, then we can describe and understand the disorder and are in a position to predict and intervene to control the disorder. Discovering causal relationships is therefore a basic goal, and this discovery is often accomplished by conducting research with internal and external validity. *Internal validity* refers to the extent to which conclusions can be drawn about the causal effects of one variable on another (i.e., the effect of the independent variable on the dependent variable). *External validity* is the extent to which one can generalize the results of the research to the populations and settings of interest. Both kinds of validity are necessary. Researchers need to construct rigorous research designs that will allow one to draw causal inferences and to conduct sufficient research to know the extent to which the findings apply (or do not apply) to different populations and settings. The latter task is particularly important in allowing one to know how universally valid or applicable the research is.

The scientific principles of internal and external validity are differentially enforced and encouraged. In practice, attention is paid to internal validity, and external validity is often assumed but not tested. Far more papers submitted for publication are probably rejected because of design flaws, inability to control for confounding or extraneous variables, and so on, than for possible external validity problems.

Table 9.2   Consequences of Selective Enforcement of Scientific Principles

Internal validity elevated over external validity
    Attention paid to internal rather than external validity
Assumed generality of findings
Low knowledge base for ethnic minority populations
    Few empirical findings
    Need to conduct baseline studies
    Validity of existing theories and assessment tools unknown
Problems in ethnic research productivity
    Research costly and difficult to conduct
Papers submitted for publication considered preliminary
    Justification for funding more difficult to argue
Fewer publications on ethnic minorities

The assumption of the generality of findings and the dominance of internal over external validity are evident in much of the psychological research being conducted. Let us provide three examples. First, much psychological research has been conducted on college students, and major theories of human beings have been developed on college students. Impressive is the rigor and ingenuity of research designs to enhance internal validity. Yet a number of researchers have pointed to limitations in the generality of findings derived from the use of college students who do not represent mainstream Americans in educational attainments, age, ethnicity, social class, attitudes, and values (Kazdin, 1999; Sears, 1986). Second, psychological research is relatively mature in the United States compared to other parts of the world. Theories of human beings, measurement tools, and research methods are developed by this research. Americans are the primary subjects of the research. However, Americans represent only about 5% of the world's population. This means that theories and findings selectively derived from one country representing about 5% of the world's population are used to generate universal theories. This is neither good practice nor good science. It points to the lack of interest in external validity.

Finally, the dominance of internal over external validity is apparent in the mental health field, where a distinction is made between efficacy, which has been considered the gold standard for outcome research, and effectiveness research. Efficacy studies are investigations that examine the outcomes of mental health interventions, often by using experimental methods, control over the influence of extraneous variables, and laboratory-like settings. On the other hand, effectiveness research examines outcomes of mental health interventions in a naturalistic setting (such as a mental health clinic) where random assignment of clients, clear-cut experimental manipulations, matched experimental and control groups, and so forth, may not be possible. Whereas efficacy research may employ strict exclusion criteria in the selection of clients to study, this may not be the case in effectiveness research. For example, in an efficacy study of a treatment for schizophrenia, exclusionary criteria might include comorbidity, current use of psychotropic medication, and non-White race. That is, clients who have multiple disorders, are using medication, and are members of an ethnic minority group may be excluded from the study to eliminate variables not being studied. However, such a practice would limit the applicability or generality of the findings. On the other hand, effectiveness research studies treatment outcomes in more real-life situations, where patients may have multiple disorders, may be taking medication, and may be members of various racial groups.

Effects on Ethnic Research

The relative inattention to external validity means that researchers are not particularly motivated to test the generality of their research findings. Generality is simply assumed. In such a situation, researchers may feel little need to devote resources to studying ethnic groups. The assumption of generality is actually antithetical to science because conclusions in science are built on facts and evidence, not assumptions or biases. Scientists should be skeptical and base conclusions on research findings or logical deductions. In the absence of evidence, beliefs or hypotheses should be tested. Because much of the psychological research is not based on ethnic minority populations, it is actually unclear whether a particular theory or principle is applicable, whether an intervention has the same phenomenological meaning for different cultural groups, or whether measures or questionnaires are valid for these populations. The responsibility is placed on those who are interested in ethnic minority groups to show whether research findings that are based on mainstream Americans but assumed to be universal are applicable to ethnic minority populations. When the research is not applicable, ethnic researchers have to conduct basic or descriptive research to establish baseline knowledge or test the cultural adequacy of research measures and designs. This entire process results in fewer publications, more descriptive and pilot studies rather than sophisticated investigations, and lower probability of receiving research funding for ethnic rather than mainstream populations.

Guyll and Madon (2000) believe that the notion of selective enforcement of scientific principles is a serious charge that is leveled against the scientific community. They contend that (a) current practices in science are not biased against ethnic research, (b) ethnic minority research that replicates research on the mainstream population will be judged as being less important, (c) ethnic research that is inconsistent with existing theories is considered only as a weak challenge, and (d) it is parsimonious to assume that theories developed on White populations have generality to other populations. In essence, Guyll and Madon argue that their propositions are based on "theoretical conservatism." Theoretical conservatism is an approach that is not biased against ethnic minority research. However, ethnic minority research is likely to be considered relatively unimportant because if the research supports the theory, it is considered a replication. Replications are often not highly valued. Guyll and Madon further maintain that if ethnic research findings contradict the theory, then the challenge to the theory is weak because alternative explanations exist for obtaining different findings across theories. Novel theoretical claims based on new research often lack a strong empirical foundation. They are especially vulnerable to subsequent refutation by contradictory evidence or by the discovery of an internal flaw. Finally, they believe that precluding generalizations from one population to another would encourage a Balkanization of psychological science, requiring the testing of all populations before validating the universality of a theory.

The position adopted by Guyll and Madon (2000) can be challenged on several fronts (Sue, 2000). It is not clear if their characterization of theoretical conservatism is accurate. However, if one accepts their notion of theoretical conservatism, it seems to run counter to scientific conservatism. As noted earlier, science requires evidence and a skeptical attitude. The assumption that a theory is universally valid, in the absence of cross-cultural validation, seems to violate the scientific principles that require evidence for conclusions and skepticism in thinking. It is not consistent with scientific principles to make generalizations without evidence. Consistent with rigorous science is the careful testing of theories and their generality, especially because there are many instances when theoretical formulations based on one population fail to be validated with other populations (Sue, 1999). It is true that requiring the cross-validation of theories with different populations will entail much effort. However, even if not all populations can be subjected to research, the goal is to construct a nomological net that supports a theory in question. Psychological theories are difficult to "prove." Our science is largely based on probability. Through research, one can increase the probability of being theoretically sound. The real task is to study different populations, form a nomological net, and increase one's confidence in the validity of a proposed theory. Inclusion of ethnic populations in research is therefore important and consistent with good scientific practice.

Toward Solutions

As we have tried to indicate, two main problems have hindered the development of ethnic research: (a) the methodological and conceptual difficulties in conducting such research and (b) the practice in psychological science of ignoring the importance of external validity in research. How can these two problems be addressed?

First, as revealed in Table 9.1, cultural considerations are critical in all phases of research. Therefore, the training of researchers

with expertise in ethnic minority and cross-cultural research is important. Graduate and postdoctoral training programs should offer opportunities to learn about the methodological and conceptual problems in ethnic research and the means to conduct rigorous ethnic research. Recently, some excellent textbooks have been published that provide a basic introduction into race/ethnic minority research (e.g., see Walsh et al., 2000). Second, the importance of ethnic and cross-cultural research in validating the universality or applicability of theories, methodologies, and measures should be emphasized. In fact, all theories as well as measures should be rated as to their cross-cultural adequacy. For example, if Theory A is grounded in research on only one population, it should be considered as a local (emic) theory until tested and validated with other populations. On the other hand, Theory B, which has been tested and validated with many different populations, should be viewed as being more robust, rigorous, and stringent in meeting research criteria and more applicable to human beings in general than Theory A. It is indeed impressive for a researcher to not only create theories and measures but also demonstrate their meaningfulness for a variety of populations. In reviewing manuscripts for publication, journal editors have a responsibility to require research to demonstrate cross-cultural validity. These actions will do much to increase the importance of ethnic and cross-cultural research. They are good for science.

REFERENCES

Brislin, R. W. (1993). *Understanding culture's influence on behavior*. New York: Harcourt Brace.

Graham, S. (1992). "Most of the subjects were White and middle class": Trends in published research on African Americans in selected APA journals, 1970-1989. *American Psychologist, 47,* 629-639.

Guyll, M., & Madon, S. (2000). Ethnicity research and theoretical conservatism. *American Psychologist, 55,* 1509-1510.

Iwamasa, G. Y., & Smith, S. K. (1996). Ethnic diversity in behavioral psychology: A review of the literature. *Behavior Modification, 20,* 45-59.

Jones, J. M. (1997). *Prejudice and racism.* San Francisco: McGraw-Hill.

Kazdin, A. E. (1999). Overview of research design issues in clinical psychology. In P. C. Kendall, J. N. Butcher, & G. N. Holmbeck (Eds.), *Handbook of research methods in clinical psychology* (pp. 3-30). New York: John Wiley.

Mertens, D. M. (1998). *Research methods in education and psychology.* Thousand Oaks, CA: Sage.

Padilla, A. M., & Lindholm, K. J. (1995). Quantitative educational research with ethnic minorities. In J. A. Banks & C. A. McGee-Banks (Eds.), *Handbook of research on multicultural education* (pp. 97-113). New York: Macmillan.

Rogler, L. H. (1989). The meaning of culturally sensitive research in mental health. *American Journal of Psychiatry, 146,* 296-303.

Sears, D. O. (1986). College sophomores in the laboratory: Influences of a narrow data base on social psychology's view of human nature. *Journal of Personality and Social Psychology, 51,* 515-530.

Sue, S. (1999). Science, ethnicity, and bias: Where have we gone wrong? *American Psychologist, 54,* 1070-1077.

Sue, S. (2000). The practice of psychological science. *American Psychologist, 55,* 1510-1511.

Sue, S., Kurasaki, K. S., & Srinivasan, S. (1999). Ethnicity, gender, and cross-cultural issues in clinical research. In P. C. Kendall, J. N. Butcher, & G. N. Holmbeck (Eds.), *Handbook of research methods in clinical psychology* (pp. 54-71). New York: John Wiley.

Takeuchi, D. T., Chung, R. C., Lin, K. M., Shen, H., Kurasaki, K., Chun, C., & Sue, S. (1998). Lifetime and twelve-month prevalence rates of major depressive episodes and dysthymia among Chinese Americans in Los Angeles. *American Journal of Psychiatry, 155,* 1407-1414.

Trimble, J. (1988). Putting the etic to work: Applying social psychological principles in cross-cultural settings. In M. H. Bond (Ed.), *The cross-cultural challenge to social psychology* (pp. 109-121). Newbury Park, CA: Sage.

Walsh, M., Smith, R., Morales, A., & Sechrest, L. (2000). *Ethnocultural research: A mental health researcher's guide to the study of race, ethnicity, and culture.* Cambridge, MA: Health Services Research Institute.

CHAPTER 10

Acculturation Research
Current Issues and Findings

GERARDO MARÍN
PAMELA BALLS ORGANISTA
KEVIN M. CHUN
University of San Francisco

Acculturation is arguably the most important moderating variable or construct considered when conducting research or assessing the impact of interventions that involve ethnic minority individuals. As is true with other multidisciplinary concepts (e.g., culture, ethnicity), acculturation as a construct suffered from unclear and incomplete definitions, improper and ill-defined measurement approaches, and overextended applications. Nevertheless, during the past two decades, social scientists have renewed their interest in exploring the relation between acculturation and a person's attitudes, behaviors, and values and better defining and understanding the construct and its implications. From early attempts at describing acculturation as a social process of change (e.g., Redfield, Linton, & Herskovitz, 1936; Social Science Research Council, 1954), the field has shifted to our contemporary concern for understanding acculturation as a psychological (and therefore more individual) process (e.g., Berry, 1980, 1997; Graves, 1967; Padilla, 1980b).

As can be expected from this increased attention to acculturation, the number of publications related to acculturation has exploded. Indeed, a number of reviews or analyses of acculturation have appeared since Padilla's (1980a) seminal book, including a number of chapters and books (e.g., Berry & Sam, 1997; Chun, Balls Organista, & Marín, 2003; Kim & Abreu, 1995;

AUTHORS' NOTE: Preparation of this chapter was partially supported by Grants 6RT-0407 and 6PT-6001 from the California Tobacco-Related Research Program and from The Pew Charitable Trusts. The opinions expressed in this report are those of the authors and do not necessarily reflect the views of The Pew Charitable Trusts.

LaFromboise, Coleman, & Gerton, 1993; Landrine & Klonoff, 1996). Given the proliferation of recent publications, including the comprehensive analysis edited by Chun and his colleagues (2003), this chapter will not present an extensive review of the literature on acculturation. Instead, this chapter provides a summary of general themes centered on conceptualization, measurement, and application of acculturation paradigms, particularly within psychology.

HISTORY OF ACCULTURATION AS A CONSTRUCT

Initially, acculturation was a construct used by researchers to better understand the modernization and Westernization processes that various cultures and communities were undergoing during the 19th century. More recently, acculturation has become important in understanding the experiences of ethnic and cultural minorities as international migrations and political conflicts support the creation of multicultural societies.

In the United States, acculturation became a construct of significance toward the early part of the 20th century as social scientists tried to explain the process of cultural diffusion and personal change taking place as large numbers of immigrants reached the country from Europe, China, Japan, Mexico, and other countries. The rapid industrialization of the country and the need for agricultural workers and construction workers, together with politically and economically unstable foreign nations, gave rise to significant migratory currents into the United States. Whether arriving through Ellis Island or through Angel Island or walking across the Rio Grande, those early 20th-century immigrants found a nation with a relatively short history that exhibited a defined cultural set of values inherited, in part, from the colonizing nations of Europe. These more recent immigrants joined the large number of Africans whose physical and intellectual efforts have contributed to this country's growth after enduring forced migration as slaves.

Defining Acculturation

Earlier researchers defined *acculturation* as "those phenomena which result when groups of individuals having different cultures come into continuous first-hand contact with subsequent changes in the original culture patterns of either or both groups" (Redfield et al., 1936, p. 149). A few years later, a group of scholars meeting under the auspices of the Social Science Research Council (1954) suggested a more complex definition of acculturation as

> cultural change that is initiated by the conjunction of two or more autonomous cultural systems. . . . Its dynamics can be seen as the selective adaptation of value systems, the process of integration and differentiation, the generation of developmental sequences, and the operation of role determinants and personality factors. (p. 974)

Thus, the "accomodational" experiences of some 20th-century European immigrants became the defining pattern for our early understanding of the acculturation process (Olmedo, 1980). This initial conceptualization gave rise to paradigms such as the "melting pot" to define "American" culture and to promote assimilation into the host culture as the end goal of the acculturative process. More recently, theorists (e.g., Berry, 1980, 1997, 2001) have argued that acculturation occurs along various dimensions rather than one dimension, moving from monoculturalism (of origin) toward assimilation. In particular, Berry's (1980, 1997, 2003) conceptualization of acculturation as a multidirectional process has been an important contribution to the psychological understanding of acculturation.

Berry (1980) suggested that acculturation occurs when two fairly autonomous cultural groups come in contact with each other. He further argued that the process can be conflictual and difficult for individuals who face a variety of possible adaptation strategies. Furthermore, Berry stated that there are at least four types of outcomes to the acculturative process:

Assimilation (when the individual gives up the cultural identity of origin and wishes positive relationships with the host culture)

Separation (when the original culture is retained and no positive relationships with the original culture are desired)

Integration (when the individual desires to retain the culture of origin as well as maintain positive relationships with the host culture)

Marginalization (where there is no retention of the original culture and no desire to have positive relationships with the host culture)

Berry further suggested that as a dynamic process, acculturation must be viewed as a gradual change in a number of areas (or dimensions) that affect the individual (e.g., language, cognitive style, personality, identity, attitudes, and acculturative stress). In this sense, any of the acculturative outcomes (e.g., integration, assimilation) can be identified through changes in one of many influential areas (e.g., language use, personal identity).

Inherent in many of the models for acculturation described above is the notion that biculturalism is indeed possible and frequent among individuals exposed to two or more cultures. Indeed, a number of recent studies have shown that biculturalism is not only frequent but also quite beneficial to individuals (LaFromboise et al., 1993). Chapter 20 in this *Handbook* reviews recent literature on biculturalism.

Although definitions of acculturation have emphasized different aspects of the construct, a contemporary understanding of acculturation would probably include the following aspects: (a) continuous and long-term contact with one or more different cultures or subcultures; (b) continuity and change of attitudinal and behavioral patterns along multiple cultural/ethnic dimensions; (c) fluidity of the acculturative process, implying that individuals are in constant movement along the cultural/ethnic dimensions; and (d) a process that involves various strategies and varied outcomes, including conflict and adaptation. In short, as Trimble (2003) suggested, acculturation is a "multidimensional process generating several definitive outcomes" (p. 7).

ASSESSMENT OF ACCULTURATION

To better understand the unique challenges and transformations that ethnic minorities experience as they are exposed to a new culture, one must have sound measures available to assess their acculturation status. In the past few years, as definitions of acculturation have improved (e.g., Berry, 1997; Padilla, 1980b) and the bi- or multidimensionality of acculturation has been acknowledged (e.g., Berry, 1990), measurement has become more sophisticated and grounded in theory (e.g., Cuellar, Arnold, & Maldonado, 1995; Marín & Gamba, 1996). However, there are still many challenges involved in assessing such a complex phenomenon. For instance, most published acculturation scales require respondents to choose among terms that assess the unidirectional movement of individuals from traditional culture to majority culture (Marín & Gamba, 1996; Zane & Mak, 2003). Although this problem is recognized by some researchers (Cuellar et al., 1995; Marín, 1992; Szapocznik & Kurtines, 1980), it remains a major difficulty plaguing most acculturation scales.

Researchers who are aware of unidirectionality and therefore try to produce bidirectional scales still propose scoring techniques (e.g., subtracting an "Asian" score from a "non-Hispanic White" score) that reflect an erroneous zero-sum perception of acculturation (Rogler, Cortes, & Malgady, 1991). Indeed, certain researchers (e.g., Choney, Berryhill-Paapke, & Robbins, 1995) state that this type of assessment represents a "deficit model" approach in which it is assumed that movement toward the White (or majority) culture represents health, whereas the other direction is more related to pathology.

Fortunately, there exists a new generation of acculturation measures, albeit small in number, designed to assess the various dimensions of acculturation by measuring two or more cultures independent of each other (e.g., Cuellar et al., 1995; Marín & Gamba, 1996). This type of approach assumes that one's adaptation to the new culture does not negate the possibility of retaining all or part of one's culture of origin.

Primary Indices of Acculturation

Several different indices are assessed by some of the most frequently used acculturation measures. The most popular index of acculturation is language, including assessment of primary language spoken or written (e.g., Cultural Life Styles Inventory [CLSI]) (Mendoza, 1989), language preference (e.g., Acculturation Rating Scale for Mexican Americans–Revised [ARSMA-R]) (Cuellar et al., 1995), and language proficiency (e.g., the Bidimensional Acculturation Scale) (Marín & Gamba, 1996). In addition, certain instruments measure language use within various social contexts (e.g., with family or colleagues at work).

Another popular index of acculturation is preference for social affiliation (e.g., CLSI) (Mendoza, 1989). These measures can include questions about people with whom the individual chooses to socialize or types of activities the individual likes to engage in while socializing with others. Related to

social affiliation are other indices that tap into an individual's association with his or her native culture or the host culture through self-identification, cultural pride, or perceived acceptance by a particular cultural group.

Cultural practices, beliefs, and values are also assessed by a small number of acculturation instruments (e.g., ARSMA-R) (Cuellar et al., 1995). A focus on engagement in cultural practices and knowledge about cultural beliefs and values may be particularly important for groups that present unique challenges in determining acculturation status. For example, many popular measures devised to assess acculturation in some ethnic groups (e.g., Asian Americans and Latinos) include questions about English-language use or proficiency, length of U.S. residence, immigration status, and observance of cultural holidays. Although some of these indices are appropriate measures for certain ethnic groups, these types of questions can be particularly difficult to apply to other sizable and diverse ethnic groups such as African Americans (Snowden & Hines, 1999) and American Indians (Choney et al., 1995).

Zane and Mak (2003) recently conducted a content analysis of 19 of the most frequently cited measures used to assess acculturation among three major ethnic groups in the United States—specifically, Asian Americans, Hispanics, and African Americans. Their analysis revealed that the majority of scales focused on the acculturation process among Hispanic Americans, with fewer scales available for measuring acculturation among Asian/Pacific Islanders and even less designed for African Americans. In addition, there appeared to be significant variation in the areas that the acculturation scales measure. Although some scales overlapped in terms of the areas assessed, other scales showed little or no overlap in content. This variation raised the concern as to whether the measures tap into similar characteristics of acculturation across the various ethnic groups. Even when

Zane and Mak (2003) analyzed measures designed to assess the same ethnic groups (e.g., Hispanics or Asian Americans), they still noted a lack of content overlap.

Challenges for Future Assessment of Acculturation

It is common for acculturation scales and indices to include demographic indicators or correlates of acculturation (e.g., generation of respondents) as part of the acculturation scale, which may spuriously increase the validity of the scale. An additional limitation of most acculturation scales is the reliance on one or very few domains or dimensions of acculturation to measure a complex multidimensional process. In some cases, the use of one type of variable or index has been dictated by data reduction techniques (e.g., when language use explains a large proportion of variance), whereas in other studies, researchers have simply chosen to use proxy measures (e.g., language of interview, place of birth, generational status). Although it seems certain that language-related dimensions are powerful correlates of acculturation, researchers often have failed to acknowledge the fact that some accuracy has been sacrificed by limiting the number of indexes measured.

Other problems with most acculturation scales include the fact that most investigators seldom use data reduction techniques to psychometrically derive their acculturation scales (Marín & Gamba, 1996). Often, researchers use items that are assumed to measure a given acculturative dimension (e.g., language use, patterns of media use, peer's ethnicity), and the scores derived from these items are used as if the items actually formed a scale. In most of these cases, the reader is not provided information on the internal consistency of the "scale," and likewise, validity indicators are often missing or not reported.

As stated earlier, certain ethnic groups such as African Americans and American Indians remain underresearched in the acculturation literature. To rectify this limitation, researchers must direct more attention toward the formulation of theory that will guide the construction of measures. Greater attention must be given toward identifying central themes that comprise these diverse ethnic groups' values, beliefs, and traditions. These issues must be addressed to advance the field toward larger scale, more sophisticated and inclusive studies that will lead to greater insight into the relationship between acculturation and psychological distress and adjustment.

One final comment regarding current acculturation scales is in order: There are very few appropriate acculturation scales for children. One effort is Marín and colleagues' Short Acculturation Scale for Hispanics (SASH) (Marín, Sabogal, VanOss Marín, Otero-Sabogal, & Pérez-Stable, 1987) that has been adapted for youth—SASH-Y (Barona & Miller, 1994). The SASH-Y shows excellent psychometric characteristics but produces unidirectional acculturation scores. Research in the near future should produce better acculturation scales that are appropriate for research with children.

ACCULTURATION IN RELATION TO PSYCHOLOGICAL DISTRESS

The scope of topics in acculturation research has grown in tandem with the development of new measures and investigative strategies. In particular, an increasing number of studies have examined acculturation processes in relation to risk for psychological distress and the experience and expression of symptoms. As noted earlier, much of the acculturation research on psychological distress focuses on new immigrants and refugees and their potential risk for psychological symptomatology and disorders. To this end, researchers have attempted to identify single indices or composite measures of acculturation that predict anxiety, depression, substance abuse, and other mental illnesses. Various status indices (e.g., English-language proficiency, language preference, years of residency in the United States, generational status) and cultural participation and affiliation indices (e.g., desire to return to one's homeland, participation in one's culture of origin, ethnic composition of social networks) have received considerable attention in the literature as possible correlates of psychological distress. Past findings, which are mostly based on Asian American and Latino immigrant and refugee populations, have generally pointed to three distinct paradigms—immigration stress, social stress, and selective migration—that highlight the complex relationship between acculturation and psychological distress.

Often, investigations of psychological distress begin with an a priori assumption that recently arrived immigrants encounter significant acculturative stress that predisposes them to psychological problems. This notion, which forms the basis of the immigration stress paradigm, was first widely discussed as "culture shock" by such notable sociologists as Park (1928) and Stonequist (1935) in the early half of the 20th century. An impressive body of studies has since offered empirical support for this paradigm by showing a negative relationship between acculturation levels and psychological distress, psychosocial dysfunction, and physical health problems (Chun et al., 2003; Lee & Zane, 1998; Myers & Rodriguez, 2003). The most poignant illustrations of these relationships are witnessed for Southeast Asian refugees, beginning with pioneering studies of the Vietnamese (e.g., Lin, Tazuma, & Masuda, 1979), Cambodians (e.g., Kinzie et al., 1990), Hmong (Westermeyer, 1989), Laotians (Kroll et al., 1989), and other early comparative analyses of these refugee communities (e.g., Gong-Guy, 1987; Mollica, Wyshak, & Lavelle, 1987; Rumbaut, 1985). These and subsequent studies have generally supported

the notion that acculturative stress may exacerbate or increase one's risk for various disorders and adjustment difficulties. In particular, low English-language proficiency has been identified as one of the most consistent predictors of anxiety and depressive symptoms for these groups.

Still, it is often difficult to discern the actual contribution of acculturative stress to psychological problems due to the lack of information on premorbid functioning for study samples. This can be highly problematic because most Southeast Asian refugees have experienced multiple premigration, migration, and encampment stressors and traumas that may heighten the negative effects of acculturative stress. This is particularly true for the Hmong and Cambodians, who have endured extensive loss of life and material possessions, persecution and torture, and life-threatening escape from their native countries (Abueg & Chun, 1996). Also, certain sociodemographic variables (e.g., age, sex, educational background, socioeconomic status) and personality traits (e.g., hardiness) often moderate the effects of acculturative stress, leading to varied adjustment patterns. Therefore, it is not surprising that researchers have yet to identify robust and consistent predictors of distress (with the possible exception of English-language proficiency) across diverse refugee and immigrant groups. For instance, past findings show that limited years spent in the United States and foreign birth both predict greater psychological distress (Abe & Zane, 1990), whereas other findings indicate that this relationship is insignificant when socioeconomic status is controlled (Ying, 1988). Such conflicting findings may also result from methodological variance, as witnessed by the use of different assessment tools and multiple operational definitions of acculturation and psychological distress. In addition, past research indicates that acculturation may differentially affect distinct measures of psychological distress and adjustment. For example, Sue and Zane (1985) found that recently arrived Chinese immigrant students report higher levels of anxiety yet surprisingly show higher academic achievement compared to Chinese students who have been U.S. residents for longer periods. Sue and Zane thus cautioned that multiple measures of adjustment and psychological distress are required when examining the effects of acculturative stress.

The social stress paradigm also has received wide attention in the literature, particularly for Latino populations. According to this paradigm, higher levels of acculturation are associated with psychological distress and mental health problems. As noted in previous literature reviews (e.g., Balls Organista, Organista, & Kurasaki, 2003), this phenomenon may stem from the gradual erosion of "traditional Latino culture" or supportive family networks that guard against distress. In addition, Latinos who are long-term U.S. residents may be more susceptible to mental health problems due to prolonged exposure to racial discrimination and social stratification and new cultural norms that may encourage substance use.

Support for the social stress paradigm is found across a broad range of studies. Most notably, investigations using epidemiological data from the Epidemiologic Catchment Areas (ECA)–Los Angeles study (Burnam, Hough, Karno, Escobar, & Telles, 1987), the National Comorbidity Study (Ortega, Rosenheck, Alegria, & Desai, 2000), and the Mexican American Prevalence and Services Survey (Vega et al., 1998) report a positive relationship between acculturation levels and psychological distress. Burnam and his colleagues (1987) found that U.S.-born Mexican Americans evidence higher lifetime prevalence rates of psychiatric and substance use disorders than their Mexican-born counterparts. Likewise, Ortega and his colleagues (2000) more recently reported high prevalence rates

of psychiatric disorders and substance use for more acculturated Mexican Americans, Puerto Ricans, and "other" Hispanics. In this latter study, variables related to proficient use of the English language proved to be the most consistent predictors of psychological distress.

Recent studies of cognitive expectancies for alcohol use provide further insights into the social stress paradigm. For instance, Marín (1998) found that more acculturated Mexican Americans (as measured by language preference and use) tended to report more positive and fewer negative expectancies for drinking compared to their less acculturated counterparts. Such changes in expectancies may partially explain past reports that highly acculturated Hispanic women are more likely to drink compared to those who are less acculturated (Caetano, 1998). Still, researchers have cited a number of important caveats to these findings; namely, acculturation and substance use should not be reduced to a simple linear relationship but should instead be viewed as a complex interaction between individual characteristics and sociocultural and historical factors (Caetano & Clark, 2003).

Finally, researchers also have considered the selective migration paradigm to explain the relationship between acculturation and psychological distress. This paradigm holds that newer immigrants inherently possess unique, adaptive personal traits that guard against mental illness. Consequently, it is hypothesized that newer immigrants represent a particularly resilient group and therefore experience less psychological distress than their American-born counterparts. This paradigm was offered as a possible explanation to the aforementioned early ECA findings that showed higher lifetime prevalence rates of psychiatric disorders among U.S.-born Mexican Americans relative to those who were foreign born (Burnam et al., 1987). However, more recent reports showing comparable prevalence rates of distress for Mexican American immigrants and Mexican nationals refute the selective migration paradigm (Balls Organista et al., 2003). Also, past studies with Asian Americans generally show that newer immigrants and refugees are at greater risk for adjustment difficulties than U.S.-born Asian Americans as previously noted.

The experience and expression of psychological distress have also been investigated in relation to acculturation. In regards to experience, past findings suggest that acculturation affects cognitive and emotional interpretations of distress. For instance, Ying (1990) found that newer Chinese American immigrants held distinct explanatory models or emic constructions of major depression that included both physiological and emotional components. According to Ying, such models are embedded in Chinese health beliefs that implicate both somatic and psychological processes in the etiology of this disorder. However, these cultural health beliefs may transform during acculturation. This was evidenced for a community sample of Chinese Americans who did not frequently cite biological or organic factors as possible causes for mental disorders (Loo, Tong, & True, 1989). Interestingly, the majority of Chinese Americans in this latter study had resided in the United States for a much longer period of time (10 years or more) compared to those in Ying's study (an average of 2.7 years). Finally, acculturation may shape experiences of social distress as well. In this case, Okazaki (1997) found that less acculturated Chinese American college students were more likely to report greater avoidance of and higher distress in social situations than their peers with higher acculturation levels. Okazaki posited that Asian Americans with lower acculturation levels are more likely to endorse interdependent self-construals that increase their sensitivity to social situations.

Symptom expression may also vary according to acculturation levels, as witnessed by somatization and culture-bound syndromes. Past studies of somatization have shown that newer immigrants and refugees may initially report more physical symptoms such as headaches, mild abdominal pains, physical tension, and general malaise when experiencing psychological distress (Chun, Eastman, Wang, & Sue, 1998). This is not entirely surprising given that they may hold both somatic and psychological interpretations of distress as previously noted. Somatization may also represent a culturally acceptable way to express distress, especially in cultures where shame and stigma are attached to mental illness. Still, it is important to note that somatization is not solely associated with "traditional" health beliefs and cultural values among newer immigrants. Instead, treatment settings (i.e., medical vs. psychotherapeutic) (Cheung, 1987) and methods of diagnostic inquiry and assessment (e.g., structured vs. open-ended interviews) (Lin, 1989) may also contribute to somatic symptom presentations.

Finally, the relationship between acculturation and the expression of psychological distress can also be seen in culture-bound syndromes. Inclusion of these syndromes (e.g., *hwabyung* among Koreans, *koros* among Malaysians and Chinese, and *ataques de nervios* among Puerto Ricans) in the appendix of the *Diagnostic and Statistical Manual of Mental Disorders* (*DSM-IV*) (American Psychiatric Association, 1994), along with new research on these disorders, attests to their growing significance in the field. Moreover, they clearly demonstrate how symptoms may be intimately tied to unique religious and cultural belief systems that are often overlooked by current Western diagnostic nosology. Instances of sudden nocturnal death syndrome (SUNDS) underscore this point. The cause of this syndrome, which is mostly seen among young adult Hmong men, still defies clear scientific explanations. Interestingly, researchers have suggested that acculturative stress may play an important role in this disorder given that most who are inflicted with SUNDS have spent relatively few years in the United States and have faced significant postmigration stressors (Adler, 1998). Thus, acculturation figures prominently in symptom expression when considering its potential to elicit stress reactions and influence cultural health beliefs.

Despite the growing number of acculturation studies pertaining to psychological distress, some fundamental questions remain: What are the exact mechanisms involved with increased risk for psychological distress? Why do past findings support the social stress paradigm for Mexican Americans but not for Asian American groups? Alternatively, why is there more support for the immigration stress paradigm for Asian American populations than for Latinos? Are certain cultural health beliefs more salient than others in shaping the experience and expression of psychological distress? Do developmental skills and abilities mediate the relationship between acculturation and psychological adjustment?

CONCLUSION

Despite several current limitations highlighted in this overview, researchers are ideally poised to make significant strides in understanding the influence of acculturation on people's behavior and consequent adjustment: Conceptualizations and measures are more refined, and patterns of acculturation's effects are becoming more distinct. As our world cultures continue to come in closer proximity and convergence, efforts must continue to document the importance of this construct as a testament to psychology's commitment to human welfare. Any future effort in this regard must nevertheless use appropriate measurements and culturally appropriate theories to properly identify the relationship between acculturation and people's behaviors, attitudes, and values. Continued use of faulty measures and monolithic theoretical constructs can only delay our understanding of the phenomenon by producing spurious relationships and results of limited validity and generalization.

REFERENCES

Abe, J. S., & Zane, N. W. S. (1990). Psychological maladjustment among Asian and White American college students: Controlling for confounds. *Journal of Counseling Psychology, 37,* 437-444.

Abueg, F. R., & Chun, K. M. (1996). Traumatization stress among Asians and Asian Americans. In A. J. Marsella, M. J. Friedman, E. T. Gerrity, & R. M. Scurfield (Eds.), *Ethnocultural aspects of posttraumatic stress disorder: Issues, research, and clinical applications* (pp. 285-300). Washington, DC: American Psychological Association.

Adler, S. R. (1998). Refugee stress and folk belief. In P. Balls Organista, K. M. Chun, & G. Marín (Eds.), *Readings in ethnic psychology* (pp. 260-269). New York: Routledge.

American Psychiatric Association. (1994). *Diagnostic and statistical manual of mental disorders* (4th ed.). Washington, DC: Author.

Balls Organista, P., Organista, K. C., & Kurasaki, K. (2003). The relationship between acculturation and ethnic minority mental health. In K. M. Chun, P. Balls Organista, & G. Marín (Eds.), *Acculturation: Advances in theory, measurement, and applied research* (pp. 139-161). Washington, DC: American Psychological Association.

Barona, A., & Miller, J. A. (1994). Short Acculturation Scale for Hispanic Youth (SASH-Y): A preliminary report. *Hispanic Journal of Behavioral Sciences, 16,* 155-162.

Berry, J. W. (1980). Acculturation as a variety of adaptation. In A. M. Padilla (Ed.), *Acculturation: Theory, models and some new findings* (pp. 9-25). Boulder, CO: Westview.

Berry, J. W. (1990). Psychology of acculturation. In J. Berman (Ed.), *Cross-cultural perspectives: Nebraska symposium on motivation* (pp. 201-234). Lincoln: University of Nebraska Press.

Berry, J. W. (1997). Immigration, acculturation and adaptation. *Applied Psychology, 46,* 5-68.

Berry, J. W. (2003). Conceptual approaches to acculturation. In K. M. Chun, P. Balls Organista, & G. Marín (Eds.), *Acculturation: Advances in theory, measurement, and applied research* (pp. 17-37). Washington, DC: American Psychological Association.

Berry, J. W., & Sam, D. (1997). Acculturation and adaptation. In J. W. Berry, M. H. Segall, & I. Kagitcibasi (Eds.), *Handbook of cross-cultural psychology: Vol. 3. Social behavior and applications* (pp. 291-326). Boston: Allyn & Bacon.

Burnam, M. A., Hough, R. L., Karno, M., Escobar, J. I., & Telles, C. A. (1987). Acculturation and lifetime prevalence of psychiatric disorders among Mexican Americans in Los Angeles. *Journal of Health and Social Behavior, 28,* 89-102.

Caetano, R. (1998). Drinking and alcohol-related problems among minority women. In P. Balls Organista, K. M. Chun, & G. Marín (Eds.), *Readings in ethnic psychology* (pp. 188-203). New York: Routledge.

Caetano, R., & Clark, C. L. (2003). Acculturation, alcohol consumption, smoking, and drug use among Hispanics. In K. M. Chun, P. Balls Organista, & G. Marín (Eds.), *Acculturation: Advances in theory, measurement, and applied research* (pp. 223-239). Washington, DC: American Psychological Association.

Cheung, F. M. (1987). Conceptualization of psychiatric illness and help-seeking behavior among Chinese. *Culture, Medicine, and Psychiatry, 11,* 97-106.

Choney, S. K., Berryhill-Paapke, E., & Robbins, R. R. (1995). The acculturation of American Indians: Developing frameworks for research and practice. In J. G. Ponterotto, J. M. Casas, L. A. Suzuki, & C. M. Alexander (Eds.), *Handbook of multicultural counseling* (pp. 73-92). Thousand Oaks, CA: Sage.

Chun, K. M., Balls Organista, P., & Marín, G. (Eds.). (2003). *Acculturation: Advances in theory, measurement, and applied research.* Washington, DC: American Psychological Association.

Chun, K. M., Eastman, K. L., Wang, G. C. S., & Sue, S. S. (1998). Psychopathology. In L. C. Lee & N. W. S. Zane (Eds.), *Handbook of Asian American psychology* (pp. 457-484). Thousand Oaks, CA: Sage.

Cuellar, I., Arnold, B., & Maldonado, R. (1995). Acculturation Rating Scale for Mexican Americans–II: A revision of the original ARSMA scale. *Hispanic Journal of Behavioral Sciences, 17,* 275-304.

Gong-Guy, E. (1987). *The California Southeast Asian mental health needs assessment* (Contract No. 85-76282A-2). Sacramento: California State Department of Mental Health.

Graves, T. D. (1967). Acculturation, access, and alcohol in a tri-ethnic community. *American Anthropologist, 69,* 306-321.

Kim, B. S. K., & Abreu, J. M. (1995). Acculturation measurement: Theory, current instruments, and future directions. In J. G. Ponterotto, J. M. Casas, L. A. Suzuki, & C. M. Alexander (Eds.), *Handbook of multicultural counseling* (pp. 394-424). Thousand Oaks, CA: Sage.

Kinzie, J., Boehnlein, J. K., Leung, P. K., Moore, L. J., Riley, C., & Smith, D. (1990). The prevalence of posttraumatic stress disorder and its clinical significance among Southeast Asian refugees. *American Journal of Psychiatry, 147,* 913-917.

Kroll, J., Habenicht, M., Mackenzie, T., Yang, M., Chan, S., Vang, T., Nguyen, T., Ly, M., Phommasouvanh, B., Nguyen, H., Vang, Y., Souvannasoth, L., & Cabugao, R. (1989). Depression and posttraumatic stress disorder in Southeast Asian refugees. *American Journal of Psychiatry, 146,* 1592-1597.

LaFromboise, T., Coleman, H. L. K., & Gerton, J. (1993). Psychological impact of biculturalism: Evidence and theory. *Psychological Bulletin, 114,* 395-412.

Landrine, H., & Klonoff, E. A. (1996). *African American acculturation.* Thousand Oaks, CA: Sage.

Lee, L. C., & Zane, N. W. S. (Eds.). (1998). *Handbook of Asian American psychology.* Thousand Oaks, CA: Sage.

Lin, K. M., Tazuma, L., & Masuda, M. (1979). Adaptational problems of Vietnamese refugees: I. Health and mental health status. *Archives of General Psychiatry, 36,* 955-961.

Lin, N. (1989). Measuring depressive symptomatology in China. *Journal of Nervous and Mental Disease, 177*(3), 121-131.

Loo, C., Tong, B., & True, R. (1989). A bitter bean: Mental health status and attitudes in Chinatown. *Journal of Community Psychology, 17,* 283-296.

Marín, G. (1992). Issues in the measurement of acculturation among Hispanics. In K. Geisinger (Ed.), *Psychological testing of Hispanics* (pp. 235-251). Washington, DC: American Psychological Association.

Marín, G. (1998). Expectancies for drinking and excessive drinking among Mexican Americans and non-Hispanic Whites. In P. Balls Organista, K. M. Chun, & G. Marín (Eds.), *Readings in ethnic psychology* (pp. 204-222). New York: Routledge.

Marín, G., & Gamba, R. J. (1996). A new measurement of acculturation for Hispanics: The Bidimensional Acculturation Scale for Hispanics (BAS). *Hispanic Journal of Behavioral Sciences, 18,* 297-316.

Marín, G., Sabogal, F., VanOss Marín, B., Otero-Sabogal, R., & Pérez-Stable, E. J. (1987). Development of a short acculturation scale for Hispanics. *Hispanic Journal of Behavioral Sciences, 9,* 183-205.

Mendoza, R. H. (1989). An empirical scale to measure type and degree of acculturation in Mexican-American adolescents and adults. *Journal of Cross-Cultural Psychology, 20,* 372-385.

Mollica, R., Wyshak, G., & Lavelle, J. (1987). The psychosocial impact of war trauma and torture on Southeast Asian refugees. *American Journal of Psychiatry, 144,* 1567-1572.

Myers, H. F., & Rodriguez, N. (2003). Acculturation and physical health in racial and ethnic minorities. In K. M. Chun, P. Balls Organista, & G. Marín (Eds.), *Acculturation: Advances in theory, measurement, and applied research* (pp. 163-185). Washington, DC: American Psychological Association.

Okazaki, S. (1997). Sources of ethnic differences between Asian American and White American college students on measures of depression and social anxiety. *Journal of Abnormal Psychology, 106*(1), 52-60.

Olmedo, E. L. (1980). Quantitative models of acculturation: An overview. In A. M. Padilla (Ed.), *Acculturation: Theory, models, and some new findings* (pp. 27-45). Boulder, CO: Westview.

Ortega, A. N., Rosenheck, R., Alegria, M., & Desai, R. A. (2000). Acculturation and the lifetime risk of psychiatric and substance use disorders among Hispanics. *Journal of Nervous and Mental Disease, 188*(11), 728-735.

Padilla, A. M. (Ed.). (1980a). *Acculturation: Theory, models and some new findings.* Boulder, CO: Westview.

Padilla, A. M. (1980b). The role of cultural awareness and ethnic loyalty in acculturation. In A. M. Padilla (Ed.), *Acculturation: Theory, models and some new findings* (pp. 47-84). Boulder, CO: Westview.

Park, R. E. (1928). Human migration and the marginal man. *American Journal of Sociology, 5,* 881-893.

Redfield, R., Linton, R., & Herskovitz, M. J. (1936). Memorandum on the study of acculturation. *American Anthropologist, 38,* 149-152.

Rogler, L. H., Cortes, D. E., & Malgady, R. G. (1991). Acculturation and mental health status among Hispanics. *American Psychologist, 46,* 585-597.

Rumbaut, R. (1985). Mental health and the refugee experience: A comparative study of Southeast Asian refugees. In T. C. Owan (Ed.), *Southeast Asian mental health: Treatment, prevention, services, training, and research* (pp. 433-486). Rockville, MD: National Institute of Mental Health.

Snowden, L. R., & Hines, A. M. (1999). A scale to assess African American acculturation. *Journal of Black Psychology, 25,* 36-47.

Social Science Research Council. (1954). Acculturation: An exploratory formulation. *American Anthropologist, 56,* 973-1002.

Stonequist, E. V. (1935). The problem of the marginal man. *American Journal of Sociology, 7,* 1-12.

Szapocznik, J., & Kurtines, W. (1980). Acculturation, biculturalism and adjustment among Cuban-Americans. In A. M. Padilla (Ed.), *Acculturation: Theory, models and some new findings* (pp. 139-159). Boulder, CO: Westview.

Sue, S., & Zane, N. W. S. (1985). Academic achievement and socioemotional adjustment among Chinese university students. *Journal of Counseling Psychology, 32,* 570-579.

Trimble, J. (2003). Introduction: Social change and acculturation. In K. M. Chun, P. Balls Organista, & G. Marín (Eds.), *Acculturation: Advances in theory, measurement, and applied research* (pp. 3-13). Washington, DC: American Psychological Association.

Vega, W. A., Kolody, B., Aguilar-Gaxiola, S., Alderete, E., Catalano, R., & Caraveo-Anduaga, J. (1998). Lifetime prevalence of *DSM-III-R* psychiatric disorders among urban and rural Mexican Americans in California. *Archives of General Psychiatry, 55,* 771-782.

Westermeyer, J. (1989). Psychological adjustment of Hmong refugees during their first decade in the United States: A longitudinal study. *Journal of Nervous and Mental Disease, 177,* 132-139.

Ying, Y. (1988). Depressive symptomatology among Chinese-Americans as measured by the CES-D. *Journal of Clinical Psychology, 44,* 739-746.

Ying, Y. (1990). Explanatory models of major depression and implications for help-seeking among immigrant Chinese-American women. *Culture, Medicine, and Psychiatry, 14,* 393-408.

Zane, N., & Mak, W. (2003). Major approaches to the measurement of acculturation among ethnic minority populations: A content analysis and an alternative empirical strategy. In K. M. Chun, P. Balls Organista, & G. Marín (Eds.), *Acculturation: Advances in theory, measurement, and applied research* (pp. 39-60). Washington, DC: American Psychological Association.

CHAPTER 11

Instrument Development
Cultural Adaptations for Ethnic Minority Research

MILAGROS BRAVO

University of Puerto Rico

Research on ethnic minorities requires instrumentation that is sensitive to cultural variations. Psychological research on minorities usually involves comparisons among different ethnic groups. These comparisons demand instruments capable of identifying similar psychological phenomena in dissimilar groups. A challenge to the researcher who is studying diverse ethnic groups or cultures is to ensure that the assessment tools are equivalent across groups. Only by achieving this equivalence will it be possible to compare substantive results not confounded by instrumentation artifacts. Attaining this equivalence to study ethnic minorities in the United States sometimes requires translations into languages other than English, for example, to study Hispanics, Asian Americans, or Native Americans. For all ethnic groups, even for those whose native language is English, such as African Americans, cultural adaptations are necessary. This chapter describes conceptual and methodological challenges involved in the use of structured instruments in the study of ethnic minorities. It presents a comprehensive model to translate and adapt research instruments for its use in an ethnic group or culture other than that in which the instrument was originally developed. Within the model, techniques usually used to attain equivalency across languages and cultures are described. Some of the difficulties involved in the process are discussed and illustrated.

AUTHOR'S NOTE: I would like to thank Dr. Glorisa Canino, from the Behavioral Science Research Institute at the Medical Sciences Campus of the University of Puerto Rico, for her permission to use material from previous articles in which we have collaborated. I want also to express my appreciation to Maritza Rubio-Stipec, Michel Woodbury-Fariña, and Roberto Lewis-Fernández for the opportunity to discuss these issues when collaborating in previous publications. I would also like to thank Dr. Peter Guarnaccia, from Rutgers University, for some valuable suggestions for this chapter and Drs. Blanca Ortiz-Torres and Jeannette Roselló, from the University of Puerto Rico, for the careful reviews of this document.

CONCEPTUAL CONSIDERATIONS

Culture serves as a web that structures human thought, emotion, and interaction (Canino & Guarnaccia, 1997). It is a dynamic process in which social transformations, social conflicts, power relationships, and migrations affect views and practices. Culture is the product of group values, norms, and experiences as well as of individual innovations and life histories. Although ethnic minorities share a common context with mainstream culture, each group has unique cultural characteristics that permeate their lives. These characteristics are the product of the continued interaction of their culture of origin with the dominant or majority culture. Cultures and subcultures vary not only by national, regional, or ethnic background but also by age, gender, and social class. Ethnic minorities also vary by whether the studied group is composed of migrants or natives to the host country. All these considerations must be taken into account when studying ethnic minorities.

Most investigators agree on the value of cross-ethnic and cross-cultural research findings and on the need to make research culturally sensitive (Canino, Lewis-Fernández, & Bravo, 1997). It has been emphasized that the goal of cultural sensitivity is to increase the scientific accuracy of the research rather than merely promoting multicultural political correctness (Rogler, 1999a). However, there is disagreement as to the degree of cultural or ethnic modifications that should be incorporated into research instruments.

Cross-cultural studies can be approached from two different perspectives, which together have been called the *emic-etic paradigm* (Brislin, Lonner, & Thorndike 1973). The emic perspective involves the evaluation of the studied phenomenon from within the culture and its context, aiming to explain the studied phenomenon's significance and its interrelationship with other intracultural elements "from the inside." This approach attempts to describe the internal logic of a culture, its singularity, considering this a necessary step prior to any valid cross-cultural analysis. The etic perspective, on the other hand, is basically comparative. It involves the evaluation of a phenomenon from "outside the culture," aiming to identify and compare similar phenomena across different cultural contexts.

Both perspectives have been criticized in the pertinent literature (Canino et al., 1997). Critics argue that cross-cultural research based on the emic approach neglects the problem of observation bias. The lack of methodological homogeneity across studies of different cultures can result in the inability to disentangle methodological from substantive factors when variability in cross-cultural comparisons is observed. For example, it may hinder the test of causal hypotheses across cultures. Although a thorough understanding of concepts relevant to one culture is obtained by using this approach, these concepts are not necessarily comparable to those of other cultures. On the other hand, the etic approach has been criticized for emphasizing reliability at the expense of validity. It may impose the appearance of cross-cultural homogeneity that is artifactual to the use of a constricted conceptualization embedded in the instrumentation. This limitation has been called the "cultural fallacy" (Kleinman & Good, 1985). Several investigators have devised strategies that attempt to integrate emic and etic perspectives into one overall research methodology that is both culturally valid and generalizable (see Canino et al., 1997, for examples from mental health research). Similarly, the instrument adaptation model presented in this chapter aims to respond to both the etic and emic perspectives. Its main purpose is to produce instruments that search for the equivalents of psychological phenomena across linguistically and culturally different populations, thus enabling comparisons inherent to the etic perspective. However, it aims to do it in a culturally sensitive way that makes possible the identification of unique cultural characteristics within groups.

INSTRUMENT ADAPTATION MODEL

Culturally sensitive research involves a continuing and incessant process of substantive and methodological adaptations designed to mesh the process of inquiry with the cultural characteristics of the group being studied (Rogler, 1989). An essential component of such an approach is the development and adaptation of culturally appropriate research instruments. Most psychological research instruments are developed in English in the context of the U.S. mainstream culture. Their use with ethnic minorities requires a careful and thorough adaptation process to produce cross-cultural equivalency. In some instances, it involves translation into another language, but in all cases, it entails cultural adaptations to guarantee its pertinence, applicability, and validity in each ethnic group. The adequacy of an instrument in a given culture or subculture does not guarantee its validity in another one (Brislin et al., 1973).

The model presented frames the cultural adaptation of an instrument in the context of the process of establishing validity of a measure (Flaherty, 1987; Flaherty, Gaviria, & Pathak, 1988). It postulates that equivalence between cross-language and cross-cultural versions of an instrument can be achieved by obtaining evidence about their equivalence on five dimensions: (a) semantic, (b) content, (c) technical, (d) criterion, and (e) conceptual equivalence. This model is generally consonant with recent guidelines developed by the International Testing Commission for cross-culturally adapting educational and psychological tests (Hambleton, 1994). In the Spanish-speaking Caribbean island of Puerto Rico, we have used this comprehensive

model to translate and adapt a number of research instruments for studying mental health in both adult and children populations (Bravo, Canino, Rubio-Stipec, & Woodbury-Fariña, 1991; Bravo, Woodbury-Fariña, Canino, & Rubio-Stipec, 1993; Canino & Bravo, 1994). The difficulties and examples presented in the chapter mainly come from this work, but the issues involved are considered to be sufficiently general in character that they can apply to instrument adaptations involving other research topics as well as other cultural and ethnic groups.

Semantic Equivalence

Semantic equivalence requires that the meaning of each item in the instrument is similar in the language of each cultural group. When an already existing instrument is involved, a thorough process of translation is required to attain it. The translation of research instruments for use with ethnic minorities is a difficult and costly endeavor. Sometimes it has been avoided in large-scale surveys by excluding minorities who do not speak English. Besides the obvious bias that this practice entails (i.e., a subgroup of the population with unique characteristics is excluded, and thus the sample is not truly representative of the whole population), it forces minority people who speak some English to answer in their nonpreferred language. Although many people from ethnic minorities speak English, most feel more at ease speaking about emotional or behavioral topics in their native language. Furthermore, many do not have an adequate command of the English language to understand the linguistic nuances of a structured instrument, thus hampering its comprehension. Therefore, the conscientious study of ethnic minorities whose native language is not English requires the translation of research instruments. Even for those minorities whose native language is English (e.g., African Americans), some linguistic adaptations may be necessary to make the instruments more understandable and adequate. Processes described in this chapter are also appropriate for this purpose.

Attaining semantic equivalence is not an easy task. Latin American writer Octavio Paz has said that as the number of translations in the modern era has increased, skepticism about it has also increased in the philosophical, literary, and linguistic critique (Bravo, Canino, & Bird, 1987). Contrary to earlier times in which faith in translations was based on religious beliefs about the universality and lack of temporality of divine truth, at the present time it is considered that all text is relative and belongs to a specific time and place. Within this context, the modern translator does not search for the impossible identity but for the difficult similarity, intending to produce similar effects with different means.

Moreover, most research instruments are not developed with their translatability in mind (Draguns, 1980), although guidelines for using translatable language on research instruments were formulated some time ago. To ease translation of English into other languages, Brislin et al. (1973) formulated the following rules: (a) Use short, simple sentences; (b) employ the active rather than the passive voice; (c) repeat nouns instead of using pronouns; (d) avoid metaphors and colloquialisms; (e) avoid the subjunctive mode (e.g., use of *could* or *would*); (f) avoid adverbs and prepositions telling "where" or "when"; (g) avoid possessive forms; (h) use specific rather than general terms (e.g., *cows, pigs* instead of *livestock*); (i) avoid words that indicate vagueness about some event or thing (e.g., *probably, frequently*); and (j) avoid sentences with two different verbs if the verbs suggest different actions. Even when using these rules, some terms or verbal forms may not have adequate equivalents in other languages.

The best procedure to enhance equivalence in translations has been labeled *decentering* because it is not centered on any one culture or language (Brislin et al., 1973). It involves changing the original source version of an instrument if, during the translation process, it is identified that some terms or verbal forms do not have acceptable equivalents in the translated language. Therefore, both the original and translated versions of the instrument are open to revision to increase equivalence across languages. Through iterations of translations and back-translations, appropriate wording in the source and target languages is achieved. When developing instruments for use in diverse ethnic groups, this procedure is the best alternative because when versions of an instrument are decentered, they are in an equal linguistic partnership: The wording in each language is familiar and salient to respondents in the cultural groups involved (Rogler, 1999a). However, because this alternative is not commonly used in the development of instruments, even when its use with ethnic minorities is considered, instruments usually have to be translated as they are.

Cross-language equivalency of research instruments requires a comprehensive process that involves not only translation but also thorough testing in alternative languages. A combination of translation and back-translation techniques is the first step in the process. It involves translating the instrument into the target language and then translating it back to the original source language by someone other than the original translator (Brislin et al., 1973). A bilingual committee then compares the original and the back-translated versions. Members of this committee must be knowledgeable about the constructs that the instruments assess, as well as the population to be studied. They must check if the instrument's items retain their original intent and that the language used is appropriate for the age and education level of the targeted population. It is important to consider language usage in the particular targeted group because the same language can be spoken in different ways by different groups. If semantic differences are observed, the version in the target language is altered. The process is repeated until the meaning of each item in the instrument is similar in both languages.

Although it is a useful technique, back-translation entails certain dangers. To promote similarity between the back-translated version and the original one, one could force the instrument in the target language to conform to the grammatical structure of the source language. For example, in the case of an instrument in English that is translated into Spanish, English syntax could be imposed into the translated version. This results in awkward wording that is difficult to understand by speakers of the target language. Rogler (1999b) presented some examples reported in the literature on the presence of this error on instruments used to survey Latinos or Hispanics in the United States, undermining the findings generated. Translation errors identified included errors of grammar or syntax, poorly constructed sentences, use of double negatives, and literal translations of colloquial expressions, among others. The objective of a translation is to produce easy-to-read, smooth, and natural-sounding wording that is still faithful to the original. To achieve this, a professional translator could be involved in the process of developing the first translation and revising the final one to guarantee that the translated version conforms to the rules and use of the target language. Another alternative is to involve a monolingual committee, representative of the study population, in the process of revising the work produced during back-translation (World Health Organization [WHO], 1998).

Yet the previously described process is still not sufficient to attain semantic equivalence. Field testing of the instrument is essential. In those places where bilingual participants, who are similar to those to be studied but equally proficient in both languages, are available, the instrument should be administered to these participants in both languages.

Results from both administrations are then compared. If bilingual participants equally proficient in both languages are not available, the instrument is administered in the target language, but feedback from interviewers or debriefing of participants is obtained. Feedback from interviewers should include whether they felt each item was understood, if respondents' comments and reactions were consonant with the item's intent, and whether respondents looked engaged, distracted, or fatigued. The debriefing should ask respondents what they understand each question to be asking, whether they could repeat it in their own words, what came to their minds when they heard a particular phrase or term, and how they chose their answer (WHO, 1998). This information is best obtained on in-depth individual interviews, but focus groups are also an alternative.

The importance of field testing for attaining semantic equivalence is illustrated in the following example. In the translation and adaptation process of the Diagnostic Interview Schedule for Children (DISC), the translation of the phrase "to worry a lot" for the assessment of anxiety presented difficulties that were not envisioned by the bilingual research committee (Bravo et al., 1993). The Spanish literal equivalent "to worry a lot" is *preocuparse mucho*. Yet, the interviewers who field-tested the translated instrument noticed that the wording had an unintended interpretation. When parents were asked whether their children worried a lot about school, many proudly answered, "Of course he [or she] worries a lot [*se preocupa mucho*], he [or she] is a very good student," conveying the message that the child had shown an appropriate and desirable behavior. After analyzing the situation, the bilingual committee concluded that the word in Spanish can have a negative connotation similar to the English word *worry*, but it can also have a positive one more consonant with that of the English word *concern*. The item was changed to *se preocupa demasiado,* the literal equivalent of "worries too much," to convey the connotation that the behavior was to be out of the normal and desirable range. This kind of equivalence cannot be achieved by using a back-translation process. The purpose of semantic equivalence goes beyond what can be accomplished with this process. As Rogler (1999b) stated, "In research, translation similarity can be considered sufficient when translation has no consequences for the variance in the response's replies, which is contributed by the language of the instrument" (p. 428). The focus is then on semantic and cultural equivalence rather than on linguistic or literal translation.

If the instrument to be translated and adapted is to be used in several countries, with people of varied ethnicity or even with diverse subgroups within an ethnic minority, the revision by an international or culturally diverse committee is recommended. This step was included in the development of the latest Spanish version of the DISC, the DISC IV (Bravo et al., 2001). An intercultural committee, sponsored by the National Institute of Mental Health (NIMH), was composed of people from different Spanish-speaking countries (Spain, Mexico, and Venezuela) and U.S. Hispanic groups (from Mexican, Central American, and South American origin), as well as Puerto Rico. The main goal of this committee was to ensure that the final translated version was applicable to diverse Spanish-speaking groups and comprehensible to people of varied educational levels. Each committee member carefully reviewed the initial version of the instrument translated and adapted in Puerto Rico, and consensus was reached about the appropriate wording of items. When a term common to all groups was not found, several ethnic variations or regionalisms were included in parentheses so the appropriate word could be selected in each place. For example, to translate the phrase "how often," three phrases in Spanish had to be included: *cuán a menudo, con qué*

frecuencia, and *qué tan seguido.* In this way, an instrument appropriate to a wide variety of Spanish-speaking groups was developed.

Content Equivalence

Content equivalence refers to whether the content of each item is relevant to each cultural group or population under study, that is, if it evaluates a phenomenon that occurs in and is noted as real by members of the ethnic or cultural groups. A committee composed of people who know one or preferably both cultural groups well can attain content equivalence through careful revision. A procedure similar to rational analysis, which is usually employed to obtain evidence about content validity in the development of an instrument, should be employed. That is, a panel of judges, usually composed of experts in the construct to be assessed, decides whether the instrument's items reflect the concept under study. However, this procedure is sufficient in the judgment of items only when researchers and respondents share the symbolic systems of the same culture (Rogler, 1999a). When researchers and respondents have little or no cultural symbolism in common, it is not sufficient. In this case, detailed cultural observations must supplement it.

These cultural observations should be used for two purposes. First, it should determine whether the construct that the original instrument measures is pertinent to the target cultural group. Second, it should determine whether its operationalization is appropriate. Differences not only across groups but also within the same ethnic group (e.g., socioeconomic or age differences) must be considered in both processes. These determinations sometimes can be made in the selection of the instrument to use in a particular population, even before it is translated, but at other times they are revealed through pilot testing.

Rogler, Malgady, and Rodríguez (1989) described an instance when the irrelevance of a construct was identified at this stage. They had started by trying to measure spousal relationships through decision-making questionnaires. During the initial phase of the study, it became apparent that the items of the instrument they were considering did not apply to impoverished Puerto Rican couples in New York. The items inquired about decision making regarding where to go on vacation, which school the children should attend, the purchasing of insurance policies, and so on. They thought about changing the content of the items but retaining the operationalization of spousal relationships through decision making. After pretesting these new items, it became clear that the construct of decision making for these families was irrelevant because the margin of choice in their lives was slim. In another study using an impoverished island sample, the alternative, identified through ethnographic observations, was to assess changes in marital relationships through gender-based division of labor (Rogler, 1999b). This example serves to illustrate how a higher level construct that an instrument evaluates (i.e., marital relationship) can be defined by using a more pertinent lower-level construct (i.e., gender division of labor) instead of another lower-level one that was found to be culturally inappropriate (i.e., decision making). These examples illustrate the importance of (a) determining whether the construct that the original instrument measures is pertinent to the target cultural group and (b) identifying an alternative construct, if possible, that can be used to assess the higher-order construct that is the main focus of study. Moreover, it also illustrates the need to take into consideration other variables, besides culture, when making these decisions. The decision-making construct was not appropriate for these families, not necessarily because they were Puerto Rican but because they were at the bottom of a socially stratified system struggling to satisfy their most basic needs. This situation can be applicable to poor

people from any ethnic minority or even majority group. It illustrates that cultural aspects as well as other factors such as socioeconomic conditions must be considered on the revision of instruments. As previously stated, cultures and ethnic groups vary not only by national, regional, or ethnic background but also by age, gender, and social class.

Content equivalence should be carefully examined, especially in instruments that aim to assess deviations from "normal" behavior. For example, an examination of an instrument designed to measure family functioning revealed that its operationalization of what constitutes "normal" family functioning was not pertinent for Puerto Rican families. The instrument in question, the Family Adaptability and Cohesion Scale (FACES) (Olson, Portner, & Bell, 1982), contained several items that ran counter to its cultural norms and practices. The respondent was asked to rate the frequency by which, for example, children had a say in their discipline and could help solve family problems, whether household responsibilities shifted from person to person, or whether family members consulted other family members on their decisions. The Puerto Rican family, especially in the low socioeconomic class, is predominantly hierarchical, with marked division of labor around sex role stereotypes, and children usually have little participation in decision making. "Normal" family functioning can therefore not be measured along concepts that inquire about sharing in decision making and responsibilities and egalitarian sex role definitions. Again, this characteristic could be more related to the slim margin of decision making that living in poverty can entail than to cultural factors.

A similar problem was identified regarding an instrument that measures social adaptation in children. *Adaptation* is defined in terms of the way the person's role performance conforms to the expectations of his or her reference group. Measures are thus based on behaviors or roles that are normative to a given society or context (Katsching, 1983). Given this contextual definition, one would expect the construct to vary across different cultural and/or socioeconomic groups. We have evidence from a 1985 Puerto Rican children survey (Bird et al., 1988) that supports this statement. Even after matching children for age, sex, and socioeconomic status, differences between Puerto Rican and Anglo children were observed in the Child Behavior Checklist's social competence scores. Puerto Rican parents and teachers scored youth as considerably lower in the social competence items of this scale as compared to the Anglo sample. The adolescents also scored themselves lower in social competence. A closer inspection showed that reports on items that assess use of spare time, such as involvement in sports, hobbies, organizations, or part-time jobs, were significantly lower for Puerto Rican children, contributing to their lower social competence scores. The lack of resources in poor-income neighborhoods that is common in the island, as well as the high unemployment rates that limit the availability of jobs particularly for the younger age groups, probably accounts for these findings rather than the conclusion that Puerto Rican children are less socially adapted. Moreover, Puerto Rican children more frequently endorsed an item that measured frequency of contacts with friends and getting along with family and siblings. The latter results may reflect the importance that the Puerto Rican culture gives to close family ties and good interpersonal relations (Canino, 1982). In these situations, the content of items that are not relevant to the specific group to be studied must be substituted for others that are more culturally appropriate. In this case, although the lower-order construct of "use of spare time" can be retained to define a dimension of the higher-order construct of "social adaptation," it must be operationalized in a more culturally consonant way.

Whether the construct that the instrument measures is pertinent to the target group can also vary by geographical location. The DISC has some items designed to assess seasonal depression. Children and parents are asked whether they had experienced the symptoms characteristic of a dysphoric mood when days were shorter (late fall and winter) as compared to when days were longer (spring and summer). In Puerto Rico, people looked puzzled when asked in this manner. In a tropical island, there are no marked differences in the length of days during the year or striking environmental differences among the various seasons. To convey a similar idea in a more contextually appropriate way, we reworded the item to ask about seasons *cuando obscurece más temprano (de octubre a marzo)* and *cuando obscurece más tarde (de abril a septiembre)*— literally, this means, "when it grows dark sooner (from October to March)" or "it grows dark later (from April to September)." However, even after changing these items to make more sense in our context, we found that none of the children interviewed experienced seasonal depression. We wondered whether it was the result of the translation and adaptation or because it is unlikely to occur in a place where there are no marked seasonal changes. Results from the testing of the DISC, done through field trials carried out in collaboration with three North American sites, showed a pattern consistent with the latter. The prevalence of seasonal depression was higher in two communities of the Northeast of the United States, lower in a Southern community, and nonexistent in Puerto Rico (Canino & Bravo, 1999). This empirical finding was consistent with the arguments presented in the international committee's meetings. Although some members coming from the continental United States considered the construct and the original items appropriate for their sites, those coming from places nearer the equator (e.g., Venezuela) argued that it was not pertinent to their context.

These examples illustrate the importance of operationalizing and assessing constructs in a culturally appropriate way, after determining whether the construct is adequate for the ethnic groups involved. To carry out these tasks, researchers sometimes must use ethnographic methods, as illustrated in some of the examples presented above. Their use is intended to avoid the imposition of the appearance of cross-cultural homogeneity that is artifactual to the use of a constricted conceptualization embedded in the instrumentation ("cultural fallacy") (Kleinman & Good, 1985). Through a combination of psychometric empirical studies and ethnographic inquiry, this bias can be surmounted (in the mental health literature, e.g., see Carstairs & Kapur, 1976; Kinzie et al., 1982; Manson, Shore, & Bloom, 1985).

TECHNICAL EQUIVALENCE

Technical equivalence is attained if it can be documented that the measuring techniques used are similarly appropriate—that is, produce similar effects—in the different cultures involved. Sometimes differences identified between cultures that have used the same assessment instrument could be due to differences in the assessment technique being used rather than the content of the instrument. It is thus important that the technical equivalence of the instrument is assessed before the onset of the study. A careful consideration of the capabilities of the targeted respondents and their familiarity with the instrument's format and administration technique is needed. A bicultural committee familiar with the population under study can do this revision. However, field testing is essential. The use of these techniques is illustrated in what follows.

To study drug use, researchers should use self-administered instruments to minimize response bias due to social desirability. However, the lack of appropriate reading and writing skills is a source of inaccuracy when studying inner-city minority populations in which functional illiteracy is prevalent. It is thus necessary to maintain the anonymity of self-reports for sensitive information of this nature and at the same time address the problem of functional illiteracy. For this purpose, Turner, Lessler, and Gfroerer (1992) have developed a computerized audio system in which the respondent is not required to read the item but must answer the question posed by the audio system by pressing a key on the computer. These technological advances, although encouraging, must be carefully assessed to evaluate their appropriateness across and within ethnic groups. For example, this technology could be appropriate for youth familiar with computers or similar technology but not for those unfamiliar with them. Moreover, it could be appropriate for youth but not for older respondents.

Maximizing anonymity through self-report techniques as described earlier might not be sufficient for certain populations. Ethnic minorities and other socially disadvantaged populations may be more prone to deny behaviors such as use of drugs, physical abuse, sexual activity, or other antisocial behaviors because they think they could get into trouble with the authorities. In fact, there is evidence that a significantly greater proportion of African Americans than non-Hispanic Whites admit that they would not be honest in reporting their illicit drug use, even if they did hypothetically engage in this type of behavior (Mensch & Kandel, 1988). The lower rates of drug use among African American populations reported in national surveys sponsored by the National Institute of Drug Abuse may be the result of underreporting.

Data thus suggest that the assessment of sensitive or antisocial behaviors through self-reports will need to be supplemented with other types of assessment to avoid significant underreporting. This is especially so in populations in which this type of behavior is greatly censured or in groups who are at a disadvantage in the society surveyed. The use of key informants and other data sources (e.g., police and medical records or hair or urine analyses for biological detection of drug use) might be advisable. In addition, use of interviewers who live in the participants' community or prior consistent contact of interviewers with community leaders might be necessary to avoid underreporting of sensitive information.

Testing the reliability of an adapted instrument is an additional way for determining whether the assessment technique is appropriate for the particular group studied. If it is not, inconsistent answers are likely to be obtained. Moreover, reliability results from the adapted instrument that are similar to those obtained with the original version constitute more evidence of the technical equivalence of the instrument in both cultures and ethnic groups studied. Other more complex statistical techniques have been developed in the education field to test technical equivalence among different language versions of structured instruments (see, e.g., Hambleton, 1993).

Criterion Equivalence

Criterion equivalence implies that the interpretation of the results obtained from the measure is similar when evaluated in accordance with the established norms of each culture. It involves techniques similar to those used to assess criterion validity of a measure. However, it is very important that the criterion that serves as a validator is culturally appropriate. Again, the similarity between the observed validity results using the adapted version and those obtained with the original instrument attests to the criterion equivalence among both versions of the instrument.

The criterion equivalence of the Spanish versions of various diagnostic instruments has been established in Puerto Rico by comparing the diagnoses they produce against the clinical judgment of well-trained and experienced Puerto Rican clinicians, which is used as an external criterion (see, e.g., Bravo et al., 1993; Canino et al., 1987; Rubio-Stipec, Bird, Canino, & Gould, 1990). Because the reliability and validity of clinical judgments have sometimes been questioned, certain procedures have been employed to make the judgments more accurate. These include using the structured interview schedule to organize the interview, requiring that clinicians evaluate the presence of each diagnostic criterion (instead of only the disorder as a whole), and using a best estimate diagnosis (BED). The BED involves the consensus judgment of at least two clinicians about the presence of a disorder in a case (for more details, see Canino & Bravo, 1999). Relatively similar results to those obtained with the English versions of the diagnostic instruments have been obtained when similar comparisons were made, attesting to the criterion equivalence of the instruments' versions.

Results from comparisons between the diagnoses produced by the instruments and those given by clinicians have also been used to enhance the adapted instruments. For example, in the validity study of the Diagnostic Interview Schedule (DIS) (Robins, Helzer, Croughan, & Ratcliff, 1981), an overdiagnosis of schizophrenia relative to the clinical judgment was observed. Looking for the cause of this bias, it was identified that certain culturally syntonic experiences were likely to be scored as a positive psychotic symptom by the instrument yet were not considered as such by experienced Puerto Rican clinicians. The reported experiences were usually religious or spiritual in nature with strong influences from Catholic, Pentecostal, and Spiritism (*Espiritismo*) belief systems (see Garrison, 1977). These beliefs are common to large segments of the Puerto Rican population (Hohmann et al., 1990) and are prominent in Latin American cultures and literature (see, e.g., Allende, 1986). These experiences usually involve seeing or hearing dead relatives or religious figures (e.g., saints, the Virgin Mary, Jesus Christ) and having premonitions of events to occur. Under certain circumstances, these experiences are culturally valued and even considered a "special gift." As a result of these findings, in the instrument used for the epidemiological study, we introduced some additional items to fine-tune the assessment of these experiences. These items gather information about how acceptable and common the reported experience is for the interviewed persons and their relatives or friends ("Have you talked about these experiences with your family, friends, or peers?" "What did they say about them?" "Do you think these experiences happen only to you?"). The answers to these questions, in addition to the description of the experience that was also collected by the instrument, were used by Puerto Rican clinicians to decide whether the experience should be considered psychotic or a culturally syntonic behavior (Guarnaccia, Guevara-Ramos, González, Canino, & Bird, 1992). The addition of these features to the diagnostic instrument increased its criterion equivalence because it made the diagnoses derived from it more similar to the clinical judgments used as the culturally consonant validation criterion.

Conceptual Equivalence

Conceptual equivalence requires that the same theoretical construct be evaluated in the different cultures involved. Procedures similar to those used to attain construct validity of instruments can be used. One of the strategies is to use factor analysis to check the similarities in factor structures among versions of the same instrument. Another strategy is to determine the relationship of the construct with other relevant concepts derived from theory or previous research to test whether hypothesized relationships are confirmed.

We used the latter strategy in the Spanish translation and adaptation of the DISC. We hypothesized that children classified by the DISC as disordered would have higher levels of impairment (as measured by the Children's Global Assessment Scale) (Shaffer, Gould, & Brasic, 1983), lower levels of adaptive functioning (Beiser, 1990), and more school problems (dropping out, absenteeism, failure, detention, suspension, attending special classes) as compared to children who did not meet DISC diagnostic criteria. These hypothesized relationships were generally confirmed (Bravo et al., 1993). Results thus suggested that the adapted instrument was evaluating phenomena associated with dysfunction in social, psychological, and academic dimensions in children and adolescents, a finding that would be expected from an instrument appropriately evaluating psychiatric disorders in our context.

Cross-Cultural Comparisons

The presented model aims to produce equivalent instruments for varied languages and contexts. Once methodological artifacts have been minimized, comparisons across cultures or ethnic groups may yield illuminating findings, especially if many and varied cultures are involved. That is the case for the Diagnostic Interview Schedule (Robins et al., 1981), which has been used across many diverse sites in Asia, Europe, and North America (see Helzer & Canino, 1992; Weissman et al., 1994; Weissman et al., 1997; Weissman, Bland, Canino, Faravelli, et al., 1996; Weissman, Bland, Canino, Greenwall, et al., 1996). Interesting discrepancies and similarities have been observed (Rubio-Stipec & Bravo, 1999).

Some disorders varied widely in lifetime prevalence (i.e., alcoholism, 0.45%-23%; major depression, 1.5%-19%), but most showed more consistent rates (i.e., bipolar disorder, 0.3%-1.5%; social phobia, 0.5%-2.6%; panic disorder, 0.4%-2.9%; and obsessive compulsive disorder, 1.9%-2.5%). Reasonably consistent age of onset was observed for all studied disorders: social phobia (mid-teens to early 20s), bipolar disorder (late teens to mid-20s), alcoholism (early to mid-20s), panic disorder (early 20s to mid-30s), obsessive compulsive disorder (early 20s to mid-30s), and major depression (mid-20s to early 30s). Consistencies in symptomatic expression across sites were also observed for some disorders, such as alcoholism (rank order correlation of symptoms > .80 within North American sites and within Asian sites), but not for others, such as obsessive compulsive disorder (predominance of obsessions over compulsions for some sites and the opposite pattern for others).

Moreover, consistent gender distributions have been generally identified: Major depression, panic disorder, and social phobia tended to be female prevalent; alcoholism tended to be male prevalent; and bipolar and panic disorders tended to be gender balanced. The magnitude of female-to-male ratios were similar for some disorders (i.e., bipolar disorder, 0.3:1 to 1.2:1; social phobia, 1.4:1 to 1.6:1) but varied widely for others (i.e., major depression [F:M, 1.6:1 to 3.5:1], panic disorder [F:M, 1.3:1 to 5.8:1], and alcoholism [M:F, 4:1 to 25:1]). The male-to-female ratio was particularly high for alcoholism in the Asian and Hispanic cultures compared with Western and Anglo-Saxon cultures (12-25 vs. 4-6 times greater in males) as well as for Mexican American immigrants to the United States (25:1) compared to Mexican Americans native to the United States (4:1). This result suggests that an important societal effect, such as social stigma attached to drinking among females, may be present. It also illustrates the advantage of studying immigrant and native ethnic minorities in the context of larger multinational comparisons to elucidate observed patterns.

A caveat, however, is warranted at this point. Various limitations have been identified in the cross-cultural use of the DIS that may undermine the studies' findings (Rogler, 1999b). They include the overinclusiveness of some items and the absence of equivalent culturally significant symptoms of mental distress when applied to other cultures (for studies of the Hopi, see, e.g., Manson et al., 1985). The previously reviewed articles that reported DIS data do not usually describe in detail the process of translating and adapting the instrument to other languages and cultures. Therefore, it is not possible to judge whether a culturally sensitive process was used, and thus the resulting instruments cannot be considered culturally equivalent to the original. Therefore, interpretation of findings must take this into account. However, if the comparisons are culturally valid, they are a step in the process of understanding the role of culture in the development and course of disorders.

DISCUSSION

A major undertaking for psychology is the comparison of psychological phenomena across cultural or ethnic boundaries. This line of inquiry is embedded in the current interest on emphasizing the role of culture as an integral part of the study of cognition, emotions, intentions, and behaviors (Sinha, 1996). Psychology had been "culture blind" in the past. This tradition implied not only the denial of the influence of culture on human development but also the hegemony of a Euro-American worldview in the production of theories to explain it. According to Berry (1996), the reaction to this "culture-blind" tradition has been twofold. First, it was characterized by the emergence of conceptualizations and studies that consider culture a factor in the explanation of behavior. Second, it was represented by cross-cultural studies designed to compare the influence of various cultures on particular human behaviors. This cultural perspective is a reflection of debates and transformations in the philosophy of science, as well as the increasing recognition that knowledge is socially constructed (Cole, 1996).

Consonant with this philosophical transformation, Rogler (1999b) has used the concept of procedural norms, taken from the analysis of science as an institutional structured social process, to identify sources of persistent cultural insensitivity in research. Procedural norms are "canons of research that tell scientists what should be studied and how, and they are taught to successive generations of researchers" (p. 424). The procedural norms this author identified are (a) obtaining evidence about content validity based on experts' rational analysis of concepts, (b) using translations that try to conform to the exact terms used in standardized instruments, and (c) uncritically transferring concepts across cultures. These issues have been addressed in this chapter, and some solutions to tackle them have been proposed. They are, respectively, (a) including cultural observations besides the rational analysis of concepts to attain content equivalence, (b) targeting semantic or cultural equivalence rather than linguistic or literal translation, and (c) determining whether the construct that the original instrument evaluates is pertinent to the target cultural or subcultural group through detailed cultural observations and pilot testing.

However, these methodological procedures, as well as others described before, may produce an instrument that is somewhat or markedly different from the original one. Although most investigators agree on the value of cross-ethnic and cross-cultural research findings and on the need to make research culturally sensitive, there is disagreement as to the degree to which cultural or ethnic diversity should be incorporated into research instruments (Canino et al., 1997). Specifically, how much local cultural diversity can be incorporated into an established instrument before the degree of alteration renders the instrument incapable of measuring the original constructs for which it was designed?

This dilemma is difficult to tackle and is at the root of the emic-etic paradigm. On one hand, cross-cultural comparisons require similarities in observations, but the phenomena observed in each cultural group must be culturally valid for the comparison to be worthwhile.

In what follows, I propose two sets of guidelines to enhance valid cross-ethnic or cross-cultural comparisons derived from the experience of using the adaptation model previously presented and the analysis of pertinent literature. One set of rules applies to the case when a cross-ethnic collaborative process is used to develop the instrument from the start. The suggested steps are as follows.

First, include researchers from varied ethnic and cultural groups in the development of any instrument that is foreseen to be widely used. In this way, constructs and their operationalizations that are appropriate to multiple groups are considered and incorporated. Second, employ translatable English following Brislin et al.'s (1973) rules. Third, translate the instrument to other pertinent languages and use a decentering process to attain semantic equivalence across languages. Fourth, obtain evidence about the content validity of the instrument in the different languages and cultures by using experts' rational analysis. Fifth, pilot-test the different versions in diverse groups; special attention should be given to low-education and low-socioeconomic status (SES) populations because they are not likely to be represented in the panel of experts, regardless of ethnic group. Cultural observations should be added at this point to ensure that the constructs evaluated, or their operationalizations, as well as the administration procedures are appropriate. Sixth, evaluate the psychometric properties of each language version and targeted population to obtain evidence about their reliability and validity as well as their construct and conceptual equivalence. The whole process is not centered on any one culture or language; all language versions are subject to modifications at any step to attain cross-cultural equivalency. This is the ideal situation, but it is not likely to occur frequently due to the costs, effort, and coordination involved.

The other set of guidelines applies to translations and adaptations of an established instrument. First, examine carefully whether the instrument's constructs and dimensions, as well as its operationalization, are appropriate to the target group (content equivalence). Perform cultural observations (e.g., ethnography, culturally sensitive in-depth interviews or focus groups) in the target populations, besides rational analysis, when studying a population not familiar to the researchers, even within the same ethnic group (e.g., low-education or low-SES people). If lack of pertinence is identified beforehand, resources involved in translation and pretesting could be spared. However, this check for cultural pertinence should continue throughout the whole process of instrument development, especially in the translation and pretesting phases. Second, translate the instrument, but when translating, conform to semantic or cultural equivalents, not the exact terms of standardized instruments. Third, when some cultural discordance is identified within the instrument, substitute for culturally concordant equivalents. If the assessed higher-order construct (e.g., social adaptation) and its lower-order dimension (e.g., use of spare time) are considered culturally appropriate but not its operationalization (e.g., participation in organized sports), work at the item level to attain cultural equivalency; that is, the best alternative is to substitute each item for a pertinent operationalization (e.g., participating in informal sport games). When revising items, delete them only after being absolutely sure that no cultural equivalents are possible. If the addition of items is necessary, the analysis of data with and without the added items is sometimes appropriate. Fourth, if the discordance is of a higher magnitude—that is, at the level of the assessed higher-order construct (e.g.,

marital relations) or a lower-order dimension used to define it (e.g., decision making)—work at the dimension or instrument level is required. In this case, substitute culturally inappropriate lower-level constructs (e.g., decision making) for other lower-level appropriate ones (e.g., gender-based division of labor) to define the same higher-level construct in the instrument (decision making). Even in this case, try to maintain the same instrument format, if appropriate, and the same approximate length. Analytical difficulties in the comparison may result, however. An alternative is to develop equivalent cutoff points for each ethnic or cultural group—for example, culturally equivalent scores of "good" marital relations between the decision-making and the division-of-labor operationalizations. Fifth, test the psychometric properties of the new adapted version in the targeted population to obtain evidence about their reliability and validity as well as their construct and conceptual equivalence. Comparison of results with those obtained using the original version is warranted. Finally, write a thorough description of the methods used to translate and adapt the instrument, and publish it to let readers judge the adequacy of the process.

From what is presented above, it follows that the culturally sensitive perspective advocated in this chapter entails difficult endeavors because multiple methodological challenges must be overcome. On one hand, cross-cultural comparisons require equivalency in observations in the different cultures or ethnic groups, enabling researchers to disentangle whether the differences observed across groups are due to differences in the methods and measures employed or to true ethnic or cultural differences. On the other hand, for the comparisons to be worth the effort, instruments should be translated and adapted in a thorough and culturally sensitive way to avoid the cultural fallacy of imposing the appearance of cross-cultural homogeneity that is artifactual to the use of a constricted conceptualization embedded in the instrument (Kleinman & Good, 1985). The use of careful and comprehensive adaptation concepts and methods, similar to those described and illustrated in this chapter, is thus recommended to attain both goals. As previously stated, culturally sensitive research involves a continuing and incessant process of substantive and methodological adaptations designed to mesh the process of inquiry with the cultural characteristics of the groups being studied (Rogler, 1989). It is a difficult but worthwhile endeavor because the scientific accuracy of the research depends on it.

REFERENCES

Allende, I. (1986). *House of spirits*. New York: Bantam.

Beiser, M. (1990). *Flower of two soils: Final report*. Report submitted for NIMH Grant No. 5-ROI-MH96678 and Canada Health and Welfare NHRDP Grant No. 6610-1322-04.

Berry, J. W. (1996). On the unity of the field: Variations and commonalities in understanding human behavior in cultural context. *Interamerican Journal of Psychology, 30*(1), 89-98.

Bird, H. R., Canino, G., Rubio-Stipec, M., Gould, M. S., Ribera, J., Sesman, M., Woodbury, M., Huertas-Goldman, S., Pagán, A., Sanchez-Lacay, A., & Moscoso, M. (1988). Estimates of the prevalence of childhood maladjustment in a community survey in Puerto Rico. *Archives of General Psychiatry, 45,* 1120-1126.

Bravo, M., Canino, G., & Bird, H. (1987). La traducción y adaptación del esquema de entrevista diagnóstica DIS en Puerto Rico [The translation and adaptation of the Diagnostic Interview Schedule in Puerto Rico]. *Acta Psiquiátrica y Psicológica de Latinoamérica, 33,* 27-42.

Bravo, M., Canino, G., Rubio-Stipec, M., & Woodbury-Fariña, M. (1991). A cross-cultural adaptation of a diagnostic instrument: The DIS adaptation in Puerto Rico. *Culture, Medicine and Psychiatry, 15,* 1-18.

Bravo, M., Ribera, J., Rubio-Stipec, M., Canino, G., Shrout, P., Ramírez, R., Fábregas, L., Alegría, M., Bauermeister, J., Taboas, A. M., & Rivera-Medina, E. (2001). Test-retest reliability of the Spanish version of the Diagnostic Interview Schedule for Children (DISC-IV). *Journal of Abnormal Child Psychology, 29*(5), 433-444.

Bravo, M., Woodbury-Fariña, M., Canino, G., & Rubio-Stipec, M. (1993). The Spanish translation and cultural adaptation of the Diagnostic Interview Schedule for Children (DISC) in Puerto Rico. *Culture Medicine and Psychiatry, 17*(3), 329-344.

Brislin, R. W., Lonner, W. J., & Thorndike, R. M. (1973). *Cross-cultural research methods*. New York: John Wiley.

Canino, G. (1982). The Hispanic woman: Sociocultural influences on diagnoses and treatment. In R. Becerra, M. Karno, & J. Escobar (Eds.), *Mental health and Hispanic Americans: Clinical perspectives* (pp. 117-138). New York: Grune & Stratton.

Canino, G., Bird, H., Shrout, P., Rubio-Stipec, M., Bravo, M., Martínez, R., Sesman, M., & Guevara, L. M. (1987). The prevalence of specific psychiatric disorders in Puerto Rico. *Archives of General Psychiatry, 44,* 727-735.

Canino, G., & Bravo, M. (1994). The adaptation and testing of diagnostic and outcome measures for cross-cultural research. *International Review of Psychiatry, 6,* 281-286.

Canino, G., & Bravo, M. (1999). The translation and adaptation of diagnostic instruments for children in cross-cultural research. In D. Shaffer, C. P. Lucas, & J. E. Richters (Eds.), *Diagnostic assessment in child psychopathology* (pp. 285-298). New York: Guilford.

Canino, G., & Guarnaccia, P. (1997). Methodological challenges in the assessment of Hispanic children and adolescents. *Applied Development Science, 1*(3), 124-134.

Canino, G., Lewis-Fernández, R., & Bravo, M. (1997). Methodological challenges in cross-cultural mental health research. *Transcultural Psychiatry, 34*(2), 163-184.

Carstairs, G. M., & Kapur, R. (1976). *The great universe of Kota.* Berkeley: University of California Press.

Cole, M. (1996). *Cultural psychology: A once and future discipline.* Cambridge, MA: Belknap.

Draguns, J. G. (1980). *Psychological disorders of clinical severity: Vol. 6. Psychopathology.* Boston: Allyn & Bacon.

Flaherty, F. A., Gaviria, F. M., & Pathak, D. (1988). Developing instruments for cross-cultural psychiatric research. *Journal of Nervous and Mental Diseases, 176,* 257-263.

Flaherty, J. A. (1987). Appropriate and inappropriate research methodologies for Hispanic mental health. In M. Gaviria (Ed.), *Health and behavior: Research agenda for Hispanics* (pp. 177-186). Chicago: University of Illinois Press.

Garrison, V. (1977). The Puerto Rican syndrome in espiritismo and psychiatry. In V. Crapanzano & V. Garrison (Eds.), *Case studies in spirit possession* (pp. 383-449). New York: Wiley-Interscience.

Guarnaccia, P. J., Guevara-Ramos, L. M., González, G., Canino, G., & Bird, H. (1992). Cross-cultural aspects of psychotic symptoms in Puerto Rico. *Research in Community Mental Health, 7,* 99-110.

Hambleton, R. K. (1993). Translating achievement tests for use in cross-national studies. *European Journal of Psychological Assessment, 9,* 57-68.

Hambleton, R. K. (1994). Guidelines for adapting educational and psychological tests. A progress report. *European Journal of Psychological Assessment, 10,* 229-244.

Helzer, J. E., & Canino, G. (1992). Comparative analysis of alcoholism in ten cultural regions. In J. E. Helzer & G. Canino (Eds.), *Alcoholism—North America, Europe and Asia: A coordinated analysis of population from ten regions* (pp. 289-306). Oxford, UK: Oxford University Press.

Hohmann, A., Richport, M., Marriot, B., Canino, G., Rubio-Stipec, M., & Bird, H. (1990). Spiritism in Puerto Rico: Results of an island-wide community study. *British Journal of Psychiatry, 156,* 328-335.

Katsching, H. I. E. (1983). Methods for measuring social adjustment. In T. Helgason (Ed.), *Methodology in evaluation of psychiatric treatment* (pp. 205-218). New York: Cambridge University Press.

Kinzie, J. D., Manson, S. M., Vinh, D. T., Tolan, N. T., Anh, B., & Pho, T. N. (1982). Development and validation of Vietnamese-Language Depression Rating Scale. *American Journal of Psychiatry, 139,* 1276-1281.

Kleinman, A., & Good, B. (Eds.). (1985). *Culture and depression.* Berkeley: University of California Press.

Manson, S. M., Shore, J. H., & Bloom, J. D. (1985). The depressive experience in American Indian communities: A challenge for psychiatric theory and diagnosis. In A. Kleinman & B. Good (Eds.), *Culture and depression.* Berkeley: University of California Press.

Mensch, B. S., & Kandel, D. B. (1988). Underreporting of substance use in a national longitudinal youth cohort. *Public Opinion Quarterly, 52,* 100-124.

Olson, D. H., Portner, J., & Bell, R. O. (1982). *FACES II: Family adaptability and cohesion evaluation scales.* St. Paul: Family Social Science, University of Minnesota.

Robins, L. N., Helzer, J. E., Croughan, J., & Ratcliff, K. S. (1981). The NIMH Diagnostic Interview Schedule: Its history, characteristics and validity. *General Psychiatry, 38,* 381-389.

Rogler, L. H. (1989). The meaning of culturally sensitive research in mental health. *American Journal of Psychiatry, 146,* 296-303.

Rogler, L. H. (1999a). Implementing cultural sensitivity in mental health research: Convergence and new directions, Part I. *Psychline, 3*(1), 5-11.

Rogler, L. H. (1999b). Methodological sources of cultural insensitivity in mental health research. *American Psychologist, 54*(6), 424-433.

Rogler, L. H., Malgady, R. G., & Rodríguez, O. (1989). *Hispanics and mental health: A framework for research.* Malabrar, FL: Kriger.

Rubio-Stipec, M., Bird, H., Canino, G., & Gould, M. (1990). The internal consistency and concurrent validity of a Spanish translation of the Child Behavior Checklist. *Journal of Abnormal Child Psychology, 18*(4), 393-406.

Rubio-Stipec, M., & Bravo, M. (1999). Structured diagnostic instruments in cross-cultural psychiatric epidemiology: The experience in Hispanic communities and other groups. In J. M. Herrera, W. B. Lawson, & J. J. Sramel (Eds.), *Cross-cultural psychiatry* (pp. 87-98). New York: John Wiley.

Shaffer, D., Gould, M. S., & Brasic, J. (1983). A Children's Global Assessment Scale (C-GAS). *Archives of General Psychiatry, 40,* 1228-1231.

Sinha, D. (1996). Culturally rooted psychology in India: Dangers and developments. *Interamerican Journal of Psychology, 30*(1), 99-110.

Turner, C., Lessler, J., & Gfroerer, J. (1992). Future directions for research and practice. In C. F. Turner, J. T. Lessler, & J. C. Gfroerer (Eds.), *Survey measurement of drug use: Methodological studies* (pp. 299-306). Rockville, MD: National Institute on Drug Abuse, U.S. Department of Health and Human Services.

Weissman, M. M., Bland, M. B., Canino, G. J., Greenwald, S., Hwu, H. G., Lee, C. K., Newman, S. C., Oakley-Browne, M. A., Rubio-Stipec, M., Wickramaratne, P. J., Wittchen, H. U., & Yeh, E. K. (1994). The cross-national epidemiology of obsessive compulsive disorder. *Journal of Clinical Psychiatry, 55*(3), 5-10.

Weissman, M. M., Bland, R., Canino, G., Faravelli, C., Greenwald, S., Hwu, H. G., Joyce, P. R., Karam, E. G., Lee, C. K., Lellouch, J., Lépine, J. P., Newman, S., Oakley-Browne, M. A., Rubio-Stipec, M., Wells, J. E., Wickramaratne, P., Wittchen, H. U., & Yeh, E. K. (1997). The cross-national epidemiology of panic disorder. *Archives of General Psychiatry, 54,* 305-309.

Weissman, M. M., Bland, R., Canino, G., Faravelli, C., Greenwald, S., Hwu, H. G., Joyce, P. R., Karam, E. G., Lee, C. K., Lellouch, J., Lépine, J. P., Newman, S., Rubio-Stipec, M., Wells, J. E., Wickramaratne, P., Wittchen, H. U., & Yeh, E. K. (1996). Cross-national epidemiology of major depression and bipolar disorder. *Journal of the American Medical Association, 276,* 293-299.

Weissman, M. M., Bland, R. C., Canino, G. J., Greenwall, L., Lee, C. K., Newman, S. C., Rubio-Stipec, M., & Wickramaratne, P. J. (1996). The cross-national epidemiology of social phobia: A preliminary report. *International Journal of Clinical Psychopharmacology, 11,* 9-14.

World Health Organization (WHO). (1998). *Procedures for the development of new language versions of the WHO Composite International Diagnostic Interview (WHO-CIDI).* Geneva: Author.

Part III

SOCIAL AND DEVELOPMENTAL PROCESS

CHAPTER 12

Social and Psychological Perspectives on Ethnic and Racial Identity

JOSEPH E. TRIMBLE
Western Washington University

JANET E. HELMS
Boston College

MARIA P. P. ROOT
Seattle, Washington

In September 1931, distinguished anthropologist Margaret Mead ventured from New York City to study the way sex roles are characterized in different cultural groups. After a long journey across the United States and the Pacific Ocean, she and her then husband, Reo Fortune, landed in New Guinea. Her meticulously and carefully conducted ethnographic study provided her with sufficient information to publish in 1935 the now-classic book, *Sex and Temperament in Three Primitive Societies,* where she describes the contrasting personalities of men and women from three New Guinea villages. The first group she contacted and studied lived in the Prince Alexander Mountains located in New Guinea's northwestern corner. In a letter dated April 20, 1932, Mead states, "We still have not decided what to call this mountain people for they have

AUTHORS' NOTE: The senior author wants to extend his deepest gratitude to the administration and research staff at the Radcliffe Institute for Advanced Study, Harvard University, for providing him with the time, resources, and support that allowed him to conduct research for the preparation and writing of this chapter. In addition, he wishes to extend his warm appreciation to his Radcliffe research junior partners, Harvard College seniors Peggy Ting Lim and Maiga Miranda, who conducted research and provided him with wonderful, thought-provoking commentary and advice for many topics covered in this chapter.

no name for themselves, just friendly little nicknames or names for sections of a community, like man-o-bush or 'poisonous snakes'" (Mead, 2001, p. 125). After much thought, Mead eventually chose to refer to them as the Arapesh or Mountain Arapesh.

Currently, it may be difficult to comprehend the possibility that any society or ethnocultural group does not have an identity or label to use to refer to it in some collective manner. Such a discovery by Margaret Mead challenges conventional beliefs that all collectives, societies, and ethnocultural groups have distinct names for the collective or refer to themselves in some designated manner, such as "people" in their language. The fundamental principle of any identity theory suggests that all groups have a label or name for themselves. Thus, how does an outsider ask whether it is possible that a small remote collective living in New Guinea in the 1920s would not know what to call themselves? Is it possible that identity is an "etic-bound" construct not universally valued and expressed by all societies and cultures? Certainly, additional questions can be phrased concerning Mead's finding, and those are left for further speculation and articulation.

Nonetheless, interest in collective and individual identity theory has generated considerable discussion and research in the past 60 years. Within the past 30 years, specific attention has been devoted to the construct and its relationship to ethnic and racial groups. The following chapter is a summary of the definitions, theories, research findings, speculations, controversies, and challenges presented by the study of the structural, functional, and dynamic characteristics of ethnic and racial identity.

The topic may appear to be limited in scope, but in fact, it is a broad and expansive one. Since 1887, according to the citations found in the PsycINFO electronic database, slightly more than 3,000 articles have been written on the topic of ethnic and racial identity; two thirds of those articles have been written since 1990. *Sociological Abstracts* indicates that 3,648 articles have been written on the topic since 1963, and an anthropology electronic database indicates that 1,149 were written from that field's perspective, although no specific time frame was provided. The literature search suggests that interest in the topic is multidisciplinary and has accelerated considerably since 1990. The accelerated interest indicates that we must stop and take stock of the topic and its future direction; also, the content and emphasis of publications dedicated to the topic are changing strongly, pointing to the need for a summary of the findings and discussions.

OVERVIEW

A plethora of theories and models of ethnic and racial identity exist. Varying in emphasis, they generally define a dynamic, multifaceted construct (cf. Mio, Trimble, Arredondo, Cheatham, & Sue, 1999). Ethnic and racial identity can include personal identity, notions of belonging, knowledge of the reference group, and shared values. Its expression or belonging may change across situations, points in time, and within the same people (Stephan & Stephan, 1989; Trimble, 1988; Trimble & Mahoney, 2002; Waters, 1990). The literature suggests that at least three layers of context influence how these components of ethnic identity manifest time context (history and generation), space (size of community), and place (geography or region). Finally, a reflexive process affected by the continuous impact of events and experiences drives enculturation in part through experiences that range from stressful to traumatic as part of acculturative stress (Bernal & Knight, 1993; Berry, 1975), reflected in our constructs of the process of acculturation and assimilation. Furthermore, cross-culturally, ethnic identification derives from social and political processes (Romanucci-Ross &

DeVos, 1995; Roosens, 1989). Despite the challenge to conceptualize ethnic identity, it eludes definitive measurement. At best, measurement presents a partial picture of someone's ethnic identity. Consider the following examples of three people who all identify as Filipino American in some situations.

Example 1. Annabel is second generation, raised in the Virginia Beach area of Virginia. Her mother and father are both college educated, born in the Philippines. They obtained their graduate degrees in the United States in the early 1970s in nursing and dentistry, respectively. They socialize with the significant Filipino community in their area, many of whom are professionals and have immigrated post-1965. Annabel, an attorney, now lives in Washington, D.C., and works in a medium-sized law firm. Except for visits home, she seldom participates in organized Filipino community events.

Example 2. Patrick immigrated with his parents in the early 1980s for safety reasons because of his father's ties with the Marcos government as an attorney. His mother had never worked outside the home prior to fleeing the Philippines. Now, in the United States, both his parents work, his father as a grossly underemployed stock clerk in a grocery store and occasional law clerk, his mother as a janitor in an elementary school. Now a young adult, Patrick lives in Los Angeles and struggles to finish college. He became a citizen at 22 years of age. He is involved with the Filipino immigrant community and still speaks Tagalog some portion of every day.

Example 3. Tony is second generation, born in Seattle. His father worked the field as a migrant worker up and down the West Coast. His mother was also from a Filipino migrant farm family. Tony, now almost 70, has proudly identified as Filipino American.

He was part of the first significant generation of American-born Filipinos to forge the meaning of *Filipino American.* College educated, he was the first in his family to obtain this level of education. He has worked in mainstream university and government institutions, always advancing the agenda of minorities.

Although applied initially to the concept of race, sociologist Robert Parks (1937) observed the complex interactive dimensions of identity. He maintained,

> Race relations, like many if not most other relations among human beings, must be conceived as existing in three dimensions rather than as we ordinarily conceive it, in two . . . between individuals and between groups of individuals. . . . Changes may be, or seem to be, merely fortuitous. At other times, they assume a cyclical or secular form. All three types of change are involved in the processes of growth and all three are more or less involved in what we may describe as the "race relation cycle." . . . At any time and place . . . once initiated, inevitably continues until it terminates in some predestined racial configuration, and one consistent with an established social order of which it is a part. (pp. xiii-xiv)

Ethnicity has both a private and social construction. Ironically, the confusion between race and ethnicity in part stems from social assignments to ethnic groups based on some markers of origins, behavior, and phenotype versus personal identification. When the former are thought to arise from biologically based markers, more mistakes are likely to be made in social assignment as factors of change over time, person, and location are not factored into personal identification processes. Moreover, ethnic and racial identity is a form of self-determination as expressed through a self-declaration. The declaration, however, may not be recognized by others. Thus, a person or group of people can suffer real damage, real distortion, if the people of society mirror back to them a confining or demeaning or contemptible picture of themselves. Nonrecognition or misrecognition can inflict harm, can be a form of oppression, imprisoning someone in a false, distorted and reduced mode of being. (Taylor, 1992, p. 25)

Individuals may privately know who they are, but certain social forces and groups can and do deny or limit self-declaration.

ETHNIC GLOSS

Before the topic of ethnic identity is considered in more detail, attention must be given to the manner in which researchers, among many others, specify and describe ethnic and culturally distinct populations. As one scans the ethnic and racial identity literature, it becomes readily apparent that a number of studies focus on American Indians (or Native Americans), African Americans (Blacks), Asian and Pacific Americans, Mexican Americans and Puerto Ricans, and other ethnic-specific or ethnocultural groups. Occasionally, researchers provide greater specificity concerning their respondents in their titles and abstracts by giving reference to a geographic or geocultural region or city in the United States. Others will distinguish their respondents along urban and rural lines, whereas others, when referring to an American Indian group, will specify the tribe (e.g., Dine, Lakota, Hopi, or one of the Pueblos in New Mexico). Nonetheless, most studies in the ethnic/racial social and behavioral science literature provide descriptions of ethnic and cultural groups that tend to rely on the use of broad "ethnic glosses"—superficial, almost vacuous, categories that serve only to separate one group from another (Trimble, 1991). Use of such "glosses" gives little or no sense of the richness and cultural variation within these groups, much less the existence of numerous subgroups characterized by distinct lifeways

(*ethos*) and thoughtways (*eidos*). Furthermore, the use of broad "ethnic glosses" to describe a cultural or ethnic group in a research venture may be poor science. Apart from the fact that such sweeping references to ethnic groups are gross misrepresentations, their use can violate certain tenets concerning external validity (the ability to generalize findings across subgroups within an ethnic category) and erode any likelihood of an accurate and efficient replication of research results.

In selecting ethnic samples for social and behavioral science studies, researchers almost tacitly assume that the respondents share a common understanding of their own ethnicity and nationalistic identification. It is as though the researcher believes that African Americans, American Indians, Hispanics, and others share some modal characteristic that at one level sets them apart from another comparative sample, such as "Whites" (Trimble, 1988).

Mounting evidence suggests that the assumption may be invalid. Marín and Marín (1982) illustrated how the use of an ethnic category, in this case, Hispanic, can disrupt a well-intended sampling strategy. The researchers were interested in the health records of some 500 patients at a clinic in East Los Angeles, California, an area known for its high concentration of people with Hispanic origins. Because of the location of the clinic, they expected to find mostly Hispanics in their sample. Much to their surprise, they found that some patients with Spanish surnames actually checked the "White" and "other" ethnic category on the medical form. On examining the "other" category, they found that 3% of the patients wrote in specific ethnic identifiers such as "Mexican American" and "Chicano." All in all, some 13% chose to identify themselves in a way that differed from what one might expect from a person with a Spanish surname. Indeed, the use of "Hispanic" as a means to identify a sample is insufficient because the category can mean quite different things to people. Heath (1978) pointedly argued that "categories of people such as those compared under the rubric of 'ethnic groups' are often not really meaningful units in any sociocultural sense" (p. 60). Heath went on to add "that the ways in which people define and maintain the 'social boundaries' between or among self-identified categories are often far more important and revealing of sociocultural dynamics" (p. 60).

Use of broad-brush ethnic categories does have a useful purpose at one level. Researchers and policy planners can use the results to differentiate groups to highlight salient characteristics. In a crude way, it is a good deal easier to discuss differences between ethnic and cultural groups by using the "gloss." As such, planners, legislators, and decision makers find it convenient to balance and present the findings and problems of one or more ethnic groups against other groups. Use of the ethnic gloss at this level is tolerable. Most definitions of ethnic identity rely on an identifiable group to form the basis of the construct. Reliance on a group orientation not only views identity as static but also provides little credence to individual-level variations and influences created by situational or contextual circumstances. In short, psychological and situational characteristics are not found in typical definitions and conceptualizations of ethnic identity.

DEFINITIONS OF CONSTRUCTS

A construct such as ethnic identity generates many viewpoints. To understand the complications, one must consider the meanings of race and ethnicity. Feagin (1978) defined a racial group as one in which "persons inside or outside the group have decided what is important to single out as inferior or superior, typically on the basis of real or alleged physical characteristics subjectively selected" (p. 7). An ethnic group, maintained Feagin, is one "which is socially distinguished or set apart, by others and/or by itself, primarily on the basis of cultural or nationality characteristics" (p. 9). Thompson (1989) elaborated on the term *ethnic* and chose to view it as a culturally distinct population that can be set apart from other groups. Such groups, Thompson argued, engage in behaviors "based on cultural or physical criteria in a social context in which these criteria are relevant" (p. 11).

Although there are numerous "White" and "non-White" ethnic groups in the Americas, more often than not, non-White ethnics are designated as minority groups. At one level, the term *minority* implies that a "majority group" exists that assumes a position of dominance within a given country. To an extent, the term *minority group* has racist overtones and implies that a particular group has been and continues to be the victim of collective discrimination. Most notably in North America, an ethnic minority group may be defined as

(1) subordinate segments of complex state societies; (2) [having] special physical or cultural traits which are held in low esteem by the dominant segments of the society; (3) self-conscious units bound together by the special traits which their members have and by the special disabilities which these bring; (4) [one where] membership is transmitted by a rule of descent which is capable of affiliating succeeding generations even in the absence of readily apparent special cultural or physical traits; and (5) [people who] by choice or necessity tend to marry within the group. (Wayley & Harris, 1958, p. 10)

Ethnic and *racial identity* are overlapping constructs, but their distinctiveness flows from the emphasis placed on the seemingly interchangeable terms. Phinney (2000) defined ethnic identity as

a dynamic, multidimensional construct that refers to one's identity, or sense of self, in ethnic terms, that is in terms of a subgroup within a larger context that claims a common ancestry and shares one or more of the following elements: culture, race, religion, language, kinship, or place of origin. (p. 254)

Compare her definition of the construct with one offered by Bram (1965). He defined the construct as

> a form of self-conceptualization by a person which may be accepted or rejected by the social world around him. It may be forced on him by coercion and is of limited predictive value for his own ancestry or that of his descendants. It varies in meaning across persons and through history and is interchangeable with national identity. (p. 242)

The definitions are similar, but the emphasis of the source of the identity varies. Helms (1990) maintained that "'racial identity' refers to a sense of group or collective identity based on one's perception that he or she shares a common racial heritage with a particular racial group" (p. 3). The terms *ethnic, racial,* and *cultural* all share a common meaning but only from the perspective that people congregate around common core characteristics. The source of the core characteristics can be criteria established and deeply held by the in-group and out-groups, which can also set their own criteria for designating and differentiating one group from another. Thompson (1989) was highly critical of the labeling process and drew attention to theoretical and practical matters befallen "those who have had the fortune or, in most cases, the misfortune of being labeled 'ethnics' in the modern world" (p. 42). Helms (1990) concurred, to an extent, as she found it rather confusing "since one's racial-group designation does not necessarily define one's racial, cultural, or ethnic characteristics" (p. 7). In her work on Black and White identities, Helms preferred to emphasize "race" as an organizing construct. To distinguish one group or individual from another by appealing to race, ethnicity, or culture is an attempt to be distinctive. Labeling a group as a distinct cultural (racial or ethnic) unit, however, tends to promote stereotypes and leads to overgeneralizations, further compounding the complexity of the problem. It is not uncommon for outsiders to believe that identifiable members of a racial group act as a single unitary whole—a group mind—and that they are more homogeneous than heterogeneous. Such labeling leads to blanket-type statements, such as "_____(fill in the blank) are all the same." Many Americans use similar statements when referring to such nationalistic groups as Japanese, Mexicans, Nigerians, and Saudi Arabians, among many others—many Americans actually use the blanket-type statement to refer to all Asians, often claiming that they cannot differentiate a Japanese from a Korean, Chinese, Laotian, or Indonesian, and so on.

Numerous debates emerging in the literature challenge many of the theories espoused to explain the complex meaning and nature of ethnic identity. Pierre van den Berghe (1981) and Richard Thompson (1989) are two whose perspectives on the topic stir up some controversy. Thompson has taken issue with van den Berghe's "pop sociobiological" view of ethnic and race relations. van den Berghe has advocated a primordialist position about ethnicity, in which one's sense of attachment and belongingness is tied to an ancestral origin. Unlike sociologist Edward Shils and anthropologist Glifford Geertz, early proponents of the primordialist theory, van den Berghe has held that sociobiological principles and tenets must be used to tighten loose theoretical ends. Thompson has taken on the primordialist position—a viewpoint that is used to explain and justify emerging "ethnic consciousness" movements—by appealing to other more seemingly social structural perspectives such as assimilationism, capitalism, and neo-Marxism. He is critical of these perspectives, too. Thompson also laid out a sequence of interesting topics that any theory of ethnicity must accommodate: (a) ethnic and racial classifications, (b) ethnic and racial sentiments, and (c) ethnic and racial social organization. Put another way, humans typically develop systems to categorize and classify themselves and others, attach significance and meaning to the classification, and use racial and ethnic classifications for organizational criteria.

Race and ethnicity share histories of constructions of social relations that have served economic, social, and political purposes to separate classes and even castes, often starkly observed in colonial projects (Forbes, 1990; Young, 1995). Rules are invented that must be internalized and tend to be highly illogical. Nevertheless, *race* and *ethnicity* are not synonymous. However, their juxtaposition uses physically visible differences or socially constructed imaginings of character or characteristics as shorthand markers of ethnicity. With racially visible groups other than European-originated persons, race has been used as a biological marker for signaling ethnicity. Whereas ethnic options—and even ethnic divestment—are possible for European-originated persons (Waters, 1990), these choices are constrained for persons who are identified racially as other than White.

RACE

Sociologist Pierre van den Berghe (1967) noted that

> the human group that defines itself, and/or is defined by other groups is different by virtue of innate or immutable characteristics. These physical characteristics are in turn assumed to be intrinsically related to moral, intellectual and other non-physical attributes or abilities. A race, therefore, is a group that is socially defined on the basis of physical criteria. (p. 18)

The social construction of race that is embedded in U.S. history is captured formally every 10 years by the formal census. The rules for racial classification over the decades demonstrate the social construction of race. Rules of *hypodescent*, assignment to the race of lower social status or greater social stigma, have prevailed. For example, until 1989, biracial babies with a White parent were assigned

to the racial status of the non-White parent; babies of two parents of color were assigned the race of the father. As of 1989, all infants are designated by their mothers' race (Waters, 1994). In 1978, the Federal Office of Management and Budget designated that racial data be collected according to five mutually exclusive racial categories: Black, White, Asian/Pacific Islander, American Indian/Alaska Native, and other. People were to enact the rules of hypodescent by designating themselves as people in their community would identify them. These categories also set the framework for civil rights protections. All of these racial designations assume rules of hypodescent to perpetuate monoracial affiliation that protects Whiteness (Root, 1996). Later, Hispanic was created as an ethnic group, but it actually serves as a pseudo-racial group in daily life because all the other racial groups are also used as "ethnic glosses," which eliminates the possibility of describing their actual ethnicity. By 1990, people were allowed to identify themselves as they personally wanted to be identified. By 2000, racial categories had changed: Asian and Pacific Islander were now two separate categories, and people were allowed to check more than one racial category in response to the race category. Six racial categories now existed, although they were no longer deemed mutually exclusive. With the 2000 census, the racial system was further challenged. Despite the option for multiple checkoffs to the racial question and placing the Hispanic origin question before the race question, 42% of Hispanics still checked "other" for race (U.S. Bureau of the Census, 2001). In addition, more than 4,119,000 individuals chose to mark "American Indian and Alaska Native" along with one or more "race" categories. The "race alone or in combination" count is much higher than the "race alone" count of 2,475,956. The discrepancy raises the question about which count is more accurate or representative of the "true" Indian population (cf. Trimble, 2000). Similar findings occurred for other ethnic and racial groups in the United States.

The racial system in this country has functioned as a caste system to create barriers to protect Whiteness; thus, in this sense, it is a political construction intended initially to serve a few. Although Root (2001) noted that some racially designated groups are now experiencing a shift from caste to class, particularly if they do not live in enclaves but do operate fluidly and skillfully as bicultural, caste remnants remain, particularly for persons of African descent. Caste regulates sexual relations and, subsequently, status, privileges, and social mobility (Montague, 1997). This backdrop for understanding the necessity for racial construction in this country is important for understanding some of the complexity in ethnic identity construction and choice.

ETHNICITY

Waters (1990) observed that the common assumption about ethnic identity is that it is inherited versus dynamic, socially constructed, and even chosen. She also observed that a tension exists in the construction of ethnic identity between freedom to choose and constraint based on one's socially ascribed race. Although many persons of European mixed stock can opt for which ethnicity to declare—if any—this freedom does not pertain to persons of other origins who have been constructed as racially non-White in the United States. Waters (1990) further observed that White persons even have the option to divest themselves of an ethnicity and declare themselves American.

On the other hand, some of the declarations of ethnicity by White Americans are only symbolic, with little knowledge or attachment to their grandparents' origins. Waters (1990) described a respondent in her study who wanted a "thick culture" that was flexible. She described this process as resulting in symbolic ethnicity because

it gives middle-class Americans at least the appearance of both: conformity and individuality; community with social change. And as an added bonus—which almost ensures its appeal to Americans—the element of choice is there also. This partly explains the patterns in the choices [White] people make about their ethnic identities. When given a choice, whites will choose the most "ethnic" of the ancestries in their backgrounds. (p. 154)

The symbolic identity has little social cost or stigmatization and even provides individual satisfaction.

Symbolic identity stands in contrast to nonsymbolic ethnicity, the experience of racial minorities. Waters (1990) noted that as persons of European ancestry invoke symbolic ethnicity and equate it with enjoyment and lack of constraint, the understanding of the racially juxtaposed or constrained ethnic options for racial minorities will be less understood.

Seldom discussed is the role of maternal or paternal lineage in determining one's ethnic identity, particularly when one inherits more than one ethnic lineage. Ethnic options may be directed by patrilineal rules when ethnicity is mixed, even if both parents are of European stock. Several large-scale survey studies (e.g., the Census Bureau's Reinterview Study and the Michigan National Election Study) demonstrated people's tendency to choose paternal ancestry over maternal ethnicity when multiple ethnicities were involved (cf. Waters, 1990, pp. 20-22). Furthermore, ethnicities are often traced through surnames, which still are governed by patrilineal rules.

Because intergroup prejudices still pertain in the United States, nonsymbolic identity is tied largely to minority or disenfranchised status by racial group belonging and economic disenfranchisement. The social tensions that further maintain ethnicity as a defining characteristic for many residents of the United States stem from a greater gap in inequality between those who operate the wealth and those who live at poverty lines. Necessarily, individual and group processes combined provide more comprehensive models by which to understand ethnic identity.

CULTURAL IDENTITY

A little attention also should be given to the term *cultural identity*. It, too, is a complex term and is probably the most difficult to define. There are a number of complications owing to theoretical differences; however, the definition of *culture* (*cultural*) presents the biggest problem. Anthropologists and cross-cultural psychologists claim that there are more than 165 different definitions of *culture* (Kroeber & Kluckhohn, 1952). In defining *culture,* one must consider not only what exists but also what is desirable. Cultures are not merely an amalgam of specific behaviors because they include, in addition to activities of a standard nature, consistent cognitive, perceptual, motivational, and affective patterns and a distinctive array of artifacts of human alterations of the environment. Cultures also are continuous, cumulative, and progressive (White, 1947).

Thus, culture can be a way of life attributed to a distinct collective of humans who reside in a particular geographic locale, but however broad this definition may be, it is not without flaws. For the sake of brevity, we can appeal to Brown's (1991) definition. He maintained that

> culture consists of the conventional patterns of thought, activity, and artifact that are passed on from generation to generation in a manner that is generally assumed to involve learning rather specific programming. Besides being transmitted "vertically" from generation to generation, culture may also be transmitted "horizontally" between individuals and collectivities. (p. 40)

Primordialists and sociobiologists undoubtedly would have something to say about this concise and somewhat learning-centered version.

EGO AND ETHNIC DEVELOPMENT THEORIES

Ethnic identity is closely aligned to ego identity and self-esteem. The social status of a group also can influence self-esteem; if an ethnic group has experienced a long, oppressive history of prejudice and discrimination, then group members could experience a devalued sense of self (Tajfel, 1981). The self-image, however, is significantly influenced by one's evaluation of the group—if the evaluation is positive, then commitment is strong, contentment is high, and involvement in ethnic behaviors and practices is significant, therefore allowing one to achieve a strong secure identity with the group (Phinney, 1991). But if the evaluation is negative, then involvement, preferences, contentment, and commitment will be minimal in these instances; multiethnic individuals will seek ways to pass as members of other groups or denigrate the value of the group by forging relations with related subgroups.

Using ego involvement, the group evaluation process, and Eriksen's model (Stevens, 1983) as a foundation, Phinney (1989) developed the Ethnic Identity Development Measure (EIDM). Essentially, individuals (especially adolescents) can experience one of four identities:

1. diffused identity, in which individuals express little or no interest in their identity;

2. foreclosed identity, in which a person shows some interest in his or her ethnicity and parental influences have been internalized;

3. moratorium identity, in which an individual continues to explore his or her ethnic identity but in the process may be experiencing some degree of confusion; and

4. achieved identity, in which one's identity has been successfully integrated into his or her self-concept.

Individuals' self-esteem is the mainstay of the theory and can be influenced by any one of their developmental stages.

Writing more than 30 years ago, Cross (1971) developed the first of a series of his iterations of Nigrescence theory. Like Phinney's (1989) model, it rests on a developmental sequence composed of five stages:

1. Preencounter, in which the process of identification is formed and directed to a group;

2. Encounter, in which individuals decide they need a change in their sense of ethnic self-awareness that is influenced by significant events;

3. Immersion-Emersion, in which old and new identities create a struggle for the individuals;

4. Internalization, in which the newly adopted identity becomes accepted; and

5. Internalization-Commitment, the ultimate stage in which ethnicity is salient and is an integral part of one's daily life.

Similar to Phinney's (1989) model, levels of self-esteem are related to Cross's (1971) stages, and consequently esteem levels are lowest at the Preencounter stage and change accordingly to a peak positive level at the Internalization-Commitment stage.

Owing to the mounting research on ethnic identity models, especially for Helms's racial identity model (Helms, 1989a, 1990) and the addition of several alternative models, Cross (1991) was compelled to revise his levels. Cross now believes that social situations can act as a moderating variable; one's identity in some situations may be reinforcing and contribute to positive ego functioning, but in other situations, identification with a group may be of little consequence. Cross also learned that identity may not be salient for some individuals; they know they are Black or American Indian or some other group, and they feel no need to explore its meaning. Cross found that self-esteem is not necessarily correlated with one's identity, which is a consistent finding in the field (cf. Bates, Trimble, & Beauvais, 1997; Trimble,

1987, 2000; Trimble & Mahoney, 2002). To accommodate new thoughts and research findings, Cross revised his levels by expanding the meaning of the Preencounter and Internalization levels; the salience of one's identity serves to sharpen the meaning of the two levels. The revised model accounts for those individuals for whom ethnicity is central to their sense of self and for those whose ethnicity is not important to them.

In recent years, a good deal of attention has been devoted to the salience of ethnic identity for Blacks (African Americans), in part stimulated by the works of Cross and Helms. Mays (1986) described in a compelling article the various historical forces that shaped the identity of Blacks. Using a psychological framework, she emphasized the influences that various social and economic forces have had on an ethnic population that was essentially powerless to effect change. Ethnic and group identity among Blacks has been strong and robust. The strength of that identity was supported in the results of a national survey of Black Americans by Broman, Neighbors, and Jackson (1988), in which the older and least educated Blacks expressed the strongest identity.

The literature on Black identity quite often suggests that some African Americans hold differing opinions about who and what they are. Parham and Helms (1985) and Parham (1989) explored the process of psychological Nigrescence among different Black populations in an effort to support and extend Cross's (1971) model of psychological Nigrescence. In one study, the authors found that pro-White/anti-Black and pro-Black/anti-White student attitudes were associated with personal distress. Awakening Black attitudes were positively associated with the process of self-actualization and negatively associated with inferiority feelings and anxiety levels. Their findings hold some importance for cross-cultural counselors.

Undoubtedly, identity is a major portion of what it means to be an African American in a multicultural society. Aries and Moorehead (1989) found among a sample of Black adolescents that ethnicity was most important in forming an overall identity. In a related finding, Looney (1988) demonstrated that an interesting relationship existed between ego development and Black identity: Individuals with a strong ego will define who and what they are, but those with a weak ego will allow others to define them. White and Burke (1987) supported a similar relationship; that is, identity salience, commitment, and self-esteem are associated with ethnic identity among Black and White youth. In their study, Black respondents who expressed strong ethnic identity also reported a high sense of self-esteem. Identity can also be influenced by the sociocultural context in which one is reared, socialized, and educated. Baldwin, Duncan, and Bell (1987) found that Black identity was higher among Black students who attended a predominantly Black university than Blacks who attended a predominantly White school. Moreover, the researchers found that identity was high among those who attended all-Black elementary schools and were older in years. Therefore, the context in which individuals find themselves reinforces and strengthens their sense of belongingness and their identity. However, there are questions about the extent to which socioeconomic status relates to ethnic identity among African Americans (Carter & Helms, 1988). Finally, it should be noted that the exploration and meaningfulness of ethnic identity appear to be more important for ethnic minority youth than White youth (Phinney & Alipuria, 1990). Related to this conclusion is the likelihood that self-esteem also may be of importance for ethnic minorities, although the findings on this topic are inconclusive (see Trimble, 1987; Trimble & Mahoney, 2002).

Rowe, Bennett, and Atkinson (1994) also proposed an intriguing and compelling ethnic identity model that eventually may prove useful. Their model deserves attention in part because it challenges the other models' oppressive-adaptive orientation, their reliance on attitudes about out-groups, and their dependence on identity formation as a developmental sequence. Rowe, Bennett, and Atkinson lean heavily on Phinney's (1989) stages to form their two-part consciousness levels. The three counseling psychologists constructed their theoretical model to account for White (Euro-American) racial consciousness; however, their status can be generalized to other groups. The model's component elements are (a) unachieved racial consciousness that includes an avoidance, dependent, and dissonant typology and (b) achieved racial consciousness that includes a dominative, conflictive, reactive, and integrative typology. Rowe et al. maintained that the "key element in the process . . . is the role of dissonance," in which "dissonance between previously held attitudes and new attitudes and feelings resulting from some recent, intense, and/or significant life event" can influence movement between the phases (p. 142). The model awaits empirical validation.

PRINCIPLES OF HELMS'S RACIAL IDENTITY MODEL

Racial identity theory addresses the psychological processes that individuals develop in response to societal socialization, in which they are treated as though they belong to mutually exclusive racial groups. Although some theorists (e.g., Phinney, 1996) use *ethnic identity* and *racial identity* synonymously, other theorists argue that ethnic identity pertains to a self-conception based on own-group cultural customs, traditions, and behavioral practices that one learns to function adaptively in one's kinship group(s) (Betancourt & Lopez, 1993; Helms & Talleyrand, 1997). Racial identity, however, refers to the psychological mechanisms that people develop to function effectively in a society where some people enjoy social and political advantage because of their or their ancestors' (presumed) physical appearance, but others suffer disadvantage and lower status for the same reasons. Thus, racial identity is essentially imposed by political and economic forces and typically is based on easily recognizable characteristics, whereas ethnic identity is chosen and may be invisible to people who are not members of the relevant ethnic group.

In U.S. society, racial survival issues differ depending on whether one's ascribed racial group is advantaged or disadvantaged. Traditionally, formal racial identity models have focused on the identity formation of indigenous Black Americans because theorists assumed that they experienced considerable traumatic racial socialization (e.g., racism) but no ethnic cultural socialization at all—especially if they were Black (Cross, 1971; Eriksen, 1968). On the other hand, models of ethnic identity formation and acculturation typically have been used to describe the racial socialization effects for Asian and Pacific Islanders and Latina/Latino Americans, but their experiences of traumatic racial socialization have been disregarded (Alvarez & Helms, 2001; Takaki, 1993).

Moreover, until recently (Helms, 1984, 1989b), the racial identity of White people was an unexplored domain. Instead, when race was discussed with respect to White people, their feelings and attitudes about members of other racial groups rather than their own group or themselves were the focus of most theoretical models pertaining to White people. Thus, many models and measures of White racism exist and continue to be quite influential in the social psychology literature (Dovidio, Kawakami, Johnson, Johnson, & Howard, 1997), but models of White identity are becoming more available (Hardiman, 1982; Helms, 1984, 1990).

Although various models of Black, White, and people of color models of identity are now becoming the focus of research and theory (Hutnik, 1991), in this section, we focus on Helms's models of racial identity. This is because her models were the first to treat racial identity as a construct that could be measured at the individual as well as systemic levels (Cross, Parham, & Helms, 1991). They were also the first to incorporate emic measures of identity. *Emic,* in this case, refers to identity issues that are specific to the racial socialization experiences of members of each group according to the conditions of oppression or advantage in society that characterize their ascribed racial group(s).

Both Helms's people of color and White racial identity models have in common the assumption that the development of a healthy racial self-conception involves transcending the internalized racism inherent in U.S. socialization. For people of color, internalized racism manifests as self- or group-devaluing messages to the effect that oneself and members of one's ascribed racial group are not as good as "pure" White people or members of that group (Takaki, 1993; Zinn, 1980). For White people, internalized racism manifests as internalized socialization messages to the effect that oneself and members of the White group are superior to people of color and, consequently, deserve to have privileged status relative to them. As a consequence, for people of color, development of a healthy "nonracist" identity involves transcending messages intended to communicate inferiority, whereas for Whites, it involves transcending messages intended to communicate superiority and privilege.

Helms (1997) proposed that transcendence for all groups occurs via a developmental process in which, increasingly, more cognitively and emotionally complex schemas for processing racial information potentially become available to the person. She suggested that schemas are the observable or measurable aspects of identity but that statuses are the dynamic or motivational forces that define the schemas. Other theorists use "stages" rather than "statuses" as labels for the motivational forces as Helms formerly did (Helms, 1984, 1990; Phinney, 1990; Sellers, Chavous, & Cooke, 1998). However, regardless of how the processes or their exact content are labeled, most contemporary theories share the following assumptions: (a) identity development is a person-level intrapsychic process that occurs within a particular type of social (racial) context, (b) the developmental process involves efforts to define oneself relative to one's racial group(s), and (c) "better" development occurs as the person acquires the capacity to overcome self-limiting constraints imposed by either one's own group or society more generally. It is probably also the case that most racial identity theories are self-schema theories in that one's self-perceptions relative to one's own group are thought to have broad implications for other aspects of personality development and interpersonal behavior. In this respect, they are similar to other self-schema theories in social psychology (e.g., Iran-Nejad & Winsler, 2000).

In Helms's (1997) people of color racial identity model, the developmental process consists of six statuses and parallel schemas: Conformity, Dissonance, Immersion, Emersion, Internalization, and Integrative Awareness. These processes are assumed to be interrelated and dynamic rather than static. Conformity is characterized by the person's incapacity to perceive the adverse effects of racial socialization on herself or himself and the unthinking internalization of negative socialization messages about those of her or his own racial group(s) that are defined as "not White." The nature of Dissonance is ambivalent awareness of the racial self or one's own group. Immersion is characterized by psychological and (if possible) physical withdrawal into one's own group, idealization of one's group of color, and denigration of the White group(s) and its culture. Internal commitment and interpersonal affiliation with one's group(s) of color and its culture characterize Emersion. Internalization involves ongoing

efforts to respond objectively to own-group/ White-group racial issues from the perspective of one who is positively committed to his or her own group. Integrative Awareness is the process of integrating various demographic identities (e.g., gender, sexual orientation) into one's self-conception as well as one's conception of others (Helms & Cook, 1999).

Six racial identity statuses and related schemas also define Helms's (1990, 1997) White racial identity model. The statuses are Contact, Disintegration, Reintegration, Pseudo-Independence, Immersion-Emersion, and Autonomy. As is the case with respect to her people of color and Black models of racial identity, the statuses are not disjunctive. Rather, they are conceived as dynamic, interrelated hypothetical processes, which are expressed through observable or measurable schemas. Contact is characterized by a lack of self-awareness with respect to one's own or the White group's privileged racial status in society. The process of Disintegration involves ambivalent identification with the White racial group and confusion about the implications of membership in the group for oneself. Reintegration status is characterized by psychological and physical separation of oneself from all people and things perceived to be "not White" and idealization of the White group. Pseudo-Independence is characterized by an intellectualized understanding of White privilege and oneself as a beneficiary of it. Immersion-Emersion is the process of redefining Whiteness to avoid benefiting from White privilege and attempting to replace "bad" White people with other White people who share a similar racial consciousness. The Autonomy status defines an ongoing process of recognizing racial as well as other forms of oppression and attempting to eradicate them.

The parallel or co-related schemas for racial identity statuses are hypothesized to be multidimensional. In other words, they may be expressed in several ways. For example, for people of color, possible characteristics of the Conformity schema are obliviousness, distortion, and minimization. For White people, possible characteristics of the Contact schema are obliviousness, denial, and avoidance. Both models are summarized in Helms (1997) and Helms and Piper (1994); Helms and Cook (1999) provided real-life examples of each.

SOCIAL INTERACTION THEORY

Because schematic behaviors are often visible to other people, the perceived behaviors may become the catalysts for other people's racial reactions. That is, perceived racial identity reactions stimulate the perceiver's racial identity reactions in response to them. Alternatively, people may use the "appearance" of a stimulus person as the catalyst for their racial identity reactions to the person. Helms (1984, 1997; Helms & Cook, 1999) developed racial identity social interaction theory to describe the qualitative dimensions of various types of race-related interpersonal interactions (e.g., groups, dyads).

Racial identity interaction theory is intended to pertain to two or more individuals of either the same or different races. It assumes that the individuals involved in the interaction are of different social statuses because of race or ethnicity, social role (e.g., parent-child, teacher-student), numerical representation, or other characteristics by which society accords different levels of social power to people. The theoretical constructs are described from the viewpoint of the person or persons with the least social power in the interaction. Also, the model assumes that within the context of the interaction, a person may wield a different level of social power than he or she possesses in interactions external to the interaction.

Thus, three types of racial identity social interactions are progressive, regressive, and parallel. Crossed interactions are subcategories of progressive or regressive interactions.

Each type of interaction is characterized by specific behavior and emotional themes, which are described in considerable detail in Helms (1990, 1997) and Helms and Cook (1999, chap. 7).

Briefly, parallel interactions are defined as placid, harmonious relations whose nature is determined by the characteristics of the schemas that are being expressed. For example, interactions may be parallel because each participant is using a schema that involves addressing racial issues (e.g., Autonomy–Integrative Awareness, Autonomy-Autonomy). They may also be parallel because each participant is using a schema that involves not addressing racial issues (e.g., Contact-Conformity, Conformity-Conformity).

Progressive interactions potentially occur when the participant with the most social power is able to use more developmentally sophisticated schemas to respond to racial events than the participant with less social power. These interactions typically are invigorating, collaborative, and cooperative.

Regressive interactions occur when the participant with greater social power uses more immature racial identity schemas to respond to perceived racial catalysts than the participant with less social power. These types of interactions typically are combative as each participant struggles for power. If they are also crossed (i.e., the racial identity schemas used by participants are opposites on all dimensions), then the interactions may also be hostile or antagonistic.

MEASUREMENT OF RACIAL IDENTITY

Measurement of racial identity constructs provides some as yet unresolved dilemmas at both the individual and interaction levels. Racial identity at the individual level typically is measured via ostensible "attitudinal" measures. Because interaction theory proposes that characteristics of the individuals within any given situation determine the quality of the interaction, individual-level measures typically have been used to study interactions. Therefore, it might be useful to discuss some of the measurement issues that are perhaps unique to racial identity measurement as it involves individuals and interactions.

Individual

Racial identity theories typically describe the race-related developmental issues of individuals. Individuals potentially develop the capacity to process racial information better or differently than they could when their response repertoire was limited to less developmentally mature statuses of development. Thus, for example, when a White person is capable of using Immersion-Emersion (e.g., sensitization) as a primary schema for processing racial information, then, according to Helms's (1996) theory, they cannot also use Contact (e.g., obliviousness) as a primary schema. Various pairs of developmental constructs (e.g., schemas, stages) operate in opposition to each other in Helms's racial identity theories as well as in other theories (e.g., Hutnik, 1991; Phinney, 1990). Use of some schemas involves different kinds of repression or suppression of racial cues (i.e., Contact, Conformity), whereas others involve different kinds of sensitization to such cues (e.g., Reintegration, Immersion-Emersion).

According to racial identity theories, an individual should not use both repressing and sensitizing schemas equivalently. Therefore, scales assessing the use of repressing and sensitizing schemas have to be inversely related at the level of the individual respondent, if they adequately reflect racial identity constructs. Consequently, Helms (1999) pointed out that racial identity theoretical constructs are ipsative. The term *ipsative* typically is used in psychometric theory to refer to measures that yield scale scores that are interdependent at the level of the individual (Hicks, 1970). That is, when a person's score on one scale is high, her or his score on another scale has to be low when a measure is ipsative. Ordinarily, ipsativity is caused by structural properties of measures such as response format (e.g., forced choice) or scoring procedures (e.g., subtracting mean total scores from each individual scale). Ipsativity, in the case of measuring racial identity constructs, does not occur because response format or scoring procedures typically consist of summated Likert-type or bipolar attitudinal scales. However, Helms (1999) pointed out that if developmental racial identity constructs are conceptual opposites, they are ipsative (i.e., interdependent) by definition, regardless of the structure of the measure's items or scoring procedures.

An implication of her observation for assessing individuals is that combinations of scale scores (e.g., profiles) rather than single scales (i.e., highest scores) are necessary to adequately capture their characteristics. However, there are virtually no well-accepted psychometric procedures available for evaluating the psychometric properties of measures whose constructs and, therefore, scales are interrelated.

Measurement theory in psychology assesses psychometric characteristics of measures from large samples and makes inferences from these large groups to the individual rather than examining characteristics of individuals per se (Nunnally, 1978). Thus, properties of scale scores such as reliability and validity coefficients typically are summary statistics derived from large groups. Use of traditional psychometric analyses is problematic when a measure is ipsative or partially ipsative for several reasons. Because scale scores must be interrelated to adequately reflect the theory on which they are based, reliability coefficients also must be interrelated such that when the reliability of one scale is high, the reliability of its conceptual opposite has to be low (cf. Tenopyr, 1988). Rather than recognizing this statistical artifact as a spurious effect, researchers have often used such findings as evidence that racial identity scales were not functioning properly and erroneously discarded or revised measures based on such findings (Behrens, 1997; Swanson, Tokar, & Davis, 1994).

If a measure is ipsative, regardless of the reason for its ipsativity (i.e., theory, scoring procedures), then some of its scales will be inversely related to each other for reasons previously discussed. In such cases, if factor analysis is used to study the psychometric properties of the scales, then bipolar factors will be identified. These factors merely indicate that within the sample, some people use one type of racial identity schema whereas others in the sample use the opposite schema.

Several theorists and researchers have recommended statistical procedures that can be used when factor analysis is counterindicated (Cohen & Cohen, 1975; Cornwell & Dunlap, 1994; Guilford, 1952; Johnson, Wood, & Blinkhorn, 1988). Recommended strategies include theory-driven hierarchical regression analyses in which scales are successively entered in an order derived from theoretical principles, Q-type factor analyses, cluster analyses, and configural or profile analyses in which people rather than scales or items are the variables. Although racial identity measures have been the focus of many psychometric studies, researchers typically have used traditional psychometric criteria to evaluate the scales regardless of whether such criteria were appropriate.

Interactions

Assessment of the dynamics of racial identity social interactions has been the least investigated area of racial identity theory. When assessing the racial identity themes of social interactions, measurement problems occur because no measures have been developed to date that assess climates from a racial identity theoretical perspective. Therefore, researchers either study these processes qualitatively or attempt to classify interactions based on scale scores of the individuals involved in the interactions (Ladany, Inmani, Constantine, & Hofheinz, 1997). Yet given that patterns of scores rather than single scores best describe a person, the assessment problem with respect to interactions is how to combine the patterns of individuals to effectively reflect the nature of interactions involving them.

THE MEASUREMENT OF ETHNIC IDENTITY

Ethnic groups can be viewed as units of analysis. To identify and discover the ethnic perspective of an ethnocultural group, Berry (1985) suggested that one should first consider compiling an inventory. The investigator should carefully explore the concept of a group's ideas about ethnic identification, which essentially involves a cognitive orientation and values expressions from a cognitive-behavioral orientation. Determining one's ethnicity provides researchers with data that enable them to define clustered homogeneous subgroups. Identifying value orientations, in addition, provides data that reveal the extent to which a respondent endorses traditional indigenous values against those more representative of a dominant culture that serves as the major acculturating agent. Presumably a native-oriented, nonacculturated individual would endorse and act out native-oriented values, and one who expressed the least ethnic identification would espouse values more in line with the group to which he or she affiliates. Once data are accumulated on the two variables, researchers can then proceed to conduct ethnic group-specific and comparative cross-cultural studies by introducing other variables of interest. Furthermore, data on the two variables could extend the measurement procedure to a deeper, more definitive level, assuming a relatively homogeneous sample of members is obtained from a particular subgroup or for a generalized category of the unit as a whole.

HIERARCHICAL NESTING AND IDENTITY

A hierarchical nesting respondent identification procedure produces a rather subjective interpretation of one's ethnicity and value orientation. In fact, the method comes close to the main premises of symbolic interactionism, which are

> 1) humans act toward things on the basis of the meanings that the things have for them; 2) the meaning of the things is derived from, or arises out of, the social interaction that one has with one's fellows; and 3) the meanings are handled in, and modified through, an interpretative process used by the person in dealing with the things he encounters. (Blumer, 1969, p. 2)

In more specific terms, one's ethnicity and expression of values are centralized meanings particular to the individual and therefore have intrinsic importance in their own right. The main premise of symbolic interactionism closely resembles Triandis's (1972) notion of subjective culture; however, he takes a more collective rather than an individual approach. "By subjective culture," Triandis says, "we mean a cultural group's characteristic way of perceiving its social environment" (p. 3). The variables of the subjective culture approach are essentially attributes of cognitive domains and are analyzed by extracting consistently generated responses, which generates a map outlining the group's characteristics. Use of both perspectives comes close to emergent thinking of the *neoideographic approach,* a term probably first introduced by Zavalloni (1980). The approach actually emphasizes the person element in the Person × Situation schema advocated by the interactional school of personality. The importance of a neoidiographic perspective lies in the manner in which an individual interprets and internalizes lifeways and converts them to thoughtways, both of which become the source of one's identity. Zavalloni emphasized that neoidiographic data take the form of "psychological processes that are idiosyncratic and individual rather than central tendencies in an aggregate" (p. 109). Data, therefore, take the form of "idiosyncratic cognitive productions" such as those elicited by free-association procedures. It can be argued that ethnic identification is a subjective experience designed "to express affiliation, allegiance or oneness" with a preferred group (Casino, 1981, p. 16). Equally important is the notion that ethnic identity is contextual, in that it

> is a product of *social transaction* [italics added] insofar as one assumes an ethnic identity by claiming it and demonstrating the conventional signs of membership. A claimant is always subject to the response of others who may concur with or deny the claim. (Casino, 1981, p. 18)

Efforts at establishing ethnic identity typically occur at an *exonymic* level, where the researcher presents a set of fixed attitude-like statements to the respondents. Often, the ethnic identity scale resembles a pseudo-etic set of items. What emerges is an outsider-produced level of identity, the exonymic, and not the respondent's *autonymic* definition. Ethnic actors indeed embody an ethnic consciousness (Klineberg & Zavalloni, 1969) that is closely aligned with the culturalogical elements of the group with which they affiliate. The ultimate test, of course, is "the 'authentic' union of personal identity (the autonym) with communal identity" (Casino, 1981, p. 17). Therefore, it is logical to assume that a concordance would exist between the autonymic and the exonymic, in which importance is placed on the individual's own categories and intentions for self-identification. Yet it would be foolhardy to assume that one's criteria would not line up with those of the group; often, however, the criteria developed by researchers do not align with the group's criteria and hence may well be conceived as "pseudo-exonymic" or, worse yet, an "ethnic gloss."

Nesting the ethnic identity of an individual from a neoidiographic process and following the symbolic interactionist approach can serve to refine the identification of ethnic group samples. It makes sense, then, that merely identifying respondents on the basis of outward physical appearances and their present residence is hardly an "authentic" representation of the cultural group in question.

Neoidiographic ethnic identification involves more than merely nesting oneself in a hierarchical scheme. More often than not, individuals will use rather "ethnolocal" speech patterns and gestures to promote the authenticity of their claim. If outward physical appearances do not mesh or there is the sense that the other party doubts the identity claim, ethnic actors will tend to exaggerate and give emphasis to mannerisms and speech idiosyncrasies known to be particular (or peculiar) to the group in question. Such emphasis of ethnolocal mannerisms often occurs when people from the same ethnic group gather in geographic areas other than their homelands or communities of common origin. The somewhat stylized ritual can be referred to as *situational ethnicity*, in which ethnic actors take the occasion to reaffirm their ethnicity, often to the dismay and puzzlement of outsiders. Including these ethnic specific mannerisms in a measure of ethnic identification, although a worthy research effort in its right, would be awkward, time-consuming, and possibly redundant.

MULTIDIMENSIONALITY OF MEASUREMENT

Santiago-Rivera (1999) pointed out that ethnic identity is multidimensional and consists of the following components: self-identification or the label individuals give themselves; knowledge about one's own culture, including language, customs, values, beliefs, and norms; attitudes and feelings about group membership; and language fluency. Note that particularly if a single component is chosen, what is being measured may be very circumscribed and not comparable between studies. Measurement, because it is typically done at a single point in time, attempts to capture a dynamic construct with methods intended for static concepts. For example, given that ethnic identity can be situational and change within a person across time or context, the measurement captures a moment or stage in time and poses a general context within which to answer questions. Nevertheless, several researchers have attempted to develop scales that capture several components of the first four approaches (e.g., Felix-Ortiz, 1994, for Latinos measuring self-identification, knowledge, preferences, and behaviors; Suinn, Ahuna, & Khoo, 1992, for Asians assessing self-identification, preferences, and behaviors; and Phinney, 1992, for any multiple-group identification emphasizing the cognitive and affective components).

The assessment and measurement of ethnic identification must account for people's natal background, subjective preferences, the behavior they are likely to engage in that reflects their ethnic and cultural interests, and the extent to which various situations and contexts influence their pronouncement and enactment of their ethnicity. Use of a single construct such as natality or one's self-declaration is insufficient to capture the full effect that identity has on our lives. In keeping with this position, Trimble (1995) developed a four-part ethnic identity measurement model that includes natal, subjective, behavioral, and situational measurement domains. Use of a subjective label is one small part of the measurement process. The depth of one's identification can be expanded to include measures of acculturative

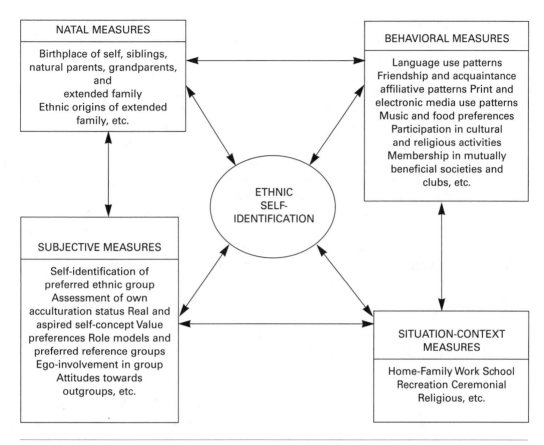

Figure 12.1 Ethnic Self-Identification Measurement Domains

status, ego involvement, value preferences, role models, and preferred reference groups, and participation in cultural and religious activities, among many other variables. Figure 12.1 shows the interactive nature of the four domains and some variables that might be considered for each one. The situational setting domain presents unusual methodological and measurement challenges as the list of situations that one finds himself or herself in on any given day can vary considerably. Moreover, certain situations may be prescriptive, so one may find it necessary to shift the degree to which he or she identifies with a group to accommodate the unwitting ethnic rules of the setting that consists of members of another ethnic group. Often referred to as situational ethnicity, the possibility that one may shift to accommodate bicultural or multicultural ethnic demands presents extraordinary measurement problems that cannot be captured in a typical survey format.

Ethnic identity can be conveyed by a self-label. This self-identification can be symbolic or nonsymbolic. In contrast to early assumptions that such self-labels are absolutely correlated with reference group recognition of an individual, these components are separated. Measurement is simple and occurs by selecting a label from a list, using narrative studies, or having children selecting pictures or dolls to identify themselves.

Affective, attitudinal, and value endorsement constitutes another way of trying to establish ethnic identity. In essence, this conceptual approach to identity attempts to measure similarity to some static notion of ethnicity and a sense of belonging and affiliation. Direct questions about affiliation; questionnaires asking about activities, food preferences, and social affiliations; and questionnaires or scales attempting to measure ethnic pride are characteristic of measurement. Betancourt and Lopez (1993) and Phinney (1996) have emphasized the importance of measuring cultural values rather than having single items to confirm or disconfirm ethnicity.

Intellectual knowledge about the group with whom one identifies constitutes another means of determining the degree of ethnic identity. This cognitive knowledge can be measured through questionnaires and narrative interviews assessing knowledge of history, traditions, and how one has used this information to construct, strengthen, and understand one's ethnicity.

Worldview and relational orientation of self within and between the reference ethnic community serves as a different approach to understanding ethnic identity. Questionnaires are usually used to assess orientation to the family (*familialism*), individualism, and collectivism. Work in this area suggests that the latter two concepts are very complex and are contextually and class driven. Collectivism, in contrast to individualism, puts the group's well-being and goals above the individual. These orientations have drastic implications for the value a group or individual places on interdependence versus independence, the age and orientation to attachment and separation, and motives for affiliation (Markus & Kitayama, 1991). However, Singelis, Triandis, Bhawuk, and Gelfand (1995) have noted that horizontal and vertical aspects exist within collectivism. Vertical collectivism is class driven. Those with wealth and status in otherwise collectivistic cultures operate very much from day to day with an individualistic orientation.

Most measures of ethnic identity provide little or no opportunity to assess the variable and fluctuating nature of the concept. One's identification with an ethnic group is not static or immutable. It can and does change over time as a function of varied circumstances and social contexts. In some situations, people tacitly identify with significant others who are associated with the contexts, and then there are other settings where an individual may act quite differently because the ethnic makeup may be quite different. When individuals vary their behavior, they may more or less vary their level of group association from a weak-nominal, almost passive, level to a strong-committed, active one. Hence, it may be that one's intensity of ethnic identification fluctuates with a particular social context or situation. According to Weinreich (1986), one's ethnic identity is "situated in a specific social context [and] is defined as that part of the totality of one's self construal" (p. 299). Weinreich has been exploring the variable nature of situated identities through the use of identity structure analysis (ISA), a method that permits the operationalization of "a person's conflicted identification with another, so that the relative magnitudes of self's various identification conflicts may be estimated" (p. 300). As a result of his extensive work on the subject, Weinreich strongly suggested that

> (1) individuals can indeed be somewhat different beings according to which ethnic context they cue into; (2) when cued into the one ethnicity, the values characteristics of the "alternative" ethnicity may be emphasized; and (3) in . . . linguistic contexts, the identity structures of individuals are essentially the same kind of complex amalgamation of identification elements across . . . ethnicities. (pp. 305-306)

ISA involves the use of a complex array of measurement items and therefore could be time-consuming. It, too, necessitates dealing with specific situations one encounters to determine one's level of identification. Nonetheless, the arguments for using an abridged version of ISA in the field are compelling (Weinreich & Saunderson, 2002).

Oetting and Beauvais (1991) proposed an orthogonal cultural identification theory and a correspondent measurement tool to assess cultural identity. Their approach is built on the assumption that cultural identity is not a linear phenomenon and follows the four-part ethnic identity measurement model developed by Trimble (1995) (cf. Bates et al., 1997). They argued that cultural dimensions are independent of one another and that an increasing identification with one culture does not produce a decreasing identification with another culture. One could, for example, highly identify with two cultural groups and conversely not identify with any group. Hence, the researchers would argue that an individual could conceivably identify with two, three, and even four cultural groups and not in the least be disoriented or confused about their cultural identification.

Oetting and Beauvais (1991) developed a set of items that allows an individual to "independently express identification or lack of identification" with several cultural groups (p. 663). They claimed that "in large-scale surveys of adults, only two basic items may be needed to assess identification with any one culture reasonably well: (1) Do you live in the . . . way of life? and (2) Are you a success in the . . . way of life?" (p. 664). Other issues can be added to assess such things as family identification and tradition, participation in cultural events, language preferences, and parental identification to expand the scale's measurement domains and its presumed effectiveness.

The Orthogonal Cultural Identity Scale has been used to determine the relationship between cultural identity and drug use. Results have been mixed. Bates et al. (1997) found that a moderately strong identification with American Indian culture among fourth

to sixth graders predicted less drug use; however, no relationship was found for adolescents. In another study, Oetting and Beauvais (1990) found that Hispanic adolescent females with high cultural identity were less likely to use drugs, particularly marijuana.

Strengthening our understanding of ethnic minority respondents using measures of identification is no small matter. Smith (1980) reminds us that "(1) ethnicity is a difficult attribute to measure; and (2) ethnic identification does not start with given nationalities, but rather begins with whether a person has an ethnicity to identify with" (p. 92). Indeed, efforts to develop ethnic identity scales tacitly assume that people have an ethnicity that they can call their own. Phinney (1991) presented a model that presents the variable components that define ethnic identity. The model is a continuum with one end representing a high, strong, secure, or achieved level of identity and the other a low, weak, or diffuse identity. The former continuum would describe a person with a strong identity as one who has high self-identification, is involved in ethnic behaviors and practices, evaluates his or her own group positively, is committed to belonging to the group, and is happy with membership. Phinney's model typifies the approach taken by most who develop ethnic identity measures. Weinreich's (1986) work with ISA would be an exception.

What follows is a brief overview of the approaches taken to measure the construct over the years. The literature on the topic is extensive; hence, the following reflects a small portion of what is available.

Language has been used both as indices of core ethnic identity and acculturation (Giles, 1977). However, ties with one's ethnic group of choice may be maintained despite loss of language or fluency. Language is thought to be core because of the way in which it is a lens for a worldview.

Some studies have attempted to assess ethnic identity using multiple components from the previous variable list but examine changes in identity over time with age and life circumstance. These range from large-scale studies to small ones but often involve an interview to illuminate the process of this dynamic aspect of ethnicity.

Socialization experiences of mixed-race and transracial adoptees can influence ethnic identity and awareness of one's own natal culture. McRoy, Zurcher, Lauderdale, and Anderson (1984) found that the degree to which families discussed racial identity issues can affect transracial youths' perception of themselves when compared to members of their own ethnic group; hence, identities varied as a function of the cultural composition of a family's network. In a related finding, McRoy and Freeman (1986) emphasized that racial conception and racial evaluation can influence a child's racial identity and that attention should be given to the two processes in working with racially mixed families. Andujo (1988) also found that socioeconomic factors could influence an adopted child's ethnic identity. To adequately describe and account for the development of racial identity, Poston (1990) argued that the following measurement areas must be considered: personal identity, choice of group categorization, enmeshment/denial, appreciation, and integration.

A number of studies point to a potential relationship between intermarriage and adoption and degrees of ethnic identity both among married partners, offspring, and added family members. Judd (1990) found that in families with parents who have different religious affiliations, material influences can serve to maintain or enhance a youth's religio-ethnic identity, especially if the child follows the mother's religious preference. In a related study, Parsonson (1987) found that children's ethnic identities are stronger when parents come from the same ethnic group.

Immigration and relocation are potent forms of sociocultural change. A few researchers have conducted studies to examine the effects of resettlement on ethnic identity, especially among Asian American populations. Bromley (1988) drew attention to the identity formation problems occurring among Southeast Asian adolescent refugees, especially those who were unaccompanied to the United States. She pointed out that four distinct conditions have affected identity development among this age group—specifically, exposure to overwhelming tension-producing situations, failure in values, withdrawal from channels that promote identity formation, and inadequate coping mechanisms. Westermeyer, Neider, and Callies's (1989) decade-long study of relocated Hmong in Minnesota supports some of Bromley's contentions. Essential to the maintenance of culture among the refugees was the maintenance of traditional values—a finding that seems to be a consistent theme in the literature (cf. Wooden, Leon, & Toshima, 1988).

Identity formation is especially significant among adolescents. As part of the process, ethnic minorities often are saddled with the additional matter of affirming and internalizing their cultural background into the formation process. Phinney and Tarver (1988) found that more than a third of their eighth-grade respondents actively engaged in a search for their ethnic identity; the search was especially evident for Black females. The authors also found that Blacks tended to focus on their own ethnic background, whereas White youth were more concerned about relationships with other groups. Forming a solid identity with one's own ethnic group, however, can be accompanied by some behavioral and personal problems. Grossman, Wirt, and Davids (1985) found among samples of Chicano and Anglo youth that ethnic esteem mediates with self-esteem. Chicano youth expressed strong ethnic esteem but demonstrated low self-esteem and low behavioral adjustment patterns. Gonzalez (1988), in a related study, found that high-achieving Chicano women who expressed strong ethnic esteem tended to be a threat to Chicano males; the threat perception tended to create distress for the women. Maintenance of ethnic identity, therefore, creates a conflict between achievement and the desire to maintain close interpersonal and cultural relations with men. Conflicts among adolescent Hispanic women extend into many spheres and become so overwhelming that suicide may result. Identity and acculturative status problems can be a contributing factor (Zayas, 1987).

Caetano (1986) developed a useful four-fold measure of ethnic identification to assess drinking patterns and alcohol problems among a sizable household sample of Hispanics. Respondents in his survey were asked a series of demographic and ethnic identification questions that focused on (a) ethnicity of family of origin, (b) own or subjective ethnic identification, (c) country of ancestors, and (d) respondent's country of birth. Results from his study show that different ethnic identifiers are useful in assessing levels of alcohol consumption among Hispanics, as there were significant differences among drinking patterns. Caetano commented that "ethnicity of family of origin seems to be the most encompassing definition, followed by national group, and there is a good level of agreement between these two rubrics" (p. 341). However, he cautioned that "the search for a standard definition of Hispanic ethnicity does not seem to be near its end . . . [and that] researchers should consider multiple ways to identify this ethnic group" (p. 342).

Teske and Nelson (1973) developed two scales to assess identity among Mexican Americans. One scale measured identity and consisted of 16 items, and the other assessed interaction with others and contained 19 items. Reliability coefficients for the two scales were quite high, suggesting that the overall combined item pool could be used

with confidence. Garcia (1982) extended the notion of identity among Chicanos to include measures of political consciousness along with ones for ethnic consciousness. He found that the two constructs were not highly correlated and suggested that ethnicity may be more related to self-identification.

Elements of cognitive social learning, cognitive development, and self-esteem theories were included in a study of ethnic identity among Mexican American children (Bernal, Knight, Garza, Ocampo, & Cota, 1990). Using a "Who am I?" approach that ties identity with self-concept, Bernal et al. (1990) demonstrated that age-related developmental shifts occurred among Mexican American children. Shifts in changing identities, therefore, may influence the social settings and persons who are likely to have an impact on the child.

Researchers have resorted to the use of less obtrusive measures in an effort to tap ethnic identity. Most researchers are acutely aware of the seminal doll selection technique developed by Clark and Clark (1947). Basically, Black children showed a preference for White dolls, suggesting that the youth identified more with Whites than Blacks. Their work, especially the methodology and conclusions, has been questioned by other researchers (see Katz & Zalk, 1974; Stephan & Rosenfield, 1978). Use of the technique persists. For example, although aware of the flaws, Vaughan (1986) demonstrated that Maori children in New Zealand select pictures and dolls that represent their image of their group within the dominant culture. The article also contains a solid review of the literature on using picture and doll tests. Fine and Bowers (1984) replicated the design and procedure of the Clark and Clark studies. Their findings revealed that young female Blacks were more likely to identify with Black dolls than young Black males. The socioeconomic and political climate, the authors suggest, may contribute to their findings; such factors must be considered when results from doll selection techniques are used. For instance, Gopaul-McNicol (1988) found that samples of Black preschool youth from New York City and Trinidad preferred the White doll over a Black one. The racial contexts in which the techniques are used also must be considered. Pfeffer (1984) used a Draw-A-Person procedure with Yoruba (Nigerian) children as a measure of ethnic identity. Findings revealed that the Yoruba youth avoided use of dark colors when coloring the skin; results from a comparable Black sample in the United States were quite different.

Acculturation and Ethnic Identity Measures

Ethnicity is learned through a process of enculturation. In this process, an abstract concept of ethnicity must be learned through direct instruction and interaction within the reference group; at a more advanced level, the social and political meaning and construction of ethnicity, like race, is instructed by relations between groups (Bernal & Knight, 1993; Berry, 1975). Unfortunately, as racial identity is constructed in part through a process of stressful and traumatic experience (Root, 2001), ethnic identity is influenced by a process of acculturative stress. Both assimilation and acculturation reflect processes rather than static points. They are processes that reflect tension and intergroup interaction. Trimble (1988, 1996) has proposed an ecological framework to understand the process of ethnic identity development in American Indians that is composed of exogenous variables, person variables, situations, and acculturative patterns filtered through worldviews, cognitive appraisals, and behavioral perceptions.

Acculturation historically referred to relinquishing ethnic group ways and adopting the host culture's way. Thus, to be assimilated, one must acculturate. Whereas acculturation has been discussed as a unidirectional process, the ratio of one group to another may allow for a bidirectional influence. For example, Le Vine and Padilla (1980) suggested that there may be mutual influences in some of the southwest regions due to the large historical and population size of persons of Mexican descent. Similarly, Trimble (1988) noted that mutual influence has a salient impact on groups, influencing identity and acculturation in various contextual settings.

The bulk of the research in psychological acculturation tends to emphasize person characteristics that emerge from contact with and participation in some lifestyle facet of the contact or dominant culture. A selected review of the literature indicates that many of the variable domains included in identity measures can be found in acculturation scales and measures. In compiling a variable domain, a researcher is likely to ask informants to respond to a series of items that assess the number of elements they use or borrow from the dominant culture, those elements of their own culture that they continue to use, and the level of participation in activities found in both cultural contact groups. An example of a contact measure is the 8-variable scale developed by Berry, van de Koppel, et al. (1986) for use in Central Africa. The scale tapped such contact-specific information as number of local languages spoken, property and material ownership, employment status, clothing, and religiosity. Responses to the scale were collapsed to a single score from which an inference about one's acculturative status was derived. Rauch, Bowler, and Schwarzer (1987) developed a 3-item culture contact scale to assess acculturation effects on the self-esteem of three American ethnic minority groups. Although Rauch et al. found significant differences for self-esteem between the groups, they also reported an extremely low correlation between contact and self-esteem ($r = .12$), suggesting that contact may not influence one's sense of self.

Triandis, Kashima, Shimada, and Villareal (1986) used a participatory measure of acculturation to assess the existence of cultural differences among a sample of Hispanic and non-Hispanic navy recruits. Triandis et al. used a 4-item index, including items that assessed length of residence in the United States, media acculturation, number of non-Hispanic coworkers, and number of non-Hispanic friends and romantic partners. Summing the four indices created a single acculturation score. The study's Hispanic participants were grouped according to the single culture index into low-, medium-, and high-acculturation categories. The authors concluded that "one can use indexes of acculturation to establish the existence of cultural differences" (p. 67). Pumariega (1986) also used a 15-item contact and participation acculturation scale to explore the relationship between socioeconomic status (SES) and eating attitudes among Hispanic adolescent girls. His results showed that the more one moves toward a contact culture, the greater is one's vulnerability for developing an eating disorder. Pumariega also found that SES is not correlated with acculturative status, suggesting that one's occupational and educational status may not be useful in understanding the influences of cultural contact and participation.

Hispanic populations, more than any other ethnic group, appear to be the focus of interest among a few acculturation researchers. Franco (1983) developed a 10-item acculturation scale for Mexican American children that is filled out by a child's teacher, counselor, or someone who knows the child well. Franco included items to tap peer associations, ethnic identity, and language preference. Martinez, Norman, and Delaney (1984) also developed a scale for Hispanic children. The acculturation measure contains 23 items and assesses food preferences,

Spanish usage among self and significant others, and general cultural exposure. Both scales reportedly have a high reliability. Montgomery and Orozco (1984) cross-validated an acculturation scale developed for use with Mexican Americans by Cuellar, Harris, and Jasso (1980). A factor analysis of the items generated four dimensions: language preference, ethnic identity and generation removed from Mexico, ethnicity of friends and associates, and extent of direct contact with Mexico. Their findings tend to support the general item content of related Hispanic acculturation measures. Mainous (1989), however, suggested that self-concept, conceived of as role identity, should be included in Mexican American acculturation scales. His 9-item index yielded three factor dimensions: language, self-definition as an insider, and self-definition as an outsider.

Mendoza (1989) developed an elaborate Cultural Life Style Inventory to assess acculturative status among Mexican American adolescents and adults. The inventory taps five factor dimensions: intrafamily language usage, extrafamily language usage, social affiliations and activities, cultural identification and pride, and cultural resistance, incorporation, and shift. Note again that the scale contents capture much of the same information developed in other scales.

Richman, Gaviria, Flaherty, Birz, and Wintrob (1987) developed a 21-item scale that tapped five dimensions—language (6 items), customs (4 items), ethnic identity (1 item), sociability (4 items), and discrimination (6 items)—for use among Huahuapuquien Indian migrants in Lima, Peru. The multifaceted scale was used to assess the acculturative process within the Peruvian social-structural context. Of importance is the researchers' attempt to assess the effects of discrimination on adaptation.

Suinn, Rickard-Figueroa, Lew, and Vigil (1987) developed an acculturation scale for assessing Asian acculturation; the scale contents were modeled after several scales developed for use with Hispanics. Atkinson and Gim (1989) modified the Suinn-Lew scale and administered it to three different Asian American groups. Results show that most acculturated students were likely (a) to recognize the need for professional psychological help, (b) to be tolerant of the stigma associated with psychological help, and (c) to be open to discussing their problems with a psychologist. Moreover, the researchers were able to validate the Suinn-Lew scale in an applied setting.

Two studies are reported in the literature that draw attention to the development of more generalized acculturation scales that transcend ethnic-specific measures. Oakland and Shermis (1989) analyzed the factor structure of the Sociocultural Scales of the System of Multicultural Pluralistic Assessment. Their analysis supported the existence of four subscales, one of which was urban acculturation. The latter subscale is a measurement domain that heretofore has received little attention in the acculturation field. An American International Relations Scale developed by Sodowsky and Plake (1991) represents the current state of the art in measuring acculturation. The researchers maintain that the following moderator variables influence the acculturation process: (a) generation status, (b) education and income, (c) age, (d) years of residence in the United States, (e) ethnic density of neighborhood, (f) country of birth, and (g) job skills, religion, kinship structures, and purposes of immigration. Their 34-item scale has been expanded to include 43 items and is referred to as the Majority-Minority Relations Survey (Sodowsky, Lai, & Plake, 1991). Results from their early work with the scale are favorable and suggest that a valid, generalizable, and reliable scale has been developed to assess acculturation attitudes of Asian Americans and Hispanics.

Most measures of contact-participation acculturation generate a single average or cumulative score. To some extent, the single-unit scales have proven to be reliable and hence useful largely because certain researchers have been able to discriminate between and among cultural groups and predict outcomes such as mental health, alcohol and drug use, and eating disorders. The use of a single score is presumptive because it considers all that fall at or about the unit to be relatively homogeneous. That may not be the case.

Berry, Trimble, and Olmedo (1986) agreed that "not every person in the acculturating group will necessarily enter into the acculturation process in the same way or to the same degree" (p. 296). Not every individual from his or her culture will respond to the elements presented by the dominant culture. Individual variations in the adaptation, adjustment, and internalization of another culture's folkways and mores can be mediated by resistance, fear, anxiety, allegiance to one's own culture, and the level of perceived acceptance in one's own and the dominant culture. Moreover, an individual may make specific accommodations in certain settings and situations but in others cling to and maintain traditional and conventional own-culture behaviors. Consequently, one's adjustments and accommodations, combined with the rejection of acceptable behavioral patterns, generate a good deal of variation in acculturative styles. The process of changing and adapting to another culture is not a unidirectional process in which one progresses "solely from the host groups to the newcomer groups" (Richman et al., 1987, p. 841).

Questions concerning the unidirectional issue and individual variations in acculturative styles, combined with the use of single-unit measures of acculturation, are beginning to emerge in the literature. Berry (1990) has taken the position, for example, that acculturation can be viewed as a multilinear phenomenon rather than a single dimension. Building his argument on the assumptions that (a) an individual may prefer to remain culturally as he or she has been and (b) that the same individual may prefer to have variable and selective contact and participation with those of other cultures, Berry developed a framework that identifies four varieties of acculturation—namely, integration, assimilation, separation, and marginalization. Using a Likert-type scale format, Berry developed a series of items that ultimately generate four separate cumulative scores, thus providing a more inclusive understanding of one's attitude toward acculturation and one's position in the process.

Padilla (1980) proposed an acculturation framework that embraces elements of the contact-participation dimension and one's perceived loyalty to his or her own culture. Padilla used 11 dimensions (e.g., language preferences, name preference for children) to measure loyalty and 15 dimensions to assess cultural awareness. Padilla concluded that "cultural awareness is the more general component" and "ethnic loyalty is the more tenuous" (p. 65).

Padilla's (1980) two-factor model formed the basis of a multifactorial acculturation model developed by Richman et al. (1987), who agreed that

> the process of acculturation in Peru is composed of a more complex set of sub-components, each of which may have very different social meanings, covary separately for different social status groups, and have differing consequences for psychological distress or well being. (p. 842)

As a consequence of their observations of the various Peruvian cultural groups, Richman et al. (1987) created an overall acculturation scale containing five subscales, including language use; ethnic customs that encompassed music, food preferences, and dress; ethnic identification; sociability preferences; and perceived discrimination. The scale generates six distinct scores. Scale results are useful in identifying variations across age and generation levels and changes among certain individuals

that are bidirectional and characterized by inequality.

The measurement of the acculturation process tends to emphasize person characteristics in which information is compiled to identify one's preferences, tendencies, and elements of another culture that internalize into one's lifestyle orientation. Despite the changes occurring in acculturation measures and concepts, problems abound. Escobar and Vega (2000), for example, forcefully challenged the meaning and measurement of acculturation on the grounds that it has become a "catchall" for anything that has to do with social and individual change involving people from different ethnocultural groups. Similarly, Suarez-Orozco (2001) has pointed out that assimilation and acculturation themes predict that change is "directional, unilinear, nonreversible, and continuous" (p. 8), but that is not what occurs with immigrant populations. Berry, Trimble, and Olmedo (1986) admitted that a good deal of confusion surrounds the measurement of acculturation, owing largely to confusion surrounding the conceptualization of acculturation itself. To achieve a partial remedy to the confusion, Berry suggested that any comprehensive study should approach the topic from a multivariate perspective. From this perspective, researchers should compile information about an acculturating group's general mode of adaptation, experiences with cultural contact and conflict, and the contact and conflict experiences of the individual.

A multivariate perspective as recommended by Berry (1983) and amplified by Olmedo (1979) would indeed provide useful information about the source of influences as the acculturation process is experienced. However, such knowledge would provide us with information only about a person's style, preferences, behavior, and orientation. Ethnographic and case-directed interviews of acculturating individuals generate observations that point to the fact that the context in which acculturation occurs and the situations one encounters often dictate unique behaviors that in themselves are situation specific. Given the observations, it would seem reasonable to propose that more attention should be given to the situations and the contexts in which acculturation occurs.

As individuals experience a new culture, they will undoubtedly encounter new and varied situations. For those interested in the acculturative process, it makes sense to focus on the individuals' perceptions of any situation they encounter, the behavior they choose to evoke, and their cognitive appraisals of the effect the situation holds for them. Interactionists—that is, those who study the person-situation interaction—recognize that individuals often will select the situations they encounter. Many situations may not be selected simply because people do not know what to do or how to react. Individual variations in situation selection may be directly related to acculturative status. Hence, the selection of situations may shed some insights on the types of situations selected and consequently further our understanding of the acculturative process.

The advancement of our understanding of the acculturative process interest should focus on how individuals vary or are similar in the selection of situations. This would include an effort to identify how one selects and organizes situations, the motivations involved in the selection process, the perceived ability to perform, and the general feelings elicited by the situation and the behavioral consequences. Argyle (1978) identified four structural variables that appear useful in investigating the situation selection process: choice of situations, grouping of situations, motivation/emotion, and ability.

Including a situational measurement domain in assessing the acculturative process can serve to uncover a relationship between one's identity and one's choice of situations. Foote (1951) suggested that one's identity can

be a function of that person's performance in situations and hence can be motivational. He added that a problematic situation calls for performance of a particular act, in which consummations and consequences are more or less anticipated, thereby releasing the energy appropriate to performing it. Successful encounters with problematic situations, especially those experienced in another culture, can assist in strengthening one's sense of confidence and building a bicultural or multicultural sense of identity.

SOME CONCLUDING THOUGHTS

Studies of ethnicity, racial identity, ethnic consciousness, ethnic self-identification, and the measurement of the constructs are part of a complex, intertwined multidisciplinary process. The complexity is confounded by the increased interest in the constructs across many academic disciplines; the levels of analysis particular to each discipline further complicate matters because the units and methods of inquiry often conflict with one another. Although the definitions of the constructs may resemble one another, ethnic and racial identity theories differ from one another both within and between disciplines. Indeed, the "invention of ethnicity is an interdisciplinary field . . . [as are] attempts to understand the processes that give ethnic debates such a virulent centrality in the modern world" (Sollors, 1989, p. xx).

From all indications, the literature and findings from the 2000 census indicate that Americans are probing deeply into their biological ancestry and cultural backgrounds to identify a source for meaning and structure in their lives. From the discoveries, one constructs a "symbolic identity." "If you wish to understand persons—their development and their relations with significant others," maintained Strauss (1959), "you must be prepared to view them as embedded in historical context" (p. 164). In the course of constructing and maintaining the identity, common historical symbols are identified, shared, and passed along to future generations. The symbols also can serve as a public affirmation of one's ethnic claim. Along with the declaration and discovery, individuals are openly expressing pride and respect for their ancestries and their ethnic orientations.

Many of the literature findings suggest that ethnic and racial declarations are not private acts "but are usually if not predominantly public concerns, problematic situations, and issues of public contention as well as private debate" (Strauss, 1959, p. 26). Identity declarations at some point require external validation, and therefore the judgments of others play a major role in the transaction. Ordinarily, people construct their identities within the context of their biological background and the sociopolitical context in which they are socialized. Many people declare their ethnic and racial heritage to place themselves in the social order and seek out settings and situations for confirmation (Harre, 1989). Quite often, people construct their identity and image to fit preferred sociocultural contexts and, along with self-declaration, construct the situations and contexts to fit the preferred image (Fitzgerald, 1993). The identity process, no matter how conceived and measured, is not static and invariant—people change, and their identities and sense of self-satisfaction change accordingly.

Erik Eriksen (1968) undoubtedly has contributed immensely to the ongoing debate about identity development and formation. He maintained that identity was located in the self or core of the individual, and one's communal culture—self-esteem and one's sense of affiliation and belongingness—is deeply affected by the process. Identity, then, is inextricably linked to self-understanding and therefore can be posited "as the academic metaphor for self-in-context" (Fitzgerald,

1993, p. ix). Without a context, identity formation and self-development cannot occur.

To further an understanding of identity, most social and psychological theorists must contend with the concept of self. To approach a modicum of understanding of the self process, one must provide plausible if not reasonable explanations for the following domains: physical traits and characteristics, personal experiences and their memory, personal behaviors, "what belongs to me and what I belong to," the person I believe myself to be, and "who and what others tell me I am" (Cirese, 1985). Explanations for these domains consume volumes; indeed, studies of the personal, social, and situational self present a most challenging and daunting task. Adding ethnicity and racial constructs to the inquiry further complicates the exploration.

Future studies and developments in the field of ethnic and racial identity must continue to examine and advance understanding of developmental and self influences such as those advanced by Cross (1991), Helms (1990), and Phinney (1989). In addition, situational and contextual correlates must be examined because ethnic and racial declarations can be influenced by settings. Referred to as "situational ethnicity," people often will modify or amplify their declarations to fit the settings or contexts where others are perceived as potent sources of self and ethnic validation. People will change their speech patterns, often speaking in a dialect or the language (lingua franca) particular to the setting. Moreover, behavioral mannerisms, gestures, physical positioning of the body relative to others, and clothing styles will be adjusted. The extent to which there are modifications may be a function of an individual's need to be accepted and perceived as a member of the group who has not forgotten his or her heritage and cultural background. Similarly, some people may become "more ethnic or native" in ethnic-specific contexts because they are most comfortable with the self-presentation.

There is one final important point that bears attention and recognition. Self-identification and self-declarations are powerful phenomena that strongly influence personality, one's sense of belonging, one's quality of life, and one's sense of connectedness with others who share similar identities. The powerful nature of identity can readily be seen in the civil strife and struggles of nations and ethnic groups in Africa and Eastern Europe, along with the growing preoccupation with ethnic differences in North America, especially in Quebec. At the core of these struggles is the assertion that individuals have a right to their identity within the context of a common cultural orientation. On that point, Forbes (1990) argued that people have a right to state who and what they are; hence, we must recognize that there are multiple approaches to achieving and asserting identity. And with this in mind, we "must recognize that all ethnic groups and units can change genes, while yet remaining whole and retaining their identity" (Forbes, 1990, p. 48).

REFERENCES

Alvarez, A. N., & Helms, J. E. (2001). Racial identity and reflected appraisals as influences on Asian Americans' racial adjustment. *Cultural Diversity and Ethnic Minority Psychology, 7,* 217-231.

Andujo, E. (1988). Ethnic identity of transethnically adopted Hispanic adolescents. *Social Work, 33*(6), 531-535.

Argyle, M. (1978). *The psychology of interpersonal behaviour* (3rd ed.). Harmondsworth, UK: Penguin.

Aries, E., & Moorehead, K. (1989). The importance of ethnicity in the development of identity of Black adolescents. *Psychological Reports, 65*(1), 75-82.

Atkinson, D., & Gim, R. (1989). Asian-American cultural identity and attitudes toward mental health services. *Journal of Counseling Psychology, 36*(2), 209-212.

Baldwin, J., Duncan, J., & Bell, Y. (1987). Assessment of African self-consciousness among Black students from two college environments. *Journal of Black Psychology, 13*(2), 27-41.

Bates, S., Trimble, J., & Beauvais, F. (1997). American Indian alcohol involvement and ethnic identification. *Substance Use and Misuse, 32*(14), 2013-2031.

Behrens, J. T. (1997). Does the White Racial Identity Attitude Scale measure racial identity? *Journal of Counseling Psychology, 44,* 3-12.

Bernal, M., & Knight, G. (Eds.). (1993). *Ethnic identity: Formation and transmission among Hispanics and other minorities.* Albany: State University of New York Press.

Bernal, M., Knight, G., Garza, C., Ocampo, K., & Cota, M. (1990). The development of ethnic identity in Mexican-American children. *Hispanic Journal of the Behavioral Sciences, 12*(1), 3-24.

Berry, J. (1975). Ecology, cultural adaptation, and psychological differentiation: Traditional patterning and acculturative stress. In R. Brislin, S. Bochner, & W. Lonner (Eds.), *Cultural perspectives in learning* (pp. 207-228). Beverly Hills, CA: Sage.

Berry, J. (1983). Acculturation: A comparative analysis of alternative forms. In R. Samuda & S. L. Woods (Eds.), *Perspectives in immigrant and minority education* (pp. 65-77). New York: Lanham.

Berry, J. (1985). Cultural psychology and ethnic psychology: A comparative analysis. In I. Lagunes & Y. Poortinga (Eds.), *From a different perspective: Studies of behavior across cultures* (pp. 3-15). Lisse, the Netherlands: Swets & Zeitlinger.

Berry, J. (1990). Psychology of acculturation. In J. Berman (Ed.), *Nebraska symposium on motivation* (Vol. 37, pp. 201-234). Lincoln: University of Nebraska Press.

Berry, J., Trimble, J. E., & Olmedo, E. (1986). Assessment of acculturation. In W. J. Lonner & J. W. Berry (Eds.), *Field methods in cross-cultural research* (pp. 291-324). Newbury Park, CA: Sage.

Berry, J., van de Koppel, J., Senechal, C., Annis, R., Bahuchet, S., Cavalli-Sforza, L., & Witkin, H. (1986). *On the edge of the forest: Cultural adaptation and cognitive development in Central Africa.* Lisse, The Netherlands: Swets & Zeitlinger.

Betancourt, H., & Lopez, S. R. (1993). The study of culture, ethnicity, and race in American psychology. *American Psychologist, 48*(6), 629-637.

Blumer, H. (1969). *Symbolic interactionism: Perspective and method.* Englewood Cliffs, NJ: Prentice Hall.

Bram, J. (1965). Change and choice in ethnic identification. *Transactions of the New York Academy of Sciences, 28*(2), 242-248.

Broman, C., Neighbors, H., & Jackson, J. (1988). Racial group identification among Black adults. *Social Forces, 67*(1), 146-158.

Bromley, M. (1988). Identity as a central adjustment issue for the Southeast Asian unaccompanied refugee minor. *Child and Youth Care Quarterly, 17*(2), 101-114.

Brown, D. E. (1991). *Human universals.* Philadelphia: Temple University Press.

Caetano, R. (1986). Alternative definitions of Hispanics: Consequences in an alcohol survey. *Hispanic Journal of Behavioral Sciences, 8,* 331-344.

Carter, R., & Helms, J. (1988). The relationship between racial identity and social class. *Journal of Negro Education, 57*(1), 22-30.

Casino, E. (1981). *Introduction to ethnicology: Ways of talking about ethnicity.* Unpublished manuscript, University of Hawai'i at Manoa.

Cirese, S. (1985). *Quest: A search for self.* New York: Holt, Rinehart & Winston.

Clark, K. B., & Clark, M. (1947). Racial identification and preferences in Negro children. In T. M. Newcomb & E. L. Hartley (Eds.), *Readings in social psychology* (pp. 169-178). New York: Holt.

Cohen, J., & Cohen, P. (1975). *Applied multiple regression/correlation analyses for the behavioral sciences.* Hillsdale, NJ: Lawrence Erlbaum.

Cornwell, J. M., & Dunlap, W. P. (1994). On the questionable soundness of factoring ipsative data: A response to Saville & Willson (1991). *Journal of Occupational and Organizational Psychology, 67,* 89-100.

Cross, W. (1991). *Shades of black: Diversity in African American identity.* Philadelphia: Temple University Press.

Cross, W. E., Jr. (1971). The Negro-to-Black conversion experience: Toward a psychology of Black liberation. *Black World, 20*(9), 13-27.

Cross, W. E., Jr., Parham, T. A., & Helms, J. E. (1991). The stages of Black identity development: Nigrescence models. In R. L. Jones (Ed.), *Black psychology* (pp. 319-338). Berkeley, CA: Cobb & Henry.

Cuellar, I., Harris, L., & Jasso, R. (1980). An acculturation scale for Mexican-American normal and clinical populations. *Hispanic Journal of Behavioral Sciences, 2,* 199-217.

Dovidio, J. F., Kawakami, K., Johnson, C., Johnson, B., & Howard, A. (1997). On the nature of prejudice: Automatic and controlled processes. *Journal of Experimental Social Psychology, 33*(5), 510-540.

Eriksen, E. (1968). *Identity, youth, and crisis.* New York: Norton.

Escobar, J., & Vega, W. (2000). Mental health and immigration's AAAs: Where are we and where do we go from here? *Journal of Nervous and Mental Disorders, 188*(11), 736-740.

Feagin, J. R. (1978). *Racial and ethnic relations.* Englewood Cliffs, NJ: Prentice Hall.

Felix-Ortiz, M. (1994). A multidimensional measure of cultural identity for Latino and Latina adolescents. *Hispanic Journal of Behavioral Sciences, 16,* 99-116.

Fine, M., & Bowers, C. (1984). Racial self-identification: The effects of social history and gender. *Journal of Applied Social Psychology, 14*(2), 136-146.

Fitzgerald, T. K. (1993). *Metaphors of identity: A culture-communication dialogue.* Albany: State University of New York Press.

Foote, N. (1951). Identification as the basis for a theory of motivation. *American Sociological Review, 16,* 14-21.

Forbes, J. D. (1990). The manipulation of race, caste and identity: Classifying AfroAmericans, Native Americans and Red-Black people. *Journal of Ethnic Studies, 17,* 1-51.

Franco, J. (1983). An acculturation scale for Mexican-American children. *Journal of General Psychology, 108*(2), 175-181.

Garcia, J. (1982). Ethnicity and Chicanos: Measure of ethnic identification, identity, and consciousness. *Hispanic Journal of Behavioral Sciences, 4*(3), 295-314.

Giles, H. (1977). *Language, ethnicity, and intergroup relations.* London: Academic Press.

Gonzalez, J. (1988). Dilemmas of the high-achieving Chicana: The double-bind factors in male/female relationships. *Sex Roles, 18*(7-8), 367-380.

Gopaul-McNicol, S. (1988). Racial identification and racial preference of Black preschool children in New York and Trinidad. *Journal of Black Psychology, 14*(2), 65-68.

Grossman, B., Wirt, R., & Davids, A. (1985). Self-esteem, ethnic identity and behavioral adjustment among Anglo and Chicano adolescents in west Texas. *Journal of Adolescence, 8*(1), 57-68.

Guilford, J. P. (1952). When not to factor analyze. *Psychological Bulletin, 49,* 26-37.

Hardiman, R. (1982). *White identity development: A process oriented model for describing the racial consciousness of White Americans.* Unpublished doctoral dissertation, University of Massachusetts, Amherst.

Harre, R. (1989). Language games and the texts of identity. In J. Shotter & J. J. Gergen (Eds.), *Texts of identity* (pp. 20-35). Newbury Park, CA: Sage.

Heath, D. B. (1978). The sociocultural model of alcohol use: Problems and prospects. *Journal of Operational Psychiatry, 9,* 55-66.

Helms, J. (1984). Toward a theoretical model for explaining the effects of race on counseling: A Black and White model. *The Counseling Psychologist, 12,* 153-165.

Helms, J. (1989a). Considering some methodological issues in racial identity counseling research. *The Counseling Psychologist, 17*(2), 227-252.

Helms, J. (1989b). Eurocentrism strikes in strange ways and in unusual places. *The Counseling Psychologist, 17*(4), 643-647.

Helms, J. (Ed.). (1990). *Black and White racial identity: Theory, research, and practice.* Westport, CT: Greenwood.

Helms, J. E. (1996). Toward a methodology for measuring and assessing "racial" as distinguished from "ethnic" identity. In G. R. Sodowsky & J. Impara (Eds.), *Multicultural assessment in counseling and clinical psychology* (pp. 143-192). Lincoln, NE: Buros Institute of Mental Measurements.

Helms, J. E. (1997). Implications of Behrens (1997) for the validity of the White Racial Identity Attitude Scale. *Journal of Counseling Psychology, 44*(1), 13-16.

Helms, J. E. (1999). Another meta-analysis of the White Racial Identity Attitude Scale's Cronbach alphas: Implications for validity. *Measurement & Evaluation in Counseling & Development, 32*(3), 122-137.

Helms, J. E., & Cook, D. A. (1999). *Using race and culture in counseling and psychotherapy: Theory and process.* Needham, MA: Allyn & Bacon.

Helms, J. E., & Piper, R. E. (1994). Implications of racial identity theory for vocational psychology. *Journal of Vocational Psychology, 44,* 124-138.

Helms, J. E., & Talleyrand, R. M. (1997). Race is not ethnicity. *American Psychologist, 52*(11), 1246-1247.

Hicks, L. (1970). Some properties of ipsative, normative, and forced-choice normative measures. *Psychological Bulletin, 74*(3), 167-184.

Hutnik, N. (1991). *Ethnic minority identity: A social psychological perspective.* Oxford, UK: Oxford University Press.

Iran-Nejad, A., & Winsler, A. (2000). Bartlett's schema theory and modern accounts of learning and remembering. *Journal of Mind and Behavior, 21*(1-2), 5-35.

Johnson, C. E., Wood, R., & Blinkhorn, S. F. (1988). Spuriouser and spuriouser: The use of ipsative personality tests. *Journal of Occupational Psychology, 61,* 153-162.

Judd, E. (1990). Intermarriage and the maintenance of religio-ethnic identity: A case study. *Journal of Comparative Family Studies, 21*(2), 251-268.

Katz, P., & Zalk, S. (1974). Doll preferences: An index of racial attitudes? *Journal of Educational Psychology, 66,* 663-668.

Klineberg, O., & Zavalloni, M. (1969). *Tribalism and nationalism.* The Hague, the Netherlands: Mouton.

Kroeber, A., & Kluckhohn, C. (1952). Culture: A critical review of concepts and definition. *Papers of the Peabody Museum of American Archeology and Ethnology, 47*(1).

Ladany, N., Inmani, A., Constantine, M., & Hofheinz, E. (1997). Supervisee multicultural case conceptualization ability and self-reported multicultural competence as functions of supervisee racial identity and supervisor focus. *Journal of Counseling Psychology, 44,* 284-293.

Le Vine, E., & Padilla, A. (1980). *Crossing cultures in therapy: Pluralistic counseling for the Hispanic.* Belmont, CA: Wadsworth.

Looney, J. (1988). Ego development and Black identity. *Journal of Black Psychology, 15*(1), 41-56.

Mainous, A. (1989). Self-concept as an indicator of acculturation in Mexican Americans. *Hispanic Journal of Behavioral Sciences, 11*(2), 178-189.

Marín, G., & Marín, B. V. (1982). Methodological fallacies when studying Hispanics. In L. Bickman (Ed.), *Applied social psychology annual* (Vol. 3, pp. 99-117). Beverly Hills, CA: Sage.

Markus, H. R., & Kitayama, S. (1991). Culture and the self: Implications for cognition, emotion, and motivation. *Psychological Review, 98*(2), 224-253.

Martinez, R., Norman, R., & Delaney, H. (1984). A Children's Hispanic Background Scale. *Hispanic Journal of Behavioral Sciences, 6*(2), 103-112.

Mays, V. (1986). Identity development of Black Americans: The role of history and the importance of ethnicity. *American Journal of Psychotherapy, 40*(4), 582-593.

McRoy, R., & Freeman, E. (1986). Racial identity issues among mixed-race children. *Social Work in Education, 8*(3), 164-174.

McRoy, R., Zurcher, L., Lauderdale, M., & Anderson, R. (1984). The identity of transracial adoptees. *Social Casework, 65*(1), 34-39.

Mead, M. (1935). *Sex and temperament in three primitive societies.* New York: Morrow.

Mead, M. (2001). *Letters from the field, 1925-1975.* New York: HarperCollins.

Mendoza, R. (1989). An empirical scale to measure type and degree of acculturation in Mexican-American adolescents and adults. *Journal of Cross-Cultural Psychology, 20*(4), 372-385.

Mio, J., Trimble, J., Arredondo, P., Cheatham, H., & Sue, D. (Eds.). (1999). *Keywords in multicultural interventions: A dictionary.* Westport, CT: Greenwood.

Montague, A. (1997). *Man's most dangerous myth: The fallacy of race* (6th ed.). Walnut Creek, CA: AltaMira Press.

Montgomery, G., & Orozco, S. (1984). Validation of a measure of acculturation for Mexican Americans. *Hispanic Journal of Behavioral Sciences, 6*(1), 53-63.

Nunnally, J. C. (1978). *Psychometric theory* (2nd ed.). New York: McGraw-Hill.

Oakland, T., & Shermis, M. (1989). Factor structure of the sociocultural scales. *Journal of Psychoeducational Assessment, 7*(4), 335-342.

Oetting, E. R., & Beauvais, F. (1990). Adolescent drug use: Findings of national and local surveys. *Journal of Consulting and Clinical Psychology, 58*(4), 385-394.

Oetting, E. R., & Beauvais, F. (1991). Orthogonal cultural identification theory: The cultural identification of minority adolescents. *International Journal of Addictions, 25*(5A-6A), 655-685.

Olmedo, E. (1979). Acculturation: A psychometric perspective. *American Psychologist, 34*, 1061-1070.

Padilla, A. (1980). *Acculturation: Theory, models and some new findings.* Boulder, CO: Westview.

Parham, T. (1989). Cycles of psychological Nigrescence. *The Counseling Psychologist, 17*(2), 187-226.

Parham, T., & Helms, J. (1985). Relation of racial identity attitudes to self-actualization and affective states of Black students. *Journal of Counseling Psychology, 32*(3), 432-440.

Parks, G. (1937). Forward. In R. Adams (Ed.), *Interracial marriage in Hawaii* (pp. i-xvii). New York: Macmillan.

Parsonson, K. (1987). Intermarriages: Effects on the ethnic identity of the offspring. *Journal of Cross-Cultural Psychology, 18*(3), 363-371.

Pfeffer, K. (1984). Interpretation of studies of ethnic identity: Draw-A-Person as a measure of ethnic identity. *Perceptual and Motor Skills, 59*(3), 835-838.

Phinney, J. (1989). Stages of ethnic identity development in minority group adolescents. *Journal of Early Adolescence, 9*(1-2), 34-49.

Phinney, J. (1990). Ethnic identity in adolescents and adults: Review of research. *Psychological Bulletin, 108*, 499-514.

Phinney, J. (1991). Ethnic identity and self esteem: A review and integration. *Hispanic Journal of Behavioral Sciences, 13*(2), 193-208.

Phinney, J. (1992). The multigroup ethnic identity measure: A new scale for use with diverse groups. *Journal of Adolescent Research, 7*, 156-176.

Phinney, J. (1996). When we talk about American ethnic groups, what do we mean? *American Psychologist, 51*(9), 918-927.

Phinney, J. (2000). Ethnic identity. In A. E. Kazdin (Ed.), *Encyclopedia of psychology* (pp. 254-259). New York: Oxford University Press.

Phinney, J., & Alipuria, L. (1990). Ethnic identity in college students from four ethnic groups. *Journal of Adolescence, 13*(2), 171-183.

Phinney, J., & Tarver, S. (1988). Ethnic identity search and commitment in Black and White eighth graders. *Journal of Early Adolescence, 8*(3), 265-277.

Poston, W. (1990). The Biracial Identity Development Model: A needed addition. *Journal of Counseling and Development, 69*(2), 152-155.

Pumariega, A. J. (1986). Acculturation and eating attitudes in adolescent girls: A comparative and correlational study. *Journal of the American Academy of Child Psychiatry, 25*(2), 276-279.

Rauch, S., Bowler, R., & Schwarzer, R. (1987, August). *Acculturation effects on personality characteristics in three minority groups.* Paper presented at the meeting of the American Psychological Association, New York.

Richman, J., Gaviria, M., Flaherty, J., Birz, S., & Wintrob, R. (1987). The process of acculturation: Theoretical perspectives and an empirical investigation in Peru. *Social Science Medicine, 25*(7), 839-847.

Romanucci-Ross, L., & DeVos, G. (1995). *Ethnic identity: Creation, conflict and accommodation.* Walnut Creek, CA: AltaMira Press.

Roosens, E. (1989). *Creating ethnicity*. Newbury Park, CA: Sage.

Root, M. P. P. (1996). The multiracial experience: Racial borders as a significant frontier in race relations. In M. P. P. Root (Ed.), *The multiracial experience: Racial borders as the new frontier* (pp. xiii-xxviii). Thousand Oaks, CA: Sage.

Root, M. P. P. (2001). *Love's revolution: Interracial marriage*. Philadelphia: Temple University Press.

Rowe, W., Bennett, S., & Atkinson, D. (1994). White racial identity models: A critique and alternative proposal. *The Counseling Psychologist, 22*(1), 129-146.

Santiago-Rivera, A. L. (1999). Ethnic identity. In J. Mio, J. Trimble, P. Arredondo, H. Cheatham, & D. Sue (Eds.), *Keywords in multicultural interventions: A dictionary* (pp. 107-108). Westport, CT: Greenwood.

Sellers, R. M., Chavous, T. M., & Cooke, D. (1998). Racial ideology and racial centrality as predictors of African American college students' academic performance. *Journal of Black Psychology, 24*(1), 8-27.

Singelis, T. M., Triandis, H. C., Bhawuk, D. P. S., & Gelfand, M. J. (1995). Horizontal and vertical dimensions of individualism and collectivism: A theoretical and measurement refinement. *Cross-Cultural Research, 29*(3), 240-275.

Smith, T. W. (1980). Ethnic measurement and identification. *Ethnicity, 7,* 78-95.

Sodowsky, G., Lai, E., & Plake, B. (1991). Moderating effects of sociocultural variables on acculturation attitudes of Hispanics and Asian Americans. *Journal of Counseling Development, 70,* 194-204.

Sodowsky, G., & Plake, B. (1991). Psychometric properties of the American International Relations Scale. *Educational and Psychological Measurement, 51,* 207-216.

Sollors, W. (Ed.). (1989). *The invention of ethnicity*. New York: Oxford University Press.

Stephan, W., & Rosenfield, D. (1978). Effects of desegregation on racial attitudes. *Journal of Personality and Social Psychology, 36*(8), 795-804.

Stephan, W., & Stephan, W. G. (1989). After intermarriage: Ethnic identity among mixed heritage Japanese-Americans and Hispanics. *Journal of Marriage and the Family, 51,* 505-519.

Stevens, R. (1983). *Erik Eriksen: An introduction*. New York: St. Martin's.

Strauss, A. L. (1959). *Mirrors and masks: The search for identity*. Glencoe, IL: Free Press.

Suarez-Orozco, M. (2001). Everything you ever wanted to know about assimilation but were afraid to ask. In R. Shweder, M. Minow, & H. Markus (Eds.), *The free exercise of culture* (pp. 1-30). New York: Russell Sage Foundation.

Suinn, R., Ahuna, C., & Khoo, G. (1992). The Suinn-Lew Asian Self-Identity Acculturation Scale: Concurrent and factorial validation. *Educational and Psychological Measurement, 52,* 1041-1046.

Suinn, R., Rickard-Figueroa, K., Lew, S., & Vigil, P. (1987). The Suinn-Lew Self-Identity Acculturation Scale. *Educational and Psychological Measurement, 47*(2), 401-407.

Swanson, J. L., Tokar, D. M., & Davis, L. E. (1994). Content and construct validity of the White Racial Identity Attitude Scale. *Journal of Vocational Behavior, 44,* 198-217.

Tajfel, H. (1981). *Human groups and social categories*. Cambridge, UK: Cambridge University Press.

Takaki, R. (1993). *A different mirror: A history of multicultural America*. Boston: Little, Brown.

Taylor, C. (1992). *Multiculturalism and "the politics of recognition."* Princeton, NJ: Princeton University Press.

Tenopyr, M. L. (1988). Artifactual reliability of forced-choice scales. *Journal of Applied Psychology, 73,* 749-751.

Teske, R., & Nelson, B. (1973). Two scales for the measurement of Mexican-American identity. *International Review of Modern Sociology, 3*(2), 192-203.

Thompson, R. H. (1989). *Theories of ethnicity: A critical appraisal.* New York: Greenwood.

Triandis, H. (1972). *The analysis of subjective culture.* New York: John Wiley.

Triandis, H., Kashima, Y., Shimada, E., & Villereal, M. (1986). Acculturation indices as a means of confirming cultural differences. *International Journal of Psychology, 21*(1), 43-70.

Trimble, J. (1987). Self-understanding and perceived alienation among American Indians. *Journal of Community Psychology, 15,* 316-333.

Trimble, J. (1988). Multilinearity of acculturation: Person-situation interactions. In D. Keats, D. Munro, & L. Mann (Eds.), *Heterogeneity in cross-cultural psychology* (pp. 173-186). Berwyn, PA: Swets & Zeitlinger.

Trimble, J. (1991). Ethnic specification, validation prospects and future of drug abuse research. *International Journal of the Addictions, 25*(2), 149-169.

Trimble, J. (1995). Toward an understanding of ethnicity and ethnic identification and their relationship with drug use research. In G. Botvin, S. Schinke, & M. Orlandi (Eds.), *Drug abuse prevention with multiethnic youth*, (pp. 3-27). Thousand Oaks, CA: Sage.

Trimble, J. (1996). Acculturation, ethnic identification and the evaluation process. In A. H. Bayer, F. L. Brisbane, & A. Ramirez (Eds.), *Advanced methodological issues in cultural competent evaluation for substance abuse prevention* (Cultural Competence Series 6, Pub. [SMA]96-3110). Washington, DC: Center for Substance Abuse Prevention, Department of Health and Human Services.

Trimble, J. (2000). Social psychological perspectives on changing self-identification among American Indians and Alaska Natives. In R. H. Dana (Ed.), *Handbook of cross-cultural/multicultural personality assessment* (pp. 197-222). Mahwah, NJ: Lawrence Erlbaum.

Trimble, J., & Mahoney, W. (2002). Gender and ethnic differences in adolescent self-esteem: A Rasch measurement model analysis. In P. D. Mail, S. Heurtin-Roberts, S. E. Martin, & J. Howard (Eds.), *Alcohol use among American Indians: Multiple perspectives on a complex problem* (National Institute on Alcohol Abuse and Alcoholism Research Monograph No. 37). Bethesda, MD: National Institute on Alcohol Abuse and Alcoholism.

U.S. Bureau of the Census. (2001). *Census of the population: General population characteristics, 2000.* Washington, DC: Government Printing Office.

van den Berghe, P. (1967). *Race and racism: A comparative perspective.* New York: John Wiley.

van den Berghe, P. (1981). *The ethnic phenomenon.* New York: Elsevier.

Vaughan, G. M. (1986). Social change and racial identity: Issues in the use of picture and doll measures. *Australian Journal of Psychology, 38*(3), 359-370.

Waters, M. C. (1990). *Ethnic options: Choosing identities in America.* Berkeley: University of California Press.

Waters, M. C. (1994, April). *The social construction of race and ethnicity: Some examples from demography.* Paper presented at American Diversity: A Demographic Challenge for the Twenty-First Century, Center for Social and Demographic Analysis Conference, SUNY, Albany, NY.

Wayley, C., & Harris, M. (1958). *Minorities in the new world: Six case studies.* New York: Columbia University Press.

Weinreich, P. (1986). The operationalisation of identity theory in racial and ethnic relations. In J. Rex & D. Mason (Eds.), *Theories of race and ethnic relations* (pp. 299-320). Cambridge, UK: Cambridge University Press.

Weinreich, P., & Saunderson, W. (Eds.). (2002). *Analysing identity: Cross-cultural, societal and clinical contexts*. London: Routledge/Taylor & Francis/Psychology Press.

Westermeyer, J., Neider, J., & Callies, A. (1989). Psychosocial adjustment of Hmong refugees during their first decade in the United States: A longitudinal study. *Journal of Nervous and Mental Disease, 177*(3), 132-139.

White, C., & Burke, P. (1987). Ethnic role identity among Black and White college students: An interactionist approach. *Sociological Perspectives, 30*(3), 310-331.

White, L. (1947). Culturological vs. psychological interpretations of human behavior. *American Sociological Review, 12,* 686-698.

Wooden, W., Leon, J., & Toshima, M. (1988). Ethnic identity among Sansei and Yonsei church-affiliated youth in Los Angeles and Honolulu. *Psychological Reports, 62*(1), 268-270.

Young, R. J. C. (1995). *Colonial desire: Hybridity in theory, culture, and race*. New York: Routledge.

Zavalloni, M. (1980). Values. In H. C. Triandis & R. W. Brislin (Eds.), *Handbook of cross-cultural psychology: Social psychology* (Vol. 5, pp. 73-120). Boston: Allyn & Bacon.

Zayas, L. (1987). Toward an understanding of suicide risks in young Hispanic females. *Journal of Adolescent Research, 2*(1), 1-11.

Zinn, H. (1980). *A people's history of the United States*. New York: Harper & Row.

CHAPTER 13

Constructing Race
and Deconstructing Racism
A Cultural Psychology Approach

JAMES M. JONES
University of Delaware

Whether race is considered a biologically invariant quality of human beings or a socially constructed taxonomy of human kinds, it captures the human tendency to form hierarchies of human groups and to enforce them. Furthermore, whether race stands for human differences associated with skin color, socioeconomic status, geographical region, cultural attributes, or even ethnic qualities (e.g., Jews in Hitler's Germany), its role in society is a stratifying one, with characteristics (however defined) of those in power on top and those who are subordinate on the bottom. DuBois (1903) captured this hierarchical reality famously in his dictum, "The problem of the twentieth century is the problem of the color line" (p. 3).

Race as a biological concept stands on emaciated legs and has all but been toppled over (cf. Jones, 1997). One cannot find reliable biological differences (e.g., blood types) that correspond to known racial classifications. Nor do taxonomies by race, based on modern scientific standards, support the phenotypic judgments we make about racial groups. That is, people who may look alike do not necessarily share genetic markers. It is popular to say now that there is greater variability *within* so-called racial groups than there are differences *between* them.

Without belaboring this point, we come quickly to the modern-day mantra that race is "socially constructed." Sometimes it seems that merely uttering the phrase strips race of its pernicious, hierarchy-enhancing (cf. Sidanius & Pratto, 2001) properties. But it is simply not so. To argue that a socially constructed race is fundamentally different from a biologically derived race is pragmatically vacuous. Social hierarchies based on race are and have always been supported by instruments of society and culture, whatever the underlying assumptions of race are.

So to state the implications of these points simply, *race matters*. Race matters in the psychology of people who live in highly racialized societies such as the United States. Race matters in the culture of this society as well, filled as it is with symbols of race and racism and the beliefs that define and support them. In this chapter, I will do three things: First, I will examine the evidence for the psychological representation of race and the behavioral expressions of racism. Second, I will suggest ways in which targets of racism react to their target status and present a model of TRIOS (an acronym for the psychological processes associated with Time, Rhythm, Improvisation, Orality, and Spirituality) that helps organize these responses for African Americans. Third, I will put these analyses in the context of cultural psychology by which culture and psyche are intertwined.

RACISM IS A MULTILEVELED PHENOMENON

Racism can be defined:

at an individual level, whereby a person has beliefs about the inherent superiority of his or her own racial group over others, leading to antipathy toward other racial groups;

at an institutional level, whereby systematic racial inequalities result from institutional practices by individual design (intentional) or as a standard of practice (unintentional); and

at a cultural level, whereby one dominant racial group has the power and tendency to impose cultural standards on others so that it achieves superior access, outcomes, and social judgments relative to subordinate racial groups. (Jones, 1972, 1997)

Racism presupposes three related psychosocial concepts: *race,* which we have already discussed as a socially meaningful human categorization that is easily hierarchicalized;

racialism, which refers to the belief that race explains human behavior so that differences in behavior can be understood on the basis of differences in race; and *racialization,* the societal projects that both define and reflect the meanings of race and confer operational status in everyday life. It is in fact through racialization that the important qualities of race are constructed.

As depicted here, racism is woven into the cultural fabric of the United States. There are three important consequences of this universality. First, all groups, regardless of their racial classification, are socialized into a society in which these racialized meanings are well known. Thus, racism is part of the psyche of everyone. Second, this universality of racism makes it an accessible construct for explaining social structure, interpersonal relations, and psychological characteristics. Third, despite this universality, its effects on those in dominant positions may be fundamentally different from the effects on those in subordinate positions. Let's briefly consider the nature of these three consequences of racism for its targets.

Race as a Central Feature of American Society. Jones (1997, Figure 17.1) describes a model by which race is woven into the cultural fabric of the society and is transmitted through cultural symbols, beliefs and values, political structures, and behaviors through social institutions, where it becomes socialized into the psyches of U.S. citizens.

Racism Is a Universal Context for Its Targets. When you belong to a group that is targeted for oppression, discrimination, and bias, that bias is a potential explanatory variable in your life. One may be sensitized to the possibility that negative treatment is likely or, when it occurs, that it is based on your racial classification. This leads to the constant use of cognitive resources associated with what Crocker and Major (1989) called "attributional ambiguity"—that is, the ambiguity associated with attributing one's treatment to an objective appraisal of one's behavior or to built-in racial biases by the other person. In a culture where racial denigration has hundreds of years of normative sanction, it is easy to see how this would continue to influence social perception of its targets. Furthermore, continued evidence of racial bases (racial profiling, social audit studies that document outright discrimination, and racial disparities in health, economic well-being, and educational attainment) (cf. Jones, 1997) brings the historical pattern into contemporary relief.

The universality of racism as an accessible construct has several psychological consequences (Jones, in press). First, racism is an accessible, explanatory construct with motivational consequences. There are two types of motivational consequences of the universal context of racism:

In *self-protective motivations*, one seeks to detect the occurrence of, protect oneself from, avoid if anticipated, and conquer if confronted with racism. Needless to say, this takes a lot of energy.

In *self-enhancing motivations*, one sustains, defends, and enhances one's self-worth and humanity.

I argue that both of these motivational tendencies are triggered by the universal context of racism, but the self-protective, more than the self-enhancing, motives have been the subject of theory and research on race.

Second, psychological tensions result from individual-level versus group-level dynamics. Three sets of conflicted force fields can be identified: (a) Personal identity versus reference group orientation captures the relative importance of personal uniqueness versus group belonging needs at a moment in time (Brewer, 1991), (b) racial identity versus superordinate identity reflects the relative importance at a moment in time of in-group distinctiveness versus superordinate group belonging, and (c) instrumentality versus expressiveness pits the desire for self-expression against the perceived requirements for mainstream success. Belonging to a marginalized minority group creates the potential for conflicts and tensions in each of these domains. How targets resolve these psychological tensions or conflicts substantially influences their range of behavioral and attitudinal options in a universal racism context.

Racism Is Not Necessarily Accessible for Perpetrators of Bias. One of the problems of racism is that its existence, expression, and consequences vary between those who most frequently perpetrate it and those who are most frequently its targets. Although it is acutely accessible for targets, it is much less so for perpetrators, people we conventionally call prejudiced (cf. Gaertner & Dovidio, 1986). The general concepts of modern (McConahay, 1986), aversive (Dovidio, Kawakami, & Gaertner, 2002), or symbolic (Sears, 1998) racism all identify the same psychological dynamic: People deflect their true prejudices away from race onto other neutral objects (a bus, a principle, a policy). By so doing, they convince themselves that they are not racially prejudiced. Despite these protestations, scientific research is able to illuminate ways in which these beliefs are contradicted by attitudes, emotions, or behaviors. The following are a few brief descriptions of research that illustrate these points.

Bargh and his colleagues (Bargh, 2001; Bargh, Chen, & Burrows, 1996) have shown that racial stereotypes can prime racially biased behavior even when their presence is unconscious. In one test of this idea (Bargh et al., 1996), White undergraduates searched a computer screen for particular patterns in a tedious, lengthy exercise. While they were performing this task, they were presented with computer-generated faces whose exposure was below their threshold of detection (subliminally). Half of the participants saw the faces of Whites, and half saw the faces of Blacks. After about 45 minutes, an error message was flashed suggesting that the data had been lost due to a computer failure. Participants were instructed that they would have to begin over from the beginning. The experimenter was summoned, and after checking the equipment, he informed them they would have to begin again. A hidden video camera captured their responses when they first learned from the computer they would have to begin again, and the experimenter rated their anger when he informed them of the same thing. The problem was fixed, though, and they did not have to redo the task. Independent judges who were unaware of the variations in faces seen rated the videotapes on anger and hostility. The data from both sources showed the same result: Those participants who were primed with Black faces were rated as more angry and hostile than those who saw White faces. The explanation for this finding is that the Black faces primed the racial stereotype associated with Blacks, which includes hostility and aggressiveness (cf. Devine & Baker, 1991). Thus, the presence of Blacks in one's environment "can" trigger an emotional response, mediated by perceptual processes, which increases the likelihood that events will be interpreted in a more negative or hostile way. If those same targets are the object of those judgments, then racial biases may be directed at those who may have innocently stimulated a degree of hostility unrelated to any behavior in which they have engaged.

Another illustration comes from a study by Darley and Gross (1983) but does not involve race. College students evaluated the performance of a young 10-year-old student named Hannah. For half of the participants, Hannah was described as low socioeconomic status (SES). For the other half, she was upper SES. First, participants rated Hannah on how well they thought she would do academically. For the most part, they were not confident that they could make this judgment reliably and were reluctant to do so. They then were shown a videotape of Hannah taking a test. After viewing the video, they were asked to rate how well Hannah did on the test. Now there were significant differences in these judgments based on whether the participants thought Hannah was upper or lower SES. Her performance was judged significantly better when she was upper class than lower class. Moreover, after seeing the video, all judges were confident in their assessment. The fact that they saw the identical video (and hence Hannah's performance did not vary at all) leaves us with clear evidence that their expectation, based on SES, was the significant determinant of their assessments. The fact that they were confident in their judgments suggests that they believed that having seen her behave in a testing situation, they now could make an objective assessment. That they were biased by the SES information was transparent to the judges. So, Hannah now is subject to perceptual and judgmental biases based on her SES. Similar forms of this sort of self-fulfilling prophecy effect have been demonstrated for race (cf. Word, Zanna, & Cooper, 1974).

A final illustration comes from a clever study by Dovidio et al. (2002). Derived from the aversive racism model, Dovidio et al. assessed participants' racial attitudes in two ways. An explicit measure, as we are most familiar with, assesses racial attitudes via a paper-and-pencil assessment. The authors used the Brigham Attitudes Toward Blacks Scale (cf. Brigham, 1993) to measure explicit prejudicial attitudes and a lexical decision-making reaction time procedure to measure implicit racial attitudes. They found that participants' assessment of the friendliness of interracial interactions was related to their "explicit" racial attitudes, but the perceptions of observers followed more closely their "implicit" racial attitudes. Because the two measures were uncorrelated, this meant that Whites were largely unaware of how their nonverbal behavior signaled racial biases that were detected by others with whom they were interacting.

Racism Can Influence Targets in a Variety of Ways. Although perpetrators of racism are often unaware of their bias, targets are acutely aware. This awareness can take on different forms. One, as we saw earlier, is attributional ambiguity, a psychological vigilance that asks if unfavorable or even favorable treatment is based on race or a more "objective appraisal" of the situation. The net effect of attributional ambiguity is that others' assessments are discounted. This can be both good and bad. It can be good when a prejudicial judgment is discounted and not internalized as a blow to one's self-worth (cf. Crocker & Major, 1989). However, at the same time, a positive evaluation may also be discounted (tokenism, affirmative action obligation) so that one is not able to benefit from a positive outcome. Racism, then, creates a chronic ambiguity in interpersonal and institutional settings, the net effect of which is to leave a person either having to handle a substantial amount of ambiguity or adopting a strategy that would protect him or her from this uncertainty. Sometimes the strategy may impose a certain rigidity of options that diminishes both the opportunity path and the psychological enjoyments that come with success.

A well-researched and compelling line of reasoning comes from Steele's (1998) research on stereotype threat. Stereotype threat describes the context in which a person is performing an evaluative task (e.g., taking a test) in a situation for which there exists well-known negative stereotypes about the social group (e.g., African American) to which that person belongs. In this situation, a person may feel the personal threat of a group stereotype, resulting in anxiety that his or her performance may corroborate the negative stereotype. For Blacks, for whom most of the research has been done, this has been shown to account for poor test-taking outcomes. Steele and Aronson (1995) had Blacks and Whites take a difficult version of the Advanced Graduate Record Exam under one of two conditions. The first experimental condition described the test as a reliable assessment of their actual ability (stereotype threat condition). The second condition was described as difficult and challenging but one that would not assess their true ability. Differences in these two instructional sets had no effect for White test takers, but for African Americans, their performance was significantly poorer when the test was perceived to be diagnostic of their ability than when it was not. Absent the stereotype threat arousal, no racial differences in performance were found. Variations on this paradigm suggest that the decline in performance is due to heightened anxiety associated with attachment to one's racial group that is the target of the negative stereotype. More recent data suggest that this underperformance is greater when a person has a strong academic motivation to succeed and a strong racial identity (Steele, personal communication, 2001).

The explanation for stereotype threat effects suggests that one strategy for coping with the threat is protective disidentification with the stigmatized domain. This means that when one is faced with a high probability of confirming a negative group stereotype in a given performance domain, he or she may "disidentify" with that domain, which means that one's self-esteem is disconnected from performance. In this case, poor performance or negative judgments cannot influence one's self-esteem. Osborne (1995) illustrated the effects of such a process in a national data sample of high school students. He assessed the correlation between self-esteem and grade point average (GPA) among Black and White students in the 8th and 10th grades. His assumption was that the lower the correlation between self-esteem and GPA, the greater the evidence for disidentification processes in academic domains. In a sample of nearly 25,000 students, he found that the correlation between self-esteem and GPA *increased* slightly from 8th to 10th grade for White males (+.02) and decreased slightly for White females (–.01). However, the correlation decreased substantially more for Black females (–.05) and most dramatically and significantly for Black males (–.12). This suggests both a race effect (Blacks show greater tendencies toward academic disidentification as they progress in secondary school than Whites) and a race-by-gender interaction (Black males increase disidentification, whereas White males decrease it as they progress in school).

The net effect of stereotype threat is a double whammy. If you engage in academics seriously and try really hard, anxiety and the threat factor may actually undermine your performance. If you take the alternative course and disidentify with academics, then your grades still suffer and the default consequence is underperformance. Steele (1998) has shown that major interventions that disconnect the negative stereotypes from academic expectancies are the best way to remove these negative effects.

RACISM-STRESS PARADIGM

Another consequence of racism is that it generates both acute and chronic stress. One source of stress is the cognitive load that is associated with resolving attributional ambiguity, protecting self-esteem, and detecting and defusing stereotype threat environments. Another kind of issue comes from simply trying to determine how best to acculturate to mainstream society when one comes from a marginalized culture (cf. LaFromboise, Coleman, &

Gerton, 1993). If mainstream society is a source of discrimination and negative stereotypes but also the place for opportunities and possibilities for achieving success and material well-being, an approach-avoidance situation results. LaFromboise et al. (1993) offered an excellent analysis of "bicultural adaptation" by which one may acquire competence in a second culture. Whether you are born in the United States or elsewhere, residential segregation and cultural marginalization are such that participation in mainstream society has most frequently been represented by an acculturation model. LaFromboise et al. offered four options: assimilation, acculturation, alternation and multiculturalism, and fusion. The first, assimilation, is not viable because one loses support of one's culture of origin but inevitably finds oneself marginalized in the new mainstream culture. Acculturation shares certain aspects of assimilation in that the acculturated self is seen as more distant from the culture of origin and closer to the acquiring culture. This again leaves one vulnerable to lost social support from one's original culture and continued marginalization from the acquiring culture. Multiculturalism is ideally a promising strategy, and we now speak in positive terms about a multicultural agenda. We have not, however, figured out how to take into account the myriad multicultural possibilities and to divvy up opportunities and rewards equitably across a growing number of cultural groups. Fusion represents what we have traditionally considered the melting pot ideology and has been criticized for the loss of cultural identity and the tendency to fuse into the most dominant cultural group at the expense of less dominant cultural origins. Finally, LaFromboise et al. preferred the alternation model, which mirrors bilingualism in that one who is competent in two different cultures can demonstrate those competencies in the appropriate contexts and time, thereby maximizing the benefits of one's culture of origin and the opportunities of an acquired culture. Whatever we may think of these options and others that are not spelled out here, we are clearly talking about a complex calculus of personal and group dynamics with varying psychological, emotional, and behavioral consequences. This complexity is one of the consequences of navigating a society that is defined in critical ways by an essential quality of racism.

Clark, Anderson, Clark, and Williams (1997) have provided a detailed and well-articulated theory of the connection between racism and stress and their associated effects. The consequences are not merely psychological or attitudinal but physiological and physical. Detecting hostility in a given context commands cognitive resources that are then unavailable to process other relevant information. Furthermore, the physiological preparation for fight or flight puts the autonomic nervous system on high alert, which, if repeatedly activated, can lead to chronically elevated cardiovascular reactivity. The cumulative consequences of these dynamic reactions to racism are a stressful psychological and physical life.

Race Becomes Culture

Race is historically defined as a biological marker of group differences. However, the psychological meaning and social significance of race ensure that race plays a significant role in the differential experiences of people who belong to different races. As a result, group differences, which may have initially been predicated in part on real cultural differences, now blur the boundaries between culture and race. Thus, when we talk about racism, we are also talking about cultural biases as well. The use of the term *cultural racism* (Jones, 1972, 1997) is meant to convey the intersection of race and culture as a way of understanding the problems we associate with racism. Criteria that suggest this intersection include the following:

1. Culture can be defined as both an antecedent and a consequent of behavior.

2. Isolation by SES, geography, education, language, and age all provide singular influences on experience that mark recurring patterns of behavior over time (i.e., culture or subcultures).

3. Reactions to racial biases and stereotypes *produce* the very racial differences that the stereotypes presuppose (cf. Word et al., 1974).

TRIOS: A THEORY OF CULTURE AND PSYCHE

There are many different ways to think about culture. I borrow from Kroeber and Kluckhohn's (1952) definition that culture consists of (a) patterned ways of thinking, feeling, and reacting that are transmitted by and through symbols; (b) the core of traditional ideas and the values attached to them; and (c) the products of action and the conditioning elements of future actions. By these criteria, culture is the following:

Psychological—patterns of thinking, feeling, behaving, and valuing

Symbolic—representations of meaningful psychological patterns

Historical—cultural elements selectively derived and transmitted over time

Dynamic—cultural elements that both shape meaning and are transformed by events and actions

With this basic orientation, I argue that contemporary African American culture is continuous with its African origins. The dynamic cultural transmission involves the dual mechanisms of *reactivity* and *evolution*. Reactivity is the set of adaptation-coping sequences that develop to address the ecological challenges that members of the cultural group face. Evolution is the unfolding and elaboration of the core cultural elements as they are modified by the reactivity sequences. The result is simultaneous processes of continuity and change.

To make this set of theoretical assumptions practical, one needs to

1. specify the cultural elements of origin,

2. describe the ecological challenges,

3. trace the reactivity processes and their influence on these original cultural elements, and

4. describe the current set of core cultural elements and how they function in a contemporary context.

For the present purposes, I will stipulate that TRIOS can define those psychologically meaningful origins. Furthermore, these TRIOS elements have mediated reactivity to the ecological challenges faced by Africans in the 17th- and 18th-century Diaspora. Over time, the TRIOS elements also have defined both the evolution of African cultural origins in the Diaspora and their dynamic change as a result of reactivity processes.

TRIOS, then, is a worldview that directs as well as reflects culture. The psychological correlates of this cultural conception diverge from one constructed on the principles of a European-derived materialistic individualism. TRIOS is the nexus from which we trace the dynamics of African-European cultural contact in America.

Ecological Challenges in the New World

The ecological challenges of slavery engaged the patterns of TRIOS in adapting-coping sequences. In this oppressive environment, the opportunities for expression, social organization, and control demanded each of the TRIOS elements. Creole or pidgin languages emerged to enable oral communication among people who may have spoken somewhat different languages or dialects (cf. George, 1998). Improvisation was a means of creating linguistic meanings that were privileged among the native speakers and thus shielded them from adverse consequences when speech was heard by a person hostile to their well-being. Expression of the human spirit was made possible through music, song, and dance. Social organization was necessarily improvised, as were strategies for controlling self-protective collective actions. The cultural patterns became practical means of coping, adapting, and surviving. Thus, humanity was preserved through employing known and deep cultural principles and practices.

TRIOS: PSYCHOLOGICAL PRINCIPLES AND HYPOTHETICAL POSSIBILITIES

As a cultural worldview, each TRIOS dimension reflects human capacity developed from the fabric of experience, necessity, belief, and evolutionary success. Psychological concepts are derived from a particular cultural history and the problems and issues it defines. Thus, mainstream psychology is inspired by European American cultural concerns and worldview. TRIOS offers an alternative origination of basic psychological ideas, situated in the context of African psychological culture and its elaboration in the Diaspora.

Because the dimensions of TRIOS are qualities and capacities of people, they are not unique to African Americans. As cultural phenomena of a psychological nature, they may organize psychological processes, including perception, values, beliefs, preferences, behavioral style, attachments, interpersonal dynamics, temporal orientation, and a variety of motives, including those for achievement. TRIOS rests on two related organizing principles: (a) All TRIOS concepts are driven by and responsive to context, thus

Table 13.1   Descriptive Summaries of TRIOS Dimensions and Sample Items to Assess Them

Dimension Name	Description	Sample Item
Time	*Focuses attention on the present; immediacy of goals or behavior	I try to live one day at a time.
	*Setting goals and planning for the future	I make extensive plans for the future.
	*Emotion-laden thoughts about the past	I think about the past a lot.
Rhythm	*An internal rhythmic process with external dynamic properties—flow, entrainment	I always try to get in synch with surroundings.
	*Importance of and preference for physical expression	Music and dance are important forms of personal expression.
Improvisation	*Creative problem solving in conflicted contexts	When something disrupts my goals, I often figure out how to achieve them anyway.
	*Personally characteristic expressiveness or style	I have a personal style that is all my own.
Orality	*Preference for verbal exchange that is face-to-face	I always try to deal with people straight up and face-to-face.
	*Words, speech. and humor are fundamental modes of personal expression	I often feel that my experiences are not "real" until I tell someone about them.
	*Means of creating and maintaining social bonds	In my social group, laughter often holds us together.
	*Means of communicating cultural values, knowledge, and expectations	The most important things I know come more from stories I have heard than things I have read.
Spirituality	*Belief in a higher power or forces	Belief in God or a greater power helps me deal with the circumstances of my life.
	*Control and responsibility are shared with these forces	There are forces that influence my life that I cannot explain.

making TRIOS a theory of context, and (b) the driving energy in this context analysis is the prevailing premise of being-in-the-world.

With the help of graduate students in a seminar on cultural psychology of African Americans, 100 items tapping the five dimensions of TRIOS were written. Table 13.1 provides a summary description of each dimension, as well as a sample item that taps it. The items were given to a large and ethnically and racially diverse sample that varied in age, gender, and geographical location.

The following is an overview of preliminary findings.

The Sample

Responses from 1,351 participants were subjected to an exploratory factor analysis (EFA). Of the sample, two thirds were women and one third were men. A little over 40% were White, 21% were Black, 19% were Latin, and 11% were Asian. The age range was 14 to 62, with the average for each group between 20 and 21 years.

Early Findings

The Structures of TRIOS

The omnibus five-factor EFA reproduced the TRIOS dimensions extremely well. In order of extraction, the dimensions were Spirituality, Improvisation, Time (present orientation), Rhythm, and Orality. They accounted for 30% of the variance, and all but Rhythm had modest but acceptable levels of reliability. But although this does suggest that we can produce a factor structure that corresponds pretty well to the five separate dimensions of TRIOS, there is a more interesting story.

We conducted separate EFAs for each ethnic/racial group as a preliminary look at the possibility that these structures might vary with interesting results. For the Black sample, the first factor extracted included items that tapped all five of the TRIOS dimensions. Table 13.2 summarizes this factor structure. The nine items that comprise TRIOS reflect each dimension. One of the unanswered questions was whether TRIOS was best represented as five separate factors, each of which had a specific structure and relationship to behavior, or if TRIOS was somehow a self-organizing strategy or worldview that cohered in some integrative way. The Black EFA suggests that for this sample, the latter seems to be an appropriate characterization. For none of the other ethnic/racial groups was this true. For the remainder of this article, the composite TRIOS factor for Blacks is labeled TRIOS-C and represents the integrative TRIOS worldview as discussed in preceding sections. TRIOS will be used when referring to the generalized model of adaptation and coping derived from the African legacy. Those who score high on TRIOS-C are self-expressive, have a strong sense of personal uniqueness, live in the present, and deal with people directly. They are confident that they can handle any interpersonal situation that may arise, and this confidence, combined with a belief in a spiritual universe that puts their own lives in perspective, should inspire confidence and a personal sense of satisfaction and well-being. In short, TRIOS-C is a personal blueprint for adaptation, coping, and personal well-being. That it comes from Blacks and not from other racial ethnic groups provides some support for the derivation of TRIOS as an African-inspired worldview that has evolved over time. What remains to be shown is the functional utility of TRIOS as a mediator of important behavioral outcomes.

The five factors for the Black EFA are largely unrelated. TRIOS-C correlates significantly with Spirituality, but no other correlations are significant. Of particular interest, though, is Factor 2, Orality-in-the-Now. The primacy of verbal exchange combines with a focus on the now. This "now focus" is different from the present orientation of the composite TRIOS because it is defined by the lack of future visibility and lack of confidence in the future. The future is a blank, and planning for it is a waste of time. Thus, Orality-in-the-Now can be described as a truncated time horizon in which immediate interpersonal relationships and interactions define the self. We will return to an interesting difference between TRIOS and Orality-in-the-Now later.

Ethnic/Racial Differences in TRIOS

Now that we have this structure, the first question is how racial-ethnic groups compare. We expected that Blacks as a group would endorse the TRIOS items more than other racial/ethnic groups. A Race × Sex × Age multivariate analysis of variance was conducted on all five TRIOS factors. For all factors except Rhythm, the main effect of race was significant.

Blacks scored highest on Orality-in-the-Now and Spirituality. Blacks along with Latinos also scored higher than Whites and

Table 13.2 Preliminary Results of Exploratory Factor Analysis (Oblim rotation) for the Black Sample of Respondents

Item	F1 TRIOS-C Composite	F2 Orality-in-the-Now	F3 Improvisation	F4 Rhythm	F5 Spirituality
Music and dance are important forms of personal expression.	**0.54**	-0.07	0.01	0.19	0.00
Belief in God or a greater power helps me deal with the circumstances of my life.	**0.52**	0.11	0.14	-0.26	**-0.47**
I have a personal style that is all my own.	**0.48**	-0.11	-0.24	0.09	-0.03
I try to live one day at a time.	**0.46**	0.07	-0.07	-0.10	-0.01
It is very important that how I behave makes a distinctive statement of who I am.	**0.45**	-0.21	0.16	0.31	-0.12
When something disrupts my goals, I often figure out how to achieve them anyway.	**0.45**	-0.21	-0.17	-0.14	-0.16
I enjoy things more for what they are than what they could be.	**0.43**	0.00	-0.21	0.28	0.00
I always try to deal with people straight up and face-to-face.	**0.39**	-0.15	-0.27	-0.18	-0.23
I often feel that my experiences are not "real" until I tell someone about them.	0.12	**0.57**	-0.07	0.11	0.03
I have always preferred listening to a book on tape rather than reading it.	-0.03	**0.50**	-0.06	-0.13	-0.12
It is better to live the present moment to the fullest than to plan for the future.	0.05	**0.45**	0.03	-0.01	-0.04
When I try to envision the future, I draw a blank.	0.19	**0.45**	0.18	0.18	0.12
Preparing for the future is often a waste of time.	-0.02	**0.44**	-0.03	-0.09	0.05
When I feel that people who do not know me are making my life difficult, I can always find ways to handle the situation.	-0.05	-0.06	**-0.55**	-0.01	-0.17
When things do not go as planned, I can devise another plan right on the spot.	0.11	0.07	**-0.49**	-0.16	-0.02
I can figure many ways out of almost any situation.	0.00	0.06	**-0.47**	0.13	-0.05
When a situation arises, I usually know two to three different ways to handle it.	-0.06	-0.01	**-0.47**	-0.16	-0.19
It's good to have a plan, but it's more important to be able to roll with the punches.	-0.17	0.11	**-0.45**	0.08	0.13
I always try to put my personal mark on things.	0.29	0.01	**-0.38**	0.08	-0.02

Item	F1 TRIOS-C Composite	F2 Orality-in-the-Now	F3 Improvisation	F4 Rhythm	F5 Spirituality
I often feel anxiety when I am late.	-0.03	0.00	-0.06	**0.43**	-0.13
I always try to get in synch with my surroundings.	0.27	0.25	-0.09	**0.42**	0.03
Sometimes I can't do things because the timing is all wrong.	-0.02	0.08	0.01	**0.38**	-0.14
When I am late for a meeting, I feel terrible.	0.09	0.01	0.14	0.37	-0.08
There is a higher force that directs my path in life.	0.00	-0.19	-0.04	0.20	**-0.69**
Sometimes you just have to put your life in the hands of a higher power.	-0.10	0.03	-0.01	0.01	**-0.56**
Belief in a higher power is important to me.	0.35	0.05	-0.07	-0.03	**-0.50**
Belief in God or a greater power helps me deal with the circumstances of my life.	0.13	0.10	0.08	0.00	**-0.37**
Eigenvalue	6.21	3.75	2.68	2.46	2.15
% variance	10.53	6.36	4.55	4.16	3.64
Cronbach's alpha	0.64	0.56	0.64	0.38	0.80
Number of items	9	8	6	4	4

NOTE: Bold numbers are the nonstandardized beta weights above .37 used to define each of the TRIOS factors.

Asian Americans on TRIOS-C and on Improvisation. We expected Blacks to score higher than other groups, and generally this is what we found. But it is interesting also to note that Latinos scored very high on the TRIOS-C factor and on Improvisation. It is also interesting to note that Asians scored very low on Improvisation, and Whites scored very low on Spirituality. The interesting possibility here is that because race is not mentioned at all in any single item of the scale, these ethnic/racial differences may reflect true cultural differences in experience, values, worldview, and behavioral preferences.

There were some sex and age main effects and, on some variables, two-way and three-way interactions. In each case where sex differences were obtained (TRIOS-C; Rhythm and Spirituality), women scored higher than men did.

TRIOS Begets Forgiveness

There is growing evidence that the ability to forgive may have important health benefits. Witvliet, Ludwig, and Vander Laan (2001) argued that how we respond to interpersonal offenses can affect our physical and probably psychological well-being. If one has been offended, failure to forgive (harboring a grudge, rehearsing the hurt) may erode health, but forgiving the offense (empathizing with the humanity of the offender and simply forgiving him or her) may enhance health. Participants were asked to recall a real instance of an interpersonal offense, then to actively imagine either a forgiving or unforgiving response to it, while their physiological processes were monitored. Unforgiving thoughts prompted more aversive emotion and elevated heart rate, skin conductance, and blood pressure compared to when they imagined forgiving responses.

If targets of discrimination are more likely to experience offensive encounters, would their likelihood of forgiveness actually bestow health benefits? Furthermore, if, as I have suggested, TRIOS is a mechanism for adaptation and personal control, would TRIOS levels be related to more effective coping with interpersonal stress? Orality-in-the-Now can be thought to reflect a world in which one's social and psychological self is defined moment to moment by virtue of interpersonal interactions and their outcomes. A threat or transgression is harder to forgive when it penetrates the core of one's being than when it can be deflected by a greater complexity and broader worldview, as seen in the composite TRIOS. So, we hypothesized that TRIOS would be positively related to forgiveness, but Orality-in-the-Now would be negatively related.

Tangney, Boone, Fee, and Reinsmith (2002) have developed a measure of the "propensity to forgive." It consists of 16 vignettes in which another has offended or harmed you in some way (e.g., borrowed your car and wrecked it, stood you up for lunch, slept with your lover) or you have harmed another. Participants are asked how likely they might forgive the other or themselves. How long would it take? How angry would they be? How much would they blame the other person or themselves? The scoring produces several different indices of the propensity to forgive, which we combined into a single forgiveness index. We gave the forgiveness scale to 123 University of Delaware White undergraduates along with the TRIOS scale. TRIOS-C was positively related to forgiveness ($r = .33$, $p < .05$), whereas Orality-in-the-Now was negatively related to forgiveness ($r = -.08$, ns). Although the negative correlation was not significant, it was significantly different from the correlation with TRIOS-C.

Three interesting points emerge. One is that TRIOS-C and Orality may represent quite different worldviews and thus be connected to a rather different set of behavioral, value, and attitudinal tendencies. The second is that because the respondents were all White, it is possible that TRIOS-C could serve as a nonreactive measure of general prosocial orientation and hence a reduced level of prejudice. But it is also possible that Black participants would respond differently. Third, if forgiveness is a health benefit, it may be more about self and less about the other. In the context of racism, forgiveness is not absolution for transgressions but is self-focused on personal well-being. As Mamie Mobley said of the killers who mutilated and murdered her son, Emmett Till, in 1954 but were later acquitted by an all-White jury, "What they had done is not for me to punish and it was not for me to go around hugging hate to myself because that would destroy me"(Terkel, 1992, p. 21).

CONCLUSION

Racism is a problem for people who perpetrate it, targets who are victimized by it, and the society that houses and enables it. Racism is woven deeply into the psychological fabric of America and its citizens. Research clearly shows that that although enormous progress has been made, there remain subtle vestiges of its most pernicious consequences. Much of the psychological research on race has focused on the antecedents to hostile racial attitudes and their consequences in behavior. However, much less attention has been paid to the consequences of being a target of such bigotry and discrimination. A growing body of research on this topic, a sample of which was reviewed here, suggests we may well come to learn a great deal about the capacity of people to create functional lives in the face of threatening and ambiguously hostile environments. The subtle challenges are laid out in a variety of elegant experimental studies. The cumulative adaptations of people who have been targets of racism are captured in the theory of TRIOS, which, although developed in the context of racism against African Americans, may hold a more general significance for any social group targeted for discriminatory treatment. Our ongoing research and theory development should capitalize on increasingly well-developed theory and research on racism from both the perpetrator and target perspectives. The result will be a better understanding of the psychological dynamics of coping with racism, as well as the positive adaptive and expressive qualities of people in their cultural contexts.

REFERENCES

Bargh, J. A. (2001). The perception-behavior expressway: Automatic effects of social perception on social behavior. In M. P. Zanna (Ed.), *Advances in experimental social psychology* (Vol. 33, pp. 1-40). San Diego: Academic Press.

Bargh, J. A., Chen, M., & Burrows, L. (1996). Automaticity of social behavior: Direct effects of trait constructs and stereotype activation on action. *Journal of Personality and Social Psychology, 71*(2), 230-244.

Brewer, M. B. (1991). The social self: On being the same and different at the same time. *Personality and Social Psychology Bulletin, 17*, 475-482.

Brigham, J. (1993). College students' racial attitudes. *Journal of Applied Social Psychology, 23*, 1933-1967.

Clark, R., Anderson, N. B., Clark, V. R., & Williams, D. R. (1997). Racism as a stressor for African-Americans: A biopsychosocial model. *American Psychologist, 54*(10), 805-816.

Crocker, J., & Major, B. (1989). Social stigma and self-esteem: The protective properties of stigma. *Psychological Review, 96,* 608-630.

Darley, J. M., & Gross, P. G. (1983). A hypothesis-confirming bias in labeling effects. *Journal of Personality and Social Psychology, 44,* 20-33.

Devine, P.G., & Baker, S. (1991). Measurement of racial stereotype subtyping. *Personality and Social Psychology Bulletin, 17,* 44-50.

Dovidio, J. F., Kawakami, K., & Gaertner, S. L. (2002). Implicit and explicit prejudice and interracial interaction. *Journal of Personality and Social Psychology, 82* (1).

DuBois, W. E. B. (1903). *Souls of Black folk.* Chicago: A. C. McClurg.

Gaertner, S. G., & Dovidio, J. F. (1986). The aversive form of racism. In J. F. Dovidio & S. G. Gaertner (Eds.), *Prejudice, discrimination and racism* (pp. 61-90). Orlando, FL: Academic Press.

George, N. (1998). *Hip hop America.* New York: Viking.

Jones, J. M. (1972). *Prejudice and racism.* Reading, MA: Addison-Wesley.

Jones, J. M. (1997). *Prejudice and racism* (2nd ed.). New York: McGraw-Hill.

Jones, J. M. (in press). TRIOS: A psychological theory of the African legacy in American culture. *Journal of Social Issues.*

Kroeber, A. L., & Kluckhohn, C. (1952). *Culture: A critical review of concepts and definitions.* New York: Random House.

LaFromboise, T., Coleman, H. L. K., & Gerton, J. (1993). Psychological impact of biculturalism: Evidence and theory. *Psychological Bulletin, 114,* 395-412.

McConahay, J. B. (1986). Modern racism, ambivalence, and the modern racism scale. In J. F. Dovidio & S. G. Gaertner (Eds.), *Prejudice, discrimination and racism* (pp. 91-126). Orlando, FL: Academic Press.

Osborne, J. W. (1995). Academics, self-esteem, and race: A look at the underlying assumptions of the disidentification hypothesis. *Personality and Social Psychology Bulletin, 21,* 449-455.

Sears, D. O. (1998). Racism and politics in the United States. In J. Eberhardt & S. Fiske (Eds.), *Confronting racism: The problem and the response* (pp. 76-100). Thousand Oaks, CA: Sage.

Sidanius, J., & Pratto, F. (2001). *Social dominance.* New York: Cambridge University Press.

Steele, C. M. (1998). A threat in the air: How stereotypes shape the intellectual test performance of African-Americans. *American Psychologist, 52,* 613-629.

Steele, C. M., & Aronson, J. (1995). Stereotype threat and the intellectual test performance of African Americans. *Journal of Personality and Social Psychology, 69,* 797-811.

Tangney, J. P., Boone, A. L., Fee, R., & Reinsmith, C. (2002). *Individual differences in the propensity to forgive: Measurement and implications for psychological and social adjustment.* Unpublished manuscript, George Mason University.

Terkel, S. (1992) *Race: How Blacks and Whites think and feel about the American obsession.* New York: the New Press.

Witvliet, C. V., Ludwig, T. E., & Vander Laan, K. L. (2001). Granting forgiveness or harboring grudges: Implications for emotions, physiology, and health. *Psychological Science, 12*(2), 117-123.

Word, C. O., Zanna, M. P., & Cooper, J. (1974). The nonverbal mediation of self-fulfilling prophesies in interracial interaction. *Journal of Experimental Social Psychology, 10,* 109-120.

CHAPTER 14

Implicit Attitudes and Stereotyping

SAERA R. KHAN
University of San Francisco

O ver the past several decades, psychologists have attempted to discern the relation between the conscious and unconscious and how these systems create and maintain categories for efficiently processing information (for further information, see Lakoff, 1987). Social cognition researchers are especially interested in documenting the process by which an activated construct produces social behavior. This assessment of the relation between implicit and explicit attitudes holds great promise in providing answers for many social problems. In particular, the past century has borne witness across the globe to both large- and small-scale acts of violence stemming from ethnic hatred. The recent Bosnian Muslim and Rwandan genocides are stark reminders of how negative prejudice can quickly escalate to violence. Psychologists want to understand how the seeds of hatred, prejudice, and stereotypes influence judgment and, in turn, behavior.

Although U.S. race relations have appreciably improved over the past several decades, both racial tension and prejudice continue to exist inside and outside of the United States (Dovidio & Gaertner, 1986; Kinder, 1986; Nier, Mottola, & Gaertner, 2000). From a researcher's perspective, understanding the structure of racial attitude and its underlying factors may reveal viable solutions for reducing racial conflict. Unfortunately, theories or models of racial attitude and it relationship to behavior have become increasingly complex with improved research tools and techniques. Since 1990, at least 11 different racial attitude measures have been published in the United States (Biernat & Crandall, 1999). Many of these scales are constructed to measure at least one of the dimensions of racial attitude (e.g., endorsement of stereotypes, support or opposition to federal aid policies).

Furthermore, researchers must now reckon with the difficulties of appropriately measuring explicit racial attitudes while also documenting the role of implicit attitudes (e.g., Dasgupta, McGhee, Greenwald, & Banaji, 2000; Greenwald & Banaji, 1995). The rapid growth in technology and methodology in the past 10 years has increased our appreciation of the prominence of implicit attitudes and stereotyping within the mind's toolbox. Exploring the structure of their relation is yielding insights into this phenomenon. However, many questions remain. Understanding the strength and shortcomings of current cross-cultural research in this area will inspire future research. This chapter seeks to provide an overview of the research on implicit racial attitudes. Also, unresolved issues, such as the relation between implicit and explicit attitudes, and the need for a unifying theory as well as future directions for research will be discussed.

OVERVIEW OF EXPLICIT ATTITUDES

Before discussing racial attitudes in depth, an extremely brief overview of attitude is needed. Attitudes are most generally referred to as one's enduring evaluation of a particular entity. In particular, one's affective reaction underlies the evaluation. This definition has been disputed; there is a debate over the unidimensional versus multidimensional structure of attitude (for a review, see Eagly & Chaiken, 1993). Although research has been equivocal on this issue, understanding racial attitudes from both perspectives has yielded valuable insights. From the unidimensional perspective, racial attitude can be thought of as one's favorable or unfavorable evaluation of a particular racial/ethnic group. From the tripartite perspective, attitudes are classified into three components: cognition, affect, and behavior (Katz & Stotland, 1959; Rosenberg & Hovland, 1960; see also Eagly & Chaiken, 1993). Responses stemming from a person's favorable or unfavorable beliefs, thoughts, or knowledge about the attitude object form the cognitive component. Affective responses stem from positive or negative feelings or emotions toward the attitude object. There is some disagreement in the literature regarding the need to make these components of attitude conceptually distinct (e.g., Fishbein & Azjen, 1975; Rosenberg, 1960; Zajonc & Markus, 1982; Zanna & Olson, 1994). Nevertheless, recent empirical work has been successful in distinguishing between affective and cognitive components of attitude (e.g., Breckler & Wiggins, 1989; Crites, Fabrigar, & Petty, 1994; Jackson et al., 1996; Stangor, Sullivan, & Ford, 1991). For instance, Haddock, Zanna, and Esses (1993) found that distinguishing between stereotypic beliefs, affect, symbolic beliefs, and prior personal experience significantly predicted both high and low authoritarians' explicit attitudes toward homosexuals. In most current research, both implicit and explicit racial attitudes are conceptualized as unidimensional. Nevertheless, for both models, stereotypes consist of trait associations with a particular group. Although an immense amount of information has been uncovered through the unidimensional framework, revisiting the tripartite model might shed some light on several unresolved issues, such as the link between implicit and explicit attitudes. This point will be revisited in the conclusion. Prior to this, however, distinctions must be established between implicit and explicit attitudes.

Measurement of Explicit Attitudes

Explicit attitudes refer to one's conscious beliefs. Self-report measures are thought to capture one's attitude toward a particular object or group. In early attitude research, respondents reported their evaluation or feelings on a Likert-type scale ranging from *strongly agree* to *strongly disagree*. For example, questionnaires reflecting what is referred to as "old-fashioned racism" asked respondents to what extent they agreed with statements such as, "Blacks are generally more aggressive than Whites" (McConahay, 1986; see also Lambert, Cronen, Chasteen, & Lickel, 1996).

Assessing racial attitude with blatant measures became problematic as society experienced a shift in values. In the United States, the advent of the civil rights era increased social consciousness and encouraged egalitarian norms that rendered simple self-report measures (face-valid scales) as outdated and inaccurate. Many viewed segregation and other racist practices as antiquated and inconsistent with their egalitarian values. Still others, despite holding negative racial attitudes, were unwilling to report them due to normative pressures to appear nonprejudiced (Dovidio & Fazio, 1992). In response to this concern, instruments such as the Modern Racism Scale (MRS) were developed to unobtrusively measure racial prejudice (McConahay, 1986). The questions were worded so that people unknowingly revealed their true beliefs. According to this measure and surveys, there has been a dramatic decline in racial prejudice and endorsement of stereotypes over the past two decades (Devine & Elliot, 1995; Judd, Park, Ryan, Brauer, & Kraus, 1995). Unfortunately, other research suggests that the decline in prejudice may be related in part to faulty measures of racial attitude (e.g., Crosby, Bromley, & Saxe, 1980; Fazio, Jackson, Dunton, & Williams, 1995). For example, the MRS is not unobtrusive as once thought and has met with accusations that it confounds political conservatism and racism (Sniderman & Tetlock, 1986a, 1986b). In other words, respondents who are simply conservative can be classified as racist by this measure. Also, if the measurement of explicit attitudes via self-report were truly reliable, then we might happily conclude that a vast majority of Americans no longer hold any negative prejudices against ethnic minorities. Of course, the continuing humiliating acts of prejudice (Feagin, 1991) experienced by many ethnic minorities along with shocking reports of violent racial incidents remind us that the eradication of racism is not complete. The knowledge that self-report measures were not solely sufficient motivated researchers to develop novel research techniques for measuring attitudes.

OVERVIEW OF IMPLICIT ATTITUDES AND STEREOTYPES

Interest in implicit attitudes has experienced a revival, with mounting evidence from cognitive, memory, and social research suggesting a distinction between implicit and explicit attitudes (Jacoby, Yonelinas, & Jennings, 1997; Shiffrin & Schneider, 1977). Implicit attitudes are defined as "introspectively unidentified (or inaccurately identified) traces of past experience that mediate favorable or unfavorable feeling, thought, or action toward social objects" (Greenwald & Banaji, 1995, p. 8). Research regarding automatic processing is analogous to implicit processing of information (e.g., Bargh, Chaiken, Govender, & Pratto, 1992; Fazio, Sanbonmatsu, Powell, & Kardes, 1986; Greenwald, McGhee, & Schwartz, 1998). Implicit or automatic processes are characterized as unconscious, uncontrollable, unintentional, and efficient. In contrast, explicit or controlled processes are described as conscious, controllable, intentional, and effortful (Bargh, 1989, 1994; Wegner & Bargh, 1998). The precise relation between these two types of attitude is disputed. However, recent evidence suggests there is flexibility within and perhaps overlap between both types of attitude (Bargh, 1989, 1994, 1996; Zbrodoff & Logan, 1986).

Implicit Stereotyping

A great deal of research and theory has focused on understanding implicit racial attitudes and its relation to using stereotypes for judgment (e.g., Devine, 1989; Dovidio, Kawakami, Johnson, Johnson, & Howard, 1997; Fazio et al., 1995; Greenwald & Banaji, 1995; Nesdale & Durkin, 1998; von Hippel, Sekaquaptewa, & Vargas, 1997;

Wittenbrink, Judd, & Park, 1997). Stereotypes are the cognitive companion of prejudice and are generalized group-based traits used to judge individual members of a group (Ashmore & Del Boca, 1981). (For a detailed review on prejudice, sexism, and racism, please refer to Chapter 10 of this *Handbook*.) Just as implicit attitudes exist, implicit stereotypes do as well. *Implicit stereotypes* are defined as "introspectively unidentified (or inaccurately identified) traces of past experience that mediate attributions of qualities to members of a social category"(Greenwald & Banaji, 1995, p. 15). Features or traits consistent with the group stereotype can become unconsciously activated on encountering a member of that group (Greenwald & Banaji, 1995; Hamilton & Sherman, 1994; Smith, Fazio, & Cejka, 1996; cf. Gilbert & Hixon, 1991). Allport's (1954) definition of prejudice is analogous to racial attitude in that it focuses on the affective reaction toward outgroup members. Thus, stereotypes and attitude may be conceptually distinct but are related in influencing overall judgment and behavior (Eagly & Mladinic, 1989; cf. Gardner, 1973).

Devine's (1989) groundbreaking studies on automatic and controlled processing and their relation to stereotyping provided the catalyst for much of the recent work in this area. Research on automatic and controlled processing has proceeded along the lines of the work on implicit and explicit processing; both seek to distinguish processing that occurs inside and outside one's awareness and control. According to Devine, both high- and low-prejudiced persons exhibit racial stereotyping at the unconscious level but exhibit differences in judgment at the conscious level. Thus, if a low-prejudiced person is somehow unwilling or unable to exert mental effort when processing information about another person, stereotypes will be used for judgment. Critics of Devine's work argue that the primes used in her work

mingled negative stereotypes with category activation and that stereotypical judgments are not inevitable at the unconscious level for those low in prejudice (Fazio et al., 1995; Lepore & Brown, 1997). Nevertheless, she demonstrated how the activation of implicit stereotypes influenced behavior.

Measurement of Implicit Attitudes

The development of response latency measures by cognitive psychologists introduced a novel way of measuring implicit attitude. In particular, semantic priming procedures have reliably demonstrated that paired associations facilitate responses. People are faster to respond to pairs of words, images, or even concepts that are already associated in memory than those that are not. Activation of implicit attitude occurs too rapidly for it to be solely driven by conscious processes, but it can be measured by these techniques (Banaji & Hardin, 1996; Bargh et al., 1992; Fazio et al., 1986). The logic of using response latency measures is that perceivers typically rely on highly accessible constructs activated from memory for judgment than newly constructed associations not consistent with our attitudes. This method of measurement is powerful because people can be unaware of or reluctant to articulate their beliefs. Thus, when using these measures for assessing racial attitudes, we can indirectly measure people's underlying attitudes toward concepts without directly asking them.

Research on Implicit Attitudes and Stereotyping

Over the past 15 years or so, numerous studies have been published on implicit attitudes and stereotyping. It is impossible to review all of them, but a few noteworthy studies employing different methods to assess implicit attitudes will be discussed. Special attention will be paid to the development and application of the implicit association test (Greenwald & Banaji, 1995; Greenwald et al., 1998). The Implicit Association Test (IAT) has been used extensively to document racial implicit attitudes (e.g., Greenwald et al., 1998; Neumann & Seibt, 2001; Neumann, Totzke, Popp, & Fernandez, 2000; Ottaway, Hayden, & Oakes, 2001; Rudman, Greenwald, Mellott, & Schwartz, 1999).

Response time measures (Dovidio, Evans, & Tyler, 1986; Gaertner & McLaughlin, 1983) and semantic priming methodology (Devine, 1989) are alternative ways to measure racial attitude. The basic premise of priming studies is that the prior presentation of a stimulus can influence the interpretation of novel information (Bruner, 1957). The primed information (e.g., words or images) activates a construct in memory that remains accessible while perceiving novel information. Higgins, Rholes, and Jones (1977) demonstrated that participants judge a character in a story in more favorable terms if they were recently primed with positive traits than if they were primed with negative traits.

Priming participants with words designed to activate the category for a particular group allows an assessment of implicit racial attitudes. Presumably, not only is the category activated, but the attitude toward that group is as well (Fazio et al., 1986). For example, to activate attitude toward Black people, Lepore and Brown (1997) subliminally presented White British participants with words or group labels associated with the racial category. High-prejudiced participants subsequently rated an ambiguously described person as aggressive and unreliable, whereas low-prejudiced people judged the same person in more favorable terms. Thus, the mere presentation of semantic group labels successfully activates the category and attitude toward that group.

Along similar lines, Fazio et al. (1995) employed faces instead of labels for their priming task. In addition, the study compared participants' responses toward African Americans obtained by the Modern Racism Scale and a priming task. White American participants completed the MRS scale and at a later session were presented with Black and White male and female faces on a computer screen. Immediately after the presentation of a face, participants judged the valence of an adjective word flashed on the screen (good vs. bad). The participants showed relatively faster judgments when White faces preceded positive adjectives and Black faces preceded negative adjectives. Also, MRS scores were not correlated with participants' responses on the priming task and were influenced by the presence of a White or Black experimenter. Most important, this study provided a severe blow to the claims made that the MRS is an unobtrusive measure of prejudice.

In another study, Wittenbrink et al. (1997) used a semantic priming task in which White American participants were first subliminally primed with the word *Black* or *White* and then asked to judge whether a string of letters presented on a computer screen constituted a real word or not (i.e., word or not word). The actual words were positive and negative stereotypical traits of Whites and Blacks. Participants also completed several explicit measures of prejudice. Participants' responses were facilitated when negative stereotypical words were preceded by the Black prime and the positive stereotypical words preceded the White prime. The explicit measures were highly correlated with each other and with implicit prejudice. Unlike Fazio et al.'s (1995) study, this experiment provides evidence that implicit attitudes are indeed related to explicit attitudes.

Research Using the Implicit Association Test

Implicit Association Test. Greenwald et al. (1998) developed the IAT as a measure of implicit attitudes. Participants' attitudes are inferred by their response latencies in categorizing psychologically congruent and incongruent paired target concepts (e.g., White + pleasant; Black + pleasant). Response latencies should be faster when categorizing implicitly associated concepts compared to pairs that are not associated a priori. For the critical trials, two concepts are assigned to a single response key (e.g., Black names and pleasant words), whereas the other two contrasting concepts are assigned to a different response key (e.g., White names and unpleasant words). Participants are asked to quickly press the response key that correctly categorizes the stimulus word presented on the screen. The IAT effect is calculated by subtracting the response latency of the congruent paired concept from the incongruent paired concept. The IAT employs numerous methodological controls for variables that could influence response latencies.

Research Studies Employing the IAT. The first published studies using the implicit association test demonstrated its validity in measuring implicit associations between affect or valence (pleasant vs. unpleasant) and categories (Greenwald et al., 1998). In Experiment 2, Korean American and Japanese American college students categorized typical Korean and Japanese surnames according to their ethnic group by pressing the appropriate computer key that was also used to differentiate pleasant or unpleasant words. Two paper-and-pencil questionnaires were used to assess explicit attitudes. For the feeling thermometer measure, participants rated their warmth or coolness toward the in-group and out-group. Participants also rated each group along a 7-point scale, anchored at each end by polar-opposite adjective pairs (e.g., *beautiful-ugly*). Next, participants answered questions assessing cultural immersion in their respective ethnic group. The results revealed IAT effects for both groups. That is, Korean

Americans' responses were faster when the category Korean shared the same response key as *pleasant* and Japanese with *unpleasant*. Japanese Americans showed the same effect for their own group. An additional effect was found for cultural immersion. Those participants reporting greater immersion in their culture showed larger IAT effects than those acculturated to the United States. Neither of the explicit measures revealed this difference among participants.

Experiment 3 was conducted similarly to the previous experiment, except that White American male and female college students categorized Black and White names along with pleasant and unpleasant words. Participants showed a clear implicit preference for Whites over Blacks on this measure. Explicit attitude measures did not reveal this preference, nor did these measures predict IAT responses.

Criticisms of Implicit Attitude Research. In response to Greenwald et al.'s study (1998) as well as others using the IAT, critics argued that Whites' unfamiliarity with African Americans as well as the African American names used in Experiment 3 may account for the large IAT effects obtained. Studies conducted by Ottaway et al. (2001) and Dasgupta et al. (2000) attempt to rule out some of these alternative explanations. Ottaway and colleagues controlled for subjective familiarity and frequency for Black, White, and Hispanic names. Dasgupta et al. (2000) statistically controlled for name familiarity and used pictures of unfamiliar Blacks and Whites as well as names for their stimuli. Both studies reduced the overall magnitude of the IAT effect but still demonstrated Whites' implicit preference for their own group over Blacks and Hispanics.

Employing these methodological and statistical controls rules out one version of familiarity, but more studies examining different concepts of familiarity remain necessary. Familiarity with names is not equivalent to familiarity with group members, nor is unfamiliarity with particular White and Black faces equivalent to unfamiliarity with the category and its actual members. It is important to keep in mind that the amount and type of actual social interaction may play a large role in moderating implicit attitudes. Social context must not be neglected. Recently, Dovidio, Kawakami, and Gaertner (2000) reported that intergroup contact along with recategorization into a common group identity reduced implicit stereotyping.

Thus far, it is unclear whether implicit and explicit attitudes are related. Some studies reveal a correlation between implicit and explicit measures of prejudice (e.g., Wittenbrink et al., 1997), but others do not (Fazio et al., 1995; Greenwald et al., 1998). These mixed findings may be due to differences in methodologies employed (for further discussion, see Brauer, Wasel, & Niedenthal, 2000). At this point, we do know that both implicit and explicit racial attitudes do exist and can be measured. According to Dovidio et al. (1997), explicit attitudes should not diminish in relevance, nor should we view implicit attitudes as somehow more "true" than explicit attitudes. Rather, each type of attitude might influence different aspects of behavior. Advancement of research and theory is clearly needed in this area so that we may better understand these relationships as well as the possibility of modifying attitudes and behaviors.

IMPLICIT LEARNING

Social psychologists have paid much greater attention to establishing the ubiquity of implicit attitudes as opposed to documenting their development. Unlike explicit learning, implicit learning is largely unconscious, unintentional, and not limited by cognitive capacity (Berry & Broadbent, 1988; Broadbent, 1989; Hayes & Broadbent,

1988; O'Brien-Malone & Maybery, 1998; Reber, 1992). Although the information is acquired unconsciously, whether the conscious has access to implicit knowledge is unclear (Hasher & Zacks, 1979, 1984; Lewicki, Hill, & Czyzewska, 1992; Reber, 1989). Two primary models account for implicit learning. Schneider and Shiffrin's (1977) model describes how information becomes implicit through frequent activation of associated constructs in memory. In this case, stereotypes become implicit through activation on frequent encounters with a stimulus from a particular category. For example, if a male perceiver associates the trait passive with female, the two concepts of *female* and *passive* will eventually become implicitly associated if frequently used when interacting with females.

Alternatively, Hasher and Zack's (1979) model posits that an explicit learning stage is not always necessary; implicit learning is hardwired and part of our information-processing system. Moreover, these innate processes "should be widely shared and minimally influenced by differences in age, culture, education, early experience, and intelligence" (Hasher & Zacks, 1979, p. 360). Differences in opinion among cognitive psychologists do exist concerning the boundary conditions of this type of implicit learning (for further discussion on this issue, see O'Brien-Malone & Maybery, 1998). In general, this model points to the extreme difficulties in tracing how the actual content or associations forming the basis of implicit stereotypes are developed. In fact, racial and gender stereotypes may be formed early in childhood just as other social categories are created.

What is potentially most disturbing about implicit learning is that we often do not and cannot anticipate what information people use to form these associations. In their essay, Miller and Swift (2000) recount a popular riddle to demonstrate this point:

A man and his young son were in an automobile accident. The father was killed and the son, who was critically injured, was rushed to the hospital. As attendants wheeled the unconscious boy into the emergency room, the doctor on duty looked down at him and said, "My God, it's my son!" What was the relationship of the doctor to the injured boy?

That people are stumped when solving this riddle reflects the difficulty when thinking of a woman as a doctor. In a cognitive sense, people are implicitly associating *doctor* and *male*.

A personal example illustrates this point. While playing with a toy car, my 3-year-old twin nephews stated that dads always sit in the driver's seat and moms sit beside them. Worried that somehow they were making a larger inference about gender hierarchical relationships, I suggested that Mom can drive the car and Dad can sit in the passenger's seat. Their refusal to accept my suggestion was especially puzzling given their reality. Eventually, I realized that it was not necessarily the media or another child's influence that led to their conclusion. Their father always drove the car when both parents were present. Thus, their perception of Mom's driving as more of an exception to the rule (she drives only when Dad is not around) than the norm is rooted in their experience. What can never be determined is how this information (and other examples we unwittingly provided) entered their unconsciousness and the sorts of implicit associations made.

Implications for Implicit Learning

We can see how associations are made without deliberate intent or awareness by the perceiver or communicator. Economic and social realities might provide one way for the formation of racially implicit associations by majority perceivers. In the United States, Hispanic and African Americans are underrepresented in the middle and upper socioeconomic classes. The majority of middle- and upper-class Whites live in rural or suburban areas away from economically disadvantaged minorities. For many Whites, interactions with African Americans or Hispanics are often in the context in which the minority member is a low-paying service provider. Limited interactions such as these as well as negative media portrayals of minorities might provide the foundation for implicit associations. Unbeknownst to both groups of perceivers, an implicit association might be formed between the racial/ethnic group category and a negative trait, such as poverty. Now, the overall valenced association formed for the minority group is negative or unpleasant. This negatively valenced association may lead to the storage of other unpleasant traits within this category. How negative traits tend to be associated with other irrelevant negative traits is analogous to the halo effect (Thorndike, 1920). The halo effect describes the tendency to form impressions of others by associating positive traits with other unrelated positive traits on the basis of limited information. Just as some people benefit from the halo effect (e.g., physically attractive persons), others may suffer from the opposite effect (for a more complete discussion on the halo effect and implicit attitudes, see Greenwald & Banaji, 1995). Thus, seeing or interacting with out-group members in a limited or impersonal fashion may facilitate undesired implicit attitudes that are subsequently activated on encountering members of the group. In no way is the obvious role of plain racism in the formation of implicit attitudes or stereotypes ruled out. What is being argued, however, is that in addition to racism, well-meaning people do acquire information and form personally deplorable associations without awareness or intent. The extent to which these associations are used for judgment and behavior of any real consequence is debatable.

In-Group Implicit Associations

Extending this argument further, the notion of implicitly learning prejudice is provocative because it implies that all of us, including ethnic minorities, may have learned to associate negative concepts with minority groups and positive concepts for the powerful majority group. Although published research on minority members' own implicit racial stereotypes does not exist, a closely related study by Jost, Pelham, and Carvallo (2000) provides evidence of out-group favoritism in Hispanics and Asian Americans. In this study, Hispanic and Asian American students preferred to participate in a "getting acquainted" study with a White stranger than someone whom they believed belonged to their own ethnic group. Although this study did not strictly examine implicit processes, their behavioral measurement was unobtrusive and unlikely to have aroused suspicions by participants. Another series of studies examining gender and racial groups demonstrates how group status affects implicit associations made by majority perceivers. In these studies, groups accustomed to having more power (i.e., males and Whites) over their respective out-groups showed varying favorable and unfavorable implicit attitudes as the power dynamic changed in the experiment (Richeson, 2000).

Research examining implicit gender stereotypes reveals different results. Male and female participants associated favorable gender stereotypes for the self and their own gender group (Rudman, Greenwald, & McGhee, 2001). According to this study, our self-esteem needs may protect us from implicitly stereotyping our own in-group. Given these mixed results, a closer look at the social stigma attached to particular group identities and its relation to implicit self-stereotyping is needed (for research on stigma and social groups, see Crocker, 1999; Dovidio, Major, & Crocker, 2000; Swim & Stangor, 1998).

The Role of Language

The acquisition and use of language can be viewed as another primary force by which implicit associations are formed. According to the noted linguist Edward Sapir (1963), language reflects the societal hierarchy and provides psychological status to subgroups. In this case, the powerful group creates terms used to describe less powerful groups. Feminists argue that our use of *man* to describe all humankind is a blatant reminder of patriarchal structure rather than a term of convenience without cognitive ramifications. In fact, research by Banaji and Hardin (1996) and McConnell and Fazio (1996) demonstrated that gender primes automatically activate stereotyping for both males and females. Thus, the mere presentation of a word, such as *nurse,* automatically activates the concept of female. Moreover, generic masculine terms such as *human* also produced an automatic activation of the concept male. Thus, group labels do carry an association with power status and favorability.

Allport (1954) noted the sway of language as well in his chapter titled "Linguistic Factors." In this chapter, he describes how ethnic labels used by majority perceivers to describe out-group members are often tainted with negative connotations. In fact, he concludes, "Prejudice is due in large part to verbal realism" (Allport, 1954, p. 187). An example of language evolving to reflect a shift in societal values and hierarchy is the ethnic/racial labels used to refer to African Americans. These labels changed as African Americans gained societal power and the rest of society decided that offensive labels are no longer acceptable. Although there is no single agreed-on term, African Americans, Native Americans, and other groups understand that reclaiming their right to choose their group labels is a rejection of subordination. In fact, choosing one's own group label may have even greater implications than once thought. Labels may serve as markers for which category will be activated and used by the perceiver. For example, in Germany, the label *Black* does not carry a negative connotation, as does *foreigner*. Neumann et al. (2000) used the IAT to examine how Germans react to the same exemplars identified by different category labels. White German students show an implicit preference for Whites over Blacks when the category label for Blacks was "foreigners." However, no such preference was found for the Black versus White IAT when the category label was "Black." One far-reaching implication of these results is that arguments over the "political correctness" of certain types of language should not be dismissed as petty and trivial. Terms deemed as politically correct may potentially activate different categories than their politically incorrect counterparts.

CONCLUSIONS

Social and cognitive psychologists' interdisciplinary efforts have benefited the entire field of psychology. Theoretical and methodological advancements have provided the foundation for interesting and important research. With these advancements, the primary research goal must remain the development and advancement of theories with these new tools. Novice and experienced researchers should address whether their findings fit into existing theoretical frameworks or whether modifying or creating new theories is required. Along similar lines, the structure of attitude as well as the relation between implicit and explicit attitude needs additional scrutiny. At this point, two contrasting models account for the relation (or lack thereof) between the two types of attitude, and both are empirically supported

(Brauer et al., 2000). However, improvement in both types of attitude measures is most likely necessary to form any conclusions. Revisiting the tripartite model for measuring both types of attitude might be one improvement. Conceptualizing both types of attitude as unidimensional may have erroneously led to an emphasis of one component of attitude over the others. For example, some explicit measures tap into more of the cognitive than the affective component, whereas the reverse exists in some implicit measures (Baggenstos, Khan, & Ottaway, 2001).

Finally, the crucial link is establishing the connection between implicit racial attitude and social behavior. Dovidio et al. (1997) showed that implicit activation influenced largely uncontrollable behaviors (e.g., blinking and visual contact). These results encourage further investigation of these types of effects. Establishing the boundary conditions for when implicit and explicit attitudes influence judgment and behavior will provide the foundation for developing successful interventions aimed at reducing prejudice.

It is difficult to form general conclusions about the link between implicit attitudes and behaviors because of the varying methodologies used. The area would greatly benefit from researchers systematically investigating the differences in results obtained by the use of different methodologies. One key difference in the various methodologies employed in these studies is whether or not participants are aware of the activation of implicit attitude. Classic priming studies have documented the effects of awareness on behavior. Awareness of primes can lead participants to adjust and correct for the activation, which can lead to contrast instead of assimilation effects (e.g., Herr, Sherman, & Fazio, 1983). Bargh and others demonstrated that subliminal activation of constructs influenced controllable social behaviors (Bargh, Chen, & Burrows, 1996). In this case, participants did not "correct" for the activation in their behaviors because they were unaware of the attitude activation itself. Studies using the IAT demonstrate how despite awareness of activation, participants' performance on a largely uncontrollable task (i.e., computer response time task) is still influenced by implicit activation of attitude. In this case, awareness does not help participants to "correct" for the influence of activation in their judgments. Implicit attitude research would benefit from integrating theories and research examining stereotype activation and inhibition (e.g., Bodenhausen & Macrae, 1998; Bodenhausen, Macrae, & Garst, 1998; Lambert, Chasteen, Khan, & Manier, 1998). Specifically, future research needs to examine whether the awareness of the activation of implicit attitudes influences overt and covert controllable behaviors in social interactions.

In any case, understanding prejudice and stereotyping at the implicit level is of incredible import. If implicit attitudes influence judgment and behavior outside the perceiver's awareness, then perhaps it explains why there is often disagreement between majority and minority perceivers regarding the specific acts and prevalence of racial discrimination today. Members of minority groups continue to feel the brunt of racial discrimination in both subtle and flagrant forms. The continual development of new methods for assessing subtle forms of prejudiced behaviors and attitudes may ultimately reduce the difference between racial groups in their perception of the frequency and extent of racial prejudice and discrimination. Members of the majority racial group often fail to appreciate the full effects of their unintentional racism (e.g., aversive racism) (Dovidio & Gaertner, 1999). For prejudice intervention techniques to succeed, recognition of one's own prejudices and a commitment to eliminating them must occur (Kawakami, Dovidio, Moll, Hermsen, & Russin, 2000; Moskowitz, Gollwitzer, Wasel, & Schaal, 1999). It is hoped that this program of research will encourage the development of equitable racial attitudes and behavior by capitalizing on people's strong egalitarian values and their genuine desire to be nonprejudiced.

REFERENCES

Allport, G. W. (1954). *The nature of prejudice*. Cambridge, MA: Addison-Wesley.

Ashmore, R. D., & Del Boca, F. K. (1981). Conceptual approaches to stereotypes and stereotyping. In D. L. Hamilton (Ed.), *Cognitive processes in stereotyping and intergroup behavior* (pp. 1-35). Hillsdale, NJ: Lawrence Erlbaum.

Baggenstos, D., Khan, S. R., & Ottaway, S. A. (2000, April). Cognitive and affective components of racial attitudes: Evidence from implicit and explicit measures. Presented at the annual convention of the Western Psychological Association, Portland, OR.

Banaji, M. R., & Hardin, C. D. (1996). Automatic stereotyping. *Psychological Science, 7,* 136-141.

Bargh, J. A. (1989). Conditional automaticity: Varieties of automatic influence in social perception and cognition. In J. S. Uleman & J. A. Bargh (Eds.), *Unintended thought* (pp. 3-51). New York: Guilford.

Bargh, J. A. (1994). The four horsemen of automaticity: Awareness, intention, efficiency, and control in social cognition. In R. S. Wyer & T. K. Srull (Eds.), *Handbook of social cognition* (2nd ed., Vol. 1, pp. 1-40). Mahwah, NJ: Lawrence Erlbaum.

Bargh, J. A. (1996). Automaticity in social psychology. In E. T. Higgins & A. W. Kruglanski (Eds.), *Social psychology: Handbook of basic principles* (pp. 169-183). New York: Guilford.

Bargh, J. A., Chaiken, S., Govender, R., & Pratto, F. (1992). The generality of the automatic attitude activation effect. *Journal of Personality and Social Psychology, 62,* 893-912.

Bargh, J. A., Chen, M., & Burrows, L. (1996). Automaticity of social behavior: Direct effects of trait construct and stereotype activation on action. *Journal of Personality and Social Psychology, 71,* 230-244.

Berry, D. C., & Broadbent, D. E. (1988). Interactive tasks and the implicit-explicit distinction. *British Journal of Psychology, 79,* 251-272.

Biernat, M., & Crandall, C. (1999). Racial attitudes. In J. P. Robinson, P. R. Shaver, & L. S. Wrightsman (Eds.), *Measures of political attitudes* (Vol. 2, pp. 297-411). San Diego: Academic Press.

Bodenhausen, G. V., & Macrae, C. N. (1998). Stereotypes activation and inhibition. In R. S. Wyer (Ed.), *Advances in social cognition* (Vol. 11). Mahwah, NJ: Lawrence Erlbaum.

Bodenhausen, G. V., Macrae, C. N., & Garst, J. (1998). Stereotypes in thought and deed: Social-cognitive origins of intergroup discrimination. In C. Sedikides, J. Schopler, & C. A. Insko (Eds.), *Intergroup cognition and intergroup behavior* (pp. 311-335). Mahwah, NJ: Lawrence Erlbaum.

Brauer, M., Wasel, W., & Niedenthal, P. M. (2000). Implicit and explicit components of prejudice. *Review of General Psychology, 4,* 79-101.

Breckler, S. J., & Wiggins, E. C. (1989). Affect versus evaluation in the structure of attitudes. *Journal of Experimental Social Psychology, 25,* 253-271.

Broadbent, D. E. (1989). Lasting representations and temporary processes. In H. L. Roediger III & F. I. M. Craik (Eds.), *Varieties of memory and consciousness* (pp. 211-227). Hillsdale, NJ: Lawrence Erlbaum.

Bruner, J. (1957). On perceptual readiness. *Psychological Review, 64,* 123-152.

Crites, S. L., Fabrigar, L. R., & Petty, R. E. (1994). Measuring the affective and cognitive properties of attitudes: Conceptual and methodological issues. *Personality and Social Psychology Bulletin, 20,* 619-634.

Crocker, J. (1999). Social stigma and self-esteem: Situational construction of self-worth. *Journal of Experimental Social Psychology, 35,* 89-107.

Crosby, F., Bromley, S., & Saxe, L. (1980). Recent unobtrusive studies of Black and White discrimination and prejudice: A literature review. *Psychological Bulletin, 87,* 546-563.

Dasgupta, N., McGhee, D. E., Greenwald, A. G., & Banaji, M. R. (2000). Automatic preferences for White Americans: Eliminating the familiarity explanation. *Journal of Experimental Social Psychology, 36,* 316-328.

Devine, P. G. (1989). Stereotypes and prejudice: Their automatic and controlled components. *Journal of Personality and Social Psychology, 56,* 5-18.

Devine, P. G., & Elliot, A. J. (1995). Are racial stereotypes really fading? The Princeton trilogy revisited. *Personality and Social Psychology Bulletin, 21,* 1139-1150.

Dovidio, J. F., Evans, N., & Tyler, R. B. (1986). Racial stereotypes: The contents of their cognitive representations. *Journal of Experimental Social Psychology, 22,* 22-37.

Dovidio, J. F., & Fazio, R. H. (1992). New technologies for the direct and indirect assessment of attitudes. In J. M. Tanur (Ed.), *Questions about questions: Inquiries into the cognitive bases of surveys* (pp. 204-237). New York: Russell Sage.

Dovidio, J. F., & Gaertner, S. L. (Eds.). (1986). *Prejudice, discrimination, and racism: Theory and research.* Orlando, FL: Academic Press.

Dovidio, J. F., & Gaertner, S. L. (1999). Reducing prejudice: Combating intergroup biases. *Current Directions in Psychological Science, 8,* 101-105.

Dovidio, J. F., Kawakami, K., & Gaertner, S. L. (2000). Reducing contemporary prejudice: Combating explicit and implicit bias at the individual and intergroup level. In S. Oskamp (Ed.), *The Claremont symposium on applied social psychology: Reducing prejudice and discrimination* (pp. 137-163). Mahwah, NJ: Lawrence Erlbaum.

Dovidio, J. F., Kawakami, J. F., Johnson, C., Johnson, B., & Howard, A. (1997). On the nature of prejudice: Automatic and controlled processes. *Journal of Experimental Social Psychology, 33,* 510-540.

Dovidio, J. F., Major, B., & Crocker, J. (2000). Stigma: Introduction and overview. In T. F. Heatherton & R. E. Kleck (Eds.), *The social psychology of stigma* (pp. 1-28). New York: Guilford.

Eagly, A. H., & Chaiken, S. (1993). *The psychology of attitudes.* Orlando, FL: Harcourt Brace.

Eagly, A. H., & Mladinic, A. (1989). Gender stereotypes and attitudes toward women and men. *Personality and Social Psychology Bulletin, 15,* 543-558.

Fazio, R. H., Jackson, J. R., Dunton, B. C., & Williams, C. J. (1995). Variability in automatic activation as an unobtrusive measure of racial attitudes: A bona fide pipeline? *Journal of Personality and Social Psychology, 69,* 1013-1027.

Fazio, R. H., Sanbonmatsu, D. M., Powell, M. C., & Kardes, F. R. (1986). On the automatic activation of attitudes. *Journal of Personality and Social Psychology, 50,* 229-238.

Feagin, J. R. (1991). The continuing significance of race: Anti-Black discrimination in public places. *American Sociological Review, 56,* 101-116.

Fishbein, M., & Azjen, I. (1975). *Belief, attitude, intention, and behavior: An introduction to theory and research.* Reading, MA: Addison-Wesley.

Gaertner, S. L., & McLaughlin, J. P. (1983). Racial stereotypes: Associations and ascriptions of positive and negative characteristics. *Social Psychology Quarterly, 46,* 23-30.

Gardner, R. C. (1973). Ethnic stereotypes: Attitudes or beliefs? *Canadian Journal of Psychology, 14*(2), 133-148.

Gilbert, D. T., & Hixon, J. G. (1991). The trouble of thinking: Activation and application of stereotypic beliefs. *Journal of Personality and Social Psychology, 60, 509-517.*

Greenwald, A. G., & Banaji, M. R. (1995). Implicit social cognition: Attitudes, self-esteem, and stereotypes. *Psychological Review, 102,* 4-27.

Greenwald, A. G., McGhee, D. E., & Schwartz, J. L. K. (1998). Measuring individual differences in implicit cognition: The implicit association test. *Journal of Personality and Social Psychology, 74,* 1464-1480.

Haddock, G., Zanna, M. P., & Esses, V. M. (1993). Assessing the structure of prejudicial attitudes: The case of attitudes toward homosexuals. *Journal of Personality and Social Psychology, 65,* 1105-1118.

Hamilton, D. L., & Sherman, T. L. (1994). Stereotypes. In R. S. Wyer & T. K. Srull (Eds.), *Handbook of social cognition* (pp. 1-68). Hillsdale, NJ: Lawrence Erlbaum.

Hasher, L., & Zacks, R. T. (1979). Automatic and effortful processes in memory. *Journal of Experimental Psychology: General, 108,* 356-388.

Hasher, L., & Zacks, R. T. (1984). Automatic processing of fundamental information: The case of frequency of occurrence. *American Psychologist, 39,* 1372-1388.

Hayes, N. A., & Broadbent, D. I. (1988). Two modes of learning for interactive tasks. *Cognition, 28,* 249-276.

Herr, P. M., Sherman, S. J., & Fazio, R. H. (1983). On the consequences of priming: Assimilation and contrast effects. *Journal of Experimental Social Psychology, 19,* 323-340.

Higgins, E. T., Rholes, W. S., & Jones, C. R. (1977). Category accessibility and impression formation. *Journal of Experimental Social Psychology, 13,* 141-154.

Jackson, L. A., Hodge, C. N., Gerard, D. A., Ingram, J. M., Ervin, K. S., & Sheppard, L. (1996). Cognition, affect, and behavior in the prediction of group attitudes. *Personality and Social Psychology Bulletin, 22,* 306-316.

Jacoby, L. L., Yonelinas, A. P., & Jennings, J. M. (1997). The relation between conscious and unconscious (automatic) influences: A declaration of independence. In J. D. Cohen & J. W. Schooler (Eds.), *Carnegie Mellon symposia on cognition: Scientific approaches to consciousness* (pp. 13-47). Mahwah, NJ: Lawrence Erlbaum.

Jost, J. T., Pelham, B. W., & Carvallo, M. R. (2000). *Non-conscious forms of system justification: Cognitive, affective, and behavioral preferences for higher status groups.* Research Paper Series Rep. No. 1626, Stanford University, Stanford, CA.

Judd, C. M., Park, B., Ryan, C. S., Brauer, M., & Kraus, S. (1995). Stereotypes and ethnocentrism: Diverging interethnic perceptions of African American and White American youth. *Journal of Personality and Social Psychology, 69,* 460-481.

Katz, D., & Stotland, E. (1959). A preliminary statement to the theory of attitude structure and change. In S. Koch (Ed.), *Psychology: A study of a science* (Vol. 3, pp. 423-475). New York: McGraw-Hill.

Kawakami, K., Dovidio, J. F., Moll, J., Hermsen, S., & Russin, A. (2000). Just say no (to stereotyping): Effects of training in the negation of stereotypic associations on stereotype activation. *Journal of Personality and Social Psychology, 78,* 871-888.

Kinder, D. R. (1986). The continuing American dilemma: White resistance to racial change 40 years after Myrdal. *Journal of Social Issues, 42,* 151-171.

Lakoff, G. (1987). *Women, fire, and dangerous things: What categories reveal about the mind.* Chicago: University of Chicago Press.

Lambert, A. J., Chasteen, A. L., Khan, S. R., & Manier, J. (1998). Rethinking our assumptions about stereotype inhibition: Do we need to correct our theories about correction? In R. S. Wyer (Ed.), *Advances in social cognition* (Vol. 11, pp. 127-144). Mahwah, NJ: Lawrence Erlbaum.

Lambert, A. J., Cronen, S., Chasteen, A., & Lickel, B. (1996). Private versus public expressions of prejudice. *Journal of Experimental Social Psychology, 32,* 437-459.

Lepore, L., & Brown, R. (1997). Category stereotype activation: Is prejudice inevitable? *Journal of Personality and Social Psychology, 72,* 275-287.

Lewicki, P., Hill, T., & Czyzewska, M. (1992). Nonconscious acquisition of information. *American Psychologist, 47,* 796-801.

McConahay, J. B. (1986). Modern racism, ambivalence, and the modern racism scale. In J. F. Dovidio & S. L. Gaertner (Eds.), *Prejudice, discrimination, and racism* (pp. 91-125). Orlando, FL: Academic Press.

McConnell, A. R., & Fazio, R. H. (1996). Women as men and people: Effects of gender-marked language. *Personality and Social Psychology Bulletin, 22,* 1004-1013.

Miller, C., & Swift, K. (2000). One small step for genkind. In E. Ashton-Jones, G. A. Olson, & M. G. Perry (Eds.), *The gender reader* (2nd ed., pp. 289-300). Boston: Allyn & Bacon.

Moskowitz, G. B., Gollwitzer, P. M., Wasel, W., & Schaal, B. (1999). Preconscious control of stereotype activation through chronic egalitarian goals. *Journal of Personality and Social Psychology, 77,* 167-184.

Nesdale, D., & Durkin, K. (1998). Stereotypes and attitudes: Implicit and explicit processes. In K. Kirsner, C. Speelman, M. Maybery, A. O'Brien-Malone, M. Anderson, & C. Macleod (Eds.), *Implicit and explicit mental processes* (pp. 219-232). Mahwah, NJ: Lawrence Erlbaum.

Neumann, R., & Seibt, B. (2001). The structure of prejudice: Associative strength as a determinant of stereotype endorsement. *European Journal of Social Psychology, 6,* 609-620.

Neumann, R., Totzke, T., Popp, C., & Fernandez, O. (2000). *Distinct attitudes despite similar targets: Comparing German students' attitudes towards "Blacks" and foreigners.* Manuscript submitted for publication.

Nier, J. A., Mottola, G. R., & Gaertner, S. L. (2000). The O. J. Simpson criminal verdict as a racially symbolic event: A longitudinal analysis of racial attitude change. *Personality and Social Psychology Bulletin, 26,* 507-516.

O'Brien-Malone, A., & Maybery, M. (1998). Implicit learning. In K. Kirsner, C. Speelman, M. Maybery, A. O'Brien-Malone, M. Anderson, & C. Macleod (Eds.), *Implicit and explicit mental processes* (pp. 37-55). Mahwah, NJ: Lawrence Erlbaum.

Ottaway, S. A., Hayden, D., & Oakes, M. (2001). Implicit attitudes and racism: Effect of word familiarity and frequency on the implicit association test. *Social Cognition, 19,* 97-144.

Reber, A. S. (1989). Implicit learning and tacit knowledge. *Journal of Experimental Psychology: General, 118,* 219-235.

Reber, A. S. (1992). The cognitive unconscious: An evolutionary perspective. *Consciousness and Cognition, 1,* 93-133.

Richeson, J. A. (2000). *Paradigms of power: Social stigma versus situational status in dyadic interactions.* Unpublished doctoral dissertation, Harvard University.

Rosenberg, M. J. (1960). A structural theory of attitude dynamics. *Public Opinion Quarterly, 24,* 319-340.

Rosenberg, M. J., & Hovland, C. I. (1960). Cognitive, affective, and behavioral components of attitudes. In C. I. Hovland & M. J. Rosenberg (Eds.), *Attitude organization and change: An analysis of consistency among attitude components* (pp. 1-14). New Haven, CT: Yale University Press.

Rudman, L. A., Greenwald, A. G., Mellott, D. S., & Schwartz, J. L. K. (1999). Measuring the automatic components of prejudice: Flexibility and generality of the implicit association test. *Social Cognition, 17,* 437-465.

Rudman, L. A., Greenwald, A. G., & McGhee, D. E. (2001). Implicit self-concept and evaluative implicit gender stereotypes: Self and ingroup share desirable traits. *Personality and Social Psychology Bulletin, 27,* 1164-1178.

Sapir, E. (1963). *Selected writings of Edward Sapir in language, culture, and personality* (D. Mandelbaum, Ed.). Berkeley: University of California Press.

Schneider, W., & Shiffrin, R. M. (1977). Controlled and automatic human information processing: I. Detection, search and attention. *Psychological Review, 84,* 1-66.

Shiffrin, R. M., & Schneider, W. (1977). Controlled and automatic human information processing: II. Perceptual learning, automatic attending, and a general theory. *Psychological Review, 84,* 127-190.

Smith, E. R., Fazio, R. H., & Cejka, M. A. (1996). Accessible attitudes influence categorization of multiply categorizable objects. *Journal of Personality and Social Psychology, 71,* 888-898.

Sniderman, P. M., & Tetlock, P. E. (1986a). Reflections on American racism. *Journal of Social Issues, 42,* 173-180.

Sniderman, P. M., & Tetlock, P. E. (1986b). Symbolic racism: Problems of motive attribution in political analysis. *Journal of Social Issues, 42*(2), 129-150.

Stangor, C. S., Sullivan, L. A., & Ford, T. E. (1991). Affective and cognitive determinants of prejudice. *Social Cognition, 9,* 359-380.

Swim, J. K., & Stangor, C. (Eds.). (1998). *Prejudice: The target's perspective.* San Diego: Academic Press.

Thorndike, E. L. (1920). A constant error in psychological ratings. *Journal of Applied Psychology, 4,* 25-29.

von Hippel, W., Sekaquaptewa, D., & Vargas, P. (1997). The linguistic intergroup bias as an implicit indicator of prejudice. *Journal of Experimental Social Psychology, 33,* 490-509.

Wegner, D. M., & Bargh, J. A. (1998). Control and automaticity in social life. In D. Gilbert, S. T. Fiske, & G. Lindzey (Eds.), *Handbook of social psychology* (4th ed., pp. 446-496). Boston: McGraw-Hill.

Wittenbrink, B., Judd, C. M., & Park, B. (1997). Evidence for racial prejudice at the implicit level and its relationship with questionnaire measures. *Journal of Personality and Social Psychology, 72,* 262-274.

Zajonc, R. B., & Markus, H. (1982). Affective and cognitive factors in preferences. *Journal of Consumer Research, 9,* 123-131.

Zanna, M. P., & Olson, J. M. (Eds.). (1994). *The psychology of prejudice: The Ontario symposium* (Vol. 7). Hillsdale, NJ: Lawrence Erlbaum.

Zbrodoff, N. J., & Logan, G. D. (1986). On the autonomy of mental processes: A case study of arithmetic. *Journal of Experimental Psychology: General, 115*(2), 118-130.

CHAPTER 15

Infant Mental Health in African American Families
A Sociocultural Perspective

SUZANNE M. RANDOLPH
SALLY A. KOBLINSKY
University of Maryland, College Park

In raising young children, families adopt child-rearing practices rooted in a culture that defines their beliefs and values, organizes their physical and social interactions, shapes their learning and coping styles, and influences their receptivity to developmental interventions. Accepting and respecting cultural diversity means recognizing that there are strengths and resources in families from *all* cultural backgrounds (Kaufmann & Dodge, 1997). Because culture and family provide a foundation for the development of children's cognitive and social competence, researchers, practitioners, and policymakers must recognize and build on cultural strengths inherent in families and communities.

Currently, there is a need to provide culturally responsive mental health services and programming to families from diverse backgrounds (Surgeon General of the United States, 2001), particularly those with young children (Randolph & Koblinsky, 2000). Culturally responsive programming incorporates "the importance of culture, the assessment of cross cultural relations, vigilance toward the dynamics that result from cultural differences, the expansion of cultural knowledge, and the adaptation of services to meet culturally unique needs" (Cross, Bazron, Dennis, & Isaacs, 1989, p. 1). Although many scholars support the importance of such programming, they also recognize serious shortcomings in the knowledge base examining how culture affects the developmental pathways of infants and toddlers (Shonkoff & Phillips, 2000).

A number of recent reports and volumes have emphasized the need to explore how cultural values and child-rearing practices influence infant and child development (Osofsky &

Fitzgerald, 2000; Shonkoff & Phillips, 2000; Zeanah, 2000). In 1996, Head Start researchers and policymakers were among the first to recommend that highest priority be given to new research that examines the challenges posed to early childhood programs such as Head Start as a result of increasing ethnic diversity, explores how ethnically diverse homes and Head Start environments interact to affect children's development, and embeds research studies within a community context (Phillips & Cabrera, 1996). The 1996 report further recognized that new pressures on low-income families to move toward economic self-sufficiency may influence the ways in which families from different cultural backgrounds are able to fulfill their parenting aspirations. Of particular importance is the need to examine how family members in multigenerational families (e.g., grandparents, aunts, and uncles) from various cultural backgrounds participate in the rearing of young children. Although the Head Start report focused largely on preschoolers in stable urban or rural family situations, the Head Start recommendations also highlight the need to consider cultural factors in providing services to children from birth to age 3, children in immigrant families, and children in migrant families. A more recent report, *From Neurons to Neighborhoods: The Science of Early Childhood Development* (Shonkoff & Phillips, 2000), further underscores these points by noting that

> the extent to which both the capacity and the resolve to learn more about the relationship between culture and early childhood development are strengthened will determine the ability to understand the rich diversity of human cognitive, social, emotional, and moral development beginning in the earliest years of life. (p. 69)

Within recent decades, the population of the United States has become increasingly culturally diverse (Fisher, Jackson, & Villarruel, 1998; Hernandez, 1999). In this chapter, we focus on African American families to illustrate how culture might influence parenting behaviors, attitudes toward mental health, and children's mental health outcomes. More specifically, we focus on low-income African American families. African American families represent only 12.9% of the U.S. population (U.S. Bureau of the Census, 2001). Yet African American children are more likely to live in poor families and experience persistent poverty than children in families from other racial/ethnic groups. For children younger than age 18, the poverty rate is 33%for African Americans, 30% for Hispanics/Latinos, and 9% for Whites. The poverty rate for young children (younger than age 6) is 37% for African Americans, 31% for Hispanics/Latinos, and 10% for Whites (National Center for Children in Poverty, 2000). For many years, poor African American families have been receiving services through programs funded by the federal government and other sources. Yet only recently have federal policymakers recognized the importance of giving mental health needs of young children a meaningful place on the national agenda (Chazan-Cohen, Jerald, & Stark, 2001; Knitzer, 2000; Mann, 1997; U.S. Department of Health and Human Services [DHHS], 2001; Yoshikawa & Knitzer, 1997). There is currently a paucity of research to guide the development of culturally appropriate interventions for these families.

Educators know relatively little about the normative development of African American children, the parenting values and behaviors of their parents, or the characteristics of the neighborhoods in which they live. In particular, relatively few studies explore the strengths and resources of African American families that reduce risks, protect children, and contribute to optimal development (Allen & Majidi-Ahi, 1989). Information is especially needed about parent and child mental health during the children's early years because the influence of a parent's (usually defined as mother's) mental health status on children's outcomes is well documented (Carnegie Task Force, 1994).

Recent brain research provides further evidence that child functioning from preschool onward hinges significantly on experiences before age 3 (Shonkoff & Phillips, 2000).

Given the limited knowledge base on the mental health of young African American children and other children of color, we explore in this chapter the sociocultural context of African American infant/toddler development in an effort to identify factors that contribute to understanding and addressing infant mental health from a sociocultural perspective. The purposes of this chapter are to increase awareness of how expectations and perceptions of infant mental health might differ by culture, discuss how the culture of the family and community can be used as a resource in addressing infant mental health issues, and increase awareness of the variations in experiences, beliefs, and practices within cultures that are important to the development of sound interventions. In addition, we provide suggestions about how practitioners can provide culturally competent mental health services and supports to infants and toddlers of color and their families. This sociocultural perspective has implications for the design of prevention programs, family and community outreach, and research and policy in childhood mental health.

This chapter is organized into three sections. The first section reviews contemporary theoretical frameworks that guide our analysis of early childhood development and other models to consider as we explore the role of culture in infant mental health. The second section reviews research that reflects the importance of understanding cultural variations in experiences, beliefs, and practices that might influence infant mental health. The third section presents a framework that can be applied to promote cultural competence in services and programs. Last, the chapter presents implications for practice, policy, and research to more appropriately address the mental health needs of infants and families of diverse backgrounds.

CONCEPTUAL FRAMEWORKS

Traditional Models. One of the most widely used conceptual models for understanding child development is the ecological approach. The social ecology model (Bronfenbrenner, 1986), also labeled a *contextualist model,* views child outcomes as dependent on characteristics of the child, parent, family, and community (or macrosystem), as well as the complex interactions among these variables. Some have argued that traditional ecological models are limited because issues in the macrosystem such as social history, social location, majority or minority status, and discrimination are excluded or so external that they make the model irrelevant. Therefore, an expanded conceptual framework—the integrative model of the development of competence in children of color—was developed by Garcia Coll et al. (1996) to account for such variables. This model considers the centrality of cultural form and meaning and extends the role of family and kin networks beyond that seen in traditional ecological models.

Macrosystem, or cultural-level, components of the integrative model include factors such as race, ethnicity, social class, and gender. The effects of social position are mediated by mechanisms such as racism and discrimination and may directly affect children through processes such as segregation or the direct experience of prejudice or, in the case of infants, indirectly through the experiences of racism or oppression of their parents. Thus, although all children in our society are exposed to similar settings, such as child care, preschool, and other early childhood environments, the impact of these environments on children of color must be considered from the standpoint of whether they inhibit, promote, or both inhibit and promote competence (Garcia Coll et al., 1996; Phillips, 1994). Inhibiting environments result from limited resources, such as the lack of mental health services in segregated neighborhoods, and from an incompatibility between the values and goals of the family and the particular environment (e.g., the child care setting or early childhood program).

A central premise of the integrative model is that families of color develop adaptive cultures—or systems of goals, values, behaviors, and social networks—that set them apart from the dominant culture. The coping mechanisms of these families, which develop in response to cultural/social stratification, are a product of both the group's cultural/political history and the demands of the immediate environment. Such demands directly influence family processes and child characteristics, which interact to influence the development of child competence. At the heart of the integrative model is the assumption that children of color cannot be judged by some universal standard but must be understood in the context of their specific ecological circumstances. Later in this chapter, we focus on a number of these contexts at the parent, family, and neighborhood levels in an effort to identify how culture may differentially contribute to outcomes among African American infants. Before presenting this review, we discuss some of the dimensions of the worldview of African Americans to better understand how these values may shape parenting behaviors and practices that have implications for infant mental health and mental health service delivery.

The Africentric Worldview. Many researchers have noted the failure of traditional social science approaches to tap the underlying cultural processes that guide the behavior of African American parents and their children (e.g., Akbar, 1974; Baldwin, 1981; Nobles, 1986). In response to this problem, several scholars have developed Africentric models for understanding African American individual, family, and community development (Akbar, 1974; Asante, 1980; Baldwin, 1981; Boykin & Toms, 1985; Hilliard, 1997; Myers, 1988; Nobles, 1986). These models recognize that strands of ancient African history, culture, and

philosophy manifest themselves in contemporary African American life and communities (Staples & Boulin Johnson, 1993). Central to these models is the notion of a *worldview,* a "complex, interacting set of values, expectations, and images of oneself and others, which guide and are guided by a person's perceptions and behavior, and which are closely related to . . . feelings of well being" (Frank, 1977, p. 27). This focus on worldview is not unique to African Americans but extends to other racial/ethnic groups in that most descriptions of these other groups also begin with identifying characteristics or preferences related to the group's region of origin (Frank, 1977; Shonkoff & Phillips, 2000).

The African worldview includes numerous dimensions that reflect ways in which African American people may think, feel, and act. Although some of these dimensions are found in other groups, it is the unique blend that defines the particular culture. It should also be noted that there are variations in the degree to which members of racial/ethnic groups adhere to the dimensions of their group's worldview. At least 10 dimensions comprise the African worldview (Boykin & Toms, 1985; Randolph & Banks, 1993) and may be helpful in interpreting African American parents' goals and behaviors, as well as the developmental outcomes among their infants.

The first dimension, *spirituality,* goes beyond religiosity to focus on the spiritual qualities of people rather than material possessions. For example, when asked what they want for their children in the future, some African American mothers may answer "to be happy" (a spiritual goal) rather than to "graduate from college" (a material goal). *Communalism* or an interpersonal orientation reflects an emphasis on group over individual goals, a preference for cooperation rather than competition, and a focus on people-related versus task-specific activities. Mothers with this communal focus may place a high value on young children learning to share their toys or engaging in play activities with other children, rather than pushing their children to "be the best" or "have the best" in the group. *Harmony* refers to the importance of integrating one's life into a whole, recognizing one's interdependency with the environment, and seeking unity rather than control.

A fourth dimension of the African worldview, *expressive communication* or *orality*, emphasizes transmitting and receiving information orally, through rhythmic communication and call and response. *Affect sensitivity to emotional cues* reflects the integration of feelings with cognitions and a synthesis of the verbal and nonverbal. For example, parents may signal children to alter their behaviors with a simple gesture or look. *Rhythmic movement* is expressed in gross motor behavior and reflects an interest in flexible yet patterned action. *Multidimensional perception* or *verve* is illustrated in the preference for stimulus variety in learning (e.g., visual, auditory, tactile, motor); both parents and children value experimentation. *Stylistic expressiveness* refers to the valuing of the individual's unique style, flair, or spontaneity of expression (e.g., the way one walks, talks, or wears an article of clothing) but is emphasized only when it facilitates group goals.

Still another Africentric dimension, *time as a social factor*, reflects the view that time is spiritual, not material or linear. For example, an event begins when the first person arrives and ends when the last person leaves, rather than at fixed points on a clock. There is also a recognition of the linkages of present time to the past and the future. Finally, *positivity* refers to the desire to see good in all situations no matter how bad they seem on the surface. This positive perspective—"making a way out of no way"—is thought to stop self-defeating behavior and generate positive problem solving.

Proponents of this model acknowledge there is much work to be done to identify African cultural dimensions that may be present in contemporary African American behavior.

However, these cultural characteristics already have been associated with positive functioning among African American school-age children (Boykin, 1983; Boykin & Allen, 2000; Boykin & Bailey, 2000), adolescents (Roberts, 1997), and adults (Gary & Berry, 1985). Moreover, parents of children who engage in racial and ethnic socialization practices that reflect Africentric values have been found to have more socially and academically competent children than those who have not adopted these practices (Greene, 1992; Spencer, 1983; Stevenson, 1994).

This chapter provides examples of how these Africentric dimensions may shape family and community perceptions of mental health, as well as parent-child interactions and family patterns of help-seeking behavior. This approach recognizes that not all African American parents may value these dimensions, so it is important to understand within-group differences in parenting beliefs that have implications for infants' mental health. Moreover, some contemporary social conditions that disproportionately affect African American families, such as poverty, HIV/AIDS, substance abuse, and community violence, may pose threats to values that have traditionally been viewed as strengths or protective factors and processes in African American families. We must be cognizant that the current state of our science limits our ability to systematically capture these Africentric values and socialization practices. A better science of African American children's early development will provide the most promising basis for addressing child mental health needs.

SOCIOCULTURAL CONTEXT OF AFRICAN AMERICAN INFANT DEVELOPMENT

Infant and toddler development in African American families is shaped by numerous factors in the ecology of the child: parents' goals, values, and behaviors; parental work demands; parental mental health; family organization; family strengths; and neighborhood contexts. A brief review of the existing literature, which focuses largely on the mother as parent, illustrates the important role of these ecological variables.

Parenting Goals, Values, and Behaviors

The parent is the most salient figure in the social world of most infants. Differences in parenting style and child-rearing strategies have been found to be associated with differences in children's cognitive and socioemotional development (e.g., Baumrind, 1972; Bradley et al., 1989). African American parents, like parents in any ethnic or cultural group, share a unique system of values and practices that overlap but differ in some ways from those of other cultures (Garcia Coll, 1990). With respect to infancy, for example, parents from different cultural groups may differ in their views concerning the fragility of newborns, their perceptions of and responses to crying, and the importance of encouraging specific developmental skills (Garcia Coll & Meyer, 1993; Lewis, 2000). For example, some researchers have speculated that the early motor maturity of African American infants is the result of mothers' frequent handling of the infants during the neonatal period (Lester & Brazelton, 1981), as well as mothers' expectations that their infants master motor tasks at earlier ages than White infants (Rosser & Randolph, 1989, 1996).

Unfortunately, researchers have conducted few comprehensive studies of the developmental expectations, socialization goals, or caregiving practices of African American parents of infants (Rosser & Randolph, 1989). Yet the growing number of young African American children living in poor, single-parent families (Children's Defense Fund, 1998) and the special child-rearing challenges of

mothers within the context of welfare reform argue for the urgency of such research. McLoyd (1994) asserts that "culturally anchored" research on racial/ethnic minority children of all ages is "a moral imperative."

Researchers have claimed that it is inappropriate to use standards of parenting derived from the study of middle-class White families to evaluate the functioning of minority, often low-income, parents and children (e.g., Levine, 1977; Ogbu, 1981). These researchers note that like other parents, minority parents attempt to foster behavioral competencies they feel children need to survive in their environment. For example, in a study of African American parenting in inner-city neighborhoods, Ogbu (1981) found that parents expressed abundant warmth in infancy, followed by an absence of warmth, inconsistent demands for obedience, and the use of physical discipline in the postinfancy period. Ogbu suggested that these strategies promoted traits that parents felt are essential for child survival, including self-reliance, resourcefulness, mistrust of authority, and ability to fight back.

To understand the socialization goals and parenting strategies of African American families, we must consider the sociocultural context in which they occur. Low-income African American mothers disproportionately experience situations that present threats to parenting, such as poor housing and violent neighborhoods (Stevenson, 1994). African American parents and other parents of color are also faced with the challenge of preparing children for environments that may be racially hostile. Yet despite these challenges, many parents succeed in raising healthy, competent children. To determine predictors of child resilience, we need to identify whether dimensions of parenting routinely addressed in the literature—such as warmth, nurturance, responsivity, and positive control—are expressed in culturally specific ways. The existing literature is limited by the fact that these parenting practices are understudied in ethnic minority populations and may not be well tapped by traditional parenting measures developed with populations of predominantly White families.

Maternal Work Demands

Another parent variable that may influence infant mental health is maternal work demands. African American women in working-class and middle-class families have a long history of labor force participation (Lerner & Noh, 2000; McLoyd, 1993; Randolph, 1995). Today, there is also a large number of low-income African American mothers with histories of receiving public assistance who are joining the workforce. Government programs such as Temporary Assistance to Needy Families (TANF) now have mandatory work requirements and lifetime limits. Many of the jobs available to low-income parents are stressful and unstable and demand variable work hours (Center for Future of Children, 1997). When work and family demands are in conflict, mothers may significantly reduce the time they have available to interact with their children (Howes et al., 1995). Moreover, demanding jobs may create psychological distress and dysfunctional parenting behaviors (McLoyd, 1990). Alternatively, the opportunity to work may provide parents with a sense of self-esteem and emotional reward, enhancing the mother's sense of competency in the child-rearing role (Howes et al., 1995). Given the potential for work involvement to be linked with child outcomes, it is important to understand the impact of work demands on specific populations of parents of infants and toddlers, such as parents moving from welfare to work, parents who migrate for seasonal employment opportunities, and immigrant parents.

Parental Mental Health

Parental mental health is a factor likely to be related to both effective parenting and child outcomes (Crnic & Acevedo, 1995; Field, 1992, 1995; McLoyd, Jayaratne, Ceballo, & Borquez, 1994; NICHD Early Child Care Research Network, 1999). Living in a low-income family and neighborhood may increase the probability of parents' emotional distress or depression because of exposure to negative situations and events, such as unpredictable income and community violence (Belle, 1990; Yu & Williams, 1999). For African Americans, parents' direct encounters with racism or discrimination are other major sources of emotional distress that have been found to relate to disrupted parenting practices, difficulties with parent-child interaction, and child adjustment problems (Johnson, 2001; Peters, 1981; Peters & Massey, 1983). Depression is a major problem among low-income women generally (Downey & Coyne, 1990; Lennon, Blome, & English, 2001). Samples of low-income African American mothers, in particular, show a high prevalence of depression (e.g., Harley, 2000; Koblinsky, Randolph, Roberts, Boyer, & Godsey, 2000). Previous research suggests that depression hinders mothers' ability to provide the nurturance, attention, and stimulation that children need to achieve developmental milestones (Downey & Coyne, 1990; NICHD Early Child Care Research Network, 1999), as well as develop a healthy self-concept and secure attachment (Cichetti, Rogosch, & Toth, 1998). When parents experience depression or emotional distress, they may lose interest in activities previously experienced as rewarding, including caring for their children (Willner, 1985). Depressed parents' preoccupation with basic survival issues reduces their physical energy, undermines their sense of competence, and diminishes their sense of self-control (Halpern, 1993). Several studies have reported a relationship between psychological distress and a reduction in the quality of parenting (e.g., Colletta, 1983; Simons, Beaman, Conger, & Chao, 1993).

Previous research has found that poor parents experiencing emotional or physical problems may provide inconsistent care for infants, pushing their children's needs into the background when they feel distressed. In an early study of Washington, D.C., parents in a public housing project, Jeffers (1967) found that parents experienced mood swings that contributed to discontinuity in the day-to-day care of infants. In another early study involving African American inner-city families in St. Louis, Rainwater (1970) discovered that low-income mothers alternated between enjoying and ignoring their children as a function of crises and other events that were demanding their attention.

A mother's temporary or persistent emotional distress reduces the attentiveness necessary to interpret and respond appropriately to infant moods and needs (Eldridge & Schmidt, 1990). Moreover, when an infant responds anxiously to a mother's depression, the child's response may overwhelm the mother, who then withdraws further in a kind of downward spiral. After a period, the infant may begin to withdraw from both the mother and other social interactions. Field, Heal, Goldstein, Perry, and Bendell (1988) found that 3- to 6-month-old infants with chronically depressed mothers appeared to internalize their mothers' psychological state, even when confronted with animated strangers. In view of the recognized importance of nurturance, consistency, and maternal validation in optimal development, there is a need to conduct additional research exploring how parents' mental health influences the developmental trajectories of low-income African American infants. Although currently understudied, the roles of African American custodial and noncustodial fathers and the influence of their mental health status on young children's development are also in need of attention. According to Knitzer (2000), "Evidence suggests that many low income fathers may have more contact with their children than the 'noncustodial' label implies, especially when their children are young" (p. 11).

Family Organization

Researchers and mental health professionals acknowledge the critical role of families in infant development. However, researchers and practitioners may need to define families in ways that more accurately describe elements of culture and ethnicity, relationships, and economic circumstances (e.g., Phillips & Cabrera, 1996; Randolph, 1995). For example, dimensions of the family sociocultural context such as income, education, language, country of origin, and acculturation should be considered. The family contexts of African American infants and other infants of color may differ from those of the majority population in several ways, and these differences may influence infant development and family interaction with the mental health system. For example, low-income African American families tend to be characterized by younger mothers, a higher percentage of single mothers, and a greater likelihood of kin residence (Dickerson, 1995; Staples & Miranda, 1980; U.S. Bureau of the Census, 1995, 2001). The presence of multiple caregivers (kin residence) may be a positive adaptation to the unpredictability that many poor families encounter (Halpern, 1993; Ornstein & Ornstein, 1985). Alternatively, infants living with multiple caregivers may experience inconsistent parenting practices that jeopardize the development of secure attachment and other positive socioemotional and cognitive outcomes.

Consideration of whether the African American family has a multigenerational configuration, with its implications for child-rearing responsibilities, will also provide better guidance about who to involve in mental health treatment strategies. Traditional approaches assume that the mother is the principal caregiver. However, knowledge of the specific family configuration may dictate that other family members should be included in parent involvement activities and educational or clinical interventions to handle an infant's special needs. Although there have been numerous studies of African American family structure, there is currently an absence of research concerning the influence of kinship on child rearing, parent-infant interaction, or developmental processes during childhood (Garcia Coll & Meyer, 1993; Jackson, 1993; Wilson, 1984). Studies of the sociocultural context of African American infant development need to explore who is parenting the infant and the impact of family configuration on infant mental health.

Family Strengths

One way in which African culture manifests itself in contemporary African American life is through family strengths. Twenty-five years ago, R. B. Hill (1997) developed a typology of African American family strengths that remains relevant today. This typology includes high achievement orientation, strong work orientation, flexible family roles, close kinship bonds, and strong religious orientation. Hill linked several positive aspects of African American family functioning and child and adult development to African cultural legacies: the resilience of low-income children, the high achievement orientation of single-parent families, the role flexibility of Black female-headed families, the low levels of substance abuse among Black youth, and the continuing influence of Black extended families. The extent to which African American family strengths serve to buffer the stressors experienced by low-income mothers with infants and toddlers is not known. However, it is presumed that mothers in families with multiple strengths are less likely to be socially isolated and better able to engage infants in warm, sensitive interactions than mothers in families with fewer strengths. More research is needed to identify the ways in which African American family strengths contribute to specific developmental outcomes among infants and toddlers.

Social Support

Social support is another aspect of family functioning with the potential to influence parenting and child development. Social support has traditionally been recognized as critical to the well-being of individuals in African American families (Hays & Mindel, 1973; R. B. Hill, 1993). Both relative and nonrelative ("fictive") kin networks have played an especially important role in providing support for poor urban African American families (Billingsley, 1968; Stack, 1974). African American families are more likely to receive child care assistance from extended kin, to perceive extended kin as significant, and to live in close proximity to extended families or in multigenerational family households than White families (Hofferth, 1984; Jayakody, Chatters, & Taylor, 1993).

The ability to form and maintain social networks can be crucial to a low-income mother's psychological well-being and parental functioning (McLoyd, 1990). Yet despite some studies showing that social support networks provide parents with child care, assistance with household tasks, and opportunities to pursue educational or employment goals (Hogan, Hao, & Parish, 1990; Letiecq, Anderson, & Koblinsky, 1996), the relationship between social support, parental functioning, and African American infant/toddler outcomes remains unclear. Moreover, some members of social networks may introduce stress into families rather than serving as a protective factor (McAdoo, 1986; Randolph, 1995). For example, nonparental caregivers may differ from parents in their attitudes about discipline or their developmental expectations for children at certain ages. Thus, before developing programs for families or individual plans for infants that rely on sources of informal support, staff should explore whether the parents' social support operates as a protective factor or a risk factor.

Neighborhood and Community Characteristics

Neighborhoods have been defined as physically bounded areas characterized by some degree of relative homogeneity and/or social cohesion. Recently, educators have stressed the importance of investigating neighborhood- and community-level variables that may affect parenting and child development. Potential variables for examination include the degree of neighborhood organization or disorganization, availability of resources, neighborhood norms and expectations for parenting and child development, and level of community violence. A few previous studies have found relationships between the quality of parenting, the availability of neighborhood resources for child rearing (Garbarino & Sherman, 1980), the perceived danger in the community (Kriesberg, 1970), and the degree of neighborhood transience and the proportion of older adults in the community (Cotterell, 1986).

Many families of color, including those of African American heritage, experience different neighborhood or other residential environments than the majority population because of their lower socioeconomic status. As a result, these families and their infants may encounter numerous problems associated with socioeconomic disadvantage, including substandard housing, seasonal migration, residential segregation, neighborhood disorganization, and high levels of community violence. Many minority neighborhoods are experiencing a loss or breakdown of the religious, social, and economic institutions that are vital to family life and provide potential routes out of poverty (Halpern, 1993). These neighborhood characteristics may contribute to survival-oriented patterns of parenting and relating to others (the "adaptive culture"), including isolation from family and friends, mistrust of neighbors (with whom parents formerly shared child care responsibilities), and restriction of infants and children from virtually all outdoor neighborhood play (Randolph, Koblinsky, & Roberts, 1997). Thus, neighborhood characteristics of low-income African American families may force parents to focus on particular dimensions of caregiving such as physical care and child protection at the expense of other behaviors such as play and language stimulation.

A basic issue in investigating the impact of sociocultural context on development is the definition of developmental or socioemotional skills and problems in infancy (Garcia Coll & Meyer, 1993). Generally, the normative standards by which child development specialists identify developmental strengths and problems reflect the dominant Anglo culture. Past traditions of using parenting and infant measures normed on Anglo families have resulted in the interpretation of differences as deficits, masked the strengths of many minority parents and children, and produced misguided intervention approaches (Garcia Coll & Meyer, 1993; Myers, Rana, & Harris, 1979). For example, a practitioner may try to reduce an African American toddler's "overactive, aggressive" behaviors, whereas parents reinforce those same behaviors because they feel they will protect the toddler in the violent neighborhood where they live. Thus, to better serve African American and other minority families, practitioners must not only seek parents' views about their infants' behaviors and their own parenting needs but must also address the challenges of the family's living environment. Devoting time to understanding important elements of infants' sociocultural environment will enable practitioners to incorporate family and community strengths in intervention efforts and honor the cultural diversity of families (Bredekamp & Copple, 1997; Phillips & Crowell, 1994).

The Macrosystem

This "adaptive culture" also includes the development of informal networks of support for child care, family assistance, and social and emotional support that could be tapped to provide services to families. The Black church has traditionally been one of these strongholds in African American communities (Billingsley & Caldwell, 1994), and "religion continues to be a vital resource for black parents in rearing their children" (S. A. Hill, 1999, p. 142). However, the church may be a less likely candidate for intervention today because of the migration of affluent African Americans from inner cities and inner-city churches, the diminishing communal orientation of many Black churches, and the decline in church attendance among African American youth (Randolph, Billingsley, & Caldwell, 1994). Sororities, fraternities, and other social or public service organizations abound in the Black community and have the potential to supply both instrumental and emotional support to needy families. Still another resource in the larger macrosystem is the system of historically Black colleges and universities, which have increasingly been recruited by federal agencies to partner with low-income communities in knowledge development and service delivery programs.

FRAMEWORK TO IMPROVE CULTURAL RESPONSIVENESS

An evolving framework that acknowledges the many influences on child development and attempts to provide more responsive mental health services for children of color is the cultural competence framework (Cross et al., 1989). Cross and his colleagues defined cultural competence as "a set of congruent behaviors, attitudes, and policies that come together in a system, agency or among professionals and enables that system, agency or professionals to work effectively in cross cultural situations'" (Cross et al., 1989, p. 13). In an effort to operationalize this concept and apply it to systems of child mental health services, Cross et al. (1989) identified five elements of culturally competent organizations:

1. They value diversity, recognizing that other cultures may exhibit certain values, behaviors, and preferences that differ from the dominant culture.

2. They have a system for cultural self-assessment, allowing them to select policies and practices that reduce barriers to participation for members of various cultural groups.

3. They are aware of the differential dynamics that occur when persons from diverse cultures interact, including differences in communication styles, help-seeking behaviors, and problem-solving styles.

4. They institutionalize cultural knowledge through the provision of cross-cultural training for staff, culturally appropriate services for clients, and the establishment of support networks of community leaders from different cultural groups.

5. They are able to adapt to diversity, adopting policies and procedures that reduce negative stereotyping and prejudice and promote greater appreciation of difference (Hernandez, Isaacs, Nesman, & Burns, 1998).

Cross et al. (1989) described a 6-point continuum of cultural competence anchored at the low end by cultural destructiveness and at the high end by advance cultural competence or proficiency. At the highest level, agencies hold families of racially/ethnically diverse backgrounds in high esteem. These agencies understand how individual, family, community, and cultural factors influence child development and parenting practices. Individual staff members at the advanced or proficient level draw on their cultural knowledge and contacts to design innovative approaches to service delivery, disseminate the lessons they have learned, and advocate effectively for children and families.

IMPLICATIONS FOR PRACTICE, POLICY, AND RESEARCH

Today there is a compelling need to develop new knowledge about families of color in order to develop culturally competent practices and policies that promote infant mental health. Although there is abundant new research to be done, the existing literature suggests a number of steps that can be taken to enhance culturally responsive programming and policies for infants, their families, and their principal caregivers.

Practice

Both ecological and sociocultural approaches to infant mental health emphasize the need to understand the infant within the context of the family, the community, and the culture. In assessing the family's well-being, practitioners working with African American and other infants of color must identify which members of the family serve as "parental figures," including parents, grandparents, other relatives, and "fictive kin." Efforts should also be made to learn about the cultural values, beliefs, and parenting goals that may influence parent/caregiver responses to infant behavior (e.g., crying, high verbal or physical activity). Equally important, mental health practitioners should attempt to identify strengths and resources in each family so that they may be used to enhance the success of intervention. For example, the emphasis on communalism and oral expressiveness in many African American families may facilitate bringing family members together in a cohesive, responsive, interdependent team to address infant needs. Early identification of family and cultural strengths, as well as challenges, will help mental health personnel to individualize services that promote infant emotional health and target problems at an early stage. Time invested in learning about the family will likewise improve the "working alliance" between the practitioner and parent(s) as they come together for the benefit of the child.

For some infants, parental factors such as maternal depression pose serious threats to mental health promotion. African American mothers may be especially vulnerable to depression because of their disproportionate exposure to poverty, racism, discrimination, and related stressors. Mental health specialists should draw on their knowledge of the values, worldviews, and life experiences of mothers from specific cultural groups to provide needed outreach and lessen the stigma often associated with mental health assistance. Practitioners working with African American mothers, for example, may employ strategies that focus on communalism, harmony, and positivity to expand social support networks, reduce isolation, and increase mothers' expression of positive affect toward their infants. Establishing a trusting relationship with the depressed mother, which includes respect for her culture and life experiences, will help her to obtain therapeutic services for herself and her child.

Practitioners should also consider maternal work demands in planning and designing mental health services for families with infants and toddlers. In some instances, work pressures such as temporary placements or frequent shift changes may interfere with optimal parenting and adherence to mental health appointments. Agencies may need to offer flexible service hours or arrangements to accommodate parents' variable work schedules. Some parents of color may encounter racism and discrimination on the job, draining their emotional reserves for parenting. Such parents may need assistance in dealing with work-related stress so that they can be more emotionally available to their children. Still other working parents may have access to job-related resources that will help them to address their children's mental health needs, such as health insurance, employee assistance, child care subsidies, or family and medical leave. In conducting mental health assessments of client families, practitioners should also include the work environment as a potential source of both assets and problems.

Culturally responsive mental health services focus not only on the family but also on the larger community. Knowledge of community factors that may compromise mental health is particularly important in working with ethnic minority families, as African American and Hispanic families are more likely to confront poverty and other adverse circumstances than White families (Shonkoff & Phillips, 2000). Practitioners must be aware of the specific challenges that families encounter in their neighborhoods and communities, including the presence of poor housing, homelessness, violence, drug activity, and other problems linked to poverty. Such information may dictate the times, places, and conditions under which families will seek mental health assistance for themselves and their children.

Community assessments should not only investigate neighborhood stressors but also identify community strengths, including the activities of health agencies, churches/mosques, educational programs (e.g., Early Head Start), community organizations (e.g., Big Brothers/ Big Sisters, Urban League), and public service sororities/fraternities. Home visitation programs, in particular, provide opportunities for practitioners to enhance infant mental health in a community context because of their focus on environmental health, quality of caregiving, cultural rituals and routines, and the family's social support system. Mental health specialists who maintain partnerships with community agencies and cultural groups will increase opportunities for families to obtain culturally sensitive assistance that promotes family stability and infant emotional health.

Policies

With our increasingly diverse society, it is especially important that public policies recognize cultural differences in child development and extend mental health outreach to more families of color. The U.S. Surgeon General's reports on mental health (Surgeon General of the United States, 2000, 2001) and the Healthy People 2010 objectives (DHHS, 2000) articulate the need to offer a wider range of mental health services to infants and parents from diverse cultural backgrounds. The Head Start performance standards (DHHS, 1995-1996) for mental health recognize the critical importance of the early parent-child relationship in emotional adjustment and provide guidelines for promoting infant mental health in a community and cultural context.

Comprehensive, community-based mental health systems are needed to address the specific problems, strengths, and resources of families within targeted communities. Mental health agencies must incorporate diversity issues and messages into their policies, services, program materials, and office décor so that families will experience respect for their individual cultures. Hiring mental health staff who reflect the cultural groups and neighborhoods served is one way to affirm commitment to culturally responsive practice. However, it should be noted that the hiring of such staff is not sufficient for cultural competence; diversity training and retraining of all agency staff, from board members to frontline workers, are essential. Policymakers should seek to ensure a broad continuum of respectful care by providing training in culturally competent mental health practices for current practitioners, early childhood educators, college students entering the mental health professions, and others involved in working with infants and toddlers. Policies may establish ways for agencies within a community network to meet regularly, exchange information, discuss referrals, and identify neighborhood resources (e.g., grandmothers who may counsel depressed mothers from the same cultural background) to address infant and parental mental health needs. The challenge is to develop and maintain a coordinated system of practitioners, educators, caregivers, and programs that value cultural diversity and support healthy emotional development of young children.

Research

Ultimately, the development of sound, culturally responsive policies and practices to promote positive infant mental health will require the expansion of basic and applied research involving African American and other families of color. Scientific evidence is needed to address the complexity of designing programs for these families and their communities and to help policymakers formulate strategies that recognize minority family strengths and challenges. Researchers must begin by expanding traditional theoretical and conceptual frameworks to incorporate the worldviews of the target populations and to acknowledge the cultural integrity of the communities to which this research, policy, and practice will be directed. This conceptual shift, or "new way of knowing," requires use of more integrative models (e.g., Garcia Coll et al., 1996), as well as a research agenda that targets more diverse populations and issues of cultural relevancy.

Future research on infant mental health must develop and employ culturally sensitive measures for tapping the parenting values, skills, and behaviors of ethnic minority families. In assessing these families, researchers must also take note of the potential heterogeneity within cultural groups. For example, African American parents living in the same neighborhood may have childhood roots in the United States, Haiti, or East Africa, bringing different beliefs and perspectives to their parenting of infants. Investigators must make efforts to learn more about family histories than the parents' racial/ethnic group. It should also be emphasized that despite the preponderant focus on poor single-parent families in this chapter, African American families are found across a wide range of socioeconomic categories and family forms. There is a particular need for studies that examine the impact of fathers and father figures on infant mental health.

Additional research is also needed to develop culturally appropriate tools for assessing parent-infant interaction and infant emotional development and mental health. Observational measures of parent-infant interaction in naturalistic settings—such as homes, child care centers, and community programs—offer opportunities to identify emotional tones, approaches to learning, and interactive styles that are more prevalent among parents or caregivers from particular cultures and that may be influencing infant mental health. Finally, there is a need to examine which types of infant mental health interventions work best for specific families and why. Such investigations may address a variety of factors, including age of the child, cultural background of the family, other family characteristics, and community strengths and stressors.

CONCLUSION

Mental health practitioners, early childhood educators, and policymakers have unique opportunities to work with families from diverse backgrounds to promote infant mental health. There is an urgent need to examine how cultural knowledge and culturally responsive health practices can be used as a resource in mental health prevention and intervention. Development of a research, policy, and practice agenda that is based on greater understanding of the worldviews, values, and life experiences of families of color will enable researchers to offer improved guidance, support, and mental health services to infants and their parents or caregivers.

REFERENCES

Akbar, N. (1974). Awareness: The key to Black mental health. *Journal of Black Psychology, 1,* 30-37.

Allen, L., & Majidi-Ahi, S. (1989). Black American children. In J. T. Gibbs & L. N. Huang (Eds.), *Children of color: Psychological interventions with minority youth* (pp. 148-178). San Francisco: Jossey-Bass.

Asante, M. (1980). *Afrocentricity: The theory of social change.* Buffalo, NY: Amulefi.

Baldwin, J. (1981). Notes on Afrocentric theory of personality. *The Western Journal of Black Studies, 5,* 172-177.

Baumrind, D. (1972). An exploratory study of socialization effects on Black children: Some Black-White comparisons. *Child Development, 43,* 261-267.

Belle, D. (1990). Poverty and women's health. *American Psychologist, 45*(3), 385-389.

Billingsley, A. (1968). *Black families in White America.* Englewood Cliffs, NJ: Prentice Hall.

Billingsley, A., & Caldwell, C. H. (1994). The social relevance of the contemporary Black church. *National Journal of Sociology, 8*(1-2), 1-23.

Boykin, A. W. (1983). On academic task performance and Afro-American children. In J. R. Spence (Ed.), *Achievements and achievement motives* (pp. 324-371). Boston: Freeman.

Boykin, A. W., & Allen, B. (2000). Enhancing African American children's learning and motivation: Evolution of the verve and movement expressiveness paradigms. In R. Jones (Ed.), *African American children, youth, & parenting.* Hampton, VA: Cobb & Henry.

Boykin, A. W., & Bailey, C. T. (2000). *Experimental research on the role of cultural factors in school relevant cognitive functioning: Home environment, cultural orientation and individual differences factors* (Center for Research on the Education of Students Placed at Risk [CRESPAR], Technical Rep. No. 43). Washington, DC: Howard University.

Boykin, W., & Toms, F. D. (1985). Black child socialization: A conceptual framework. In H. P. McAdoo & J. L. McAdoo (Eds.), *Black children: Social, educational, and parental environments* (pp. 33-51). Beverly Hills, CA: Sage.

Bradley, R. H., Caldwell, B. M., Rock, S. L., Barnard, K. E., Gray, C., Hammond, M. A., Mitchell, S., Siegel, L., Ramey, C. T., Gottfried, A. W., & Johnson, D. L. (1989). Home environment and cognitive development in the first three years of life: A collaborative study involving six sites and three ethnic groups in North America. *Developmental Psychology, 25,* 217-235.

Bredekamp, S., & Copple, C. (Eds.). (1997). *Developmentally appropriate practice in early childhood programs* (Rev. ed.). Washington, DC: National Association for the Education of Young Children.

Bronfenbrenner, U. (1986). Ecology of the family as a context for human development: Research perspectives. *Developmental Psychology, 22*(6), 723-742.

Carnegie Task Force on Meeting the Needs of Young Children. (1994, April). *Starting points: Meeting the needs of our youngest children.* New York: Carnegie Corporation.

Center for the Future of Children. (1997). Children and poverty. In R. E. Behrman (Ed.), *The future of children* (Vol .7, p. 1). Los Angeles: The David and Lucille Packard Foundation.

Chazan-Cohen, R., Jerald, J., & Stark, D. R. (2001). A commitment to supporting the mental health of our youngest children. *Zero to Three, 22*(1), 4-12.

Children's Defense Fund. (1998). *The state of America's children: Yearbook 1998.* Washington, DC: Author.

Cichetti, D., Rogosch, F. A., & Toth, S. L. (1998). Maternal depressive disorder and contextual risk: Contributions to the development of attachment insecurity and behavior problems in toddlerhood. *Development and Psychopathology, 10,* 283-300.

Colletta, N. D. (1983). At risk for depression: A study of young mothers. *Journal of Genetic Psychology, 142,* 301-310.

Cotterell, J. (1986). Work and community influences on the quality of child rearing. *Child Development, 57,* 362-374.

Crnic, K., & Acevedo, M. (1995). Everyday stresses and parenting. In M. H. Bornstein (Ed.), *Handbook of parenting: Vol. 4. Applied and practical* parenting (pp. 277-297). Mahwah, NJ: Lawrence Erlbaum.

Cross, T. L., Bazron, B. J., Dennis, K. W., & Isaacs, M. R. (1989). *Towards a culturally competent system of care: A monograph on effective services for minority children who are severely emotionally disabled.* Washington, DC: CASSP Technical Assistance Center, Georgetown University Child Development Center.

Dickerson, B. (Ed.). (1995). *African American single women: Understanding their lives and their families.* Thousand Oaks, CA: Sage.

Downey, G., & Coyne, J. (1990). Children of depressed parents: An integrative review. *Psychological Bulletin, 108*(1), 50-76.

Eldridge, A., & Schmidt, E. (1990). The capacity to parent: A self psychological approach to parent-child psychotherapy. *Clinical Social Work Journal, 18*(4), 339-351.

Field, T. (1992). Infants of depressed mothers. *Development and Psychopathology, 4,* 49-66.

Field, T. (1995). Psychologically depressed parents. In M. H. Bornstein (Ed.), *Handbook of parenting: Vol. 4. Applied and practical parenting* (pp. 85-99). Mahwah, NJ: Lawrence Erlbaum.

Field, T., Heal, B., Goldstein, S., Perry, D., & Bendell, D. (1988). Depressed behavior even with nondepressed adults. *Child Development, 59,* 1569-1579.

Fisher, C. B., Jackson, J. F., & Villarruel, F. A. (1998). The study of African American and Latin American children and youth. In W. Damon & R. M. Lerner (Eds.), *Handbook of child psychology: Vol. 1: Theoretical models of human development* (5th ed., pp. 1145-1207). New York: John Wiley.

Frank, J. D. (1977). *Persuasion and healing.* New York: Schoken.

Garbarino, J., & Sherman, D. (1980). High-risk neighborhoods and high-risk families: The human ecology of child maltreatment. *Child Development, 51,* 88-198.

Garcia Coll, C. (1990). Developmental outcome of minority infants: A process-oriented look into our beginnings. *Child Development, 61,* 270-289.

Garcia Coll, C., Lamberty, G., Jenkins, R., McAdoo, H. P., Crnic, K., Wasik, B. H., & Vazquez Garcia, H. (1996). An integrative model for the study of developmental competencies in minority children. *Child Development, 67,* 1891-1914.

Garcia Coll, C., & Meyer, E. C. (1993). The sociocultural context of infant development. In C. H. Zeanah, Jr. (Ed.), *Handbook of infant mental health* (pp. 56-69). New York: Guilford.

Gary, L., & Berry, G. (1985). Predicting attitudes toward substance use in a Black community: Implications for prevention. *Community Mental Health Journal, 21,* 42-51.

Greene, B. A. (1992). Racial socialization as a tool in psychotherapy with African American children. In L. Vargus & J. D. Koss-Chioino (Eds.), *Working with culture* (pp. 63-81). San Francisco: Jossey-Bass.

Halpern, R. (1993). Poverty and infant development. In C. H. Zeanah, Jr. (Ed.), *Handbook of infant mental health* (pp. 73-86). New York: Guilford.

Harley, T. L. (2000). *Parenting behaviors of depressed and nondepressed homeless and housed mothers of young children.* Unpublished master's thesis, University of Maryland, College Park, MD.

Hays, W. C., & Mindel, C. H. (1973). Extended kinship relations in Black and White families. *Journal of Marriage and the Family, 35,* 51-56.

Hernandez, D. J. (Ed.). (1999). *Children of immigrants: Health, adjustment, and public assistance.* Washington, DC: National Academy Press.

Hernandez, M., Isaacs, M. R., Nesman, T., & Burns, D. (1998). Perspectives on culturally competent systems of care. In M. Hernandez & M. R. Isaacs (Eds.), *Promoting cultural competence in children's mental health services* (pp. 1-25). Baltimore: Brookes.

Hill, R. B. (1993). Dispelling myths and building strengths: Supporting African American families. *Family Resource Coalition Report, 1,* 3-5.

Hill, R. B. (1997). *The strengths of African American families: Twenty-five years later.* Washington, DC: R&B Publishers.

Hill, S. A. (1999). *African American children: Socialization and development in families.* Thousand Oaks, CA: Sage.

Hilliard, A. G. (1997). *SBA: The reawakening of the African mind.* Gainesville, FL: Makare.

Hofferth, S. L. (1984). Kin networks, race, and family structure. *Journal of Marriage and the Family, 46,* 791-806.

Hogan, D. P., Hao, L., & Parish, W. L. (1990). Race, kin networks, and assistance to mother-headed families. *Social Forces, 68,* 797-812.

Howes, C., Sakai, L. M., Shinn, M., Phillips, D., Galinsky, E., & Whitebook, M. (1995). Race, social class, and maternal working conditions as influences on children's development. *Journal of Applied Developmental Psychology, 16,* 107-124.

Jackson, J. (1993). Multiple caregiving among African Americans and infant attachment: The need for an emic approach. *Human Development, 36*(2), 87-102.

Jayakody, R., Chatters, L. M., & Taylor, R. J. (1993). Family support to single and married African American mothers: The provision of financial, emotional, and child care assistance. *Journal of Marriage and Family, 55,* 261-281.

Jeffers, C. (1967). *Living poor.* Ann Arbor, MI: Ann Arbor Press.

Johnson, D. J. (2001). Parental characteristics, racial stress, and racial socialization processes as predictors of racial coping in middle childhood. In A. M. Neal-Barnett, J. Contreras, & K. Kerns (Eds.), *Forging links: African American children clinical developmental perspectives* (pp. 57-74). New York: Praeger.

Kaufmann, R. K., & Dodge, J. M. (1997). *Prevention and early interventions for young children at risk for mental health and substance abuse problems and their families: A background paper.* Unpublished manuscript, Georgetown University, Washington, DC.

Knitzer, J. (2000). *Promoting resilience: Helping young children and parents affected by substance abuse, domestic violence, and depression in the context of welfare reform* (Children and Welfare Reform Issue Brief No. 8). New York: National Center for Children in Poverty. Retrieved August 10, 2001, from www.nccp.org

Koblinsky, S. A., Randolph, S. M., Roberts, D. D., Boyer, W., & Godsey, E. (2000, June). *Parenting skills of depressed and non-depressed African American mothers and female caregivers of Head Start children in violent neighborhoods.* Paper presented at a symposium on mental health at Head Start's Fifth National Research Conference, Washington, DC.

Kriesberg, L. (1970). *Mothers in poverty: A study of fatherless families.* Chicago: Adline.

Lennon, M. C., Blome, J., & English, K. (2001, April). *Depression and low-income women: Challenges for TANF and welfare-to-work policies and programs.*

Paper presented at the Research Forum on Children, Families and the New Federalism at the National Center for Children in Poverty, Mailman School of Public Health, Columbia University, New York. Retrieved August 10, 2001, from www.nccp/org

Lerner, J. V., & Noh, E. R. (2000). Maternal employment influences on early adolescent development: A contextual view. In R. D. Taylor & M. C. Wang (Eds.), *Resilience across contexts: Family, work, culture, and community* (pp. 121-145). Mahwah, NJ: Lawrence Erlbaum.

Lester, B., & Brazelton, T. B. (1981). Cross-cultural assessment of neonatal behavior. In H. Stevenson & D. Wagner (Eds.), *Cultural perspectives on child development*. San Francisco: Freeman.

Letiecq, B. L., Anderson, E. A., & Koblinsky, S. A. (1996). Social support of homeless and permanently housed low-income mothers with young children. *Family Relations, 45,* 265-272.

Levine, R. A. (1977). Child rearing as a cultural adaptation. In P. H. Leiderman, S. R. Tulkin, & A. Rosenfeld (Eds.), *Culture and infancy* (pp. 15-27). New York: Academic Press.

Lewis, M. (2000). The cultural context of infant mental health: The developmental niche of infant-caregiver relationships. In C. H. Zeanah (Ed.), *Handbook of infant mental health* (pp. 91-107). New York: Guilford.

Mann, T. L. (1997). Promoting the mental health of infants and toddlers in Early Head Start: Responsibilities, partnerships, and supports. *Zero to Three, 18*(2), 37-40.

McAdoo, H. P. (1986). Strategies used by Black single mothers against stress. In M. Simms & J. Malveaux (Eds.), *Slipping through the cracks: The status of Black women* (pp. 153-156). New Brunswick, NJ: Transaction Books.

McLoyd, V. C. (1990). The impact of economic hardship on Black families and children: Psychological distress, parenting, and socioemotional development. *Child Development, 61,* 311-346.

McLoyd, V. C. (1993). Employment among African American mothers in dual earner families: Antecedents and consequences for family life and child development. In J. Frankel (Ed.), *The employed mother and the family context.* New York: Springer.

McLoyd, V. C. (1994). Research in the service of poor and ethnic/racial minority children: A moral imperative. *Family and Consumer Science Research Journal, 23,* 56-66.

McLoyd, V. C., Jayaratne, T., Ceballo, R., & Borquez, J. (1994). Unemployment and work interruption among African American single mothers: Effects on parenting and adolescent socioemotional functioning. *Child Development, 65,* 562-589.

Myers, H. F., Rana, P. G., & Harris, M. (1979). *Black child development in America, 1927-1977.* Westport, CT: Greenwood.

Myers, L. J. (1988). *Understanding an Afrocentric world view: Introduction to an optimal psychology.* Dubuque, IA: Kendall/Hunt.

National Center for Children in Poverty. (2000). *Children in poverty* (Fact sheet). Retrieved August 10, 2001, from www.nccp.org.

NICHD Early Child Care Research Network. (1999). Chronicity of maternal depressive symptoms, maternal sensitivity, and child functioning at 36 months. *Developmental Psychology, 35*(5), 1297-1310.

Nobles, W. W. (1986). *African psychology: Toward its reclamation, reascension, and revitalization.* Oakland, CA: Black Family Institute.

Ogbu, J. (1981). Origins of human competence: A cultural ecological perspective. *Child Development, 52,* 413-429.

Ornstein, A., & Ornstein, P. (1985). Parenting as a function of the adult self: A psychoanalytic developmental perspective. In E. J. Anthony & G. Pollock (Eds.), *Parental influences in health and disease.* Boston: Little, Brown.

Osofsky, J., & Fitzgerald, H. (Eds.). (2000). *Handbook of infant mental health* (Vol. 1.). New York: John Wiley.

Peters, M. F. (1981). Parenting in Black families with young children: A historical perspective. In H. P. McAdoo (Ed.), *Black families* (pp. 211-224). Beverly Hills, CA: Sage.

Peters, M. F., & Massey, G. C. (1983). Chronic vs. mundane stress in family stress theories: The case of the Black families in White America. *Marriage and Family Review, 6,* 193-218.

Phillips, C. B. (1994). The movement of African-American children through socio-cultural contexts. In B. L. Malory & R. S. New (Eds.), *Diversity and developmentally appropriate practices: Challenges for early childhood education* (pp. 137-154). New York: Teachers College Press.

Phillips, D. A., & Cabrera, N. J. (Eds.). (1996). *Beyond the blueprint: Directions for research on Head Start's families.* Washington, DC: National Academy Press.

Phillips, D. A., & Crowell, N. A. (Eds.). (1994). *Cultural diversity and early education: Report of a workshop.* Washington, DC: National Academy Press.

Rainwater, L. (1970). *Behind ghetto walls: Black life in a federal slum.* Chicago: Aldine.

Randolph, S. M. (1995). African American children in single mother families. In B. Dickerson (Ed.), *African American single mothers: Understanding their lives and families* (pp. 117-145). Thousand Oaks, CA: Sage.

Randolph, S. M., & Banks, H. D. (1993). Making a way out of no way: The promise of Afrocentric approaches to HIV prevention. *Journal of Black Psychology, 19,* 204-214.

Randolph, S. M., Billingsley, A., & Caldwell, C. H. (1994). Studying Black churches and family support in the context of HIV/AIDS. *National Journal of Sociology, 8*(1-2), 109-130.

Randolph, S. M., & Koblinsky, S. A. (2000, October). *The sociocultural context of infant mental health in African American families.* Paper presented at the U.S. Department of Health and Human Services, Administration for Children and Families, Administration on Children, Youth, and Families, Head Start Forum on Mental Health, Alexandria, VA.

Randolph, S. M., Koblinsky, S. A., & Roberts, D. D. (1997). Studying the role of family and school in the development of African American preschoolers in violent neighborhoods. *Journal of Negro Education, 65,* 282-294.

Roberts, D. D. (1997). *Racial/ethnic identity as a buffer to discrimination among low-income African American adolescents: An examination of academic performance.* Unpublished doctoral thesis, Temple University.

Rosser, P. L., & Randolph, S. M. (1989). Black American infants: The Howard University normative study. In J. K. Nugent, B. M. Lester, & T. B. Brazelton (Eds.), *The cultural context of infancy: Vol. 1. Biology, culture, and infant development* (pp. 133-165). Norwood, NJ: Ablex.

Rosser, P. L., & Randolph, S. M. (1996). The Developmental Milestones Expectations Scale: An assessment of parents' expectations for infants' development. In R. L. Jones (Ed.), *Handbook of tests and measurements for Black populations* (pp. 31-38). Berkeley, CA: Cobb & Henry.

Shonkoff, J., & Phillips, D. (Eds.). (2000). *From neurons to neighborhoods: The science of early childhood development.* Washington, DC: National Academy Press.

Simons, R. L., Beaman, J., Conger, R. D., & Chao, W. (1993). Stress, support, and antisocial behavior trait as determinates of emotional well-being and parenting practices among single mothers. *Journal of Marriage and the Family, 55,* 385-398.

Spencer, M. B. (1983). Children's cultural values and parental child rearing strategies. *Developmental Review, 3,* 351-370.

Stack, C. B. (1974). *All our kin: Strategies for survival in a Black community.* New York: Harper & Row.

Staples, R., & Boulin Johnson, L. (1993). *Black families at the crossroads: Challenges and prospects.* San Francisco: Jossey-Bass.

Staples, R., & Miranda, A. (1980). Racial and cultural variations among American families: An analytic review of the literature on minority families. *Journal of Marriage and the Family, 42,* 887-904.

Stevenson, H. C. (1994). Racial socialization in African American families: The art of balancing intolerance and survival. *The Family Journal: Counseling and Therapy for Couples and Families, 2,* 190-198.

Surgeon General of the United States. (2000). *Mental health: A report of the surgeon general.* Retrieved September 1, 2000, from www.surgeongeneral.gov/library/mentalhealth

Surgeon General of the United States. (2001). *Culture, race, and ethnicity: A supplement to Mental Health: A report of the surgeon general.* Retrieved September 1, 2001, from www.surgeongeneral.gov/library/mentalhealth

U.S. Bureau of the Census. (1995). *The Black population in the United States: March 1994 and 1993.* Washington, DC: Author.

U.S. Bureau of the Census. (2001). *America's families and living arrangements: March 2000* (Current Population Reports P20-537). Washington, DC: Author. Retrieved August 2001 from www.census.gov

U.S. Department of Health and Human Services (DHHS). (1995-1996). *National Head Start Bulletin, 1,* 57.

U.S. Department of Health and Human Services (DHHS). (2000). *Healthy People 2010: With understanding and improving health and objectives for improving health* (2 vols., 2nd ed.). Washington, DC: Government Printing Office. Retrieved August 21, 2001, from www.health.gov/healthypeople/Document/html/

U.S. Department of Health and Human Services (DHHS). (2001). *National action agenda for children's mental health.* Washington, DC: National Institute of Mental Health.

Willner, P. (1985). *Depression: A psychobiological synthesis.* New York: John Wiley.

Wilson, M. N. (1984). Mothers' and grandmothers' perception of parental behavior in three-generational Black families. *Child Development, 55,* 1333-1339.

Yoshikawa, H., & Knitzer, J. (1997). *Lessons from the field: Head Start mental health strategies to meet changing needs.* New York: National Center for Children in Poverty, Joseph L. Mailman School of Public Health, Columbia University.

Yu, Y., & Williams, D. R. (1999). Socioeconomic status and mental health. In C. S. Aneshensel & J. C. Phelan (Eds.), *Handbook of the sociology of mental health* (pp. 151-166). New York: Kluwer Academic/Plenum.

Zeanah, C. H. (Ed.). (2000). *Handbook of infant mental health.* New York: Guilford.

CHAPTER 16

Achievement Gap Between Black and White Students

Theoretical Analysis With Recommendations for Remedy

JEROME TAYLOR
University of Pittsburgh

MALICK KOUYATÉ
Center for Family Excellence

T he purpose of this chapter is to offer a measurement perspective on how to understand and eliminate the persisting achievement gap between Black and White students. We start out by describing the nature of this achievement gap, which provides the foundation for introducing our measurement perspective for understanding it. From this perspective, we evaluate a sample of educational reforms developed to narrow if not eliminate the gap. On the basis of this review with critique, we offer recommendations for remedy anchored around a new standard of achievement: A minimum of 70% of African American children should perform at or above the 50th percentile rank on standardized tests of reading and math. In the next section, we uncover the reasons why.

AUTHORS' NOTE: We express our thanks to the Richard K. Mellon Foundation, the Buhl Foundation, the Pittsburgh Child Guidance Foundation, the Poise Foundation, Lamar Advertising, the Pittsburgh School District, the city of Pittsburgh, and the Commonwealth of Pennsylvania for their financial support, which made possible the development and implementation of program and policy initiatives later described in this chapter. We are also grateful to the Committee on Common Causation, whose members provided formative input in the development of this chapter. We also thank Dr. Joan Vondra of the University of Pittsburgh's School of Education for providing stimulating and insightful comments on a previous draft of this chapter. However, the authors alone accept full responsibility for all attributions made and for whatever shortcomings remain.

NATURE OF THE GAP

From national and regional surveys of student achievement, Steele (1997) noted that (a) African American students in most school districts are about two full grade levels behind their non-Black counterparts by sixth grade, (b) racial differences in SAT scores are as large if not larger in middle and upper classes as in the lower class, (c) about 62% of African American students who start college do not finish, and (d) the GPA of African Americans who complete college is about two thirds of a letter grade lower than other graduating students. Thus, racial disparities in achievement would appear to cut across developmental levels and socioeconomic status within the African American community. These achievement disparities are not without social, economic, and health consequences.

Educational achievement and attainment have long been associated with salutary outcomes of a wide range: lower juvenile delinquency, better occupational outcomes, higher lifetime incomes, better mental health, higher marital satisfaction, longer life span, lower fertility rates, and lower risks of teenage pregnancy, school dropout, gang involvement, welfare dependence, and drug and alcohol abuse (Hoge & Andrews, 1996; *International Encyclopedia of Economics of Education*, 1995; Vazsonyi & Flannery, 1997). Moreover, educational achievement and attainment contribute to the economic health of nations, to the development and differentiation of labor markets, and to the general quality of national life (*International Encyclopedia of Economics of Education*, 1995).

In relation to current interests now being expressed in health disparities by race, it is important to point out that low literacy serves as a barrier to adequate health care because it prevents patients from fully engaging in the process of care (Miles & Davis, 1995). To effectively manage one's health, individuals must demonstrate *functional literacy*; that is, they need to be able not only to read and write but also to understand and act on that understanding (P. P. Lee, 1999). Moreover, recent studies demonstrate that low literacy is associated with poorer self-reported health (Baker, Parker, Williams, Clark, & Nurss, 1997) and increased utilization of hospital services (Marwick, 1997). In addition, individuals with low literacy are less likely to know essential information about their chronic conditions, including hypertension, diabetes, and asthma (Williams, Baker, Hoing, Lee, & Nowian, 1998; Williams, Baker, & Parker, 1998); less likely to understand discharge instructions following an emergency department visit (Jolly, Scott, Feied, & Sanford, 1993; Spandorfer, Karras, Hughes, & Caputo, 1995); and more likely to report medication errors because they are unable to read prescription labels (Baker, Parker, & Williams, 1996). Such findings may partly explain why individuals with low literacy are more likely to be hospitalized, even after adjusting for demographic characteristics, socioeconomic status, and overall health (Baker, Parker, Williams, & Clark, 1998). Poor understanding of the symptoms of early disease states may result in delayed treatment seeking, and even when treatment is sought, the individual's ability to participate in medical care decision making may be severely limited.[1]

Thus, educational underachievement has individual and communal consequences that carry local as well as national significance. And because participation in our global economy is conditioned by educational and technological competencies that nation-states bring to the table, educational underachievement in our inner cities carries implications for our national positioning within the international marketplace. Facing these realities of the new millennium, our educational goal for African American students must be particularly high for three additional reasons:

- Structural changes in local, national, and international economies will demand more educational and technological competence in the 21st century than in the 20th century. Academic underachievement will be more costly in the 21st century than in the 20th century.
- Local, state, and national educational policies supporting racial preferences will most likely pass into oblivion during the 21st century. Students starting behind run the risk of being left behind.
- The intractability of racial stereotyping may well require a higher standard of minority achievement; that is, African American students may need to perform better than their European American peers to attain economic and social parity in our society. Unfair though this may be, we believe this conclusion is more true than false.

Against this backdrop of market demands and historical realities, it would not seem unreasonable or unwise to argue that a minimum of 70% of African American students should perform at or above the 50th percentile rank on nationally or regionally standardized tests of reading and math. Against this expectation of our new standard, the gap is wide indeed. Distressing also is the achievement gap for other minorities: Hispanic, American Indian, and Alaskan minorities (National Center for Educational Statistics, 2002a, 2002b). Although typically Asian American students have been positively stereotyped and frequently described as "smart and quiet" in the classroom, a study based on the National Center for Education Statistics revealed that about 24% of eighth-grade Asian Americans failed to achieve basic achievement levels in math (Huang, 1995), and their 10th-grade dropout rate more than doubled between the periods 1980-1982 and 1990-1992 (McMillen, Kaufman, & Whitener, 1994).

UNDERSTANDING THE GAP

Using components of variance theory, student performance level on a given test (St^2) is composed of systematic and relevant variance (Sr^2), systematic and irrelevant variance (Si^2), and error variance (Se^2). Structurally,

$$St^2 = Sr^2 + Si^2 + Se^2. \qquad (1)$$

Suppose we are interested in actual math achievement scores (St^2), as estimated by the Iowa Test of Basic Skills, which is a nationally standardized test of student achievement.

The component Sr^2 would refer to that component of students' *actual* scores (St^2) attributable to students' *real* level of math achievement. Clearly, equating *actual* with *real* level of math achievement is indefensible because the *actual* score is influenced also by remaining components Se^2 and Si^2.

The component Se^2 refers to impermanent sources of variation that contribute unsystematically to *actual* scores (St^2). Illness, distraction, distemper, indifference, and other transitory variables may deflect accurate estimation of *actual* performance (St^2). These variables therefore contribute to error component Se^2. The component Si^2 would refer to variables other than *real* math achievement that contribute systematically to *actual* scores (St^2).

In understanding the achievement gap between Black and White, our lead question, then, is this: Which variables contribute to components Sr^2 and Se^2 as well as Si^2 to begin with? We explore three possibilities.

CASTELIKE MINORITIES THEORY

In a series of international studies, Ogbu and Fordham (1986) reported that oppressed persons whose social mobility is restricted by tacit and explicit codes of discrimination often exhibit castelike qualities: (a) They experience disillusionment with opportunities for economic enhancement, (b) they show diminution of effort and perseverance, (c) they expect schooling is not worth the effort, and (d) they blame the system for their failures. In these societies, there is a 15-point IQ gap between the majority population and castelike minorities—the Maoris of New Zealand, the Baraku of Japan, the Harijans of India, the Oriental Jews of Israel, the West Indians of Great Britain, and Blacks of the United States. Structurally, these consistent disparities are attributable to the castelike positioning of minorities (Si^2), which undermines their actual performance (St^2) and may erode their real ability (Sr^2). Because the maintenance of brain cells and neural connections underlying cognitive processes depends in part on one's willingness to take on analytically challenging tasks such as reading, math, and science or hobbies such as creating art, solving puzzles, playing chess, or mastering an instrument (Kandel & Hawkins, 1995), a sociocultural environment that discourages or dissuades commitment to these active engagements may well diminish the neurological substrate that nurtures and sustains real ability (Sr^2). Interestingly, there also is evidence that active engagements of the sort described may have protective implications for cognitively impairing disorders—head injury (Powell, Zahner, & Micheli-Tzanakou, 1995) and Alzheimer's disease (Friedland, Fritsch, et al., 2001). Our basic argument, then, is that persons victimized by negative social stereotyping are at triple risk—cognitively, psychologically, and neurologically—which carries untoward implications for Sr^2, Si^2, and thus St^2. We note also that even deeply rooted positive stereotypes may be costly to their recipients. S. J. Lee (1996) noted, for example, that positive stereotypes mask individual differences among Asian American students, which often serves to isolate them from other ethnic groups. Thus, social and interethnic relations may suffer because of implicit comparisons based on positive stereotypes.

DIAGNOSTIC THREAT THEORY

Steele (1997) defined stereotype threat as the fear of being judged or treated stereotypically in the identified domain. For African Americans, this threat is related to the domain of intellectual performance. In particular, when African Americans are evaluated within this domain, negative emotions are triggered (Se^2), which undermines actual performance (St^2). At Stanford University, for example, Steele and his colleagues found that Black students solving demanding Graduate Record Examination items under the assumption that performance was diagnostic of ability did significantly less well than White students who tackled the same items under identical assumptions. When the diagnostic threat was removed, there were no significant differences between Black and White students. Diagnostic threat, then, appears to impair actual performance (St^2) without eroding real ability (Sr^2). That diagnostic threat entails the risk of inflating error component Se^2 would seem to accommodate Howard and Hammond's (1985) conclusion that competitive engagement activates feelings of inferiority, which impairs cognitive performance. A further implication is that the situation of academic "insiders and outsiders" based on intense achievement-oriented competition virtually ensures dysfunctional race relations among Black, White, and Asian students, which might further exacerbate diagnostic threat experienced by African Americans in culturally diverse settings.

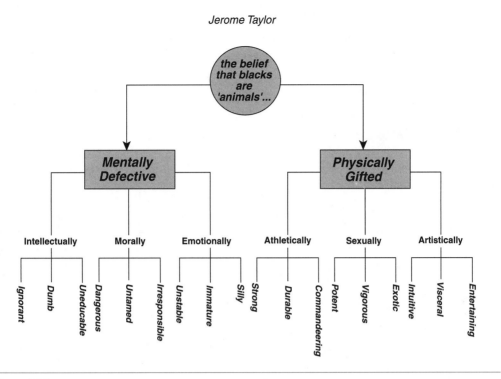

Jerome Taylor

Figure 16.1

INTERNALIZED RACISM THEORY

In research summarized by Taylor and Obiechina (in press), about one in three Blacks endorse racist stereotypes about Blacks as mentally defective (intellectually, morally, emotionally) and physically gifted (athletically, sexually, artistically). Figure 16.1 provides a conceptual representation of these expectations that we have found are joined together by the latent belief that "Blacks are animals," which apparently is used to "explain" why Blacks are mentally defective and physically gifted (Taylor & Zhang, 1990). In studies conducted over the past 15 years, Black endorsement of racist stereotypes about Blacks has ranged from a low of 15% in a sample of married couples to 50% in a sample of single-parent mothers living in four public housing

communities. We note that internalized racism in Blacks is associated with poorer structural outcomes as indexed by educational, income, and career attainment (Murrell, 1989) and with lower IQ scores as estimated from the Weschler Intelligence Scale for Children (see Taylor & Obiechina's [in press] description of Asbury, Adderly-Kelly, & Knuckle, 1987). Quite possibly, then, internalized racism (Si^2) undermines actual performance (St^2) and, over time, may erode real ability (Sr^2) for reasons identified in our discussion of the castelike minority theory.

On an adult sample of Barbadians, we are now evaluating a new loss of bearing construct that consists of two indicators—internalized racism (endorsement of beliefs that Blacks are mentally defective and physically gifted) and spiritual disintegration (evidence

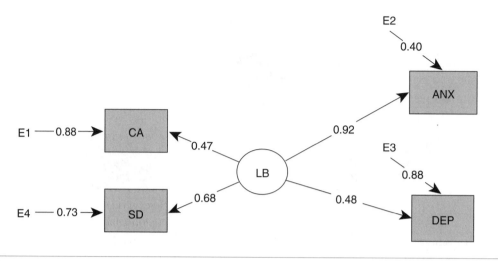

Figure 16.2

of self-absorption associated with a diminished sense of hope and connection to community). Accounting for 85% of the variance in anxiety and 23% of the variance in depressive symptoms (Figure 16.2), our loss of bearing construct may be linked to situational or global performance impairments of the sort noted by Steele (1997). To the extent that these results are replicated, it would appear that anxiety—estimated from such items as, "I have trouble concentrating or I often feel uneasy inside"—may be a primary affective response to loss of bearing. To what extent, then, could attention disorders or hyperactivity problems, so often diagnosed in African American children, express loss of bearing that is nurtured consciously or unselfconsciously by family, peers, school, media, and public policies? And to what extent is loss of bearing a personal response to systemic oppression conveyed through subtle to overt forms of discrimination (cf. Taylor, 1980)? This implication could apply as well to poor children of other minorities. The study by Cherulnik and Sounders (1984), for example, found that people living in poor neighborhoods are perceived in general as "dangerous, noisy, timid, superstitious, gullible, irresponsible, lazy, and less intelligent, energetic, and ambitious." These classist expectations may affect poor children of whatever ethnicity.

Extending the findings associated with the preceding theories, the structural model presented in Figure 16.3 proposes key modifications in the components of variance model summarized by equation (1). This reformulated proposal shares with the original model (1) the assumption that three factors affect actual achievement—Si^2, Sr^2, and Se^2. In addition, this reformulation assumes that systematic but irrelevant variables affecting Si^2—castelike identity, diagnostic threat, internalized racism—predict error variance (Se^2) and real achievement (Sr^2).[2] On one hand, it is assumed that sizable variations in castelike identity, diagnostic threat, and internalized racism will inflate error variance (Se^2). This expectation is consistent with Steele's (1997) findings that actual achievement of African American students is conditioned situationally by the salience of

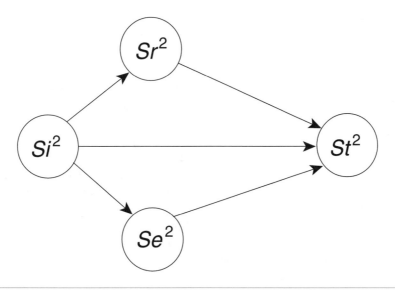

Figure 16.3

diagnostic threat. On the other hand, it is assumed that castelike identity, diagnostic threat, and internalized racism will affect the real achievement of Black students; that is, cognitive expectations of incompetence, affective responses to oppression, and neurological consequences of intellectual disengagement may have progressively erosive effects on real achievement (Sr^2). Taylor and Franklin (1994) discussed how prophecy fulfillment may in part mediate these implications.

In general, we argue that to the extent poor White or ethnically marginalized children identify with stereotypes that discourage intellectual striving, their performance also will be affected in the manner hypothesized for Black students. We anticipate, then, that we can close the achievement gap in racially, ethnically, sexually, or economically marginalized children through program and policy initiatives that are effective in (a) diminishing sources of error variance, (b) diminishing sources of systematic but irrelevant variance that suppress real and

actual achievement, or (c) using curriculum or pedagogical reforms that contribute directly to student achievement. Within this context, we shall use the term *culturally competent* to refer to program and policy initiatives that accomplish (a), (b), and (c). Educational program and policy initiatives that ignore, minimize, or controvert these considerations shall be referred to as *culturally incompetent*. We now examine efforts to close the achievement gap in relation to this standard of cultural competence.

CLOSING THE GAP

In this section, we evaluate two contrasting models for closing the achievement gap between Black and White children. The first is structured around values offering the promise of enhancing academic readiness and achievement excellence, and the second is structured around curriculum and pedagogical reforms directed toward the same end.

Axiological Models[3]

Axiology generally refers to the study of fundamental values, preferences, or truths. Identifying what parents value for the future of their children is thus an appropriate field of application for this construct, and identifying values from social tradition or historical sources is another. Although both models are reviewed, we provide special attention to the former, which was designed expressly as a culturally competent model.

Values for Life

From a large number of interviews with Black and White mothers and fathers of low and middle income, we have identified seven values parents consider crucial to the healthy development of their children (Taylor, Turner, & Lewis, 1999). In what follows, we identify positive and negative polarities of these values—with negative expressions (italicized) representing sources of systematic but irrelevant variance Si^2 that undermine academic readiness and achievement and positive expressions (nonitalicized) representing sources of systematic but irrelevant variance Si^2 that promote academic readiness and achievement:

1. Learning orientation: Analytic, savvy, smart, creative, and inventive; asks questions, wants to know how things work; remembers, identifies, compares, contrasts, generalizes; sees connections between different areas of learning; enjoys helping others learn; open to working with others around learning tasks versus *doesn't analyze things, shows little creativity, is bored easily, asks few questions; unfocused; doesn't seek or express relationships between different areas of learning; uncooperative with others on learning tasks; poor memory for stories or events read or heard; disinterested in how things work; refuses to answer questions; seldom names objects in the environment.*

2. Self-confidence: Tends to explore, probe, investigate; is attentive and enthusiastic when new lessons, materials, or challenges are introduced; eager to explore new places, meet new people, or examine new ideas leading to constructive opportunities; daring in constructive ways; excited about living—upbeat about social as well as academic competence versus *inattentive, withdrawn, apathetic, unenthusiastic, overly shy, reclusive, doubtful, uninterested, unsure of oneself, unexpressive; unwilling to try anything new and different; disengaged and unmotivated.*

3. Self-persistence: Sticks with task until it is finished; able to hang in there when the going is frustrating or rough; maintains focus in face of distractions; patient in figuring things out; seeks out challenging or difficult subjects or tasks; overcomes obstacles in solving problems; bounces back from frustrations; has surprisingly long and sustained attention span versus *gives up, easily distracted, avoids challenges, readily frustrated, impatient while solving problems; unwilling to try after frustrated, unable to see alternatives; unable to move forward—gets stuck; refuses to complete project started; moves to another activity when frustrated; flits from activity to activity without completing anything.*

4. Self-esteem: Expresses pleasure over newly acquired understanding or skill; maintains cool in face of teasing or stereotyping; shares accomplishments in new understandings or skills with others; expresses positive interest in others' accomplishments; feels good about who she or he is; able to deal with negative as well as positive aspects of self and others versus *critical of others, negative attitude toward self and others; negative about who she or he is, talks negatively about others; depressed with self; loses cool when teased; apathetic about accomplishments, unwilling to share them with others.*

5. Self-reliance:[4] Able to think and act alone when necessary; resists temptations to mischief; avoids physically and emotionally hazardous situations; thinks before acting; stands up for what is fair; responds appropriately to racist, classist, or sexist stereotypes versus *overly dependent on others, follows more than leads, easily tempted to do wrong, gets into dangerous or potentially harmful situations, acts without thought, does not speak up for what is right, fails to challenge others who are doing wrong; goes along with racist, classist, or sexual stereotypes; easily misled; easily led to do negative things.*

6. Love and respect: Respects differences; avoids racist, classist, or sexist teasing or joking; displays special regard for those older and carries sense of responsibility for those younger; encourages those who feel down; goes to the aid of those in distress; expresses and receives constructive love versus *disrespects others; shows intolerance for differences; ridicules or makes fun of others; goes along with or initiates racist, classist, or sexist stereotypes; low regard for older persons; little sense of responsibility for those younger; makes fun of people who are down; abandons or ignores those in need; unsociable; antisocial.*

7. Interpersonal skills: Sensitive to feelings of others; accurately reads feelings and moods of others; expresses thoughts and feelings constructively; exercises self-discipline, patience, and control in managing conflict; is capable of leading others constructively; seeks and considers constructive council; takes constructive criticism without crumbling or withdrawing *versus insensitivity to feelings of others; misreads feelings and moods of others; unable to express thoughts and feelings constructively; unable to control own behavior in conflict situations; unable to lead others constructively; difficulty asking for help; unable to take constructive criticism; crumbles in face of constructive criticism.*

For students K-8, the behavioral expression of each value is estimated by teacher ratings on the VAL-OE Inventory (Johnson & Taylor, 1998).[5] We use the moniker *values for life* to refer to this set of seven values identified by parents themselves—not by expert opinion, privileged reflection, historical analysis, or think tank deliberations, although we acknowledge there are parallels between what parents propose and competence constructs such as self-persistence, self-esteem, self-confidence, intrinsic motivation, attachment security, impulse control, prosocial skills, and internal locus of control proposed by developmental theorists. Given these origins of values for life, parents may be more open to working with schools or community organizations committed to promoting their adoption and expression. We believe these values—embraceable by racially, ethnically, and economically diverse groups—are generally promotive of academic readiness and achievement for four reasons.[6]

First, *values for life have self-regulatory implications* (Taylor & Kouyaté, in preparation); that is, they structure cognitive and motivational processes that control the articulation and achievement of goals relevant to academic readiness and achievement outcomes. Students high in learning orientation, self-confidence, and self-persistence may be more likely to employ self-regulatory strategies that help them acquire, organize, and use knowledge efficiently (Fromm, 1976; Langer, 1997; Shore & Dover, 1987; Sternberg & Davidson, 1983). Students high in self-esteem bring a disposition that allows them to celebrate academic successes and learn from academic failures. Students high in self-reliance may be better able to resist the siren call of unremitting temptations that undermine academic excellence, and students high in interpersonal skills and love and respect may be more committed to relationship maintenance with teachers, parents, and mentors whose input is vital to excellence in academic readiness and achievement outcomes. In general, instructional and correlational studies provide consistent evidence for the importance of self-regulatory processes in understanding motivational, volitional, and behavioral dispositions underlying skill performance and maintenance (Bouffard & Vezeau, 1998; Bouffard-Bouchard, Parent, & Larivée, 1993; Bransford et al., 1982; Ferrari & Sternberg, 1998; Lefebvre-Pinard, 1985; Markus, Cross, & Wurk, 1990; Markus, Niedenthal, & Nurius, 1986; McCombs & Marzano, 1990; Pinard, 1986; Taylor & Kouyaté, in preparation).

Second, *values for life have hermeneutical implications* (Taylor, Obiechina, & Harrison, 1998), providing cognitive frameworks for interpreting a range of events, from commonplace to traumatic. Is a new lesson unit on fractions interpreted as an interesting challenge (high self-confidence) or an imposing barrier (low self-confidence)? Is a free trial offer of a street drug interpreted as a harmful event (high self-reliance) or an irrepressible opportunity (low self-reliance)? Is a drive-by murder interpreted as a cause for mourning (high love and respect) or justified because of one gang's dissn' another (low love and respect)? We are interested particularly in hermeneutical applications offering transformative appraisal, interpretation, and management of daily hassles or life events (Quintás, 1989). For the student gripped with a sense of mourning over a drive-by murder, is there an effort to join or form a community organization to provide political and cultural remedy to this problem? For the student open to a new lesson unit on fractions, is there an effort to talk with other students about the new material or to apply new concepts on fractions to articles at home or in the neighborhood? For the

student who has been offered a street drug, is there an effort to talk with parents, pastors, or community leaders about the availability of drugs in the neighborhood? Our view is that students who adopt values for life will be more likely to engage in constructive and transformative appraisals and interpretations that lead to more habitable environments supportive of excellence in academic readiness and achievement outcomes.

Third, *values for life help to protect children from harmful effects of negative experiences.* However difficult or traumatic situations may be, there often is hope for persons armed with the will and skill to bounce back. As a self-righting and growth process (Higgins, 1994), resiliency is viewed as the capacity to bounce back, withstand hardship, repair oneself (Wolin & Wolin, 1993), and successfully adapt in the face of adversities—poverty, parental illness, and parenting abnormalities (Block, 1994; Block & Block, 1980; Herrenkohl, Herrenkohl, & Egolf, 1994). We now examine theoretical and empirical bases for our claim that values for life enlarge students' capacity for emotional resiliency, thus helping to protect them from harmful effects of negative experiences. To the degree resilience is related to values for life, we should find evidence of the latter wherever there is evidence of the former. We now examine this linkage in a representative sample of studies. In an investigation of 206 *economically disadvantaged children,* Cicchetti, Rogosch, Lynch, and Holt (1993) found that self-esteem was more important than intelligence in predicting level of adjustment. *Among children with histories of abuse and neglect,* resilient children were described by Block and Block (1980) as reflective, attentive, persistent, dependable, planful, calm, relaxed, and responsive to reason—all attributes that correspond to learning orientation, self-confidence, self-persistence, and self-reliance. *For stressors and adversities associated with psychopathology in 50% to 67% of children exposed to them* (Rutter, 1985; Werner, 1989), the following attributes characterize the 33% to 50% who overcame these odds:

cognitive skills (learning orientation) (Garmezy, 1991; Radke-Yarrow & Sherman, 1990; Werner & Smith, 1982);

reflectiveness in dealing with new situations (interpersonal skills, self-reliance) (Garmezy, 1991);

positive responsiveness to others (love and respect, interpersonal skills) (Garmezy, 1991; Werner & Smith, 1982);

alertness, curiosity, and enthusiasm (self-confidence) (Radke-Yarrow & Sherman, 1990);

multiple interests and goal-setting behavior (learning orientation, self-confidence, self-persistence, self-reliance) (Werner & Smith, 1982); and

internal locus of control and high self-esteem (self-esteem) (Moran & Eckenrode, 1992).

For stressors and adversities associated with school failure, Christiansen, Christiansen, and Howard (1997) identified several factors that characterize resilient children who do well:

(a) They approach problems proactively, seeking positive change and believing they can bring it about (self-esteem, self-persistence).

(b) They are often good-natured, gaining the positive attention of others (interpersonal skills, love and respect).

(c) They are able to confront and overcome negative situations to their advantage (self-persistence).

(d) They have a sense of control over their lives, which provides a degree of order and structure (self-confidence, self-persistence, self-esteem).

We conclude that the adoption of values for life may well help students living in communities at risk survive and even thrive in the face of negative life experiences.

Fourth, *positive expressions of values for life would seem to prevent or remedy internalization of stereotypes that undermine academic readiness and achievement.* Consulting Figure 16.1 in relation to our description of positive and negative polarities of values for life, the stereotype that Blacks are intellectually inferior is countered by the values of learning orientation, self-confidence, self-persistence, and self-esteem; the stereotype that Blacks are morally deficient is controverted by the values of love and respect and self-reliance; the expectation that Blacks are emotionally immature is countered by each of the seven values; and the stereotype that Blacks are sexually gifted may be countered by the values of love and respect, interpersonal skills, self-persistence, and self-reliance.

In general, then, we believe that normalizing[7] the behavioral expression of values for life directly counters the social stereotyping, diagnostic threat, and internalized racism we previously associated with variance component Si^2 as well as components Sr^2 and Se^2. For these reasons, we conclude that reform initiatives promoting values for life are culturally competent under the definition.

The question that remains is whether values for life are empirically associated with academic readiness and achievement. Figure 16.4 examines the association between values for life and standardized reading and math scores obtained on a sample of 72 second- and third-grade African American students attending an inner-city public school (Taylor & Michie, in preparation). In the first row, the first number (2.5) indicates that students rated above the median on love and respect were two and a half times more likely to score at or above the national average in math than students rated below the median

Values	ITBS: Math	SAT 9: Reading
Love & Respect	2.5	7.0
Interpersonal Skills	3.5	28.0
Learning Orientation	2.5	>6.0
Self-Confidence	2.5	7.0
Self-Persistence	8.0	2.5
Self-Esteem	5.3	7.0
Self-Reliance	8.0	2.5

Figure 16.4

on love and respect. The second number (7.0) means that students rated above the median on love and respect were seven times more likely to score at or above the national average in reading than students rated below the median on love and respect. In general, students rated as above the median on the values were a minimum of two and a half times more likely to score at or above average on math and reading achievement than students rated below the median on the values. Students rated as above the median on self-esteem were five to seven times more likely to score above average on math and reading than students rated below the median on self-esteem. Self-persistence and self-reliance may be especially important in promoting high levels of achievement in math achievement. Love and respect, interpersonal skills, learning orientation, and self-confidence may be especially important in promoting reading achievement. Finally, we note on each value that students scoring above the median tended to have a higher percentile rank in math—an overall average percentile rank of 53.12 for students at or above the median and 32.23 for students below the median, a net percentile rank difference of 20.89. Also, we found on each value that students scoring

at or above the median tended to have a higher percentile rank in reading—an overall average percentile rank of 45.65 for students above the median and 27.05 for students below the median, a net percentile rank difference of 18.

Figure 16.5 summarizes results of the relationship between two of the values—self-confidence and self-persistence—and standardized reading and math scores obtained on a random sample of fourth- and fifth-grade students attending an all-Black inner-city public school. These two values accounted for about 29% of the variance in reading and math achievement on the Iowa Test of Basic Skills. Associated with $R = .54$, we note that this might be an underestimation of the true relationship because of a 2- to 4-month lag between values for life ratings and achievement testing.

An even more powerful documentation of association would be evidence that a reform initiative designed to enhance the behavioral expression of values for life actually improved academic readiness and achievement outcomes in students living in communities at risk. Figure 16.6 provides a summary of the classroom component of this values for life initiative (Taylor,

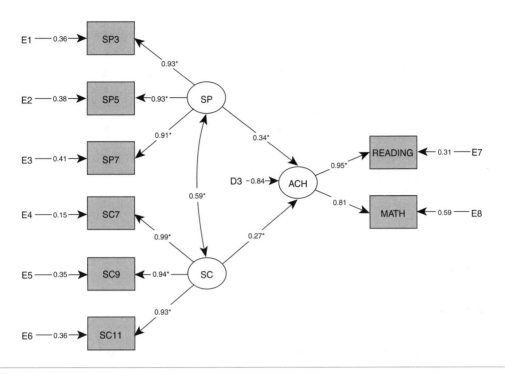

Figure 16.5

Johnson, & Michie, 1998) implemented at all-Black McKelvy Elementary School serving children K-5 who for the most part live in a public housing community.[8]

Do values for life initiatives affect achievement outcomes? We summarize achievement outcome data that we requested and received from the Pittsburgh School District. For the period from 1998 to 1999, comparative data were available only for second through fifth grades because no district assessments were administered to first graders in 1998. For second graders: In math (Iowa Test of Basic Skills [ITBS]), 25% in 1998 and 62% in 1999 scored at or above the national norm—a net increase of 37% performing at or above the national norm. In reading (Stanford Achievement Test 9 [SAT 9]), 21% in 1998 and 29% in 1999 scored at or above the national norm—a net increase of 8%. For third graders: In math (ITBS), 45% in 1998

and 59% in 1999 scored at or above the national norm—a net increase of 15%. In reading (SAT 9), 21% in 1998 and 50% in 1999 scored at or above the national norm—a net increase of 29%. For fourth grade: In math skills (New Standards [NS]), 24% in 1998 and 27% in 1999 achieved standard—a net increase of 3%. In math concepts (NS), 0% in 1998 and 44% in 1999 fully achieved standard—a net increase of 44%. In math problem solving (NS), 0% in 1998 and 0% in 1999 fully achieved standard—a net increase of 0%. In basic reading (NS), 35% in 1998 and 45% in 1999 fully achieved standard—a net increase of 10%. In reading understanding and analysis (NS), 17% in 1998 and 17% in 1999 fully achieved standard—a net increase of 0%. For fifth grade: In math (Pennsylvania State System of Assessment [PSSA]), 4% in 1998 and 16% in 1999 scored at or above the state norm—a

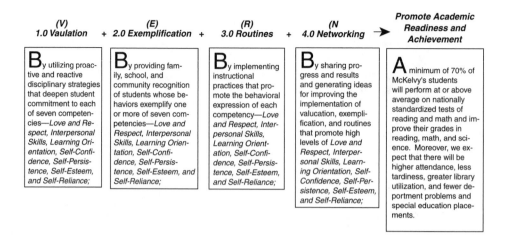

(V) 1.0 Vaulation	+	(E) 2.0 Exemplification	+	(R) 3.0 Routines	+	(N 4.0 Networking	→	Promote Academic Readiness and Achievement
By utilizing proactive and reactive disciplinary strategies that deepen student commitment to each of seven competencies—*Love and Respect, Interpersonal Skills, Learning Orientation, Self-Confidence, Self-Persistence, Self-Esteem, and Self-Reliance;*		**B**y providing family, school, and community recognition of students whose behaviors exemplify one or more of seven competencies—*Love and Respect, Interpersonal Skills, Learning Orientation, Self-Confidence, Self-Persistence, Self-Esteem, and Self-Reliance;*		**B**y implementing instructional practices that promote the behavioral expression of each competency—*Love and Respect, Interpersonal Skills, Learning Orientation, Self-Confidence, Self-Persistence, Self-Esteem, and Self-Reliance;*		**B**y sharing progress and results and generating ideas for improving the implementation of valuation, exemplification, and routines that promote high levels of *Love and Respect, Interpersonal Skills, Learning Orientation, Self-Confidence, Self-Persistence, Self-Esteem, and Self-Reliance;*		**A** minimum of 70% of McKelvy's students will perform at or above average on nationally standardized tests of reading and math and improve their grades in reading, math, and science. Moreover, we expect that there will be higher attendance, less tardiness, greater library utilization, and fewer deportment problems and special education placements.

Figure 16.6

net increase of 12%. In reading (PSSA), 12% in 1998 and 9% in 1999 scored at or above the state norm—a net decrease of 3%. *With exceptions noted for fourth-grade math problem solving and fifth-grade reading achievement, the rate of net increases at the end of 2001 exceeded net increases reported for the previous 2 years.*

Do values for life initiatives affect academic readiness? From student information reports, we found that in-school suspensions were lower in 2001 than in the previous 2 years. Also, attendance was up and tardiness down in 2001 relative to the 2 previous years.

In conclusion, values for life may have salutary effects on academic readiness and achievement outcomes. However, longitudinal studies coupled with cross-site evaluations with control schools are critical to a final judgment. In the absence of such studies, we summarize results of companion investigations that may have some bearing on the potential efficacy of values for life initiatives.

In day care and Head Start applications of a values for life initiative, we found evidence of (a) significant increases in the behavioral expression of all values and (b) significant increases in the personal-social, adaptive, gross motor, communication, and cognitive components of the Batelle Development Inventory (Taylor, Thomas, & Bagley, 1999; Taylor et al., 1994). In a related study, we explored the relationship between quality of the caregiving environment and quality of socioemotional development. Four caregiving environments were identified: (a) children enrolled in values for life child care center, (b) children of parents at low risk of abuse and neglect, (c) children of parents who were high in neglect, and (d) children of parents who were high in abuse. We found that children in values for life child care were significantly more advanced in socioemotional development than all remaining groups (Taylor & Bartolomucci, 1996).

In a series of studies conducted on college students by the senior author's undergraduate students, Strothers (1997) found that fellow undergraduates scoring at or above the median on learning orientation reported more positive attitudes toward taking technical courses such as calculus, chemistry, and biology than students scoring below the median on learning orientation. Lawrence (1999) and Lundy (1997) also found that college students at or above the median in self-reliance reported better study skills, higher achievement motivation, and more time dedicated to study than students below the median in self-reliance.

Character Education

The teaching of moral values and civic virtues with the aim of creating a more compassionate and responsible society is rapidly becoming a mainstay of popular, professional, and political interest. Currently, more than 100 Web sites describe models or feature reports on character education models that typically promote traits such as honesty, courage, kindness, compassion, responsibility, perseverance, fairness, and respect (Bennett, 1988; Wynne & Walberg, 1986). Typically, teachers spend 10 to 15 minutes introducing and discussing the featured trait of the week and its implications for students. In some applications, biographies, fables, stories, or quotations are used in introducing the featured trait that is then infused into daily lesson plans. Often these strategies are combined with efforts to involve parents, community, and the media. In relation to our preceding analysis, we now identify seven points of difference between values for life and character education initiatives.

1. Differences in origin: Although values undergirding character education initiatives are generally assumed to be correct by virtue of history and tradition, values for life are reflections of parental aspirations for their children. One could make an a priori case that the former might be less intrinsically motivating than the latter. To the extent that the mobilization of parent, teacher, and community is critical in closing the racial achievement gap, this difference may be of considerable psychological significance. This coalescing of communal interest may be critically important in countering negative influences associated with systematic but irrelevant variance component Si^2.

2. Differences in grounding: Values featured in character education models are directed toward creating a civil society, whereas values for life are directed toward promoting a spiritually integrative way of being—a sense of hope, a vital connection to community, and a capacity for transcendence (Taylor, Rogers, & Thomas, in preparation). Hope is the antidote to despair, connection is the antidote to alienation, and transcendence is the antidote to victimization by racism, classism, sexism, and materialism. We therefore believe values for life may be more proficient in countering negative factors defined on variance component Si^2.

3. Differences in theory: The social theory underlying character education is fragmentary at best, whereas values for life are based on an elaboration of the theory of reasoned action (Fishbein & Ajzen, 1975), arguably the most successful theory for understanding and predicting social behaviors of a wide range (Evans & Taylor, 1995). Our expectation that the underlying theory of values for life may be more effective in promoting the adoption and expression of featured values than the underdeveloped theory underlying character education will need to be evaluated in future studies. To the extent that our expectation is supported empirically, we would expect that values for life are a more proficient corrective of negative factors defined on variance component Si^2.

4. Differences in curriculum: The curriculum of character education might best be described as multicultural. It features biographies, fables, or quotations drawn from national and world literature that include but

are not structured intentionally around African and African American contributions that illustrate featured values. Because of the ubiquity of racial images that promote internalized racism and spiritual disintegration, the theory of values for life in its current application is structured primarily but not exclusively around African and African American biographies, aphorisms, folktales, and images. Because our studies indicate that about 50% of parents living in public housing communities may identify with racist stereotypes (Taylor & Obiechina, in press), and because most parents served by our values for life initiative live in public housing communities, we believe that it may be especially important to expose African American children to materials and images that counter stereotypes that Blacks are mentally defective and physically gifted. In so doing, we expect that values for life will counter negative influences of factors defined on Si^2 more than character education initiatives will.

5. Differences in scheduling: In some applications of character education, a different value is featured every week, whereas in values for life, a different value is featured about every 30 days. Given the complexity of values, we question whether the shorter period of time used by character education initiatives is sufficient to promote adoption of the featured value. In consequence, we would expect that the likelihood of countering negative influences defined on Si^2 would be less under character education than values for life. Moreover, we expect that the relatively short term for implementing character education initiatives is unlikely to have as persuasive effects on risk reduction and self-regulatory or hermeneutical processes as values for life initiatives.

6. Differences in measurement: Currently, there are no reliable and valid measures of values underlying character education initiatives, whereas there are reliable and valid measures of values for life for preschoolers, elementary school students, and adolescents and adults. Availability of these measures makes it possible to examine whether values for life instructional methods and curriculum are effective in promoting the adoption and expression of featured values. Of course, the absence of measures for character education makes it impossible to evaluate whether instructional methods and curriculum materials have expected effects on values formation and expression.

7. Differences in evaluation: On the Internet, there is abundant reference to anecdotal reports of social and behavioral improvements associated with character education reforms. There is appreciably less attention given to the evaluation of enhancements in reading and math. In contrast, the evaluation of social, behavioral, and achievement outcomes is an integral part of values for life initiatives that we have found are associated with student achievement—variance component Si^2.

These differences notwithstanding, there are conceptual continuities and design challenges shared by character education and values for life. Conceptually, there is overlap in many of the descriptors associated with each system: perseverance, fortitude, patience, and self-discipline (self-persistence); caring and understanding (interpersonal skills); compassion, respect, and generosity (love and respect); and courage and fairness (self-reliance). These conceptual continuities as well as their distinctiveness will be examined in a subsequent paper. From a design perspective, character education and values for life share a common failing: Thus far, both have used one of the weakest quasi-experimental designs— pretesting and posttesting without randomized or nonequivalent controls. Thus, both of these axiological initiatives are vulnerable to subject, situational, and historical confounds that may well include Hawthorne and Pygmalion effects. These issues must be addressed in future research.

Curriculum Models

In this section, we review six curriculum and pedagogical reform initiatives intended to decrease the achievement gap between Blacks and Whites and between haves and have-nots.

Early Title I School Reforms

Title I of the 1965 Elementary and Secondary Act was developed to provide supplemental assistance to local education agencies serving areas with concentrations of children from low-income families to expand and improve their educational programs. Since its inception nearly 35 years ago, more than $100 billion have been spent (Borman, D'Agostino, Wong, & Hedge, 1998). This enormous investment notwithstanding, the federal government has sponsored only two systematic, longitudinal, and nationally representative studies on the educational efficacy of Title I.

The congressionally mandated Sustained Effort Study, conducted from 1976 through 1979, is the largest investigation ever undertaken of elementary education. Carter (1984) and his associates collected data on a nationally representative sample of 300 elementary schools involving as many as 120,000 students. Although Carter found that Title I students outperformed other needy children not enrolled in compensatory programs, there was little evidence that Title I was successful in closing the reading and math achievement gap between disadvantaged and more advantaged students. The reader should note that in an earlier version of Part A of Title I, funds could be used only for supplementary educational services for eligible children who were failing or at risk of failing state standards. The current version of Part A of Title I permits use of funds to upgrade educational enrichment throughout the school to raise achievement levels of all students.

In the second congressionally mandated Prospects Study conducted over a 4-year period beginning in 1991, a nationally representative sample of 40,000 first, third, and seventh graders was evaluated. Findings detailed in three reports again indicate that Title I programs have not been successful in closing the reading and math achievement gap between disadvantaged and more advantaged students (Borman et al., 1998). In particular, exposure to the program through third grade did not significantly diminish achievement gaps existing in first grade (Borman et al., 1998; Carter, 1984).

Overall, it would appear that earlier applications of Title I have not been successful in removing the achievement gap between Black students who tended to be more economically disadvantaged than White students. This may be because earlier applications of Part A of Title I could be used only for supplementary educational services for eligible children. Or could it be that earlier Title I initiatives failed to address issues of social stereotyping, diagnostic threat, or internalized racism? Can there really be a reform effort that closes the achievement gap between Blacks and Whites or the haves or have-nots without addressing these issues that contribute negatively to variance components Si^2 and Se^2? We believe the answer is no to the degree that commitment to student transformation and curriculum reform are uncoupled priorities.

Whole-School Reforms

The New American Schools Development Corporation was founded in 1991 by business and foundation leaders interested in promoting school transformation. In February 1992, a nationally distributed request for proposals drew nearly 700 submissions, from which 11 proposals for whole-school reform were selected. Of the 11 initially funded, 9 of these survived the first two phases of implementation: Atlas Communities, Audrey Cohen College, Community Learning Centers, Co-NECT Schools, Expeditionary Learning Outward Bound, Los Angeles Learning Center, Modern Red Schoolhouse, the National Alliance for Restructuring Education, and Roots & Wings (Bodilly, 1996). All models entailed whole-school reforms in curriculum and pedagogical practices as well as governance routines and procedures. Of these 9 well-funded program initiatives, described at some length in Stringfield, Ross, and Smith (1996), only 4 reported program effects on reading or math achievement outcomes: Co-NECT, Modern Red School House, the National Alliance for Restructuring Education, and Roots & Wings. Of this number, only 1—Roots & Wings—met a rigorous standard of improving achievement gains in reading and math (Slavin & Fashola, 1998). But even here as with other whole-school reform initiatives that include direct instruction (Bereiter & Engelmann, 1996, core knowledge (Hirsch, 1987), accelerated schools (Hopfenberg & Levin, 1993; Levin, 1987), school development programs (Comer, 1980, 1988), consistency management and cooperative discipline (Freiberg, Prokosch, & Treister, 1990), coalition of essential schools (Sizer, 1984, 1992, 1996, and the Paideia proposal (Adler, 1982), there is scant evidence that these models have been consistently successful in eliminating the achievement gap between Black and White students, even following 2 to 4 years of implementation (see Goldberg & Richards, 1996; Slavin & Fashola, 1998; Slavin & Madden, 1999;

Slavin, Madden, & Wasik, 1996, who profile the impact of these various reform initiatives on student achievement).

To their credit, whole-school initiatives have combined curriculum and pedagogical reform with innovative governance structures and processes. With the exception of the talent development model (Boykin, 2000), which aims at student transformation and curriculum reform, these models have not embraced issues of social stereotyping, diagnostic threat, or internalized racism (Si^2) that we have argued affect real (Sr^2) and actual (St^2) achievement as well as the variance component for error (Se^2). We therefore question whether these curriculum and pedagogical reforms alone can eliminate the achievement gap between Black and White students.

Independent Schools Reform

From Rattery's (1990) database, there were about 400 independent African American schools serving 52,000 mixed-income students. About 80% of these schools were owned or operated by African Americans, about one half of these by churches. Although many of these schools do not stress or even endorse an Afrocentric view, all stress high academic achievement. There is, however, little systematic data on how students representing this pool of 400 schools perform on standardized tests of reading and math.

Effective Schools Reform

The focal concern of effective schools reform has been with the description of schools producing high achievement among low-income students (Brookover, 1985; Cole-Henderson, 2000; Edmonds, 1979; Purkey & Smith, 1982; Sizemore, 1983, 1985; Weber, 1971). Among other things, these researchers uniformly identify strong administrative leadership, an orderly school climate, high expectations for student success, a focus on academic skills acquisition, frequent monitoring and testing of student progress, maximum time-on-task, and an organizational culture supportive of collegial exchange and academic excellence. To the degree these characteristics are normalized, near or above-average achievements in reading and math have been reported (for examples of detailed descriptions of these schools, see Cole-Henderson, 2000; Collins, 1990; Sizemore, 1983, 1985; Weber, 1971).

Because of the strategy of frequent monitoring and testing of student performance, these schools directly address the issue of diagnostic threat (Steele, 1997), which theoretically should reduce the magnitude of error (as reflected in variance component Se^2), and their uniformly high expectation of success is likely to counter negative influences associated with variance component Si^2. The integration of monitoring results with lesson planning also represents a pedagogical feature of effective schools that may influence actual performance directly (St^2).

Afrocentric School Reforms

Major proponents of African-centered education have sought to undo hegemonic claims of European constructions of history and culture by reconstructing history and culture from an African perspective (Asante, 1987; Harris, 1992; Hilliard, 1984; C. D. Lee, 1992; Pine & Hilliard, 1990). In Detroit, which would seem to be the capital of Afrocentric reform, 21 schools endorse this model, which (a) stresses interpretation of history and culture from African perspective, (b) emphasizes the promotion of self-esteem, (c) maintains open buildings 6 days

a week from 7:30 a.m. to 7:30 p.m., (d) extends the school year from 180 days to 200 days, (e) pairs adults with children from single-parent families, (f) insists on parental involvement, and (g) emphasizes the importance of in-service training on Afrocentric perspective and methods. It would appear that results are mixed, with some schools reporting student achievement above and others below city and state averages (Butty, 1996). Although there are several different models of Afrocentric education, all share a commitment to exposing children to the cultural and sociopolitical history of Africans on the Continent and in the Diaspora through an African-centered lens. This commitment informs the approach to the teaching of reading and math. To this degree, we would anticipate a salutary impact on the variance component Si^2. Whether curriculum and pedagogical methods associated with these models have a salutary impact on variance components St^2 and Se^2 is not readily apparent from published studies of Afrocentric educational reforms. The extent to which parental self-selection of these programs influences achievement outcomes remains an unaddressed evaluation challenge for Afrocentric reforms as it does for religious school reforms.

Religious School Reforms

Here we limit our attention to Catholic schools, which feature close supervision, high expectations, sense of community, and instruction in moral values. Studies of the effects of Catholic instruction on high school students have generally revealed that (a) African Americans and Hispanics have higher levels of math and reading achievement than in private and public schools, (b) low-income students achieve greater gains in math and reading than in private and public schools, (c) the level of dropouts for African American students in Catholic schools is 4.6% in contrast to 14.3% in private schools and 17.2% in public schools, (d) reading and math achievement is about the same in children of single-parent as two-parent households in Catholic but not in public schools, and (e) students in Catholic schools experience larger gains in the last 2 years of high school than in public school (Coleman & Hoffer, 1987; Coleman, Hoffer, & Kilgore, 1982a, 1982b; Hill, Foster, & Gendler, 1990; Marsh, 1991). Moreover, a study of more than 54 Catholic schools where 70% of the students were poor and minority revealed that many of these children transferring in with deficits in reading and math later performed above national norms in some areas and were within 6 months of national norms in other areas (Blum, 1985).

In addition to structured and demanding curriculum affecting St^2 directly, we speculate that the normalization of high expectations and personal regard for students of different ethnic and social backgrounds may contribute even more to the reduction of social stereotyping and internalized racism that otherwise undermine academic readiness and student achievement (variance component Si^2).

RECOMMENDATIONS FOR REMEDY

From the measurement perspective organizing and motivating this chapter, eliminating the achievement gap between Black and White students would require reducing negative effects of social stereotyping and internalized racism (Si^2), which also are expected to affect real (Sr^2) and actual (St^2) achievement as well as errors in responding during test-taking (Se^2). In our formulation of program

or policy initiatives for families at risk, we generally use the concept of design redundancy, which entails specifying more than one way of affecting a particular outcome—St^2, in the present instance. In this spirit, St^2 also can be enhanced by reducing error variance associated with diagnostic threat (Se^2) or by implementing curriculum and pedagogical reforms that affect performance directly (St^2). These theoretical implications structure our approach to prospective remedies.

Reducing Effects of Social Stereotyping and Internalized Racism (Si^2)

Racism is still the bane of American society (Taylor, 1980; Taylor & Grundy, 1996). Its ubiquity is expressed at every level—in public policy, in the electronic and print media, and in a variety of holding environments, including schools, churches, families, peers, and human and medical service organizations. Although we tend to bristle at the thought that we are anything other than a civil society, the record points in an embarrassingly different direction. Even among academics, one survey suggests that the majority believe that Blacks are genetically inferior (Snyderman & Rothman, 1988).

That African Americans are victimized by the ubiquity of racism is suggested from our research, which indicates that between 15% and 50% of African Americans identify with White racist concepts of Blacks as mentally defective and physically gifted (Taylor & Obiechina, in press). For low-income single parents whose children are often at higher risk of academic under-achievement, the level of internalization may be closer to 50%. In general, we believe that the effects of racism are often underestimated in the development of program and policy initiatives designed to close the achievement gap characterizing Black and White students. This neglect is regrettable because evidence indicates that internalized racism is associated with health risks of a wide range: *mental* (Brown, 1976; Franklin, 1986; Taylor, 1999; Taylor, Henderson, & Jackson, 1991; Taylor & Jackson, 1990a, 1990b, 1991; Tomes, Brown, Semenya, & Simpson, 1990), *social* (Taylor, 1990; Taylor & Zhang, 1990), and *physical* (Tull et al., 1999). Thus, the challenge is to protect African American children from negative effects of racism while challenging them to academic, social, and cultural standards that controvert racist claims.

Based on our review, reforms that feature the expectation that all children can and will learn provide a fundamental antidote to the stereotype that Blacks are intellectually inferior. Effective school reform would provide one example, Catholic school reform another, Success for All a third, and Afrocentric school reform a fourth. A fifth, values for life, also nurtures self-regulatory, hermeneutical, and protective processes that help students manage and transform daily hassles and life events. Earlier versions of Title I have not been successful in lifting or translating high expectations, and the jury is still out on the extent to which latter-day versions of Title I and for-profit initiatives are able to do so. Also, the extent to which traditional character education reforms promote high expectations that counter effects of internalized racism is unclear. In relation to these observations, we recommend support of reform initiatives that (a) infuse expectations of above-average achievement—a minimum of 70% of African American children will perform at or above the 50th percentile rank on standardized tests of reading and math; (b) counter racist claims that Blacks are mentally defective and physically gifted; and (c) enhance emotional

resilience and self-regulatory and interpretive skills that help students manage or transform challenging environments that otherwise undermine academic readiness and success.

Enhancing Achievement Performance Directly (St^2)

We believe that whole-school reforms that entail curriculum and pedagogical innovations represent efforts to increase achievement outcomes directly (i.e., not through Si^2 or Se^2). Marva Collins's (1990) use of great books and Shakespeare to accelerate achievement levels of African American students suggests that use of comparably challenging materials may have similarly accelerative effects on achievement outcomes. Or the use of pedagogical reforms such as instructional routines used in values for life or cooperative learning featured in success for all may be effective in engaging students' interests in curriculum materials. *Our recommendation, then, favors reform initiatives that use (a) highly challenging, developmentally sequenced, and affectively engaging curriculum and (b) instructional pedagogy that enhances students' engagement with curriculum materials.*

Reducing Effects of Diagnostic Threat (Se^2)

Variations in actual achievement (St^2) depend in part on the relative presence or absence of diagnostic threat (Steele, 1997), which contributes to error variance Se^2. To the degree that we can help students manage diagnostic threat, estimates of their actual achievement should be less erroneous. In this connection, it would seem that weekly testing programs featured in effective schools may go a long way toward attenuating student evaluation anxieties about testing in general—including annual testing on state or nationally standardized tests in reading and math. This observation leads to our first recommendation for reducing Se^2: Weekly testing in reading and math should be used to evaluate student progress and inform the development of subsequent lesson plans.

But we think it is possible to reduce error variance even further by enhancing students' performance efficacy ("I can do this X") and outcome efficacy ("Doing X leads to outcome Y"), where X represents completing seatwork and homework assignments and Y represents doing well on weekly exams. Recasting these efficacy expectations as Bayesian analogues, Taylor (1998) discovered that there may be three forms of structured feedback that offer promise of increasing performance and outcome efficacy: Teachers would need to present (a) evidence of change on weekly exams over time, (b) evidence of completed seatwork or homework assignments, and (c) evidence showing that completed seatwork or homework assignments are linked to changes on weekly exams over time. Together, this provision of *structured feedback* is expected to enhance students' sense of empowerment—the expectation that they can do X, which leads to Y. We believe that students' co-ownership of responsibility for reading and math outcomes Y will have a general stabilizing effect on test-taking disposition, which we anticipate will reduce error variance Se^2. These considerations, then, lead to our second recommendation for reducing Se^2: Use structured feedback to enhance students' sense of performance and outcome efficacy.

FINAL THOUGHTS

Many families in inner-city communities experience deepening despair over the future of their children. The challenge of academic underachievement is one expression of this problem, which often is alloyed with concerns over juvenile delinquency, teenage pregnancy, drug experimentation, gang involvement, and general perils of street life in the neighborhood and beyond. It is within this context of urban realities that our concept of "design redundancies" introduced previously becomes all the more urgent and appropriate. Reaching our new standard—70% of African American children performing at or above the 50th percentile on standardized tests of reading and math—will entail access to educational reforms that affect each component of our measurement model: St^2, Si^2, and Se^2. Only those reforms that embrace these components in their design and implementation can be called culturally competent.

Implementation of culturally competent reforms will require overcoming institutional coquettishness about racial matters, promoting designer openness in collaborating with other designers, and shifting current evaluation paradigms to accommodate our new standard—from reporting only gain scores in relation to nonequivalent controls (the usual case) to reporting the percentage of African American students scoring at or above the 50th percentile rank in reading and math (the rare case). Only then can we evaluate reform efficacy in relation to our new standard for the new millennium—70/50[9]—and only then can we evaluate the responsiveness of reform initiatives to educational needs and aspirations of the African American community.

Finally, the African American community itself needs to create new centers of accountability for educational excellence. Civil rights and social advocacy organizations along with church conventions, adjudicatories, and coalitions having vested interests in the cultural future of African

Americans must be brought to the table. These vested guardians and purveyors of our cultural interests should receive "report cards" that profile the achievement of reform initiatives against our new standard, and they should be involved as well in the initial selection and ongoing evaluation of reform initiatives serving inner-city communities. As the expectation of excellence is normalized in relation to reforms that produce it, we expect to improve the social, mental, and physical well-being of African Americans and the nation as a whole.[10]

NOTES

1. The authors express their appreciation to Dr. Charlotte Brown, a member of the Committee of Common Causation and a staff member of the University of Pittsburgh's Western Psychiatric Institute and Clinic, who first called our attention to the health implications of literacy.

2. We recognize the technical difficulty of estimating this structural model. Nonetheless, the conceptual implications of this reformulation have heuristic implications that may contribute to strategies for closing the gap. This is a matter we take up in the next section on "closing the gap."

3. The Committee on Common Causation, which the senior author chairs, hypothesizes that values—our axiological view—are related to a wide range of social, mental, and physical health outcomes. In the present application, educational disparities would be represented as a major social health issue.

4. This value, coupled with subsequent values of love and respect and interpersonal skills, may also have special significance for current public concern over school violence in general or gun violence in particular. Indeed, our values for life peer support initiative was recognized in 2000 by the governor of Pennsylvania as one of the top three violence prevention programs in the state. Our thanks to Dr. Sekai Turner, member of the Committee on Common Causation and faculty member of Psychology in Education at the University of Pittsburgh, for developing this initiative (Turner, Lyons, & Smith, 2000).

5. We also have developed measures to evaluate the behavioral expression of values for life in preschoolers (VAL-O Inventory) and in adolescents and adults (VAL-R Inventory).

6. We believe also that normalization of values for life will diminish risks of conduct disorders, juvenile delinquency, gang formation, school violence, teenage pregnancy, and drug dependence.

7. Making commonplace.

8. Unfortunately, due to shifting demographics associated with declining enrollments, the Pittsburgh School District recently decided to close McKelvy Elementary School.

9. This is a truncated representation of our new standard: "70% over the 50th percentile in reading and math."

10. The basis for this expectation was introduced in the section "Nature of the Gap."

REFERENCES

Adler, M. J. (1982). *The Paideia proposal: An educational manifesto.* New York: Macmillan.

Asante, M. K. (1987). *The Afrocentric idea.* Philadelphia: Temple University Press.

Asbury, C. A., Adderly-Kelly, B., & Knuckle, E. P. (1987). Relationship among WISC-R performance categories and measured ethnic identity in Black adolescents. *Journal of Negro Education, 56,* 172-183.

Baker, D. W., Parker, R. M. & Williams, M. V. (1996). The health care experience of patients with low literacy. *Archives of Family Medicine, 5,* 329-334.

Baker, D. W., Parker, R. M., Williams, M. V., & Clark, W. S. (1998). Health literacy and the risk of hospital admission. *Journal of General Internal Medicine, 13,* 791-798.

Baker, D. W., Parker, R. M., Williams, M. V., Clark, W. S., & Nurss, J. (1997). The relationship of patient reading ability to self-report health and use of health services. *American Journal of Public Health, 87,* 1027-1030.

Bennett, W. J. (1988). Moral literacy and the formation of character-experience of patients with low literacy. *Archives of Family Medicine, 5,* 329-334.

Bereiter, C., & Engelmann, S. (1996). *Teaching disadvantaged children in the preschool.* Englewood Cliffs, NJ: Prentice Hall.

Block, J. (1994). Studying personality the long way. In D. C. Funder, R. D. Parke, C. Tomlinson-Keasey, & K. Widman (Eds.), *Studying lives through time: Personality development.* Washington, DC: American Psychological Association.

Block, J., & Block, J. H. (1980). The role of ego-control and ego resiliency in the organization of behavior. In W. A. Collins (Ed.), *Development of cognition, affect, and social relations.* Hillsdale, NJ: Lawrence Erlbaum.

Blum, V. (1985, May). Private elementary education in the inner city. *Phi Delta Kappan,* pp. 643-646.

Bodilly, S. J. (1996). *Lessons from the New American Schools Development Corporation's Development Phase.* Washington, DC: RAND.

Borman, G. D., D'Agostino, J. V., Wong, K. K., & Hedge, L. V. (1998). The longitudinal achievement of chapter 1 students: Preliminary evidence from the Prospects Study. *Journal of Education for Students Placed at Risk, 3,* 363-400.

Bouffard, T., & Vezeau, C. (1998). The developing self-system and self-regulation of primary school children. In M. Ferrari & R. Sternberg (Eds.), *Self-awareness: Its nature and development.* New York: Guilford.

Bouffard-Bouchard, T., Parent, S., & Larivée, S. (1993). Self-regulation on a concept-formation task among average and gifted students. *Journal of Experimental Child Psychology, 56,* 115-134.

Boykin, A. W. (2000). The talent development model of schooling: Placing students at promise for academic success. *Journal of Education for Students Placed at Risk, 5,* 3-25.

Bransford, J. D., Stein, B. S., Vye, N. J., Franks, J.J., Auble, P. M., Nezynski, K. J. & Perfetto, G. A. (1982). Difference in approaches to learning: An overview. *Journal of Experimental Psychology: General, 111,* 390-398.

Brookover, W. B. (1985). Can we make schools effective for minority students? *Journal of Negro Education, 54,* 257-268.

Brown, A. B. (1976). *Personality correlates of the Developmental Inventory of Black Consciousness.* Unpublished master's thesis, University of Pittsburg, Pittsburg, PA.

Butty, D. C. (1996, May 19). Afrocentrism generates mixed results in Detroit and debate across the nation. *The Detroit News,* p. 85.

Carter, L. F. (1984). The sustaining effects study of compensatory and elementary education. *Educational Researcher, 13,* 4-13.

Cherulnik, P. D., & Sounders, S. B. (1984). The social contents of place schemata: People are judged by the places where they live and work. *Population and Environment, 7,* 211-233.

Christiansen, J., Christiansen, J. H., & Howard, (1997). Using protective factors to enhance resilience and school for at-risk students. *Intervention in School and Clinic, 3,* 86-89.

Cicchetti, D., Rogosch, F. A., Lynch, M., & Holt, K. D. (1993). Resilience in maltreated children: Processes leading to adaptive outcome. *Development and Psychopathology, 5,* 629-647.

Cole-Henderson, B. (2000). Organizational characteristics of school that successfully serve low-income urban African American students. *Journal of Education for Students Placed at Risk, 5*(1-2), 77-91.

Coleman, J., & Hoffer, T. (1987). *Public and private high schools: The impact of communities.* New York: Basic Books.

Coleman, J., Hoffer, T., & Kilgore, S. (1982a). Achievement and segregation in secondary schools: A further look at private and public school differences. *Sociology of Education, 55,* 162-182.

Coleman, J., Hoffer, T., & Kilgore, S. (1982b). Cognitive outcomes in public and private schools. *Sociology of Education, 55,* 65-76.

Collins, M. (1990). *Marva Collins' way.* Los Angeles: J. P. Tarcher.

Comer, J. (1980). *School power.* New York: Free Press.

Comer, J. (1988). Educating poor minority children. *Scientific American, 259,* 42-48.

Edmonds, R. (1979). *A discussion of the literature and issues related to effective schooling.* East Lansing, MI: National Center for Research on Teacher Learning. (ERIC Document Reproduction Service No. ED170394)

Evans, J. P., & Taylor, J. (1995). Why are contemporary gangs more violent than earlier gangs? An exploratory application of the theory of reasoned action. *Journal of Black Psychology, 21,* 71-78.

Ferrari, M., & Sternberg, R. (1998). *Self-awareness: Its nature and development.* New York: Guilford.

Fishbein, M., & Ajen, I. (1975). *Belief, attitude, intention, and behavior: An introduction to theory and research.* Reading, MA: Addison-Wesley.

Franklin, A. T. (1986). *Influence of economic, social, religious, and cultural factors on depression in single Black women with male friends.* Unpublished doctoral dissertation, University of Pittsburgh, Pittsburgh, PA.

Freiberg, H. J., Prokosch, N., & Treister, E. S. (1990). Turning around five at-risk elementary schools. *School Effectiveness and School Improvement, 1*(1), 5-25.

Friedland, R. P., Fritsch, T., Smyth, K. A., Koss, E., Lerner, A. J., Chen, C. H., Petot, G. J., & Debanne, S. M. (2001). Patients with Alzheimer's disease have reduced activities in midlife compared with healthy control-group members. *Proceedings of the National Academy of Sciences, 98*(6), 3440-3445.

Fromm, E. (1976). *To have or to be?* New York: Harper & Row.

Garmezy, N. (1991). Resilience and vulnerability to adverse developmental outcomes associated with poverty. *American Behavior Scientist, 34,* 416-430.

Goldberg, B., & Richards, J. (1996). Co-NECT schools. In S. Stringfield, S. Ross, & L. Smith (Eds.), *Bold plans for school restructuring: The New American Schools Development Corporation Designs.* Mahwah, NJ: Lawrence Erlbaum.

Harris, M. D. (1992). Africentrism and curriculum: Concepts, issues, and prospect. *Journal of Negro Education, 61*(3), 301-316.

Herrenkohl, E. C., Herrenkohl, R. C., & Egolf, B. (1994). Resilient early school-age children from maltreating homes: Outcomes in late adolescence. *American Journal of Orthopsychiatry, 64,* 301-309.

Higgins, G. O. (1994). *Resilient adults: Overcoming a cruel past.* San Francisco: Jossey-Bass.

Hill, P., Foster, G., & Gendler, T. (1990). *High schools with character.* Santa Monica, CA: RAND.

Hilliard, A. (1984). Democratizing the common school in a multicultural society. *Educational and Urban Society, 16,* 262-273.

Hirsch, E. D. (1987). *Cultural literacy: What every American needs to know.* New York: Random House.

Hoge, D., & Andrews, D. A. (1996). An investigation of risk and protective factors in a sample of youth offenders. *Journal of Child Psychology, 37,* 419-424.

Hopfenberg, W. S., & Levin, H. M. (1993). *The accelerated schools resource guide.* San Francisco: Jossey-Bass.

Howard, J., & Hammond, R. (1985, September 9). The hidden obstacles to Black success: Rumors of inferiority. *New Republic,* pp. 17-21.

Huang, S. L. (1995, April). *Comparing the learning environment of resilient and non-resilient Asian American students.* Paper presented at the annual meeting of the American Educational Research Association, New York.

International encyclopedia of economics of education. (1995). New York: Pergamon.

Johnson, Y. E., & Taylor, J. (1998). *The VAL-OE Inventory for K-5 elementary school students.* Pittsburgh, PA: The Village, Center for Family Excellence.

Jolly, B., Scott, J., Feied, C., & Sanford, S. (1993). Functional illiteracy among emergency department patients: A preliminary study. *Annals of Emergency Medicine, 22,* 573-578.

Kandel, E. R., & Hawkins, R. D. (1995). Neuroscience, memory, and language. In R. D. Broadwell (Ed.), *Decade of the brain* (pp. 45-58). Washington, DC: Government Printing Office.

Langer, E. J. (1997). *The power of mindful learning.* Boston: Perseus.

Lawrence, L. (1999). *Relationship between self-reliance and indicators of academic excellence.* Unpublished manuscript, Department of Africana Studies, University of Pittsburgh, Pittsburgh, PA.

Lee, C. D. (1992). Profile of an independent Black institution: African-centered education at work. *Journal of Negro Education, 61*(2), 160-177.

Lee, P. P. (1999). Why literacy matters: Links between reading ability and health. *Archives of Ophthalmology, 117*(1), 100-103.

Lee, S. J. (1996). *Unraveling the "model minority" stereotype: Listening to Asian American youth.* New York: Teachers College Press.

Lefebvre-Pinard, A. (1985). Taking charge of one's cognitive activity: Moderator of competence. In E. D. Neimark, R. De Lisi, & J. L. Newman (Eds.), *Moderators of competence* (pp. 191-211). Hillsdale, NJ: Lawrence Erlbaum.

Levin, H. M. (1987). Accelerated schools for disadvantaged students. *Educational Leadership, 44*(6), 19-21.

Lundy, B. (1997). *Relationship between self-reliance and study habits.* Unpublished manuscript, Department of Africana Studies, University of Pittsburgh, Pittsburgh, PA.

Markus, H., Cross, S., & Wurk, E. (1990). The role of the self-system in competence. In R. J. Sternberg & J. Kolligan, Jr. (Eds.), *Competence considered* (pp. 205-225). New Haven, CT: Yale University Press.

Markus, H., Niedenthal, P., & Nurius, P. (1986). On motivation and the self-concept. In R. M. Sorrentino & E. T. Higgins (Eds.), *Handbook of motivation and cognition: Foundations of social behavior* (pp. 96-121). New York: Guilford.

Marsh, H. (1991, May). Public, Catholic single-sex, and Catholic coeducational high schools: Their effect on achievement, affect, and behaviors. *American Journal of Education,* pp. 320-356.

Marwick, C. (1997). Patients' lack of literacy may contribute to billions of dollars in higher hospital costs. *JAMA, 278,* 971-972.

McCombs, B. L., & Marzano, R. J. (1990). Putting self in self-regulated learning: The self as agent integrating will and skill. *Educational Psychologist, 25,* 51-69.

McMillin, M.M., Kaufman, P., & Whitener, S.D. (September 13, 1994). *Dropout rates in the U.S. (1993).* U.S. Department of Education, Office of Educational Research and Improvement, National Center for Education Statistics, Publication NCES 94-669.

Miles, S., & Davis, T. (1995). Patients who can't read: Implications for the health care system. *JAMA, 274,* 1719-1720.

Moran, P. B., & Eckenrode, J. (1992). Protective personality characteristics among adolescence victims of maltreatment. *Child Abuse and Neglect, 16,* 743-754.

Murrell, A. J. (1989, August). *Social support and ethnic identification as predictors of career and family roles of Black women.* Paper presented at the 21st Annual Convention of the Association of Black Psychologists, Fort Worth, TX.

National Center for Educational Statistics (2002a). Comparisons of average reading scales scores by race/ethnicity. http://nces.ed.gov/nationsreportcard/reading/scorerace8.asp.

National Center for Educational Statistics (2002b). *Racial/ethnic gaps in average mathematics scores, grades 4, 8, and 12: 1990-2000.* http://nces.ed.gov/nationsreportcard/mathematics/results/scale-ethnic-compare.asp.

Ogbu, J. U., & Fordham, S. (1986). Black students' school success: Coping with the burden of "acting White." *The Urban Review, 18,* 176-206.

Pinard, A. (1986). "Prise de conscience" and taking charge of one's own cognitive functioning. *Human Development, 29,* 341-354.

Pine, G. J., & Hilliard, A. G., III. (1990). Rx for racism: Imperatives for America's schools. *Phi Delta Kappan, 71,* 593-600.

Powell, A. L., Zahner, D., & Micheli-Tzanakou, E. (1995). The protective effects of education on simulated brain injury. *Journal of Neurotrauma, 12*(5), 957-960.

Purkey, S., & Smith, M. (1982). *Effective schools: A review.* Madison: Wisconsin Center for Education Research. (ERIC Document Reproduction Service No. 221-534)

Quintás, A. L. (1989). *The knowledge of values: A methodological introduction.* Lanham, MD: University Press of America.

Radke-Yarrow, M., & Sherman, T. (1990). Hard growing: Children who survive. In J. Rolf, A. S. Masten, D. Cichetti, K. Neucherlein, & S. Weintraub (Eds.), *Risk and protective factors in the development of psychopathology.* New York: Cambridge University Press.

Rattery, J. (1990). African-American achievement: A research agenda emphasizing independent schools. In K. Lomotey (Ed.), *Going to school: The African-American experience.* Albany, NY: State University of New York Press.

Rutter, M. (1985). Resilience in the face of adversity: Protective factors and resistance of psychiatric disorder. *British Journal of Psychiatry, 147,* 598-611.

Shore, B. M., & Dover, A. C. (1987). Metacognition, intelligence and giftedness. *Gifted Child Quarterly, 31,* 37-39.

Sizemore, B. (1983). *An abashing anomaly: The high achieving predominantly Black elementary school* [Executive summary]. Pittsburg, PA: University of Pittsburgh, Department of Black Community Education, Research, and Development.

Sizemore, B. (1985). Pitfalls and promises old effective schools research. *Journal of Negro Education, 54,* 269-288.

Sizer, T. (1984). *Horace's compromise: The dilemma of the American high school.* Boston: Houghton Mifflin.

Sizer, T. (1992). *Horace's school.* New York: Houghton Mifflin.

Sizer, T. (1996). *Horace's hope.* New York: Houghton Mifflin.

Slavin, R. E., & Fashola, O. S. (1998). *Show me the evidence! Proven and promising programs for America's schools.* Thousand Oaks, CA: Corwin Press.

Slavin, R. E., & Madden, N. A. (1999). *Roots & Wings. Effects of whole-school reform on student achievement.* Center for Research on the Education of Students Placed at Risk (CRESPAR), Report No. 36.

Slavin, R. E., Madden, N. A., & Wasik, B. A. (1996). Roots and Wings. In S. Stringfield, S. Ross, & L. Smith (Eds.), *Bold plans for school restructuring: The New American Schools Development Corporation Designs.* Mahwah, NJ: Lawrence Erlbaum.

Snyderman, M., & Rothman, S. (1988). *The IQ controversy: The media and public policy.* New Brunswick, NJ: Transaction Books.

Spandorfer, J., Karras, D., Hughes, L., & Caputo, C. (1995). Comprehension of discharge instructions by patients in an urban emergency department. *Annals of Emergency Medicine, 25,* 71-74.

Steele, C. M. (1997). A threat in the air: How stereotypes shape intellectual identity and performance. *American Psychologist, 52,* 613-629.

Sternberg, R. J., & Davidson, J. E. (1983). Insight in the gifted. *Educational Psychologist, 73,* 1-16.

Stringfield, S., Ross, S., & Smith, L. (Eds.). (1996). *Bold plans for educational reform: The New American Schools Development Corporation Designs.* Hillsdale, NJ: Lawrence Erlbaum.

Strothers, P. (1997). *Relationship between learning orientation and attitudes toward taking technical courses.* Unpublished manuscript, Department of Africana Studies, University of Pittsburgh, Pittsburgh, PA.

Taylor, J. (1980). Dimensionalization of racialism. In R. L. Jones (Ed.), *Black psychology* (3rd ed.). Hampton, VA: Cobb & Henry.

Taylor, J. (1990). Relationship between internalized racism and marital satisfaction. *Journal of Black Psychology, 16,* 45-53.

Taylor, J. (1998). *The village—Transforming school culture Part II: Focus on teachers.* Pittsburgh, PA: Center for Family Excellence.

Taylor, J. (1999). Toward a purposeful systems approach to parenting. In R. L. Jones (Ed.), *African American children, youth and parenting.* Hampton, VA: Cobb & Henry.

Taylor, J., & Bartolomucci, E. (1996). Measuring separation-individuation processes. In R. L. Jones (Ed.), *Handbook of tests and measurements for Black population* (Vol. 2, pp. 71-86). Hampton, VA: Cobb & Henry.

Taylor, J., & Franklin, A. (1994). Psychosocial analysis of Black teenage pregnancies: Implications for public and cultural policies. *Policy Studies Review, 13,* 157-164.

Taylor, J., & Grundy, C. (1996). Measuring Black internalization of White stere types about Blacks: The Nadanolitization Scale. In R. L. Jones (Ed.), *Handbook of tests and measurements for Black populations* (Vol. 2). Hampton, VA: Cobb & Henry.

Taylor, J., Henderson, D., & Jackson, B. B. (1991). A holistic model for understanding and predicting depressive symptoms in African American women. *Journal of Community Psychology, 19,* 306-320.

Taylor, J., & Jackson, B. B. (1990a). Factors affecting alcohol consumption in Black women: Part I. *International Journal of the Addictions, 25,* 1287-1300.

Taylor, J., & Jackson, B.B. (1990b). Factors affecting alcohol consumption in Black women: Part II: *International Journal of the Addictions, 25,* 1415-1427.

Taylor, J., & Jackson, B. B. (1991). Evaluation of a holistic model of mental health symptoms in African American women. *Journal of Black Psychology, 18,* 19-45.

Taylor, J., Johnson, Y. C., & Michie, S. (1998). *The Village: Closing the Achievement Gap.* Center for Family Excellence, Inc., Pittsburgh, PA.

Taylor, J., & Kouyaté, M. (in preparation). *Values for life in the arts: Theoretical and pedagogical foundations.*

Taylor, J., & Michie, S. (in preparation). *Association between values for life and student achievement.*

Taylor, J., & Obiechina, C. (in press). Cultural alienation: Analytical and empirical implications. *Journal of Black Studies.*

Taylor, J., Obiechina, C., & Harrison, S. (1998). Toward a psychology of liberation and restoration: Answering the challenge of cultural alienation. In R. L. Jones (Ed.), *African American mental health* (pp. 283-301). Hampton, VA: Cobb & Henry.

Taylor, J., Rogers, J., & Thomas, L. (in preparation). *Normalizing values for life to promote spiritual integration.*

Taylor, J., Thomas, L., & Bagley, E. (1999). *Introducing values for life childcare.* Pittsburgh: Center for Family Excellence.

Taylor, J., Turner, S., & Lewis, M. (1999). Valucation: Definition, theory, and methods. In R. L. Jones (Ed.), *Advances in African American psychology* (pp. 51-80). Hampton, VA: Cobb & Henry.

Taylor, J., Turner, S., Underwood, C., Franklin, A., Jackson, E., & Staff, V. (1994). Values for life: Preliminary evaluation of the educational component. *Journal of Black Psychology, 20,* 210-233.

Taylor, J., & Zhang, X. (1990). Cultural identity in maritally distressed and nondistressed black couples. *The Western Journal of Black Studies, 14,* 205-213.

Tomes, E., Brown, A., Semenya, K., & Simpson, J. (1990). Depression in Black women of low socioeconomic status: Psychological factors and nursing diagnosis. *Journal of National Black Nurses Association, 4,* 37-46.

Tull, E. S., Wickramasurioya, T., Taylor, J., Smith-Barnes, V., Brown, M., Champagnie, G., Daye, K., Donaldson, K., Solomon, N., Walker, S., Fraiser, H., & Jordan, O. W. (1999). Relationship of internalized racism to abdominal obesity and blood pressure in Afro-Caribbean women. *Journal of the National Medical Association, 91,* 447-452.

Turner, S., Lyons, P., & Smith, K. (2000). *The village: Peer support groups.* Pittsburgh, PA: Center for Family Excellence.

Vazsonyi, A. T., & Flannery, D. J. (1997). Early adolescent delinquent behaviors: Associations with family and school domains. *Journal of Early Adolescence, 17,* 271-293.

Weber, G. (1971, October). *Inner-city children can be taught to read: Four successful schools* (Council on Basic Education Occasional Paper No. 18). New York: Clearinghouse on Urban Education.

Werner, E. (1989). Vulnerability and resilience: A longitudinal perspective. In M. Bambring, E. Losel, & H. Skowronek (Eds.), *Children at risk: Assessment, longitudinal research and intervention.* New York: de Gruyter.

Werner, E., & Smith, R. (1982). *Vulnerable but invincible: A longitudinal study of resilient children and youth*. New York: McGraw-Hill.

Williams, M. V., Baker, D. W., Hoing, E. G., Lee, M. L., & Nowian, A. (1998). Inadequate literacy is a barrier to asthma knowledge and self-care. *Chest, 114*, 1008-1015.

Williams, M. V., Baker, D. W., & Parker, R. M. (1998). Relationship of functional health literacy to patients' knowledge of their chronic disease. *Archives of Internal Medicine, 158*, 166-172.

Wolin, S. J., & Wolin, S. (1993). *The resilient self: How survivors of troubled families rise above adversities*. New York: Villard.

Wynne, E. A., & Walberg, H. J. (1986). Pupil character and academics: Concurrent priorities. *NASSP Bulletin, 70*, 59-66.

CHAPTER 17

Assessment of Psychometric Intelligence for Racial and Ethnic Minorities

Some Unanswered Questions

ELEANOR ARMOUR-THOMAS
Queens College

The validity of conventional tests of intelligence for racial and ethnic minorities has remained one of the most enduring and contentious issues in psychoeducational assessment. At the heart of the seemingly unending debate is whether intelligence as measured by standardized tests is a universal phenomenon and therefore could be subjected to legitimate comparisons between and among cultural groups. Despite the furor, conventional tests of intelligence continue to be used for educational purposes. For example, test scores predict school grades, standardized academic achievement, and some aspects of job performance (Greenfield, 1997; Neisser et al., 1996), and they are used as a major factor in placement in gifted and talented and special education programs (Suzuki & Valencia,

1997). But in a democratic and multicultural society such as the United States, it is very difficult to avoid a misunderstanding of test results for populations whose cultural frame of reference is different from the population on whom intelligence tests were initially normed. Indeed, since its inception, critics have voiced concerns about the use and interpretation of results of standardized measures of intelligence for some racial and ethnic minorities, particularly those socialized beyond the pale of the mainstream or dominant culture of the United States (e.g., African Americans, Latinos, and Native Americans).

Some problems in assessment for these populations concern conceptual issues regarding the construct of intelligence itself, whereas others are more methodological in nature and relate to the standardization criteria used in intelligence test construction, administration, and validation. It is crucial that these challenges are not only understood but that steps are also taken to ensure greater cultural sensitivity by test developers, researchers, and practitioners who work with children from culturally diverse backgrounds.

The thesis of this chapter is that any standardized test of intelligence, oftentimes called an IQ test, only has validity for the cultural group(s) for whom it was developed. This chapter opens with a brief revisitation of a perspective of intelligence that I refer to as *psychometric* intelligence. Although other conceptions of intelligence have emerged in recent years—for example, Gardner's (1983) multiple intelligences, Sternberg's (1985) triarchic theory of intelligence, and Goleman's (1995) emotional intelligence—the psychometric perspective is singled out for particular attention because the majority of conventional tests of intelligence are based on psychometric methodologies. Moreover, it is the validity of such tests that has been suspect for some racial and ethnic minority groups in the United States. Next, the interdependency of culture and human cognition is explored, the discussion of which forms the backdrop for challenging assumptions and raising unanswered questions about psychometric intelligence for some racial and ethnic minority children in the United States. This chapter ends with recommendations for researchers and professional practitioners for promoting greater cultural sensitivity in the assessment of cognitive abilities, oftentimes used interchangeably with the construct *intelligence*.

PSYCHOMETRIC INTELLIGENCE . . . A WORK IN PROGRESS

Psychometric intelligence is used here to refer to the mental operations underlying performance on a set of cognitive tasks identified through factor analysis. Factor analysis is a mathematical procedure that analyzes the intercorrelations among different kinds of cognitive tasks. The results of the analysis reveal sources of observable individual differences in performance that psychometricians call *factors,* each of which is presumed to represent a mental or cognitive ability. Factors may differ in terms of *number* (e.g., Horn's [1991] nine abilities; Spearman's [1927/1981] two-factor theory; Thurstone's [1938] seven primary abilities) or *structure* (e.g., Carroll's [1993] three-stratum theory; Guilford's structure of the intellect model [1982]; Vernon's [1971] hierarchical model). Examples of psychometric abilities include memory; quantitative, inductive, and deductive reasoning; comprehension; knowledge; visual spatialization; visual and auditory processing; and speed of cognitive processing. There is a strong empirical evidence for the psychometric ability model (see, e.g., Carroll, 1993), which serves as a reference for the analysis and interpretation of most conventional tests of intelligence, such as the third edition of the Wechsler Intelligence Scale for Children (Wechsler, 1991), the fourth edition of the Stanford-Binet Intelligence Scale (Thorndike, Hagen, & Sattler, 1986), the Woodcock-Johnson Psycho-Educational Battery—Revised (Woodcock & Johnson, 1989), and the Kaufman Adolescent and Adult Intelligence Test (Kaufman & Kaufman, 1993).

A major assumption of the psychometric view of intelligence that has influenced the development of these measures is that individual differences in intellectual functioning can be understood in terms of these "factors of the mind" that are unaffected by culture. Recently, Salovey and Mayer (1994) articulated this assumption that seems to undergird any measure of psychometric intelligence: "Intelligence, as defined by Western psychology, is the property of the individual, and that individual, idiocentric or allocentric, can have his or her intelligence gauged by abilities at manipulating symbols" (p. 310).

An even more compelling justification for the use of psychometric intelligence came from a group of well-known researchers considered as experts on intelligence and intelligence testing. In a position paper titled "Mainstream Science on Intelligence," developed in 1994 and reprinted in the journal *Intelligence* (Gottfredson, 1997), they signed a statement that

> intelligence is a very general mental capability that . . . can be measured, and individual tests measure it well. . . . Intelligence tests are not culturally biased against American blacks, or other native-born, English-speaking peoples in the U.S. Rather, IQ scores predict equally accurately for all such Americans, regardless of race and social class. (p. 17)

This claim, though, has not gone unchallenged by other well-known researchers who question whether any standardized measure of intelligence, psychometric or otherwise, can be used with populations whose cultural frame of reference is substantively different from the cultural group(s) for whom the test was initially developed and validated. For example, as early as 1970, the Association of Black psychologists (Williams, 1970) called for a moratorium on intelligence testing for racial minorities, with charges that test data

> label black children as uneducable; place black children in special classes; potentiate inferior education; assign black children to lower education tracks than whites; deny black children higher educational opportunities; and destroy positive intellectual growth and development of black children. (p. 5)

Today, criticisms of IQ tests are as strong as the condemnation of it more than 30 years ago. For example, Dent (1996) argued that the cultural content of standardized intelligence tests unfairly penalizes some ethnic minorities:

> Asking an African American child who has lived in the inner-city, a Hispanic youngster, brought up in a barrio, or a refugee child who recently arrived from another country questions that reflect White American middle-class values and experiences will reveal little about that child's cognitive ability or intellectual functioning. (p. 110)

Finally, recent reviews (e.g., Gresham & Witt, 1997; Reschley, 1997) have found little justification for the use of intelligence tests in schools, with claims that (a) IQ measures are no better at identifying low-achieving students or students with low cognitive abilities and learning disabilities than what could be obtained from teacher judgments, and (b) no empirical evidence shows that recommendations from IQ tests do in fact lead to better educational intervention for children.

Despite the voluminous research and widespread practice of psychometric tests of intelligence, I consider them "works in progress" because neither test developers, researchers, nor professional practitioners have given sufficient attention to aspects of culture that matter when assessing children from diverse backgrounds. If differences due to culture are real but unexamined or if no meaningful benefits can be shown for all children who obtain low IQ scores, might not the psychometric principles on which tests are based be reasonably questioned? In a later section, I try to show how continuing cultural insensitivity in intellectual assessment for some racial and ethnic minorities will guarantee that test development, research, and practice based on psychometric methodologies will remain "a work in progress."

CULTURE AND COGNITION

I take the position that *intelligence,* however defined, is a culture-dependent construct because it develops and finds expression in the shared ways of life of a social group. The position is neither new nor original and is consistent with a fundamental assumption in Vygotskian theory that human development is inseparable from culturally and socially organized activities (Vygotsky, 1978). This premise has undergirded much of the cross-cultural research in cognitive development and behavior in the past 20 years and should guide test development and administration as well. The term *cognition* is used to describe those mental or cognitive processes that any culture considers necessary for solving problems, representing information, understanding, making decisions, reasoning, and remembering. Because these processes are similar to "factors of the mind" as defined in psychometric tests of intelligence, they are used interchangeably with terms such as *mental abilities* or *intellectual abilities*. Admittedly, this is a rather narrow conception of intelligence but one that has informed the majority of widely used conventional tests of intelligence.

In previous research, my colleague and I (Armour-Thomas & Gopaul-McNicol, 1998) suggested a biocultural perspective for assessing intelligence, and the current conceptualization about culture and cognition draws heavily from and builds on that work. Although cognitions underlying behavior deemed "intelligent" may be identified through psychometric procedures, they do not function as abstract thought. Rather, they are inextricably wedded to a cultural group's (a) values and beliefs about what and how these processes are to be applied to cognitive tasks important and relevant to the cultural group's way of life, (b) the language style used by its members for communicating about matters pertaining to the development and manifestation of cognitive skills, and (c) the symbol system that the cultural group uses to embody cognitive tasks of interest.

CULTURAL ATTRIBUTES

Although definitions of culture abound in the psychological literature, I examined those that include measurable characteristics or attributes with relevance for understanding human behavior. This decision finds support among a growing number of researchers who study the role of culture in psychology (e.g., Betancourt & Lopez, 1993; Laboratory of Comparative Human Cognition, 1986; Gauvain, 1995; Greenfield, 1997; Helms, 1992; Phinney, 1996; Rohner, 1984; Triandis et al., 1980; van de Vijver & Leung, 1997). In keeping with this criterion, the following four attributes of culture are singled out for further discussion: values and beliefs, language style, and symbol system.

Values and Beliefs

Values refer to the social norms or conventions that define the standards and expectations for behaviors that, according to Berry (1976), members of a social group regard as proper, right, and natural. Values also include unspoken but shared understandings of a social group about the goal of an activity, the "right" strategies for pursuing it, and judgments of what constitutes "appropriate" performance of goal attainment. In keeping with this definition, the cognitive processes or "factors of the mind" underlying intelligent behavior cannot operate in isolation but rather are tied in large measure to the values of a social group.

Beliefs are emotionally charged mind-sets that reflect a tacit consensus of assumptions that members of a social group form about themselves and others as a consequence of their collective experiences and understandings. Beliefs are closely associated with values in that they are deeply embedded in the standards against which behavior is perceived and judged. Like values, beliefs are also included in a definition of *worldview,* which Mbti (1970) defined as an attitude of mind or perceptions that influence the way people think, act, and speak in various situations of life. Along these lines, how intelligence is defined and who has how much or little of it are strongly influenced by the beliefs of a social group.

Language Styles

The term *language styles* describes the courtesies and conventions governing the different ways a social group communicates ideas, feelings, and thoughts among its members in various situations. The context-specific nature of language styles means that the norms of communication may differ from one setting to the next; consequently, what is considered as an appropriate style of social interaction in one context may be culturally incorrect in another. These idiosyncratic ways of using language do have relevance for human cognition to the extent that individuals who engage in cognitive tasks understand and can apply the rules of social engagement. In adult-child communication, what types of questions are commonly asked by adults and what are the expectations of children in responding to them? Is the interactional format for communication mutually understood by adults and children? Are some of the questions relevant for the communication medium in which cognitive tasks are negotiated?

Symbol System

A symbol system describes the technologies or modes of representation that embody cognitive tasks of any given cultural group. Some cognitive tasks are represented in linguistic, pictorial, figural, and numerical domains, whereas others are represented in symbolic media such as maps, charts, manipulatives, and tools. Vygotsky (1978) was among the first cultural psychologists to call attention to the psychological functions of ancient tools such as tying knots that were used as mnemonic devices to help retrieve information from memory or counting on fingers as a support in higher intellectual functioning involved in basic arithmetic operations. The efficacy with which children are able to engage in cognitive tasks that produce intelligent behavior depends to some extent on the familiarity or the amount of practice they have had with the symbol system in which such tasks are represented.

LEARNING EXPERIENCES IN CULTURAL NICHES

What is the mechanism by which these attributes of culture, as described in the previous section, become linked to human cognition in ways that result in intelligent behavior? To answer this question, I elaborate on two concepts my colleague and I (Armour-Thomas & Gopaul-McNicol, 1998) discussed in our biocultural perspective of intelligence: "learning experiences" and "cultural niche."

A *learning experience* with relevance for cognition describes an encounter with at least four critical ingredients: (a) an adult, capable peer, or anyone who is a significant other in a person's life who provides structure, guidance, and direction for the developing person; (b) the cognitive task or activity of interest to be engaged; (c) a process of social interaction for engaging the cognitive task or activity; and (d) the desired goal to be attained from task or activity engagement. The cultural attributes as described in the previous section are embodied in learning experiences, thus making it impossible to separate cognition from culture. For example, to minimize misunderstanding, the significant other more than likely will use a familiar language style when communicating with the child about the cognitive task or activity of interest. Engagement in the cognitive task or activity is likely to be more efficient if it is represented in a symbol system familiar to the child. Moreover, what constitutes the "right" cognitive strategies during task engagement or "good" performance after task completion are value-laden judgments communicated by the significant other to the child.

The second concept, a *cultural niche,* refers to a highly specialized area in the environment that contains critical ingredients for children's healthy growth and development. The use of the term here is similar to terms used by other researchers who have studied the role of culture in cognitive development. For example, Super and Harkness (1986) and Gauvain (1995) used the term *developmental niche* to discuss cultural influences of children's cognitive development. Earlier, Bronfenbrenner (1979) coined the term *ecological niches* to draw attention to the importance of properties and conditions of some physical and social contexts in fostering cognitive growth. What accounts for a cultural niche's psychological significance, in my judgment, is not merely its physical or social address but the nature and quality of the learning experiences embedded with it and to which the developing person is exposed in a consistent and systematic manner over time. It is the *routinization* of learning experiences within cultural niches that accounts for the development of cognitive potentials along particular trajectories toward particular end states. Contexts such as the home, community, the school, and peer groups may be conceived as cultural niches to the extent that they provide the kinds of learning experiences conducive to cognitive growth and development.

THE CHALLENGE TO DEVELOP AND ADMINISTER CULTURALLY SENSITIVE ASSESSMENT

The United States is a nation of different racial and ethnic groups, each with its own distinctive culture. Thus, one can speak of the culture of Black or White Americans to describe cultural differences between two racial groups. Or one can speak of the culture of African Americans, Anglo-Americans, Native Americans, Latinos, and Asian and Pacific Islander Americans to describe cultural differences between or among ethnic groups. Although there are many cultural attributes of various racial or ethnic groups, I have focused only on those measurable aspects of culture that have relevance for intellectual functioning: shared values, beliefs, language style, and a symbol system.

Attention to these cultural attributes suggests a number of questions for designers of intelligence tests: Does intelligence have the same valued meaning among the various racial and ethnic groups assessed? Is the stimulus embodying the intelligence task familiar to all racial and ethnic groups assessed? Finally, is the language style used in test item development and administration similarly appropriate for all racial and ethnic groups assessed? Essentially, these questions are about cultural equivalence—whether the various racial and ethnic groups in our society share similar values and beliefs, language styles, and symbol system(s) associated with intelligence. In the section that follows, I explore the difficulties inherent in developing and administering a standardized intelligence test to meet the criterion of cultural equivalence.

Does Intelligence Have the Same Meaning Across Racial/Ethnic Groups?

In developing a standardized test of intelligence, test developers assume that there is agreement on the meaning of the construct *intelligence* that is being measured within and across racial and ethnic groups. It is also assumed that during administration of an intelligence test, both examiner and examinee would have a common understanding as to what constitutes an intelligent question and what constitutes an intelligent answer. However, these assumptions about construct equivalences are not necessarily applicable for some racial and ethnic groups in the United States. For example, Okagaki and Sternberg (1991) interviewed native-born Anglo-American and Mexican American parents as well as immigrant parents from Cambodia, Mexico, the Philippines, and Vietnam about their beliefs about child rearing and intelligence. Findings indicated that parents had different views about what characterizes an intelligent first-grade child. For the Asian parents, noncognitive factors (e.g., motivation, social skills, and self-management skills) were more important than cognitive skills such as problem-solving skills, creative skills, and verbal skills. The Mexican American and Mexican immigrant parents equally valued noncognitive factors and cognitive skills in their conception of intelligence. In contrast, the Anglo-American parents thought that cognitive skills were more important to their conception of intelligence than factors such as motivation and hard work.

In another study, Gopaul-McNicol (1993) found that some immigrant children in the United States with a Caribbean background experienced difficulty in completing tasks on psychometric intelligence tests because slow but careful execution of a task was valued in their culture. Even when requested by the examiner for a quick response, such children ignored the request and continued to work methodically and cautiously. Their approach to cognitive tasks is not unlike Ugandan villages that use words such as *careful, slow,* and *active* to define intelligence (Wober, 1972).

More than 30 ago, Messick and Anderson (1970) claimed that the same test may measure different cognitive processes among minority children from low-income backgrounds than it measures among White middle-class children. More recent investigations have found profile differences in intellectual abilities among racial and ethnic groups.

Some studies reported that Asian Americans performed better on visual and quantitative reasoning than on verbal subtests on an intelligence measure. In other studies, it was found that Native Americans also tended to show relatively better performance on the visual reasoning subtest than on the verbal subtests. Although not ruling out other explanations, it is possible that the observed ethnic differences in intellectual performance may be attributable to different cultural values about what it means to be intelligent. If this is the case, an intelligence measure may be assessing different notions of valued intellectual abilities in different racial and ethnic groups and, in so doing, invalidating its results for these groups.

Are There Stereotypical Beliefs About Intelligence?

Much has been written over the years about the damaging effects of prejudice and discrimination to which some racial and ethnic groups have been subjected in the United States. One negative impact of discrimination with relevance to performance on intelligence tests has to do with the concept of *stereotype threat,* which Steele (1997) defined as

> the event of a negative stereotype about a group to which one belongs becoming self-relevant, usually as a plausible interpretation for something one is doing, for an experience one is having, or for a situation one is in, that has relevance to one's self-definition. (p. 617)

According to Steele (1997), some African American students have internalized the stereotypical belief or myth of intellectual inferiority that has been so pervasive in much of the heated debates about racial differences in IQ scores within and outside the academy. When told that an IQ test was diagnostic of their abilities, these students tend to perform less well than their Anglo-American peers for whom such information holds no threat.

Ogbu (1992) provided a different perspective on how beliefs associated with Black and White culture can negatively affect the performance of some African Americans and other ethnic minorities of color who share similar beliefs. According to Ogbu, opposition and ambivalence are distinguishing attributes of Black culture in its relation to White or mainstream culture that have emerged in response to their subordination and exploitation by the dominant group in U.S. society. These aspects of Black culture are reflected in the belief among some African Americans that the cultural frame of reference is substantively different from the White cultural frame of reference. Moreover, these elements are embodied in an oppositional cultural system with mechanisms for protecting and maintaining the identity of its members. One of the mechanisms with relevance for academic (or intellectual functioning) is *cultural inversion*—the tendency of members of one social group (e.g., Black Americans) to consider certain forms of behavior, symbols, and events as inappropriate for them because these elements are *not* valued by members of another group (e.g., White Americans).

Many questions may be raised about stereotypical beliefs that are relevant in the administration of an intelligence test: How many children from racial groups recommended for psychoeducational evaluation, of which the IQ test is a central component, are vulnerable to the stereotype threat? How many of them hold beliefs that an IQ test is a product of White or mainstream culture and should therefore not be taken seriously? How many examiners who administer the IQ test to children from racial and ethnic minority groups hold *caste thinking* about them? To the extent that examiners and/or examinees hold stereotypical beliefs during the administration of an intelligence test, it will clearly violate the assumption of equivalence of testing conditions that will be necessary for making comparative judgments of intellectual abilities between Black and White ethnic groups.

Are Cultural Attributes Comparable Between Racial/Ethnic Groups?

One of the difficulties in developing a measure of intelligence that is culturally sensitive is figuring out how to ensure comparability of those aspects of culture that have implications for intellectual functioning represented among the racial and ethnic groups included in the standardization sample. The United States is a multicultural society and, as such, reflects attributes of cultures of diverse racial and ethnic groups. Some individuals within each group, though, may choose to retain some aspects of their ancestral culture while identifying with aspects of the dominant culture to which they have acculturated. A customary practice in instrument development is to ask participants to identify themselves by choosing from among social categories such as race and ethnicity. Given the heterogeneity of beliefs and values that must inevitably be embedded within any racial or ethnic group, how do test designers ensure that all members within each group that make up the representative sample have had equivalent culturally relevant experiences? The problem is further complicated by the comingling of cultural attributes with other dimensions of human diversity, such as socioeconomic status and regionality.

For example, some years ago, Williams (1975) developed the BITCH 100 (Black Intelligence Test of Cultural Homogeneity), a vocabulary test from which words were selected from the dictionary of Afro-American slang. African American high school students scored significantly higher than their Anglo-American peers, a finding that the author attributed to the possibility that the Anglo group had less opportunity to learn the words than the African American group. Because socioeconomic status was uncontrolled in this study, it may well be that the items favored a particular social class within the African American group or a region in which they live rather than African Americans as a cultural group.

Are Conventions of Discourse Comparable Between Racial/Ethnic Groups?

An assumption in any standardized measure of intelligence developed in the United States is that the format of test questions is similarly understood by all U.S.-born racial and ethnic groups to whom the test is administered. In addition, it is also assumed that all respondents know the cultural convention about when and how to respond to an examiner's question. In describing the convention underlying every cognitive test, Greenfield (1997) stated that "the test question assumes that a questioner who already has a given piece of information can sensibly ask a listener for the same information" (p. 1119). However, this particular convention of discourse may be a function of formal schooling and child-rearing practices among some racial and ethnic groups from middle-class backgrounds. For example, in a study conducted in the southern United States, Heath (1989) examined the linguistic conventions of African American and Anglo-American adults and their children. It was found that Anglo-American parents questioned their children a great deal in a manner similar to what is found in a formal testing context. In contrast, the African American parents infrequently questioned their children and hardly ever used testlike questions. In another study, Miller-Jones (1989) described the interactions between a 5-year-old lower-middle-class African American and an examiner in a standardized IQ testing context in which it was obvious that both the child and the examiner were responding to different expectations regarding communication conventions.

There is tremendous language style variations within and across racial and ethnic groups in the United States (African Americans, Latinos, Asian Americans, and Anglo-Americans), many of whom have distinctive conventions of discourse (for further discussion on this issue, see Butcher & Pancheri, 1976; Hamayan & Damico, 1991; van de Vijver & Leung, 1997). Validity of test scores will be compromised if members of racial and ethnic groups use communicative conventions different from what is assumed by any standardized IQ test. In my judgment, it is virtually impossible to design and administer a test that meets the criterion of communication convention equivalence in a linguistically diverse society such as the United States.

Do Racial/Ethnic Groups Have Comparable Familiarity With Symbol System?

To make valid comparisons between two groups on any standardized intelligence measure, test developers must ensure familiarity of symbols or stimuli used to represent test items. This is very difficult to do because children have had differential exposure to cultural practices in which certain symbols are used to embody cognitive tasks. For example, an early cross-cultural study (Gay & Cole, 1967) used bowls of rice and geometric blocks to assess classification skills between schooled and unschooled Liberians and U.S.-schooled children. It was found that the unschooled Liberians experienced greater difficulty sorting geometric shapes than did the U.S.-schooled children. However, when the materials to be classified were changed to rice, the results were reversed. The U.S. children showed greater difficulty in sorting rice than the Liberians. In another study, Serpell (1979) compared the performance of English and Zambian children on a pattern reproduction task embodied in three symbolic media: clay, paper and pencil, and strips of wire. The English children performed better with the paper-and-pencil medium, whereas the Zambian children performed better in the wire medium. When a medium familiar to both groups (clay) was used, both groups performed equally well on the same task. Also, Lantz (1979) compared the classification skills of Indian children using grains, seeds, and colors. It was found that children showed better skills when grains and seeds were used than when the same task used an array of colors. Finally, numerous researchers (Hatano, 1982; Stigler, 1984; Stigler, Barclay, & Aiello, 1982) have examined Japanese abacus experts who used the abacus as a tool for arithmetic operations. The researchers found that the experts were able to do mental arithmetic calculations with the abacus as accurately as without it. It appeared that the experts created a representation of the problems using a "mental abacus" that enhanced skills of remembering digits forward or backward.

These studies underscored the importance of the medium in which cognitive tasks are embedded and demonstrate how differential familiarity with the medium can account for differences in cognitive functioning. At least two questions can be raised from these studies, with implications for the standardized assessment of intelligence of children from different racial and ethnic backgrounds in the United States: Is the symbol system(s) used in the test sufficiently familiar to *all* children to whom the IQ test is administered? If not, how much variation in intellectual performance between racial and ethnic groups can be explained in terms of differential familiarity with the symbol system used in the test?

FUTURE DIRECTIONS FOR THE ASSESSMENT OF INTELLIGENCE

When considered from the perspective of cultural psychology, any standardized test of intelligence is a reflection of the values, beliefs, language styles, and symbol system of a particular cultural group. But as I have tried to show in the previous section, it is extremely difficult to design and administer a valid *standardized* test of intelligence for culturally diverse groups in a democratic society. Moreover, inattention to cultural issues in test construction and administration leaves unknown the contribution of culture in interpretations for observed differences in intellectual performance between Anglo-American and racial and ethnic minority groups. Despite these concerns, psychometric tests of intelligence continue to have widespread use in psychoeducational evaluations of racial and ethnic minority groups in the United States, and claims about its inappropriateness for these populations have been met with spirited resistance (see Frisby, 1999, for the latest defense of psychometric intelligence). I submit that until efforts are made to adequately address the culture question in psychometric assessments of intelligence, the controversy and debate surrounding its questionable validity for racial and ethnic minorities in the United States will continue. In the section that follows, I propose some suggestions for making intellectual assessments more culturally sensitive in the areas of research and practice.

PSYCHOMETRIC ASSESSMENT RESEARCH

The primary research challenge in studies seeking to compare intelligence within and across racial and ethnic groups in the United States has to do with validity of results: whether the interpretation for observed differences in performance on any psychometric test of intelligence is legitimate for racial and ethnic minorities. Threats to validity derive from incomplete answers to the following questions: Does the construct *intelligence* have the same meaning for the racial and ethnic groups investigated as it does for the researcher? Are the subjects selected for comparative study truly independent? Are the items that make up the test equivalent for the groups studied? Are alternative explanations ruled out for the differences observed when comparing the results of racial and ethnic groups? These questions are consistent with rudimentary principles of science, and I argue that researchers in the psychometric tradition have unevenly adhered to them in their investigations of intelligence of racial and ethnic minorities in the United States. There are at least four areas in research that, if addressed, could enhance the validity of results of psychometric intelligence tests.

Conceptual Definition of Construct

The absence of consensus with respect to the *meaning* of intelligence among some racial and ethnic minorities in the United States makes it difficult to explain their high or low performance on an intelligence test. To be sure, defenders of psychometric intelligence would argue otherwise by citing studies that used factor-analytic procedures to demonstrate the equivalence of the construct of intelligence between groups on the same psychometric test (see Jensen, 1980; Keith et al., 1995; Mishra, 1981; Valencia, 1995, for construct validity studies between White Mexican American and African American groups). But a posteriori statistical procedures, no matter what their scientific credibility is, yield insufficient proof of construct equivalence. These methods must be complemented by a priori procedures to establish construct familiarity between or within the racial or ethnic group to be studied.

Before administering any psychometric intelligence test, the researcher needs to ascertain rather than assume that the groups to be studied share the same values and beliefs about the construct of intelligence as their counterparts on whom the test was

initially normed. Absent such evidence, the researcher has three options:

1. Develop a test consistent with a conception of intelligence as agreed on by the groups under investigation. As Greenfield (1997) pointed out, such a decision is not made at an individual level but rather at a cultural level in terms of social norms of the groups.

2. Modify an existing psychometric test in an effort to accommodate legitimate cultural differences among members of the group.

3. Measure the cultural attributes that are likely to influence the performance on the psychometric test.

The last two options are elaborated on in subsequent paragraphs.

Measurement of Cultural Attributes

A comparative study of intelligence using a psychometric test may still proceed without conceptual consensus of intelligence. However, in the interest of scientific fairness and to avoid misattribution for observed differences between racial or ethnic groups studied, the researcher must take steps to rule out a cultural explanation. This can be done by developing additional measures of cultural attributes to be used in conjunction with the psychometric test. For example, if there is a possibility that stereotype threat may be a factor in the observed differences in psychometric test scores of African Americans and Anglo-Americans, interviews or questionnaires could be administered to determine whether that is the case. Similarly, if there is a possibility that differences in performance between Asian Americans and Mexican Americans may be due, in part, to differential levels of acculturation to U.S. mainstream culture, an acculturation scale can be developed or may be administered to these groups. Moreover, specific behaviors indicative of values associated with the ancestral culture of these social groups may be clinically observed during the administration of the psychometric test.

A common practice in validity studies is to minimize as much as possible alternative explanations for observed differences in performance on a measure used with culturally diverse populations.

Similarly, the hypothesis that differences in performance between Asian Americans and Mexican Americans are related to acculturation to U.S. mainstream culture could be validated by measuring the cultural values, language usage, and symbolic modes of representation associated with cognitive functioning in *both* the ancestral culture of the group and the U.S. culture.

Modification of Existing Psychometric Test

It was argued earlier that differential language style during administration of a psychometric test and/or differential familiarity with the stimuli used in test items could lead to misunderstanding and invalidate the results of the test for some racial and ethnic groups. Without a doubt, proponents of psychometric tests of intelligence with culturally diverse populations would be quick to point to empirical research that shows the absence of situational bias in test administration (Jensen, 1980; Mishra, 1980, 1983; Oplesch & Genshaft, 1981) and content validity of test items (Jensen, 1980; Koh, Abbatiello, & McLoughlin, 1984; Mishra, 1981; Pugh & Boer, 1989; Sandoval, Zimmerman, & Woo-Sam, 1983) in refuting these claims. However, I raise the concern again about the insufficiency of a posteriori statistical procedures in "proving" the validity of a psychometric measure for all English-speaking racial and ethnic minorities in the United States. Efforts must also be made to ensure cultural equivalence *before* and *during* administration of a psychometric test of intelligence developed and administered to groups for whom the conventions of language usage

and the symbols used in test items may be unfamiliar. I elaborate on this issue in a subsequent section, but the interested psychometric researcher may refer to a number of excellent references on the topic of equivalence in assessments for culturally diverse populations (e.g., Butcher, 1982; Cole, Gay, Glick, & Sharp, 1971; Helms, 1992; Laboratory of Comparative Human Cognition, 1986; Lonner, 1981; van de Vijver & Leung, 1997).

Categorization of Subjects

In typical studies using a psychometric test of intelligence to examine similarities or differences in cognitive ability, researchers use terms such as *White* and *Black* to categorize subjects into racial groups. They may also use a continent, or a country of origin, paired with "American" to classify members of ethnic groups (e.g., African American, Asian American, Mexican American). But these socially derived categories mask psychologically relevant cultural attributes that may be similar or different across and within racial and ethnic groups. After all, most social groups in the United States, irrespective of the social category to which they are assigned or to which they self-select, share some aspects of the mainstream culture of the United States while simultaneously retaining others from their ancestral culture. What these cultural attributes are and their significance for intellectual behavior depend, in part, on the racial or ethnic groups selected for study and the kinds of socialization experiences members would have had in cultural niches such as the home, the school, and the peer group. By not assessing or controlling for these cultural attributes, researchers run the risk of attributing differences or similarities to race or ethnicity that may in actuality be due to culture differences or similarities in values, beliefs, language style, or symbol usage. In the interest of scientific objectivity and to avoid misunderstanding psychometric test results of two racial or ethnic groups, psychometric researchers must at least make the effort to unbundle and measure the cultural attributes within and between the groups under investigation. (See Armour-Thomas & Gopaul-McNicol, 1998; Betancourt & Lopez, 1993; Helms, 1992; Phinney, 1996; Rohner, 1984, for further discussion of the problem of comingling of culture with other dimensions of human diversity such as race, ethnicity, and socioeconomic status.)

PSYCHOMETRIC ASSESSMENT PRACTICES

The use of a psychometric test of intelligence and the interpretation of its results for certain racial and ethnic minorities are sources of unending controversy both within and outside the academic community. Critics may be hard-pressed to argue against the use of these measures for understanding individuals' intellectual strengths and weaknesses to make intervention more responsive to their needs. However, the overrepresentation of some racial and ethnic minorities in special education classes and underrepresentation of these groups in gifted and talented programs have fueled suspicion that the test provides an inaccurate diagnosis of their cognitive strengths and weaknesses. Moreover, the tacit interpretations of their performance in terms of genetic inferiority or cultural deprivation are suspect due to the questionable methodologies in psychometric test construction and administration used with these groups as discussed earlier. In light of these concerns, what options are open to professional practitioners such as school psychologists, who are required to use a psychometric test of intelligence as part of their psychoeducational assessment regimen? The following recommendations are offered as strategies for enabling greater cultural sensitivity before, during, and after the administration of a psychometric test of intelligence. Central to these recommendations is a

hope for an assessment system rather than a single test for assessing intelligence.

Before Assessment

To protect against premature labeling and probable misattribution for cognitive performance to be analyzed later, the professional practitioner should gather background data of potential cultural significance prior to the administration of a psychometric test. Consider some of the procedures that may be used for this purpose.

An observational protocol could be developed to collect qualitative data on the examinee in contexts or cultural niches such as the classroom, cafeteria, and playground. As indicated earlier, cultural experiences within these environments may differ for some racial and ethnic minority children, and these experiences could have either a positive or negative impact on their cognitive functioning. The practitioner would need to pay particular attention to the nature and quality of the interactions between examinee and teacher, coach, or adult in the school setting as well as peers. Observation in multiple contexts is also important to ascertain whether there is behavior inconsistency with respect to cognitive functioning from one context to the next.

The professional practitioner may conduct a case history interview with significant others in the examinee's life (e.g., parent or guardian, minister, coach, teacher, community social worker) to gather information of cultural significance for cognitive functioning. Examples include specific beliefs about intelligence, language styles, conception of time, and developmental and educational history. A written questionnaire about these cultural factors may also be given to significant adults in the examinee's life.

During Assessment

There is good reason to believe that the administration of a psychometric test of intelligence under standardized conditions provides an incomplete picture of the cognitive strengths and weaknesses of some children from racial and ethnic minority backgrounds. Differential familiarity of test stimuli, different patterns of language usage, and different values about time in answering questions are some of the cultural variables that could affect behavior during assessment. Ignoring or trivializing their importance could lead to the misunderstanding and, in turn, misattribution of test results for some children for whom culture matters. There are many clinical strategies a professional practitioner can use to ensure cultural sensitivity during the administration of a psychometric test. Techniques that deviate from standardized procedures are commonly defined as "testing to the limits" in the psychoeducational literature.

One technique may involve suspending the time allotted on the psychometric test items to see whether the examinee may eventually obtain the right answer. Another might be to teach items to the examinee to establish familiarity with the test format or stimuli and then readminister the psychometric items to see if the examinee's performance improves. A third technique might include giving the examinee a paper and pencil to ascertain whether he or she could solve psychometric items requiring mental computation. Yet another procedure may involve contextualizing vocabulary items on the psychometric test to determine whether the examinee understands the meaning of words. Finally, the professional practitioner may try to make items on the psychometric test equivalent to the examinee's cultural experience by matching selected items to the examinee's culture. A more comprehensive discussion of these strategies is found in Armour-Thomas and Gopaul-McNicol (1998).

After Assessment

Prior to writing up the report, the professional practitioner analyzes the results of the psychometric test using the clinical data obtained before and during assessment as well as the psychometric data. One primary question of interest is the following: To what extent is the psychometric score obtained due to cultural factors? It is extremely important that the professional practitioner rule out these factors before attributing observed low or high scores to factors intrinsic to the individual.

To the extent that cultural factors did affect the test results, another question of interest would need to be answered: What culture-relevant recommendations can be made to the classroom teacher, parent, and mental health worker that are likely to improve the cognitive functioning of the examinee? (For examples for writing a culturally sensitive psychological report, see Armour-Thomas & Gopaul-McNicol, 1998; Gopaul-McNicol & Armour-Thomas, 2002.)

CONCLUSION

The psychometric model has been dominant in psychology for almost 100 years since Alfred Binet designed the first intelligence test. It has contributed insightful notions of the structure of the human intellect, about which numerous comparative studies have been conducted and measures of intelligence developed and used with diverse groups. In this chapter, I have argued that incomplete attention or neglect to matters of culture as it pertains to some racial and ethnic minorities in the United States has raised doubts about the validity of psychometric intelligence research and test practices for this population. I believe that a rigid adherence to the continuing use of psychometric measures of intelligence in research and practice, irrespective of cultural considerations, creates an unhealthy tension in a multicultural society committed in principle to the twin ideals of equity and social justice. After all, genuine respect for cultural diversity in a democracy allows those who identify with a particular culture the right to develop and express intelligence in accordance with the values, beliefs, symbols, and language systems of their particular social group. It also allows them the choice of adopting the cultural attributes of another social group or switching cultural frames of reference, depending on the salience of experiences they would have had in one cultural niche or another. What this means is that the "one size fits all" approach of standardized assessment of intelligence must give way to an assessment system in which the psychometric IQ test is important but is only one measure on the assessment menu. The recommendations proposed in this chapter are intended to encourage greater cultural sensitivity in intelligence research and test practices for those racial and ethnic minorities in the United States who have been disadvantaged by psychometric intelligence tests.

REFERENCES

Armour-Thomas, E., & Gopaul-McNicol, S. (1998). *Assessing intelligence: A biocultural perspective.* Thousand Oaks, CA: Sage.

Berry, J. W. (1976). *Human ecology and cognitive style.* New York: Sage-Halsted.

Betancourt, H., & Lopez, S. R. (1993). The study of culture, ethnicity and race in American psychology. *American Psychologist, 48*(6), 629-637.

Bronfenbrenner, U. (1979). *Toward the ecology of human development.* Cambridge, MA: Harvard University Press.

Butcher, J. N. (1982). Cross-cultural research methods in clinical psychology. In P. C. Kendall & J. N. Butcher (Eds.), *Handbook of research methods in clinical psychology* (pp. 273-308). New York: John Wiley.

Butcher, J. N., & Pancheri, P. (1976). *A handbook of cross-national MMPI-2 and MMPI-A interpretation.* Minneapolis: University of Minnesota Press.

Carroll, J. B. (1993). *Human cognitive abilities: A survey of factor-analytic studies.* New York: Cambridge University Press.

Cole, M., Gay, J., Glick, J. A., & Sharp, D. W. (1971). *The cultural context of learning and thinking.* New York: Basic Books.

Dent, H. E. (1996). Non-biased assessment or realistic assessment? In R. L. Jones (Ed.), *Handbook of tests and measurement for Black populations* (Vol. 1, pp. 103-122). Hampton, VA: Cobb & Henry.

Frisby, C. L. (1999). Straight talk about cognitive assessment and diversity. *School Psychology Quarterly, 14*(3), 195-207.

Gardner, H. (1983). *Frames of mind: The theory of multiple intelligences.* New York: Basic Books.

Gauvain, M. (1995). Thinking in niches: Sociocultural influences on cognitive development. *Human Development, 38,* 25-45.

Gay, J., & Cole, M. (1967). *The new mathematics and an old culture.* New York: Holt, Rinehart & Winston.

Goleman, D. (1995). *Emotional intelligence: Why it can matter more than IQ.* New York: Bantam.

Gopaul-McNicol, S. (1993). *Working with West Indian families.* New York: Guilford.

Gopaul-McNicol, S., & Armour-Thomas, E. (2002). *Assessment and culture: Psychological tests with minority populations.* New York: Academic Press.

Gottfredson, L. S. (1997). Mainstream science on intelligence: An editorial with 52 signatories, history, and bibliography. *Intelligence, 24,* 13-23.

Greenfield, P. M. (1997). You can't take it with you: Why ability assessments don't cross cultures. *American Psychologist, 52*(10), 1115-1124.

Gresham, F. M., & Witt, J. C. (1997). Utility of intelligence tests for treatment planning, classification and placement decisions: Recent empirical findings and future directions. *School Psychology Quarterly, 12,* 249-267.

Guilford, J. P. (1982). *The nature of human intelligence.* New York: McGraw-Hill.

Hamayan, E. V., & Damico, J. S. (Eds.). (1991). *Limiting bias in the assessment of bilingual students.* Austin, TX: PRO-ED.

Hatano, G. (1982). Cognitive consequences of practice in culture specific procedural skills. *Quarterly Newsletter of Comparative Human Cognition, 4,* 15-17.

Heath, S. B. (1989). Oral and literate traditions among Black Americans living in poverty. *American Psychologist, 44,* 367-373.

Helms, J. E. (1992). Why is there no study of cultural equivalence in standardized cognitive ability testing? *American Psychologist, 47*(9), 1083-1101.

Horn, J. L. (1991). Measurement of intellectual capabilities: A review of theory. In K. S. McGrew, J. K. Werder, & R.W. Woodcock (Eds.), *WJ-R technical manual.* Chicago: Riverside.

Jensen, A. R. (1980). *Bias in mental testing.* New York: Free Press.

Kaufman, A. S., & Kaufman, N. L. (1993). *K-ABC: Kaufman Assessment Battery for Children.* Circle Pines, MN: American Guidance Service.

Keith, T. Z., Fugate, M. H., DeGraff, M., Diamond, C. M., Shadrach, E. A., & Stevens, M. L. (1995). Using multi-sample confirmatory factor analysis to test for construct bias: An example using the K-ABC. *Journal of Psychoeducational Assessment, 13,* 347-364.

Koh, T., Abbatiello, A., & McLoughlin, C. S. (1984). Cultural bias in WISC subtest items: A response to Judge Grady's suggestion in relation to the PASE case. *School Psychology Review, 13,* 89-94.

Laboratory of Comparative Human Cognition. (1986). Culture and intelligence. In R. J. Sternberg (Ed.), *Handbook of human intelligence* (pp. 642-719). Cambridge, MA: Cambridge University Press.

Lantz, D. A. (1979). A cross-cultural comparison of communication abilities: Some effects of age, schooling and culture. *International Journal of Psychology, 14,* 171-183.

Lonner, W. J. (1981). Issues in testing and assessing in cross-cultural counseling. *The Counseling Psychologist, 13,* 599-614.

Mbti, J. (1970). *African religions and philosophy.* Garden City, NJ: Anchor.

Messick, S., & Anderson, S. (1970). Educational testing, individual development and social responsibility. *The Counseling Psychologist, 2*(2), 93-97.

Miller-Jones, D. (1989). Culture and testing. *American Psychologist, 44,* 360-366.

Mishra, S. P. (1980). The influence of examiners' ethnic attributes on intelligence test scores. *Psychology in the Schools, 17,* 117-122.

Mishra, S. P. (1981). Reliability and validity of the WRAT with Mexican-American children. *Psychology in the Schools, 18,* 154-158.

Mishra, S. P. (1983). Effects of examiners' prior knowledge of subjects' ethnicity and intelligence on the scoring of responses to the Stanford-Binet Scale. *Psychology in the Schools, 20,* 133-136.

Neisser, U., Boodoo, G., Bouchard, T. J., Boykin, A. W., Brody, N., Ceci, S. J., Halpern, D. F., Loehlin, J. C., Perloff, R., Sternberg, R. J., & Urbina, S. (1996). Intelligence: Knowns and unknowns. *American Psychologist, 51,* 77-101.

Ogbu, J. U. (1992). Understanding cultural diversity and learning. *Educational Researcher, 21*(3), 5-14.

Okagaki, L., & Sternberg, R. J. (1991). Cultural and parental influences. In L. Okagaki & R. L. Sternberg (Eds.), *Directors of development: Influences on the development of children's thinking* (pp. 101-120). Hillsdale, NJ: Lawrence Erlbaum.

Oplesch, M., & Genshaft, J. L. (1981). Comparison of bilingual children on the WISC-R and the Escala de Inteligencia Wechsler Para Ninos. *Psychology in the Schools, 18,* 159-163.

Phinney, J. S. (1996). When we talk about American ethnic groups what do we mean? *American Psychologist, 51*(9), 918-927.

Pugh, G. M., & Boer, D. P. (1989). An examination of culturally appropriate items for the WAIS-R Information subtest with Canadian subjects. *Journal of Psychoeducational Assessment, 7,* 131-140.

Reschley, D. J. (1997). Diagnostic and treatment utility of intelligence tests. In D. P. Flanagan, J. L. Genshaft, & P. L. Harrison (Eds.), *Contemporary intellectual assessment: Theories, tests, and issues* (pp. 437-456). New York: Guilford.

Rohner, R. P. (1984). Toward a conception of culture for cross-cultural psychology. *Journal of Cross-Cultural Psychology, 15,* 111-138.

Salovey, P., & Mayer, J. (1994). Some final thoughts about personality and intelligence. In R. J. Sternberg & P. Ruzgis (Eds.), *Personality and intelligence* (pp. 303-318). New York: Cambridge University Press.

Sandoval, J., Zimmerman, I. L., & Woo-Sam, J. M. (1983). Cultural differences on WISC-R verbal items. *Journal of School Psychology, 21,* 383-386.

Serpell, R. (1979). How specific are perceptual skills? A cross-cultural study of pattern reproduction. *British Journal of Psychology, 70,* 365-380.

Spearman, C. (1981). *The abilities of man: Their nature and measurement.* New York: AMS. (Original work published 1927)

Steele, C. M. (1997). A threat in the air: How stereotypes shape intellectual identity and performance. *American Psychologist, 52*(6), 613-629.

Sternberg, R. J. (1985). *Beyond IQ: A triarchic theory of intelligence.* New York: Cambridge University Press.

Stigler, J. W. (1984). "Mental abacus": The effect of abacus training on Chinese children's mental calculation. *Cognitive Psychology, 16,* 145-176.

Stigler, J. W., Barclay, C., & Aiello, P. (1982). Motor and mental abacus skills: A preliminary look at an expert. *Quarterly Newsletter of the Laboratory of Comparative Human Cognition, 4,* 12-14.

Super, C. M., & Harkness, S. (1986). The development niche: A conceptualization at the interface of child and culture. *International Journal of Behavioral Development, 9,* 545-569.

Suzuki, L. A., & Valencia, R. R. (1997). Race-ethnicity and measured intelligence. *American Psychologist, 52,* 1103-1114.

Thorndike, R. L., Hagen, E. P., & Sattler, J. M. (1986). *Stanford-Binet Intelligence Scale* (4th ed.). Itasca, IL: Riverside.

Thurstone, L. L. (1938). *Primary mental abilities.* Chicago: University of Chicago Press.

Triandis, H., Lambert, W., Berry, J., Lonner, W., Heron, A., Brislin, R., & Draguns, J. (Eds.). (1980). *Handbook of cross-cultural psychology* (Vols. 1-6). Boston: Allyn & Bacon.

Valencia, R. R. (1995). Stability of the Kaufman Assessment Battery for Children for a sample of Mexican American children. *Journal of School Psychology, 23,* 189-193.

van de Vijver, F., & Leung, K. (1997). *Methods and data analysis for cross-cultural research*. Thousand Oaks, CA: Sage.

Vernon, P. E. (1971). *The structure of human abilities*. London: Methuen.

Vygotsky, L. S. (1978). *Mind in society: The development of higher psychological processes*. Cambridge, MA: Harvard University Press.

Wechsler, D. (1991). *Wechsler Intelligence Scale for Children* (3rd ed.). San Antonio, TX: The Psychological Corporation.

Williams, R. (1970). Danger: Testing and dehumanizing Black children. *Clinical Child Psychology Newsletter, 9*(1), 5-6.

Williams, R. (1975). The BITCH 100: A culture specific test. *Journal of Afro-American Issues, 3*, 103-106.

Wober, M. (1972). Culture and the concept of intelligence: A case in Uganda. *Journal of Cross-Cultural Psychology, 3*, 327-328.

Woodcock, R. W., & Johnson, M. B. (1989). *Woodcock-Johnson Psycho-Educational Battery—Revised*. Chicago: Riverside.

Part IV

STRESS
AND ADJUSTMENT

CHAPTER 18

Stress, Coping, and Minority Health

Biopsychosocial Perspective
on Ethnic Health Disparities

HECTOR F. MYERS
University of California, Los Angeles, and
Charles R. Drew University of Medicine & Science

TENE T. LEWIS
University of California, Los Angeles

TYAN PARKER-DOMINGUEZ
University of Southern California

Current epidemiological evidence indicates a persistent disparity in health status, morbidity, and mortality among racial/ethnic minorities relative to Caucasians. Regardless of the health and social status criteria used, African Americans, Hispanics, Native Americans, and many South Pacific and Southeast Asian groups carry a disproportionate burden of morbidity and mortality and are overrepresented among those suffering from the greatest social disadvantage (Flack et al., 1995; National Center for Health Statistics [NCHS], 2000). The social imperative we face today is to identify those factors that contribute to or maintain these persistent health disparities and to design innovative interventions to close the gaps. Driven by the dual forces of immigration and a higher birth rate among racial/ethnic minorities, the U.S. population is projected to include a plurality of persons of color by the year 2025. If the current health trends continue unabated,

AUTHORS' NOTE: Preparation of this chapter was supported in part by Grants Nos. MH 54965 and HL51519-06 to the first author.

the overall health status of the United States will decline, along with the attendant increases in health care costs and declines in the quality of life for all Americans.

In this chapter, we provide a select and integrative review of the literature on the role of stress as a contributor to disease risk and expression and psychosocial resources such as coping and social support as stress moderators in helping to account for the ethnic health disparities. This review is informed by a multidimensional biopsychosocial perspective, and we argue that at the core of ethnic health disparities is differential exposure and vulnerability to psychosocial stresses moderated by inadequate access to and control over essential material, psychological, and social resources. We also argue that this disadvantageous stress-resource imbalance is created by social status–defining attributes of race/ethnicity and social class that define the social hierarchy and life opportunities. The stress-disease relationship is further enhanced and maintained through debilitating social environments and is mediated through biological, behavioral, and psychological pathways. The interplay of these factors is hypothesized to result in cumulative biobehavioral vulnerability over the life span, which accounts, at least in part, for the cross-generational persistence of the health disparities that is documented in the epidemiologic literature.

This chapter is organized into four sections. First, we briefly review the evidence of ethnic health disparities, with specific emphasis on cardiovascular disease, diabetes, and birth outcomes. Second, we review current models of stress and disease relationships, paying particular attention to research on exposure to generic life stresses that all persons face, as well as the additional burden of status-related stresses that persons of color face. Third, we discuss the role of social resources, especially appraisal and coping styles (i.e., cognitive schemas, proactive vs. avoidant coping), social supports, psychological dispositions (i.e., perceived personal and collective control; dispositional optimism/pessimism), and sociocultural factors (i.e., acculturation and acculturative stress, religiosity) that can either exacerbate or moderate stress vulnerability. Finally, we discuss the implications of this review and suggest directions for future research.

ETHNIC HEALTH DISPARITIES

Current evidence indicates that the health of the United States has improved significantly in the past decade. However, this improvement has not been uniform, with Caucasians enjoying a significant health advantage over other racial/ethnic groups. Unfortunately, efforts to capture the full extent of the health status differences between groups continue to be hampered by the uneven availability of health data by ethnic groups. For example, although there is considerable research on the health of African Americans, Hispanics, and Asians relative to Caucasians, there is comparatively less health data on Native Americans. This problem becomes even more evident when subgroup comparisons are investigated. For example, although Asians overall are a healthier group than other ethnic minority groups, several subgroups suffer significant health disadvantages compared to other ethnic groups.

Despite these constraints, however, current epidemiologic evidence indicates significant and persistent ethnic group differences on virtually all major health status indicators (NCHS, 2000; Williams & Collins, 1995). Three health conditions—cardiovascular disease (CVD), diabetes, and birth outcomes—illustrate these differences.

Ethnic Differences in Cardiovascular Disease

The life expectancy of the U.S. population has increased, but African Americans, Native Americans, Hispanics, Native Hawaiians, and Southeast Asians evidence shorter life expectancies and excess death rates from all causes compared to Caucasians. CVD continues to be the primary cause of death, and stroke is the third leading cause of death in the United States (NCHS, 2000). Although CVD is the leading cause of death for all ethnic groups, the prevalence rates for coronary heart disease (CHD), stroke, and hypertension vary significantly across groups (NCHS, 1995). Caucasians have the highest rate of CHD of all groups, with African Americans second, Hispanics and Native Americans next, and Asians/Pacific Islanders (APIs) with the lowest overall rates. However, the overall rates for Hispanics and APIs are deceptive because they conceal important within-group differences in risk. Puerto Ricans have CHD rates similar to African Americans, and Native Hawaiians and some Southeast Asian groups have CHD rates similar to Hispanics.

Caucasians and African Americans have comparable rates of stroke that are higher than other ethnic groups. However, African Americans have the highest rate of stroke-related mortality and the highest rates of hypertension and related sequelae of all ethnic groups. Thus, although approximately 35% of African Americans are diagnosed with essential hypertension, only 23% of Hispanics, 22% of Caucasians, 12% of American Indians, and 9% of APIs suffer from this disease. These differences in CVD rates are largely explained by socioeconomic differences, especially as these are expressed in differences in behavioral risk factors (e.g., high cholesterol, physical inactivity, excess weight, smoking, less access to adequate health care, and exposure to chronic environmental and sociocultural stresses) (American Heart Association, 2002; Myers, Kagawa-Singer, Kumanyika, Lex, & Markides, 1995; Pickering, 1999; Williams, 1999).

Ethnic Differences in Diabetes

More Americans than ever are suffering from non-insulin-dependent diabetes mellitus (NIDDM), which is the seventh leading cause of death in the United States (NCHS, 2000). Like hypertension, this disease is prevalent but often goes unrecognized and untreated, with an estimated 34% of those affected being undiagnosed and untreated (Centers for Disease Control and Prevention [CDC], 1997). This disease is associated with a variety of disabling conditions, including enhanced risk for end-stage renal disease, blindness, lower extremity amputations, gum disease, CHD, stroke, complications of pregnancy, functional limitations, and increased mortality. Minorities are disproportionately affected compared to Caucasians, women are more affected than men, American Indians have the highest prevalence of any group (Carter, Pugh, & Monterrosa, 1996), Hispanics and African Americans are comparable (10.6% and 10.8%, respectively), but the rates among African Americans have increased 33% in the past decade (CDC, 1997).

There is substantial within-group variability in prevalence of this disease. Among American Indians, the Pima and Papago Indians have the highest prevalence of diabetes in the world, with rates around 50%. Among Hispanics, Puerto Rican men and Mexican American women have some of the highest rates, whereas the rates are lowest among Cuban women. Also, and unlike in other diseases where APIs enjoy a significant health status benefit, prevalence rates of diabetes are higher in some API groups (e.g., Koreans, Filipino, and Chinese in Hawaii) than in other minority groups (Carter et al., 1996).

Not only is NIDDM more prevalent among ethnic minorities, but also minorities suffer disproportionately from the complications secondary to this disease. As a whole, ethnic minorities are twice as likely to experience blindness secondary to diabetes than Caucasians; African American diabetics are 6.6 times, Mexican American diabetics are up to 7 times, and American Indian diabetics are 6.3 times more likely to suffer from end-stage renal disease than non-Hispanic Caucasian diabetics. In addition, African Americans are significantly more likely to have amputations secondary to diabetes than Caucasians and Hispanics, and except for APIs, ethnic minorities with diabetes are at higher risk for mortality from this disease than Caucasians (Carter et al., 1996).

Ethnic Differences in Birth Outcomes

There is also ample evidence of a persistent disparity in birth outcomes between African Americans and all other groups (NCHS, 1993). This discrepancy is evident on most maternal or child outcome measures used. African American women are more likely to die from ectopic pregnancies and are three times more likely than Caucasians to die in hospitals following hysterectomies. Compared to Caucasians, African Americans have rates of low birth weight (LBW = 5 lbs., 8 oz.) and preterm delivery (PTD = < 37 weeks' gestation) that are almost twice as high (i.e., 13% vs. 7% and 10% vs. 18%) (CDC, 1999; Paneth, 1995; Schoendorf, Hogue, Kleinman, & Rowley, 1992). African American mothers also experience three times the rate of very low birth weight (VLBW = < 3 lbs., 4 oz.) babies and four times the rate of very early delivery (i.e., < 28 weeks' gestation). Also, African American infants are three times as likely to die of causes attributable to perinatal events and twice as likely to die in the first month of life (IM = 14.1 vs. 6.0 deaths per 1,000 live births in 1998) than Caucasian infants (Guyer et al., 1999; Schoendorf et al., 1992).

This African American–Caucasian differential is further complicated by the paradoxical finding that the infant mortality rate is lower among infants born to African American teens compared to Caucasians and older African American women (Geronimus, 1992). Also, although the low birth weight and infant mortality rates are higher in less educated and poorer women of all ethnic groups, the African American–Caucasian differential in LBW and in infant mortality is smaller among the less educated and larger among the most educated (Kleinman, Fingerhut, & Prager, 1991; Shiono, Rauh, Park, Lederman, & Suskar, 1997). This suggests that African American women derive less reproductive benefit from upward mobility than Caucasian women.

The birth outcome picture is even more interesting when the data on Hispanics are examined. For example, although Hispanic women share many of the socioeconomic deprivations, burdens of morbidity, and lifestyle risk factors as many African American women (and, in some cases, may be worse off because of the added stresses of immigrant status), Hispanic women as a whole have birth outcomes that are comparable to those of Caucasian women. Thus, despite being significantly poorer on average and having a poorer health behavior profile than Caucasian women, Hispanic women have comparable IM, LBW, VLBW, and PTD rates as Caucasians (Guyer et al., 1999; Kleinman et al., 1991). A number of sociocultural explanations have been offered to account for these counterintuitive findings, including the protective effects of low acculturation and the availability of large and effective social networks of support that counteract other risk factors (Scribner & Dwyer, 1989).

Obstetrical outcome data are more limited for the other ethnic groups, but the available evidence suggests that controlling for socioeconomic status (SES), the birth outcomes for Native American women are only slightly worse than for non-Hispanic Caucasian women, and the outcomes for Asian/Pacific Islanders are more favorable overall. However, there are important subgroup differences in each case, with Puerto Rican, Hawaiian, and Filipino women having poorer outcomes on average than other non-Caucasian women, except African Americans. In summary, current epidemiologic evidence documents the persistent health status differences in the U.S. population, with ethnic minorities, especially African Americans, Native Americans, Native Hawaiians, and Southeast Asians, carrying a disproportionate burden of morbidity and mortality. These data also demonstrate, however, that there are substantial within-group differences in vulnerability to specific diseases and their sequelae, and factors such as lower socioeconomic status, obstacles to accessing health care, and health behaviors are likely to contribute to the persistence of these differences.

WHAT ACCOUNTS FOR THE ETHNIC HEALTH DISPARITIES?

Health outcomes, whether they are chronic conditions such as CVD and NIDDM or discrete events such as the birth of an infant, are the by-product of the complex interaction of many factors. Research has identified individual difference factors that predict illness, including biological predispositions, behavioral lifestyle, psychological characteristics, and environmental and psychosocial factors. Different hypotheses have been offered to account for the excess burden of disease among racial/ethnic groups, both overall and for specific disorders. Factors such as differences in intracellular ion transfer mechanisms (i.e., salt metabolism) (Cooper & Borke, 1993; Grim & Wilson, 1993), differences in autonomic stress reactivity (Anderson & McNeilly, 1993; Saab et al., 1997), and differences in psychosocial risk factors (Myers & McClure, 1993) have been offered to account for African American–Caucasian differences in essential hypertension. Others have suggested differences in genetic susceptibility (Bogardus & Lillioja, 1992), as well as

differences in lifestyles and other psychosocial factors (e.g., level of acculturation) to account for the observed Native American, Hispanic, African American, and Caucasian differences in diabetes (Carter et al., 1996). Similar multidimensional hypotheses have been offered to account for African American, Caucasian, and Hispanic differences in adverse birth outcomes (Kleinman et al., 1991; Rini, Dunkel-Schetter, Sandman, & Wadhwa, 1999).

Others have identified psychological factors such as repressive coping style, pessimism, hostility, and depression as mediators of stress and disease generally, as well as more socioculturally mediated coping styles such as John Henryism (James, 1994), religiosity/spirituality (Arcury, Quandt, McDonald, & Bell, 2000; Levin & Taylor, 1993; Magana & Clark, 1995), "controlarse" (i.e., self-control) (Cohen, 1985), and "saving face" behaviors (Hom & Amada, 1985) to account for health status and help-seeking differences among persons of color.

There is also substantial evidence that ethnic group differences in health status are attributable to differences in individual health behaviors such dietary intake, exercise, smoking, use of abusable substances, and patterns of health care access and utilization (Myers et al., 1995). However, as noted by Taylor, Repetti, and Seeman (1997), these psychosocial and behavioral risk factors are "nested within geographic, developmental, occupational and social environments" (p. 413), and environmental effects on health cannot be adequately explained by these individual characteristics. We extend this argument even further by noting that predictors of health and health differentials between groups are nested in a sociopolitical context that is shaped by race/ethnicity and social class (Williams, Lavizzo-Mourey, & Warren, 1994). Macrosocial factors such as poverty and social status influence health through a variety of intermediary mechanisms, including individual health behaviors, access to adequate medical care, access to and control of psychosocial resources, and exposure to chronic life stresses (Baum, Garofalo, & Yali, 1999; Krieger, Rowley, Herman, Avery, & Phillips, 1993; Myers et al., 1995; Taylor & Seeman, 1999; Williams et al., 1994). We give special attention in this review to the evidence that racial/ethnic minorities, as a group, are generally exposed to more chronic and insidious stresses and report more distress, disease, and dysfunction than Caucasians (Krieger et al., 1993; Williams, 1999).

CONCEPTUAL MODEL

Unfortunately, there is little synergy between the biological, psychosocial, and behavioral explanations that have been offered to account for the ethnic disparities in health. Therefore, we offer an integrative biopsychosocial model that is firmly grounded in theories of stress and disease as a useful conceptual tool for integrating these disparate literatures and advancing our understanding of ethnic group differences in health and disease. At the outset, we argue that models of stress must be expanded to account for racially mediated social hierarchies and the mechanisms or pathways through which they contribute to differences in health and functional status. The proposed model, which is depicted in Figure 18.1, makes explicit that race/ethnicity, social class, and environments (i.e., community, family, work, etc.) are independent contributors to chronic stress burden, which includes both generic life stresses and ethnicity-related stresses. This chronic burden of stress is hypothesized as contributing to disease through a biological pathway that includes the triggering of physiological response mechanisms (i.e., allostasis), constitutional predispositions or vulnerabilities, and allostatic load (i.e., wear and tear on the system). This allostatic load, in turn, contributes over time to cumulative vulnerability, and this ultimately results in disease and dysfunction.

The model acknowledges, however, that the stress–biological processes–disease pathway is influenced or moderated by a number of psychosocial and behavioral factors, including psychological characteristics (e.g., personality dispositions), lifestyle factors (e.g., diet, exercise, smoking, substance use), stress appraisal and coping strategies used, and the availability of social resources. Therefore, it is all of these factors operating synergistically over time that results in differential health status and health trajectories for the different racial/ethnic and social class groups. In-depth coverage of all aspects of this conceptual model is beyond the scope of this chapter, so special emphasis is given to discussing the role of chronic stress and allostatic load as predictors of disease, as well as stress appraisal, coping, and social supports as psychosocial moderators of the stress-illness relationship.

THE STRESS-HEALTH LINK: CHRONIC BURDEN AND ALLOSTATIC LOAD

Stress is generally defined as "environmental demands that tax or exceed the adaptive capacity of an organism, resulting in biological and psychological changes that may be detrimental and place the organism at risk for disease" (Cohen, Kessler, & Gordon, 1995, p. 3). Models of stress and disease often distinguish between stress exposure, which involves confrontation with an environmental demand or stressor; stress appraisal, which involves estimating the relative threat of stressors by weighing demands against available resources; and stress response, which involves emotional, physiological, and behavioral responses to the appraised stressor (Lobel, Dunkel-Schetter, & Scrimshaw, 1992).

Hans Selye (1956) first proposed the notion that stress exposure may have a damaging effect on physical health. He proposed the general adaptation syndrome (GAS), in which

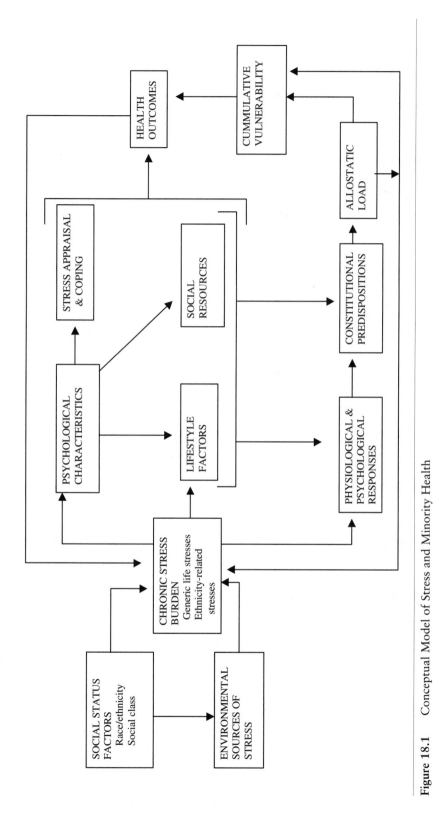

Figure 18.1   Conceptual Model of Stress and Minority Health

SOURCE: Adapted from models by Clark, Anderson, Clark, and Williams (1999); Myers and Rodriguez (2002); and Taylor, Repetti, and Seeman (1997).

individuals respond to stressful events with nonspecific physiological responses that, over time, produce wear and tear on the system. Selye argued that repeated cycling through the stress response would eventually lead to damage to the organism (McEwen, 1998). More recently, McEwen and Stellar (1993) coined the term *allostasis* to refer to the normal fluctuations of the autonomic nervous system, the hypothalamic-pituitary-adrenal (HPA) axis, and the metabolic, cardiovascular, and immune system that maintain stability and "provide protection to the body by responding to internal and external stress." The most common allostatic responses involve the activation of the sympathetic nervous system and the HPA axis and the resulting release of stress hormones. A normal stress response involves the activation of these systems (i.e., stress hormones mobilize the body for action by increasing heart rate, blood pressure, and respiration and also mobilize the immune system to protect against infection). These normal reactions are subsequently inactivated once the stressors are removed or reduced. However, when inactivation is insufficient or incomplete, there is prolonged exposure to stress hormones, which over time results in an increase in *allostatic load,* which refers to the physiological costs of overtaxing these systems.

According to McEwen (1998), allostatic load is increased under four conditions: (a) frequent stress exposure, which promotes frequent exposure to stress hormones; (b) inadequate habituation to stressful experiences, which also results in prolonged exposure to stress hormones; (c) inability to recover, in which physiological arousal and reactivity continue even after the stressor has been removed or terminated; and (d) an inadequate response to stress because of system fatigue or dysfunction, which triggers pathological compensatory responses in other systems. A good example of this model is essential hypertension, which is conceptualized as a disease that results from the dysregulation of blood

pressure control mechanisms due to persistent and pathological autonomic hyperreactivity to stress (Manuck, Kasprowicz, & Muldoon, 1990). Similar evidence linking stress to a variety of pregnancy outcomes has been demonstrated (Dunkel-Schetter, Wadhwa, & Stanton, 2000; Hoffman & Hatch, 1996). For example, prospective studies that assess stress exposure, appraisal, and response over time have demonstrated that higher prenatal life event stress is associated with several adverse birth outcomes, including lower infant birth weight and shorter gestational length (Wadhwa, Sandman, Porto, Dunkel-Schetter, & Garite, 1993), and with a higher preterm delivery rate in a sample of socioeconomically disadvantaged pregnant women (Lobel et al., 1992). Other studies suggest that maternal corticotropin-releasing hormone (CRH) levels in late pregnancy may mediate the stress-birth outcome relationship by affecting preterm labor and gestational length (Wadhwa, Porto, Garite, Chicz-DeMet, & Sandman, 1998). Similarly, Sandman, Wadhwa, Chicz-DeMet, Dunkel-Schetter, and Porto (1997) reported that maternal stress in late pregnancy is associated with gestational length, birth weight, and maternal plasma levels of ACTH and cortisol. However, several psychosocial factors, especially social support from partners and other members of the social network, have positive effects on maternal and fetal outcomes (Collins, Dunkel-Schetter, Lobel, & Scrimshaw, 1993; Norbeck & Anderson, 1989), including birth weight and fetal growth (Feldman, Dunkel-Schetter, Sandman, & Wadhwa, 2000).

Overall, the literature in this area demonstrates that stress is significantly associated with pregnancy outcomes independent of biomedical and sociodemographic risk factors (Dunkel-Schetter et al., 2000) and that social support, personal resources, and other psychosocial factors may also play an important role during pregnancy. However, when investigating ethnic disparities, it is clear that stressors associated with minority status are also important and that the sociopolitical context of a woman's life must be considered.

STRESS AND ETHNIC DISPARITIES IN HEALTH

A growing number of studies have specifically tested the hypothesis that ethnic differences in physical health may be due, at least in part, to differential exposure to chronic and acute life stressors (Geronimus, 1992; Myers, 1982; Williams, Yu, Jackson, & Anderson, 1997). Ethnic minorities, especially those from the lower social classes, often report a greater number of negative life events (Ituarte, Kamarck, Thompson, & Bacanu, 1999; Myers, 1982), report greater and more frequent exposure to "generic life stressors" (i.e., stressors that are a usual part of modern life—financial, occupational, relationships, parental, etc.), perceive these events as more stressful, and report greater psychological distress from these stressful life experiences (Collins et al., 1998; Myers, 1982) than their Caucasian counterparts. As such, therefore, they are likely to be particularly vulnerable to the long-term effects of high allostatic load because of their relative social position. Chronic stressors due to financial strain, inadequate housing, crowding, and violence may all contribute to more frequent activation of stress-response systems and prolonged exposure to stress hormones (Anderson, McNeilly, & Myers, 1992).

Studies have also shown greater exposure and greater reactivity to stress linked to ethnic differences in pregnancy outcomes. For example, Orr et al. (1996) found that exposure to high psychosocial stressors is related to low birth weight for African Americans. In their study of ethnic differences in birth weight, Shiono et al. (1997) reported that living in public housing and believing that one's health is largely determined by chance are negatively related to birth weight and that having a stable residence is associated with higher birth weight. Furthermore, Zambrana, Dunkel-Schetter, Collins, and Scrimshaw (1999) found that prenatal stress, drug use and smoking, and attitudes toward the pregnancy account for ethnic differences in birth weight between African Americans and Hispanics.

Therefore, the evidence suggests that ethnic differences in exposure to generic life stressors account for some of the ethnic disparities in health. However, such a simple differential stress burden explanation underestimates the true complexity of the minority stress-health relationships. By virtue of their marginal social status, many of the life stresses attributable to lower social class are exacerbated by race because of the dynamics of racism and discrimination (Krieger et al., 1993). In other words, race conditions social class such that exposure to generic life stressors are not only greater among the lower classes, but at each equivalent level of SES, racial/ethnic minorities experience higher stress burdens and poorer health outcomes (Krieger et al., 1993; Williams, 1999; Williams & Rucker, 1996). This race-SES relationship can have direct effects on health through the additional stress burden and higher allostatic load, as well as indirect effects through structural barriers of access to health care and other social resources (i.e., housing, employment, safety), acceptance of societal stigma of inferiority (i.e., acceptance of minority status), high-risk and unhealthy lifestyles (Myers et al., 1995), and negative affective states (e.g., depression, hostility, dispositional pessimism) (Clark, Anderson, Clark, & Williams, 1999; Krieger et al., 1993; Williams, 1999; Williams, Spencer, & Jackson, 1999).

In addition to its role as a conditioner of generic life stresses, race/ethnicity also contributes to greater stress burden through additional stresses that are specifically related to being a member of an ethnic minority group. For example, in a recent study examining the effects of social class, racism, and stress on self-reported physical and mental health of 520 Caucasians and 586 African Americans in Detroit, Williams and his colleagues (1997) found that both race-related stressors and general life stressors significantly account for racial differences in physical health status. Similar results were found in three studies testing this hypothesis in minority college students and young adults. Smedley, Myers, and Harrell (1993); Boyce (1997); and Rodriguez, Myers, Morris, and Cardoza (2000) demonstrated that minority status stresses make a significant additional contribution to the level of experienced psychological distress beyond that accounted for by generic life stresses that all students and young adults experience. These studies also indicated that African American students evidence greater sensitivity to race-related stressors than Chicano, Latino, and Filipino students (Smedley et al., 1993) and that being the numerical majority in a large university does not reduce the additional burden of minority-status stresses experienced by Latino students (Rodriguez et al., 2000).

These and other studies distinguished several ethnicity-related stressors that merit special recognition. These include racism and discrimination, acculturative stresses, own-group conformity pressures, stereotype threat, constant threat awareness, the pioneer syndrome, and incongruent efficacy expectations.

Racism

Racism involves the power of the majority group to institute and force conformity to its particular cultural norms (Clark et al., 1999), and it is the most obvious additional source of stress faced by racial/ethnic minorities. *Racism* is defined as "beliefs, attitudes, institutional arrangements, and acts that tend to denigrate individuals or groups because of phenotypic characteristics or ethnic group affiliation" (Clark et al., 1999, p. 805). In their recent review of the extant literature on racism and its effects on African Americans, Clark et al. (1999) discussed the empirical evidence that racism has substantial pathogenic psychological and physical effects. They acknowledged that both intergroup and intragroup racism and attitudinal (i.e., prejudice) and behavioral (i.e., overt discrimination) racism are significant stressors and offer a biopsychosocial model to account for its health effects (for a detailed discussion of these issues, see Clark et al., 1999).

It is important to acknowledge, however, that there is substantial individual and group variability in the experience of racism and discrimination, with the quantity and severity of racism a person experiences depending to some degree on his or her phenotypic characteristics (i.e., skin color, hair, other physical features) and social mannerisms (e.g., clothing, speech, social skills, etc.) (Dressler, 1993; Williams, 1997). Those who look, sound, and behave more "White" (i.e., biculturals, biracials, and persons with a blended identity) are more likely to be accepted and less likely to experience overt discriminatory experiences than those with more ethnically distinct features, accents, and behaviors (Clark et al., 1999). Similarly, there is considerable anecdotal and some empirical evidence of group differences in reported risk of exposure to discrimination, with African Americans and Hispanics, especially those who are darker, poorer, and male, reporting more overt experiences with discrimination than other racial/ethnic groups (e.g., "driving while Black," assumptions that young African American and Hispanic males are likely to be gang members, sentencing differences as a function of race, etc.) (Holmes, Hosch, Daudistel, Perez, & Graves, 1993; Zatz, 1984).

However, such blatant acts of racial prejudice and discrimination are less commonplace today and have a direct impact on the lives of fewer minority individuals. What is more common and more insidious are the new, more subtle, and aversive forms of racism that have evolved (i.e., micro insults) in which ethnic minorities continue to experience discrimination, even from educated and politically liberal Caucasian Americans who support racial equality and consider themselves to be non-prejudiced (e.g., making exclusionary decisions in college admissions, employment, treating successful minorities as exceptions that prove the rule of minority inferiority, etc.) (Dovidio & Gaertner, 2000).

Of course, institutionalized racism continues to exist in the form of structural constraints and barriers to access and control over essential resources (e.g., residential segregation, education to a standard of mediocrity rather than preparation for social mobility, limited access to good-quality health care, etc.), and its impact is especially evident for those who are both non-White and poor. These structural barriers have reemerged in the current efforts to systematically dismantle affirmative action programs in higher education and employment while failing to implement any alternative programs that would ensure equal access to these key social resources.

One of the methodological challenges facing research on the experience and impact of racism on health is the fact that racism is often a "perceived stressor" (i.e., the subjective experience of prejudice or discrimination). Clark et al. (1999) argued that traditional models of stress focus primarily on more "objective" stressors such as life events, role strains, and daily hassles and, in doing so, may ignore or underestimate the importance of exposure to more subtle racism because it involves some degree of subjectivity. However, as noted by Lazarus and Folkman (1984), it is the subjective appraisal of events as stressful that determines the magnitude of a stress response. Therefore, it is reasonable to expect greater psychological and physiological reactivity and greater allostatic load in those who report greater exposure to both objectively measurable chronic and episodic stressors as well as subjectively

experienced greater exposure to racism-related stresses (Armstead, Lawler, Gorden, Cross, & Gibbons, 1989; Fang & Myers, 2001; Krieger & Sidney, 1996).

It is also likely that ethnic individuals and groups will differ in the degree to which they have developed "racial" filters, cognitive schemas, or scripts that mediate how they interpret and respond to experiences that may be "racially meaningful." Some groups (e.g., African Americans and Hispanics) may have more sensitive racial filters and scripts that predispose them to interpret a wider range of experiences and events, especially those that are more ambiguous, as "racially meaningful" and to react to them. This would increase the impact such events may have on their health and well-being.

It is also true that there are substantial individual differences in response to stressors, including racism-related stressors, and factors such as constitutional factors, coping skills and resources, and psychological and behavioral factors are likely to partially mediate or moderate their effects on health and well-being (Contrada et al., 2000; Krieger & Sidney, 1996). Unfortunately, although there is considerable debate about racism and its effects, there continues to be inadequate attention given to investigating factors that might moderate or mediate the effects of exposure to racism. Also, most of the work in this area is focused on African Americans and Hispanics, with limited attention given to exposure to racism in other ethnic groups.

Acculturative Stress and Own-Group Conformity

There is a substantial and growing body of research on acculturation and its effect on psychological and physical health (for a comprehensive review of this literature, see Berry, 1998). Berry (1997) argued that investigations of relationships between acculturation and adjustment (and health) need to consider the influences of social and personal variables from the society of origin (i.e., social class, sex roles, opportunity structures for social mobility, etc.), the society of settlement (i.e., receptivity of cultural differences), and phenomena that exist both prior to (e.g., trauma) and during the process of acculturation. Despite continued debates about how to conceptualize and measure acculturation, the preponderance of the evidence suggests that acculturation to the majority society is associated with both benefits and costs. For example, research indicates that recent Hispanic and Asian immigrants evidence better mental and physical health than U.S.-born members of the same group (Rogler, Cortes, & Malgady, 1991; Vega et al., 1998). However, this initial advantage is lost during the early phases of acculturation, primarily through stresses associated with acculturation (i.e., learning a new language, exposure to immigrant-related discrimination, changes in social roles, family disintegration) (Balcazar, Peterson, & Krull, 1997; Nicholson, 1997) and health behaviors (Myers et al., 1995). Contrada et al. (2000) also noted that own-group conformity pressures, defined as "the experience of being pressured or constrained by one's ethnic group's expectations specifying appropriate or inappropriate behavior for the group" (p. 138), are independent of discrimination and are an additional source of stress for those who are upwardly mobile and acculturating (e.g., minority college students).

Fortunately, those who achieve bicultural status appear to regain the health losses due to acculturation (i.e., they integrate into majority society yet retain their ethnic identity and cultural roots) (Cortes, Rogler, & Malgady, 1994; LaFromboise, Coleman, & Gerton, 1995; Moyerman & Forman, 1992; Roysircar-Sodowsky & Maestas, 2000).

Therefore, minority group members must weigh the potential gains of acculturation and assimilation to the majority culture against the potential loss of legitimacy within the minority community. Those who choose to fully immerse themselves in the majority culture (i.e., become assimilated) run the risk of being ostracized or marginalized within their own group. Those who fully immerse themselves in their own communities (i.e., remain enculturated) become culturally isolated and generally fail to take full advantage of the opportunities afforded in the larger society, thus effectively precluding their likelihood of social mobility. On the other hand, those who develop a bicultural identity appear to be better able to handle the conflicting cultural demands of both their community of origin and majority society because although they understand what it takes to be successful in the majority culture, they also retain their own cultural roots, enabling them to navigate both cultural worlds.

Constant Threat Awareness

Many ethnic minorities are aware of their minority status, either consciously or otherwise. As a result, they are often on guard, gauging how they are perceived and treated by Whites and by other ethnic groups. With each new social encounter, an automatic "sizing up" process occurs in which the potential for racial conflict is estimated and behavior is adjusted accordingly to reduce risk. This state of heightened intergroup vigilance, hyperreactivity, and preemptive coping is psychologically taxing and is likely to increase the risk for psychological distress and other disorders. This hypothesis receives partial support in studies of Black-White differences in 24-hour ambulatory blood pressure, which suggest that the significantly higher mean blood pressures among African Americans may be the result of maintaining an unconscious state of heightened physical arousal even during sleep (Williams et al., 1994).

The Pioneer or Solo Experience

Another ethnicity-related stressor faced by socially mobile ethnic minorities is the experience of being the first or only one of their group who enters into a predominantly Caucasian setting. Although accomplishing educational and career goals is a source of considerable personal pride, being the first or only one of the group brings several additional stresses. These pioneers often perceive that they carry the weight of the group's collective success (i.e., their successes and failures influence the future opportunities of others from their group) and often have the added responsibility of being the interpreter and/or defender of the actions of others from the group. In addition, they are also expected by the group to be their advocate and role model. Individual personality characteristics, support and other resources available for coping, and cultural factors will influence how these often conflicting pressures are handled and their relative effect on health and functioning.

Incongruent Efficacy Expectations

The spirit of rugged individualism and individual success due to hard work and determination is central to the American cultural ethos. However, the promise of hard work paying off in rich rewards (i.e., expectation of efficacy) is not realized as often for members of minority communities. The continual frustration of not succeeding despite constant effort may be not only psychologically demoralizing (i.e., can lead to disinvestments) but also physiologically costly. Research by Sherman James and colleagues testing his John Henryism hypothesis, which he defines as prolonged, effortful coping with difficult psychosocial stressors despite limited resources, indicates that this coping style confers specific additional risk for high blood pressure to low-SES African American men but not to Caucasian men or to women (for a review of these studies, see James, 1994).

STRESS APPRAISAL, COPING, AND HEALTH OUTCOMES

The impact stress has on health is moderated by a number of psychosocial factors, principal among which are appraisal, coping, and social supports.

Appraisal

The impact that exposure to chronic stress has on health is moderated by how one interprets or appraises and responds to the stressful experience. Stress appraisal involves the weighing of one's resources against the demands of the stressor to determine how large a threat the stressor is to well-being. Resources encompass personality factors such as self-esteem and self-efficacy, as well as demographic and social factors, such as monetary resources and social support. For ethnic minorities, stress appraisal involves not only the subjective examination of resources versus demands but also the filtering of stressful experiences through one's unique cultural lens. For example, women of all ethnic groups have served as the traditional center of families and are responsible for the emotional, physical, and spiritual well-being of its members (Reid & Bing, 2000). For African American women and other women of color, however, this has also included sharing or carrying the major responsibility for the economic viability of the family, coping with their own stressful life experiences, and moderating the impact of life stresses on the members of the family (Chisholm, 1996; hooks, 1993; Robinson, 1983). Acceptance of this "strong woman" image is an additional burden of stress, and cultural expectations that they should be able to handle life challenges may hinder some minority women from seeking outside assistance with problems. On the other hand, fulfilling strong traditional roles may contribute to their resiliency, resourcefulness, and flexibility in dealing with stressful situations (Reid & Bing, 2000). Among some ethnic groups (e.g., Hispanics and Asians), challenging life situations may be deemed the result of fate so that coping focuses on acceptance of the challenge rather than acting actively to change the situation. Also, Asian cultures are often described as holding a collective versus individualistic worldview (Markus & Kitayama, 1999). For these groups, life stresses are more likely to be perceived as a threat to the entire family or community system rather than only to the individual, and more collective coping efforts are expected and reinforced.

Furthermore, and as noted earlier, ethnic minority individuals and groups may also differ in the extent and salience of racial filters and scripts that influence their relative "sensitivity" to stressful racial cues and degree of reactivity to racially meaningful events. These individual and group differences in appraisal also apply to life stresses generally. Several studies have suggested that ethnic minorities may minimize or downplay the significance of stressful events and experiences. This may be interpreted as a response bias (e.g., denial, minimization) and a form of defensive reappraisal and coping. However, it may also be the result of habituation to a chronic stressor to which one has become familiar and for which one has developed a way of coping that reduces the impact of the stressor (e.g., less distress in the face of limited financial resources). It should be noted, however, that even though psychological accommodation can be protective against distress, exposure to the stressors still has physiologic effects and costs, and it is the latter that might contribute over time to the cumulative vulnerability that results in adverse health outcomes.

Coping

The impact that exposure to chronic stresses has on health is also moderated by how one copes with these experiences. The relative effectiveness of coping efforts is determined by the type of coping used (i.e., active vs. passive), the type of stressor (i.e., controllable vs. uncontrollable), the match between type of stressor and the coping response used, and the availability of adequate resources for coping (e.g., adequate knowledge, access to treatment, etc.) (Lazarus, 1993). Coping is defined as the strategies one engages in to manage demands that are perceived as taxing or exceeding one's available resources (Lazarus & Folkman, 1984). These strategies can be cognitive, emotional, or behavioral and may be adaptive or maladaptive. An important distinction is usually made between active- or approach-oriented coping strategies and avoidant coping strategies. Active- or approach-oriented coping strategies are those cognitive, behavioral, or emotional responses that involve actively engaging the stressor to control, resolve, or remove it or to control the thoughts and emotions that the stressor elicits. Conversely, avoidant coping strategies are cognitive, emotional, and behavioral strategies that distance the person from the stressor. Most studies have found that active- or approach-oriented coping strategies, such as positive attitudes (Taylor et al., 1992), physical exercise (Norvell, Martin, & Salamon, 1991), and assertiveness (Salamon et al., as cited in Taylor, 1995), are associated with positive physical and psychological adjustment. These active coping efforts are especially effective with stressors that are controllable (e.g., preparing for a major test or competition, avoiding money problems by budgeting funds, etc.). On the other hand, avoidant coping strategies (e.g., denial, distraction, wishful thinking) can be helpful in the short run as a means of controlling emotional reactivity, especially with uncontrollable stressors (e.g., diagnosis of a serious illness), but they are usually less effective in the long run and are associated with greater psychological distress and risk of disease and dysfunction (Antoni, Schneiderman, Esterling, &

Ironson, 1994; Namir, Wolcott, Fawzy, & Alumbaugh, 1987).

Recent studies on coping as a moderator of stress and disease have identified several specific strategies such as emotional expression, cognitive processing, finding meaning, and realistic acceptance that are implicated in disease outcomes as diverse as risk for CVD (i.e., emotional repression, reactive hostility) (Siegman, 1994) and immune dysfunction, disease progression, and time to death in HIV/AIDS (Kemeny & Gruenewald, 2000). However, because most of these studies have been conducted on middle-class Caucasians, relatively little is known about how these strategies affect physical health and well-being in ethnic minorities.

Coping in Ethnic Minorities

In a theoretical discussion of issues surrounding coping in women, Banyard and Graham-Bermann (1993) argued that "coping occurs in a context shaped by social forces based on gender, race, class, age and sexual orientation. These forces exert a powerful influence both on how a stressful situation is appraised and on judgments made about what coping resources are available" (p. 311). They further argued that coping as it is traditionally measured is largely influenced by education and income, such that those with more resources typically cope "better." In this respect, an individual's social position and the environments associated with the same can constrain his or her resources and choice of coping strategies (Taylor et al., 1997). Members of marginalized groups, either because of ethnicity, social class, and/or gender, may face special challenges to active coping. Limitations in finances, knowledge, and access to requisite technical expertise or other resources, as well as cultural, social, or psychological barriers, may discourage active coping. For example, assertiveness in minority men and women is often misperceived as aggressiveness or arrogance and responded to with fear or punishment (i.e., put them in their place). On the other hand, passive compliance (i.e., going along to get along), although useful in deflecting threats, does not usually yield the desired goals (e.g., earned rewards) and has been shown to confer greater health risks (Krieger & Sidney, 1996).

Ethnic minority status can also influence the effectiveness of certain coping strategies, especially when SES is considered. For example, the work by James and colleagues (James, 1994) on John Henryism illustrates this relationship. *John Henryism* is defined as active, effortful coping with adversity marked by attitudes that reflect (a) efficacious mental and physical vigor, (b) a strong commitment to hard work, and (c) a single-minded determination to succeed. When compared to higher SES African Americans and Caucasians from all SES groups, John Henryism has been shown to predict higher blood pressure and greater risk for hypertension only in African American men with low socioeconomic resources (Dressler, Bindon, & Neggers, 1998; James, 1994). Thus, John Henryism is relatively benign for high-SES African Americans and Caucasians. However, for African American men with limited resources, the benefits of effortful coping (i.e., economic survival) are tempered by increased health risks.

Given that ethnic minorities are often confronted with chronic stressors that are not easily ameliorated, it is not surprising that effortful, active coping strategies such as John Henryism have mixed results. Such coping strategies would not effect change and may in fact produce high levels of frustration, which might account for the higher levels of blood pressure seen in these individuals. Unfortunately, the literature in this area has not focused on those coping strategies that would be adaptive for ethnic minorities with few resources. It is very likely that healthy functioning in the face of chronic stress exposure from low SES requires the development of a different array of active and passive coping strategies than is the case for those with more socioeconomic resources.

An emerging body of literature indicates that African American and Hispanic women often use religion as a way of coping with chronic stressors (Levin, Chatters, & Taylor, 1995; Mattis, 1997). For example, when faced with uncontrollable events such as illness or death, ethnographic studies and first-person accounts indicate that African American women often use prayer and meditation to cope with the stress and anxiety that they experience (Villarosa, 1994; Wade-Gayles, 1995). In a study of Black and White elderly women with medical problems, Conway (1985) found that the majority (64%) of Black women employed prayer as a coping strategy, compared to only one third of their White counterparts. A study on coping in women with HIV found that Latinas and African American women engaged in prayer and "rediscovery of self" more often than any other coping strategy (Kaplan, Marks, & Mertens, 1997). Recent studies of African American and Hispanic women suffering from chronic illness have found that religious coping is associated with less depression and anxiety but is not associated with physical health outcomes (Alferi, Culver, Carver, Arena, & Antoni, 1999; Woods, Antoni, Ironson, & Kling, 1999). In this respect, religious coping may be effective in reducing the psychological distress associated with chronic stressors but may not be effective in ameliorating the negative effects of chronic stressors on health outcomes.

Unfortunately, most of the literature on coping in ethnic minorities has focused on ethnic-specific coping strategies, such as John Henryism and religiosity, whereas the mainstream coping literature has largely ignored ethnic minority populations and discussions of cultural differences. An integration of the two literatures is greatly needed.

For example, a great deal of recent research has centered on the effects of emotion-focused coping on physical and mental health outcomes (Stanton, Danoff-Burg, Cameron, & Ellis, 1994; Stanton et al., 2000). Emotion-focused coping strategies typically involve expressing or processing feelings around a particular stressful experience. Emotions may be expressed privately (e.g., journal writing) or interpersonally (e.g., talking and sharing feelings with others). Several studies have found that emotional expression has a positive effect on health outcomes, whereas emotional suppression has negative health effects (Gross, 1998; Pennebaker & Seagal, 1999).

These findings have particular implications for ethnic minorities because there are important cultural differences in norms surrounding the expression and experience of emotions. For example, several researchers have speculated that Latinas are socialized to be emotionally expressive, whereas African American women are socialized to present a "strong Black woman" image to others (hooks, 1993). Thus, it is likely that Latinas may be more likely to engage in emotionally expressive coping strategies than African American women. However, it is not clear who would benefit the most from expressing their emotions. African American women may benefit less from expressing emotions, if it is not viewed as culturally appropriate; on the other hand, African American women may benefit *more* from expressing emotions because they may be experiencing negative health consequences from suppressing their emotions. There is some support for this notion in a study conducted by Nancy Krieger (1990), who investigated the effects of discrimination on women. She found that African American women who reported that they usually accepted and kept quiet about unfair treatment were 4.4 times more likely to report hypertension than women who expressed their feelings to others (Krieger, 1990). However, the tendency to use more affect control strategies among Asians does not appear to be as maladaptive, perhaps because it is more culturally congruent (Tsai & Levenson, 1997).

SUMMARY AND IMPLICATIONS

In this chapter, we reviewed some of the evidence of the persistent racial health disparities and offered an integrated biopsychosocial model of stress and disease to account for these disparities. Specific emphasis was given to the contribution of ethnicity-related stresses, including racism and discrimination, as an independent source of stress that adds to the overall stress to higher allostatic load and to greater cumulative vulnerability for ethnic minorities, especially those who are low SES. We also acknowledge that there are substantial individual and group differences in exposure to stresses, as well as in response to these stresses, and that factors such as appraisal, coping, and access to support resources are important moderators of stress and risk for adverse health outcomes. Future studies are needed that investigate the major hypotheses in the extant literature on stress and disease with ethnically diverse populations and identify those factors that are most predictive of health and illness.

Finally, in our efforts to account for ethnic health disparities, we continue to overlook those racial/ethnic minorities who remain resilient despite being at high socioecological risk. A small but growing body of evidence suggests that factors such as parental warmth and family structure, biculturalism, strong ethnic/tribal identity, supportive family/social network, a resilient perspective, and an activist social perspective are all associated with greater resilience (Klassen, 1997; McCubbin, Thompson, Thompson, & Fromer, 1998; McCubbin, Thompson, Thompson, & Futrell, 1998; Myers & Taylor, 1998; Rogler et al., 1991). Research pursuing these hypotheses has the potential not only to clarify what factors confer risk but also to suggest directions for interventions to close these gaps by developing those attributes that enhance resilience.

REFERENCES

Alferi, S. M., Culver, J. L., Carver, C. S., Arena, P. L., & Antoni, M. H. (1999). Religiosity, religious coping, and distress: A prospective study of Catholic and Evangelical Hispanic women in treatment for early-stage breast cancer. *Journal of Health Psychology, 4*(3), 343-356.

American Heart Association. (2002). *Heart facts 2002: All Americans.* Chicago: Author.

Anderson, L. P. (1991). Acculturative stress: A theory of relevance to Black Americans. *Clinical Psychology Review, 11,* 685-702.

Anderson, N. B., & McNeilly, M. (1993). Autonomic reactivity and hypertension in Blacks: Toward a contextual model. In J. C. S. Fray & J. G. Douglas (Eds.), *Pathophysiology of hypertension in Blacks* (pp. 107-139). New York: Oxford University Press.

Anderson, N. B., McNeilly, M., & Myers, H. F. (1992). Autonomic reactivity and hypertension in Blacks: Toward a contextual model. In E. H. Johnson, W. D. Johnson, & S. Julius (Eds.), *Personality, elevated blood pressure and essential hypertension* (pp. 197-216). New York: Hemisphere.

Antoni, M. H., Schneiderman, N., Esterling, B., & Ironson, G. (1994). Stress management and adjustment to HIV-1 infection. *Homeostasis in Health & Disease, CIANS-Homeostasis: Czechoslovakia, 35*(3), 149-160.

Arcury, T. A., Quandt, S. A., McDonald, J., & Bell, R. A. (2000). Faith and health self-management of rural older adults. *Journal of Cross-Cultural Gerontology, 15*(1), 55-74.

Armstead, C. A., Lawler, K. A., Gorden, G., Cross, J., & Gibbons, J. (1989). Relationship of racial stressors to blood pressure responses and anger expression in Black college students. *Health Psychology, 8,* 541-556.

Balcazar, H., Peterson, G. W., & Krull, J. L. (1997). Acculturation and family cohesiveness in Mexican American pregnant women: Social and health implications. *Family & Community Health, 20,* 16-31.

Banyard, V. L., & Graham-Bermann, S. A. (1993). Can women cope? A gender analysis of theories of coping with stress. *Psychology of Women Quarterly, 17,* 303-318.

Baum, A., Garofalo, J. P., & Yali, A. M. (1999). Socioeconomic status and chronic stress: Does stress account for the SES effects on health? In N. E. Adler, M. Marmot, B. S. McEwen, & J. Stewart (Eds.), *Socioeconomic status and health in industrial nations: Social, psychological, and biological pathways* (pp. 131-144). New York: New York Academy of Sciences.

Berry, J. W. (1997). Immigration, acculturation, and adaptation. *Applied Psychology: An International Review, 46*(1), 5-34.

Berry, J. W. (1998). Acculturation and health: Theory and practice. In S. S. Kazarian & D. R. Evans (Eds.), *Cultural clinical psychology: Theory, research & practice* (pp. 39-57). New York: Oxford University Press.

Bogardus, C., & Lillioja, S. (1992). Pima Indians as a model to study the genetics of NIDDM. *Journal of Cell Biochemistry, 48,* 337-343.

Boyce, C. A. (1997). Racial stressors for African Americans. *Dissertation Abstracts International, 57*(12-B).

Carter, J. S., Pugh, J. A., & Monterrosa, A. (1996). Non–insulin dependent diabetes mellitus in minorities in the United States. *Annals of Internal Medicine, 125,* 221-232.

Centers for Disease Control and Prevention (CDC). (1997). *National diabetes fact sheet: Diabetes at highest levels in the U.S.: Minority populations especially affected.* Atlanta, GA: Author.

Centers for Disease Control and Prevention (CDC). (1999). Achievements in public health, 1900-1999: Healthier mothers and babies. *Morbidity & Mortality Weekly, 48*(38), 849-858.

Chisholm, J. F. (1996). Mental health issues in African-American women. *Annals of the New York Academy of Sciences, 789,* 161-179.

Clark, R., Anderson, N. B., Clark, V. R., & Williams, D. R. (1999). Racism as a stressor for African Americans: A biopsychosocial model. *American Psychologist, 54*(10), 805-816.

Cohen, L. M. (1985). "Controlarse" and the problems of life among Latino Immigrants. In W. A. Vega & M. R. Mirandal (Eds.), *Stress & Hispanic mental health: Relating research to service delivery* (pp. 202-218). Rockville, MD: National Institute of Mental Health.

Cohen, S., Kessler, R. C., & Gordon, L. U. (1995). Strategies for measuring stress in studies of psychiatric and physical disorders. In S. Cohen, R. C. Kessler, & L. U. Gordon (Eds.), *Measuring stress: A guide for health and social scientists* (pp. 3-26). New York: Oxford University Press.

Collins, J. W., David, R. J., Symons, R., Handler, A., Wall, S., & Andes, S. (1998). African-American mothers' perceptions of their residential environment, stressful life events, and very low birthweight. *Epidemiology, 9*(3), 286-289.

Collins, N. L., Dunkel-Schetter, C., Lobel, M., & Scrimshaw, S. C. (1993). Social support in pregnancy: Psychosocial correlates of birth outcomes and postpartum depression. *Journal of Personality and Social Psychology, 65*(6), 1243-1258.

Contrada, R. J., Ashmore, R. D., Gary, M. L., Coups, E., Egeth, J. D., Sewell, A., Ewell, K., Goyal, T. M., & Chasse, V. (2000). Ethnicity-related sources of stress and their effects on well-being. *Current Directions in Psychological Science, 9*(4), 136-139.

Conway, K. (1985). Coping with the stress of medical problems among Black and White elderly. *International Journal of Aging & Human Development, 21,* 39-48.

Cooper, R. S., & Borke, J. L. (1993). Intracellular ions and hypertension in Blacks. In J. C. S. Fray & J. G. Douglas (Eds.), *Pathophysiology of hypertension in Blacks* (pp. 181-213). New York: Oxford University Press.

Cortes, D. E., Rogler, L. H., & Malgady, R. G. (1994). Biculturality among Puerto Rican adults in the United States. *American Journal of Community Psychology, 22,* 707-721.

Dovidio, J. F., & Gaertner, S. L. (2000). Aversive racism and selection decisions: 1989 and 1999. *Psychological Science, 11*(4), 315-319.

Dressler, W. W. (1993). Social and cultural dimensions of hypertension in Blacks: Underlying mechanisms. In J. C. S. Fray & J. G. Douglas (Eds.), *Pathophysiology of hypertension in Blacks* (pp. 69-89). New York: Oxford University Press.

Dressler, W. W., Bindon, J. R., & Neggers, Y. H. (1998). John Henryism, gender, and arterial blood pressure in an African American community. *Psychosomatic Medicine, 60,* 620-624.

Dunkel-Schetter, C. (1998). Maternal stress and preterm delivery. *Prenatal and Neonatal Medicine, 3,* 39-42.

Dunkel-Schetter, C., Wadhwa, P., & Stanton, A. L. (2000). Stress and reproduction: Introduction to the special section. *Health Psychology, 19*(6), 507-509.

Fang, C. Y., & Myers, H. F. (2001). Hostility and cardiovascular reactivity to racial stressors. *Health Psychology, 20*(1), 64-70.

Feldman, P. J., Dunkel-Schetter, C., Sandman, C. A., & Wadhwa, P. D. (2000). Maternal social support predicts birthweight and fetal growth in human pregnancy. *Psychosomatic Medicine, 62*(5), 715-725.

Flack, J. M., Amaro, H., Jenkins, W., Kunitz, S., Levy, J., Mixon, M., & Yu, E. (1995). Panel I: Epidemiology of minority health. *Health Psychology, 14*(7), 592-600.

Geronimus, A. T. (1992). The weathering hypothesis and the health of African American women and infants: Evidence and speculations. *Ethnicity & Disease, 2,* 207-221.

Grim, C. E., & Wilson, T. W. (1993). Salt, slavery and survival: Physiological principles underlying the evolutionary hypothesis of salt-sensitive hypertension in Western Hemisphere Blacks. In J. C. S. Fray & J. G. Douglas (Eds.), *Pathophysiology of hypertension in Blacks* (pp. 25-49). New York: Oxford University Press.

Gross, J. J. (1998). Antecedent-and response-focused emotion regulation: Divergent consequence for experience, expression, and physiology. *Journal of Personality and Social Psychology, 64,* 224-237.

Guyer, B., Hoyert, D. L., Martin, J. A., Ventura, S. J., MacDorman, M. F., & Strobino, D. M. (1999). Annual summary of vital statistics—1998. *Pediatrics, 104*(6), 1229-1246.

Hoffman, S., & Hatch, M. C. (1996). Stress, social support, and pregnancy outcome: A reassessment based on recent research. *Paediatric and Perinatal Epidemiology, 10*(4), 380-405.

Holmes, M. D., Hosch, H. M., Daudistel, H. C., Perez, D. A., & Graves, J. B. (1993). Judges' ethnicity and minority sentencing: Evidence concerning Hispanics. *Social Science Quarterly, 74*(3), 496-506.

Hom, A., & Amada, G. (1985). Overcoming the problem of face-saving: Outreach services to Chinese students. In G. Amada (Ed.), *Mental health on the community college campus* (2nd ed., pp. 83-91). Landham, MD: University Press of America.

hooks, b. (1993). *Sisters of the Yam: Black women and self-recovery*. Boston: South End.

Ituarte, P. H., Kamarck, T. W., Thompson, H. S., & Bacanu, S. (1999). Psychosocial mediators of racial differences in nighttime blood pressure dipping among normotensive adults. *Health Psychology, 18*(4), 393-402.

James, S. A. (1994). John Henryism and the health of African-Americans. *Culture, Medicine & Psychiatry, 18*(2), 163-182.

Kaplan, M. S., Marks, G., & Mertens, S. B. (1997). Distress and coping among women with HIV infection: Preliminary findings from a multiethnic sample. *American Journal of Orthopsychiatry, 67*(1), 80-91.

Kemeny, M. E., & Gruenewald, T. L. (2000). Affect, cognition, the immune system and health. *Progress in Brain Research, 122,* 291-308.

Klassen, H. M. (1997). The development of resilience in American Indian adolescents. *Dissertation Abstracts International, 57*(n7-A), 2857.

Kleinman, J. C., Fingerhut, L. A., & Prager, K. (1991). Differences in infant mortality by race, nativity status, and other maternal characteristics. *American Journal of Diseases of Childhood, 145,* 194-195.

Krieger, N. (1990). Racial and gender discrimination: Risk factors for high blood pressure? *Social Science & Medicine, 30*(12), 1273-1281.

Krieger, N., Rowley, D. L., Herman, A. A., Avery, B., & Phillips, M. T. (1993). Racism, sexism, and social class: Implications for studies of health, disease, and well-being. *American Journal of Preventive Medicine, 9*(Suppl. 6), 82-122.

Krieger, N., & Sidney, S. (1996). Racial discrimination and blood pressure: The CARDIA study of young Black and White adults. *American Journal of Public Health, 86,* 1370-1378.

LaFromboise, T., Coleman, H. L. K., & Gerton, J. (1995). Psychological impact of biculturalism: Evidence and theory. In N. R. Goldberger & J. B. Veroff (Eds.), *The culture and psychology reader* (pp. 489-535). New York: New York University Press.

Lazarus, R. S. (1993). Coping theory and research: Past, present, and future. *Psychosomatic Medicine, 55*(3), 234-247.

Lazarus, R. S., & Folkman, S. (1984). *Stress, appraisal & coping*. New York: Springer.

Levin, J. S., Chatters, L. M., & Taylor, R. J. (1995). Religious effects on health status and life satisfaction among Black Americans. *Journals of Gerontology, Series B: Psychological Science & Social Sciences, 50*(3), S154-S163.

Levin, J. S., & Taylor, R. J. (1993). Panel analysis of religious involvement and well-being in African Americans: Contemporaneous vs. longitudinal effects. *Journal for the Scientific Study of Religion, 37*(4), 695-709.

Lobel, M., Dunkel-Schetter, C., & Scrimshaw, S. (1992). Prenatal maternal stress and prematurity: A prospective study of socioeconomically disadvantaged women. *Health Psychology, 11*(1), 32-40.

Magana, A., & Clark, N. M. (1995). Examining a paradox: Does religiosity contribute to positive birth outcomes in Mexican American populations? *Health Education Quarterly, 22*(1), 96-109.

Manuck, S. B., Kasprowicz, A. L., & Muldoon, M. F. (1990). Behaviorally-evoked cardiovascular reactivity: Potential associations. *Annals of Behavioral Medicine, 12*(1), 17-29.

Markus, H. R., & Kitayama, S. (1999). Culture and the self: Implications for cognition, emotion, and motivation. In R. F. Baumeister (Ed.), *The self in social psychology* (pp. 339-371). Philadelphia: Psychology Press.

Mattis, J. (1997). Spirituality and religiosity in the lives of Black women. *African American Research Perspectives, 3,* 56-60.

McCubbin, H. I., Thompson, E. A., Thompson, A. I., & Fromer, J. E. (Eds.). (1998). *Resiliency in Native American and immigrant families.* Thousand Oaks, CA: Sage.

McCubbin, H. I., Thompson, E. A., Thompson, A. I., & Futrell, J. A. (Eds.). (1998). *Resiliency in African American families.* Thousand Oaks, CA: Sage.

McEwen, B. S. (1998). Stress, adaptation, and disease: Allostasis and allostatic load. *Annals of the New York Academy of Sciences, 840,* 33-44.

McEwen, B. S., & Stellar, E. (1993). Stress and the individual: Mechanisms leading to disease. *Archives of Internal Medicine, 153,* 2093-2101.

Moyerman, D. R., & Forman, B. D. (1992). Acculturation and adjustment: A meta-analytic study. *Hispanic Journal of Behavioral Sciences, 14,* 163-200.

Myers, H. F. (1982). Stress, ethnicity & social class: A model for research on Black populations. In E. E. Jones & S. Korchin (Eds.), *Minority mental health* (pp. 118-148). New York: Holt, Rinehart & Winston.

Myers, H. F., Kagawa-Singer, M., Kumanyika, S. K., Lex, B. W., & Markides, K. S. (1995). Panel III: Behavioral risk factors related to chronic diseases in ethnic populations. *Health Psychology, 14*(7), 613-621.

Myers, H. F., & McClure, F. H. (1993). Psychosocial factors in hypertension in Blacks: The case for an interactional perspective. In J. C. S. Fray & J. G. Douglas (Eds.), *Pathophysiology of hypertension in Blacks* (pp. 90-106). New York: Oxford University Press.

Myers, H. F., & Rodriguez, N. (2002). Acculturation & health in racial/ethnic minorities. In K. Chun, P. B. Organista, & G. Marín (Eds.), *Acculturation: Advances in theory, measurement & applied research.* Washington, DC: American Psychological Association.

Myers, H. F., & Taylor, S. (1998). Family contributions to risk and resilience in African American children. *Journal of Comparative Family Studies, 29*(1), 215-229.

Namir, S., Wolcott, D. S., Fawzy, F. I., & Alumbaugh, M. J. (1987). Coping with AIDS: Psychological and health implications. *Journal of Applied Social Psychology, 17,* 309-328.

National Center for Health Statistics (NCHS). (1993). Advance report of final natality statistics, 1991. *Monthly Vital Statistics Report, 42*(Suppl.), 37, 39.

National Center for Health Statistics (NCHS). (1995). *Healthy People 2000: Progress report for heart disease and stroke.* Hyattsville, MD: U.S. Department of Health and Human Services.

National Center for Health Statistics (NCHS). (2000). *Health, United States, 2000 with adolescent health chartbook.* Hyattsville, MD: U.S. Department of Health and Human Services.

Nicholson, B. L. (1997). The influence of pre-emigration and postemigration stressors on mental health: A study of Southeast Asian refugees. *Social Work Research, 21*(1), 19-31.

Norbeck, J. S., & Anderson, N. J. (1989). Psychosocial predictors of pregnancy outcomes in low-income Black, Hispanic, and White women. *Nursing Research, 38*(4), 204-209.

Norvell, N., Martin, D., & Salamon, A. (1991). Psychological and physiological benefits of passive and aerobic exercise in sedentary middle-aged women. *Journal of Nervous & Mental Disease, 179*(9), 573-574.

Orr, S. T., James, S. A., Miller, C. A., Barakat, B., Daikoku, N., Pupkin, M., Engstrom, K., & Huggins, G. (1996). Psychosocial stressors and low birthweight in an urban population. *American Journal of Preventive Medicine, 12*(6), 459-466.

Paneth, N. (1995). The problem of low birthweight. *The Future of Children, 5*(1), 19-34.

Pennebaker, J. W., & Seagal, J. D. (1999). Forming a story: The health benefits of narrative. *Journal of Clinical Psychology, 55*(10), 1243-1254.

Pickering, T. (1999). Cardiovascular pathways: Socioeconomic status and stress effects on hypertension and cardiovascular function. In N. E. Adler, M. Marmot, B. S. McEwen, & J. Stewart (Eds.), *Socioeconomic status and health in industrial nations: Social, psychological, and biological pathways* (pp. 262-277). New York: New York Academy of Sciences.

Reid, P. T., & Bing, V. M. (2000). Sexual role of girls and women: An ethnocultural lifespan perspective. In C. B. Travis & J. W. White (Eds.), *Sexuality, society, and feminism* (pp. 141-166). Washington, DC: American Psychological Association.

Rini, C. K., Dunkel-Schetter, C., Sandman, C. A., & Wadhwa, P. D. (1999). Psychological adaptation and birth outcomes: The role of personal resources, stress, and sociocultural context in pregnancy. *Health Psychology, 18*(4), 333-345.

Robinson, C. R. (1983). Black women: A tradition of self-reliant strength. *Women and Therapy, 2*(2/3), 135-144.

Rodriguez, N., Myers, H. F., Morris, J. K., & Cardoza, D. (2000). Latino college student adjustment: Does an increased presence offset minority-status and acculturative stresses? *Journal of Applied Social Psychology, 30*(7), 1523-1550.

Rogler, L., Cortes, D. E., & Malgady, R. G. (1991). Acculturation and mental health status among Hispanics: Convergence and new directions of research. *American Psychologist, 6*, 585-597.

Roysircar-Sodowsky, G., & Maestas, M. V. (2000). Acculturation, ethnic identity, and acculturative stress: Evidence and measurement. In R. H. Dana (Ed.), *Handbook of cross-cultural and multicultural personality assessment* (pp. 131-172). Mahwah, NJ: Lawrence Erlbaum.

Saab, P. G., Llabre, M. M., Schneiderman, N., Hurwitz, B. E., McDonald, P. G., Evans, J., Wohlgemuth, W., Hayashi, P., & Klein, B. (1997). Influence of ethnicity and gender on cardiovascular responses to active coping and inhibitory-passive coping challenges. *Psychosomatic Medicine, 59*(4), 434-446.

Sandman, C. A., Wadhwa, P. D., Chicz-DeMet, A., Dunkel-Schetter, C., & Porto, M. (1997). Maternal stress, HPA activity, and fetal/infant outcomes. *Annals of the New York Academy of Sciences, 814*, 266-275.

Schoendorf, K. C., Hogue, C. J. R., Kleinman, J. C., & Rowley, D. (1992). Mortality among infants of Black as compared with White college-educated parents. *New England Journal of Medicine, 326*, 1522-1526.

Scribner, R., & Dwyer, J. H. (1989). Acculturation and low birthweight among Latinos in the Hispanic HANES. *American Journal of Public Health, 79*, 1263-1267.

Selye, H. (1956). *The stress of life.* New York: McGraw-Hill.

Shiono, P. H., Rauh, V. A., Park, M., Lederman, S. A., & Suskar, D. (1997). Ethnic differences in birthweight: Lifestyle and other factors. *American Journal of Public Health, 87*(5), 787-793.

Siegman, A. W. (1994). Cardiovascular consequences of expressing and repressing anger. In A. W. Siegman & T. W. Smith (Eds.), *Anger, hostility, and the heart* (pp. 173-197). Hillsdale, NJ: Lawrence Erlbaum.

Smedley, B. D., Myers, H. F., & Harrell, S. P. (1993). Minority-status stresses and the college adjustment of ethnic minority freshmen. *Journal of Higher Education, 64*(4), 434-452.

Stanton, A. L., Danoff-Burg, S., Cameron, C. L., & Ellis, A. P. (1994). Coping through emotional approach: Problems of conceptualization and confounding. *Journal of Personality and Social Psychology, 66*(2), 350-362.

Stanton, A. L., Danoff-Burg, S., Cameron, C. L., Bishop, M., Collins, C. A., Kirk, S. B., Sworowski, L. A., & Twillman, R. (2000). Emotionally expressive coping predicts psychological and physical adjustment to breast cancer. *Journal of Consulting & Clinical Psychology, 68*(5), 875-882.

Taylor, S. E. (1995). *Health psychology* (3rd ed.). New York: McGraw-Hill.

Taylor, S. E., Kemeny, M. E., Aspinwall, L. G., Schneider, S. G., Rodriguez, R., & Herbert, M. (1992). Optimism, coping, psychological distress, and high-risk sexual behavior among men at risk for acquired immunodefieciency syndrome (AIDS). *Journal of Personality and Social Psychology, 63*(3), 460-473.

Taylor, S. E., Repetti, R. L., & Seeman, T. E. (1997). Health psychology: What is an unhealthy environment and how does it get under the skin? *Annual Review of Psychology, 48*, 411-447.

Taylor, S. E., & Seeman, T. E. (1999). Psychosocial resources and the SES-health relationship. In N. E. Adler, M. Marmot, B. S. McEwen, & J. Stewart (Eds.), *Socioeconomic status and health in industrial nations: Social, psychological, and biological pathways* (pp. 210-225). New York: New York Academy of Sciences.

Tsai, J. L., & Levenson, R. W. (1997). Cultural influences of emotional responding: Chinese American and European American dating couples during interpersonal conflict. *Journal of Cross-Cultural Psychology, 28*(5), 600-626.

Vega, W. A., Kolody, B., Aguilar-Gaxiola, S., Alderete, E., Catalano, R., & Caraveo-Anduaga, J. (1998). Lifetime prevalence of *DSM-III-R* psychiatric disorders among urban and rural Mexican Americans in California. *Archives of General Psychiatry, 55*, 771-782.

Villarosa, L. (Ed.). (1994). *Body & soul: The Black women's guide to physical health and emotional well-being: A National Black Women's Health Project book*. New York: HarperCollins.

Wade-Gayles, G. (Ed.). (1995). *My soul is a witness: African-American women's spirituality*. Boston: Beacon.

Wadhwa, P. D., Porto, M., Garite, T., Chicz-DeMet, A., & Sandman, C. A. (1998). Maternal corticotropin-releasing hormone levels in the early third trimester predict length of gestation in human pregnancy. *American Journal of Obstetrics and Gynecology, 179*(4), 1079-1085.

Wadhwa, P. D., Sandman, C. A., Porto, M., Dunkel-Schetter, C., & Garite, T. (1993). The association between prenatal stress and infant birthweight and gestational age at birth: A prospective investigation. *American Journal of Obstetrics and Gynecology, 169*, 858-865.

Williams, D. R. (1997). Race and health: Basic questions, emerging directions. *Annals of Epidemiology, 7*(5), 322-333.

Williams, D. R. (1999). Race, socioeconomic status, and health: The added effects of racism and discrimination. In N. E. Adler, M. Marmot, B. S. McEwen, & J. Stewart (Eds.), *Socioeconomic status and health in industrial nations: Social, psychological, and biological pathways* (pp. 173-188). New York: New York Academy of Sciences.

Williams, D. R., & Collins, C. (1995). Socioeconomic and racial differences in health. *Annual Review of Sociology, 21*, 349-386.

Williams, D. R., Lavizzo-Mourey, R., & Warren, R. C. (1994). The concept of race and health status in America. *Public Health Reports, 109*(1), 26-41.

Williams, D. R., & Rucker, T. (1996). Socioeconomic status and the health of racial minority populations. In P. M. Kato & T. Mann (Eds.), *Handbook of diversity issues in health psychology* (pp. 407-423). New York: Plenum.

Williams, D. R., Spencer, M. S., & Jackson, J. S. (1999). Race, stress, and physical health: The role of group identity. In R. J. Contrada & R. D. Ashmore (Eds.),

Self, social identity, and interdisciplinary explorations (pp. 71-100). New York: Oxford University Press.

Williams, D. R., Yu, Y., Jackson, J. S., & Anderson, N. B. (1997). Racial differences in physical and mental health: Socio-economic status, stress and discrimination. *Journal of Health Psychology, 2*(3), 335-351.

Woods, T. E., Antoni, M. H., Ironson, G. H., & Kling, D. W. (1999). Religiosity is associated with affective status in symptomatic HIV-infected African-American women. *Journal of Health Psychology, 4*(3), 317-326.

Zambrana, R. E., Dunkel-Schetter, C., Collins, N., & Scrimshaw, S. C. (1999). Mediators of ethnic-associated differences in infant birthweight. *Journal of Urban Health, 76*(1), 102-116.

Zatz, M. S. (1984). Race, ethnicity, and determinate sentencing: A new dimension to an old controversy. *Criminology: An Interdisciplinary Journal, 22*(2), 147-171.

CHAPTER 19

Depression in Ethnic Minorities

Latinos and Latinas, African Americans, Asian Americans, and Native Americans

EMILY SÁEZ-SANTIAGO
GUILLERMO BERNAL
University of Puerto Rico

This chapter examines the recent literature related to depression in ethnic minority groups. First, we present information about the status of depression in the general population, including the prevalence rates and risk factors for this disorder. Then, we review the literature on depression and ethnicity/race to evaluate whether ethnicity or race has a relationship with depression. The theoretical approach that informs the interpretation of the findings from the literature on depression and ethnic minorities is based on the notion that people are more vulnerable to develop depression as a result of their subordinated and defeated status (as is the case of members of minority groups). Finally, we present the available prevalence rates and other epidemiological information of depression in the four ethnic minority groups in the United States: Latinos and Latinas, African Americans, Asian Americans, and Native Americans. The available epidemiological information on depression in the general population for White/Caucasian and ethnic minority samples is examined.

Depression has been identified as one of the most serious health problems in the general population around the world. In a report made by the World Health Organization (WHO), depression was ranked fourth among the leading diseases, after respiratory infections, diarrheal diseases, and conditions during the perinatal period (Murray & Lopez, 1997). In

AUTHORS' NOTE: The work reported in this chapter was supported in part by National Institute of Mental Health (NIMH) grants R24 MH 49368, by the Latino Research Program Project PO1MH59876, and by an NIMH National Service Award F31 MH 1925. We are grateful to Jeannette Rosselló and Amy Fontenot for their review of this manuscript. Correspondence concerning this chapter should be addressed to Guillermo Bernal or Emily Sáez-Santiago at the University of Puerto Rico, CUSEP, P. O. Box 23174 UPR Station, San Juan, PR, 00931-3174.

fact, by the year 2020, depression is expected to be the most serious health problem (second only after heart disease) affecting the world population. Major depression is a psychiatric disorder that can generate a considerable impairment in the person's functioning, comparable to—or sometimes worse than—that caused by a chronic medical condition (Cross-National Collaborative Group, 1992). But despite the impairment associated with this disorder, major depression can be treated successfully in 80% to 90% of the cases (Regier et al., 1988). However, only one in three individuals who suffer from a depressive disorder actually seeks treatment for depression. When treatment is sought, outcome is poor because too often, depression is not well recognized and treated. Taking these factors into consideration, depression is a serious worldwide health problem.

PREVALENCE OF MAJOR DEPRESSION

Reviews of several epidemiological studies (Lehtinen & Joukamaa, 1994) carried out around the world from 1965 to 1992 suggested that the prevalence rate for depression varied from 2.6% to 5.5% for men but fluctuated between 6.0% and 11.8% for women. When the full diagnosis of major depression was not considered and only depressive symptoms were measured, the prevalence rates were higher. These investigators found that the prevalence of depressive symptoms ranged from 13% to 19%. When evaluating prevalence by gender, depressive symptoms were more prevalent in women than in men, varying from 10% to 19% in men and from 18% to 34% in women.

In the United States, the National Comorbidity Survey (NCS) included a national community sample between 15 and 54 years of age. The prevalence of current major depression was 4.9% (Blazer, Kessler, McGonagle, & Swartz, 1994). The lifetime prevalence estimated in this study was 17.1%. The prevalence of current major depression was 5.9% in women and 3.8% in men, whereas the lifetime prevalence was estimated as 21.3% for women and 12.7% for men. These prevalence rates found in the NCS for major depression were higher than in the previous national epidemiological studies carried out in the United States. For example, the lifetime prevalence of depression in the Epidemiologic Catchment Area (ECA) study, which included a representative sample from five communities, was 5.8% for residents of the United States 18 years or older (Regier et al., 1988). The differences in prevalence rates between the NCS and ECA studies are probably due to methodological considerations. For example, the higher prevalence rate of major depression in the NCS compared with the ECA may be due to the use of the Composite International Diagnostic Interview (CIDI), which is a more sensitive instrument than the Diagnostic Interview Schedule (DIS) used in the ECA. The NCS methodology required a probing for symptoms of depression where each respondent had three chances to answer to questions. In this sense, the NCS may have had a higher proportion of true lifetime depression cases; as a consequence, the prevalence was higher. Another reason for the discrepancy between the two studies is the fact that the NCS used a national sample that might have yielded higher prevalence than adjusted rates from local surveys, as were the sampling methods in the ECA. Finally, the sample in the NCS included younger persons than the ECA, so the prevalence in the NCS was expected to be higher given that the higher rates for depression were among younger people.

The literature suggests that the prevalence rates for major depression have changed throughout the past decades. The Cross-National Collaborative Group (1992) pointed out that rates of major depression have been increasing since World War II. The group reviewed nine epidemiological surveys and three family studies from different parts of the world in which a higher rate of depression in females than in males was persistently established over time. In addition, the findings point toward an increase in prevalence rates for younger persons. This particular change began around 1930 and has been identified especially in persons 25 years of age. These trends have been explained by taking into account the evolution in historical, social, economic, and environmental contexts. More specifically, the Cross-National Collaborative Group mentioned several changes throughout time that have been associated with the rate of depression, such as mortality, fertility, marital stability, alcohol and other drug abuse, composition of the labor force, urbanization, changes in family structures, and possible toxic exposures or occult infectious agents. Gastpar (1986) offered other reasons for the increase of prevalence in depression, which include increases in (a) life expectancy, especially in females; (b) urban populations in comparison with rural areas; (c) mental health services; and (d) new and possibly more effective treatments. After considering these changes and the findings of several studies, which establish that depression is more frequent in older women and in persons living in urban areas, it became clear that an increase in the prevalence of depression might be related to those factors. Alternatively, the accessibility to psychological and psychiatric services could help to identify more clinical cases of major depression. Another explanation for the increasing prevalence of depression is the different definitions this disorder has had throughout time and the criteria used to identify depression.

RISK FACTORS FOR DEPRESSION

Several factors are strongly associated with the occurrence of symptoms of depression: female gender; low levels of education; being separated, divorced, widowed, or never married; and unemployment (Blazer et al., 1994). Major depression is more common in women than in men—with usually an approximate ratio of 2:1 but could be one and a half to three times more common in women than in men (Kessler, McGonagle, Swartz, & Blazer, 1993). Also, depression is higher in persons who are separated, divorced, or widowed and in persons of low socioeconomic status (Lehtinen & Joukamaa, 1994). Although these risk factors have been validated in many studies, other investigators have not established significant relationships between them and depression. For example, according to the fourth edition of the *Diagnostic and Statistical Manual of Mental Disorders* (American Psychiatric Association [APA], 1994), "The prevalence rates for major depressive disorder appear to be unrelated to ethnicity, education, income, or marital status" (p. 341). Thus, there are divergent views in the literature questioning the relationship between ethnicity/race and depression, suggesting that the establishment of some variables as risk factors, such as ethnicity and race, for depression are debatable. The dispute between the association among the risk factors mentioned above and depression clearly shows that there is a need for more research in this area with greater methodological sophistication.

ETHNICITY AND RACE: IS THERE A RELATIONSHIP WITH DEPRESSION?

The inclusion of ethnicity and race as variables in the epidemiological research has been increasing (Senior & Bhopal, 1994). In particular, many investigators are recognizing that particular characteristics of ethnicity and race influence the psychological well-being of every person (Cuéllar & Roberts, 1997; National Advisory Mental Health Council, 1998). In fact, in a report by the NIMH Basic Behavioral Science Task Force of the National Advisory Mental Health Council (1998), social, cultural, and environmental aspects were considered as central in shaping what we are and the way in which we function. More specifically, the report identified several important findings from the literature on ethnicity and mental health. Among these are that (a) cultural beliefs about the nature of mental illness influence the person's view of the course and treatment of any condition, (b) there are differences in how individuals from different cultural backgrounds experience and manifest symptoms of mental illness, and (c) diagnoses of mental disorders vary across cultures and, moreover, among subcultures. Although these results are widely accepted, many clinicians and researchers obviate cultural issues in the diagnosis and treatment of mental disorders.

But despite the recognition of ethnicity and race as important variables in the study of mental health, there are problems with the use of ethnicity and race in research. Senior and Bhopal (1994) identified four methodological issues with the use of ethnicity as a variable in research: (a) the difficulties of measurements, (b) the heterogeneity of the population to be studied as an ethnic group, (c) the lack of clarity in the research question, and (d) the ethnocentric bias that affects the interpretation of the data. Bhopal and Rankin (1999) suggested that the definition of the term *ethnicity* is often not well defined and that superficial labels are used to describe the population studied. Too often, *ethnicity* is used synonymously with *race* (Bhopal & Rankin, 1999; Edwards, 1992; Okazaki & Sue, 1998; Pfeffer, 1998; Senior & Bhopal, 1994). However, ethnicity and race are two different concepts. The concept of ethnicity is multifactorial in nature (Crews & Bindon, 1991), involving shared common cultural traditions, such as ancestry, psychological factors, common language, shared values, and sometimes a shared religion (Anand, 1999; Senior & Bhopal, 1994). Although ethnicity is a social construct, race refers to biological aspects that differentiate humanity by the physical characteristics of a person (Senior & Bhopal, 1994). Race is defined as "observable physiognomic features such as skin, color, hair type and color,

eye color, stature, facial features, and so forth" (Okazaki & Sue, 1998, p. 27).

Another problem with the use of ethnicity as a variable in research is the lack of acceptable and accurate parameters to define whether a person belongs to one particular ethnic group. There are two common techniques used in research to identify belonging to particular ethnic groups (Aspinall, 1997). One is self-identification, in which the person determines her or his ethnic group identity without taking into consideration if an observer finds the identification ambiguous. The other technique used is ethnic identification through the judgments of a community of scientific observers. Both methods have problems. Self-definition involves a self-perception mediated by social pressure and psychological needs; thus, this process of identification is completely subjective. The determination of ethnicity by a group of observers implies the classification among preidentified categories, obviating ethnic groups that are not frequently recognized groups. Moreover, the classification of persons in one ethnic group might reduce or completely eliminate the heterogeneity or variations within groups. In addition, this process of classification could represent a violation of the person's right to self-identification.

Ethnocentric bias is important to consider as part of the conceptualization of ethnicity as a variable. Ethnocentric bias refers to the tendency to view one's own ethnic group or culture as the gold standard against which other ethnic groups are evaluated (Senior & Bhopal, 1994). In other words, as Dana (1998) pointed out, ethnocentrism is the belief that one's worldview is the reality. Ethnocentric bias could affect the development of all phases of research, including the formulation of hypotheses, the process of data collection, and the interpretation of the outcomes. As Rogler (1999) stated, research issues intertwine with the dispositions and feelings of the researcher, so the research methodology and explanations of its findings may be based on the investigator's worldview of different ethnic groups. In the United States, the White Anglo-Saxon Protestant culture is considered the dominant cultural group. Ethnic minorities are identified as such not on the basis of their numeric size but rather for the convergence of historical and political processes (Williams & Harris-Reid, 1999). For example, with Native Americans, there is a history of genocide and conquest. With African Americans, slavery, segregation, and discrimination are part of the legacy of survival. Puerto Ricans and Mexican Americans share a legacy of being conquered and subordinated. Certain Asian American groups also share a legacy of discrimination and subordination. Thus, exposure to discrimination, low socioeconomic status, and the legacy of genocide, slavery, or social, economic, and political subordination are tied to the identity of ethnic minorities.

Despite the methodological and conceptual challenges with these variables, ethnicity and race appear to influence depressive disorders. In the epidemiological surveys carried out in the United States, using a national sample and other nonrepresentative samples, important differences in depression among ethnic groups are reported. Differences have been found in prevalence rates, risk factors, and symptoms for different ethnic groups. Although ethnicity per se may not contribute directly to explaining the variance in depression, some experiences and characteristics related to a particular ethnicity are risk factors for depressive disorders (Cuéllar & Roberts, 1997).

The ECA was the first large-scale probabilistic study of psychiatric epidemiology. The data obtained as part of the ECA study showed some interesting differences in depression prevalence rates among the ethnic groups studied. In this investigation, the lifetime prevalence of major depression was 4.8% for Whites, 2.9% for African Americans, 4.3% for Latinos, and 3.4% for Asian Americans (Zhang & Snowden, 1999). Although prevalence was slightly higher for Whites than for Latinos and Asians, the differences were not

significant. But these prevalence rates differed significantly between African Americans and Whites, suggesting that African Americans were less likely than Whites to report depression. In a more recent epidemiological study—the National Comorbidity Survey (NCS)—higher prevalence rates for all ethnic groups were reported. The lifetime prevalence was 17.9% for Whites, 11.9% for African Americans, and 17.7% for Latinos (Blazer et al., 1994). Also, in the NCS study, major depression was lower in African Americans than in Whites and Latinos, and the prevalence rates did not differ between these last two ethnic groups. It is important to note that the prevalence rates for either Asian Americans or Native Americans were not estimated in the NCS because these groups were not part of the sample. In addition, the NCS African American sample was small, and the Latino sample consisted of only English-speaking Latinos/Latinas (M. Alegría, personal communication, January 20, 2001).

Two risk factors for depressive symptoms are common in ethnic minority groups: racism and discrimination. Racism is defined by Clark, Anderson, Clark, and Williams (1999) as "beliefs, attitudes, institutional arrangements and acts that tend to denigrate individuals or groups because of phenotypic characteristics or ethnic group affiliation" (p. 805). Another definition, provided by Williams and Harris-Reid (1999), points out that racism "includes ideologies of superiority to and negative attitudes and beliefs about outgroups, as well as differential treatment of members of those groups by individual and societal institutions" (p. 310). Racism can be manifested in one of three ways: individual, institutional, and cultural (Jones, 1997, cited in Rollock & Gordon, 2000). There is an understanding that racism is transmitted by generations through individuals and institutions. Racist beliefs and acts can be executed by members of a different ethnic group or by members of the same ethnic group. Typically, racism occurs in relationships between members of oppressed and nonoppressed groups, with subordinated groups being the target of discrimination and abuse.

Racism and discrimination are part of daily life for many people of color, and its presence can generate stress that can lead to emotional distress (Clark et al., 1999; National Advisory Mental Health Council, 1998; Williams & Harris-Reid, 1999). When a person perceives an act as racist, his or her psychological and physiological stress responses are exacerbated. Constitutional (which refer to physical and medical aspects such as skin tone and history of hypertension), sociodemographic, psychological, and behavioral factors and coping strategies mediate in these responses to perceived discriminations (Clark et al., 1999).

Acculturation, acculturative stress, and migration are other variables that are consistently associated with depression in ethnic minority groups. Ethnic minority groups face stressors based on differences in cultural values and practices from the mainstream majority culture (National Advisory Mental Health Council, 1998). Additional stressors that affect immigrants are related to feelings of isolation, the challenges of economic survival in a new socioeconomic system, and difficulties with the new language (Williams & Harris-Reid, 1999). People's adaptation and their levels of acculturation are determined by the way they cope with the conflicts generated by the demands of their native culture and those of the U.S. dominant culture. Acculturation refers to the adoption of beliefs, values, and practices of the host culture (Comas-Díaz & Grenier, 1998). According to the National Advisory Mental Health Council (1998), members of the ethnic minority groups use four broad coping strategies to handle acculturative stress: (a) assimilation (being absorbed into the dominant cultural group), (b) acculturation (acquiring the prominent elements of the dominant culture), (c) biculturalism (becoming proficient in two cultural systems and switching between them as the situation requires), and (d) multiculturalism (maintaining cultural identity but working with other groups to achieve mutual goals) (National Advisory Mental Health Council, 1998). Other researchers use different categorizations to identify the acculturation strategies. For example, Berry (1998) presented the following four strategies: assimilation (wish to keep their cultural identity and are immerged in the dominant one), separation (want to maintain their cultural values and avoid interaction with others), integration (maintain their culture but interact with others), and marginalization (have little interest in own culture and in having relationships with others). Comas-Díaz and Grenier (1998) mentioned that the process of acculturation could be manifested as un-acculturation, assimilation, marginalization, biculturalism, and transculturation. *Unacculturated* immigrants remain immersed in their culture of origin, whereas *transculturation* refers to the development of a hybrid culture between the original and the host one.

The report of the National Advisory Mental Health Council (1998) pointed out that too often, adaptation to the dominant culture contributes to mental health status and that in this process, the person accommodating to the dominant culture could be subordinated and marginalized. Recently, Vega (2000) found in the Mexican American Prevalence and Services Survey (MAPSS) that Mexican Americans born in the United States had rates of *DSM-III-R* (APA, 1987) diagnosis similar to the general population in United States. Although the findings are not conclusive, more recent immigrants had better mental health outcomes than more acculturated immigrants. In other words, the more acculturated immigrants had worse mental health outcomes. This provocative finding might be interpreted as resulting from feelings of self-depreciation and isolation from the traditional support systems as the person assimilates to the dominant culture (Williams & Harris-Reid, 1999). A review of several studies on acculturation and assimilation suggests both positive and negative relationships between high acculturation and psychological distress (Williams & Harris-Reid, 1999). The implication here is that optimal mental health status could be reached when the person obtains a balance between his or her native cultural norms and those of the host culture; moves away from this equilibrium often lead to psychological distress.

DEPRESSION IN SUBORDINATED AND DEFEATED GROUPS

Sloman and Gilbert's (2000) theory of mood disorders posits that different species develop affective disorders as a response to their subordinated and defeated status. This evolutionary approach is framed as the social competition hypothesis of depression. Within this model, it is understood that certain strategies to cope with loss and failure can lead to psychopathology, particularly depression. Within this framework, depression is an adaptive response to subordination, exploitation, and defeat (Gilbert, 2000). Unwinnable situations lead to feelings of helplessness and the sense that no matter how hard one struggles, it is not possible to win, escape, or change the situation. Similar to the learned helplessness model, if one concludes that working harder to win or change the situation is futile, then the only adaptive response is to accept the situation and acknowledge that the other is more powerful. As a consequence of accepting the reality of overwhelming odds, a dominant-subordinate relationship in which the depressed person feels weak, inferior, and submitted is developed or maintained. This response to conflictive situations is most likely to be generated under conditions of social adversity and lack of control. Gilbert (2000) pointed out three sources of defeat and

subordination that can precede the depressive states: loss of or low resources, internal and external sources of attack, and social putdown. The first source—loss of or low resources—refers to failure to achieve or maintain highly valued goals and resources. The second refers to internal sources of attack; this includes negative cognitions of self-attacking, judgment, unfavorable social comparisons that lead to feelings of inferiority, and fear of failure. The third source refers to external attack and social putdown, which includes being the subject of hostile and abusive acts in an environment where one is labeled as inferior, shamed, humiliated, subordinated, neglected, and marginalized.

When a person experiences such socially adverse situations, his or her reactions may be mediated by the defeated and arrested defensive strategies, depending on his or her mood state. The nondepressive person shows assertiveness, turning the anger generated by the conflictive situation into benefit. If the struggle does not look favorable, the person has the capacity to take "flight" and feels relief at escaping. Then, the nondepressed person can accept compromises or give in (affiliative subordinate). However, the depressed person handles the situation in a different way. He or she wants to fight harder but always expects to lose, and when the strategy of flight might be the best alternative, the person blocks himself or herself from escape and feels guilt, fear, and more subordination for leaving. As a result, the depressed person feels weak, inferior, and submitted, reinforcing symptoms of depression (Gilbert, 2000).

The coping strategies used by people in conflictive situations are grouped and identified as the involuntary defeat strategy (IDS). The IDS is described as a genetically programmed strategy that is automatically activated when a person recognizes that defeat in social competition is inevitable (Sloman, 2000). This strategy serves as an adaptive function, allowing the recognition that one has lost the encounter and promotes the accommodation to occupy a subordinated role. Sloman (2000) explained that the IDS has three specific functions: (a) an executive function that creates a sense of incapacity that contributes to the loss of motivation to continue the fight, (b) a signaling function to alert the rival that he or she does not represent a threat and also to let others know that he or she is "out of action" and the struggle is over, and (c) a facilitative function that leads to escape or submission and then acceptance. The IDS ends after the acceptance phase, when the person redirects his or her efforts to other issues. In summary, the general function of the IDS is to de-escalate conflict, but when de-escalation does not occur and conflict persists, depressive symptoms are developed or exacerbated. The effectiveness of the IDS in each person is determined by several factors, which include (a) resource value (value that the person gives to the resource that is the object of the struggle), (b) group interaction variables (group pressure from others who want to continue the fight), (c) entrapment (perceptions of the inability to escape or move associated with ineffective IDS), and (d) personality and psychodynamic factors.

Taking into consideration this IDS model of depression, the person in a subordinated position is at risk for depression. Demographic variables such as poverty, unemployment, discrimination, gender, race, and ethnicity have been linked to psychological distress, including depression, and actually may be a proxy for the experience of subordination and defeat. To the extent that the person does not have the resources to change his or her adverse circumstances or perceives the situation as impossible to change, depression becomes an adaptive response. If the problem is perceptual, the person may not see how to change these adverse circumstances. In these cases, depression is developed and maintained by distorted cognitions that negatively affect the person's self-esteem; as a consequence, the person becomes unable to handle conflicts. However, if the problem is related to aspects of the social context that may not have an immediate solution, the IDS model helps to explain why depressive disorders are more prevalent in subordinated groups in our society, such as women, children, the poor, less educated groups, and ethnic minority groups. As we mentioned earlier, ethnic minorities in the United States confront the added stresses of poverty, racism, discrimination, and acculturation. Ethnic minorities with a history of subordination and conquest may have fewer resources to change or escape subordinated situations, are more vulnerable to depression, and may be likely to have a defeat response. In this way, the cycle that leads to depression is perpetuated in many Latinos/Latinas, African Americans, Asian Americans, and Native Americans living in the United States.

DEPRESSION IN LATINOS AND LATINAS

Latinos and Latinas in the United States

Latinos and Latinas now number 35.3 million persons, representing 12.5% of the whole U.S. population (U.S. Bureau of the Census, 2001). The Latino community is a diverse and heterogeneous population. Of these 35.3 million, 62.6% are Mexican Americans, 11.1% are Puerto Ricans, 4.9% are Cubans, 13.8% come from Central and South America, and 7.6% include people from Spain and other people who do not trace their origin to a particular Latin American country.

Latinos and Latinas migrate to the United States for different reasons. These migrations are determined by social, economic, and political factors (Bernal & Enchautegui-de-Jesús, 1994; Dana, 1998). For example, migrations from Mexico were stimulated by the demand for cheap labor in the United States, in combination with the high unemployment and low wages in Mexico (Bernal & Enchautegui-de-Jesús, 1994), drawing primarily people from low socioeconomic levels. Also, people with low socioeconomic status mainly constituted Puerto Rican emigrations. The large migration wave of Puerto Ricans who emigrated to the United States occurred during the 1940s and 1950s and was motivated by a government policy to ameliorate the poverty and overpopulation in Puerto Rico (Bernal & Flores-Ortiz, 1984). In contrast, Cubans emigrated mostly for political reasons. The initial waves of Cubans who entered the United States were persons from high and middle socioeconomic groups and came as refugees seeking political asylum, although recent emigrations were from lower socioeconomic groups and were also propitiated by economic motivations (Bernal & Enchautegui-de-Jesús, 1994). Latinos and Latinas from other countries such as Argentina, Chile, and Nicaragua came to the United States in particular periods as political refugees.

Another important sociopolitical factor to consider in understanding the diverse experiences of Latino and Latina migrants in the United States is the history of conquest of their native countries (Bernal, Bernal, Martinez, Olmedo, & Santisteban, 1983). Motivated by the expansionist policy called "Manifest Destiny," the United States invaded and occupied Mexican lands in 1845. As a consequence of the Mexican-American War, the Treaty of Guadalupe Hidalgo was signed in 1848, in which Mexico received $15 million from the United States and ceded 45% of its national territory, including the territories now known as Texas, New Mexico, Arizona, and California. Puerto Rico has had a similar history of conquest. With the Spanish-American War in 1898, Puerto Rico, Cuba, and the Philippines were invaded by the United States, but unlike the other countries, Puerto Rico did not achieve its independence. Actually, Puerto Rico remains a territory of the United States. Mexican Americans and Puerto Ricans share a common legacy of subordination and defeat, although this is not the case for Cubans.

In general, the Latino and Latina population living in the United States is poor. According to census data (U.S. Bureau of the Census, 2001), Hispanic families are more likely to live below poverty levels than non-Hispanic families. Among Latino and Latina subgroups, Puerto Ricans have the lowest median income, followed by Mexican Americans, Central and South Americans, other Latinos/Latinas, and Cubans. In terms of age, Cubans are the oldest group, followed by other Latinos/Latinas, Central and South Americans, Puerto Ricans, and the youngest group, Mexican Americans. These differences among Latino and Latina subgroups must be taken into account when mental health status is evaluated. It is well-known that historical and sociodemographic variables play an essential role in a person's psychological adjustment.

In summary, although there are some differences among Latino and Latina subgroups living in the United States, these ethnic groups share some similarities, such as poverty, inadequate housing, a high proportion of single-parent families, acculturative stress, and discrimination (Dana, 1998). In addition, Latinos and Latinas share the Spanish language and cultural traits such as *personalismo*, familism (*familismo*), and sympathy (*simpatía*) (Bernal & Enchautegui-de-Jesús, 1994; Dana, 1998).

Prevalence of and Risk Factors for Depression

As mentioned earlier, the prevalence of major depression in Latinos and Latinas in the United States has been estimated at 4.3% in the ECA and 17.7% in the NCS. In both epidemiological studies, the Latino and Latina population had the second-highest prevalence rate of depression. Although Whites had a slightly higher prevalence, the difference was not statistically significant, so the prevalence rate of major depression in Latinos and Latinas was actually higher than for Whites. This finding shows that depression is higher in Latinos and Latinas than in other ethnic minority groups in the United States. When studies that used self-rating scales were reviewed, higher prevalence of depression was found. In these cases, prevalence rates fluctuated between 27.8% and 44% (Muñoz, Boddy, Prime, & Muñoz, 1990; Vera et al., 1991) (see Table 19.1 for detailed information).

The prevalence rate of depression among Latino and Latina subgroups has been estimated only for Mexicans Americans, Puerto Ricans, and Cuban Americans. No other study of depression in "other" Latinos and Latinas was identified in the literature reviewed for this chapter. We found two studies that evaluated depression in Mexican Americans, Puerto Ricans, and Cuban Americans—namely, the ECA and the Hispanic Health and Nutrition Examination Survey (HHNES). Although these are two different investigations, both studies used the Center for Epidemiological Studies Depression Scale (CES-D) and the Diagnostic Interview Schedule (DIS), so we can make some comparisons of the study results. The findings of these studies suggest that Puerto Ricans manifest higher depression levels, followed by Cuban Americans and Mexican Americans. In fact, the prevalence rate of depression in Puerto Ricans is considerably higher than in the other two groups, being 7.19% for Puerto Ricans, 3.15% for Cuban Americans, and 2.3% for Mexican Americans (Golding & Lipton, 1990; Narrow, Rae, Moscicki, Locke, & Regier, 1990; Potter, Rogler, & Moscicki, 1995) (see Table 19.1).

In terms of the risk factors associated with depression in Latinos and Latinas, the same variables related to depression in the general population were identified. Depressive symptoms in Latinos and Latinas were associated with being a woman or youth, being unemployed, and having an unmarried status, a low level of education, and a low income. Consistently, the investigations on major depression with Latinos and Latinas have found gender differences, with depressive disorders occurring in more women than men (Cuéllar & Roberts, 1997; Golding & Lipton, 1990; Narrow et al., 1990; Potter et al., 1995; Vera et al., 1991). However, in a study that included a sample of Mexican migrant farmworkers in California, the investigators found that depressive symptoms were higher in men than in women (Alderete, Vega, Kolody, & Aguilar-Gaxiola, 1999). The investigators offered the following three possible reasons to explain this finding: (a) the unusual strains imposed on men and women alike by the harshness of seasonal agricultural work, (b) the incorporation of particularly hardy and resilient women into the farmworker pool, and (c) the CES-D scale (the instrument used in this study) reflected the individuals' response to situational stress and not a full diagnosis of depression. In addition, several studies validated the other risk factors for depression: having a low level of education (Golding & Lipton, 1990; Munet-Vilaró et al., 1999; Vera et al., 1991), having a low income (Golding & Lipton, 1990; Vera et al., 1991), being unemployed (Munet-Vilaró et al., 1999; Narrow et al., 1990; Vera et al., 1991), being unmarried (Alderete et al., 1999; Golding & Lipton, 1990; Potter et al., 1995), and being young (Alderete et al., 1999; Golding & Lipton, 1990; Potter et al., 1995).

Other risk factors associated with major depression in Latinos and Latinas were health status, perceived control of daily stressful events, acculturation status, discrimination, and language difficulties. Prevalence rate of depression was higher in Latinos and Latinas with poor health status, lack of self-control at times of stressful events (Munet-Vilaró et al., 1999), legal problems, high acculturation level, high discrimination, and language problems (Alderete et al., 1999).

(text continued on p. 414)

Table 19.1 Depression in Latinos/Latinas: Authors, Study, Samples, Primary Measure, Prevalence Rates, and Relevant Findings

Study (Source)	Sample	Measure	Prevalence	Other Relevant Findings
Muñoz, Boddy, Prime, and Muñoz (1990)	100 Hispanic patients at Logan Heights Family Health Center in San Diego, CA (ages 17-79 years)	Spanish version of the 20-item SDS (Self-Rating Depression Scale)	44% of the patients had mild or severe depressive symptoms	
Los Angeles Epidemiological Catchment Area (NIMH) (Golding & Lipton, 1990)	1,244 Mexican American and 1,149 non-Hispanic Whites born in the United States, residents of Los Angeles County (age 18 years or older)	Center for Epidemiological Studies Depression Scale (CES-D) and Diagnostic Interview Schedule (DIS)	2.3% of Mexican Americans and 2.7% of non-Hispanic Whites	Depressive symptoms in Mexican Americans have a strong, positive relationship with being young, having a low income, and being unmarried.
The Hispanic Health and Nutrition Examination Survey (Narrow, Rae, Moscicki, Locke, & Regier, 1990)	865 Cuban American adults (ages 20-74 years), residents of Dade County, FL	Center for Epidemiological Studies Depression Scale (CES-D) and Diagnostic Interview Schedule (DIS)	Lifetime prevalence of 3.15%; 6-month prevalence of 2.12%; 1-month prevalence of 1.50%	Significantly high levels of depression in women and unemployed persons.
The Hispanic Health and Nutrition Examination Survey and a project of use of mental health services in Puerto Rico (Vera et al., 1991)	1,267 Puerto Ricans living in New York City and 1,658 Puerto Ricans living in poor areas on the island (ages 20-64 years in both samples)	Center for Epidemiological Studies Depression Scale (CES-D)	28.12% of Puerto Ricans living in New York and 28.56% of Puerto Ricans living on the island	Being a woman, having a low educational level, being unemployed, and having a low income are predictors of high depressive symptoms for both samples.
The Hispanic Health and Nutrition Examination Survey (Potter, Rogler, & Moscicki, 1995)	1,140 Puerto Ricans from the New York City metropolitan area, adults older than 19 years of age	Center for Epidemiological Studies Depression Scale (CES-D) and Diagnostic Interview Schedule (DIS)	27.81% of the entire sample had high levels of depression; 32.96% of women and 19.20% of men had severe depression symptoms as	Never-married persons and persons with disrupted marriages had higher levels of depressive symptoms. Higher rates of depression were found in respondents

(text continued on p. 414)

Table 19.1 (Continued)

Study (Source)	Sample	Measure	Prevalence	Other Relevant Findings
			measured by CES-D. Six-month prevalence of depression (using the DIS) was 7.19% for entire sample, 9.15% for females, and 3.90% for males. The 1-month prevalence was 5.93%, 7.60%, and 3.14%, for the entire sample, women, and men, respectively.	from the youngest age group (20-24 years). Writing Spanish better than English was associated with a lower risk for depression.
Hispanic Health and Nutrition Examination Survey (HHANES) (Canabal & Quiles, 1995)	1,519 Puerto Ricans 20 years old and older from New York City area and parts of New Jersey and Connecticut	CES-D	Mean depression score of 13.32.	Poverty and unemployment had the strongest relationship with depression, more than acculturation or other variables. When the economic factors were controlled, acculturation appears not to be a significant variable in the explanation of depression.
Cuéllar and Roberts (1997)	1,271 Latino students of English classes in the University of Texas; 65% were Mexican Americans, 24% included other Latino groups, and 11%	DSD26 Depression Scale, a shortened version of the DSM scale for depression	The prevalence rate for depression was 3.2%.	Females manifested more depressive symptoms than males. Socioeconomic status played an important role for major depression. Ethnicity and acculturation were not as influential for depression

Study (Source)	Sample	Measure	Prevalence	Other Relevant Findings
	identified themselves as Mexican National. The average age was 21 years.			as other sociodemographic variables (such as SES and gender).
Miranda and Umhoefer (1998)	282 Latinos/Latinas with an average age of 31 years, members of two community social services agencies in a metropolitan area of Georgia	Beck Depression Inventory (BDI)	Mean score on BDI was 29.40 ($SD = 8.79$) for the group with low acculturation, 9.02 ($SD = 11.63$) for the bicultural group, and 27.51 ($SD = 13.81$) for the highly acculturated group.	
Munet-Vilaró, Folkman, and Gregorich (1999)	673 Latino immigrants living in the United States; 520 Mexicans living in Mexico City, and 650 Puerto Ricans living in Puerto Rico	Center for Epidemiological Studies Depression Scale (CES-D)	The CES-D adjusted mean was 24.08 for Latino immigrants, 21.39 for Puerto Ricans, and 18.06 for Mexicans.	Higher CES-S score in women, younger and less educated respondents, and persons who reported lack of control over daily stressful events.
Alderete, Vega, Kolody, and Aguilar-Gaxiola (1999)	1,001 male and female Mexican migrant farmworkers from rural central California, ages 18 to 59 years	Center for Epidemiological Studies Depression Scale (CES-D)	The mean CES-D score for the entire sample was 10.8; 21.1% of males and 19.7% of females showed high levels of depression.	Higher prevalence of depression was found in widowed, separated, and divorced people. The same was found for people with lower age, less social support, legal status problems, and high acculturation, discrimination, and language conflicts.

However, Miranda and Umhoefer (1998) found that depression was more likely in the group with a low acculturation level.

DEPRESSION IN AFRICAN AMERICANS

African Americans are estimated as numbering approximately 35 million people (U.S. Bureau of the Census, 2001). As with other ethnic groups, African Americans comprise a large population with many within-group differences. There are important differences in terms of socioeconomic levels, residence in urban or rural areas, cultural variables, and degree of racial/cultural identity. More than half of all African Americans are poor (Dana, 1998). Most African Americans live below the poverty line, with some being part of the lower and middle classes (Gilbert & Kahl, 1987). Moreover, African American females are overrepresented as heads of households and in general, tend to stay in poverty longer than Whites do (Rodríguez, Allen, Frongillo, & Chandra, 1999). The unemployment rate for African Americans is more than double the rate for the White population (U.S. Department of Labor, 2002). Considering the residential area, most African Americans live in urban areas in segregated neighborhoods (Dana, 1998).

Racial and cultural identity are important issues for the African American community. Racial identity in African Americans is denominated as *Afrocentrism* or *Africentrism,* which refers to "a set of shared beliefs, values, behaviors, and standards concerning the social reality and priorities of African-Americans in the American society" (Dana, 1998, p. 98). Afrocentrism/Africentrism gives emphasis to the perception of psychological and sociopolitical dimensions in which members of the African American community are immersed. This degree of cultural and racial identification helps to characterize the African American population in terms of values and roles compatible with Afrocentric values versus adaptation to a White cultural orientation. In contrast to other ethnic minority groups, African Americans share similarities with the White dominant population such as language and certain behavior patterns (Anderson, 1991). Yet there are important differences between African Americans and Whites in terms of discrimination and racism. Sanders (1996) pointed out that one third of a community sample of African Americans reported an experience of racism that generated psychological distress.

Prevalence of and Risk Factors for Depression

Epidemiological studies report a lower prevalence rate of depression in African Americans when compared with other ethnic groups. The prevalence of depression in African Americans was 2.9% in the ECA study (Zhang & Snowden, 1999) and 11.9% in the NCS study (Blazer et al., 1994). It is notable that the prevalence of depression in African Americans differed statistically from the prevalence in Whites, who had the highest prevalence in both surveys. Also, it is important to note that two studies reviewed for this chapter reported a mean score under the cutoff level for depression (Brown, Gary, Greene, & Milburn, 1992; Munford, 1994), so we may infer that the samples for both studies had a low index of depression. However, other investigations reported higher levels of depression in African American samples than in White samples (Jones-Webb & Snowden, 1993; Rodríguez et al., 1998) (see Table 19.2). These studies indicated that sociodemographic variables and not particular race characteristics could explain those differences in prevalence rates. For example, Rodríguez and colleagues (1998) suggested that in general, African Americans are employed in jobs that

Table 19.2   Depression in African Americans: Authors, Study, Samples, Primary Measure, Prevalence Rates, and Relevant Findings

Study (Source)	Sample	Measure	Prevalence	Other Relevant Findings
Dressler and Badger (1985)	285 African Americans from a small southern city (ages 17 years and older)	A modified version of the Hopkins Symptoms Checklist depression subscale	20.4% adults scored as having high depressive symptoms.	Females and single, divorced, separated, and unemployed people reported more depressive symptoms. An inverse relationship between income and depression was found.
Brown, Gary, Greene, and Milburn (1992)	927 African American adults from Norfolk, VA (ages 18 years and older)	Center for Epidemiological Studies Depression Scale (CES-D)	Mean score on CES-D was 13.98 for women and 12.45 for men ($SD = 10.11$ and 8.77, respectively).	High levels of depressive symptoms in women and in unmarried persons. Depression is related to economic difficulties. Increases in age, income, and education were associated with low levels of depression. Patterns of social affiliation (family ties, religious involvement, and voluntary associations) are inversely related to depression.
1984 National Alcohol Survey (Jones-Webb & Snowden, 1993)	1,947 African Americans and 1,777 White adults	Center for Epidemiological Studies Depression Scale (CES-D)	In the African American sample, 25% of women and 15% of men had high depressive levels. For Whites, 19% of women and 11% of men had high depression scores.	For African Americans, depressive symptoms were higher in females; respondents between 30 and 39 years of age; those who had widowed, separated, or divorced; people in a lower social class; those who

(Continued)

Table 19.2 (Continued)

Study (Source)	Sample	Measure	Prevalence	Other Relevant Findings
				identified with a non-Western religion; and the unemployed, retired people, homemakers, and those living in the north-central region or the West.
Munford (1994)	146 African American students at North Carolina Central University and 83 adults from Durham and New Bern, NC (ages 18-75 years)	Beck Depression Inventory (BDI)	Mean score on BDI was 6.60 for entire sample ($SD = 6.67$), 6.40 for students ($SD = 6.23$), and 6.95 for adults in community ($SD = 7.39$).	Depression was strongly related to low self-esteem. Pro-White/anti-Black racial identity attitudes were positively associated with depression, but experiencing the value of their race and culture was inversely related to depression. No significant differences by gender or social class were found in levels of depression.
Brown, Ahmed, Gary, and Milburn, (1993)	865 African Americans (ages 20 years and older) from Norfolk, VA	Diagnostic Interview Schedule (DIS)	3.1% for 1-year prevalence of major depression	Age was significantly related with depression (high prevalence in those 20-29 years = 5.6%). The self-assessed health status was a good predictor for depression (persons in poor health were 7.30 times more likely to have depression, compared to 3.03 times for persons in good health).

Study (Source)	Sample	Measure	Prevalence	Other Relevant Findings
				Experiencing many stressful life events during the past year increased the odds for depression.
National Survey of Families and Households (Rodríguez, Allen, Frongillo, & Chandra, 1998)	1,369 African Americans and 6,660 Whites (ages 17-65 years)	Depression index developed from the responses to 15 items of the Center for Epidemiological Studies Depression Scale (CES-D)	For employment status and work satisfaction, the mean scores for African American women ranged from 14.2 for part-time employed and satisfied with job and 33.85 for unemployed and not looking for work. The mean scores for men fluctuated from 11.4 for retired and 18.81 for full-time employed.	In both subsamples (African Americans and Whites), women reported more depressive symptoms than men. In most employment groups, with the exception of nonworking and welfare recipients, African Americans reporter higher levels of depression than Whites. Being the head of the family was associated with more depression in African American women but not with White women. For African American women, nonstatistical differences were found for depressive levels among the employment groups.

do not offer health and mental health benefits. In addition, they do not have enough confidence in medical professionals, so the preventive health care services are limited.

Typically, gender, age, employment status, household income, marital status, self-esteem, and stressful life events are variables associated with the manifestation of depressive symptoms. The reviewed articles about the African American population evaluated all of these associations (see Table 19.2). Additional risk factors for depression have been suggested in the reviewed studies, pointing to the concept of African Americans' cultural identity. One of these investigations found that patterns of social affiliation are inversely associated with depression in an African American sample (Brown et al., 1992). The investigators included family ties, religious involvement, and voluntary associations as patterns of social affiliations. They described these patterns of social affiliations as specific sociocultural adaptations to cope with stressful life events that affect all minority groups. In another study, Munford (1994) evaluated the relationship between racial identity attitudes and depression in African Americans. Racial identity was understood as a cognitive developmental process composed of four stages: (a) Preencounter, (b) Encounter, (c) Immersion/Emersion, and (d) Internalization. The first stage—Preencounter—refers to pro-White and anti-Black racial identity attitudes. In the Encounter stage, the person has experiences that challenge his or her view of "Blackness." The Immersion/Emersion stage occurs when the person recognizes the meaning and value of his or her race and culture. In the Internalization stage, the person feels proud of and safe with his or her race and identity. The findings of the study show that Preencounter and Encounter attitudes were positively related to depression, and Internalization attitudes were negatively related to depression.

DEPRESSION IN ASIAN AMERICANS

Asian Americans have had a rapid growth rate in the U.S. population. The 2000 census showed that 10.6 million Asians/Pacific Islanders live in the United States (U.S. Bureau of the Census, 2001). The 1990 census showed that among Asian Americans, there are 32 different cultural groups with pronounced differences among them. Asian Americans have different ethnic identities, religion, history, language, and cultural traditions. The Asian groups include Chinese, Japanese, Koreans, Filipinos, Vietnamese, Cambodian, Hmong, Laotian, and Thai, among others. In 1990, the largest Asian groups in the United States were Filipinos, Chinese, Koreans, Japanese, Vietnamese, and Asian Indians, and each group is as numerous as the others. Like other U.S. immigrants, many of the Asian immigrants migrated for political and economic reasons. Specifically, males working for gold mines, agriculture, and the railroad constituted the first wave of Chinese immigration to the United States (in the 1840s) (Loo & Young Yu, 1998). In the 1920s, the migration of intellectuals began. In the case of Vietnamese, the first major immigration was in 1975, when 132,000 people arrived as political refugees. After that year, many Vietnamese migrated to the United States for political reasons. Other Asian people (Laotians, Cambodians) migrated seeking political asylum. Despite the differences among Asian groups, the incorporation of Asians to the United States was characterized by labor exploitation, segregation, and discriminatory legislation (Loo & Young Yu, 1998). Moreover, there are common bonds shared by Asian groups as part of the U.S. experience: (a) facing the problems of migration, (b) acculturation, (c) acculturative stress, (d) discrimination, and (e) language barriers (Dana, 1998).

Prevalence of and Risk Factors for Depression

The ECA was the only study identified that included a subsample of Asian Americans to compare the presence of psychiatric disorders among ethnic groups in the United States. In this epidemiological study, Asian Americans had a prevalence of 3.4% for major depression (Zhang & Snowden, 1999). After African Americans, Asian Americans had the lowest prevalence rate of depression. However, many other studies have reported that Asian American groups have had a higher prevalence of depression than Whites (Aldwin & Greenberger, 1987; Hymes & Akiyama, 1991). Although we did not identify investigations comparing depression in Asian Americans with other ethnic groups in the literature review made for this chapter, it is important to point out that the indexes of depression in Asian Americans are higher than those found in studies with other ethnic groups. Among the articles reviewed, one study with a Vietnamese sample reported a CES-D mean score of 29.75 (Tran, 1993), which is a high score indicating more-depressive symptoms (see Table 19.3). This mean score is close to the mean score in the studies of Latinos/Latinas, who have the second-highest prevalence of depression. Takeuchi et al. (1998) presented two hypotheses to explain the seemingly contradictory findings of both high and low rates of depression in Asian Americans: Depression will be high because many Asian Americans have had to experience difficult transitions in adjusting to American society. Alternatively, low rates of depression may be explained by the fact that Asian Americans are likely to express their problems in behavioral or somatic forms rather than in emotional terms. Other reasons for the discrepancy in prevalence may be due to differences in methodological aspects of the study.

As in other ethnic groups, depression in Asian Americans is associated with gender, age, marital status, employment status, and income. All of these variables, with the exception of age, are associated with depression in Asian Americans in basically the same form across different ethnic groups (see Table 19.3). Interestingly, depression in Chinese Americans is more likely to be manifested in older age groups than in younger groups, which is the case for many other populations. Specifically, one study that included a sample of Chinese Americans in Los Angeles found that people between ages 50 and 65 had more-depressive symptoms (Takeuchi et al., 1998). In addition to age, other variables are considered risk factors for depression in members of Asian American communities. As well as for other immigration groups, acculturation is a critical factor for the development of major depression in Asian Americans. For example, Chinese Americans with a high acculturation level had a higher rate of depression than those with a low acculturation level (Takeuchi et al., 1998). In this study, high acculturation meant greater exposure to American lifestyles, and it was measured by language use, ethnicity of the workplace, and the types of foods eaten. The findings of other research that evaluated several variables in a sample of Vietnamese showed that acculturation stresses had the strongest relationship with depression (Tran, 1993). Tran (1993) also reported that premigration stresses, nightmares, and proficiency in speaking English are variables that contribute to the variance of depression in the study sample. The relationship of English-speaking ability and depression in Vietnamese was also found in other studies, in which poor English proficiency was associated with the affective disorder (Hinton et al., 1998).

Table 19.3 Depression in Asian Americans: Authors, Study, Samples, Primary Measure, Prevalence Rates, and Relevant Findings

Study (Source)	Sample	Measure	Prevalence	Other Relevant Findings
Flaskerud and Hu (1994)	5,126 Chinese, Japanese, and Korean outpatients of the Los Angeles County mental health system	DSM-III diagnostic criteria for major depression	12% for a 5-year prevalence.	
Chinese American Psychiatric Epidemiology (Takeuchi et al., 1998)	1,747 Chinese Americans (ages 18–65) living in Los Angeles County	Composite International Diagnostic Interview (CIDI)	6.9% lifetime prevalence; 3.4% had a major depression episode in the past year.	Depression was higher in the oldest group (ages 50–65) than the younger age groups. No significant difference in depression was found by sex for the entire sample, but when acculturation levels were taken into consideration, females in the high-acculturation group were more likely than males to have depression. Negative life events have a strong relationship with depression.
Tran (1993)	147 Vietnamese adults (ages 20 and older) living in a metropolitan area in the Northeast region	Center for Epidemiological Studies Depression Scale (CES-D)	Mean score on CES-D was 29.75 ($SD = 5.94$).	60% of the variance in depression was explained by premigration stresses, nightmares, acculturation stresses, personal efficacy, age, gender, marital status, and English ability. Acculturation stresses had the strongest relationship with depression.
Hinton et al. (1998)	3,401 Vietnamese adult males (age 18 or older) from San Francisco/Alameda and Santa Clara Counties in California and from Houston, Texas	Hopkins Symptom Checklist Depression Subscale (HSC-D)	9.8% in San Francisco/Alameda, 8.2% at Santa Clara, and 8.6% at Houston had high depression scores.	High depression scores are more likely to occur in unemployed or disabled individuals, veterans, men with poor English proficiency, and men with income below the poverty line.

DEPRESSION IN NATIVE AMERICANS

The 2000 census estimated that 2.5 million of the U.S. population are American Indian and Alaska Native/Native American (U.S. Bureau of the Census, 2001). Native Americans comprise many nations and tribes with unique cultural customs and languages. Native Americans are considered an ethnic minority group with a high need in social, health, and mental health domains (Renfrey, 1998). One issue affecting this population is the changing profile of Native Americans over time. Changes in demographic characteristics have occurred as a result of the growth due to lower rates of mortality and a slower reduction in fertility (Parker et al., 1997). The process of acculturation and life stress events compound these changes. According to Dana (1998), five issues characterize Native American communities: (a) marginal cultural orientation status (which results from fragmented and confused lifestyles, coerced assimilation, racism, and discrimination), (b) damaged sense of self, (c) relationship problems, (d) chronic alcohol and drug abuse, and (e) lack of skills (inadequate development of academic and life skills needed for appropriate functioning in the dominant society). In terms of mental health, Parker and colleagues (1997) pointed out that the most prevalent mental disorders in this population are depression, anxiety, adjustment reactions, and alcohol abuse.

Prevalence of and Risk Factors for Depression

The study of major depression—and mental health—in Native Americans has been limited. Our literature review yielded only two articles that evaluated depression in Native Americans (see Table 19.4).

Furthermore, the two epidemiological studies with national representative samples cited earlier (the ECA and the NCS) did not include Native American communities in their analyses.

The two studies reviewed for this chapter confirm that depression is one of the most common mental disorders among Native Americans. In one study, Parker and colleagues (1997) found that major depression was the most frequent diagnosis in the sample, which included outpatients of a clinic at the Albuquerque Indian Hospital. The Native Americans who participated in this study had the following tribal affiliations: Navajo, Pueblo (with different Pueblos cited), Oklahoma-based tribes (nine tribes cited), Montana-based tribes, South Dakota–based tribes, Apache, and Oneida. The prevalence of major depression estimated in this study was 12%. The other study (Somervell et al., 1993), however, reported that 20% of the entire sample had higher levels of depression as measured by the CES-D. Due to methodological differences in both samples, the comparisons between the study results are not appropriate.

CONCLUSIONS

Major depression is one of the principal mental diseases affecting people around the world and across a wide range of cultures. In the United States, the national epidemiological studies found that prevalence of depression varies among ethnic groups. But despite these variations in prevalence rates of depression in different ethnic groups, we cannot conclude that there is a direct relationship between depression and ethnicity or race. In addition, Aneshensel, Clark, and Frerichs (1983) found in a study with a sample of Whites, Blacks, and Latinos/Latinas that the core of depressive disorders would appear to

Table 19.4 Depression in Native Americans: Authors, Study, Samples, Primary Measure, Prevalence Rates, and Relevant Findings

Study (Source)	Sample	Measure	Prevalence	Other Relevant Findings
Somervell et al. (1993)	120 adults (ages 20 years and older), residents of a coastal Indian village in the state of Washington	Center for Epidemiological Studies Depression Scale (CES-D) and the Schedule for Affective Disorders and Schizophrenia, Lifetime version (SADS-L)	20% of the sample scored high depression levels on the CES-D.	
Parker et al. (1997)	100 outpatients from a primary care clinic at the Albuquerque Indian Hospital, NM. Participants were 18 years of age and older.	Primary Care Evaluation of Mental Disorders (PRIME-MD)	12% had major depression.	Depression was the most frequent diagnosis in this sample.

be shared by the three ethnic groups. It is important to point out that the perception and expression of depressive symptoms vary from culture to culture (Kim, 1995; Tabora & Flaskerud, 1994). In addition, we could not identify any study demonstrating that depression is associated with a specific ethnic characteristic per se. However, there is ample evidence that symptoms of depression are strongly related to many aspects that characterize the circumstances and contexts in which members of particular ethnic groups are immersed. It may be that ethnicity serves as a proxy for other variables such as socioeconomic status, identity, cultural values, subordination, defeat, discrimination,

and acculturation. Understanding the meaning of ethnicity and its relationship to depression is an important challenge to the field.

As stated earlier, the risk factors for depression include being poor, female, young, unmarried, and unemployed. It is a fact that these risk factors form part of the lives of many individuals who are part of ethnic minority groups in the United States. For example, Latino/Latina and African American communities have a high prevalence of young single females living below the poverty level; thus, one would expect that these ethnic minority groups should have a higher prevalence of depression. Furthermore, despite these sociodemographic characteristics, ethnic minority groups in the United States have to face difficult circumstances associated with depressive symptoms. These circumstances are linked to acculturation (and/or adaptation) and discrimination. Acculturation to the lifestyle of the dominant culture can generate serious distress if a person does not have the adequate skills to handle the requirements made by the mainstream culture. Also, discrimination and the perception of discrimination lead to psychological problems. Difficulties with the acculturation process and discrimination place people in a subordinated, defeated position and—as discussed earlier—could trigger the use of involuntary defeat strategies, increasing the risk of depression.

The epidemiological findings for depression in minority communities are probably less than accurate. The studies conducted in the United States privileged the White population. It is important to note that ethnic minority populations were underrepresented in these epidemiological studies, and thus the comparison between ethnic groups is not adequate. Further research is needed to address this issue. It is important to note that two research projects (National Latino and Asian American Study, Margarita Alegría, principal investigator [PI]; National Survey of African Americans, James Jackson, PI) are currently focusing on three ethnic minority groups. One of the objectives in these projects is estimating prevalence rates of psychiatric disorders in the minority community, taking into account the limitations of the previous national epidemiological surveys.

In addition to having an overrepresentation of Whites in the national epidemiological studies, most of the research on depression conducted in the United States has been focused on the White community. Also, Whites/Anglo-Americans have been established as a comparison parameter. As a result, the diagnostic criteria, assessment techniques, test interpretations, and therapeutic approaches developed for the Anglo-American populations have been applied to the minority groups without much

consideration of language and culture. In the majority of cases, cultural influences have not been taken into consideration.

Given the estimate that by the year 2050, one of every two individuals will be non-White and/or Latino (U.S. Bureau of the Census, 1999), it becomes critical to have the knowledge base to offer mental health treatment and preventive services to ethnic minorities. One way to achieve this goal is by studying ethnic minority populations to understand each group, their prevalence rates, and the association of depression and other disorders to risk factors. As evidenced in this chapter, some investigators (Jackson, Alegría, Manson, Takeuschi, Sue) have focused their research efforts on specific minority groups, yet there is much work to be done.

Clearly, there are important methodological challenges in the study of depression with ethnic minorities. Perhaps the greater challenge is the definition of ethnicity and our understanding of processes related to the ethnic minority experience. It is well recognized that each ethnic minority group is constituted by a diversity of many communities, which represent a broad spectrum of cultural values and customs. It is important to consider the heterogeneity and uniqueness of specific ethnic groups so that such findings can be generalized to the entire community. This was the problem case with the ECA study, in which Mexican Americans comprised the Hispanic category in its majority. Another limitation in comparing prevalence rates of depression was the variety of instruments used to measure depressive symptoms. Many studies use self-report instruments to measure levels of depression. Unlike diagnostic interviews, the data obtained by scales do not yield a diagnosis for depression. The literature reviewed showed that most studies reported scores for depression, and only a few studies reported the prevalence of major depression, thus limiting our analysis. Finally, a serious limitation in the study of depression in ethnic minority groups is the relatively small samples, which again limit the generalizability of the findings.

Considering the need for more research on depression and ethnic minorities groups in the United States, as well as the importance of developing more rigorous studies that allow the generalizations, we recommend that future studies consider the following:

1. Conceptualize the research process from a culturally sensitive or multicultural perspective, beginning with the formulation of the research question, the design of methods, the selection and development of instruments, and the analytic strategies for the results (Bernal, Bonilla, & Bellido, 1994; Rogler, 1989).

2. Develop studies on the meaning and on the phenomenology of the ethnic minority experience to explore the possible association with depression.

3. Develop studies on the definition of ethnicity for specific minority groups and studies that explore the relationship of other variables such as SES, acculturation, acculturative stress, migration, ethnic identity, subordination, and so on, to examine the relationship of these to depression.

4. Enlarge and diversify the inclusion of ethnic subgroups to represent the entire ethnic group.

5. Use valid and reliable diagnostic instruments to measure major depression in each ethnic subgroup (such instruments should be culturally adapted and administered in the preferred language of the person).

6. Develop cultural sensitivity in researchers working with ethnic minority communities.

REFERENCES

Alderete, E., Vega, W. A., Kolody, B., & Aguilar-Gaxiola, S. (1999). Depressive symptomatology: Prevalence and psychosocial risk factors among Mexican migrant farmworkers in California. *Journal of Community Psychology, 27*, 457-471.

Aldwin, C., & Greenberger, E. (1987). Cultural differences in the predictors of depression. *American Journal of Community Psychology, 15*, 789-813.

Alegría, M., & Canino, G. (2000). Women and depression. In L. Sherr & J. S. St. Lawrence (Eds.), *Women, health and the mind* (pp. 185-210). Chichester, UK: Wiley.

American Psychiatric Association (APA). (1987). *Diagnostic and statistical manual of mental disorders* (3rd ed., rev.). Washington, DC: Author.

American Psychiatric Association (APA). (1994). *Diagnostic and statistical manual of mental disorders* (4th ed.). Washington, DC: Author.

Anand, S. S. (1999). Using ethnicity as a classification variable in health research: Perpetuating the myth of biological determinism, serving socio-political agendas, or making valuable contributions to medical sciences? *Ethnicity & Health, 4*, 241-244.

Anderson, L. P. (1991). Acculturative stress: A theory of relevance to black Americans. *Clinical Psychology Review, 11*, 685-702.

Aneshensel, C. S., Clark, V. A., & Frerichs, R. R. (1983). Races, ethnicity, and depression: A confirmatory analysis. *Journal of Personality and Social Psychology, 44*, 385-398.

Aspinall, P. J. (1997). The conceptual basis of ethnic group terminology and classifications. *Social Science Medicine, 45,* 689-698.

Bernal, G., Bernal, M. E., Martinez, A. C., Olmedo, E. L., & Santisteban, D. (1983). Hispanic mental health curriculum for psychology. In J. C. Chunn II, P. J. Dunston, & F. Ross-Sheriff (Eds.), *Mental health and people of color: Curriculum development and change* (pp. 65-93). Washington, DC: Howard University Press.

Bernal, G., Bonilla, J., & Bellido, C. (1994). Ecological validity and cultural sensitivity for outcome research. *Journal of Abnormal and Child Psychology, 23,* 67-82.

Bernal, G., & Enchautegui-de-Jesús, N. (1994). Latinos and Latinas in community psychology: A review of the literature. *American Journal of Community Psychology, 22,* 531-557.

Bernal, G., & Flores-Ortiz, Y. (1984). *Latino families: Sociohistorical perspectives and cultural issues* [Monograph]. San Francisco: Bay Area Spanish Speaking Therapists Association.

Berry, J. W. (1998). Acculturation and health. In S. S. Kazarian & D. R. Evans (Eds.), *Cultural clinical psychology: Theory, research, and practice* (pp. 39-57). New York: Oxford University Press.

Bhopal, R., & Rankin, J. (1999). Concepts and terminology in ethnicity, race and health: Be aware of the ongoing debate. *British Dental Journal, 186,* 483-484.

Blazer, D. G., Kessler, R. C., McGonagle, K. A., & Swartz, M. S. (1994). The prevalence and distribution of major depression in a national community sample: The National Comorbidity Survey. *American Journal of Psychiatry, 151,* 979-986.

Brown, D. R., Ahmed, F., Gary, L. E., & Milburn, N. G. (1993). Major depression in a community sample of African Americans. *American Journal of Psychiatry, 152,* 373-378.

Brown, D. R., Gary, L. E., Greene, A. D., & Milburn, N. G. (1992). Patterns of social affiliation as predictors of depressive symptoms among urban Blacks. *Journal of Health and Social Behavior, 33,* 242-253.

Canabal, M. E., & Quiles, J. A. (1995). Acculturation and socioeconomic factors as determinants of depression among Puerto Ricans in the United States. *Social Behavior and Personality, 23,* 235-248.

Clark, R., Anderson, N. B., Clark, V. R., & Williams, D. R. (1999). Racism as a stressor for African Americans: A biopsychosocial model. *American Psychologist, 54,* 805-816.

Comas-Díaz, L., & Grenier, R. J. (1998). Migration and acculturation. In J. Sandoval, C. L. Frisby, K. F. Geisinger, J. D. Scheuneman, & J. R. Grenier (Eds.), *Test interpretation and diversity: Achieving equity in assessment* (pp. 213-239). Washington, DC: American Psychological Association.

Crews, D. E., & Bindon, J. R. (1991). Ethnicity as a taxonomic tool in biomedical and biosocial research. *Ethnicity & Disease, 1,* 42-49.

Cross-National Collaborative Group. (1992). The changing rate of major depression: Cross-national comparisons. *Journal of the American Medical Association, 268,* 3098-3105.

Cuéllar, I., & Roberts, R. E. (1997). Relations of depression, acculturation, and socioeconomic status in a Latino sample. *Hispanic Journal of Behavioral Sciences, 19,* 230-238.

Dana, R. H. (1998). *Understanding cultural identity in intervention and assessment.* Thousand Oaks, CA: Sage.

Dressler, W. W., & Badger, L. W. (1985). Epidemiology of depressive symptoms in Black communities: A comparative analysis. *Journal of Nervous and Mental Disease, 173,* 212-220.

Edwards, N. C. (1992). Important considerations in the use of ethnicity as a study variable. *Canadian Journal of Public Health, 83,* 31-33.

Flaskerud, J. H., & Hu, L. (1994). Participation in and outcome of treatment for major depression among low income Asian-Americans. *Psychiatry Research, 53,* 289-300.

Gastpar, M. (1986). Epidemiology of depression (Europe and North America). *Psychopathology, 19,* 17-21.

Gilbert, D., & Kahl, J. A. (1987). *The American class structure: A new synthesis.* Chicago: Dorsey.

Gilbert, P. (2000). Varieties of submissive behavior as forms of social defense: Their evolution and role in depression. In L. Sloman & P. Gilbert (Eds.), *Subordination and defeat: An evolutionary approach to mood disorders and their therapy* (pp. 3-45). Englewood Cliffs, NJ: Lawrence Erlbaum.

Golding, J. M., & Lipton, R. I. (1990). Depressed mood and major depressive disorder in two ethnic groups. *Journal of Psychiatric Research, 24,* 65-82.

Hinton, L., Jenkins, C. N. H., McPhee, S., Wong, C., Lai, K. Q., Le, A., Du, N., & Fordham, D. (1998). A survey of depressive symptoms among Vietnamese-American men in three locales: Prevalence and correlates. *Journal of Nervous and Mental Disorders, 186,* 677-683.

Hymes, R. W., & Akiyama, M. M. (1991). Depression and self-enhancement among Japanese and American students. *Journal of Social Psychology, 13,* 321-334.

Jones-Webb, R. J., & Snowden, L. R. (1993). Symptoms of depression among Blacks and Whites. *American Journal of Public Health, 83,* 240-244.

Kim, M. T. (1995). Cultural influences on depression in Korean Americans. *Journal of Psychosocial Nursing, 33,* 13-18.

Kessler, R. C., McGonagle, K. A., Swartz, M., & Blazer, D. G. (1993). Sex and depression in the National Comorbidity Survey: I. Lifetime prevalence, chronicity and recurrence. *Journal of Affective Disorders, 29,* 85-96.

Lehtinen, V., & Joukamaa, M. (1994). Epidemiology of depression: Prevalence, risk factors and treatment situation. *Acta Psychiatrica Scandinavia, 377,* 7-10.

Loo, C. M., & Young Yu, C. (1998). Heartland of gold: A historical overview. In C. M. Loo (Ed.), *Chinese Americans: Mental health and quality of life in the inner city* (pp. 29-53). Thousand Oaks, CA: Sage.

Miranda, A. O., & Umhoefer, D. L. (1998). Depression and social interest differences between Latinos in dissimilar acculturation stages. *Journal of Mental Health Counseling, 20,* 159-171.

Munet-Vilaró, F., Folkman, S., & Gregorich, S. (1999). Depressive symptomatology in three Latino groups. *Western Journal of Nursing Research, 21,* 209-224.

Munford, M. B. (1994). Relationship of gender, self esteem, social class, and racial identity to depression in Blacks. *Journal of Black Psychology, 20,* 157-174.

Muñoz, R. A., Boddy, P., Prime, R., & Muñoz, L. (1990). Depression in the Hispanic community: Preliminary findings in Hispanic general medical patients at a community health center. *Annals of Clinical Psychiatry, 2,* 115-120.

Murray, C. J. L., & Lopez, A. D. (1997). Global mortality, disability, and the contribution of risk factors: Global Bureau of Disease Study. *Lancet, 349,* 1436-1442.

Narrow, W. E., Rae, D. S., Moscicki, E. K., Locke, B. Z., & Regier, D. A. (1990). Depression among Cuban Americans: The Hispanic Health and Nutrition Examination Survey. *Social Psychiatry and Psychiatric Epidemiology, 25,* 260-268.

National Advisory Mental Health Council. (1998). Basic behavioral science research for mental health: Sociocultural and environmental processes. In P. Balls Organista, K. M. Chun, & G. Marín (Eds.), *Readings in ethnic psychology* (pp. 43-58). New York: Routledge.

Okazaki, S., & Sue, S. (1998). Methodological issues in assessment research with ethnic minorities. In P. Balls Organista, K. M. Chun, & G. Marín (Eds.), *Readings in ethnic psychology* (pp. 26-40). New York: Routledge.

Parker, T., May, P. A., Maviglia, M. A., Petrakis, S., Sunde, S., & Gloyd, S. V. (1997). PRIME-MD: Its utility in detecting mental disorders in American Indians. *International Journal of Psychiatry in Medicine, 27,* 107-128.

Pfeffer, N. (1998). Theories of race, ethnicity and culture. *British Medical Journal, 317,* 1381-1384.

Potter, L. B., Rogler, L. H., & Moscicki, E. K. (1995). Depression among Puerto Ricans in New York City: The Hispanic Health and Nutrition Examination Survey. *Social Psychiatry and Psychiatric Epidemiology, 30,* 185-193.

Regier, D. A., Hirschfeld, R. M. A., Goodwin, F. K., Burke, J. D., Lazar, J. B., & Judd, L. L. (1988). The NIMH Depression Awareness, Recognition, and Treatment Program: Structure, aims, and scientific bias. *American Journal of Psychiatry, 145,* 1351-1357.

Renfrey, G. (1998). Cognitive-behavior therapy and the Native American client. In P. Balls Organista, K. M. Chun, & G. Marín (Eds.), *Readings in ethnic psychology* (pp. 335-352). New York: Routledge.

Rodríguez, E., Allen, J. A., Frongillo, E. A., & Chandra, P. (1999). Unemployment, depression, health: A look at the African-American community. *Journal of Epidemiology Community Health, 335-342.*

Rogler, L. M. (1989). The meaning of culturally sensitive research in mental health. *American Psychologist, 146,* 296-303.

Rogler, L. H. (1999). Methodological sources of cultural insensitivity in mental health research. *American Psychologist, 54,* 424-433.

Rollock, D., & Gordon, E. W. (2000). Racism and mental health into the 21st century: Perspectives and parameters. *American Journal of Orthopsychiatry, 70,* 5-13.

Sanders Thompson, V. L. (1996). Perceived experiences of racism as stressful life events. *Community Mental Health Journal, 32,* 223-233.

Senior, P. A., & Bhopal, R. (1994). Ethnicity as a variable in epidemiological research. *British Medical Journal, 309,* 327-330.

Sloman, L. (2000). How the involuntary defeat strategy relates to depression. In L. Sloman & P. Gilbert (Eds.), *Subordination and defeat: An evolutionary approach to mood disorders and their therapy* (pp. 47-67). Englewood Cliffs, NJ: Lawrence Erlbaum.

Sloman, L., & Gilbert, P. (Eds.). (2000). *Subordination and defeat: An evolutionary approach to mood disorders and their therapy.* Englewood Cliffs, NJ: Lawrence Erlbaum.

Somervell, P. D., Beals, J., Kinzie, J. D., Boehnlein, J., Leung, P., & Manson, S. M. (1993). Criterion validity of the Center for Epidemiological Studies Depression Scale in a population sample from an American Indian village. *Psychiatry Research, 47,* 255-266.

Tabora, B., & Flaskerud, J. H. (1994). Depression among Chinese Americans: A review of the literature. *Issues in Mental Health Nursing, 15,* 569-584.

Takeuchi, D. T., Chung, R., Lin, K., Shen, M., Kurasaki, K., Chun, C., & Sue, S. (1998). Lifetime and twelve-month prevalence rates of major depressive episodes and dysthymia among Chinese Americans in Los Angeles. *American Journal of Psychiatry, 155,* 1407-1414.

Tran, T. V. (1993). Psychological traumas and depression in a sample of Vietnamese people in the United States. *Health & Social Work, 18,* 184-194.

U.S. Bureau of the Census. (1999). *Projections of the total resident population by 5-year age groups, race, and Hispanic origin with special age categories: Middle series, 2050 to 2070.* Washington, DC: U.S. Bureau of the Census, Population Division, Statistical Information Staff.

U.S. Bureau of the Census. (2001). *Overview of race and Hispanic origin.* Retrieved from www.census.gov/population/www/cen2000/briefs.html

U.S. Department of Labor (2002). Unemployed persons by marital status, race, age, and sex. U.S. Department of Labor, Household Data Annual Averages. Retrieved November 12, 2002, from the World Wide Web: ftp://ftp.bls.gov/pub/special.requests/lf/aat24.txt

Vega, W. (2000, May). *Hispanic mental health research and disparities in services.* Oral presentation at the Disparities in Latino Mental Health Care meeting, Los Angeles.

Vera, M., Alegría, M., Freeman, D., Robles, R. R., Ríos, R., & Ríos, C. F. (1991). Depressive symptoms among Puerto Ricans: Island poor compared with residents of New York City area. *American Journal of Epidemiology, 134,* 502-510.

Williams, D. R., & Harris-Reid, M. (1999). Race and mental health: Emerging patterns and promising approaches. In A. V. Horwitz & T. Scheid (Eds.), *A handbook for the study of mental health: Social context, theories, and systems* (pp. 295-314). New York: Cambridge University Press.

Zhang, A. Y., & Snowden, L. R. (1999). Ethnic characteristics of mental disorders in five U.S. communities. *Cultural Diversity and Ethnic Minority Psychology, 5,* 134-146.

CHAPTER 20

Anxiety Disorders Among Ethnic Minority Groups

GAYLE Y. IWAMASA
University of Indianapolis

SHILPA M. PAI
Oklahoma State University

According to the fourth edition of the *Diagnostic and Statistical Manual of Mental Disorders (DSM-IV)* (American Psychiatric Association, 1994), anxiety disorders involve conditions in which an individual experiences anxiety, fear, apprehension, increased arousal, and avoidance behavior to the extent that it interferes with daily functioning. Although the *DSM-IV* does include sections on "Specific Culture, Age, and Gender Features" for each anxiety disorder, the information provided is very general (except for the mention of *taijin-kyofu-sho,* which is discussed later in this chapter). Thus, clinicians are not provided with specific information or resources in the consideration of anxiety symptoms among various cultural groups.

Good and Kleinman (1985) reviewed the cross-cultural literature on anxiety disorders and concluded that although different terminology may be used, anxiety disorders are universal. However, they did point out that the expression of anxiety symptoms is influenced by culture-specific factors. For example, some cultures may have disorders of the "nerves," "fright disorders," or "neurasthenia," which all include anxiety symptoms. Comparability of these disorders with the *DSM-IV* diagnostic classification is often difficult because although some symptoms may overlap, others do not.

The purpose of this chapter is to briefly summarize the existing research on anxiety disorders among the four major ethnic minority groups in the United States. Treatment will briefly be discussed, but readers are encouraged to refer to Part 6 of this book, as treatment issues are discussed in more depth than they can be in this chapter. As may be expected, the amount of research on the mental health of ethnic minorities is woefully inadequate. Thus, when appropriate, brief summaries of research on anxiety disorders from a more broad-based cultural perspective will be provided, as it is possible that such culture-specific disorders may be seen among U.S. ethnic minorities, particularly among immigrants. Indeed, some of the disorders discussed in this chapter have already been documented in the U.S. mental health literature.

PREVALENCE OF ANXIETY DISORDERS AMONG ETHNIC MINORITIES

Guarnaccia (1997) reviewed the prevalence of anxiety disorders among selected ethnic minority groups based on the Epidemiologic Catchment Area (ECA) studies (Reiger et al., 1984). Guarnaccia cited data from the Los Angeles ECA site, which, unfortunately, only included information comparing Mexican Americans born in Mexico and the United States (Karno et al., 1989). Those results indicated that U.S.-born Mexican Americans had higher rates of anxiety disorders as compared to those born in Mexico. Guarnaccia also presented comparison data from the Baltimore and St. Louis ECA sites (Brown, Eaton, & Sussman, 1990) between Black and White Americans. At both sites, Black Americans had higher prevalence rates of phobias as compared to White Americans.

Guarnaccia (1997) noted that cultural differences in the prevalence of anxiety disorders are difficult to explain because it is possible that the range of experiences and, perhaps, the diagnostic criteria of anxiety disorders are culturally bound and may need modification. For example, *DSM* definitions emphasize excessive worry and apprehension and lack emphasis on somatic symptoms. Clearly, more epidemiological data on the prevalence of anxiety symptomatology and disorders among ethnic minority individuals are needed.

THE CONCEPTUALIZATION OF ANXIETY

The influence of culture on the conceptualization of disease and illness has been addressed in the work of Kleinman, Eisenberg, and Good (1978). Their explanatory model of illness (EMI) specifically addresses the influence of culture on help-seeking behavior. The EMI defines *disease* as a Western concept of biological malfunctioning, whereas *illness* is a personal or cultural reaction to disease. Therefore, illness is shaped by how culture influences the perception, labeling, experience, and coping with disease. As a result, Kleinman et al. hypothesized that culture will influence the presentation of symptoms, which therefore influences one's expectations for treatment and thus help seeking. The implication, as suggested by Kleinman et al.'s EMI, is that mental health providers and other health care workers will provide inappropriate treatment, or no treatment at all, without knowledge of their patients' conceptualization of illness. In addition, compliance with treatment recommendations is likely to be diminished if the patient and health care provider have differing EMIs of the patient's difficulties. Related to anxiety, a clinician who is not aware of how his or her EMI may differ from that of the client will likely not be able to develop a culturally sensitive treatment plan and thus will not adequately explain the rationale for whatever treatment recommendations he or she may have. It is reasonable to assume that clients will not follow treatment recommendations that they do not see as being helpful.

The issue of how one conceptualizes anxiety and anxiety disorder symptoms is particularly important for ethnic minority individuals. Unfortunately, this issue has received little attention in the empirical literature, and as a result, not much is known about how various ethnic minority groups experience and express psychological distress in general and anxiety specifically. Culturally appropriate clinical assessment of anxiety is apt to be challenging, yet mental health professionals must be aware of those challenges and adjust their assessment methods accordingly.

ASSESSMENT ISSUES

Although Part IV of this book covers issues related to diagnosis and assessment, a few comments will be made here due to their importance. Factors such as language, cultural and motivational differences, and interpersonal expectations may complicate the assessment process, and special considerations may be necessary to provide appropriate assessment and diagnosis of ethnic minority individuals (Butcher, Nezami, & Exner, 1998).

Dana (1993) conducted comprehensive reviews of a variety of assessment measures used with multicultural populations. He outlined the use of both *etic* assessment (assumption of universality of constructs) and *emic* assessment (culture specific) with ethnic minorities and emphasized that a combination of a general with a more individualized approach to assessment is often needed and provides more comprehensive and important information. In addition to the domains discussed by Butcher et al. (1998), Dana also discussed the need to consider the issues of differing worldviews (i.e., one's group identity, individual identity, beliefs, and values), ethnic identity, and racism in conducting assessment.

Use of Translators in Assessment

To address the needs of individuals for whom English is not their first language, some mental health professionals have turned to using translators. Although the use of translators in psychological assessment grew in the 1990s, clinicians must be aware of the potential problems using translators may cause. Unless the translator is a mental health worker familiar with diagnostic classification systems, symptomatology, and certain cultural expressions, the risk of misinterpretation and inaccurate information is very high.

Given the lack of staff who are fluent in a variety of languages, many agencies resort to using family members as translators—often the client's child or even grandchild. This mode of assessment may not only be in direct opposition to specific cultural roles family members have but may actually violate such roles. For example, in many cultures, elder family members are held in high regard and viewed as wise and knowing. Thus, placing a child or grandchild in the position of having to question an elder regarding symptoms of psychological distress and to also provide the recommendations of the mental health professional is likely to be disrespectful, shameful, and embarrassing to the older adult. This influences the increased likelihood of a poor client-provider relationship, the gathering of inaccurate information, inappropriate treatment recommendations, and poor compliance with treatment.

Factors Influencing the Development of Anxiety Among Ethnic Minorities

Although specific ethnic group issues in the expression and experience of anxiety will be covered in this chapter, a number of general factors likely influence the development of anxiety symptoms among ethnic minority individuals. First, the impact of racism and discrimination experienced by many ethnic minorities is likely to be an influential factor and thus should be assessed as a potential risk factor for the development of anxiety symptoms. When assessing an individual's anxiety symptoms, clinicians not only would benefit from acknowledging the possibility that such experiences might contribute to anxiety but also should inquire about any specific experiences or perceptions of racism and/or discrimination an ethnic minority client may have. This assessment should also include inquiry about parental and other familial experiences of racism and discrimination that the client may have vicariously experienced. Indeed, transgenerational effects of trauma have been documented by international scholars in children of Holocaust survivors (Solomon, 1998) and Aboriginal people in Australia (Rafael, Swan, & Martinek, 1998). In the United States, Sorscher and Cohen (1997) have documented transgenerational trauma in children of Holocaust survivors, and Nagata (1991) documented the transgenerational impact of the internment of Japanese Americans during World War II. Given the history of racism and discrimination of many ethnic minority groups, it is reasonable to believe that many ethnic minority individuals have experienced the transgenerational transmission of racism and discrimination, and this may serve as a risk factor in the development of anxiety symptoms and disorders.

In assessing anxiety among ethnic minority individuals, mental health professionals must recognize the great heterogeneity among each ethnic minority group. Among Asian Americans, Latinos, and Black/African Americans, there exists a vast array of nationalities, ethnicities, languages, religious/spiritual beliefs and practices, generational status, and so on. Among American Indians, there are numerous tribes, each with different values, languages, practices, and so on (Bigfoot & Braden, 1998; John, 1998; McDonald, 2000). For newer immigrants, huge differences may exist in terms of reasons for immigrating to the United States, their familiarity with American values and customs, the immigration process, and adaptation experiences once arriving in the United States, which all may influence the development of anxiety. For example, refugees from Cambodia, Haiti, and certain Central American countries are likely to be at higher risk for the development of anxiety as compared to immigrants who left their countries during relatively peaceful periods (e.g., Korean immigrants). A thorough review of these issues is beyond the scope of this chapter. Thus, readers are referred to Iwamasa's (1997) summary of the literature related to increased anxiety symptoms among Asian immigrants, which are likely to be applicable to other ethnic minority immigrants as well.

Acculturation level and ethnic and racial identity are additional personal characteristics on which ethnic minorities will vary. Although frequently related to generational status (Iwamasa, Pai, Hilliard, & Lin, 1998; Suinn, Rickard-Figueroa, Lew, & Vigil, 1987), acculturation level may vary across generations and, among first-generation individuals, may be affected by length of residence in the United States. In addition, mental health researchers have increasingly examined the role of ethnic and racial identity and its relation to various psychological concepts (Casas & Pytluk, 1995; Choney, Berryhill-Paapke, & Robbins, 1995; Cross, 1995; Marsella, Johnson, Johnson, & Brennan, 1998; Sodowsky, Kwan, & Pannu, 1995; White & Parham, 1990; Yamada, Marsella, & Yamada, 1998). Some of the research on the relationship of these processes and identities, as well as the development of psychological distress in general and anxiety disorders in particular, has been equivocal. For example, as discussed later in this chapter, McNeil, Kee, and Zvolensky (1998) found that ethnic identity was related either to decreases or increases in anxiety, depending on the context. In addition, Christensen (1999) examined the influence of ethnic identity and family relationships on the psychological well-being of Native American elders. The results revealed that a stronger familial support was related to fewer anxiety and psychosomatic symptoms. However, ethnic identity was not found to significantly relate to psychological well-being.

In addition, the huge, increasing number of biethnic/biracial individuals also must be considered. Root (1992, 1998, 1999) and LaFromboise and colleagues (LaFromboise, Coleman, & Gerton, 1993; LaFromboise, Heyle, & Ozer, 1999), among others, have discussed the difficulties with ethnic identity development that some racially mixed individuals may face, such as feeling ostracized and discriminated by members of both ethnic groups, which might also increase the risk of developing psychological distress. Again, issues related to the development of identity among these individuals have increasingly been associated with various psychological concepts and processes (Kerwin & Ponterotto, 1995).

These are just a few of the shared risk factors among ethnic minority groups that should be included in any assessment of anxiety symptoms. Clinicians should be familiar with these issues as well as with ethnic-specific issues and should integrate questions about them in the assessment process.

State-Trait Anxiety Inventory

Specific to anxiety, in his review, the only assessment device Dana (1993) discussed was the multicultural application of the State-Trait Anxiety Inventory (STAI) (Spielberger, 1976). According to Spielberger (1989), the STAI has been translated into more than 40 different languages and dialects, generally following an idiomatic rather than literal equivalence approach. Idiomatic translation may be a more accurate reflection of the underlying meaning of a phrase as compared to a literal translation. Unfortunately, psychometric data were not provided, thus making it difficult to ascertain the utility of these translated versions. Dana's evaluation of the STAI's Spanish versions indicated that these versions are useful tools in assessing anxiety symptoms among Spanish-speaking adults. However, he did emphasize that clinicians must consider "local" and community norms in the interpretation of scores. For example, age, gender, socioeconomic status, and nationality will vary among Latinos and thus should be considered in interpreting level of distress.

Developed in 1986 for use in Hong Kong, the Chinese version of the STAI (C-STAI) revealed high item-total correlations and alpha coefficients (Chan, 1990). Shek's (1993) comparison of the C-STAI to other psychological measures (i.e., Beck Depression Inventory [BDI], General Health Questionnaire, Leeds Scales for the Self-Assessment of Anxiety and Depression) revealed concurrent validity and a significant correlation between A-State and A-Trait.

Clinician Self-Assessment

In addition to the client factors discussed above, a brief discussion of clinician factors must be made. Mental health professionals must begin to acknowledge the role of their own worldview, knowledge base and experience with other cultural groups, possible biases, and stereotypes and prejudices that might influence the process of assessment. In addition to didactic knowledge, mental health professionals must take some responsibility for acquiring the skills needed to provide culturally appropriate assessment. Minimally, this would include the clinician's own self-assessment of thoughts and feelings related to people of different cultural backgrounds. In addition, mental health professionals should also strive to understand the context in which ethnic minorities live. For example, clinicians could consider what it might be like for a potential client to face lifelong discrimination and racism through a combination of personal experience and vicarious, observed experiences. Indeed, the need for emphasis on multicultural competence among mental health professionals not only is warranted but is an ethical obligation (Sue, Bingham, Porche-Burke, & Vasquez, 1999).

ASIAN AMERICANS/
PACIFIC ISLANDERS

The November 1, 1999, U.S. census population estimates indicated that approximately 4% of the population was Asian American/Pacific Islander (U.S. Bureau of the Census, 2000). The Census Bureau also reported that as a collective group, Asian Americans are one of the fastest-growing ethnic and cultural groups in the United States. Indeed, the population estimates of Asian Americans and Pacific Islanders increased by .4% in just 4½ years. As mentioned previously, Asian Americans/Pacific Islanders (AA/PIs) are a very heterogeneous group comprising more than 25 ethnic groups collapsed into one category based on their common heritage in Asia and the Pacific Islands, similar appearance, and cultural values.

As indicated earlier, prevalence data on anxiety disorders among AA/PI individuals do not exist. Thus, the extent of anxiety problems among AA/PIs is unknown. In a review of the literature on depression and anxiety among Asian American older adults, Iwamasa and Hilliard (1999) found only two studies that focused on anxiety and Asian American older adults, and both focused on Japanese Americans. Yamamoto et al.'s (1985) study found that among Japanese American elders, anxiety disorders were less frequent as compared to other disorders such as depression and organic brain disorder. Nine percent of their participants met criteria for panic disorder. Iwamasa, Hilliard, and Osato (1998) conducted interviews with Japanese American elders and found that although many individuals defined anxiety and depression similar to the diagnostic criteria of *DSM,* some of the participants conceptualized anxiety using depressive symptoms and vice versa. These results highlight the notion that how AA/PIs conceptualize anxiety may be different from other ethnic groups' conceptualization. For some AA/PI individuals, they may describe a person as being anxious using depressive symptoms and a depressed person as someone with anxiety symptoms.

Culture-Specific Considerations

In the assessment of anxiety symptoms among AA/PI individuals, clinicians should consider the following issues in terms of the roles they may play in mediating anxiety: focus on family, focus on community, respect for elders, communication style, interpersonal harmony and cooperation (collectivistic orientation), sex roles, ethnic identity, language, acculturation, generational status, immigration status, religiosity/spirituality, age, education level, occupational status, socioeconomic status (SES), and access to health care. Some of these values/behaviors may actually serve as protective factors against the development of some anxiety symptoms. For example, Lin, Ensel, Simeone, and Kuo (1979) found that social support was significantly and negatively related to illness symptoms in a Chinese American sample in Washington, D.C. Similarly, Viswanathan, Shah, and Ahad (1997) revealed that family involvement and social support may facilitate the therapeutic process but also may produce additional anxiety (e.g., disagreeing with an authority figure). Given that family and community are important Asian cultural values, this may actually work to decrease the development of anxiety and other distress symptoms in Asian Americans. This highlights one of the resources available to health care providers—using family and community to support treatment.

However, some aspects about traditional Asian values might also increase the likelihood of the development of an anxiety disorder. For example, values within the Asian Indian culture such as dependency, unassertiveness, and submissiveness may contribute to social phobias, especially within the American culture, which promotes assertiveness and less rigid social boundaries (Viswanathan et al., 1997).

Culture-Specific Disorders

Dhat. Evidence of *dhat* syndrome, a sexual neurosis, has been found within the Indian subcontinent (Viswanathan et al., 1997). This syndrome is characterized by a fear of losing semen (*dhat*) through urine, which leads to a loss of physical and mental energy. Individuals present with several somatic symptoms such as weakness, fatigue, palpitations, sleeplessness, and physical and mental exhaustion (Bhatia & Malik, 1991). Although not technically an anxiety disorder, *dhat* syndrome is included here because of its psychological sequelae. Treatment includes sexual counseling and treatment of the associated disorders. Research and evidence of this syndrome have primarily occurred in India. Thus, mental health providers in the United States may observe *dhat* syndrome only in first-generation Asian Indians.

Hwa-Byung. Lin (1983) described three cases of *hwa-byung,* a Korean folk illness experienced by patients and their families to be a physical affliction, despite the fact that its manifestations include both physiological and psychological symptoms. From a Western perspective, *hwa-byung* appears to be a mixture of depression and anxiety. In addition, the patient often recognizes interpersonal conflicts and anger as precipitating factors to the somatic complaints. Each patient described by Lin also identified an epigastric mass that was not identified on physical examination. Symptoms of the disorder included (a) repressed or suppressed anger of long duration; (b) various somatic complaints (e.g., panic attacks, psychomotor retardation, tiredness, loss of appetite, weight loss, indigestion, dizziness, insomnia); (c) feelings of helplessness, resentfulness, and

guilt; (d) tension; (e) pressure or compression in the epigastrium; and (f) fear of impending death despite medical reassurance. With these patients, antidepressants were prescribed, and with two of the patients, supportive psychotherapy also was used. Lin reported these treatments as being effective in treating the symptoms. A follow-up study of 109 Korean Americans, ages 18 years and older, in the metropolitan Los Angeles area, found that 11.9% reported having suffered from *hwa-byung* (Lin et al., 1992). Thus, it appears that the incidence of *hwa-byung* may increase as the population of Korean Americans increases and as clinicians become more aware of the symptoms. See Iwamasa (1997) for a more thorough review of this disorder.

Koro. This syndrome, documented in Chinese and Asian Indian cultures, is characterized by an intense fear that the penis will shrink or disappear into the abdomen as a punishment for sins (Al-Issa & Oudji, 1998; Viswanathan et al., 1997). Symptoms include anxiety related to sexual functioning of organs, heart palpitations, sweating, vertigo, fear of death, and guilt and shame associated with masturbation and sexual activity. Among the Chinese, *koro* is referred to as *shuk* (dwindling/withdrawal) *yang* (male genitals) (Al-Issa & Oudji, 1998). Treatment of *koro* in India and China includes psychotherapy and tranquilizers (Viswanathan et al., 1997). Although not yet documented in the United States, this disorder may exist in first-generation Indian and Chinese men.

Taijin-Kyofu-Sho. Taijin-kyofu-sho (TKS) has been described by Kirmayer (1991) as the Japanese equivalent to social phobia. *DSM-IV* describes social phobia as marked and persistent fear of one or more social or performance situations in which the person is exposed to unfamiliar people or scrutiny by others. The individual fears he or she will act in a humiliating or embarrassing way, and exposure to the feared social situation provokes anxiety; thus, the situation is avoided.

TKS is described in Japan as a neurotic disorder of extraordinary intense anxiety and tension in social settings, in which people have a fear of being looked down upon, making others feel unpleasant, and being disliked, such that it leads to withdrawal or avoidance of social relations (Tseng, Asai, Kitanishi, McLaughlin, & Kyomen, 1992). Behaviors that might lead to the intense anxiety include blushing, concerns about emitting offensive odors, staring inappropriately, and improper facial expressions. An individual might not actually be doing these behaviors, but instead, the anxiety is a result of the fear that others perceive that he or she is engaging in the behaviors. In most incidences, individuals often describe a single circumscribed fear. The four subtypes of TKS are (a) transient type (temporary, usually occurs in adolescents); (b) neurotic type; (c) severe type, which often includes delusions or ideas of reference; and (d) secondary type, which is a phobia that occurs concomitantly with schizophrenia.

Kleinknecht, Dinnel, Tanouye-Wilson, and Lonner (1994) described the major difference between social phobia and TKS as being the focus of the social anxiety. With social phobia, anxiety is due to concern that the person will embarrass *himself* or *herself*. With TKS, the concern is that the person will do something that will offend or embarrass *others*. As discussed earlier, traditional Asian cultural values emphasize the importance of the group over the individual. One can see how the emphasis on interpersonal relations among the Japanese could result in intense anxiety in those who may lack adequate coping skills or who have low levels of self-confidence. Thus, one might experience anxiety symptoms as a result of the cultural emphasis on interpersonal harmony. A more thorough discussion of TKS may be found in Iwamasa (1997).

BLACKS AND AFRICAN AMERICANS

The November 1, 1999, U.S. census population estimates indicated that approximately 12.8% of the population was Black/African American (U.S. Bureau of the Census, 2000). As with AA/PIs, the population of Blacks/African Americans is increasing, albeit at a slower rate of .2% in the past 4½ years. Although they comprise a significant portion of the U.S. population, unfortunately, the anxiety literature on the prevalence, expression, and help-seeking patterns of this population is quite limited (Heurtin-Roberts, Snowden, & Miller, 1997).

The prevalence rates of anxiety disorders have been reported to be higher in African Americans than in other populations. For example, African Americans are three times more likely to have simple phobias than Caucasians, experience panic disorders more than other populations, and have higher comorbidity rates with anxiety and other illnesses (Snowden, 1999). African American children also experience more general fears and reality-based fears than other children (Heurtin-Roberts et al., 1997).

Culture-Specific Considerations

Historically, African Americans have been misdiagnosed and mistreated by the mental health professional (Neal-Barnett & Smith, 1997). As such, active help seeking among African Americans is quite limited. Thus, mental health professionals should be aware of the potential distrust of the field that many African Americans may have toward them and consider those issues in conducting assessment and treatment. Neal-Barnett and Smith (1997) also discussed the need to inform and educate African Americans on the signs and symptoms of anxiety disorders.

As with other ethnic minority groups, it has been suggested that the presentation of anxiety symptoms differs in African Americans because it is influenced by culture. For example, a cultural theme related to a blood imbalance (e.g., thickening or thinning of blood) that leads to emotional distress has been reported (Heurtin-Roberts et al., 1997). Anxiety folk disorders related to this blood imbalance include *falling-out,* "*high-pertension,*" *high blood,* and *nerves.* Evidence for this cultural expression of anxiety has been found in the United States, the Caribbean, and South America. Panic disorder also appears to co-occur frequently with diagnoses of hypertension among African Americans (Neal, Nagle-Rich, & Smucker, 1994; Neal & Turner, 1991). Other culturally related anxiety symptoms may include hallucinations and delusions, and themes of victimization, violence, and paranoia have been found (Heurtin-Roberts et al., 1997).

Kleinman et al.'s (1978) warning that inappropriate treatment will occur without knowledge of a patient's conceptualization is quite salient given that the misdiagnosis of African Americans has led to high rates of hospitalization and prescription of antipsychotic medications (Al-Issa & Oudji, 1998). Snowden (1999) also reported that African Americans express somatic complaints (i.e., headaches, dizziness, weakness, pounding heart, hot flashes, and chills) that are believed to be symptoms of underlying disorders and contribute to the overall distress level. Following this presentation of somatic symptoms, research has revealed that African Americans are more likely to use medical services rather than mental health services (Heurtin-Roberts et al., 1997).

With regard to specific anxiety disorders, Neal-Barnett and Smith (1997) found that in general, African Americans seldom endorse generalized anxiety disorder symptoms. In one study of African American women, Neal-Barnett and Smith discovered that although some symptoms were exhibited, diagnostic criteria for generalized anxiety disorder were not met. The authors hypothesized that Africans Americans may experience life as full of generalized anxiety and thus learn to cope with it. In addition, concerning social anxiety disorder, Neal-Barnett and Smith reported that African Americans are more likely to experience social anxiety in the presence of other Blacks than with Caucasians. This heightened anxiety may be due to a fear of not attaining an African American "standard" or fitting in with the African American culture. For African Americans who experience social anxiety in the presence of Caucasians, the authors suggested that racism may play a role.

As previously mentioned, African Americans experiencing anxiety symptoms are more likely to present to medical services. African Americans experiencing obsessive-compulsive disorder commonly present to dermatology clinics (Neal-Barnett & Smith, 1997). Despite this help-seeking pattern, the authors noted that the presentation of obsessive-compulsive disorder is similar to the *DSM-IV* diagnosis. To provide appropriate diagnosis and treatment, Neal-Barnett and Smith suggested modifying structured interviews to include information on extended family, spirituality, victimization, exposure to violence, and sleep paralysis. In general, limited information exists on the presentation, conceptualization, and treatment of anxiety disorders with African Americans.

For Caribbean Americans, Gopaul-McNichol and Brice-Baker (1997) discussed the difficulties inherent in assessing anxiety symptoms, as Caribbean Americans are likely to be resistant to mental health intervention. Specifically, the concept of time ("anytime is Caribbean time") and the need to keep "secrets" within the family (and resolve problems within the family) were discussed as major impediments to traditional therapy. Gopaul-McNichol and Brice-Baker also discussed potential risk factors for the development of anxiety symptoms and disorders among Caribbean Americans, such as immigration experiences, racism, and witchcraft.

Although practice of voodoo, *espiritismo,* and *santeria* are often viewed as protective factors, fear of evil spirits or being the target of an evil spell may precipitate panic attacks.

Culture-Specific Disorders

Brain-Fag Syndrome. Prince first defined this syndrome in 1960, and its existence was confirmed in several regions of Africa (Al-Issa & Oudji, 1998). The basis of this disorder is an intense fear of failure as educational achievement is highly valued within the African family. This syndrome was observed in university students in Africa after intense study periods. Symptoms included (a) pain in the back of the neck, (b) frontal headache, (c) burning sensations of the scalp and head, (d) difficulty in attention and thinking, and (e) inability to understand what one reads and amnesia of what has just been studied. More recently, Prince (1985) attributed the brain-fag syndrome to "the forbidden knowledge theory." He reported that African students attending Western schools perceived themselves as betraying their ancestors (they reported dreams of their ancestors beating them). Prince noted that these individuals were less acculturated into Western society. Thus, this disorder may be more likely to be documented among immigrant African Americans. More research is necessary to further investigate this syndrome.

Isolated Sleep Paralysis. Bell, Hildreth, Jenkins, and Carter (1988) described isolated sleep paralysis among African Americans as a recurrent condition often referred to as "the witch is riding you," which occurs upon awakening or when falling asleep. Individuals report being unable to move and may experience hallucinations or feelings of impending danger. When the paralysis subsides, individuals often report panic symptoms. The relationship of isolated sleep paralysis to panic disorder is not yet clear, but some believe it serves as a precursor to the development of panic disorder (Neal et al., 1994).

NATIVE AMERICANS

The November 1, 1999, U.S. census population estimates indicated that approximately .9% of the population was American Indian, Eskimo, and Aleut (U.S. Bureau of the Census, 2000). In addition to the aforementioned ethnic groups, Bigfoot and Braden (1998) suggested that the Native American population also include Native Alaskans and Native Hawaiians.

American Indians share a history of oppression, depression, anxiety, and shame (Bigfoot & Braden, 1998). Yet McNeil et al. (1998) noted the paucity of empirical information on the nature, assessment, and impact of anxiety on American Indians. This information is salient given that anxiety is associated with poor health and substance abuse. Tribal surveys have revealed that more than 50% of participants reported anxiety problems followed by substance abuse and depression. In addition, many Native American children and adolescents have also been found to meet criteria for an anxiety disorder (McNeil, Porter, Zvolensky, Chaney, & Kee, 2000).

Culture-Specific Considerations

Forty-eight percent of the American Indian/Eskimo/Aleut population continues to reside in the most rural areas of the United States as compared to other ethnic minority groups, who are more likely to live in urban areas. This population is characterized as younger, less educated, and poorer than the general population. Approximately 31.6% of American Indians live below the poverty line as compared to a national average of 13.1% (Bigfoot & Braden, 1998). Limited access to medical facilities, medical professions, and funding sources have also contributed to the poor health of American Indians. For example, tuberculosis, diabetes, and fetal alcohol syndrome are higher in Native Americans than in other populations. Native Americans may also be characterized by their adherence to traditional culture, language, family structure, social functions, and health practices (Norton & Manson, 1996). Again, provided that this population is very heterogeneous, the information presented in this section is intended to serve as general guidelines and is not necessarily applicable to all Native Americans.

Researchers have highlighted the importance of examining anxiety, as the cultural abuses (i.e., forced relocation, genocide) suffered by American Indians may have led to culturally related anxiety. For example, McNeil et al.'s (1998) study of Navajo college students examined the relationship between ethnic identity (self-concept related to social group membership and emotional response to the membership) and culturally related anxiety. A strong ethnic identity may decrease the development of anxiety as an individual has more access to tribal support systems. However, a strong ethnic identity may also contribute to the development of anxiety due to culturally related anxiety and interacting with the majority culture. No significant relationship between ethnic identity and anxiety was found. In addition, no gender differences were revealed with respect to culturally related anxiety.

More recently, McNeil et al. (2000) developed the Native American Cultural Involvement and Detachment Anxiety Questionnaire (CIDAQ), a 20-item culturally related anxiety measure. The CIDAQ includes three subscales: Social Involvement With Native Americans and Alaska Natives, Economic Issues, and Social Involvement With the Majority (Caucasian) Culture. The measure, which was normed on a pan-Indian sample and a homogeneous sample (Navajo), had good internal consistency and appeared to tap into culturally related anxiety. The authors reported that future research should continue to assess the psychometric properties of the CIDAQ.

With regard to help seeking and treatment, research has revealed that compared to other Americans, American Indians are less aware of available psychological services. For those

aware of services, they fail to pursue therapy due to cultural and ethnic differences (LaFromboise, 1988). This may be because American Indians' view of therapy significantly differs from the dominant culture (LaFromboise, Trimble, & Mohatt, 1990). Specifically, expectations, goals, and attitudes toward therapy may differ. These differences include but are not limited to a spiritual and holistic view of mental health, inclusion of the Indian community, attribution of psychological problems to weakness or lack of discipline to maintain cultural values, ceremonial rituals, and consultation with medicine men.

American Indians may also fear that therapists will attempt to change values rather than problem solve or suggest treatments in conflict with American Indian culture. In addition, the historical mistreatment of American Indians and racism also may provide a barrier in developing trust in therapy (LaFromboise et al., 1990). For successful therapy, LaFromboise et al. (1990) recommended increasing access to traditional treatments and integrating traditional healing methods into culturally appropriate therapy. The authors specifically noted the merits of using a skills-training paradigm (social learning theory) or a network approach (inclusion of clan, family, and friends) in working with American Indians.

Bigfoot-Sipes, Dauphinais, LaFromboise, and Bennett (1992) investigated help-seeking patterns with a high school sample of American Indians and Metis (mixed Indian and Caucasian ancestry). Research revealed that American Indians with a strong adherence to their culture preferred counselors of the same ethnicity and sex. American Indian girls appeared to prefer female American Indian counselors. In addition, the nature of the problem (personal vs. academic) also influenced therapist preference. For personal problems, same-sex counselors were preferred, whereas similar age and education were preferred for academic problems. Similar to other ethnic groups, this research highlights the importance of assessing acculturation level in working with American Indians.

Culture-Specific Disorders

Kayak-Angst. This syndrome, characterized as an acute panic state, has been evidenced among the Inuit. Symptoms include vertigo, dazed feelings, spatial disorientation, "violent vegetative reaction," and "panic-stricken anguish." Al-Issa and Oudji (1998) reported that *kayak-angst* has been observed while Inuit seal hunters wait (immobile) in a boat for hours. The symptoms appear to be relieved when an affected individual is assisted and surrounded by others. The limited information on this culture-specific syndrome clearly warrants future research.

LATINOS/HISPANICS

The November 1, 1999, U.S. census population estimates indicated that approximately 11.6% of the population was of Hispanic origin (of any race) (U.S. Bureau of the Census, 2000). According to census projections, this population is the fastest-growing ethnic minority group in the United States, with a 2.6% increase in just 9 years. As discussed earlier, this population is highly heterogeneous, composed of individuals collapsed into one category based on their common heritage in South and Central America, Puerto Rico and Cuba, and Spain.

Culture-Specific Considerations

The underutilization of mental health services by Hispanic Americans has been associated with language and cultural differences. Research has revealed that Hispanics' reliance on family, religion, and folk remedies may account for the limited utilization of mental health services (Salman, Diamond, Jusino, Sanchez-LaCay, & Liebowitz, 1997). In addition, Hispanics have culturally defined labels for behaviors that also contribute to the limited use of mental health services. Due to this underutilization of mental health services, the family may serve as the primary caregiver and buffer individuals from the embarrassment and stigma associated with mental illness. In addition, as with AA/PIs, some of these cultural values may actually serve as protective factors in the development of anxiety. However, use of mental health facilities was found to increase when bilingual individuals were available to work with Hispanic clients (Salman et al., 1997).

Glover, Pumariega, Holzer, Wise, and Rodriguez's (1999) study revealed that anxiety disorders are more prevalent in Mexican American adults than in other populations. They also noted a high prevalence rate (13.8%-21%) among Mexican American adolescents. The researchers noted that a relationship between culture and symptomatic expression may exist. Based on their research, Glover et al. hypothesized that Mexican American adolescents with higher levels of anxiety may be attempting to balance two cultures. They specifically noted that female adolescents may be attempting to balance gender roles and experience more internal emotional distress and somatic symptoms. Applicable to other ethnic minority groups, Glover et al. noted the importance of examining the relationship between acculturation and anxiety.

Tran (1997) investigated the effects of ethnic identification and gender with respect to several social stress variables, including anxiety. Participants were Cuban American, Mexican American, and Puerto Rican American older adults. Results revealed that a high percentage of these three groups experienced anxiety. Results also revealed that individuals with lower SES, increased physical difficulties, and poorer health experienced more anxiety than their counterparts. With regard to gender, across the three groups, more women (46.2%) reported anxiety than men (33.8%). In examining within-group gender differences, Puerto Rican men experienced more anxiety than both Cuban and Mexican American men. In contrast, Puerto Rican women experienced less anxiety than both Cuban and Mexican American women. The results of Tran's study demonstrate the importance of examining both ethnicity and gender when researching psychological disorders with ethnic minority populations.

CULTURE-SPECIFIC DISORDERS

Ataques de Nervios. Ataques de nervios was reported in 1955, as observed in Puerto Rican army recruits. Since then, *ataques de nervios* also has been documented in the general Puerto Rican adult population, among Caribbean Hispanics, and also in areas of Latin America (Guarnaccia, 1997). *Ataques* is viewed as a normative stress-related reaction that commonly occurs at funerals, accidents, and familial conflicts. Symptoms of this disorder include crying, shaking, palpitations, numbness, shouting, swearing, striking others, and falling to the ground with convulsive body movements (Al-Issa & Oudji, 1998; Salman et al., 1997). Guarnaccia, Rivera, Franco, and Neighbors (1996) have also highlighted the role of strong anger, loss of impulse control, and dissociative features as significant features of the phenomenology of *ataques.*

Salman et al. (1997) referred to this syndrome as a folk label used to describe a loss of emotional control. In their clinical sample, the authors discovered that some of these *ataques* were diagnosable anxiety and affective disorders. They also noted subtypes of *ataques,* each possessing a specific symptom pattern and correlating with a psychological disorder. Thus, Salman et al. reported that *ataques* may be helpful clinical markers for identifying psychological disorders.

Nervios. The Hispanic population has referred to *nervios* as a level of distress related to physical symptoms, emotional conditions, and familial changes. As compared to *ataques, nervios* are more chronic, low grade, and transient (Salman et al., 1997). Symptoms include headache, insomnia, lack of appetite, trembling, and disorientation (Al-Issa & Oudji, 1998). Recent studies have revealed that left untreated, *nervios* may develop into diagnosable psychological disorders.

TREATMENT ISSUES

Part VI of this book focuses on clinical interventions in depth. However, some treatment issues are discussed here as they relate specifically to anxiety symptoms. As discussed earlier, Kleinman et al.'s (1978) construct of EMI will likely influence treatment. Thus, as few ethnic minority individuals are likely to seek out traditional mental health services when experiencing anxiety problems, the possibility that they will seek informal or medical sources of help are fairly high (Cheung, 1991; Dinges & Cherry, 1995).

Psychopharmacology

In the medical field, ethnic differences with regard to psychopharmacology have been noted, yet concern still exists as to whether those who prescribe medications take culture and ethnicity into consideration in prescribing medications, both type and dosage (Lawson, 1996, 1999; Sramek, 1996). Although ethnic differences in response to psychotropic medications have been documented and discussed in the psychopharmacology literature (Lin, 1986, 1995; Ramirez, 1996), little information on the use of psychiatric medications among ethnic minorities is available in the multicultural mental health literature. What little research exists demonstrates the need for caution in the use of medications among ethnic minority populations (Al-Issa & Oudji, 1998). For example, some studies have revealed that African Americans are more sensitive to several psychotropic drugs than Caucasians. African Americans have also been found to have a quicker reaction to tricyclic antidepressants than Caucasians. Finally, Asian Americans are generally prescribed smaller dosages (one half to two thirds less) of benzodi-azapines as compared to Caucasians. More information on the use of psychotropic medications for anxiety among ethnic minorities must be provided in the mental health literature.

Incorporation of Spirituality, Religion, and Healing Practices

As stated in this chapter and throughout this book, for many ethnic minorities, seeking help from professional mental health professionals is not the first-line approach when experiencing psychological distress. Many ethnic minority individuals have strong spiritual or religious beliefs and may turn to their spiritual and religious leaders when seeking help. For example, Bigfoot and Braden (1998) noted that American Indians may conduct ceremonies and rituals for healing, and prayers may be offered to assist families. In general, American Indians maintain their cultural traditions (e.g., respect for elderly, role of extended family, traditional gatherings), and thus the mental health professional must be made aware to provide culturally appropriate assessment and treatment of this population. This specific example demonstrates the need to consider ethnic minority individuals' social support networks and the context of their lives in the development of culturally appropriate treatment plans. Readers are encouraged to consult Koss-Chioino (1995), who provides an excellent review of traditional and folk approaches to psychological distress and suggestions on incorporating such practices into traditional psychotherapy.

FUTURE DIRECTIONS

This chapter has provided a brief summary of the existing research on anxiety disorders among ethnic minority populations. Clearly, more research is needed to help mental professionals fully understand the experiences of ethnic minority individuals in psychological distress. More epidemiological data on anxiety disorders (and other mental disorders, in general) are needed on all ethnic minority groups. Health care providers and mental health professionals must also begin to consider the applicability of the culture-specific disorders contained in this chapter for immigrant individuals. As has been noted, some of these disorders have already been documented in the United States, and thus it is quite possible that the other disorders likely exist as well; but because health care providers lack knowledge about them, they are left unidentified and untreated, resulting in unnecessary psychological distress. In conducting this research, further data are needed on the effects of factors specific to ethnic minorities such as racism and discrimination, accessibility to services, language barriers, and culture-specific conceptualizations of anxiety. Finally, in the research on anxiety among ethnic minorities, within-group differences such as ethnic identity, acculturation, generational status, and sex and gender roles must be examined to further assist us in understanding the complex issues faced by ethnic minority people.

CONCLUDING COMMENTS

Anxiety disorders are thought to be some of the most common psychological disorders among the general population of the United States. However, given the lack of epidemiological and empirical data on ethnic minority people in the United States, the extent of anxiety disorders among ethnic minorities is unclear. It is hoped that this brief summary of the mental health literature, demonstration of the lack of research on anxiety disorders among ethnic minorities, and presentation of the unique cultural issues among ethnic minority populations will serve as a wake-up call to researchers. Much more research is needed to provide culturally appropriate and effective services to this increasing and very diverse population.

REFERENCES

Al-Issa, I., & Oudji, S. (1998). Culture and anxiety disorders. In S. S. Kazarian & D. R. Evans (Eds.), *Cultural clinical psychology* (pp. 127-151). New York: Oxford University Press.

American Psychiatric Association. (1994). *Diagnostic and statistical manual of mental disorders* (4th ed.). Washington, DC: Author.

Bell, C. C., Hildreth, C. J., Jenkins, E. J., & Carter, C. (1988). The relationship of isolated sleep paralysis and panic disorder to hypertension. *Journal of the National Medical Association, 80,* 289-294.

Bhatia, M. S., & Malik, S. C. (1991). *Dhat* syndrome: A useful diagnostic entity in Indian culture. *British Journal of Psychiatry, 159,* 691-695.

Bigfoot, D. S., & Braden, J. (1998). *Upon the back of a turtle: A cross-cultural curriculum of federal criminal justice personnel* [Training manual]. Oklahoma City: Center on Child Abuse and Neglect (CCAN), University of Oklahoma Health Sciences Center.

Bigfoot-Sipes, D. S., Dauphinais, P., LaFromboise, T. D., & Bennett, S. K. (1992). American Indian secondary school students' preference for counselors. *Journal of Multicultural Counseling & Development, 20*(3), 113-122.

Brown, D. R., Eaton, W. W., & Sussman, L. (1990). Racial differences in prevalence of phobic disorders. *Journal of Nervous and Mental Disease, 178,* 434-441.

Butcher, J. N., Nezami, E., & Exner, J. (1998). Psychological assessment of people in diverse cultures. In S. S. Kazarian & D. R. Evans (Eds.), *Cultural clinical psychology* (pp. 61-105). New York: Oxford University Press.

Casas, J. M., & Pytluk, S. D. (1995). Hispanic identity development: Implications for research and practice. In J. Ponterotto, J. M. Casas, L. Suzuki, & C. Alexander (Eds.), *Handbook of multicultural counseling* (pp. 155-180). Thousand Oaks, CA: Sage.

Chan, M. A. (1990). Development and evaluation of a Chinese translation of the State-Trait Anxiety Inventory and the Beck Depression Inventory (Doctoral dissertation, Fuller Theological Seminary School of Psychology, 1991). *Dissertation Abstracts International, 51*(11), 5631.

Choney, S. K., Berryhill-Paapke, E., & Robbins, R. R. (1995). The acculturation of American Indians: Developing frameworks for research and practice. In J. Ponterotto, J. M. Casas, L. Suzuki, & C. Alexander (Eds.), *Handbook of multicultural counseling* (pp. 73-92). Thousand Oaks, CA: Sage.

Christensen, M. L. (1999). *The role of ethnic identity and family support in the psychological well-being of American Indian elders: A comparison of men and women in reservation and urban settings.* Unpublished doctoral dissertation, Loyola University, Chicago.

Cross, W. E. (1995). The psychology of Nigrescence: Revising the Cross model. In J. Ponterotto, J. M. Casas, L. Suzuki, & C. Alexander (Eds.), *Handbook of multicultural counseling* (pp. 93-122). Thousand Oaks, CA: Sage.

Dana, R. H. (1993). *Multicultural assessment perspectives for professional psychology.* Boston: Allyn & Bacon.

Dinges, N. G., & Cherry, D. (1995). Symptom expression and the use of mental health services among American ethnic minorities. In J. F. Apote, R. Y. Rivers, & J. Wohl (Eds.), *Psychological interventions and cultural diversity* (pp. 40-56). Boston: Allyn & Bacon.

Glover, S. H., Pumariega, A. J., Holzer, C. E., Wise, B. K., & Rodriguez, M. (1999). Anxiety symptomatology in Mexican-American adolescents. *Journal of Child and Family Studies, 8*(1), 47-57.

Good, B. J., & Kleinman, A. M. (1985). Culture and anxiety: Cross-cultural evidence for the patterning of anxiety disorders. In A. H. Tuma & J. Maser (Eds.), *Anxiety and the anxiety disorders* (pp. 297-324). Hillsdale, NJ: Lawrence Erlbaum.

Gopaul-McNichol, S., & Brice-Baker, J. (1997). Caribbean Americans. In S. Friedman (Ed.), *Cultural issues in the treatment of anxiety* (pp. 81-98). New York: Guilford.

Guarnaccia, P. J. (1997). A cross-cultural perspective on anxiety disorders. In S. Friedman (Ed.), *Cultural issues in the treatment of anxiety* (pp. 3-20). New York: Guilford.

Guarnaccia, P. J., Rivera, M., Franco, F., & Neighbors, C. (1996). The experiences of ataques de nervios: Towards an anthropology of emotions in Puerto Rico. *Cultural, Medicine, and Psychiatry, 20,* 343-367.

Heurtin-Roberts, S., Snowden, L., & Miller, L. (1997). Expressions of anxiety in African Americans: Ethnography and epidemiological catchment area studies. *Culture, Medicine, and Psychiatry, 21,* 337-363.

Iwamasa, G. Y. (1997). Asian Americans. In S. Friedman (Ed.), *Cultural issues in the treatment of anxiety* (pp. 99-129). New York: Guilford.

Iwamasa, G. Y., & Hilliard, K. M. (1999). Depression and anxiety among Asian American elders: A review of the literature. *Clinical Psychology Review, 19,* 343-357.

Iwamasa, G. Y., Hilliard, K. M., & Osato, S. S. (1998). Conceptualizing anxiety and depression: The Japanese American older adult perspective. *Clinical Gerontologist, 19,* 77-93.

Iwamasa, G. Y., Pai, S. M., Hilliard, K. M., & Lin, S. (1998). Acculturation of Japanese Americans: Use of the SL-ASIA with a community sample. *Asian American and Pacific Islander Journal of Health, 6,* 25-34.

John, R. (1998). Native American families. In C. H. Mindel, R. W. Habenstein, & R. Wright (Eds.), *Ethnic families in America: Patterns and variations* (pp. 361-381). Upper Saddle River, NJ: Prentice Hall.

Karno, M., Golding, J. M., Burnham, M. A., Hough, R. L., Escobar, J. I., Wells, K. M., & Boyer, R. (1989). Anxiety disorders among Mexican Americans and non-Hispanic Whites in Los Angeles. *Journal of Nervous and Mental Disease, 177,* 202-209.

Kerwin, C., & Ponterotto, J. G. (1995). Biracial identity development: Theory and research. In J. Ponterotto, J. M. Casas, L. Suzuki, & C. Alexander (Eds.), *Handbook of multicultural counseling* (pp. 1199-1217). Thousand Oaks, CA: Sage.

Kirmayer, L. J. (1991). The place of culture in psychiatric nosology: *Taijin Kyofusho* and *DSM-III-R. Journal of Nervous and Mental Disease, 179,* 19-28.

Kleinknecht, R. A., Dinnel, D. L., Tanouye-Wilson, S., & Lonner, W. J. (1994). Cultural variation in social anxiety and phobia: A study of *Taijin Kyofusho. The Behavior Therapist, 17,* 175-178.

Kleinman, A., Eisenberg, L., & Good, B. (1978). Culture, illness, and care: Clinical lessons from anthropologic and cross-cultural research. *Annals of Internal Medicine, 88,* 251-258.

Koss-Chioino, J. (1995). Traditional and folk approaches among ethnic minorities. In J. F. Apote, R. Y. Rivers, & J. Wohl (Eds.), *Psychological interventions and cultural diversity* (pp. 145-163). Boston: Allyn & Bacon.

LaFromboise, T. (1988). American Indian mental health policy. *American Psychologist, 43*(5), 388-397.

LaFromboise, T., Coleman, H. K., & Gerton, J. (1993). Psychological impact of biculturalism: Evidence and theory. *Psychological Bulletin, 114,* 395-412.

LaFromboise, T., Heyle, A. M., & Ozer, E. J. (1999). Changing and diverse roles of women in American Indian cultures. In L. A. Peplau, S. C. Debro, R. C. Veniegas, & P. L. Taylor (Eds.), *Gender, culture, and ethnicity: Current research about women and men* (pp. 48-61). Mountain View, CA: Mayfield.

LaFromboise, T., Trimble, J. E., & Mohatt, G. V. (1990). Counseling intervention and American Indian treatment. *The Counseling Psychologist, 18*(4), 628-654.

Lawson, W. B. (1996). The art and science of psychopharmacotherapy of African Americans. *Mt. Sinai Journal of Medicine, 63,* 301-305.

Lawson, W. B. (1999). The art and science of ethnopharmacotherapy. In J. H. Herrera, W. B. Lawson, & J. J. Sramek (Eds.), *Cross-cultural psychiatry* (pp. 67-73). New York: John Wiley.

Lin, K. M. (1983). *Hwa-byung*: A Korean culture-bound syndrome? *American Journal of Psychiatry, 140,* 105-107.

Lin, K. M. (1986). Ethnicity and psychopharmacology. *Cultural Medical Psychiatry, 10,* 151-165.

Lin, K. M. (1995). Ethnicity and psychopharmacology: Bridging the gap. *Psychiatric Clinics of North America, 18,* 635-647.

Lin, K. M., Lau, J. K., Yamamoto, J., Zheng, Y. P., Kim, H. S., Cho, K. H., & Nakasaki, G. (1992). Hwa-byung: A community study of Korean Americans. *Journal of Nervous and Mental Disease, 180,* 386-391.

Lin, N., Ensel, W. M., Simeone, R. S., & Kuo, W. (1979). Social support, stressful life events, and illness: A model and empirical test. *Journal of Health and Social Behavior, 20,* 108-119.

Marsella, A. J., Johnson, F. A., Johnson, C. L., & Brennan, J. (1998). Ethnic identity in second-(Nisei), third-(Sansei), and fourth-(Yonsei) generation Japanese-Americans in Hawai'i. *Asian American and Pacific Islander Journal of Health, 6,* 46-52.

McDonald, J. D. (2000). A model for conducting research with American Indian participants. In Council of National Psychological Associations for the Advancement of Ethnic Minority Interests (Ed.), *Guidelines for research in ethnic minority communities* (pp. 12-15). Washington, DC: Council of National Psychological Associations for the Advancement of Ethnic Minority Interests (CNPAAEMI).

McNeil, D. W., Kee, M., & Zvolensky, M. J. (1998). Culturally related anxiety and ethnic identity in Navajo college students. *Cultural Diversity and Ethnic Minority Psychology, 5*(1), 56-64.

McNeil, D. W., Porter, C. A., Zvolensky, M. J., Chaney, J. M., & Kee, M. (2000). Assessment of culturally related anxiety in American Indians and Alaska Natives. *Behavior Therapy, 31,* 301-325.

Myers, L. J., Abdullah, S., & Leary, G. (2000). Conducting research with persons of African descent. In Council of National Psychological Associations for the Advancement of Ethnic Minority Interests (Ed.), *Guidelines for research in ethnic minority communities* (pp. 5-8). Washington, DC: Council of National Psychological Associations for the Advancement of Ethnic Minority Interests (CNPAAEMI).

Nagata, D. K. (1991). Transgenerational impact of the Japanese-American internment: Clinical issues in working with children of former internees. *Psychotherapy, 28,* 121-128.

Neal, A. M., Nagle-Rich, L., & Smucker, W. D. (1994). The presence of panic disorder among African American hypertensives: A pilot study. *Journal of Black Psychology, 20,* 29-35.

Neal, A. M., & Turner, S. M. (1991). Anxiety disorders research with African Americans: Current status. *Psychological Bulletin, 109,* 400-410.

Neal-Barnett, A. M., & Smith, J. (1997). African Americans. In S. Friedman (Ed.), *Cultural issues in the treatment of anxiety* (pp. 154-174). New York: Guilford.

Norton, I. M., & Manson, S. M. (1996). Research in American Indian and Alaska Native communities: Navigating the culture universe of values and process. *Journal of Consulting & Clinical Psychology, 64*(5), 856-860.

Prince, R. (1985). The concept of culture-bound syndromes: Anorexia nervosa and brain-fag. *Social Science & Medicine, 21,* 197-203.

Rafael, B., Swan, P., & Martinek, N. (1998). Intergenerational aspects of trauma for Australian Aboriginal people. In Y. Danieli (Ed.), *International handbook of multigenerational legacies of trauma* (pp. 327-339). New York: Plenum.

Ramirez, L. F. (1996). Ethnicity and psychopharmacology in Latin America. *Mt. Sinai Journal of Medicine, 63,* 330-331.

Reiger, D. A., Myers, J. K., Kramer, M., Robins, L. N., Blazer, D. G., Hough, R. L., Eaton, W. W., & Locke, B. Z. (1984). The NIMH Epidemiologic Catchment Area program. *Archives of General Psychiatry, 41,* 934-941.

Root, M. P. P. (1992). *Racially mixed people in America.* Newbury Park, CA: Sage.

Root, M. P. P. (1998). Multiracial Americans: Changing the face of Asian America. In L. C. Lee & N. W. S. Zane (Eds.), *Handbook of Asian American psychology* (pp. 261-287). Thousand Oaks, CA: Sage.

Root, M. P. P. (1999). The biracial baby boom: Understanding ecological constructions of racial identity in the 21st century. In R. H. Sheets & E. R. Hollins (Eds.), *Racial and ethnic identity in school practices: Aspects of human development* (pp. 67-89). Mahwah, NJ: Lawrence Erlbaum.

Salman, E., Diamond, K., Jusino, C., Sanchez-LaCay, A., & Liebowitz, M. R. (1997). Hispanic Americans. In S. Friedman (Ed.), *Cultural issues in the treatment of anxiety* (pp. 59-80). New York: Guilford.

Shek, D. T. (1993). The Chinese version of the State-Trait Anxiety Inventory: Its relationship to different measures of psychological well-being. *Journal of Clinical Psychology, 49*(3), 349-358.

Snowden, L. R. (1999). African American folk idiom and mental health services use. *Cultural Diversity and Ethnic Minority Psychology, 5*(4), 364-370.

Sodowsky, G. R., Kwan, K., & Pannu, R. (1995). Ethnic identity of Asians in the United States. In J. Ponterotto, J. M. Casas, L. Suzuki, & C. Alexander (Eds.), *Handbook of multicultural counseling* (pp. 123-154). Thousand Oaks, CA: Sage.

Solomon, Z. (1998). Transgenerational effects of the Holocaust: The Israeli research perspective. In Y. Danieli (Ed.), *International handbook of multigenerational legacies of trauma* (pp. 69-83). New York: Plenum.

Sorscher, N., & Cohen, L. J. (1997). Trauma in children of Holocaust survivors: Transgenerational effects. *American Journal of Orthopsychiatry, 67,* 493-499.

Spielberger, C. D. (1976). The nature and measurement of anxiety. In C. D. Spielberger & R. Diaz-Guererro (Eds.), *Cross-cultural anxiety* (Vol. 1, pp. 1-11). Washington, DC: Hemisphere.

Spielberger, C. D. (1989). *State-Trait Anxiety Inventory: A comprehensive bibliography.* Palo Alto, CA: Consulting Psychologists Press.

Sramek, J. J. (1996). Ethnicity and antidepressant response. *Mt. Sinai Journal of Medicine, 63,* 320-325.

Sue, D. W., Bingham, R. P., Porche-Burke, L., & Vasquez, M. (1999). The diversification of psychology: A multicultural revolution. *American Psychologist, 54,* 1061-1069.

Suinn, R. M., Rickard-Figueroa, K., Lew, S., & Vigil, P. (1987). The Suinn-Lew Asian Self-Identity Acculturation Scale: An initial report. *Educational and Psychological Measurement, 47,* 401-407.

Tran, T. V. (1997). Ethnicity, gender, and social stress among three groups of elderly Hispanics. *Journal of Cross-Cultural Gerontology, 12,* 341-356.

Tseng, W., Asai, M., Kitanishi, K., McLaughlin, D. G., & Kyomen, H. (1992). Diagnostic patterns of social phobia: Comparison in Tokyo and Hawaii. *Journal of Nervous and Mental Disease, 80,* 380-385.

U.S. Bureau of the Census. (2000). *Resident population estimates of the United States by sex, race, and Hispanic origin: April 1, 1990 to November 1, 1999.* Retrieved from www.census.gov/population/esimates/nation/intfile3-1.txt

Viswanathan, R., Shah, M. R., & Ahad, A. (1997). Asian-Indian Americans. In S. Friedman (Ed.), *Cultural issues in the treatment of anxiety* (pp. 175-195). New York: Guilford.

White, J. L., & Parham, T. A. (1990). *The psychology of Blacks: An African-American perspective.* Englewood Cliffs, NJ: Prentice Hall.

Yamada, A., Marsella, A. J., & Yamada, S. Y. (1998). The development of the ethno-cultural identity behavioral index: Psychometric properties and validation with Asian Americans and Pacific Islanders. *Asian American and Pacific Islander Journal of Health, 6,* 35-44.

Yamamoto, J., Machizawa, S., Araki, F., Reece, S., Steinberg, A., Leung, J., & Cater, R. (1985). Mental health of elderly Asian Americans in Los Angeles. *American Journal of Social Psychiatry, 1,* 37-46.

CHAPTER 21

Drug Abuse

Etiology and Cultural Considerations

FRED BEAUVAIS
EUGENE OETTING
Colorado State University

The use and abuse of psychoactive chemicals has been one of the more weighty social issues of the past half century. Drug use has permeated many segments of society and, in addition to inherent deleterious effects, has become intertwined with a large number of other social problems, including street gangs, organized crime, the spread of AIDS, school dropout, and violence. Drug abuse clearly affects all segments of society, and ethnic minority populations have not escaped involvement with drugs and the consequences of drug use.

Drug use is circumscribed by a variety of cultural, social, economic, and other demographic factors, which must be taken into account for a full understanding of the complexity of the problem. For instance, some use of crack cocaine occurs throughout the United States, but heavy use of crack cocaine, addiction to crack cocaine, and the violence and promiscuous sex associated with its use occur predominantly in inner cities and among ethnic minorities, particularly African Americans. The social isolation, prejudice, and the socioeconomic conditions in the ghetto and barrio environments where crack cocaine is most heavily used undoubtedly play a large part in that pattern of use. By contrast, the most recent surge in "club drugs," such as ecstasy and ketamine, and their use at raves is occurring primarily among White American middle-class and suburban youth and reflects the changing lifestyles and values of those more affluent youth.

In each of these examples, ethnicity is a component in the use of the drug, but ethnicity is only one element in the overall social, economic, and cultural environment that is actually determining drug use. This complex pattern is typical of the kinds of links we expect to find between ethnicity and drug use. Ethnicity and ethnic identification are related to drug use, but the relationships are not simple;

they are complex interactions that involve the entire social/cultural environment.

The purpose of this chapter is to examine some of the more global issues that are currently of interest in the cross-cultural study of substance abuse. Space certainly limits the level of detail that can be presented, but it is hoped that what is covered will provide some insight into the major topics of concern. A description of the differential rates of drug use by ethnic groups will set the stage for a discussion of etiological factors. Subsequent sections will focus on the current, high level of interest in the role of acculturation and cultural identification in substance use. The final sections will provide some guidance on developing culturally sensitive interventions, with a special emphasis on spirituality and the need to intimately involve ethnic communities in the development of interventions.

ETHNICITY AND DRUG USE

Rates of Drug Use in Ethnic Minority Populations

Although public stereotypes about ethnicity and drug use have not actually been studied, it is likely that those stereotypes include the belief that ethnic minorities use drugs more than non-minorities. Actually, general population studies, using broadly defined ethnic glosses, reveal that with the exception of American Indians, drug use among U.S. ethnic minority adolescents is equal to or lower than that of nonminority youth (see, e.g., Johnston, O'Malley, & Bachman, 2000; U.S. Department of Health and Human Services [DHHS], 2000).

The lowest drug use rates are found among Asian Americans, followed by African Americans and Hispanics, with higher rates among White American youth. American Indians are the only broadly defined ethnic group that consistently shows higher rates of drug use than White American youth; Beauvais and coworkers (Beauvais, 1992, 1996;

Beauvais & LaBoueff, 1985; Beauvais, Oetting, & Edwards, 1985) have tracked drug use of American Indian youth who live on reservations for the past 25 years. Consistently, over that time, rates of drug use have been much higher than those of other American youth. A number of surveys have found that youth of mixed ethnic origin have the highest rates of drug use of all adolescents (DHHS, 2000).

Among young people, gender differences in drug use are small for most ethnic groups; adolescent males and females are likely to use drugs at about the same rates. The exception has been Hispanic youth, where males typically have had higher rates of use than females. In a very recent study, however, Swaim (personal communication, October 15, 2000) has found that those gender differences may be disappearing among Mexican American youth.

Differences in drug use rates among minority populations seem to hold up across the life span with one exception. During adolescence, African Americans have lower drug use rates than the national average. However, there is a crossover as African Americans move into young adulthood and beyond; drug use among African Americans appears to increase until it is higher than that found for other ethnic groups (Biafora & Zimmerman, 1998; DHHS, 2000). There are no data-based explanations for this postadolescent increase in proportional use among African Americans. There is some speculation that the lower rates of drug use among African American youth occur because African American families exert more effective control over the behavior of their children (Griesler & Kandel, 1998; Peterson, Hawkins, Abbot, & Catalano, 1994). It is possible that as African Americans move into adulthood, some of them lose that extra family-based protection. It is also possible that African American youth suffer greater social and economic problems as they move from adolescence into young adulthood than other youth. If these young adults are subject to particularly high economic stress and discrimination and if, because of financial and social limitations, they are still living in disadvantaged neighborhoods where there is high exposure to peers who are using drugs, it may explain the higher relative levels of drug use (Biafora & Zimmerman, 1998). It would be useful to have a better understanding of what the early protective factors are among African Americans and how they operate and how those factors change with the move to young adult status. It would be valuable to both enhance these protective influences among other youth and to reduce whatever risk factors are appearing among older African American youth.

As might be suspected, ethnicity and socioeconomic status are often confounded. The issue has been characterized as follows:

> Drug problems of minorities in disadvantaged environments probably do not generalize to minority youth in other environments. In ghettos, barrios or Indian reservations, prejudice is compounded by social isolation, poverty, unemployment, deviant role models and sometimes by gang influence. The result includes heavy drug involvement, but these pockets of high minority drug use probably are not well represented in general population surveys and are not typical of other American minority youth. (Oetting & Beauvais, 1990, p. 391)

American Indian youth offer a good example of how rates of drug use can vary under differing socioeconomic conditions. Beauvais (1992) reported that the rates of use for Indian adolescents who live on reservations, where economic stress can be severe, are quite a bit higher than for Indian youth living in non-reservation environments. Indian youth, living on reservations, experience the same social isolation, prejudice, poverty, and lack of opportunity found in the ghettos and barrios of America's inner cities and share the same high levels of drug use. Indian youth living off reservations also have high rates of drug use, but not as high as those found among reservation youth. This is not surprising because many of those nonreservation Indian youth actually live, part of the time, on reservations, and many other Indian youth suffer from the same kinds of social and economic problems as their reservation counterparts. The failure to partial out socioeconomic effects leaves the impression that high rates of substance abuse are a function of minority status rather than of economic and social disadvantage.

Consequences of Drug Use

Even though many ethnic minority groups have lower rates of drug use, it has been consistently found that ethnic minority populations endure much more severe consequences from their use (Rebach, 1992). These findings suggest that drug consequences are not produced merely by the use of drugs but are produced by a combination of drug use and psychosocial conditions. For instance, the generally lower socioeconomic status of ethnic minorities may make the consequences of drug use worse for minorities. Other social and psychological factors may also interact with drug use to produce more severe consequences. Resources for treatment of drug-produced health problems are likely to be more difficult to obtain in impoverished ethnic minority neighborhoods, and there may, in addition, be cultural barriers that make treatment for substance use and its medical consequences less available.

There are definitely more legal consequences for drug use among minority populations (Rebach, 1992). A major factor that has produced more severe legal consequences for minorities is the difference in penalties for possessing crack cocaine and for possessing powder cocaine. Although both are cocaine, the legal penalties for possession of crack are often far more severe than those for powder cocaine, and African Americans are more likely to use crack, whereas White Americans are more likely to use powder cocaine. Another factor has been police profiling. Police in many areas have stopped and searched the cars of ethnic minorities far more often than those of nonminorities, leading to more arrests of minorities. There is also speculation that there may be differential application of statutes by ethnic status; for the same evidence of a crime, minorities are more likely to be arrested and, once arrested, are likely to be charged with a more serious offense (Wallace, Bachman, O'Malley, & Johnston, 1995).

Ethnic Glosses and Drug Use

A major limitation of most studies of ethnic minority substance abuse is the use of broad glosses to define ethnic minorities, terms such as *Hispanic, African American,* or *Asian* (Trimble, 1990-1991). The use of these broad classifications provides some useful information about general trends in minority drug use but has obscured important differences among subgroups of ethnic populations. For instance, reporting the drug use of Hispanics or Latinos covers up very large cultural differences. Those broad ethnic glosses include major subgroups that have very different levels and styles of drug involvement. Cuban Americans, Puerto Rican Americans, Mexican Americans, and Americans with roots in South and Central America have different cultural, socioeconomic, and political backgrounds and are located in different geographic areas of the country. For example, Cuban Americans live primarily in the Southeast, with their highest density in Florida. They tend to be urban dwellers. They are, on average, better off socioeconomically and have different medical/cultural beliefs than Mexican Americans. Mexican Americans live primarily in the Southwest. Many live in rural communities, and their average income level is much below that of Cuban Americans. Even within these groups, there will be major economic and social differences that produce different types of drug use. The Mexican Americans living in large city barrios will certainly grow up with a different cultural experience and different types of drug involvement than those living in rural migrant worker communities.

Similarly, because it negates a stereotype, it is useful to know that, overall, African American adolescents have somewhat lower rates of drug use, but it does not tell us much about the actual drug use of very different African American populations. The cultural surround and the drug use of African Americans in an inner city, for instance, are vastly different from that of rural African Americans in small southern towns.

Another example involves the general perception that Asians have one of the lowest levels of drug use in the United States. There are many different Asian groups, with different languages, different socioeconomic levels, and different cultural beliefs. Although the data on many Asian subpopulations are sparse, there is evidence of extremely variable rates of use, with some Asian groups showing very high rates of use (Nagasawa, Qian, & Wong, 1999).

It should be clear that the proper interpretation of comparative drug use rates must include a thorough knowledge of the populations that are being studied. This is often not the case, and the resulting publications can lead to inappropriate generalizations. It is incumbent on researchers to make clear the nature and limitations of the groups that are being described. For example, a sample description might state, "The study population consisted of largely Mexican American youth living in a small, rural, southwestern community where the majority population was Mexican American." Further descriptors should then include the predominant immigration history, socioeconomic conditions, and educational and employment opportunity. Without this type of detailed information, it is easy to form stereotypes about meaningless aggregations of minority populations.

CAUSATIVE FACTORS IN ETHNIC MINORITY DRUG USE

Drug use behavior emerges during adolescence and, in some instances, even earlier. Kandel (1999) found that it is rare for an individual to begin use of drugs after the age of 19 or 20. To understand the origins of drug abuse, then, we must examine the many factors that come together during this formative time. The main question is the degree to which the differing cultural backgrounds of some ethnic minorities may influence their decision to begin using drugs, thus setting them apart from the general population. If the basic causes of drug use are similar across cultures, the underlying principles for prevention and treatment may be generalizable across cultures. If the causes differ greatly for particular cultures, then preventive interventions would have to be focused specifically on the causes that are related to drug use within those individual cultures.

Genetics and Ethnicity

Some myths about the causes of ethnic minority drug use should be discarded. For example, discussion of drug and alcohol use among ethnic minorities often brings up the issue of genetic influences. There has been an assumption, for instance, that American Indians have a genetic predisposition to alcoholism. Despite a substantial amount of genetic research, no such link for a population-based characteristic has been found for American Indians (Long & Lorenz, 2000).

There are genetic differences in response to alcohol and drugs and in the potential for becoming addicted to drugs. These do run in families. But these genetic influences are factors that produce familial transmission in all ethnic groups. For example, the rate of familial transmission of alcoholism among American Indians resembles that found in the general population. High rates of alcoholism among some American Indian groups cannot be blamed on a genetic propensity. Without direct evidence demonstrating clear genetic differences between ethnic groups, it is best to assume that there is as much genetic variation within minority populations as there is between minority and non-minority populations. Genetic differences do not explain drug use among ethnic minorities.

Cultural/Ceremonial Use of Drugs

Another myth that should be eliminated is the idea that drug use among ethnic minority adolescents is related to what are perceived as exotic, unusual, or distinctive elements in ethnic minority cultures. For example, American Indian alcohol abuse and other types of intoxication have been postulated by some as being a substitute for the American Indian vision quest, a cultural practice among some tribes (Mail & McDonald, 1980). Similarly, the use of peyote in religious ceremonies by some Indian people has been invoked to account for the high use of mind-altering drugs by Indian adolescents. Another simplistic explanation for drug use behavior among Mexican American males is that boisterous and aggressive use of drugs and alcohol is just another expression of culturally accepted "machismo" or stereotyped dominating male behavior.

The popular appeal of these types of cultural explanations is that they provide simple answers to a difficult and complex problem. A deeper analysis shows that they just do not work. One limitation is that they involve inappropriate generalizations across the minority ethnic group. For instance, vision quests occur among some Indian tribes and not among others, but the rates of adolescent drug use are similar across all reservation tribes (Beauvais, 1992). A more serious limitation is that these explanations stereotype and distort the meaning and cultural significance of the traditional behavior. For example, the highly ritualized and controlled use of peyote by members of the Native American church bears no resemblance to out-of-control group drinking or to

Indian adolescent use of drugs for recreational purposes. Likewise, instead of being a primary source of alcohol abuse, machismo is a very complex cultural expectation for male behavior that includes a great deal of family responsibility and respect for women, factors that strongly mitigate against certain forms of drunken behavior (Gilbert, 1989).

Secular and Temporal Causes of Drug Use

So what are the actual forces that determine drug use among ethnic minority youth? Do they differ from those for other American youth? If so, the trends over time in drug use for minority and nonminority youth might differ as well. Johnston et al. (2000) have been following the trends in drug use rates among American adolescents since 1974 and have found a quite orderly pattern. Drug use rose through the early 1980s and then began a 10-year decline. In 1992, use began to rise again, with indications that it may be leveling off again beginning in 1997. Importantly, although the levels of use among ethnic minorities may differ from that of youth in general, their pattern of increases and decreases in rates of use over time parallels that for other American youth. Johnston et al. found that the changes in drug use rates over time for Hispanic and Black students followed essentially the same trends as that for nonminority youth, whereas Beauvais (1996) found that trends across time for American Indian students paralleled those for other American youth. In essence, a general American "adolescent drug culture" appears to be driving the drug use behavior of all American youth, including ethnic minorities.

Johnston (1990) described a number of societal forces that may impinge on the lives of young people and that could be influencing drug use changes over time. He speculated that these forces may include drug availability, attitudes toward the law, perception of drug harmfulness, and historical forces such as the aftermath of foreign wars. The parallel trends in drug use of ethnic minority and nonminority youth argue that these temporal and secular forces influence drug use in essentially the same way for all American youth, ethnic minorities and nonminorities. Prevention programs that target these factors are, therefore, likely to be useful for both minority and nonminority youth.

Ethnicity and Individual Risk and Protective Factors

Those general societal forces alter trends in drug use over time, but at any one point in time, within any ethnic group, some young people get involved with drugs and others do not. There are personal and social characteristics that are risk and protective factors for drug use and that determine whether a youth will use drugs. Conceptually, it is important to recognize that risk factors are not simply the absence of protective factors; that is, they are not the opposite ends of a continuum. For instance, although poverty may be a risk factor for some youth, the lack of poverty is not necessarily a protective factor. In fact, youth with more available income are slightly more likely to use drugs. Likewise, high levels of chronic anger may predispose a youth to drug use, but the lack of an angry disposition may not be predictive of nonuse.

Do ethnic minority youth have different personal and social risk factors for drug use than nonminority youth? Unfortunately, the literature does not provide a clear answer to that question. One problem in trying to answer this question is that risk factors do not operate alone and cannot be studied individually. A consistent research finding is that it is the total number of risk factors that predicts substance use. For instance, Newcomb, Maddahian, and Bentler (1986) found that adolescents with seven or more risk factors, regardless of the type of risk factor, were nine times more likely to be heavy users of hard drugs compared with their overall study sample. This general finding holds true for both minority and nonminority youth: Moncher, Holden, and Trimble (1990) found this same result for American Indian youth and Newcomb (1995) for Latino adolescents.

The need to study the multiple interactions of risk factors produces problems in comparing findings across studies of ethnic groups. Newcomb (1995) reviewed a number of studies looking at ethnic differences in risk factors for drug use and found highly variable and, in some instances, contradictory findings. He concluded that this was the result of using different study groups within ethnic populations (e.g., rural vs. urban Hispanics). But other problems in comparison are produced because measures of risk and protective factors differ greatly across studies. One study may use only one or two items to assess a particular risk factor, whereas another study uses several items or even several short scales to assess a latent variable. The relatively high correlations among risk factors can also produce analysis problems when examining multiple predictors. If the measures of peer influence, for example, are weak, they may not add significantly to the variance predicted by family influence because of the correlations between family and peer influence.

Overall, it is likely that ethnic minority and nonminority youth share the same major risk and protective factors for drug use, although they are probably weighted differently for different ethnic groups and, possibly, even for subgroups within ethnic groups that live under different sociodemographic conditions. Newcomb (1995) categorized risk factors under four headings: *culture and society* (e.g., economic deprivation), *interpersonal* (e.g., family conflict), *psychobehavioral* (e.g., academic failure), and *biogenetic* (e.g., inherited susceptibility). Additional factors include age and emotional problems. These four areas are likely to influence drug use in all ethnic groups.

If there is one protective factor that appears to stand out for ethnic minority populations,

it is the influence of the family. Although primary socialization theory proposes that the family is a strong risk and protective factor for all ethnic groups (Oetting & Donnermeyer, 1998), the family appears to have a somewhat greater influence on ethnic minority youth throughout the life span. Minority youth routinely express a greater closeness to the family and are more likely to turn to family in times of crisis. The existence of large, extended families in many minority populations increases the power of the family.

The drug use of both minority and nonminority adolescents is influenced by both peers and the family, but the relative strength of family influence may be greater for some ethnic minority youth. For instance, in developing a model for the relative impact of family and peers on the use of drugs, Swaim, Oetting, Jumper-Thurman, Beauvais, and Edwards (1993) found a somewhat attenuated path between peers and drug use for American Indians compared to White adolescents, whereas family assumed greater influence. The same proportionally greater family influence has been observed for other ethnic populations (Catalano et al., 1992; Vega, Gil, & Kolody, 1998). These findings have strong implications for the prevention of drug abuse. Capitalizing on the influence of the inherent strength of the family system could strengthen prevention programs for ethnic minority groups, especially those for adolescents. Such programs need to include elements that specifically incorporate the family into the prevention activities. Szapocznik et al. (1988) have had considerable success with treatment programs for drug-using Cuban American youth by using not only the family but the extended family as well.

For some ethnic minority youth, there are also differences in the relative effects of school success as a protective factor and of school failure as a risk factor. For example, it is likely that in every ethnic group, school dropouts have higher rates of drug use

(Chavez, Oetting, & Swaim, 1994), but *dropout* has a very different meaning in different ethnic groups. In a fairly typical southwestern urban area, for example, there were, proportionally, very few White American female dropouts, and those few dropouts were highly deviant. Among Mexican American females, a much larger proportion had dropped out of school, but the general level of deviance among these girls was much lower. Dropout had a very different cultural and social meaning for White American and Mexican American females in this community (Chavez et al., 1994). As another example, gang members are often school dropouts, but in a Southern California community, an Asian gang that is involved in drug use and other deviant behaviors prides itself on success in school (Austin, personal communication, July 1995).

In general, youth who do well in school are also socialized normatively in other aspects of their lives and are less likely to have deviant friends and engage in other deviant acts. However, for a variety of historical reasons, some groups of minority youth have less of an investment in the educational system. For them, school success is not as available as a protective factor, and if the school environment is hostile, the school may even become a risk factor.

Although the risk and protective factors for drug use are likely to be essentially the same for ethnic minorities and nonminorities, the relative weights of various factors may differ. Prevention and treatment for ethnic minorities can be improved by taking these differences into account.

CULTURAL IDENTIFICATION, ACCULTURATION, AND DRUG USE

A third area of difference for minority youth is the very fact that they are culturally different from the mainstream society. Ethnic minority youth typically have to reconcile those cultural differences. This is simply not an issue for non-minority youth. Acculturation and cultural identification have important implications for whether or not young people begin drug use, but this is a very complicated area. Depending on a host of other variables, being culturally different can be a risk factor or a protective factor, or it may have little bearing on drug use.

Acculturation Stress and Drug Use

Many writers have attributed drug use among minority youth to acculturation stress, the stress that is produced by trying to adapt to two cultures or trying to move toward the majority culture (for a review, see Rodriguez, 1995). This theory has not held up well, in part because many youth do not experience stress from the acculturation process, primarily because stress is not a primary factor in producing adolescent drug use. Adolescent drug use is a social behavior; it is not the result of self-medication for stress.

There is, however, some evidence that drug addiction is linked to the use of drugs to deal with emotions. Individuals do not start using drugs for emotional reasons; they start drug use for social reasons because they are engaged in a lifestyle that involves drug use and because their friends are using drugs (Oetting, Deffenbacher, & Donnermeyer, 1998). Most of these adolescent social users do not become addicted to drugs, but some move on to become addicts. As heavy drug users move toward drug addiction, they learn to use drugs under all kinds of circumstances, including using drugs to relieve stress. Although it has not been studied, it is possible that the experience of acculturation stress plays a role in this process and that, therefore, acculturation stress is related to the movement from drug use as a social behavior to drug addiction. The addict may learn to use drugs to reduce stress related to cultural adaptations as well as learning to use drugs to deal with other emotional hassles and crises.

Acculturation and Drug Use

Short of addiction, most drug use is a social behavior, and cultural values, attitudes, and beliefs influence social behaviors. There has been a fair amount of research on the effects of acculturation on substance use (i.e., a minority person accommodating to the larger culture). In general, it appears that drug and alcohol use will tend to move toward the levels found in the mainstream culture over time. The most complete studies of acculturation have probably been on the use of alcohol by Mexican females immigrating to the United States. Women emigrating from Mexico have much lower drug use rates than Mexican American or Anglo-American women (Gilbert, 1989). This protective effect, however, tends to weaken with successive generations in this country. The more that Mexican American females are identified with Anglo culture, the more alcohol they use (Caetano, 1988; Gilbert, Mora, & Ferguson, 1994; Trotter, 1985). Men who emigrate from Mexico show a slightly different pattern. The norm in Mexico is for infrequent heavy drinking, whereas the norm in the United States is characterized by more frequent drinking but in smaller quantities. Unfortunately, with increasing time in the United States, these patterns tend to combine into frequent heavy drinking.

Increasing drug and alcohol use with successive generational status in the United States has been found in other ethnic populations, but the explanations for this finding are elusive. On one hand, it would appear that simple modeling or social learning theory might account for an increase in use that would match that currently existing in the United States. But Blane (1977) found that Italian American immigrants developed a drinking style that included elements of their old culture and of the new culture. In general, as acculturation progresses, immigrants seem to follow any of a number of patterns. They can maintain the use patterns of their original culture. They can assimilate the drinking and drug use behaviors of the majority group. They can develop a new style that incorporates elements of both their traditional culture and the majority group. Trimble (1996) argued that generational status alone is not sufficient to account for cultural variables among immigrants. He stated that there is likely a wide range of levels of identification with one's traditional culture among immigrants that needs to be factored in.

Cultural Identification and Drug Use

One attempt at disentangling the many factors has been the search for a connection between cultural identification and drug use, particularly among adolescents. The hypothesis driving this search has been that adolescents who more closely identify with a traditional culture, with its proscription against drug use, will use fewer drugs. Alternately, it is postulated that the loss of culture is a major cause of drug use. A number of studies have attempted to find such a direct link but have been unable to do so, although there is evidence for indirect links (Beauvais, 1998). For instance, Whitbeck (personal communication, June 10, 2000) has found that American Indian youth with high Indian cultural identification feel that they are discriminated against more than those with lower levels of Indian cultural identification. High perceived discrimination, in turn, is correlated with higher levels of drug use. However, high Indian cultural identification is also related to better success in school, which leads to lower drug use. Perceived discrimination and school success are both related to Indian identification but have opposite effects on drug use that cancel each other out when a direct link is sought between drug use and cultural identification. Vega, Gil, and Wagner (1998) found that a high level of cultural identification was a protective factor against drug use for foreign-born Hispanics in Florida, but it was a risk factor for U.S.-born Hispanics. There are likely a host of other factors that also mediate the relationship between cultural identification and drug use in both positive and negative directions.

Oetting and Donnermeyer (1998) have proposed some theoretical reasons why a direct link between cultural identification and drug use is unlikely to be found. They proposed that adolescents are socialized mainly from three primary sources: family, peers, and school. Different social behaviors may be influenced differentially by these socialization sources. For example, the family may be the primary source of culture and of its transmission to children. A child may be strongly attached to family, and if that family adheres to its traditional background, this will be passed on to the child. Drug-using values, however, are not socialized through the family; they are socialized through peers. Cultural identification and drug use norms, therefore, derive from different primary socialization sources. It is possible then, to have a youth who is "traditional" and at the same time uses drugs. This combination would lead to the lack of a correlation between cultural identification and drug use. It could also produce changes in the correlation between cultural identification and drug use over time. For instance, there may be a negative link between drug use and strong cultural identification in the younger years when a child is still bonded primarily with the family, but that link could disappear when, during adolescence, peers become the predominant source of influence on many different behaviors, including drug use.

The situation may be somewhat different with adults. It is frequently observed within ethnic minority populations that adult alcoholics who become sober will engage in a cultural transformation as a central part of their search for sobriety. They rediscover their cultural roots, and treatment is often marked by extensive and intensive engagement in cultural rituals. It should be recognized, however, that these adults are at a very different developmental stage than adolescents; for the most part, they have disengaged from adolescent peer influences and are influenced by family members, clan relatives, and other adult peer sources. Developmentally, they may also have grown to the point where they are less dependent on the influence of others and are much more able to make independent decisions about their life and behavior.

If culture is to make a difference in the lives of young people, creative ways need to be developed to make it much more central to their lives and to lessen the dependence on deviant peer norms. One route to this would be the development of an adolescent culture that is broadly supportive of traditional values wherein there are a significant number of peers who would endorse those values. It is difficult to ask an adolescent to engage in behaviors or to espouse values that are not rewarded or accepted among a broad spectrum of friends.

CULTURAL INTERVENTIONS

Despite the similarities with other youth in patterns of rates of use, a great deal of attention has been given to the question of whether cultural elements within minority communities may operate in specific ways to affect drug-using behavior. At the broadest level, it is generally agreed that most cultures eschew drug abuse and in one form or another will sanction both use and abuse. Given that adolescent drug use is present in these communities, however, it is clear that these sanctions are not always effective. Nonetheless, there is likely to be a prevailing belief in many minority communities that drug abuse can be prevented or treated by the invocation of traditional cultural beliefs, practices, and values. This turns out to be an incredibly complex issue.

There is a strong consensus in the drug prevention field that any type of intervention should be cast in terms that are congruent with the values, beliefs, and practices of minority cultures (Resincow, Soler, & Braithwaite, 2000). This includes such things as language, traditional stories, the use of elders as teachers, and traditional crafts. Although currently no research indicates that the inclusion of traditional culture produces more effective interventions (Dent, Sussman, Ellickson, & Brown, 1996), it does greatly increase the acceptance of such programs within the community. Without community acceptance, no program can be maintained, and so incorporation of these elements in prevention and treatment programs is recommended.

One of the more serious barriers in addressing substance abuse across cultures is the lack of understanding of how psychoactive substance are viewed within various cultures. This encompasses both the meaning of drug use and the value judgment of whether drug use is good or bad. Drug abuse researchers and practitioners generally proceed from the assumption that most drug and alcohol use is harmful, and all efforts should be put forward to eliminate or minimize its use. It is further assumed that those who use drugs hold the same perspective that use is bad and that they are simply choosing to act in deviant ways. Although this may be a general perception of all drug users, it is often a thinly veiled stereotype that attributes deviancy to all those not of the majority culture. There may, in fact, be culturally influenced attitudes toward drugs that help explain some of the patterns that are found. O'Nell and Mitchell (1996), for instance, studied attitudes toward heavy use of alcohol in one American Indian tribe and found that alcohol use was perceived as a problem only to the extent that it interfered with fulfilling traditional responsibilities such as taking care of elders. The amount of alcohol consumed was not the criterion for alcohol abuse, so two individuals could be consuming the same amount: One would be perceived as having a problem, but the other would not.

Inaccurate perceptions of cultural attitudes toward drug use are not unique to ethnic minority groups. Although substance use agencies view any adolescent alcohol use or drug use as deviant, that is not necessarily true for many residents of American communities. Adolescent alcohol use is not only tolerated by adults; it is often viewed as a rite of passage and is expected, if not directly encouraged. Adolescent tobacco use is tolerated in many tobacco-growing communities and in many subcultures in the rest of the United States. Marijuana use is more likely to be hidden, but many parents would not be particularly shocked to find that their children have tried marijuana. It is likely that many culturally determined attitudes affect perceptions of substance use, and it is important to understand these values and beliefs and how they differ in neighborhoods and communities, as well as how they differ in ethnic minority subgroups.

SPIRITUALITY

A central element of traditional ethnic cultures is that of spirituality and the effects of spirituality on behaviors such as substance use. At the community level, nearly every discussion of substance use prevention and treatment will involve discussion of the need for increased attention to spirituality. Among Indian tribes, traditional elders and medicine people are very clear that substance abuse and related problems cannot be understood without inclusion of spirituality. Religion, prayer, and the connection to God are important elements in many Hispanic cultures. Spiritual connections in Asian cultures often link closely to extended historical family. Churches in African American communities play a prominent role in the control of drug and alcohol abuse. Curiously, however, spirituality has received very little attention from the research community. Only recently have there been efforts at the national funding level to address this central issue. This is a very sensitive issue that is difficult to approach from the perspective of Western scientific methods. Nonetheless, given the exceedingly strong beliefs among those at the community level that spirituality is at the core of preventing and treating substance abuse problems, spirituality should be included in the agenda in all communities, particularly in ethnic minority communities.

COMMUNITY INVOLVEMENT

Although good drug abuse prevention programs can be as effective as many other public health activities, their effects have been, at best, modest (Botvin, 1995). A major reason may be that the potency of most interventions does not match the gravity of the problem. It is unreasonable to expect, for instance, that a once-a-week classroom intervention for 12 weeks will do much to influence a group of youth who bring 12 years of prior socialization to the classes and who spend 25 hours with their friends for every hour in a drug prevention class. Furthermore, most of the existing interventions also focus only on the individual and ignore the powerful influence of the social context within which the individual exists. There is growing consensus that effective interventions must be long lasting and involve multiple sources of influence in the individual lives (Botvin, 1995; May, 1992). They must involve many different parts of the community. Inclusion of the community in the design of intervention programs may help ensure that the interventions are relevant, are potent, and include a wide range of socialization sources.

Research on minority drug abuse problems has suffered from the same limitation of the failure to include the local "voice." Research hypotheses, methods, and interpretations are typically generated from the "outside" and, as such, lack validity regarding the actual situation within minority communities (Baldwin, 1999; Beauvais & Trimble, 1992). Over the years, minority communities have witnessed a procession of research efforts that most often fail to address the existing and serious problems that community members live with on a day-to-day basis. Resistance to such research is growing. The more fruitful route appears to lie in collaborative research projects that begin with problem identification at the local level and involvement of community members in the research project. This approach not only ensures community acceptance of the research effort but also leads to better science through more accurate interpretation of research results.

USEFUL TOPICS FOR INQUIRY

This general presentation of drug use issues among ethnic minority populations suggests that there are a number of questions, the answers to which would be helpful in addressing the topic of substance abuse. Quite clearly, these are not exhaustive, but it is hoped that they describe some of the more salient areas of research.

An overriding issue is the need for new models of how to conduct such research. Our current approaches have not been particularly effective in elucidating such overarching influences as spirituality and the impact of cultural traditions on substance use. Furthermore, the typical "top-down" model, wherein research at the community level is formulated and conducted by outside researchers, needs to be inverted to incorporate the cultural knowledge of ethnic minority communities.

There should be continued efforts to unravel the posited links between acculturation and cultural identification and drug use. Of particular interest would be the study of the influences that lead to increased drug use as ethnic immigrants spend more time in the majority culture. Also of interest would be the nature and mechanism for the putative buffering effects of traditional culture on substance use.

Although the data reveal distinct trends in adolescent drug use over time, there is little understanding of which larger social forces influence these trends. This is of interest for all adolescent drug use because the trends are similar across ethnic populations. A fuller understanding of these phenomena would also help explain how culture moderates the rates of use between and within ethnic populations.

A final area of inquiry would be a more extensive study of the meaning of substance abuse within and between cultures. There is a common, value-laden assumption that drug use is something to be universally avoided and that the goal is to eradicate any use of mind-altering substances. It is not at all clear that this perception is shared by all populations and that there may be culturally bound drug-related behaviors that are acceptable.

SUMMARY

Drug use is a serious problem among all American youth, including ethnic minority youth. Inner-city ghettos and barrios and Indian reservations may have high levels of drug use, suggesting that there is high drug use among minorities. It is true that when an ethnic minority group is socially isolated, impoverished, and uneducated and has little opportunity, that group is likely to have high rates of drug use. But the same principle holds true for nonminorities; when a group of White Americans is severely disadvantaged, drug use rates are also likely to be high. With the exception of American Indians, a large proportion of whom live under severe disadvantaged conditions, ethnic minority youth in general do not use drugs any more than other American youth.

Ethnic minority drug use is not produced by ethnic genetic differences or by traditional ethnic cultural practices that involve psychoactive drugs. Over time, the rates of adolescent drug use change. The changes are essentially the same among minority and nonminority youth, indicating that the secular and temporal factors that produce drug use are essentially the same for minority and nonminority youth. The major factors that produce temporal changes in drug use over time are the attitudes of American youth toward drugs, drug use, and drug users, and those changes influence both ethnic minority and nonminority youth.

The risk and protective factors that lead individuals toward drug use are also very similar for ethnic minority and nonminority youth, although their relative importance may differ. For example, family influence may be somewhat stronger and peer influence somewhat weaker in some ethnic groups, but both family and peer influence are present in all ethnic groups. Similarly, school success is a protective factor and school failure a risk factor for essentially all ethnic groups, but ethnic minorities may have different attitudes toward education that influence school adjustment and the links between school adjustment and drug use.

Although acculturation stress has been shown to produce emotional, social, and economic problems, it probably does not directly produce adolescent drug use because adolescents, for the most part, take drugs for social, not emotional, reasons. On the other hand, acculturation stress may influence drug addiction because addicts do learn to use drugs to deal with emotional problems.

Because drug use is a social behavior, cultural values and attitudes and the process of acculturation do influence drug use. As an ethnic group becomes acculturated to the majority culture, it generally tends to move toward the drug use behaviors of the majority culture. Specific patterns of cultural adaptation, however, may appear that include retention of some ethnic minority cultural norms or adaptation of those norms, blending them with norms of the majority culture.

The level of cultural identification with either the minority culture or the nonminority culture is related to drug use but not in any simple manner. Among adolescents, cultural identification is primarily derived from the family, whereas drug use norms are more likely to be derived from a different source—peers—so cultural identification may be only loosely related to drug use. A high level of cultural identification can also influence different processes, some of which produce a risk of drug use and others that protect against drug use.

Culture does play an important role in prevention and treatment. Prevention and treatment programs must be culturally congruent, or they will not be acceptable to ethnic minority communities and will not be supported and maintained. They must be in tune with cultural values and beliefs, or they will not influence their intended targets. Prevention, treatment, and research on drug use in ethnic minority communities should be a collaborative effort with heavy community involvement.

REFERENCES

Baldwin, J. (1999). Conducting drug abuse prevention research in partnership with Native American communities: Meeting challenges through collaborative approaches. In M. De La Rosa, B. Segal, & R. Lopez (Eds.), *Conducting drug abuse research with minority populations: Advances and issues* (pp. 77-92). New York: Haworth.

Beauvais, F. (Ed.). (1992). Indian adolescent drug and alcohol use: Recent patterns and consequences [Special Issue]. *American Indian and Alaska Native Mental Health Research, 5*(1).

Beauvais, F. (1996). Trends in drug use among American Indian students and dropouts, 1975-1994. *American Journal of Public Health, 86,* 1594-1598.

Beauvais, F. (1998). Cultural identification and substance abuse in North America: An annotated bibliography. *Substance Use and Misuse, 33,* 1315-1336.

Beauvais, F., & LaBoueff, S. (1985). Drug and alcohol abuse intervention in American Indian communities. *International Journal of the Addictions, 20,* 139-171.

Beauvais, F., Oetting, E. R., & Edwards, R. W. (1985). Trends in drug use of Indian adolescents living on reservations: 1975-1983. *American Journal of Drug and Alcohol Abuse, 11,* 209-229.

Beauvais, F., & Trimble, J. E. (1992). The role of the researcher in evaluating American Indian alcohol and other drug abuse prevention programs. In M. Orlandi (Ed.), *Cultural competence for evaluators: A guide for alcohol and other drug abuse prevention practitioners working with ethnic/racial communities* (pp. 173-201). Rockville, MD: Office of Substance Abuse Prevention.

Biafora, F., & Zimmerman, R. (1998). Developmental patterns of African-American adolescent drug use. In W. Vega & A. Gil (Eds.), *Drug use and ethnicity in early adolescence* (pp. 149-175). New York: Plenum.

Blane, H. (1977). Acculturation and drinking in an Italian American community. *Journal of Studies on Alcohol, 38*, 1324-1345.

Botvin, G. (1995). Drug abuse prevention in school settings. In G. Botvin, S. Schinke, & M. Orlandi (Eds.), *Drug abuse prevention with multiethnic youth* (pp. 169-192). Thousand Oaks, CA: Sage.

Caetano, R. (1988). Alcohol use among Hispanic groups in the U.S. *American Journal of Drug and Alcohol Abuse, 14*, 292-308.

Catalano, R., Morrison, D., Wells, E., Gilmore, M., Iritani, B., & Hawkins, D. (1992). Ethnic differences in family factors related to early drug initiation. *Journal of Studies on Alcohol, 53*, 208-217.

Chavez, E., Oetting, E., & Swaim, R. (1994). Dropout and delinquency: Mexican American and Caucasian, non-Hispanic youth. *Journal of Clinical Child Psychology, 23*, 47-55.

Dent, C., Sussman, S., Ellickson, P., & Brown, P. (1996). Is current drug abuse prevention generalizable across ethnic groups? *American Behavioral Scientist, 39*, 911-918.

Gilbert, M. (1989). Alcohol related practices, problems and norms among Mexican Americans. In *Alcohol use among U.S. ethnic minorities: Proceedings of a conference on alcohol use and abuse among ethnic minority groups, September 1985* (pp. 115-134). Rockville, MD: National Institute on Alcohol Abuse and Alcoholism.

Gilbert, M., Mora, J., & Ferguson, L. (1994). Alcohol related expectations among Mexican-American women. *International Journal of the Addictions, 29*, 1127-1147.

Griesler, P., & Kandel, D. (1998). Ethnic differences in correlates of adolescent smoking. *Journal of Adolescent Health, 23*, 167-180.

Johnston, L. (1990). Toward a theory of drug epidemics. In L. Donohew, D. Sypher, & W. Bukoski (Eds.), *Persuasive communication and drug abuse prevention* (pp. 93-132). Hillsdale, NJ: Lawrence Erlbaum.

Johnston, L., O'Malley, P., & Bachman, J. (2000). *Monitoring the future: National survey on drug use, 1975-1999: Vol. I. Secondary students.* Bethesda, MD: National Institute on Drug Abuse.

Kandel, D. (1999). Developmental stages of involvement in substance use. In P. Ott & R. Tarter (Eds.), *Sourcebook on substance abuse: Etiology, epidemiology, assessment, and treatment* (pp. 50-74). Boston: Allyn & Bacon.

Long, J., & Lorenz, J. (2000). Genetic polymorphism and American Indian origins, affinities and health. In E. Rhoades (Ed.), *American Indian health: Innovations in health care, promotion and policy* (pp. 122-137). Baltimore: Johns Hopkins University Press.

Mail, P., & McDonald, D. (1980). *Tulapai to tokay: An annotated bibliography of alcohol use and abuse among Native Americans of North America.* New Haven, CT: HRAF Press.

May, P. (1992). Alcohol policy considerations for Indian reservations and border-town communities. *American Indian and Alaska Native Mental Health Research, 4*, 5-59.

Moncher, M., Holden, G., & Trimble, J. (1990). Substance abuse among Native-American youth. *Journal of Consulting and Clinical Psychology, 58*, 408-415.

Nagasawa, R., Qian, Z., & Wong, P. (1999, August). *Theory of segmented assimilation and patterns of drug and alcohol use among Asian Pacific youths.* Paper presented at the meeting of the American Sociological Association, Chicago.

Newcomb, M. (1995). Drug use etiology among ethnic minority adolescents. In G. Botvin, S. Schinke, & M. Orlandi (Eds.), *Drug abuse prevention with multiethnic youth* (pp. 105-129). Thousand Oaks, CA: Sage.

Newcomb, M., Maddahian, E., & Bentler, P. (1986). Risk and protective factors for drug use among adolescents: Concurrent and longitudinal analyses. *American Journal of Public Health, 76,* 525-531.

Oetting, E., & Beauvais, F. (1990). Adolescent drug use: Findings of national and local surveys. *Journal of Consulting and Clinical Psychology, 58,* 385-394.

Oetting, E., Deffenbacher, J., & Donnermeyer, J. (1998). Primary socialization theory: The role played by personal traits in the etiology of drug use and deviance: II. *Substance Use and Misuse, 33,* 1337-1366.

Oetting, E., & Donnermeyer, J. (1998). Primary socialization theory: The etiology of drug use and deviance: I. *Substance Use & Misuse, 33,* 995-1026.

O'Nell, T., & Mitchell, C. (1996). Alcohol use among American Indian adolescents: The role of culture in pathological drinking. *Social Science & Medicine, 42,* 565-578.

Peterson, P., Hawkins, D., Abbot, R., & Catalano, R. (1994). Disentangling the effects of parental drinking, family management and parental alcohol norms on current drinking by Black and White adolescents. *Journal of Research on Adolescents, 4,* 203-227.

Rebach, H. (1992). Alcohol and drug use among American minorities. In J. Trimble, C. Bolek, & S. Niemcryk (Eds.), *Ethnic and multicultural drug abuse: Perspectives on current research* (pp. 23-58). New York: Haworth.

Resnicow, K., Soler, R., & Braithwaite, R. (2000). Cultural sensitivity in substance use prevention. *Journal of Community Psychology, 28,* 271-290.

Rodriguez, O. (1995). Causal models of substance abuse among Puerto Rican adolescents. In G. Botvin, S. Schinke, & M. Orlandi (Eds.), *Drug abuse prevention with multiethnic youth* (pp. 130-146). Thousand Oaks, CA: Sage.

Swaim, R., Oetting, E., Jumper-Thurman, P., Beauvais, F., & Edwards, R. (1993). American Indian adolescent drug use and socialization characteristics: A cross-cultural comparison. *Journal of Cross-Cultural Psychology, 24,* 53-70.

Szapocznik, J., Perez-Vidal, A., Brickman, A., Foote, F., Santisteban, D., & Hervis, O. (1988). Engaging adolescent drug abusers and their families in treatment: A strategic structural systems approach. *Journal of Consulting and Clinical Psychology, 56,* 552-557.

Trimble, J. (1990-1991). Ethnic specification, validation prospects and future of drug abuse research. *International Journal of the Addictions, 25*(2), 149-169.

Trimble, J. (1996). Acculturation, ethnic identity and the evaluation process. In A. Bayer, F. Brisbane, A. Ramirez, M. Orlandi, & L. Epstein (Eds.), *Advanced methodological issues in culturally competent evaluation for substance abuse prevention* (pp. 13-61). Rockville, MD: Center for Substance Abuse Prevention.

Trotter, R. (1985). Mexican American experience with alcohol: South Texas examples. In L. Bennet & G. Ames (Eds.), *The American experiences with alcohol* (pp. 279-296). New York: Plenum.

U.S. Department of Health and Human Services (DHHS). (2000). *1999 national household survey on drug abuse.* Rockville, MD: Substance Abuse and Mental Health Services Administration, U.S. Department of Health and Human Services.

Vega, W., Gil, A., & Kolody, B. (1998). Pathways to drug use. In W. Vega & A. Gil (Eds.), *Drug use and ethnicity in early adolescence* (pp. 71-93). New York: Plenum.

Vega, W., Gil, A., & Wagner, E. (1998). Cultural adjustment and Hispanic adolescent drug use. In W. Vega & A. Gil (Eds.), *Drug use and ethnicity in early adolescence* (pp. 125-148). New York: Plenum.

Wallace, J., Bachman, J., O'Malley, P., & Johnston, L. (1995). Racial/ethnic differences in adolescent drug use: Exploring possible explanations. In G. Botvin, S. Schinke, & M. Orlandi (Eds.), *Drug abuse prevention with multiethnic youth* (pp. 59-80). Thousand Oaks, CA: Sage.

CHAPTER 22

Examining the Impact of Violence on Ethnic Minority Youth, Their Families, and Communities

Issues for Prevention Practice and Science

LE'ROY E. REESE
Centers for Disease Control and Prevention,
National Center for Injury Prevention and Control

ELIZABETH M. VERA
Loyola University Chicago

LA MAR HASBROUCK
Centers for Disease Control and Prevention,
National Center for Injury Prevention and Control

Interpersonal violence and suicide have exacted a tremendous toll on the citizens of the United States over the past several decades. The impact of violence in general and interpersonal violence in particular has, however, had a disproportionate impact on the quality of life of ethnic and racial minority groups (i.e., African, Asian, Hispanic, and Native Americans) in this country (Hill, Soriano, Chen, & LaFromboise, 1994). For example, homicide has been the leading cause of death for African American and Latino youth between the ages of 10 and 24 for the past decade (National Center for Health Statistics [NCHS], 1998). In 1998, the year for which the most recent data are available, African American males, ages 15 to 24, accounted for approximately 50% (2,739 of 5,506) of the homicide victims in that age group, although they only represent 6% of that age demographic (NCHS, 1998). What these trends suggest is that public health efforts to reduce racial and ethnic health disparities must also include attention to intentional injury.

The goals of this chapter include describing the prevalence of interpersonal violence in ethnic minority communities in the United States, focusing on children and adolescents. We also examine risk factors for youth interpersonal violence. Next, we attend to some of the complexities of violence prevention and intervention in these communities while reviewing strategies that have demonstrated varying degrees of empirical efficacy in the reduction of youth aggression and violence. Last, we discuss the impact of violence on minority communities in the United States and offer recommendations that advance the science and practice of violence prevention and health promotion for these communities. Space limitations prevent an exhaustive discussion of all the relevant issues regarding the impact of violence on the identified groups, as well as differences and similarities between and within these groups. Thus, what we offer here is an overview of the effects and experience of violence in these communities.

As a public health issue, violence and its various manifestations (e.g., suicide, child abuse, partner violence) is a complex phenomenon. Our focus here is on youth interpersonal violence, even though suicide is a more common form of violence across the human life span. We define *interpersonal violence* as behavior(s) that a person or persons engage in for the purpose of intentionally causing physical and/or psychological injury or death to another person or group (Powell, Mercy, Crosby, Dahlberg, & Simon, 1999). The critical difference between interpersonal violence and suicide is that in suicide, the intentional behavior is self-directed.

Beyond understanding the differences between the various forms of violence, we also suggest that there are a variety of developmental and contextual considerations important to the occurrence of violence (Bronfenbrenner,

1979; McLoyd, 1998). Many of these considerations have their origins in the early life experiences of children and adolescents. Thus, although the focus of this chapter is on minority youth and violence, we contend that many of the developmental antecedents for the various forms of adult violence (e.g., intimate partner violence and child abuse and neglect) begin during childhood and adolescence (Menard, 2001). In addition to these developmental considerations, we emphasize the significant influence of ecological factors. In particular, we highlight the influence of poverty, the disproportionate impact of violence on the poor, and the disproportionate representation of ethnic and racial minorities among the poor, particularly for Latino ethnic groups and African Americans. In sum, we assert that to truly comprehend the impact of violence on the psychological health and well-being of minority communities, we must understand ecological factors such as these.

EPIDEMIOLOGY OF MINORITY YOUTH VIOLENCE

In this section, we describe the prevalence of violent victimization occurring among ethnic and racial minority groups in the United States. In 1997, there were 2,901 homicide deaths among youth ages 10 to 19 years. This corresponded to an overall rate of 7.6 per 100,000 youth. Youth from 15 to 19 years of age accounted for the majority (2,618) of homicide deaths among teens and represented 13% of homicide deaths for all Americans, despite making up only 7% of the total U.S. population. Following an epidemic period that began in the mid-1980s and peaked in 1993, there has been a significant decrease in the rates of youth homicides. In addition, arrests among youths for violent crimes are at the lowest level in a decade, and aggressive behavior in schools has also been declining (Brener, Simon, Krug, & Lowry, 1999). Although encouraging, these decreases are still unacceptably high and have not declined to preepidemic levels observed prior to the mid-1980s. An important caveat to the interpretation of the data reported here is that although the decreases in youth homicide are important, they should not be viewed as a commentary on the scope of youth violence (U.S. Department of Health and Human Services [DHHS], 2001).

Time Trends

There have been three important contemporary time periods with regard to youth violence. The most problematic of these periods has been the "epidemic period" between 1983 and 1994. In the period prior to this, murder rates were relatively low (5.0 per 100,000 in 1983), and the period following the 1993 peak in homicide rates (11.3 per 100,000) is the other notable time period in light of the recent decreases in youth homicides. Homicide rates among youth from 1994 through 1997 showed a significant downward trend. Much of the decrease in the homicide rates was attributable to a decrease in firearm-related homicides. Specifically, the use of firearms was responsible for more than 80% of the increase in youth homicides observed during the epidemic period, whereas the nonfirearm homicide rate remained relatively unchanged.

Arrest rates for nonfatal violent crime among adolescents roughly followed the patterns described above. For example, arrests for violent crimes (i.e., rape, robbery, aggravated assault) for youth younger than age 18 increased in 1989 to its highest level since the 1960s. This rate continued to increase each year thereafter, until it reached a peak in 1994. The rapid increase of 62% from 1988 to 1994 was followed by a rapid decline. By 1997, violent crime arrests among youth were at their lowest level in the 1990s (Ringel, 1997). Most of the improvements in nonfatal violent injuries were due to declines in aggravated assault rates, the driving force

behind the overall growth of arrests for violent crimes during the epidemic period (Snyder & Sickmund, 1999).

Geographic Variation

In 1998, the violent victimization rates (rape, robbery, and assault combined) for all persons 12 years and older were highest in the western United States (46.7 per 1,000 persons) and lowest in the South and Northeast (31.0 per 1,000). These rates were also highest in urban areas (46.3 per 1,000) and lowest in rural areas, at 27.6 per 1,000 population (Rennison, 1999). The homicide rates for youth ages 10 to 19 years, for both overall homicide and firearm-related homicide, were highest in the southern and western parts of the United States (8.8 and 8.2 per 100,000, respectively) and lowest in the Northeast in 1997 (5.4 per 100,000). These patterns mirrored the national patterns for homicide among all persons.

Age and Gender

There were 19,846 persons murdered in the United States in 1997. This corresponds to an annual age-adjusted rate of 8.0 per 100,000 population, making homicide the 13th leading cause of death in America (Hoyert, Kocknek, & Murphy, 1999). Young people accounted for a substantial proportion of these deaths. Thirteen percent (2,618) of these deaths occurred among young persons ages 15 to 19 years. The 2,618 deaths from homicide among persons ages 15 to 19 years made homicide the second leading cause of death for adolescents and young adults. Conversely, only 1% (283) of homicides occurred among children ages 10 to 14 years. The 283 homicide deaths among children ages 10 to 14 years made homicide the fourth leading cause of death for that age group (Hoyert et al., 1999).

From 1982 through 1997, the highest overall homicide rates for adolescents ages

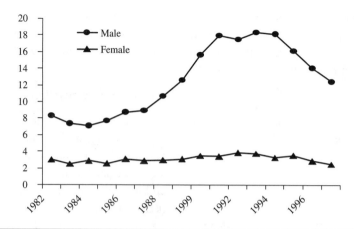

Figure 22.1 Rates of Homicide Among 10- to 19-Year-Olds, United States, 1982-1997

SOURCE: NCHS (1998) mortality data.

10 to 19 years occurred among males. In 1997, males made up 84% of all homicides among adolescents ages 10 to 19 years. The homicide rate was 12.4 per 100,000 for male youths and 3.0 per 100,000 among females. From 1982 to 1997, the rate for females remained relatively stable, decreasing by 17% from 3.0 per 100,000 in 1982 to 2.5 per 100,000 in 1997. Rates for males fluctuated significantly during this 16-year period, increasing by 50%, from 8.3 per 100,000 in 1982 to 12.4 per 100,000 in 1997.

Race and Ethnicity

For African Americans and Latinos between 15 and 19 years old, homicide ranked as the number one cause of death in 1997 and has been the leading cause of death for these groups for the past decade. In 1997, more than half of the 2,618 homicides (1,438) among persons ages 15 to 19 years occurred among African Americans. Homicide rates vary significantly by race and ethnicity.

Among youth 10 to 19 years, African Americans and Latinos had the highest rates of victimization by homicide, whereas Whites and Asian/Pacific Islanders had the lowest rates. Homicide rates for American Indians were higher than those of Whites and Asian/Pacific Islanders. In 1997, African American male youths had the highest homicide rate of 45.6 per 100,000, whereas White females had the lowest, with a rate of 1.7 per 100,000.

The Age × Race × Gender comparison reflects important demographic differences in homicide rates. As Figure 22.4 shows, African American males ages 15 to 19 years had the highest homicide rates, followed by Hispanic males ages 15 to 19 years. Rates for American Indians and Asian/Pacific Islanders were too small to make similar comparisons.

OTHER MEASURES OF THE PROBLEM

Given the rates of adolescent violence in the larger society and the recent multiple-victim school shootings, school safety has become a growing public concern. A recent national study conducted by the Centers for Disease Control and Prevention (CDC) and the U.S. Departments of Education and Justice,

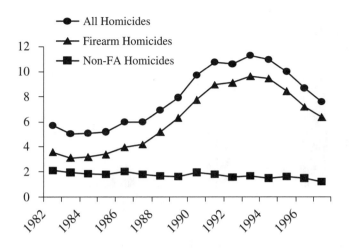

Figure 22.2   Rates of Homicide Among 10- to 19-Year-Olds by Sex, United States, 1982-1997

SOURCE: NCHS (1998) mortality data.

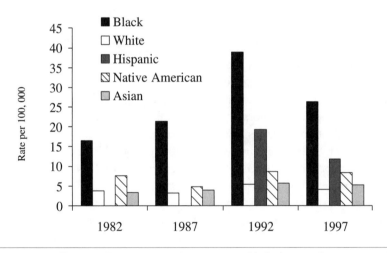

Figure 22.3   Rates of Homicide Among 10- to 19-Year-Olds by Race/Ethnicity, United States, 1982-1997

SOURCE: NCHS (1998) mortality data.

however, found that fewer than 1% of homicides among school-age children (5-19 years) had occurred on or near school grounds or at a school-related event (Anderson, Kaufman, Simon, Barrios, & Paulozzi, 2001; Kachur et al., 1996). This rate has remained constant through June 1999, suggesting that

schools are generally safe for young people (CDC, 2000a, 2000b).

Moreover, self-reported violent behaviors at schools appear to be decreasing. A recent study by Brener et al. (1999), who examined trends in nonfatal violent behaviors among adolescents in the United States between

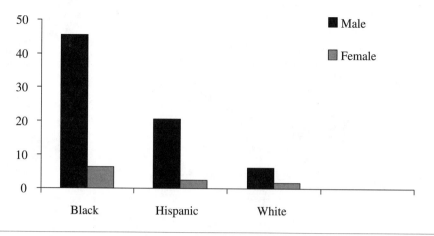

Figure 22.4 Rates of Homicide Among 15- to 19-Year-Olds by Race/Ethnicity and Gender
SOURCE: NCHS (1998) mortality data.

1991 and 1997, found that the percentage of students who reported carrying a weapon decreased 30% between 1993 and 1997, the percentage who carried a weapon on school grounds decreased by 28%, and the percentage of students who carried a gun away from school decreased by 25%. The authors noted that high school students became less likely to carry guns but not other weapons (e.g., knife, club). The proportion of students surveyed who were threatened with violence or injured with a weapon on school property in 1997 did not change from 1993 (7.4% and 7.3%, respectively).

Physical fighting, a common form of interpersonal violence among adolescents, also decreased between 1991 and 1997 according to adolescent self-reports. Further analysis showed that the decrease in fighting from 1991 to 1997 was the result of a decrease in fighting among White and African American students but not among Latino students or students of other racial or ethnic groups (Brener et al., 1999). Notably, these declines in school-related weapon carrying, assault, and fighting occurred during the "post-epidemic" period.

DATA SOURCES

Data for victims of homicide from 1982 to 1997 were analyzed using the National Center for Health Statistics (NCHS) annual mortality tapes from the CDC. Data on assault victimization are from the annual reports of the National Crime Victimization Survey (NCVS), conducted by the U.S. Department of Justice. NCVS obtains information about crimes (excluding homicide) from an ongoing, nationally representative sample of persons older than age 12 years residing in U.S. households. The category "crimes of violence" include rapes, personal robbery, and assault (simple and aggravated).

RISK FACTORS FOR YOUTH VIOLENCE

Although a thorough discussion of all risk and protective factors for youth violence is beyond the scope of this chapter, we highlight what we consider some of the more critical factors (see DHHS, 2001, for a thorough review). At the outset, however, we assert that many risk factors discussed here are developmental in nature. Specifically, some of these risk factors have a greater impact on youth earlier in life, whereas others have a more pronounced effect later in life (i.e., adolescence). For example, the family has a greater impact on a child prior to adolescence, whereas peers have a greater influence on an adolescent's behavior as the influence of the family decreases. Equally important to the developmental nature of various risk factors is understanding the impact of a child's social ecology in influencing behavior and that many risk factors are embedded in these ecologies (Bronfenbrenner, 1979). The cumulative effect of these factors is that youth are often directed toward trajectories that promote prosocial development or increase risk for violence and other risk behaviors, although research continues to clarify these developmental pathways (see Dahlberg & Potter, 2001; DHHS, 2001).

Generally, there is agreement that some risk factors generalize across the developmental stages of childhood and adolescence in influencing violent or other acting-out behaviors. Examples include exposure to violence in the home and community (Edelson, 1999; Osofosky, 1999), violent victimization (Menard, 2001; Wilson, 1996), and abject poverty and community underemployment (McLoyd, 1998). Beyond this, however, many risk factors tend to have a reciprocal and additive influence on one another such as the case with individual risk factors, which can often be exacerbated or positively managed based on family, peer, and community influences.

Early and Late Childhood

A number of risk factors for violence have a greater impact on younger children than adolescents. An important example includes early involvement in aggressive and other disruptive behaviors (Maguin et al., 1995).

Children who engage in aggression at earlier ages are more likely to persist in aggressive behavior than youth who first engage in these behaviors later in life. Other risk factors for younger children include the influence of the family and other primary caregivers. Specifically, parents who are ineffective in their parenting practices (e.g., poor supervision, inconsistent use of discipline or modeling negative/aggressive behavior) create risk for their children (Loeber & Stouthamer-Loeber, 1987; Wells & Rankin, 1988). Child abuse and neglect is another family risk factor that can put younger children at significant risk for aggressive behavior (Smith & Thornberry, 1995).

Adolescence

During adolescence, the influence of the family decreases as a young person develops more meaningful relationships outside the home, and delinquent peers can become a significant arbiter in influencing a young person's aggressive behavior (Maguire & Pastore, 1998). Another powerful influence on aggressive behavior is gangs, as adolescents involved in gangs are significantly more likely to become involved in violent behavior than non-gang-affiliated youth (Howell, 1998). Last, adolescents who are social isolates and outcasts with limited social supports also tend to be at greater risk for aggressive behavior.

Although not discussed here, a current focus of etiologic research in youth violence focuses on identifying and examining protective factors or influences that buffer the influence of risk factors on youth. Future efforts, particularly those focused on minority communities, require greater attention to understanding those protective factors that allow the vast majority of youth who might otherwise be considered at risk due to contextual factors such as poverty from engaging in aggressive or violent behavior.

THE ROLE AND IMPACT OF VIOLENCE IN ETHNIC MINORITY COMMUNITIES

Because perpetration of and victimization by violence is overrepresented in ethnic minority communities, researchers have tried to determine whether there are culturally specific functions or reasons for violence in these communities. This question has been difficult to answer for a number of reasons. One of the more important reasons is that socioeconomic status (i.e., poverty) is frequently confounded by race and ethnicity. Specifically, there is a disproportionate representation of people of color residing in communities that are under-resourced and poor (McLoyd, 1998; U.S. Bureau of the Census, 1999). In impoverished communities, there tends to be higher levels of community violence, rundown, and over-crowded housing, combined with unemployment and/or underemployment (Wilson, 1996). At times, illegal drug economies and/or the presence of gangs can be sources of community violence and may influence the occurrence of domestic violence and other forms of family violence. Often, then, when violence has been studied in racial and ethnic minority communities, it has focused on poor communities. If the stressors that accompany living in poverty are at the core of elevated levels of violence, then making attributions about culture and violence becomes quite complicated. Further complicating efforts to understand violence in minority groups are the effects of racism and discrimination that many members of ethnic and racial minority groups report experiencing personally and occupationally (Clark, Anderson, Clark, & Williams, 1999). For example, the chronic stress associated with discrimination can influence participation in risk behaviors such as violence. This discussion is not intended as a justification for violent behavior; instead, our goal is to attempt to highlight its complexity in poor minority communities.

One aspect of understanding violence that is pertinent to racial and ethnic minority communities, regardless of socioeconomic issues, is the sociopolitical histories of violence inherent to the experiences of African Americans, Native Americans, Asian Americans, and Latinos in the United States. The enslavement of Africans for more than half a century in this country (and others) was characterized by a complete disregard for human life exhibited through the regular use of violence (including rape) as a means of coercion and control (Ani, 1994). The legacy of slavery for African Americans in the 20th century was characterized by the continuation of violence in the form of lynchings, segregation laws, de facto discrimination, and the assassination of prominent civil rights leaders. Thus, the history of African Americans in the United States is interwoven with experiences of violence that continue to this day.

Native Americans have had a similar experience to that of African Americans. The genocidal effects of colonization on the indigenous people of the Americas in many cases led to the extermination or near elimination of entire tribes by European colonizers (Feagin & Feagin, 1996; Yung & Hammond, 1994). The involuntary movement of those who survived (and their descendants) to reservations throughout the United States resulted in a ghettoization of native peoples, who often live with limited resources brought on by abject poverty and underemployment influencing the presence of substance abuse and violence among native peoples.

Latinos have a history in this country similar to both the experiences of Native Americans and African Americans as a result of their history of colonization. Although peoples of Latin American descent were never technically enslaved, they were subjected to forced religious conversions and exploited by sharecropping systems (i.e., indentured servitude) during the colonization of the Americas, where the use of violence was commonplace (Feagin & Feagin, 1996; Soriano, 1994). The use of lynching, segregation laws, and other forms of systematic marginalization also existed for Latinos prior to the civil rights movement (Martinez, 1991).

Unfortunately, the Asian American community's experience shares several common elements with those of other minority groups in the United States. Whether one considers the aftermath of wars, which forced many Asian ethnic groups to flee to the United States, or the use of internment camps for Japanese Americans during World War II (Feagin & Feagin, 1996), violence and coercion have had a significant effect on the Asian community, although their rates of homicidal victimization are lower than other minority groups (Chen & True, 1994).

The experience of violence by ethnic and racial minorities is not just a historical footnote; it is a contemporary problem (e.g., incidents of police brutality, the reemergence of White supremacist groups). Thus, violence and ethnic/racial minority communities are not new to one another. This said, however, the phenomenon of violence by and within communities of color is equally disturbing.

"Black on Black" violence, as an example of within-group violence, has been discussed by Bell and Jenkins (1994) and Yung and Hammond (1994), among others. In particular, Yung and Hammond reported that young Black men were most likely to be murdered by associates, and young Black women were most likely to be the victims of violence inflicted by boyfriends or spouses. Such findings suggest that there is a serious problem within the Black community, as well as other ethnic minority communities, in which the experience of violence is not just coming from outside the community directly but from within it as well. In exploring phenomena such as that described above, it is important to avoid overly simplistic and inaccurate stereotypes (i.e., Blacks are more prone to be violent).

Is it possible that the use of violence within these communities is a replication or imitation of the violence and coercion first introduced to these communities by the historical experiences of violence and marginalization? Alternatively, is it possible that the presence and promulgation of violence are a function of the effects of internalized oppression and/or the devaluing of life resulting from centuries of oppression? Such hypotheses are difficult if not impossible to test empirically, despite their reasonableness and the desire to test them. The research literature has discussed the dynamics of racism and oppression within communities of color in a manner suggesting that it is unreasonable and short-sighted to divorce the examination of risk behaviors such as violence from the historical and contemporary experience of these groups (Clark et al., 1999; Fanon, 1967).

Racism has been linked to a variety of health-compromising conditions due to the chronic stress it imposes on the lives of racial minority group members (Clark et al., 1999). Hill et al. (1994) discussed how racism and discrimination adversely affect the mental health of ethnic and racial minorities, highlighting the frustration resulting from institutionalized racism (e.g., low-paying jobs, poor-quality education, lack of economic mobility) and how such experiences may be linked to expressions of violence. This assertion has been supported by the literature that has linked poverty, more so than race, to the prediction of violence (DHHS, 2001; Hill et al., 1994; Menard, 2001). Critical to accurately disaggregating the relationship of race and socioeconomic status to violence is understanding the disproportionate representation of minorities among the poor, particularly for African Americans and certain Latino ethnic groups (U.S. Bureau of the Census, 1999; Wilson, 1987).

Wilson (1987) and McLoyd (1990), among others, have articulated how it is that community destabilization and the psychological distress associated with living amid racism and poverty influence the emergence of violent behavior in individuals. One example includes how interpersonal relationships are affected by the distress of being marginalized (e.g., parental discipline of children may become more corporal in nature, domestic conflict may escalate into violence). In addition, riskier means of economic activities (e.g., drug economies) may sometimes be pursued because traditional tracks of economic stability (e.g., higher education, job advancement) may be less available in disenfranchised communities (Hill et al., 1994). As a result of such considerations, the experience of violence may be more common as are more negative contacts with law enforcement agencies.

It is important to qualify the preceding discussion by saying that the overwhelming majority of ethnic and racial minorities, whether poor, middle class, or affluent, are not involved in violent interpersonal relationships or pseudo-occupations that involve violence. To characterize either group (racial and ethnic minorities or the poor) in such a way is irresponsible. To understand the conditions that may result in greater rates of violent perpetration and victimization in ethnic minority communities, one must consider inequities in social conditions and the risk factors embedded in these conditions. There is sufficient evidence to suggest that greater percentages of racial and ethnic minority group members, compared to their European American counterparts, live in poverty relative to their representation in the general population (U.S. Bureau of the Census, 1999). It is also true that having inadequate resources for food, shelter, education, and leisure activities undoubtedly is related to a poorer quality of life. Menard (2001) reported data from the Youth Development Survey, indicating that poorer children are more likely to be victimized by violence and such victimization can influence risk for later violent perpetration. Indeed, in his analyses of this longitudinal data set, he found that victimization puts respondents at significantly greater

risk for violent perpetration than did not being victimized. Thus, it may be the case that changing the social conditions in which many racial and ethnic minority families reside will be related to a decrease in a number of health, mental health, and interpersonal problems such as violence experienced by these communities. Summarily, we assert the need for scientists seeking to understand violence in ethnic minority communities to not confuse the culture of these groups with the experience or perpetration of violence, but instead to understand this phenomenon within the historical and contemporary experiences of these groups. This is particularly notable when the rates of youth violence in the United States are compared to other countries, with the United States significantly outpacing other countries, suggesting that there is more violence in the United States in general and not just within minority communities.

Perhaps a more insidious problem that links conditions of poverty and racism to violence is the mainstream cultural norm that links an individual's sense of worth to certain external criteria and material objects (Myers, 1988). This is especially problematic in a society such as the United States, where specific skin color, hair texture, and body type are the preferred physical traits, and material possessions (e.g., expensive homes and luxury items) are associated with "success" and "happiness," and persons in possession of these elements are "valued" differently than citizens who do not possess such characteristics. Given such observations, it is easy to see why people living in poverty may develop negative self-esteem, poor self-images, and pessimistic future outlooks (Myers, 1988). If one is taught (via societal or familial messages) to dislike or hate oneself and those similar to you, the devaluing of such lives becomes tenable and may encourage attitudes supportive of violent behavior.

Fortunately, we know that a number of factors such as a positive sense of self and an optimistic worldview can serve as protective factors for youth violence and a host of other mental health problems (Masten & Coatsworth, 1998). Racial and ethnic minority children are considered more resilient (i.e., less affected by environmental stressors) when they have a greater sense of self-control, self-efficacy, and a positive identity. Positive ethnic identity (or valuing one's ethnic heritage) has also been found to be associated with more positive academic and mental health outcomes in ethnic and racial minorities and is considered by some as a safeguard against involvement in aggressive behavior (Jagers, 1997; Spencer, Dobbs, & Swanson, 1988). Spencer, Cole, DuPree, Glymph, and Pierre (1993) also found that academic achievement of African American youth is predicted by a number of family variables, including perceptions of family conflict. School engagement and achievement have frequently been identified as having the potential to serve a protective function in the prevention of youth violence and victimization (Reese, Crosby, & McKinney, 2001).

Hill et al. (1994) discussed the types of ethnic socialization that may serve as protective factors for ethnic minority children, including a strong sense of family and community, a heightened awareness of the effects of racism, a valuing of relationships, and a belief in the interconnectedness among living things. They argued that ethnic minority children who hold these values and beliefs may be less likely to turn to violence as a means of solving problems or expressing negative emotions (see also Jagers, 1997; Myers, 1988).

Last, beyond the issues raised in this section, the fact remains that interpersonal violence has exacted a tremendous toll on minority communities within the United States, as Figure 22.5 shows.

Specifically, when the impact of mortality caused by homicide is operationalized in terms of years of life lost, the impact of violence on minority communities is clear. For 1998, African Americans accounted for more than 48% of the years of life lost while only accounting for approximately 13% of the population. Similarly, Hispanics accounted for 18% of years lost to homicide while accounting for 11% of the population.

PREVENTION STRATEGIES

Traditionally, "prevention" has been seen as a tripartite concept consisting of primary, secondary, and tertiary approaches and, more recently, as universal, indicated, and targeted. Primary prevention, according to Conyne (1987), refers to intentional programs that target groups of people who are currently unaffected by a particular problem for the purposes of helping them continue to function in healthy ways, free from disturbance. Secondary prevention targets populations exhibiting early-stage problems to forestall the development of more serious difficulties (e.g., working with aggressive kindergartners to curb later violent episodes). Secondary prevention efforts typically rely on early detection methods such as schools or the legal system to identify at-risk youth (Durlak, 1997).

Tertiary prevention aims to reduce the duration or consequences of established problems or disorders (e.g., working with juvenile offenders who are in jail). In many instances, tertiary prevention interventions are difficult to differentiate from traditional rehabilitation. The Committee on Prevention of Mental Disorders (Munoz, Mrazek, & Haggerty, 1996) recommended that the term *prevention* be reserved for only those interventions that occur prior to the onset of a diagnosable disorder or specific risk behavior. Interventions that occur after the onset are considered treatment.

Preventive interventions can be categorized as either person or environment centered (Baker & Shaw, 1987; Durlak &

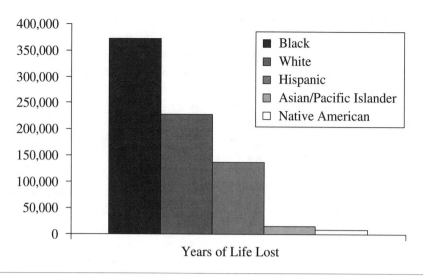

Figure 22.5   Years of Life Lost Due to Homicide by Race/Ethnicity, 1998

SOURCE: NCHS (1998) mortality data.

Wells, 1997). Person-centered interventions are targeted directly to the target population (e.g., teaching anger management skills to impulsive children). Environment-centered interventions seek to modify the child's social context (e.g., programs that modify parental child-rearing techniques or teachers' classroom management techniques). Programs that contain both person-centered and environment-centered intervention strategies to address issues of violence, versus either alone, are likely to be the most successful (Catalano, Berglund, Ryan, Lonczak, & Hawkins, 1998; Durlak, 1997; Munoz et al., 1996). This is an important distinction given the earlier discussion detailing the role that environmental factors play in creating risk for violent behavior.

Identifying children who are in greatest need of preventive intervention is an important issue. Part of the challenge in this area involves the settings in which preventive interventions are typically delivered. School-based programs are probably most common for prevention efforts (Catalano et al., 1998; Guerra,

Tolan, & Hammond, 1994), but often the children at greatest risk for perpetration of violence either attend school irregularly or are dropouts. Thus, having access to youth determined to be most "at risk" is difficult, unless there have been consequences for their behavior (e.g., getting arrested) that can be used to encourage their participation in prevention and treatment programs. An additional difficulty with school-based prevention programs is that often the caregivers for these children, who also require prevention services, are not included as program participants. Last, efforts to work with the most at-risk youth is exacerbated by the observation that often these youth are unwilling participants, which can prohibit maximum benefit of interventions (Guerra et al., 1994).

Although identifying youth in greatest need of preventive interventions is critical, there remains considerable debate about whether psychologists and other public health professionals should focus solely on identifying and decreasing the impact of specific risk factors. An alternative approach would be to focus on increasing social competencies and other general and protective factors, which could reduce child and adolescent mental disorders and risk behaviors across the board (Albee, 1996). Much of this debate is connected to the assumptions made about the functions of risk behaviors in youth. For example, Jessor and Jessor's (1977) problem behavior theory, a dominant theoretical view, suggests that diverse problem behaviors such as drug abuse, delinquent behavior, and sexual activity have similar functions (e.g., gaining peer acceptance, coping with stress). Because such behaviors tend to bring about similar reinforcement or serve common purposes, they tend to come in "packages." This does not necessarily mean that drug abuse and academic dysfunction, for example, always co-occur, but samples of youth with one behavior are more likely to have higher rates of other risk behaviors than youth similar in age and gender (Kazdin, 1993). As an example, Farrrell, Danish, and Howard (1992) investigated the relationship between five adolescent problem behaviors (cigarette smoking, alcohol use, marijuana use, delinquency, and sexual intercourse) in seventh and ninth graders and found positive relationships existing among those behaviors. A confirmatory factor analysis also supported the hypothesis that a common factor underlies adolescent problem behaviors. Thus, there would seem to be support for programs that target interrelated problems in youth.

Guerra et al. (1994) argued that youth violence regularly co-occurs with other youth problems such as delinquent activity, school dropout, and other unhealthy behaviors. Practitioners and prevention scientists guided by this multiproblem philosophy would argue that helping youth develop the skills and abilities to meet their needs in ways that promote social and behavioral competence would be more beneficial than developing programs aimed at specific risk behaviors. Furthermore, because risk factors for youth violence are also associated with other problems such as

substance abuse, the types of interventions designed often have common features that have demonstrated empirical efficacy in reducing other risk behaviors.

To illustrate some of the typical approaches to violence prevention, we have reviewed programs that include person-centered, environment-centered, and person-in-environment components. Evaluation in violence prevention is so new that it is difficult to say with certainty what is the most effective way to implement programs or which programs are most effective. However, the following represent some of the most well-known efforts as well as some that have demonstrated consistent effects in reducing youth violence with minority groups. A critical feature of many of the most effective prevention programs is sensitivity to the cultural worldview of the targeted population. Indeed, the Blueprint initiative coordinated by the Center for the Study and Prevention of Violence, which highlights violence prevention programs with demonstrated empirical efficacy, suggests *cultural sensitivity* broadly defined is central to effective violence prevention.

Hammond's (1991) Positive Adolescents Choices Training (PACT) is an example of a skill-based secondary prevention program focused on aggression and violence in African American familial and peer relationships. Using the *Dealing With Anger* videotapes that depict scenarios using contemporary African American actors, this program highlights the process of violence escalation, social perspective taking, negotiation, and self-regulation skills in the prevention of aggressive and violent behavior. A preliminary outcome study of the 20-session program, using an experimental and a control group, found that control group participants were referred to juvenile courts more frequently for violent offenses at a 3-year follow-up than participants in the experimental condition (Hammond & Yung, 1993).

The Viewpoints Training Program (Guerra & Panizzion, 1986) is an example of a tertiary treatment program that uses cognitive-behavioral methods for changing youth beliefs and attitudes about violent behavior by enhancing problem-solving skills. In a study with incarcerated youth, Guerra and Slaby (1990) found that program participants had greater decreases in aggression than control group participants. The decrease was directly related to the targeted variables of the treatment program, thus providing some support for its promise as an effective intervention for youth with a history of violent behavior.

The Providing Alternative Thinking Strategies (PATHS) is a school-based skills program that addresses a number of youth development constructs (Greenberg, 1996). These constructs include emotional, social, behavioral, and moral competencies; prosocial norms and behavior; and resiliency. The focus of this program is on enhancing each participant's ability to effectively self-manage emotions and behavior while using effective interpersonal problem-solving skills.

Evaluations of the PATHS program using a quasi-experimental design (i.e., with intervention and control groups) with both "normally" adjusted and high-risk students are promising (Greenberg & Kusche, 1997). For the normally adjusted participants (compared to control group participants), significant improvements were seen in defining complex feelings, reasoning, and social perspective taking. Also, there were improvements in interpersonal problem solving and decreases in aggressive solutions. For the at-risk participants, improvements were seen (compared to control group participants) in ability to identify feelings, improved social perspective taking, and self-efficacy in the management of feelings. In addition, there were significant improvements in frustration tolerance, assertiveness, and social skills (Catalano et al., 1998). A 1-year follow-up showed a sustained effect of the program on problem-solving skills, social perspective taking, and lower reported aggression. A 2-year follow-up showed that both the normally adjusted and high-risk participants reported lower rates of conduct problems.

The above overview provides selected examples of different types of prevention programs that have been developed and subjected to various states of evaluative rigor. Beyond these examples, there are programs that take a person-in-environment approach and have been identified by prevention experts as exemplary in the sustained prevention of youth violence. Of the examples discussed here, each involves efforts to affect the family ecology in which the child or children exists by working with caregivers and family members. Each of these programs and their evaluations are described in detailed elsewhere (see Center for the Study and Prevention of Violence in Reese, Vera, Simon, & Ikeda, 2000).

Olds, Hill, Mihalic, and O'Brien's (1998) home visitation program is an example of an effective primary prevention program that works with low-income pregnant women experiencing their first pregnancy whose children are thought to be at risk for poor developmental and health outcomes. The focus of this program is on providing health care services and health-related education, with the goal of reducing the likelihood of adverse health outcomes and the risks of child neglect while improving family functioning. Evaluations with both rural European American women and inner-city African American women found similar results. Specifically, evaluations from this program indicate that as the number of health services offered to pregnant women increased, these children had fewer problems when they became teenagers (e.g., less arrests, drug use, and child abuse). In addition, the mothers themselves had fewer difficulties, as evidenced by decreased smoking, reports of increased social support, and general positive adjustment (see Kitzman et al., 1997; Olds & Kitzman, 1993).

At the other end of the continuum of family interventions is multisystemic therapy (MST), which works with youth already engaged in criminal behavior (e.g., drug use and violence). The theoretical underpinnings of this approach are to change the family ecology of the targeted child by developing an individualized treatment plan that focuses on reducing behavioral deficits and improving the protective features and functioning of the youth and family (Henggeler, Mihalic, Rone, Thomas, & Timmons-Mitchell, 1998). The treatment strategies employed in MST are all empirically based approaches that are implemented in a manner that allows the therapist or family collaborator to be responsive to the needs of the child in a holistic manner (i.e., individually, family). The goals include being sensitive to the influences of the youth's social ecology while simultaneously attempting to influence aspects of that ecology (i.e., family) (see Henggeler et al., 1998, for a complete description).

Evaluations of MST have occurred with diverse youth populations, including violent youth. These evaluations have shown that MST is more effective than individual psychotherapy, and more specifically randomized trials have reported significant decreases in criminal activity and drug abuse and improved family relations that have been sustained between 2 and 4 years (Henggeler et al., 1998).

Children and adolescents, especially those with histories of aggression and limited social skills, need to learn a number of skills related to nonviolence. These include knowing how to solve problems assertively and communicate with others nonaggressively, as well as receiving support from family members and peers who do not reinforce or model violence or abuse. With regard to environmental contexts, children need to be provided with safe, organized activities in which they can participate regularly and that nurture prosocial attributes. Equally important, however, is that often the caregivers and peers of these children require intervention. Specifically, the risk factor literature elaborates in some detail how risk for aggression and violence can be and often is embedded within families and peer groups, and each can represent differing levels of risk depending on the age and developmental stage of the child. Although no "cure-all" exists for all youth and their ecological circumstances, being sensitive and responsive to the prevention needs of families and peers is critical to effective violence prevention.

FUTURE DIRECTIONS

Effective violence prevention and health promotion in marginalized communities are complex because "violence," whether interpersonal or psychological, does not occur in a vacuum. As this volume has attempted to highlight, often a variety of ecological considerations (e.g., poverty, poor-quality education, underemployment, and discrimination) bear directly on the occurrence of violence. A current reality in the United States is that minorities in general, especially minority youth, tend to be disproportionately affected by violence and its risk factors. Beyond the influence of contemporary risk factors, a challenge of effective violence prevention lies in understanding the sociopolitical histories and realities of minority groups in the United States. As Akbar (1996) and others have discussed, a limitation of Western behavioral science is the realization that individual as well as collective behavior can be influenced by historical as well as contemporary factors (e.g., enslavement, discrimination).

Due to the disproportionate impact of violence and other health and social problems on ethnic and racial minorities, prevention scientists and practitioners must be careful not to inappropriately assign these problems or their influences (e.g., poverty) to the culture or cultural practices of these groups.

Although it is important to examine the cultural values and behaviors of any group to a given outcome of interest, it is equally important to understand the influence of factors external to that group, and clearly this is needed with respect to understanding violence in minority communities. As the U.S. Surgeon General's report on youth violence (DHHS, 2001) highlights, race and ethnicity may serve as a risk marker but is not in itself a risk factor for aggression and is often mitigated by socioeconomic status.

Given the assertion above, it becomes important to challenge stereotypes sometimes evidenced in prevention research that inaccurately portray minority youth as having a greater disposition for violent behavior. As important is the development of interventions that are culturally responsive to the target populations if positive and sustained effects of prevention interventions are expected (Dumas, Rollock, & Prinz, 1999; Mercy & Hammond, 2001). Practically, developing culturally responsive prevention programs means efforts by psychologists and other public health professionals to understand the worldview of the constituents with whom they work (e.g., Lerner, 1995) in a manner that stretches the paradigms of Western science and health practice.

Perhaps the most significant challenge to supporting the positive development of minority youth in the United States exists in confronting and changing the environmental constraints that serve as risk factors for violence (Mercy & Hammond, 2001). The literature suggests that person-in-environment prevention strategies are more effective than strategies that only focus on individual-level change. Thus far, such strategies have focused on changing family ecologies and, more recently, school ecologies. What is needed now, given what we know about how risk factors can be embedded within a community, is for prevention strategies to be expanded to include "community" as both participant and

foci of change while simultaneously considering individual, family, and school contexts. Given the complexity of such challenges, it is imperative that multidisciplinary approaches be employed. It is here that professionals in public health, the faith community, psychology, medicine, economics, law, education, and other relevant fields must contribute efforts toward understanding and developing solutions to prevent violence and its disproportionate impact on minority communities. Such approaches may allow violence to be reframed in a manner truly reflective of its complexity while empowering families and communities. For example, economically depressed communities may be more likely to experience violence, underemployment, lower academic achievement, and other problems reflective of the reciprocal nature of co-occurring risk factors and behaviors (Bandura, 1997; Jessor & Jessor, 1977).

Beyond the issues identified above, a number of efforts can be made to prevent violence among minority youth. The Centers for Disease Control and Prevention and the U.S. Surgeon General's Office recently published documents describing "best practices" in the prevention of youth violence that detail strategies with proven efficacy (CDC, 2000a, 2000b; DHHS, 2001). Early interventions that focus on promoting social and behavioral competencies should be encouraged that support parents and other child caregivers (Reese et al., 2000). Also important to the prevention of violence is developing policies that promote the use of "best practice" approaches reflecting what is known to be effective in the prevention of youth violence. As Dodge (2001) suggested, one of the most important bridges yet to be crossed is for effective prevention science to inform effective public policy.

In sum, the influence of violence on minority youth, their families, and communities has been profound. At present, a number of scholars and policymakers seek to understand and be responsive to the violence prevention needs of these communities through a variety of prevention and health promotion mechanisms. Efforts to disaggregate the impact of violence on the quality of life of these communities are difficult, yet the impact of violence has been clear relative to family stability, years of life lost, visibility in the job market, educational achievement, and other outcomes of adjustment and well-being. As a public health priority, psychologists and other concerned scientists and practitioners must fully embrace the complexities of violence and its developmental nature across the life span if we are to optimally assist those disproportionately affected by its occurrence.

REFERENCES

Akbar, N. (1996). *Breaking the chains of psychological slavery.* Tallahassee, FL: Mind Productions and Associates.

Albee, G. W. (1996). Revolutions and counterrevolutions in prevention. *American Psychologist, 51,* 1130-1133.

Anderson, M., Kaufman, J., Simon, T. S., Barrios, L., & Paulozzi, L. (2001). School associated violent deaths in the United States: 1994-1999. *Journal of the American Medical Association, 286,* 2695-2702.

Ani, M. (1994). *Yurugu: An African-centered critique of European cultural thought and behavior.* Trenton, NJ: Africa World Press.

Baker, S. B., & Shaw, M. C. (1987). *Improving counseling through primary prevention.* Columbus, OH: Merrill.

Bandura, A. (1997). Exercise of personal and collective efficacy in changing societies. In A. Bandura (Ed.), *Self-efficacy in changing societies.* New York: Cambridge University Press.

Bell, C., & Jenkins, E. (1994). Community violence and children on Chicago's southside. *Psychiatry, 56,* 46-54.

Brener, N. D., Simon, T. R., Krug, E. G., & Lowry, R. (1999). Recent trends in violence-related behaviors among high school students in the United States. *Journal of the American Medical Association, 282,* 440-446.

Bronfenbrenner, U. (1979). *The ecology of human development.* Cambridge, MA: Harvard University Press.

Catalano, R. F., Berglund, M. L., Ryan, J. A. M., Lonczak, H. C., & Hawkins, J. D. (1998). *Positive youth development in the United States: Research findings on evaluations of positive youth development programs.* Washington, DC: Department of Health and Human Services, National Institute for Child Health and Human Development.

Centers for Disease Control and Prevention (CDC). (2000a). *Best practices of youth violence prevention: A sourcebook for community action.* Atlanta, GA: Author.

Centers for Disease Control and Prevention (CDC). (2000b). Fact sheet on school violence. National Center for Injury Prevention and Control. Retrieved from www.cdc.gov/ncipc/factsheets/schoolsvi.htm

Chen, S. A., & True, R. H. (1994). Asian/Pacific Islanders. In L. Eron, J. Gentry, & P. Schlegel (Eds.), *Reason to hope: A psychosocial perspective on violence and youth.* Washington, DC: American Psychological Association.

Clark, R., Anderson, N. B., Clark, V. R., & Williams, D. R. (1999). Racism as a stressor for African Americans. *American Psychologist, 54,* 805-816.

Conyne, R. K. (1987). *Primary preventive counseling.* Muncie, IN: Accelerated Development.

Dahlberg, L. L., & Potter, L. B. (2001). Youth violence: Developmental pathways and prevention challenges. *American Journal of Preventative Medicine, 20,* 3-21.

Dodge, K. (2001). The science of youth violence prevention: Progressing from developmental epidemiology to efficacy to effectiveness in public policy. *American Journal of Preventative Medicine, 20,* 63-70.

Dumas, J., Rollock, D., & Prinz, R. (1999). Cultural sensitivity: Problems and solutions in applied and preventative intervention. *Applied & Preventative Psychology, 8,* 175-196.

Durlak, J. A. (1997). *Successful prevention programs for children and adolescents.* New York: Plenum.

Durlak, J. A., & Wells, A. M. (1997). Primary prevention mental health programs for children and adolescents: A meta-analytic review. *American Journal of Community Psychology, 25,* 115-152.

Edelson, J. L. (1999). Children's witnessing of adult domestic violence. *Journal of Interpersonal Violence, 14,* 839-870.

Fanon, F. (1967). *Black skin, white mask.* New York: Grove.

Farrell, A. D., Danish, S. J., & Howard, C. W. (1992). Relationship between drug use and other problem behaviors in urban adolescents. *Journal of Consulting and Clinical Psychology, 60,* 705-712.

Feagin, J. R., & Feagin, C. B. (1996). *Racial and ethnic relations.* Upper Saddle River, NJ: Prentice Hall.

Greenberg, M. T. (1996). *The PATHS project: Preventive intervention for children: Final report to NIMH.* Seattle: University of Washington, Department of Psychology.

Greenberg, M. T., & Kusche, C.A. (1997, April). *Improving children's emotional regulation and social competence: The effects of the PATHS curriculum.* Paper presented at the annual meeting of the Society for Research in Child Development, Washington, DC.

Guerra, N., & Panizzion, A. (1986). *Viewpoints training program.* Santa Barbara, CA: Center for Law-Related Education.

Guerra, N. G., & Slaby, R. G. (1990). Cognitive mediators of aggression in adolescent offenders: 2. Intervention. *Developmental Psychology, 26,* 269-277.

Guerra, N. G., Tolan, P. H., & Hammond, R. (1994). Prevention and treatment of adolescent violence. In L. Eron, J. Gentry, & P. Schlegel (Eds.), *Reason to hope: A psychosocial perspective on violence and youth* (pp. 383-404). Washington, DC: American Psychological Association.

Hammond, R. (1991). *Dealin with anger: Givin' it, takin' it, workin' it out: Leader's guide.* Champaign, IL: Research Press.

Hammond, R., & Yung, B. (1993). *Evaluation and activity report: Positive adolescent choices training.* Unpublished grant report, U.S. Maternal and Child Health Bureau, Washington, DC.

Henggeler, S. W., Mihalic, S. F., Rone, L., Thomas, C., & Timmons-Mitchell, J. (1998). *Blueprints for violence prevention: Multisystemic therapy.* Boulder: University of Colorado.

Hill, H. H., Soriano, F. I., Chen, S. A., & LaFromboise, T. D. (1994). Sociocultural factors in the etiology and prevention of violence among ethnic minority youth. In L. D. Eron, J. H. Gentry, & P. Schlegel (Eds.), *Reason to hope: A psychosocial perspective on violence and youth* (pp. 59-97). Washington, DC: American Psychological Association.

Howell, J. A. (1998). Promising programs for youth gang violence prevention and intervention. In R. Loeber & D. P. Farrington (Eds.), *Serious and violent juvenile offenders: Risk factors and successful interventions* (pp. 284-312). Thousand Oaks, CA: Sage.

Hoyert, D. L., Kocknek, K. D., & Murphy, S. L. (1999). *Deaths: Final data for 1997* (National Vital Statistics Reports, Vol. 47, No. 19). Hyattsville, MD: National Center for Health Statistics, Centers for Disease Control and Prevention.

Jagers, R. J. (1997). Afrocultural integrity and the social development of African American children: Some conceptual, empirical, and practical considerations. In R. J. Watts & R. J. Jagers (Eds.), *Manhood development in urban African American communities* (pp. 7-34). Binghamton, NY: Haworth.

Jessor, R., & Jessor, S. L. (1977). *Problem behavior and psychological development: A longitudinal study of youth*. San Diego: Academic Press.

Kachur, S. P., Stennies, G. M., Powell, K. E., Modzeleski, W., Stephens, R., Murphy, R., et al. (1996). School-associated violent deaths in the United States, 1992-1994. *Journal of the American Medical Association, 275,* 1729-1733.

Kazdin, A. E. (1993). Adolescent mental health: Prevention and treatment programs. *American Psychologist, 48,* 127-141.

Kitzman, H., Olds, D. L., Henderson, C. R., Hanks, C., Cole, R., Tatelbaum, R., McConnochie, K. M., Sidora, K., Luckey, D. W., Shaver, D., Engelhardt, K., James, D., & Barnard, K. (1997). Effect of prenatal and infancy home visitation by nurses on pregnancy outcomes, childhood injuries, and repeated childbearing: A randomized controlled trail. *Journal of the American Medical Association, 278,* 644-652.

Lerner, R. M. (1995). *America's youth in crisis: Challenges and options for programs and policies*. Thousand Oaks, CA: Sage.

Loeber, R., & Stouthamer-Loeber, M. (1987). Prediction. In H. C. Quay (Ed.), *Handbook of juvenile delinquency* (pp. 325-382). New York: John Wiley.

Maguin, E., Hawkins, J. D., Catalano, R. F., Hill, K., Abbott, R., & Herrenkohl, T. (1995, November). *Risk factors measured at three ages for violence at age 17-18*. Paper presented at the meeting of the American Society of Criminology, Boston.

Maguire, K., & Pastore, A. L. (1998). *Sourcebook of criminal justice statistics 1997*. Washington, DC: U.S. Department of Justice, Bureau of Justice Statistics.

Martinez, E. (1991). *Five hundred years of Chicano history*. Albuquerque, NM: Southwest Organizing Project.

Masten, A. S., & Coatsworth, J. D. (1998). The development of competence in favorable and unfavorable environments: Lessons from research on successful children. *American Psychologist, 53,* 185-204.

McLoyd, V. C. (1990). The impact of economic hardship on Black families and children: Psychological distress, parenting, and socioemotional development. *Child Development, 61,* 311-346.

McLoyd, V. C. (1998). Socioeconomic disadvantage and child development. *American Psychologist, 53,* 185-204.

Menard, S. (2001). *Short and long term consequences of violent victimization*. Boulder, CO: Institute for Behavioral Sciences.

Mercy, J. A., & Hammond, W. R. (2001). Learning to do violence prevention well. *American Journal of Preventative Medicine, 20,* 1-2.

Munoz, R. F., Mrazek, P. J., & Haggerty, R. J. (1996). Institute of Medicine report on prevention of mental disorders: Summary and commentary. *American Psychologist, 51,* 1116-1122.

Myers, L. J. (1988). *Understanding an Afrocentric world view: Introduction to an optimal psychology*. Dubuque, IA: Kendall.

National Center for Health Statistics (NCHS). (1998). *Vital statistics mortality data, underlying cause of death, 1997*. Hyattsville, MD: U.S. Department of Health and Human Services, Centers for Disease Control and Prevention.

Olds, D. L., Hill, P. L., Mihalic, S. F., & O'Brien, R. A. (1998). *Blueprints for violence prevention: Prenatal and infancy home visitation by nurses.* Boulder: University of Colorado.

Olds, D., & Kitzman, H. (1993). Review of research on home visiting for pregnant women and parents of young children. *The Future of Children, 3,* 53-92.

Osofosky, J. D. (1999). The impact of violence on children. *The Future of Children, 9,* 33-49.

Powell, K. E., Mercy, J. A., Crosby, A. E., Dahlberg, L. L., & Simon, T. R. (1999). Public health models of violence and violence prevention. *Encyclopedia of Violence, Peace, and Conflict, 3,* 175-187.

Reese, L. E., Crosby, A. E., & McKinney, K. (2001, April). *Macro-level correlates of homicide among African American males: Examining educational attainment and poverty as risk factors for homicide.* Paper presented at the Fifth National Conference on Family and Community Violence Prevention, Los Angeles.

Reese, L. E., Vera, E. M., Simon, T. R., & Ikeda, R. M. (2000). The role of families and care givers as risk and protective factors in preventing youth violence. *Clinical Child and Family Psychology, 3,* 61-77.

Rennison, C. M. (1999). *Criminal victimization 1998: Changes 1997-98 with trends 1993-98* (Pub. No. NCJ176353). Washington, DC: Bureau of Justice Statistics.

Ringel, C. (1997). *Criminal victimization 1996: Changes 1995-96* (Pub. No. NCJ-165812). Washington, DC: Bureau of Justice Statistics.

Smith, C., & Thornberry, T. P. (1995). The relationship between childhood maltreatment and adolescent involvement in delinquency. *Criminology, 33,* 451-481.

Snyder, H. N., & Sickmund, M. (1999). *Juvenile offenders and victims: 1999 national report.* Washington, DC: U.S. Department of Justice, Office of Justice Programs, Office of Juvenile Justice and Delinquency Prevention.

Soriano, F. (1994). U.S. Latinos. In L. Eron, J. Gentry, & P. Schlegel (Eds.), *Reason to hope: A psychosocial perspective on violence and youth* (pp. 119-132). Washington, DC: American Psychological Association.

Spencer, M. B., Cole, S. P., DuPree, D., Glymph, A., & Pierre, P. (1993). Self-efficacy among urban African American early adolescents: Exploring issues of risk, vulnerability, and resilience. *Development and Psychopathology, 5,* 719-739.

Spencer, M. B., Dobbs, B., & Swanson, D. P. (1988). Afro-American adolescents: Adaptational processes and socioeconomic diversity in behavioral outcomes. *Journal of Adolescence, 11,* 117-137.

U.S. Bureau of the Census. (1999). *Poverty in the United States.* Washington, DC: U.S. Department of Commerce, Economics and Statistics Administration.

U.S. Department of Health and Human Services. (2001). *Youth violence: A report of the surgeon general.* Rockville, MD: Author.

Wells, L. E., & Rankin, J. H. (1988). Direct parental controls and delinquency. *Criminology, 26,* 263-285.

Wilson, W. J. (1987). *The truly disadvantaged.* Chicago: University of Chicago Press.

Wilson, W. J. (1996). *When work disappears: The world of the new urban poor.* New York: Vintage.

Yung, B., & Hammond, W. R. (1994). Native Americans. In L. Eron, J. Gentry, & P. Schlegel (Eds.), *Reason to hope: A psychosocial perspective on violence and youth* (pp. 133-144). Washington, DC: American Psychological Association.

Part V

CLINICAL INTERVENTIONS

CHAPTER 23

Cross-Cultural Counseling
Developing Culture-Centered Interactions

PAUL B. PEDERSEN
University of Hawaii

Cross-cultural counseling is any broadly defined psychological helping relationship in formal or informal settings where the provider assesses, understands, and/or evaluates a client's behavior in that client's cultural context where those behaviors were learned and displayed. Because all behavior is learned and displayed in a cultural context—and if culture is defined broadly to include demographic, status, and affiliation as well as ethnographic variables—then all counseling can be described as cross-cultural.

If culture is made central to counseling, then behavior can be measured more accurately, personal identity becomes more clear, the consequences of problems are better understood, and situations become more meaningful in their cultural contexts. Culture-centered interventions depend on an inclusive definition of culture and a broad definition of the counseling process. The search for models that tolerate the complexity of a culture-centered perspective includes non-Western alternatives as multiculturalism evolves into a "fourth force" or dimension in contemporary counseling theory.

Culture controls our lives and defines reality for each of us, with or without our permission and/or intentional awareness. A culture-centered perspective recognizes each person's cultural context as central and not marginal, fundamental and not exotic. Some conventional approaches have been "behavior centered" without recognizing how culture shapes and directs our behaviors. Other approaches have been "person centered" without recognizing the role of culture in shaping the person's perception of reality. Still other approaches have been "problem centered" without recognizing the role those problems serve in a culturally defined context. The culture-centered approach to counseling interventions is directly focused on the culturally learned assumptions that direct our behaviors, define our personality, and negotiate with our problems (Pedersen, 2000a; Pedersen & Ivey, 1993).

A HISTORICAL PERSPECTIVE OF MULTICULTURAL COUNSELING

Although mental health problems are similar across cultures, the appropriate response to those problems through various forms of counseling has been very diversified. The increase of urbanized, modernized, and industrialized societies and the corresponding breakdown of family and village support systems on a global scale have increased the appropriateness of counseling for managing social and individual problems.

The functional precursors of mental health services have been documented in a wide variety of cultures, although usually not differentiated as a separate specialty outside the Euro-American context. The labels of *counseling* and *therapy* are relatively new, but the functions described by those labels have a long history. A comprehensive history of counseling interventions would need to go back to the beginning of recorded social relationships. We now know (a) that formal counseling and therapy have spread with the worldwide rise of industrialization, urbanization, and modernization; (b) that "talk therapy" is only one alternative counseling intervention in a global context; (c) that counseling is the treatment of choice for a relatively small number of people worldwide; and (d) that counseling and therapy are becoming more responsive to the culturally defined context of people worldwide (Pedersen, 2000a; Ponterotto, Casas, Suzuki, & Alexander, 1995; Sue & Sue, 1999).

The Western and Non-Western Context of Counseling

Counseling has conventionally relied on a "Westernized" description of the self that presumes a separate independent and autonomous individual guided by traits, abilities, values, and motives that distinguish that individual from others. Western cultures are described by Berry, Poortinga, Segall, and Dasen (1992) as more *idiocentric,* emphasizing competition, self-confidence, and freedom, whereas collectivistic cultures are more *allocentric,* emphasizing communal responsibility, social usefulness, and acceptance of authority. Westernized beliefs grew out of a naturalistic understanding of the physical world describing human behavior in objective expressions rather than more subjective and internalized sensations (Taylor, 1989).

The clash between Western and non-Westernized thinking styles is evident in majority-minority cultural relationships. Counseling and therapy have a history of protecting the status quo against change, as perceived by minority cultures. These attitudes are documented in scientific racism (Sue & Sue, 1999) and Euro-American ethnocentrism. Cultural differences were explained by a "genetic deficiency" model that promoted the superiority of dominant cultures. This was modified to a "cultural deficit" model that described minorities as deprived or disadvantaged by their culture. Minorities were underrepresented among professional counselors and therapists, the topic of multiculturalism was trivialized at professional meetings, minority views were underrepresented in the research literature, and consequently, the counseling profession was discredited among minority populations.

The conflict between Western and non-Western perspectives is not necessary. Walsh (1989) described the relationship between Asian and Western psychologies as complementary to one another. Asian and Western psychologies both focus on development, with the Asian systems focused on advanced stages of development in a more transpersonal focus and Western systems focused on psychopathology and physical/mental development.

From a multiple-state-of-consciousness model, the traditional Western approach is recognized as a relativistically useful model provided that, because of the limitations imposed by state-specific relevancy, learning and understanding, it is not applied inappropriately to perspectives and states of consciousness and identity outside its scope. (Walsh, 1989, p. 549)

Pathologizing mystical experiences would be an example of Western models going beyond their boundaries in some cultures.

The recent emphasis on "indigenous psychology" (Kim & Berry, 1993) and the increased attention to psychology in non-Western cultures have resulted from (a) increased international contact, (b) redefinition of postcolonial relationships, (c) internationalization of the social sciences, (d) radicalization of special interest groups, (e) a methodological paradigm shift toward qualitative methods, (f) activism of contemporary social sciences, (g) increased interdisciplinary cooperation, (h) increased awareness of cultural diversity, and (i) increased international educational exchanges (Sloan, 1990). By positioning the cultural context as central to the counseling process, a new theoretical explanation of human behavior emerges.

> We are living in a time when the conventional wisdom about human nature and the nature of society is under attack. Technology has run amok; many now question our ability to bring technology under manageable control. Bureaucracy—a social structure originally established to provide for personal growth—now stifles human development and generates a philosophy that human nature is lazy, irresponsible and extrinsically motivated. The communal movement has challenged a pessimistic drift in our society. Through study of the movement's assumptions, aims, procedures and outcomes, we may gain an understanding of the future of philosophies of human nature. (Wrightsman, 1992, p. 293)

Sampson (1993) suggested that psychology and counseling have at best accommodated "add-on" eclectic strategies in response to culturally different perspectives without fundamentally transforming conventional frameworks of understanding:

> Psychology is accused of using a framework of understanding that implicitly represents a particular point of view, that of currently dominant social groups, all the while acting as though its own voice were neutral, reflecting reason rationality, and with its ever expanding collection of empirical data, perhaps truth itself. (p. 1221)

The legitimacy of counseling as a science requires more than additional data or even more inclusive samples of objective data in defense of objective positivism. It requires the inclusion of more subjective, constructivist, and contextual perspectives based on the sociocultural context of culturally different people.

The Contemporary Context of Multicultural Counseling

Morris Jackson (1995) provided a concise description of the contemporary historical perspective for multicultural counseling. Although the functions of counseling have been applied around the world, the term *multicultural* is more of an American phenomenon, at least in its origination as a label. Many of the early writings about multicultural counseling were done primarily by Black American minority authors, leading up to the civil rights movement, women's rights issues, and the forced recognition of other special interest groups in America and in response to segregation, exclusion, prejudice, and injustice toward those groups. More extensive discussions of these early authors are available elsewhere (M. L. Jackson, 1995; Pedersen, 1997, 2000a; Sue & Sue, 1999).

During the 1960s, there was a revolution going on in American society that was related, in part, to the opposition to the war in Vietnam, the civil rights movement, increased attention to feminism, and a questioning of established authority generally. This was the beginning of multicultural counseling as a visible perspective. Professional counseling organizations such as the American Personnel and Guidance Association (APGA) and the

American Psychological Association (APA) began to recognize the injustices of a mono-cultural perspective. Multiculturalism developed a militancy during this time that has continued up to the present time, as advocates of "minority groups" agitated for a more fair and equitable treatment by society.

During the 1970s, there was increased attention to ethnocultural minority issues and the different perspectives of special interest groups, and multicultural counseling organizations were established. Almost all of the counseling professionals working toward the establishment of multicultural counseling were themselves minority group members, writing about their own cultural groups and from their own perspective.

During the 1980s and 1990s, there was an explosion of literature about multicultural counseling, and the topic became more recognized among majority culture liberals, such as the present author. With increased publications and visibility of multicultural counseling, the movement gained power to influence the American Counseling Association (ACA) and APA as well as other professional organizations. There was a realization that multicultural counseling was not only advocating the welfare of minority groups but also the validity of counseling as a discipline. Because all behaviors are learned and displayed in a cultural context, accurate assessment, meaningful understanding, and appropriate intervention require attention to the client's cultural context. This generic application of multicultural counseling to the whole field of counseling has profound implications for the future. If we are to take culture and multiculturalism seriously as a generic "fourth force" perspective to complement—but not compete with—psychodynamic, behavioral, and humanistic perspectives, then multicultural counseling will become a permanent feature of counseling (Pedersen, 1991, 1998).

The Future Context of Multicultural Counseling

Culture promises to make our lives more complicated in teaching, administration, research, and direct service. We must develop tools to manage this necessary complexity and not ignore it as we have in the past. Lifton's (1993) "protean self," in contrast with the "fundamentalist self," demonstrates complexity with reference to the Greek god Proteus, who was constantly changing form. The postmodern person is a "shape-shifter" with multiple identities as a source of strength so that tolerance of ambiguity rather than dissonance reduction becomes the psychological ideal (Geleick, 1987). In the postmodern world, discontinuous change seems to be a permanent feature (Rosenau, 1992), but for the affirmative postmodernists, at least, it promotes the search for meaning through complex patterns.

Complexity theory in the social sciences grew out of chaos theory in the physical sciences as it seeks to redefine conventional categories. Those who advocate complexity theory

> believe that they are forging the first rigorous alternative to the kind of linear, reductionistic thinking that has dominated science since the time of Newton—and that has now gone about as far as it can go in addressing the problems of our modern world. (Waldrop, 1992, p. 13)

Barton (1994) described a new paradigm for understanding systems described in terms of nonlinear and self-organizing dynamics. Butz (1992a, 1992b, 1993) applied chaos theory to the experience of anxiety in psychotherapy and systems theory in family therapy in a multicultural context, reviewing the dozens of publications in print that apply chaos theory to counseling and therapy. Chaos is the starting point for most psychotherapies, in which the therapist becomes the guide and companion for encountering chaos in the client's life. Western cultures have tended to disregard or resolve chaos and thus lack conceptual tools for dealing with this level of complexity. We might well look to non-Western cultures to find conceptual tools for managing the complexity and recognizing the simplicity of each cultural context.

CURRENT AND ENDURING CONTROVERSIES

There are many controversies in cross-cultural counseling about how interventions should be done in multicultural contexts. Although there are no conclusive and final answers to any of these controversies, it is important to be informed on the issues being debated.

Is Counseling Culturally Encapsulated?

Wrenn (1962) first introduced the concept of cultural encapsulation. This perspective assumes five basic identifying features. First, reality is defined according to one set of cultural assumptions. Second, people become insensitive to cultural variations among individuals and assume their own view is the only right one. Third, assumptions are not dependent on reasonable proof or rational consistency but are believed true regardless of evidence to the contrary. Fourth, solutions are sought in technique-oriented strategies and quick or simple remedies. Fifth, everyone is judged from the viewpoint of one's self-reference criteria without regard for the other person's separate cultural context. There is evidence that the profession of counseling is even more encapsulated now than it was when Wrenn wrote his original article (Wrenn, 1985).

The former president of the American Psychological Association, George Albee (1994), described how completely psychology in the United States has been encapsulated in the past hundred years:

> Most of the early leaders in psychology embraced ideological views that stressed the natural superiority of a white male patriarchy, the acceptance of Social Darwinism, the inferiority of women and of the brunette races. Calvinism stressed economic success as the hallmark of salvation and psychology concurred. Anti-semitism and homophobia were standard. Eugenics spokesmen urged the elimination of the unfit and inferior and opposed welfare programs, decent wages and safe working conditions. (p. 22)

Some of these biased views continue to be supported in the psychological literature, although in more subtle forms.

Examples of cultural encapsulation are evident in the counseling literature when the following assumptions are presumed to be true and accepted (Pedersen, 2000a):

1. All persons are evaluated according to a hypothetical "normal" standard of behavior across cultural contexts.

2. Individualism is presumed to be more appropriate than a collectivist perspective.

3. Professional boundaries are narrowly defined and interdisciplinary cooperation is discouraged.

4. Psychological health is described primarily in abstract jargon with little or no attention to the unique cultural context.

5. Dependency is considered to be an undesirable or even neurotic condition.

6. The client's support systems are not normally considered in the analysis of an individual person's psychological health.

7. Only linear-based "cause-effect" thinking is accepted as appropriate.

8. The individual is usually expected to "adjust" to fit the system, even when the system is wrong.

9. The historical roots of a person's cultural context are disregarded or minimalized in counseling.

10. The counselor presumes herself or himself to be relatively free of racism and cultural bias.

Cultural encapsulation does exist. Counseling has a reputation in many minority communities as having been used as an oppressive instrument by those in power to maintain the status quo (Sue & Sue, 1999). Ponterotto and Casas (1991) contended that "the majority of traditionally trained counselors operate from a culturally biased and encapsulated framework which results in the provision of culturally conflicting and even oppressive counseling treatments" (pp. 7-8).

Are Counseling Measures and Assessments Culturally Biased?

Lonner and Ibrahim (1996) pointed out how assessment measures used in counseling have been culturally biased. They concluded that an accurate assessment would need to meet certain criteria: (a) The client's worldview, beliefs, values, and culturally unique assumptions need to be understood; (b) the client's culture-specific norm grouping needs to be generated; and (c) a combination of approaches using clinical judgment as well as standardized or objective measures needs to be derived. At the same time, standardized assessment measures raise problems of (a) the distinction between constructs and criteria, (b) the establishment of equivalence, (c) the effect of verbal or nonverbal stimuli, (d) the role of response sets, (e) the tendency to infer deficits from test score differences, and (f) other examples of embedded bias. Kohlberg's measures of moral development, for example, are biased toward an individualistic norm reflecting the values of an urban, middle-class group (Segall, Dasen, Berry, &

Poortinga, 1990) and with a bias favoring the male perspective (Gilligan, 1982, 1987).

Cultural bias in the use of tests and measurements are likely to result in overdiagnosis, underdiagnosis, or misdiagnosis. Although it is generally accepted that biases exist in the use of counseling tests and measures (Dana, 1993; Paniagua, 1994; Samuda, 1998), this does not necessarily mean that those tests and measures cannot or should not be used. The search first for "culture-free" tests and later for "culture-fair" tests has not been successful (Irvine & Berry, 1993; Lonner & Ibrahim, 1996). Flaherty, Gaviria, and Pathak (1988) suggested that any culture-fair test would need to fulfill five validity criteria of (a) content equivalence across cultures, (b) semantic equivalence across cultures, (c) technical equivalence, (d) criterion equivalence, and (e) conceptual equivalence. Escobar (1993) contended that no test or assessment can fulfill these five criteria.

Lonner (1990) demonstrated that (a) testing and assessment are not familiar procedures in much of the non-Western world; (b) psychological constructs and concepts are not universally valid; (c) the basis of comparison across cultures is often not equivalent; (d) test stimuli are more frequently in the verbal rather than visual mode, even though language conveys strong bias; and (e) test score differences frequently imply a "deficit" in one or another culture by the language used to describe those differences.

Should Culture Be Defined Broadly or Narrowly?

The broad definition of culture presumes that the salient features of a person's cultural identity may include demographic variables (age, gender, place of residence, etc.), status variables (social, educational, economic, etc.), and affiliations (formal and informal) in addition to ethnographic variables of nationality and ethnicity. According to the broad definition, some aspects of all counseling are multicultural, given the complexity of culturally defined salience as it adapts to each changing cultural context. The culture-centered perspective is generic, and a broad definition of culture becomes an important metaphor for counseling.

Culture-centered counseling must be sensitive to the client's comprehensive cultural context. Segall et al. (1990) described culture as the ecological forces that move and shape nature: "Given those characteristics of culture it becomes possible to define it simply as the totality of whatever all persons learn from other persons" (p. 26). If culture is part of the environment and all behavior is shaped by culture, then culture-centered counseling is a response to all broadly defined culturally learned patterns. Cultural psychology (Shweder, 1990) presumes that each human behavior gives meaning to the environment, which changes people in response to that sociocultural environment. Cultural traditions and social practices regulate, express, and change patterns of human behavior. "Cultural psychology is the study of the ways subject and object, self and other, psyche and culture, person and context, figure and ground, practitioner and practice live together, require each other and dynamically, dialectically and jointly make each other up" (Shweder, 1990, p. 73).

Goldstein (1994) explained that the prescriptive mismatch of services occurred as a result of cultural differences between lower social class clients and typically middle-class change agents:

> Both may be of the same race, ethnicity, age, gender and city of residence. But if they are from different social classes they are from different cultures. Further, they are from different cultures in ways that directly bear upon the form and efficacy of the intervention most appropriately offered. (p. 160)

Sampson (1993) described the political implications of a person's many cultural identities. Identity politics is based on the culturally learned perspectives of people seeking to be in control of their own identities, despite being denied that opportunity.

> The clear message is that current forms of cultural and psychological practice deny certain groups any possibility of being heard in their own way, on their own terms, reflecting their own interests and specificities and that this condition does not reflect mere chance but rather reflects the operation of the power in charge to dictate the terms by which psychological and social reality will be of those encountered. (Sampson, 1993, p. 1220)

Although the broad definition of culture presents the danger of "watering down" culture, the narrow definitions of culture also present a serious danger. Sue (1990) warned against the dangers of a narrow definition of culture in (a) fostering technique-oriented shortcuts, (b) developing rigid counseling styles, (c) applying the self-reference criterion to good counseling, and (d) perpetuating stereotypes.

Can You Measure Ethno-Racial-Cultural Identity?

One useful area of counseling research that has grown out of the ethnocultural perspective has been the measurement of racial/ethnic identity (Ponterotto et al., 1995). This research was based on a conceptual framework proposed by Thomas (1971) on a six-stage "Negromachy" and independently by Cross (1971) on a four-stage "Nigresence" framework of Black identity development. B. Jackson (1975) also introduced a Black identity development with four stages at about the same time. The first stage emphasized passive acceptance, the second emphasized active resistance, the third involved redirection, and the fourth was internalization of identity. Marcia (1980) based his research on Erikson's stages of crisis in ego identity formation through diffusion, foreclosed identity, and finally, achieved identity. Delworth (1989) used Marcia's work to look at gender-related aspects of identity development. Others have looked at a great variety of different special interest group members' identity development using the same framework.

Helms's (1985) stage model is probably the best-known contemporary example. This model is based on five assumptions.

1. Minority groups develop model personality patterns in response to White racism.

2. Some styles of identity are healthier than others.

3. Cultural identity requires new attitudes toward cognitive, affective, and behavioral processes.

4. Styles of identity are distinguishable.

5. Cultural interaction is influenced by the participant's cultural identity.

Helms (1990) went on to trace racial consciousness of Blacks from the less healthy White-defined models to more healthy self-defined models. Each stage is a worldview related to maturation. In the first pre-encounter stage, the Black idealizes White standards and ignores or is assimilated into a White society. In the second encounter stage, the Black is confronted with racial injustice. The third immersion stage follows as an internalized but stereotyped Black perspective. The fourth stage of internalization moves toward a positive Black identity. The fifth stage involves commitment to the positive internalized perspective.

Cross (1991) has recently modified his earlier model toward a more inclusive direction. Cross's recent framework follows his earlier work in the first three stages. In the fourth stage of internalization, however, a thoughtful salience shifts from a convergent nationalistic to a bicultural or multicultural perspective, so that racial identity is matched divergently to other identity concerns about religious, gender, career, class, and role orientations. In the fifth stage of internalization-commitment, there is a long-term transition of Black identity into a more broadly defined life plan focused on a wide range of potentially salient identities.

Should Culture-Centered Counseling Emphasize Similarities or Differences?

To distinguish universal and shared aspects of all cultures from unique and particular aspects of a single culture, Pike (1966) borrowed from the linguistic term *phonemics* (*emic*), referring to sounds unique in a particular language, and the linguistic term *phonetics* (*etic*), or universal language sounds. This emic-etic distinction has led some counselors to focus on cultural similarities, whereas others have focused on cultural differences, ignoring the essential complementarity of these two aspects.

The applications of culture-centered counseling are always unique and universal at the same time. Brewer (1991) described social identity as derived from a tension between nomothetic similarity and unique individuation at the same time. Brewer documented the importance of this dual emphasis in "uniqueness theory" and other models of individuation. "In general these models assume that individuals meet these needs by maintaining some intermediate degree of similarity between the self and relevant others" (Brewer, 1991, p. 477).

Segall et al. (1990) also emphasized the interaction of similarities and differences. A counselor begins with an "imposed etic," applying one's own culture as though it were a universal rule, while refining and adapting those rules in practice to identify cultural differences. As a result, the two cultures are distinguished by their differences, and a "derived etic" describing their similarities is constructed. The emic approach has been associated with relativism, whereas the etic approaches have been associated with universalism. Berry et al. (1992) distinguished the relativist from the universalist position in cross-cultural psychology, pointing out the complementary implications of each for culture-centered counseling interventions.

Are Professional Ethical Guidelines Adequate to Guide Culture-Centered Counselors?

Too often, the culture-centered counselor has to choose between following professional ethical guidelines or acting in an ethical manner (Casas & Thompson, 1991). All professional counselor associations with ethical guidelines emphasize the ethical responsibility of counselors to know their clients' cultural values before delivering a mental health service to those clients. However, professional guidelines continue to support the perspective of a dominant culture (Pedersen, 1994), sometimes requiring the counselor to demonstrate "responsible disobedience" (Pedersen & Marsella, 1982) to the formal ethical guidelines. The trend toward ethical consciousness in culture-centered counseling is credited to demographic changes favoring minority groups, increased visibility of ethnic minorities, pressure by civil rights and human rights groups worldwide, and the economic incentives to attract minority clients (Casas, 1984). The support for more adequate multicultural ethical guidelines has continued with heightened group consciousness, government-mandated affirmative action, court-ordered integration, and bicultural educational alternatives.

The ethical imperative has been overshadowed by the need to fix blame. This polarization of society into majority versus minority orientation has resulted in moral exclusion demonstrated through psychological distancing, displacing responsibility, demonstrating group loyalty, and normalizing violence. This can occur through overt and malicious action or through covert support and passive disregard. "As severity of conflict and threat escalates, harm and sanctioned aggression become more likely. As harm doing escalates, societal structures change, the scope of justice shrinks, and the boundaries of harm doing expand" (Opotow, 1990, p. 13). Moral exclusion is one obvious example of institutional racism.

Professional ethical guidelines have sometimes protected providers against culturally different consumers (Axelson, 1999; Corey, Corey, & Callanan, 1993; LaFromboise, Foster, & James, 1996; Ponterotto & Casas, 1991). The APA's (1992) ethical guidelines provide numerous examples of how cultural biases are implicit within the principles themselves (Pedersen, 2000a). The APA's ethical standards are even more blatant in their cultural bias, beginning with Standard 1.08, which presumes that differences of age, gender, race, ethnicity, national origin, religion, sexual orientation, disability, language, and socioeconomic status are not always significant in all psychological interventions! The presumption of generalized and abstract standards or guidelines for ethical behavior is that all counselors of good will share the same cultural assumptions, despite the considerable evidence to the contrary (Pedersen, 2000b). Seeking safety in abstractions has allowed the individual counseling provider to project her or his own self-referenced cultural assumptions into the professional guidelines at the expense of culturally different clients.

What Training Models Are Culture Centered?

Culture-centered training results in movement from simple to more complex thinking about multicultural counseling relationships. A trained counselor depends less on stereotypes and is better prepared to comprehend the influence of a cultural context on the counseling process. The trained counselor has a wider range of response alternatives to meet the needs of each cultural context. The trained counselor can describe each cultural context from the contrasting viewpoints of culturally different participants. The trained counselor can identify and understand the "source" or basic underlying cultural assumptions of a problem. The trained counselor can keep track of the "salient" culture for a client as it changes over time and place. The trained counselor can account for her or his own culturally learned assumptions in the counseling process (Midgette & Meggert, 1991).

Several multicultural training models have been suggested. Ridley, Mendoza, and Kanitz (1994) described multicultural counseling training (MIT) as a framework that moves from training philosophy to learning objectives, instructional strategies, program designs, and evaluation that matches instructional strategies with learning objectives. Landis and Brislin (1983) described training alternatives that divide experiential/discover approaches from didactic/expository approaches and culture-general from culture-specific perspectives. Sue, Arredondo, and McDavis (1992) described a three-stage developmental sequence from awareness to knowledge to skill (AKS) as a hierarchy of multicultural counseling competencies. A needs assessment of these AKS competencies is available in Pedersen (2000a).

AWARENESS-ORIENTED TRAINING

Culture is within the person and difficult to separate from other learned competencies. Developing an awareness of culturally learned assumptions is therefore essential for any intentional counselor as a professional obligation (Sue, Ivey, & Pedersen, 1996). The achievement of multicultural awareness through education and training is not a trivial goal. Understanding the basic underlying assumptions that control both counselor and client is fundamental for accurate and appropriate counseling interventions.

The Intrapersonal Cultural Grid in Figure 23.1 provides a framework for describing the degree of awareness necessary for culture-centered counselors. On one dimension, the "cultural teachers" or social system variables of demographic (age, gender, place of residence, etc.), status (social, educational, economic, etc.), affiliation (formal and informal), and ethnographic variables (ethnicity, nationality, language, religion, etc.) are combined to suggest the complex, dynamic, and potentially salient cultural identities and roles that control both the counselor and the client's behavior. Salience is assumed to continuously change across social system variables, depending on the cultural context in each situation, with some social system variables becoming more salient and others less salient all the time.

The Intrapersonal Cultural Grid combines personal features of behavior (what you did), expectation (why you did it), and value (where you learned to do it) with social system variables (Pedersen, 1997). The Intrapersonal Cultural Grid is an open-ended framework to increase awareness of the "teachers" of our culture who have taught us the cultural rules that regulate each of our many behaviors. Each behavior is guided by culturally learned expectations that regard that behavior as appropriate in a particular situation. Each culturally learned expectation is an extension of culturally learned basic and fundamental values that are not negotiable and cannot be compromised. Each value is learned from teachers in the different social systems as these systems become salient. The personal behavior combined with the social systems contextual orientation provides an awareness of how culture controls behavior through culture-centered training.

Within-Person Cultural Grid

PERSONAL VARIABLES

Cultural Teachers	Where You Learned to Do It	Why You Did It	What You Did
1. Family relations relatives fellow countrypersons ancestors shared beliefs			

2. Power relationships
social friends
sponsors and
   mentors
subordinates
supervisors and
   superiors			

3. Memberships coworkers organizations gender and age groups workplace colleagues			
4. Nonfamily relationships friendships classmates neighbors people like me			

Figure 23.1   The Intrapersonal "Within-Person" Cultural Grid

KNOWLEDGE-ORIENTED TRAINING

Developing an accurate and appropriate cultural awareness is not enough. It is essential to assemble the facts and information identified by those culturally learned assumptions as important for culture-centered counseling.

The facts and information become important tools for change, based on cultural assumptions. Counselors who have developed an appropriate awareness will know what facts they need and will be motivated to gather that information before proceeding in their counseling interventions. The second step is that of gathering knowledge and developing an informed comprehension or understanding of the client in her or his cultural context. Without an appropriate foundation of awareness, the facts and information gathered will have no meaning (Sue et al., 1992; Sue et al., 1998).

A counselor who has the required knowledge, understanding, and comprehension of the clients' cultural context will be better prepared to be genuine and authentic in a variety of cultural settings. Having mastered these competencies of knowledge can help the counselor be more accurate and competent with every client, regardless of that client's cultural context. Absence of understanding, on the other hand, is likely to inhibit effectiveness.

Sue and Sue (1999) pointed out a pervasive and enduring bias in the knowledge being taught at most counselor education programs. First, although there is much rhetoric about the importance of multiculturalism in counselor education programs, there is little evidence of including culture-centered knowledge into the curriculum. Cultural information has usually been relegated to a separate course rather than integrated throughout the curriculum. Second, there has not been a systematic approach to the teaching of culture-centered counseling skills. Until culture-centered constructs are recognized as generic and central to all counseling, the changes are likely to be cosmetic and superficial. Third, media-based training packages need to be developed to demonstrate the broad and important role of culture in counselor education. These supporting materials for a counselor education curriculum need to be developed to demonstrate and illustrate specific strategies for inclusion in counseling. Fourth, there is a presumption that multiculturalism in counselor education is merely accumulating additional knowledge about other cultures, without regard to the underlying assumptions or the consequent skills that are necessary.

SKILL-ORIENTED TRAINING

The third level of educating a culture-centered counselor requires an effective and skilled ability to make appropriate changes in a variety of culturally different contexts. This third level is the most difficult and presumes a successful development first of cultural awareness and second of cultural knowledge about the client's cultural context.

The Interpersonal Cultural Grid in Figure 23.2 describes how both cultural similarities and differences can be mobilized in culture-centered counseling. Culture teaches us that similar behaviors have different meanings, and different behaviors might have the same meaning. It is important for the counselor to interpret behaviors accurately in terms of the expectations and values attached to the behaviors by the client. If two persons share the same positive expectation of trust, respect, caring, success, or safety, it is not always necessary for them to display the same behaviors.

In the first quadrant, two individuals display the same behaviors (what was done) and the same positive expectations (why it was done) in a congruent and harmonious relationship. There is no conflict or disharmony in this aspect of the relationship, but there is also relatively little challenge or learning taking place.

In the second quadrant, two individuals have different behaviors but share some of the same positive expectations of trust, respect, and fairness, for example. This describes the typical cross-cultural conflict in which one or both persons misinterpret the other's behavior by assuming their own self-reference criteria. If the skilled counselor can help both persons find common ground in their shared positive expectations, both persons may become more tolerant of behavior differences, and both will be more accurate in interpreting the other person's behavior and/or may learn new behaviors appropriate

BETWEEN-PERSONS CULTURAL GRID

WHAT WAS DONE?

	PERCEIVED POSITIVE ACTION	PERCEIVED NEGATIVE ACTION
WHAT WAS DONE?		
WHY WAS IT DONE?		

Figure 23.2 The Interpersonal "Between-Persons" Cultural Grid

to both persons' shared positive expectations for trust, respect, caring, safety, or success.

In the third quadrant, both individuals display the same behaviors, but their expectations are now negative or different. One or both persons are forced to behave in a particular way, but they resent the imposition. When a culture-centered intervention has failed to find common ground of shared positive expectations, the conflict is likely to migrate to this third quadrant. The conflict in this third cell is more disguised and hidden—by the similar pretended behaviors—but more destructive of personal relationships because of the different or negative expectations.

In the fourth quadrant, the two individuals have both different behaviors and different or negative expectations. They are at war with one another and may not even be interested in finding common ground. In the absence of culture-centered counseling, conflict is likely to migrate from the second to the third and ultimately to the fourth quadrant. A skilled culture-centered counselor might be able to move the conflict back to the second quadrant, where differences of behavior are safe and even desirable, as long as both persons trust and respect each other through shared positive expectations.

The culture-centered approach suggests that individual change must be sensitive to the cultural context in which that change occurs. Change is perceived as linked to the cultural context in such a way that training and education themselves become a treatment modality. The influence between a culture-centered counselor and client becomes reciprocal in this cultural context, with both counselor and client contributing to the construction of a shared context that is both complex and dynamic. Culture-centered counselors are able to generate a wide variety of intentional verbal and nonverbal responses appropriate to the cultural context. Through training, the culture-centered counselor is able to manage more complexity, send and receive verbal and nonverbal messages more accurately, and perceive each client from the viewpoint of the client's cultural context.

CONCLUSION

Gielen (1994) contended that American psychology routinely neglects international research, even when the research is in English, in contrast with the hard sciences, which include international research. Rosensweig

(1992) estimated that about 40% to 45% of all psychological researchers live outside the United States and that the more international researchers are vastly underrepresented in U.S. professional psychological journals. Psychology is growing faster outside than within the United States, and in the very near future, more published research will be done abroad than in the United States, threatening to isolate monocultural domestic psychological perspectives.

If mainstream "textbook" counseling is to become more global and less culturally biased, several changes will be required (Gielen, 1994). First, textbooks need to incorporate examples from a variety of cultures. Second, textbooks need to introduce cross-cultural perspectives throughout the text. Third, psychological theories need to be routinely contextualized in a culture-centered framework. Fourth, psychological theories need to be consistently understood in their historical context. Fifth, U.S. journals need to invite more international editors, authors, and advisers to participate. Sixth, U.S. journals need to cite more relevant foreign publications. Seventh, textbooks might be jointly written by authors from different cultures. Eighth, institutional support and funding for collaborative research across cultural and national boundaries need to become more available.

Culture-centered counseling will be guided more by adapting to culturally different clients than by theory. Theoretical structures will need to be extrapolated from examples of success with culturally different clients. It will be important to remember that the counseling audience of the future is a globally defined population. Solutions to problems of culture-centered counseling will rely on both Western and non-Western cultures. By moving from practice to theory in the field of counseling, we can become responsive to cultural similarities and differences in each cultural context. By making culture central to the counseling process, this chapter has attempted to demonstrate the ways that culture can facilitate the quality of counseling and the effectiveness of counselors. Attempts to disregard the cultural context, on the other hand, will lead counselors toward abstract projections of their own self-referenced criteria and the fatal illusion of a monocultural fantasy.

REFERENCES

Albee, G. W. (1994). The sins of the fathers: Sexism, racism and ethnocentrism in psychology. *International Psychologist, 35*(1), 22.

American Psychological Association (APA). (1992). Ethical principles of psychologists and code of conduct. *American Psychologist, 47*(12), 1561-1597.

Axelson, J. A. (1999). *Counseling and development in a multicultural society* (3rd ed.). Pacific Grove, CA: Brooks/Cole.

Barton, S. (1994). Chaos, self-organization and psychology. *American Psychologist, 49*(1), 5-14.

Berry, J. W., Poortinga, Y. H., Segall, M. H., & Dasen, P. J. (1992). *Cross cultural psychology: Research and applications.* Cambridge, UK: Cambridge University Press.

Brewer, M. B. (1991). The social self: On being the same and different at the same time. *Personality and Social Psychology Bulletin, 17*, 475-482.

Butz, M. R. (1992a). Chaos, an omen of transcendence in the psychotherapeutic process. *Psychological Reports, 71*, 827-843.

Butz, M. R. (1992b). The factual nature of the development of the self. *Psychological Reports, 71,* 1043-1063.

Butz, M. R. (1993). Systemic family therapy and symbolic chaos. *Humanity and Society, 17*(2), 200-223.

Casas, J. (1984). Policy training and research in counseling psychology: The racial/ethnic minority perspective. In S. Brown & R. Lent (Eds.), *Handbook of counseling psychology* (pp. 785-831). New York: John Wiley.

Casas, J., & Thompson, C. E. (1991). Ethical principles and standards: The racial ethnic minority perspective. *Counseling and Values, 35,* 186-195.

Corey, G., Corey, M. S., & Callanan, P. (1993). *Issues and ethics in the helping professions* (4th ed.). Pacific Grove, CA: Brooks/Cole.

Cross, W. (1971). The Negro-to-Black conversion experience. *Black Worlds, 20,* 13-17.

Cross, W. (1991). *Shades of black.* Philadelphia: Temple University Press.

Dana, R. H. (1993). *Multicultural assessment perspectives for professional psychology.* Boston: Allyn & Bacon.

Delworth, U. (1989). Identity in the college years: Issues of gender and ethnicity. *Journal of the National Association of Student Personnel Administrators, 26,* 162-166.

Escobar, J. E. (1993). Psychiatric epidemiology. In A. C. Gaw (Ed.), *Culture, ethnicity and mental illness* (pp. 43-73). Washington, DC: American Psychiatric Press.

Flaherty, J. H., Gaviria, F. M., & Pathak, D. (1988). Developing instruments for cross-cultural psychiatric research. *Journal of Nervous and Mental Disease, 176,* 257-263.

Geleick, J. (1987). *Chaos making a new science.* New York: Viking-Penguin.

Gielen, U. P. (1994). American mainstream psychology and its relationship to international and cross-cultural psychology. In A. L. Comunian & U. P. Gielen (Eds.), *Advancing psychology and its applications: International perspectives* (pp. 26-40). Milan, Italy: Franco-Angeli.

Gilligan, C. (1982). *In a different voice.* Cambridge, MA: Harvard University Press.

Gilligan, C. (1987). Moral orientation and moral development. In E. F. Kittay & D. T. Myers (Eds.), *Woman and moral theory* (pp. 19-33). Totowa, NJ: Rowman & Littlefield.

Goldstein, A. (1994). Teaching prosocial behavior to low-income youth. In P. Pedersen & J. Carey (Eds.), *Multicultural counseling in schools* (pp. 157-176). Boston: Allyn & Bacon.

Helms, J. E. (1985). Cultural identity in the treatment process. In P. Pedersen (Ed.), *Handbook of cross-cultural counseling and therapy* (pp. 239-245). Westport, CT: Greenwood.

Helms, J. E. (1990). *Black and White racial identity: Theory, research and practice.* Westport, CT: Greenwood.

Irvine, S. H., & Berry, J. W. (1993). *Human assessment and cultural factors.* New York: Plenum.

Jackson, B. (1975). Black identity development. In L. Golubschick & B. Persky (Eds.), *Urban social and educational issues* (pp. 158-164). Dubuque, IA: Kendall-Hall.

Jackson, M. L. (1995). Multicultural counseling: Historical perspectives. In J. G. Ponterotto, J. M. Casas, L. A. Suzuki, & C. M. Alexander (Eds.), *Handbook of multicultural counseling* (pp. 3-16). Thousand Oaks, CA: Sage.

Kim, U., & Berry, J. W. (1993). Introduction. In U. Kim & J. W. Berry (Eds.), *Indigenous psychologies: Research and experience in cultural context* (pp. 1-29). Newbury Park, CA: Sage.

LaFromboise, T. D., Foster, S., & James, A. (1996). Ethics in multicultural counseling. In P. Pedersen, J. Draguns, W. Lonner, & J. Trimble (Eds.), *Counseling across cultures* (4th ed., pp. 47-72). Thousand Oaks, CA: Sage.

Landis, D., & Brislin, R. W. (1983). *Handbook of intercultural training: Vol. I. Issues in theory and design.* New York: Pergamon.

Lifton, R. J. (1993). *The protean self.* New York: Basic Books.

Lonner, W. (1990). An overview of cross-cultural testing and assessment. In R.W. Brislin (Ed.), *Applied cross-cultural psychology* (pp. 56-76). Newbury Park, CA: Sage.

Lonner, W. J., & Ibrahim, F. A. (1996). Appraisal and assessment in cross-cultural counseling. In P. Pedersen, J. Draguns, W. Lonner, & J. Trimble (Eds.), *Counseling across cultures* (4th ed., pp. 293-322). Thousand Oaks, CA: Sage.

Marcia, J. E. (1980). Identity in adolescence. In J. Adelson (Ed.), *Handbook of adolescent psychology* (pp. 159-187). New York: John Wiley.

Midgette, T. E., & Meggert, S. S. (1991). Multicultural counseling instruction: A challenge for faculties in the 21st century. *Journal of Counseling & Development, 70*(1), 38-46.

Opotow, W. (1990). Moral exclusion and injustice: An introduction. *Journal of Social Issues, 46*(1), 1-20.

Paniagua, F. A. (1994). *Assessment and treating culturally diverse clients: A practical guide.* Thousand Oaks, CA: Sage.

Pedersen, P. (1991). Multiculturalism as a fourth force in counseling. *Journal of Counseling and Development, 70*(1), 5-25.

Pedersen, P. (1994). *A handbook for developing multicultural awareness* (2nd ed.). Alexandria, VA: American Counseling Association.

Pedersen, P. (1997). *Culture-centered counseling interventions: Striving for accuracy.* Thousand Oaks, CA: Sage.

Pedersen, P. (1998). *Multiculturalism as a fourth force.* Philadelphia: Brunner/Mazel.

Pedersen, P. (2000a). *A handbook for developing multicultural awareness* (3rd ed.). Alexandria, VA: American Counseling Association.

Pedersen, P. (2000b). *Hidden messages in culture-centered counseling: A triad training model.* Thousand Oaks, CA: Sage.

Pedersen, P., & Ivey, A. E. (1993). *Culture-centered counseling and interviewing skills.* Westport, CT: Greenwood/Praeger.

Pedersen, P., & Marsella, A. C. (1982). The ethical crisis for cross-cultural counseling and therapy. *Professional Psychology, 13,* 492-500.

Pike, R. (1966). *Language in relation to a united theory of the structure of human behavior.* The Hague, the Netherlands: Mouton.

Ponterotto, J. G., & Casas, J. M. (1991). *Handbook of racial/ethnic minority counseling research.* Springfield, IL: Charles C Thomas.

Ponerotto, J. G., Casas, J. M., Suzuki, L. A., & Alexander, C. M. (Eds.). (1995). *Handbook of multicultural counseling.* Thousand Oaks, CA: Sage.

Ridley, C. R., Mendoza, D. W., & Kanitz, B. E. (1994). Multicultural training: Reexamination, operationalization and integration. *The Counseling Psychologist, 22*(2), 227-289.

Rosenau, P. M. (1992). *Post-modernism and the social sciences.* Princeton, NJ: Princeton University Press.

Rosensweig, M. R. (1992). Psychological science around the world. *American Psychologist, 39,* 877-884.

Sampson, E. E. (1993). Identity politics: Challenges to psychology's understanding. *American Psychologist, 48*(12), 1219-1230.

Samuda, R. J. (1998). *Psychological testing of American minorities.* Thousand Oaks, CA: Sage.

Segall, M. H., Dasen, P. R., Berry, J. W., & Poortinga, Y. H. (1990). *Human behavior in global perspective: An introduction to cross-cultural psychology.* New York: Pergamon.

Shweder, R. A. (1990). Cultural psychology—What is it? In J. W. Stigler, R. A. Shweder, & G. Herdt (Eds.), *Cultural psychology: Essays on comparative human development* (pp. 73-112). New York: Cambridge University Press.

Sloan, T. S. (1990). Psychology for the Third World? *Journal of Social Issues, 46*(3), 1-20.

Sue, D. W. (1990). Culture specific techniques in counseling: A conceptual framework. *Professional Psychology, 21,* 424-433.

Sue, D. W., Arredondo, P., & McDavis, R. J. (1992). Multicultural counseling competencies and standards: A call to the profession. *Journal of Counseling and Development, 70,* 477-486.

Sue, D. W., Carter, R. T., Casas, J. M., Fouad, N. A., Ivey, A. E., Jensen, M., LaFromboise, T., Manese, J. E., Ponterotto, J. G., & Vasquez-Nutall, E. (1998). *Multicultural counseling competencies.* Thousand Oaks, CA: Sage.

Sue, D. W., Ivey, A. E., & Pedersen, P. B. (1996). *A theory of multicultural counseling and therapy.* Pacific Grove, CA: Brooks/Cole.

Sue, D. W., & Sue, D. (1999). *Counseling the culturally different: Theory and practice* (3rd ed.). New York: John Wiley.

Taylor, C. (1989). *Sources of the self: The making of the modern identity.* Cambridge, MA: Harvard University Press.

Thomas, C. (1971). *Boys no more.* Beverly Hills, CA: Glencoe.

Waldrop, M. M. (1992). *Complexity: The emerging science at the edge of order and chaos.* New York: Touchstone.

Walsh, R. (1989). Toward a synthesis of Eastern and Western psychologies. In A. A. Shiekh & K. S. Shiekh (Eds.), *Eastern and Western approaches to healing* (pp. 542-555). New York: John Wiley.

Wrenn, C. G. (1962). The culturally encapsulated counselor. *Harvard Educational Review, 32,* 444-449.

Wrenn, C. G. (1985). Afterward: The culturally encapsulated counselor revisited. In P. Pedersen (Ed.), *Handbook of cross-cultural counseling and therapy* (pp. 323-329). Westport, CT: Greenwood.

Wrightsman, L. S. (1992). *Assumptions about human nature: Implications for researchers and practitioners.* Newbury Park, CA: Sage.

CHAPTER 24

Cross-Cultural Career Counseling

FREDERICK T. L. LEONG
The Ohio State University

PAUL J. HARTUNG
Northeastern Ohio Universities College of Medicine

As the field of psychology increases its recognition of the importance of cultural differences, scholars have begun to challenge Western-based models of career counseling and their relevance to culturally different clients (see Leong, 1995). Many of these scholars have gone on to reformulate existing career theories with greater attention to issues of culture and context in career development and counseling. Another trend has been for scholars and practitioners within the fields of vocational psychology and career development to propose more culturally appropriate models for racial and ethnic minorities. These models have been advanced in efforts to improve the process and outcome of career counseling and career intervention for clients of diverse racial and ethnic minority backgrounds by situating counseling in a cultural context (Fouad & Bingham, 1995; Leong, 1993; Leong & Brown, 1995; Leong & Hartung, 1997).

Effective career counseling with racial and ethnic minorities, as with all clients, necessarily occurs within a cultural context (Fouad, 1995; Fouad & Arbona, 1994). Counselors must attend to important cultural variables such as values, ethnic identity, language, interpersonal communication style, and time orientation for the career counseling and intervention process to be appropriate and for that process to yield desirable outcomes (Fouad, 1995; Leong, 1993, 1995; Leong & Hartung, 1997). Because racial and ethnic minority individuals are more likely to seek formal counseling for educational and work-related concerns, career counselors stand uniquely positioned to deliver services that incorporate culturally appropriate processes and goals (Leong, 1993; Sue & Sue, 1990). Doing so might thereby increase the likelihood that racial and ethnic minority clients will seek additional mental health services when the need arises.

In recent years, scholars within the fields of vocational psychology and career development have increasingly come to explicitly adopt the belief that career counseling must take place within a cultural context. Consequently, they have examined the validity and viability of career counseling models and methods for a culturally diverse workforce—a workforce that includes growing numbers of people representing various racial and ethnic minority groups (Fitzgerald & Betz, 1994; Fouad, 1995; Leong, 1995; Savickas, 1995a, 1995b). Scholars have considered the extent to which existing career choice and development theories explain, predict, and describe the career development and vocational behavior of racial and ethnic minority group members (see, e.g., Fitzgerald & Betz, 1994; Leong, 1995; Savickas, 1995a, 1995b). Some have argued that extant career development theories and career counseling models have little value at all in this realm and are limited mostly to use with college-educated, White, male, middle-class individuals. Such a claim derives support from those who quickly note that most research on career theories, and in psychology generally, involves White college undergraduate students (Fitzgerald & Betz, 1994; Triandis, 1994). In this regard, Leong and Brown (1995) asserted that "the central problem with most, if not all of the majority career theories is their lack of cultural validity for racial and ethnic minorities in this country" (p. 145).

An important response to the cultural validity problem in career theory and counseling practice within the past decade has been increased scholarly productivity aimed at both better conceptualizing the career choice and development process and developing culturally relevant career counseling models and intervention methods. This scholarship has produced textbooks (e.g., Leong, 1995; Savickas & Walsh, 1996), chapters (e.g., Fitzgerald & Betz, 1994; Fouad, 1995; Fouad & Bingham, 1995;

Leong & Brown, 1995; Subich, 1996; Vondracek & Fouad, 1994), and a number of articles in special issues and sections of journals, including *The Career Development Quarterly* (Leong, 1991; Savickas, 1993), *Journal of Vocational Behavior* (Tinsley, 1994), and *Journal of Career Assessment* (Walsh, 1994). The growing body of multicultural career development and counseling literature has done much to enhance conceptual and, to some degree, empirical knowledge of cultural, socioeconomic, gender, and environmental factors that influence career development and vocational behavior.

Recent statements of career theories also demonstrate progress in attending to issues of culture and context in career development and counseling. For example, Super, Savickas, and Super (1996) described how the constructs of roles and values make life span and life space theory more relevant to women and diverse cultural and ethnic groups. Similarly, Young, Valach, and Collin (1996) embedded issues of culture within the fabric of their contextual explanation of career. Much scholarship has also focused on examining the relevance and usefulness of career counseling models and interventions for individuals representing diverse racial and ethnic minority groups (see, e.g., Betz & Fitzgerald, 1995; Bowman, 1993; Subich, 1996). Nancy Betz's (1993) conclusion that "there is much to be done in the area of multicultural career counseling" (p. 55) still holds true, yet significant work has begun to advance knowledge and awareness of the career counseling process with racial and ethnic minorities.

Work in this vein has led to the development or adaptation of several distinct models of cross-cultural career counseling. These models have been advanced in efforts to improve the process and outcome of career counseling and career intervention for clients of diverse racial and ethnic minority backgrounds by situating counseling in a cultural context (Fouad & Bingham, 1995; Leong, 1993; Leong & Brown, 1995; Leong & Hartung, 1997). One such model, which we describe more fully elsewhere in this chapter, adapted a conceptual framework for cross-cultural career assessment and counseling using an integrative tripartite approach (Leong & Hartung, 1997). Like models of similar purpose that we will review below, the integrative-sequential model recognizes how culture influences what individuals identify as career problems, whether they seek professional help for any work- or career-related problems that have been identified, and how counselors evaluate those problems to identify culturally appropriate interventions.

In addition to counseling models, some specific approaches to career intervention have been described that support and advance culturally sensitive career counseling. These approaches include contextual (Collin, 1996; Young & Valach, 1996; Young et al., 1996), personal construct (Savickas, 1995a), and narrative (Cochran, 1997) strategies for assisting individuals to make improved career decisions. Each of these strategies emphasizes clients' subjective and personal career realities.

In this chapter, we examine several recently developed models useful for conducting cross-cultural career counseling. Although there have been numerous empirical studies of career development among racial and ethnic minority students, many of these findings have already been reviewed elsewhere (e.g., Leong, 1995, Leong & Brown, 1995). We decided that a review of these newer intervention models might help spark additional research. These models were chosen for review here because they embed cultural variables and issues throughout the career counseling process.

The first model seeks to locate career counseling in a comprehensive sequential cultural context that illustrates the influence of cultural factors across all stages of the career counseling help-seeking process. The second model was developed specifically for cross-cultural

career counseling, drawing primarily from the cross-cultural and multicultural counseling literature (e.g., Sue & Sue, 1990). The third model represents an elaboration of an existing developmental career assessment and counseling approach designed to increase its relevance for use in cross-cultural career counseling contexts. The fourth and final model proposes a cultural accommodation approach to cross-cultural counseling in general but can be readily adapted to career counseling clients.

INTEGRATIVE-SEQUENTIAL MODEL OF CAREER COUNSELING SERVICES

We begin with a model that adopted a broad contextual perspective in analyzing the career counseling enterprise with racial and ethnic minorities. This model adopted a conceptual framework for cross-cultural career assessment and counseling by using an integrative-sequential approach (Leong & Hartung, 1997). Like models of similar purpose that we will review below, the integrative-sequential model recognizes how culture influences what individuals identify as career problems, whether they seek professional help for any identified work- or career-related problems, and how counselors evaluate those problems to identify culturally appropriate interventions.

Given this set of assumptions, here is the probable scenario using Leong and Hartung's (1997) sequential model for career counseling services with racial and ethnic minority clients. We will use the example of Asian American clients to illustrate this model. In the first stage of this model, where the emergence of career problems occurs in the ethnic minority community, Asians and Asian Americans are likely to have different conceptualizations of their career problems in contrast to White Americans by virtue of their collectivistic orientation. White Americans with individualistic values are likely to possess a conception of their "self" as autonomous, distinct, and self-contained. Independent thinking and action are the hallmarks of a mature and actualized individual. Obviously, such beliefs will also color how they conceptualize their career problems. Having a sense of self that is connected and defined greatly by group norms and expectations, Asians and Asian Americans are less likely to view their career decision-making problems as purely personal ones. They are much more likely than White Americans to experience tensions between personal interests/goals/aspirations and family duty/obligations and social responsibilities. At the same time, the high power distance and hierarchical relationships in existence in the families of these individuals make the expression and sharing of such tensions highly complex and problematic. In light of such a conception of career problems, Asians and Asian Americans are therefore much more likely to believe that these problems are too complicated to be resolved simply by talking with someone else about them.

For those who eventually do seek career counseling, such a belief is often confirmed because most of the White European American career counselors they encounter are likely to approach their career problems with a conception of the self as an autonomous and separate entity. Indeed, many of these counselors will perceive these clients as being quite immature because they appear not to have "fully individuated" from their families of origin as they should have. This moves us to the second stage in Leong and Hartung's (1997) model, namely, help seeking. Being collectivistic and having an interdependent self-construal, the clients will very likely view their "personal career problems" as being embedded in a complex social network of obligations and responsibilities that transcends the notion that a career choice is simply a personal choice based on individual interests, aptitudes, and abilities. Such a conceptualization, combined with the tendency for collectivistic persons to distrust out-group members, will make Asians and Asian Americans very reluctant to seek help with their career problems. This culturally based reluctance to seek professional help is also further supported by the important influence of in-group members, such as families and peers, on collectivistic persons. This social inhibition toward seeking professional assistance for problems, career or emotional ones, should be quite robust among collectivistic clients because it is multiply determined and supported by numerous cultural values and beliefs. All of this results in a very high threshold that has to be passed before an Asian or Asian American person with collectivistic values will seek career counseling.

For those for whom the threshold has been passed, other problems may occur when career counseling services are sought. The social inhibition described above is now accompanied by a considerable amount of ambivalence as the Asian or Asian American client enters into career counseling. Already fearful that the White American career counselor may not fully understand the complexity of his or her problems, the client brings with him or her a high level of cultural mistrust and cultural stereotypes. More often than not, these stereotypes are confirmed. Here is a not too unreasonable scenario: A White European American counselor trained in Western-based models of career counseling engages the client and begins the career assessment phase. This is the third stage in Leong and Hartung's (1997) sequential model. Being an individualistic counselor with an independent self-construal operating on the ethnocentric assumption that the client should be similar in self-conception, he or she concludes from the assessment that the client exhibits evidence of career immaturity and too much dependence on others in the career decision-making process. As this conceptualization is "tactfully" communicated to the client, the counselor does not realize that he or she is misunderstanding his or her Asian or Asian American client and quite possibly alienating him or her by applying a social cognitive schema that simply does not fit. We would propose that if we were to conduct career counseling process studies with such dyads (collectivistic Asian client and individualistic White career counselor), we would find many instances of such culturally dystonic experiences for the client, which in turn would result in negative therapeutic encounters and premature termination from career counseling. With his or her fears and stereotypes confirmed, the client decides not to come for the next appointment with this counselor and instead prematurely terminates from counseling.

Western-based models of career counseling have long been criticized for their Eurocentric bias. Specifically, this translates into the tendency to conceptualize career maturity from a purely individualistic orientation, thereby relegating persons with a collectivistic orientation to the diagnosis of being career immature. Some recent research has begun to demonstrate empirically the individualistic bias in such career assessment models. For example, an early study found that Asian American college students exhibited a more dependent decision-making style and lower career maturity than European American students (Leong, 1991). Leong (1991) went on to question the validity of these findings because the same Asian Americans who exhibited dependent decision-making styles and lower career maturity did not exhibit lower levels of vocational identity, as measured by Holland, Daiger, and Power's (1980) My Vocational Situation inventory. Motivated by this discrepancy, Hardin, Leong, and Osipow (2001) conducted a study demonstrating that the definition and measurement of career maturity may be less valid for Asian Americans because it fails to accurately distinguish between independence, interdependence, and dependence. Hardin et al. (2001) believed that Asian Americans, who tend to be more collectivistic and more likely to possess interdependent self-construals than European Americans,

are actually considered dependent (not interdependent) and erroneously classified as less career mature in current assessment models such as the Career Maturity Inventory.

To investigate this possibility, Hardin et al. (2001) administered several instruments, including the Career Maturity Inventory (CMI) (Crites, 1978) and the Self-Construal Scale (SCS) (Singelis, 1994), to 235 self-identified non-Hispanic, White European American and 182 self-identified Asian American college students. Consistent with previous research (Leong, 1991; Luzzo, 1992), the Asian American participants exhibited less mature career choice attitudes, as measured by the CMI, than their European American counterparts. However, these results were moderated by self-construal. Specifically, interdependence, not independence, was found to be most associated with career choice attitudes. Those participants who had high interdependent self-construals, regardless of the level of their independent self-construals, had less mature career choice attitudes, as measured by the CMI, than those participants who had lower interdependent self-construals. No differences in maturity of career choice attitudes were observed based on level of independence. Furthermore, the three subscales on which the Asian Americans were found to exhibit less mature career choice attitudes than the European Americans (Compromise, Independence, and Involvement) were also the three subscales found to be most related to interdependence. Specifically, those participants who were high in interdependence had lower scores on these subscales than participants who were low in interdependence. Thus, it appears that the CMI is biased toward a definition and measurement of career maturity based on independent self-construals and that persons high on interdependent self-construals, such as collectivistic Asians, will be categorized as career immature in this model.

For those clients who make it to the fourth stage of Leong and Hartung's (1997) model, where actual career counseling begins, other challenges present themselves. The same collectivistic tendency to view out-group members as very different and not to be readily trusted exists in the counseling phase as in the assessment phase. Such clients are also likely to expect a high power distance and hierarchical relationship with the counselor. The counselor's attempt to use a nondirective and egalitarian approach is likely to produce puzzlement and even discomfort among these clients. In addition, collectivistic Asian or Asian American clients with interdependent self-construals will have very strong ties to families and friends. Attempts by the counselor to help the client "mature and individuate from the families and friends" to "become an independent, self-sufficient person capable of making his or her own decisions" will often result in more culturally dystonic experiences for this client. This is likely to lead to negative outcomes for the final phase in Leong and Hartung's (1997) model, namely, counseling outcomes and return to the community.

The major advantage of this model is the adoption of a comprehensive perspective of the natural history in which career services are sought. With a stage-oriented sequential process, this model allows for an in-depth exploration of the possible cultural factors that might influence the career counseling enterprise from problem conception, problem emergence, and help seeking to intervention and outcome. By separating out the career counseling into different stages, this model allows us to examine different facets of that natural history. For example, if racial and ethnic minority groups exhibit differential rates of help seeking for career and vocational problems, as they currently do for mental health problems (see Leong, 2001), are there cultural differences in problem conception (vis-à-vis career problems) that would help us understand the differential rates in help seeking? The current model proposes that the client's career problem does not begin and end with the career counselor but instead has a natural history that exists prior to help seeking and extends beyond the termination of counseling.

A CULTURALLY APPROPRIATE CAREER COUNSELING MODEL

Asserting the centrality of culture in effective career counseling, Fouad and Bingham (1995) articulated a culturally appropriate career counseling model. Their seven-step model extends prior work by Ward and Bingham (1993), who sought to develop a culturally sensitive model for use in career assessment with ethnic minority women. The model rests on the fundamental assumption that counselors must consider and attend to a wide array of important cultural variables in the career counseling process and when designing career interventions with racial and ethnic minorities. These cultural variables include, for example, racial identity development, discrimination, family and gender role expectations, and various worldview dimensions. Let us consider each step of the model proposed by Fouad and Bingham in turn.

Step 1: Establish a Culturally Appropriate Relationship. Issues of culture are considered throughout each step of the counseling process, which begins in Step 1 with the counselor establishing a culturally appropriate relationship. For many ethnic minority individuals who may prize the relationship more than any other component of counseling, this step may be the most crucial (Bingham & Ward, 1996). As in any client-counselor relationship, establishing rapport is important to successful engagement of the client in the counseling process. With racial and ethnic minorities, it becomes particularly important for the counselor to attend to issues of culture that may influence the client's perception of the counseling process and their expectations for its outcome. Different clients will likely approach the relationship with a counselor differently as a function of their cultural values and beliefs. These differences may surface during counseling in verbal and nonverbal behaviors, such as level of self-disclosure and degree of eye contact, and in the clients' expectations of the counselor. Fouad and Bingham (1995) noted, for example, that Asian American clients might expect the counselor to take an authoritative or expert role, whereas Hispanic clients may expect the counselor to self-disclose and share personal information. In this opening phase of cross-cultural career counseling, counselors must demonstrate flexibility in adjusting their style to appropriately connect with the client, suspend their own stereotypes and biases, and accommodate to the needs and expectations of the client relative to the role the client desires the counselor to assume in the relationship.

Step 2: Identify Career Issues. Step 2 of the culturally appropriate career counseling model involves identifying career issues that clients present. This step centers on determining what the client defines as a "career issue," and therefore it is important for the counselor to conceive career issues in the broadest sense. Clients must be allowed and encouraged to explore whatever problems and concerns they are experiencing across a broad range of cognitive, emotional, behavioral, environmental, and other domains. The counselor facilitates this process through open-ended questions and prompts aimed to help the client broadly examine and then specify what the client perceives and defines as career issues. To further assist in this process, Bingham and Ward (1997) described the Career Counseling Checklist and the Decision Tree as career assessments to help clients broaden their cultural perspectives on the world of work and to assist counselors in determining the need for counseling and when to address racial and ethnic issues. Fouad and Bingham (1995) also advised that in this step of the counseling process especially, counselors should help clients to explicitly define any external barriers to their career choice and development such as employer, coworker, or institutional prejudice, racism, and discrimination.

Step 3: Assess the Effects of Cultural Variables. Having established a culturally appropriate relationship and identified the client's career concerns and perceived barriers in Steps 1 and 2, Step 3 moves to assessing the effects of cultural variables on the client's career issues and decisions. The outcome of this step should be a clear understanding of how cultural variables influence the client's career decision making and development. Fouad and Bingham (1995) depicted various spheres of influence of cultural variables using a concentric circles diagram. The individual self, including biological and genetic factors, occupies the core circle, with gender, family, racial or ethnic group, and the dominant (majority) group emanating outward from and exerting an influence on this core of the person. In counseling, the model asserts the importance of examining the full range of these variables to determine what particular spheres may be affecting the client. For example, gender role expectations may inhibit some women from exploring traditionally male-dominated occupations. Family-based norms of duty, obligation, and deference to parents may affect the career decision-making process for various ethnic minorities. On another level, structural factors such as stereotyping, racism, and discrimination that limit racial and ethnic minority group members' participation in particular occupations can and do significantly affect and inhibit career development and work adjustment for these individuals. By working with clients to assess and pinpoint the particular cultural issues that affect their career development, appropriate treatment goals and interventions can be designed.

Step 4: Set Counseling Goals. In a 1993 article, Leong described the importance of setting culturally appropriate goals in cross-cultural career counseling. Leong cautioned counselors against directing clients toward culturally inappropriate goals due to their own prejudices and stereotyping. For example, a counselor may become frustrated with a racial or ethnic minority client's lack of English-language proficiency, which may in turn dilute the career counseling services the client receives as the counselor believes the client cannot benefit from counseling. Counselors might also steer racial and ethnic minority clients toward occupations based on stereotypical beliefs about what those clients might be best suited for (e.g., Asian Americans in science occupations or Hispanic Americans in service-oriented occupations). Fouad and Bingham (1995) concurred with Leong's assessment and therefore included as Step 4 of their model the importance of establishing counseling goals consistent with the client's worldview, cultural value orientation, and cultural practices. Vital to this step of the process is the counselor underscoring the collaborative nature of the counseling relationship. This translates into the counselor actively working in partnership with the client to set goals that the client wants, that the client can realistically achieve, and that respect the client's cultural background.

Step 5: Design Culturally Appropriate Counseling Interventions. In Step 5, the focus of counseling centers squarely on interventions. With a trusting relationship and appropriate goals established, client and counselor work in tandem to select and implement culturally relevant counseling interventions designed to promote attainment of the mutually agreed-on goals set in the previous step. Reviewing the scant literature on career interventions with racial and ethnic minorities up to 1993, Bowman delineated several areas and types of interventions for counselors to consider using with racial and ethnic minority clients. Among her recommendations, she suggested that counselors (a) use group rather than individual interventions for clients with more collectivistic and relational cultural value orientations, (b) incorporate the family in the counseling and decision-making process, (c) use role models working in nontraditional occupations that appropriately reflect the racial and ethnic identity of the client and that promote the client's awareness of previously unconsidered options, (d) use career information materials in ways appropriate to the client's language and cultural background (see Hartung, 1996, for more discussion of this point), and (e) enlist counselors of the same ethnicity as the client to deliver the intervention.

Step 6: Make a Decision. Readiness to make a career-related decision in Step 6 occurs only after the client and counselor have successfully completed the previous five steps (Bingham & Ward, 1996; Fouad & Bingham, 1995). On reaching Step 6, clients would be expected to be involved in decision making related to their specific career concerns and goals, initially implementing their plans, and moving toward closure of the counseling process. There may arise at this point a need to revisit earlier steps to reconsider or reappraise the client-counselor relationship, revise and reestablish counseling goals, or redesign intervention strategies. The model suggests here that it is incumbent on the counselor to remain sensitive and open to the possibility of again working through previously "completed" steps.

Step 7: Implement and Follow Up. Counseling draws to a close in Step 7, with the client becoming more highly involved in implementing decisions and plans toward ultimate goal attainment. Fouad and Bingham (1995) discussed how, at this step, the counselor may need to encourage the client to seek further counseling despite any feelings on the part of the client that doing so would somehow indicate that the client failed and possibly result in the client's "loss of face." The counselor must, when necessary, convey clearly to the client that returning to counseling occurs frequently among clients and represents an opportunity to reevaluate and improve on the gains already made.

A DEVELOPMENTAL APPROACH TO CROSS-CULTURAL CAREER COUNSELING

Taking a different approach to conceptualizing the cross-cultural career counseling process, Hartung et al. (1998) elaborated the career-development assessment and counseling model (C-DAC) (Super, 1983) for use in career counseling with racial and ethnic minorities. Rather than developing an entirely new model, Hartung et al. decided to extend the C-DAC model as an existing conceptual scheme with the goal of making it more relevant in cross-cultural counseling contexts. They argued that counselors who take a developmental career assessment and counseling approach would benefit from using this elaborated framework by increasing their awareness, knowledge, and skills relative to the influence of cultural factors on racial and ethnic minority career development and vocational behavior throughout the counseling process.

The C-DAC Model. Developmental career assessment and counseling systematically bridges career theory and practice. Integrating differential, developmental, and phenomenological methods, the C-DAC model uses a comprehensive career assessment battery to help clients explore their roles, developmental stages and tasks, career attitudes and knowledge, values, and interests within their unique life contexts. Hartung et al. (1998) elaborated on the C-DAC model to formally appraise cultural identity in Step 1 of

the model and to consider cultural identity concerns throughout the career assessment and counseling process. This would help counselors more clearly understand how cultural factors influence individuals' career development and vocational behavior.

The four-step C-DAC approach begins in Step 1 with a *preview* of the client's record and an initial interview to assess role salience and formulate a preliminary counseling plan. Central to this first step, counselors determine through dialogue and formal assessment the importance of work to the client relative to life roles in other areas (e.g., study, home and family, community, and leisure). Ascertaining the client's level of work role salience indicates to the counselor whether further career assessment and counseling will be meaningful (high career salience) or not (low career salience). Clients high in career salience show readiness for further career assessment. Clients low in career salience may, depending on their unique life status, need help either orienting to the world of work prior to further assessment or exploring and preparing for other life roles.

Step 2, *depth-view,* comprises formal assessment of career choice readiness and adaptability, interests, and values. Here the counselor first administers instruments to formally assess important career choice process variables, including the client's developmental career stage, career concerns, and level of career maturity or career adaptability. Step 2 thus begins with measurement of the client's readiness for career decision-making activities such as identifying and exploring occupational interests and work values. If the client's scores indicate a high level of career choice readiness, the counselor interprets this to mean that the client is prepared to maximally benefit from interest, values, and other career choice content assessments. If the client attains low scores on career choice readiness assessments, the counselor interprets this to mean that the client is less apt to be able to benefit from such content assessments (see Savickas,

2000, for a discussion of career choice content and career choice process assessments).

Data assessment in Step 3 reviews all information gathered. This includes data obtained from both the informal assessment conducted in the preview stage and formal assessment completed in the depth-view stage. *Counseling* in Step 4 explores what the data mean for the client. Taken together, the four steps of the C-DAC approach incorporate the following five dimensions of career assessment and counseling interventions designed to promote successful career decision making:

- Role salience: the relative importance of work and nonwork roles
- Career development: assessing developmental stages and tasks
- Career choice readiness: career planning attitudes and knowledge
- Values and interests: desired outcomes of work and preferred occupations
- Tentative decision making, plan formation, and initial implementation

Hartung et al. (1998) recommended extending the C-DAC model to infuse assessments and interventions that address the following sixth dimension:

- Cultural identity development

Incorporating this sixth dimension was designed to make cultural identity a core component of the C-DAC model, foster cultural relevance in implementing each step of the model, and specify culturally sensitive assessments and counseling interventions as part of the assessment and counseling process. Hartung et al. (1998) recommended including in the assessment and counseling process culture-sensitive assessments such as the Multicultural Career Counseling Checklist (MCCC) (Bingham & Ward, 1996; Ward & Bingham, 1993) and the Career Counseling Checklist (CCC) (Bingham & Ward, 1996; Ward & Bingham, 1993).

Hartung et al. (1998) thus elaborated the model to formally appraise cultural identity in Step 1 and to consider cultural identity concerns throughout the counseling and assessment process. They recommended adding to the model assessments and interventions that address cultural identity development as a significant variable affecting career exploration, choice, development, and adjustment. In so doing, counselors might take better account of cultural factors, such as those described in Step 3 of Fouad and Bingham's (1995) model, that influence each C-DAC step and attend to how those factors promote or inhibit racial and ethnic minority career development. The elaboration further recognizes the influence of such factors as acculturation, cultural value orientations (individualism and collectivism), and external career barriers (e.g., stereotypes, prejudice, and discrimination) on racial and ethnic minority career development and vocational behavior.

Including cultural identity as a core C-DAC element should prompt career counselors to be aware of their own attitudes about clients who are culturally different from themselves. For example, Hartung et al. (1998) suggested that counselors might examine their own career development and take a C-DAC battery of instruments. This would effectively create a parallel process that might enhance a counselor's empathy for the career process of the client.

Hartung et al. (1998) argued that making cultural identity a core component of the C-DAC model would augment the differential, developmental, and personal construct components of the approach. Infusing this important dimension takes into account cultural variables that influence each of the other components as well as the entire career decision-making and development process. To effectively use the C-DAC model, counselors must also recognize the role of cultural variables that influence the counseling process for both the client and themselves. Counselors need to remain cognizant of such factors as acculturation, cultural value orientations, and external career obstacles (e.g., stereotypes, prejudice, and discrimination) that may act as significant moderators of racial and ethnic minority career development and vocational behavior. For example, assessing the client's acculturation level in Step 1 would guide the counselor in determining whether and how to modify subsequent steps (e.g., in terms of selecting, sequencing, and interpreting assessment instruments). Major issues related to ethnic minority vocational behavior and career development relative to their acculturation levels include occupational segregation, stereotyping, discrimination, prestige, mobility, attitudes, aspirations and expectations, stress, satisfaction, choice, and interest (Leong, 1995; Leong & Serafica, 1995).

Using the C-DAC model within this elaborated framework recognizes that the individual client and counselor both can be conceptualized from the universal, group, and individual perspectives. All three perspectives are important, and using any one vantage point without the other two reveals only part of the problem and part of the solution. Counselors must consider all three perspectives to accurately understand clients' career development. Doing so should give the C-DAC model incremental validity above and beyond its use when emphasizing only one dimension.

AN INTEGRATIVE AND MULTIDIMENSIONAL MODEL OF CAREER COUNSELING

Lamenting the lack of comprehensive and integrative theoretical models for cross-cultural counseling, Leong (1996) proposed a multidimensional and integrative model of cross-cultural counseling. This integrative model has recently been extended to career counseling (Leong & Hardin, in press; Leong & Tang, in press). Leong (1996) used Kluckhohn and Murray's (1950) tripartite framework in proposing that cross-cultural counselors and therapists need to attend to all three major dimensions of human personality and identity—namely, the universal, the group, and the individual dimensions. The universal dimension is based on the knowledge base generated by mainstream psychology and the "universal laws" of human behavior that have been identified (e.g., the universal "fight or flight" response in humans to physical threat). The group dimension has been the domain of both cross-cultural psychology and ethnic minority psychology and the study of gender differences. The third and final dimension concerns unique individual differences and characteristics. The individual dimension is more often covered by behavioral and existential theories in which individual learning histories and personal phenomenology are proposed as critical elements in the understanding of human behavior. Leong's (1996) integrative model proposes that all three dimensions are equally important in understanding human experiences and should be attended to by the counselor in an integrative fashion.

Leong (1996) used a famous quote from Kluckhohn and Murray's (1950) influential chapter on "The Determinants of Personality Formation," published in their book *Personality in Nature, Society, and Culture,* as the beginning point for his integrative model. The quote was as follows: "Every man is in certain respects: a) like all other men, b) like some other men, and c) like no other man" (p. 35). In this quote, Kluckhohn and Murray are pointing out that some of the determinants of personality are common features found in the genetic makeup of all people. This addresses the biological aspect of the biopsychosocial model generally used in today's medical sciences. For certain other features of personality, however, Kluckhohn and Murray (1950) stated that most men are like some other men, showing the importance of social grouping, whether that grouping is based on culture, race, ethnicity, gender, or social class. Last, they said that "each individual's modes of perceiving, feeling, needing, and behaving have characteristic patterns which are not precisely duplicated by those of any other individual" (p. 37). Each person's individuality, often the focus of social learning theories and models, is thus expressed in the last part of the quote. It accentuates the fact that all persons have distinct social learning experiences that can influence their values, beliefs, and cognitive schemas.

The integrative model of cross-cultural counseling proposed by Leong (1996) has as one of its fundamental bases the notion that the individual client must exist at three levels: the universal, the group, and the individual. The problem with much of the past research in the field of cross-cultural counseling is that the focus has been on only one of the three levels, ignoring the influence of the other levels in the counseling situation. Leong's (1996) integrative model includes all three dimensions of personality as well as their dynamic interactions and thus will have better incremental validity than any model that focuses on only one of the three levels. The integrative model for cross-cultural counseling and psychotherapy was conceived to provide a more complex and dynamic conception of human beings.

Cross-cultural career counseling that is based on Leong's (1996) integrative model would be an eclectic approach that seeks to apply knowledge from all three dimensions to understand and assist the client with his or her career problems and developmental tasks (see Leong & Hardin, in press; Leong & Tang, in press). For example, career counselors using this model would recognize that work is universal but that its meaning is embedded in a cultural context that shapes and colors its nature and experience. Instead of mindlessly applying Western-based models of career

counseling to all clients coming through their doors, career counselors using the integrative model would carefully select theories and models from both the universalist (mainstream psychology) and the cross-cultural and racial/ethnic minority psychology literature to guide their counseling with culturally different students. At the same time, these counselors also realize that theories and models from the universal and group dimensions will never fully capture or represent the unique experiences of individuals. Instead, they will recognize the complexity of the individual and seek to integrate all three dimensions of knowledge to guide their work with students.

To illustrate how the integrative model of cross-cultural career counseling would work, we would like to use an example cited by Leong and Tan (2002). They chose Super's (1957) model of career development to illustrate the value and utility of the integrative model. Although Leong and Tan had chosen Super's model to illustrate Leong's (1996) integrative model, the integrative model is equally applicable to other career models and constructs. According to Leong and Tan,

> One important component of Super's (1957) model is the concept of career maturity. According to Super, an individual's level of career maturity will influence his or her ability to handle the career developmental tasks at his or her appropriate stage. Those with high levels of career maturity would progress smoothly in their career development while those with low levels of career maturity would experience considerable difficulties. In using this model, school counselors would actually be intervening at the universal dimension within the integrative model, assuming that career maturity is a universal concept and is therefore applicable to all clients including those who are culturally different. And yet, research is beginning to show that such an assumption may not be correct. (p. 248)

Leong and Tan (2002) went on to observe that

a school counselor who is trying to help a culturally different student by simply adopting Super's model and proceeds to assess the student's career maturity level with the Career Maturity Inventory (Crites, 1965) may actually be making an error if he or she does not understand the cultural relativity inherent in the concept and measurement of career maturity. This is because the concept of the self varies significantly across cultures and the Group dimension within the integrative models needs to be taken into account. According to Markus and Kitayama (1991), Asian Americans, with more collectivistic values, may conceive of the self as interdependent, whereas persons from individualistic cultures may view the self as independent. According to this model, the independent self has the core need to strategically express or assert the internal attributes of the self while the interdependent construal formulates self in relation to others (Markus & Kitayama, 1991). Being unique is very critical for the independent self and fitting-in is very important for the interdependent self. The basis of self-esteem for the independent self is the ability to express the self and to validate internal attributes. For the interdependent self, the basis of self-esteem is the ability to adjust, restrain self, and maintain harmony with social context (Markus & Kitayama, 1991). Such differences in self-conception may make career decision-making a much more interpersonal process for collectivists than for individualists. For the latter, career decision making may be an individual matter based mainly on personal interests, values, and aspirations, while for the former, career decision-making may be a familial matter based on group interests, values, and needs. (pp. 248-249)

Some research has already begun to demonstrate the value of self-construal as a culture-specific variable in our analysis of the career psychology of Asian Americans. In a research project examining ethnic differences in career maturity between Asian Americans and White Americans, Leong (1991) found an interesting anomaly. Using Crites's (1978) measure of career maturity, Leong (1991) found that although Asian Americans showed less mature career choice attitudes than their European American counterparts, the two groups did not differ in terms of vocational identity, as measured by Holland et al.'s (1980) My Vocational Situation. He concluded that these results indicated that Asian Americans and European Americans approached the career decision-making process differently, yet still arrived at similarly crystallized vocational identities. On the basis of these results, Leong (1991) introduced the concept of cultural relativity in the construct of career maturity. He suggested that rather than automatically assuming that Asian Americans actually have lower career maturity, researchers and counselors need to carefully investigate possible ways in which cultural differences moderate the meaning of career maturity.

Leong and Tan (2002) argued that the concept of independence may be culturally relative and needs to be understood in context. They criticized Crites's (1965) theory of career maturity, based on Super's (1957) theory of vocational development and the basis of the CMI, for its assumption that their construct of independence in career decision making is universal and an equally crucial component of career mature attitudes for all cultural groups with the same external referents. However, this emphasis on independence, to the exclusion of other alternatives such as interdependence, may underlie the cultural differences discussed above between Asian and European Americans in their approaches to the career decision-making process. Once again, the study by Hardin et al. (2001) illustrates the cultural relativity in Crites's (1978) CMI. They found that interdependence, not independence, was most associated with career choice attitudes. Those participants who had high interdependent self-construals, regardless of the level of their independent self-construals, had less mature career choice attitudes, as measured by the CMI, than those participants who had lower interdependent self-construals.

No differences in maturity of career choice attitudes were observed based on the level of independence. Furthermore, the three sub-scales on which the Asian Americans were found to exhibit less mature career choice attitudes than the European Americans (Compromise, Independence, and Involvement) were also the three subscales found to be most related to interdependence. Specifically, those participants who were high in interdependence had lower scores on these subscales than participants who were low in interdependence.

In view of these findings, a counselor who applies only the universal dimension and administers a career maturity scale to Asian American clients without attending to the group dimension may actually be committing a diagnostic error. As shown by the research studies cited above, current measures of career maturity are biased against an interdependent (collectivistic) construal of the self and therefore favor independent self-construal, which is dominant in Western societies. Using such measures without modifications may inappropriately diagnose Asian American clients as "career immature" when in actuality they are not.

A basic premise of the integrative model is that we need to mindfully question the "assumed" universality of the constructs (e.g., career maturity) within Western models of career counseling and use cultural differences to help us identify "group-level" (i.e., cultural in the present case) variables that would fill the gaps in our current dominant models. Universality should not be assumed but instead systematically examined in comparative cross-cultural studies to identify possible group-level differences or moderator effects. Where cultural relativity is found, emic or culture-specific constructs may be sought to help better explain the phenomenon or account for the "anomalies" within Western models. At the same time, it should

not be assumed that culture accounts for vast amounts of variance in the vocational behavior of racial and ethnic minority groups without empirical verification. Clearly, both cultural validity and cultural specificity types of research in vocational psychology need to continue (Leong & Brown, 1995). In the meantime, recognizing and attending to both the universal and group dimensions and their complex interactions within a unique individual make for a cross-culturally competent counselor.

CONCLUSION

We have reviewed four recent models of cross-cultural career counseling with racial and ethnic minority clients. The development of models such as those reviewed in this chapter bodes well for the future of vocational psychology and career intervention. Incorporating important cultural variables, such as these models attempt to do, helps the field move closer to its goal of cultural validity in career theory, research, and practice with individuals representing diverse racial and ethnic backgrounds. Our goals for this chapter have been to (a) provide an overview of the current models to readers outside of vocational psychology who may not be familiar with these models, (b) share these cross-cultural career counseling models with practitioners who are in great need for such models, and (c) encourage psychologists and other social scientists to pursue empirical research to test the validity and utility of these models. Finally, in the not-too-distant future, as these theories become more established and research evidence begins to accumulate either to challenge or support these models, other scholars may begin to attempt to compare and contrast these models and perhaps even develop models that seek to integrate these disparate models into one.

REFERENCES

Betz, N. E. (1993). Toward the integration of multicultural and career psychology. *Career Development Quarterly, 42,* 53-55.

Betz, N. E., & Fitzgerald, L. F. (1995). Career assessment and intervention with racial and ethnic minorities. In F. T. L. Leong (Ed.), *Career development and vocational behavior of racial and ethnic minorities* (pp. 263-279). Mahwah, NJ: Lawrence Erlbaum.

Bingham, R. P., & Ward, C. M. (1996). Practical applications of career counseling with ethnic minority women. In M. L. Savickas & W. B. Walsh (Eds.), *Handbook of career counseling theory and practice* (pp. 291-314). Palo Alto, CA: Davies-Black.

Bingham, R. P., & Ward, C. M. (1997). Theory into assessment: A model for women of color. *Journal of Career Assessment, 5,* 403-418.

Bowman, S. (1993). Career intervention strategies for ethnic minorities. *Career Development Quarterly, 42,* 14-25.

Cochran, L. (1997). *Career counseling: A narrative approach.* Thousand Oaks, CA: Sage.

Collin, A. (1996). New relationships between researchers, theorists, and practitioners: A response to the changing context of career. In M. L. Savickas & W. B. Walsh (Eds.), *Handbook of career counseling theory and practice* (pp. 377-399). Palo Alto, CA: Davies-Black.

Crites, J. O. (1965). Measurement of vocational maturity in adolescence: I. Attitude test of the vocational development inventory. *Psychological Monographs: General & Applied, 79*(2, Whole No. 595).

Crites, J. O. (1978). *Career maturity inventory: Theory and research handbook.* Monterey, CA: CTB/McGraw-Hill.

Fitzgerald, L. F., & Betz, N. E. (1994). Career development in cultural context: The role of gender, race, class, and sexual orientation. In M. L. Savickas & R. W. Lent (Eds.), *Convergence in career development theories: Implications for science and practice* (pp. 103-117). Palo Alto, CA: Consulting Psychologists Press.

Fouad, N. A. (1995). Career behavior of Hispanics: Assessment and career intervention. In F. T. L. Leong (Ed.), *Career development and vocational behavior of racial and ethnic minorities* (pp. 165-191). Mahwah, NJ: Lawrence Erlbaum.

Fouad, N. A., & Arbona, C. (1994). Careers in a cultural context. *Career Development Quarterly, 43,* 96-104.

Fouad, N. A., & Bingham, R. P. (1995). Career counseling with racial and ethnic minorities. In W. B. Walsh & S. H. Osipow (Eds.), *Handbook of vocational psychology: Theory, research, and practice* (2nd ed., pp. 331-365). Mahwah, NJ: Lawrence Erlbaum.

Hardin, E. E., Leong, F. T. L., & Osipow, S. H. (2001). Cultural relativity in the conceptualization of career maturity. *Journal of Vocational Behavior, 58,* 36-52.

Hartung, P. J. (1996). Work illustrated: Attending to visual images in career information materials. *Career Development Quarterly, 44,* 234-241.

Hartung, P. J., Vandiver, B. J., Leong, F. T. L., Pope, M., Niles, S. G., & Farrow, B. (1998). Appraising cultural identity in career-development assessment and counseling. *Career Development Quarterly, 46,* 276-293.

Holland, J. L., Daiger, D. C., & Power, P. G. (1980). *My Vocational Situation.* Palo Alto, CA: Consulting Psychologists Press.

Kluckhohn, C., & Murray, H. A. (1950). Personality formation: The determinants. In C. Kluckhohn & H. A. Murray (Eds.), *Personality in nature, society, and culture* (pp. 35-48). New York: Knopf.

Leong, F. T. L. (1991). Guest editor's introduction: Special issue on career development of racial and ethnic minorities. *Career Development Quarterly, 42,* 196-198.

Leong, F. T. L. (1993). The career counseling process with racial/ethnic minorities: The case of Asian Americans. *Career Development Quarterly, 42,* 26-40.

Leong, F. T. L. (1995). *Career development and vocational behavior of racial and ethnic minorities.* Hillsdale, NJ: Lawrence Erlbaum.

Leong, F. T. L. (1996). Challenges to career counseling: Boundaries, cultures, and complexity. In M. L. Savickas & W. B. Walsh (Eds.), *Handbook of career counseling theory and practice* (pp. 333-345). Palo Alto, CA: Davies-Black.

Leong, F. T. L. (2001). Guest editor's introduction to the special issue: Barriers to providing effective mental health services to racial and ethnic minorities. *Mental Health Services Research, 3,* 179-180.

Leong, F. T. L., & Brown, M. T. (1995). Theoretical issues in cross cultural career development: Cultural validity and cultural specificity. In W. B. Walsh & S. H. Osipow (Eds.), *Handbook of vocational psychology: Theory, research, and practice* (2nd ed., pp. 143-180). Mahwah, NJ: Lawrence Erlbaum.

Leong, F. T. L., & Hardin, E. (in press). Career psychology of Asian Americans: Cultural validity and cultural specificity. In G. Hall & S. Okazaki (Eds.), *Asian American psychology: The science of lives in context.* Washington, DC: American Psychological Association.

Leong, F. T. L., & Hartung, P. J. (1997). Career assessment with culturally-different clients: Proposing an integrative-sequential conceptual framework for cross-cultural career counseling research and practice. *Journal of Career Assessment, 5,* 183-202.

Leong, F. T. L., & Serafica, F. (1995). Career development of Asian Americans: A research area in need of a good theory. In F. T. L. Leong (Ed.), *Career development and vocational behavior of racial and ethnic minorities* (pp. 67-102). Hillsdale, NJ: Lawrence Erlbaum.

Leong, F. T. L., & Tan, V. L. M. (2002). Cross-cultural career counseling in schools. In P. Pedersen & J. C. Carey (Eds.), *Multicultural counseling in schools: A practical handbook* (2nd ed., pp. 234-254). Boston: Allyn & Bacon.

Leong, F. T. L., & Tang, M. (in press). A cultural accommodation approach to career assessment with Asian Americans. In K. Kurasaski, S. Sure, & S. Okazaki (Eds.), *Asian American mental health: Assessment, theories and methods.* Dordrecht, the Netherlands: Kluwer.

Luzzo, D. A. (1992). Ethnic group and social class differences in college students' career development. *Career Development Quarterly, 41,* 161-173.

Savickas, M. L. (Ed.). (1993). Special section: A symposium on multicultural career counseling. *Career Development Quarterly, 42*(1), 3-55.

Savickas, M. L. (1995a). Constructivist counseling for career indecision. *Career Development Quarterly, 43,* 363-373.

Savickas, M. L. (1995b). Current theoretical issues in vocational psychology: Convergence, divergence, and schism. In W. B. Walsh & S. H. Osipow (Eds.), *Handbook of vocational psychology: Theory, research, and practice* (2nd ed., pp. 1-34). Mahwah, NJ: Lawrence Erlbaum.

Savickas, M. L. (2000). Assessing career decision making. In C. E. Watkins & V. Campbell (Eds.), *Testing and assessment in counseling practice* (2nd ed., pp. 429-477). Hillsdale, NJ: Lawrence Erlbaum.

Savickas, M. L., & Walsh, W. B. (Eds.). (1996). *Handbook of career counseling theory and practice.* Palo Alto, CA: Davies-Black.

Singelis, T. M. (1994). The measurement of independent and interdependent self-construals. *Personality and Social Psychology Bulletin, 20,* 580-591.

Subich, L. M. (1996). Addressing diversity in the process of career assessment. In M. L. Savickas & W. B. Walsh (Eds.), *Handbook of career counseling theory and practice* (pp. 277-289). Palo Alto, CA: Davies-Black.

Sue, D. W., & Sue, D. (1990). *Counseling the culturally different: Theory and practice* (2nd ed.). New York: John Wiley.

Super, D. E. (1957). *The psychology of careers.* New York: Harper & Row.

Super, D. E. (1983). Assessment in career guidance: Toward truly developmental counseling. *Personnel and Guidance Journal, 61,* 555-562.

Super, D. E., Savickas, M. L., & Super, C. M. (1996). The life-span, life-space approach to careers. In D. Brown & L. Brooks (Eds.), *Career choice and development: Applying contemporary theories to practice* (3rd ed., pp. 121-178). San Francisco: Jossey-Bass.

Tinsley, H. E. A. (Ed.). (1994). Racial identity and vocational behavior [Special issue]. *Journal of Vocational Behavior, 44*(2).

Triandis, H. C. (1994). Cross-cultural industrial and organizational psychology. In H. C. Triandis, M. D. Dunnette, & L. M. Hough (Eds.), *Handbook of industrial and organizational psychology* (2nd ed., pp. 102-172). Palo Alto, CA: Consulting Psychologists Press.

Vondracek, F. W., & Fouad, N. A. (1994). Developmental contextualism: An integrative framework for theory and practice. In M. L. Savickas & R. W. Lent (Eds.), *Convergence in career development theories: Implications for science and practice* (pp. 207-214). Palo Alto, CA: Consulting Psychologists Press.

Walsh, W. B. (Ed.). (1994). Career assessment with racial and ethnic minorities [Special issue]. *Journal of Career Assessment, 2*(3).

Ward, C. M., & Bingham, R. P. (1993). Career assessment of ethnic minority women. *Journal of Career Assessment, 1,* 246-257.

Young, R. A., & Valach, L. (1996). Interpretation and action in career counseling. In M. L. Savickas & W. B. Walsh (Eds.), *Handbook of career counseling theory and practice* (pp. 361-375). Palo Alto, CA: Davies-Black.

Young, R. A., Valach, L., & Collin, A. (1996). A contextual explanation of career. In D. Brown, L. Brooks, & Associates (Eds.), *Career choice and development* (3rd ed., pp. 477-512). San Francisco: Jossey-Bass.

CHAPTER 25

Cognitive-Behavioral Therapy

Concepts, Issues, and Strategies for Practice With Racial/Ethnic Minorities

MILDRED VERA
DORYLIZ VILA
MARGARITA ALEGRÍA
University of Puerto Rico

Therapists are faced with significant challenges in attempting to provide services that take into consideration the cultural and social contexts of racial/ethnic minorities. Most models that guide the practice of psychotherapy were developed based on the constructions and ideologies of middle-class mainstream American culture, with limited or biased consideration toward the client's race or ethnicity (Hays, 1995). During the past decades, increased attention has been focused on the need that therapists appreciate the diverse and complex experiences confronted by their racial/ethnic minority clients (Bhugra & Bhui, 1998; Fábrega, 1987; Kleinman, 1988; Manson, Shore, & Bloom, 1985; Rogler, Malgady, Costantino, & Blumenthal, 1987; Sue & Sue, 1987). However, although it is important to be aware of the cultural differences of racial/ethnic minorities, therapists should not fall into the trap of stereotyping clients, depriving them of their individual experiences. In the psychotherapeutic process, therapists need to deal with making decisions about how and when to incorporate social and cultural elements in their interventions with racial/ethnic minorities (Falicov, 1998). Yet there is a dearth of information to guide them in this process.

In this chapter, we examine diverse strategies that can help cognitive-behavioral therapists

AUTHORS' NOTE: Preparation of this chapter was supported in part by Grant No. MH59876 from the National Institutes of Mental Health.

become more responsive to the needs and experiences of their racial/ethnic minority clients. First, we start discussing different frameworks available to clinicians when addressing the cultural context of racial/ethnic minorities. Next, we review the historical background and basic assumptions of cognitive-behavioral therapy. Specifically, we examine the strengths and limitations intrinsic to these assumptions for providing treatment to racial/ethnic minorities. Finally, guided by an inclusive framework, we discuss several strategies for integrating cultural elements in the practice of cognitive-behavioral therapy with racial/ethnic minorities.

CULTURAL FRAMEWORKS AND PSYCHOTHERAPY

Universal and Particular Positions

Although the role of culture in human behavior has been widely acknowledged throughout history, the study of culture has been largely ignored in mainstream psychology (Betancourt & López, 1993). Most of the practice of psychotherapy up to the 1980s, including cognitive-behavioral models, was guided by the assumption that constructs and principles developed in the United States with Euro-Americans applied to individuals everywhere. Culture and ethnicity were not considered relevant for understanding basic psychological processes. According to Goldberg (1994), this emphasis on monoculturalism emerged in the United States late in the 19th century and became ingrained into the American culture by the middle of the 20th century. Within this perspective, ethnoracial minorities were approached from an assimilationist melting pot model, which meant "giving up all those 'un-American' values . . . renouncing—often in clearly public ways—one's subjectivity, who one literally was: in name, in culture, and, as far as possible, in color" (Goldberg, 1994, pp. 4-5). This approach toward racial/ethnic

minorities provided the backdrop under which behavioral therapy originated in the United States approximately five decades ago. Cultural differences were seen as irrelevant, prevailing among behavioral therapists in a cultural universalist position.

Most psychological concepts are based on universal assumptions, sustaining the use of similar methods, constructs, measures, and treatments across cultural groups. Contextual and cultural influences experienced by racial/ethnic minorities are seen as one of many factors in the individual's background. Emphasis is placed on the equivalencies across cultures while differences are minimized. Therapists within this universalist position view culture as marginal, sustaining that effective treatments will follow the same course for all cultures. At the other end, therapists with a particularist orientation highlight individual differences rather than similarities. They argue that no generalizations can be made about the individual's relationship with the larger culture, placing more importance on the particular experiences of each individual. Overall, both the universalist and particularist positions provide limited attention to the cultural context of racial/ethnic minority clients (Falicov, 1998).

Culturally Specific Position

As the population of the United States expanded to include ethnic minorities from non-European origins, the dominance of the monoculturalist perspective began to be challenged during the second half of the 20th century. Furthermore, the civil rights and countercultural movements of the 1960s initiated a shift from the prevailing reductive assimilative standard toward a new emphasis on multiculturalism (Goldberg, 1994). During these past decades, cultural diversity has gained unparalleled importance in psychology, with increased demands for greater attention to the inclusion and protection of values and worldviews of the many racial/ethnic minority groups living in the United States (Abe-Kim & Takeuchi, 1996; Guarnaccia & Rodríguez, 1996; Lewis-Fernández & Kleinman, 1995; Rogler et al., 1987; Sue & Zane, 1987). Consequently, the assumed universality and generalizability of theories among racial/ethnic minorities have been questioned (Dana, 1998; López, 1997; Orr, 1996; Tharp, 1991). It has been raised that interventions developed primarily for Euro-Americans may only represent Western cultural perspectives about emotional distress and healing that are adopted as universally valid (Bhugra & Bhui, 1998). These categories of experience may be valid for some cases; however, concerns arise that the therapist might undertake the majority view as the standard of health and interpret cultural deviations as problematic or dysfunctional (Dana, 1998).

The culturally specific perspective emphasizes the relevance of characteristic traits associated with specific racial/ethnic minority groups. A shared set of norms, beliefs, attitudes, and values are attributed to the members of a social group. Proponents suggest that interventions should be tailored to the specific racial/ethnic group, calling for the need to derive culturally based modalities or treatment variations (Tharp, 1991). This position is credited with raising awareness of the need to provide culturally competent mental health services to racial/ethnic minorities. However, despite this contribution, several shortcomings were identified by Falicov (1998). Concerns have been raised that the characteristics attributed to specific racial/ethnic groups provide limited space for cultural differences, which may make these groups appear more similar than they actually are. Furthermore, the racial/ethnic generalizations supported by this approach also give the impression that cultural meanings are fixed and unchanging, failing to portray the complexity of human experiences. Another limitation presented is

that the practice of attributing broad generalizations to describe different racial/ethnic groups contributes to homogenizing and stereotyping cultural diversity. The culturally specific position also demands from the provider a high degree of information for each racial/ethnic group, limiting the possibility that therapists provide care to members of other racial/ethnic groups. Overall, these concerns pose the threat that therapists within this approach unintentionally fall into the tendency of stereotyping their clients and end with formulas to treat them that do not address the complex interactions of class, gender, religion, and other cultural contexts of racial/ethnic minorities (Falicov, 1998).

Multidimensional Ecosystemic Comparative Approach

Rather than have therapists choose between the universal, particular, or culturally specific positions, the advantage of integrating elements from these perspectives is recognized (Bravo, Canino, Rubio-Stipec, & Woodbury-Fariña, 1991; Tharp, 1991). The multidimensional ecosystemic comparative approach (MECA) elaborated by Falicov (1998) is proposed as an alternative to conventional frameworks to help clinicians go beyond particular therapeutic orientations to address the cultural context of racial/ethnic minorities. This approach sustains that therapists must be able to appreciate human similarities that unite people (universalist position) while considering and respecting cultural differences related to race, ethnicity, class, and gender (culture-specific position). It is essential in this process that therapists also incorporate a particularist perspective, which recognizes and respects the uniqueness of each client.

The MECA emphasizes that therapists should address cultural elements from three perspectives: multidimensional, ecosystemic, and comparative. The multidimensional perspective highlights that culture develops over time through membership and participation in multiple contexts. These contexts, associated with language, race, ethnicity, religion, family structure, socioeconomic status, and others, contribute to an individual's cultural makeup. Within this perspective, it is crucial that clinicians be attentive to the influences of the multiple interrelated contexts within which their clients interact. This approach sustains that the combination of these multiple contexts, rather than any particular context exclusively, is what affects the molding of an individual's culture.

The ecosystemic perspective of culture within MECA examines the diversity of ecological contexts in which the individual lives and works. The exploration of this dimension of culture facilitates that therapists gain a better perspective of the client's total ecological field, including experiences of discrimination or conflict that can be experienced by racial/ethnic minorities, as well as support systems that might be available within the community.

The MECA also highlights the importance of comparing the multiple cultural contexts inherent to both the client and provider. By examining these contexts (e.g., ethnicity, race, language, social class, occupation), similarities and differences between the client and provider can be identified and clarified, facilitating the therapeutic work. For example, although the client and provider may belong to different ethnic groups, they may share the same educational level and socioeconomic position, making them similar in other aspects. It is emphasized that the therapist should focus on examining differences and similarities only for those aspects of culture that are relevant to the therapist's evaluation and approach.

Although culture is usually seen as marginal to psychological theory and practice, the MECA sustains that an individual's cultural heritage can have a strong influence on his or her perspective of health, illness, and healing. Therefore, it favors that cultural elements be addressed at every step of the psychotherapeutic process. However, although this approach recognizes the relevance of the cultural collective experiences shared by members of a particular racial/ethnic group, these interpretations should not be so tightly constructed that individual differences and personal interpretations are undervalued in the therapeutic relationship.

COGNITIVE-BEHAVIORAL THERAPY

Historical Perspective

Cognitive-behavioral therapy is not a homogeneous or uniform approach; rather, within this broad framework, there exists a diverse set of related theoretical orientations and clinical techniques that arose from a multiplicity of influences (Dobson & Shaw, 1995). Behaviorism provided the conceptual framework for the initial theoretical developments. Within this framework, psychology was defined as the science of behavior, limiting the extent of psychological exploration to directly observable events and behaviors (Craighead, Craighead, & Ilardi, 1995). On the basis of this orientation, in the late 1950s, clinical psychologists initiated the development of therapeutic methods following the predominant learning theories of the period. Until this time, most of the support for therapeutic interventions had been based on clinical data derived from psychoanalysis. Behavioral therapists challenged this practice, developing therapeutic methods based on learning theory. Classical conditioning principles provided the basis for the technique of systematic desensitization, useful for treating conditions such as phobias. Intervention strategies directed at influencing behavior through positive and negative reinforcement were derived from the operant conditioning stimulus-response (S-R) model. The rubric of behavior therapy clusters diverse therapeutic procedures initiated independently by various clinicians (Lazarus,

1958; Skinner, 1953; Wolpe, 1958). Kazdin (1982) explained that the differences among the various behavioral approaches and treatment techniques were mostly overlooked, with the purpose of presenting a relatively unified front against the traditional disease model of abnormal behavior. They also excluded any reference to the role of thinking processes, attitudes, and values in treatment procedures as a reaction against the insight-oriented psychoanalytic approaches dominant at that time (Corey, 1996).

Despite the clinical and experimental advances achieved by behavior therapists, the field experienced a significant reformulation in the late 1960s and 1970s. The initial developments in behavior therapy had limited the role of psychology to the study of observable behaviors, indicating that covert, private behavior, such as thoughts, were not a proper object of scientific inquiry. The main reason to justify this position was that nobody besides the cognizer could verify the accuracy of the data. However, during this period, the importance of cognitive and affective processes in changing behavior began to attract increasing attention among clinicians. Social learning theory, derived from the work of Bandura (1969), had a major impact in the integration of cognitive and symbolic processes into behavior therapy. He introduced the principles of observational learning or modeling that invoked cognitive explanations for learning from watching and listening to other people. His findings supported the reformulation of learning theory to include the cognitive mediation of behavior.

These developments, as well as the existing discontentment with the prevailing S-R learning model and the emergence of computer analogues to human thought processes, are credited with influencing the initiation of the "cognitive revolution" in psychological research (Craighead et al., 1995). The cognitive revolution had a strong impact on behavior therapy by recognizing the central role of cognitive processes in the mediation of behavior change, thereby validating cognitions as a target for intervention. It has also been credited with providing the support for the transformation of behavior therapy into cognitive-behavioral therapy. Consequently, since the early 1970s, the behavioral movement has provided a rightful position to thought processes, giving cognitive factors a central role in the understanding and treatment of behavioral problems. Techniques developed during the past decades particularly emphasize cognitive and affective processes in behavior change (Mahoney, 1991; Meichenbaum, 1985).

Basic Characteristics and Assumptions

Contemporary cognitive-behavioral therapy includes diverse theoretical orientations, methodological approaches, and intervention procedures. It is not a monolithic approach but rather includes a set of related clinical methods and techniques developed from a multiplicity of influences (Craighead et al., 1995). Dobson and Shaw (1995) indicated that between 12 and 17 distinct therapeutic models are estimated to be included within this broad framework. Furthermore, they specified that the field of cognitive-behavioral therapy is still in a state of growth and maturation.

However, limited attention has been given to the application of cognitive-behavioral techniques across racial/ethnic minority cultures (Bhugra & Bhui, 1998). In the following, we discuss some of the central concepts and assumptions identified by several authors (Corey, 1996; Spiegler & Guevremont, 1998) within the heterogeneity of approaches in contemporary cognitive-behavioral therapy. In addition, we examine the strengths and limitations of these assumptions to provide culturally appropriate psychotherapy to racial/ethnic minorities.

View of Human Nature

Initial behavioral therapies held a strict mechanistic and deterministic view of human nature, whereby all behaviors were based on a stimulus-response model of learning. Individuals were seen as passive agents subjected to environmental forces with no influence over their surroundings, a view that was energetically rejected by cognitive therapists. Studies of language behavior (Chomsky, 1959), memory, and observational learning (Bandura, 1969) sustained that individuals are not merely passive recipients of new information but have an active role as producers of their environment through symbolic cognitive processes. Attention was focused on the mediating role of cognitive factors and the subjective reaction of people to the environment. Different from behavioral approaches, cognitive-behavioral therapists included cognition as both a mechanism and a target of clinical change and substituted environmental determinism with the idea of reciprocal determinism between the individual and the environment (Craighead et al., 1995). The basic assumption is that the individual's perception of these events is what mediates his or her response and adaptation to different circumstances rather than the events themselves (Dobson & Shaw, 1995).

Strengths for Use With Racial/Ethnic Minorities. Although other theoretical orientations are more prone to attribute fault mainly to the individual, cognitive-behavioral approaches pay more attention to environmental conditions that contribute to the problems experienced by racial/ethnic minorities (Corey, 1996). The shift from environmental determinism to an increased consideration of the environmental factors that interact with behaviors and thoughts is a major strength of cognitive-behavioral therapy for conducting interventions with racial/ethnic minorities (Casas, 1995).

Cognitive-behavioral therapy's emphasis on interventions that center on specific behaviors, thoughts, and emotions is another strength, particularly when therapy takes place in a client's second language (Hays, 1995). When therapy is dependent on the use of abstract theoretical constructs, as in the case of other theoretical models, the potential for misunderstandings can increase (Casas, 1988). The clarity of direction and purpose of cognitive-behavioral interventions strongly contribute to minimize this risk.

View of Emotional Disturbance

The fundamental model underlying cognitive-behavioral approaches sustains that individuals with an emotional disorder have dysfunctional cognitive structures that lead to faulty thoughts and misconceptions in specific situations. Cognitive-behavioral therapists focus on correcting faulty cognitions and self-signals to assist individuals in making alternative interpretations of events in their daily living (Beck, 1976). Dobson and Shaw (1995) pointed out that although the earlier expositions of cognitive-behavioral therapy (Beck, Rush, Shaw, & Emery, 1979) focused on the assessment and modification of automatic thoughts and dysfunctional attitudes, in more recent work, cognitive-behavioral theorists have emphasized the role of cognitive schemas and constructivistic processes (Beck, Freeman, & Associates, 1990; Young, 1990).

The constructivistic model in the field of cognitive therapy has focused on placing more importance on the subjective framework and interpretations of the client rather than on the objective foundation of faulty beliefs (Corey, 1996). The position held by constructivists (Guidano, 1987, 1991; Guidano & Liotti, 1983) is that a permanent, external reality does not exist. Reality is seen as a constructed entity that is the result of subjective and social experience; therefore, the reality presented by the client is accepted without questioning its rationality or accuracy (Dobson & Shaw, 1995; Neimeyer, 1993). From this perspective, individuals are dysfunctional to the degree that their experience is disturbing to them or is inconsistent with social experience. Dobson and Shaw (1995) and others (Kovacs & Beck, 1977; Young, 1990) have focused on the role of cognitive schemas as the structures that may facilitate distorted thoughts. Patients with a disorder are seen as having cognitive schemas that contribute to the negative thinking that takes place in specific situations. They described cognitive schemas as "abstract aspects of cognitive functioning, hypothetically based on experience and residing in long-term memory, that affect a number of cognitive processes, including attention, information processing, encoding, and recall" (Dobson & Shaw, 1995, p. 161). Under this model, they sustained that the central point of treatment is to identify the nature, strength, coherence, and viability of the cognitive schemas that the client employs and explore alternative schemas that are more emotionally, cognitively, and behaviorally adaptive.

Strengths and Limitations for Use With Racial/Ethnic Minorities. A major criticism of the main cognitive-behavioral approaches for use with racial/ethnic minorities is that although the impact of the social context on individuals' development is recognized, there is still the expectation that individuals must change their subjective experience of reality and improve their ability to adapt to the existing environmental conditions (Casas, 1995). A significant contribution of the constuctivist orientation within cognitive-behavioral therapy is that it allows clients to explore their beliefs and provide their own reinterpretations of significant life events within the framework of their own cultural values and worldview (Corey, 1996). Within this approach, the client's reality is accepted without questioning its accuracy or rationality (Weishaar, 1993). Clients are stimulated to examine their way of thinking so they can explore the impact their beliefs have on their behaviors. An advantage of the constructivist viewpoint for working with racial/ethnic minorities is that therapists can facilitate that clients modify painful beliefs and interpretations without imposing their values and interpretations (Corey, 1996).

Action-Oriented Approach

Cognitive-behavioral therapy promotes diverse action-oriented methods to help individuals change their actions and thoughts. Clients are provided with skills and techniques for self-change, so they can actively participate in dealing with their problems and assume responsibility for their behaviors. They are expected to take an active role in dealing with the situations that affect their lives and fully participate in making decisions about their treatment.

Strengths and Limitations for Use With Racial/Ethnic Minorities. Given the focus on client empowerment, this action-oriented approach appears potentially helpful for racial/ethnic minority clients (Casas, 1995; Hays, 1995). Cognitive-behavioral therapy recognizes that people have the ability to control their thoughts and emotions and can use their skills to deal with their life situations. In this process, therapists have been cautioned that when dealing with racial/ethnic minorities, they should not seek to control them but rather allow them to develop skills and self-control in terms of their own behavior (Casas, 1995). According to Hays (1995), this environment of respect for the client's abilities and particular life situations promotes a collaborative relationship in which individual and cultural differences are recognized rather than denied.

Among the potential limitations of cognitive-behavioral approaches for racial/ethnic minorities is the lack of attention to the client's history. It is argued that by focusing on the present, therapists from another culture or generation may not gain relevant information about cultural differences in the client's upbringing and life experiences (Hays, 1995). Corey (1996) sustained that cognitive-behavioral therapists can pay attention to the clients' past without getting lost in this past and falling into a fatalistic stance about their clients' earlier experiences. Concerns have also been raised about the emphasis placed by cognitive-behavioral approaches on the orientation toward future goals. According to Casas (1995), the focus on a linear time perspective is strongly influenced by Euro-American White middle-class values. He indicated that this futuristic orientation can prove confusing and alien to members of other cultural groups, such as Native Americans, who sustain a circular perspective of time.

Reliance on Empirically Tested Procedures

Cognitive-behavioral therapy has a strong conviction on the principles of the scientific method. No other therapeutic process has been subjected to as much research as cognitive-behavioral therapy (Spiegler & Guevremont, 1998). Therapeutic procedures are described in clear and objective terms to ease replication. Goals and expected outcomes are clearly defined and measured to facilitate empirical testing and appropriate revisions. A substantial body of research provides compelling evidence on the efficacy of cognitive-behavioral therapy for diverse mental health conditions. In study after study, cognitive-behavioral therapy has been shown to be as effective as medications in treating both depression and anxiety.

Strengths and Limitations for Use With Racial/Ethnic Minorities. The integration of assessment procedures during all phases of the therapeutic process has been identified as a strength of cognitive-behavioral therapy for providing treatment to racial/ethnic minorities (Hays, 1995; Kirk, 1989). The

emphasis placed on documenting the client's progress from his or her perspective, as well as the inclusion of process and outcome measures, is indicative of the therapist's respect for the client's opinions. Hays (1995) pointed out that although this strength is important for all therapeutic relationships, it is of particular importance when the racial/ethnic background of the therapist and client differs. However, concerns have been raised about the appropriateness of the assessment methods used when treating racial/ethnic minority clients. Most conventional measures of clinical outcomes and symptom reduction do not consider cultural and contextual differences. The validity and reliability of the assessment methods chosen for clients with different cultural backgrounds need to be evaluated when providing treatment to racial/ethnic minorities.

Research findings show that cognitive-behavioral therapy is definitely an effective treatment for depression (Spiegler & Guevremont, 1998), but few studies include racial/ethnic minorities in their samples (Hays, 1995). The design and implementation of interventions for improving depression treatment mainly have been carried out with Anglo populations. As a result, racial/ethnic minority populations are vastly underrepresented in both efficacy and effectiveness studies (Alvidrez, Azocar, & Miranda, 1996). Table 25.1 includes cognitive-behavioral therapy studies that provide information about the proportion of racial/ethnic minority participants. For most studies, the sample of racial/ethnic minorities is so limited that study findings cannot be reported for specific minority groups. Recent effectiveness research studies on the use of cognitive-behavioral therapy for depression (Miranda & Muñoz, 1994; Wells, 1997) have begun to include Spanish-speaking Latinos. However, these studies must be viewed as the first step of a larger program of bringing the benefits of clinical developments in effectiveness studies to all groups

Table 25.1 Summary of Major Studies Related to the Use of Cognitive-Behavioral Therapies With Minority Groups

Reference	Title	Study Sample	Condition Treated
Alan, Montoya, Nelson, and Spence (1995)	Effectiveness of Adjunct Therapies in Crack Cocaine Treatment	228 participants: 92.5% African American 3.2% White 4.3% Latino	Drug use
Agras, Walsh, Fairburn, Wilson, and Kraemer (2000)	A Multicenter Comparison of Cognitive-Behavioral Therapy and Interpersonal Psychotherapy for Bulimia Nervosa	219 participants: 77% White 11% Latino 6% African American 5% Asian	Bulimia nervosa
Bell, Richard, and Dayton (1996)	Effects of Drug User Treatment on Psychosocial Change: A comparison of In-Treatment and Out-of-Treatment Cocaine Users	486 participants: 87% African American 6% European American 7% Latino	Drug use
Comas-Diaz (1981)	Effects of Cognitive Behavioral Group Treatment on Depressive Symptomatology of Puerto Rican Women	26 participants: 100% Latino	Depression
Dai et al. (1999)	Cognitive Behavioral Therapy of Minor Depressive Symptoms in Elderly Chinese Americans: A Pilot Study	30 participants: 100% Chinese	Minor depression
Miranda et al. (2001)	Can Quality Improvement Interventions Improve Care and Outcomes for Depressed Minorities? Results of a Randomized Controlled Trial	1,269 participants: 61.31% White 31.36% Latino 7.33% African American	Depression
Muñoz et al. (1995)	Prevention of Depression With Primary Care Patients: A Randomized Controlled Trial	150 Participants 35.1% White 24.3% Latino 23.7% African American 10.1% Asian 6.8% Other	Depression
Organista, Muñoz, and Gonzalez (1994)	Cognitive-Behavioral Therapy for Depression and Minority Outpatients: Description of a Program and Exploratory Analyses	175 participants: 34.6% White 44.4% Latino 18% African American 3% Asian	Depression
Sanderson, Raue, and Wetzler (1998)	The Generalizability of Cognitive Behavior Therapy for Panic Disorder	30 participants: 43% White 53% Latino 3% African American	Panic disorder with agoraphobia

(Continued)

Table 25.1 Continued

Reference	Title	Study Sample	Condition Treated
Satterfield (1998)	Cognitive Behavioral Group Therapy for Depressed, Low-Income, Minority Clients: Retention and Treatment Enhancement	23 participants: 35% White 12% Latino 47% African American 6% Other	Depression
Williams et al. (2000)	Treatment of Dysthymia and Minor Depression in Primary Care	415 participants: 78% White 12% Latino 9% African American 1% Other	Dysthymia and minor depression

in society. Increased research efforts, with sufficient sample sizes, are needed to explore the appropriateness of cognitive-behavioral interventions for diverse racial/ethnic minority populations.

Collaborative Partnership Between Therapist and Client

Beck (1987) emphasized that a relationship of collaboration is a fundamental element in cognitive-behavioral therapy. It is recognized that a good therapeutic relationship contributes to the clients' receptivity to treatment. In addition to characteristics such as empathy, warmth, and nonjudgmental acceptance, the therapist must also be creative and active, have the ability to engage clients in treatment, and be skilled and knowledgeable in the use of cognitive-behavioral strategies aimed at facilitating the client's process of self-discovery (Corey, 1996). Contrary to traditional psychoanalytic orientations, the therapist takes an active part in cognitive-behavioral therapy. Therapists work collaboratively with clients by helping them understand how their thoughts influence their feelings and actions (Neimeyer, 1993). A high level of skills and rapport is required to facilitate the process of self-disclosure and establish a collaborative relationship with the client.

Strengths and Limitations for Use With Racial/Ethnic Minorities. Providing cognitive-behavioral therapy that is responsive to clients of varying racial/ethnic backgrounds is a challenging task (Iwamasa, 1996; Martin, 1995). In establishing a collaborative relationship, the therapist must take into account unique aspects of the client's cultural identity (Fudge, 1996; Tanaka-Matsumi & Higginbotham, 1994). A strength of this orientation in dealing with racial/ethnic minorities is the emphasis on the need that therapists respect their clients' underlying values. The importance of this is especially highlighted in the case where the therapist and client are from different cultural backgrounds and do not share the same worldview.

Even though cognitive-behavioral therapy takes into consideration social and cultural elements that affect the life of clients, it has not openly addressed the impact that racism and other forms of oppression have on racial/ethnic minority clients (Hays, 1995). Among the potential limitations of cognitive-behavioral therapy is that the values of marginalized groups might be overlooked because they are not well known or are suppressed by therapists of dominant cultural groups (Hays, 1995). Furthermore, concerns have been raised on the need to be aware of the therapy's subtle biases. For example, Euro-American middle-class values, which emphasize self-control and personal autonomy, although highly valued in the United States, may not have the same relevance for other racial/ethnic groups. Failure to adequately address the values of racial/ethnic minority clients might limit the therapist's ability to engage clients in treatment and establish an effective collaborative relationship.

STRATEGIES FOR ADDRESSING CULTURAL ELEMENTS IN COGNITIVE-BEHAVIORAL THERAPY WITH RACIAL/ETHNIC MINORITIES

During recent years, there has been a growing movement that supports the adaptation of current psychological models to address the needs of diverse racial/ethnic minority groups (Bhugra & Bhui, 1998; Corey, 1996). This perspective favors that the base of contemporary theories be broadened to include a focus on cultural differences. The MECA, previously discussed, provides a framework for guiding the integration of cultural elements into the practice of cognitive-behavioral therapy with racial/ethnic minorities. This framework favors that cultural elements be incorporated at every step of the therapeutic process: the therapist's observations, how the problem is conceptualized, and the intervention. Within this perspective, it is crucial that the therapist be attentive to the client's cultural interpretations of health, illness, and healing. On the basis of the three main components of the MECA, we discuss in this section the relevance of the outline for cultural formulation in facilitating the integration of cultural elements in the practice of cognitive-behavioral therapy with racial/ethnic minorities. Specifically, we embrace a holistic inclusive approach in which the assessment,

diagnosis, and treatment center on the client's emotions, thoughts, social context, and cultural identity.

Outline for Cultural Formulation

The outline for cultural formulation of the fourth edition of the *Diagnostic and Statistical Manual of Mental Disorders (DSM-IV)* was designed to assist clinicians in conducting a systematic evaluation of the individual's cultural context, the role of cultural elements in the manifestation and interpretation of symptoms and dysfunction, and the impact that cultural differences between the clinician and the client may have on the therapeutic relationship (American Psychiatric Association, 1994, 2001). This outline was developed with the purpose of making culture more central to the *DSM-IV*. The main aim was to facilitate the use of a cultural perspective in the process of clinical interviewing and diagnostic formulation to complement the *DSM-IV* (Lewis-Fernández, 1996). Consonant with the inclusive multidimensional ecosystemic comparative framework, emphasis is placed on intracultural as well as cross-cultural elements, focusing particularly on the interactions of class, race, ethnicity, gender, and other intracultural factors (Lewis-Fernández, 1996). Overall, the cultural formulation outline allows therapists to complement and broaden standard assessment and diagnostic work. In the following, we discuss the dimensions addressed in the cultural formulation outline and examine their relevance for helping clinicians take into account the impact of the individual's cultural context on the practice of cognitive-behavioral therapy (see Appendix 25.1 for a summary).

Cultural Identity. The first dimension of the cultural formulation involves the identification of the individual's cultural reference groups. It is commonly assumed that members of racial/ethnic minority groups share the same beliefs and behavioral norms. These assumptions contribute to simplistic and unfounded ideas about ethnicity, even to the stereotyping of cultural heritage. The multidimensional component of the inclusive multidimensional ecosystemic comparative framework, proposed to guide the integration of cultural variations that are relevant to the theory and practice of cognitive-behavioral therapy, recognizes that each person "is raised in a 'plurality of cultural groups' that exert a 'multiplicity of influences' depending on the degree of contact with each subcultural context" (Falicov, 1998, p. 14). The combination of these multiple contexts and the individual's particular experiences is what defines the individual's culture rather than any of these separately. Therefore, to avoid stereotypes, clinicians must assess the individuals' level of involvement with their culture of origin and with their host culture. Differences in cultural identity may be noted in language preference, religion, educational level, social class, and gender status. Although the clinician's knowledge about the individual's culture can be of help to inform him or her about relevant cultural factors, to effectively assess cultural identity, the clinician must treat each individual as a unique case, exploring directly his or her cultural identity (Castillo, 1997).

Cultural Explanations of the Individual's Illness. Multiple complex factors have been identified as significant elements in the initiation, maintenance, and treatment of mental illnesses. To effectively address the needs of our clients, we need to assess these different elements and their interactions, taking into consideration the cultural nature of human emotions (Castillo, 1997). This information is crucial because of the impact that cultural concepts have on structuring individual and collective realities. As discussed earlier, the constructionist perspective within cognitive-behavioral therapy (Guidano, 1987, 1991; Guidano & Liotti, 1983) sustains that an external reality does not exist as such; rather, reality is seen as a constructed entity that is the result of subjective and social experiences. Cognitive schemas are identified as relevant structures in mediating the process between sensory stimuli and a dysfunctional emotional response (Dobson, 1986; Dobson & Shaw, 1995; Young, 1990). Castillo (1997) stated that "because cultural schemas provide the cognitive structure for the appraisal of sensory stimuli, the meaning of events and norms of behavioral responses for adult human emotions are not uniform across cultures" (p. 56). Consequently, he sustained that the assessment of cultural schemas and personal cognitive patterns that support dysfunctional emotional responses is essential for viewing those emotions within a wider context to identify the sources of distress and possible strategies for emotional healing. He proposed Levy's (1984) three-stage cognitive model of emotion as a guide for understanding human emotions. The first stage of this model, *initial appraisal,* sustains that the meaning of events is determined by the individual's cognitive assessment of the situation based on the cultural schemas guiding norms of behavior. The next stage, *emotional feeling,* involves the bodily sensations and physiological alterations experienced by the individual in response to his or her cognitive evaluation of the situation. The last stage involves the culture-based behavioral response that takes place as a response to the previous stages. For the assessment of the cultural aspects of emotion, Castillo (1997) suggested the following six aspects developed by Shweder (1985). The first aspect involves examining if any particular emotions may be present in the client's cultural group that may not be common in Western culture. Next, the clinician should explore if there are variations in the emotions elicited by particular situations. For example, the death of a baby might evoke different emotional responses from members of different cultural groups. A third aspect that needs to be examined is the meaning that the emotion experienced by the client has for his or her cultural group. When assessing pathology, it is also very important to evaluate what emotions are acceptable or unacceptable for a person of a particular social position. For example, in some cultures, the expression of lust and sexual aggressiveness by a man is seen as appropriate, but it is considered deviant or pathological if manifested by a woman. Other relevant aspects involve assessing the idioms of distress, means of expression for communicating an emotion, and methods of dealing with unexpressed emotions.

Cultural Factors Related to Psychosocial Environment and Levels of Functioning. The ecosystemic component of the MECA maintains that therapists who emphasize explanations based on a racial/ethnic perspective can unintentionally work against the individual by overlooking influences from the social context. Focusing on the individual's psychosocial context, the third dimension of the cultural formulation outline, facilitates that clinicians take into consideration the impact of social and environmental stressors. Discrimination and intolerance have been strongly ingrained in the history and experience of racial/ethnic minorities in the United States. By conducting an integrated assessment that considers the individual's social ecological context, level of impairment, and related stressors, cognitive-behavioral therapists significantly contribute to increase their ability to provide culturally attuned psychotherapy to racial/ethnic minorities.

Cultural Elements of the Relationship Between the Individual and the Clinician. The fourth dimension in the cultural outline encourages that differences between the therapist's and client's culture and social status be examined. This dimension recognizes the need to acknowledge the impact that the therapist's subjectivity and practice models

have on understanding cultural descriptions provided by the client. This can have a significant impact on the clinician's assessment and understanding of the problem presented by the client. Consonant with the comparative component of the MECA, this dimension of the cultural formulation outline promotes that clients' and therapists' cultural similarities and differences be drawn out and used to enhance the therapeutic work. This allows descriptions and comparisons of the multiple cultural contexts, ethnicity, race, social class, occupation, and language inherent to both the client and provider.

Overall Cultural Assessment for Diagnosis and Care. The last dimension of the outline for cultural formulation entails generating a comprehensive diagnosis and treatment plan that reflects the individual's needs, reached as a result of the agreement between the therapist, client, and, when relevant, the client's family. Consistent with cognitive-behavioral therapy principles, it is emphasized that clients have an active role in making decisions about their treatment. Generating a treatment plan based on the negotiated consensus of the problem will allow all parties to collaborate in following the planned treatment (Castillo, 1997). Furthermore, a good collaborative relationship will significantly contribute to clients assuming responsibility for their behaviors and participating in the process of improving their lives.

CONCLUSION

Further expansion of cognitive-behavioral therapy is anticipated over the next few years in view of the rising costs of health care and the increased participation of psychologists in health issues. Although it is estimated that more than a third of the U.S. population consists of racial/ethnic minorities, cognitive-behavioral therapy, as well as other mainstream psychotherapeutic models, has provided limited or biased consideration to racial/ethnic minority cultures. Increasingly, therapists will be providing mental health services to clients of diverse racial/ethnic backgrounds. To reach this growing group, mental health professionals need to expand familiar cognitive-behavioral therapy models developed mainly with middle-class Anglo-Americans and examine the diverse and complex experiences of their racial/ethnic minority clients.

As we have discussed, significant advances during the past few years have been accomplished in the design of frameworks and outlines that can help cognitive-behavioral therapists become more responsive to specific issues of cultural diversity. The multidimensional ecosystemic comparative framework provides a guide for clinicians to integrate the clients' cultural context in the practice of cognitive-behavioral therapy with racial/ethnic minorities. The outline for cultural formulation facilitates this process by helping clinicians make culture more central in the assessment and diagnosis of racial/ethnic minorities. However, so far, most of these efforts have been limited to providing general guidelines for addressing cultural elements when intervening with clients of diverse racial/ethnic backgrounds. Currently, there is scarce evidence documenting efforts aimed at incorporating these guidelines into the practice of cognitive-behavioral therapy with racial/ethnic minorities.

The inclusion of an outline for cultural formulation as an appendix, rather than in the main text in the American Psychiatric Association's (1994, 2001) *DSM-IV*, denotes a limited commitment of mainstream psychology to provide culturally appropriate mental health services and could influence some not to use this outline as widely as it is warranted. An impetus among cognitive-behavioral therapists to encourage a more widespread dissemination and adoption of the elements of the cultural formulation outline in the assessment and

treatment of racial/ethnic minorities is strongly needed. This can be accomplished by developing improved treatment manuals and protocols that incorporate the components of the cultural formulation outline to provide better practical guidelines for the assessment and treatment of racial/ethnic minorities.

It is our contention that although the main concepts and principles of cognitive-behavioral therapy show significant strengths for providing treatment to racial/ethnic minorities, limited attention has been paid by cognitive-behavioral therapists to specific issues of race, ethnicity, and cultural diversity. Many clinicians and researchers are relatively unprepared to deal with diverse racial/ethnic minority populations. The training of mental health professionals needs to be enhanced, and it is important that cognitive-behavioral therapists develop a better understanding of the multiple cultural issues that can influence the treatment of racial/ethnic minorities. Furthermore, research that incorporates cultural constructs and examines the applicability and effectiveness of cognitive-behavioral therapy for racial/ethnic minorities is critically needed. Concerns arise about the usefulness and outcomes of cognitive-behavioral therapy with racial/ethnic minorities if the current neglect continues in this field.

APPENDIX 25.1

SUMMARY OF DIMENSIONS AND ASSESSMENT AREAS OF THE OUTLINE FOR CULTURAL FORMULATION

A. Cultural identity—identification of the individual's cultural reference groups, defined by the combination of the individual's multiple contexts (i.e., social class, language preference, race, education level) and particular experiences

B. Cultural explanations of the individual's illness

Meaning of events determined by the individual's cognitive assessment of the situation based on cultural schemas guiding behavioral norms

Relevant areas to assess:

Emotions present in client's cultural group that are not common in Anglo-American culture

Variations in the emotions that are elicited by a particular situation (i.e., death of baby)

Meaning that the emotion experienced has for the client's cultural group

Acceptable and unacceptable emotions for a person of a particular social position (i.e., manifestations of sexual aggressiveness by a man vs. a woman)

Means of expression for communicating an emotion

Methods of dealing with unexpressed emotions

C. Cultural factors related to psychosocial environment and levels of functioning

Integrated assessment that takes into consideration the individual's socioecological context, level of impairment, and sources of stress, such as poverty, discrimination, immigrant status, and other forms of disqualification

D. Cultural elements of the relationship between the individual and the clinician

Examine similarities and differences between the therapist's and client's multiple cultural contexts, such as ethnicity, race, social class, and language

Acknowledge the impact that the therapist's subjectivity and practice models may have on the understanding of cultural descriptions provided by the client

E. Overall cultural assessment for diagnosis and care

Comprehensive diagnosis and treatment plan reached as a result of agreement between the therapist, client, and family members, when relevant

REFERENCES

Abe-Kim, J., & Takeuchi, D. T. (1996). Cultural competence and quality of care: Issues for mental health services delivery in managed care. *Clinical Psychology: Science and Practice, 3,* 273-295.

Agras, S., Walsh, T., Fairburn, G., Wilson, T., & Kraemer, H. (2000). A multicenter comparison of cognitive-behavioral therapy and interpersonal psychotherapy for bulimia nervosa. *Archives of General Psychiatry, 57,* 459-466.

Alan, J. R., Montoya, I. D., Nelson, R., & Spence, R. T. (1995). Effectiveness of adjunct therapies in crack cocaine treatment. *Journal of Substance Abuse Treatment, 12*(6), 401-413.

Alvidrez, J., Azocar, F., & Miranda, J. (1996). Demystifying the concept of ethnicity for psychotherapy researchers. *Journal of Consulting and Clinical Psychology, 6*(5), 903-908.

American Psychiatric Association. (1994). *Diagnostic and statistical manual for mental disorders* (4th ed.). Washington, DC: Author.

American Psychiatric Association. (2001). *Diagnostic and statistical manual for mental disorders* (4th ed., text rev.). Washington, DC: Author.

Bandura, A. (1969). *Principles of behavior modification.* New York: Holt, Rinehart & Winston.

Beck, A. T. (1976). *Cognitive therapy and emotional disorders.* New York: International Universities Press.

Beck, A. T. (1987). Cognitive therapy. In J. K. Zeig (Ed.), *The evolution of psychotherapy* (pp. 149-178). New York: Brunner/ Mazel.

Beck, A. T., Freeman, A., & Associates. (1990). *Cognitive therapy of personality disorders.* New York: Guilford.

Beck, A. T., Rush, A. J., Shaw, B. F., & Emery, G. (1979). *The cognitive therapy of depression.* New York: Guilford.

Bell, D., Richard, A., & Dayton, C. (1996). Effects of drug user treatment on psychosocial change: A comparison of in-treatment and out-of-treatment cocaine users. *Substance Use & Misuse, 39,*1083-1100.

Betancourt, H., & López, S. R. (1993). The study of culture, ethnicity and race in American psychology. *American Psychologist, 48*(6), 629-637.

Bhugra, D., & Bhui, K. (1998). Psychotherapy for ethnic minorities: Issues, context and practice. *British Journal of Psychotherapy, 14*(3), 310-326.

Bravo, M., Canino, G., Rubio-Stipec, M., & Woodbury-Fariña, M. (1991). A cross-cultural adaptation of a psychiatric epidemiology instrument: The Diagnostic Interview Schedule Adaptation in Puerto Rico. *Culture, Medicine and Psychiatry, 15,* 1-18.

Casas, J. M. (1988). Cognitive behavioral approaches: A minority perspective. *The Counseling Psychologist, 16,* 106-110.

Casas, J. M. (1995). Counseling and psychotherapy with racial/ethnic minority groups in theory and practice. In B. Bongar & L. E. Beutler (Eds.), *Comprehensive textbook of psychotherapy: Theory and practice* (pp. 311-335). New York: Oxford University Press.

Castillo, R. J. (1997). *Culture & mental illness.* Pacific Grove, CA: Brooks/Cole.

Chomsky, N. (1959). A review of verbal behavior by B. F. Skinner. *Language, 35,* 26-58.

Comas-Diaz, L. (1981). Effects of cognitive and behavioral group treatment on the depressive symptomatology of Puerto Rican women. *Journal of Consulting and Clinical Psychology, 49,* 627-632.

Corey, G. (1996). *Theory and practice of counseling and psychotherapy.* Pacific Grove, CA: Brooks/Cole.

Craighead, W. E., Craighead, L. W., & Ilardi, S. S. (1995). Behavior therapies in historical perspective. In B. Bongar & L. E. Beutler (Eds.), *Comprehensive textbook of psychotherapy: Theory and practice* (pp. 159-172). New York: Oxford University Press.

Dai, Y., Zhang, S., Yamamoto, J., Ao, M., Belin, T., Cheung, F., & Hifumi, S. (1999). Cognitive behavioral therapy of minor depressive symptoms in elderly Chinese Americans: A pilot study. *Community Mental Health Journal, 35,* 537-542.

Dana, R. H. (1998). Problems with managed mental health care for multicultural populations. *Psychology Reports, 83,* 283-294.

Dobson, K. S. (1986). The self-schema in depression. In L. Hartman & K. Blankstein (Eds.), *Perception of self in emotional disorder and psychotherapy* (pp. 187-218). New York: Plenum.

Dobson, K. S., & Shaw, B. F. (1995). Cognitive therapies in practice. In B. Bongar & L. E. Beutler (Eds.), *Comprehensive textbook of psychotherapy: Theory and practice* (pp. 159-172). New York: Oxford University Press.

Fábrega, H. (1987). Psychiatric diagnosis: A cultural perspective. *Journal of Nervous and Mental Disease, 175,* 383-394.

Falicov, C. J. (1998). *Latino families in therapy*. New York: Guilford.

Fudge, R. C. (1996). The use of behavior therapy in the development of ethnic consciousness: A treatment model. *Cognitive and Behavioral Practice, 3*, 317-335.

Goldberg, D. T. (1994). Introduction: Multicultural conditions. In D. T. Goldberg (Ed.), *Multiculturalism: A critical reader* (pp. 1-33). Boston: Blackwell.

Guarnaccia, P. J., & Rodríguez, O. (1996). Concepts of culture and their role in the development of culturally competent mental health services. *Hispanic Journal of Behavioral Sciences, 18*(40), 419-443.

Guidano, V. (1987). *Complexity of the self*. New York: Guilford.

Guidano, V. (1991). *The self in process: Towards a post-rationalist cognitive therapy*. New York: Guilford.

Guidano, V., & Liotti, G. (1983). *Cognitive processes and emotional disorders*. New York: Guilford.

Hays, P. A. (1995). Multicultural applications of cognitive-behavior therapy. *Professional Psychology: Research and Practice, 26*(3), 309-315.

Iwamasa, G. Y. (1996). Introduction to the special series: Ethnic and cultural diversity in cognitive and behavioral practice. *Cognitive and Behavioral Practice, 3*, 209-213.

Kazdin, A. E. (1982). History of behavior modification. In A. S. Bellack, M. Hersen, & A. E. Kazdin (Eds.), *International handbook of behavior modification and therapy* (pp. 3-32). New York: Plenum.

Kirk, J. (1989). Cognitive-behavioral assessment. In K. Hawton, P. M. Salkovskis, J. Kirk, & D. M. Clark (Eds.), *Cognitive behavior therapy for psychiatric Problems: A practical guide* (pp. 13-51). Oxford, UK: Oxford University Press.

Kleinman, A. (1988). *Rethinking psychiatry: From cultural category to personal experience*. New York: Free Press.

Kovacs, M., & Beck, A. T. (1977). Cognitive-affective processes in depression. In C. E. Izard (Ed.), *Motions in personality and psychopathology* (pp. 214-247). New York: Plenum.

Lazarus, A. A. (1958). New methods in psychotherapy: A case study. *South African Medical Journal, 32*, 660-664.

Levy, R. I. (1984). Emotion, knowing, and culture. In R. A. Schweder & R. A. Le Vine (Eds.), *Culture, theory: Essays on mind, self, and emotion* (pp. 189-208). Cambridge, UK: Cambridge University Press.

Lewis-Fernández, R. (1996). Cultural formulation of psychiatric diagnosis. In B. J. Good & M. Good (Eds.), *Culture, medicine and psychiatry, 20*(2), 133-144.

Lewis-Fernández, R., & Kleinman, A. (1995). Cultural psychiatry: Theoretical, clinical, and research issues. *Psychiatric Clinics of North America, 18*, 433-438.

López, S. R. (1997). Cultural competence in psychotherapy: A guide for clinicians and their supervisors. In C. E. Watkins, Jr. (Ed.), *Handbook of psychotherapy supervision* (pp. 570-588). New York: John Wiley.

Mahoney, M. J. (1991). *Human change processes: The scientific foundations of psychotherapy*. New York: Basic Books.

Manson, S. M., Shore, J. H., & Bloom, J. D. (1985). The depressive experience in American Indian communities: A challenge for psychiatric theory and diagnosis. In A. Kleiman & B. Good (Eds.), *Culture and depression: Studies in the anthropology and cross-cultural psychiatry of affect and disorder* (pp. 331-368). Berkeley: University of California Press.

Martin, S. (1995). Ethnic issues deeply entwined in family therapy. *APA Monitor, 26*, 38.

Meichenbaum, D. (1985). *Stress inoculation training*. New York: Pergamon.

Miranda, J., & Muñoz, R. (1994). Intervention for minor depression in primary care patients. *Psychosomatic Medicine, 56*, 136-141.

Miranda, J., Wells, K. B., Duan, N., Jackson-Triche, M., Lagomasino, I., & Sherbourne, C. (2001). *Can quality improvement interventions improve care and outcomes for depressed minorities? Results of a randomized, controlled trial.* Manuscript in preparation.

Muñoz, R., Ying, Y., Bernal, G., Pérez-Stable, E., Sorensen, J., Hargreaves, W., Miranda, J., & Miller, L. (1995). Prevention of depression with primary care patients: A randomized controlled trial. *American Journal of Community Psychology, 23,* 200-222.

Neimeyer, R. A. (1993). An appraisal of constructivist psychotherapies. *Journal of Consulting and Clinical Psychology, 61,* 221-234.

Organista, K., Muñoz, R., & Gonzalez, G. (1994). Cognitive-behavioral therapy for depression and minority outpatients: Description of a program and exploratory analyses. *Cognitive Therapy and Research, 18,* 241-259.

Orr, R. D. (1996). Treating patients from other cultures. *American Family Physician, 53*(6), 2004-2006.

Rogler, L. H., Malgady, R. G., Costantino, G., & Blumenthal, R. (1987). What do culturally sensitive mental health services mean? The case of Hispanics. *American Psychologist, 42*(6), 565-570.

Sanderson, W., Raue, P., & Wetzler, S. (1998). The generalizability of cognitive behavior therapy for panic disorder. *Journal of Cognitive Psychotherapy: An International Quarterly, 12,* 323-330.

Satterfield, J. (1998). Cognitive behavioral group therapy for depressed, low-income, minority clients: Retention and treatment enhancement. *Cognitive and Behavioral Practice, 5,* 65-80.

Shweder, R. A. (1985). Menstrual pollution, soul loss, and the comparative study of emotions. In A. Kleiman & B. Good (Eds.), *Culture and depression: Studies in the anthropology and cross-cultural psychiatry of affect and disorder* (pp. 182-215). Berkeley: University of California Press.

Skinner, B. J. (1953). *Science and human behavior.* New York: Free Press.

Spiegler, M. D., & Guevremont, D. C. (1998). *Contemporary behavior therapy.* Pacific Grove, CA: Brooks/Cole.

Sue, D., & Sue, S. (1987). Cultural factors in the clinical assessment of Asian Americans. *Journal of Counseling and Social Psychology, 55,* 479-487.

Sue, S., & Zane, N. W. S. (1987). The role of culture and cultural techniques in psychotherapy: A critique and reformulation. *American Psychologist, 42,* 37-45.

Tanaka-Matsumi, J., & Higginbotham, H. N. (1994). Clinical application of behavior therapy across ethnic and cultural boundaries. *The Behavior Therapist, 17,* 123-126.

Tharp, R. G. (1991). Cultural diversity and treatment of children. *Journal of Consulting and Clinical Psychology, 59*(6), 799-812.

Weishaar, M. E. (1993). *Aaron T. Beck.* London: Sage.

Wells, K. B. (1999). The design of Partners in Care: Evaluating the cost-effectiveness of improving care for depression in primary care. *Social Psychiatry and Psychiatric Epidemiology, 34,* 20-29.

Williams, J., Barrett, J., Oxman, T., Frank, E., Katon, W., Sullivan, M., Cornell, J., & Sengupta, A. (2000). Treatment of dysthymia and minor depression in primary care. *Journal of American Medical Association, 284,* 1519-1526.

Wolpe, J. (1958). *Psychotherapy by reciprocal inhibition.* Stanford, CA: Stanford University Press.

Young, J. (1990). *Cognitive therapy for personality disorders: A schema-focused approach.* Sarasota, FL: Professional Resource Exchange.

CHAPTER 26

Drug Abuse Treatments With Racial/Ethnic Clients

Toward the Development of Culturally Competent Treatments

FELIPE GONZÁLEZ CASTRO
Arizona State University

JEANNE L. OBERT
MATRIX Institute on Addictions

RICHARD A. RAWSON
UCLA Integrated Substance Abuse Programs

COURTNEY V. LIN
RON DENNE, JR.
Arizona State University

GENERAL ISSUES IN DRUG ABUSE TREATMENT

This chapter presents a sociocultural perspective on drug abuse treatment with members of the major ethnic/racial populations of the United States: Hispanics/Latinos, African Americans, Asian Americans, and Native American Indians. Unfortunately, at present, conventional drug abuse treatment programs have not been culturally appropriate or gender specific to meet the needs of diverse groups of people of color who have become addicted to tobacco, alcohol, and/or to illicit drugs. Today and into the future, there will be a growing need and demand for culturally relevant interventions (both prevention and treatment) as delivered by culturally competent staff (both professional and paraprofessional). Accordingly, clear approaches to the provision of such services are needed. These approaches include the following:

1. improved conceptualization (both in theory and in practice) and the development of culturally relevant interventions,

2. the use of an empirical evaluation (both research and program evaluation) to evaluate the efficacy of these interventions,

3. the development of new or expanded theories and models that *explicitly* include and test the potential effects of specific cultural factors as these may affect the efficacy of treatments for drug abuse, and

4. upgrading the level of cultural competence of organizations and their staff so that they are able to provide culturally relevant and culturally proficient interventions in a cost-effective manner.

The present chapter address these and other related issues with the aim of contributing toward the development of culturally responsive drug abuse treatments for various people of color.

NIDA Principles of Drug Addiction Treatment

The National Institute on Drug Abuse (NIDA) has developed a research-based guide that describes 13 principles and related issues in the effective treatment of drug abuse (National Institute on Drug Abuse, 1999). These principles are the following:

1. no single treatment is appropriate for all individuals;

2. treatment needs to be readily available;

3. effective treatment attends to the client's multiple needs and not just to drug treatment;

4. continual assessment and modification of the treatment plan are necessary;

5. remaining in treatment is crucial to treatment effectiveness;

6. behavioral treatments are essential for effective outcomes;

7. medications, especially in combination with counseling, are important for many patients;

8. for patients with coexisting mental and drug abuse disorders, both should be treated;

9. medical detoxification is only a first step in a full treatment;

10. treatment does not need to be voluntary to be effective;

11. possible drug use during treatment must be monitored continuously;

12. patient behaviors that risk infectious diseases such as HIV/AIDS should be addressed in treatment; and

13. recovery often involves multiple episodes of treatment.

From these principles, it is clear that treatment for drug abuse must address the complex of psychiatric, legal, familial, personal, and other factors that will influence progress toward full recovery from drug abuse and dependence. Thus, treatment program staff must attend to co-occurring psychiatric disorders and health problems, including HIV infection, because each of these forms of comorbidity will complicate the process of recovery. Moreover, for many racial/ethnic minority clients, the drug treatment program must also take into account salient sociocultural and community factors that can prompt high-risk behavior. Unfortunately, many of these factors constitute stressors, including the effects of cravings, that can easily prompt a return to illicit drug use, even among clients who express the most sincere intentions to avoid ever using drugs again.

General Treatment Approaches

In the 1990s, general treatment approaches for dependence on cocaine, heroin, and other illicit substances typically involved treatment referral to an inpatient or outpatient treatment program, with additional referrals as needed to therapeutic communities and to self-help groups.

Inpatient Treatment. In the past, inpatient treatments have typically followed the "Minnesota model," a program of treatment that lasts 14 to 28 days, depending on the extent of insurance coverage. The treatment components of typical hospital-based inpatient programs have included (a) detoxification, (b) an overview of the Alcoholics Anonymous 12-step philosophy, (c) group therapy in which the individual is confronted with psychological issues involved in addiction, (d) brief individual therapy aimed at personalizing issues and developing an understanding of one's unique process of addiction and recovery, and (e) self-management approaches, such as anger management and time management, designed to help the individual recover health and focus on improving patterns of living.

Under today's managed care environment, there remain only a few inpatient treatment programs. Their cost for inpatient services have typically ranged from $15,000 to $25,000 for a single course of treatment lasting 2 to 4 weeks, with most of these costs being paid by the client, given that today insurance companies will seldom pay for such inpatient treatment services (Rawson & Obert, 2001). In response to this limitation, a few shorter-term, acute hospitalized care programs have been developed that provide detoxification, assessment, and short-term medical treatment to drug abuse patients who have withdrawal symptoms that are severe enough to require intensive short-term medical and nursing care (Rawson & Obert, 2001).

Outpatient Treatment. By contrast, outpatient treatment typically involves sessions offered once a week or more during the early stages of the recovery. Most outpatient treatment programs incorporate cognitive-behavioral approaches, including relapse prevention education, 12-step program activities, family involvement, psychoeducation, and alcohol and drug testing (Rawson & Obert, 2001).

A typical outpatient treatment program has several phases, including an initial 1-month-long phase that includes detoxification if needed, a drug use assessment, an orientation to treatment, and early recovery treatment activities. This phase is followed by a second phase of approximately 5 months that consists of the core of the treatment program. A third phase may include a follow-up program that focuses on skill building to further reduce the risk of relapse and to promote a more complete recovery from addiction.

Both for inpatient and outpatient treatments, an *aftercare* phase is often involved that seeks to ensure that prior treatment gains have been and will be maintained. Aftercare can include continued treatment sessions on an outpatient basis or referral to a residential treatment program in cases where the individual is still not able to return to active recovery within the community.

Residential Treatment/Therapeutic Communities. Residential treatment involves the client in a longer-term sheltered environment for 6 months or more. This isolation keeps the client away from drugs and immerses that client in a complete therapeutic environment. In the past, successfully recovered addicts have been employed as counselors and as role models or "parental figures." More recently, these therapeutic communities have added traditional medical and other professional staff (Rawson & Obert, 2001). In these drug-free environments, former substance abusers live, work, and socialize while receiving multimodal treatments (e.g., detoxification, individual therapy, family therapy, group therapy, and self-help groups). These therapeutic communities may also provide transitional services to facilitate the recovering addict's reintroduction into the community (Comer, 1995).

Treatment goals of therapeutic communities are to produce lasting lifestyle changes by treating "the whole person." The aim is to develop a new and positive social identity that emphasizes being drug free and crime free. Treatment community interventions include addiction education, the development of personal and life skills, and skills training for seeking a new job, especially for clients who have had a poor history of employment. Thus, this approach not only emphasizes "rehabilitation" but also "habilitation," the learning of new life skills never before acquired by addicts, many of whom have life histories involving greatly arrested social and emotional development (Nielsen, Scarpitti, & Inciardi, 1996).

Self-Help Organizations. In addition, the inclusion of or referral to Alcoholics Anonymous (AA), Narcotics Anonymous (NA), and/or Cocaine Anonymous (CA) is a regular feature of many inpatient and outpatient programs. Self-help groups provide peer support with spiritual and moral components to help people overcome substance abuse and dependence (Moos & Finney, 1983). Meetings take place one or more times per week, and certain members who participate as "sponsors" are available to help 24 hours a day. These self-help groups encourage members to live substance free, "one day at a time." They urge their members to accept that they are powerless over disease and that only through permanent abstention will they be able to live normal lives (Alcoholics Anonymous, 1976).

Conceptualizing Issues of Culture, Race, and Ethnicity

Understanding Culture, Race, and Ethnicity in Drug Abuse Treatment. The concept of *culture* is rich yet complex, but it is also often amorphous when used in relation to drug abuse treatment. However, culture is important to a people because it gives them a sense of identity, purpose, and direction (Locke, 1998). Drug abuse counselors can benefit from considering two components of culture: (a) *objective culture,* which refers to social norms or rules established by family and/or environments that define appropriate conduct, and (b) *subjective culture,* which refers to a person's own beliefs, attitudes, values, expectations, and introjected norms (rules) regarding appropriate conduct. Thus, people's current subjective cultural views shape their ethnic identity, as well as their current ways of thinking. Such thinking is typically the product of the integration of the views from one or more cultures, and it influences a person's current life preferences and behavioral choices.

The concept of *race* is often used as a biological trait variable, despite the contemporary recognition that race is more of a socially defined variable than a biological one (Sue et al., 1998). In contrast to race, *ethnicity* refers to a group or collectivity of people who have a "common ancestral origin" and thus share many cultural characteristics in common (Harwood, 1981; Sue et al., 1998). Wyatt (1991) has indicated that *ethnicity,* as opposed to *race,* more aptly reflects a people's cultural values and behavioral patterns that relate to risk behaviors and to the risk of disease.

Finally, *minority status* refers to a subgroup of people within a larger society that has experienced differential and unequal treatment, often in the form of collective discrimination (Sue et al., 1998). Each of the major racial/ethnic minority groups in the United States has suffered historically from discrimination that still yields collective memories and life situations (e.g., living on a reservation) that shape their collective identities, lifestyles, sense of mutual belongingness, and overall experience of being a racial/ethnic minority person—a person of color.

Development of Cultural Capacity. The goal of increasing the cultural capacity of an organization and its staff is an important health services strategy for the new millennium, one that is aimed at improving relevance and quality of health services. Cultural capacity is evaluated within three areas: knowledge, attitudes, and skills (Orlandi, Weston, & Epstein, 1992; Sue et al., 1998). The acquisition of progressively greater depth of cultural capacity involves a greater ability to work effectively with various people of color. Cultural capacity is conceptualized as a progressive gradient with the following levels: cultural destructiveness (–3), cultural incapacity (–2), cultural blindness (–1), cultural sensitivity (+1), cultural competence (+2), and cultural proficiency (+3) (Castro, 1998).

The most negative level of cultural capacity is described as *cultural destructiveness,* which involves low levels of knowledge and skills and, beyond this, a negative, rejecting, and active discrimination. *Cultural incapacity* involves the philosophy that separate and equal facilities are a way of addressing the need for health services to minority clients. The approach, although seeming fair, often involves passive discrimination. *Cultural blindness,* although seemingly fair and impartial, nonetheless involves an attitude that *discounts* the importance of cultural issues. *Cultural sensitivity,* the first positive level of cultural capacity, involves a positive attitude and an acknowledgment of the importance of cultural issues. However, under cultural sensitivity, knowledge level solely involves an *awareness* of cultural issues. Accordingly, this limited level of knowledge is consistent with the perception of "ethnic glosses" (Trimble, 1995) and with stereotypical thinking wherein

the person is aware of cultural traits but is unable to understand the meaning of observed cultural beliefs and behaviors.

Cultural competence moves beyond sensitivity in the capacity to appreciate and understand the rich within-group variability that occurs within any diverse racial/ethnic group. Under cultural competence, the clinician also understands the conditional and contextual relationships that occur daily within complex "real-world" situations faced by their clients. Finally, *cultural proficiency* involves a progression to a deeper level of analysis and understanding that is characterized by the capacity to detect and understand *cultural nuances* and more complex aspects of a culture. This deeper capacity involves the ability to accurately distinguish *cultural paradoxes* from *contradictions* and to distill correct meaning from complex beliefs and behaviors that occur among members of a cultural group. A counselor may become culturally competent in working with members of one cultural group while lacking competence with members of another culture group; level of cultural capacity is specific for each cultural group. For each drug abuse counselor or therapist, the quest toward cultural proficiency in cultural skills development should be a lifelong "professional odyssey" (Castro, 1998).

Conceptualizing Ethnocultural Factors. Nemoto and colleagues (1998) have pointed out that drug and AIDS problems among racial/ethnic clients are products of historical forces that still exert their effects today. This constitutes a "historical ripple effect" that influences the current beliefs and behavior of today's clients, even if these clients are themselves unaware of these ripple effects. Thus, drug abuse counselors must understand clients and their families within the context of these historical forces (Locke, 1998; Nemoto et al., 1998).

An important treatment question in the contemporary drug abuse treatment environment, which unfortunately remains for the most part "culturally blind," is how basic inpatient, outpatient, and aftercare programs should be modified to address the unique needs of various racial/ethnic minority clients. An aid in conceptualizing within-group variability of client cultural identity is the work of Ramirez (1999). Ramirez proposed that people's *cultural styles* can be conceptualized along a continuum ranging from traditionalism to modernism (Ramirez, 1999; Ramirez & Castañeda, 1974). Under a traditional cultural orientation, strong family identification and loyalty are emphasized. By contrast, under a modernistic cultural orientation, individualism and independence are more highly valued. As a social context, ethnic clients residing in the United States live within a "modernized" Eurocentric culture that mostly emphasizes Protestant ethics involving individual initiative, upward social mobility, consumerism, and freedom of expression and action. Accordingly, dominant culture personal attributes associated with a greater level of "acculturation" into this environment include having a strong sense of individualism, small nuclear families, a limited involvement with one's nuclear and extended family, personal choice in relationships, social status that is attained by individual effort, and nonadherence to traditional moral constraints imposed by conservative family norms (Jackson & Lopez, 1999).

As noted previously, at present, very few drug treatment programs nationally have incorporated *cultural factors* as an integral part of their treatment and recovery programs. (Castro & Hernandez-Alarcon, 2002). For example, among less acculturated (low acculturated and bicultural) Hispanics/ Latinos, cultural issues such as traditional family dynamics, the role of ethnic identity in recovery, and the availability of culturally relevant strategies to avoid relapse constitute important areas involving cultural factors that have not been yet should be incorporated into a culturally relevant drug treatment program for Hispanic/Latino clients. It is noteworthy here that a subgroup of *highly acculturated* Hispanic clients may *not* require the addition of culturally relevant intervention components. Conversely, bilingual/bicultural and low-acculturated Hispanic clients may well benefit from the meaningful life context for recovery offered by a culturally relevant intervention that aims to develop an understanding of how a "new cultural self" may facilitate recovery from addiction.

In an analysis of ethnocultural factors that affect substance abuse among racial/ethnic minority persona, Terrell (1993) identified three substantive ethnocultural areas: (a) the acculturation experience; (b) sources of stress, coping, and social supports; and (c) beliefs and attitudes regarding substance abuse. Terrell also noted that many prevention interventions *do not* take into account the role that cultural differences may play in drug use initiation and its progression. By implication, this same inattention appears in the area of drug abuse treatment. As noted by Terrell, at present, a few strategic approaches have been proposed to promote culturally relevant interventions for ethnic clients. However, still missing are the specific culturally relevant program components, especially as organized in the form of a treatment manual that outlines specific cultural activities and how to evaluate their treatment efficacy under a well-conceptualized program evaluation protocol.

Ethnic Family Systems. The extent to which family involvement is essential to the recovery process may vary in relation to the cultural norms that prevail within a given family. Many traditional and low-acculturated members of the Asian Pacific Islander (API) cultures (Chinese, Japanese, Korean, Thai, Vietnamese, Cambodian, etc.) have been socialized to accept certain "Pan-Asian ideals" that emphasize respect for authority and social hierarchies (Dana, 1993). This exposure to strong group-oriented norms would produce extreme stress if failing to live up to family or group expectations or if bringing shame to the family. Thus, among low-acculturated/ traditional members of these cultures, to be involved in treatment without the permission and support of their families would be unrealistic. Also, these clients would be concerned over the stigma of "losing face" because the very act of admitting to having a problem with alcohol or drugs is a source of shame, and this concern would serve as a barrier to treatment seeking among many API clients (Ja & Aoki, 1993). Accordingly, within this cultural context, treatment programs must find ways to educate family members about treatment in a culturally relevant manner that involves connecting with these families despite the stigma while also engendering family support for the recovering person (Ja & Aoki, 1993).

Many people of color and their cultures, including American Indians, African Americans, and Hispanics/Latinos, give considerable attention and high value to interpersonal relationships, a pattern of behavior that may describe these cultures as "relational cultures." Through their language and rules regarding proper conduct in relationships, members of these cultures attend closely to personal ways of relating to others, a pattern described as "field dependence" (Ramirez, 1999; Ramirez & Castañeda, 1974). This level of attention to nuances in family relationships is based in part on their upbringing within an extended family network that often includes aunts, sisters, cousins, and grandparents, each of whom has an important role in sustaining the family's well-being. However, in relation to such family closeness, some of these clients and their families can also be distrustful of persons outside their immediate family circle. Moreover, a value of "keeping it within the family" imposes a resistance to revealing problems publicly and fosters a resistance to intrusions into their privacy by persons from outside their cultural sphere (Szapocznik & Kurtines, 1989).

Along these lines, among many African American families, relationships with both nuclear family members (parents and siblings) and extended family members (relatives, friends, church clergy, and various fictive kin) are very important (Paniagua, 1998). Thus, during treatment, the social influence of both biological and nonbiological members of the client's family (including fictive kin) should be examined in understanding the role of the family in the process of recovery and relapse prevention among African American clients.

Similarly, many American Indian communities and their residents have experienced the historical ripple effect of the U.S. government's efforts at assimilating them into the American culture (Olson & Wilson, 1986). In part, this assault on their indigenous culture has generated some negative health and social consequences, including excessive alcohol use. For many years, their experiences with alcohol and drugs appeared to be quantitatively and qualitatively more harsh than for any other group in the United States (Indian Health Service, 1995; Wing, Crow, & Thompson, 1995). Effective drug treatment approaches with American Indians appear to be those that are holistic and that include traditional values, beliefs, ceremonies, and processes (Freese, Obert, Dickow, Cohen, & Lord, 2000). Incorporating these elements for American Indian clients involves bringing into treatment their respected ancestors and families.

Within traditional family systems, conservative cultural expectations, values, and attitudes may well influence the way in which the recovering addict is accepted back into the family setting and how that individual will be supported in his or her efforts at recovery from substance abuse. An ethnic family's history of experiences with drug problems may serve as an important factor that determines how the family system will help or hinder the recovering addict's efforts to remain sober and drug free. For example, among young heroin-addicted Mexican American females, Moore (1990) noted that multigeneration drug-using families had developed a system of support that allows the recovering young woman to return home and function adaptively in the street and in the family environment. By contrast, young Mexican American women from more conservative "traditional" families that had never before contended with drug problems had families that were less able to provide sufficient support and, to the contrary, expressed negative reactions to their young daughters' illicit drug use.

Most recovering addicts feel stigmatized regarding their addiction and are very sensitive to rejection from society and family. A return to a punitive, enmeshed, nonsupportive, rejecting, guilt-inducing family system will set the stage for failure in recovery and promote drug relapse (Szapocznik & Kurtines, 1989). By contrast, an overly permissive family system may also set the stage for relapse by not setting appropriate limits and by not fostering with the recovering addict a sense of responsibility to the family and the community. Clearly, a balance in family supportive style is needed to reduce the risk of relapse.

Future drug treatment and recovery research should examine the effects of an *overly punitive* and of an *overly permissive* ethnic family system in the recovery of a drug-using family member. It should also consider the drug addict's preparedness for recovery within the context of more traditional values espoused by many ethnic family systems. Within this context, further research is needed to understand the factors within traditional indigenous cultural beliefs and values that facilitate recovery from drug abuse and those that hinder recovery.

Gender Expectations and Roles. A second culturally related issue for racial/ethnic minority clients involves differences in gender expectations and roles as these may influence the process of the client's involvement in treatment and recovery (Castro & Gutierres, 1997). Although illicit drug use is seldom acceptable in traditional ethnic cultures, alcohol and drug use by males has been tolerated or reluctantly

accepted. By contrast, strong ostracism and rejection are typical reactions within traditional ethnic families to female drug use. Families not prepared to help their female drug-addicted family member may well impose more punitive demands that may prompt a return to drug use in the form of relapse.

Currently, most treatment programs nationally include little or no information on how various types of racial/ethnic families can be helped in providing needed support for their recovering women. Gutierres and Todd (1997) reported that as compared with men, women are less likely to successfully complete drug treatment programs often because conventional programs are insensitive to the needs of women. These investigators thus called for the design of *women-sensitive* programs that include gender-relevant components, such as child care, that address the specific needs of recovering women.

An example of a strong woman-sensitive approach is the PROTOTYPES program of Southern California (V. Brown, personal communication, August 30, 2000). This program consists of a residential treatment community that provides integrated care for women affected by the co-occurring problems of (a) domestic violence/victimization, (b) substance abuse, and (c) mental disorder. Within this nurturing and supportive organizational culture, professional and peer women counselors offer several treatment services that include outreach, screening, substance abuse counseling, trauma-supportive services, and peer counseling. These services are designed to be culturally and gender relevant for various women who have had a long history of victimization and multiple life problems that include mental disorder and substance abuse.

Sexual Orientation. Nemoto and colleagues (1998) have noted that the little-understood process of acculturation often occurs in relation to more than one culture. For example, a gay API client may acculturate to each of three cultural groups: to the Asian, to the mainstream American, and to the gay culture. Given this complex social and personal process of identity formation, it is important for the therapist to understand the client's level of involvement in each of these cultures and the nuances that accompany various patterns of this involvement; the counselor must develop cultural competence in understanding the total life context in which these clients live their lives. This involvement might be measured in part by the client's frequency of contacts with members of each culture, as well as by the client's avowed sense of "belongingness" to each of these cultures. Here, it must also be recognized that racial/ethnic minority lesbian, gay, and bisexual (LGB) clients often face the added psychological stress of negotiating among the complex and at times conflicting beliefs, values, and norms from both the mainstream and the minority cultures (Committee on Lesbian, Gay, and Bisexual Concerns, 2000).

ILLICIT DRUG USE IN ETHNIC/RACIAL POPULATIONS

Sociocultural Context to Illicit Drug Use

General Issues for People of Color. Given the significant social and cultural forces that shape the lives of many ethnic clients, the use of illicit drugs, progression to addiction, recovery, and risk of relapse must be examined within an *integrative sociocultural context*. Accordingly, the drug abuse counselor or therapist must recognize that persistent poverty, unemployment and underemployment, low educational attainment, and acculturation stressors are some of the many factors that compromise the life chances of many racial/ethnic minority clients (Enchautegri, 1995). Other factors include barriers to health care such as lack of health insurance and language discrepancies between provider and client/patient (Giachello, 1994; Molina, Zambrana, & Aguirre-Molina, 1994).

Various accounts regarding the role of "culture" in thought and behavior depict "culture" as a core source of information and beliefs that influences the thinking and behavior of various ethnic persons. Here, for each of the four major racial/ethnic groups in the United States, a few specific cultural themes are identified as important core cultural factors that influence an ethnic person's beliefs and behavior.

Culturally Specific Issues for Hispanics. For Hispanics, important cultural themes include *familism, simpatia, personalismo, respeto, confianza,* and *dignidad* (Locke, 1998). *Familism* refers to a strong emphasis placed on family unity. This prompts a way of relating to others called *simpatia,* agreeableness and deference to the wishes of others, which aims to maintain harmony within the family (Marín & Marín, 1991). This deference occurs often at the expense of deferring one's own wishes in favor of the needs of other family members. However, this concern for the well-being of others within the family may also create conflict avoidance, which at times can extend to denying the existence of a significant family problem such as the abuse of alcohol and other drugs.

Regarding interpersonal relations, *personalismo,* the value of genuine interpersonal relationships, motivates persons to treat others with respect (*respeto*), although only the most intimate relationships rise to the level of full and complete trust (*confianza*). The value of personal integrity in relationships also prompts a concern for maintaining a sense of self-worth and dignity (*dignidad*). These patterns of interpersonal relationships are idyllic, although aspects of these patterns are visible to varying degrees in the daily interactions of various Hispanic individuals.

Culturally Specific Issues for African Americans. For African Americans, the following are some major cultural themes. Many African Americans are concerned about continued instances of racism, discrimination, economic disadvantage, and inequality of treatment in various social areas. These concerns exist as a legacy of the historical effects of slavery and continued and overt discrimination that lasted into the 1960s. Another major cultural theme is the importance of the extended family network that serves as a source of kinship, belongingness (We-ness), and social support. As a coping strategy, there is the acceptance of life's harsh realities with aims to "keep on keepin' on." Such coping includes the significance of African spirituality as a source of vitality for life's activities, including religion, art, and music. Some politically active African Americans have emphasized the importance of *Afrocentrism,* an attitude of cultural pride that serves as a source of identity, self-worth, dignity, and motivation to endure despite adversity (Dana, 1998; Locke, 1998). Although considerable within-group variability exists among African Americans in the extent to which they acknowledge these themes and are concerned about them on a day-to-day basis, the counselors' understanding of these themes provides a cultural context for understanding an individual African American client's life situation when in need of drug abuse treatment.

Culturally Specific Issues for Asian Americans. For Asian Americans, major cultural themes center on a set of traditional "Pan-Asian values," derived from Confucianism, Taoism, and Buddhism (Dana, 1993). These hemes include the observation of obligations, loyalty, and respect conferred to family and group; a high regard for social hierarchies; and obedience to social norms in order to enact correct action. This also involves the avoidance of incorrect action that brings shame to self and family (a loss of face). There

is also a strong value of education and achievement, an ethic of hard work, and the avoidance of complaint even if experiencing pain (suffering in silence) (Dana, 1998; Locke, 1998). Adherence to these strong cultural norms on the part of many Asian Americans leads to the notion that Asian Americans are a "model minority," one that is successful academically and socially. Although many Asian Americans have been successful in this society, Asian American scholars have noted that this notion is often stereotypical because there are also many and growing numbers of Asians and Pacific Islanders (API) who do suffer from various social problems, including substance abuse (Ja & Aoki, 1993).

Culturally Specific Issues for American Indians. For American Indians, these cultural themes include the living of a holistic lifestyle and a Being orientation that gives reverence to nature, time, and mystical experiences. Many American Indians value natural learning and the avoidance of coercion and punishment as a way of promoting learning and child rearing. American Indians have an oral tradition whereby learning occurs via storytelling. Many have a reverence for the group and group unity and for the value of giving as a way of contributing to the survival of the group. There is also a reverence for spiritual well-being and natural processes in which the person should seek to live in harmony with natural elements and not seek to control them.

Regarding the family, traditional American Indians value old age and the wisdom of the elders. They value ancestral worship and a preference for cooperation over competition. Moreover, humility and modesty are seen as virtues that favor integration as a member of the group rather than emphasizing the achievements of an individual (Dana, 1998; Locke, 1998).

Today, many American Indian elders are concerned about the loss of Indian culture among the young that has been occurring as some Indian youth leave the reservation in the quest for economic advancement, as well as among Indian youth in cities who lack contact with their Indian traditions. As with other racial/ethic minority groups, considerable within-group variability exists in terms of the degree to which a particular American Indian client identifies with Indian ways and observes them on a day-to-day basis.

The Process of Drug Addiction for Racial/Ethnic Clients

Illicit drug use and addiction develop in various ways and are influenced by multiple factors (Newcomb & Bentler, 1988). The concepts of the problem behavior syndrome (Jessor & Jessor, 1977) and conduct disorder (American Psychiatric Association, 1994) constitute two related behavioral syndromes involving impulsive and maladaptive behaviors that lie at the core of the high risk for drug and alcohol abuse (Santisteban, Szapocznik, & Kurtines, 1995). Among these impulsive youth, dropping out of school is a related high-risk outcome that is also associated with antisocial and nonconformist attitudes; affiliation with deviant peers, including gangs; and the use of "gateway drugs" (alcohol and cigarettes) in early adolescence. Among Mexican American adolescents, rates of school dropout are especially high, thus setting the stage for street life and the use of illicit drugs. Among some Hispanic adolescents, illicit drug use may also be affected by sociodemographic factors such as low level of education and poor school grades (Schinke et al., 1992). Relative to other youth, those youth who had earned grades of C and under in school and whose mothers had failed to complete high school were observed to be more likely to use illicit drugs.

Among Hispanic and other minority youth, other factors such as acculturation stressors, identity conflicts, economic disillusionment, and unique community or cultural prompts within a ghetto neighborhood may impose additional and unique social or environmental influences that may also prompt drug use and abuse (Castro, Boyer, & Balcazar, 2000).

Among API populations, drug abuse is not often viewed from the popular Western perspective of being a chronic relapsing condition for which the primary problem involves the person's inability to cope with the world. In the Thai culture, as in many other Asian and Buddhist cultures, drug use is regarded as a response to either availability, cultural acceptance of drug use, peer and familial pressure to use (or lack of pressure to not use), performance enhancement at work, and/or factors such as poverty, depression, social isolation, boredom, or risk taking (Rawson & Obert, 2001).

When a person becomes a user of illicit drugs, life focus narrows such that a large portion of that person's waking hours is focused on procuring that drug (Peele & Brodsky, 1991). Both the habitual and the pharmacological effects of illicit drug use force the person to continue using to avoid the discomforts of withdrawal and/or cravings. Criminal behavior involving various illegal acts to procure money to maintain one's drug addiction can also become a central feature of that person's daily activities. Depending on the type of drug used and route of administration (e.g., snorting, smoking, or injection), it is now well known that sharing needles also promotes the risk of HIV infection.

After years of drug use, entry into treatment occurs when the individual's significant others, or that individual himself or herself, realize that the problem has gotten out of control or when the individual has been referred to mandatory treatment by the courts. At that point, the addicted individual may have lost or compromised work, social relations, and health, thus creating an acute need for treatment. As noted, some drug-addicted individuals, however, are unwilling to enter treatment voluntarily and thus are brought in under coercion from the courts or from insistent family members. Entry into treatment under coercion raises questions about the client's preparedness for treatment.

Regarding preparedness for treatment, Prochaska and Prochaska (1999) developed the transtheoretical approach, which defines five stages of preparedness for behavior change. These stages are as follows: (a) *precontemplation,* a state in which the person cannot change without special help; (b) *contemplation,* a state in which the person is not sure whether he or she wants to change; (c) *preparation,* a state in which the person wishes to change but does not know how to change; (d) *action;* and (e) *maintenance.* Clients entering treatment in these early stages of readiness have traditionally been termed *in denial* or *unmotivated.* Program personnel have traditionally believed that these clients could not be treated successfully until they experienced the full consequences of their use and were ready for treatment. Miller and Rollnick (1991) have articulated a manner of interacting with clients in these early stages of readiness for treatment. This approach, *motivational interviewing,* has been shown to be more effective than waiting for the natural process of preparedness to occur, beginning treatment regardless of readiness, or confronting the individual with the program expectations. For various ethnic minority clients, little is known about the factors that promote effective treatment and recovery and how these are similar or different from the factors for effective recovery among nonminority Euro-American clients.

Cultural Issues in Drug Abuse Treatment With Ethnic Clients

Culturally Responsive Assessment and Treatment Planning. Clients who enter a drug treatment program are often users of multiple drugs and alcohol and often have a history of legal and family problems. These patterns have also been observed among various ethnic

minority drug addicts. Maddox and Desmond (1992) reported on a 10-year longitudinal study of 95 male methadone maintenance clients and a comparison group of 77 male opiate users who were eligible for but not admitted to a methadone maintenance program. The majority of these clients in both groups (more than 87%) were Mexican Americans. Among these participants, more than 50% had come from broken families, more than 33% had disciplinary problems in school, and more than 60% had been arrested prior to their first use of opioids. Also, these clients had more than 14 years of opioid use prior to treatment entry, more than 67% had a problem with alcohol abuse before admission (or eligibility) to methadone maintenance, their mean age at first admission (or eligibility) to methadone maintenance treatment was 33 to 34 years of age, and they had been in prior drug treatments an average of three or more times prior to seeking methadone treatment.

These Mexican American heroin addicts were similar to many other heroin addicts in that they have undergone a series of social, legal, and other drug problems that preceded or occurred concurrently with their heroin abuse. Thus, their *level of severity* of drug abuse and related sociocultural problems was high, suggesting that a more intense program of recovery would be needed to modify their addiction to heroin, as well as to improve their personal and social capacity to remain off heroin and other illicit drugs (Simpson, Joe, Fletcher, Hubbard, & Anglin, 1999).

Culturally Responsive Treatment Planning. In one of the few culturally oriented studies of heroin addicts, Jorquez (1984) found that many Mexican American heroin addicts reject conventional forms of treatment. Jorquez suggested that treatment of Chicano heroin addicts should include a recognition of the difficulties involved in permanently eliminating addiction to heroin while helping the *tecato,* the Chicano heroin addict, to avoid discouragement and a perceived lack of progress in treatment. Jorquez also asserted that important psychosocial issues must also be addressed to provide a more complete and successful program for a full drug rehabilitation of these Mexican American/Chicano heroin users.

Regarding gender issues, Gutierres and Todd (1997) found that a high percentage of their American Indian female clients completed a certain treatment (87%) as compared with their Mexican American peers (56%) and Anglo American peers (58%). This higher completion rate for the American Indian clients was attributed to the culturally sensitive residential program that was provided for the American Indian women, a program that included traditional healing practices, a sweat lodge ceremony, a talking circle, and a program accommodation for these women that encouraged them to bring their children into the therapeutic community.

Relapse Prevention and Promoting Effective Treatment Outcomes

For users of illicit drugs such as cocaine and heroin, relapse after undergoing drug treatment involves a return to drug use at pretreatment levels in terms of frequency and quantity of use (Brownell, Marlatt, Lichtenstein, & Wilson, 1986). Regarding important aspects of relapse, Marlatt and Gordon (1985) made an important distinction between a lapse and a relapse in their relapse prevention theory (RPT). Marlatt and Gordon defined a *lapse* as a brief episode of drug use (a slip) that is followed by an expeditious return to abstinence. By contrast, a *relapse* is a full-blown return to use for an extended period of time and typically at the original levels of use (quantity and frequency) or beyond. Besides amount and duration of use, the critical factor that governs whether a lapse progresses to a relapse is the attributional process by which the addicted person evaluates the *meaning* of an episode of

drug use. Under this self-evaluation process, if an episode of use is followed by feelings of guilt and failure, the "abstinence violation effect," then the individual is likely to continue drug use (Marlatt & Gordon, 1985).

In the treatment of cocaine- and heroin-addicted patients, the goal of relapse prevention is attained via skills training in recognizing, avoiding, and exerting control over events that produce relapse (Marlatt & Gordon, 1985). Thus, a complete program for relapse prevention in the clinical setting should address at least seven key areas: (a) addressing client ambivalence in treatment motivation, (b) reducing drug availability, (c) coping with high-risk situations, (d) overcoming cravings related to conditioned cues, (e) avoiding "apparently irrelevant decisions," (f) providing lifestyle modification toward healthier behaviors, and (g) coping with the abstinence violation effect (Carroll, Rounsaville, & Keller, 1991).

In an extension of Marlatt and Gordon's (1985) RPT, Walton, Castro, and Barrington (1994) developed an eight-level index of lapse/relapse outcomes (abstinence, three levels of lapse, and four levels of relapse). In this index, the major measurable distinction between lapses and relapses was that a lapse is generally an "isolated" episode of use in which such instances are separated by at least 1 week, whereas relapses are "clustered" episodes of use, binges that occur two or more times within the period of 1 week. These patterns of use aid in the classification of users as "lapsers" and "relapsers."

It has been observed that persons who ultimately remain lapsers as compared with persons who go on to become relapsers make different cognitive attributions. A lapse is seen as a "unique" event, one that is not likely to occur for other drugs (a specific attribution), whereas a relapse is seen as an event likely to occur for other drugs as well (a global attribution) (Walton et al., 1994). Thus, as compared with clients who achieve total abstinence, clients who experience a full-blown relapse also develop feelings of loss of control and self-blame. In a spiraling process, these negative views about self are perpetuated across time and, in turn, contribute to a greater likelihood of continuing to use.

In preventing relapse among persons addicted to cocaine, education and training have focused on the identification of "triggers," events, or situations (i.e., *cues*) that prompt or initiate a return to drug use. These cues, events, or triggers can include *cravings* that can occur when the recovering addict observes drug paraphernalia or receives encouragement from others to use drugs as before. Learning to recognize and avoid triggers greatly reduces the potential for relapse. When avoiding triggers is not possible, clients can be taught to use visualization techniques to reduce the power of the craving process and avoid careening out of control (Obert et al., 2000). Skills such as "thought stopping," avoidance of triggers, and time scheduling are critical elements for clients to learn who are being treated primarily in outpatient modalities. These are the techniques that, when successfully executed, provide the structure within which recovery can succeed. Being able to develop these skills allows the client to operate in the "real world" during treatment and to begin to gain a sense of personal control, empowerment, and success.

However, relapse avoidance is not always an individual or a rational process. Regarding the influence of dual diagnosis (the co-occurrence of mental disorder with illicit drug use), Carroll et al. (1991) indicated that many users of cocaine (and users of heroin) also have coexisting Axis I and Axis II psychiatric disorders (such as depression or antisocial personality disorder). The presence of mental disorder complicates the process of coping with stressors, which prompts a return to drug use. Drug-addicted persons who experience psychiatric complications cannot cope exclusively on their own but instead are in need of stable and supportive sources of encouragement and support from family and friends.

To date, little work has been conducted on how the principles of RPT and the complications of psychiatric disorder may apply to various racial/ethnic minority clients. Besides the need for the individual addict to make a formal commitment to sobriety/drug avoidance, a requirement for successful relapse prevention may also involve enhancing the ethnic minority client's self-concept by building ethnic pride and personal pride and also by mobilizing family support. Given the importance of the family in minority cultures, family issues may require an added focus in treatment to promote effective relapse prevention among recovering minority drug addicts (Castro & Barrington, 1993). Instilling pride in family and ethnic heritage, where such pride may have been compromised by drug involvement, may foster a new and positive concept of self. Thus, in minority families, this self-concept may include an emerging view of the self as a member of the family who must be responsible in avoiding drugs to contribute to the well-being of the family (Szapocznik, 1995).

In addition, establishing a new circle of friends (a sober reference group) and advising family on how to be supportive while also setting limits on maladaptive behavior are two critical systems-oriented interventions that place family members in the role of confidants who support the drug-addicted person's recovery (Castro, Sharp, Barrington, Walton, & Rawson, 1991). Prompts by even one confidant that discourage heroin and other drug use can serve as a potent deterrent to relapse (Castro & Tafoya-Barraza, 1997). As noted, the role of significant others may be stronger for ethnic/racial clients who place a strong cultural value on harmony (*simpatia*) in social and family relations (Marín & Marín, 1991). In summary, the presence of one or more significant others who discourage drug use would appear to be an important factor in successful relapse prevention among racial/ethnic minority clients.

FUTURE DIRECTIONS IN RESEARCH AND TREATMENT

Treatment Outcome Research With Ethnic Clients

General Research Considerations. Typical group comparison studies found in the research literature often use a categorical variable (e.g., Caucasian, Black, Hispanic) to categorize members of a sample into a racial/ethnic category. By doing so, they treat all minority persons subsumed under that category (e.g., Asian Americans as if they were "all alike") in the trait of "ethnicity." This level of analysis constitutes "ethnic gloss" (Trimble, 1995), which involves a shallow level of analysis. In essence, this resorts to a group average and ignores subgroup variability on this dimension of "ethnicity." This simplistic level of analysis is often problematic, especially when a group is extremely diverse, as is the case for Asians and Pacific Islanders, which include more than 32 distinct groups or nationalities, and American Indians, which include more than 505 federally recognized and 365 state-recognized tribal groups (Ja & Aoki, 1993; Locke, 1998).

Cultural competence in instrumentation and data analysis requires the use of variable conceptualizations and measures that are compatible with the perceptions and needs of members of a target population in terms of language, cultural idioms, and usage. Furthermore, such instruments should directly examine clients' experiences, including their beliefs and perceptions regarding how well they are being understood by the service provider or researcher (Nemoto et al., 1998).

Acculturation Effects. For work with various ethnic clients, level of acculturation has been a useful, albeit a limited, indicator of within-group variability. Beyond this, level of acculturation should be examined as a *moderator variable* in future studies that examine and test models that relate predictors and moderators to important outcomes in prevention and in treatment (Jessor, Van den Bos, Vanderryn, Costa, & Turbin, 1995). Such studies would be aided by the further development of culturally sound theory, conceptualization, and measurement of acculturation and other related indicators of within-group variability (Kim, Atkinson, & Yang, 1999; Klonoff & Landrine, 2000; Rogler, Cortés, & Malgady, 1991). Conceptually, the use of moderator variables (Baron & Kenny, 1986) is important in moving from a stage of "cultural sensitivity" to "cultural competence" in research methodology with racial/ethnic minority clients. Such variables that can serve as ordered indicators of within-group variability for any racial/ethnic minority group include level of acculturation, Afrocentricity, traditional versus nontraditional orientation, and immigrant versus U.S. native-born status. A general aim in the use of such moderator variables with racial/ethnic populations is to identify important subgroups that can be ordered and understood in relation to an important dimension of within-group variability.

Zane and Huh-Kim (1998) indicated that several variables, including level of acculturation, generational status, nationality or ethnic group, place of birth, and gender, should be considered when analyzing patterns of alcohol and drug use among Asian American clients. Moreover, as discussed by Oetting and Beauvais (1991), the level and extent of cultural identification or enculturation (the reciprocal process to acculturation) are not clearly conveyed by a *single* continuum. That is, a person can be acculturated or enculturated in varying degrees to the mainstream culture while also identifying in varying degrees with his or her own racial/ethnic minority culture. Moreover, some racial/ethnic minority persons can report identifying with two or more racial or ethnic backgrounds and thus having a multiple racial/ethnic identity. These are all real yet challenging cultural issues that must be considered in total when designing and implementing culturally competent research.

Moreover, there is a growing view that ethnic individuals who develop into truly *bicultural* persons have developed stronger social skills to cope with the competing and at times conflicting demands of each of the two cultures (Felix-Ortiz & Newcomb, 1985). By contrast, a person who is "acultural" or "culturally marginalized" may not have the skills to access resources and support in either culture (LaFromboise, Coleman, & Gerton, 1993). For this and other reasons, a bicultural person may well be better adjusted and capable of achieving a more positive treatment outcome (Castro et al., 2000). By contrast, many drug-addicted persons have experienced arrested social and personal development, often remaining "acultural" or "culturally marginalized" throughout their lives. For these persons, the prognosis for full drug rehabilitation is less favorable, unless a treatment program specifically addresses these important needs. Future research needs to develop psychometrically sound methods of assessing level of acculturation and cultural identification, especially when it involves the multiple identities observed among certain drug-using clients (e.g., a gay, bicultural Asian American male).

General Clinical Interventions

In the process of relapse prevention, developing skills for recognizing and avoiding cues that trigger a return to drug use operate as a form of personal empowerment. More research is needed to identify culturally relevant factors that may influence the *process* of relapse among racial/ethnic minority clients. Among these clients, potential moderators of relapse may include the person's level of cultural identifications and how he or she relates to various ethnic cultural values and traditions. It appears that acculturation to mainstream American culture can have both positive and negative effects. It is often difficult to predict under what conditions a client's high level of acculturation will facilitate or impede positive treatment outcomes. More process-oriented and qualitative research is needed to clarify the ways in which the process of acculturation might contribute to the risk of illicit drug use among racial/ethnic minority clients and how it might influence treatment outcomes.

Currently, it is hypothesized that the availability of culturally relevant treatment activities (i.e., programs that promote cultural identity and pride) and certain types of traditionalism (e.g., family loyalty and social responsibility) may help reduce the risks of illicit drug use among certain racial/ethnic minority clients (Castro & Gutierres, 1997). However, only the conduct of controlled treatment outcome studies that explicitly examine these issues of culture and identity will provide scientific evidence that will confirm or refute this hypothesis. Within this context, how basic inpatient, outpatient, residential treatment, and other aftercare programs may need to be modified to accommodate the unique needs of various racial/ethnic minority clients remains an interesting and important treatment question.

Developing Culturally Responsive Drug Abuse Treatments

Regarding research methodology, issues of sampling are important in reaching hidden and stigmatized subpopulations or sectors within a given racial/ethnic population (Nemoto et al., 1998; Stueve, O'Donnell, Duran, San Doval, & Blome, 2001). Here it is noted that few group differences would be expected when comparing the acculturated or assimilated members of any racial/ethnic minority group with members of the White mainstream Westernized U.S. population. More remarkable cultural differences would be expected in examining the subgroup of members within any racial/ethnic minority group that are *hidden* and *hard to access* (e.g., African American male-to-female transgender persons who are addicted to cocaine) (Nemoto et al., 1998).

In the process of cultural program adaptation, a dynamic tension exists between sensitivity to the unique cultural needs of such cultural subgroups and the competing need to provide members of that subgroup with new learning, thus "acculturating" them to adopt certain contemporary "Western" behaviors that promote survival and success within this society. In this process, the treatment program developer must (a) recognize the adaptive challenges of acculturation to U.S. mainstream cultural norms and (b) recognize and respect the need and desire of many racial/ethnic minority people to retain aspects of their ethnic traditions that have great personal significance to them.

Thus, "universal" drug treatment programs that ignore issues of culture can be described as "culturally blind" and will likely be insensitive to one or more specific needs of a given racial/ethnic minority client (Ja & Aoki, 1993). Such needs depend on the background and identity of a specific minority client. However, such needs include (a) feelings of being discriminated, alienated, or not feeling accepted; (b) identity conflicts in addition to the typical adolescent or young adult developmental issues; (c) value conflicts imposed by social processes that force acculturation or conformity with mainstream American lifeways; and (d) racial/ethnic family dynamics that can inadvertently interfere with treatment and can promote relapse (Locke, 1998; Ramirez, 1999).

Culturally competent relapse prevention efforts must also address issues of family support for the recovering addict. In working with ethnic minority drug addicts, it is important to offer an integrated program of treatment (LaFromboise, Trimble, & Mohatt, 1990) that,

for certain ethnic minority clients, includes treatment in their native language and treatment that includes cultural, psychological, and spiritual activities that are important to them. Thus, clinic administrators must recognize the need for such treatments and thus to develop a parallel treatment track. Alternately, a less costly approach is to offer a set of *treatment components* or *modules* that address these relevant and specific cultural issues. Such modules can be designed as supplements to a conventional treatment program. Various relevant and effective approaches can be designed, provided that clinic staff recognize the importance of sociocultural issues and make a commitment to address these in a therapeutic manner.

Agency-Level Planning

1. Initially, preparing to provide effective services locally involves conducting a needs assessment, whether large or small, to identify the unique profile of needs of clients from the local community who are current or prospective clients (McKenzie & Smeltzer, 2001). Agency staff can determine whether the agency is now receiving a sizable percentage of clients from a special subgroup (e.g., low-acculturated, Spanish-speaking adolescents referred to drug abuse treatment by the courts) or clients who present specific treatment issues not now addressed by the current treatment program.

2. Next, an important factor is hiring and training staff who are culturally competent to provide drug abuse treatment within the local community. This involves increasing the cultural capacity of these staff members by providing training on knowledge, attitudes, and skills that promote cultural sensitivity, competence, and, beyond this, cultural proficiency.

Program-Level Planning

3. Next, it will be important to examine the "universal" or currently offered drug abuse treatment program for sources of "cultural

incongruence" in program assumptions or practices. That is, areas of "nonfit" should be examined to consider the development of treatment modules that provide greater "cultural congruence" (i.e., a better fit) in treatment offered to members of a targeted subgroup of clients.

4. In a *cultural adaptation phase,* it will be important to collect empirical data from consumers, expert consultants, and community key informants. These are community leaders who can represent the views of a specific cultural subgroup. These persons can be invited as one-time consultants, or they can serve a term on an agency advisory board. These people would help to plan and evaluate new models or other modifications to the current treatments in response to the unique cultural needs of an identified subgroup of clients.

5. Next, there is a need to conduct a small but viable *formative evaluation* that provides evaluative feedback on a short-term basis. Such quick feedback helps in revising the activities or modules that have been developed. At the end of this cycle, the aim is to develop a local "best practice" that enhances treatment and that is effective in reducing relapse and in improving other treatment outcomes.

6. Finally, it will be important to develop a *treatment manual* that provides a clinically grounded and stable yet revisable protocol that clearly, in step-by-step fashion, outlines what the therapist should do in offering this culturally relevant treatment. The aim is to standardize this culturally enhanced treatment that could now serve as an "evidence-based practice," one that uses culturally competent activities that have been tested for cultural relevance and effectiveness with members of the local targeted subgroup of clients (Center for Substance Abuse Treatment, 2001).

In summary, an agency's concerted efforts in attending *actively* to issues of culture within their current drug abuse treatment program constitute a commitment toward cultural competence in service delivery. This effort can enhance services to members of specific cultural subgroups. In other words, the very act of attending and taking concerted action serves as a concrete expression of this commitment toward cultural competence. It is hoped that more agencies will conduct a closer and systematic examination of their current drug treatment services in efforts to upgrade them with the infusion of culturally competent interventions that aim to improve quality of care and treatment outcomes for their racial/ethnic minority clients.

REFERENCES

Alcoholics Anonymous. (1976). *Alcoholics anonymous: The story of how many thousands of men and women have recovered from alcoholism* (3rd ed.). New York: Alcoholics Anonymous World Services.

American Psychiatric Association. (1994). *Diagnostic and statistical manual of psychiatric disorders* (4th ed.). Washington, DC: Author.

Baron, R. M., & Kenny, D. A. (1986). The moderator-mediator variable distinction in social psychological research: Conceptual, strategic, and statistical considerations. *Journal of Personality and Social Psychology, 51,* 1173-1182.

Brownell, K. D., Marlatt, G. A., Lichtenstein, E., & Wilson, G. T. (1986). Understanding and preventing relapse. *American Psychologist, 41,* 765-782.

Carroll, K. M., Rounsaville, B. J., & Keller, D. S. (1991). Relapse prevention strategies for the treatment of cocaine abuse. *American Journal of Drug and Alcohol Abuse, 17,* 249-265.

Castro, F. G. (1998). Cultural competence training in clinical psychology: Assessment, clinical intervention, and research. In A. S. Bellack & M. Hersen (Eds.), *Comprehensive clinical psychology: Sociocultural and individual differences* (Vol. 10, pp. 127-140). Oxford, UK: Pergamon.

Castro, F. G., & Barrington, E. H. (1993, July). *Client-treatment matching with a focus on ethnic identity.* Invited workshop presented at the 36th Annual Institute of Alcohol and Drug Studies, Texas Commission on Alcohol and Drug Abuse, Austin, TX.

Castro, F. G., Boyer, G. R., & Balcazar, H. G. (2000). Healthy adjustment in Mexican American and other Hispanic adolescents. In R. Montemayor, G. R. Adams, & T. P. Gullota (Eds.), *Adolescent diversity in ethnic, economic and cultural contexts* (pp. 141-178). Thousand Oaks, CA: Sage.

Castro, F. G., & Gutierres, S. (1997). Drug and alcohol use among rural Mexican Americans. In E. B. Robertson, Z. Sloboda, G. M. Boyd, L. Beatty, & J. Kozel (Eds.), *Rural substance abuse: State of knowledge and issues* (NIDA Research Monograph Series No. 168, pp. 498-533). Rockville, MD: National Institute on Drug Abuse.

Castro, F. G., & Hernandez-Alarcon, E. (2002). Integrating cultural variables into drug abuse prevention and treatment with racial/ethnic minorities. *Journal of Drug Issues, 32,* 783-810.

Castro, F. G., Sharp, E. V., Barrington, E. H., Walton, M., & Rawson, R. (1991). Drug abuse identity in Mexican Americans: Theoretical and empirical considerations. *Hispanic Journal of Behavior Sciences, 13,* 209-225.

Castro, F. G., & Tafoya-Barraza, H. M. (1997). Treatment issues with Latinos addicted to cocaine and heroin. In J. G. Garcia & M. C. Zea (Eds.), *Psychological interventions and research with Latino populations* (pp. 191-216). Boston: Allyn & Bacon.

Center for Substance Abuse Treatment. (2001). *Changing the conversation—November 2000* (DHHS Pub. No. (SMA) 00-3480). Rockville, MD: Author.

Comer, R. (1995). *Abnormal psychology* (2nd ed.). New York: Freeman.

Committee on Lesbian, Gay, and Bisexual Concerns. (2000). Guidelines for psychotherapy with lesbian, gay, and bisexual clients. *American Psychologist, 55,* 1440-1451.

Dana, R. H. (1993). *Multicultural assessment perspectives for professional psychology.* Boston: Allyn & Bacon.

Dana, R. H. (1998). *Understanding cultural identity in intervention and assessment.* Thousand Oaks, CA: Sage.

Enchautegri, M. E. (1995). *Policy implications of Latino poverty.* Washington, DC: The Urban Institute.

Felix-Ortiz, M., & Newcomb, M. D. (1985). Cultural identity and drug use among Latino and Latina adolescents. In G. Botvin, S. Schinke, & M. A. Orlandi (Eds.), *Drug abuse prevention with multiethnic youth* (pp. 147-165). Beverly Hills, CA: Sage.

Freese, T. E., Obert, J., Dickow, A., Cohen, J., & Lord, R. (2000). Methamphetamine abuse: Issues for special populations. *Journal of Psychoactive Drugs, 32,* 177-182.

Giachello, A. L. M. (1994). Issues of access and use. In C. W. Molina & M. Aguirre-Molina (Eds.), *Latino health in the U.S.: A growing challenge* (pp. 83-111). Washington, DC: American Public Health Association.

Gutierres, S. E., & Todd, M. (1997). The impact of childhood abuse on treatment outcomes of substance users. *Professional Psychology: Research and Practice, 28,* 348-354.

Harwood, A. (1981). *Ethnicity and medical care.* Cambridge, MA: Harvard University Press.

Indian Health Service. (1995). *Trends in Indian health.* Rockville, MD: U.S. Department of Health and Human Services.

Ja, D., & Aoki, B. (1993). Substance abuse treatment: Cultural barriers in the Asian American community. *Journal of Psychoactive Drugs, 25,* 61-71.

Jackson, V. H., & Lopez, L. (1999). *Cultural competency in managed behavioral healthcare.* Providence, RI: Manisses Communications Group.

Jessor, R., & Jessor, S. L. (1977). *Problem behavior and psychosocial development: A longitudinal study of youth.* New York: Academic Press.

Jessor, R., Van den Bos, J., Vanderryn, J., Costa, F. M., & Tubin, M. S. (1995). Protective factors in adolescent problem behavior: Moderator effects and developmental change. *Developmental Psychology, 31,* 923-933.

Jorquez, J. S. (1984). Heroin use in the barrio: Solving the problem of relapse or keeping the Tecato Gusano asleep. *American Journal of Drug and Alcohol Abuse, 10*(1), 63-75.

Kim, B. S. K., Atkinson, D. R., & Yang, P. H. (1999). The Asian Values Scale: Development, factor analysis, validation, and reliability. *Journal of Counseling Psychology, 46,* 342-352.

Klonoff, E. A., & Landrine, H. (2000). Revising and improving the African American Acculturation Scale. *Journal of Black Psychology, 26,* 235-261.

LaFromboise, T., Coleman, H. L. K., & Gerton, J. (1993). Psychological impact of biculturalism: Evidence and theory. *Psychological Bulletin, 114*(3), 395-412.

LaFromboise, T. D., Trimble, J. E., & Mohatt, G. V. (1990). Counseling intervention and American Indian tradition: An integrative approach. *The Counseling Psychologist, 18,* 628-654.

Locke, D. C. (1998). *Increasing multicultural understanding: A comprehensive model* (2nd ed.). Thousand Oaks, CA: Sage.

Maddox, J. F., & Desmond, D. P. (1992). Ten-year follow-up after admission to methadone maintenance. *American Journal of Drug and Alcohol Abuse, 18*(3), 289-303.

Marín, G., & Marín, B. V. (1991). *Research with Hispanic populations.* Newbury Park, CA: Sage.

Marlatt, G. A., & Gordon, J. (1985). *Relapse prevention: Maintenance strategies in the treatment of addictive behaviors.* New York: Guilford.

McKenzie, J. F., & Smeltzer, J. L. (2001). *Planning, implementing and evaluating health promotion programs: A primer* (3rd ed.). Boston: Allyn & Bacon.

Miller, W. R., & Rollnick, S. (1991). *Motivational interviewing: Preparing people to change addictive behavior.* New York: Guilford.

Molina, C. W., Zambrana, R., & Aguirre-Molina, M. (1994). The influence of culture, class, and environment on health care. In C. W. Molina & M. Aguirre-Molina (Eds.), *Latino health in the U.S.: A growing challenge* (pp. 23-43). Washington, DC: American Public Health Association.

Moore, J. (1990). Mexican American women addicts: The influence of family background. In R. Glick & J. Moore (Eds.), *Drugs in Hispanic communities* (pp. 127-153). New Brunswick, NJ: Rutgers University Press.

Moos, R. H., & Finney, J. W. (1983). The expanding scope of alcoholism treatment evaluation. *American Psychologist, 38,* 1036-1044.

National Institute on Drug Abuse. (1999). *Principles of drug addiction treatment* (NIH Pub. No. 99-4180). Rockville, MD: Author.

Nemoto, T., Wong, F. Y., Ching, A., Chng, C. L., Bouey, P., Hendrickson, M., & Sember, R. E. (1998). HIV seroprevalence, risk behaviors, and cognitive factors among Asian and Pacific Islander American men who have sex with men: A summary and critique of empirical studies and methodological issues. *AIDS Education and Prevention, 10*, 31-47.

Newcomb, M. D., & Bentler, P. M. (1988). *Consequences of adolescent drug use: Impact on the lives of young adults.* Newbury Park, CA: Sage.

Nielsen, A. L., Scarpitti, F. R., & Inciardi, J. A. (1996). Integrating the therapeutic community and work release for drug-involved offenders. *Journal of Substance Abuse Treatment, 13*, 349-358.

Obert, J. L., McCann, M. J., Marinelli-Casey, P. M., Weiner, A., Minsky, S., Brethen, P., & Rawson, R. (2000). The matrix model of outpatient stimulant abuse treatment: History and description. *Journal of Psychoactive Drugs, 32*(2), 157-164.

Oetting, E. R., & Beauvais, F. (1991). Orthogonal cultural identification theory: The cultural identification of minority adolescents. *International Journal of the Addictions, 25*(5A-6A), 655-685.

Olson, J. S., & Wilson, R. (1986). *Native Americans in the twentieth century.* Urbana: University of Illinois Press.

Orlandi, M., Weston, R., & Epstein, L. G. (1992). *Cultural competence for evaluators: A guide for alcohol and other drug abuse prevention practitioners working with ethnic/racial communities.* Rockville, MD: Office of Substance Abuse Prevention.

Paniagua, F. A. (1998). *Assessing and treating culturally diverse clients: A practical guide.* Thousand Oaks, CA: Sage.

Peele, S., & Brodsky, A. (1991). *The truth about addiction and recovery: The life process program for outgrowing destructive habits.* New York: Simon & Schuster.

Prochaska, J. O., & Prochaska, J. M. (1999). Why don't continents move? Why don't people change? *Journal of Psychotherapy Integration, 9*, 83-102.

Ramirez, M. (1999). *Multicultural psychotherapy: An approach to individual and cultural differences* (2nd ed.). Boston: Allyn & Bacon.

Ramirez, M., & Castañeda, A. (1974). *Cultural democracy, bicognitive development and education.* New York: Academic Press.

Rawson, R. A., & Obert, J. L. (2001). *The substance abuse treatment system in the U.S.: What is it? What does it do? Myths and misconceptions.* Manuscript under review.

Rogler, L. H., Cortés, D. E., & Malgady, R. G. (1991). Acculturation and mental health status among Hispanics: Convergence and new directions for research. *American Psychologist, 46*(6), 585-597.

Santisteban, D., Szapocznik, J., & Kurtines, W. (1995). Behavioral problems among Hispanic/Latino youth: The family as moderator of adjustment. In J. Szapocznik (Ed.), *A Hispanic/Latino family approach to substance abuse prevention* (DHHS Pub. No. (SMA) 95-3034, pp. 19-39). Rockville, MD: Center for Substance Abuse Prevention.

Schinke, S., Orlandi, M., Vaccaro, D., Espinoza, R., McAlister, A., & Botvin, G. (1992). Substance among Hispanic and non-Hispanic adolescents. *Addictive Behaviors, 17*, 117-124.

Simpson, D. D., Joe, G. W., Fletcher, B. W., Hubbard, R. L., & Anglin, D. D. (1999). A national evaluation of treatment outcomes for cocaine dependence. *Archives of General Psychiatry, 56*, 507-514.

Stueve, A., O'Donnell, L. N., Duran, R., San Doval, A., & Blome, J. (2001). Time-space sampling in minority communities: Results with young Latino men who have sex with men. *American Journal of Public Health, 91*, 922-926.

Sue, D. W., Carter, R. T., Casas, J. M., Fouad, N. A., Ivey, A. E., Jensen, M., LaFromboise, T., Manese, J. E., Ponterotto, J. G., & Vasquez-Nutall, E. (1998). *Multicultural counseling competencies: Individual and organizational development*. Thousand Oaks, CA: Sage.

Szapocznik, J. (1995). *Hispanic/Latino family approach to substance abuse prevention* (DHHS Pub. No. (SMA) 95-3034). Rockville, MD: Center for Substance Abuse Prevention.

Szapocznik, J., & Kurtines, W. M. (1989). *Breakthroughs in family therapy with drug abusing and problem youth*. New York: Springer.

Terrell, M. D. (1993). Ethnocultural factors and substance abuse toward culturally sensitive treatment models. *Psychology of Addictive Behaviors, 7*, 162-167.

Trimble, J. (1995). Toward an understanding of ethnicity and ethnic identity, and their relationship to drug use research. In G. Botvin, S. Schinke, & M. Orlandi (Eds.), *Drug abuse prevention with multiethnic youth* (pp. 3-27). Thousand Oaks, CA: Sage.

Walton, M. A., Blow, F. C., & Booth, B. M. (2000). A comparison of substance abuse patients' and counselors' perceptions of relapse risk: Relationship with actual relapse. *Journal of Substance Abuse Treatment, 19*, 161-169.

Walton, M. A., Castro, F. G., & Barrington, E. H. (1994). The role of attributions in abstinence, lapse, and relapse following substance abuse treatment. *Addictive Behaviors, 19*, 319-331.

Wing, D. M., Crow, S. S., & Thompson, T. (1995). An ethonursing study of Muscogee (Creek) Indians and effective health care practices for treating alcohol abuse. *Family and Community Health, 18*, 52-64.

Wyatt, G. E. (1991). Examining ethnicity versus race in AIDS related sex research. *Social Sciences and Medicine, 33*, 37-45.

Zane, W. S., & Huh-Kim, J. (1998). Addictive behaviors. In L. Lee (Ed.), *Handbook of Asian American psychology* (pp. 527-554). Thousand Oaks, CA: Sage.

CHAPTER 27

Mental Health Issues for African Americans

WILLIAM B. LAWSON
Howard University School of Medicine

More than a decade and a half ago, a federal report showed that African Americans and other racial and ethnic minorities have higher rates of morbidity and mortality across the life span (Malone, 1985). That report and subsequent studies have shown that these health disparities are in part a result of less access to treatment. More recently, the U.S. surgeon general released a report showing that many Americans have limited access to mental health services (U.S. Department of Health and Human Services, 1999). African Americans have less access, which could contribute to poorer outcomes (U.S. Department of Health and Human Services, 2001).

DIAGNOSIS

Historically, African Americans have been more likely than Caucasians to receive the clinical diagnosis of schizophrenia (Adebimpe, 1981; Jones & Gray, 1986). This disorder generally has the worst prognosis of any psychiatric disorder. On the other hand, affective or mood disorders appear to be underdiagnosed in African Americans. The prognosis for these disorders is usually more favorable. These ethnic differences in diagnosis may be a consequence of "true" differences in prevalence, a consequence of misdiagnosing or diagnostic error, or a result of a difference in phenomenology rather than prevalence (i.e., African Americans with the same disorder as Caucasians may have different presenting symptoms) (Neighbors, 1984).

Currently, there are no reliable biological markers for mental disorders. Consequently, verbal report and careful observation must remain the mainstay of treatment. Nevertheless, structured interviews or assessment instruments with predetermined questions can lead to reliability and validity outcomes that are as good as many general medical treatments or outcomes. When structured interviews are used (i.e., when the interview questions are predetermined), racial differences tend to disappear (Jones & Gray, 1986). Large-scale studies such as the Epidemiological Catchment Area study (a five-city door-to-door survey using a structured interview to determine diagnoses) and the National Comorbidity Study (NCS) (a recent national randomized survey using a structured interview that could generate *DSM-III-R* [American Psychiatric Association, 1987] diagnoses) found few consistent ethnic differences when socioeconomic status was controlled (Kessler et al., 1994; Robins, Locke, & Regier, 1991). The NCS reported that African Americans had a lower prevalence of most mental disorders, including schizophrenia, when compared with non-Hispanic Whites (Kessler et al., 1994). However, that study did not survey institutional settings such as jails or inpatient psychiatric facilities, where minorities are often overrepresented. Most important, the differences, although statistically significant, were consistently small. Nevertheless, such findings suggest that previously reported ethnic differences in diagnoses were in large part due to diagnostic errors in prevalence.

AFFECTIVE DISORDERS

As noted earlier, African Americans are often overdiagnosed with schizophrenia at the expense of affective disorders (Adebimpe, 1994). This practice continues despite widespread usage of the fourth edition of the *Diagnostic and Statistical Manual of Mental Disorders* (*DSM-IV;* American Psychiatric Association, 1994) and despite evidence from epidemiological studies cited above. Many clinicians continue to believe that affective disorders are uncommon in African Americans (Jones & Gray, 1986). Diagnosis of bipolar affective disorder is often missed in African Americans, leading to a delay in the initiation of appropriate antimanic treatment. African Americans with clear evidence of bipolar disorder are more likely to receive a diagnosis of schizophrenia and less likely to receive lithium therapy (Bell & Mehta, 1980, 1981; Mukherjee, Shukla, & Woodline, 1983). Depressive disorders are often underdiagnosed as much as 50% of the time

(Brown, Feroz, Gary, & Milburn, 1995; Skaer, Selar, Robison, & Galin, 2000; Sussman, Robins, & Earls, 1987).

Many of these individuals may also be misdiagnosed. African Americans with psychotic depression are more likely to be misdiagnosed with schizophrenia (Raskin, Crook, & Herman, 1975). We also reported that Latinos with psychotic depression are at increased risk for being misdiagnosed as having schizophrenia (Lawson, 1990; Lawson, Herrera, & Costa, 1992). African Americans tend to score differently on the Minnesota Multiphasic Personality Inventory (MMPI), showing more paranoid-type symptoms (Adebimpe, Gigardet, & Harris, 1979). More suspiciousness is seen compared to non-Hispanic White populations, which some have interpreted as a "healthy paranoia" (Jones & Gray, 1986). Affective disorders are more likely to present with psychotic symptoms, mania may present with more irritable symptoms, and depression may present with suspiciousness (Adebimpe, 1981; Adebimpe, Hedlund, Cho, & Wood, 1982). African Americans with bipolar disorder are more likely to show psychotic symptoms such as hallucinations (Strakowski, McElroy, Keck, & West, 1996).

Manic subtypes such as mixed mania, rapid cyclers, and mania with psychotic features may be more common than pure mania (Bowden, 1995). The underrecognition of these may certainly play a role in misdiagnosis. Bipolar I, which is characterized by irritability and impulsivity as much as euphoria, will often lead to correctional referrals as well as misdiagnosis. Bipolar II, which is characterized by major depressive disorders but hypomanic rather then manic episodes, may be diagnosed as major depression and treated by non–mental health medical and nonmedical providers. Unfortunately, there is virtually no literature on these subtypes in African Americans.

Cultural factors may play a role in misdiagnosis by confusing the unwary clinician. Cultural differences may be interpreted as psychopathology (Adebimpe, 1994). Africans and perhaps African Americans are less likely to complain of guilt when they have an affective disorder (German, 1972).

Guilt appears to be a western European concept that focuses on individual responsibility and assumes a more individualistic view of the world. People from tribal cultures emphasize communal rather than individual responsibility. Shame rather than guilt is more likely to be experienced (German, 1972). Often, the diagnosis of major depression is missed in African Americans. African Americans with major depression are diagnosed only 50% of the time (Brown et al., 1995; Sussman et al., 1987). Probably a much smaller percentage is adequately treated. Part of the reason may be a failure to recognize symptoms as psychopathology or as depression. African Americans often may not express sadness when depressed (Jones & Gray, 1986). Rather, somatic symptoms or anger may be expressed rather then depressive complaints, although vegetative signs may be the same, regardless of ethnicity. Another factor may be an unwillingness of African Americans to express depressive symptoms because of a fear of hospitalization (Sussman et al., 1987).

African Americans may have a similar prevalence of mental disorders but could present with different symptoms that would contribute to the misdiagnosis of schizophrenia and increased likelihood of antipsychotic use. A consistent finding is the greater likelihood of psychotic symptoms in African Americans for a range of different affective and anxiety disorders. Mania may also present with more irritable symptoms, which could be misinterpreted as psychosis. African Americans with depression may show more paranoid symptoms on the MMPI (Adebimpe et al., 1979). Suspiciousness is often seen compared with non-Latino White populations, which some have interpreted as a "healthy paranoia" (Jones & Gray, 1986). Consequently, antipsychotics may be used more frequently in African

Americans because they are seen as being needed to treat psychotic symptoms.

ANXIETY DISORDERS

Disorders of anxiety are also likely to be misdiagnosed in African Americans. Panic disorder and phobic disorders are often underdiagnosed in African Americans (Brown, Eaton, & Sussman, 1990; Neal & Turner, 1991; Paradis, Hatch, & Friedman, 1994). Epidemiological studies suggest that these disorders may have the same prevalence or may occur more frequently in ethnic minorities (Kessler et al., 1994; Robins et al., 1991). Obsessive-compulsive disorder is rarely diagnosed in African Americans (Friedman, Paradis, & Hatch, 1994; Paradis et al., 1994). Obsessions can be easily mistaken for hallucinations or delusions, and compulsions may be considered the result of command hallucinations. Posttraumatic disorder, the anxiety disorder that results from exposure to a stressful event or series of events, is often underdiagnosed in African Americans despite studies of combat veterans showing that African Americans may be more likely to report posttraumatic stress disorder (Allen, 1986, 1996; Penk, Robinowitz, Dorsett, Bell, & Black, 1988). The symptoms of posttraumatic stress disorder (PTSD) have been mistaken for psychotic symptoms. Flashbacks in PTSD may be mistaken for hallucinatory experiences. The emotional blunting may be mistaken for a flattened affect or the hyperreactivity for psychotic excitement. As a result, patients are at risk for being misdiagnosed with schizophrenia (Allen, 1986).

Symptom presentation may differ in African Americans with combat-related PTSD (Allen, 1986, 1996; Parson, 1985; Penk & Allen, 1991). As with affective disorders, African Americans have scored higher on the MMPI scales for paranoid and psychotic symptoms (Penk et al., 1988; Penk et al., 1989). A later study found higher levels of psychotic symptoms and paranoid ideation for Blacks versus Whites with PTSD using the MMPI-2. The original MMPI was criticized for being normed on midwestern Caucasians, but the MMPI-2 was normed on diverse ethnic groups (Frueh, Smith, & Libet, 1996).

SCHIZOPHRENIA

As noted earlier, schizophrenia tends to be over-diagnosed in African Americans (Adebimpe, 1994). Moreover, paranoid schizophrenia often is the subtype diagnosed most often (Lawson, Yesavage, & Werner, 1984). Presumably, the tendency to see African Americans as overly suspicious extends to the subtyping of schizophrenia. African Americans with schizophrenia may be seen as more violent when they are actually not (Lawson et al., 1984). The reasons are unknown but may include an overgeneralization of the high African American homicide rate or confusion over the "healthy paranoia" for hostility. Finally, many African Americans may have their illness confused with criminality and being jailed. As noted above, the prison system has become a major provider of mental health services, and African Americans are disproportionately in that system (Lawson, 1986b).

TREATMENT

African Americans with schizophrenia or other severe mental disorders are often treated differently in the mental health system. They are more likely to be hospitalized, to be involuntarily committed, and to be placed in seclusion or restraints (Flaherty & Meagher, 1980; Lawson, Hepler, Holladay, & Cuffel, 1994; Lindsey, Paul, & Mariotto, 1989; Paul & Menditto, 1992; Soloff & Turner, 1982; Strakowski et al., 1995). Most studies do not find differences in

behavior or psychopathology that may account for these differences.

Medication is also prescribed differently. African Americans are more likely than Caucasians to receive, per nurses' request, medication and higher doses of antipsychotic medication (Chung, Mahler, & Kakuna, 1995; Flaherty & Meagher, 1980; Lawson, 1986a; Strakowski, Shelton, & Kolbrener, 1993). We noted earlier that African Americans with nonpsychotic illness often receive antipsychotics (Strickland et al., 1991). Antidepressants, however, are prescribed less often for African Americans (Blazer, Hybels, Simonsick, & Hanlon, 2000; Olfson et al., 1998; Skaer et al., 2000). The underprescribing of antidepressants is due in part to the underdiagnosis of depression (Skaer et al., 2000). Certainly, the overdiagnosis of psychosis plays a role, whether from different presentations of the illness, lack of cultural competence, or misinterpretation of nonpsychotic symptoms as psychosis. African Americans are more likely to be on depot (i.e., long-acting injectable) medication, suggesting a history of noncompliance and lack of investment in mental health treatment (Price, Glazer, & Morgenstern, 1985; Segal, Bola, & Watson, 1996).

Therapist attitudes may directly affect prescribing. Segal and associates (1996) reported that therapists' feelings about the patients affected their prescribing of medication for patients with schizophrenia. Consistent with previous reports, African Americans were found to receive more psychiatric medication, more doses of antipsychotic medications, more injections of antipsychotic medication, and higher 24-hour dosages compared to Caucasians. However, prescribing patterns were related to a rating of the physician's willingness to engage patients in treatment. In contrast, rated unwillingness to engage was associated with excessive medicating. Presumably, social distance (i.e., most of the providers were Caucasian) increased the likelihood that patients would get more medication.

Inappropriate medication may have adverse consequences. Pharmacokinetic and clinical studies suggest that African Americans may need less antidepressant, antipsychotic, and antimanic medications (Rudorfer & Robins, 1982; Ziegler & Biggs, 1977). As a result, they may experience more side effects when given doses appropriate for Caucasians. Antidepressants may not be as well tolerated either (Mendoza, Smith, & Lin, 1999). More side effects are reported with usual therapeutic doses and blood levels of lithium (Strickland, Lin, Fu, Anderson, & Zheng, 1995). The sometimes irreversible movement disorder of tardive dyskinesia is seen up to twice as often in African Americans (Glazer, Morgenstern, & Doucette, 1994; Morgenstern & Glazer, 1993).

African Americans may not have access to certain treatments. Newer medications appear to have fewer side effects and to be better tolerated by African Americans (Tran, Lawson, Andersen, & Shavers, 1999). Consequently, some of the problems with medications' side effects can be avoided with newer treatments. However, access to newer medications is limited. African Americans are less likely to have access to the atypical antipsychotic clozapine, which has a superior efficacy and movement disorder side effect profile compared to typical antipsychotics (Moeller, Chen, & Steinberg, 1995). Contrary to popular beliefs, African American children are less likely to be prescribed stimulants for attention deficit disorder, although inappropriate use is still possible (Hoagwood, Jensen, Feil, Vitiello, & Bhatara, 2000; Safer & Malever, 2000). Specific serotonin reuptake inhibitors (SSRIs), which are generally safer and better tolerated then older tricyclic antidepressants, are also less likely to be prescribed to African Americans (Melfi, Croghan, & Hanna, 1999; Melfi, Croghan, Hanna, & Robinson, 2000).

Availability of psychotherapy may also be limited for African Americans. African Americans are more likely to be referred for medication alone (Flaherty & Meagher, 1980).

They are terminated sooner from treatment by Caucasian therapists, especially if the therapist is racially biased (Chung et al., 1995; Flaherty & Meagher, 1980; Yamamoto, James, Bloombaum, & Hattem, 1967). Conversely, patients with African American providers stay in treatment longer, suggesting that therapist attitude and social distance can affect outcome (Rosenheck, Fontana, & Cottrol, 1995).

GENERAL ISSUES OF ACCESS

As noted earlier, the experience of African Americans in the mental health system often appears to be punitive rather than therapeutic. Consequently, fear of treatment should not be surprising. Fear of hospitalization probably contributes to delayed treatment for depression (Sussman et al., 1987). Fear of psychostimulants also may play a role in the lack of availability of these agents, perhaps to the detriment of African American parents (Safer & Krager, 1992). The social distance described above certainly contributes to the unwillingness of African Americans to seek initial treatment in the mental health system for mental disorders (Neighbors, 1984). Another factor is the widespread awareness of the Tuskegee study (Roy, 1995), which was a federally sponsored study begun in the 1930s in which African American men diagnosed with syphilis had treatment withheld without their knowledge. Only newspaper exposés in the 1970s ended the study. Partially as a consequence, psychotropic medication and mental health treatment are often viewed with suspicion.

Costs are a significant barrier for African Americans. New treatments tend to be more costly than standard agents as pharmaceutical manufactures try to recoup development costs for drugs that are patent protected. Such costs can limit their availability (Griffith, 1990). African Americans often have limited incomes or are underinsured. African Americans' median income is 60% and family wealth is one tenth of Caucasians', and nearly a quarter of African Americans live below the poverty line (O'Hare, Pollard, & Mann, 1991). As a result, African Americans are more likely to be uninsured, depend on public facilities for care, or depend on public insurance programs such as state disability or Medicaid (Snowden & Cheung, 1990). Medicaid and public facilities tend to have restrictive formularies that can limit the availability of psychotherapy and newer pharmaceutical agents.

There is now general agreement that disparities in health care exist for racial and ethnic minorities. Clearly, disparities in access to care exist in mental health as well. Improved treatments in psychotherapy and medications have greatly improved the outcome of mental disorders and removed some ethnic disparities. Bold efforts are needed to further improve the access of African Americans to quality mental health care. Despite extensive efforts, diagnostic deficiencies and limited access to treatment continue to exist for African Americans.

REFERENCES

Adebimpe, V. R. (1981). Overview: White norms and psychiatric diagnosis of Black patients. *American Journal of Psychiatry, 138,* 279-285.

Adebimpe, V. R. (1994). Race, racism, and epidemiological surveys. *Hospital Community Psychiatry, 45,* 27-31.

Adebimpe, V. R., Gigardet, J., & Harris, E. (1979). MMPI diagnosis of Black psychiatric patients. *American Journal of Psychiatry, 135,* 85-87.

Adebimpe, V. R., Hedlund, J. L., Cho, D. W., & Wood, J. P. (1982). Symptomatology of depression in Black and White patients. *Journal of the National Medical Association, 74,* 185-190.

Allen, I. M. (1986). Posttraumatic stress disorder among Black Vietnamese veterans. *Hospital Community Psychiatry, 37,* 55-61.

Allen, I. M. (1996). PTSD among African Americans. In A. J. Marsella, M. J. Friedman, E. T. Gerrity, & R. M. Scurfield (Eds.), *Ethnocultural aspects of posttraumatic stress disorder: Issues, research, and clinical applications* (pp. 209-238). Washington, DC: American Psychological Association.

American Psychiatric Association. (1987). *Diagnostic and statistical manual of mental disorders* (3rd ed., rev.). Washington, DC: Author.

American Psychiatric Association. (1994). *Diagnostic and statistical manual of mental disorders* (4th ed.). Washington, DC: Author.

Bell, C. C., & Mehta, H. (1980). The misdiagnosis of Black patients with manic-depressive illness. *Journal of the National Medical Association, 72,* 141-145.

Bell, C. C., & Mehta, H. (1981). Misdiagnosis of Black patients with manic-depressive illness: Second in a series. *Journal of the National Medical Association, 73,* 101-107.

Blazer, D. G., Hybels, C. F., Simonsick, E. M., & Hanlon, J. F. (2000). Marked differences in antidepressant use by race in an elderly community sample: 1986-1996. *American Journal of Psychiatry, 157,* 1089-1094.

Bowden, C. L. (1995). Predictors of response to divalproex and lithium. *Journal of Clinical Psychiatry, 56*(Suppl. 3), 25-30.

Brown, D. R., Eaton, W. W., & Sussman, L. (1990). Racial differences in prevalence of phobic disorders. *Journal of Nervous Mental Disorders, 178,* 434-441.

Brown, D. R., Feroz, A., Gary, L. E., & Milburn, N. G. (1995). Major depression in a community of African Americans. *American Journal of Psychiatry, 152,* 373-378.

Chung, H., Mahler, J. C., & Kakuna, T. (1995). Racial differences in the treatment of psychiatric inpatients. *Psychiatric Services, 46,* 586-591.

Flaherty, J. A., & Meagher, R. (1980). Measuring racial bias in inpatient treatment. *American Journal of Psychiatry, 137,* 679-682.

Friedman, S., Paradis, C. M., & Hatch, M. (1994). Characteristics of African-American and White patients with panic disorder and agoraphobia. *Hospital & Community Psychiatry, 45*(8), 798-803.

Frueh, B. C., Smith, D. W., & Libet, J. M. (1996). Racial differences on psychological measures in combat veterans seeking treatment for PTSD. *Journal of Personality Assessment, 66,* 41-53.

German, G. A. (1972). Aspects of clinical psychiatry in Sub-Saharan Africa. *British Journal of Psychiatry.*

Glazer, W. M., Morgenstern, H., & Doucette, J. (1994). Race and tardive dyskinesia among outpatients at a CMHC. *Hospital & Community Psychiatry, 45,* 38-42.

Griffith, E. E. H. (1990). Clozapine: Problems for the public sector. *Hospital & Community Psychiatry, 41,* 837.

Hoagwood, K., Jensen, P. S., Feil, M., Vitiello, B., & Bhatara, V. S. (2000). Medication management of stimulants in pediatric practice settings: A national perspective. *Journal of Developmental and Behavioral Pediatrics, 21,* 322-331.

Jones, B. E., & Gray, B. A. (1986). Problems in diagnosing schizophrenia and affective disorders among Blacks. *Hospital & Community Psychiatry, 37,* 61-65.

Kessler, R. C., McGonogle, K. A., Zhao, S., Nelson, C. B., Hughes, M., Eshleman, S., Wittchen, H.-U., & Kendler, K. S. (1994). Lifetime and 12 month prevalence of *DSM III-R* psychiatric disorders in the United States. *Archives of General Psychiatry, 51,* 8-19.

Lawson, W. B. (1986a). Clinical issues in the pharmacotherapy of African-Americans. *Psychopharmacology Bulletin, 32,* 275-281.

Lawson, W. B. (1986b). Racial and ethnic factors in psychiatric research. *Hospital & Community Psychiatry, 37,* 50-54.

Lawson, W. B. (1990). Biological markers in neuropsychiatric disorders: Racial and ethnic factors. In E. Sorel (Ed.), *Family, culture, and psychobiology.* New York: Levas.

Lawson, W. B., Hepler, N., Holladay, J., & Cuffel, B. (1994). Race as a factor in inpatient and outpatient admissions and diagnosis. *Hospital & Community Psychiatry, 45,* 72-74.

Lawson, W. B., Herrera, J. M., & Costa, J. (1992). The dexamethasone suppression test as an adjunct in diagnosing depression. *Journal of the Association for Academic Minority Physicians, 3,* 17-19.

Lawson, W. B., Yesavage, J. A., & Werner, R. D. (1984). Race, violence, and psychopathology. *Journal of Clinical Psychiatry, 45,* 294-297.

Lindsey, K. P., Paul, G. L., & Mariotto, M. J. (1989). Urban psychiatric commitments: Disability and dangerous behavior of Black and White recent admissions. *Hospital & Community Psychiatry, 40,* 286-294.

Malone, T. (Chair). (1985). *Report of the secretary's task force on Black and minority health.* Washington, DC: U.S. Department of Health and Human Services.

Melfi, C. A., Croghan, T. W., & Hanna, M. P. (1999). Access to treatment for depression in a Medicaid population. *Journal of Health Care for the Poor and Underserved, 10,* 201-215.

Melfi, C. A., Croghan, T. W., Hanna, M. P., & Robinson, R. L. (2000). Racial variation in antidepressant treatment in a Medicaid population. *Journal of Clinical Psychiatry, 61,* 16-21.

Mendoza, R. P., Smith, M. W., & Lin, K.-M. (1999). Ethnicity and the pharmacogenetics of drug-metabolizing enzymes. In J. M. Herrara, W. B. Lawson, & J. J. Sramek (Eds.), *Cross cultural psychiatry.* Chichester, UK: Wiley.

Moeller, F. G., Chen, Y. W., & Steinberg, J. L. (1995). Risk factors for clozapine discontinuation among 805 patients in the VA hospital system. *Annals of Clinical Psychiatry, 7,* 167-173.

Morgenstern, H., & Glazer, W. M. (1993). Identifying risk factors for tardive dyskinesia among chronic outpatients maintained on neuroleptic medications: Results of the Yale Tardive Dyskinesia Study. *Archives of General Psychiatry, 50,* 723-733.

Mukherjee, S., Shukla, S., & Woodline, J. (1983). Misdiagnosis of schizophrenia in bipolar patients: A multi-ethnic comparison. *American Journal of Psychiatry, 140,* 1571-1574.

Neal, A. M., & Turner, S. M. (1991). Anxiety disorders research with African Americans: Current status. *Psychological Bulletin, 109,* 400-410.

Neighbors, H. W. (1984). The distribution of psychiatric morbidity in Black Americans: A review and suggestion for research. *Community Mental Health Journal, 20,* 169-181.

O'Hare, W. P., Pollard, K. M., & Mann, T. L. (1991). African Americans in the 1990's. *Population Bulletin, 46,* 1-40.

Olfson, M., Marcus, S. C., Pincus, H. A., Zito, J. M., Thompson, J. W., & Zardin, D. A. (1998). Antidepressant prescribing practices of outpatient psychiatrists. *Archives of General Psychiatry, 55,* 310-316.

Paradis, C. M., Hatch, M., & Friedman, S. (1994). Anxiety disorders in African Americans: An update. *Journal of the National Medical Association, 86,* 609-612.

Parson, E. R. (1985). Ethnicity and traumatic stress: The intersecting point in psychotherapy. In C. R. Figley (Ed.), *Trauma and its wake: The study and treatment of posttraumatic stress disorder.* New York: Brunner/Mazel.

Paul, G. I., & Menditto, A. A. (1992). Effectiveness of inpatient treatment programs for mentally ill adults in public psychiatric facilities. *Applications of Preventive Psychology, 1,* 41-63.

Penk, W., Robinowitz, R., Black, J., Dolan, M., Bell, W., Doresett, D., Ames, M., & Noriega, I. (1989). Ethnicity: Post-traumatic stress disorder (PTSD) differences among Black, White, and Hispanic veterans who differ in degrees of exposure to combat in Vietnam. *Journal of Clinical Psychology, 45,* 729-735.

Penk, W., Robinowitz, R., Dorsett, D., Bell, W., & Black, J. (1988). Posttraumatic stress disorder: Psychometric assessment and race. In T. Miller (Ed.), *A primer on diagnosing and treating Vietnam combat-related post traumatic stress disorders.* New York: International Universities Press.

Penk, W. E., & Allen, I. M. (1991). Clinical assessment of post-traumatic stress disorder (PTSD) among American minorities who served in Vietnam. *Journal of Traumatic Stress, 4,* 41-66.

Price, N., Glazer, W., & Morgenstern, H. (1985). Demographic predictors of the use of injectable versus oral antipsychotic medications in outpatients. *American Journal of Psychiatry, 142,* 1491-1492.

Raskin, A., Crook, T. H., & Herman, K. D. (1975). Psychiatric history and symptom differences in Black and White depressed inpatients. *Journal of Consulting and Clinical Psychology, 43,* 73-80.

Robins, L. N., Locke, B., & Regier, D. A. (1991). An overview of psychiatric disorders in America. In L. N. Robins & D. A. Regier (Eds.), *Psychiatric disorders in America: The Epidemologic Catchment Area Study* (pp. 328-366). New York: Free Press.

Rosenheck, R., Fontana, A., & Cottrol, C. (1995). Effect of clinician-veteran racial pairing in the treatment of post traumatic stress disorder. *American Journal of Psychiatry, 152,* 555-563.

Roy, B. (1995). The Tuskegee syphilis experiment: Biotechnology and the administrative state. *Journal of the National Medical Association, 87,* 56-67.

Rudorfer, M. V., & Robins, E. (1982). Amitriptyline overdose: Clinical effects on tricyclic antidepressant plasma levels. *Journal of Clinical Psychiatry, 43,* 457-460.

Safer, D. J., & Krager, J. M. (1992). Effect of a media blitz and a threatened lawsuit on stimulant treatment. *Journal of the American Medical Association, 268,* 1004-1007.

Safer, D. J., & Malever, M. (2000). Stimulant treatment in Maryland public schools. *Pediatrics, 106,* 533-539.

Segal, S. P., Bola, J., & Watson, M. (1996). Race, quality of care, and antipsychotic prescribing practices in psychiatric emergency services. *Psychiatric Services, 47,* 282-286.

Skaer, T. L., Selar, D. A., Robison, L. M., & Galin, R. S. (2000). Trends in the rate of depressive illness and use of antidepressant pharmacotherapy by ethnicity/race: An assessment of office-based visits in the United States, 1992-1997. *Clinical Therapy, 22,* 1575-1589.

Snowden, L. R., & Cheung, F. K. (1990). Use of inpatient mental health services by members of ethnic minority groups. *American Psychology, 45,* 347-355.

Soloff, P. A., & Turner, S. M. (1982). Patterns of seclusion: A prospective study. *Journal of Nervous Mental Disorders, 169,* 37-44.

Strakowski, S. M., Lonczak, H. S., Sax, K., West, S. A., Crist, A., Mehta, R., & Thienhaus, O. J. (1995). The effects of race on diagnosis and disposition from a psychiatric emergency service. *Journal of Clinical Psychiatry, 56,* 101-107.

Strakowski, S. M., McElroy, S. L., Keck, P. E., Jr., & West, S. A. (1996). Racial influences on diagnosis in psychotic mania. *Journal of Affective Disorders, 39,* 157-162.

Strakowski, S. M., Shelton, R. C., & Kolbrener, M. L. (1993). The effects of race and comorbidity on clinical diagnosis in patients and psychosis. *Journal of Clinical Psychiatry, 54,* 96-102.

Strickland, T. L., Lin, K.-M., Fu, P., Anderson, D., & Zheng, Y. (1995). Comparison of lithium ratio between African-American and Caucasian bipolar patients. *Biological Psychiatry, 37,* 325-330.

Strickland, T. L., Ranganath, V., Lin, K.-M., Poland, R. E., Mendoza, R., & Smith, M. W. (1991). Psychopharmacologic considerations in the treatment of Black American populations. *Psychopharmacology Bulletin, 27,* 441-448.

Sussman, L. K., Robins, L. N., & Earls, F. (1987). Treatment-seeking for depression by Black and White Americans. *Social Science Medicine, 24,* 187-196.

Tran, P. V., Lawson, W. B., Andersen, S., & Shavers, E. (1999). Treatment of the African American patient with novel antipsychotic agents. In J. M. Herrera, W. B. Lawson, & J. J. Sramek (Eds.), *Cross cultural psychiatry* (pp. 131-138). Chichester, UK: Wiley.

U.S. Department of Health and Human Services. (1999). *Mental health: A report of the surgeon general—executive summary*. Rockville, MD: U.S. Department of Health and Human Services, Substance Abuse and Mental Health Services Administration, National Institutes of Health.

U.S. Department of Health and Human Services. (2001). *A supplement to Mental Health: A report of the surgeon general*. Rockville, MD: U.S. Department of Health and Human Services, Substance Abuse and Mental Health Services Administration, National Institutes of Health.

Yamamoto, J., James, Q. C., Bloombaum, M., & Hattem, J. (1967). Racial factors in patient selection. *American Journal of Psychiatry, 124,* 630-636.

Ziegler, V. E., & Biggs, J. T. (1977). Tricyclic plasma levels: Effect of age, race, sex and smoking. *Journal of the American Medical Association, 238,* 2167-2169.

Part VI

APPLIED AND PREVENTIVE PSYCHOLOGY

CHAPTER 28

Interventions With Ethnic Minority Populations

The Legacy and Promise of Community Psychology

MARY H. CASE

W. LAVOME ROBINSON

DePaul University

Since its inception in 1965, the field of community psychology has developed into a powerful framework for how psychologists can conceptualize, develop, and implement research and intervention protocols within ethnic populations. This chapter provides a brief history and overview of the tenets of community psychology, emphasizing a commitment to prevention, ecological validity, cultural pluralism, cultural specificity, and contextualism. By describing seminal research conducted in minority populations, we highlight evidence-based work carried out in community psychology to date and suggest challenges and starting points for future research opportunities. Toward this end, this chapter seeks to emphasize community psychology's role in prevention science and health promotion for ethnic minority populations. By exploring the psychological tenets and action initiatives of community psychology, we hope this chapter will foster a greater

realization of the ideological goals of this increasingly relevant field of psychology.

AN OVERVIEW: THE HISTORY OF COMMUNITY PSYCHOLOGY

Community psychology traces its roots back to May 1965, at the Swampscott Conference in Swampscott, Massachusetts. Psychologists attending this conference embraced "a call" for a new perspective within psychology and shared a collective vision for the future direction of the field. This vision would necessitate a shift from traditional treatment models, deemed largely ineffectual for large segments of society, toward a new focus on the prevention of psychological disorders. This shift toward prevention was coupled with the crucial recognition that ecological and contextual factors frequently contribute to the development, maintenance, and exacerbation of psychological disorders, a recognition based largely on the work of Kurt Lewin (1951) and later Urie Bronfenbrenner (1979). The newly formed group of psychologists also believed that a greater understanding of salient contextual factors might provide potential answers for the prevention and amelioration of psychological disorders (Duffy & Wong, 1995). The synergism of a dualistic approach of prevention and contextualism became the core philosophical underpinning of the emerging field of community psychology.

Community psychology emerged amid not only controversy and conflict regarding the limited effectiveness of psychotherapy but also as part of a notable historical movement. This time in history represented vast societal changes. First, the impact and height of the civil rights movement of the 1950s and 1960s led to increasing social awareness of the inequalities evident in social institutions and the untenable circumstances plaguing members of ethnic minority groups. Second, the substantial moral outrage over the U.S. involvement in Vietnam represented an unprecedented challenge to the previously unquestioned authority of institutions, such as governmental agencies. Community psychology responded to these events by constructing a model of psychology cognizant of the reality of such events and their impact on human behavior. Community psychologists remain resolute in their commitment to action-oriented strategies that consider the larger sociopolitical context in which problems develop among members of diverse populations. They also emphasize that individuals' historical and cultural realities necessitate a more flexible and possibly "grassroots" approach to providing services and conducting research. As is discussed throughout this chapter, it is perhaps these aspects of community psychology—a recognition of the contextual forces in the development of behavior and a more flexible approach to services—that hold the greatest promise when working with ethnic minorities.

Today, in addition to the establishment of the Society for Community Research and Action (SCRA), an international society, community psychology is a recognized division of the American Psychological Association, Division 27. Furthermore, a spate of books has been published within the past 35 years to both define and explicate the application of community psychology. The vitality of the field is further evidenced by the proliferation of several mainstream journals primarily devoted to the dissemination of scholarly works in the area of community psychology (e.g., the *Journal of Community Psychology*, the *American Journal of Community Psychology*, the *Journal of Community and Applied Social Psychology*, and the *Journal of Primary Prevention*). Such first-tier journals have been referenced as devoting a greater percentage of their publications to issues pertaining to ethnic minority members than other psychological journals.

Indeed, one of the most defining features of community psychology is a historical and unwavering commitment to understanding diversity. Having abandoned the ahistorical, acultural, acontextual tradition of psychology, community psychologists increasingly acknowledge the centrality of diversity and focus on the unique settings in which individuals exist and experience life, working to determine how these contexts shape the individual, the family, and the larger community, as well as the dynamic interaction that results when these multiple systems interface.

Throughout the evolution and development of community psychology, other key ideologies have been concurrently integrated within the original framework of prevention and contextualism, such as (a) spirit of participatory collaboration (Kelly, 1990; Robinson, 1990; Strother, 1987); (b) focus on adaptation, strengths, and resiliency among individuals (Duffy & Wong, 1995); (c) commitment to social change and the empowerment of individuals and communities (Zimmerman &

Rappaport, 1988); (d) interdisciplinary approaches to addressing psychological problems and root social ecological triggers (Kelly, 1990; Strother, 1987); and (e) focus on settings and communities in understanding psychological phenomena (Davidson & Cotter, 1991; Sarason, 1974). Each of these central tenets of community psychology, as illustrated in upcoming sections, has provided a framework for existing research of ethnic minority populations, as well as an opportunity for future research and improved services.

A FOCUS ON PREVENTION

Within community psychology, the development and implementation of prevention interventions represent highly evolved areas of thought and prolific research contributions. Community psychology posits that in comparison to traditional rehabilitative models of treatment, the prevention of psychological disorders offers a more effective approach to reducing psychological distress. From this perspective, primary prevention programs—programs aimed at intervening *before* problems occur—offer the optimal strategy for success. Emory Cowen (1980) commented on the inherent difficulty in trying to "undo" psychological damage and alternatively proposed the use of broad-based prevention programs targeting individuals prior to the onset of symptomatology. In instances when such programs are nonexistent or unsuccessful, secondary prevention programs—programs targeting the initial signs of psychological distress—are recommended. Finally, and only if both of the above approaches are unsuccessful, tertiary programs—programs similar to traditional rehabilitative treatment—should be implemented and carried out.

The limitations of traditional rehabilitative models of treatment are well documented, particularly among ethnically diverse populations (Baker & Bell, 1999; Cowen, 1980;

Rosado, 1980; Tolman & Reedy, 1998). Community psychology's focus on prevention offers a more optimal framework for members of diverse ethnic groups for several reasons. Unlike traditional treatment models that are historically informed by the needs and research findings of White, middle-class individuals (Caplan, 1994; Rossello & Bernal, 1996), community psychology's approach to prevention has been increasingly characterized by greater flexibility and cultural sensitivity, prerequisites necessary to attend to and resonate with the lives of individuals experiencing and surviving racism, oppression, and marginalization. Many well-meaning mental health professionals trained in traditional treatment paradigms provide services to ethnic minority individuals virtually unaware of these complex contextual factors and the associated cultural traditions specific to these populations. They are even less likely to understand how such factors affect psychological well-being. Not surprisingly, many members of ethnic minority groups report that traditional psychological treatments are not well suited to their problems (U.S. Public Health Services, 2000). Ironically, it is often these individuals who possess the most extraordinary stressors and the least financial resources and thus stand in the greatest need of services. As Kaniasty and Norris (2000) stated, "Relative need is not the sole or even the strongest predictor of *who* gets help" (p. 576). In response to these realities, community psychology's redirected focus on prevention, characterized by a commitment to recognizing ecological factors and a need for greater flexibility, has and continues to offer a sense of optimism for research and intervention with ethnic minority groups.

The research of Ortiz-Torres, Serrano-Garcia, and Torres-Burgos (2000) exemplifies the importance of intervention models informed by cultural values and traditions. A long-standing tradition among Latino women is to not discuss sexual issues or assert themselves sexually. This "sexual silence" has been hypothesized in Latino culture to contribute to the growing contraction of HIV/AIDS (Diaz, 1998). Yet when Ortiz-Torres et al. examined traditional and customary approaches to HIV/AIDS reduction among Latinas (e.g., approaches focusing on assertiveness skills), Latina women reported that insisting that Latino male partners use a condom—a commonly encouraged assertiveness skill—was subversive and untenable. Although a traditionally trained psychologist might view the failure of these programs as resistance on the part of the participants, the authors proposed that such cultural nuances inform intervention efforts, ultimately achieving greater intervention effectiveness among various cultural groups.

Another strength of community psychology stems from the field's emphasis on outreach and prevention in the promotion and application of proactive, anticipatory, community-based models of intervention. Rather than waiting in one's office for the arrival of individuals already struggling with existing symptoms, community psychologists seek out at-risk and/or disempowered individuals *prior* to the onset of psychological disorders. Thus, prevention efforts typically occur within indigenous community settings where individuals may generally feel more comfortable, an alternative to the traditional office visit. This approach is particularly important for ethnic minorities, many of whom display significant ambivalence over seeking out psychological services (Bloom & Padilla, 1979; Napoles-Springer et al., 2000; Padgett, Patrick, Burns, & Schlesinger, 1995). Kaniasty and Norris (2000) discussed the importance of cultural values in relation to one's comfort in seeking out social support networks. These authors maintained that members of collectivistic groups, groups that place value on working together and in harmony with others, are often less likely to seek out social support from established social institutions. For example,

Tolman and Reedy (1998) described how Native Americans are particularly reticent to use traditional Western health care, viewing it as ineffectual for their problems. This reticence is based largely on their belief that illness (e.g., psychological or physical) is emblematic of disharmony with oneself, one's community, and nature (Tolman & Reedy, 1998). African Americans also have historically demonstrated high reliance on community networks (White & Parham, 1990). This reliance and community cooperation have served as a mainstay of survival through years of oppression and racism (Hatchett & Jackson, 1993; White & Parham, 1990). As such, African Americans frequently seek out extended family members, neighbors, and clergy for social support (Ball, 1983; Ulbricht, Warheit, & Zimmerman, 1989; Weeks & Cuellar, 1981). Similarly, Rodriguez and O'Donnell (1995) suggested that "cultural scripts" of *familism* and *simpatia* (values of strong family and interpersonal relationships) among Latinos and Latinas underlie their reticence in seeking outside help. Of concern, however, is that despite such a strong commitment to and reliance on families, many researchers report that members of ethnic minority groups frequently express discomfort in sharing their distress and problems with family members (Eckenrode, 1983; Golding & Baezconde-Garbanati, 1990; Keefe, Padilla, & Carlos, 1978; Weeks & Cuellar, 1981) and subsequently report receiving inadequate support for their difficulties (Silverstein & Waite, 1993; Weeks & Cuellar, 1981). In fact, despite pervasive stereotypes suggesting the existence of cohesive family systems among Asian Americans, Asian American youth actually have reported less common feelings of acceptance and warmth within their families as compared to Euro-American youth. These findings underscore the essential need for appropriate and effective services among ethnic minorities that both incorporate the strengths of such cultural values while also recognizing the limitations within these systems. By examining the meaning and complexity of relevant cultural values such as family and community reliance, community psychology is able to integrate these values within its outreach and prevention/intervention efforts, establishing services that consumers deem as more sensitive, engaging, less stigmatizing, and beneficial.

GOALS OF EMPOWERMENT

The empowerment of ethnic minority individuals and communities is yet another hallmark of community psychology (Rappaport, 1987). Proposed by the Cornell University Empowerment Group (1989), a widely accepted definition of *empowerment* among community psychologists is "an intentional, ongoing process centered in the local community involving mutual respect, critical reflection, caring, and group participation through which people lacking an equal share of valued resources gain greater access to and control over those resources" (p. 2). This definition encompasses the spirit, complexity, and multileveled struggle for enhancing empowerment.

One of the most common empowerment strategies used by community psychologists involves working in collaboration with members of a community. As described earlier in this chapter, community psychologists emphasize the importance of learning from the individuals and communities with which they work. Commonly, the phrase "coupling with the host environment" has been adopted (Trickett, McConahay, Phillips, & Ginter, 1985) to describe the multifaceted collaborative approach involved in research and intervention efforts with communities. This collaborative process is often a novel and unique experience for many ethnically diverse groups. Thus, by reducing barriers, increasing familiarity and comfort in an egalitarian manner, and including participants in the

entire process, identified goals are reached more expeditiously and a sense of shared ownership of the process ensues. In contrast to a traditional and hierarchical view of psychology in which the psychologist is viewed as the "expert," community psychologists are guided by the belief that community members are equal contributors to the social construction of knowledge (Serrano-Garcia, 1994). Encouraged to fully participate at all stages of a project, community members become empowered to implement and sustain change.

A primary feature of the collaborative process involves an earned trust and reciprocity between researcher and community members. As Robinson (1990) stated, "The research relationship must be one of sharing, parity, respect, courtesy, and joint collaboration" (p. 193). This process is characterized by a mutual negotiation that continually addresses the concerns and needs of the community. Without these basic conditions, collaboration remains only an illusion.

Another essential aspect of the collaboration process involves the active participation of community members. Active participation and the expression of one's thoughts frequently have been linked to perceived fairness by group members (Tyler & Lind, 1990; van den Bos, Lind, Vermunt, & Wilke, 1997). van den Bos et al. (1997) maintained that this perception of fairness is directly related to the individual's feeling that he or she has been treated with dignity, politeness, and respect.

Several more broadly based empowerment programs have been implemented targeting ethnic minority groups. One such example, the Meyerhoff Scholastic Program (MSP), was designed to provide a multisystem approach for talented African Americans seeking future careers in the field of science (Meyerhoff Scholastic Program, 1995). The process integrated group studying, peer counseling, economic support, advising, administrative support, parental involvement, and summer bridge programs before students began their freshman year. These students, when compared to other talented African American youth not included in the multisystem program, were found by Hrabowski and Maton (1995) to have significantly elevated grades, increased retention in college, and a 50% increase in likelihood of going on to receive a Ph.D.

Another exemplary empowerment program developed by Fagan and Stevenson (1995) entailed a self-help parenting program co-led by African American fathers. The program, grounded in the empowerment approach, includes central themes such as enhancing and believing in control over one's destiny, challenging racism, exploring the meaning of fatherhood, identifying methods of working as a community toward oppression, teaching issues around violence to children, fostering a sense of pride in the Black culture, and helping children to navigate the realities of racism. The authors reported that not only did participants report higher levels of self-esteem, but they also demonstrated an increased ability to meet the needs of their children. Baldwin (1999) designed a substance abuse and HIV/AIDS prevention partnership structured so that, similar to the program described above, indigenous Native American individuals would implement the program. The author discussed how this approach, based in the traditions and culture of Native Americans, led to higher levels of participation within the program, increased empowerment of individuals within the community, and resulted in more successful outcomes for participants.

Despite the design and success of such empowerment-based programs, significant controversy exists over the effectiveness and practicality of empowerment approaches among socially marginalized group members (Gibbs & Fuery, 1994, Riger, 1993; Trickett, 1994). Riger (1993) expressed two significant criticisms of the empowerment approach. First, she argued that empowerment emphasizes the *feeling* of power or efficacy while overlooking the concrete needs of power or resources. Thus, although psychologists may be capable of establishing a sense of efficacy among individuals, Riger argued that empowerment programs offer members of disadvantaged, marginalized groups an illusion of power incommensurate with the reality of their environment and larger sociopolitical context. Second, she maintained that the empowerment perspective is based on an individualistic, male-dominated approach for independence and autonomy. Thus, she posited that empowering members of a community will ultimately lead to upheaval within existing power structures and further noncollectivistic interactions within society. She concluded that these interventions result in an outcome that is inconsistent with a sense of collaboration and community thereby at odds with the core beliefs inherent to community psychology.

In response to these criticisms, community psychologists in recent years have examined existing efforts to empower members of ethnically diverse communities. Many researchers maintain that by targeting larger sociopolitical contexts and protecting the spirit of collaboration and community empowerment, efforts will produce meaningful and sustained change. For example, Speer and Hughey (1995) suggested that when considering issues of empowerment, the researcher needs to focus on larger social problems rather than intervening at an individual level. Similarly, Trickett (1994) reminded us that empowerment interventions possess genuine potential only if they target meaningful contexts that specifically contribute to an ultimate goal or accomplishment, rather than simply providing individuals with a sense of greater efficacy. Moreover, he emphasized the importance of implementing interventions in such a way as to ensure a self-sustaining system of resources even after the intervention is completed (Altman, 1995; Trickett, 1997). Finally, Bond and Keys (1993) discussed the potential to simultaneously empower community organizations as well as individuals and families through work with other disciplines and social groups. This potential for coempowerment, presented by these authors, addresses concerns that empowerment strategies will only result in power struggles.

The focus on greater social change continues to be a key factor in empowerment efforts. Historically, community psychologists have recognized the need to implement social change aimed at the sociopolitical context in which ethnic minority communities exist (Seidman, 1988; Serrano-Garcia, Lopez, & Rivera-Medina, 1987). These types of changes represent some of the greatest challenges for the field while holding the greatest potential for empowerment within the field. A model example of such a program is evident in the work of Balcazar, Keys, and Suarez-Balcazar (2001). These researchers designed a capacity-building empowerment program for Latinos with disabilities. The authors discussed the fact that Latinos living with disabilities have historically not been included in efforts to design and shape disability agendas and determine disability rights. Thus, the goal of the program was to increase their input in relevant policy issues and then assist these individuals to establish partnerships with local advocacy organizations. Ultimately, these partnerships allowed individuals to participate actively in such organizations and to further their needs, even after the intervention had officially ended. The program addresses the multifaceted and complex issues associated with empowerment as discussed by Riger (1993) while also establishing policy skills that will empower these individuals in the future, even after researchers have returned the program to the community.

Strategies for empowerment among ethnic minorities offer exceptional opportunities to elicit meaningful change for disenfranchised and marginalized members of society, change that resonates throughout multiple systems and complex environments. Although not without risk, empowerment approaches offer the very skills and resources essential to success that are frequently withheld by members of the majority culture. By attempting to establish greater equity between and within society, community psychologists attempt to increase options and opportunities among individuals frequently lacking a venue through which to increase resources and meet their goals.

A FOCUS ON STRENGTHS AND ADAPTIVE COPING

In concert with a focus on prevention and a spirit of collaboration and commitment to empowerment, community psychologists strive to identify the strengths and adaptive behaviors used by the individual, family, or community. Community psychologists maintain that individual behavior is not adequately evaluated as adaptive or nonadaptive unless serious consideration has been given to the contexts within which the individuals exist and to the interactions between the individuals and their respective settings.

A community psychology approach focuses on the avoidance of labeling and pathologizing individuals' behaviors, a pitfall frequently found in more traditional psychological approaches (Cowen, 1980). Historically, this has represented a particular concern for members of ethnically diverse cultures. All too frequently, unfamiliar behaviors and rituals unique to a culture have erroneously been interpreted as a sign of mental illness. The errors have resulted in members of ethnic minority populations being misdiagnosed and overpathologized when employing traditional models of psychological health, subsequently leading to inappropriate and even unwarranted intervention strategies. By focusing on avoiding psychological discomfort in contrast to uncovering pathology and identifying differences as potentially adaptive, community psychological approaches circumvent many of the above-mentioned hazards.

Research suggests that the majority of existing literature pertaining to ethnic minority individuals focuses on negative behavioral outcomes (Luster & McAdoo, 1994; Taylor, Hinton, & Wilson, 1995). Nonetheless, Leavitt and Saegert (1990) found that low-income community members, particularly ethnic minority members, demonstrate many important and significant sources of strength that are useful in understanding psychological distress and behavior. In fact, Work, Cowen, Parker, and Wyman (1990) found that some members of the most impoverished neighborhoods within cities demonstrate remarkable resiliency. Miller (1999) emphasized the need to uncover and examine these unique strengths employed by nonmajority groups and understand how these factors shape behavior. By understanding these areas of strength and resiliency, community psychologists are better able to design and implement intervention strategies that use the natural resiliency of participants or to encourage the adoption of such skills among members of the community. Crucial to a comprehensive understanding of adaptive and resilient behaviors, community psychologists recognize that many behaviors defined as adaptive in one portion of society, or in a particular neighborhood, may be viewed as maladaptive, dysfunctional, or dangerous in another. For example, many members of ethnic groups have developed a cognitive style referred to by majority cultures as "suspicious"; however, given their historical experiences, this cautious approach to new experiences represents a healthy, adaptive survival technique. Similarly, research findings suggest that many African American women have taken on an independent, assertive, outspoken attitude after their experiences of racism and oppression (Sanchez-Hucles, 1997). Although these qualities may serve them well in some settings in their community and within interpersonal relationships, they may be viewed critically in White, male-dominated employment settings (Sanchez-Hucles, 1997). An Asian American individual who values privacy and limited self-disclosure may be viewed by a traditional psychologist as repressed, inhibited, or unassertive rather than having adopted a set of beliefs and behaviors that allow the individual to function within the Asian American culture (Sue, 1999).

Community psychologists recognize the need to understand such complex aspects of individuals' behavior, determining the potential adaptive quality of such characteristics and subsequently integrating these factors into the design of interventions. Furthermore, through increased awareness and understanding of particular competencies within specific ecological contexts, community psychologists may encourage the development of these skills for other members of a group not currently engaging in such behaviors. Thus, community psychologists attempt not only to understand the unique competencies used by resilient members of the group but also to disseminate such information to other individuals who might benefit from such skills.

Community psychologists have researched several areas of resiliency among ethnic minority individuals. One example, the significance of family systems, represents a compelling venue for community psychologists to examine strength and resiliency factors. Several aspects of families have been linked to resiliency, such as (a) strong kinship bonds (Hall & King, 1982; Johnson, 1995; Tseng, 1985; Weiner, 1983), (b) investment in family (Colomba, Santiago, & Rossello, 1999; Hall & King, 1982), (c) adaptability of family roles (Hall & King, 1982), (d) promotion of a strong achievement orientation (Johnson, 1995), and (e) use of native language (Johnson, 1995).

Parenting qualities also have been explored to determine what leads to resiliency among youth. Maton, Hrabowski, Freeman, and Greif (1998) found that among ethnic minority groups, a complex group of family qualities buffer youth from negative peer, social, and neighborhood factors. These processes include parental engagement in academic activities, strict discipline, consistent nurturing, and community connectedness. The extended family also has played a significant role in buffering individuals against psychological distress (Wilson, Kohn, Curry-El, & Hinton, 1995). Wilson and Tolson (1990) examined the structure, function, and interactions of African American family systems. Their findings support the potential benefits of extended family structures both for children and mothers. These extended systems appeared to allow mothers increased opportunities for self-enhancement and provided young children with many indirect benefits of multiple caregivers.

Community psychology also has found that religiosity or appreciation of spirituality within the family may buffer individuals from psychological difficulties and reduce the likelihood of engaging in risk behaviors (Benson, Donahue, & Erickson, 1989; Brown & Gary, 1994; Caldwell, Greene, & Billingsley, 1992). Specifically, participation in religious groups and church has been found to represent a significant area of strength among members of ethnic groups (Constantine, 1999). Cook (2000) reported that ethnic minority teenagers attending church were less likely to experience stress and less likely to have psychological problems than other ethnically diverse teens. African American churches have historically upheld a tradition of empowering members of its community by meeting social needs (e.g., providing food and clothing), designing educational programs, promoting civil rights awareness, and allowing for the expression of African American experiences (Caldwell et al., 1992; Gilkes, 1980; Morris & Robinson, 1996; Taylor & Chatters, 1989).

A commitment to examining resiliency often leads to a more positive approach to working with ethnic minority populations while optimizing strengths already existent within diverse communities. Rather than assuming that resiliency is a universal phenomenon, community psychologists recognize the unique strengths that diverse individuals possess and examine these buffering effects within their particular environments. The interactions among these factors take center stage and offer essential information for working with ethnically diverse populations.

A FOCUS ON COMMUNITY

The potential implications and positive impact of community represent a fundamental tenet of community psychology (Sarason, 1974). Sarason (1974) described a *sense of community* as the

> perception of similarity to others, an acknowledged interdependence with others, a willingness to maintain this interdependence by giving to or doing for others what one expects from them, the feeling that one is part of a larger dependable and stable structure. (p. 157)

This sense of community is related to a sense of resiliency and subjective well-being among community members (Davidson & Cotter, 1991). As such, individuals possessing a strong sense of community are believed to be more open to ideas and programs that enhance the environment of the entire community (Duffy & Wong, 1995).

Unfortunately, evidence is mounting to suggest that a strong sense of community has declined within some segments of society (Hill, 1996; Jason & Kobayashi, 1995). Some researchers have discussed the essential nature of community and the negative impact of the "breakdown of moral net," meaning that community members have no regard or concern for other members of the community. It is this breakdown that community psychologists struggle to avoid or repair in the process of encouraging psychological health.

Reflecting his strong belief that sense of community is a central component to the success of all programs, Sarason (1972) proposed that each intervention be evaluated based on whether it enhances or impairs a sense of community. Sarason's perspective is particularly relevant in light of research findings that point to the positive impact of increased sense of community on intervention/prevention strategies. For example, Maton and Salem (1995) found that fostering a sense of community is positively related to participants' achievement of personal goals within intervention programs. Similarly, many community psychologists report that a sense of community is directly related to increased involvement in community activities and interventions (Chavis & Wandersman, 1990; Maton & Rappaport, 1984). In fact, Davidson and Cotter (1989) found that a sense of community is predictive of increased voter turnout, interaction with public officials, and involvement in public policy efforts.

Specifically, among ethnic minority groups, the importance of community is underscored by research highlighting ethnic minority groups' preexisting devotion to, reliance on the existence of, and resiliency secondary to a sense of community (Chavis & Wandersman, 1990; Thomason, 2000). Furthermore, ethnic groups have historically demonstrated a more collectivist, less individualistic approach to problem solving and interacting with others in comparison to their White counterparts (Markus & Kitayama, 1994; Thomason, 2000). Given these findings, a focus on community offers a logical and optimal approach to working with ethnic minority populations.

Numerous research studies demonstrate the effectiveness of community-based and community-enhancing interventions among ethnic minority communities. Recognizing the belief among Native Americans that the treatment of ill or psychologically distressed individuals is a community issue, LaFromboise (1988) involved community groups in a wellness program and found this approach to be more successful for participants than other non-community-based programs. Similarly, several alcohol prevention programs developed specifically for the Native American community have shown greater success relative to traditional models of service (Rowe, 1997). For example, Edwards, Seaman, Drews, and Edwards (1995) developed a drug and alcohol prevention program for Native Americans based on community connectedness. Findings suggest that community efforts of healing and social responsibility contribute to improvement of social and behavioral problems. Guillory, Willie, and Duran (1988) implemented the Alkali Lake Band among a Native American tribe, which reduced its alcoholism rate from 95% to 5%. The authors stated that the basis of the program was "creating a community culture which no longer tolerated alcoholism as individual behavior, while concurrently revitalizing traditional culture" (p. 30).

A commitment to community allows psychologists not only to implement initial change in the context of communities but also to reinforce and sustain change through the participation of community members (Levine, 1998). Comer (1985) found in his development of full-service schools—schools providing family crisis intervention, social skills training, and specialized services for children and families in need of extra help, all with a focus on the local community—that the academic success of children, the morale of teachers and school, and the amount of community involvement in the school improved dramatically after several years. In this and similar full-service schools, community empowerment and parent involvement helped to sustain change even after grant money and formal interventions were withdrawn (Holtzman, 1997).

As evidenced by these studies, using the value of community offers a particularly effective approach to working with ethnic populations.

Continuing such efforts will allow for a greater understanding of the complexity of such successes and how they may be replicated in future implementations. Furthermore, the interaction of community and psychological well-being is recognized by psychologists as the core framework by which all other interventions are envisioned and implemented. Only in concert with the powerful force of community might the continuing goals of community psychology be realized.

FUTURE DIRECTIONS

The challenges set forth at the Swampscott Conference in 1965 encompass a complex and challenging set of goals, undoubtedly more challenging than community psychologists might ever have imagined. As evidenced throughout this chapter, the process of integrating culture and social context into community psychology represents an evolutionary, fluid, and ongoing endeavor. Despite notable and undeniable accomplishments within the field, numerous challenges still face community psychologists in adequately addressing the needs of ethnic minority populations. Such challenges represent a real opportunity to build on the success of community psychology and expand the range of efficacy within the field.

One such challenge involves ensuring a more substantial commitment to ethnic minority interests within the community psychology literature. Researchers have argued that despite the field's stated concern for ethnic minority populations, community psychology as a whole continues to exclude disenfranchised members of society from the community psychology research and literature base (Linney, 1990; Mulvey, 1988; Seidman, 1988; Serrano-Garcia et al., 1987). Almost half of the studies reviewed in Durlak and Wells's (1997) prevention meta-analysis do

not mention the race or ethnicity of the participants. Furthermore, Loo, Fong, and Iwamasa (1988) reported that 86% of community psychology articles failed to address issues of enhancing a sense of cultural identity among ethnic minority individuals. Moreover, Novaco and Monahan (1980), Arnold and colleagues (1999), and Bernal and Enchautegui-de-Jesus (1994) all suggested that despite community psychology's stated commitment to collaboration and empowerment, a significant portion of the research literature targeting ethnic minorities fails to reflect these basic tenets.

Another concern is that African American and Latino/Puerto Rican groups, as a whole, represent an inordinately greater proportion of the existing literature targeting ethnic minorities compared to Asian Americans or Native Americans (Bernal & Enchautegui-de-Jesus, 1994; Nagayama Hall & Maramba, 2001; Sue, Sue, Sue, & Takeuchi, 1995). Despite this comparative discrepancy, findings by Bernal and Enchautegui-de-Jesus (1994) suggest that only 69 articles in the community psychology literature from 1973 to 1992 represent research targeting Latinos. Researchers argue that Asian American populations are often erroneously viewed as the "model minority" and consequently not the focus of intervention strategies and research efforts (Sue et al., 1995). Native Americans, on the other hand, may represent "samples of inconvenience" and consequently lack research attention by community psychologists (Trickett, 1997). These types of research omissions place ethnic minorities at risk for again becoming the recipients of nonexistent or ill-informed intervention strategies when they stand in need of appropriate services. Criticisms such as these alert community psychologists of the continuing need to reexamine their research efforts and goals, adapting their efforts accordingly.

Another future challenge involves a greater focus on *intragroup* differences within ethnic minority populations (Serrano-Garcia & Bond, 1994; Trickett, 1996). Despite the apparent and significant diversity within ethnic groups, psychologists continue to examine ethnic minority individuals as if they exist as homogeneous entities, overlooking the subtle, or not-so-subtle, unique patterns and qualities evidenced by members within larger groups. Future research will need not only to examine these variations but also to determine how these differences lead to particular values, behaviors, and psychological well-being. Similarly, differences in acculturation, bicultural competence, and racial identity will demand further examination within ethnic subgroups to determine how this information may inform intervention strategies targeting particular members of ethnic groups (LaFromboise & Rowe, 1983; Moncher, Holden, & Trimble, 1990).

Efforts to increase and enhance culturally relevant research methods are also necessary for community psychologists to better realize their goals. Many researchers (Bernal, Bonilla, & Bellido, 1995; Hughes, Seidman, & Williams, 1993) maintain that community psychology as a whole has not demonstrated a notable commitment to the design of culturally anchored research strategies and methods. Sue et al. (1995) argued that internal validity has thus far overshadowed external validity, leading to inaccurate perceptions of ethnic minority individuals and inconclusive or erroneous support for the effectiveness of treatment interventions. This overemphasis on internal validity can be rectified in several ways. These include engaging in efficacy *and* effectiveness studies (Clarke et al., 1995), considering ecological factors that shape behaviors and the success of interventions (Bernal et al., 1995), and engaging in quantitative as well as qualitative research (Banyard & Miller, 1998; Hughes & DuMont, 1993; Jarrett, 1995; Jorgensen, 1989; Jensen, Hoagwood, &

Trickett, 1999; Watts, 1993). Research practices such as these reduce the tendency to generalize or make assumptions based on inadequate findings or inappropriate comparisons.

Several ethical issues remain at the center stage of debate among community psychologists. Serrano-Garcia (1994) discussed her belief that if community psychologists are sincerely committed to social advocacy and empowerment, they must examine the methods by which they themselves engage in inequities within the system. These inequities, she argues, are best examined through an identification of the disparity between what we as community psychologists embrace as our belief system in comparison to actual behaviors engaged in as researchers and individuals.

Ultimately, as a field, community psychology will need to remain steadfast in its commitment to the tenets described in this chapter. The idealism that marked the early stages of community psychology holds an invaluable and powerful resource; however, idealism is insufficient in the face of human suffering, and community psychologists need to remain accountable for meeting the challenges set forth by the field. Furthermore, they must recognize and acknowledge the impact of environmental factors on their own behaviors and subsequently avoid societal pressure to overlook and discount the needs of marginalized members of society. Toward this end, community psychologists themselves may benefit from securing a narrative, one that speaks to the experiences, observations, and realities encountered in the course of engaging in research with ethnic minorities. This narrative not only holds power to express the needs of many members of society presently unable to speak but also establishes a history for community psychology and a plan that adequately meets the needs of all individuals.

REFERENCES

Altman, D. G. (1995). Sustaining interventions in community systems: On the relationship between researchers and communities. *Health Psychology, 14,* 526-536.

Arnold, D. H., Ortiz, C., Curry, J. C., Stowe, R. M., Goldstein, N. E., Fisher, P. H., Zeljo, A., & Yershova, K. (1999). Promoting academic success and preventing disruptive behavior disorders through community partnership. *Journal of Community Psychology, 27*(5), 589-598.

Baker, F. M., & Bell, C. C. (1999). Issues in the psychiatric treatment of African Americans. *Psychiatric Services, 50,* 362-368.

Balcazar, F. E., Keys, C. B., & Suarez-Balcazar, Y. (2001). Empowering Latinos with disabilities to address issues of independent living and disability rights: A capacity-building approach. *Journal of Prevention & Intervention in the Community, 21*(2), 53-70.

Baldwin, J. A. (1999). Conducting drug abuse prevention in partnership with Native American communities: Meeting challenges through collaborative approaches. *Drugs & Society, 14,* 77-92.

Ball, R. E. (1983). Family and friends: A supportive network for low-income American black families. *Journal of Comparative Family Studies, 14,* 51-65.

Banyard, V. L., & Miller, K. E. (1998). The powerful potential of qualitative research for community psychology. *American Journal of Community Psychology, 26,* 485-505.

Benson, P. L., Donahue, M. J., & Erickson, J. A. (1989). Adolescence and religion: A review of the literature from 1970 to 1986. In L. M. Lynn & D. O. Moberg (Eds.), *Research in the social scientific study of religion: A research annual* (Vol. 1, pp. 153-181). Stanford, CT: JAI.

Bernal, G., Bonilla, J., & Bellido, C. (1995). Ecological validity and cultural sensitivity for outcome research: Issues for the cultural adaptation and development of psychosocial treatments with Hispanics. *Journal of Abnormal Child Psychology, 23,* 67-82.

Bernal, G., & Enchautegui-de-Jesus, N. (1994). Latinos and Latinas in community psychology: A review of the literature. *American Journal of Community Psychology, 22,* 531-558.

Bloom, D., & Padilla, A. M. (1979). A peer interviewer model in conducting surveys among Mexican-American youth. *Journal of Community Psychology, 7,* 129-136.

Bond, M. A., & Keys, C. B. (1993). Empowerment, diversity, and collaboration: Promoting synergy on community boards. *American Journal of Community Psychology, 21,* 37-57.

Bronfenbrenner, U. (1979). *The ecology of human development: Experiments by nature and design.* Cambridge, MA: Harvard University Press.

Brown, D. R., & Gary, L. E. (1994). Religious involvement and health status among African-American males. *Journal of the National Medical Association, 86,* 825-831.

Caldwell, C. H., Greene, A. D., & Billingsley, A. (1992). The Black church as a family support system. Instrumental and expressive function. *National Journal of Sociology, 6,* 21-40.

Caplan, R. B. (1994). The need for quality control in primary prevention. *Journal of Primary Prevention, 15*(1), 15-29.

Chavis, D., & Wandersman, A. (1990). Sense of community in the urban environment: A catalyst for participation and community development. *American Journal of Community Psychology, 18,* 55-81.

Clarke, G., Hawkins, W., Murphy, M., Sheeber, L. B., Lewinsohn, P. M., & Seeley, J. R. (1995). Targeted prevention of unipolar depressive disorder in an at-risk sample of high school adolescents: A randomized trial of a group cognitive intervention. *Journal of the American Academy of Child and Adolescent Psychiatry, 34,* 312-321.

Colomba, M. V., Santiago, E. S., & Rossello, J. (1999). Coping strategies and depression in Puerto Rican adolescents: An exploratory study. *Cultural Diversity & Ethnic Minority Psychology, 5,* 65-75.

Comer, J. P. (1985). The Yale-New Haven Primary Prevention Project: A follow-up study. *Journal of the American Academy of Child Psychiatry, 24,* 154-160.

Constantine, M. G. (1999). Racism's impact on counselors' professional and personal lives: A response to the personal narratives on racism. *Journal of Counseling & Development, 77,* 68-72.

Cook, K. V. (2000). "You have to have somebody watching your back, and if that's God, then that's mighty big": The church's role in the resilience of inner-city youth. *Adolescence, 35,* 717-730.

Cornell University Empowerment Group. (1989). [Special issue]. *Networking Bulletin, 1*(2).

Cowen, E. L. (1980). The wooing of primary prevention. *American Journal of Community Psychology, 8,* 258-284.

Davidson, W. B., & Cotter, P. R. (1989). Sense of community and political participation. *Journal of Community Psychology, 17,* 199-125.

Davidson, W. B., & Cotter, P. R. (1991). The relationship between sense of community and subjective well-being: A first look. *Journal of Community Psychology, 19,* 246-253.

Diaz, R. M. (1998). *Latino gay men and HIV: A cultural guide to AIDS education and prevention.* New York: Routledge.

Duffy, K. G., & Wong, F. Y. (1995). *Community psychology.* Boston: Allyn & Bacon.

Durlak, J. A., & Wells, A. M. (1997). Primary prevention mental health programs for children and adolescents: A meta-analytic review. *American Journal of Community Psychology, 25,* 115-152.

Eckenrode, J. (1983). The mobilization of social support: Some individual constraints. *American Journal of Community Psychology, 11,* 509-528.

Edwards, E. D., Seaman, J. R., Drews, J., & Edwards, M. E. (1995). A community approach for Native American drug and alcohol prevention programs: A logic model framework. *Alcoholism Treatment Quarterly, 13,* 43-62.

Fagan, J., & Stevenson, H. (1995). Men as teachers: A self-help program on parenting for African American men. *Social Work With Groups, 17,* 29-42.

Gibbs, J. T., & Fuery, D. (1994). Mental health and well-being of Black women: Toward strategies of empowerment. *American Journal of Community Psychology, 22,* 559-582.

Gilkes, C. T. (1980). The Black church as a therapeutic community: Suggested areas for research into the Black religious experience. *Journal of Interdenominational Theological Center, 8,* 29-44.

Golding, J. M., & Baezconde-Garbanati, L. A. (1990). Ethnicity, culture, and social resources. *American Journal of Community Psychology, 18,* 465-486.

Guillory, B., Willie, E., & Duran, E. (1988). Analysis of a community organizing case study: Alkali Lake. *Journal of Rural Community Psychology, 9,* 27-35.

Hall, E. H., & King, G. C. (1982). Working with the strengths of Black families. *Child Welfare, 61,* 536-544.

Hatchett, S., & Jackson, J. (1993). African American extended kin systems. In H. P. McAdoo (Ed.), *Family ethnicity: Strength in diversity* (pp. 90-108). Newbury Park, CA: Sage.

Hill, J. L. (1996). Psychological sense of community: Suggestions for future research. *Journal of Community Psychology, 24,* 431-438.

Holtzman, W. H. (1997). Community psychology and full-service schools in different cultures. *American Psychologist, 52,* 366-380.

Hrabowski, F., III, & Maton, K. I. (1995). Enhancing the success of African-American students in the sciences: Freshman year outcomes. *School Science and Mathematics, 95,* 19-27.

Hughes, D., & DuMont, K. (1993). Using focus groups to facilitate culturally anchored research. *American Journal of Community Psychology, 21,* 775-806.

Hughes, D., Seidman, E., & Williams, N. (1993). Cultural phenomena and the research enterprise: Toward a culturally anchored methodology. *American Journal of Community Psychology, 21,* 687-703.

Jarrett, R. L. (1995). Growing up poor: The family experiences of socially mobile youth in low-income African-American neighborhoods. *Journal of Adolescent Research, 10,* 110-135.

Jason, L. A., & Kobayashi, R. B. (1995). Community building: Our next frontier. *Journal of Primary Prevention, 15,* 1995-1208.

Jensen, P. S., Hoagwood, K., & Trickett, E. J. (1999). Ivory towers or earthen trenches? Community collaborations to foster real-world research. *Applied Developmental Science, 3,* 206-212.

Johnson, A. C. (1995). Resiliency mechanisms in culturally diverse families. *Family Journal-Counseling & Therapy for Couples & Families, 3,* 316-324.

Jorgensen, D. L. (1989). *Participant observation: A methodology for human studies.* Newbury Park, CA: Sage.

Kaniasty, K., & Norris, F. H. (2000). Help-seeking comfort and receiving social support: The role of ethnicity and context of need. *American Journal of Community Psychology, 28,* 545-581.

Keefe, S. E., Padilla, A. M., & Carlos, M. L. (1978). The Mexican American extended family as an emotional support system. *Spanish Speaking Mental Health Research Center Monograph Series, 7,* 49-67.

Kelly, J. G. (1990). Changing contexts and the field of community psychology. *American Journal of Community Psychology, 18,* 769-792.

LaFromboise, T. (1988). American Indian mental health policy. *American Psychologist, 43,* 388-397.

LaFromboise, T., & Rowe, W. (1983). Skills training for bicultural competence: Rationale and application. *Journal of Counseling Psychology, 30,* 589-595.

Leavitt, J., & Saegert, S. (1990). *From abandonment to hope: Community-households in Harlem.* New York: Columbia University Press.

Levine, M. (1998). Prevention and community. *American Journal of Community Psychology, 26,* 189-206.

Lewin, K. (1951). *Field theory in social science.* New York: Harper & Row.

Linney, J. A. (1990). Community psychology into the 1990s: Capitalizing opportunity and promoting innovation. *American Journal of Community Psychology, 18,* 1-17.

Loo, C., Fong, K. T., & Iwamasa, G. (1988). Ethnicity and cultural diversity: An analysis of work published in community psychology journals, 1965-1985. *Journal of Community Psychology, 16*(3), 332-349.

Luster, T., & McAdoo, H. P. (1994). Factors related to the achievement and adjustment of young African-American children. *Child Development, 65,* 1080-1094.

Markus, H., & Kitayama, S. (1994). The cultural construction of self and emotion: Implications for social behavior. In S. Kitayama & H. Markus (Eds.), *Emotion and culture* (pp. 39-130). Washington, DC: American Psychological Association.

Maton, K. I., Hrabowski, F. A., III, & Greif, G. L. (1998). Preparing the way: A qualitative study of high-achieving African American males and the role of the family. *American Journal of Community Psychology, 26*(4), 639-668.

Maton, K. I., & Rappaport, J. (1984). Empowerment in a religious setting: A multivariate investigation. *Prevention in Human Services, 3,* 37-72.

Maton, K. I., & Salem, D. A. (1995). Organizational characteristics of empowering community settings: A multiple case study approach. *American Journal of Community Psychology, 23,* 631-655.

Meyerhoff Scholastic Program (MSP). (1995). *Promotional literature.* Baltimore: Meyerhoff Program.

Miller, D. B. (1999). Racial socialization and racial identity: Can they promote resiliency for African American adolescents? *Adolescence, 34,* 493-501.

Moncher, M. S., Holden, G., & Trimble, J. E. (1990). Substance abuse among Native-American youth. *Journal of Consulting & Clinical Psychology, 58,* 408-415.

Morris, J. R., & Robinson, D. T. (1996). Community and Christianity in the Black church. *Counseling and Values, 41,* 69.

Mulvey, A. (1988). Community psychology and feminism: Tensions and commonalities. *Journal of Community Psychology, 16,* 70-83.

Nagayama Hall, G. C., & Maramba, G. G. (2001). In search of cultural diversity: Recent literature in cross-cultural and ethnic minority psychology. *Cultural Diversity & Ethnic Minority Psychology, 7,* 12-26.

Napoles-Springer, A. M., Grumbach, K. A., Alexander, M., Moreno-John, G., Forté, D., Rangel-Lugo, M., & Pérez-Stable, E. J. (2000). Clinical research with older African Americans and Latinos: Perspectives from the community. *Research on Aging, 22,* 668-691.

Novaco, R, W., & Monahan, J. (1980). Research in community psychology: An analysis of work published in the first six years of the *American Journal of Community Psychology. American Journal of Community Psychology, 8,* 131-145.

Ortiz-Torres, B., Serrano-Garcia, I., & Torres-Burgos, N. (2000). Subverting culture: Promoting HIV/AIDS prevention among Puerto Rican and Dominican women. *American Journal of Community Psychology, 28,* 859-881.

Padgett, D., Patrick, C., Burns, B., & Schlesinger, H. (1995). Use of mental health services by Black and White elderly. In D. Padgett (Ed.), *Handbook on ethnicity, aging, and mental health* (pp. 145-164). Westport, CT: Greenwood.

Rappaport, J. (1987). Terms of empowerment/exemplars of prevention: Toward a theory for community psychology. *American Journal of Community Psychology, 15,* 121-148.

Riger, S. (1993). What's wrong with empowerment? *American Journal of Community Psychology, 21,* 279-292.

Robinson, W. L. (1990). Data feedback and communication to the host setting. In P. Tolan, C. Keys, F. Chertak, & L. Jason (Eds.), *Researching community psychology: Issues of theory and methods.* Washington, DC: American Psychological Association.

Rodriguez, O., & O'Donnell, R. M. (1995). Help-seeking and use of mental health services by the Hispanic elderly. In D. K. Padgett (Ed.), *Handbook on ethnicity, aging, and mental health* (pp. 165-184). Westport, CT: Greenwood.

Rosado, J. (1980). Important psychocultural factors in the delivery of mental health services to lower-class Puerto Rican clients: A review of recent studies. *Journal of Community Psychology, 8,* 215-226.

Rossello, J., & Bernal, G. (1996). Adapting cognitive-behavioral and interpersonal treatments for depressed Puerto Rican adolescents. In E. D. Hibbs & P. S. Jensen (Eds.), *Psychosocial treatments for child and adolescent disorders: Empirically based strategies for clinical practice* (pp. 157-185). Washington, DC: American Psychological Association.

Rowe, W. E. (1997). Changing ATOD norms and behaviors: A Native American community commitment to wellness. *Evaluation & Program Planning, 20,* 323-333.

Sanchez-Hucles, J. (1997). Jeopardy not bonus status for African American women in the workforce: Why does the myth of advantage persist? *American Journal of Community Psychology, 25,* 565-580.

Sarason, S. B. (1972). *The creation of settings and the future societies.* San Francisco: Jossey-Bass.

Sarason, S. B. (1974). *The psychological sense of community: Prospects for a community psychology.* San Francisco: Jossey-Bass.

Seidman, E. (1988). Back to the future, community psychology: Unfolding a theory of social intervention. *American Journal of Community Psychology, 16,* 3-24.

Serrano-Garcia, I. (1994). The ethics of the powerful and the power of ethics. *American Journal of Community Psychology, 22,* 1-20.

Serrano-Garcia, I., & Bond, M. (1994). Empowering the silent ranks: Introduction. *American Journal of Community Psychology, 22,* 433-445.

Serrano-Garcia, I., Lopez, M. M., & Rivera-Medena, E. (1987). Toward a social-community psychology. *Journal of Community Psychology, 15,* 431-446.

Silverstein, M., & Waite, L. J. (1993). Are Blacks more likely than Whites to receive and provide social support in middle and old age? Yes, no, and maybe so. *Journals of Gerontology, 48,* S212-S222.

Speer, P. W., & Hughey, J. (1995). Community organizing: An ecological route to empowerment and power. *American Journal of Community Psychology, 23,* 729-748.

Strother, C. R. (1987). Reflections on the Stanford conference and subsequent events. *American Journal of Community Journal, 15,* 519-522.

Sue, S. (1999). Science, ethnicity, and bias: Where have we gone wrong? *American Psychologist, 54,* 1070-1077.

Sue, S., Sue, D. W., Sue, L., & Takeuchi, D. T. (1995). Psychopathology among Asian Americans: A model minority? *Cultural Diversity & Mental Health, 1,* 39-51.

Taylor, L. C., Hinton, I. D., & Wilson, M. N. (1995). Parental influences on academic performance in African-American students. *Journal of Child & Family Studies, 4,* 293-302.

Taylor, R. J., & Chatters, L. M. (1989). Family, friend, and church support networks of Black Americans. In R. L. Jones (Ed.), *Black adult development and aging* (pp. 310-320). Berkeley, CA: Cobb & Henry.

Thomason, T. C. (2000). Issues in the treatment of Native Americans with alcohol problems. *Journal of Multicultural Counseling & Development, 28,* 243-253.

Tolman, A., & Reedy, R. (1998). Implementation of a culture-specific intervention for Native American communities. *Journal of Clinical Psychology in Medical Settings, 5,* 381-392.

Trickett, E. J. (1994). Human diversity and community psychology: Where ecology and empowerment meet. *American Journal of Community Psychology, 22,* 582-592.

Trickett, E. J. (1996). A future for community psychology: The contexts of diversity and the diversity of contexts. *American Journal of Community Psychology, 24,* 209-230.

Trickett, E. J. (1997). Ecology and primary prevention: Reflections on a meta-analysis. *American Journal of Community Psychology, 25,* 197-205.

Trickett, E. J., McConahay, J. B., Phillips, D., & Ginter, M. A. (1985). Natural experiments and the educational context: The environment and effects of an alternative inner-city public school on adolescents. *American Journal of Community Psychology, 13,* 617-643.

Tseng, W. S. (1985). Cultural aspects of family assessment. *International Journal of Family Psychiatry, 6,* 19-31.

Tyler, T. R., & Lind, E. A. (1990). Intrinsic versus community-based justice models: When does group membership matter? *Journal of Social Issues, 46,* 83-94.

Ulbricht, P., Warheit, G., & Zimmerman, R. (1989). Race, socioeconomic status, and psychological distress: An examination of differential vulnerability. *Journal of Health and Social Behavior, 30,* 131-146.

U.S. Public Health Services. (2000). *Mental health: A report of the surgeon general.* Washington, DC: Author.

van den Bos, K., Lind, E. A., Vermunt, R., & Wilke, H. A. M. (1997). How do I judge my outcome when I do not know the outcome of others? The psychology of the fair process effect. *Journal of Personality & Social Psychology, 72,* 1034-1046.

Watts, R. J. (1993). Community action through manhood development: A look at concepts and concerns from the frontline. *American Journal of Community Psychology, 21,* 333-359.

Weeks, J. R., & Cuellar, J. B. (1981). Isolation of older persons: The influence of immigration and length of residence. *Research on Aging, 5,* 369-388.

Weiner, R. S. (1983). Utilizing the Hispanic family as a strategy in adjustment counseling. *Journal of Non-White Concerns in Personnel & Guidance, 11,* 133-137.

White, J. L., & Parham, T. A. (1990). The struggle for identity congruence in African Americans. In G. H. Jennings (Ed.), *Passages beyond the gate: A Jungian approach to understanding the nature of American psychology at the dawn of the new millennium* (pp. 246-253). Needham Heights, MA: Simon & Schuster.

Wilson, M. N., Kohn, L. P., Curry-El, J., & Hinton, I. D. (1995). The influence of family structure characteristics on the child-rearing behaviors of African American mothers. *Journal of Black Psychology, 21*(4), 450-462.

Wilson, M. N., & Tolson, T. F. (1990). Familial support in the Black community. *Journal of Clinical Child Psychology, 19*(4), 347-355.

Work, W. C., Cowen, E., Parker, G. R., & Wyman, P. A. (1990). Stress resilient children in an urban setting. *Journal of Primary Prevention, 11,* 3-17.

Zimmerman, M. A., & Rappaport, J. (1988). Citizen participation, perceived control, and empowerment. *American Journal of Community Psychology, 16,* 725-750.

CHAPTER 29

Honoring the Differences

*Using Community
Readiness to Create Culturally
Valid Community Interventions*

PAMELA JUMPER-THURMAN
RUTH W. EDWARDS
BARBARA A. PLESTED
EUGENE OETTING
Colorado State University

More and more frequently, we hear that it takes a village to raise a child. Although that may be true, the village must be ready to assume that responsibility or it will not happen. Mobilizing and thereby changing a community system requires vision, voices, and commitment. Addressing any community social problem is a multifaceted task with many potential pitfalls. Changing national policy rarely has immediate local effects and may never have public support. Locally initiated efforts are not always successful either. They may also lack community investment. There are many good programs that have met with failure for any number of reasons. Often, in these days of competitive time-limited grant funding, there is no sustainability of a program when funding sources end. Programs generally have a beginning and an end. With vision, however, prevention efforts can be far-reaching and sustainable. Daniel Quinn (1996) suggested that "if the world is to be saved, it will be saved by people with changed minds, people with a new vision—yet if the time isn't right for a new idea, it will fail. If, however, the time is right, an idea can sweep the world like wildfire. The measures of change are not the ease or difficulty with which they can be effected but the readiness or unreadiness of the entity needing change."

In our experience, successful local prevention and intervention efforts must be conceived from models that are community specific, culturally relevant, and consistent with the level of readiness of the community to implement an intervention. Communities vary greatly from one another. Resources also vary from community to community, as do strengths, challenges, and political climates. It isn't really surprising, then, that what works in one community may not be even minimally effective in another community. Readiness is an important factor because differences in readiness indicate what can be done and what needs to be done. But each community also needs to use its own knowledge of its assets and limitations, its culture and characteristics, and its values and beliefs to build policies and programs that are congruent with the community's characteristics and that meet the community's needs.

Intervening in ethnic minority communities adds further challenges. We all know that there is no one "promising practice" that works for all African Americans, Native Americans, Alaskan Natives, Asian Americans, and Latinos, just as there is no intervention guaranteed successful for majority culture communities. In fact, even the concept of "promising practice" seriously limits the scope of premises and ideas for interventions in ethnic communities. Simply substituting language and/or pictures of ethnic people in posters and flyers does not make a culturally competent program. A lot of vision, thought, and experience must be incorporated into an intervention effort to maximize potential for success.

Many Americans carry the gifts and strengths of their cultural traditions (Center for Substance Abuse and Prevention, 1994). These cultural backgrounds influence the way we dress, the food we eat, the music we listen to, the festivals we celebrate, the way we think, and so much more (Center for Substance Abuse and Prevention, 1994). The challenge is in defining culture. It is often viewed as language, ethnicity, race, or even religion, and although it draws on all of these elements, it is not synonymous with any of them (Center for

Substance Abuse and Prevention, 1994). Complicating the issue are the many stereotypes and misconceptions about racial and ethnic groups that exist. In developing strategies for intervention in any community, it is important that the information used to justify the efforts is accurate and that the local community is deeply involved in the development.

Acknowledging that there are differences within each ethnic group that are as great or greater than differences between ethnic groups is also critically important in developing successful intervention strategies. There are 478 tribes recognized by the Bureau of Indian Affairs (BIA) and 52 tribes without official status with the BIA, and 142 Native languages are still spoken (Heinrich, Corbine, & Thomas, 1990). Each tribal group has a different language, different customs, and different traditions. The political structures vary, as do the religious and spirituality structures, the ceremonies, and many more aspects. The terms *American Indian* or *Native American* fail to recognize the richness of all these differences. This is true for other ethnic groups as well.

The take-home lesson for this chapter is that *every* community is different and *every* community has a culture. In fact, it is virtually impossible to completely understand the culture of a specific, individual community from outside that community. Yet to be effective, we must base intervention strategies on the culture or cultures existing within that specific community. Recognizing this does not disempower us; nor does it imply that successful intervention is impossible. Rather, it gives us a strong tool for creating interventions that have greater potential for success. We are armed with the knowledge that culture can be a tool to build resiliency within the community. The interventions developed around local culture have a greater chance to be "owned" by the community. The motivation, direction, planning, and action must all involve a high level of community participation—a community vision! Generating this high level of community involvement, however, is not an easy task. Attitudes toward a specific problem vary considerably across communities. One community may be highly motivated to do something about that problem, whereas another community may not even recognize that it is a problem.

Several tools are needed to meet these challenges. First, a general but very practical method must be used to determine where a community stands on a particular social issue (i.e., how ready the community is to get involved in doing something about a problem). Second, we need an ethical method for changing the community, for moving it to the point where it can develop strategies to solve the problem. Third, we need methods that ensure that what is done is consistent with the culture of the community. Fourth, we need a method that leads to development and maintenance of programs that are effective. Such tools have been developed at the Tri-Ethnic Center for Prevention Research using the theory of community readiness.

COMMUNITY READINESS

Community readiness theory (Donnermeyer et al., 1997; Plested, Jumper-Thurman, Edwards, & Oetting, 2000; Oetting et al., 1995; Plested, Smitham, Jumper-Thurman, Oetting, & Edwards, 1999; Thurman, Plested, Edwards, & Oetting, 2001) provides a practical step-by-step framework for making culturally valid changes in communities. Community readiness is a research-based theory that provides a basic understanding of the intervention process in communities. The Edwards et al. (2000) article provides the most recent and comprehensive review of the development of the theory and includes all of the instruments needed to apply the model. The theory allows us to accurately describe the developmental level of a community relative to a specific issue or problem. The theory defines the developmental

stages that have to be worked through to move the community toward implementing and maintaining efforts to reduce the problem. It provides specific guidelines at each stage for the type and intensity level of strategies that may lead to movement to the next stage. It provides direction to the community on how to achieve the necessary community involvement to create a vision that can lead to change. These guidelines are stated broadly so as to allow specific cultural values and beliefs to be taken into account and to optimize use of local assets and resources. They include development of an understanding of local barriers and obstacles to progress and, in fact, embrace those barriers as part of the nature of the community. Although it is important to note that the model is a research-based tool, the real validation of the model comes from the many communities that have discovered the utility of the model and have claimed it as their own. Development of the model has been greatly enhanced by input from these communities, which have provided feedback that has allowed us to make modifications to make it even more useful. It truly is a model that has successfully made the journey from research to practice.

Table 29.1 lists and defines the stages of community readiness. Although each stage is qualitatively distinct and describes particular characteristics that are likely to be present if the community is at that stage of readiness, there is an underlying continuum. Movement toward each next stage of readiness is not a sudden leap; it is a thoughtful progression. One stage is not necessarily better than another; rather, the point of identifying stages is to direct the development of appropriate strategies. Each stage is a journey to the next, and the events that mark the journey provide more direction to reach realization of the vision. The community may be reasonably comfortable at whatever stage of readiness exists at the outset, and change is almost always associated with at least some anxiety and resistance. Although there is a conscious effort to induce change, it is particularly important to recognize that change cannot be instantly produced—it must be thoughtfully planned and executed and involve the people of the community. Resistance to change is part of the nature of most individuals as well as communities as entities. Identification of the stage of readiness provides definition for strategy development and shapes the direction of the intervention.

It is important to recognize that different segments of the community may be at different stages of readiness. This is to be expected and only offers more insight into the process. The model allows for these differences and encourages the use of differing strategies for the differing segments of a community. The community readiness model provides a clear structure for bringing all segments of the community to the same page. Understanding of the stages and what defines them is essential to understanding the further implications of community readiness and how the theory can be applied to produce change in communities (see Table 29.1).

CULTURE AND THE STAGES OF COMMUNITY READINESS

Community readiness theory is certainly not culture free. It is strongly grounded in research assumptions about effective community action that are characteristic of a Western viewpoint. It was created based on a Western assumption of how concrete planning occurs. It defines what types of actions will be needed—actions such as changes in policy, education, training, communication through media, and so on—that rely on essentially Western methods. The theory also makes the Western-style assumption that continued progress will involve scheduling meetings, networking across agencies or groups, obtaining and committing resources, and so on, in a Western style of structure. All of these assumptions are deeply grounded in the values and beliefs of Western society.

The utility of the model, however, goes far beyond Western culture. The methods used to implement change in community readiness are all translatable to the differing styles of communication, values, experience, networking, and policy change of the various cultures of a community. The decision as to the specific interventions used and the avenues chosen are based on the fundamental principle that community change is and should be in the hands of the community. Because of this, although community readiness theory is not culture free, it is, more important, culture embracing. It encourages the development of creative cultural strategies. For example, the higher stages of readiness involve evaluation, and in most of our papers on community readiness theory, that evaluation is described in terms of Western culture and society. This generally means that evaluation will be data based and will assess whether the program was effective based on "the numbers." It should be recognized that once changes in readiness are in the hands of a community team, a Western form of evaluation may not be culturally appropriate. The community team is encouraged within this model to implement more culturally appropriate evaluations that are equally effective and hold greater import for that specific community. For instance, in some traditional American Indian tribes, evaluation planned by a community team might draw more from the oral tradition of accurately "telling the story" of a program's implementation and its struggles and successes. It may use "talking circles" rather than focus groups and present information in a more circular structure rather than the standard linear structure favored by Western culture. This is not only more culturally

Table 29.1   Community Readiness Stage Definitions

1. *No awareness.* The issue is not generally recognized by the community or the leaders as a problem. "It's just the way things are." Community climate may unknowingly encourage the behavior, although the behavior may be expected of one group and not another (i.e., by gender, race, social class, age, etc.).

2. *Denial.* There is usually some recognition by at least some members of the community that the behavior itself is or can be a problem, but there is little or no recognition that this might be a *local* problem. If there is some idea that it is a local problem, there is a feeling that nothing needs to be done about this locally. "It's not our problem." "We can't do anything about it." Community climate tends to match the attitudes of leaders and may be passive or guarded.

3. *Vague awareness.* There is a general feeling among some in the community that there is a local problem and that something ought to be done about it, but there is no immediate motivation to do anything. There may be stories or anecdotes about a problem, but ideas about why the problem occurs and who has the problem tend to be stereotyped and/or vague. No identifiable leadership exists, or leadership lacks energy or motivation for dealing with this problem. Community climate does not serve to motivate leaders.

4. *Preplanning.* There is clear recognition on the part of at least some that there is a local problem and that something should be done about it. There are identifiable leaders, and there may even be a committee, but efforts are not focused or detailed. There is discussion but no real planning of actions to address the problem. Community climate is beginning to acknowledge the necessity of dealing with the problem.

5. *Preparation.* Planning is going on and focuses on practical details. There is general information about local problems and about the pros and cons of efforts (actions or policies), but it may not be based on formally collected data. Leadership is active and energetic. Decisions are being made about what will be done and who will do it. Resources (people, money, time, space, etc.) are being actively sought or have been committed. Community climate offers modest support of the efforts.

6. *Initiation.* Enough information is available to justify efforts (activities, actions, or policies). An activity or action has been started and is under way, but it is still viewed as a new effort. Staff are in training or have just finished training. There may be great enthusiasm among the leaders because limitations and problems have not yet been experienced. Improved attitude in community climate is reflected by modest involvement of community members in the efforts.

7. *Stabilization.* One or two efforts or activities are running, supported by administrators or community decision makers. Programs, activities, or policies are viewed as stable. Staff are usually trained and experienced. There is little perceived need for change or expansion. Limitations may be known, but there is no in-depth evaluation of effectiveness, nor is there a sense that any recognized limitations suggest a need for change. There may or may not be some form of routine tracking of prevalence. Community climate generally supports what is occurring.

8. *Confirmation/expansion.* There are standard efforts (activities and policies) in place, and authorities or community decision makers support expanding or improving efforts. Community members appear comfortable in using efforts. Original efforts have been evaluated and modified, and new efforts are being planned or tried to reach more people, those more at risk, or different demographic groups. Resources for new efforts are being sought or committed. Data are regularly obtained on the extent of local problems, and efforts are made to assess risk factors and causes of the problem. Due to increased knowledge and desire for improved progress, community climate may challenge specific efforts but is fundamentally supportive.

(Continued)

Table 29.1 Continued

9. *Professionalization.* Detailed and sophisticated knowledge of prevalence, risk factors, and causes of the problem exists. Some efforts may be aimed at general populations, but others are targeted at specific risk factors and/or high-risk groups. Highly trained staff are running programs or activities, leaders are supportive, and community involvement is high. Effective evaluation is used to test and modify programs, policies, or activities. However, community members should continue to hold efforts accountable for meeting community needs, although fundamentally they are supportive.

congruent but is also a valuable lesson for scientists who view culture as bound into Western scientific values. They tend to focus more on rather limited, data-based measures of program "success." They should learn from these tribes and expand their concept of evaluation to include assessing what the community values and identifies as important factors rather than what scientific theory may view as "success."

MAKING CHANGES WHILE MAINTAINING CULTURAL INTEGRITY

Some groups have raised the issue that community change may threaten cultural integrity. There has been concern that entities might attempt to use the community readiness approach as a tool of manipulation. This is not a concept implicit in community readiness theory. Although it is a powerful approach and attempts could be made to use the framework to attempt to impose change on a community, use of the model mandates community investment in the process. Change is not easy, and if there is no community investment, change will not occur. In fact, the methods of intervention recommended at each stage would have to be altered significantly if the model were to be used for manipulation. It would be unlikely that such intervention methods would involve the community in the

process, making the success of such manipulation improbable, if not impossible. Certainly, it was not our intent in developing community readiness theory that it should be used in this way. The cultural validity of interventions developed using the community readiness model is virtually guaranteed because even in the earliest stages of readiness, the interventions and movement toward change are placed in the hands of concerned community members. The community, therefore, determines whether the goal is valid within their culture and develops the approaches to achieving that goal within their own framework of cultural values and beliefs.

An understanding of whatever issue is being addressed and the nature of the community can be developed using the model even for communities in the very early stages of readiness. At the "no awareness" stage, the community at large does *not* recognize the issue as a problem. With the exception of one person or a small group of people, there is essentially no motivation within the community for change. But that one person or small group of people *can* and have made a difference in their community. Initiating change, then, requires efforts aimed at gaining more investment from the community. The following case study illustrates the utility of the model when a community is at the stage of no awareness, but one person acting makes a critical difference.

This particular case study has several interesting facets that made the situation quite challenging. The community is located in a remote are in the Northwest. It is a subsistence community, meaning that there are no jobs or industry but rather only fishing and hunting and a sense of community that gets the people through the long, hard months of winter. Only about 25 families lived in the community, and of those, most suffered from problems with alcohol and drugs. Drunken behavior was commonplace in the community and had, in fact, become a way of life for most families. One woman, who had left the community years earlier, decided she wanted to return to her home to fill a helping professional position. When she arrived back in the community, she was greatly saddened by all of the drunken behavior and loss of culture. Unable to find support to improve conditions from within her community, she decided to seek help from outside resources. She happened to cross paths with our center by attending some workshops held on the community readiness model. Those workshops caught her attention and, as she said later, "gave her hope that changes could be made and that she could make them."

Because the model offers a structure to follow, it is a tool that can be used by anyone wishing to make community change. This woman knew she needed to get community members involved in identifying and owning the problem, identifying potential barriers in their own language and context, and collaborating in the development of interventions that are culturally consistent with their population. At first, she reported that it seemed to be an insurmountable task. But she persevered and followed the structure of the model, step-by-step.

This woman determined that her community, due to its isolation and long history of alcohol abuse, was in the stage of no awareness. She used the strategies recommended for that stage (i.e., one-on-one visits with other community members for informal talks about her concerns, talking with other mothers who

had concerns for their children growing up in a toxic environment, and attending small, existing groups to just sit and talk informally). As she garnered more support, she also began to count the incidents of public drunkenness and the number of people who seemed to have problems with alcohol use. She kept track and then shared the information with her church group and businesses. She posted some of those "statistics" in public places to create more awareness. It wasn't long until she began to have more support from other mothers, teens, and businesses.

Today, she believes her community has moved up to the fifth stage—preparation. More than 20 people have gone into treatment, peer support groups are now active in the community, and the youth have begun community cleanup activities as part of their sobriety movement. One woman began this change. We know that effective community prevention must be based on involvement of multiple systems and utilization of within-community resources and strengths, but it takes only one committed individual to get it started. Margaret Mead said, "Never doubt that a small group of thoughtful, committed citizens can change the world; indeed, it's the only thing that ever has."

This case illustrates the point made above about how it would be difficult to use the community readiness model in a manipulative fashion. There is a self-correcting factor built in. Although one person may be imposing his or her values up to a certain point, once the community is involved in resolving its own issues, further movement will not occur unless there is a much broader base in the community wanting change.

The challenge of imposing values also exists at the denial stage because intervention of one or a few is often needed to move the community to the vague awareness stage, where it may be able to take charge of its own problems. However, the issue of imposed values becomes less prominent at this stage. Denial can mean that the community at large does not recognize that the problem exists. Someone in the community needs to collect data or provide confirmation that the problem does exist. Once that evidence is available, the community will gradually recognize that the issue may be a problem. Denial can also mean that the community recognizes the problem but is disempowered to do anything about it. This could result from grief, trauma, apathy, or helplessness. Providing information and structure that suggest something *can* be done may be enough to alleviate that difficulty and mobilize the community to action.

At any other stage of readiness, there is at least some recognition by a significant portion of the community that there is a problem and that it may be possible to do something about that problem. At and above the vague awareness stage, there is also the greater potential to form a community team to work on the issue. However, the goals still need to be accepted as legitimate by that team, or movement toward those goals will not take place without challenge.

DIMENSIONS OF COMMUNITY READINESS

Community readiness theory proposes that readiness has six dimensions: community efforts (programs, activities, policies, etc.), community knowledge of the efforts, leadership (includes appointed leaders and influential community members), community climate, community knowledge about the issue, and resources related to the issue (people, money, time, space, etc.). These dimensions are very comprehensive in nature and provide an excellent community assessment as well as a diagnostic guide to provide information as to what type of intervention is needed in which area. For example, the dimension of leadership may be one or two stages lower than efforts. This information would tell a community that it needs to begin interventions with its leadership in order to bring about greater systemic mobilization. Or community knowledge of efforts may be lower than the other stages. This would indicate that interventions are needed appropriate to their stage to raise awareness of what has already been done in the community to address the issue. The dimensions, however, are sufficiently correlated such that one aspect of community readiness is not generally more than two stages removed from the other dimensions. Another example might be that if a school develops or initiates a drug abuse prevention program but community climate (parents and youth) does not support that program, resources to maintain the program will not continue to be available, and after a while, the program will disappear. At any stage of readiness, one or more dimensions may lag or may be slightly ahead, but at each stage, each dimension needs to be evaluated and efforts expended to bring any lagging behind up with the rest so that progress can be made toward the next stage.

When progress is blocked or barriers are encountered, the community team can reassess each dimension and the overall stage of community readiness. It could be that the team tried to initiate interventions appropriate for stages beyond the stage where the community is currently. If this is the case, they can simply move back a stage and make sure that they have developed all dimensions of readiness to the next stage before trying to move on. In some cases, although the community might have been at one stage at one time, circumstances such as changing leadership, other community issues requiring focus, closing of a program, or loss of a key resource may have required the community to revert to an earlier stage of readiness. In such a case, strategies for interventions would need to change to reflect this changed level of readiness.

CULTURE AND THE DIMENSIONS OF COMMUNITY READINESS

The dimensions are not culture specific, but they have to be carefully interpreted within the context of the culture of each community, and it may be that different dimensions assume particular cultural importance at different stages of readiness. For instance, if the culture is strongly authoritarian, with top-down decision making, and the community is at the preparation stage of readiness, leadership can impose ideas, and leadership will therefore be the most important factor in initiating any new efforts. This may be the case in some religious communities. But even in an authoritarian culture, the other dimensions are certainly not meaningless. In an authoritarian culture, the community may bow to the will of leadership, but if an effort is going to be effective within the community, eventually community climate has to support the goals and the means taken to achieve those goals.

Another culture may not have authoritarian leaders but will have powerful cultural leaders. For example, elders or spiritual leaders serve this function in some American Indian tribes. In these cultures, there are individuals who are looked to for their approval and acceptance of any actions that the community eventually takes. At every stage of readiness, therefore, if it is necessary to move the dimension of community climate, that change must start with and involve the cultural leaders.

Another cultural style occurs in highly collaborative cultures, where all decision making is essentially a group function. Some of the specific statements about the leadership dimension are not as appropriate in these cultures because in these communities, leadership takes a different form. There are, however, still key people—informal leaders or individuals who are listened to and who hold a great deal of influence with the community at large. This may be the town barber or beautician, or it could be clergy or some other credible person who talks and interacts with many people on a daily basis. These individuals hold the pulse of the town and serve as informal leaders. As long as the community team is flexible and aware of these unique cultural elements, growth and movement will occur.

DEFINING COMMUNITY

Rappaport and Simkins (1991) discussed the context of community involving a set of themes, beliefs, and ideas about past and present members of the community. They recognized the power in these beliefs. That power comes from the repetition, internalization, and enactment of community stories and is derived from the community's historical sense of itself. This is an important factor that defines the community and should guide the types of interventions to be used. The historical sense of the community holds strong importance when intervening in ethnic communities. For example, we cannot minimize the tremendous impact that historical issues have had on native people in general. In taking a look at American Indians today, we can see the effects of grief and loss passed down from generation to generation in native communities—effects such as higher rates of substance use, violent crimes, conflicted parenting roles, loss of cultural traditions in some cases, higher suicide rates, higher poverty rates, and higher rates of certain diseases. The grief, loss, and trauma must be acknowledged when working in these communities. Native people are not the only group with these tragic histories, and such issues are not only in the past. However, we also know that cultural traditions hold strong resiliency factors that should guide intervention and media messages in these same communities.

Therefore, it is important to really think about the history of the community and to define the boundaries of community.

Community readiness is a general theory that applies successfully to any group, but it makes most sense as an intervention method when applied to a reasonably focused target audience and focused on a specific issue.

The definition of *community* also depends on the problem or issue being considered and the systemic level where the problem needs to be attacked. A community of place is where residents experience their society and culture. Towns and neighborhoods are communities of place. However, organizations have also successfully used the community readiness model. As an example, one organization employed community readiness to determine if its board of directors and staff were ready to embrace the concept of cultural competency. After a thorough assessment, this organization formed a committee to begin the intervention process at the level of readiness for the board as well as the staff. The assessment was very informative, and the intervention moved quickly and successfully toward establishing cultural competency within the organization. Community readiness theory applies to either a community of place or a community of interest. It's all in the definition.

The definition of the problem also helps in defining the nature of the community. Although youth drug use is definitely a community problem, school personnel may be the first to recognize the problem and therefore the first to begin some type of intervention. The school may want to reach further into the community system and pull in other entities such as parents, agencies, local government, and law enforcement to support their effort. Action on a problem has to involve the whole community, and depending on the size and demographic makeup of the community, different strategies may be needed to intervene in the different subgroups. In this case, separate assessments could be conducted with the various subgroups to more effectively identify what strategies hold the most potential for success. This would then ensure that the efforts for each subgroup would be culturally reliable and thus bring about change throughout all components of the community.

ASSESSING COMMUNITY READINESS

Key Informants. Community readiness is assessed by interviewing key members of the community, using a series of questions that ask about what is occurring in that community. Responses to these questions are then used to rate the community on each of the six dimensions of readiness. Selecting the key informants is an important task. It is important to consider the community's cultural and physical context. A key informant is someone who knows about the problem or issue of concern—not necessarily a leader or decision maker. It is best to choose people who have resided in the community for at least 5 years so that they are more likely to know the nature and structure of the community. Different key informants might be used for different problems, but key informants are all going to be people who are involved in community affairs, know what is going on, and are familiar with the culture of the community. Four to six key individuals can be interviewed to obtain reliable information. Of course, more interviews can be conducted if the team wishes to do so and if it seems important politically to do so. Some communities have conducted 10 to 15 interviews in an effort to be inclusive and not omit anyone who may be a key stakeholder with regard to any component of potential interventions. It is important to note that this data-gathering method is *not* random sampling. Rather, it is an accepted and reliable method of assessment that is derived from established ethnographic methods.

It is not usually necessary to develop a strong personal relationship to obtain accurate data about most problems, although some issues relating to behaviors viewed as highly deviant may require a high level of trust between interviewers and key informants. Telephone interviews are usually adequate to assess community readiness, although in some cultures, there are important key informants who cannot or should not be reached by telephone for a variety of reasons. In those cases, a personal interview is necessary.

The Interview. With a semistructured interview, information can be obtained from key informants systematically. The questions are structured so that they obtain information about a variety of key facets or dimensions within a community to reach conclusions about a very specific problem or issue. Although the interview must be adapted for each specific issue (because the dimensions remain the same no matter what the issue), these adaptations are easy to make. For instance, we have used the model within communities to assess readiness to address drug abuse prevention, alcohol abuse prevention, prevention of intimate partner violence, prevention of HIV/AIDS, prevention of head injury, and so on. The informants do not rate readiness themselves and, in fact, do not need to know anything about the theory of community readiness to participate in the interview. Anchored rating scales have been developed that help achieve accurate and detailed ratings.

Attention to Cultural Context. It is critical to take culture into account in doing a community readiness assessment. Although it is, of course, not possible to know about all of the specific cultural elements of each community, we must at least try to be sensitive to the cultural issues that we know exist in some groups. Some of the interview questions may need to be adapted to language or be phrased appropriately to a particular cultural context. The interviewing style may also have to be adapted to respect cultural differences. For instance, for older interviewees or in particular ethnic groups, it may be necessary to allow more silence after asking the question before

offering prompts. Some American Indian and Alaska Native people want to give more thought to a question before answering, and there may be what seem to the Western ear long periods of silence. The interviewer needs to be aware of this cultural difference and allow the person a respectful time to formulate his or her response.

USING THE COMMUNITY READINESS MODEL TO INCREASE READINESS

The stages of community readiness are consistent, in some ways, with stages of personal development. Once we know at what developmental stage a person may be, we have a fairly good idea of how he or she will characteristically respond to certain situations. We know what the next stage of development should be and what changes must take place if the person is to move to that stage of development. We also know that if we try to train the person in behaviors, attitudes, or cognitive styles that are well above his or her current stage of development, that training will either fail or the learning will be temporary and soon disappear.

Likewise, when we know the current operating stage of community readiness, we know how the community is responding to a specific problem. We also know what the next stage of readiness entails and how we can move the community toward that stage. If we try to move too fast, skip over stages, or even try to move too suddenly to the next stage, our chances of success decrease.

When the community readiness model is used to enhance readiness within the community, people can develop good ideas about culturally valid ways to move their community to the next stage. Those ideas are based on approaches and techniques suggested by the model for each stage that many communities have used with success; even more important, because they come from within the community, they are likely to be appropriate to that community's unique cultural context. It is important to recognize that even small cultural differences can be critically important in this evolution.

CULTURE AND STRATEGIES FOR CHANGING COMMUNITY READINESS

Table 29.2 provides information on strategies appropriate for each stage. Action to change readiness at the stage of *no awareness*, when members of a community may not realize that a behavior is a problem, generally starts with one or more persons recognizing the need for change. They must then identify key people important to creating change and work with them to create awareness of the problem. Knowledge of local context and local culture is essential in selecting influential people who may be sympathetic toward viewing the behavior as a problem. Typical interventions may include visiting families and neighbors in a one-on-one setting to increase awareness of the existence or extent of the problem. Informal and brief but impassioned presentations might be made in existing small groups (Sunday school, social groups, small circles of friend, community organizations, etc.). Phone calls may be another effective intervention at this stage. Media can be used, but with care. Small mentions about the issue may be made in church bulletins or local newsletters, but caution should be exercised in using media at this stage. One reason is that if there is no awareness of the issue, such efforts are a waste of time because they generally will not even be noticed or acknowledged by members of the community. Media attention might even create problems or resistance by threatening or seemingly targeting certain elements of the community before the community is able to embrace the issue as a community problem at a later stage of readiness.

At the denial stage, the focus is on creating awareness that there *is* a problem in *this* community and that, indeed, it might be possible to do something about it. There is sometimes enough recognition of the problem by at least a few people so that a small team or group can be formed, but it is essential to work carefully in selecting the team. At this stage, an influence or resource must help the team recognize that there is a local problem and that there are possibilities for doing something about it. Generally, descriptions of local incidents are likely to create more awareness for a community than statistics or data at this stage. It is also possible to use critical events (such as a major car accident involving alcohol to promote sobriety), although such incidents must be used carefully and with great sensitivity. Community members may be grieving, and it is important to make certain that any efforts be done compassionately with all families considered. These types of critical incidents are very powerful if used sensitively and can mobilize a community quickly.

At the vague awareness stage, community teams may be able to use interventions that include small-group events that are cosponsored by a church or civic organization (such as potlucks or potlatches) to increase community awareness and begin initiating action. Other specific interventions appropriate for this stage include use of newspaper editorials or articles and printing of local information in local media. It is important to be creative in considering the use of media and the cultural context in which the information is presented. National or statewide data may still make little impression on local residents, particularly when there are ethnicity differences involved. However, local survey data can be used to great advantage (e.g., results of school surveys, phone surveys,

Table 29.2   Community Readiness Strategies

1. No awareness
   Goal: To raise awareness of the issue
   - One-on-one visits with community leaders and members
   - Visit existing and established small groups to inform them of the issue
   - Make one-on-one phone calls to friends and potential supporters

2. Denial
   Goal: Raise awareness that the problem or issue exists in this community
   - Continue one-on-one visits and encourage those you have talked with to assist
   - Discuss descriptive local incidents related to the issue
   - Approach and engage local educational/health outreach programs to assist in the effort with flyers, posters, or brochures
   - Begin to point out media articles that describe local critical incidents
   - Prepare and submit articles for church bulletins, local newsletters, club newsletters, and so on
   - Present information to local related community groups

3. Vague awareness
   Goal: Raise awareness that the community can do something
   - Present information at local community events and unrelated community groups
   - Post flyers, posters, and billboards
   - Begin to initiate your own events (potlucks, potlatches, etc.) to present information on the issue
   - Conduct informal local surveys/interviews with community people by phone or door-to-door
   - Publish newspaper editorials and articles with general information but relate information to local situation

4. Preplanning
   Goal: Raise awareness with concrete ideas to combat condition
   - Introduce information about the issue through presentations and media
   - Visit and invest community leaders in the cause
   - Review existing efforts in community (curriculum, programs, activities, etc.) to determine who benefits and what the degree of success has been
   - Conduct local focus groups to discuss issues and develop strategies
   - Increase media exposure through radio and television public service announcements

5. Preparation
   Goal: Gathering existing information with which to plan strategies
   - Conduct school drug and alcohol surveys
   - Conduct community surveys
   - Sponsor a community picnic to kick off the effort
   - Present in-depth local statistics
   - Determine and publicize the costs of the problem to the community
   - Conduct public forums to develop strategies
   - Use key leaders and influential people to speak to groups and participate in local radio and television shows

6. Initiation
   Goal: Provide community-specific information
   - Conduct in-service training for professionals and paraprofessionals
   - Plan publicity efforts associated with start-up of program or activity
   - Attend meetings to provide updates on progress of the effort
   - Conduct consumer interviews to identify service gaps and improve existing services
   - Begin library or Internet search for resources and/or funding

(Continued)

Table 29.2 Continued

7. Stabilization
   Goal: Stabilize efforts/program
   - Plan community events to maintain support for the issue
   - Conduct training for community professionals
   - Conduct training for community members
   - Introduce program evaluation through training and newspaper articles
   - Conduct quarterly meetings to review progress, modify strategies
   - Hold special recognition events for local supporters or volunteers
   - Prepare and submit newspaper articles detailing progress and future plans
   - Begin networking between service providers, community systems

8. Confirmation/expansion
   Goal: Expand and enhance services
   - Formalize the networking with qualified service agreements
   - Prepare a community risk assessment profile
   - Publish a localized program services directory
   - Maintain a comprehensive database
   - Develop a local speakers bureau
   - Begin to initiate policy change through support of local city officials
   - Conduct media outreach on specific data trends related to the issue

9. Professionalization
   Goal: Maintain momentum and continue growth
   - Engage local business community and solicit financial support from them
   - Diversify funding resources
   - Continue more advanced training of professionals and paraprofessionals
   - Continue reassessment of issue and progress made
   - Use external evaluation and use feedback for program modification
   - Track outcome data for use with future grant requests
   - Continue progress reports for benefit of community leaders and local sponsorship

focus groups, small and specific public forums, etc.). It is important to present data about the community as a whole, however. Breaking down data and comparing ethnicities or other identifiable groups can be extremely detrimental to a community-wide effort, and we strongly caution against doing this. One exception to this would be if data contradict local stereotypes that assign the problem or issue to a specific subgroup. Even in such an instance, however, comparisons should be made with great caution.

At the preplanning stage, community teams focus on raising awareness with some concrete ideas about how to begin making changes. One primary goal is to gather information about what is already being done, who is doing it, and how these efforts are being accepted within the community. For example, when the problem is adolescent methamphetamine use, a valid and reliable school drug and alcohol survey can be initiated at the preparation stage so that accurate local data are available. These surveys can also serve as a diagnostic on where to begin interventions (i.e., at what age does use begin, where is use taking place, how easily is the substance obtained, etc.). Community telephone surveys could also be initiated to gain information about community attitudes and beliefs related to methamphetamine use, and in-depth local statistics can be gathered. Presenting information about the peripheral effects of methamphetamine use and how it is made also may be important to engage environmentalists and others who may think they have no vested interest in local methamphetamine use. This process broadens the base of concerned members of the community and increases the likelihood for success of efforts to prevent methamphetamine use. A key intervention at this stage may include conducting local focus groups or small public forums to put the problem in context and identify strengths and resources. Media interventions should still focus on local information, although they may begin to pull in some national data that can be used as a comparison. Stories should be developed about the various programs/curricula that are available for use so that people are aware of them and can comment with a broader knowledge base.

For communities in the stage of preparation, the goal is to gather existing information with the intention to make final decisions, plan strategies, and select and train people who may be involved in any interventions. The community team also makes decisions about whether to use preexisting curricula and educational materials. The team should consider what has been found elsewhere to work or not to work, as well as give careful thought to the demands of their unique cultural context. At this stage, it is helpful for the local teams to get as much information as possible (Internet, conferences, etc.) about the kinds of things that have worked in other communities similar to theirs. They can also begin to select ways to make their efforts culturally relevant to their community. More diverse focus groups, public forums, or call-in radio or television talk shows can be used to gain input from a wider representation of the community. When the efforts that are going to be started require it, either trained personnel are recruited or people are selected for the task and their training is started.

Communities at the initiation stage have selected culturally valid policies, programs, and activities and are putting them in place.

Community teams are encouraged to view resources broadly and to try to find local resources that can be maintained over the long haul. They know their community, and they know their resources and what types of activities or programs are appropriate for their community. To move to this stage, they have gained the support of leaders and of many community members. They can now focus their work toward getting policies in place and begin to conduct training for professionals, paraprofessionals, and community members. Another intervention at this level may be to conduct consumer interviews to gain more information about improving services and identify service gaps. Computer searches can be completed to identify potential resources that match community needs.

For communities in the stabilization stage, the goal is to stabilize or institutionalize their efforts. The interventions allow for planning of community-wide events that are likely to be attended by community members now, as opposed to when the community was at an earlier stage, because more people are invested in the process. Training can be offered to community professionals as well as community members, and the idea of evaluation can be introduced and adapted to the particular cultural context for determining the impact of the team's efforts and identifying other areas in which improvements are needed. Information about how well the efforts are working can be distributed to the public through appropriate local media. Special recognition events for local support—businesses, agencies, or volunteers—can be held to spark more interest in support. If there are programs based on grant funds or temporary funds, it is appropriate at this stage to try and find ways to maintain these programs with local resources. Formal networking between programs should be established. The community at this stage is generally applying the community readiness model to other important issues as well.

Communities at the confirmation/expansion stage focus on expanding and enhancing the services and policies they now have. Focus groups at this stage are geared more toward consumer satisfaction and identification of service gaps or needed modifications. For the rare community that has achieved the final stage, professionalism, interventions are aimed at maintaining the momentum and continuing growth. These communities maintain a very high level of data collection and analyses, track trends with sophisticated media, maintain and increase local business sponsorship of community events, and use external evaluation for consistent feedback and program modification. There is regular publication and dissemination of their learning to other programs and diversification of funding resources. For ethnic minority communities, this stage is frequently linked with efforts to transfer what they have learned to other ethnic minority communities who need their programs. In doing so, they may become community readiness trainers themselves.

All community groups or teams do not need to engage in all of the described activities; the teams are expected to have a good basis for knowing what is needed in their community, what is culturally appropriate and inappropriate, and what kinds of actions they are going to want to take. The community readiness model helps teams to recognize that when they appear to be blocked from moving forward to initiate or advance these programs, it usually means that they have misjudged the stage of readiness or ignored one or more dimensions of readiness. If this is the case, it is easy to move back and use strategies for earlier stages.

In summary, effective and sustainable community mobilization must be based on involving multiple systems within the community and using the unique resources and strengths of that community. Efforts must consider historical issues and be culturally

valid and accepted as long term in nature. The community readiness model takes these factors into account and provides a practical tool that communities can use to focus and direct their efforts toward a desired result, maximizing their resources and minimizing discouraging failures.

It is hoped that the communities that use this method will provide feedback to the authors on their experience with the model. In many ways, this model has evolved and been improved because of the feedback provided by those using it. Many communities have maintained contact with the Tri-Ethnic Center for Prevention Research, reporting on their experiences using the community readiness model. Most have experienced few difficulties in moving forward through the stages. For those communities that have not moved forward, the reasons are varied, but consistent themes have been political changes within the communities, tribes, or villages and/or personnel changes. For some, a critical community crisis has arisen that has forced the problem originally being addressed into the background as the community dealt with an even more immediate problem. The majority of communities that have used the model, however, have experienced success in developing and applying their strategies. Furthermore, many communities have indicated that they will continue to use the model not only to monitor their progress and develop their future plans regarding the issue they first addressed using the model but also to assist them in creating their own vision and addressing other community problems of concern.

The way you get meaning into your life is to devote yourself to loving others, devote yourself to your community around you, and devote yourself to creating something that gives you purpose and meaning.

—Morrie Schwartz, *Tuesdays With Morrie* (Albom, 1997, p. 127)

REFERENCES

Albom, M. (1997). *Tuesdays with Morrie: An old man, a young man, and life's greatest lesson.* New York: Bantam.

Center for Substance Abuse and Prevention Communication Team's Technical Assistance Bulletin Series. (1994). *Following specific guidelines will help you assess cultural competence in program design, application and management.* Washington, DC: Substance Abuse and Mental Health Services Administration.

Donnermeyer, J. F., Oetting, E. R., Plested, B. A., Edwards, R. W., Jumper-Thurman, P., & Littlethunder, L. (1997). Community readiness and prevention programs. *Journal of Community Development, 28*(1), 65-83.

Edwards, R. W., Jumper-Thurman, P., Plested, B. A., Oetting, E. R., & Swanson, L. (2000). Community readiness: Research to practice. *Journal of Community Psychology, 28*(3), 291-307.

Heinrich, R. K., Corbine, J. L., & Thomas, K. R. (1990). Counseling Native Americans. *Journal of Counseling & Development, 69,* 128-133.

Oetting, E. R., Donnermeyer, J. F., Plested, B. A., Edwards, R. W., Kelly, K., & Beauvais, F. (1995). Assessing community readiness for prevention. *International Journal of the Addictions, 30*(6), 659-683.

Plested, B. A., Jumper-Thurman, P., Edwards, R., & Oetting, E. R. (1998). Community readiness: A tool for community empowerment. *Prevention Researcher, 5*(2).

Quinn, D. (1996). *The story of B.* New York: Bantam.

Rappaport, J., & Simkins, R. (1991). Healing and empowering through community narrative. In K. Pargament, K. Maton, & R. Hess (Eds.), *Research, vision and action* (pp. 29-50). Binghamton, NY: Haworth.

Thurman, P. J., Plested, B. A., Edwards, R. W., & Oetting, E. R. (2001). Using the community readiness model in native communities. In J. Trimble & F. Beauvais (Eds.), *Health promotion and substance abuse prevention among American Indian and Alaska Native communities: Issues in cultural competence* (CSAP Monograph, Cultural Competence Series No. 9, DHHS Pub. No. (SMA) 99-3440, pp. 129-158). Rockville, MD: National Institute on Drug Abuse.

CHAPTER 30

Challenges of HIV Prevention in Diverse Communities

Sex, Culture, and Empowerment

BARBARA VANOSS MARÍN

University of California, San Francisco

HIV has been a particular scourge in communities of color since the epidemic began 20 years ago (Centers for Disease Control and Prevention [CDC], 1995, 1999; Selik, Castro, & Pappaioanou, 1988). The CDC estimates that approximately 75% of new HIV infections in the United States are occurring in communities of color (CDC, 2000). For communities already facing marginalization, poverty, and racism, HIV is certainly an unfair addition to their multiple disadvantages. In another way, HIV can be seen as the extension or outgrowth of those circumstances.

In communities of color, the underlying causes of HIV risk take the form of disempowerment or oppression, whether that be sexual abuse, homophobia, racism, or rigid gender role expectations. For prevention programs to be effective, they must address the larger context of HIV risk for community members. In this chapter, I will (a) present a review of the HIV prevention intervention literature for people of color and describe the key factors needed to develop successful interventions, (b) discuss the evidence for disempowerment as a risk factor for HIV, and (c) describe several recent culturally appropriate empowerment interventions to prevent HIV in communities of color.

KEY FACTORS IN SUCCESSFUL HIV PREVENTION INTERVENTIONS

In 1995, I was asked by the Office of Technology Assessment to develop a report about HIV prevention interventions for ethnic minorities (Marín, 1995). A search of the scientific literature was conducted of studies in which at least 50% of the sample was an ethnic minority group. No studies of Asian/Pacific Islanders or Native Americans were found. Of the 41 reports involving 39 different interventions, only 30 reported behavioral outcomes (e.g., condom use); the rest reported only knowledge or attitude changes. Of these 30 studies, only 8 reported large behavioral effects and 4 reported large effects in randomized trials. These 4 represent the best evidence that HIV prevention interventions can be effective with people of color. Obviously, such interventions are not easy to develop, given that so few interventions in the published literature showed convincing behavioral effects.

To learn as much as possible about what makes some interventions effective and others less effective, I compared these four studies (Jemmott, Jemmott, & Fong, 1992; Kelly et al., 1994; O'Donnell, San Doval, Duran, & O'Donnell, 1995; St. Lawrence, Brasfield, Jefferson, Alleyne, & O'Bannon, 1995) to the others on several dimensions. There were four key differences between these studies and the others reviewed: (a) preliminary work on the intervention, (b) formal behavior change theory, (c) skills practice and supportive discussion, and (d) targeting of the intervention.

Preliminary Work on the Intervention. Successful HIV prevention interventions reported substantial amounts of preliminary work on the intervention. To develop interventions for African American and Latino patients at sexually transmitted disease (STD) clinics, O'Donnell et al. (1995) conducted about 200 qualitative interviews with African American and Latino men and women who attended the clinic to identify their relevant gender roles and responsibilities regarding the introduction of condom use in primary and nonprimary relationships and their norms, attitudes, and values regarding condoms, as well as interviews with staff to increase feasibility of the intervention. The resulting videos reflect the family closeness and concerns about a family member's health typical among the Latinos, the language and vocabulary of people who go to the clinic, and the worries they have about using condoms, as well as

culturally appropriate ways to overcome specific barriers to condom use.

More than 10 years ago, while conducting studies with African American adolescents, John and Loretta Sweet Jemmot (Jemmott & Jemmott, 1990) showed the importance of hedonistic beliefs for this group. Those adolescents who believed that condoms and pleasure were compatible were more likely to use them. On the basis of this preliminary work, they developed an intervention for African American adolescent males (Jemmott et al., 1992) that emphasizes pleasurable ways to put on and use a condom. Subsequent work has shown that such carefully constructed interventions can be effective for at least 12 months (Jemmott, Jemmott, & Fong, 1998).

In work at a comprehensive community primary care clinic in a low-income neighborhood, Kelly et al. (1994) used careful pretesting with low-literacy clients to ensure comprehension of questionnaire items. Focus groups were used to identify role-playing situations that would be difficult for the women being targeted (e.g., initiating a discussion about condom use, postponing sex because the partner did not have a condom, or refuting a partner's concern that condoms imply a lack of trust). In addition, the intervention was designed to allow the women to take an active role in supporting each other's change efforts. This approach maximizes the cultural relevance of the intervention.

Working with African American adolescents, St. Lawrence et al. (1995) also used careful pretesting to revise their measures. Focus groups were used to develop scripts for high-risk situations, such as coercion to engage in unwanted sexual activity. Subsequently, the scenarios were rated by a separate group of students to determine whether they had encountered such a situation and whether the situation had been difficult for them to handle. Intervention sessions included a video specifically prepared for African American youth, values clarification about sexual decisions and pressures the youth faced, and discussion of past situations in which they had conceded to unwanted pressures.

In the process of developing these successful interventions, so much was learned that separate articles were often published describing the preliminary work (e.g., O'Donnell, San Doval, Duran, & DeJong, 1994). In marked contrast, none of the less successful interventions even mentioned preliminary work on the intervention or measures.

Formal Behavior Change Theory. All of the successful interventions that I reviewed used formal behavior change theory to develop their interventions. These interventions had used different theories of behavior change, including Social Cognitive Theory; the Theory of Reasoned Action; Information, Motivation, and Behavior Theory; and the AIDS Risk Reduction Model. So it is not the particular theory that is important but rather using theory when developing the components of an intervention. Although a few of the less successful interventions also cited theories, most did not, meaning that the intervention team had not articulated a vision of how or why individuals would change their behavior. Many less successful interventions implicitly assumed that providing information about the person's HIV risk and how to use condoms would result in change.

Skills Practice and Supportive Discussion. Less successful interventions often relied on a more didactic approach, but successful ones had high levels of participant involvement. Participants practiced suggesting a condom to an intransigent partner, as well as putting one on. Whether discussion was only 20 minutes, following the STD video (O'Donnell et al., 1995), or involved five 90-minute sessions (Kelly et al., 1994), it was caring and non-judgmental. The researchers observed the

gentle reminders that clients gave each other that they cannot be sure if a partner is safe or that they don't deserve an abusive partner. In some cases, participants would offer their home to someone else in an unsafe situation. High levels of interaction ensure that the topics discussed have relevance to the participants.

Targeting of the Intervention. Successful interventions were more likely to match the gender and ethnicity of participants and facilitators. Of those showing success in a randomized trial, 3 of 4 matched the participants and facilitators on ethnicity, whereas only 14 of the other 35 studies matched on ethnicity. Often these other interventions were given to groups of mixed ethnicity. Matching on gender and ethnicity means that the facilitator is more likely to share the cultural background, language, and worldview of the participants. This greater understanding allows for more skillful intervention and rapport in group discussions. The concerns of that particular group can be addressed while their worldview and culture are honored. Instead of being invisible, misunderstood, or fearful to speak, participants can feel at home.

Based on this literature review, the key processes in HIV prevention intervention development are the following: (a) Consider what is known and use or develop theory about the process of behavior change, (b) involve the participant in skills practice and supportive discussion, (c) match gender and ethnicity of intervenors and clients for maximum effect, and (d) use preliminary work to obtain in-depth understanding of factors and context that are limiting behavior change as well as values and beliefs that might motivate change. By having a thorough understanding of forces that disempower people from making sexually healthy and responsible decisions, many individuals can address these forces.

HIV RISK AND DISEMPOWERMENT

Disempowerment occurs when someone feels overpowered, out of control, or disabled by some circumstance in their lives. Disempowerment can occur due to an outside force, such as racism, abuse, or homophobia, but sadly, these phenomena often become accepted and internalized by the individual. Individuals who have experienced disempowering circumstances may feel or be unable to protect themselves in certain sexual situations. A number of factors related to HIV risk can reduce an individual's power: homophobia, sexual abuse, traditional gender roles, racism, poverty, sexual silence, and differences in age of partners.

Homophobia. One of the groups hardest hit by the HIV epidemic has been gay men, and gay men of color have been hardest hit of all (CDC, 1995). This situation is particularly difficult because of the serious stigmatization of homosexual behaviors in communities of color. In African American and Latino communities, homophobia is often expressed as a conspiracy of silence, which may be particularly disempowering. Asians are also noted to be highly homophobic, with homosexuality bringing shame and loss of face on the household. Most Asian cultures also place high value on sons marrying and having children (Choi, Yep, & Kumekawa, 1998).

Those who experience greater levels of homophobia report more sexual risk behavior. In Rafael Diaz's (1998) landmark book, he reported on his in-depth interviews with 75 Latino gay men. He recounted the shame associated with homosexuality, the belief that a gay man is hurting his family by being gay, and the sense of loneliness and isolation many Latino gay men feel. He also made the links between the homophobia that men experience and internalize and their HIV risk. Confirming this vision, in his recent survey of 900 Latino gay men in New York, Miami, and Los Angeles, Diaz found that the majority of men had experienced high levels of homophobia as children or adults. Those reporting higher levels of experienced homophobia also reported higher levels of sexual risk than men experiencing less homophobia (Diaz, Ayala, & Marín, 2000).

A comparison of risky and protected sexual encounters of gay men revealed striking differences in the emotional states of the men during the different encounters (Diaz, 1999b). Characteristics of risky encounters included a painful emotional need prior to the encounter, sex that was disconnected from one's emotions, abuse of drugs or alcohol to facilitate sex that is seen as frightening or undesirable, and perceptions of low sexual control. Societal homophobia plays an important role in creating the disconnections between people and their sexual desires, by causing men to view same-sex activities as disgusting, which can translate into self-loathing. The alarmingly high suicide rates among homosexual adolescents are likely a direct result of this rejection of self.

Sexual Abuse. Childhood sexual abuse is surprisingly widespread, being reported by more than one in every four women and one in eight men (Finkelhor, Hotaling, Lewis, & Smith, 1990). Although some studies suggest that it is not necessarily more prevalent among ethnic minorities (Finkelhor, 1993), other evidence questions this view, at least among men (Doll et al., 1992; Hernandez, Lodico, & DiClemente, 1993; Holmes & Slap, 1998).

Sexual abuse in childhood has been associated with risky sexual behavior in men and women, gay and straight adults. These behaviors include earlier sexual initiation; higher levels of rape and revictimization; greater numbers of sexual partners; less protection from pregnancy, HIV, and STDs; and more drug and alcohol use (Browning & Laumann,

1997; Greenberg et al., 1999; Hernandez et al., 1993; Jinich et al., 1998; Roosa, Tein, Reinholtz, & Angelini, 1997). Groups commonly associated with high HIV risk, such as injection drug users, homeless, runaways, and sex workers, all report disproportionate levels of childhood sexual abuse.

There are multiple ways that childhood sexual abuse can lead to more risk in adulthood (Allers, Benjack, White, & Rousey, 1993). For many, abuse (and this may include physical and emotional abuse) results in a need for dissociation from the painful feelings that arise. Thus, many heavy drug and alcohol users report histories of abuse. Abused children often run away, leading to lives of homelessness or prostitution. Because the abuser is someone who is more powerful, both physically and psychologically than the child, abuse violates the child's boundaries. In many cases, this will lead to poor boundaries and to poor partner selection, as adults may see abuse as love. Revictimization, in the form of domestic violence and adult rape, is a common sequela of abuse (Allers et al., 1993).

Traditional Gender Roles. Gender role beliefs can be disempowering to both men and women (Marín, Gómez, Tschann, & Gregorich, 1997). In many cultures, sex is seen as a place for men to prove their masculinity (Diaz, 1998; Marín & Gómez, 1996). To prove manhood, men may seek multiple sexual partners, take various risks, or avoid showing fear or sadness. In a large study of young men in the United States, traditional attitudes toward masculinity were associated with having more sexual partners in the past year, a less intimate relationship with the current sexual partner, and a greater belief that relationships between men and women are adversarial (Pleck, Sonenstein, & Ku, 1993). In addition, these attitudes are associated with less condom use (Pleck et al., 1993). The need to prove one's masculinity

(and women's expected role of acquiescing to men's desires) sets up two oppressive forces: homophobia and sexual coercion.

In many cultures, the need to prove masculinity combines with the belief that sexual desire and sexual activity are out of men's control, a belief held by both women and men. As a consequence, sexual violence may be condoned if women "tease." Sexual coercion is common and may be seen in some cultures as the expected male activity (Caceres, Marín, & Hudes, 2000; Koss & Oros, 1982). Men who endorse traditional gender roles and masculinity ideology are more likely to engage in sexual coercion (Marín et al., 1997) and less likely to recognize it as rape (Luddy & Thompson, 1997). In our work with Latinos, those who expressed traditional gender role beliefs tended to be less acculturated than less traditional men (Marín et al., 1997). The correlation of gender role beliefs and acculturation suggests that these are cultural values that may be modifiable as people acculturate or through intervention.

Another way that traditional gender role beliefs may be oppressive is their role in promoting discomfort about sex (Marín et al., 1997; Pleck et al., 1993). Among Latinos, both women and men endorse the belief that women should not know as much about sex as men, a belief that promotes embarrassment and discomfort with sex. A survey of Latino unmarried adults in the United States found that 44% felt uncomfortable having sex with the lights on (Marín & Gómez, 1999). It is difficult to put a condom on in the dark.

Sexual Silence. In Western society, sexual behavior is viewed with discomfort and is considered titillating, immoral, and dangerous by turns. Societal beliefs that sex should not be talked about have produced high levels of teen pregnancy in the United States, along with massive funding for programs promoting abstinence until marriage. Sexual abuse and rape are often underreported and denied by those involved. Homosexual behavior is hidden, and even longtime partners may be unrecognized by families. Sexual silence results in lack of access to needed information or protection, emotional pain, and a lack of validation of one's feelings and identity.

In Asian cultures, sex is considered an inappropriate, even taboo, topic for discussion. This sexual silence combines with taboo subjects of death and disease and makes HIV extremely stigmatized (Chin & Kroesen, 1999) and sexual discussion very difficult.

Racism. Racism and discrimination are pervasive forces in the United States. They harm health in various ways, including increased distress, higher blood pressure, and increased depression (Krieger, 1999). Racism forms the social context of people's lives, the "depleted soil" in which people of color grow (Clark, Anderson, Clark, & Williams, 1999; Jones, 2000). One would expect racism to have pervasive and oppressive effects on sexuality. In defining one race as better, more attractive, or more powerful, people of color suffer. For example, among young African American girls, poor ethnic identity is associated with greater sexual risk and more drug use (Belgrave, Marín, & Chambers, 2000). Diaz et al. (2000) have found multiple ways that racism affects the daily lives of Latino gay men. In their study of 900 Latino gay men, they found that men who reported more risky sex had experienced more racism as adults and as children and more often reported being turned down for sex due to their race, having lovers who were more interested in their race than in them, and feeling uncomfortable in a White gay club (Diaz et al., 2000).

Poverty. Poverty and the lack of sufficient resources can create situations in which sexual safety is less important than survival. Homeless youth will often engage in survival sex, which can be abusive (Rotheram-Borus, Reid, & Rosario, 1994). Sex without a condom pays better than sex with a condom. But poverty also leads to a sense of hopelessness, which in turn can lead people to early and unprotected sexual encounters.

Age Differences. Disempowerment can be subtle at times. Recently, there has been growing concern about the role of older men in impregnating young teens and preteens (Darroch, Landry, & Oslak, 1999). In a sexual relationship, age difference is likely to be important, making the older man the one who wields more power. Data from sixth-grade students indicate that having an older boyfriend or girlfriend is associated with reporting unwanted sexual advances and with having sex (Marín, Coyle, Gómez, Carvajal, & Kirby, 2000). Latino couples are particularly likely to involve older men with young women. Interestingly, the girls involved in these relationships usually report them as wanted and desirable, although some report regrets after they end (Elstein & Davis, 1997; Phillips, n.d.). So the oppressive nature of these relationships may not be readily apparent to those involved.

Summary. People can be "kept down" or disempowered by a number of forces in society or circumstances in their lives, including racism, homophobia, poverty, and abuse. These circumstances, which often are more common for communities of color, result in increased HIV risk for several reasons. Poverty, racism, and homophobia can lead to a sense of alienation or estrangement from society. The resulting lack of community feeling, sense of lone- liness, and low self-esteem may create a sense of not caring about others or about the consequences of one's actions. The use of alcohol and drugs to ease the pain of abuse or low self-esteem may also lead to sexual risk. Hopelessness is an important consequence of poverty and abuse and may result in lack of concern for oneself or others. Oppressive forces such as traditional gender roles reinforce the belief that men cannot control their sexual impulses and that sex is not to be discussed. These beliefs, held by both men and women, can invite the use of force in sexual situations by some men.

HIV PREVENTION INTERVENTIONS

As we saw earlier, HIV prevention interventions for communities of color are difficult to develop, requiring extensive preliminary work, careful attention to theory, and thoughtful implementation. To be effective, such interventions must address the unique culture and contexts of each ethnic group. In addition, such interventions must address the disempowering forces in people's lives. There are many ways that individuals can be disempowered in their sexual lives. Although the primary mechanism is often experiences of childhood sexual or physical abuse, other factors such as homophobia, racism, and gender roles can also contribute. For gay men of color who are at highest risk in the current U.S. HIV epidemic (CDC, 1995, 2000), the sources of disempowerment (homophobia, racism, poverty, and often sexual abuse) are multiple.

EXAMPLES OF EMPOWERMENT INTERVENTIONS

Three recently published interventions provide examples of methods for empowering people in the sexual domain and beyond. One (Shain et al., 1999) focuses on high-risk women, another on adolescents (Allen, Philliber, & Herrling, 1997), and the other

on Latino gay men (Diaz, 1998). Each addresses the specific forms of disempowerment being experienced by that group, and each was developed based on a thorough understanding of the needs and strengths of the group. Each has different things to teach us about how to develop such interventions.

High-Risk Women. Women experiencing sexually transmitted diseases are often disempowered because the disease is frequently caused by their partners' behavior rather than their own (Finer, Darroch, & Singh, 1999). The intervention for women discussed below is actually two interventions, one for African American women and one for Latino women. These women were identified through STD clinics and participated in a randomized trial comparing the intervention to a control condition (n = 617). The intervention consisted of three small-group sessions lasting 3 to 4 hours each. A key finding of this research is that those who attended the intervention condition had fewer sexually transmitted diseases at follow-up than those in the control condition (16% vs. 27%), and this reduction was even greater at 12 months than at 6 months after the intervention. This increasing effect over time is a very unusual finding and suggests that the women continued to change their lives in helpful ways long after the intervention had ended.

The intervention itself incorporates the key factors of successful interventions that were identified earlier. It was based on extensive preliminary work, including 25 focus groups, 102 in-depth interviews, and 13 pretests of the intervention itself. It used the AIDS Risk Reduction Model as a theoretical guide while adapting certain elements to reflect the situation of the women to be served. The intervention involved nonjudgmental discussion of the issues of importance to the women and practice of needed skills, such as communicating and negotiating about sex and erotic application of condoms. Facilitators were matched with clients on both gender and ethnicity.

The intervention itself incorporated many aspects of culturally sensitive interventions as defined by Bernal, Bonilla, and Bellido (1995), who identified factors that must be considered in doing culturally sensitive mental health treatment research. Many of these factors are applicable to the development of HIV prevention interventions. Eight factors were clearly addressed by the intervention developed by Shain and her colleagues (1999): language, persons, metaphors, content, concepts, goals, methods, and context.

Language refers not only to whether English or Spanish was available, depending on the needs of the women, but also to the use of culturally syntonic language, that is, the idioms and understandings of sexuality and risk that are common to high-risk women from these ethnic groups. Using culturally appropriate language may include using street terms for sexual activity. Also, because language is the bearer of culture, group leaders who speak Spanish should be familiar with cultural issues, such as the greater sexual discomfort common to Latino women.

Persons refers to the ethnic/racial similarities or differences between the intervenor and client. In this case, all group leaders were members of the same ethnic group as the clients. This match provides comfort and understanding and is probably a key factor in establishing the openness that is needed for frank discussion to take place.

Metaphors refers to the symbols and concepts of the population in question. In this case, for example, the intervention took advantage of a common phrase used in African American communities, the idea of doing something "behind" someone. Usually, this refers to the idea of doing something after someone else, as in eating off the same plate after someone else has finished, and it is seen as inappropriate. The designers of the intervention used this term to discuss the idea of having sex with someone who has had multiple partners, having sex "behind" those partners.

Content refers to cultural knowledge, values, and customs. In this intervention, the Latino concern for family was repeatedly used as a way to motivate the women to protect themselves and those they loved. Another content area that was addressed was the belief that women could assess their partners' risk by looking. This common belief was challenged in a nonjudgmental way.

Intervention *concepts* refers to the ways that the clients are conceptualized by the intervenors. In this case, rather than pathologize the clients, the intervenors saw them as being actively engaged in defining their sexual reality.

Treatment *goals* must be shared by clients and intervenors to maximize the effectiveness of an intervention. Instead of the usual goal of condom use at each intercourse occasion, the intervention was also designed to reduce untreated infections. This goal was more in line with the women's needs and stated desires, and it had a direct impact on the methods used.

Methods refers to the types of activities involved in the intervention. In this case, a variety of methods made this intervention more culturally sensitive and context specific. For one, meals, an important cultural metaphor for family and caring, were provided to increase bonding. In service of the goal of reducing untreated infections, the intervention addressed easy methods of recognizing whether one's partner currently has an STD lesion.

Finally, *context* involves a careful consideration of the specific contexts of the women's lives. In this case, it became important to address the concern of the African American women that there are low numbers of available men. Although the intervenors could not offer ready solutions to this problem, the inclusion of this topic among the points for discussion allowed the women to consider the issue and demonstrated the concern and cultural knowledge of intervention developers.

This intervention illustrates clearly the importance and effectiveness of carefully developing approaches that address the problems and contexts of the clients. Many of these women struggled with multiple sources of disempowerment, including racism, abuse, and traditional gender role beliefs. Yet this short-term intervention was effective in reducing their exposure to sexually transmitted diseases. It gave women the tools of empowerment, such as the skill to identify untreated STDs in their partners, as well as the relationship skills to assert themselves more effectively. Shain et al. (1999) hypothesized that the delayed effect of the intervention could be due to the time it took for women to get out of unhealthy relationships, a clear sign of their increased empowerment.

Marginalized Adolescents. Adolescents in inner-city environments face multiple sources of disempowerment, including poverty, lack of job opportunities, and racism. These factors can lead to a sense of hopelessness. Most HIV prevention interventions directed at young people focus exclusively on sexual behavior and do not address the context of hopelessness that can undermine the motivation to act safely.

An unusual program has been developed and evaluated that takes a different approach to adolescent risk (Allen et al., 1997). It involves a structured volunteer community service experience. Students spend 20 to 30 hours per year volunteering at a community agency, such as nursing homes and hospitals, walkathons, and peer tutoring. Also, each week, they discuss the experience in the classroom. Sexual behavior and school achievement were not part of the classroom discussion, yet these behaviors were affected by the intervention. In a randomized study, 25 sites nationwide randomized either interested students or classrooms to treatment ($n = 342$)

and control ($n = 352$) groups. The students in this study were disadvantaged, and 67% were African American. After 12 months, the differences between treatment and control were striking—half as many students had been suspended from school, failed a course, or had a pregnancy (4% vs. 10%) in the treatment group than in the control group.

Why is this program effective at preventing pregnancy when it does not address sexual behavior? Allen et al. (1997) hypothesized that problem behaviors may have a common underlying cause. A program that enhances students' sense of autonomy and competence may affect their relationship skills as well as provide them with the belief that they have a future and the motivation to stay in school and avoid pregnancy. The authors also believed that helping may be therapeutic for the helper. In detailed analyses of the program, they found that those students who responded well to the program felt safe, listened to, and respected during the program. So a sense of one's own competence is an essential ingredient for adolescent growth and empowerment.

Latino Gay Men. Gay men of color struggle with the racism and homophobia of the larger society as well as their internal sense of shame or guilt. These oppressors, along with high rates of sexual abuse, have been shown to be strongly related to risky sexual behavior (Diaz et al., 2000). In response to this situation, Rafael Diaz has developed a program that addresses the underlying factors associated with HIV risk in Latino gay men (Diaz, 1998).

As with the other successful programs described here, this intervention is based on extensive in-depth interviews, a theoretical framework to explain risk (Diaz, 1998), and solid cultural understanding of the men who receive it. Although not formally evaluated as the others have been, the program has been ongoing in San Francisco for more than 4 years and is well attended. Informal evaluation suggests that important changes occur as a result of participation (Diaz, 1999a).

The program is designed to reduce internalized homophobia, increase sexual self-observation, and provide social support and a sense of family. It uses small-group discussion with guided questions. Many men report that it provides the only opportunity they have to discuss their sexuality and relationships in a nonsexual context. The program combats the secrecy and shame that homophobia induces, and it gives men an opportunity to discuss their sexual behavior and consider changes. This self-observation combats the common belief that sexual impulses and actions are not under their control, a belief with roots in oppressive traditional gender roles.

EFFECTS OF DISEMPOWERMENT

Rosenfeld and Lewis (1993) indicated that the effects of childhood sexual abuse include depression, feelings of isolation, shame, low self-esteem, and feelings of loss of control. Other forms of disempowerment discussed above such as homophobia, racism, and traditional gender roles can produce similar results. All of these effects impede responsible and healthy sexual behavior by causing a person to seek sex to alleviate other painful feelings and limiting his or her ability to set limits and choose partners and situations wisely.

To combat disempowerment, individuals must be helped to recognize how their painful feelings (shame, loneliness) and experiences (discrimination) may motivate and support unhealthy behavior. In addition, programs may be able to build self-esteem and a sense of competence and worth by offering opportunities for people to promote change in their communities.

SUMMARY

It is no coincidence that ethnic minorities in the United States have the highest rates of HIV incidence and prevalence as well as experience multiple forms of disempowerment, including racism, poverty, and homophobia. The disempowerment can be addressed in culturally appropriate ways, and a few programs have successfully reduced HIV risk by addressing the culture and context of risk and building self-knowledge, skills, autonomy, and self-esteem. Effective programs require extensive development and testing to make them sensitive to the language, metaphors, values, and context of clients. Effective programs can empower clients to overcome gender role stereotypes, hopelessness, poverty, homophobia, and racism.

REFERENCES

Allen, J., Philliber, S., & Herrling, S. (1997). Preventing teen pregnancy and academic failure: Experimental evaluation of a developmentally-based approach. *Child Development, 64*(4), 729-742.

Allers, C., Benjack, K., White, J., & Rousey, J. (1993). HIV vulnerability and the adult survivor of childhood sexual abuse. *Child Abuse & Neglect, 17,* 291-298.

Belgrave, F., Marín, B. V., & Chambers, D. (2000). Cultural, contextual and interpersonal predictors of risky sexual attitudes among urban African American females in early adolescence. *Cultural Diversity and Ethnic Minority Psychology, 6*(3), 309-322.

Bernal, G., Bonilla, J., & Bellido, C. (1995). Ecological validity and cultural sensitivity for outcome research: Issues for the cultural adaptation and development of psychosocial treatments for Hispanics. *Journal of Abnormal Child Psychology, 23*(1), 67-82.

Browning, C. R., & Laumann, E. O. (1997). Sexual contact between children and adults: A life course perspective. *American Sociological Review, 62,* 540-560.

Caceres, C., Marín, B. V., & Hudes, E. S. (2000). Sexual coercion among youth and young adults in Lima, Peru. *Journal of Adolescent Health, 27,* 361-367.

Centers for Disease Control and Prevention (CDC). (1995). Update: Trends in AIDS among men-who-have-sex-with-men—United States, 1989-1994. *Morbidity and Mortality Weekly Report, 44*(21), 401-404.

Centers for Disease Control and Prevention (CDC). (1999). AIDS cases diagnosed in 1997 and 1998 by sex, race/ethnicity, age at diagnosis, and risk exposure. *HIV/AIDS Surveillance Supplemental Report, 5*(3), 1-12.

Centers for Disease Control and Prevention (CDC). (2000). *HIV prevention strategic plan through 2005.* Atlanta, GA: Division of HIV, Center for HIV, STD, and TB Prevention.

Chin, D., & Kroesen, K. W. (1999). Disclosure of HIV infection among Asian/Pacific Islander American women: Cultural stigma and support. *Cultural Diversity and Ethnic Minority Psychology, 5*(3), 222-235.

Choi, K., Yep, G. A., & Kumekawa, E. (1998). HIV prevention among Asian and Pacific Islander men who have sex with men: A critical review of theoretical models and directions for future research. *AIDS Education and Prevention, 10*(Suppl. A), 19-30.

Clark, R., Anderson, N. B., Clark, V. R., & Williams, D. R. (1999). Racism as a stressor for African Americans. *American Psychologist, 54*(10), 805-816.

Darroch, J. E., Landry, D., & Oslak, S. (1999). Age differences between sexual partners in the United States. *Family Planning Perspectives, 31*(4), 160-167.

Diaz, R. (1998). *Latino gay men and HIV: Culture, sexuality and risk behavior.* New York: Routledge.

Diaz, R. (1999a). *Behavioral risk assessment: Hermanos de Luna y Sol program.* San Francisco: Mission Neighborhood Health Center.

Diaz, R. (1999b). Trips to Fantasy Island: Contexts of risky sex for San Francisco gay men. *Sexualities, 2*(1), 89-112.

Diaz, R. M., Ayala, G., & Marín, B. V. (2000). Latino gay men and HIV: Risk behavior as a sign of oppression. *Focus: A Guide to AIDS Research and Counseling, 15*(7), 1-4.

Doll, L. S., Joy, D., Bartholow, B. N., Harrison, J. S., Bolan, G., Douglas, J., et al. (1992). Self-reported childhood and adolescent sexual abuse among adult homosexual and bisexual men. *Child Abuse & Neglect, 16*(6), 855-864.

Elstein, S. G., & Davis, N. (1997). *Sexual relationships between adult males and young teen girls: Exploring the legal and social responses.* Washington, DC: American Bar Association, Center on Children and the Law.

Finer, L., Darroch, J., & Singh, S. (1999). Sexual partnership patterns as a behavioral risk factor for sexually transmitted diseases. *Family Planning Perspectives, 31*(5), 228-236.

Finkelhor, D. (1993). Epidemiological factors in the clinical identification of child sexual abuse. *Child Abuse & Neglect, 17,* 67-70.

Finkelhor, D., Hotaling, G., Lewis, I. A., & Smith, C. (1990). Sexual abuse in a national survey of adult men and women: Prevalence characteristics, and risk factors. *Child Abuse & Neglect, 14,* 19-28.

Gant, L. M., Green, W., Stewart, P. A., Wheeler, D. P., & Wright, E. M. (1998). HIV/AIDS and African Americans: Assumptions, myths and realities. In

P. A. S. Gant & V. J. Lynch (Eds.), *Social workers speak out on the HIV/AIDS crisis: Voices from and to African-American communities* (pp. 1-12). Westport, CT: Praeger.

Greenberg, J., Hennessy, M., Lifshay, J., Kahn-Krieger, S., Bartelli, D., Downer, A., & Bliss, M. (1999). Childhood sexual abuse and its relationship to high-risk behavior in women volunteering for an HIV and STD prevention intervention. *AIDS and Behavior, 3*(2), 149-156.

Hernandez, J. T., Lodico, M., & DiClemente, R. J. (1993). The effects of child abuse and race on risk-taking in male adolescents. *Journal of the National Medical Association, 85*(8), 593-597.

Holmes, W. C., & Slap, G. B. (1998). Sexual abuse of boys: Definition, prevalence, correlates, sequelae, and management. *Journal of the American Medical Association, 280*(21), 1855-1862.

Jemmott, J., III, Jemmott, L. S., & Fong, G. T. (1998). Abstinence and safer sex HIV risk-reduction interventions for African American adolescents. *Journal of the American Medical Association, 279*(19), 1529-1536.

Jemmott, J., III, Jemmott, L. S., & Fong, J. (1992). Reductions in HIV risk-associated sexual behaviors among Black male adolescents: Effects of an AIDS prevention intervention. *American Journal of Public Health, 82*(3), 372-377.

Jemmott, L. S., & Jemmott, J., III. (1990). Sexual knowledge, attitudes and risky sexual behavior among inner-city Black male adolescents. *Journal of Adolescent Research, 5,* 346-369.

Jinich, S., Paul, J. P., Stall, R., Acree, M., Kegeles, S., Hoff, C., & Coates, T. J. (1998). Childhood sexual abuse and HIV risk-taking behavior among gay and bisexual men. *AIDS and Behavior, 2*(1), 41-51.

Jones, C. P. (2000). Levels of racism: A theoretical framework and a gardener's tale. *American Journal of Public Health, 90*(8), 1212-1215.

Kelly, J., Murphy, D. A., Washington, C., Wilson, T., Kobb, J., Davis, D., Ledezma, G., & Davantes, B. (1994). The effect of HIV/AIDS intervention groups for high-risk women in urban clinics. *American Journal of Public Health, 84*(12), 1918-1922.

Koss, M. P., & Oros, C. J. (1982). Sexual Experiences Survey: A research instrument investigating sexual aggression and victimization. *Journal of Consulting and Clinical Psychology, 50*(3), 455-457.

Krieger, N. (1999). Embodying inequality: A review of concepts, measures, and methods for studying health consequences of discrimination. *International Journal of Health Sciences, 29*(2), 295-352.

Luddy, J. G., & Thompson, E. H. (1997). Masculinities and violence: A father-son comparison of gender traditionality and perceptions of heterosexual rape. *Journal of Family Psychology, 11*(4), 462-477.

Marín, B. (1995). *Analysis of AIDS prevention among African Americans and Latinos in the United States.* Washington, DC: American Psychological Association Office on AIDS.

Marín, B. V., Coyle, K., Gómez, C. A., Carvajal, S., & Kirby, D. (2000). Older boyfriends and girlfriends increase risk of sexual initiation in young adolescents. *Journal of Adolescent Health, 27,* 409-418.

Marín, B. V., & Gómez, C. (1996). Latino culture and sex: Implications for HIV prevention. In M. C. Zea & J. García (Eds.), *Psychological interventions and research with Latino populations* (pp. 73-93). Needham Heights, MA: Allyn & Bacon.

Marín, B. V., & Gómez, C. A. (1999). Latinos and HIV: Cultural issues in AIDS prevention. In P. T. Cohen, M. A. Sande, & P. A. Volberding (Eds.), *The AIDS knowledge base* (3rd ed., pp. 917-924). Philadelphia: Williams & Wilkins.

Marín, B. V., Gómez, C., Tschann, J., & Gregorich, S. (1997). Condom use in unmarried Latino men: A test of cultural constructs. *Health Psychology, 16*(5), 458-467.

O'Donnell, L., San Doval, A., Duran, R., & DeJong, W. (1994). Reducing AIDS and other STDs among inner-city Hispanics: The use of qualitative research in the development of video-based patient education. *AIDS Education & Prevention, 6,* 140-153.

O'Donnell, L., San Doval, A., Duran, R., & O'Donnell, C. (1995). Video-based sexually transmitted disease patient education: Its impact on condom acquisition. *American Journal of Public Health, 85*(6), 817-822.

Phillips, L. M. (n.d.). *Unequal partners: Exploring power and consent in adult-teen relationships.* Morristown: Planned Parenthood of Greater Northern New Jersey.

Pleck, J. H., Sonenstein, F. L., & Ku, L. C. (1993). Masculinity ideology: Its impact on adolescent males' heterosexual relationships. *Journal of Social Issues, 49*(3), 11-29.

Roosa, M. W., Tein, J., Reinholtz, C., & Angelini, P. (1997). The relationship of childhood sexual abuse to teenage pregnancy. *Journal of Marriage and the Family, 59,* 119-130.

Rosenfeld, S., & Lewis, D. (1993). The hidden effect of childhood sexual abuse on adolescent and young adult HIV prevention: Rethinking AIDS education, program development, and policy. *AIDS and Public Policy Journal, 8*(4), 181-186.

Rotheram-Borus, M., Reid, H., & Rosario, M. (1994). Factors mediating changes in sexual HIV risk behaviors among gay and bisexual male adolescents. *American Journal of Public Health, 84*(12), 1938-1946.

Selik, R., Castro, K., & Pappaioanou, M. (1988). Racial/ethnic differences in risk of AIDS. *American Journal of Public Health, 78,* 1539-1545.

Shain, R. N., Piper, J. M., Newton, E. R., Perdue, S. T., Ramos, R., Champion, J. D., & Guerra, F. A. (1999). A randomized, controlled trial of a behavioral intervention to prevent sexually transmitted disease among minority women. *New England Journal of Medicine, 340,* 93-100.

St. Lawrence, J., Brasfield, T., Jefferson, K., Alleyne, E., & O'Bannon, R. A., III. (1995). Cognitive behavioral intervention to reduce African-American adolescents' risk for HIV infection. *Journal of Consulting and Clinical Psychology, 63*(2), 221-237.

CHAPTER 31

Reducing Prejudice and Racism Through Counselor Training as a Primary Prevention Strategy

PAUL B. PEDERSEN
University of Hawaii

Reducing prejudice and racism is too often perceived as a secondary or tertiary prevention strategy, in reaction to events that have already occurred. This chapter will describe the reduction of prejudice and racism through three counselor training approaches as a "primary" prevention strategy. Inaccurate attributions that result from prejudice and/or racism translate into defensive disengagement by counselors and their clients, each trying to protect the truth as he or she perceives it. By preventing mental health providers from making inaccurate assumptions about other cultures in the first place, multicultural counselor training can protect both the providers and consumers from misattributions. Ponterotto and Pedersen (1993) presented a model for improving interracial and interethnic relations that emphasizes the need for training programs to be preventive, developmental, and long term. This chapter will seek to build on the Ponterotto and Pedersen foundation.

Cultural, racial, and ethnic prejudice depends on preconceived judgments about individuals from selected groups that are not based on actual experience with the individuals who are prejudged. These prejudices are generalized beliefs assumed without evidence to be true despite disconfirming information to the contrary. Prejudice is a learned response to attitudes and beliefs of individuals based on misinterpretations of experience, and because it is learned, it can also be unlearned.

Racism is defined by Ridley (1995) as "any behavior or pattern of behavior that tends to systematically deny access to opportunities or privileges to members of one racial group while perpetuating access to opportunities and privileges to members of another racial group" (p. 28). Racism is typically directed against minority members at the institutional as well as the individual level in overt or covert forms. When racist behavior is based on race-based prejudices, it is intentional, but often racism can be unintentional when individuals are unaware of the effects their behaviors have on others (Ridley, Espelage, & Rubinstein, 1997).

The reduction of prejudice and racism begins with appropriate teaching and training approaches. This chapter will identify teaching and training techniques that have been widely used in teaching about racial prejudice, broadly defined to include populations identified by ethnographic, demographic, status, and formal or informal affiliations. These approaches will include (a) the triad training model for hearing the positive and negative internal dialogue of a culturally different client in counseling; (b) a synthetic culture laboratory for finding common ground without giving up cultural integrity among Alpha (high power distance), Beta (strong uncertainty avoidance), Gamma (high individualism), and Delta (strong masculine) synthetic cultures based on Geert Hofstede's (1980, 1986) 55-country database; and (c) the development of multiculturally skilled group-work leaders through the application of Ivey's (Ivey, Pedersen, & Ivey, 2001) microcounseling model to the cultural group context. The appropriateness of structured and experiential exercises for identifying culturally learned assumptions and cultural patterns will be emphasized throughout.

THE TRAINED COUNSELOR

Culture-centered training results in movement from simple to more complex thinking about multicultural counseling relationships. A trained counselor depends less on stereotypes and is better prepared to comprehend the influence of a cultural context on the counseling process. The trained counselor has a wider range of response alternatives to meet the needs of each cultural context. The trained counselor can describe each cultural context from the contrasting viewpoints of culturally different participants. The trained counselor can identify and understand the "source" or basic underlying cultural assumptions of a problem. The trained counselor can keep track of the "salient" culture for a client as it changes over time and place. The trained counselor can account for her or his own culturally learned assumptions in the counseling process (Midgette & Meggert, 1991).

Several multicultural training models have been suggested. Ridley, Mendoza, and Kanitz (1994) described multicultural counseling training (MIT) as a framework that moves from training philosophy to learning objectives, instructional strategies, program designs, and evaluation-matching instructional strategies with learning objectives. Cushner and Brislin (1997) described training alternatives, which divide experiential/discover approaches from didactic/expository approaches and culture-general from culture-specific foci. Sue et al. (1998) described a three-stage developmental sequence that moves from awareness of culturally learned assumptions to knowledge of culturally relevant facts and finally to appropriate skills to bring about positive changes. Pedersen (2000a) described a five-stage program for developing multicultural awareness, knowledge, and skill through (a) needs assessment, (b) the definition of specific objectives and design techniques, (c) training approaches, and (d) evaluation strategies.

The first stage of training is increased awareness. Culture is within the person and difficult to separate from other learned competencies. Developing an awareness of culturally learned assumptions is therefore essential for any intentional counselor as a professional obligation (Pedersen, 2000a; Sue, Ivey, & Pedersen, 1996).

The Intrapersonal Cultural Grid in Figure 31.1 provides a framework for describing the degree of awareness necessary for culture-centered counselors. On one dimension, the social system variables of (a) ethnographic (nationality, ethnicity, etc.), (b) demographic (age, gender, place of residence, etc.), (c) status

Social System Variables CultureTeachers	VALUES: Where You Learned to Do It	EXPECTATIONS: Why You Did It	BEHAVIOR: What You Did
Ethnographic 　Nationality 　Ethnicity 　etc.			
Demographic 　Gender 　Age 　Residence 　etc.			
Status 　Social 　Educational 　Economic 　etc.			
Affiliations 　Formal 　Informal			

Figure 31.1　The Intrapersonal Cultural Grid

(social, educational, economic, etc.), and (d) formal or informal affiliations to ideas and/or organizations emerge as "culture teachers" in our lives. On the other dimension, there are categories for (a) "what you did: BEHAVIOR," (b) "why you did it: EXPECTATIONS," and (c) "where you learned to do it: VALUES." The Intrapersonal Cultural Grid is an open-ended framework to increase our awareness of the "culture teachers" who have taught us the "rules" that regulate our behaviors. Each behavior is guided by many culturally learned expectations with regard to that behavior in a particular situation. Each culturally learned expectation is an extension of many culturally learned values, and each value was learned from the many culture teachers in our social systems. The interaction of behavior-expectations-values with the social system variables demonstrates the complexity of understanding prejudice and racism in the cultural context

where it was learned and is displayed. The same behavior may have different meanings, and different behaviors might have the same meaning depending on the cultural context.

The second stage of training is increased knowledge. It is essential to assemble the facts and information on which culturally learned assumptions are based before attempting to change the assumptions. Counselors who have developed an appropriate awareness will know what facts they need and will be motivated to gather that information before proceeding with their counseling intervention. This second step of gathering knowledge and developing an informed comprehension provides a database for understanding one's own and other cultures as meaningful (Sue, Arredondo, & McDavis, 1992). Sue and Sue (1999) pointed out a pervasive and enduring bias in the knowledge being taught about multiculturalism in counselor education programs.

The third level of training requires a skilled and intentional ability to make appropriate changes in each multicultural context. The third level is the most difficult and presumes a successful development, first, of cultural awareness and, second, of cultural knowledge about the client's cultural context (Pope-Davis & Coleman, 1997; Sue et al., 1998). Change is perceived as linked to the cultural context in such a way that training and education themselves become a treatment modality. The counselor, client, and their culture teachers contribute to the construction of a shared context, which is both complex and dynamic. Culture-centered counselors are able to generate a wide variety of intentional verbal and nonverbal responses appropriate to the cultural context.

We know that behaviors are learned in a cultural context and are displayed in a cultural context, so it makes sense that accurate assessment, meaningful understanding, and appropriate intervention require that counselors be educated to have the awareness, knowledge, and skill appropriate to their own and their clients' context. Every test and theory in counseling was developed to fit the precise needs of a particular cultural context, so it should not surprise us when a particular test or theory is less than an exact fit with radically different cultural contexts (Dana, 1998; Paniagua, in press; Samuda, 1998). The search for culture-free and culture-fair tests has failed. We are left with a mandate to train counselors in translating the data from culturally biased tests and theories to their clients' cultural context. Even those of our colleagues who react negatively to the infusion of multiculturalism in the curriculum are probably in favor of accurate assessment, meaningful understanding, and appropriate interventions.

The training process begins by asking the right questions. An approach for infusing multicultural questions into the counselor education curriculum can easily be developed as an integrative seminar. Students can bring their syllabuses for the other classes they are taking into the seminar. The class discussion will focus on preparing the students to generate questions about the relevance of culture into their other classes for discussion in those other classes; in that way, a culture-centered perspective is infused throughout the other courses in counselor education. Pedersen, Carter, and Ponterotto (1996) have compiled a list of several hundred unanswered questions by 30 multicultural specialists that could enrich a classroom discussion.

THE TRIAD TRAINING MODEL

The importance of self-talk (Ellis, 1987), internal dialogue (Meichenbaum, 1986), and self-instructional training (Capuzzi & Gross, 1995) has been carefully documented in cognitive therapies. Siegrist (1995) reviewed the extensive literature on inner speech as it relates to cognition, Nutt-Williams and Hill (1996) demonstrated the importance of self-talk to individual therapy, and Penn and Frankfurt (1994) demonstrated the importance of inner conversation to family therapy. The greater the cultural difference, however, the less likely a counselor is to accurately perceive the client's inner conversation (Pedersen, 2000b). However, we can assume that part of the client's inner dialogue is negative and part is positive.

The triad training model involves a role-played interview between a culturally different counselor and a three-person coached team of client, pro-counselor, and anti-counselor. The anti-counselor seeks to explicate the negative messages that a client from that culture might be thinking but not saying, whereas a pro-counselor seeks to explicate the positive messages in the client's mind. Although either an anti-counselor or a pro-counselor may be used without the other, the combined influence allows one to hear the client's internal-dialogue "hidden messages" in both their positive and negative aspects. The pro-counselor and anti-counselor provide continuous, direct, and immediate feedback to both the client and the counselor during the counseling process. Many of the sources of resistance, such as prejudice and racism, consequently become explicit and articulate to the culturally different counselor during the role-play.

It is important to understand the role of the pro-counselor and the anti-counselor. The culturally similar anti-counselor is deliberately subversive in attempting to exaggerate mistakes by the counselor and negative reactions by the client during the interview. There are several ways the anti-counselor can articulate resistance. The anti-counselor can build on the need to keep the problem, encourage the client's ambivalence, distract or sidetrack the counselor, keep the conversation superficial, obstruct communication, annoy the counselor, make the counselor defensive, and exaggerate differences between the counselor and client to keep them apart. The triad training model encourages the direct examination of hidden negative messages a counselor or client might be thinking but not saying to articulate examples of prejudice and racism in the safety of the role-play. The counselor is then able to articulate examples of prejudice and racism and better deal with those negative messages when they come up during actual interviews.

The pro-counselor attempts to articulate the hidden positive messages that might also be included in a client's internal dialogue. The culturally similar pro-counselor helps both the counselor and the client articulate the counseling process as a potentially helpful activity. The pro-counselor functions as a facilitator for the counselor's effective responses. The culturally similar pro-counselor understands the client better than the culturally different counselor and is thus able to provide relevant background information to the counselor during the interview. The pro-counselor is not a cotherapist but an intermediate resource person who can guide the counselor through

suggesting specific strategies and information that the client might otherwise be reluctant to volunteer. In these ways, the pro-counselor can reinforce the counselor's more successful strategies in coping with prejudice and racism, both verbally and nonverbally. The pro-counselor might restate or positively reframe what the client or counselor said, keep the interview focused on the primary problem, offer verbal and nonverbal approval, reinforce important insights, highlight positive statements, and suggest alternative strategies.

The advantages and directions for using the triad training model in preservice or in-service education are detailed in Pedersen (2000b). Cultural differences tend to exaggerate and magnify the likelihood of inappropriate counseling interventions. Providing immediate feedback to trainees regarding cultural differences, prejudice, racism, and other hidden messages in role-played counseling interviews creates the opportunity to prevent those negative factors from interfering with real counseling interviews later.

Research on the triad training model has not been extensive, but results thus far have been encouraging. Research (Pedersen, 2000b) suggests that it increases counselor awareness, knowledge, and skill. The evidence of increased awareness is reported in the positive evaluation of in-service training, favorable comparisons with interpersonal process recall (IPR) training on awareness, self-reports of increased awareness, and increased identification of negative thoughts in cross-cultural counseling. The evidence of increased knowledge includes increased receptivity to multicultural information about clients, a more articulate description of culturally different values, self-reports of increased sensitivity to different populations, and increased knowledge about a client's host culture. The evidence of increased skill includes increased frequency of good verbal counseling statements, increased confidence for working with client populations unfamiliar with counseling, self-reports of greater effectiveness in family therapy, and more favorable feedback from Black students working with White counselors.

The more sociocultural differences there are between a counselor and client, the more difficult it will be to accurately anticipate the influence of prejudice and racism in what the counselor or client is thinking but not saying. The triad training model is a method in which immediate and continuous debriefing occurs during the role-played cross-cultural interview itself. The triad training model is a means of learning to hear and deal with specific examples of prejudice and racism in multicultural counseling.

THE SYNTHETIC CULTURE LABORATORY

The literature on the use of simulations in training is extensive. Crookall and Saunders (1989) and Crookall and Arai (1995) discussed intercultural applications of simulations. Most simulation games include learning about interpersonal effectiveness among their objectives, recognizing that members of different cultures seldom have safe opportunities to interact with contrasting cultures in the real world. Bringing different cultures together in a simulation provides an opportunity to examine issues of prejudice and racism as they result in misunderstandings with minimum risk (Greenblat, 1989).

Hofstede and Pedersen (1999) have developed a laboratory simulation based on synthetic cultures:

> A synthetic culture is one that does not exist in reality and, moreover, does not pretend to resemble a real national culture. Synthetic cultures exist only in the training or game context. By playing these synthetic stereotypes or extreme examples, the participants will become better able to recognize and be prepared to deal with the more subtle elements of these stereotyped tendencies in themselves and others in the real world. (p. 417)

The database was derived from more than 70,000 subjects from more than 55 countries, developed by Hofstede (1980, 1986).

Pedersen and Ivey (1993) described how a synthetic culture laboratory can be used for both preservice and in-service training to identify examples of prejudice and racism. The objectives of the synthetic culture laboratory are as follows:

1. to identify culture as an internalized and learned perspective by which experiences are organized into meaningful patterns;

2. to identify stereotyped and culturally biased learning patterns and their consequences in the safety of a simulated interaction;

3. to identify participants' awareness of their own positive and negative feelings about other cultural perspectives;

4. to increase participants' skill for identifying common ground and shared values with persons from different cultures, without sacrificing integrity;

5. to increase participants' awareness of controversies and societal issues across cultural perspectives regarding "outsiders."

Participants are introduced to the four synthetic cultures of Alpha (high power distance), Beta (strong uncertainty avoidance), Gamma (high individualism), and Delta (strong masculine). The organization of the laboratory follows a series of steps.

First, participants have 30 minutes to select one of the four synthetic cultures, learn the one page of rules, discuss the problems created by "outsiders," and select a team of two or three consultants for each synthetic home culture who will visit the other three synthetic host cultures, in turn, to help them deal with their own problems caused by outsiders. By the end of 30 minutes, each of the four synthetic culture groups should have been socialized into their new synthetic culture identity and be able to respond appropriately according to the rules of that synthetic culture.

Second, the first rotation will require sending a team of consultants from each synthetic home culture to each synthetic host culture (e.g., Alpha team goes to Beta) for a 10-minute consultation in which the host and home culture participants interact in the role of their respective synthetic culture identities. After the 10-minute interaction, time will be called, and both home and host cultures will step out of their roles to debrief and discuss whether they were able to find common ground on the problem of outsiders, without either host and/or home culture participants giving up their cultural integrity. After debriefing, the consulting teams will return to their synthetic home culture to report back on what they learned about prejudice and racism, which can increase their success in future consultations.

Third, the second rotation will repeat the procedure of the first rotation, matching the team of consultants with a different host culture (e.g., Alpha team goes to Gamma).

Fourth, the third rotation will follow the same pattern as the first and second rotations with a different host culture (e.g., Alpha team goes to Delta).

Fifth, each synthetic culture group will report back to the larger group about what they learned from the laboratory. Specific emphasis will be given to the advice they have for outsiders coming into cultures resembling their synthetic host culture in the real world and feedback to the other three synthetic culture groups about what they liked and did not like about cultures resembling those synthetic host cultures.

Sixth, instructions for debriefing the synthetic culture laboratory are given in Pedersen and Ivey (1993), Hofstede and Pedersen (1999), and Hofstede, Pedersen, and Hofstede (2001). Hofstede and Pedersen (1999) identified 10 synthetic cultures in an enlarged version of the Hofstede dimensions

of national culture, which can be used for training or simulations. Other examples besides the synthetic culture laboratory are also described, including both face-to-face and electronically mediated settings.

The synthetic culture laboratory provides a safe place to take risks in increasing the counselor's self-awareness of his or her own cultural bias, increasing the counselor's awareness of alternative "real-world" cultural systems in a framework of contrasting alternatives, and socializing the counselor into a new and different synthetic culture together with people from a variety of other diverse real-world cultural backgrounds. Each counseling microskill such as giving feedback, asking questions, summarizing, encouraging, paraphrasing, reflecting feelings, reflecting meanings, confronting, focusing, and influencing is accomplished differently in each cultural context. The synthetic culture laboratory provides the counselor a chance to rehearse the different words and behaviors that are appropriate to each of the contrasting synthetic culture contexts (Pedersen & Ivey, 1993).

MULTICULTURAL GROUP MICROSKILLS

We learn about our cultures in a group context, beginning with the family, and multicultural issues are present in every group. Ivey et al. (2001) organized their book on intentional group counseling around the central issue of our multicultural memberships in groups throughout our lives:

> We are all multicultural human beings; our very selfhood and identity are embedded in the language we speak, our gender, our ethnic/racial background and our individual life path and experience. Because all behaviors are learned and displayed in a cultural context, we bring our own cultural experiences into our group through the manner in which we participate. The multicultures cannot be separated from the individual;

they are deeply embedded in our concept of self and others. (p .2)

We know that it is easier to change a person's attitudes and opinions in a group context than it is through one-on-one interaction (Corey, 2000). Social pressure from peers is a powerful force for change. All of our cultural beliefs, attitudes, and opinions—including prejudice and racism—were learned in a group context. With the increased popularity of group-work as a counseling model, it is appropriate to look at the training of culturally intentional group-work leaders as a valuable resource for reducing prejudice and racism.

If, for example, you examine how the multicultural world of the counselor is both similar and different from a client, the complex multiplicity of cultures becomes apparent. This adaptation of the cultural grid mentioned earlier examines each behavior of the client or the counselor as linked to many culturally learned expectations, each expectation as linked to many culturally learned values, and each value linked to perhaps a thousand or more of the culture teachers in our life as we remember the messages of family, friends, enemies, heroes, heroines, mentors, teachers, and fantasies we have had about the person we want to become someday. If you assume that there are only two people in the room when your client walks into your office and closes the door, you are already in trouble. There are literally thousands of people in that office hidden in the multiculturalism of the client and of the counselor.

Ivey et al.'s (2001) book uses a microskill approach to examine how our life experiences influence our worldview and the worldview of others so that we do not interpret anyone's behavior out of context. Through increased awareness of our biases and prejudices, we can become more intentional in our group leadership skills, and we can train our group members to become more intentional as well. Corey (1995) pointed out that "because of the power group counselors possess, it is possible to use this power to stifle group members instead of empowering them. Being aware of your personal biases is the first step toward guarding against unethical practices in your own group work" (p. 27).

As we become more aware of our multicultural heritage, we protect ourselves against stereotyping by recognizing both similarities as well as differences across individuals and groups, no matter how similar or different those individuals or groups might appear. There is a clear ethical mandate to understand the multicultural aspects of group-work. The American Counseling Association's (ACA, 1995) *Code of Ethics and Standards of Practice* comments, "Counselors are aware of their own values, attitudes, beliefs and behaviors and how these apply in a diverse society, and avoid imposing values on clients" (A.5.b).

The Ivey et al. (2001) approach examines each microskill used in group-work and group-work training in terms of the cultural context where that skill was learned and is being displayed. This approach attempts to demystify groups so that each microskill can be adapted accurately, meaningfully, and appropriately to each cultural context.

> If you master the basic skills of observation and intervention, you will have multiple possibilities for action when faced even with the most difficult leadership challenge. Intentionality means that you are able to flex with changing situations, develop creative new responses and constantly increase your repertoire of skills and strategies with groups. Intentionality can be expanded with the idea of cultural intentionality—the ability to work with many varying types of people with widely varying multicultural backgrounds. (Ivey et al., 2001, p. 20)

We begin learning about ourselves and our culture in the family and extended family, where we learn about power, authority, responsibility, and the other "rules" by which we live. We soon expand our memberships to include friends, peers, school, spirituality, leisure groups, and casual interactions, but we continue to apply those original culturally learned "habits" about our behavior toward others, some of which include examples of racism and prejudice.

> Each of us has learned habits—ways of thinking and behaving acquired from our past experiences—and we all have different paths through life. Participating in groups helps us discover ourselves more completely and how our habits of living are perceived by others. Group membership teaches us things about ourselves and our style that we didn't know before. (Ivey et al., 2001, p. 21)

The microskills approach seeks to systematically examine our specific habits of behavior in groups toward becoming more intentional rather than accidental or unthinking toward others. Beginning with attending behaviors, this approach builds a foundation of listening and process skills. The visual representation used is that of a pyramid, with each skill building on the previous foundation skills. Focusing, pacing, and leading are microskills that demonstrate how groups work. The basic listening sequence is a microskill for drawing out the stories of group members from there-and-then to the here-and-now. These microskills are then integrated by examining and role-playing transcripts of group interactions to practice microskills of listening, reframing, interpreting, self-disclosure, and feedback. The strategies for interpersonal influence are the most sophisticated level of microskills and help the group leaders develop their own personal style of intentional and multicultural group leadership.

The multicultural foci of this approach are not marginal to the development of generic skills in group leadership but are identified as central and essential. This model moves away from the isolation of multicultural issues to a specialized course and moves toward integrating multiculturalism into the fabric of the generic curriculum.

CONCLUSION

The generic applicability of multiculturalism can be demonstrated in basic psychological concepts. Pedersen (2000a) described at least a dozen positive advantages of reducing prejudice and racism in counseling. First, interpreting behavior out of context leads to misattribution. Second, identifying common ground across cultures facilitates win-win outcomes from conflict situations. Third, our individual identity can best be understood by learning from the culture teachers in our internal dialogue. Fourth, by examining many different perspectives in problem solving, we are less likely to overlook the best answer. Fifth, cultural diversity protects us from imposing our self-reference criteria inappropriately on others. Sixth, by learning to work with those different from ourselves, we will develop the facility for working with future cultures not yet known to us. Seventh, every social system that has imposed the exclusive will or the dominant culture as the measure of just and moral behavior has been condemned by history. Eighth, it is not just the content of our thinking but the very process of linear thinking itself that can become culturally encapsulated. Ninth, all education and learning challenge our conventional assumptions and results in some form of culture shock. Tenth, spiritual completeness requires that we complement our own understanding of ultimate reality with the understanding of others. Eleventh, cultural pluralism provides the only political alternative to chaotic anarchy or authoritarian tyranny. Twelfth, a culture-centered perspective complements and strengthens conventional theories of counseling and psychology as a fourth dimension much as the fourth dimension of time complements our understanding of three-dimensional space.

Unlearning prejudice and racism involves acquiring accurate awareness, meaningful understanding of multicultural experiences, and appropriate interventions. Sue et al. (1998) suggested four principles to guide us toward increased competence: First, we need to learn from as many sources as possible to validate our understanding; second, a balanced picture requires contact with the healthy and strong members of the target culture; third, factual understanding needs to be supplemented with experiential reality; and fourth, we must be constantly vigilant against biases in ourselves and the people around us.

We need a conceptual framework for multiculturalism as a psychological perspective. Sue et al. (1996) have attempted to develop a multicultural theory for reducing prejudice and racism in counseling based on six basic propositions. First, each Western or non-Western theory already represents a different worldview, implicitly or explicitly. Second, the comprehensive context of each client-counselor relationship must be the focus of treatment. Third, the counselor's and client's own cultural identity will influence how problems are defined and direct the goals of the counseling process. Fourth, the goal of culture-centered counseling is to expand the repertoire of helping responses available to counselors. Fifth, there are many alternative helping roles for counseling from other cultural contexts to supplement conventional counseling. Sixth, the individual, family, group, and organization can only be accurately understood in their cultural context. These propositions are intended to encourage the discussion of how cultural encapsulation by prejudice and racism can be eliminated among counselors.

Counseling is moving toward becoming a culture-inclusive science that will routinely include cultural variables in the future just as contemporary psychology routinely disregards them. We will be asking questions such as the following: Which psychological theory works best in each cultural context? What are the cultural boundaries of each psychological theory? Which psychological phenomena are more likely to occur in which cultures? We will no longer speak about cross-cultural psychology but rather understand all human behavior in the central cultural context.

REFERENCES

American Counseling Association (ACA). (1995). *Code of ethics and standards of practice.* Alexandria, VA: American Counseling Association.

Capuzzi, D., & Gross, D. R. (1995). *Counseling and psychotherapy: Theories and interventions.* Englewood Cliffs, NJ: Merrill.

Corey, G. (1995). *Theory and practice of group counseling* (3rd ed.). Pacific Grove, CA: Brooks/Cole.

Corey, G. (2000). *Theory and practice of group counseling* (5th ed.). Belmont, CA: Wadsworth.

Crookall, D., & Arai, K. (Eds.). (1995). *Simulation and gaming across disciplines and cultures: ISAGA at a watershed.* Thousand Oaks, CA: Sage.

Crookall, D., & Saunders, D. (1989). *Communication and simulation.* Clevedon, UK: Multilingual Matters.

Cushner, K., & Brislin, R. W. (1997). *Improving intercultural interactions: Modules for cross-cultural training programs* (Vol. 2). Thousand Oaks, CA: Sage.

Dana, R. H. (1998). *Understanding cultural identity in intervention and assessment.* Thousand Oaks, CA: Sage.

Ellis, A. (1987). The evolution of rational-emotive therapy (RET) and cognitive behavior therapy (CBT). In J. K. Zeig (Ed.), *The evolution of psychotherapy* (pp. *000-000*). New York: Brunner/Mazel.

Greenblat, C. S. (1989). Extending the range of experience. In D. Crookall & D. Sunders (Eds.), *Communication and simulation* (pp. 269-283). Clevedon, UK: Multilingual Matters.

Hofstede, G. (1980). *Culture's consequences: International differences in work-related values.* Beverly Hills, CA: Sage.

Hofstede, G. (1986). Cultural differences in teaching and learning. *International Journal of Intercultural Relations, 10,* 301-320.

Hofstede, G. J., & Pedersen, P. B. (1999). Synthetic cultures: Intercultural learning through simulation games. *Simulation & Gaming, 30*(4), 415-440.

Hofstede, G. J., Pedersen, P. B., & Hofstede, G. (2001). *Synthetic cultures: A training model.* Yarmouth, ME: Intercultural Press.

Ivey, A. E., Pedersen, P. B., & Ivey, M. B. (2001). *Intentional group counseling: A microskills approach.* Pacific Grove, CA: Brooks/Cole.

Meichenbaum, D. (1986). Cognitive behavior modification. In F. H. Kanfer & A. P. Goldstein (Eds.), *Helping people change* (pp. 346-381). New York: Pergamon.

Midgette, T. E., & Meggert, S. S. (1991). Multicultural counseling instruction: A challenge for faculties in the 21st century. *Journal of Counseling and Development, 70*(1), 38-46.

Nutt-Williams, E., & Hill, C. E. (1996). The relationship between self-talk and therapy process variables for novice therapists. *Journal of Counseling Psychology, 43,* 170-177.

Paniagua, F. A. (in press). *Diagnosis in a multicultural context: A casebook for mental health professionals.* Thousand Oaks, CA: Sage.

Pedersen, P. (2000a). *Handbook for developing multicultural awareness* (3rd ed.). Alexandria, VA: American Counseling Association.

Pedersen, P. (2000b). *Hidden messages in culture-centered counseling: A triad training model.* Thousand Oaks, CA: Sage.

Pedersen, P., Carter, R. T., & Ponterotto, J. G. (1996). The cultural context of psychology: Questions for accurate research and appropriate practice. *Cultural Diversity and Mental Health, 2,* 205-216.

Pedersen, P., & Ivey, A. E. (1993). *Culture-centered counseling and interviewing skills.* Westport, CT: Greenwood.

Penn, P., & Frankfurt, M. (1994). Creating a participant text: Writing multiple voices, narrative multiplicity. *Family Process, 33,* 217-231.

Ponterotto, J. G., & Pedersen, P. B. (1993). *Preventing prejudice: A guide for counselors and educators.* Newbury Park, CA: Sage.

Pope-Davis, D., & Coleman, H. (1997). *Multicultural counseling competencies.* Thousand Oaks, CA: Sage.

Ridley, C. R. (1995). *Overcoming unintentional racism in counseling and therapy: A practitioner's guide to intentional intervention.* Thousand Oaks, CA: Sage.

Ridley, C. R., Espelage, D. L., & Rubinstein, K. J. (1997). Course development in multicultural counseling. In D. B. Pope-Davis & H. L. K. Coleman (Eds.), *Multicultural counseling competencies: Assessment, education and training and supervision* (pp. 131-158). Thousand Oaks, CA: Sage.

Ridley, C. R., Mendoza, D. W., & Kanitz, B. E. (1994). Multicultural training: Reexamination, operationalization and integration. *The Counseling Psychologist, 22*(2), 227-289.

Samuda, R. J. (1998). *Psychological testing of American minorities: Issues and consequences* (2nd ed.). Thousand Oaks, CA: Sage.

Siegrist, M. (1995). Inner speech as a cognitive process mediating self consciousness and inhibiting self deception. *Psychological Reports, 76*(1), 259-265.

Sue, D. W., Arredondo, P., & McDavis, R. J. (1992). Multicultural competencies/standards: A pressing need. *Journal of Counseling and Development, 70*(4), 477-486.

Sue, D. W., Carter, R. T., Casas, J. M., Fouad, N. A., Ivey, A. E., Jensen, M., LaFromboise, T., Manese, J. E., Ponterotto, J. G., & Vasquez-Nutall, E. (1998). *Multicultural counseling competencies: Individual and organizational development.* Thousand Oaks, CA: Sage.

Sue, D. W., Ivey, A. E., & Pedersen, P. B. (1996). *A theory of multicultural counseling and therapy.* Belmont, CA: Brooks/Cole.

Sue, D. W., & Sue, D. (1999). *Counseling the culturally different: Theory and practice* (3rd ed.). New York: John Wiley.

CHAPTER 32

Prevention of Substance Abuse Among Ethnic Minority Youth

A. KATHLEEN BURLEW
TONYA HUCKS
University of Cincinnati

RANDI BURLEW
University of Michigan

CANDACE JOHNSON
University of Cincinnati

Drug use among adolescents continues to be a national concern. The percentage of high school seniors who acknowledged that they had tried an illicit drug increased from 55% to 66% between 1975 and 1981 (Johnston, O'Malley, & Bachman, 2000). After a decline to a low of 41% by 1992, the rate rose again to 54% by 1997 and has remained at that level (Johnston et al., 2000). The specific drugs with the highest percentage of youth reporting lifetime use in 2000 are alcohol (80.3%), marijuana (48.8%), cigarettes (62.5%), smokeless tobacco (23.1%), and amphetamines (15.6%) (Johnston et al., 2000). Moreover, the age of first use is lowering. As many as 20% of sixth graders report that they have tried an illicit drug (Jani, 1999).

The use of alcohol and drugs at an early age has been shown to be associated with both immediate and long-term consequences. The immediate consequences include school failure (Ensminger & Slusarcick, 1992; Rhodes & Jason, 1990), increased delinquent activity (Ellickson, McGuligan, Adams, Bell, & Hays, 1996; Johnston et al., 2000), adolescent pregnancy, and other health risks (Dawkins & Dawkins, 1983; Emshoff, Avery, Raduka, Anderson, & Calvert, 1996; Segal & Stewart, 1996). The long-term consequences can include later unemployment and increased risk of participation in violent activities, including homicide (Dawkins & Dawkins, 1983; Emshoff et al., 1996; Segal & Stewart, 1996). Moreover, those adolescents who experiment early with substances are at greater risk for future drug (Anthony & Petronis, 1995; Hawkins, Catalano, & Miller, 1992; Robins & Przyeck, 1985) or alcohol problems (Grant & Dawson, 1997; Hawkins et al., 1997).

Until recently, much of the research on prevention focused on White adolescents. However, a growing body of literature has become available more recently on ethnic minority youth. The goal of this chapter is to review the body of prevention work on ethnic minority youth. Specifically, this review will focus on the following areas: (a) prevalence and consequences of drug and alcohol use; (b) theoretical issues useful for understanding drug use and prevention among ethnic minority youth; (c) the relation of ethnic identity to drug use; (d) promising approaches to prevention, including culturally tailored interventions; (e) methodological and analytical issues in conducting research on alcohol and drug use among ethnic minority youth; and (f) areas for future research.

PREVALENCE AND CONSEQUENCES OF DRUG ABUSE AMONG ETHNIC YOUTH

Two major national studies, the Monitoring the Future Study (MTF) (Johnston, O'Malley, & Bachman, 1998) and the National Household Survey on Drug Abuse (www. samhsa.gov/oas/NHSDA/1999/chapter2.htm),

document the prevalence of drug abuse among adolescents. In particular, both studies provide information on the prevalence of drug abuse of ethnic minority groups.

The MTF is one of the most comprehensive sources for information on adolescent alcohol and drug abuse. The study began tracking the patterns of African American, Latino, and White 12th graders in 1975. In 1991, the survey expanded to collect information on drug abuse reported by 8th and 10th graders along with 12th graders. The MTF reported that, contrary to popular opinion, African American seniors (32.7%) reported lower rates of illicit drug use than White (42.8%) seniors. The rate for Latino (44.8%) seniors was very close to the rate for White seniors. Similarly, the 30-day prevalence rate for alcohol use among African American (30.0%) and Latino (51.2%) seniors was lower than the rate for White (55.1%) seniors. These findings from the MTF study are consistent with other findings that demonstrate that White children typically begin to use alcohol and other drugs earlier than Latino or African American youth (Swan, 1995).

Similar to the MTF study, the National Household Survey on Drug Abuse (www. samhsa.gov/oas/NHSDA/1999/chapter2.htm) has been collecting information on the prevalence of the abuse of alcohol and other drugs since 1971. This study collects data on nearly 70,000 individuals age 12 and older of African American, Latino, American Indian and Alaska Native, Asian American, biracial, and White backgrounds. In contrast to previous years, the 1999 survey provided information on the drug use trends according to age groups.

The NHSDA survey reported similar levels of drug use among Whites (10.9%) and African Americans (10.7%) between the ages of 12 and 17. Although 11.4% of Latino youth reported illicit drug use, this figure may not consider intragroup variations in the rate of drug abuse among various subgroups within the Latino community. For example, the Healthy People 2000 study suggested that Mexican American males consume larger amounts of alcohol than males in other Latino groups, such as Cuban Americans and Puerto Ricans (U.S. Department of Health and Human Services [DHHS], 2000).

The NHSDA survey reported that the highest rate of drug abuse was among American Indian and Alaska Native youth (19.6%). In a related study, Beauvais and Segal (1992) found that American Indian and Alaska Native youth had very high rates of drug abuse. Although this finding is consistent with previous research that suggests that American Indian and Alaska Native youth demonstrate more drug abuse and have an earlier initiation pattern into marijuana and tobacco than other groups (Beauvais, 1992a, 1992b, 1996), the drinking patterns among the 500+ tribes vary widely (Caetano, Clark, & Tam, 1998). For example, Stillner, Kraus, Leukefeld, and Hardenbergh (1999) reported that previous-month alcohol use was lower for Alaska Native parents between the ages of 26 and 34 in the Bering Sea than the 1995 national rate reported by the National Household Study.

The NHSDA survey reported that Asian Americans reported less illicit drug usage (8.4% in past 30 days) than any other group. However, previous research suggests that older males, particularly Japanese and Filipino men from a high social status, consume more alcohol than any other group of Asian Americans (DHHS, 2000). Moreover, the Healthy People 2000 report suggests that, as the number of Asian American immigrants continues to increase, so will the prevalence of alcohol use within that group.

Although drug and alcohol abuse may be less prevalent among certain ethnic/racial groups than their White counterparts (Bachman et al., 1991; Barnes & Welte, 1986; Johnston, O'Malley, & Bachman,

1995; Maddahian, Newcomb, & Bentler, 1988), the consequences associated with drug abuse may be even more pronounced among these groups than among Whites (Dawkins & Dawkins, 1983; Emshoff et al., 1996; Grace, 1992). For example, previous studies have suggested that substance abuse is associated with adolescent pregnancy, high unemployment rates, disruption of education and family life, violence and homicide, and suicide among African Americans (Dawkins & Dawkins, 1983; Emshoff et al., 1996). In addition, African American as well as Latino males have a high risk of developing acute and chronic alcohol-related diseases, such as heart disease and various cancers of the digestive tract (DHHS, 2000).

The consequences of substance abuse are high for American Indians and Alaska Natives as well. According to the Healthy People 2000 report, 4 out of 10 American Indian and Alaska Native deaths were alcohol related from 1978 to 1980 and again from 1983 to 1985. The same report also suggested that the high rate of fetal alcohol syndrome is another devastating consequence for American Indian and Alaska Natives. In addition, Beauvais (1992a, 1992b) suggested that drug abuse has led to unstable relationships with parents and peers among American Indian and Alaska Native youth.

THEORETICAL PERSPECTIVES ON DRUG ABUSE AMONG ETHNIC YOUTH

Various theoretical perspectives have been developed over the years to explain the substance use patterns described in the previous sections. Several of these seem especially applicable to understanding drug abuse among ethnic minorities. This section will focus on three of these theoretical perspectives— namely, risk and resilience, social ecology, and orthogonal cultural identification.

Risk and Resilience

One of the most promising models for understanding factors associated with drug use is a risk and resilience approach. *Risk factors* are factors that increase the likelihood that the youth will engage in substance abuse. *Resilience factors* promote healthy adaptation despite risk and adversity (Wolin & Wolin, 1995). In fact, it has been suggested that resilience factors act as a buffer between risk factors and outcome (Brook, Cohen, Whiteman, & Gordon, 1992; Newcomb & Felix-Ortiz, 1992; Stacy, Newcomb, & Bentler, 1992). For instance, positive family bonding (a resilience factor) may buffer the relationship between substance-abusing friends (a risk factor) and possible drug use (Johnson, 2001). Hawkins et al. (1992) suggested that risk factors might be categorized into the following four domains:

Personal/individual—uncontrollable (e.g., age and gender) and controllable personal characteristics (drug attitudes, perceptions of harm, impulsivity, hostility, alienation from the dominant values of the culture, and rebelliousness)

Family—includes poor family management, discipline and supervision, parental use of alcohol and drugs, and permissive drug attitudes among parents

Peer group—negative influence of peers, especially involvement with peers who use alcohol and drugs and who engage in other problem behaviors

Community—includes community norms that permit substance use, poverty, and cultural disenfranchisement

In addition, Hawkins et al. (1992) identified the following six categories of protective or resilience factors:

Personal/individual—These factors include temperament (e.g., emotional stability, positive sense of self) and social competence.

Family—Protective family characteristics include high levels of warmth, a basic sense of trust, high parental expectations, and clear rules and expectations for children.

School—The key school factors that promote resilience are a caring and supportive environment, clear standards and rules for appropriate behavior, and high expectations.

Peer group—The peer group characteristic that best promotes adaptation is an involvement in a peer group that promotes positive group activities and norms.

Community—The community factors that promote healthy adaptation are similar to the school factors, such as caring and support, high expectations for youth, and opportunities for youth to participate in community activities.

Society—The protective societal factors include the presence of media that promote strong antidrug messages and limited access to substance use.

Catalano et al. (1993) examined the relation of risk factors to drug use. The set of significant risk factors included poor family management styles and family bonding; early antisocial behavior, such as violent tendencies; accessibility and availability of drugs; and opportunities for involvement in school activities. No racial differences were evident in the relationship between these variables and the initiation of drug use. However, other studies have demonstrated racial differences in the extent to which the risk factors were present in their lives. For example, Hawkins et al. (1992) found that African American youth are exposed to more aggression than other youth; exposure to aggression is perceived as a risk factor for drug abuse. In other research, it has been suggested that the stress associated with acculturation may be a risk factor for Latino Americans (Rodriguez, 1995). For instance, the Healthy People 2000 (DHHS, 2000) report suggested that many Latino persons

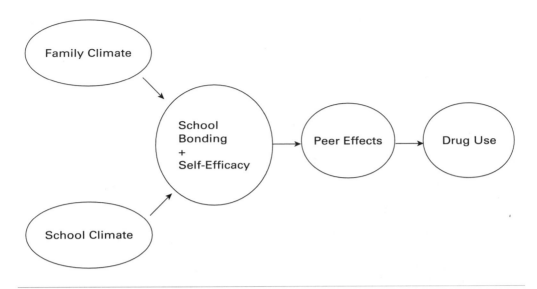

Figure 32.1   Social Ecology Model

SOURCE: Kumpfer & Turner (1990-1991).

who immigrate to the United States quickly adopt the level of alcohol consumption of their American counterparts.

The Social Ecology Model

Another theoretical perspective on drug use among ethnic minorities is the social ecology model proposed by Kumpfer and Turner (1990-1991). This theory suggests that certain social settings and environments may serve as predictors of drug use for ethnic youth. The factors discussed in the model are family climate, school climate, school bonding and self-efficacy, and peer drug use (see Figure 32.1). Similar to the risk and resilience theory, this theory hypothesizes that certain risk and protective factors predict an adolescent's drug abuse patterns. For example, the presence of a caring adult and emotional support are family protective factors, whereas parental drug abuse and family stress are

family risk factors (Kumpfer & Alvarado, 1995; Kumpfer & Bluth, in press).

Kumpfer (1994a, 1994b) used this model as a backdrop to develop the Strengthening Families Program (SFP) intervention. Research on the SFP program supports the link between family factors and adolescent drug abuse. Others have demonstrated the relationship of school (Rhodes & Jason, 1990) factors to drug outcomes. However, more research would be useful on the pattern of relationships suggested by the entire social ecology model.

Orthogonal Cultural Identification

The orthogonal cultural identification theory was based on work with American Indians and Alaska Natives along with Mexican American youth (Oetting & Beauvais, 1990). The theory suggests that identification with any culture or more than one culture is associated with better adjustment than alienation from all cultures. Moreover, cultural identification develops within the family. The theory has four assumptions: (a) Cultural identification can be assessed, (b) it is important to assess identification with any culture independently of assessing identification with any other culture, (c) identification with a culture may be a source of strength, and (d) cultural identification is strongly linked to culture-specific attitudes and behaviors (Oetting & Beauvais, 1990). Accordingly, identification with either one's ethnic subculture or identification to mainstream society is associated with positive psychosocial characteristics. Youth who identify strongly with both their ethnic subculture and the mainstream culture have the highest self-esteem, whereas those youth who identify with neither culture have the lowest self-esteem. Moreover, youth with a strong identification with either the subculture or the mainstream culture are expected to abuse less alcohol, tobacco, and other drugs than youth with only a weak identification to any culture because of greater adaptability.

In a study by Weaver (1996), researchers found that many American Indian and Alaska Native youth identify with more than one culture. In addition, the study found a correlation between cultural identification with either culture and health scales, including tobacco use (Weaver, 1996). This finding supports the orthogonal cultural identification theory. The relationship between cultural identity and drug use is discussed in the next section.

ETHNIC IDENTITY AND DRUG USE

Ethnic/racial identity[1] refers to one's identity with a subgroup that shares a common ancestry and other characteristics such as culture, race, religion, language, kinship, or place of origin (Phinney, 2000). According to Phinney (2000), ethnic/racial identity is assumed to be a multidimensional construct that may include one or more of the following elements:

1. ethnic self-identification (identifying oneself as a member of a particular ethnic group);

2. affective components (i.e., attitudes and evaluations regarding one's membership in an ethnic group such as pride and positive feelings about the group), along with a preference for ethnically related customs such as food choices or language;

3. cognitive components (i.e., knowledge about the history, customs, and traditions of the group);

4. value orientation (i.e., endorsement of the worldview of the group); and

5. processes of change (i.e., a developmental process of internalizing a psychologically healthy identity regarding oneself as a member of a particular ethnic group).

Many assumed that ethnic/racial identity would lessen over time due to acculturation. However, perhaps due to social forces such as prejudice and immigration, ethnic/racial identity remains a salient force in the lives of ethnic minorities (Phinney, 2000). Still others assume that ethnic/racial identity is an undesirable characteristic perhaps because they mistakenly perceive ethnic/racial identity as a pseudonym for a militant or anti-White ideology. However, empirical research has revealed that ethnic/racial identity has numerous positive consequences for ethnic group members such as less vulnerability to adjustment difficulties, less psychological distress, greater levels of self-actualization, and greater levels of marital satisfaction (Burlew, 2000). The relationship between a healthy ethnic/racial identity and positive drug-related outcomes for ethnic youth has been demonstrated in several studies.

Findings from studies examining the relationship between ethnic/racial identity and drug involvement among Latino populations have varied across subgroups. Some have suggested that acculturation (i.e., changes that individuals make to adapt to a new culture) plays a role. Specifically, they argue that as the level of acculturation increases, Latino youth are more likely to use drugs (Rodriguez, Recio, & De La Rosa, 1993). This relationship has been attributed to intergenerational family-adolescent conflicts (Szapocznik et al., 1986) and the stress associated with adapting to differences between the host culture and the culture of origin (Rodriguez, 1995).

Brook, Whiteman, Balka, Win, and Gursen (1998) examined the relationship between acculturation and drug use in a sample of 555 Puerto Rican males and females between the ages of 16 and 24. The youth were assigned to one of the following four categories based on their self-reported drug use: (a) no reported drug use, (b) used alcohol or tobacco only, (c) used marijuana but no other illicit drug, and (d) used illicit drugs other than marijuana. The findings revealed that those with no use or only alcohol/tobacco had higher levels of ethnic identity than those who reported more drug use. Moreover, in the same study, a strong sense of ethnic/racial identity ameliorated the effects of risk factors such as parental drug use or the availability of drug use on the adolescent's own drug use. Other studies of Latino populations have demonstrated a similar relationship between cultural identity and decreased drug use (Burnam, Hough, Karno, Escobar, & Telles, 1987; Felix-Ortiz & Newcomb, 1995; Markides, Krause, & Mendes de Leon, 1988).

The relationship between ethnic/racial identity and drug use has also been demonstrated among African American youth. For example, Resnicow, Soler, Braithwaite, Selassie, and Smith (1999) found that the more the adolescents in their sample endorsed positive attitudes about being African American, the more anti-drug attitudes they reported. In this study, 346 low-income African American adolescents were given the Racial and Ethnic Identity (REI) Scale for African American youth as well as the Adolescent Survey of Black Life. They found that pro-Black beliefs were protective factors against many negative outcomes, including pro-drug attitudes. In contrast, anti-White attitudes were associated with increased drug use. These findings were consistent with others in the literature that have found a direct relationship between pro-Black beliefs and anti-drug attitudes.

Carlton Oler (1995) reported a similar finding in another sample of African American youth. In that study, 249 fourth, fifth, and sixth graders completed a measure of racial identity developed by Banks (1984) and the Botvin Alcohol and Drug Attitude Scale (Botvin, Baker, Dusenbury, Tortu, & Botvin, 1990). The results revealed that a strong racial identity was associated with positive (intolerant) attitudes about drug use. In a study of 100 African American second graders, Townsend and Belgrave (2000) found that a positive racial identity was related to anti-drug attitudes. Similar findings were reported by Belgrave, Townsend, Cherry, and Cunningham (1997) in a study of 189 African American fourth and fifth graders. In a study of American Indians and Alaska Natives, the relationship between ethnic/racial identity and alcohol involvement was not supported (Trimble, 1995). The sample included 621 American Indian and Alaska Native adolescents from five rural, reservation, and urban settings. That study was based on Trimble's (1991) tripartite model of ethnic identification. Trimble found the following seven identity domains for American Indian self-identification: use of an American Indian or Alaska Native language, participation in American Indian or Native Alaskan traditions and ceremonies, affiliative patterns, self-identification, maternal identification, paternal identification, and acculturative status. A confirmatory factor model was performed using those domains, and the results were consistent with the Trimble tripartite model that includes natality, behavioral orientations, and subjective perceptions (Trimble, 1991). However, the findings did not reveal a relationship between ethnic identity and alcohol involvement in this sample of American Indians and Alaska Natives.

The drinking patterns of Asian Americans have been associated with both ethnicity and birthplace. Abstention rates among Asian Americans are higher among those born outside of the United States than among those born in the United States (Makimoto, 1998). This pattern is supported by the literature, which indicates that the drinking behaviors of Asian and Pacific Islanders living in the United States are more likely to reflect the adoption of the tolerant drug attitudes of the Western culture, whereas those Asians who live outside the United States may retain traditional views against drinking. The maintenance of traditional worldviews may reflect a higher level of ethnic identity.

In a study by James, Kim, and Moore (1997), alcohol use among Asian American youth was found to be related to the dynamics of adapting to Western culture. It was suggested that the transition to Western culture conflicted with the hierarchical nature of the Asian family structure, the interdependent nature of Asian family relationships, and the sense of self among young Asian Americans. The disruption of traditional family patterns and dynamics increases the risk of drug and alcohol use. The effect of acculturation on the family structure of

Asian Americans is particularly noteworthy because the literature indicates that cultural identification and effective family management styles are associated with lower rates of alcohol use in Asian American youth (James, Kim, & Armijo, 2000).

The literature reviewed in this section argues for considering culture when designing prevention programs for ethnic minority youth. Some of the major approaches to prevention are described in the next section. Although the developers of these programs usually began with a generic version of the intervention, culture was later incorporated into the subsequent versions of several of these interventions. The section on culturally tailored interventions describes several efforts to include culture in prevention programming.

APPROACHES TO PREVENTION

There is an ongoing effort to develop effective drug prevention programs for ethnic minority youth. Numerous prevention programs are being implemented throughout the United States. Although the objectives of these programs may differ with ethnicity, age, and risk factors, the common goal of drug prevention programs is to reduce the incidence of drug use and abuse (Botvin, 1995). Some prevention programs have been demonstrated to be more effective than others. Perhaps this finding supports the belief that some interventions are more closely tied than others to the empirical research on the etiology of drug use.

Drug prevention programs tend to fall into one of the following primary categories: comprehensive interventions, family-based interventions, and school-based interventions. The next few subsections will discuss each of these approaches to interventions and describe specific examples used with ethnic minorities. The three programs that are described—Project Northland, the Strengthening Families Program, and Life Skills Training—were all recently designated as exemplary programs by the U.S. Department of Education.

Comprehensive Programs

Numerous factors contribute to drug use among youth; therefore, some programs address drug use through multiple avenues of change. One comprehensive alcohol preventive intervention for youth has been fully tested (Perry & Williams, 1996). Project Northland, a community-wide research program, focuses on the prevention of alcohol use by using a multilevel, community-wide approach with youth. It was designed with primarily European youth from rural, lower-middle-class to middle-class communities. These communities were assumed to have the highest prevalence of alcohol-related problems in the state. For each year of the intervention, an overall theme was derived based on the developmental level of the group and the school organization. Social-behavioral curricula in schools, peer leadership, parental participation and education, and community-wide task force activities were all included in the intervention (Perry & Williams, 1996). The focus is on Grades 6 to 8. The objective for each grade level is different.

The objective of the sixth-grade program, "Slick Tracy," is to facilitate communication between parents and adolescents about alcohol use. The seventh-grade curriculum, "Amazing Alternatives," is aimed at enhancing refusal skills and building positive peer group influences. In the eighth grade, the youth are introduced to professional and political groups in the community that influence adolescent alcohol use. The eighth-grade curriculum is called "Powerlines."

Peer leadership is also included in the intervention. Youth whom other adolescents like and respect are selected as peer leaders. Student leaders participate in a leadership training program called T.E.E.N.S. (The Exciting and Entertaining Northland Students). These student leaders plan alcohol-free activities for seventh graders. In the standard version, this component includes a 1-day leadership training session that focuses on methods to determine seventh graders' favorite activities, budget planning for the activities, and publicizing the activities.

A community-wide task force is another component of Project Northland. In the original program, the community-wide task force activities included the passage of five alcohol-related ordinances, such as mandatory beverage service training to prevent illegal sales of alcohol to underaged youth. In addition, the task force collaborated with local businesses to establish a gold card system to provide discounts at selected businesses for youth who pledged to be alcohol and drug free.

Although this approach has proven to be successful, multilevel interventions, including both individual and environmental methods of change, are not frequently used in alcohol use prevention. Nevertheless, follow-up evaluations of this intervention demonstrate the utility of a comprehensive approach to reducing alcohol use (Perry & Williams, 1996).

Family-Based Interventions

A body of empirical literature has demonstrated the importance of family in fostering resilience (Hawkins et al., 1992; Kumpfer & Alvarado, 1995). Previous longitudinal and cross-sectional studies have demonstrated that parenting practices, such as clear no-use rules, monitoring, and limiting access to alcohol availability, play a significant role in preventing adolescent drinking. These relationships tend to be independent of race or ethnicity, yet some ethnic differences in alcohol use among youth may be attributed to variations in parenting practices (Barnes & Welte, 1986; Catalano et al., 1993).

As a result of findings linking family relationships to drug use, family-based interventions have also become an essential component in a group of drug prevention programs. Previous research has demonstrated that interventions that increase and encourage positive parenting practices can have a positive effect (Loveland-Cherry, Ross, & Kaufman, 1999; Spoth, Redmond, & Lepper, 1999). In addition to parenting practices, some researchers have postulated that family bonding may be a key social control mechanism that may lessen adolescents' risk of alcohol abuse (Bahr, Marcos, & Maughan, 1995). Although the important role of parents in drug prevention has been acknowledged, program developers continue to struggle with achieving a high degree of parental participation (Botvin, 1995).

The Strengthening Families Program (SFP), developed by Karol Kumpfer, is an example of a family-based program. The Office of Juvenile Justice and Delinquency Prevention selected the Kumpfer SFP program as one in a set of "exemplary" family programs. The ultimate goal of the program is to increase personal resiliency to drug use. The program focuses on improving family relations by strengthening family communications, increasing parent-child time together, increasing parental empathy, and increasing family planning and organization (Kumpfer, 1994a, 1994b). The intervention is based on a strong body of research indicating that family factors such as parental support (Dishion, French, & Patterson, 1995; King, Beals, Manson, & Trimble, 1992), parental supervision (Hansen et al., 1987), family conflict and involvement (Bry, 1983; Mayer, 1995), and parenting practices (Szapocznik et al., 1988) are related to adolescent substance abuse and other problem behaviors. Moreover, parents in dysfunctional,

antisocial, or drug-affected families may be limited in their capacity to respond appropriately to their children's emotional and social cues (Hans, 1995; Kumpfer, 1994a, 1994b).

The SFP intervention consists of a multicomponent 14-session program. The parents receive training in effective parenting practices (i.e., reinforcement, limit setting). The children's program is modeled after Spivack and Shure's (1979) social skills training. The Family Skills Training Program provides an opportunity for parents and children to practice their skills (with trainer support) in a structured setting. SFP is unique in that it was developed "specifically for children of alcohol- and drug-abusing parents" (Kumpfer, 1994a, 1994b).

The SFP intervention has been evaluated in a number of settings with various ethnic groups. For example, in the Utah Community Youth Activity Project, the SFP was implemented in three counties and eight agencies. The sample consisted of 703 high-risk youth between the ages of 6 and 13 and their families. Of the sample, 69% was ethnic minority, including Asians (26%), Pacific Islanders (20%), Latinos (18%), and American Indians and Alaska Natives (5%). The results revealed a significant pretest-to-posttest reduction in externalizing (i.e., problem behaviors) and internalizing (i.e., depressive symptoms, anxiety symptoms) behaviors on the Child Behavior Checklist as well as reduced levels of family conflict and higher levels of family cohesion on the Family Environment Scale.

School-Based Interventions

A large percentage of drug prevention programs are school-based interventions (Ellickson, 1995). These school-based interventions focus on helping youth develop personal and social skills that will enhance their sense of competence and decrease the likelihood of yielding to pressures to use drugs (www.LifeSkillsTraining.com). The incorporation of social influence approaches and skills training into school-based interventions has demonstrated promising results in ethnic minority populations and in economically disadvantaged communities (Harrington & Donohew, 1997; Sussman, Dent, Stacy, & Craig, 1998). On the other hand, the minimal effect sizes raise the question of whether a school-based intervention alone is sufficient for significant and long-term changes in alcohol use by adolescents without broader environmental changes (Ellickson, 1995, Gorman, 1995, 1996; Johnson et al., 1990; Moscowitz, 1989).

The Life Skills Training (LST) program is an example of a school-based program. It was designed to prevent drug use among middle school or junior high students (Botvin, 1996). The 12 program units include sessions on self-image; decision making; myths and realities about smoking, alcohol, and marijuana; advertising; coping with anxiety; and communication, social, and assertiveness skills. Although the original program was tested on White children, the intervention was later evaluated using a Latino and an African American sample. The study testing the effectiveness of the LST intervention among Latino youth was conducted among 471 seventh graders attending eight public schools in the New York metropolitan area. Half of the schools were randomly assigned to receive the intervention, and the other half became the control group. The results revealed that the youth in the intervention reported less tobacco use and more knowledge about the consequences of smoking than the control group.

Culturally Tailored Interventions

The demonstrated link between racial/ethnic identity and positive outcomes for youth was discussed earlier in the section on racial/ethnic identity and drug use. That body of work paved the way for research on the utility of culturally tailored interventions (Chipunga et al., 2000; Emshoff et al., 1996). Perhaps culturally tailored programs work because the activities are consistent with the cultural and risk characteristics of the targeted group (Chipunga et al., 2000).

Several alternative approaches exist for designing culturally tailored programs. We refer to these types as culturally enhanced (CE) and culturally based (CB) programs.

Culturally Enhanced Programs. CE programs modify a standard version to make it more culturally appropriate. These programs incorporate the same messages of the standard version but alter names, scenarios, stories, and other activities to be more culturally familiar.

The cultural version of the Botvin Life Skills Training program is an example of a CE program. Early research first documented the efficacy of the standard LST intervention with White middle-class youth (Botvin & Botvin, 1992). Later, a "culturally focused" version was developed for African Americans. This version differed from the universal version in several specific ways: (a) The materials were closely scrutinized to determine if the reading level was appropriate, (b) visual images were added to portray African American youth, and (c) the examples, role-play scenarios, and language were infused with themes consistent with the African American experience. However, the objective was to develop a "culturally focused" version that had the same messages as the universal version. Studies of the culturally tailored version of this program have shown that this approach is effective for African American youth (Botvin, Batson, et al., 1989).

Later, the materials were modified to increase their appropriateness for Latino students. Data gathered through focus groups as well as input from consultants, teachers, and students were used to make the program more culturally tailored for Latino youth (Botvin, Dusenbury, Baker, James-Ortiz, & Kerner, 1989). This time, the sample included 3,501 students from 47 public and parochial schools in New York City. Schools were assigned to either the intervention or the control condition. The results revealed a significant reduction in smoking among those Latino youth in the intervention relative to those in the control group at the end of the 7th grade. Moreover, the intervention group continued to demonstrate the efficacy of the program even during the 10th grade.

Culturally Based Programs. CB programs go beyond merely altering the manner in which the message of the generic program is presented to make it more culturally consistent. Specifically, CB programs develop curricula that incorporate cultural strengths. An underlying assumption in this second type of cultural tailoring is that it would be useful to incorporate some of the positive teachings (values) of a particular culture (cultural strengths) into the intervention. The SUPER STARS program (Emshoff et al., 1996) is an example of that form of cultural tailoring. The universal version of that intervention was modified to include activities to stress cultural pride and identity, exposure to important events in the history of African Americans, and exposure to cultural values expressed in cultural rituals (e.g., Nguzo Saba or the Seven Principles of Kwanzaa). After completing the culturally based program, youth reported both that they had more knowledge about drugs and that they were more likely to say no to drugs in the face of peer pressure (Carlyle & Emshoff, 1992). This type of cultural tailoring is more similar to the type of activities included in rites of passage and other culturally based interventions.

Our own program was a culturally based, Africentric program conducted with African American youth. The youth were sixth graders when they entered our program. Interested youth and their families attended a social gathering that served as an orientation to the program. At that session, the participants were randomly assigned to participate in either the intervention or the control group. For approximately 10 to 12 weeks, the participants attended three separate sessions. The drug education/prevention curriculum provided information about the consequences of drug use. However, several of the sessions included discussions on the incongruency between African American belief systems and drug use. The second session each week was aimed at promoting self-esteem through cultural awareness. The SETCLAE (Self-Esteem Through Culture Leads to Academic Achievement) curriculum developed by Jawanza Kunjufu was used for this session. The Saturday enrichment sessions included arts and crafts, plays, skits, storytelling, field trips, and community projects. Relative to the control group, the program participants reported more favorable school bonding, racial/cultural pride, and resistance to peer pressure to use drugs. In addition, male participants, relative to male members of the control group, had better school attendance and reported more favorable self-discipline and fewer problem behaviors.

CSAP MODEL PROGRAMS

The Center for Substance Abuse Prevention (CSAP) plays a critical role in the development, evaluation, and dissemination of research on prevention programs. CSAP funding has made it possible for researchers throughout the country to develop and evaluate numerous prevention programs that have demonstrated positive outcomes for both short- and long-term periods. The heterogeneity of these programs indicates the need for programming that meets the needs of diverse groups.

To date, CSAP has identified 20 interventions as model programs. To be considered a "model" program, a program must be rated acceptable on several criteria, including the incorporation of theory, the fidelity of the implementation of the intervention, quality of the process evaluation, the adequacy of the sampling strategy and implementation, low attrition, positive outcomes, appropriate treatment of missing data, outcome data collection, analysis, the use of designs that eliminate other plausible threats to validity (excluding attrition), integrity, utility, replications, dissemination, and cultural and age appropriateness (Substance Abuse and Mental Health Services Administration [SAMHSA], 2001). The wide range of techniques used to target particular populations has contributed to the success of these prevention programs. For example, the Dare to Be You program in Colorado addresses resilience factors rather than substance abuse itself (SAMHSA, 2001). The Keep a Clear Mind program is aimed at strengthening parent-child communication (SAMHSA, 2001). These two CSAP model programs are described below.

Dare to Be You

The Dare to Be You program was designed by Colorado State University for the parents of children between the ages of 2 and 5. It was implemented in four ethnically diverse settings, including the Ute Mountain Ute community (95% American Indian and Alaska Native), the San Luis Valley (64% Hispanic), Colorado Springs (53% White), and Montezuma County (84% White). The aim of the program was to strengthen resiliency factors in children by (a) promoting self-concept, satisfaction with the parenting

role, internal locus of control, and satisfaction with the social support network among parents while enhancing their relationship with children and the knowledge of child development; (b) training parents to replace harsh punishment with more appropriate control techniques; and (c) improving behavior, interactions with parents, and developmental milestones for preschool children at risk for alcohol and drug use.

The parent training program consists of 24 hours of weekly training over a 3- to 4-month period aimed at increasing parental knowledge of child development, personal sense of worth, effective discipline strategies, personal and parental efficacy, and appropriate child-rearing practices. Separately, the children participate in activities to bolster self-worth and self-responsibility while improving communication, problem-solving, and reasoning skills. A follow-up workshop series is added to reinforce the skills obtained during the intervention phase. When the program was implemented in Colorado, the retention was amazingly high. More than 95% of the participants completed all program components during the first year, and more than 75% completed yearly follow-up surveys. The results also revealed significant and lasting increases in parental competence and parental role satisfaction.

Keep a Clear Mind

The Keep a Clear Mind (KACM) program was developed by the University of Arkansas with a grant from the U.S. Department of Education. This home-based prevention program was developed for fourth- to sixth-grade children and their families. Both home activities and school activities were used in the implementation of this program. Home activities were sent to the families, including weekly newsletters that provided parents with information on various drugs, strategies for communicating with their children about drugs, and suggestions for helping children avoid drugs. The home activities addressed the primary goals of increasing parent-child communications related to substance use prevention and encouraging the youth to develop refusal skills for gateway drug use (SAMHSA, 2001). The classroom component included activities that focus on reducing susceptibility to peer pressure for drug experimentation. This prevention program posits that individual, family, peer, protective, and risk factors need to be addressed. Follow-up evaluations revealed that KACM participants had a higher frequency of endorsing a no-use position and a more realistic view of drug use consequences than non-KACM participants. The evaluation also revealed that the parents of these participants also had a more realistic view of drug use among youth and its harmful consequences.

RESEARCH ISSUES

The growing numbers of available prevention programs for ethnic minority and other youth summon the need to evaluate the efficacy of various types of intervention. To conduct effective evaluations, researchers must develop methodology sound enough for them to feel confident in interpreting the results. A major concern regarding the research on ethnic minorities in general and prevention programs in particular is the assumption of the universality of the American mainstream experience. That supposition too often leads researchers to assume incorrectly that the theories, procedures, measures, and analytical strategies used to conduct evaluations of White samples can be blindly applied to the evaluations of ethnic minorities. A comprehensive discussion of this issue is beyond the scope of this chapter. However, this issue is discussed more fully in the chapter titled "Research With

Ethnic Minorities: Conceptual, Methodological, and Analytical Issues" (see Chapter 8, this volume). Various conceptual issues associated with the universality assumption have been discussed throughout this chapter, such as the utility of designing intervention programs that are consistent with prevalence rates along with the specific risk and resilience factors associated with specific ethnic/racial groups. However, in this section, methodological and analytical issues and areas for future research will be discussed.

Methodological Issues

Several methodological issues pose challenges for the prevention researcher. These include recruitment, measurement, sampling, the validity of self-report, and within-group heterogeneity. Although these are certainly issues when conducting research on White youth as well, the issues themselves are slightly different in samples of ethnic minorities.

Recruitment and Retention

The NIH Revitalization Act of 1993 (P.L.103-43) (*Federal Register*, 1994) mandated the recruitment of women and minorities in clinical research and especially clinical trials. One outgrowth of that act was the development of a document titled "Outreach Notebook for the NIH Guidelines for the Inclusion of Women and Minorities as Subjects in Clinical Research." Perhaps one explanation for the difficulty of including ethnic minorities is the skepticism of ethnic minority communities about the value of research in their lives (Call, Otto, & Spenner, 1982). The poor relationships that the research community has fostered with ethnic minority communities may be a source of this skepticism. For example, one explanation for the skepticism among American Indian and Alaska Native tribes is that the tribes have rarely been invited to participate in anything other than the data collection process. Consequently, ethnic minorities may be reluctant to participate in studies in which the results are likely to be interpreted by outsiders using theories that are not always consistent with American Indian and Alaska Native culture (Baldwin, 1999).

Measurement

The tendency to assume that measures developed and standardized on other subgroups are appropriate for research on ethnic minorities is another example of the assumption of the universality of the American mainstream. Several issues may affect whether a measure is equivalent in different cultural contexts. If the group to which the scale is to be applied does not speak the same language as the group on whom the scale was developed, researchers run the risk of failing to achieve what Brislin (1993) called translation equivalence. In addition, researchers must also consider whether a scale has metric equivalence for a given minority group. Reliability and validity measures may change from one group to another. Finally, conceptual equivalence refers to whether the underlying trait is the same in the two groups (Allen & Walsh, 2000).

Several strategies have been proposed to assess whether a measure is appropriate for a given ethnic group. Assessing internal consistency is a common method used by researchers to assess whether a measure is reliable in a different group. However, other analyses need to be conducted to ensure that the traits being measured in the original and the new group are equivalent. These include factor analysis, regression, and item response theory (Allen & Walsh, 2000).

Increasing the Accuracy of Self-Report

Self-report is the most common method of collecting social behavioral research on drug use. However, the validity of self-report is a concern for prevention research for all groups, not just ethnic minorities. Strategies that may improve the accuracy of self-report of sensitive information have been examined. These strategies include anonymity, the use of a self-generated identification code, and the bogus pipeline technique.

A self-generated identification code is an anonymous code generated from information available to the participant but not to the researcher (Kearney, Hopkins, Mauss, & Warheith, 1984). Specifically, each participant is requested to use the same instructions to create the same confidential identification code at each data collection. For example, the first letter of the mother's maiden name might be used to generate the first digit. The next digit might be based on the respondent's birthplace. Using that information, the participant can generate a code that the researcher cannot use to identify the respondent. However, when that participant uses those same instructions to generate the same code at a second data collection, the researcher can match the data collected at the two time points. If the same instructions are provided at the beginning and end of an intervention, the researcher can match a participant's data at the two data points and still provide the participants with anonymity.

Evans, Hansen, and Mittlemark (1977) developed a procedure called the bogus pipeline (BPL) in which the participant is led to believe the information that she or he provides about drug use will be verified by a biochemical test. In reality, the information is not verified. That explains why it is called a "bogus" pipeline. The utility of the bogus pipeline has been widely discussed elsewhere (Aguinis, Pierce, & Quigley, 1995; Roese & Jamieson, 1993). Previous research has demonstrated that the BPL has improved the accuracy of the information provided on both alcohol and marijuana use (Hingson et al., 1986; Lowe, Windsor, Adams, Morris, & Reese, 1986). However, little research is available on the utility of these strategies among ethnic minorities.

Within-Group Heterogeneity

The heterogeneity within specific ethnic minority groups is another issue that should be considered when developing a sampling plan. For example, past research often treated American Indians and Alaska Natives as a heterogeneous group (Baldwin, 1999). However, the American Indian and Alaska Native community consists of more than 500 tribes who speak more than 200 languages. Although they are often studied as a group, drinking patterns among the different tribes vary significantly (Caetano et al., 1998). For example, the Navajo tribes view alcohol consumption as acceptable, whereas the Hopi consider drinking to be irresponsible.

The Problem With Race Comparison Analyses

A common strategy for analyzing research with ethnic minority youth and children is to use a race comparison approach (Graham, 1992; McLoyd, 1998; McLoyd & Randolph, 1985). In race comparison studies, race (or ethnicity) is the independent variable, and the objective is to compare ethnic groups on one or more dependent variables. The pitfalls of this strategy include the failure to consider that sociodemographic variables may account for some differences that masquerade as ethnic group differences. A second pitfall is the faulty assumption that mean differences reflect actual differences and not methodological errors.

Such problems have led several researchers to conclude that race comparison research is inappropriate except in a small number of specific situations (Azibo, 1988; Steinberg & Fletcher, 1998). Nevertheless, the issue of whether a specific intervention has a differential impact across ethnic/racial groups is certainly a valid concern. Assuming one has addressed the issues associated with

measurement equivalence, Steinberg and Fletcher (1998) suggested that one appropriate use of race in multiethnic prevention studies is to include race as a moderator of the relationship between an independent (i.e., assignment to the intervention or the comparison group) and a dependent variable (i.e., drug outcomes). In this case, one is addressing whether the impact of the intervention on the outcome variables differs according to race/ethnicity (moderator).

The need to address the within-group heterogeneity in the sampling plan was mentioned earlier. However, within-group heterogeneity also requires attention at the analysis stage. Specifically, if a researcher has successfully recruited a heterogeneous sample of a specific ethnic group, then the analyses should consider whether the outcomes differ for different subgroups.

AREAS FOR FUTURE RESEARCH

Too often, the research for the ethnic minority community reflects the research agenda for White youth. However, a number of issues unique to the ethnic minority community warrant further attention. First, the underutilization of available services among ethnic minorities is an issue that has been documented elsewhere (Makimoto, 1998). Although the factors that may influence utilization rates are complex, providing prevention services in a culturally consistent manner may be related to utilization. For example, Makimoto (1998) reported that participation rates increase significantly if bilingual and bicultural staff persons are available to provide services to Asian Americans.

Little research is available on the dynamics of why culturally tailored interventions may improve outcomes. Such research is crucial for designing future programs that effectively incorporate culture. One possibility is that adolescents who have more positive perceptions regarding their own ethnic group are more likely to hold positive opinions about themselves and, ultimately, to avoid drug use because they take their futures more seriously. However, an alternative explanation is that the efficacy of culturally tailored programs is due to the inculcation of a specific set of positive cultural values. The first explanation argues for prevention programming that showcases the accomplishments of the African American community. However, the second explanation would suggest the development of programs that provide more socialization to a set of important values. More research is necessary to address issues such as these.

A number of other topics warrant further research for understanding the etiology of substance abuse among ethnic minority youth. A sample of these topics include the relation of ethnic/racial identity to substance abuse and the impact of the concentration of liquor stores in ethnic minority communities. These are topics that may not be critical for understanding drug use among White youth but demand more research for understanding the drug behaviors of ethnic minorities. However, future research aimed at determining the best way to collect substance abuse information from youth will be useful for future research with all adolescents, not just ethnic minority youth.

CONCLUSIONS

This chapter has highlighted some of the important issues related to studying and understanding ethnic minority drug use. The prevalence rates vary across ethnic minority groups. Contrary to popular belief, studies have demonstrated that the prevalence of drug abuse among ethnic minorities is similar to or less than the rate for their White counterparts. However, the consequences of drug abuse appear to be more pronounced among ethnic minority groups than White youth.

Several theoretical perspectives have been used to explain drug abuse among ethnic minorities. Some have focused on the risk and resilience factors associated with drug use, such as social settings and environments, whereas other perspectives have asserted that drug use may be related to cultural identification.

As our understanding of drug-related issues continues to increase, there is an ongoing effort to make this knowledge practical through the development of various prevention programs. The major types of prevention programs include family-based, school-based, and comprehensive programs, which incorporate the community in prevention efforts. Several prevention programs have been recognized as "model programs" because of their success in the prevention of drug use among various ethnic groups. The continued success of these model programs and future prevention programs will require researchers and program developers to address the various methodological issues that surface when conducting research on ethnic minorities.

NOTE

1. Although convincing arguments have been made for differentiating between ethnic and racial identity, we use the term *ethnic/racial identity* to convey that we are not differentiating between the two terms in this particular discussion.

REFERENCES

Aguinis, A., Pierce, C., & Quigley, B. (1995). Enhancing the validity of self-reported alcohol and marijuana consumption using a bogus pipeline: A meta-analytic review. *Basic and Applied Social Psychology, 16*, 515-527.

Allen, J., & Walsh, J. (2000). A construct-based approach to equivalence: Methodologies for cross-cultural/multicultural personality assessment research. In R. Dana (Ed.), *Handbook of cross-cultural and multicultural personality assessments*. Mahwah, NJ: Lawrence Erlbaum.

Anthony, J. C., & Petronis, K. R. (1995). Early-onset drug use and risk of later drug problems. *Drug & Alcohol Dependence, 40*(1), 9-15.

Azibo, D. (1988). Understanding the proper and improper usage of the comparative research framework. *Journal of Black Psychology, 15*, 81-91.

Bachman, J. G., Wallace, J. M., O'Malley, P. M., Johnston, L. D., Kurth, C. L., & Neighbors, H. W. (1991). Racial/ethnic differences in smoking, drinking, and illicit drug use among American high school seniors, 1976-1989. *American Journal of Public Health, 81*, 372-377.

Bahr, S. J., Marcos, A. C., & Maughan, S. L. (1995). Family, educational and peer influences on the alcohol use of female and male adolescents. *Journal Studies on Alcohol, 56*, 457-469.

Baldwin, J. (1999). Conducting drug abuse prevention research in partnership with Native American communities: Meeting challenges through collaborative approaches. *Drugs & Society, 14*(1/2), 77-92.

Banks, J. (1984). Black youth in predominantly White suburbs: An exploratory study of their attitudes and self-concepts. *Journal of Negro Education, 53*(1), 3-17.

Barnes, G. M., & Welte, J. W. (1986). Adolescent alcohol abuse: Subgroup differences and relationships to other problem behaviors. *Journal of Adolescent Research, 1*, 79-94.

Beauvais, F. (1992a). Comparison of drug use rates for reservation Indian, non-reservation Indian, and Anglo youth. *American Indian & Alaska Native Mental Health Research, 5*(1), 13-31.

Beauvais, F. (1992b). The consequences of drug and alcohol use for Indian youth. *American Indian & Alaska Native Mental Health Research, 5*(1), 32-37.

Beauvais, F. (1996). Trends in drug use among American Indian students and dropouts, 1975, 1994. *American Journal of Public Health, 86*(11), 1594-1598.

Beauvais, F., & Segal, B. (1992). Drug use patterns among American Indian and Alaskan Native youth: Special rural population. *Drugs & Society, 7*(1/2), 77-94.

Belgrave, F. Z., Townsend, T. G., Cherry, V. R., & Cunningham, D. M. (1997). The influence of an Africentric world-view and demographic variables on drug knowledge, attitudes, and use among African American youth. *Journal of Community Psychology, 25*(5), 421-433.

Botvin, G. (1995). Principles of prevention. In R. H. Coombs & D. M. Ziedonis (Eds.), *Handbook on drug abuse prevention: A comprehensive strategy to prevent the abuse of alcohol and other drugs* (pp. 9-44). Needham Heights, MA: Allyn & Bacon.

Botvin, G. (1996). *Life skills training: Promoting health and personal development: Year 1 teacher's manual*. Princeton, NJ: Princeton Health Press.

Botvin, G. J., Baker, E., Dusenbury, L., Tortu, S., & Botvin, E. (1990). Preventing adolescent drug abuse through a multi-modal cognitive behavioral approach: Results of a 3-year study. *Journal of Consulting and Clinical Psychology, 58*, 437-446.

Botvin, G., Batson, H., Witts-Vitale, S., Bess, V., Baker, E., & Dusenbury, L. A. (1989). A psychosocial approach to smoking prevention for urban Black youth. *Public Health Reports, 104*, 573-582.

Botvin, G., & Botvin, E. (1992). School-based and community-based prevention approaches. In J. H. Lowinson, P. Ruiz, & R. B. Millman (Eds.), *Substance abuse: A comprehensive textbook* (2nd ed., pp. 910-927). Baltimore: Williams & Williams.

Botvin, G., Dusenbury, L., Baker, E., James-Ortiz, S., & Kerner, J. (1989). A skills training approach to smoking prevention among Hispanic youth. *Journal of Behavioral Medicine, 12,* 279-296.

Brislin, R. W. (1993). *Understanding culture's influence on behavior.* New York: Harcourt Brace.

Brook, J. S., Cohen, P., Whiteman, M., & Gordon, A. S. (1992). Psychosocial risk factors in the transition from moderate to heavy use or abuse of drugs. In M. D. Glantz & R.W. Pickens (Eds.), *Vulnerability to drug abuse* (pp. 359-388). Washington, DC: American Psychological Association.

Brook, J. S., Whiteman, M., Balka, E. B., Win, P. T., & Gursen, M. D. (1998). Drug use among Puerto Ricans: Ethnic identity as a protective factor. *Hispanic Journal of Behavioral Sciences, 20*(2), 241-254.

Bry, B. H. (1983). Empirical foundations of family-based approaches to adolescent substance abuse. In T. J. Glynn, C. G. Leukefeld, & J. P. Ludford (Eds.), *Preventing adolescent drug abuse: Intervention strategies* (DHHS Pub. No. (ADM)83-1280). Washington, DC: Government Printing Office.

Burlew, A. K. (2000). Racial identity. In A. Kazdin (Ed.), *Encyclopedia of psychology* (pp. 1110-1113). Washington, DC: American Psychological Association.

Burnam, M., Hough, R. L., Karno, M., Escobar, J., & Telles, C. (1987). Acculturation and lifetime prevalence of psychiatric disorders among Mexican Americans in Los Angeles. *Journal of Health and Social Behavior, 28,* 89-102.

Caetano, R., Clark, C., & Tam, T. (1998). Alcohol consumption among racial/ethnic minorities. *Alcohol Health and Research World, 22*(4), 233-241.

Call, V. R. A., Otto, L. B., & Spenner, K. I. (1982). *Tracking respondents: A multimethod approach.* Lexington, MA: Lexington Books.

Carlyle, B., & Emshoff, J. (1992). The SUPER II program: An early intervention program. *Journal of Community Psychology,* 10-21.

Catalano, R. F., Hawkins, J. D., Krenz, C., Gilmore, M., Morrison, D., Wells, E., & Abbott, R. (1993). Using research to guide culturally appropriate drug abuse prevention. *Journal of Consulting and Clinical Psychology, 61*(5), 804-811.

Chipunga, S., Hermann, J., Sambrano, S., Nistler, M., Sale, E., & Springer, J. (2000). Prevention programming for African American youth: A review of strategies in CSAP's national cross-site evaluation of high risk youth programs. *Journal of Black Psychology, 26,* 360-386.

Dawkins, A. J., & Dawkins, M. P. (1983, Winter). Alcohol and other drugs as cripplers: A crucial problem in the Black community. *Urban League Review,* pp. 36-45.

Delgado, M. (1999). Involvement of the Hispanic community in ATOD research. *Drugs & Society, 14*(1/2), 93-105.

Dishion, T. J., French, D., & Patterson, G. R. (1995). The development and ecology of antisocial behavior. In D. Cicchetti & D. Cohen (Eds.), *Manual of developmental psychopathology: Vol. 2. Risk, disorder, and adaptation* (pp. 421-471). New York: John Wiley.

Ellickson, P. L. (1995). Schools. In R. H. Coombs & D. M. Ziedonis (Eds.), *Handbook on drug abuse prevention: A comprehensive strategy to prevent the abuse of alcohol and other drugs* (pp. 93-120). Needham Heights, MA: Allyn & Bacon.

Ellickson, P. L., McGuligan, K. A., Adams, V., Bell, R. M., & Hays, R. D. (1996). Teenagers and alcohol misuse in the United States: By any definition, it's a big problem. *Addiction, 91*(10), 1489-1503.

Emshoff, J., Avery, E., Raduka, G., Anderson, D. J., & Calvert, C. (1996). Findings from super stars: A health promotion program for families to enhance multiple protective factors. *Journal of Adolescent Research, 11,* 68-96.

Ensminger, M., & Slusarcick, A. (1992). Paths to high school graduation or dropout: A longitudinal study of a first grade cohort. *Sociology of Education, 65,* 95-113.

Evans, R. I., Hansen, W. B., & Mittlemark, M. B. (1977). Increasing the validity of self-reports of smoking behavior in children. *Journal of Applied Psychology, 1,* 399-403.

Federal Register. (1994, March 28). *59,* 14508-14513.

Felix-Ortiz, M., & Newcomb, M. (1995). Cultural identity and drug use among Latino and Latina adolescents. In G. Botvin, S. Schinke, & M. Orlandi (Eds.), *Drug abuse prevention with multiethnic youth* (pp. 147-165). Thousand Oaks, CA: Sage.

Gorman, D. M. (1995). On the difference between statistical and practical significance in school-based drug abuse prevention. *Drugs, Education, Prevention and Policy, 2*(3), 275-283.

Gorman, D. M. (1996). Do school-based social skills training programs prevent alcohol use among young people? *Addiction Research, 4*(2), 191-210.

Grace, C. (1992). Practical consideration for program professionals and evaluators working with African-American communities. In M. A. Orlandi (Ed.), *Cultural competence for evaluators: A guide for alcohol and other drug abuse prevention practitioners working with ethnic/ racial communities* (OSAP Cultural Competence Series No. 1, DHHS Pub. No. (ADM) 92-1884, pp. 55-74). Rockville, MD: U.S. Department of Health and Human Services.

Graham, S. (1992). "Most of the subjects were white and middle class": Trends in published research on African Americans in selected APA journals 1970-1989. *American Psychologist, 47,* 629-639.

Grant, B. F., & Dawson, D. A. (1997). Age at onset of alcohol use and its association with *DSM-IV* alcohol abuse and dependence: Results from the National Longitudinal Alcohol Epidemiological Survey. *Journal of Substance Abuse, 9,* 103-110.

Hans, S. (1995). Diagnosis in etiologic and epidemiologic studies. In C. Jones & M. De La Rosa (Eds.), *National Institute on Drug Abuse technical review: Methodological issues: Etiology and consequences of drug abuse among women* (pp. *000-000*). Silver Spring, MD: National Institute on Drug Abuse.

Hansen, W. B., Graham, J. W., Sobel, J. L., Shelton, D. R., Flay, B. R., & Johnson, C. A. (1987). The consistency of peer and parent influences on tobacco, alcohol, and marijuana use among young adolescents. *Journal of Behavioral Medicine, 10,* 559-579.

Harrington, N. G., & Donohew, L. (1997). Jump Start: A targeted substance abuse prevention program. *Health Education & Behavior, 24*(5), 568-586.

Hawkins, J. D., Catalano, R. F., & Miller, J. Y. (1992). Risk and protective factors for alcohol and other drug problems in adolescence and early adulthood: Implications for substance abuse prevention. *Psychological Bulletin, 112*(1), 64-105.

Hawkins, J. D., Graham, J. W., Maguin, E., Abbott, R., Hill, K. G., & Catalano, R. F. (1997). Exploring the effects of age of alcohol use initiation and psychosocial risk factors on subsequent alcohol misuse. *Journal of Studies on Alcohol, 58*(3), 280-290.

Hingson, R., Zuckerman, B., Amaro, H., Frank, D. A., Kayne, H., Sorenson, J. R., Mitchell, J., Parker, S., Morelock, S., & Timperi, R. (1986). Maternal marijuana use and neonatal outcome: Uncertainty posed by self-reports. *American Journal of Public Health, 76*(6), 667-669.

James, W., Kim, G., & Armijo, E. (2000). The influence of ethnic identity on drug use among ethnic minority adolescents. *Journal of Drug Education, 30*(3), 265-280.

James, W. H., Kim, G. K., & Moore, D. D. (1997). Examining racial and ethnic differences in Asian adolescent drug use: The contributions of culture, background, and lifestyle. *Drugs: Education, Prevention, & Policy, 4*(1), 39-51.

Jani, S. (1999). *Drug abuse among our children: A growing national crisis* (U.S. Senate Committee No. MOF00109942). Washington, DC: Government Printing Office.

Johnson, C. (2001). *Adolescent drug use: The role of parental and peer factors in the sixth and seventh grades.* Unpublished master's thesis, University of Cincinnati, Cincinnati, OH.

Johnson, C. A., Pentz, M. A., Weber, M. D., Dwyer, J. H., Baer, N., MacKinnon, D. P., Hansen, W. B., & Flay, B. R. (1990). Relative effectiveness of comprehensive community programming for drug abuse prevention with high-risk and low-risk adolescents. *Journal of Consulting and Clinical Psychology, 58*(4), 447-456.

Johnston, L. D., O'Malley, P. M., & Bachman, J. G. (1995). *National survey results on drug use from the Monitoring the Future study, 1975-1994: Vol. 1. Secondary school students.* Rockville, MD: National Institute on Drug Abuse.

Johnston, L. D., O'Malley, P. M., & Bachman, J. G. (1998). *National survey results on drug use from the Monitoring the Future study, 1975-1997* (2 vols). Rockville, MD: National Institute on Drug Abuse.

Johnston, L. D., O'Malley, P. M., & Bachman, J. G. (2000). *Monitoring the Future national survey results on drug use, 1975-1999: Vol. 1: Secondary school students* (NIH Pub. 00-4690). Rockville, MD: National Institute on Drug Abuse.

Kearney, K., Hopkins, R., Mauss, A., & Warheith, R. (1984). Self-generated identification codes for anonymous collection of longitudinal questionnaire data. *Public Opinion Quarterly, 48,* 370-378.

King, J., Beals, J., Manson, S. M., & Trimble, J. E. (1992). A structural equation model of factors related to substance use among American Indian adolescents. *Drugs & Society, 6*(3-4), 253-268.

Kumpfer, K. L. (1994a). *Implementation manual for the Strengthening Families program.* Unpublished manuscript, Salt Lake City, UT.

Kumpfer, K. L. (1994b, December). *Predictive validity of resilience for positive life adaptation.* Paper presented at the conference, "The Role of Resilience in Drug Abuse, Alcohol Abuse, and Mental Illness," National Institute on Drug Abuse, Washington, DC.

Kumpfer, K. L., & Alvarado, R. (1995). Strengthening families to prevent drug use in multi-ethnic youth. In G. Botvin, S. Schinke, & M. Orlandi (Eds.), *Drug abuse prevention with multi-ethnic youth* (pp. 255-294). Thousand Oaks, CA: Sage.

Kumpfer, K. L., & Bluth, B. (in press). Transactional parent/child relationships and impact on resilience for substance abuse. In J. Johnson & D. K. McDuff (Eds.), *The chronicity of substance abuse.* Baltimore: Harcourt Brace.

Kumpfer, K. L., & Turner, C. W. (1990-1991). The social ecology model of adolescent substance abuse: Implications for prevention. *International Journal of the Addictions, 25*(4A), 435-463.

Loveland-Cherry, C. J., Ross, L. T., & Kaufman, S. R. (1999). Effects of home-based family interventions on adolescent alcohol use and misuse. *Journal of Studies on Alcohol, 13*(Suppl.), 94-102.

Lowe, J. B., Windsor, R. A., Adams, B., Morris, J., & Reese, Y. (1986). Use of a bogus pipeline method to increase accuracy of self-reported alcohol consumption among pregnant women. *Journal of Studies on Alcohol, 47*(2), 173-175.

Maddahian, E., Newcomb, M. D., & Bentler, P. M. (1988). Adolescent drug use and intention to use drugs: Concurrent and longitudinal analyses of four ethnic groups. *Addictive Behaviors, 13,* 191-195.

Makimoto, K. (1998). Drinking patterns and drinking problems among Asian-Americans and Pacific Islanders. *Alcohol Health and Research World, 22*(4), 270-275.

Markides, K., Krause, N., & Mendes de Leon, C. (1988). Acculturation and alcohol consumption among Mexican Americans. *American Journal of Public Health, 78,* 1178-1181.

Mayer, G. R. (1995). Preventing antisocial behavior in the schools. *Journal of Applied Behavioral Analysis, 28*(4), 467-478.

McLoyd, V. C. (1998). Changing demographics in the American population: Implications for research on minority children and adolescents. In V. McLoyd & L. Steinberg (Eds.), *Studying minority adolescents* (pp. 3-28). Mahwah, NJ: Lawrence Erlbaum.

McLoyd, V. C., & Randolph, S. M. (1985). Secular trends in the study of Afro-American children: A review of *Child Development,* 1936-1980. *Monographs of the Society for Research in Child Development, 50,* 78-92.

Moscowitz, J. M. (1989). The primary prevention of alcoholic problems: A critical review of the research literature. *Journal of Studies on Alcohol, 50*(1), 54-88.

Newcomb, M. D., & Felix-Ortiz, M. (1992). Multiple protective and risk factors for drug use and abuse: Cross-sectional and prospective findings. *Journal of Personality & Social Psychology, 63*(2), 280-296.

Oetting, G. R., & Beauvais, F. (1990). Orthogonal cultural identification theory: The cultural identification of minority adolescents. *International Journal of the Addictions, 25*(5A-6A), 655-685.

Oler, C. (1995). *Spirituality, racial identity, and intentions to use alcohol and other drugs among African American youth.* Unpublished doctoral dissertation, University of Cincinnati, Cincinnati, OH.

Perry, C. L., & Williams, C. L. (1996). Project Northland: Outcomes of a community wide alcohol use prevention program during early. *American Journal of Public Health, 86, 956-965.*

Phinney, J. (2000). Ethnic identity. In A. Kazdin (Ed.), *Encyclopedia of psychology.* Washington, DC: American Psychological Association.

Resnicow, K., Soler, R., Braithwaite, R., Selassie, M., & Smith, M. (1999). Development of a racial and ethnic identity scale for African American adolescents: The survey of Black life. *Journal of Black Psychology, 25*(2), 171-188.

Rhodes, J., & Jason, L. (1990). A social stress model of substance abuse. *Journal of Consulting and Clinical Psychology, 58*(4), 395-401.

Robins, L. N., & Przyeck, T. R. (1985). Age of onset of drug use as a factor in drug and other disorders. In C. L. Jones & R. J. Battjes (Eds.), *Etiology of drug abuse* (pp. 178-192). Rockville, MD: National Institute on Drug Abuse.

Rodriguez, O. (1995). Causal models of substance abuse among Puerto Rican adolescents. In G. Botvin, S. Schinke, & M. Orlandi (Eds.), *Drug abuse prevention with multi-ethnic youth* (pp. 130-146). Thousand Oaks, CA: Sage.

Rodriguez, O., Recio, J. L., & De La Rosa, M. (1993). Integrating mainstream and subcultural explanations of drug use among Puerto Rican youth. In M. De La Rosa & J. L. Recio (Eds.), *Drug use among minority youth: Advances in research and methodology* (NIDA Research Monograph No. 130, pp. 8-31). Washington, DC: U.S. Department of Health and Human Services.

Roese, N., & Jamieson, D. (1993). Twenty years of bogus pipeline research: A critical review and meta-analysis. *Psychological Bulletin, 114,* 363-375.

Segal, B., & Stewart, J. (1996). Substance use and abuse in adolescence: An overview. *Journal of Research in Crime and Delinquency, 31,* 3-31.

Spivack, G., & Shure, M. (1979). Interpersonal cognitive problem solving and primary prevention: Programming for preschool and kindergarten children. *Journal of Clinical Child Psychology, 8*(2), 89-94.

Spoth, R., Redmond, C., & Lepper, H. (1999). Alcohol initiation outcomes of universal family-focused preventive interventions: One- and two-year follow-ups of a controlled study. *Journal of Studies on Alcohol, 13*(Suppl.), 103-111.

Stacy, A. W., Newcomb, M. D., & Bentler, P. M. (1992). Interactive and higher-order effects of social influences on drug use. *Journal of Health & Social Behavior, 33*(3), 266-241.

Steinberg, L., & Fletcher, A. (1998). Data analytic strategies in research on ethnic minority youth. In V. McLoyd & L. Steinberg (Eds.), *Studying minority adolescents* (pp. 279-294). Mahwah, NJ: Lawrence Erlbaum.

Stillner, V., Kraus, R., Leukefeld, C., & Hardenbergh, D. (1999). Drug use in very rural Alaska villages. *Substance Use and Misuse, 34,* 579-593.

Substance Abuse and Mental Health Services Administration (SAMHSA). (2001). *CSAP's model programs* [Online]. Available: www.samhsa.gov/centers/csap/modelprograms/default.htm

Sussman, S., Dent, C. W., Stacy, A. W., & Craig, S. (1998). One-year outcomes of Project Towards No Drug Abuse. *Preventive Medicine, 27,* 632-642.

Swan, N. (1995). Targeting prevention messages: Research on drug-use risk and protective factors is fueling the design of ethnically appropriate prevention programs for children. *NIDA Notes, 10*(1), 1-3.

Szapocznik, J., Perez-Vidal, A., Brickman, A. L., Foote, F. H., Santisteban, D., Hervis, O., & Kurtines, W. M. (1988). Engaging adolescent drug abusers and their families in treatment: A strategic structural systems approach. *Journal of Consulting and Clinical Psychology, 56*(4), 552-557.

Szapocznik, J., Santisteban, D., Rio, A., Perez-Vidal, A., Kurtines, W., & Hervis, O. (1986). Bicultural effectiveness training (BET): An intervention modality for families experiencing intergenerational/intercultural conflict. *Hispanic Journal of Behavioral Sciences, 8,* 303-330.

Townsend, T., & Belgrave, F. (2000). The impact of personal identity and racial identity on drug attitudes and use among African American children. *Journal of Black Psychology, 26*(4), 421-436.

Trimble, J. (1991). Ethnic specification, validation prospects, and the future of drug use research. *International Journal of the Addictions, 25,* 149-170.

Trimble, J. (1995). Toward an understanding of ethnicity and ethnic identity, and their relationship with drug research. In G. Botvin, S. Schinke, & M. Orlandi (Eds.), *Drug abuse prevention with multiethnic youth* (pp. 3-27). Thousand Oaks, CA: Sage.

U.S. Department of Health and Human Services. (2000). *Healthy People 2000: National health promotion and disease prevention objectives* (DHHS Pub. No. (PHS) 91-50212). Washington, DC: Author.

Weaver, H. N. (1996). Social work with American Indian youth using the orthogonal model of cultural identification: Families in society. *Journal of Contemporary Human Services, 77*(2), 98-107.

Wolin, S. J., & Wolin, S. (1995). *The resilient self: How survivors of troubled families rise above adversity.* New York: Villard.

Author Index

Abbatiello, A., 368
Abbott, R., 449, 471, 634, 642
Abdul-Adil, J., 69
Abe, J., 45, 46
Abe, J. S., 213
Abe-Kim, J., 523
Abeles, N., 131, 170
Abell, W., 23, 50
Aber, L., 183
Abrams, J. C., 121
Abreu, J. M., 208
Abueg, F. R., 213
Acevedo, M., 313
Acree, M., 612
Adams, B., 647
Adams, D., 15, 43, 54
Adams, E. M., 157
Adams, V., 634
Adderly-Kelly, B., 331
Adebimpe, V. R., 561, 562,
    563, 564
Adler, M. J., 344
Adler, S. R., 216
Adorno, T. W., 27
Agbayani, A., 19
Agbayani-Siewart, P., 18, 48
Agras, S., 529
Aguilar-Gaxiola, S., 214, 388,
    410, 413
Aguinis, A., 647
Aguirre-Molina, M., 547
Ahad, A., 434, 435
Ahmed, F., 416
Ahuna, C., 256
Aiello, P., 366
Ajamu, A., 130
Ajzen, I., 341
Akbar, N., 45, 70, 73, 310, 479
Akintunde, O., 148, 151, 152
Akiyama, M. M., 419
Alan, J. R., 529
Albee, G., 67, 74
Albee, G. W., 121, 477, 491
*Albermarle Paper Co.
    v. Moody,* 32
Albom, M., 606
Alcoholics Anonymous, 542
Alderete, E., 214, 388, 410, 413
Aldwin, C., 419

Alegría, M., 214, 225, 402,
    410, 411
Alexander, C. M., 129, 173,
    488, 493
Alexander, M., 576
Alexander-Snow, M., 105, 110,
    111, 113
Alferi, S. M., 392
Alfonso, V. C., 128
Alipuria, L., 249
Al-Issa, I., 435, 437, 438, 440, 441
Allen, B., 311
Allen, I. M., 563
Allen, J., 187, 188, 189,
    614, 616, 647
Allen, J. A., 4, 5, 414, 417
Allen, L., 183, 308
Allen, W. R., 46
Allende, I., 229
Allers, C., 612
Alleyne, E., 609
Allport, G. W., 294, 299
Altmaier, E. M., 120
Altman, D. G., 578
Alumbaugh, M. J., 391
Alvarado, R., 637, 641
Alvarez, A. N., 250
Alvidrez, J., 528
Amada, G., 381
Amaro, H., 45, 377, 647
American Counseling Association
    (ACA), 628
American Heart Association, 379
American Psychiatric Association
    (APA), 215, 403, 406, 429,
    531, 534, 549, 562
American Psychological
    Association (APA), 29, 34,
    40, 41, 77, 81, 84, 85, 86,
    96, 97, 120, 149, 151, 167,
    168, 171, 172, 495
American Psychological
    Association (APA), Office
    of Ethnic Minority Affairs,
    40, 41
American Psychological
    Association (APA), Office of
    Program Consultation and
    Accreditation, 39

American Psychological
    Association (APA), Research
    Office, 44
American Psychological
    Association (APA) Council of
    Representatives, 43
Ames, M., 563-564
Amir, Y., 2
Anand, S. S., 404
Andersen, S., 565
Anderson, D., 565
Anderson, D. J., 634, 635,
    643, 644
Anderson, E. A., 315
Anderson, L. P., 128, 130, 414
Anderson, M., 469
Anderson, N. B., 5, 46, 128,
    130, 282, 381, 383, 385,
    386, 387, 405, 406, 472,
    473, 613
Anderson, N. J., 384
Anderson, R., 260
Anderson, S., 363
Andes, S., 385
Andrews, D. A., 328
Andrews, L. B., 170
Andujo, E., 260
Aneshensel, C. S., 421
Angelini, P., 612
Anglin, D. D., 550
Anh, B., 228
Ani, M., 67, 70, 472
Annis, R., 262
Anthony, J. C., 634
Antoni, M. H., 390, 392
Ao, M., 529
Aoki, B., 545, 548, 553, 555
APA Division 45 & Microtraining
    Associates, Inc., 135
Applebaum, M., 191
Arai, K., 626
Araki, F., 434
Arcury, T. A., 381
Arena, P. L., 392
Argyle, M., 266
Aries, E., 249
Armijo, E., 640
Armour-Thomas, E., 360, 361,
    369, 370

657

Subject Index

About the Editors

Guillermo Bernal, Ph.D., is Professor of Psychology and Director of the University Center for Psychological Services and Research at the University of Puerto Rico, Río Pideras campus (UPR-RP). He received his doctorate in Psychology (Clinical) from the University of Massachusetts Amherst in 1978. He has published more than 85 journal articles and chapters in the areas of Latino mental health, family and marital therapy, drug abuse, and treatment outcome research. His books include *A Family Like Yours: Breaking the Patterns of Drug Abuse* (with James L. Sorensen) and *Psicoterapia: El reto de evaluar efectividad ante el nuevo milenio.* His current research is in the efficacy and effectiveness of treatments for depression in adolescents and in primary care patients. Bernal directs the NIMH Career Opportunities in Research (COR) Program at UPR-RP that trains honor undergraduates in biopsychosocial research. He also directs the NIMH Minority Infrastructure Support Program (M-RISP) designed to develop the research infrastructure and advance research with faculty and graduate students at UPR-RP. Bernal is a Fellow of the American Psychological Association (APA) Divisions 45, 27, and 12, and he is active on the Advisory Board of the APA Minority Fellowship Program Advisory Board (1993-present). He was President of the Clinical Psychology of Ethnic Minorities (Section 6, Division 12, 1996-1997) and the Society for the Psychological Study of Ethnic Minority Issues (Division 45, 1995-1996). Currently he is an APA Council Representative for Division 45. In 1998, the Association of Psychologists of Puerto Rico recognized his contributions to psychology with a Psychologist of the Year Award. APA Division 12 (section 6) recognized his contributions to training with a Mentor Award (1999), and he recently received a mentoring award from the National Science Network on Drug Abuse.

Joseph Trimble, Ph.D. (University of Oklahoma, Institute of Group Relations, 1969), is a Professor of Psychology at Western Washington University and a Senior Scholar at the Tri-Ethnic Center for Prevention Research at Colorado State University. Throughout his 30-year career, he has focused his efforts on promoting psychological and sociocultural research with indigenous populations, especially American Indians and Alaska Natives. For the past 18 years, he has been working on drug abuse prevention research models for American

Indian youth. He has held offices in the International Association for Cross-Cultural Psychology and the American Psychological Association; he holds Fellow status in three divisions in the APA (Divisions 9, 27, and 45). He is a past president of the Society for the Psychological Study of Ethnic Minority Issues (Division 45 of the APA) and a council member for the Society for the Psychological Study of Social Issues (Division 9 of the APA). In 1994, he received a Lifetime Distinguished Career Award from the American Psychological Association's Division 45 for his research and dedication to cross-cultural and ethnic psychology. He is the recipient of three awards at Western Washington University: the Outstanding Teacher-Scholar Award in 1985, the Excellence in Teaching Award in 1987, and the Paul J. Olscamp Outstanding Research Award in 1999. In 2001, he was awarded the Eleventh Annual Janet E. Helms Award for Mentoring and Scholarship in Professional Psychology at the Teachers College, Columbia University, 18th Annual Roundtable on Cross-Cultural Psychology and Education. He has presented more than 170 papers, invited addresses, and invited lectures at professional meetings and has generated more than 130 publications and technical reports on cross-cultural topics in psychology and higher-education research.

A. Kathleen Burlew is a Professor of Psychology at the University of Cincinnati. She completed her doctoral work in psychology at the University of Michigan. She has coauthored or coedited three other books, including *Reflections on Black Psychology, Minority Issues in Mental Health,* and *African American Psychology: Theory, Research, and Practice.* She was appointed to the Board of Psychology for the state of Ohio in 2001. She also served as editor of the *Journal of Black Psychology* until 2001.

Frederick T. L. Leong is a Professor of Psychology at The Ohio State University. He obtained his Ph.D. from the University of Maryland with a double specialty in Counseling and Industrial/Organizational Psychology. He has authored or coauthored 85 articles in various counseling and psychology journals and 45 book chapters. He is the coeditor of *The Psychology Research Handbook: A Guide for Graduate Students and Research Assistants* (1996) (with James Austin) and *The Career Development and Vocational Behavior of Racial and Ethnic Minorities* (1995). His latest book is an edited volume titled *Contemporary Models in Vocational Psychology: A Volume in Honor of Samuel H. Osipow* (2001) (with Azy Barak). He is a Fellow of the American Psychological Association (Divisions 1, 2, 17, 45, and 52) and the recipient of the 1998 Distinguished Contributions Award from the Asian American Psychological Association and the 1999 John Holland Award from the APA Division of Counseling Psychology. His major research interests are in vocational psychology (career development of ethnic minorities), cross-cultural psychology (particularly culture and mental health and cross-cultural psychotherapy), and organizational behavior.

About the Contributors

Margarita Alegría, Ph.D., is Director of the Center for Multicultural Mental Health Research at Cambridge Health Alliance. As Professor of Health Services and director of the Center for Sociomedical Research and Evaluation at the School of Public Health, Puerto Rico, she has devoted her career to researching mental health services for Latinos and other ethnic populations. She is currently the Principal Investigator of two National Institute of Mental Health-funded research studies. The Latino Research Program Project (LRPP) focuses on research to improve the mental health care of Latino populations. The National Latino and Asian American Study (NLAAS) estimates the prevalence of psychiatric disorders and the use of mental health services among Latinos and Asians in the United States. The NLAAS also plans to make comparisons to non-Latino whites and African Americans. Dr. Alegría also serves on the board of directors for the Children's Foundation and the Felisa Rincón De Gautier Foundation. Her published works focus on the areas of mental health services research, conceptual and methodological issues with minority populations, risk behaviors, and disparities in service delivery.

Eleanor Armour-Thomas is Professor of Educational Psychology at Queens College, Professor in the Ph.D. Program in Educational Psychology at the Graduate School and University Center of the City University of New York, and Chair of the Department of Secondary Education at Queens College. In 1983, she received her doctorate in educational psychology (schooling) from Teachers College, Columbia University and continued her postdoctoral studies at Yale University. She received the Ted Bernstein Award from the New York Association of School Psychology in 1985 and became a National Academy of Education/ Spencer Fellow in 1987. Her research and development interests and publications center on teacher and student cognition related to classroom learning with a focus on intellectual assessment of children from culturally diverse backgrounds and assessment of teaching in mathematics at the high school level.

Fred Beauvais, Ph.D., is a Senior Research Scientist at the Tri-Ethnic Center for Prevention Research and Assistant Professor in the Department of Psychology at Colorodo State University. He has been the Principal Investigator on a number of NIH grants addressing social issues among ethnic minority youth in the United States. His particular interest has been in working with American Indian communities to understand and reduce substance abuse problems. He has also been active in developing new models of research that are based on community collaboration, incorporate the voice of the community, and address ethical issues in cross-cultural research.

Mark A. Bolden is a counseling psychology doctoral student in the Department of Human Development and Psychoeducational Studies at Howard University in Washington, DC. He earned an M.A.E. (2001) in counseling psychology from Seton Hall University in South Orange, New Jersey. He was an APA Minority Fellowship Program Mental Health and Substance Abuse Research Fellow (2001), and a Penn State University Minority In Research Training Fellow (2002). He is the editorial assistant for the *Journal of Black Psychology* and research assistant with his *jegna* (mentors) Dr. Shawn O. Utsey and Dr. Kathy Sanders-Phillips. During 2001-2002, he served as president of the Counseling Psychology Student Association in the Counseling Psychology Program at Howard University. His research interests include time orientations, substance abuse, spirituality, Africentricity, coping, resilience and health behaviors of people of African descent.

Milagros Bravo, Ph.D., is Professor of Research and Program Evaluation in the Graduate School of Education at the University of Puerto Rico, Río Piedras Campus. She is also a researcher at the Behavioral Sciences Research Institute at the Medical Sciences Campus. She has authored or coauthored numerous articles on the translation and cultural adaptation of research instruments.

Randi Burlew received an M.A. in psychology from the University of Michigan. She currently is pursuing a Ph.D. in clinical psychology at the University of Michigan. Her dissertation is on affective sharing in African American friendships.

Mary H. Case studied clinical psychology at DePaul University in Chicago, Illinois, and continues to work at DePaul in the role of Project Director. Her primary research interests include the primary prevention of depression, risk and resiliency factors among inner-city youths, and the cultural adaptation of intervention/prevention programs.

Felipe Gonzalez Castro, M.S.W., Ph.D., is Professor of Clinical Psychology in the Department of Psychology at Arizona State University. He has conducted research in the areas of health promotion and health education with Hispanics and with other ethnic/racial minorities in the United States. In this work, he has investigated aspects of the process of acculturation and assimilation as these relate to mental and physical health among Mexican Americans and other Hispanics, the effects of drug abuse treatment, and relapse prevention among users of cocaine and methamphetamine. His current work includes the study of the intergenerational (parent-youth) transmission of multiple risk behaviors, including drug abuse and HIV/AIDS risks among Mexican American drug-using fathers and their adolescent children. This work examines the interrelated issues involved in the development of a drug-user identity, gender identity (machismo), and ethnic identity as each relate to drug use and other antisocial behaviors.

Kevin M. Chun, Ph.D., is Associate Professor of Psychology and Asian American Studies at the University of San Francisco, Senior Investigator at the University of California, San Francisco, and Alumni Scholar at the National Research Center on Asian American Mental Health at the University of California, Davis. His research focuses on processes of adaptation and health among Asian American immigrants and refugees. His publications include *Acculturation: Advances in Theory, Measurement, and Applied Research* and *Readings in Ethnic Psychology: African Americans, American Indians, Asian Americans and Hispanics/Latino,* which he coedited with Pamela Balls Organista and Gerardo Marín.

Ron Denne, Jr., is a graduate student in the School Psychology Program at San Diego State University. He earned a B.A. degree in psychology from the Department of Psychology, Arizona State University. He participated as a research assistant on a study of the cognitive and behavioral determinants of relapse among stimulant users and has presented his findings at a national meeting of the Society for Prevention Research.

Ruth W. Edwards, Ph.D., is a research scientist and Co-Director at the Tri-Ethnic Center for Prevention Research at Colorado State University. She has served as principal investigator for numerous federally funded research grants. She was the principal investigator of a NIDA grant to develop the American Drug and Alcohol Survey, used by more than 200 school systems each year to assess drug and alcohol use. She is a member of the research team that developed community readiness theory. Her research interests include community interventions (particularly in rural and ethnic communities), causes and correlates of substance use, and violence and victimization among women and adolescents.

Carol A. Gernat is a doctoral candidate in counseling psychology at Seton Hall University in South Orange, New Jersey.

Paul J. Hartung, Ph.D., is Associate Professor of Behavioral Sciences at Northeastern Ohio University's College of Medicine, Rootstown, and Associate Professor of Counselor Education at the University of Akron, Ohio. His scholarship focuses on work-nonwork integration, career decision making, life span vocational development, multicultural career psychology, physician career development, and communication in medicine. He serves on the editorial boards of *The Career Development Quarterly* and the *Journal of Career Assessment.*

La Mar Hasbrouck, M.D., M.P.H., is a medical epidemiologist with the Division of Violence Prevention at the National Center for Injury Prevention and Control, Atlanta, Georgia. His research has focused on the epidemiology of youth violence, racial disparities in homicide deaths by police, and the role of homicide in the life expectancy differences between Black and Whites. He was the primary CDC scientist for the development and release of the U.S. Surgeon General's Report on Youth Violence (2001), coauthoring the epidemiology chapter of the report. In addition to his research, he lectures regularly at Morehouse College and School of Medicine and is Assistant Clinical Professor at Emory University School of Medicine.

Janet E. Helms, Ph.D., is Professor of Counseling Psychology and founding Director of the Institute for the Study and Promotion of Race and Culture at Boston College. She is a Fellow in Divisions 17 (Counseling Psychology) and 45 (Ethnic Diversity) of the American Psychological Association. She is also co-chair of the Joint Committee on Psychological Testing Practices. She has authored or coauthored more than 50 articles, chapters, and books focused on the treatment and assessment of racial and ethnic cultural populations. These include *Black and White Racial Identity: Theory, Research, and Practice,* in which she developed the most widely used measures of racial identity development, and *Using Race and Culture in Counseling and Psychotherapy* (with Donelda Cook), in which she offers racially and culturally responsive treatment strategies.

Bertha Garrett Holliday is a community psychologist and Director of the American Psychological Association's (APA) Office of Ethnic Minority Affairs, where she supports APA's involvement in both a variety of initiatives related to increasing the participation of ethnic minorities in psychology, and public policy issues affecting the well-being of communities of color throughout the world. She is interested in African American child and family socialization, research and program evaluation, and mental health. Her professional roles have included researcher, professor, program evaluator, program administrator, and Congressional Fellow. She holds degrees from the University of Chicago, Harvard University, and the University of Texas at Austin and engaged in postdoctoral study at Cornell University.

Angela L. Holmes is a clinical psychology graduate student at the University of the District of Columbia (UDC) who currently works as a senior intern in the Office of Ethnic Minority Affairs at the American Psychological Association (APA). Her research interests are in the areas of the biological processes and neuropsychology. She is a member of Psi Chi (The National Honor Society in Psychology), the American Psychological Association, and the American Psychological Association of Graduate Students. She is the recent recipient of a UDC graduate fellowship.

Tonya Hucks is a graduate student in the clinical psychology doctoral program at the University of Cincinnati. She received a master's degree in psychology from the University of Cincinnati. She is interested in HIV/AIDS prevention, substance abuse, cross-cultural issues, and serious mental illness research.

Gayle Y. Iwamasa is Associate Professor in the Clinical-Community Psychology Program at DePaul University. Her research and clinical interests are in multicultural mental health across the life span, with an emphasis on anxiety and mood disorders. She is the recipient of several research grants and has received several awards, including the Asian American Psychological Association's Early Career Award for Distinguished Contributions and the Society for the Psychological Study of Ethnic Minority Issues (Division 45) of the American Psychological Association's Emerging Professional Award.

Candace Johnson, M.A., is a graduate student in the clinical psychology doctoral program at the University of Cincinnati. She plans to pursue a career in substance abuse–related research and substance abuse treatment. Her research interests include minority mental health, substance-abusing women, adolescent drug use, and mental health treatment.

James M. Jones is Professor of Psychology at the University of Delaware and Director of the Minority Fellowship Program at the American Psychological

Association. He earned his Ph.D. in Social Psychology from Yale University (1970). He was on the faculty of the Social Relations Department at Harvard University (1970-1976) when he published the first edition of *Prejudice and Racism* (1972) and spent a year in Trinidad and Tobago on a Guggenheim Fellowship studying Calypso humor. This work led to the development of the TRIOS model of the psychology of African American culture. He is a social psychologist and serves on several editorial boards, including the *International Journal of Intercultural Relations* and the *Journal of Black Psychology*. He was awarded the 1999 Lifetime Achievement Award from the Society for the Psychological Study of Ethnic Minority Issues (Division 45) of the American Psychological Association and the 2001 Kurt Lewin Award from the Society for the Psychological Study of Social Issues (Division 9).

Pamela Jumper-Thurman, Ph.D., is a member of the Western Cherokee Tribe and is a Research Associate with the Tri-Ethnic Center for Prevention Research at Colorado State University. She has 15 years of experience in mental health and substance abuse research as well as in direct services. Her research interests are in the areas of cultural issues and health disparities, violence and victimization, rural women's concerns, and solvent abuse among youth. She also serves as Principal Investigator for several funded projects for the NIDA, CDC, and NIJ. She is a member of the research team that developed community readiness theory and is very committed to collaborative community research.

Saera R. Khan, Ph.D., is Assistant Professor of Psychology at the University of San Francisco. Her research explores how motivation and information processing influence the use of stereotypes when judging others. Her goal is to gain a comprehensive view of stereotyping by examining the process from the perspective of the perceiver, as well as the target (i.e., the individual belonging to the stereotyped group). Her most recent publication, "Perceptions of 'Rational Discrimination': When Do People Attempt to Justify Race-Based Prejudice?" appeared in *Basic and Applied Social Psychology*. She earned her doctorate from Washington University.

Sally A. Koblinsky is Professor and Chair of the Department of Family Studies at the University of Maryland, College Park. She is author or coauthor of more than 50 articles and chapters that focus on parenting and child development issues, including community violence, homeless families, adolescent pregnancy prevention, and school-age child care. She has received funding from the federal government and private foundations for more than 25 community-based research and intervention projects involving at-risk families. She was co-director of a U.S. Department of Education grant examining the role of families and Head Start in promoting positive developmental outcomes for preschoolers in violent neighborhoods. She is currently Principal Investigator of a USDHHS Center for Substance Abuse Prevention grant examining the effectiveness of a culturally specific parenting program in fostering the development of preschoolers in African American families at risk for substance abuse.

Jessica Kohout is Director of the Research Office at the American Psychological Association. The Research Office focuses on collecting, analyzing, and disseminating data on the demographics, employment, and education of psychologists. She earned her Ph.D. in sociology from the University of Denver in 1985. She has worked at the APA since 1987 and has been its director since 1991.

Malick Kouyaté, Ed.D., received his doctorate degree in Administrative and Policy Studies from the School of Education, University of Pittsburgh in 1999. Prior to that he was an instructor at the University of Conakry, Guinea (1980-1991), Head of the Educational Science Unit at the National Pedagogic Institute in Guinea (1985-1992), and Deputy Coordinator of Guinea's Educational Adjustment Program (1996-1998). Interested in values as they relate to character education, mindful learning, and spirituality, Dr. Kouyaté, along with Dr. Jerome Taylor, currently focuses on designing pedagogical methods for fostering Values for Life promotion.

William B. Lawson, M.D., Ph.D., is Professor and Chair of the Department of Psychiatry at Howard University School of Medicine. He was named as one of "America's Leading Black Doctors" by Black Enterprise Magazine, received the Jeanne Spurlock Award from the American Psychiatric Association, and received the E.Y. Williams Clinical Scholar of Distinction Award from the Psychiatry and Behavioral Sciences Section of the National Medical Association, and a Multicultural Workplace Award from the Veterans Administration. He has received state, federal, and foundation support for pharmacological research and to develop new and effective treatments. He has over 80 publications on topics including severe mental illness and its relationship to psychopharmacology, substance abuse, and racial and ethnic issues. He has a longstanding concern about ethnic disparities in mental health treatment, and he has been an outspoken advocate for assess to services of the severely mentally ill.

He is directing a program with the National Institute of Mental Health intramural program to research mood and anxiety disorders in African Americans and other ethnic minorities. He received his Ph.D. in psychology from the University of New Hampshire and his M.D. degree from the University of Chicago. He completed a fellowship in clinical psychopharmacology at the National Institute of Mental Health intramural program.

Tené T. Lewis, C.Phil., is a doctoral candidate in the department of clinical psychology at UCLA. Her research interests are in the area of clinical health psychology with an emphasis on the health of ethnic minority women. Her major line of inquiry is focused on examining how chronic and traumatic stressors contribute to excess disease morbidity and mortality in African American women and other women of color.

Courtney V. Lin is a doctoral student in clinical psychology at Arizona State University. She graduated summa cum laude from the University of San Diego with a BA in Psychology. Her thesis is on the impact of social influences (i.e, mothers, fathers, older brothers, older sisters, and friends) who smoke on Latino youth self-efficacy to avoid tobacco in the future, and how that relationship is moderated by youth grade, gender, and linguistic acculturation. She has worked for Early Head Start providing individual and group therapy to Latino teen parents in Spanish and English. She has also been involved in conducting an intervention in Spanish and English for Mexican American 7th-grade students and their families that was designed to reduce high school dropout rates and improve mental health outcomes. She is a recipient of an APA Minority Fellowship in Mental Health and Substance Abuse Services. She is interested in pursuing a university faculty position and hopes to continue her work with Latino families.

Barbara VanOss Marín, PhD, is Professor of Medicine at the Center for AIDS Prevention Studies, University of California San Francisco. Her primary interests over the past 20 years have been promoting healthy behaviors among Latinos in culturally appropriate ways and mentoring scientists of color. She has also emphasized use of appropriate research methods with communities of color. Her current research interests include identifying the cultural issues related to AIDS prevention in the Hispanic community and analyzing results from a survey of condom use in 1600 unmarried Hispanic adults in 10 states, looking at such predictors as self-efficacy to use condoms, sexual comfort, sex role traditionalism, and sexual coercion. She is currently analyzing a project designed to develop, implement and evaluate a sex education/HIV prevention program for middle schools with large proportions of Latinos and is director of the Collaborative HIV Prevention Research in Minority Communities program that provides funding and mentoring for individuals doing HIV prevention research with ethnic minority communities. She is also a guest researcher at the Centers for Disease Control at the National Center for HIV, STD and TB Prevention. She holds degrees from Loyola University of Chicago in applied social psychology and did a postdoctoral fellowship at UCSF in Health Psychology. She has published numerous research articles on HIV prevention in the Latino community, has written a report on HIV prevention interventions for ethnic minorities for the Office of Technology Assessment and consults frequently with others interested in HIV prevention research in communities of color

Gerardo Marín, Ph.D., is Professor of Psychology and Senior Associate Dean in the College of Arts and Sciences at the University of San Francisco. He has written more than 135 publications on topics that are relevant to Hispanics, including cultural norms and attitudes, risk behaviors, culturally appropriate methodology, and acculturation. He is the author of two widely used acculturation scales for Hispanics and was the editor of the recent *Surgeon General's Report on Smoking* regarding four ethnic minority groups. In 1991, he coauthored the book *Research With Hispanic Populations* with Barbara VanOss Marín and is the author of the forthcoming book *Culturally Appropriate Research*. He is an APA Fellow and has been a reviewer for various publications, including *American Psychologist, Journal of Personality and Social Psychology, Hispanic Journal of Behavioral Sciences, American Journal of Community Psychology, Journal of Cross-Cultural Psychology, and Journal of Community Psychology.*

Leonardo M. Marmol, Ph.D., is Professor and Chair of the Department of Graduate Psychology at Seattle Pacific University in Seattle, Washington. Born in

Havana, Cuba, he holds B.A. and M.A. degrees from Pepperdine University and a Ph.D. in clinical psychology from the San Francisco campus of the California School of Professional Psychology. After practicing independently in San Francisco for 17 years, he went into full-time academic teaching and adminsitration. For several years, he has been conducting research on the use of neuropsychological instruments with ethnic minority persons.

Jeffery Scott Mio, Ph.D., is Director of the M.S. in Psychology Program in the Behavioral Sciences Department at California State Polytechnic University, Pomona. He is interested in the teaching of multicultural issues, the development of allies, and how metaphors are used in political persuasion. He received his Ph.D. in Clinical Psychology from the University of Illinois, Chicago, in 1984. A third-generation Japanese American (Sansei), he honors his parents, George and Ruby Mio, for their support throughout the years, and his grandparents, Jenmatsu and Orie Mio, who helped instill his values.

Hector F. Myers, Ph.D., is Professor of Psychology at UCLA and Director of the Research Center on Ethnicity, Health, and Behavior at the Charles R. Drew University of Science & Medicine. His primary research interest is psychosocial and biobehavioral factors that contribute to the persistent health disparities between Whites, African Americans, and other persons of color. His specific focus is on testing biopsychosocial models of hypertension, CVD, HIV/AIDS, and depression, and behavioral interventions that can close these health gaps. He has published more than 100 articles and book chapters on this topic.

Yolanda Flores Niemann, Ph.D., is Associate Professor of Comparative American Cultures and Director of Latina/o Outreach at Washington State University, Tri-Cities. She is also an Affiliate Faculty in Women's Studies and Graduate Faculty in American Studies. She has served on the Washington State Governor's Commission on Hispanic Affairs and is the Program Chair for the Division of the Study of Ethnic Minority Issues for the American Psychological Association (APA), as well as Chair of the Workshop Committee for the Division for the Social Psychological Study of Social Issues of APA. Her training was in general psychology, with an emphasis in social psychology and a minor in management. Her research interests include effects of stereotypes across various domains, including identity and risky behavior, the psychological effects of tokenism, overcoming obstacles to Latina/o higher education, identity issues from Mexican to Mexican American, and the use of stereotypes as justification for discrimination. She is the author of *Black-Brown Relations and Stereotypes* (forthcoming) and has numerous publications in refereed journals and edited books, including *Journal of Applied Psychology, Personality and Social Psychology Bulletin, Sociological Perspectives, Hispanic Journal of Behavioral Sciences, Journal for the Theory of Social Behavior, The Western Journal of Black Studies, and Frontiers: A Journal of Women Studies.*

Jeanne L. Obert, M.F.T., M.S.M., is the Executive Director of the Matrix Institute on Addictions in Los Angeles, California. She is a marital and family therapist who is interested in the familial, social and cultural determinants of recovery from substance abuse. She is one of the long-term partners who developed the Matrix Model, and she led the development of the manualized version of the Matrix Model. She has also been active in studying the effectiveness of this model when applied with U. S. American Indian populations. In addition, she has traveled to various treatment centers in Thailand, where several agencies nationally have adopted the Matrix program for use with several addicted populations within their country.

Eugene Oetting, Ph.D., is Professor of Psychology and Scientific Director of the Tri-Ethnic Center for Prevention Research at Colorado State University. His research has focused on the etiology and prevention of the psychosocial problems of children, adolescents, and young adults from underserved ethnic minority populations, including drug use, dropout, crime, violence, and work adjustment. A major goal has been theory development based on research findings. He has been instrumental in the creation of the alert trance state, the work adjustment hierarchy, the counseling "cube," peer cluster theory, community readiness theory, and, most recently, primary socialization theory.

Pamela Balls Organista, Ph.D., is Associate Professor of Psychology at the University of San Francisco. She completed her doctorate in clinical psychology at Arizona State University and her postdoctorate in the Department of Psychiatry at the University of California–San Francisco. Her research interests include prevention interventions and ethnic minority health issues. Publications include *Readings in Ethnic Psychology: African Americans, American Indians, Asian Americans, and Hispanics/Latinos* and *Acculturation: Advances in Theory, Measurement, and Applied Research*, which she coedited with professors Kevin M. Chun and Gerardo Marín, and several articles on migrant laborers and AIDS, and on stress and coping in primary care patients. She was the founding faculty coordinator of the Ethnic Studies Certificate Program at the University of San Francisco, and in 1998 was appointed the Director of Academic Advising in the College of Arts and Sciences at the University of San Francisco.

Shilpa M. Pai is Assistant Professor of Clinical Psychology in the Department of Psychology at Appalachian State University, Boone, North Carolina. She received her doctorate in clinical psychology from Oklahoma State University in 2002. She completed her internship at the University of Washington School of Medicine, specializing in public behavioral health and justice policy. Her research and clinical focus is on conducting culturally appropriate therapy.

Tyan Parker-Dominguez, Ph.D., is Assistant Professor in the Graduate School of Social Work at the University of Southern California. Her research focuses on stress and pregnancy and the persistent racial disparity in adverse birth outcomes. She earned M.S.W. and M.P.H. degrees from the University of California, Berkeley. She is a member of the American Public Health Association—Maternal and Child Health and Social Work Sections, the Society for Social Work and Research, the National Association of Social Workers, and the National Black Women's Health Project.

Paul B. Pedersen is Professor Emeritus at Syracuse University and Visiting Professor in the Department of Psychology, University of Hawaii. He has authored, coauthored, or edited 39 books, 67 chapters, and 93 articles on multicultural counseling and communication. He is a Fellow in Divisions 9 (Social Issues), 17 (Counseling), 45 (Ethnic Minorities), and 52 (International) of the American Psychological Association. He has taught at universities in Indonesia, Malaysia, and Taiwan for 8 years and was in Taiwan on a Senior Fulbright for a year. His Web site is http://soeweb.syr. edu/chs/pedersen/index.html.

Barbara A. Plested, Ph.D., is a research associate at the Colorado State University Tri-Ethnic Center for Prevention Research and has worked extensively in the provision of direct services to special populations as well as in collaborative research. She has 15 years of both administrative and therapeutic service experience in both mental health and substance abuse. In this capacity, a primary role has been administrative, including the development of policy and procedure, quality assurance issues, and direct treatment. She is a member of the research team that developed community readiness theory and has published widely on the topic of community work, inhalant prevention, and treatment and violence prevention.

Randolph G. Potts, Ph.D., is Assistant Professor of Psychology at Holy Cross College and a practicing psychologist in Hartford, Connecticut. He is a member of the Council of Directors of the Benjamin E. Mays Institute in Hartford and a founder of the Rites of Passage Program at Osborn Correctional Institute in Somers, Connecticut. He earned a doctorate in Clinical-Community Psychology from DePaul University in 1994. He is a member of the Association of Black Psychologists and is an APA Minority Fellowship recipient (1990-1993).

Suzanne M. Randolph is Associate Professor of Family Studies at the University of Maryland, College Park. She earned a Ph.D. in developmental psychology from the University of Michigan at Ann Arbor. She is co-principal investigator for a USDHHS/SAMHSA/CSAP-funded study evaluating the Effective Black Parenting program with Head Start parents at risk for substance abuse and for the NICHD Study of Early Child Care and Youth Development. She is an evaluator for the Pathways to Prevention program, an infant mental health training project sponsored by the Early Head Start National Resource Center at ZERO TO THREE. She is also on the evaluation work group for the CDC Minority AIDS Initiative fielded by the MayaTech Corporation of Silver Spring, Maryland. She was Principal Investigator for a Head Start community violence prevention study funded by the U.S. Department of Education and a Robert Wood Johnson–funded evaluation of the Opening Doors program to reduce sociocultural barriers to health care. She was a member of the National Academy of Sciences Panel on Evaluation Methods for Assessing the Impact of Welfare Reform. She is a member of the Advisory Panel for the National Technical Assistance Center for Children's Mental Health at Georgetown Child Development Center, the social environment work group of the National Children's Study.

Richard A. Rawson, Ph.D., is Associate Director of the UCLA Integrated Substance Abuse Programs. He is also the Co-Principal Investigator of the CSAT Methamphetamine Treatment Project. He is the originator of the Matrix Model, which was originally implemented with heroin-using clients over 25 years ago. He then expanded the Matrix Model for use with clients addicted to cocaine and/or methamphetamine, and to other illicit drugs.

Le'Roy E. Reese, Ph.D., is a Senior Fellow in the Division of Violence Prevention at the Centers for Disease Control and Prevention. He joined the CDC after spending several years codirecting a prevention research team that conducted school and community-based prevention research in Chicago. The foci of Dr. Reese's research and clinical practice address the prevention of health-compromising behavior among children, adolescents, and their families in underresourced communities and the promotion of wellness and broad-based social and behavioral competencies. In particular, he is interested in the role of culture in promoting the psychological health and adjustment of ethnic minority communities in the United States.

W. LaVome Robinson, Ph.D., is Professor of Psychology at DePaul University, in Chicago, Illinois. She received her Ph.D. in clinical psychology from the University of Georgia. Her chief research interests are (a) the development and evaluation of school-based prevention and treatment programs and (b) mental health promotion for African American adolescents, with a primary focus on depression preventionand the cultural adaptation of interventions. Much of her research revolves around school-based health center models of service delivery and evaluation.

Maria P. P. Root, Ph.D., is a psychologist in Seattle, Washington. She has edited two award-winning books on multiracial identity that were used in the U.S. Bureau of the Census's deliberation on the historical change to the 2000 census. She focuses her publications on the intersections of racial, gender, and generational identity in her ecological framework for understanding racial identity. She is the recipient of regional and national awards for her work.

Emily Sáez is a Ph.D. candidate in clinical psychology at the Department of Psychology, University of Puerto Rico, Río Piedras Campus. Since 1993, she has been involved in clinical research, beginning as an undergraduate research assistant in the University Center for Psychological Services and Research. She received an NIMH Career Opportunities in Research Fellowship. Her research interests include depression and conduct disorder in Puerto Rican adolescents, family environment, and coping strategies. She was the recipient of an individual predoctoral National Service Research Award from NIMH to study the relationship between family environment, depression, and conduct disorder among Puerto Rican Adolescents. She completed her clinical internship at Bellevue Hospital in New York City and is currently finalizing her dissertation project on depression and conduct disorder in Puerto Rican adolescents.

Jamie Smith is a graduate student in counseling psychology at The Ohio State University. Her research interests include career development, professional identity, and group dynamics. In addition to research, she is a counselor in the college counseling center, teaches psychology courses through Ohio State and Johns Hopkins University, and serves as a campus representative for the American Psychological Association of Graduate Students.

Leslie Sue Ph.D., J.D., is Director of the Public Service Center at Butte College, California. The center consists of programs in the Administration of Justice, Fire Technology, Hazardous Materials Training, Construction Inspection Technology, and the Police and Fire Academies. He earned an Ed.D. from Nova Southeastern University, Florida, and a J.D. from Greenwich University, Hawaii. He has served in a variety of public service positions including police officer, environmental health inspector, U.S. Air Force Security Police Chief, Special Agent of the FBI, tribal court associate judge, and professor of law. His research interests are in the public safety occupations relating to workplace stress, police and fire academy performance, corporate espionage, and Asian American matriculation into law enforcement career paths. He has written articles on police stress, corporate security and technology advancement, corporate espionage, and competency-based education. He is a member of the American Bar Association and the International Association of Chiefs of Police.

Stanley Sue, Ph.D., is Professor of Psychology, Psychiatry, and Asian American Studies at the University of California, Davis, and a Ph.D. in Psychology from UCLA (1971). From 1981-1996, he was Professor of Psychology at UCLA, where he was also Associate Dean of the Graduate Division. From 1971-1981, he served on the psychology faculty at the University of Washington. He also served as Director of the National Research Center on Asian American Mental Health, a NIMH-funded research center, from 1988-2001, and was Director of the Asian American Studies Program from 1996-2001. In recognition of his mental health research, he has received a number of awards: 1990 Distinguished Contributions Award for Research on Ethnic Minorities from the Society for the Psychological Study of Ethnic Minority Issues of APA; 1990 Distinguished Contributions Award from the Asian American Psychological Association; 1996 Distinguished Contribution Award for Research in Public Policy from the American Psychological Association; 1998 Distinguished Scientific Achievement Award from the California Psychological Association.

Jerome Taylor is Associate Professor of Africana Studies at the University of Pittsburgh. He received his Ph.D. from Indiana (Bloomington, IN) and postdoctoral training in child and family psychology at the Messinger Clinic. He currently is Executive Director of the Center for Family Excellence, Inc., formerly known as the Institute for the Black Family. Dr. Taylor has published numerous articles that explore the role of cultural, religious, and structural factors on the mental and physical health of African American people, and has developed and implemented a holistic approach to values-based parenting and education. Over three decades, this Values for Life model has been infused into prevention, research, family preservation, and family reunification initiatives.

Shawn O. Utsey is Associate Professor in the Counseling Psychology Program, Department of Human Development and Psychoeducational Studies at Howard

University. He is also Editor-in-Chief of the *Journal of Black Psychology* and has been a member of the Association of Black Psychologists since 1990. He earned an M.A. in rehabilitation counseling from New York University and a Ph.D. in counseling psychology from Fordham University. His research program is aimed at examining the stressful effects of racism on African Americans, white racism and white Americans, and the role of Africanisms and related cultural factors on the psychological well-being of African Americans. He is the author of the widely used Index of Race-Related Stress and the Africultural Coping Systems Inventory.

Elizabeth M. Vera is an Associate Professor at Loyola University Chicago. She received her Ph.D. from The Ohio State University in Counseling Psychology. Areas of scholarly interest include resiliency and prevention with urban youth, the effects of similarity and difference in multicultural interactions, and ethnic identity development in children.

Mildred Vera, Ph.D., is Professor in the Department of Health Services Administration at the School of Public Health, University of Puerto Rico. She is a clinical psychologist with more than 15 years of experience in basic and applied research in health-related issues of Latinos. This research has been supported by grants from the National Institute of Mental Health, the National Institute on Drug Abuse, and the National Institute of Allergy and Infectious Diseases, among others. She has a strong interest in racial ethnic minority research and has published in the areas of mental health care among the poor, gender and mental health services use, and HIV and drug prevention research with Latino populations. Her current mental health services research project focuses on the feasibility, acceptability, and cultural relevance of established depression interventions and the development and adaptation of culturally targeted mental health interventions for Latinos.

Doryliz Vila is Project Director at the Center for Evaluation and Sociomedical Research of the University of Puerto Rico. She has been the director of several research projects, including the National Latino and Asian American Study, funded by the National Institute of Mental Health. Her research interests include child and family health, family adaptation, family-centered interventions, bereavement, and mental health. She completed her master's degree in health services research and evaluation from the Graduate School of Public Health, University of Puerto Rico.

Roderick J. Watts is a community psychologist, a licensed clinical psychologist, and Associate Professor of Psychology at Georgia State University in Atlanta. He received his Ph.D. in Psychology from the University of Maryland, College Park (1984). He is a Fellow in the American Psychological Association and the Division of Community Psychology. As a practitioner, he has served as a program development and evaluation consultant to governmental organizations, schools, foundations, research and public policy organizations, universities, and other nonprofit organizations on a variety of projects. He has also held positions at the Consultation Center at Yale University and the Institute for Urban Affairs and Research at Howard University. He recently coedited two books: *Human*

Diversity: Perspectives on People in Context and *Manhood Development in Urban African American Communities.*

Marlene Wicherski is a survey research consultant in Cambridge, Massachusetts. Prior to her move to Cambridge and her transition to a consulting position, she worked for nearly 20 years in the American Psychological Association's Research Office, where she was involved in many of the research projects conducted by the office.